ENCYCLOPEDIA OF
HISTORICAL TREATIES
AND ALLIANCES

Second Edition

ENCYCLOPEDIA OF
HISTORICAL TREATIES AND ALLIANCES

Second Edition

Volume II: FROM THE 1930s TO THE PRESENT

Charles Phillips and Alan Axelrod

Facts On File
An imprint of Infobase Publishing

Encyclopedia of Historical Treaties and Alliances, Second Edition

Facts On File, Inc.
An imprint of Infobase Publishing
132 West 31st Street
New York NY 10001

Library of Congress Cataloging-in-Publication Data

Phillips, Charles, 1948–
    Encyclopedia of historical treaties and alliances / Charles L. Phillips and Alan Axelrod—
    2nd ed.
        p. cm.
    Includes bibliographical references and index.
    ISBN 0-8160-6075-4 (hc)
    I. Treaties—Sources. 2. Treaties—History—Encyclopedias. I. Axelrod, Alan, 1952– II. Title.

KZ1160.P48 2005
341.3'7'09—dc22   2005040003

Facts On File books are available at special discounts when purchased in bulk quantities for businesses, associations, institutions, or sales promotions. Please call our Special Sales Department in New York at (212) 967-8800 or (800) 322-8755.

You can find Facts On File on the World Wide Web at http://www.factsonfile.com

Text design by Erika K. Arroyo
Cover design by Cathy Rincon

Printed in the United States of America

VB FOF 10 9 8 7 6 5 4 3 2 1

This book is printed on acid-free paper.

CONTENTS

VOLUME 2

ALPHABETICAL LIST
OF TREATIES

Part Twelve
THE WORLD AT WAR

INTRODUCTION

At 4:30 A.M. on September 1, 1939, Adolf Hitler attacked Poland. Without bothering with the formality of declaring war, the German dictator had commenced the 20th century's second worldwide conflict.

The punitive TREATY OF VERSAILLES (1919), which had ended World War I, had limited Germany's army to 100,000 men, including 4,000 officers; deprived it of its heavy weaponry, including aircraft; and closed most of the country's military academies. The treaty had reduced the German navy to 15,000 men and prohibited it from building any new submarines. In fact, though, under General Hans von Seeckt, a Prussian military aristocrat, the ostensibly skeletal postwar German army was developed into a *Führerheer*, an army of leaders, an all-volunteer force of the very highest caliber. It would serve as the core around which a new army would be formed—when the time came.

Germany had also found ways to circumvent the armament restrictions imposed by the Versailles treaty, including an agreement with the Soviet Union—the TREATY OF RAPALLO of April 1922—which established a program of military cooperation between Germany and the USSR and which gave Germany facilities in Russia for developing the advanced ground weapons and aircraft forbidden by Versailles. In addition to and apart from the treaty, both the German army and navy undertook programs of clandestine rearmament, and the ANGLO-GERMAN NAVAL AGREEMENT of June 1935 not only allowed Germany increased tonnage in warships, but also kindled Hitler's hopes that Great Britain might actually be an ally in the war he knew was coming.

For years following the Great War, German strategists were also hard at work developing a new combat doctrine. It was called "blitzkrieg"—literally, "lightning war"—a system of weapons and tactics capable of piercing an enemy's front and then encircling and destroying all or part of its forces. Its hallmarks were great speed, great violence, and the retention of the initiative at all costs. Reconnaissance identified weak points in the front, and these *Schwerpunkt* (thrust points) were rapidly exploited by crack *Kampfgruppen* (combat teams), followed swiftly by massive attacks. The Spanish Civil War of 1936–39 gave Germany its first opportunity to test its new army and air force as well as some of the tactics of blitzkrieg, but in Poland the doctrine was given its first full-scale demonstration. As devastating as the attack was, it proved no more than an overture to a darkness yet more horrible than any the first war had brought.

On that September morning, then, without warning, Hitler's Luftwaffe (air force) struck airfields all across Poland as, almost simultaneously, a superannuated German battleship, which had been "visiting" the port of Danzig, opened fire on Polish fortifications, and the Wehrmacht (army) surged across the Polish frontier. Despite the mounting tensions that had preceded the invasion, the massiveness, swiftness, and violence of the blitzkrieg took Poland—and the world—by complete surprise. The campaign itself did not last long. On September 27 Warsaw, plagued by typhoid and starvation, fell. The next day, the town of Modlin surrendered, and 164,000 Polish soldiers were taken prisoner. A holdout, the isolated coastal fortress of Hel, caved in on October 1, and five days after that the German Tenth Army crushed the last organized Polish force at Kock. An entire nation had been invaded, and its army defeated, its cities taken in little more than a month. Such was blitzkrieg.

Two images dominated the campaign and, to the watching world, characterized the German war machine and the European "situation": great hawklike Stuka (dive-bombers) swooping in for the attack, their large, nonretractable landing gear resembling some horrible mechanical talons; and the Polish cavalry making a spectacle of mounted warriors wielding lances against those modern metallic dragons the

Panzer (tanks). These images captured well the uneven development that the Versailles peace had helped to foster in Europe; they were images of the diplomatic unpreparedness of the rest of the world in the face of the aggressive fascist nations; they were images of war at mid-century.

Britain and France, bound to Poland by a number of interwar and two postinvasion treaties—including the POLITICAL AGREEMENT BETWEEN FRANCE AND POLAND, the TREATY OF MUTUAL GUARANTEE BETWEEN FRANCE AND POLAND, the AGREEMENT OF MUTUAL ASSISTANCE BETWEEN THE UNITED KINGDOM AND POLAND, and the AGREEMENT OF MUTUAL ASSISTANCE BETWEEN POLAND AND FRANCE—declared war. And so it began again, a war sparked by nationality conflicts in east-central Europe and provoked, in part, by a German stab at continental hegemony that expanded into a global conflict touching every continent.

It was more a total war than even the first since the belligerent powers' civilians not only contributed to their war efforts but became targets for their enemies. Subject populations also became targets of their home states or their occupiers. Most horrific was Hitler's attempt to exterminate the Jews of Europe, but Germany also attacked Slavs and other ethnic, social, and political groups deemed inferior by, or a threat to, Nazi ideology, and Stalin expanded the Russian terror against the Ukrainians to the conquered Poles. Even in the Pacific, the Japanese-American conflict at times degenerated into brutal race war. Indeed, World War II all but eliminated the age-old diplomatic distinction between combatants and non-combatants, and so not only would its death toll greatly exceed that of the Great War, but civilian casualties would also vastly outnumber those of the military. Not that the combatants enjoyed the benefits of so-called civilized warfare. The Geneva Conventions of 1864, 1899, 1907, 1925, and 1929 guaranteed humane treatment of prisoners of war. In many cases these guarantees were ignored. World War II was highly uncivilized.

Yet again the war in Europe developed into a contest between a German-held Europe and an Allied coalition attacking on its periphery. Yet again the United States kept clear of the conflict until its own sovereignty was insulted by direct attack. But unlike the last war, the Italians quickly joined the Germans rather than remaining neutral, and the Soviet Union, itself soon invaded by Germany, did not collapse as Imperial Russia had. Instead, Joseph Stalin's Russia held out while France fell to the Nazis, and thus ultimately the Soviets instead of the French joined the British and the Americans in the wartime conferences of the "Big Three." Although Japan, joining the Axis powers, invaded and subjected China and Southeast Asia and provoked the entry of the United States into the war, it also managed to remain neutral toward Russia.

In turn, the anti-fascist Allies, while determined to reduce Germany to rubble, nevertheless simmered with tension over varying strategies and war aims. In fact, World War II was in many ways a label for several parallel or overlapping wars, and the central conflict in Europe overlay a three-way struggle for power among Nazism, democracy, and communism. Once Germany fell and Japan was bombed into submission, these subterranean struggles between the allies burst into the open in a new kind of war and an odd sort of diplomacy.

A Phony War, Finland, and Two Fronts

By the protocol of the mutual assistance agreement with Poland, France had promised to take the offensive two weeks after mobilizing for war. French general Maurice Gamelin launched a brief sortie into the Saar, then quickly retreated behind the Maginot Line. A couple of months later, France and Britain managed to have Hitler's fearfully solicitous ally the Soviet Union expelled from the League of Nations on December 14, but otherwise the two powers proved loath to take any initiative, engaging in what critics called "Sitzgrieg" or the "Phony War." In the meantime, Hitler—in secret contacts and an October 6 "Peace Address" to the Reichstag—did his best to persuade the British to renege on their commitment to Poland, even dangling the possibility of restoring a rump state to the hapless Poles. When British prime minister Neville Chamberlain, so often the victim of Germany's diplomatic perfidy in the past, demurred, Hitler ordered his military to prepare an attack in the west by November 12. Bad weather and the protests of the German High Command delayed action first to January 1940, then to the spring, and the Phony War dragged on.

Russia was the only major power taking truly decisive action during this period. Hitler's new ally had duly occupied its share of Poland under the HITLER-STALIN PACT, but the Soviet leader, fearing the Germans would not stop at the agreed-to line in any event, called up millions of reserve troops just in case, then fecklessly offered the Germans a larger slice of conquered territory plus extensive Russian trade in exchange for a free hand in Lithuania. Not until Molotov had signed this second German-Soviet pact, the GERMAN-SOVIET BOUNDARY AND FRIENDSHIP TREATY, on September 28 did the communist parties in the West fall in line and oppose Western military resistance to Hitler. With the communist world in a Nazi embrace, an anxious Stalin by October 10 occupied Latvia, Lithuania, and Estonia.

When Finland resisted Soviet demands for changes in its borders and the leasing of military bases, Stalin sent in the Red Army on November 30. France in turn wanted to send Allied troops to Finland via Narvik in Norway, and the United States even debated a war loan to the beleaguered country, the only nation that had paid interest on its World War I debt. But Britain resisted the French proposal as a violation of Norway's neutral rights (prompting Winston Churchill to boom, "Humanity, rather than legality, must be our guide"), and the U.S. loan never materialized.

The brave Finns fought on alone till Russia broke the Mannerheim Line in February 1940. At Helsinki on March 12, Finland ceded the Karelian Isthmus to Russia and leased a naval base on the Hagö Peninsula to the Soviets. Presaging the postwar future of central Europe, Stalin set up the Finnish Democratic Republic under a Comintern agent named Otto Kuusinen. Moreover, Finland's defeat sparked the fall of the French government. A new cabinet, under Paul Reynaud, joined Chamberlain in a plan to mine or occupy North Sea ports and thus block the Germans from taking Norway and Denmark in the wake of Russia's Scandinavian conquests.

They were too late. On April 9, the day the British laid their first mine, Hitler launched a brilliant air and sea operation, seizing ports from Oslo to Narvik and taking Denmark by blitzkrieg. Strategically, Hitler needed the North Sea bases for his U-boats, and, determined to deny him such access, for the first time the Allies fought back in earnest. British troops captured Narvik on May 27 but were forced by dire events on the Continent to evacuate the port on June 6. By the time the Nazi puppet Vidkun Quisling came to power in Norway, Winston Churchill had replaced Chamberlain as prime minister and told the British people he had "nothing to offer but blood, toil, tears, and sweat." The Phony War in Europe was at an end.

The German blow to Western Europe had come on May 10. Following General Erich von Manstein's scheme, Wehrmacht panzers shot through the rugged Ardennes Forest in south Belgium and Luxemburg aiming to bypass the Maginot Line, pierce French defenses and disrupt the enemy rear, and split Allied forces in two. The Dutch surrendered within the week, which did not stop Hermann Göring's Luftwaffe from bombing Rotterdam to ruins. By May 20 von Rundstedt's tanks, breaking out of the Ardennes at Sedan, reached Abbeville on the French coast and cut the Allied armies apart as planned. Belgium's Leopold III surrendered on the 28th, and that same day Churchill's government ordered the British Expeditionary Force to head for Dunkirk and evacuation by sea. For eight months the Allies had dithered, expanding their fronts, building up their armed forces, shoring up the useless Maginot Line, and now in a fortnight it seemed the game was up and Western Europe on the verge of toppling to the German juggernaut.

No one was more shocked than Mussolini. After years of braggadocio about the beauty and necessity of war, he had balked when the Germans first launched their invasion back in August 1939, demanding tons and tons of coal, oil, and steel before he could possibly consider honoring the "PACT OF STEEL." Partly he was stalling, since his much-touted military was a sham, corrupt and ill-prepared; partly he was politically jealous of Hitler's diplomatic and military success, and partly he was, for all his bluster, a timid warrior. Literally sickened by the tension, Mussolini at times even entertained the notion of joining the Allies, but when the Germans suggested they did not really need him, he jumped on board, saving face by claiming he was not simply affixing himself to Hitler's conquests but forging "a new Roman Empire."

In fact, Mussolini only launched his "parallel" war to participate in the spoils after it was clear the Allies had lost Europe and his rather hollow regime would not truly be tested under fire. "All we need," he told one of his generals when he declared war on France on June 10, 1940, "is a few thousand dead" to claim a seat at the peace table. Mussolini's game was clear enough to everyone. "The hand that held the dagger," said U.S. president Franklin Delano Roosevelt, pretty much summing up Europe's—and history's—judgment, "has stuck into the back of its neighbor."

Regardless of the general opinion of Mussolini's international character, it was hard to deny that his sense of timing was exquisite. The next day, June 11, the French government fled Paris for Bordeaux, and a week later Reynaud resigned as his ministers leaned toward capitulation against his wishes and despite Churchill's desperate offer of an Anglo-French political union if they continued fighting. Instead, the aged Marshal Pétain asked Germany for an armistice and on June 22 submitted to Hitler's humiliating demand that it be signed at Compiègne at the same spot and in the same railway car used for the German armistice in 1918. Under the terms of the armistice, Pétain's fascistic government, headquartered at Vichy, would administer southern France, some 40 percent of the nation, while the Nazis occupied the rest: Paris, northern France, the west coast.

Mussolini had hoped for something more, but General Charles de Gaulle, in exile in England, was broadcasting pleas to the French to fight on underground and organizing Free French forces in the sub-Sahara, so Hitler tread more lightly for fear of driving the currently collaborationist Vichy regime into the arms of the Allies. It worked: when the British attacked the French fleet, moored off Algeria, Pétain broke off with London, and Hitler even toyed with the idea of an active French alliance that would shunt the nettlesome Mussolini yet further to the rear.

Even as the English Channel became the western front, Hitler refused to give up his belief that he could somehow come to terms with Britain. For one thing, Hitler believed the Germans and the British were "racially" and geopolitically compatible, but he also saw his ultimate goal as Lebensraum (territory for housing an expansive German people), and fulfillment of that goal lay eastward. In other words, Hitler was anxious to attack Russia, and he knew his generals would resist a two-front war. Churchill had no love for the Russians either, but he despised the Nazis, and England had spent the Phony War building up its home defenses, especially its air force. Churchill's government dismissed out of hand diplomatic feelers for a separate peace with the Germans (Hitler told his general staff on May 21 that "we are seeking contact with Britain on the basis of partitioning the world").

On July 2 the frustrated Führer authorized a cross-Channel invasion dubbed Operation Sea Lion. In the massive air duel of August 1940 that came to be called the Battle of Britain, technically superior British Hurricanes and Spitfires put paid to Göring's boast that the Luftwaffe would destroy England's air defenses in four days. On September 7, Göring, in response to the Allied bombing of Berlin three days earlier, shifted the attacks from airfields to the city of London. The 10-day London Blitz not only stiffened the resolve of the British, it also took a devastating toll on Göring's air force: England shot down 60 Luftwaffe planes in a single day on September 15. Hitler put Sea Lion on hold; the British Empire fought on alone for a full year.

A stymied Hitler tried to engage Francisco Franco in a Mediterranean adventure to capture Gibraltar (along with Malta and the Suez Canal), but Spain's dictator, a Catholic contemptuous of the Nazis' and the Italian Fascists' neopaganism, found a way to remain neutral. Complaining he would rather have teeth pulled than negotiate further with Franco, Hitler tried to persuade Pétain into alliance, but the marshal continued to play his double game, promising collaboration to Hitler and reassuring Churchill that Vichy France sought a "cautious balance" between the belligerents.

Even Hitler's generals held out against his desire to launch Operation Barbarossa on the Russians as soon as possible, which he would argue would finally convince the British of their hopeless situation. Here the generals were helped by the fascist powers' loose cannon, Mussolini. Italy sought Hitler's approval to attack Yugoslavia and Greece, but Hitler insisted on Crete and Cyprus, which would aid his war on Britain. When the Royal Navy demonstrated the Italians simply did not have the ability to chase the British out of the Mediterranean, Mussolini—needing to prove he could accomplish something on his own—rashly invaded Egypt.

Instead of establishing his bellicose bona fides, the disastrous adventure much helped to destroy them in Hitler's eyes. Mussolini's blundering about the Balkans in the next few months would continue to give German generals an excuse to delay the opening of a full-scale second front to the east.

One of those urging Hitler to caution was his foreign minister, Joachim von Ribbentrop, who still believed Britain could be persuaded to give up its resistance through diplomacy. Toward that end, Ribbentrop engineered in September 1940 the AXIS PACT, sometimes called the Tripartite Pact. The idea was that this alliance between Germany, Italy, and Japan would deflect from Europe the attention of Britain's potential ally the United States, which was already doing everything it could to help Britain short of war with the LEND-LEASE AGREEMENT and anything else President Franklin Delano Roosevelt could think of for Winston Churchill, with whom he had grown friendly. The pact was also supposed to threaten the USSR with a war on two fronts and thus keep Russia from wavering in its commitment to Germany until Hitler had the chance to stab Stalin in the back. All this was intended to drive the British to despair over the prospect of facing the Nazis alone.

As it turned out, the pact did none of the above. Once the United States entered the war, it would stick strictly to a Europe-first policy. The Japanese would sign a nonaggression pact of their own with Stalin, only they, unlike Hitler, would live up to their promise of neutrality. And as for England, she was already fighting Germany alone, and Churchill was not the man to back away from a fight, whatever the odds.

What the pact did do, however, was clearly divide up the sides in the war and, when the time came, embolden the militarists in Japan to take the fateful step that would actually bring the United States into the conflict.

The Pacific War

On December 7, 1941, the Empire of Japan launched an air attack on the American fleet anchored at Pearl Harbor, Hawaii, killing 2,403 Americans, destroying 19 ships and 150 planes, and propelling the United States into World War II. The myth is that the United States was totally unprepared for war. In fact, it was as prepared as it had ever been—and far more prepared to fight than had been the case on the eve of entry into World War I. In 1932 the army had a strength of only 134,024 men and women, which doubled to 267,767 by 1940. With the threat of a two-front war imminent, a peacetime draft was instituted, and by mid-1941, months before Pearl Harbor, 1,460,998 men and women were on active duty. A vigorous shipbuilding program was also well under way, as was the fulfillment of a mandate to build 10,000 aircraft.

Yet the attack, when it came, at 7:55 Sunday morning, took Pearl Harbor's fleet completely by surprise. It shouldn't have. Even while Japanese negotiators were conducting business in Washington, ostensibly to avert war, PURPLE and MAGIC messages (Japanese diplomatic ciphers U.S. intelligence had broken) were being decoded continually. By November 24 Admiral Harold Stark had telegraphed Admiral Husband Kimmel, commanding naval forces at Pearl Harbor, "Chances of favorable outcome of negotiations with Japan very doubtful" and that "a surprise aggressive movement in any direction" was anticipated. On November 25 Stark told Kimmel that FDR and Navy secretary Cordell Hull would not be surprised if the Japanese launched a surprise attack. Before war alert messages were issued to the military on November 26, Secretary of War Henry Stimson even spoke of the strategic desirability of maneuvering the Japanese into war.

Yet, through inertia, inaction, and just plain blundering, the Pacific Fleet and an array of aircraft, including many B-17 bombers, were left as easy prey for the Japanese carrier-based dive-bombers and torpedo planes. Within two hours of the attack on Pearl Harbor came a strike against Clark Field, the principal U.S. base in the Philippines, trapping General Douglas MacArthur's Far East air force on the ground and destroying half of it. Soon Japanese troops overran the islands, capturing vast numbers of American troops and soundly beating the British in Singapore to seize control of the Pacific. These defeats were humiliating and demoralizing, and the American public wanted personal vengeance against the Japanese, even though Roosevelt's official war aims were directed first and foremost toward the defeat of Nazi Germany and the salvation of Europe.

As costly as the attack was in terms of American lives lost and matériel destroyed or damaged, it cost the Japanese and their German allies far more. Pearl Harbor instantly forged an America more unified than it ever had been or, perhaps, would ever be again. Congress immediately gave President Roosevelt his declaration of war, along with unprecedented powers to mobilize a massive war machine. On the Monday following Pearl Harbor, tens of thousands jammed recruiting offices, rushing to enlist, and the government conscripted millions more, rapidly building a fighting force of more than 16 million men and women. Overnight, it seemed, boys hardly old enough to shave or drive a car were dropping bombs on the centers of a centuries-old civilization or slogging through dense jungles in parts of the world remote from anything they recognized as civilization.

The first counterstrike against Japan came far sooner than the United States was properly prepared to deliver it, but Lieutenant Colonel James Doolittle, looking for something, anything, to lift American morale, pushed the limit. On April 18, 1942, he led 16 Army Air Force B-25s—launched as no B-25 had ever been launched before, from the deck of a flattop, the carrier *Hornet*—in a spectacular low-level bombing raid on Tokyo. Damage to the Japanese capital was minimal, and the trip (as all who flew the mission well knew) was one way. It was impossible for the B-25s to carry enough fuel to get them back to the *Hornet*, and in any case, while it might be possible to get a twin-engine bomber off a flattop, it was certainly not feasible to land one on the flight deck. The plan was to land in China, dodge the Japanese occupiers of that country, and—somehow-—get back to U.S. military control.

Astoundingly, for most of the crews, the plan worked, and the Japanese, shocked at the bombardment of their capital city, kept four fighter groups at home as they moved against the remainder of the American Pacific Fleet at Midway Island, where the Navy, under Admiral Chester Nimitz, was ready for them. This hard-fought battle was the first major defeat the Japanese suffered and was the first step in America's fight to regain control of the Pacific.

Throughout 1942 and 1943, MacArthur fought the Japanese one island at a time—slogging it out on Guadalcanal, for example, from August 7, 1942, until February 8, 1943, when the Japanese finally withdrew. Meanwhile, in Europe, the American Eighth Air Force was flying a strategic bombing campaign over France and Germany. The strategic bombing campaign was always controversial, and though it was an impressive display of Allied might, it accomplished few of its objectives—except, perhaps, to exact vengeance on the Germans, who blitzed London and other English cities with bombs, V-1 ("buzz bomb") rockets, and, later, V-2 rockets. The war in Europe, everyone knew, would be won by nothing less than full-scale invasion from the west, from the coast of France, and that did not come until June 6, 1944, D Day.

As for the Pacific, the Japanese had begun to lose the war from a strategic perspective following their defeat at the Battle of Midway in June 1942, but, of course, they fought on and on, exacting a terrible toll for every inch of sea or land yielded. By July 1944 the United States had secured island bases from which to stage B-29 bombing attacks on the Japanese mainland, and Army Air Force general Curtis LeMay, having pummeled much of Europe into ashes, started in on Japan. In October 1944 Douglas MacArthur, who had evacuated the Philippines early in the war, pledging, "I shall return," returned to Leyte and cleared the island by mid-January 1945, just as marines took Iwo Jima. Okinawa fell six months later, and the United States was poised to launch an invasion of the mainland. It would ultimately be MacArthur who dictated the terms of the Japanese surrender (see JAPANESE SURRENDER DOCUMENTS, TREATY OF PEACE WITH JAPAN, and JAPANESE–UNITED STATES SECURITY TREATY).

Fall of Fortress Europe

On June 6, 1944, the United State and Britain launched an invasion of Fortress Europe, as the German Nazis had begun to call their empire of occupation. Officially code-named Operation Overlord, the long-awaited Allied invasion—which Stalin had lobbied for more and more insistently at the major Allied war conferences—hit the beaches of France's Normandy region on the morning of what the entire world was soon calling D day. Along with Russia's recent great defeat of the Germans at Stalingrad, D day marked the turning point of World War II.

U.S. general Dwight D. Eisenhower, as Supreme Allied Commander, took charge of coordinating the invasion, originating from England via the English Channel. Eisenhower and the other Allied commanders knew that Fortress Europe was at its most formidable along these western coastal regions, but they also knew that at this stage of the war, the German army was spread thinly along the coast. If the element of surprise could be maintained, it would be possible to make a beach assault where it was least anticipated and where, therefore, German defense was at its weakest. The Germans, anticipating an invasion, were unaware of the exact invasion point and therefore broadcast 50 infantry and 10 tank (Panzer) divisions across France and the Low Countries under the command of Field Marshall Gerd von Rundstedt. To ensure that these dispersed forces could not readily be transported to the point of invasion, British-based warplanes bombed rail lines, bridges, and airfields throughout France for two months preceding the assault. Then, on June 5, the night before the Normandy landings, paratroopers were dropped inland to disrupt communications. Next naval artillery began to pound the reinforced shore batteries.

At a 4 A.M. meeting held on June 5, there were serious questions about the unsettled weather. If the weather was calm enough to land a few waves of troops, then suddenly kicked up waves too high to land more, those caught on the beaches would be doomed. On the other hand, to wait would mean losing the element of surprise, and that, too, would spell defeat.

Eisenhower pondered the dilemma, nodded to his advisers, and gave the go-ahead. At low tide, in the early morning hours of June 6, 1944, the greatest amphibious invasion in the history of the world began. Five thousand Allied ships approached the Normandy coastline, which the invaders—British, Canadian, and American—had divided into beaches code-named Gold, Juno, Sword, Utah, and Omaha. The landings on all but Omaha Beach went smoothly, and the troops encountered surprisingly light resistance. At Omaha, however, which was the key for securing the landing, American soldiers encountered withering German fire that exacted a heavy toll even before many of the landing craft had unloaded. Some landing craft sank, drowning the invaders before they reached shore. Those who did hit the beach were raked by machine gun, artillery, and mortar fire. Yet even vital Omaha Beach was eventually secured, and over the next five days, 16 Allied divisions debunked at Normandy.

Fortress Europe had been breached by a combination of advanced tactics of 20th-century warfare: the achievement of Allied air superiority over a German Luftwaffe badly reduced by four years of combat, a brilliant campaign of deception and decoy, and timeless courage and determination. Considering the strategic, technological, tactical, and human forces involved, the D day operation was perhaps the single greatest battle of all time. Certainly, given the stakes involved—nothing less than the fate of humankind, or a very large segment of it, in any case—Operation Overlord was also among the most momentous battles the world has ever seen.

For the Soviet Union, however, fighting along the eastern front of what it would come to call the Great Patriotic War, it was not the much-welcomed invasion of France by its Allies that would prove crucial in halting the German juggernaut and ultimately crushing the Nazi menace in Europe; it was the Battle of Stalingrad. In fact, the Russian dictator, Joseph Stalin, and his generals were much frustrated by the numerous delays of the invasion by their Allies in the West. From the start, the Americans had been anxious to engage the enemy on his own turf, but British leaders—veterans of the bloodletting of World War I, who knew the kind of slaughter ill-laid plans could produce—had rejected a hasty, badly prepared American plan to invade the European continent early on. Instead, the Americans enlisted in British prime minister Winston Churchill's beloved North Africa campaign at a point when Germany's eastern front against Russia had become stagnant.

The year before, while Hitler's brilliant Field Marshal Erwin Rommel, the "Desert Fox," fought the Western powers to a standstill in a daring desert offensive, the Führer went ahead with his plans to invade Russia, against the advice of his general staff. Having launched the invasion, Hitler was determined to crush the Soviets, and he ordered a drive into the Caucasus Mountains, only to be held back by rains until June 1943. Encouraged by his earlier successes, Hitler decided to mount a major attack on Stalingrad, as well as the Caucasus, when the rains let up. By fall, victory seemed certain.

Then the Russians struck back. Like Napoleon before him, Hitler became mired in the mud of the harsh Russian winter, and the Russians knew how to take advantage of such weather. In a tremendous counterstrike at Stalingrad, the Soviets encircled Hitler's Sixth Army, and more than 200,000 German troops were utterly annihilated.

In North Africa around then, the crack German Afrika Korps under the command of Rommel, in part as a result of the massive Allied bombing raids on the German homeland, fell to the British and American armies. It was about time. After suffering initial defeat, the United States had brought in one of its best commanders, General George S. Patton, who, in often contentious collaboration with British commander Field Marshal Sir Bernard Law Montgomery, ultimately defeated Rommel and pushed on from North Africa to begin the invasion of Europe by way of Italy. Patton was called back to England now that the West was in a position to launch the D day invasion. Long before D day, however, it was clear that Germany had all but lost the war in the east. Russia began its march on Berlin, fighting against desperately determined but retreating German forces.

The D day invasion was the realization of every German general's worst nightmare: a full-scale two-front war. One month after the Allies first secured a beachhead in France, Patton's Third Army managed to break out and begin an incredible dash across Europe toward Berlin. In the background, the Big Three leaders—Stalin, Churchill, and Roosevelt—were engaging in a diplomatic struggle over the potential spoils of the war, with both Churchill and Stalin realizing that whoever reached Berlin first would be in a position to dominate the peace settlement. Roosevelt, fearful of alienating Stalin, whose troops were doing a good deal of the dying in Europe, ordered Eisenhower to divert his invasion from the race on Berlin to first liberate Paris, which was of no strategic importance, as a frustrated George Patton pointed out again and again.

On July 20, 1944, worried German generals almost succeeded in assassinating Hitler. On August 25 the Allied forces liberated Paris. By the fall, they had driven the Germans back into the Fatherland.

Faced with disaster, Hitler again ignored the advice of his general staff and attempted one last, desperate counteroffensive. At the Battle of the Bulge on December 15, 1944, U.S. troops retreated for eight days before regrouping and routing the German army. Two weeks later, the Red Army crossed the Vistula. As both sides advanced toward Berlin, Hitler shot himself rather than surrender. The war in Europe was at an end. The Allies moved into Germany, dividing it up into zones of occupation, with Berlin (also divided into zones) falling entirely within the Soviet-controlled area. Just as Churchill feared, Stalin immediately began attempting to dictate the terms of the "peace." (See GERMAN ACT OF MILITARY SURRENDER, and ALLIED STATEMENTS ON THE OCCUPATION OF GERMANY.)

Aftermath

Three major developments during World War II would have a special impact on postwar diplomacy. The first, which Allied troops discovered as they carried out the occupation of a defeated Nazi Germany, defied belief. It would take a powerful hold on the postwar world's imagination and lead it to question the very notion of "civilization." Toward the end of World War II, British troops, hardened by battling their way across Europe into the heart of Nazi Germany, were horrified when they marched up to the Bergen-Belsen concentration camp in Lower Saxony, where they found emaciated and diseased Jewish prisoners, together with some 13,000 unburied corpses. They had just discovered the results of the genocidal policy the Nazis called the "final solution" to the "Jewish problem," which a stunned world—after years of investigations into the origins, operation, and unspeakable outcome of the policy, as well as manhunts for those responsible and public trials of those who were caught—would come to call the Holocaust.

The 20th century had, of course, no monopoly on unbridled intolerance and irrational hatred, but what the century did have was the political and technological means to act upon such collective psychopathologies with unprecedented viciousness, thoroughness, and bureaucratic efficiency, all on a scale that is almost inconceivably vast. Jews have been persecuted for some 1,800 years, but between 1933 and 1945, Adolf Hitler directed the murder of more Jews than had been killed in 18 centuries of pogroms and organized persecution. Some 6 million human beings, two-thirds of Europe's Jewish population, became victims of the systematic genocide of an entire race in specially designed and equipped "death camps."

During the war there had been Jewish resistance to the mass roundups and deportations to concentration camps that accompanied this policy. Most famous perhaps was the fight for the Warsaw Ghetto, but outbreaks of resistance also occurred at 17 of the Nazi concentration camps, notably Sobibor and Treblinka, and in the ghettos of Vilna, Kaunas, Minsk, and Slutsk. As many as 60,000 Jews served in partisan resistance units from North Africa to Belorussia. But it was to no avail.

Worse, the Allies, who doubtless, were unaware of the full genocidal extent of the execution programs, did nothing to prevent the murders and persecution of which they were aware. Only after the liberation of Europe, as British, Soviet, and American forces marched into camp after camp, did the horror of the deaths of 6 million Jews and of some 3 million more ethnic civilians and prisoners of war the Nazis considered "subhuman" become all too apparent.

Diplomatically, the result of the discovery was the convening of the Nuremberg Trials, which investigated the Nazi leadership as war criminals and led ultimately to the 1948 GENEVA CONVENTION ON THE PREVENTION AND PUNISHMENT OF THE CRIME OF GENOCIDE. These set a precedent for the treatment of those guilty of "crimes against humanity" that would come into play, especially after the cold war ended, in areas as remote from World War II Germany as sub-Saharan Africa and as near to it as the newly formed ethnic territories in the Balkans.

The Holocaust also had a profound affect on the Middle East. As European Ashkenazi Jews poured into Palestine at war's end, they provided an immense boost to the Zionist movement. Determined never again to suffer the fate of their relatives under the Nazis and supported in that determination by the Allies in general, they joined the political and action wings of the movement, including such underground terrorist organizations as the Irgun, and pushed Zionist agitation to new levels.

The British still administered Palestine under its World War I mandate and were in many ways responsible for the current troubles, the BALFOUR DECLARATION having had the effect of promising the Jews the same territory Britain promised the Arabs in the Great War. Now, as violence escalated between Arab and Jew in Palestine, the British passed the problem on to the newly created United Nations. There sympathy for the Jewish plight during the war was marked, and in 1948 the United Nations partitioned Palestine into Jewish and Arab sections. The Zionists immediately proclaimed the new state of Israel, sparking the first in a long series of Arab-Israeli wars, which would last beyond the coming cold war.

The second major development was the decision by U.S. president Harry S. Truman not to invade Japan but instead to order the world's first (and so far only) nuclear attacks. No political leader had ever faced that kind of decision before, and as a result of Truman's choice, on August 6, 1945, the United States unleashed on the Japanese city of Hiroshima the most destructive weapon ever devised. Three days later, U.S. Army Air Force B-29s dropped a second A-bomb on Nagasaki. The nuclear attacks forced a Japanese surrender and brought World War II to a close, even as they made possible the age of potential, and sometimes imminent, worldwide destruction called the cold war.

Since everyone mistakenly assumed that German scientists, under the leadership of the brilliant theoretical physicist Werner Heisenberg, had a head start in what became the first nuclear arms race, the weapon's creation became the object of perhaps the world's most famous secret project. Even before the war, the Hungarian-born physicist Leo Szillard, who in 1938 had first imagined that nuclear fission could produce an atomic chain reaction capable of releasing enormous amounts of energy, had prevailed upon no less a prominent scientist than Albert Einstein to speak to President Franklin Roosevelt about the destructive possibilities of such a weapon and to warn him that German scientists were perfectly capable of producing an atomic bomb. On December 6, 1941, just one day before Japan's attack on Pearl Harbor, Roosevelt signed a secret order authorizing the Manhattan Project to investigate the feasibility of nuclear weapons and to create a fission bomb. The project was headed by Brigadier General Leslie R. Groves, the army engineer who directed construction of the Pentagon.

Groves's assignment was stated in starkly simple terms: develop a bomb before the Nazis do. Groves assembled a group of scientists directed by physicist Robert J. Oppenheimer, who spent months confined to a secret base at Los Alamos, New Mexico, feverishly experimenting with the "gadget," as they called it. The scientists and their gadget were backed by the costliest engineering and manufacturing program the United States government had ever undertaken to develop a single weapon.

As it turned out, Heisenberg never had much faith in the possibility of producing the "secret weapon" Hitler often hinted was going to win him the war at the last minute, and the German atomic program meandered off toward dead-end experiments in developing a heavy-water atomic bomb. Meanwhile, the Allies had marched toward the successful construction of an implosive device that would trigger a chain-reaction in enriched uranium. Trinity, the first test of the bomb, took place in the Alamogordo desert at 0529:45 on July 16, 1945, well after Germany had been defeated and shortly following the death of Franklin Roosevelt.

It fell then to Truman to decide whether to use the weapon against the remaining enemy, the Empire of Japan. The official explanation has always been that the Japanese, even with most of their cities already reduced to rubble by massive firebombings, even with their navy and air force effectively neutralized, steadfastly refused to accept unconditional surrender. Invading the islands, it was estimated, would cost the lives of perhaps a million Allied soldiers, not to mention the toll it would take on the Japanese themselves. Fearful, too, that Japan's refusal to submit would give Soviet dictator Stalin sufficient time to enter the war against the Japanese and claim his share of the spoils of victory as he had in Europe, Truman ordered the attack.

But during the war, a small group of scientists, including in their number many of those who had played roles in theorizing about and building the bomb, had argued against its deployment, especially against civilians, and had proposed steps that could be taken to avoid the potential for a nuclear arms race in the future. Apparently however, Roosevelt—and Truman after him—had already become enamored of the advantages they along with Winston Churchill imagined would result from an American-British nuclear monopoly. Just how much a role such musings played in Truman's decision to drop the bombs is a matter of conjecture among historians, but the United States certainly seemed at the end of the war content in the belief that it and only it possessed atomic weapons.

It was false security. Unknown to Truman and the others, Klaus Fuchs, who had worked on the Manhattan Project and was among those scientists who objected to the deployment of the bombs, passed atomic secrets to the Soviets. Stalin knew all about the bomb. He had not built one yet, but he soon would, and over the succeeding decades the USSR and the United States would create thousands upon thousands of nuclear weapons, which could be launched from almost anywhere on land, at sea, or in the air. Within a few years the victors in World War II had become prisoners of their own technology, former allies turned superpower rivals who would spend 40 years locked in a cold war diplomatic dance of death called "mutually assured destruction," which they could neither really control nor bring to a good end.

The third major wartime development to have an impact on postwar diplomacy was America's commitment to playing a major role in international affairs. Unlike at Versailles after World War I, the victors in World War II held no grand peace conference to attempt a comprehensive postwar settlement. This partly had to do with the abject failure of Versailles, partly with the "total" nature of the conflict, partly with the way it ended in two completely separate victories, and partly with the irreconcilable differences in ideology and needs of the Allies themselves. Instead of a peace conference, there was only a complete surrender and a long occupation, which degenerated into the cold war.

But also unlike at Versailles, the United States did not withdraw from the international scene, instead putting its considerable power and influence behind the creation of the United Nations (see UNITED NATIONS CHARTER) and the establishment of such international agreements as the General Agreement on Tariffs and Trade (GATT). These understandings had been arrived at during wartime Allied meetings, such as the Bretton Woods Conference, when all the parties involved still needed each other to finish the business of defeating the Axis powers. Because the United States was determined to see the understandings survive the conflict, they were not marginalized and abandoned after the war as the League of Nations had been.

However weak, tentative, and ineffectual the United Nations at first appeared, it became the underpinning of a new international order still in operation today. Likewise, such financial instruments as the World Bank (see the ARTICLES OF AGREEMENT OF THE INTERNATIONAL BANK FOR RECONSTRUCTION AND DEVELOPMENT) and GATT, despite the opposition and self-imposed exclusion of the Soviets, underwrote a global market that eventually played no small role in the fall of the communist world. This new international order, much tested, often found wanting, nevertheless outlasted the bitter postwar rivalry of the world's two new superpowers, Russia and the United States, early on brewing in Berlin.

TREATIES

Mutual Defense Treaties, Military Alliances, and Nonaggression Pacts

GERMAN-SOVIET BOUNDARY AND FRIENDSHIP TREATY

TREATY AT A GLANCE

Completed
September 28, 1939, at Moscow

Signatories
Germany and the USSR

Overview
Worried that the Nazis, who had walked over Poland in less than a month after invading on September 1, 1939, would not stop at the lines agreed to in the Hitler-Stalin Pact, Joseph Stalin menacingly called up reserves to intimidate his new ally and shore up Moscow's share of the plundered Polish lands. This led to a new agreement between the two powers, aimed at alleviating potential for friction but underscoring their mutual, if denied, distrust of one another.

Historical Background

The HITLER-STALIN PACT of August 23, 1939, had shocked much of the world, not least those communists and fellow travelers in the West who had long looked to Moscow as, if nothing else, a bulwark against fascism and the Nazis. Perhaps the Nazi invasion of Poland a week later, and the Soviet move to claim its share of the fallen country, was less shocking than it was benumbing. For so long had Europe feared something like this somewhere on the Continent from the Nazis, and for so long had the Great Powers tried to avoid it by appeasement, that the actual event itself stunned France and Great Britain into months of inaction that came to be called the Phony War. What stunned the Soviets, on the other hand, was not that Germany had finally embarked for a second time on the course to world war, since they themselves had helped pave the way, but instead the swift success of the Nazi blitzkrieg.

Clearly upset by how easily the Nazis were marching across Poland, Stalin became worried that they might well not halt at the line the two powers had prearranged in the previous year's pact partitioning Ger-

many's share of Poland from Moscow's. Within 10 days of the German invasion of September 1, the Soviet leader ordered the partial mobilization of many more reserve troops than he needed to occupy the Russian-held territory, and he boasted loudly in public venues of the Red Army's "three million men." Stalin was right, of course, to distrust Hitler, who planned to not only claim all of Poland but much of western Russia as soon as his prosecution of the war against France and Britain and his cautious High Command would allow him to turn and invade his erstwhile ally.

That was a while off, though, and when Stalin told the German ambassador on September 25 that "in the final settlement of the Polish question, anything that in the future might create friction between Germany and the Soviet Union must be avoided," Hitler was perfectly willing to dicker further with Stalin for the time being to see what Germany might get out of present Soviet fears. Three days later, Soviet foreign minister Molotov signed a new German-Soviet boundary and friendship agreement, which sought to shore up the alliance and plaster over, at least for now, the mutual distrust between the coinvaders.

Terms

Basically, the treaty granted Germany a little more of conquered Poland and a generous extension of Soviet trade in exchange for a free hand in lands farther east and for smoothing the rough spots of their partitioning. The published treaty established the status quo.

The Government of the German Reich and the Government of the U.S.S.R. consider it as exclusively their task, after the collapse of the former Polish state, to re-establish peace and order in these territories and to assure to the peoples living there a peaceful life in keeping with their national character. To this end, they have agreed upon the following:

ARTICLE I

The Government of the German Reich and the Government of the U.S.S.R. determine as the boundary of their respective national interests in the territory of the former Polish state the line marked on the attached map, which shall be described in more detail in a supplementary protocol.

ARTICLE II

Both parties recognize the boundary of the respective national interests established in Article I as definitive and shall reject any interference of third powers in this settlement.

ARTICLE III

The necessary reorganization of public administration will be effected in the areas west of the line specified in Article I by the Government of the German Reich, in the areas east of this line by the Government of the U.S.S.R.

ARTICLE IV

The Government of the German Reich and the Government of the U.S.S.R. regard this settlement as a firm foundation for a progressive development of the friendly relations between their peoples.

ARTICLE V

This treaty shall be ratified and the ratifications shall be exchanged in Berlin as soon as possible. The Treaty becomes effective upon signature.

Done in duplicate, in the German and Russian languages.

Moscow, September 28, 1939.

For the Government of the German Reich:
J. RIBBENTROP.
By authority of the Government of the U.S.S.R.:
W. MOLOTOV.

The meat of the agreement came in its secret provisions.

Confidential Protocol

The Government of the U.S.S.R. shall place no obstacles in the way of Reich nationals and other persons of German descent residing in the territories under its jurisdiction, if they desire to migrate to Germany or to the territories under German jurisdiction. It agrees that such removals shall be carried out by agents of the Government of the Reich in cooperation with the competent local authorities and that the property rights of the emigrants shall be protected.

A corresponding obligation is assumed by the Government of the German Reich in respect to the persons of Ukrainian or White Russian descent residing in the territories under its jurisdiction.

Moscow, September 28, 1939.

For the Government of the German Reich:
J. RIBBENTROP
By authority of the Government of the U.S.S.R.
MOLOTOV.

Secret Supplementary Protocol

The undersigned Plenipotentiaries declare the agreement of the Government of the German Reich and the Government of the U.S.S.R upon the following:

The Secret Supplementary Protocol signed on August 23, 1939, shall be amended in Item 1 to the effect that the territory of the Lithuanian State falls to the sphere of influence of the U.S.S.R., while, on the other hand, the province of Lublin and parts of the province of Warsaw fall to the sphere of influence of Germany (cf. the map attached to the Frontier and Friendship Treaty signed today). As soon as the Government of the U.S.S.R. shall take special measures on Lithuanian territory to protect its interests, the present German-Lithuanian border, for the purpose of a natural and simple frontier delineation, will be rectified in such a way that the Lithuanian territory situated to the southwest of the line marked on the attached map should fall to Germany.

Further it is declared that the Economic Agreements now in force between Germany and Lithuania will not be affected by the measures of the Soviet Union referred to above.

Moscow, September 28, 1939.

For the Government of the German Reich:
J. RIBBENTROP
By authority of the Government of the U.S.S.R.
V. MOLOTOV.

Secret Supplementary Protocol

The undersigned plenipotentiaries, on concluding the German Russian Frontier and Friendship Treaty, have declared their agreement on the following:

Neither party will tolerate in their territories Polish agitation that affects the territories of the other party. Both will suppress in its territories all beginnings of such agitation and will inform each other concerning suitable measures for this purpose.

Moscow, September 28,1939.

For the Government of the German Reich:

J. RIBBENTROP

By authority of the Government of the U.S.S.R.

V. MOLOTOV

Consequences

Before this second German-Soviet pact, the communist parties in the West, although long under the sway of Moscow, had been hesitant to embrace the hated Nazis they had so long considered anathema, despite Stalin's newly professed friendship. Afterward, however, they moved quickly to adopt the new party line. Publicly acknowledging the alliance, they now came out in opposition to Western military resistance to Hitler. Stalin, for his own part, would henceforth be a fearful and solicitous neighbor of the Nazi empire right up to the day Hitler launched Operation Barbarossa to invade Russia.

Meanwhile, however uneasy Stalin felt about Hitler's ultimate intentions, the Soviet dictator was not going to miss this opportunity to expand his own empire. Within a fortnight of signing the new treaty, the Soviets would occupy Latvia, Lithuania, and Estonia, those lands where Stalin had sought Hitler's blessing to continue his aggression. In just over a month, the USSR would attack Finland.

Source

J. A. S. Grenville, *The Major International Treaties, 1914–1973* (New York: Stein and Day, 1975), 199–200.

AXIS PACT
(TRIPARTITE PACT)

TREATY AT A GLANCE

Completed
September 27, 1940, at Berlin

Signatories
Germany, Italy, and Japan

Overview
The Axis Pact, or the Tripartite Pact, as it is sometimes called, served as the primary treaty in the alliance of the three major fascist powers in World War II, Germany, Italy, and Japan. Throughout the war, the world called these three countries—bent on conquest and expansion—the Axis powers, whose unconditional surrender became the goal of the Allied nations.

Historical Background

By September 1940, Germany had invaded and conquered Poland, subdued France, and launched an abortive attack on Great Britain. Adolf Hitler, frustrated by his inability to get the British to come to terms and join him in dividing up the world, was contemplating an attack on the Soviet Union, still his ally under the 1939 HITLER-STALIN PACT. But Hitler's ultimate goal was expansive Lebensraum for all ethnic Germans, and that "living space" lay to the east in the vast stretches of land belonging to Russia.

Wanting to avoid a war on two fronts, the German High Command was urging their Führer to hold off the invasion until the English question was settled, which Hitler's foreign minister Ribbentrop thought could be done better diplomatically than with the force of arms. It was in this context that Ribbentrop suggested a three-power agreement with Italy and Japan. First, it would deflect the mighty United States from Europe, where its generous support was helping to keep Great Britain in the war, to the Pacific, where Japan threatened its own security more immediately. Second, when the invasion of Russia did come, as inevitably it must, the USSR would be threatened with its own two-front war. And third, seeing the U.S. and Russia thus distracted would drive the British to despair over facing Germany completely alone and bring them to the bargaining table.

Terms

The Axis Pact, which would prove to be Ribbentrop's last diplomatic achievement, clearly fixed the sides in World War II. Article 4, referring to the Hitler-Stalin Pact, recognized Russia's erstwhile status as an ally while making it clear that the USSR was no part of the current arrangement.

✧

The governments of Germany, Italy and Japan, considering it as a condition precedent of any lasting peace that all nations of the world be given each its own proper place, have decided to stand by and co-operate with one another in regard to their efforts in greater East Asia and regions of Europe respectively wherein it is their prime purpose to establish and maintain a new order of things calculated to promote the mutual prosperity and welfare of the peoples concerned.

Furthermore, it is the desire of the three governments to extend co-operation to such nations in other spheres of the world as may be inclined to put forth endeavours along lines similar to their own, in order that their ultimate aspirations for world peace may thus be realized.

Accordingly, the governments of Germany, Italy and Japan have agreed as follows:

ARTICLE 1

Japan recognizes and respects the leadership of Germany and Italy in establishment of a new order in Europe.

593

ARTICLE 2

Germany and Italy recognize and respect the leadership of Japan in the establishment of a new order in greater East Asia.

ARTICLE 3

Germany, Italy and Japan agree to co-operate in their efforts on aforesaid lines. They further undertake to assist one another with all political, economic and military means when one of the three contracting powers is attacked by a power at present not involved in the European war or in the Chinese-Japanese conflict.

ARTICLE 4

With the view to implementing the present pact, joint technical commissions, members which are to be appointed by the respective governments of Germany, Italy and Japan will meet without delay.

ARTICLE 5

Germany, Italy and Japan affirm that the aforesaid terms do not in any way affect the political status which exists at present as between each of the three contracting powers and Soviet Russia.

ARTICLE 6

The present pact shall come into effect immediately upon signature and shall remain in force 10 years from the date of its coming into force. At the proper time before expiration of said term, the high contracting parties shall at the request of any of them enter into negotiations for its renewal.

In faith whereof, the undersigned duly authorized by their respective governments have signed this pact and have affixed hereto their signatures.

Done in triplicate at Berlin, the 27th day of September, 1940, in the 19th year of the fascist era, corresponding to the 27th day of the ninth month of the 15th year of Showa [the reign of Emperor Hirohito].

Consequences

Ultimately, the pact achieved none of the three goals for which Ribbentrop had hoped. The inclusion of Japan proved not to be a distraction for the United States so much as an excuse to enter the war in Europe. After Hitler's invasion of Russia, no second front appeared in East Asia. The USSR, unlike the U.S. and Britain, did not take up arms against the Japanese. Instead, Stalin struck the 1941 PACT OF NEUTRALITY BETWEEN THE UNION OF SOVIET SOCIALIST REPUBLICS AND JAPAN and honored that treaty until Germany had fallen and the Empire of the Rising Sun was facing certain defeat (see SOVIET DENUNCIATION OF THE PACT WITH JAPAN). And London stood as firmly set on fighting Hitler the day after as the day before he concluded the Axis Pact.

Source

J. A. S. Grenville, *The Major International Treaties, 1914–1973* (New York: Stein and Day, 1975), 202–203.

PACT OF NEUTRALITY BETWEEN THE
UNION OF SOVIET SOCIALIST REPUBLICS AND JAPAN

TREATY AT A GLANCE

Completed
April 13, 1941, Moscow

Signatories
Soviet Union and Japan

Overview
In April 1941 the Soviet Union was still the putative ally of Nazi Germany, although Joseph Stalin clearly feared a surprise attack by Hitler at any moment. Anxious to avoid the two-front war that seemed likely since Germany, Italy, and Japan had signed the Axis Pact the year before, the Soviets signed a neutrality agreement with Japan, which both parties honored till the Allied defeat of the Nazis, after which Stalin denounced the Japanese pact.

Historical Background

By September 1940 Adolf Hitler's blitzkrieg had paid large dividends. Poland was a conquered and partitioned nation, France was under the Nazi thumb, and England alone stood between him and his dreams of world domination. But the British were precisely the problem. Having defeated the vaunted Luftwaffe in the Battle of Britain and survived the London Blitz, the United Kingdom defiantly resisted Hitler's blandishments to come to peace with Germany and even to join him as an ally in further conquests.

Stymied in the west, Hitler was laying plans to turn east and attack his current ally, the Soviet Union, whose western territory Hitler coveted as Lebensraum for ethnic Germans. But there, too, he was meeting resistance from a High Command that feared a two-front war and a foreign minister who thought the British might yet be induced to relent through diplomacy. With that in mind, Hitler concluded the AXIS PACT with Italy and Japan, hoping to negate the United States's potential as a British ally by turning its attention to the danger in the Pacific, to threaten Russia itself with a two-front war from Germany in its west and Japan in the east, and finally—and thereby—to convince Britain of the hopelessness inherent in her isolation.

All three of the strategic goals of the Axis Pact would ultimately be frustrated, but most immediately and most directly, the Soviet Union avoided the trap of the Axis Pact by turning to Japan and negotiating the same kind of nonaggression treaty with that power that it had once, to the shock of the world, negotiated with Germany. Nothing in the Axis Pact prevented Japan from entering into a neutrality treaty with Russia, although the implications behind the document had clearly indicated otherwise.

At that point Japan's military leaders were debating Japan's own aggressive expansion. One school of thought suggested a northern advance of the empire against the Soviet Union's maritime provinces, just as Hitler and Foreign Minister Ribbentrop had imagined; another called for a southern advance against the French, Dutch, and British colonies in Southeast Asia. The very fact that Japan signed the pact with the Soviet Union speaks for the triumph of the southern strategists, since they would want to neutralize the Russian threat in their rear before beginning a march southward.

Terms

The treaty reads as follows:

The Presidium of the Supreme Soviet of the Union of Soviet Socialist Republics and His Majesty the Emperor of Japan, guided by a desire to strengthen peaceful and friendly relations between the two countries, have decided to conclude a pact on neutrality, for which purpose they have appointed as their Representatives:

The Presidium of the Supreme Soviet of the Union of Soviet Socialist Republics—Vyacheslav Mikhailovich Molotov, Chairman of the Council of People's Commissars and People's Commissar of Foreign Affairs of the Union of Soviet Socialist Republics;

His Majesty the Emperor of Japan—Yosuke Matsuoka, Minister of Foreign Affairs, Jusanmin, Cavalier of the Order of the Sacred Treasure of the First Class, and

Yoshitsugu Tatekawa, Ambassador Extraordinary and Plenipotentiary to the Union of Soviet Socialist Republics, Lieutenant General, Jusanmin, Cavalier of the Order of the Rising Sun of the First Class and the Order of the Golden Kite of the Fourth Class,

who, after an exchange of their credentials, which were found in due and proper form, have agreed on the following:

ARTICLE ONE

Both Contracting Parties undertake to maintain peaceful and friendly relations between them and mutually respect the territorial integrity and inviolability of the other Contracting Party.

ARTICLE TWO

Should one of the Contracting Parties become the object of hostilities on the part of one or several third powers, the other Contracting Party will observe neutrality throughout the duration of the conflict.

ARTICLE THREE

The present Pact comes into force from the day of its ratification by both Contracting Parties and remains valid for five years. In case neither of the Contracting Parties denounces the Pact one year before the expiration of the term, it will be considered automatically prolonged for the next five years.

ARTICLE FOUR

The present Pact is subject to ratification as soon as possible. The instruments of ratification shall be exchanged in Tokyo, also as soon as possible.

In confirmation whereof the above-named Representatives have signed the present Pact in two copies, drawn up in the Russian and Japanese languages, and affixed thereto their seals.

Done in Moscow on April 13, 1941, which corresponds to the 13th day of the fourth month of the 16th year of Showa.

V. MOLOTOV
YOSUKE MATSUOKA
YOSHITSUGU TATEKAWA

Consequences

Hitler was not particularly sanguine about such a development. Having gone to great lengths to keep Japan out of his affairs with the Soviets, he now invited the Japanese, through Ambassador Oshima Hiroshi, to join him in the liquidation of the Soviet empire. The plan was endorsed by Japanese foreign minister Matsuoka, but it came too late, even if Hitler was completely serious, which he may not have been. On June 22, when Hitler invaded Russia, the Japanese cabinet decided to follow its original inclinations and take advantage of German victories, rather than share in them, by now moving south to establish the Greater East-Asia Co-Prosperity Sphere.

If the Japanese thus honored the neutrality treaty, so did Stalin, leaving the fighting in the Pacific to the United States and Britain until after the defeat of Nazi Germany. Once ensconced in Berlin, however, the Soviets denounced the treaty (see SOVIET DENUNCIATION OF PACT WITH JAPAN) in case Stalin wished to seek a share of the East Asian as well as the eastern European spoils of war.

Source

J. A. S. Grenville, *The Major International Treaties, 1914–1973* (New York: Stein and Day, 1975), 186.

AGREEMENT AMONG GERMANY, ITALY, AND JAPAN ON THE JOINT PROSECUTION OF THE WAR

TREATY AT A GLANCE

Completed
December 11, 1941, at Berlin

Signatories
Germany, Italy, and Japan

Overview
Concluded four days after U.S. entry into World War II, this treaty affirmed and strengthened earlier military agreements among the Axis powers.

Historical Background

In August 1940 Britain's Royal Air Force defeated Germany's Luftwaffe in one of the greatest air duels of all time, the Battle of Britain. Hitler was forced to call off, at least for the time being, Operation Sea Lion, his plan to invade and subdue the island at the heart of the world's most extensive empire.

Forced to abandon, too, his hope that England would come to terms with Germany's triumph in Europe and join him in dividing up the world, Hitler turned to his plan to conquer Russia and grab Lebensraum for the German people. With his generals resisting the opening of a second front in Operation Barbarossa and his foreign minister, Ribbentrop, still trying to persuade him that Britain could be compelled to relent through diplomacy, Hitler welcomed Ribbentrop's latest and, as it turned out, last diplomatic achievement, the Tripartite, or "Axis," Pact (see AXIS PACT) between Germany, Italy, and Japan on September 27, 1940. Evidently, Hitler's hope was that the alliance would distract American attention from Europe, threaten Russia with the same kind of war on two fronts he himself was contemplating, and force Britain to accept the grim hopelessness of facing Germany alone. Thus, within two months, on December 18, 1940, Hitler ordered his general staff to prepare for Operation Barbarossa by early spring of 1941.

Instead, during the next year Franklin Roosevelt stepped up his aid to Britain under the Lend-Lease Act (see LEND-LEASE AGREEMENT), Hitler found himself mired in the mud on the Russian front, and the Japanese surprise attack at Pearl Harbor brought the United States—and its vast potential for making war—into the conflict against the Axis powers. With the world at war now divided between Atlantic and Pacific theaters, Germany and Italy declared war on the United States on December 11, 1941, and concluded this agreement with Japan, affirming their mutual war goals and trying to ensure that none of the powers would seek a separate peace with the Americans and British.

Terms

In their unshakable determination not to lay down arms until the common war against the United States of America and Britain has been brought to a successful conclusion, the German Government, the Italian Government, and the Japanese Government have agreed upon the following provisions:

ARTICLE 1
Germany, Italy and Japan jointly and with every means at their disposal will pursue the war forced upon them by the United States of America and Britain to a victorious conclusion.

ARTICLE 2
Germany, Italy, and Japan undertake not to conclude an armistice or peace with the United States of America or Britain except in complete mutual agreement.

ARTICLE 3
After victory has been achieved Germany, Italy, and Japan will continue in closest cooperation with a view to establishing a new and just order along the lines of the Tripartite Agreement concluded by them on September 27, 1940.

ARTICLE 4

The present Agreement will come into force with its signature, and will remain valid as long as the Tripartite Pact of September 27, 1940.

The High Contracting Parties will in good time before the expiry of this term of validity enter into consultation with each other as to the future development of their cooperation, as provided under Article 3 of the present Agreement.

Consequences

This tripartite agreement among Germany, Italy, and Japan allowed Roosevelt to concentrate U.S. aid on Britain and make the war in Europe a priority even when many, perhaps the majority, of the U. S. population—still influenced, despite World War I, by a strong historical tradition of isolation from European wars—supported the war effort in order to strike back at Japan. At the same time, this agreement did not affect the nonaggression pact earlier reached by Russia and Japan (see Pact of Neutrality between the Union of Soviet Socialist Republics and Japan and Soviet Denunciation of the Pact with Japan), and thus was Stalin free when the time came to concentrate on fighting Germany along the front in eastern Europe. And, of course, Churchill never even considered reversing Britain's course and coming to terms with Nazi Germany.

Source

J. A. S. Grenville, *The Major International Treaties, 1914–1973* (New York: Stein and Day, 1975), 203.

TREATY OF ALLIANCE BETWEEN GREAT BRITAIN AND THE SOVIET UNION

TREATY AT A GLANCE

Completed
May 26, 1942, at London

Signatories
Great Britain and the Soviet Union

Overview
Despite fundamental and profound ideological differences, Great Britain and the Soviet Union allied to fight their common enemy, Nazi Germany.

Historical Background

Traditionally, the British and Russian governments were imperial competitors, with conflicting interests in the Balkans, the Middle East, and elsewhere, and were naturally suspicious of one another. Those suspicions were only heightened when the Bolsheviks took control, and Great Britain—the country that Karl Marx himself had used in *Das Kapital*, the seminal text of communism, as his "privileged" (that is, primary) model of capitalism—joined the United States and others to send troops in support of the reactionary White Army against the Red Army during the Russian civil war. Certainly, Churchill had no more love for Stalin than did Hitler. However much the world may have been shocked when Soviet premier Stalin concluded the HITLER-STALIN PACT with Germany on August 23, 1939, and gleefully joined in the dismemberment of Poland that began World War II, his actions only reinforced Britain's long-standing dislike of Russia and the Soviets.

Despite all that, the events of 1940 and 1941 drew the two powers together. First, Germany quickly and soundly trounced France and launched an air invasion of England. Although Great Britain held out against Operation Sea Lion, Hitler, still Russia's putative ally, concluded a treaty with Japan and Italy, which in effect put Britain all alone and at war with the world. Then, on June 22, 1941, in violation of the 1939 nonaggression pact, Germany invaded the Soviet Union, with at first some apparent success. Suddenly, neither Churchill nor Stalin could afford to ignore their countries' common interest. A brief Anglo-Soviet Agreement was concluded on July 12, 1941, which was elaborated in the agreement of May 26, 1942.

Terms

It is significant that the May 26, 1942 agreement was given a duration of 20 years. Clearly, it was meant to outlast the war against Germany and did embody some principles for postwar coexistence and cooperation, including the concept of an organization of nations to help preserve peace. The treaty also stipulated that neither Great Britain nor the Soviet Union would seek "territorial aggrandizement for themselves."

His Majesty The King of Great Britain, Ireland, and the British Dominions beyond the Seas, Emperor of India, and the Presidium of the Supreme Council of the Union of Soviet Socialist Republics;

Desiring to confirm the stipulations of the Agreement between His Majesty's Government in the United Kingdom and the Government of the Union of Soviet Socialist Republics for joint action in the war against Germany, signed at Moscow on the 12th July 1941, and to replace them by a formal treaty;

Desiring to contribute after the war to the maintenance of peace and to the prevention of further aggression by Germany or the States associated with her in acts of aggression in Europe;

Desiring, moreover, to give expression to their intention to collaborate closely with one another as well as with the other United Nations at the peace settlement and during the ensuing period of reconstruction on the basis of the principles enunciated in the declaration made on the 14th August 1941 by the

599

President of the United States of America and the Prime Minister of Great Britain to which the Government of the Union of Soviet Socialist Republics has adhered;

Desiring, finally, to provide for mutual assistance in the event of an attack upon either High Contracting Party by Germany or any of the States associated with her in acts of aggression in Europe. . . .

Having decided to conclude a Treaty for that purpose . . .

Part I

ARTICLE I

In virtue of the alliance established between the United Kingdom and the Union of Soviet Socialist Republics the High Contracting Parties mutually undertake to afford one another military and other assistance and support of all kinds in the war against Germany and all those States which are associated with her in acts of aggression in Europe.

ARTICLE II

The High Contracting Parties undertake not to enter into any negotiations with the Hitlerite Government or any other Government in Germany that does not clearly renounce all aggressive intentions, and not to negotiate or conclude except by mutual consent any armistice or peace treaty with Germany or any other State associated with her in acts of aggression in Europe.

Part II

ARTICLE III

(1) The High Contracting Parties declare their desire to unite with other like-minded States in adopting proposals for common action to preserve peace and resist aggression in the post-war period.

(2) Pending the adoption of such proposals, they will after the termination of hostilities take all the measures in their power to render impossible a repetition of aggression and violation of the peace by Germany or any of the States associated with her in acts of aggression in Europe.

ARTICLE IV

Should one of the High Contracting Parties during the post-war period become involved in hostilities with Germany or any of the States mentioned in Article III(2) in consequence of an attack by that State against that party, the other High Contracting Party will at once give to the Contracting Party so involved in hostilities all the military and other support and assistance in his power.

This Article shall remain in force until the High Contracting Parties, by mutual agreement, shall recognize that it is superseded by the adoption of the proposals contemplated in Article III(1). In default of the adoption of such proposals, it shall remain in force for a period of twenty years, and thereafter until terminated by either High Contracting Party, as provided in Article VIII.

ARTICLE V

The High Contracting Parties, having regard to the interests of the security of each of them, agree to work together in close and friendly collaboration after the re-establishment of peace for the organization of security and economic prosperity in Europe.

They will take into account the interests of the United Nations in these objects, and they will act in accordance with the two principles of not seeking territorial aggrandizement for themselves and of non-interference in the internal affairs of other States.

ARTICLE VI

The High Contracting Parties agree to render one another all possible economic assistance after the war.

ARTICLE VII

Each High Contracting Party undertakes not to conclude any alliance and not to take part in any coalition directed against the other High Contracting Party.

ARTICLE VIII

The present Treaty is subject to ratification in the shortest possible time and the instruments of ratification shall be exchanged in Moscow as soon as possible.

It comes into force immediately on the exchange of the instruments of ratification and shall thereupon replace the Agreement between the Government of the Union of Soviet Socialist Republics and His Majesty's Government in the United Kingdom, signed at Moscow on the 12th July 1941.

Part I of the present Treaty shall remain in force until the reestablishment of peace between the High Contracting Parties and Germany and the Powers associated with her in acts of aggression in Europe.

Part II of the present Treaty shall remain in force for a period of twenty years. Thereafter, unless twelve months' notice has been given by either party to terminate the Treaty at the end of the said period of twenty years, it shall continue in force until twelve months after either High Contracting Party shall have given notice to the other in writing of his intention to terminate it.

In witness whereof the above-named plenipotentiaries have signed the present Treaty and have affixed thereto their seals.

Done in duplicate in London on the 26th day of May, 1942, in the English and Russian languages, both texts being equally authentic.

(L.S.) ANTHONY EDEN
(L.S.) V. MOLOTOV

Consequences

Throughout the war, the British and Soviets remained profoundly mistrustful of one another, and Stalin, desperately pressed by the German invasion, continually agitated for a "second front"—an Allied attack on German forces on the European continent—which Churchill stoutly resisted. The campaign in Italy notwithstanding, this second front would not commence until the Normandy D day landings of June 1944.

In any case, the wartime strategic alliance hardly outlasted the combat, with Churchill and Stalin con-

stantly at loggerheads in the various Big Three conferences, where Franklin Roosevelt played the mediator.
When Britain, a power much diminished by the worldwide conflict, enlisted on the "free world" side of the
cold war that followed, it was in many ways simply
reverting to form. Indeed, it was Winston Churchill
who first denounced Russia's extension of its sphere of
influence in eastern Europe as the drawing of an "iron
curtain" between its client states and their more western neighbors.

Source

J. A. S. Grenville, *The Major International Treaties, 1914–1973*
(New York: Stein and Day, 1975), 212–214.

TREATY OF FRIENDSHIP AND MUTUAL ASSISTANCE AND POSTWAR COOPERATION BETWEEN THE SOVIET UNION AND CZECHOSLOVAKIA

TREATY AT A GLANCE

Completed
December 12, 1943, at Moscow

Signatories
Soviet Union and Czechoslovakia

Overview
Disillusioned by the prospects of aid and cooperation from the Western powers, Edvard Beneš, president of the Czech government in exile, concluded a treaty of friendship and alliance with the Soviet Union, which would pave the way for the postwar subjugation of Czechoslovakia by the USSR.

Historical Background

The basis for Soviet-Czech military cooperation against Germany had been established by an agreement of July 8, 1941, and Edvard Beneš subsequently determined to strengthen and expand that agreement into a full-scale treaty of friendship and alliance. Beneš sought from all the Allies a declaration that the MUNICH PACT of September 30, 1938, by which Britain and France effectively gave the Sudetenland (a region of Czechoslovakia) to Germany, was invalid because it had been concluded under duress. The British government agreed only to declare it invalid because the Germans had subsequently broken it, whereas the Soviet government was willing to recognize the Czechoslovak government in exile and Czechoslovakia in its 1937 frontiers. The Soviets willingly declared the Munich settlement illegal, null, and void.

Terms

The treaty read as follows:

The Presidium of the Supreme Soviet of the Union of Soviet Socialist Republics and the President of the Czechoslovakian Republic, desiring to modify and supplement the Treaty of Mutual Assistance existing between the Union of Soviet Social-ist Republics and the Czechoslovakian Republic and signed in Prague on May 16, 1935, and to confirm the terms of the Agreement between the Government of the Union of Soviet Socialist Republics and the Government of the Czechoslovakian Republic concerning joint action in the war against Germany, signed July 18, 1941, in London; desiring to cooperate after the war to maintain peace and to prevent further aggression on the part of Germany and to assure permanent friendship and peaceful post-war cooperation between them, have resolved to conclude for this purpose a Treaty and . . . have agreed to the following:

ARTICLE I
The High Contracting Parties, having agreed mutually to join in a policy of permanent friendship and friendly post-war cooperation, as well as of mutual assistance, engage to extend to each other military and other assistance and support of all kinds in the present war against Germany and against all those States which are associated with it in acts of aggression in Europe.

ARTICLE 2
The High Contracting Parties engage not to enter during the period of the present war into any negotiations with the Hitler Government or with any other Government in Germany which does not clearly renounce all aggressive intentions, and not to carry on negotiations and not to conclude without mutual agreement any armistice or other treaty of peace with Germany or with any other State associated with it in acts of aggression in Europe.

ARTICLE 3
Affirming their pre-war policy of peace and mutual assistance, expressed in the treaty signed at Prague on May 16, 1935, the High Contracting Parties, in case one of them in the period after

the war should become involved in military action with Germany, which might resume its policy of "Drang nach Osten," or with any other State which might join with Germany directly or in any other form in such a war, engage to extend immediately to the other Contracting Party thus involved in military action all manner of military and other support and assistance at its disposal.

ARTICLE 4

The High Contracting Parties, having regard to the security interests of each of them, agree to close and friendly cooperation in the period after the restoration of peace and agree to act in accordance with the principles of mutual respect for their independence and sovereignty, as well as of non-interference in the internal affairs of the other State. They agree to develop their economic relations to the fullest possible extent and to extend to each other all possible economic assistance after the war.

ARTICLE 5

Each of the High Contracting Parties engages not to conclude any alliance and not to take part in any coalition directed against the other High Contracting Party.

ARTICLE 6

The present Treaty shall come into force immediately after signature and shall be ratified within the shortest possible time; the exchange of ratifications will take place in Moscow as soon as possible.

The present Treaty shall remain in force for a period of twenty years from the date of signature, and if one of the High Contracting Parties at the end of this period of twenty years does not give notice of its desire to terminate the Treaty twelve months before its expiration, it will continue to remain in force for the following five years and for each ensuing five-year period unless one of the High Contracting Parties gives notice in writing twelve months before the expiration of the current five-year period of its intention to terminate it.

PROTOCOL

On the conclusion of the Treaty of Friendship, Mutual Assistance and Post-War Cooperation between the Union of Soviet Socialist Republics and the Czechoslovakian Republic the High Contracting Parties undertake that, in the event that any third country bordering on the U.S.S.R. or the Czechoslovakian Republic and constituting in this war an object of German aggression desires to subscribe to this Treaty, it will be given the opportunity, upon the joint agreement of the Governments of the U.S.S.R. and the Czechoslovakian Republic, to adhere to this Treaty, which will thus acquire the character of a tripartite agreement.

By Authority of the Presidium of the Supreme Council of the U.S.S.R.

V. MOLOTOV

By Authority of the President of the Czechoslovakian Republic

Z. FIERLINGER

Consequences

Beneš traveled to Moscow to sign the treaty and was there confronted with Russian demands for firmly aligning postwar Czechoslovakia with the Soviet Union. To this Beneš consented in an agreement of May 8, 1944. Pursuant to the treaty of alliance, the Red Army advanced into Czechoslovakia beginning in the fall of 1944. A national uprising in Slovakia had been crushed by the Nazis, and after the Soviets expelled German forces, Czech administrators were permitted to govern only with Soviet consent. Moreover, Czechoslovakia was compelled to accede to the "will" of the Ruthenians to annex their territory to the Soviet Union. Thus, the Soviet Union gained a common frontier with Hungary and Czechoslovakia.

In general, the treaty helped set the stage for the spread of the USSR's postwar sphere of influence in eastern Europe and the birth of the cold war, in which the Soviets and their communist client states would engage in a nuclear standoff with western European democracies, Great Britain, and the United States.

Source

J. A. S. Grenville, *The Major International Treaties, 1914–1973* (New York: Stein and Day, 1975), 215–216.

TREATY OF FRIENDSHIP AND MUTUAL ASSISTANCE BETWEEN THE SOVIET UNION AND THE FRENCH REPUBLIC

TREATY AT A GLANCE

Completed
December 10, 1944, at Moscow

Signatories
Soviet Union and the Provisional Government
of the French Republic

Overview
This was the first formal alliance treaty between the Allies to recognize the provisional French government of Charles de Gaulle.

Historical Background

Charles de Gaulle, who had served as undersecretary of defense and war in Paul Reynaud's wartime government, fled to England when France fell to the Nazis and the collaborationist Marshal Pétain set up his Vichy regime. From England de Gaulle broadcast to his French compatriots numerous appeals to continue the war under his leadership, and a Vichy court-martial tried and sentenced him in absentia to death, deprived him of military rank, and confiscated his property. With no political status, virtually unknown in both England and France, de Gaulle turned a handful of haphazardly recruited volunteers into the Free French Forces and gained national recognition through his judicious use of those forces, his London broadcasts, and his contacts with the resistance movement in France through both his own forces and those of the British Secret Service.

In London, however, de Gaulle's relationship with the British and, later, the United States was never a particularly happy one, and he exacerbated the problems by his political misjudgments and his Gallic touchiness. In 1943 he moved to Algiers, where he joined General Henri Giraud at the head of the French Committee of National Liberation. Waging a political war against Giraud even as the Free French fought Germany, de Gaulle succeeded on both fronts, returning in triumph from Algiers to Paris after its liberation by the Allies as president of his shadow government. Only then did he receive full recognition by the Allied powers, first among them Stalin's USSR.

Terms

The treaty concluded between the provisional government of the French Republic and the Soviet Union not only accorded Charles de Gaulle's government recognition but set forth terms of postwar cooperation, which included France's integration into the so-called United Nations, which at the time meant the wartime Allies united against Germany and Japan.

> The Presidium of the Supreme Soviet of the Union of Soviet Socialist Republics and the Provisional Government of the French Republic, determined to prosecute jointly and to the end the war against Germany, convinced that once victory is achieved, the reestablishment of peace on a stable basis and its prolonged maintenance in the future will be conditioned upon the existence of close collaboration between them and with all the United Nations; having resolved to collaborate in the cause of the creation of an international system of security for the effective maintenance of general peace and for ensuring the harmonious development of relations between nations; desirous of confirming the mutual obligations resulting from the exchange of letters of September 20, 1941, concerning joint actions in the war against Germany; convinced that the conclusion of an alliance between the U.S.S.R. and France corresponds to the sentiments and interests of both peoples, the demands of war, and the requirements of peace and economic reconstruction in full conformity with the aims which the United Nations have set themselves, have decided to conclude a Treaty to this effect and appointed as their plenipotentiaries . . .

ARTICLE I

Each of the High Contracting Parties shall continue the struggle on the side of the other party and on the side of the United Nations until final victory over Germany. Each of the High Contracting Parties undertakes to render the other party aid and assistance in this struggle with all the means at its disposal.

ARTICLE II

The High Contracting Parties shall not agree to enter into separate negotiations with Germany or to conclude without mutual consent any armistice or peace treaty either with the Hitler Government or with any other Government or authority set up in Germany for the purpose of the continuation or support of the policy of German aggression.

ARTICLE III

The High Contracting Parties undertake also, after the termination of the present war with Germany, to take jointly all necessary measures for the elimination of any new threat coming from Germany, and to obstruct such actions as would make possible any new attempt at aggression on her part.

ARTICLE IV

In the event either of the High Contracting Parties finds itself involved in military operations against Germany, whether as a result of aggression committed by the latter or as a result of the operation of the above Article III, the other party shall at once render it every aid and assistance within its power.

ARTICLE V

The High Contracting Parties undertake not to conclude any alliance and not to take part in any coalition directed against either of the High Contracting Parties.

ARTICLE VI

The High Contracting Parties agree to render each other every possible economic assistance after the war, with a view to facilitating and accelerating reconstruction of both countries, and in order to contribute to the cause of world prosperity.

ARTICLE VII

The present Treaty does not in any way affect obligations undertaken previously by the High Contracting Parties in regard to third States in virtue of published treaties.

ARTICLE VIII

The present Treaty, whose Russian and French texts are equally valid, shall be ratified and ratification instruments shall be exchanged in Paris as early as possible. It comes into force from the moment of the exchange of ratification instruments and shall be valid for twenty years. If the Treaty is not denounced by either of the High Contracting Parties at least one year before the expiration of this term, it shall remain valid for an unlimited time; each of the Contracting Parties will be able to terminate its operation by giving notice to that effect one year in advance. . . .

On the authorization of the Presidium of the Supreme Soviet of the U.S.S.R.

MOLOTOV

On the authorization of the Provisional Government of the French Republic.

BIDAULT

Consequences

Early support from Russia helped cement the strength of the Communists, who had been prominent in the French Resistance, in the postwar provisional governments, and in what had become by November 1946 the Fourth French Republic. De Gaulle headed two of those provisional governments in succession, but, irritated at the left-wing political parties forming the Fourth Republic, resigned abruptly on January 20, 1946. Hostile to the new French constitution, the French party system, and especially the French Communists' warm relationship with Moscow, despite the fact that the USSR had early recognized the republic's legitimacy in the agreement he pushed on the Allies, de Gaulle remained in opposition until 1958, when he returned to capture the leadership of the France in the wake of the crisis in Algiers.

Source
J. A. S. Grenville, *The Major International Treaties, 1914–1973* (New York: Stein and Day, 1975), 216–217.

YALTA AGREEMENT

TREATY AT A GLANCE

Completed
February 11, 1945, at Yalta, USSR (present-day Ukraine)

Signatories
Soviet Union, United States, and Great Britain

Overview
As World War II wound down in Europe, the United States and Great Britain pressed for Soviet involvement in the continuing war against Japan. This document secured a Soviet pledge to declare war.

Historical Background

As the "Big Three"—Franklin Roosevelt, Winston Churchill, and Joseph Stalin—concluded in the REPORT OF THE YALTA (CRIMEA) CONFERENCE on February 11, 1945, "Nazi Germany [was] doomed." However, the war in the Pacific, while its outcome was no longer seriously in doubt, ground on fiercely. The Japanese cause, too, was doomed, but the Japanese military continued to fight at great cost to themselves and to the Allies. Invasion of the Japanese mainland was inevitable, but the Allied experience in taking back the Japanese-held islands of the Pacific suggested that the Japanese would resist invasion virtually to the last man.

Hitherto, the Soviets had refrained from declaring war on Japan, for Stalin had everything he could do to resist provoking a German invasion of his country, and when it came, to avoid fighting his own two-front war. Having incurred the greatest losses of all the powers involved in the war, the Soviets had no desire to turn from an incalculably dear victory over Germany to help Britain and the United States finish off Japan. Franklin Roosevelt, however, persuaded Stalin to declare war on Japan "two or three months after Germany has surrendered," in return for Soviet acquisition of southern Sakhalin Island and the Kuril Islands (the territories lost in the Russo-Japanese War of 1904–05) and Soviet dominance in Outer Mongolia and Manchuria.

Terms

The Yalta Agreement read in total as follows:

Yalta Agreement on the Kuriles and Entry of the Soviet Union in the War against Japan, 11 February 1945

The leaders of the three Great Powers—the Soviet Union, the United States of America and Great Britain—have agreed that in two or three months after Germany has surrendered and the war in Europe has terminated the Soviet Union shall enter into the war against Japan on the side of the Allies on condition that:

1. The *status quo* in Outer Mongolia (The Mongolian People's Republic) shall be preserved;

2. The former rights of Russia violated by the treacherous attack of Japan in 1904 shall be restored, viz:

(a) the southern part of Sakhalin as well as the islands adjacent to it shall be returned to the Soviet Union,

(b) the commercial port of Dairen shall be internationalized, the pre-eminent interests of the Soviet Union in this port being safeguarded and the lease of Port Arthur as a naval base of the U.S.S.R. restored,

(c) the Chinese-Eastern Railroad and the South-Manchurian Railroad which provides an outlet to Dairen shall be jointly operated by the establishment of a joint Soviet-Chinese Company, it being understood that the pre-eminent interests of the Soviet Union shall be safeguarded and that China shall retain full sovereignty in Manchuria;

3. The Kuril islands shall be handed over to the Soviet Union.

It is understood that the agreement concerning Outer Mongolia and the ports and railroads referred to above will require concurrence of Generalissimo Chiang Kai-shek. The President will take measures in order to obtain this concurrence on advice from Marshal Stalin.

The Heads of the three Great Powers have agreed that these claims of the Soviet Union shall be unquestionably fulfilled after Japan has been defeated.

For its part the Soviet Union expresses its readiness to conclude with the National Government of China a pact of friendship and alliance between the U.S.S.R. and China with its armed forces for the purpose of liberating China from the Japanese yoke.

February 11, 1945

J. STALIN
FRANKLIN D. ROOSEVELT
WINSTON S. CHURCHILL

Consequences

The Yalta Agreement turned out to be a very good deal for the Soviet Union. The dreaded invasion of Japan never occurred. Instead, the United States' Manhattan Project produced atomic bombs, which were dropped on the Japanese cities of Hiroshima (August 6, 1945) and Nagasaki (August 9), devastating them. President Harry S. Truman's decision to drop the bombs was in fact partly influenced by fears of increased Soviet sway in Japan should Russia have gotten involved in an invasion.

In any case, the Soviets, who had delayed declaring war on Japan within the time frame specified by the Yalta Agreement, quickly did so now, on August 8, two days after Hiroshima. On August 10, the Japanese indicated acceptance of most of the Allied surrender terms, and five days later bowed to the final American demand, that the emperor would be subject to the Supreme Allied Commander. The Soviets reaped the benefits of the Yalta Agreement without having to fight the Japanese.

Source

J. A. S. Grenville, *The Major International Treaties, 1914–1973* (New York: Stein and Day, 1975), 230.

TREATY OF FRIENDSHIP AND ALLIANCE BETWEEN CHINA AND THE SOVIET UNION

TREATY AT A GLANCE

Completed
August 14, 1945, at Moscow

Signatories
Republic of China and the Soviet Union

Overview
After the Soviets invaded Manchuria to attack the Japanese there, they negotiated an after-the-fact alliance with Nationalist China.

Historical Background

Japan and Russia hotly contested Manchuria as an imperialist prize at the end of the 19th century. In 1898 Russia managed to acquire from China a 25-year lease of the Liaodong (Liaotung) Peninsula as well as the right to build a connecting railway from the Russian ports of Dairen and Port Arthur to the Chinese Eastern Railway. Conflict between Russian and Japanese interests in Manchuria (and Korea) ignited the Russo-Japanese War of 1904–05, which resulted in the defeat of Russia and the cession to Japan of all its interests in southern Manchuria (see TREATY OF PORTSMOUTH).

After the Chinese Revolution of 1911, Manchuria came under the nominal control of the local warlord, Zhang Zuolin (Chang Tso-lin), who granted the Japanese concessions in the region in return for military support. In 1915 China extended Japan's lease on the territory of Gunagdong (Kwangtung; at the tip of the Liaodong Peninsula) for 99 years and gave to Japan extensive civil and commercial privileges throughout Manchuria. During the long conflict following the 1911 revolution, Japan gained an increasingly strong hold over Manchuria, culminating in the creation of the puppet state of Manchukuo out of the three Manchurian provinces in 1932.

From 1932 to 1945, Manchuria was under Japanese rule, but as World War II wound down, Joseph Stalin, at the Yalta Conference (see YALTA AGREEMENT and REPORT OF THE YALTA [CRIMEA] CONFERENCE) of February 1945, demanded the restoration of all former Russian rights and privileges in Manchuria in return for Soviet entry into the Pacific war. The Allies agreed, and on August 8 the Soviet Union—seeking a say in the postwar settlement concerning the Far East—declared war on Japan; it invaded Manchuria the next day. Japan surrendered to the Allies on August 15, one day after the Soviets concluded the Treaty of Friendship and Alliance with China.

Terms

The treaty read in part as follows:

I. TREATY OF FRIENDSHIP AND ALLIANCE

The President of the National Government of the Republic of China and the Presidium of the Supreme Soviet of the Union of Soviet Socialist Republics,

Being desirous of strengthening the friendly relations which have always prevailed between the Republic of China and the Soviet Union, by means of an alliance and by good neighborly postwar collaboration;

Determined to assist each other in the struggle against aggression on the part of the enemies of the United Nations in this World War and to collaborate in the common war against Japan until that country's unconditional surrender;

Expressing their unswerving resolve to collaborate in maintaining peace and security for the benefit of the peoples of both countries and of all peace-loving nations . . . have agreed as follows:

ARTICLE 1

The High Contracting Parties undertake jointly with the other United Nations to prosecute the war against Japan until final victory is achieved. The High Contracting Parties mutually undertake to afford one another all necessary military and other assistance and support in this war.

ARTICLE 2

The High Contracting Parties undertake not to enter into separate negotiations with Japan or conclude, except by mutual consent, any armistice or peace treaty either with the present Japanese Government or any other Government or authority set up in Japan that does not clearly renounce all aggressive intentions.

ARTICLE 3

On the conclusion of the war against Japan, the High Contracting Parties undertake to carry out jointly all the measures in their power to render impossible a repetition of aggression and violation of the peace by Japan.

Should either of the High Contracting Parties become involved in hostilities with Japan in consequence of an attack by the latter against that party, the other High Contracting Party will at once render to the High Contracting Party so involved in hostility all the military and other support and assistance in its power.

This Article shall remain in force until such time as, at the request of both High Contracting Parties, responsibility for the prevention of further aggression by Japan is placed upon the "United Nations" Organization.

ARTICLE 4

Each High Contracting Party undertakes not to conclude any alliance and not to take part in any coalition directed against the other Contracting Party.

ARTICLE 5

The High Contracting Parties, having regard to the interests of the security and economic development of each of them, agree to work together in close and friendly collaboration after the reestablishment of peace and to act in accordance with the principles of mutual respect for each other's sovereignty and territorial integrity and non-intervention in each other's internal affairs.

ARTICLE 6

The High Contracting Parties agree to afford one another all possible economic assistance in the post-war period in order to facilitate and expedite the rehabilitation of both countries and to make their contribution to the prosperity of the world.

ARTICLE 7

Nothing in this Treaty should be interpreted in such a way as to prejudice the rights and duties of the High Contracting Parties as Members of the Organization of the "United Nations."

ARTICLE 8

The present Treaty is subject to ratification in the shortest possible time. The instruments of ratification shall be exchanged in Chungking as soon as possible.

The Treaty comes into force immediately upon ratification, and shall remain in force for thirty years. Should neither of the High Contracting Parties make, one year before the date of the Treaty's expiry, a statement of its desire to denounce it, the Treaty will remain in force for an unlimited period, provided that each High Contracting Party may invalidate it by announcing its intention to do so to the other Contracting Party one year in advance.

Exchange of Notes

No. 1

In connection with the signing on this date of the Treaty of Friendship and Alliance between China and the Union of Soviet Socialist Republics, I have the honour to place on record that the following provisions are understood by both Contracting Parties as follows:

1. In accordance with the spirit of the above-mentioned Treaty and to implement its general idea and its purposes, the Soviet Government agrees to render China moral support and assist her with military supplies and other material resources, it being understood that this support and assistance will go exclusively to the National Government as the Central Government of China.

2. During the negotiations on the ports of Dairen and Port Arthur and on the joint operation of the Chinese Changchun Railway, the Soviet Government regarded the Three Eastern Provinces as part of China and again affirmed its respect for the complete sovereignty of China over the Three Eastern Provinces and recognition of their territorial and administrative integrity.

3. With regard to recent events in Sinkiang, the Soviet Government confirms that, as stated in Article 5 of the Treaty of Friendship and Alliance, it has no intention of interfering in the internal affairs of China . . .

No. 3

In view of the frequently manifested desire for independence of the people of Outer Mongolia, the Chinese Government states that, after the defeat of Japan, if this desire is confirmed by a plebiscite of the people of Outer Mongolia, the Chinese Government will recognize the independence of Outer Mongolia within her existing frontiers. . . .

II. AGREEMENT BETWEEN THE CHINESE REPUBLIC AND THE UNION OF SOVIET SOCIALIST REPUBLICS ON THE CHINESE CHANGCHUN RAILWAY

The President of the National Government of the Republic of China and the Presidium of the Supreme Soviet of the U.S.S.R. being desirous of strengthening, on the basis of complete regard for the rights and interests of each of the two parties, friendly relations and economic ties between the two countries, have agreed as follows:

ARTICLE 1

After the expulsion of the Japanese armed forces from the Three Eastern Provinces of China, the main trunk lines of the Chinese Eastern Railway and the South Manchurian Railway leading from the station of Manchouli to the station of Pogranichnaya and from Harbin to Dairen and Port Arthur, shall be combined to form a single railway system to be known as "Chinese Changchun Railway," and shall become the joint property of the U.S.S.R. and the Chinese Republic and be jointly exploited by them. Only such lands and branch lines shall become joint property and be jointly exploited as were constructed by the Chinese Eastern Railway while it was under Russian and joint Soviet-Chinese management, and by the South Manchurian Railway while under Russian management, and which are intended to serve direct needs of those railways. Ancillary undertakings directly serving the needs of those railways and constructed during the above-mentioned periods shall also be included. All other railway branch lines, ancillary undertakings and lands will be the exclusive property of the Chinese Government. The joint exploitation of the above-mentioned railways shall be effected by a single administration under Chinese sovereignty as a purely commercial transport undertaking . . .

III. AGREEMENT ON THE PORT OF DAIREN

Whereas a Treaty of Friendship and Alliance has been concluded between the Chinese Republic and the Union of Soviet Socialist Republics, and whereas the U.S.S.R. has guaranteed to respect the sovereignty of China over the Three Eastern Provinces as an inalienable part of China, the Chinese Republic, in order to protect the interests of the Union of Soviet Socialist Republics in Dairen as a port for the import and export of goods, hereby agrees:

1. To proclaim Dairen a free port, open to the trade and shipping of all countries.

2. The Chinese Government agrees to allocate docks and warehouse accommodation in the said free port to be leased to the U.S.S.R. under a separate agreement.

Protocol

1. The Government of China when requested to do so by the Soviet Union shall grant the Soviet Union, freely and without consideration, a thirty years' lease of one-half of all harbour installations and equipment, the other half of the harbour installations and equipment remaining the property of China.

IV. AGREEMENT ON PORT ARTHUR

In accordance with the Sino-Soviet Treaty of Friendship and Alliance and as an addition thereto, both Contracting Parties have agreed on the following:

1. In order to strengthen the security of China and the U.S.S.R. and prevent a repetition of aggression on the part of Japan, the Government of the Chinese Republic agrees to the joint use by both Contracting Parties of Port Arthur as a naval base. . . .

V. AGREEMENT ON RELATIONS BETWEEN THE SOVIET COMMANDER-IN-CHIEF AND THE CHINESE ADMINISTRATION FOLLOWING THE ENTRY OF SOVIET FORCES INTO THE TERRITORY OF THE THREE EASTERN PROVINCES OF CHINA IN CONNECTION WITH THE PRESENT JOINT WAR AGAINST JAPAN

The President of the National Government of the Chinese Republic and the Presidium of the Supreme Soviet of the Union of Soviet Socialist Republics, being desirous that after the entry of Soviet forces into the territory of the Three Eastern Provinces of China in connection with the present joint war of China and the U.S.S.R. against Japan, relations between the Soviet Commander-in-Chief and the Chinese administration conform with the spirit of friendship and alliance existing between both countries, have agreed on the following:

1. After the entry, as a result of military operations, of Soviet troops into the territory of the Three Eastern Provinces of China, the supreme authority and responsibility in the zone of military activity in all matters relating to the conduct of the war shall, during the period necessary for conducting such operations, be vested in the Commander-in-Chief of the Soviet Armed Forces.

2. A representative of the National Government of the Chinese Republic and a staff shall be appointed in any recaptured territory, who shall:

(a) Organize and control, in accordance with the laws of China, the administration on the territory freed from the enemy;

(b) Assist in establishing cooperation in restored territories between the Chinese armed forces, whether regular or irregular, and the Soviet armed forces;

(c) Ensure the active collaboration of the Chinese administration with the Soviet Commander-in-Chief and, in particular, issue corresponding instructions to the local authorities, being guided by the requirements and desires of the Soviet Commander-in-Chief.

3. A Chinese Military Mission shall be appointed to the Headquarters of the Soviet Commander-in-Chief for the purpose of maintaining contact between the Soviet Commander-in-Chief and the representative of the National Government of the Chinese Republic.

4. In zones that are under the supreme authority of the Soviet Commander-in-Chief, the administration of the National Government of the Chinese Republic for restored territories shall maintain contact with the Soviet Commander-in-Chief through a representative of the National Government of the Chinese Republic.

5. As soon as part of a recaptured territory ceases to be a zone of direct military operations, the National Government of the Chinese Republic shall assume complete power in respect |of civil affairs and shall render the Soviet Commander-in-Chief all assistance and support through its civil and military organs.

6. All members of the Soviet armed forces on Chinese territory shall be under the jurisdiction of the Soviet Commander-in-Chief. All Chinese citizens whether civil or military, shall be under Chinese jurisdiction. . . .

Consequences

For the Nationalist Chinese, the treaty seemed an expedient means of ousting Puyi (P'u-yi), the last Qing (Manchu) emperor, whom the Japanese had set up as "chief executive" of Manchuria renamed Manchukuo. However, Premier Stalin wasted no time in exploiting the country, appropriating food, gold bullion, industrial goods, and other supplies. Even worse for the Nationalist Chinese and despite the explicit provisions of the "Exchange of Notes" subjoined to the Treaty of Friendship and Alliance, the Soviets aided Chinese Communist forces in occupying Manchuria. This greatly contributed to the Communist victory over the Nationalists in 1948.

Source

J. A. S. Grenville and Bernard Waserstein, eds., *The Major International Treaties Since 1945* (London and New York: Methuen, 1987), 51–54.

Peace Treaties and Truces

GERMAN ACT OF MILITARY SURRENDER

TREATY AT A GLANCE

Completed
May 8, 1945, at Berlin

Signatories
Supreme Commander of the Allied Expeditionary Force,
the Supreme Commander of the Red Army, and
the German High Command

Overview
With Germany being overrun by Allied armies east and west, the Nazi leadership rushed to surrender to the American forces immediately upon news that Hitler had committed suicide in his bunker in Berlin. The Nazi High Command was forced to formally surrender as well to the Russians now occupying the German capital. Germany was utterly defeated, its surrender was unconditional, and the war in Europe was at an end.

Historical Background

In February 1945 German resistance to the Allied invasion of Europe was near its end. Despite the fact that the Allied advance from the west had been stalled for six weeks by Hitler's last offensive in the Battle of the Bulge, a number of Soviet and Western leaders were already—and openly—describing the last campaigns of the war in Europe as a "land grab" aimed as much against their suspicious co-powers as against the Germans.

As D day invasion commander General Dwight D. Eisenhower moved inexorably eastward, he took pains to reassure the Soviets rushing west toward Berlin. He deflected George S. Patton's tanks, which had been moving since D day through France with surprising speed and military aplomb, from the German capital and took time to needlessly liberate Paris. What many historians consider Curtis LeMay's cruel and unnecessary firebombing of Dresden was part of the same effort to reassure a Stalin who blandly stated, "Berlin has lost its former strategic importance" while making a beeline to the city. Churchill, no fool for "Friend Joe," pleaded with the United States for a rapid thrust to take Berlin and Prague, but Eisenhower—backed by the man in charge of all Allied efforts, George Marshall—stuck to military matters alone and even recalled troops when they exceeded their already determined occupation zones in April. Meanwhile, the Soviets took Vienna, then Königsburg, and on April 25 surrounded Berlin.

Hitler in despair damned Germany itself as unworthy of his leadership and committed suicide in his Berlin bunker on April 30. Taking up command, Admiral Dönitz rushed to surrender to the Western armies, where he rightly reasoned he would get a better deal for his troops and his country. The Soviets, intent on revenge and reprisal, refused to recognize the Nazi surrender on May 7 at Eisenhower's headquarters. Instead, Germany was forced to surrender a second time on a Soviet V-E Day, May 8, in Berlin itself.

Terms

The surrender was, as the Allies had demanded from the beginning, complete and unconditional.

611

German Act of Military Surrender
May 8, 1945

1. We the undersigned, acting by authority of the German High Command, hereby surrender unconditionally to the Supreme Commander, Allied Expeditionary Force and simultaneously to the Supreme High Command of the Red Army all forces on land, at sea, and in the air who are at this date under German control.

2. The German High Command will at once issue orders to all German military, naval and air authorities and to all forces under German control to cease active operations at 2301 hours Central European time on 8th May 1945, to remain in all positions occupied at that time and to disarm completely, handing over their weapons and equipment to the local allied commanders or officers designated by Representatives of the Allied Supreme Commands. No ship, vessel, or aircraft is to be scuttled, or any damage done to their hull, machinery or equipment, and also to machines of all kinds, armament, apparatus, and all the technical means of prosecution of war in general.

3. The German High Command will at once issue to the appropriate commanders, and ensure the carrying out of any further orders issued by the Supreme Commander, Allied Expeditionary Force and by the Supreme Command of the Red Army.

4. This act of military surrender is without prejudice to, and will be superseded by any general instrument of surrender imposed by, or on behalf of the United Nations and applicable to GERMANY and the German armed forces as a whole.

5. In the event of the German High Command or any of the forces under their control failing to act in accordance with this Act of Surrender, the Supreme Commander, Allied Expeditionary Force and the Supreme High Command of the Red Army will take such punitive or other action as they deem appropriate.

6. This Act is drawn up in the English, Russian and German languages. The English and Russian are the only authentic texts.

Signed at Berlin on the 8th day of May, 1945

VON FRIEDEBURG
KEITEL
STUMPFF
On behalf of the German High Command

IN THE PRESENCE OF:

A.W.TEDDER
On behalf of the Supreme Commander
Allied Expeditionary Force
GEORGI ZHUKOV
On behalf of the Supreme High Command
of the Red Army

At the signing also were present as witnesses:

F. DE LATTRE-TASSIGNY
General Commander in Chief
First French Army
CARL SPAATZ
General, Commander United States
Strategic Air Force

Consequences

The war in Europe was over, and the Allies began jockeying for position in a postwar world.

Source
Avalon Project at the Yale Law School, "German Act of Military Surrender, May 8, 1945." Available online. URL: http://www.yale.edu/lawweb/avalon/wwii/gs7.htm. Accessed May 16, 2005.

ALLIED STATEMENTS ON THE OCCUPATION OF GERMANY

TREATY AT A GLANCE

Completed
June 5 and November 30, 1945

Signatories
United States, Great Britain, Soviet Union, and
the Provisional Government of the French Republic

Overview
At the conclusion of the European phase of World War II, the victorious Allies gave most of eastern Germany to Poland and the USSR, dividing the rest into four zones of occupation, with provisions for interzonal air flights.

Historical Background

At the end of April 1945, with General Dwight D. Eisenhower's troops in control of a liberated France and western Germany, with Allied bombs dropping on Berlin almost daily, and with his capital surrounded by Russian troops hungry for revenge, Adolf Hitler married his long-time companion Eva Braun, denounced the German people as unworthy of him, and committed suicide in his Berlin bunker. The Nazi government, now under Admiral Dönitz, surrendered not just unconditionally but twice, first at Eisenhower's headquarters on May 7 and then again to the Russians in Berlin on May 8 (see GERMAN ACT OF MILITARY SURRENDER).

Already the suspicions and strains that had plagued the Allied war effort were becoming more evident, especially the historical distrust and dislike between Britain and Russia. Churchill had already vented his worries about Stalin at Yalta (see REPORT ON THE YALTA [CRIMEA] CONFERENCE) and would do so again as the "peace" process progressed. As it was, it took the occupying powers—the United States, Britain, Russia, and France—a month to come up with their declarations for handling the defeated Nazis. They would reflect the concerns at Yalta, for example, in the references to a United Nations, which at that point meant the Allies and those countries sympathetic to their cause, in the minuet over Russia's demands for reparations, and in the way they presaged the breaking up of Europe into cold war zones and flight corridors.

Terms

The surrender, or more precisely the surrenders, of Germany restored its frontiers to their extent as of December 31, 1937—prior to the Anschluss with Austria, the acquisition of the Sudetenland, and the invasion of Poland. This contracted Germany was divided "for the purposes of occupation . . . into four zones, one to be allotted to each Power as follows: an eastern zone to the Union of Soviet Socialist Republics; a north-western zone to the United Kingdom; a south-western zone to the United States of America; a western zone to France."

Each of the four occupying nations was to designate a commander in chief with responsibility for its zone. Although Berlin was well within the Soviet zone, it likewise was to be divided into four zones of occupation:

> The area of "Great Berlin" will be occupied by forces of each of the Four Powers. An Inter-Allied Governing Authority [in Russian, *Komendatura*] consisting of four Commandants, appointed by their respective Commanders-in-Chief, will be established to direct jointly its administration.

The "control machinery" for Germany during the "period when Germany is carrying out the basic requirements of unconditional surrender" was defined in another document of June 5, 1945:

> . . . In the period when Germany is carrying out the basic requirements of unconditional surrender, supreme authority in Germany will be exercised, on

instructions from their Governments, by the British, United States, Soviet, and French Commanders-in-Chief, each in his own zone of occupation, and also jointly, in matters affecting Germany as a whole. The four Commanders-in-Chief will together constitute the Control Council. Each Commander-in-Chief will be assisted by a Political Adviser.

2. The Control Council, whose decisions shall be unanimous, will ensure appropriate uniformity of action by the Commanders-in-Chief in their respective zones of occupation and will reach agreed decisions on the chief questions affecting Germany as a whole.

3. Under the Control Council there will be a permanent Coordinating Committee composed of one representative of each of the four Commanders-in-Chief, and a Control Staff organized in the following Divisions (which are subject to adjustment in the light of experience): Military; Naval; Air; Transport; Political; Economic; Finance; Reparation, Deliveries and Restitution; Internal Affairs and Communications; Legal; Prisoners of War and Displaced Persons; Manpower. There will be four heads of each Division, one designated by each Power. The staffs of the Divisions may include civilian as well as military personnel, and may also in special cases include nationals of other United Nations appointed in a personal capacity.

4. The function of the Coordinating Committee and of the Control Staff will be to advise the Control Council, to carry out the Council's decisions and to transmit them to the appropriate German organs, and to supervise and control the day-to-day activities of the latter.

5. Liaison with the other United Nations Governments chiefly interested will be established through the appointment by such Governments of military missions (which may include civilian members) to the Control Council. These missions will have access through the appropriate channels to the organs of control.

6. United Nations organizations will, if admitted by the Control Council to operate in Germany, be subordinate to the Allied control machinery and answerable to it.

7. The administration of the 'Greater Berlin' area will be directed by an Inter-Allied Governing Authority, which will operate under the general direction of the Control Council, and will consist of four Commandants, each of whom will serve in rotation as Chief Commandant. They will be assisted by a technical staff which will supervise and control the activities of the local German organs.

8. The arrangements outlined above will operate during the period of occupation following German surrender, when Germany is carrying out the basic requirements of unconditional surrender. Arrangements for the subsequent period will be the subject of a separate agreement.

The isolation of Berlin in the Soviet zone of occupation made it necessary to establish three air corridors into Berlin (from Hamburg, Bückeburg, and Frankfurt-am-Main), which were recorded in minutes of the Thirteenth Meeting of the Control Council:

> . . . Marshal Zhukov recalled that the Coordinating Committee had approved the establishing of three air corridors, namely, Berlin-Hamburg, Berlin-Bückeburg and Berlin-Frankfort-on-Main.
>
> Field Marshal Montgomery expressed the hope that in due course the question of establishing the remaining air corridors would be settled satisfactorily.
>
> General Koenig approved the paper in principle and shared the opinion of Field Marshal Montgomery.
>
> Marshal Zhukov expressed himself confident that in due course the other air corridors would be opened. He added that he would like to make a proposal on this paper. He assumed that his colleagues would give the Soviet military authorities the right to fly along these air corridors into Western zones and would consent to put at their disposal appropriate airfields for landing Soviet ground staffs on terminal and intermediate airfields along the proposed air corridors to facilitate the servicing of Soviet aircraft. The reasons which Marshal Zhukov gave for the necessity of establishing Soviet airfields in the Western zones was the work of dismantling plants for deliveries on account of reparations when it comes to sending Soviet experts to organize that work.
>
> Field Marshal Montgomery stated that in his zone he would afford every facility for Soviet aircraft.
>
> Marshal Zhukov said that he would like to clarify his declaration: namely, he proposed that appropriate airfields should be placed at the disposal of the Soviet authorities in the Western zones, or that permission should be given for Soviet ground crews for the servicing of Soviet aircraft to be stationed at these airfields.
>
> Field Marshal Montgomery proposed to refer the proposal made by the head of the Soviet delegation to the Air Directorate for examination. He asked whether his understanding was correct that the question of the three air corridors from the Western zones to Berlin was settled and that the organization of these air corridors could be started immediately, without awaiting the results of the examination of the Soviet proposal.
>
> Marshal Zhukov observed that he considered the paper accepted and expressed the hope that the proposal of the Soviet delegation on placing airfields in the Western zones at the disposal of the Soviet authorities would meet with full sympathy on the part of his colleagues.

Consequences

While these early agreements suggest accord among the four Allies, they ultimately failed to agree on whether (or how) to reunite the four occupied zones. As World War II was replaced by the cold war, the temporary dividing lines between the Soviet zone in the east and the British, French, and U.S. zones became a permanent boundary. Late in March 1948, the Soviets, wary of the West's growing commitment to establish a separate capitalist state of West Germany, began detaining troop trains bound for West Berlin. On June 7, 1948, the Western nations officially announced their intention to create West Germany.

Two weeks later, the Soviets blockaded West Berlin, arguing that Berlin, because of its location, could not serve as the capital of West Germany. U.S. president Harry S. Truman responded by ordering the most massive airlift in history in order to keep West Berlin supplied. In this, the first great "battle" of the cold war, the West emerged victorious. After some 272,000 flights over 321 days—an unparalleled logistical achieve-ment—the Soviets backed down on May 12, 1949. Later that month, East and West Germany became separate nations, and over the next several months and years, the Soviets erected a wall between East and West Berlin. Intended to keep those under communist rule from defecting to the West, the Wall became a tangible symbol to the "free" world of Soviet tyranny throughout the cold war period.

Source

J. A. S. Grenville and Bernard Waserstein, eds., *The Major International Treaties Since 1945* (London and New York: Methuen, 1987), 186–187.

JAPANESE SURRENDER DOCUMENTS

TREATY AT A GLANCE

Completed
September 2, September 3, and September 12, 1945, at Tokyo Bay,
Japan; Baguio, Luzon, Philippine Islands; and Singapore

Signatories
United States, Great Britain, the USSR, China, and
other Allied governments and Japan

Overview
On August 6, 1945, the United States unleashed on the Japanese
city of Hiroshima the most destructive weapon ever devised. Three
days later, U.S. Army Air Force B-29s dropped a second A-bomb on
Nagasaki. The nuclear attacks forced a Japanese surrender—beginning with the first of a series of documents signed aboard the U.S.
battleship *Missouri* in Tokyo Bay on September 2—and brought
World War II to a close, even as they made possible the age of
potential, and sometimes imminent, mutual destruction called the
cold war.

Historical Background

With the entry of the United States into World War II,
Americans of course closely followed the progress of
the war both on the home front and overseas. Although
the war for them had started in the Pacific, President
Roosevelt—urged on by British prime minister Winston Churchill in a series of conferences—took as his
first priority the salvation of Europe and the defeat of
Nazi Germany.

The official war aims, however, did not fully
match the mood of the American public, which supported the war primarily as a means of taking revenge
on Japan. Not only had the Japanese caught the United
States unawares in Hawaii, but within two hours of
dropping the first bombs on Pearl Harbor, they had
also struck Clark Field, the main U.S. base in the
Philippines, trapping General Douglas MacArthur's
Far East air force on the ground and destroying about
half of it. In short order, Japan ran the American command out of the islands, captured massive numbers of
American troops who were fighting a last-ditch effort
on the Bataan Peninsula, and soundly defeated the
British in Singapore to take control of the Pacific.

Roosevelt was forced to lead public opinion
rather than to rely on it. Thus, the first counterstrike against Japan came in an action that spoke more

for the desperate needs of American morale than of
sound strategic thinking. On April 18, 1942, Lieutenant
Colonel James Doolittle led 16 Army Air Force B-25s,
launched from the U.S. Navy aircraft carrier *Hornet*, in
a spectacular low-level surprise attack against Tokyo
that wrought only minor damage, quickly repaired, and
ended in the loss of all aircraft in bad weather over
China. Most of the crews were saved, however; Americans felt better; and the shocked Japanese kept four
fighter groups home as they moved against the remainder of the American fleet at Midway Island, where the
Navy, under Admiral Chester Nimitz, was waiting for
them. The Japanese lost their first major sea battle in
the war, Americans took control of Pacific waters, and
the United States could turn its attention to its primary
goals on the other side of the world.

As the Allies commenced their terribly costly
strategic bombing campaign over Fortress Europe,
MacArthur began to slog his way across New Guinea
toward his lost command on the Philippines. All
through the summer of 1942, Nimitz's amphibious
forces leapfrogged from island to island up the Pacific
toward Japan. The Japanese put up tremendous resistance, fighting for five deadly months at Guadalcanal,
for example, before Japan evacuated the survivors.

When the Allies at last launched their much
delayed D day invasion of Europe, Nimitz's island-

hopping had brought U.S. troops face to face with the Japanese at Saipan, the main bastion protecting the empire's homeland. In a savage air battle on June 19, 1944, Japan lost 346 planes while shooting down only 50 Americans, and its navy was fatally crippled. Saipan's civilians committed mass suicide, and its 40,000-strong garrison died fighting to the last man. A month later the United States had a base for launching massive B-29 bombing raids on Japan, directed by a Curtis LeMay fresh from burning down cities in Europe. MacArthur, who returned to Leyte in October 1944, cleared the island by mid-January, just as the marines took Iwo Jima. Six months of hard fighting later, Okinawa was occupied, and Japan's fate was sealed.

Now the American leaders were faced with a momentous decision. On December 6, 1941, just one day before Japan's attack on Pearl Harbor, Roosevelt had signed a secret order authorizing the Manhattan Project to investigate the feasibility of nuclear weapons and to create a fission bomb. The project was headed by Brigadier General Leslie R. Groves, the army engineer who directed construction of the Pentagon. Groves assembled a group of scientists directed by physicist Robert J. Oppenheimer, who spent months confined to a secret base at Los Alamos, New Mexico, feverishly experimenting with the "gadget," as they called it. The scientists and their gadget were backed by the costliest engineering and manufacturing program the United States government had ever undertaken to develop a single weapon, for extracting plutonium in sufficient quantity to make a bomb required extraordinary facilities. The Allies marched toward the successful construction of an implosive device that would trigger a chain reaction in enriched uranium. Trinity, the first test of the bomb, took place in the Alamogordo desert at 0529:45 on July 16, 1945, well after Germany had been defeated and shortly following the death of Franklin Roosevelt.

It fell to Harry S. Truman to decide whether to use the weapon against the remaining enemy, the empire of Japan. Even with most of their cities already reduced to rubble by the massive firebombings, even with their navy and air force effectively neutralized, the Japanese steadfastly refused to accept unconditional surrender. Invading the islands, it was estimated, would cost the lives of perhaps a million Allied soldiers, not to mention the toll it would take on the Japanese themselves. Truman faced a U.S. public anxious to pay back the Japanese for Pearl Harbor and fully supportive of the demand for unconditional surrender, but one that would hardly have tolerated the high American casualties of an invasion if it became known he had possessed all along the technology to end the war immediately without them. He was fearful, too, that Japan's resistance to such an invasion would give Soviet dictator Joseph Stalin sufficient time to enter the war against the Japanese, as he had promised at the Yalta Conference (see YALTA AGREEMENT and REPORT OF THE YALTA [CRIMEA] CONFERENCE) and claim his share of the spoils of victory as he had in Europe.

At the same time, however, a small group of scientist—including among their number many of those who had played roles in theorizing about and building the bomb—were arguing against its deployment, especially against civilians, and proposed steps that could be taken to avoid the potential for a nuclear arms race in the future. Despite such sentiments from the scientists, Truman—and Roosevelt before him—along with Winston Churchill were not unmindful of the military and political advantages they imagined would result from an American-British nuclear monopoly. Just how much a role these various considerations played in Truman's decision to drop the bombs is a matter of much conjecture among historians, but the fact is that Truman did decide that fateful summer to deploy the weapon the United States had developed. He ordered the only nuclear attacks in world history.

On August 6, 1945, a specially equipped B-29 called the *Enola Gay* appeared in the skies over the Japanese military port of Hiroshima and dropped a single atomic bomb. The blast destroyed everything in the vicinity, burning four-and-one-half square miles, killing more than 66,000 people, and horribly injuring some 70,000 others. Joseph Stalin immediately declared war on Japan and invaded Manchuria. Three days later, Truman, to prove the first nuclear attack was no one-time fluke, dropped a second bomb on Nagasaki, killing nearly 40,000 more. Japanese emperor Hirohito summoned his cabinet to an audience, told them that to continue the war would be suicidal, and expressed his wish for Japan to accept the terms of the Potsdam Protocol with one exception: that he should remain emperor and sovereign of Japan. He then upbraided the military men present for failing to perform as they had promised him.

This may not have been completely unconditional, but it was close enough, and Truman and his advisers decided that even had the emperor not raised the issue, they would probably have kept him on under Allied supervision, if nothing else to ensure the surrender of the Japanese armies scattered across East Asia and the Pacific. The Americans replied on August 11 that the emperor and the Japanese government's authority would be subject to the Supreme Commander of the Allied powers, implying that Hirohito could remain emperor. Meanwhile, a few of the more fanatical officers attempted a coup on the palace grounds, but their revolt failed.

On August 14 Hirohito accepted the Potsdam provision and a cease-fire was sounded. On the morning of

September 2, 1945, General Douglas MacArthur, on board the battleship *Missouri*, anchored in Tokyo, received the Japanese delegation and accepted the surrender. The greatest war in history had come to an end.

Terms

Some historians have argued that if the United States had made its willingness to retain Hirohito as emperor clear earlier, even under the yoke of an Allied Supreme Commander, the Japanese might well have surrendered earlier, and there would have been no need to employ nuclear weapons. As it was, the Allies carefully employed the authority of the emperor throughout the surrender process, accepting the surrender documents from the delegation to the *Missouri* as the "First Instrument of Surrender," then carefully proclaiming the emperor's receipt of the surrender, and finally securing additional "instruments of surrender" in other parts of the Pacific theater, such as the Philippines and Singapore.

Instrument of Surrender

We, acting by command of and in behalf of the Emperor of Japan, the Japanese Government and the Japanese Imperial General Headquarters, hereby accept the provisions set forth in the declaration issued by the heads of the Governments of the United States, China, and Great Britain on 26 July 1945 at Potsdam, and subsequently adhered to by the Union of Soviet Socialist Republics, which four powers are hereafter referred to as the Allied Powers.

We hereby proclaim the unconditional surrender to the Allied Powers of the Japanese Imperial General Headquarters and of all Japanese armed forces and all armed forces under the Japanese control wherever situated.

We hereby command all Japanese forces wherever situated and the Japanese people to cease hostilities forthwith, to preserve and save from damage all ships, aircraft, and military and civil property and to comply with all requirements which my be imposed by the Supreme Commander for the Allied Powers or by agencies of the Japanese Government at his direction.

We hereby command the Japanese Imperial Headquarters to issue at once orders to the Commanders of all Japanese forces and all forces under Japanese control wherever situated to surrender unconditionally themselves and all forces under their control.

We hereby command all civil, military and naval officials to obey and enforce all proclamations, and orders and directives deemed by the Supreme Commander for the Allied Powers to be proper to effectuate this surrender and issued by him or under his authority and we direct all such officials to remain at their posts and to continue to perform their non-combatant duties unless specifically relieved by him or under his authority.

We hereby undertake for the Emperor, the Japanese Government and their successors to carry out the provisions of the Potsdam Declaration in good faith, and to issue whatever orders and take whatever actions may be required by the Supreme Commander for the Allied Powers or by any other designated representative of the Allied Powers for the purpose of giving effect to that Declaration.

We hereby command the Japanese Imperial Government and the Japanese Imperial General Headquarters at once to liberate all allied prisoners of war and civilian internees now under Japanese control and to provide for their protection, care, maintenance and immediate transportation to places as directed.

The authority of the Emperor and the Japanese Government to rule the state shall be subject to the Supreme Commander for the Allied Powers who will take such steps as he deems proper to effectuate these terms of surrender.

Signed at TOKYO BAY, JAPAN at 0904 I on the SECOND day of SEPTEMBER, 1945

MAMORU SHIGMITSU
By Command and in behalf of the Emperor
of Japan and the Japanese Government
YOSHIJIRO UMEZU
By Command and in behalf of the Japanese
Imperial General Headquarters

Accepted at TOKYO BAY, JAPAN at 0903 I on the SECOND day of SEPTEMBER, 1945, for the United States, Republic of China, United Kingdom and the Union of Soviet Socialist Republics, and in the interests of the other United Nations at war with Japan.

DOUGLAS MacARTHUR
Supreme Commander for the Allied Powers
C.W. NIMITZ
United States Representative
HSU YUNG-CH'ANG
Republic of China Representative
BRUCE FRASER
United Kingdom Representative
KUZMA DEREVYANKO
Union of Soviet Socialist Republics Representative
THOMAS BLAMEY
Commonwealth of Australia Representative
L. MOORE COSGRAVE
Dominion of Canada Representative
JACQUES LE CLERC
Provisional Government of the French Republic Representative
C.E.L. HELFRICH
Kingdom of the Netherlands Representative
LEONARD M. ISITT
Dominion of New Zealand Representative

Proclamation

Accepting the terms set forth in the Declaration issued by the heads of the Governments of the United States, Great Britain, and China on July 26th, 1945 at Potsdam and subsequently adhered to by the Union of Soviet Socialist Republics, We have commanded the Japanese Imperial Government and the Japanese Imperial General Headquarters to sign on Our behalf the Instrument of Surrender presented by the Supreme Commander for the Allied Powers and to issue General Orders to the Military and Naval Forces in accordance with the direction of the Supreme Commander for the Allied Powers. We command all Our people forthwith to cease hostilities, to lay down their arms and faithfully to carry out all the provisions of Instrument of Surrender and the General Orders issued by the Japanese Imperial General Headquarters hereunder.

This second day of the ninth month of the twentieth year of Showa . . .

[SEAL of the Empire]
Signed: HIROHITO
Countersigned: NARUHIKO-O
Prime Minister
MAMORU SHIGEMITSU
Minister of Foreign Affairs
IWAO YAMAZAKI
Minister of Home Affairs
JUICHI TSUSHIMA
Minister of Finance
SADAMU SHIMOMURA
Minister of War
MITSUMASA YONAI
Minister of Navy
CHUZO IWATA
Minister of Justice
TAMON MAEDA
Minister of Education
KENZO MATSUMURA
Minister of Welfare
KOTARO SENGOKU
Minister of Agriculture and Forestry
CHIKUHEI NAKAJIMA
Minister of Commerce and Industry
NAOTO KOBIYAMA
Minister of Transportation
FUMIMARO KONOE
Minister without Portfolio
TAKETORA OGATA
Minister without Portfolio
BINSHIRO OBATA
Minister without Portfolio

Instrument of Surrender

of the Japanese and Japanese-Controlled Armed Forces in the Philippine Islands to the Commanding General United States Army Forces, Western Pacific
Camp John Hay
Baguio, Mountain Province,
Luzon, Philippine Islands
3 September, 1945

Pursuant to and in accordance with the proclamation of the Emperor of Japan accepting the terms set forth in the declaration issued by the heads of the Governments of the United States, Great Britain, and China on 26 July 1945; at Potsdam and subsequently adhered to by the Union of Soviet Socialist Republics; and to the formal instrument of surrender of the Japanese Imperial Government and the Japanese Imperial General Headquarters signed at Tokyo Bay at 0908 on 2 September 1945:

1. Acting by command of and in behalf of the Emperor of Japan, the Japanese Imperial Government and the Japanese Imperial General Headquarters, We hereby surrender unconditionally to the Commanding General, United States Army Forces, Western Pacific, all Japanese and Japanese-controlled armed forces, air, sea, ground and auxiliary, in the Philippine Islands.

2. We hereby command all Japanese forces wherever situated in the Philippine Islands to cease hostilities forthwith, to preserve and save from damage all ships, aircraft, and military and civil property, and to comply with all requirements which may be imposed by the Commanding General, United States Army Forces, Western Pacific, or his authorized representatives.

3. We hereby direct the commanders of all Japanese forces in the Philippine Islands to issue at once to all forces under their command to surrender unconditionally themselves and all forces under their control, as prisoners of war, to the nearest United States Force Commander.

4. We hereby direct the commanders of all Japanese forces in the Philippine Islands to surrender intact and in good order to the nearest United States Army Force Commander, at times and at places directed by him, all equipment and supplies of whatever nature under their control.

5. We hereby direct the commanders of all Japanese forces in the Philippine Islands at once to liberate all Allied prisoners of war and civilian internees under their control, and to provide for their protection, care, maintenance and immediate transportation to places as directed by the nearest United States Army Force Commander.

6. We hereby undertake to transmit the directives given in Paragraphs 1 through 5, above, to all Japanese forces in the Philippine Islands immediately by all means within our power, and further to furnish to the Commanding General, United States Army Forces, Western Pacific, all necessary Japanese emissaries fully empowered to bring about the surrender of Japanese forces in the Philippine Islands with whom we are not in contact.

7. We hereby undertake to furnish immediately to the Commanding General, United States Army Forces, Western Pacific, a statement of the designation, numbers, locations, and commanders of all Japanese armed forces, ground, sea, or air, in the Philippine Islands.

8. We hereby undertake faithfully to obey all further proclamations, orders and directives deemed by the Commanding General, United States Armed Forces, Western Pacific, to be proper to effectuate this surrender.

Signed at Camp John Hay, Baguio, Mountain Province, Luzon, Philippine Islands, at 1210 hours
3 September 1945:
TOMOYUKI YAMASHITA,
General, Imperial Japanese
Army Highest Commander,
Imperial Japanese Army in the Philippines.
DENHICI OKOCHI,
Vice Admiral, Imperial Japanese
Navy, Highest Commander,
Imperial Japanese Navy in the Philippines.
By command and in behalf
of the Japanese Imperial
General Headquarters

Accepted at Camp John Hay, Baguio, Mountain Province Luzon Philippine Islands, at 1210 hours 3 September 1945:

> For the Commander-in-Chief, United States
> Army Forces, Pacific:
> EDMOND H. LEAVY,
> Major General, USA
> Deputy Commander, United States Army Forces,
> Western Pacific.

Supreme Allied Commander South East Asia Instrument of Surrender of Japanese Forces under the Command or Control of the Supreme Commander, Japanese Expeditionary Forces, Southern Regions, within the Operational Theatre of the Supreme Allied Commander South East Asia

1. In pursuance of and in compliance with:

(a) the Instrument of Surrender signed by the Japanese plenipotentiaries by command and on behalf of the Emperor of Japan, the Japanese Government and the Japanese Imperial General Headquarters at Tokyo on 2 September, 1945;

(b) General Order No. 1, promulgated at the same place and on the same date;

(c) the Local Agreement made by the Supreme Commander, Japanese Expeditionary Forces, Southern Regions, with the Supreme Allied Commander, South East Asia at Rangoon on 27 August, 1945;

to all of which Instrument of Surrender, General Order and Local Agreement this present Instrument is complementary and which it in no way supersedes, the Supreme Commander, Japanese Expeditionary Forces, Southern Regions (Field Marshall Count Terauchi) does hereby surrender unconditionally to the Supreme Allied Commander, South East Asia (Admiral The Lord Louis Mountbatten) himself and all Japanese sea, ground, air and auxiliary forces under his command or control and within the operational theatre of the Supreme Allied Commander, South East Asia.

2. The Supreme Commander, Japanese Expeditionary Forces, Southern Regions, undertakes to ensure that all orders and instructions that may be issued from time to time by the Supreme Allied Commander, South East Asia, or by any of his subordinate Naval, Military, or Air-Force Commanders of whatever rank acting in his name, are scrupulously and promptly obeyed by all Japanese sea, ground, air and auxiliary forces under the command or control of the Supreme Commander, Japanese Expeditionary Forces, Southern Regions, and within the operational theatre of the Supreme Allied Commander, South East Asia.

3. Any disobedience of, or delay or failure to comply with, orders or instructions issued by the Supreme Allied Commander, South East Asia, or issued on his behalf by any of his subordinate Naval, Military, or Air Force Commanders of whatever rank, and any action which the Supreme Allied Commander, South East Asia, or his subordinate Commanders action on his behalf, may determine to be detrimental to the Allied Powers, will be dealt with as the Supreme Allied Commander, South East Asia may decide.

4. This Instrument takes effect from the time and date of signing.

5. This Instrument is drawn up in the English Language, which is the only authentic version. In any case of doubt to intention or meaning, the decision of the Supreme Allied Commander, South East Asia is final. It is the responsibility of the Supreme Commander, Japanese Expeditionary Forces, Southern Regions, to make such translations into Japanese as he may require.

Signed at Singapore at 0341 hours (G.M.T.) on 12 September, 1945.

> SEISHIRO ITAGAKI
> (for) Supreme Commander
> Japanese Expeditionary Forces,
> Southern Regions
> LOUIS MOUNTBATTEN
> Supreme Allied Commander
> South East Asia

Consequences

During the course of the American occupation, Japan, free of costly defense spending, first began developing a world-class economy that would eventually rival that of the occupier. At the same time, defense spending for the Allied countries grew ever more expensive after the war precisely because the United States had dropped the atomic bombs on Japan and unleashed the nuclear age in world history. Immediately after the war, the United States sat for a time content in the knowledge that it and only it possessed the atomic bomb.

Unknown to Truman and Churchill, Klaus Fuchs, who had worked on the Manhattan Project and was among those scientists who objected to the deployment of the bombs, had already passed atomic secrets to the Soviets. Fuchs, one of a number of British intellectuals recruited by the Soviets beginning in the 1930s, not a few of whom happened to be in the British secret services, committed his treason even before the bomb was dropped, so that by the time of the Yalta Conference, Stalin knew all about it, although he kept his knowledge carefully hidden from his Allied counterparts at the meeting. He hadn't built an atomic bomb yet, but he soon would.

Over the succeeding decades the USSR and the United States would create thousands upon thousands of nuclear weapons, which could be launched from almost anywhere on land, at sea, or in the air. Within a few years the victors in World War II had become prisoners of their own technology, and former allies had turned superpower rivals who would spend 40 years locked in a cold war dance of death called "mutually assured destruction," which they neither could really control nor bring to a good end.

At the dawn of this cold war, the disarming of Japan appeared more problematic than it had seemed at the surrender, and as the occupation came to an end, the United States found it prudent on September 8, 1951, to conclude not only a TREATY OF PEACE WITH JAPAN but also a JAPANESE–UNITED STATES SECURITY TREATY, under which it would continue seeing to the defense of the island nation.

Source

Avalon Project at the Yale Law School. "Japanese Surrender Document." Available online. URL: http://www.yale.edu/lawweb/avalon/wwii/jmenu.htm. Accessed May 16, 2005.

PEACE TREATY BETWEEN THE ALLIES AND ITALY

TREATY AT A GLANCE

Completed
February 10, 1947, at Paris

Signatories
Allied and Associated Powers, and Italy

Overview
Three years after the Fascists surrendered and nearly two years after the Allies liberated Italy from Nazi hegemony and brought the conflict there to a close, this treaty formally ended World War II hostilities between Italy and the Allies.

Historical Background

When the British and American troops under Field Marshal Bernard Montgomery and General George Patton defeated Erwin Rommel's Afrika Korps, they opened the way for the invasion of Sicily on July 10, 1943. The rapid advance of the Allies into what Winston Churchill had called Europe's "soft underbelly" pulled the last supports from Benito Mussolini's tottering Fascist regime. Many in Mussolini's own party, including his foreign minister and son-in-law Galeazzo Ciano and his general Pietro Badoglio had already denounced him and been removed by February 1943. With the Allied invasion, a Grand Council of Fascist leaders convened on July 25 and, after a vicious debate, voted to depose Il Duce and return their country to "the King and parliament." Mussolini resigned the next day, and King Victor Emmanuel III appointed Badoglio to head a new government and issued a warrant for Mussolini's arrest.

Faced with a dilemma—Italy wanted peace but was afraid to break with Hitler and provoke a German attack—Badoglio feigned loyalty to Germany but made secret contact with Supreme Allied Commander Dwight David Eisenhower. Badoglio was hoping to time an armistice with immediate Allied occupation in order to avoid having to fight Germans, but the Americans made it clear in August that Italy's surrender had to be unconditional. Worse, Eisenhower would not promise to land as far north as Rome.

The Germans were growing suspicious as two British corps crossed the Straits of Messina unopposed, and Badoglio agreed on September 3 to Allied occupation. When the Italian surrender was announced on the 8th, Allied landings followed immediately that night in the Bay of Salerno, south of Naples. Before the week was out, Hitler's commandos parachuted into northern Italy, rescued Mussolini, and set him up as their puppet dictator. All Badoglio's efforts to exit the war proved worthless when the Allies demanded that the Italians declare war on Germany. He executed the volte-face on October 13, and Italy became an Allied "co-belligerent."

Mussolini, in German-occupied north Italy, renamed the Fascist Party the Republican Fascist Party and created the Italian Social Republic as Germany's new ally. Meanwhile, anti-Fascist parties were emerging all over Italy, merging and remerging, and launching a resistance as the Americans fought their way north, which invited Nazi reprisals against civilians in the tens of thousands. Left-wing anti-Fascist parties in the south, which had refused participation in the current regime (because they wanted the king, tainted by long association with the Fascists, to abdicate), executed their own about-face when Joseph Stalin recognized Badoglio's government. Coalitions between royalists and communists, Christian Democrats and traditional socialists, conservatives and liberals produced an uneasy provisional government of national unity in March 1944, and Rome was liberated in June.

The situation was, to say the least, complicated. Rome was declared an "open" city; the Nazis still occupied the north; American and British troops fought alongside Italian soldiers they had been fighting against only recently; communist partisans roamed the countryside; Sicily, whose well-established Mafia had aided the Allied invasion, was openly separatist; Italian colonies were up in arms. The government called for a

Constituent Assembly to write a new constitution when all of Italy had been liberated, but then fell in a crisis created by its refusal to purge Fascists from its administration with enough gusto. The government that replaced it was even more right-wing. By the spring of 1945, a general partisan uprising was under way, and Allied forces were closing in on Milan and Mussolini. Mussolini and his mistress, Clara Petacci, fled but were captured by Italian partisans. Executed by firing squad on April 28, their bodies were hung by their heels in a Milan public square.

After the entire peninsula had been liberated, long negotiations to form a government resulted in the formation of yet another coalition, this one headed by the Committee of National Liberation's Ferrucio Parri, a compromise candidate between Socialist Pietro Nenni and Christian Democrat Alcide De Gasperi. But Parri's leftist leanings led to the coalition's collapse in November 1945. De Gasperi, the ablest of the Italian political leaders emerging from the war, took control and, backed by the Allies, began formulating Italian policies along moderate lines. In May 1946 Victor Emmanuel abdicated in favor of his less compromised son, Umberto II, and a referendum on the constitution and elections to the Constituent Assembly limited its powers to drafting the constitution and ratifying treaties. With the increasing strength of the left evident, De Gasperi took conservative steps to strengthen the powers of the state and maintain law and order.

By January 1947 what would come to be called the cold war was clearly having an impact on Italian politics, and De Gasperi declared which "side" he was on by that month visiting the United States. A month later, a little over three years after Badoglio's surrender, the Italian government signed the peace treaty with the Allied powers in New York on February 10, 1947.

Terms

The preamble of this treaty acknowledged that fascism in Italy was toppled not only because of the Allied victory but also "with the assistance of the democratic elements of the Italian people." Accordingly, Italy enjoyed special status among the nations of the former Axis. While its government willed aggressive war, a large portion of its people had worked for peace.

Italy's frontiers were reestablished as they had existed on January 1, 1938, except that the conquests of Albania and Ethiopia were annulled, the Dodecanese was ceded to Greece, and certain Adriatic islands were likewise ceded to Greece and Albania. The boundary between Italy and France was also subject to adjustment. Other territorial adjustments were politically more delicate.

Section III
Free Territory of Trieste

ARTICLE 21
1. There is hereby constituted the Free Territory of Trieste, consisting of the area lying between the Adriatic Sea and the boundaries defined in Articles 4 and 22 of the present Treaty. The Free Territory of Trieste is recognized by the Allied and Associated Powers and by Italy, which agree that its integrity and independence shall be assured by the Security Council of the United Nations.

2. Italian sovereignty over the area constituting the Free Territory of Trieste as above defined, shall be terminated upon the coming into force of the present Treaty.

3. On the termination of Italian sovereignty, the Free Territory of Trieste shall be governed in accordance with an instrument for a provisional regime drafted by the Council of Foreign Ministers and approved by the Security Council. This Instrument shall remain in force until such date as the Security Council shall fix for the coming into force of the Permanent Statute which shall have been approved by it. The Free Territory shall thenceforth be governed by the provisions of such Permanent Statute. The texts of the Permanent Statute and of the Instrument for the Provisional Regime are contained in Annexes VI and VII.

4. The Free Territory of Trieste shall not be considered as ceded territory within the meaning of Article 19 and Annex XIV of the present Treaty.

5. Italy and Yugoslavia undertake to give to the Free Territory of Trieste the guarantees set out in Annex IX.

ARTICLE 22
The frontier between Yugoslavia and the Free Territory of Trieste shall be fixed as follows . . .

Section IV
Italian Colonies

ARTICLE 23
1. Italy renounces all right and title to the Italian territorial possessions in Africa, i.e. Libya, Eritrea and Italian Somaliland.

2. Pending their final disposal, the said possessions shall continue under their present administration.

3. The final disposal of these possessions shall be determined jointly by the Governments of the Soviet Union, of the United Kingdom, of the United States of America, and of France within one year from the coming into force of the present Treaty, in the manner laid down in the joint declaration of February 10, 1947, issued by the said Governments, which is reproduced in Annex XI.

Section V
Special Interests of China

ARTICLE 24
Italy renounces in favor of China all benefits and privileges resulting from the provisions of the final Protocol signed at Peking on September 7, 1901, and

all annexes, notes and documents supplementary thereto . . .

Section IV
Albania

ARTICLE 27

Italy recognizes and undertakes to respect the sovereignty and independence of the State of Albania.

ARTICLE 28

Italy recognizes that the Island of Saseno is part of the territory of Albania and renounces all claims thereto. . . .

Section VII
Ethiopia

ARTICLE 33

Italy recognizes and undertakes to respect the sovereignty and independence of the State of Ethiopia.

Important political clauses were aimed at enforcing human rights and eliminating all vestiges of fascism:

ARTICLE 15

Italy shall take all measures necessary to secure to all persons under Italian jurisdiction, without distinction as to race, sex, language or religion, the enjoyment of human rights and of the fundamental freedoms, including freedom of expression, of press and publication, of religious worship, of political opinion and of public meeting.

ARTICLE 16

Italy shall not prosecute or molest Italian nationals, including members of the armed forces, solely on the ground that during the period from June 10, 1940, to the coming into force of the present Treaty, they expressed sympathy with or took action in support of the cause of the Allied and Associated Powers.

ARTICLE 17

Italy, which, in accordance with Article 30 of the Armistice Agreement, has taken measures to dissolve the Fascist organizations in Italy, shall not permit the resurgence on Italian territory of such organizations, whether political, military or semi-military, whose purpose it is to deprive the people of their democratic rights. . . .

The Italian armed forces were strictly limited until modified "by agreement between the Allied and Associated Powers and Italy or, after Italy becomes a member of the United Nations, by agreement between the Security Council and Italy." A schedule for the withdrawal of Allied troops was established, and reparations were fixed—the Soviet Union receiving about $100 million over a seven-year period, with additional amounts going to Yugoslavia ($125 million), Greece ($105 million), Ethiopia ($25 million), and Albania ($5 million). For their part, France, Britain, and the United States agreed to forgo reparations claims.

Consequences

Despite fears in the West that Italy might go the way of eastern Europe, become communist, and fall into the orbit of the Soviet Union, the Constituent Assembly completed its work on December 22, 1947, by approving the text of a new constitution, which entered into force on January 1, 1948, and which clearly established Italy as one of the West's liberal democracies.

That did not mean, however, that Italy became a steady member of the European postwar community. Instead, it suffered through years of instability, as the republic saw six successive Christian Democratic administrations rise and fall between 1953 and 1958. While the Christian Democrats did manage to produce a Ten-Year Plan for Growth and Development, the limited maneuverability of these governments severely hampered their attempts to pass essential legislation. As laws for instituting the regions called for in the constitution, for establishing the Constitutional Court, and for replacing the Fascist codes were postponed again and again, Italy gained a reputation for corruption, violence, and political volatility that it has never completely shaken.

Source

J. A. S. Grenville, *The Major International Treaties, 1914–1973* (New York: Stein and Day, 1975), 277–281.

TREATY OF PEACE WITH JAPAN

TREATY AT A GLANCE

Completed
September 8, 1951, at San Francisco;
entered into force April 28, 1952

Signatories
Allied powers (excluding the Soviet Union, People's Republic of
China, and Taiwan, who declined to sign) and Japan

Japan had agreed to unconditional surrender after World War II by
signing the instrument of surrender aboard the USS *Missouri* in
1945. The 1951 treaty formalized these terms and defined others.

Historical Background

Following the Japanese surrender on September 2, 1945, aboard the battleship *Missouri* in Tokyo Bay, the man who received the JAPANESE SURRENDER DOCUMENTS, General Douglas MacArthur, became the Allied commander of the Japanese occupation between 1945 and 1951. Certainly autocratic if not megalomaniacal, MacArthur nevertheless proved to be a effective administrator. He directed the demobilization of the Japanese military forces, seeing to the complete expurgation of the island empire's entrenched militarists, and he guided the restoration of the Japanese economy and the drafting of a liberal constitution, which was adopted in 1946. Under his tutelage, Japan inaugurated significant reforms in land distribution, education, labor relations, public health policies, and the treatment of women.

Serving also as head of the U.S. Army's Far East command, MacArthur was called upon to take charge of United Nations forces in Korea when war broke out there in 1950. He soon ran afoul of President Harry S. Truman, who removed MacArthur from command—and from the Far East—for his insubordination and his unwillingness to fight a limited war. Thus MacArthur was gone and his influence over Japanese affairs at an end, when the peace treaty, which he had long negotiated, was finalized.

Terms

The signing of the 1951 treaty was the culmination of discussions during MacArthur's day that had already established the terms of the document. These included the establishment of territorial boundaries as they existed at the end of the war, with Japan affirming its renunciation of rights to all territories surrendered by the armistice concluded aboard the *Missouri*. Japan also renounced any special rights with regard to China. However, the treaty conveyed to the Soviet Union no special title to the Kurils and southern Sakhalin (see YALTA AGREEMENT). Nor did it turn over Taiwan to China. For these reasons, the Soviet Union and the two Chinas declined to sign the treaty, though a majority of the Allies did sign, making it universally effective.

While the treaty established the principle that Japan should pay reparations, it left the amounts for subsequent bilateral negotiations. The treaty also brought to bear the principles of the UNITED NATIONS CHARTER, to which Japan agreed to subscribe, further agreeing to follow internationally accepted fair trade and commerce practices. The treaty provided for the transition from a government of military occupation to sovereignty and independence within 90 days of the date on which the treaty came into force. Of signal importance is the absence of military clauses restricting armed forces in Japan. A central feature of the TREATY OF VERSAILLES (1919) and other World War I treaties, these were made unnecessary by the Japanese constitution, adopted in 1946, which forbade the maintenance of any Japanese armed forces (in part at the insistence of the United States, a small defense force was later created). However, in Article 5 of the present treaty, Japan agreed to accept "the obligations set forth in Article 2 of the [United Nations Charter]," and for their part, the Allied signatories recognized "that Japan as a sovereign nation possesses the inherent right of individual or collective self-defense referred to in Article 51 of the [United Nations Charter]."

Treaty of Peace with Japan, San Francisco, 8 September 1951

Whereas the Allied Powers and Japan are resolved that henceforth their relations shall be those of nations which, as sovereign equals, cooperate in friendly association to promote their common welfare and to maintain international peace and security, and are therefore desirous of concluding a Treaty of Peace which will settle questions still outstanding as a result of the existence of a state of war between them;

Whereas Japan for its part declares its intention to apply for membership in the United Nations and in all circumstances to conform to the principles of the Charter of the United Nations; to strive to realize the objectives of the Universal Declaration of Human Rights; to seek to create within Japan conditions of stability and well-being as defined in Articles 55 and 56 of the Charter of the United Nations and already initiated by post-surrender Japanese legislation; and in public and private trade and commerce to conform to internationally accepted fair practices;

Whereas the Allied Powers welcome the intentions of Japan set out in the foregoing paragraph;

The Allied Powers and Japan have therefore determined to conclude the present Treaty of Peace, and have accordingly appointed the undersigned plenipotentiaries, who, after presentation of their full powers, found in good and due form, have agreed on the following provisions:

Chapter I. Peace

ARTICLE 1

a) The state of war between Japan and each of the Allied Powers is terminated as from the date on which the present Treaty comes into force between Japan and the Allied Power concerned as provided for in Article 23.

(b) The Allied Powers recognize the full sovereignty of the Japanese people over Japan and its territorial waters.

Chapter II. Territory

ARTICLE 2

(a) Japan, recognizing the independence of Korea, renounces all right, title and claim to Korea, including the islands of Quelpart, Port Hamilton and Dagelet.

(b) Japan renounces all right, title and claim to Formosa and the Pescadores.

(c) Japan renounces all rights, title and claim to the Kurile islands, and to that portion of Sakhalin and the islands adjacent to it over which Japan acquired sovereignty as a consequence of the Treaty of Portsmouth of September 5, 1905.

(d) Japan renounces all right, title and claim in connection with the League of Nations Mandate System, and accepts the action of the United Nations Security Council of April 2, 1947, extending the trusteeship system to the Pacific islands formerly under mandate to Japan.

(e) Japan renounces all claim to any right or title to or interest in connection with any part of the Antarctic area, whether deriving from the activities of Japanese nationals or otherwise.

(f) Japan renounces all right, title and claim to the Spratly islands and to the Paracel islands.

Article 3. Japan will concur in any proposal o the United States to the United Nations to place under its trusteeship system, with the United States as the sole administering authority. . . .

Chapter III. Security

ARTICLE 5

(a) Japan accepts the obligations set forth in Article 2 of the Charter of the United Nations, and in particular the obligations

(i) to settle its international disputes by peaceful means in such a manner that international peace and security, and justice, are not endangered;

(ii) to refrain in its international relations from the threat or use of force against the territorial integrity or political independence of any State or in any other manner inconsistent with the Purposes of the United Nations;

(iii) to give the United Nations every assistance in any action it takes in accordance with the Charter and to refrain from giving assistance to any State against which the United Nations may take preventive or enforcement action.

(b) The Allied Powers confirm that they will be guided by the principles of Article 2 of the Charter of the United Nations in their relations with Japan.

(c) The Allied Powers for their part recognize that Japan as a sovereign nation possesses the inherent right of individual or collective self-defense referred to in Article 51 of the Charter of the United Nations and that Japan may voluntarily enter into collective security arrangements.

ARTICLE 6

(a) All occupation forces of the Allied Powers shall be withdrawn from Japan as soon as possible after the coming into force of the present Treaty, and in any case not later than ninety days thereafter. Nothing in this provision shall, however, prevent the stationing or retention of foreign armed forces in Japanese territory under or in consequence of any bilateral or multilateral agreements which have been or may be made between one or more of the Allied Powers, on the one hand, and Japan on the other.

(b) The provisions of Article 9 of the Potsdam Proclamation of July 26, 1945, dealing with the return of Japanese military forces to their homes, to the extent not already completed, will be carried out.

(c) All Japanese property for which compensation has not already been paid, which was supplied for the use of the occupation forces. . . .

Chapter IV. Political and Economic Clauses

ARTICLE 10

Japan renounces all special rights and interests in China, including all benefits and privileges resulting from the provisions of the final Protocol signed at Peking on September 7, 1901, and all annexes, notes and documents supplementary thereto, and agrees to the abrogation in respect to Japan of the said Protocol, annexes, notes and documents.

ARTICLE 11

Japan accepts the judgements of the International Military Tribunal for the Far East and of other Allied War Crimes Courts both within and outside Japan, and will carry out the sentences imposed thereby upon Japanese nationals imprisoned in Japan.

The power to grant clemency, to reduce sentences and to parole with respect to such prisoners may not be exercised except on the decision of the Government or Governments which imposed the sentence in each instance, and on the recommendation of Japan. In the case of persons sentenced by the International Military Tribunal for the Far East, such power may not be exercised except on the decision of a majority of the Governments represented on the Tribunal, and on the recommendation of Japan.

ARTICLE 12

[Trade arrangements] . . . .

(c) In respect to any matter, however, Japan shall be obliged to accord to an Allied Power national treatment, or most-favored-nation treatment, only to the extent that the Allied Power concerned accords Japan national treatment or most-favored-nation treatment, as the case may be, in respect of the same matter . . .

Chapter V. Claims and Property

ARTICLE 14

(a) It is recognized that Japan should pay reparations to the Allied Powers for the damage and suffering caused by it during the war. Nevertheless it is also recognized that the resources of Japan are not presently sufficient, if it is to maintain a viable economy, to make complete reparation for all such damage and suffering and at the same time meet its other obligations.

Therefore,

(a) Japan will promptly enter into negotiations with Allied Powers so desiring, whose present territories were occupied by Japanese forces and damaged by Japan, with a view to assisting to compensate those countries for the cost of repairing the damage done, by making available the services of the Japanese people in production, salvaging and other work for the Allied Powers in question. Such arrangements shall avoid the imposition of additional liabilities on other Allied Powers, and, where the manufacturing of raw materials is called for, they shall be supplied by the Allied Powers in question, so as not to throw any foreign exchange burden upon Japan. . . .

(b) Except as otherwise provided in the present Treaty, the Allied Powers waive all reparations claims of the Allied Powers, other claims of the Allied Powers and their nationals arising out of any actions taken by Japan and its nationals in the course of the prosecution of the war, and claims of the Allied Powers for direct military costs of occupation. . . .

ARTICLE 16

As an expression of its desire to indemnify those members of the armed forces of the Allied Powers who suffered undue hardships while prisoners of war of Japan, Japan will transfer its assets and those of its nationals in countries which were neutral during the war, or which were at war with any of the Allied Powers, or, at its option, the equivalent of such assets, to the International Committee of the Red Cross which shall liquidate such assets and distribute the resultant fund to appropriate national agencies, for the benefit of former prisoners of war and their families on such basis as it may determine to be equitable. . . .

Chapter VII: Final Clauses

ARTICLE 23

(a) The present Treaty shall be ratified. by the States which sign it, including Japan, and will come into force for all the States which have then ratified it, when instruments of ratification have been deposited by Japan and by a majority, including the United States of America as the principal occupying Power. . . .

ARTICLE 26

Japan will be prepared to conclude with any State which signed or adhered to the United Nations Declaration of January 1, 1942, and which is at war with Japan, or with any State which previously formed a part of the territory of a State named in Article 23, which is not a signatory of the present Treaty, a bilateral treaty of peace on the same or substantially the same terms as are provided for in the present Treaty, but this obligation on the part of Japan will expire three years after the first coming into force of the present Treaty. Should Japan make a peace settlement or war claims settlement with any State granting that State greater advantages than those provided by the present Treaty, those same advantages shall be extended to the parties to the present Treaty.

Consequences

One might say MacArthur had learned the lessons of Versailles and applied them in Japan, avoiding the punitive and carefully nurturing the economic reconstruction of the defeated country. Many Japanese would have disagreed; certainly, MacArthur's autocratic rule sometimes felt punitive, and the total disarmament forced on the Japanese under their constitution more resembled the intent of Versailles than not. MacArthur's time in Japan was an occupation, more subtle, even more benign perhaps, than the Soviets' occupation of East Germany, but an occupation nevertheless. In some ways, the peace treaty, like the SOVIET DECLARATION ON THE SOVEREIGNTY OF THE GERMAN DEMOCRATIC REPUBLIC, signaled the official end of that occupation.

On the same day that the peace treaty was signed, Japan concluded the JAPANESE–UNITED STATES SECURITY TREATY, which allowed (among other provisions) the United States to maintain military forces in Japan. This treaty was supplanted in 1960 by the TREATY OF MUTUAL COOPERATION AND SECURITY BETWEEN THE UNITED STATES AND JAPAN. The postwar arrangements between the United States and Japan proved an unexpected boon for the island kingdom. Freed of the need to maintain a costly security sector, the Japanese economy, fully industrialized before the war but saddled with none of the outmoded plants (courtesy of Allied bombing) such industrialization might have implied, eventually took off to dizzying new heights.

Source

J. A. S. Grenville and Bernard Waserstein, eds., *The Major International Treaties Since 1945* (London and New York: Methuen, 1987), 55–57.

JAPAN–UNITED STATES SECURITY TREATY

TREATY AT A GLANCE

Completed
September 8, 1951, at San Francisco;
entered into force April 28, 1952

Signatories
Japan and the United States

Overview
Concluded simultaneously with the Treaty of Peace with Japan, this security treaty provided for the "provisional" stationing of United States armed forces in Japan to maintain "international peace and security in the Far East."

Historical Background

By 1951, under General Douglas MacArthur's stewardship, Japan had already become a political and economic asset to an America engaged in the cold war, although nothing like the financial juggernaut the island would become in future decades. However, having constitutionally disarmed at the insistence of the United States as an occupying power, the Japanese without American protection were defenseless against the two neighboring Communist giants, Russia and China. In the wake of Mao Zedong's takeover of the mainland in 1949, they appeared at the time to be more a single ideological and political monolith than later proved to be the case. Especially with the coming of the Korean War in 1950, which witnessed both a massive invasion of the South by Chinese Communist troops and significant technical support for North Korea from the Soviet Union, it became important for the United States at last to sign not only a permanent peace with Japan but to reach some agreement on security.

Terms

The preamble to the security treaty implies that Japan was disarmed by the TREATY OF PEACE WITH JAPAN:

> Japan has this day signed a Treaty of Peace with the Allied Powers. On the coming into force of that Treaty, Japan will not have the effective means to exercise its inherent right of self-defense because it has been disarmed.

This is misleading, for the Treaty of Peace with Japan differed dramatically from the treaties concluding World War I (see TREATY OF VERSAILLES [1919]) in that it contained no military clauses calling for arms reduction or disarmament of the defeated nation. Such provisions were unnecessary because the Japanese constitution, adopted in 1946, forbade the maintenance of any armed forces, and it was this constitution, not the treaty of peace, that disarmed Japan. The preamble continues:

> There is danger to Japan in this situation because irresponsible militarism has not yet been driven from the world. Therefore Japan desires a Security Treaty with the United States of America to come into force simultaneously with the Treaty of Peace between the United States of America and Japan.
>
> The Treaty of Peace recognizes that Japan as a sovereign nation has the right to enter into collective security arrangements, and further, the Charter of the United Nations recognizes that all nations possess an inherent right of individual and collective self-defense.
>
> In exercise of these rights, Japan desires, as a provisional arrangement for its defense, that the United States of America should maintain armed forces of its own in and about Japan so as to deter armed attack upon Japan.
>
> The United States of America, in the interest of peace and security, is presently willing to maintain certain of its armed forces in and about Japan, in the expectation, however, that Japan will itself increasingly assume responsibility for its own defense against direct and indirect aggression, always avoiding any armament which could be an offensive threat or serve other than to promote peace and security in accordance with the purposes and principles of the United Nations Charter.

In giving the United States the right to maintain a military presence in Japan, the treaty expanded the scope of the purpose of those forces from the defense of Japan to the "maintenance of international peace and security in the Far East":

ARTICLE I

Japan grants, and the United States of America accepts, the right, upon the coming into force of the Treaty of Peace and of this Treaty, to dispose United States land, air and sea forces in and about Japan. Such forces may be utilized to contribute to the maintenance of international peace and security in the Far East and to the security of Japan against armed attack from without, including assistance given at the express request of the Japanese Government to put down large-scale internal riots and disturbances in Japan, caused through instigation or intervention by an outside Power or Powers.

Additional articles barred Japan from allowing other nations to establish military installations on its soil and defined conditions for the termination of the treaty:

ARTICLE II

During the exercise of the right referred to in Article I, Japan will not grant, without the prior consent of the United States of America, any bases or any rights, powers or authority whatsoever, in or relating to bases or the right of garrison or of maneuver or transit of ground, air or naval forces to any third Power.

ARTICLE III

The conditions which shall govern the disposition of armed forces of the United States of America in and about Japan shall be determined by administrative agreements between the two Governments.

ARTICLE IV

This Treaty shall expire whenever in the opinion of the Governments of the United States of America and Japan there shall have come into force such United Nations arrangements or such alternative individual or collective security dispositions as will satisfactorily provide for the maintenance by the United Nations or otherwise of international peace and security in the Japan area. . . .

In order to accomplish the aim of the preceding paragraph, land, sea, and air forces, as well as other war potential, will never be maintained. The right of belligerency of the State will not be recognized.

Consequences

Japan, though it had suffered tremendously at the end of the war, reaped unexpected benefits from the postwar settlements. Protected in many ways from foreign competition, freed to develop an all but entirely new industrial infrastructure, and forbidden to invest in the costly weapons and security programs that would consume so much of the superpower budgets, Japan developed a truly powerful economy, which in the coming decades became a marvel and model around the globe and made the Pacific Rim a hotbed of economic growth.

Source

J. A. S. Grenville and Bernard Waserstein, eds., *The Major International Treaties Since 1945* (London and New York: Methuen, 1987), 118–119.

Trade Agreements and Commercial Treaties

LEND-LEASE AGREEMENT

TREATY AT A GLANCE

Completed
March 11, 1941 (authorizing legislation), and February 23, 1942
(signed treaty), at Washington, D.C.

Signatories
United States and Great Britain

Overview
When British prime minister Winston Churchill informed the
newly reelected U.S. president Franklin D. Roosevelt that Great
Britain was nearly bankrupt in its war against Nazi Germany, FDR
stepped up U.S. aid from the former cash-and-carry basis to a new
lend-lease policy that England could afford. It was but one more
step in FDR's attempt to move the American public toward outright belligerent status in World War II on the side of the Allies.

Historical Background

With the outbreak of a general European war in 1939,
the majority of the American people were probably
already sympathetic toward a Great Britain that they,
over the next few months, came increasingly to view as
a lonely and brave nation holding out against the odds.
Isolationism was still a very powerful force in American politics, especially among the Republicans in Congress, but President Franklin Delano Roosevelt—
unlike Woodrow Wilson in World War I, who had
counseled neutrality in word and deed—was trying to
lead public opinion toward outright support of the
British. He laid the groundwork for his policy of carefully expanded aid to the Allies in a brilliant speech to
Congress supporting passage of the Pittman Bill. The
bill passed into law on November 4 and repealed the
arms embargo on belligerent nations, which allowed
FDR to trade with Britain and France, but only on a
cash-and-carry basis.

Roosevelt's steady march toward the Allies and his
growing personal friendship with British prime minister Winston Churchill worried Senator Arthur Vanden-
burg, who pointed out that the United States could not
"become the arsenal for one belligerent without
becoming the target for another." He was right, of

course, but not completely in tune with the mood of
the times, evident in the massive increase in defense
spending that FDR sought and received following the
fall of France in 1940. Even as Roosevelt made clearer
his desire, as he wrote Churchill, to aid the British in
every way possible consistent with public sentiment,
he cautiously explained to the American people that he
was doing so because aiding Britain was the best way to
keep out of a direct fight with the Nazis.

Roosevelt had to move cautiously since he was
in a heated reelection campaign. The Republican candidate, Wendell Willkie, charged during the campaign
that a vote for Roosevelt would mean a vote for war,
and FDR responded by promising voters that "your
boys are not going to be sent into any foreign wars,"
obscuring the fact that should Germany attack the
United States—or, for that matter, should Italy or
Japan—the conflict would no longer be a foreign war.

Shortly after Roosevelt won the election, on December 9, 1940, Churchill warned that Great Britain was
nearly bankrupt, and Roosevelt responded with the
"lend-lease" plan. Roosevelt said he wanted to "eliminate the dollar sign" by lending arms to Britain, not selling them. He argued that if your neighbor's house was
on fire, you did not offer to sell him a hose. Instead, you

lent it to him until he had put the fire out. Warning that if Britain fell, all Americans would be "living at the point of a gun," Roosevelt insisted that "we must be the great arsenal of democracy." Churchill threw in his two cents worth, challenging Americans in his own way with his usual goose-bump rhetoric: "Give us the tools and we will finish the job." Wendell Willkie, of all people, threw his support to the Lend-Lease Agreement, asking fellow Republicans to pass the act authorizing it, which they did on March 11, 1941.

Terms

Roosevelt wasted no time getting aid to Britain under his new lend-lease authority, although the ultimate Lend-Lease Agreement between the two countries would not be signed for almost another year, on February 23, 1942, long after Pearl Harbor had led the United States into the war alongside the Allies.

Whereas the Governments of the United States of America and the United Kingdom of Great Britain and Northern Ireland declare that they are engaged in a cooperative undertaking, together with every other nation or people of like mind, to the end of laying the bases of a just and enduring world peace securing order under law to themselves and all nations;

And whereas the President of the United States of America has determined, pursuant to the Act of Congress of March 11, 1941, that the defense of the United Kingdom against aggression is vital to the defense of the United States of America;

And whereas the United States of America has extended and is continuing to extend to the United Kingdom aid in resisting aggression;

And whereas it is expedient that the final determination of the terms and conditions upon which the Government of the United Kingdom receives such aid and of the benefits to be received by the United States of America in return therefor should be deferred until the extent of the defense aid is known and until the progress of events makes clearer the final terms and conditions and benefits which will be in the mutual interests of the United States of America and the United Kingdom and will promote the establishment and maintenance of world peace;

And whereas the Governments of the United States of America and the United Kingdom are mutually desirous of concluding now a preliminary agreement in regard to the provision of defense aid and in regard to certain considerations which shall be taken into account in determining such terms and conditions and the making of such an agreement has been in all respects duly authorized, and all acts, conditions and formalities which it may have been necessary to perform, fulfil or execute prior to the making of such an agreement in conformity with the laws either of the United States of America or of the United Kingdom have been performed, fulfilled or executed as required;

The undersigned, being duly authorized by their respective Governments for that purpose, have agreed as follows:

ARTICLE I

The Government of the United States of America will continue to supply the Government of the United Kingdom with such defense articles, defense services, and defense information as the President shall authorize to be transferred or provided.

ARTICLE II

The Government of the United Kingdom will continue to contribute to the defense of the United States of America and the strengthening thereof and will provide such articles, services, facilities or information as it may be in a position to supply.

ARTICLE III

The Government of the United Kingdom will not without the consent of the President of the United States of America transfer title to, or possession of, any defense article or defense information transferred to it under the Act or permit the use thereof by anyone not an officer, employee, or agent of the Government of the United Kingdom.

ARTICLE IV

If, as a result of the transfer to the Government of the United Kingdom of any defense article or defense information, it becomes necessary for that Government to take any action or make any payment in order fully to protect any of the rights of a citizen of the United States of America who has patent rights in and to any such defense article or information, the Government of the United Kingdom will take such action or make such payment when requested to do so by the President of the United States of America.

ARTICLE V

The Government of the United Kingdom will return to the United States of America at the end of the present emergency, as determined by the President, such defense articles transferred under this Agreement as shall not have been destroyed, lost or consumed and as shall be determined by the President to be useful in the defense of the United States of America or of the Western Hemisphere or to be otherwise of use to the United States of America.

ARTICLE VI

In the final determination of the benefits to be provided to the United States of America by the Government of the United Kingdom full cognizance shall be taken of all property, services, information, facilities, or other benefits or considerations provided by the Government of the United Kingdom subsequent to March 11, 1941, and accepted or acknowledged by the President on behalf of the United States of America.

ARTICLE VII

In the final determination of the benefits to be provided to the United States of America by the Government of the United Kingdom in return for aid furnished under the Act of Congress of March 11, 1941, the terms and conditions thereof shall be such as not to burden commerce between the two countries, but to promote mutually advantageous economic relations between them and the betterment of world-wide economic relations. To that end, they shall include provision for agreed action by the United States of America and the United Kingdom, open to participation by all other countries of like mind, directed to the expansion, by appropriate international and domestic measures, of production, employment, and the exchange and consumption of goods, which are the material foundations of the liberty and welfare of all peoples; to the elimination of all forms of discriminatory treatment in international commerce, and to the reduction of tariffs and other trade barriers; and, in general, to the attainment of all the economic objectives set forth in the Joint Declaration made on August 14, 1941, by the President of the United States of America and the Prime Minister of the United Kingdom.

At an early convenient date, conversations shall be begun between the two Governments with a view to determining, in the light of governing economic conditions, the best means of attaining the above stated objectives by their own agreed action and of seeking the agreed action of other like-minded Governments.

ARTICLE VIII

This Agreement shall take effect as from this day's date. It shall continue in force until a date to be agreed upon by the two Governments.

Signed and sealed at Washington in duplicate this twenty-third day of February 1942.

For the Government of the United States of America:

[SEAL] SUMNER WELLES
Acting Secretary of State of the United States of America.

For the Government of the United Kingdom of Great Britain and Northern Ireland:

[SEAL] HALIFAX
His Majesty's Ambassador Extraordinary and
Plenipotentiary at Washington.

Consequences

The Lend-Lease Agreement had the results that Roosevelt desired: it provided Britain with the goods and weapons it needed desperately to stave off the Nazi threat while inevitably drawing the United States closer to war. German attacks on American shipping had resulted in an undeclared war in the Atlantic by the time the Japanese bombed Pearl Harbor. Had that sneak attack never occurred, almost certainly the United States would nevertheless have soon entered the war over some *Lusitania*-style incident—which had sparked American entry into World War I—on the high seas.

Source

National Historical Center, "Lend Lease Act, 11 March 1941." Available online. URL: http://www.history.navy.mil/faqs/faq59-23.htm. Accessed May 16, 2005.

ARTICLES OF AGREEMENT ESTABLISHING THE INTERNATIONAL BANK FOR RECONSTRUCTION AND DEVELOPMENT

TREATY AT A GLANCE

Completed
July 22, 1944, at Bretton Woods, New Hampshire; ratified by conference members December 27, 1945, at Washington, D.C.

Signatories
Initially, the 44 nations participating in the Bretton Woods Conference; subsequently, most United Nations member nations

Overview
Under the auspices of the United Nations, the agreement established the International Bank for Reconstruction and Development, more commonly known as the World Bank, an institution designed to finance projects that further the economic development of member nations.

Historical Background

The vague postwar aims of U.S. president Franklin Delano Roosevelt did not prevent American policy makers from adopting a determined Wilsonian internationalism when they came to consider plans for reconstruction. If nothing else, they were above all certain they wanted to avoid the mistakes that had led after 1918 to economic disaster: hyperinflation, excessive tariffs, unsustainable war debts, and punitive and unrealistic reparations. In 1943, then, the United States sponsored the United Nations Relief and Rehabilitation Administration and in July 1944 presided over the creation of the International Monetary Fund and World Bank at the United Nations Monetary and Financial Conference at Bretton Woods.

The conferees determined that the dollar, returned to the gold standard and convertible at $35 an ounce, would serve as the world's reserve currency, while the pound, the franc, and other currencies would be pegged to the dollar. Reasoning that such stability would allow world trade to recover from the degradation it suffered during the war, those attending the Bretton Woods Conference also sought to ensure low tariffs and avoid a return to virulent economic nationalism through a General Agreement on Tariffs and Trade, although it would be 1948 before the GATT was actually ratified. U.S. treasury secretary Henry Morgenthau tried hard to entice the Soviets to come to Bretton Woods, but Stalin demurred, opting out of the postwar's new economic order.

Terms

The World Bank, which officially began operations in June 1946, shortly after World War II ended, could make loans directly to governments or to private enterprises guaranteed by the appropriate government.

The Governments on whose behalf the present Agreement is signed agree as follows:

INTRODUCTORY ARTICLE

The International Bank for Reconstruction and Development is established and shall operate in accordance with the following provisions:

ARTICLE I

Purposes. The purposes of the Bank are:

(i) To assist in the reconstruction and development of territories of members by facilitating the investment of capital for productive purposes, including the restoration of economies destroyed or disrupted by war, the reconversion of productive facilities to peacetime needs and the encouragement of the development of productive facilities and resources in less developed countries.

(ii) To promote private foreign investment by means of guarantees or participations in loans and other investments made by private investors; and when private capital is not available on reasonable terms, to supplement private investment by providing, on suitable conditions, finance for productive purposes out of its own capital, funds raised by it and its other resources.

(iii) To promote the long-range balanced growth of international trade and the maintenance of equilibrium in balances of payments by encouraging international investment for the development of the productive resources of members, thereby assisting in raising productivity, the standard of living and conditions of labour in their territories.

(iv) To arrange the loans made or guaranteed by it in relation to international loans through other channels so that the more useful and urgent projects, large and small alike, will be dealt with first.

(v) To conduct its operations with due regard to the effect of international investment on business conditions in the territories of members and, in the immediate post-war years, to assist in bringing about a smooth transition from a war-time to a peacetime economy.

The Bank shall be guided in all its decisions by the purposes set forth above.

Consequences

Initially the World Bank made loans to finance post–World War II reconstruction, but by the 1950s it was primarily financing economic development in Africa, Asia, the Middle East, and Latin America. In subsequent decades, the International Monetary Fund and the World Bank became something of an economic police force, insisting that governments of developing nations expand their economic bases, curb excessive inflation, and adopt sound monetary policies before extending their loans. Ironically enough, both played major roles in developing the new economies of former Iron Curtain countries after the fall of the Soviet Union in 1991.

Source
Nicholas Rengger, ed., *Treaties and Alliances of the World,* 5th ed. (London: Longman Current Affairs, 1990), 60–61.

Multinational Conventions and Agreements

ACT OF CHAPULTEPEC

TREATY AT A GLANCE

Completed
March 3, 1945, at Chapultepec Palace, Mexico City, Mexico

Signatories
Nations participating in the Inter-American Conference

Overview
This document affirmed the major tenets of President Franklin D. Roosevelt's good-neighbor policy, which defined U.S. relations to Latin America and was especially important in securing Latin American cooperation during World War II. As the cold war got under way, shoring up that policy was central to U.S. desire to combat Communist-bloc influence in the Western Hemisphere.

Historical Background

Roosevelt introduced the good neighbor concept in his inaugural address of 1933. At the end of that year, at the Pan American Conference in Montevideo, Uruguay, the United States signed a convention forbidding intervention by one state in the affairs of another. In 1934 the U.S. Marines withdrew from a two-decade occupation of Haiti, and the Roosevelt administration formally abrogated the Platt Amendment (see TREATY BETWEEN THE UNITED STATES AND CUBA), which had made an ostensibly independent Cuba a de facto U.S. protectorate. The hope in Latin America, especially when World War II emphasized the strategic importance of such a friendly policy, was that states from the Rio Grande to Cape Horn might become less vulnerable to such U.S. meddling and intimidation, might perhaps even become full partners in a strategic alliance. Instead, these hopes would be dashed by the events already under way in Europe leading to the birth of the cold war.

Terms

The Act of Chapultepec affirmed the unity and commonality of interest of the nations of the Americas and established the first multinational collective security system in the Western Hemisphere. The principal portions of the Act of Chapultepec follow:

PART I

THE GOVERNMENTS represented at the Inter-American Conference on War and Peace declare:

1. That all sovereign states are juridically equal amongst themselves.

2. That every state has the tight to the respect of its individuality and independence on the part of the other members of the international community.

3. That every attack of a state against the integrity or the inviolability of the territory, or against the sovereignty or political independence of an American state, shall, conformably to Part III hereof, be considered as an act of aggression against the other states which sign this act. In any case, invasion by armed forces of one state into the territory of another, trespassing boundaries established by treaty and demarcated in accordance therewith, shall constitute an act of aggression.

4. That in case acts of aggression occur or there may be reasons to believe that an aggression is being prepared by any other state against the integrity and inviolability of the territory, or against the sovereignty or political independence of an American state, the states signatory to this act will consult amongst themselves in order to agree upon the measures it may be advisable to take.

5. That during the war, and until the treaty recommended in Part II hereof is concluded, the signatories of this act recognize that such threats and acts of aggression, as indicated in paragraphs 3 and 4 above, constitute an interference with the war effort of the United Nations, calling for such procedures,

within the scope of their constitutional powers of a general nature and for war, as may be found necessary, including recall of chiefs of diplomatic missions; breaking of diplomatic relations; breaking of consular relations; breaking of postal, telegraphic, telephonic, radiotelephonic relations; interruption of economic, commercial, and financial relations; use of armed force to prevent or repel aggression.

6. That the principles and procedures contained in this declaration shall become effective immediately, inasmuch as any act of aggression or threat of aggression during the present state of war interferes with the war effort of the United Nations to obtain victory. Henceforth, and to the end that the principles and procedures herein stipulated shall conform with the constitutional processes of each republic, the respective governments shall take the necessary steps to perfect this instrument in order that it shall be in force at all times.

PART II

THE INTER-AMERICAN Conference on Problems of War and Peace recommends that, for the purpose of meeting threats or acts of aggression against any American republic following the establishment of peace, the governments of the American republics should consider the conclusion, in accordance with their constitutional processes, of a treaty establishing procedures whereby such threats or acts may be met by the use, by all or some of the signatories of said treaty of any one or more of the following measures: Recall of chiefs of diplomatic missions; breaking of diplomatic relations; breaking of consular relations; breaking of postal, telegraphic, telephonic, radiotelephonic relations; interruption of economic, commercial, and financial relations; use of armed force to prevent or repel aggression.

PART III

THE ABOVE DECLARATION and recommendation constitute a regional arrangement for dealing with such matters relating to the maintenance of international peace and security as are appropriate for regional action in this hemisphere. The said arrangement, and the pertinent activities and procedures, shall be consistent with the purposes and principles of the general international organization, when established.

This agreement shall be known as the Act of Chapultepec.

Consequences

Despite this document and despite such future U.S. initiatives as the creation of the Organization of American States (OAS, 1948) and the Alliance for Progress (1961). U.S.–Latin American relations often suffered during the postwar years and the decades to follow. Many in Central and South America believed that U.S. companies had not abandoned their history of economic exploitation. It also seemed to many that the United States was increasingly reacting to changes in Latin American politics, especially changes aimed at promoting social progress, solely in terms of East-West relations between the superpowers. As the cold war intensified, they believed, the U.S. tended to view all those seeking democratic reforms as Soviet-backed and communist-inspired, and to support entrenched ruling classes or dictatorial strongmen who could best protect U.S. strategic and economic interests at the expense of the common people in the countries they ruled. Especially irksome to many Latin Americans was the growing role that such agencies as the U.S. Central Intelligence Agency played behind the scenes, both in the training of state security personnel and in secret, or "covert," actions aimed at influencing the outcome of internal developments. While diplomacy remained outwardly optimistic, there was often an undercurrent of distrust and resentment that kept relations volatile, if not unstable.

Source
Nicholas Rengger, ed., *Treaties and Alliances of the World,* 5th ed. (London: Longman Current Affairs, 1990), 432.

PACT OF THE ARAB LEAGUE

TREATY AT A GLANCE

Completed
March 22, 1945, at Cairo, Egypt

Signatories
Syria, Transjordan (later Jordan), Iraq, Saudi Arabia, Lebanon, Egypt, and Yemen

Overview
This pact created the Arab League, an organization dedicated to coordinating the political actions and to safeguard the sovereignty of the Arab states.

Historical Background

The Islamic nationalism awakened during World War I came to fruition at the end of World War II. The first great wave of decolonization came when the British and the French, honoring their wartime promises, first evacuated, then recognized the sovereignty of Egypt, Transjordan, and Syria in 1946 and Iraq in 1947. The Arab League was formed in anticipation of these and future liberations (Oman and Yemen, the latter a founding member of the League, remained under British administration until the 1960s; Kuwait and the Trucial States [now the United Arab Emirates] until 1971). Allied support came in recognition of the strategic importance of the Middle East, deriving from its vast oil reserves, the Suez Canal, and its position along the south rim of the Soviet Union. While the Arab kingdoms and republics, all Islamic, were not drawn to communist ideology, the USSR hoped nevertheless to expand its influence by keeping up the pressure on Turkey and Iran and insinuating itself in the many quarrels of the region.

From the beginning and throughout the century, the most intractable of these disputes would be the Arab-Israeli conflict. For World War I had also given rise to the national aspirations of the Jews. Since the 1917 BALFOUR DECLARATION, Zionists had been waiting for the homeland the British had promised them eventually in Palestine. The old Ottoman Empire province had become a British mandate in 1922 under the League of Nations, and the Jewish population of some 60,000 had tripled by the end of the 1920s. Arab resentment against this mass immigration exploded into riots in 1929. Under the encouragement of the grand mufti of Jerusalem, an admirer of the Nazis, Arab rioting became endemic in the years 1936–39. In response, the Jews formed Haganah (Defense), which by 1939 had grown from an underground militia to a semiprofessional army that served as a cobelligerent with the British during the war against Germany.

The Holocaust spawned sympathy for Zionism worldwide, and Franklin Delano Roosevelt in his 1944 reelection campaign endorsed the founding of a "free and democratic Jewish Commonwealth." This put the United States at odds with Britain, which at war's end was seeking to maintain its hegemony in the Middle East through good relations with the Arabs. It should come as no surprise that the more radical Jewish organizations—Menachem Begin's Irgun and the Abraham Stern Group—had turned against the British occupation by 1944, nor perhaps that the Arab League, formed the following year, determined first and foremost to prevent the formation of any such Jewish state in Palestine.

Terms

The postwar formation of the League was favored and actively supported by the English, who believed that the governments destined to dominate the League would thus be well disposed toward Great Britain. However, it proved very difficult to create consensus among the League members and in the one-member, one-vote council of the League, unanimity was required in order to make any action binding.

ARTICLE 1

The League of the Arab States is composed of the independent Arab States which have signed this pact.

Any independent Arab State has the right to become a member of the League. If it desires to do so, it shall submit a request which will be deposited with the permanent Secretariat-General and submitted to the Council at the first meeting held after submission of the request.

ARTICLE 2

The League has as its purpose the strengthening of relations between the Member States; the coordination of their policies in order to achieve cooperation between them and to safeguard their independence and sovereignty; and a general concern with the affairs and interests of the Arab countries. It has also as its purpose the close cooperation of the Member States, with due regard to the organization and circumstances of each State, on the following matters:

(a) Economic and financial affairs, including commercial relations, customs, currency, and questions of agriculture and industry.

(b) Communications: this includes railroads, roads, aviation, navigation, telegraphs, and posts.

(c) Cultural affairs.

(d) Nationality, passports, visas, execution of judgments, and extradition of criminals.

(e) Social affairs.

(f) Health problems.

ARTICLE 3

The League shall possess a Council composed of representatives of the Member States of the League; each State shall have a single vote, irrespective of the number of its representatives.

It shall be the task of the Council to achieve the realization of the objectives of the League and to supervise the execution of agreements which the Member States have concluded on the questions enumerated in the preceding Article, or any other questions.

It likewise shall be the Council's task to decide upon the means by which the League is to cooperate with the international bodies to be created in the future in order to guarantee security and peace and regulate economic and social relations.

ARTICLE 4

For each of the questions listed in Article 2 there shall be set up a special committee in which the Member States of the League shall be represented. These committees shall be charged with the task of laying down the principles and extent of cooperation. Such principles shall be formulated as draft agreements, to be presented to the Council for examination preparatory to their submission to the aforesaid States.

Representatives of the other Arab countries may take part in the work of the aforesaid committees. The Council shall determine the conditions under which these representatives may be permitted to participate and the rules governing such representation.

ARTICLE 5

Any resort to force in order to resolve disputes arising between two or more Member States of the League is prohibited. If there should arise among them a difference which does not concern a State's independence, sovereignty, or territorial integrity, and if the parties to the dispute have recourse to the Council for the settlement of the difference, the decision of the Council shall then be enforceable and obligatory.

In such a case, the States between whom the difference has arisen shall not participate in the deliberations and decisions of the Council.

The Council may lend its good offices for the settlement of all differences which threaten to lead to war between two Member States, or a Member State and a third State, with a view to bringing about their reconciliation.

Decisions of arbitration and mediation shall be taken by majority vote.

ARTICLE 6

In case of aggression or threat of aggression by one State against a Member State, the State which has been attacked or threatened with aggression may demand the immediate convocation of the Council.

The Council shall by unanimous decision determine the measures necessary to repulse the aggression. If the aggressor is a Member State, his vote shall not be counted in determining unanimity.

If, as a result of the attack, the Government of the State attacked finds itself unable to communicate with the Council, the State's representative in the Council shall have the right to request the convocation of the Council for the purpose indicated in the foregoing paragraph. In the event that this representative is unable to communicate with the Council, any Member State of the League shall have the right to request the convocation of the Council.

ARTICLE 7

Unanimous decisions of the Council shall be binding upon all Member States of the League, majority decisions shall be binding only upon those States which have accepted them.

In either case the decisions of the Council shall be enforced in each Member State according to its respective fundamental laws.

ARTICLE 8

Each Member State shall respect the systems of government established in the other Member States and regard them as exclusive concerns of those States. Each shall pledge to abstain from any action calculated to change established systems of governments.

ARTICLE 9

States of the League which desire to establish closer cooperation and stronger bonds than are provided by this Pact may conclude agreements to that end.

Treaties and agreements already concluded or to be concluded in the future between a Member State and another State shall not be binding or restrictive upon other members.

ARTICLE 10

The permanent seat of the League of Arab States is established in Cairo. The Council may, however, assemble at any other place it may designate.

ARTICLE 11

The Council of the League shall convene in ordinary session twice a year, in March and in October. It shall convene in extraordinary session upon the request of two Member States of the League whenever the need arises.

ARTICLE 12

The League shall have a permanent Secretariat-General, which shall consist of a Secretary-General, Assistant Secretaries, and an appropriate number of officials.

The Council of the League shall appoint the Secretary-General by a majority of two-thirds of the States of the League. The Secretary-General, with approval of the Council, shall appoint the Assistant Secretaries and the principal officials of the League. . . .

ARTICLE 16

Except in cases specifically indicated in this Pact, a majority vote of the Council shall be sufficient to make enforceable decisions on the following matters:

(a) Matters relating to personnel.

(b) Adoption of the budget of the League.

(c) Establishment of the administrative regulations for the Council, the committees, and the Secretariat-General.

(d) Decision to adjourn the sessions.

A special "annex" to the pact empowered the Council of the League to appoint an Arab representative of Palestine. The Arabs refused to recognize the legitimacy of Israel, and they considered Israeli territory, in effect, occupied Palestine, a rightfully Arab nation that had as yet failed to achieve independence:

(I) Annex regarding Palestine

Since the termination of the last great war the rule of the Ottoman Empire over the Arab countries, among them Palestine, which had become detached from the Empire, has come to an end. She has come to be independent in herself, not subordinate to any other State.

The Treaty of Lausanne proclaimed that her future was to be settled by the parties concerned.

However, even though she was as yet unable to control her own affairs, the Covenant of the League (of Nations) in 1919 made provision for a régime based upon recognition of her independence.

Her international existence and independence in the legal sense cannot, therefore, be questioned, any more than could the independence of the other Arab countries.

Although the outward manifestations of this independence have remained obscured for reasons beyond her control, this should not be allowed to interfere with her participation in the work of the Council of the League.

The States signatory to the Pact of the Arab League are therefore of the opinion that, considering the special circumstances of Palestine, and until that country can effectively exercise its independence, the Council of the League should take charge of the selection of an Arab representative from Palestine to take part in its work.

Consequences

In the long run, not only did the League prove less than fully effective in resolving disputes between its members, it also failed to coordinate military and political action effectively during a number of armed conflicts with the Israelis, including the Arab-Israeli War of 1948–49 over the creation of the Jewish state; the Sinai War of 1956, over Egypt's nationalization of the Suez Canal; the Six-Day War of 1967, after the withdrawal of U.N. peacekeepers in the region; and the Yom Kippur War of 1973, over Israel's occupation of Arab territory gained in the Six-Day War. Egypt was ejected from the League when President Anwar Sadat suddenly concluded a separate peace with Israel in 1979, and was not readmitted for another decade.

The League was severely tested by the 1990 Iraqi invasion of Kuwait. Twelve of its 21 members condemned Iraq, and nine contributed ground forces to join the international U.S.-led coalition formed against Iraq during the 1991 Persian Gulf War—an unprecedented action for League members.

Comoros joined the League in 1993. In 2002, Libya withdrew, citing as the reason "Arab incapacity" to deal with crisis in the Middle East, referring to both the Israeli-Palestinian conflict and the war between the United States and Iraq. In March 2003, the League voted 21-1 for a resolution demanding U.S. and British withdrawal from Iraq. The lone dissenting vote was cast by Kuwait.

Source

J. A. S. Grenville and Bernard Waserstein, eds., *The Major International Treaties Since 1945* (London and New York: Methuen, 1987), 353–356.

UNITED NATIONS CHARTER

TREATY AT A GLANCE

Completed
Adopted June 25, 1945; entered into force
October 24, 1945, at San Francisco

Signatories
Fifty-one original member nations: Argentina, Australia, Belgium, Bolivia, Brazil, Belarus (Belorussia), Canada, Chile, China, Colombia, Costa Rica, Cuba, Czechoslovakia, Denmark, Dominican Republic, Ecuador, Egypt, El Salvador, Ethiopia, France, Greece, Guatemala, Haiti, Honduras, India, Iran, Iraq, Lebanon, Liberia, Luxembourg, Mexico, Netherlands, New Zealand, Nicaragua, Norway, Panama, Paraguay, Peru, Philippines, Poland, Saudi Arabia, South Africa, Syria, Turkey, Ukraine, United Kingdom, United States, Uruguay, USSR, Venezuela, and Yugoslavia

Overview
The Charter defines the international organization established at the end of World War II to replace the tragically ineffectual League of Nations.

Historical Background

In June 1945, before World War II had ended, delegates from 51 nations met in San Francisco to draft the charter of the United Nations, an attempt to stabilize world politics—more successfully than the TREATY OF VERSAILLES (1919) had done after World War I—by bringing the nations of the planet into a single, cooperative, deliberative forum with sufficient authority to resolve international disputes peacefully.

As at the end of World War I, the nations approaching the end of World War II, seeing everywhere about them the ruin of large parts of the world, desired to find some means of averting future military catastrophes. The San Francisco meeting had been scheduled by the Big Three—British prime minister Winston Churchill, United States president Franklin D. Roosevelt, and Russian president Joseph Stalin—during the February 1945 Yalta Conference in the Crimea (see REPORT OF THE YALTA [CRIMEA] CONFERENCE), called for the express purpose of discussing the final Allied assault on Germany and the postwar division of Europe.

The League of Nations, the international body formed at the end of World War I, hardly provided an encouraging model for the contemplated organization.

As World War II demonstrated, the League had failed, but the nations were prepared to try again.

Terms

Pursuant to the UNITED NATIONS DECLARATION of January 1, 1942, and subsequent meetings and discussion, two sets of conferences were held at Dumbarton Oaks, in Washington, D.C., from August 21 to September 28, 1944, and from September 29 to October 7, 1944, which produced Proposals for the Establishment of a General International Organization, outlining the main structure of the United Nations. The proposals, while comprehensive, left unresolved three major thorny issues: the voting procedures of the Security Council (principal peacekeeping arm of the organization), the membership of the organization, and the question of trusteeship over and disposition of colonial territories. The Yalta Conference partially resolved the voting procedures question (giving each permanent member of the council the right to veto any military enforcement action) and membership questions (agreeing, among other things, that the three Soviet states, Russia, Ukraine, and Belorussia, would each be admitted and that China and France would be invited along with the Big Three).

From April 25 to June 26, 1945, the San Francisco Conference took place, attended by the foreign ministers of the principal Allied powers, together with delegations of lesser nations at war with Germany. In San Francisco the delegates devised a charter that called for a General Assembly, composed of delegates from each member country, and a Security Council, made up of delegates from five permanent member nations and six other members elected for two-year terms. The permanent members of the council—the United States, the Soviet Union, Great Britain, France, and China—were given responsibility for maintaining world peace and could employ a variety of diplomatic, economic, and military measures to achieve that end. To ensure that no coalition or alliance could be formed within the Security Council, the five permanent members were bound to agree unanimously on any action. Debate over Security Council procedures was most intense, even threatening to wreck the nascent organization. The issues were resolved, and especially important were the principles established pertaining to the rights of nations to defend themselves singly or in alliance in the event that the Security Council, through lack of agreement, should be unable to act. This right, embodied in Article 51 of the United Nations Charter, was the basis for the formation of NATO and other regional alliances (see NORTH ATLANTIC TREATY).

The main purposes of the United Nations were set forth in the preamble to the Charter and in Chapter I, Article 1:

We the People of the United Nations determined
to save succeeding generations from the scourge of war, which twice in our lifetime has brought untold sorrow to mankind, and
to reaffirm faith in fundamental human rights, in the dignity and worth of the human person, in the equal rights of men and women and of nations large and small, and
to establish conditions under which justice and respect for the obligations arising from treaties and other sources of international law can be maintained, and
to promote social progress and better standards of life in larger freedom,
and for these ends
to practice tolerance and live together in peace with one another as good neighbors, and
to unite our strength to maintain international peace and security, and
to ensure, by the acceptance of principles and the institution of methods, that armed force shall not be used, save in the common interest, and
to employ international machinery for the promotion of the economic and social advancement of all peoples,
have resolved to combine our efforts to accomplish these aims

Accordingly, our respective Governments, through representatives assembled in the city of San Francisco, who have exhibited their full powers found to be in good and due form, have agreed to the present Charter of the United Nations and do hereby establish an international organization to be known as the United Nations.

Chapter I: Purposes and Principles

ARTICLE I
The Purposes of the United Nations are:
1. To maintain international peace and security, and to that end: to take effective collective measures for the prevention and removal of threats to the peace, and for the suppression of acts of aggression or other breaches of the peace, and to bring about by peaceful means, and in conformity with the principles of justice and international law, adjustment or settlement of international disputes or situations which might lead to a breach of the peace;
2. To develop friendly relations among nations based on respect for the principle of equal rights and self-determination of peoples, and to take other appropriate measures to strengthen universal peace;
3. To achieve international cooperation in solving international problems of an economic, social, cultural, or humanitarian character, and in promoting and encouraging respect for human rights and for fundamental freedoms for all without distinction as to race, sex, language, or religion; and
4. To be a center of harmonizing the actions of nations in the attainment of these common ends.

In vivid contrast to the COVENANT OF THE LEAGUE OF NATIONS, which was judicial and legalistic in tenor, the opening of the Charter set a political and morally idealistic tone.

Membership was "open to all . . . peace-loving States which accept the obligations contained in the present Charter and, in the judgement of the Organization, are able and willing to carry out these obligations" (Chapter II, Article 4). Chapter III established the "principal organs of the United Nations": the Security Council, the General Assembly, the Economic and Social Council, the Trusteeship Council, the International Court of Justice, and a Secretariat. The Charter also allowed for the subsequent creation of "subsidiary organs" as required.

As mentioned, the primary responsibility for maintaining international peace and security was assigned to the Security Council, but its effective operation was ultimately based on the highly dubious assumption that World War II's "Big Five" Allies could reach unanimity on issues of war and peace in the postwar world. The General Assembly, in which all member nations participated, was set up as a forum for debating world issues. As was the case with the League of Nations, it was believed that openly discussing disputes between nations would encourage their peaceful resolution. The Economic and Social Council was founded in the conviction that much international conflict was rooted in poverty and want and that, therefore, international efforts to raise standards of living worldwide would promote peace worldwide. Colonialism was seen as yet another frequent source of war, and accordingly, the Trusteeship Council was established to promote the peaceful independence of colonial states. The absence of common legal standards among nations also promoted war, according to the founders of the United Nations. The International Court of Justice was established to address this and provide a legally binding forum for resolving international differences peacefully. Finally, the Secretariat was established to administer the day-to-day workings and programs of the organization. It would be operated by a core of men and women who answered not primarily to their nations of citizenship but to the international community.

Chapter IV: The General Assembly

COMPOSITION

ARTICLE 9

1. The General Assembly shall consist of all the Members of the United Nations.

2. Each Member shall have not more than five representatives in the General Assembly.

FUNCTIONS AND POWERS

ARTICLE 10

The General Assembly may discuss any questions or any matter within the scope of the present Charter or relating to the powers and functions of any organs provided for in the present Charter, and, except as provided in Article 12, may make recommendations to the Members of the United Nations or to the Security Council or to both on any such questions or matters.

ARTICLE 11

1. The General Assembly may consider the general principles of cooperation in the maintenance of international peace and security, including the principles governing disarmament and the regulation of armaments, and may make recommendations with regard to such principles to the Members or to the Security Council or to both.

2. The General Assembly may discuss any questions relating to the maintenance of international peace and security brought before it by any Member of the United Nations, or by the Security Council, or by a State which is not a Member of the United Nations in accordance with Article 35, paragraph 2, and, except as provided in Article 12, may make recommendations with regard to any such question to the State or States concerned or to the Security Council or to both. Any such question on which action is necessary shall be referred to the Security Council by the General Assembly either before or after discussion.

3. The General Assembly may call the attention of the Security Council to situations which are likely to endanger international peace and security.

4. The powers of the General Assembly set forth in this Article shall not limit the general scope of Article 10.

ARTICLE 12

1. While the Security Council is exercising in respect of any dispute or situation the functions assigned to it in the present Charter, the General Assembly shall not make any recommendations with regard to that dispute or situation unless the Security Council so requests.

2. The Secretary-General, with the consent of the Security Council, shall notify the General Assembly at each session of any matters relative to the maintenance of international peace and security which are being dealt with by the Security Council and shall similarly notify the General Assembly, or the Members of the United Nations if the General Assembly is not in session, immediately the Security Council ceases to deal with such matters.

ARTICLE 13

1. The General Assembly shall initiate studies and make recommendations for the purpose of:

(a) promoting international cooperation in the political field and encouraging the progressive development of international law and its codification;

(b) promoting international cooperation in the economic, social, cultural, educational, and health fields, and assisting in the realization of human rights and fundamental freedoms for all without distinction as to race, sex, language, or religion.

2. The further responsibilities, functions, and powers of the General Assembly with respect to matters mentioned in paragraph I(b) above are set forth in Chapters IX and X.

ARTICLE 14

Subject to the provisions of Article 12, the General Assembly may recommend measures for the peaceful adjustment of any situation, regardless of origin, which it deems likely to impair the general welfare or friendly relations among nations, including situations resulting from a violation of the provisions of the present Charter setting forth the Purposes and Principles of the United Nations.

ARTICLE 15

1. The General Assembly shall receive and consider annual and special reports from the Security Council; these reports shall include an account of the measures that the Security Council has decided upon or taken to maintain international peace and security.

2. The General Assembly shall receive and consider reports from the other organs of the United Nations.

ARTICLE 16

The General Assembly shall perform such functions with respect to the international trusteeship system as are assigned to it under Chapters XII and XIII, including the approval of the trusteeship agreements for areas not designated as strategic.

ARTICLE 17

1. The General Assembly shall consider and approve the budget of the Organization.

2. The expenses of the Organization shall be borne by the Members as apportioned by the General Assembly.

3. The General Assembly shall consider and approve any financial and budgetary arrangements with specialized agencies referred to in Article 57 and shall examine the administrative budgets of such specialized agencies with a view to making recommendations to the agencies concerned.

VOTING

ARTICLE 18

1. Each member of the General Assembly shall have one vote.

2. Decisions of the General Assembly on important questions shall be made by a two-thirds majority of the members present and voting. These questions shall include: recommendations with respect to the maintenance of international peace and security, the election of the nonpermanent members of the Security Council, the election of the members of the Economic and Social Council, the election of members of the Trusteeship Council in accordance with paragraph 1(c) of Article 86, the admission of new Members to the United Nations, the suspension of the rights and privileges of membership, the expulsion of Members, questions relating to the operation of the trusteeship system, and budgetary questions.

3. Decisions on other questions, including the determination of additional categories of questions to be decided by a two-thirds majority, shall be made by a majority of the members present and voting.

ARTICLE 19

A Member of the United Nations which is in arrears in the payment of its financial contributions to the Organization shall have no vote in the General Assembly if the amount of its arrears equals or exceeds the amount of the contributions due from it for the preceding two full years. The General Assembly may, nevertheless, permit such a Member to vote if it is satisfied that the failure to pay is due to conditions beyond the control of the Member.

PROCEDURE

ARTICLE 20

The General Assembly shall meet in regular annual sessions and in such special sessions as occasion may require. Special sessions shall be convoked by the Secretary-General at the request of the Security Council or of a majority of the Members of the United Nations.

ARTICLE 21

The General Assembly shall adopt its own rules of procedure. It shall elect its President for each session.

ARTICLE 22

The General Assembly may establish such subsidiary organs as it deems necessary for the performance of its functions.

Chapter V: The Security Council

COMPOSITION

ARTICLE 23

1. The Security Council shall consist of fifteen Members of the United Nations. The Republic of China, France, the Union of Soviet Socialist Republics, the United Kingdom of Great Britain and Northern Ireland, and the United States of America shall be permanent members of the Security Council. The General Assembly shall elect ten other Members of the United Nations to be nonpermanent members of the Security Council, due regard being specially paid, in the first instance to the contribution of Members of the United Nations to the maintenance of international peace and security and to the other purposes of the Organization, and also to equitable geographical distribution.

2. The non-permanent members of the Security Council shall be elected for a term of two years. In the first election of the non-permanent members after the increase of the membership of the Security Council from eleven to fifteen, two of the four additional members shall be chosen for a term of one year. A retiring member shall not be eligible for immediate re-election.

3. Each member of the Security Council shall have one representative.

FUNCTIONS AND POWERS

ARTICLE 24

1. In order to ensure prompt and effective action by the United Nations, its Members confer on the Security Council primary responsibility for the maintenance of international peace and security, and agree that in carrying out its duties under this responsibility the Security Council acts on their behalf.

2. In discharging these duties the Security Council shall act in accordance with the Purposes and Principles of the United Nations. The specific powers granted to the Security Council for the discharge of these duties are laid down in Chapters VI, VII, VIII, and XII.

3. The Security Council shall submit annual and, when necessary, special reports to the General Assembly for its consideration.

ARTICLE 25

The Members of the United Nations agree to accept and carry out the decisions of the Security Council in accordance with the present Charter.

ARTICLE 26

In order to promote the establishment and maintenance of international peace and security with the least diversion for armaments of the world's human and economic resources, the Security Council shall be responsible for formulating, with the assistance of the Military Staff Committee referred to in Article 47, plans to be submitted to the Members of the United Nations for the establishment of a system for the regulation of armaments.

VOTING

ARTICLE 27

1. Each member of the Security Council shall have one vote.

2. Decisions of the Security Council on procedural matters shall be made by an affirmative vote of nine members.

3. Decisions of the Security Council on all other matters shall be made by an affirmative vote of nine members including the concurring votes of the permanent members; provided that, in decisions under Chapter VI, and under paragraph 3 of Article 52, a party to a dispute shall abstain from voting.

PROCEDURE

ARTICLE 28

1. The Security Council shall be so organized as to be able to function continuously. Each member of the Security Council shall for this purpose be represented at all times at the seat of the Organization.

2. The Security Council shall hold periodic meetings at which each of its members may, if it so desires, be represented by a member of the Government or by some other specially designated representative.

3. The Security Council may hold meetings at such places other than the seat of the Organization as in its judgement will best facilitate its work.

ARTICLE 29

The Security Council may establish such subsidiary organs as it deems necessary for the performance of its functions.

ARTICLE 30

The Security Council shall adopt its own rules of procedure, including the method of selecting its President.

ARTICLE 31

Any Member of the United Nations which is not a member of the Security Council may participate, without vote, in the discussion of any question brought before the Security Council whenever the latter considers that the interests of that Member are specially affected.

ARTICLE 32

Any Member of the United Nations which is not a member of the Security Council or any State which is not a Member of the United Nations, if it is a party to a dispute under consideration by the Security Council, shall be invited to participate, without vote, in the discussion relating to the dispute. The Security Council shall lay down such conditions as it deems just for the participation of a State which is not a Member of the United Nations.

Chapter VI: Pacific settlement of disputes

ARTICLE 33

1. The parties to any dispute, the continuance of which is likely to endanger the maintenance of international peace and security, shall, first of all, seek a solution by negotiation, enquiry, mediation, conciliation, arbitration, judicial settlement, resort to regional agencies or arrangements, or other peaceful means of their own choice.

2. The Security Council shall, when it deems necessary, call upon the parties to settle their dispute by such means.

ARTICLE 34

The Security Council may investigate any dispute, or any situation which might lead to international friction or give rise to a dispute, in order to determine whether the continuance of the dispute or situation is likely to endanger the maintenance of international peace and security.

ARTICLE 35

1. Any Member of the United Nations may bring any dispute, or any situation of the nature referred to in Article 34, to the attention of the Security Council or of the General Assembly.

2. A State which is not a Member of the United Nations may bring to the attention of the Security Council or of the General Assembly any dispute to which it is a party if it accepts in advance, for the purposes of the dispute, the obligations of pacific settlement provided in the present Charter.

3. The proceedings of the General Assembly in respect of matters brought to its attention under this Article will be subject to the provisions of Articles 11 and 12.

ARTICLE 36

1. The Security Council may, at any stage of a dispute of the nature referred to in Article 33 or of a situation of like nature, recommend appropriate procedures or methods of adjustment.

2. The Security Council should take into consideration any procedures for the settlement of the dispute which have already been adopted by the parties.

3. In making recommendations under this Article the Security Council should also take into consideration that legal disputes should as a general rule be referred by the parties to the International Court of Justice in accordance with the provisions of the Statute of the Court.

ARTICLE 37

1. Should the parties to a dispute of the nature referred to in Article 33 fail to settle it by the means indicated in that Article, they shall refer it to the Security Council.

2. If the Security Council deems that the continuance of the dispute is in fact likely to endanger the maintenance of international peace and security, it shall decide whether to take action under Article 36 or

to recommend such terms of settlement as it may consider appropriate.

ARTICLE 38

Without prejudice to the provisions of Articles 33 to 37, the Security Council may, if all the parties to any dispute so request, make recommendations to the parties with a view to a pacific settlement of the dispute.

Chapter VII: Action with respect to threats to the peace, breaches of the peace, and acts of aggression

ARTICLE 39

The Security Council shall determine the existence of any threat to the peace, breach of the peace, or act of aggression and shall make recommendations, or decide what measures shall be taken in accordance with Articles 41 and 42, to maintain or restore international peace and security.

ARTICLE 40

In order to prevent an aggravation of the situation, the Security Council may, before making the recommendations or deciding upon the measures provided for in Article 39, call upon the parties concerned to comply with such provisional measures as it seems necessary or desirable. Such provisional measures shall be without prejudice to the rights, claims, or position of the parties concerned. The Security Council shall duly take account of failure to comply with such provisional measures.

ARTICLE 41

The Security Council may decide what measures not involving the use of armed force are to be employed to give effect to its decisions, and it may call upon the Members of the United Nations to apply such measures. These may include complete or partial interruption of economic relations and of rail, sea, air, postal, telegraphic, radio, and other means of communication, and the severance of diplomatic relations.

ARTICLE 42

Should the Security Council consider that measures provided for in Article 41 would be inadequate or have proved to be inadequate, it may take such action by air, sea, or land forces as may be necessary to maintain or restore international peace and security. Such action may include demonstrations, blockade, and other operations by air, sea, or land forces of Members of the United Nations.

ARTICLE 43

1. All Members of the United Nations, in order to contribute to the maintenance of international peace and security, undertake to make available to the Security Council, on its call and in accordance with a special agreement or agreements, armed forces, assistance, and facilities, including rights of passage, necessary for the purpose of maintaining international peace and security.

2. Such agreement or agreements shall govern the numbers and types of forces, their degree of readiness and general location, and the nature of the facilities and assistance to be provided.

3. The agreement or agreements shall be negotiated as soon as possible on the initiative of the Security Council. They shall be concluded between the Security Council and Members or between the Security Council and groups of Members and shall be subject to ratification by the signatory States in accordance with their respective constitutional processes.

ARTICLE 44

When the Security Council has decided to use force it shall, before calling upon a Member not represented on it to provide armed forces in fulfillment of the obligations assumed under Article 43, invite that Member, if the Member so desires, to participate in the decisions of the Security Council concerning the employment of contingents of that Member's armed forces.

ARTICLE 45

In order to enable the United Nations to take urgent military measures, Members shall hold immediately available national airforce contingents for combined international enforcement action. The strength and degree of readiness of these contingents and plans for their combined action shall be determined, within the limits laid down in the special agreement or agreements referred to in Article 43, by the Security Council with the assistance of the Military Staff Committee.

ARTICLE 46

Plans for the application of armed force shall be made by the Security Council with the assistance of the Military Staff Committee.

ARTICLE 47

1. There shall be established a Military Staff Committee to advise and assist the Security Council on all questions relating to the Security Council's military requirements for the maintenance of international peace and security, the employment and command of forces placed at its disposal, the regulation of armaments, and possible disarmament.

2. The Military Staff Committee shall consist of the Chiefs of Staff of the permanent members of the Security Council or their representatives. Any Member of the United Nations not permanently represented on the Committee shall be invited by the Committee to be associated with it when the efficient discharge of the Committee's responsibilities requires the participation of that Member in its work.

3. The Military Staff Committee shall be responsible under the Security Council for the strategic direction of any armed forces placed at the disposal of the Security Council. Questions relating to the command of such forces shall be worked out subsequently.

4. The Military Staff Committee, with the authorization of the Security Council and after consultation with appropriate regional agencies, may establish regional sub-committees.

ARTICLE 48

1. The action required to carry out the decisions of the Security Council for the maintenance of international peace and security shall be taken by all the Members of the United Nations or by some of them, as the Security Council may determine.

2. Such decisions shall be carried out by the Members of the United Nations directly and through their action in the appropriate international agencies of which they are members.

ARTICLE 49

The Members of the United Nations shall join in affording mutual assistance in carrying out the measures decided upon by the Security Council.

ARTICLE 50

If preventive or enforcement measures against any State are taken by the Security Council, any other State, whether a Member of the United Nations or not, which finds itself confronted with special economic problems arising from the carrying out of those measures shall have the right to consult the Security Council with regard to a solution of those problems.

ARTICLE 51

Nothing in the present Charter shall impair the inherent right of individual or collective self-defence if an armed attack occurs against a Member of the United Nations, until the Security Council has taken measures necessary to maintain international peace and security. Measures taken by Members in the exercise of this right of self-defence shall be immediately reported to the Security Council and shall not in any way affect the authority and responsibility of the Security Council under the present Charter to take at any time such action as it deems necessary in order to maintain or restore international peace and security.

Chapter VIII: Regional arrangements

ARTICLE 52

1. Nothing in the present Charter precludes the existence of regional arrangements or agencies for dealing with such matters relating to the maintenance of international peace and security as are appropriate for regional action, provided that such arrangements or agencies and their activities are consistent with the Purposes and Principles of the United Nations.

2. The Members of the United Nations entering into such arrangements or constituting such agencies shall make every effort to achieve pacific settlement of local disputes through such regional arrangements or by such regional agencies before referring them to the Security Council.

3. The Security Council shall encourage the development of pacific settlement of local disputes through such regional arrangements or by such regional agencies either on the initiative of the States concerned or by reference from the Security Council.

4. This Article in no way impairs the application of Articles 34 and 35.

ARTICLE 53

1. The Security Council shall, where appropriate, utilize such regional arrangements or agencies for enforcement action under its authority. But no enforcement action shall be taken under regional arrangements or by regional agencies without the authorization of the Security Council, with the exception of measures against any Enemy State, as defined in paragraph 2 of this Article, provided for pursuant to Article 107 or in regional arrangements directed against renewal of aggressive policy on the part of any such State, until such time as the Organization may, on request of the Governments concerned, be charged with the responsibility for preventing further aggression by such a State.

2. The term Enemy State as used in paragraph I of this Article applies to any State which during the Second World War has been an enemy of any signatory of the present Charter.

ARTICLE 54

The Security Council shall at all times be kept fully informed of activities undertaken or in contemplation under regional arrangements or by regional agencies for the maintenance of international peace and security.

Chapter IX: International economic and social cooperation

ARTICLE 55

With a view to the creation of conditions of stability and well-being which are necessary for peaceful and friendly relations among nations based on respect for the principle of equal rights and self-determination of peoples, the United Nations shall promote:

(a) higher standards of living, full employment, and conditions of economic and social progress and development;

(b) solutions of international economic, social, health, and related problems; and international cultural and educational cooperation; and

(c) universal respect for, and observance of, human rights and fundamental freedoms for all without distinction as to race, sex, language, or religion.

ARTICLE 56

All Members pledge themselves to take joint and separate action in cooperation with the Organization for the achievement of the purposes set forth in Article 55.

ARTICLE 57

1. The various specialized agencies, established by intergovernmental agreement and having wide international responsibilities, as defined in their basic instruments, in economic, social, cultural, educational, health, and related fields, shall be brought into relationship with the United Nations in accordance with the provisions of Article 63.

2. Such agencies thus brought into relationship with the United Nations are hereinafter referred to as specialized agencies.

ARTICLE 58

The Organization shall make recommendations for the coordination of the policies and activities of the specialized agencies.

ARTICLE 59

The Organization shall, where appropriate, initiate negotiations among the States concerned for the creation of any new specialized agencies required for the accomplishment of the purposes set forth in Article 55.

ARTICLE 60

Responsibility for the discharge of the functions of the Organization set forth in this Chapter shall be vested in the General Assembly and, under the authority of the General Assembly, in the Economic and Social Council, which shall have for this purpose the powers set forth in Chapter X.

Chapter X: The Economic and Social Council

COMPOSITION

ARTICLE 61

1. The Economic and Social Council shall consist of twenty-seven Members of the United Nations elected by the General Assembly. . . .

FUNCTIONS AND POWERS

ARTICLE 62

1. The Economic and Social Council may make or initiate studies and reports with respect to international economic, social, cultural, educational, health, and related matters and may make recommendations with respect to any such matters to the General Assembly, to the Members of the United Nations, and to the specialized agencies concerned. . . .

Articles 62–66 set out in detail these functions and powers.

VOTING

ARTICLE 67

1. Each member of the Economic and Social Council shall have one vote.

2. Decisions of the Economic and Social Council shall be made by a majority of the members present and voting.

Articles 68–72 set out in detail the procedures to be followed.

Chapter XI: Declaration regarding non-self-governing territories

ARTICLE 73

Members of the United Nations which have or assume responsibilities for the administration of territories whose peoples have not yet attained a full measure of self-government recognize the principle that the interests of the inhabitants of these territories are paramount, and accept as a sacred trust the obligation to promote to the utmost, within the system of international peace and security established by the present Charter, the well-being of the inhabitants of these territories, and, to this end:

(a) to ensure, with due respect for the culture of the peoples concerned, their political, economic, social, and educational advancement, their just treatment, and their protection against abuses;

(b) to develop self-government, to take due account of the political aspirations of the peoples, and to assist them in the progressive development of their free political institutions, according to the particular circumstances of each territory and its peoples and their varying stages of advancement;

(c) to further international peace and security;

(d) to promote constructive measures of development, to encourage research, and to cooperate with one another and, when and where appropriate, with specialized international bodies with a view to the practical achievement of the social, economic, and scientific purposes set forth in this Article; and

(e) to transmit regularly to the Secretary-General for information purposes, subject to such limitation as security and constitutional considerations may require, statistical and other information of a technical nature relating to economic, social, and educational conditions in the territories for which they are respectively responsible other than those territories to which Chapters XII and XIII apply.

ARTICLE 74

Members of the United Nations also agree that their policy in respect of the territories to which this Chapter applies, no less than in respect of their metropolitan areas, must be based on the general principle of good-neighborliness, due account being taken of the interests and well-being of the rest of the world, in social, economic, and commercial matters.

Chapter XII: International trusteeship system

ARTICLE 75

The United Nations shall establish under its authority an international trusteeship system for the administration and supervision of such territories as may be placed thereunder by subsequent individual agreements. These territories are hereinafter referred to as trust territories.

ARTICLE 76

The basic objectives of the trusteeship system, in accordance with the Purposes of the United Nations laid down in Article I of the present Charter, shall be:

(a) to further international peace and security;

(b) to promote the political, economic, social, and educational advancement of the inhabitants of the trust territories, and their progressive development towards self-government or independence as may be appropriate to the particular circumstances of each territory and its peoples and the freely expressed wishes of the peoples concerned, and as may be provided by the terms of each trusteeship agreement;

(c) to encourage respect for human rights and for fundamental freedoms for all without distinction as to race, sex, language, or religion, and to encourage recognition of the interdependence of the peoples of the world; and

(d) to ensure equal treatment in social, economic, and commercial matters for all Members of the United Nations and their nationals, and also equal treatment for the latter in the administration of justice, without prejudice to the attainment of the foregoing objectives and subject to the provisions of Article 80.

ARTICLE 77

1. The trusteeship system shall apply to such territories in the following categories as may be placed thereunder by means of trusteeship agreements:

(a) territories now held under mandate;

(b) territories which may be detached from Enemy States as a result of the Second World War; and

(c) territories voluntarily placed under the system by States responsible for their administration.

2. It will be a matter for subsequent agreement as to which territories in the foregoing categories will be brought under the trusteeship system and upon what terms.

ARTICLE 78

The trusteeship system shall not apply to territories which have become Members of the United Nations, relationship among which shall be based on respect for the principle of sovereign equality.

ARTICLE 79

The terms of trusteeship for each territory to be placed under the trusteeship system, including any alteration or amendment, shall be agreed upon by the States directly concerned, including the mandatory power in the case of territories held under mandate by a Member of the United Nations, and shall be approved as provided for in Articles 83 and 85.

ARTICLE 80

1. Except as may be agreed upon in individual trusteeship agreements, made under Articles 77, 79, and 81, placing each territory under the trusteeship system, and until such agreements have been concluded, nothing in this Chapter shall be construed in or of itself to alter in any manner the rights whatsoever of any States or any peoples or the terms of existing international instruments to which Members of the United Nations may respectively be parties.

2. Paragraph I of this Article shall not be interpreted as giving grounds for delay or postponement of the negotiation and conclusion of agreements for placing mandated and other territories under the trusteeship system as provided for in Article 77.

ARTICLE 81

The trusteeship agreement shall in each case include the terms under which the trust territory will be administered and designate the authority which will exercise the administration of the trust territory. Such authority, hereinafter called the administering authority, may be one or more States or the Organization itself.

ARTICLE 82

There may be designated, in any trusteeship agreement, a strategic area or areas which may include part or all of the trust territory to which the agreement applies, without prejudice to any special agreement or agreements made under Article 43.

ARTICLE 83

1. All functions of the United Nations relating to strategic areas, including the approval of the terms of trusteeship agreements and of their alteration or amendment, shall be exercised by the Security Council.

2. The basic objectives set forth in Article 76 shall be applicable to the people of each strategic area.

3. The Security Council shall, subject to the provisions of the trusteeship agreements and without prejudice to security considerations, avail itself of the assistance of the Trusteeship Council to perform those functions of the United Nations under the trusteeship system relating to political, economic, social, and educational matters in the strategic areas.

ARTICLE 84

It shall be the duty of the administering authority to ensure that the trust territory shall play its part in the maintenance of international peace and security. To this end the administering authority may make use of volunteer forces, facilities, and assistance from the trust territory in carrying out the obligations towards the Security Council undertaken in this regard by the administering authority, as well as for local defence and the maintenance of law and order within the trust territory.

ARTICLE 85

1. The functions of the United Nations with regard t o trusteeship agreements for all areas not designated as strategic, including the approval of the terms of the trusteeship agreements and of their alteration or amendment, shall be exercised by the General Assembly.

2. The Trusteeship Council, operating under the authority of the General Assembly, shall assist General Assembly in carrying out these functions.

Chapter XIII: The Trusteeship Council

COMPOSITION

ARTICLE 86

1. The Trusteeship Council shall consist of the following Members of the United Nations:

(a) those Members administering trust territories;

(b) such of those Members mentioned by name in Article 23 as are not administering trust territories; and

(c) as many other Members elected for three-year terms by the General Assembly as may be necessary to ensure that the total number of members of the

Trusteeship Council is equally divided between those Members of the United Nations which administer trust territories and those which do not.

2. Each member of the Trusteeship Council shall designate one specially qualified person to represent it therein.

FUNCTIONS AND POWERS

ARTICLE 87

The General Assembly and, under its authority, the Trusteeship Council, in carrying out their functions, may:

(a) consider reports submitted by the administering authority;

(b) accept petitions and examine them in consultation with the administering authority;

(c) provide for periodic visits to the respective trust territories at times agreed upon with the administering authority; and

(d) take these and other actions in conformity with the terms of the trusteeship agreements.

Article 88. The Trusteeship Council shall formulate a questionnaire on the political, economic, social, and educational advancement of the inhabitants of each trust territory, and the administering authority for each trust territory within the competence of the General Assembly shall make an annual report to the General Assembly upon the basis of such questionnaire.

VOTING

ARTICLE 89

1. Each member of the Trusteeship Council shall have one vote.

2. Decisions of the Trusteeship Council shall be made by a majority of the members present and voting.

PROCEDURE

ARTICLE 90

1. The Trusteeship Council shall adopt its own rules of procedure, including the method of selecting its President. . . .

Chapter XIV: The International Court of Justice

ARTICLE 92

The International Court of Justice shall be the principal judicial organ of the United Nations. It shall function in accordance with the annexed Statute, which is based upon the Statute of the Permanent Court of International Justice and forms an integral part of the present Charter.

ARTICLE 93

1. All Members of the United Nations are *ipso facto* parties to the Statute of the International Court of Justice.

2. A State which is not a Member of the United Nations may become a party to the Statute of the International Court of Justice on conditions to be determined in each case by the General Assembly upon the recommendation of the Security Council.

ARTICLE 94

1. Each Member of the United Nations undertakes to comply with the decision of the International Court of Justice in any case to which it is a party.

2. If any party to a case fails to perform the obligations incumbent upon it under a judgement rendered by the Court, the other party may have recourse to the Security Council, which may, if it deems necessary, make recommendations or decide upon measures to be taken to give effect to the judgement.

ARTICLE 95

Nothing in the present Charter shall prevent Members of the United Nations from entrusting the solution of their differences to other tribunals by virtue of agreements already in existence or which may be concluded in the future.

ARTICLE 96

1. The General Assembly or the Security Council may request the International Court of Justice to give an advisory opinion on any legal question.

2. Other organs of the United Nations and specialized agencies, which may at any time be so authorized by the General Assembly, may also request advisory opinions of the Court on legal questions arising within the scope of their activities.

Chapter XV: The Secretariat

ARTICLE 97

The Secretariat shall comprise a Secretary-General and such staff as the Organization may require. The Secretary-General shall be appointed by the General Assembly upon the recommendation of the Security Council. He shall be the chief administrative officer of the Organization.

ARTICLE 98

The Secretary-General shall act in that capacity in all meetings of the General Assembly, of the Security Council, of the Economic and Social Council, and of the Trusteeship Council, and shall perform such other functions as are entrusted to him by these organs. The Secretary-General shall make an annual report to the General Assembly on the work of the Organization.

ARTICLE 99

The Secretary-General may bring to the attention of the Security Council any matter which in his opinion may threaten the maintenance of international peace and security.

ARTICLE 100

1. In the performance of their duties the Secretary-General and the staff shall not seek or receive instructions from any Government or from any other authority external to the Organization. They shall refrain from any action which might reflect on their position as international officials responsible only to the Organization.

2. Each Member of the United Nations undertakes to respect the exclusively international character of

the responsibilities of the Secretary-General and the staff and not to seek to influence them in the discharge of their responsibilities.

ARTICLE 101

1. The staff shall be appointed by the Secretary-General under regulations established by the General Assembly. . . .

Consequences

Given the disparity of ideology among the permanent members, unanimity was bound to be rare, and the United Nations quickly became a forum for international discussion rather than an organization that exercised military or concerted diplomatic action. The General Assembly of the new organization first met in London in 1946, but later assemblies convened at the permanent headquarters in New York City, built by an international team of architects under the general direction of the great French modernist Le Corbusier on an $8.5 million parcel of land along the East River donated by John D. Rockefeller, Jr.

At that first London meeting, bitter debate surrounded the Soviet Union's continued occupation of the Azerbaijan region of Iran and Great Britain's continued occupation of Greece. Another early issue centered on the control of atomic energy. The Atomic Energy Commission was created by the General Assembly in 1946 to explore the area of atomic control, and in June of that year, it devised a plan to outlaw all atomic weapons. The debate ended with a Soviet veto of the plan; the Soviet Union refused to allow UN-mandated inspectors inside its borders and likewise declined to relinquish its veto power over atomic matters in the Security Council by entrusting the regulation of such matters to the Atomic Energy Commission. The Soviets had their reasons: although they would not test their first atomic bomb until 1949, they were well on their way to building one, thanks in part to Soviet espionage within the wartime Manhattan Project, which developed the U.S. bombs. Meanwhile, the United States, which had dropped what at the time were the world's only nuclear devices on Japan in 1945, was secretly researching and planning to construct the many times more powerful thermonuclear hydrogen bomb, which would first be tested in 1952.

This failure to eradicate the nuclear threat was a terrific disappointment and, from the start, a crippling blow to the prestige of the United Nations. With the superpowers holding one another hostage to a policy of mutually assured destruction, the world was doomed to almost five decades of cold war, and as the members of the "atomic club" played a potentially deadly game of ideological chess, so-called third world nations found in the United Nations little more than an often hollow

debating society. And warfare—hot warfare—was by no means brought to an end, not in Korea, not in Southeast Asia, not in the Middle East. Nevertheless, as the cold war began to wind down in the 1980s, the mission of the United Nations suddenly became clear again, and the organization played a strategically central political role in the Persian Gulf War against Saddam Hussein's Iraq, which had invaded neighboring Kuwait, and in subsequent warfare in Africa and the Balkans.

The effectiveness of the United Nations in the Gulf War seemed to bode well for the future, yet the world body has seemed relatively powerless to improve conditions in the war-torn republics of the former Yugoslavia. The collapse of the cold war had left them in almost the same ethnic and national confusion of conflicting claims that prevailed at the end of World War I, which itself had failed to resolve the conflicts created by the Balkan Wars at the dawn of the century. Neither could the United Nations seem to propose an effective solution to the horrifying internal strife afflicting the African nations of Somalia and Rwanda, whose tribal struggles in many ways resembled the ethnic conflicts of the Balkans.

Hopes for an increasingly prominent role for the United Nations in resolving international conflicts were dashed by the United States when President George W. Bush decided to expand the U.S. war on terror into an invasion of Iraq. The former, aimed at the perpetrators of the September 11, 2001, attacks on the twin towers of the World Trade Center in New York City and the Pentagon outside Washington, D.C., was fought primarily in Afghanistan and enjoyed the support of most member countries of the United Nations. The latter, a hastily decided attempt to remove Saddam Hussein from power and "democratize" Iraq, was disavowed not only by most of the UN member nations but also by all the longtime U.S. allies in Western Europe save Britain (which participated in the invasion). The United States justified its invasion before the United Nations with claims that Hussein had "weapons of mass destruction." After these claims proved false, the General Assembly gave President Bush an extremely chilly reception at an appearance during his reelection campaign. Clearly there was a growing gap between international and domestic U.S. opinion on the war, which was undermining both the legitimacy of U.S. foreign policy and the general effectiveness of the United Nations. After the U.S. presidential election, though the Bush administration continued to emphasize the need for UN backing in order to effect peace in Iraq, it made clear that peace would come on American terms.

Source

United Nations, "Charter of the United Nations." Available online. URL: http://www.un.org/aboutun/charter/. Accessed December 28, 2004.

GENEVA CONVENTION ON THE PREVENTION AND PUNISHMENT OF THE CRIME OF GENOCIDE

TREATY AT A GLANCE

Completed
December 9, 1948, at Geneva, Switzerland;
entered into force January 12, 1951

Signatories
Member nations of the United Nations

Overview
When the Nuremberg trials and other war crimes tribunals revealed the horrors of the Nazi death camps, a new term was coined for the mass murder of whole classes or groups of people, *genocide,* which the United Nations moved to make a crime whether it occurred in war or peace and outside or inside a nation's borders.

Historical Background

In the wake of the horrifying discovery of Nazi death camps by Allied troops marching into occupied German territory late in World War II, the victorious Allies set up an International Military Tribunal at Nuremberg, Germany, to indict and try former Nazi leaders as war criminals. The indictments lodged four counts: crimes against peace, or the planning, initiating, and waging of wars of aggression in violation of international treaties and agreements; crimes against humanity, including exterminations, deportations, and genocides; war crimes, or violations of the laws of war; and "criminal conspiracy" to commit the crimes included in the indictments.

The tribunal rejected the major defenses offered by the defendants that only a state, and not individuals, could be found guilty of war crimes and that the acts of the tribunal itself were ex post facto, that is, that the tribunal was leveling charges of crimes that had not been declared crimes at the time they were committed. To the first, the tribunal ruled that crimes against international law were committed by men, not nations, and that only by punishing such individuals could such law be enforced. To the second, it responded that the acts committed by the Nazis had been considered criminal long before World War II.

After 216 sessions held in 1945 and 1946, the tribunal handed down verdicts in 22 of the 24 original indictments, the defendants in the other two, Robert Ley and Gustav Krupp von Bohlen, having committed suicide and gone insane, respectively. Hitler's chief aide, Martin Bormann, who was tried in absentia, and eleven others were sentenced to hang; Rudolf Hess and two others to life imprisonment; and Albert Speer and three others to from 10 to 20 years in prison.

The verdicts were in some sense anticlimactic after the story brought out piece by piece in the testimony at the trials, a story that has since become familiar as the Holocaust. Early in his political development, Adolf Hitler had riveted on the Jews as the cause of Germany's degradation. He did not tailor his anti-Semitism from whole cloth but summoned up a welter of pseudoscientific theories and allegations that had been in the air at least since the 19th century in the writings of the Anglo-German political scientist H. S. Chamberlain, who developed theories of racial purity, and the French ethnologist J. A. Gobineau, who argued the superiority of the "Aryan race." Indeed, anti-Semitism was virulent in most of Europe and a well-organized movement in Germany long before Hitler came to power.

His Nazi Party, however, made it official government policy. Between 1933 and 1938 the Nazis instituted boycotts of Jewish businesses, established Jewish quotas in Germany's professions and schools, enacted the Nuremberg Laws of 1935, banning marriage between Jews and Gentiles, and in 1933 established the first concentration camp, at Dachau, near Munich.

The camp was first intended for the detention of communists and other political undesirables. By 1935 Theodor Eicke, acting under the direction of Hitler's Gestapo chief, Heinrich Himmler, standardized the administration of the camp, which would serve as the pattern for others, including those at Buchenwald and Sachsenhausen. In 1938, after years of persecuting them, Hitler decided to "deport" all Jews from Germany and instituted mass arrests in May 1938. Dachau and the other camps were soon supplemented by additional forced-labor facilities, all intended to house the deported Jews.

On November 9 and 10, 1938, using as a pretext the assassination of Ernst von Rath, a German legation secretary in Paris, Nazi storm troopers burned 267 synagogues and arrested 20,000 Jews. Jewish homes and businesses were destroyed, and so much smashed glass littered the streets that the nocturnal orgy of destruction was given the ironically poetic name Kristallnacht, "crystal night," the night of broken glass. Following the arrests came more deportations to the camps, but not before Hitler levied an atonement fine of $400 million against the Jews to pay for the damage that had been done—to their own property.

In 1940, after Poland had been overrun, the German invaders rounded up Warsaw's more than 400,000 Jews and confined them to the ancient ghetto, which was then cut off from the rest of the city. Many died from starvation and disease, and about 300,000 more were sent to concentration camps. Then German authorities drastically contracted the size of the ghetto. On April 19, 1943, they attacked it, with 2,000 German regulars supplemented by a force of Lithuanian militiamen and Polish police and firefighters. The attackers had expected to be executing a slaughter. Instead, they were confronted by some 60,000 Jews—all those who remained in the ghetto—armed with a few pistols, rifles, machine guns, and homemade weapons. They put up a resistance as heroic as it was ultimately futile. The Nazis countered by setting fire to the ghetto block by block, then flooding and smoke-bombing the sewers, through which the ghetto inmates were attempting escape. On May 16, 1943, General Juergen Stroop reported, "The former Jewish quarter of Warsaw is no longer in existence." Stroop further reported that his men had killed about 56,000, some 20,000 in the streets of Warsaw and the remainder, presumably, in death camps.

For that is what the concentration camps had become: not places of deportation and detention, not even primarily sites for the forced labor the German war machine desperately needed, but the instruments for execution of what Hitler—ever since a January 1942 conference at Wannsee, chaired by Reinhard Heydrich, an aide to Himmler—had called the "final solution."

Auschwitz, as the Germans called the southern Polish town of Oświęcim, was the site of the camp chosen as the center of annihilation. Here 1–3 million—no one knows just how many—human beings were herded naked into gas chambers that were disguised as delousing showers and murdered with hydrocyanic gas produced by Zyklon B crystals. Other Nazi methods of execution included carbon monoxide asphyxiation, electrocution, phenol injections, immolation by flamethrower, and death by hand grenade, gunshot, beating, torture, and "medical experimentation." Victims' clothing and valuables were systematically collected, including gold dental fillings, which were melted down to finance the war machine. The bodies themselves were burned in massive crematoria constructed expressly for the purpose. The killings at Auschwitz began in March 1942 and included large numbers of Poles, Russians, and Gypsies (Rom), in addition to Jews. Concentration camps at Oranienburg, Buchenwald, Dachau, Bergen-Belsen, and elsewhere all became death camps as well.

In 1946, under the impact of revelations such as these at Nuremberg and other war crimes trials, the General Assembly of the United Nations affirmed a convention that stated "genocide is a crime under international law which the civilized world condemns." In 1948 the General Assembly approved the Convention on the Prevention and Punishment of the Crime of Genocide, which went into effect in 1951.

Terms

Unlike the Nuremberg Tribunal, which had associated genocide with war crimes, the United Nations declared that it was a crime whether committed in peace or war, and it established the principle that, even if genocide was perpetrated by a government within its own territory, it was not merely an internal matter but one of international concern.

The Contracting Parties,

Having considered the declaration made by the General Assembly of the United Nations in its resolution 96 (I) dated 11 December 1946 that genocide is a crime under international law, contrary to the spirit and aims of the United Nations and condemned by the civilized world;

Recognizing that at all periods of history genocide has inflicted great losses on humanity; and

Being convinced that, in order to liberate mankind from such an odious scourge, international co-operation is required;

Hereby agree as hereinafter provided.

ARTICLE 1
The Contracting Parties confirm that genocide, whether committed in time of peace or in time of war, is a crime under international law which they undertake to prevent and to punish.

ARTICLE 2
In the present Convention, genocide means any of the following acts committed with intent to destroy, in whole or in part, a national, ethnical, racial or religious group, as such:

(a) Killing members of the group;

(b) Causing serious bodily or mental harm to members of the group;

(c) Deliberately inflicting on the group conditions of life calculated to bring about its physical destruction in whole or in part;

(d) Imposing measures intended to prevent births within the group;

(e) Forcibly transferring children of the group to another group.

ARTICLE 3
The following acts shall be punishable:

(a) Genocide;

(b) Conspiracy to commit genocide;

(c) Direct and public incitement to commit genocide;

(d) Attempt to commit genocide;

(e) Complicity in genocide.

ARTICLE 4
Persons committing genocide or any of the other acts enumerated in Article 3 shall be punished, whether they are constitutionally responsible rulers, public officials or private individuals.

ARTICLE 5
The Contracting Parties undertake to enact, in accordance with their respective Constitutions, the necessary legislation to give effect to the provisions of the present Convention and, in particular, to provide effective penalties for persons guilty of genocide or any of the other acts enumerated in Article 3.

ARTICLE 6
Persons charged with genocide or any of the other acts enumerated in Article 3 shall be tried by a competent tribunal of the State in the territory of which the act was committed, or by such international penal tribunal as may have jurisdiction with respect to those Contracting Parties which shall have accepted its jurisdiction.

ARTICLE 7
Genocide and the other acts enumerated in Article 3 shall not be considered as political crimes for the purpose of extradition.

The Contracting Parties pledge themselves in such cases to grant extradition in accordance with their laws and treaties in force.

ARTICLE 8
Any Contracting Party may call upon the competent organs of the United Nations to take such action under the Charter of the United Nations as they consider appropriate for the prevention and suppression of acts of genocide or any of the other acts enumerated in Article 3.

ARTICLE 9
Disputes between the Contracting Parties relating to the interpretation, application or fulfilment of the present Convention, including those relating to the responsibility of a State for genocide or any of the other acts enumerated in Article 3, shall be submitted to the International Court of Justice at the request of any of the parties to the dispute.

ARTICLE 10
The present Convention, of which the Chinese, English, French, Russian and Spanish texts are equally authentic, shall bear the date of 9 December 1948.

ARTICLE 11
The present Convention shall be open until 31 December 1949 for signature on behalf of any Member of the United Nations and of any non-member State to which an invitation to sign has been addressed by the General Assembly.

The present Convention shall be ratified, and the instruments of ratification shall be deposited with the Secretary-General of the United Nations.

After 1 January 1950, the present Convention may be acceded to on behalf of any Member of the United Nations and of any non-member State which has received an invitation as aforesaid.

Instruments of accession shall be deposited with the Secretary-General of the United Nations.

ARTICLE 12
Any Contracting Party may at any time, by notification addressed to the Secretary-General of the United Nations, extend the application of the present Convention to all or any of the territories for the conduct of whose foreign relations that Contracting Party is responsible.

ARTICLE 13
On the day when the first twenty instruments of ratification or accession have been deposited, the Secretary-General shall draw up a proces-verbal and transmit a copy of it to each Member of the United Nations and to each of the non-member States contemplated in Article 11.

The present Convention shall come into force on the ninetieth day following the date of deposit of the twentieth instrument of ratification or accession.

Any ratification or accession effected subsequent to the latter date shall become effective on the ninetieth day following the deposit of the instrument of ratification or accession.

ARTICLE 14
The present Convention shall remain in effect for a period of ten years as from the date of its coming into force.

It shall thereafter remain in force for successive periods of five years for such Contracting Parties as have not denounced it at least six months before the expiration of the current period.

Denunciation shall be effected by a written notification addressed to the Secretary-General of the United Nations.

ARTICLE 15
If, as a result of denunciations, the number of Parties to the present Convention should become less than sixteen, the Convention shall cease to be in force as from the date on which the last of these denunciations shall become effective.

ARTICLE 16

A request for the revision of the present Convention may be made at any time by any Contracting Party by means of a notification in writing addressed to the Secretary-General.

The General Assembly shall decide upon the steps, if any, to be taken in respect of such request.

ARTICLE 17

The Secretary-General of the United Nations shall notify all Members of the United Nations and the non-member States contemplated in Article 11 of the following:

(a) Signatures, ratifications and accessions received in accordance with Article 11;

(b) Notifications received in accordance with Article 12;

(c) The date upon which the present Convention comes into force in accordance with Article 13;

(d) Denunciations received in accordance with Article 14;

(e) The abrogation of the Convention in accordance with Article 15;

(f) Notifications received in accordance with Article 16.

ARTICLE 18

The original of the present Convention shall be deposited in the archives of the United Nations.

A certified copy of the Convention shall be transmitted to all Members of the United Nations and to the non-member States contemplated in Article 11.

ARTICLE 19

The present Convention shall be registered by the Secretary-General of the United Nations on the date of its coming into force.

Consequences

In the years since the United Nations's adoption of the convention, genocide itself has become a controversial charge. The Vietnamese use of the convention, for example, as an excuse for torturing downed American pilots during the Vietnam War was clearly a perversion of its original purpose, despite arguments, perhaps justified, that such actions as the secret bombing of Cambodia, a nonbelligerent in the war, and the widespread, indiscriminate use of chemical defoliants and napalm by the United States contravened the laws of war. Some fringe academics came to deny that the Jewish Holocaust ever happened, despite the mountain of evidence that continues to grow refuting such claims.

With the fragmentation of postcolonial Africa and post–cold war eastern Europe and the consequent rise of tribal warfare and ethnic conflicts, genocide once again stalked the international stage under the rubric of "ethnic cleansing." By the 1990s, a permanent tribunal under United Nations auspices, set up in The Hague to issue indictments and conduct trials of those perpetrating such crimes on their former fellow citizens, was underfunded and began its work cautiously and slowly. In the late 20th century, however, the tribunal began to hand down verdicts on cases from the former Yugoslavia, raising hopes that such crimes can be punished. Also see ROME STATUTE OF THE INTERNATIONAL CRIMINAL COURT.

Source

United Nations Office of the High Commissioner for Human Rights, "Convention on the Prevention and Punishment of the Crime of Genocide." Available online. URL: http://www.unhchr.ch/html/menu3/b/p_genoci.htm. Accessed December 28, 2004.

GENEVA CONVENTION RELATIVE TO THE TREATMENT OF PRISONERS OF WAR

TREATY AT A GLANCE

Completed
August 12, 1949, at Geneva, Switzerland;
entered into force October 21, 1950

Signatories
183 nations, including all major powers

Overview
This is the most recent and virtually universally accepted convention specifying the rights of prisoners of war and setting minimum standards for their humane treatment.

Historical Background

When public officials or characters in popular war stories refer to the "Geneva Convention," they are usually talking about the 1949 Geneva Convention Relative to the Treatment of Prisoners of War. This was actually the third of four Geneva conventions, stretching back to the American Civil War. Of the 1949 agreements, Convention I, For the Amelioration of the Condition of the Wounded and Sick in Armed Forces in the Field, stipulates protections for members of the armed forces who become wounded or sick. Convention II, For the Amelioration of the Condition of Wounded, Sick and Shipwrecked Members of Armed Forces at Sea, extends these protections to wounded, sick, and shipwrecked members of naval forces. Convention IV, Relative to the Protection of Civilian Persons in Time of War, addresses the protection of civilian populations in times of war. In addition, two protocols, completed on June 8, 1977, relate to the conventions. Protocol I (Additional to the Geneva Conventions of 12 August 1949, and relating to the Protection of Victims of International Armed Conflicts) extends protection to victims of wars against racist regimes, wars of self-determination, and wars against alien oppression. Protocol II (Additional to the Geneva Conventions of 12 August 1949, and relating to the Protection of Victims of Non-International Armed Conflicts, 8 June 1977) extends protection to victims of internal conflicts in which an armed opposition controls enough territory to enable them to carry out sustained military operations. All together called the Geneva Conventions of 1949, these represent the culmination of a long history of attempts to limit and in some sense humanize wartime behavior by codifying the rules of appropriate military conduct.

Efforts to limit unnecessary cruelty in war, of course, predate even the earliest Geneva conventions. The first recorded attempt along these lines may be found in the writings of the sixth-century B.C.E. Chinese general, strategist, and military theorist Sun Tzu. As early as 200 B.C.E., in ancient India, the Hindu Laws of Manu introduced the notion of war crimes. In 1305, the English tried Scotland's national hero, Sir William Wallace (1272?–1305), on charges of having murdered civilian noncombatants in war, and in 1625 the Dutch jurist and theologian Hugo Grotius (1583–1645) wrote *On the Law of War and Peace,* which concerns the treatment of civilians in time of war. The first important modern prosecution for the mistreatment of prisoners of war came in 1865, when Confederate captain Henry Wirz (1822–65) was found guilty of murdering Union Army prisoners of war (POWs) at Georgia's infamous Andersonville prison camp. In the course of his trial, the murders were portrayed as part of an ongoing regimen and policy of flagrantly inhumane prisoner abuse. Wirz was executed.

The initial Geneva Convention was concluded in 1864, at the instigation of the International Red Cross, as an international agreement on certain standards and procedures to protect the sick and wounded in wartime (see GENEVA CONVENTION OF 1864). This began what has become the traditional role of the International Red Cross in helping to draft as well as to monitor and enforce all subsequent Geneva conventions. In 1899, new conventions were concluded at Geneva, Switzerland, limiting the use of asphyxiating gases and expanding bullets, and in 1907, a total of 13 conventions were signed, including one regulating the treatment of POWs. The 1925 Geneva Gas Protocol prohibited the use of poison gas and bacteriological warfare, and in 1929 the most detailed conventions thus far were concluded relative to the treatment of the wounded and POWs. The 1949 Geneva Convention renewed and expanded the 1929 convention of the same name and became the definitive international agreement on the handling of the wounded and the captured.

Terms

The 1949 convention is founded on the key provision of the 1929 convention, that "Prisoners of war are in the power of the hostile Government, but not of the individuals or formation which captured them. They shall at all times be humanely treated and protected, particularly against acts of violence, from insults and from public curiosity. Measures of reprisal against them are forbidden."

Like the 1929 document, the Geneva Convention of 1949 established minimum requirements for the humane and dignified treatment of POWs, including provisions governing conditions of capture; the requirement that POWs be evacuated humanely from the combat zone; a set of basic standards for POW camps; a set of rules governing the use of prisoners for labor; the right of prisoners to communicate with their families; the boundaries of discipline, punishment, and the prisoners' relations with authorities; and rules governing parole during a conflict and release upon its conclusion. Both the 1929 and 1949 conventions also define circumstances under which certain civilians may be treated as prisoners of war and thereby accorded the protection of the convention. These include "persons who follow the armed forces without directly belonging thereto, such as correspondents, newspaper reporters, sutlers, or contractors, who fall into the hands of the enemy, and whom the latter think fit to detain."

The 1949 convention expanded that of 1929 from 97 to 143 articles. The revisions generally reflected the experience of World War II, including changes in the conduct of warfare and in the general living condition of peoples. Key changes included a general revision of the language of the convention itself. Because the document was to be publicly posted in all POW camps, the 1949 convention's language was made less legalistic and more readily comprehensible to general readers. The new convention also broadened the categories of persons entitled to POW status, with the rights and protections that status confers. The new convention more precisely defined and specified acceptable conditions and places of captivity, and it more precisely defined the ways in which POWs may be legally used for the purposes of labor. Aspects of treatment as those relating to POWs' financial resources, relief received by prisoners, and judicial proceedings were clarified. Perhaps most important of all, the 1949 convention made explicit the overriding principle that all POWs are to be released and repatriated without delay after the cessation of active hostilities.

ARTICLE 2

In addition to the provisions which shall be implemented in peace time, the present Convention shall apply to all cases of declared war or of any other armed conflict which may arise between two or more of the High Contracting Parties, even if the state of war is not recognized by one of them.

The Convention shall also apply to all cases of partial or total occupation of the territory of a High Contracting Party, even if the said occupation meets with no armed resistance.

Although one of the Powers in conflict may not be a party to the present Convention, the Powers who are parties thereto shall remain bound by it in their mutual relations. They shall furthermore be bound by the Convention in relation to the said Power, if the latter accepts and applies the provisions thereof.

ARTICLE 3

In the case of armed conflict not of an international character occurring in the territory of one of the High Contracting Parties, each Party to the conflict shall be bound to apply, as a minimum, the following provisions:

(1) Persons taking no active part in the hostilities, including members of armed forces who have laid down their arms and those placed hors de combat by sickness, wounds, detention, or any other cause, shall in all circumstances be treated humanely, without any adverse distinction founded on race, colour, religion or faith, sex, birth or wealth, or any other similar criteria. To this end the following acts are and shall remain prohibited at any time and in any place whatsoever with respect to the above-mentioned persons:

(a) violence to life and person, in particular murder of all kinds, mutilation, cruel treatment and torture; (b) taking of hostages; (c) outrages upon personal dignity, in particular, humiliating and degrading treatment; (d) the passing of sentences and the carrying out of executions without previous judgment pronounced by a regularly constituted court affording all the judicial guarantees which are recognized as indispensable by civilized peoples.

(2) The wounded and sick shall be collected and cared for.

An impartial humanitarian body, such as the International Committee of the Red Cross, may offer its services to the Parties to the conflict. . . .

ARTICLE 4

A. Prisoners of war, in the sense of the present Convention, are persons belonging to one of the following categories, who have fallen into the power of the enemy:

(1) Members of the armed forces of a Party to the conflict, as well as members of militias or volunteer corps forming part of such armed forces.

(2) Members of other militias and members of other volunteer corps, including those of organized resistance movements, belonging to a Party to the conflict and operating in or outside their own territory, even if this territory is occupied, provided that such militias or volunteer corps, including such organized resistance movements, fulfil the following conditions: (a) that of being commanded by a person responsible for his subordinates; (b) that of having a fixed distinctive sign recognizable at a distance; (c) that of carrying arms openly; (d) that of conducting their operations in accordance with the laws and customs of war.

(3) Members of regular armed forces who profess allegiance to a government or an authority not recognized by the Detaining Power.

(4) Persons who accompany the armed forces without actually being members thereof, such as civilian members of military aircraft crews, war correspondents, supply contractors, members of labour units or of services responsible for the welfare of the armed forces, provided that they have received authorization, from the armed forces which they accompany, who shall provide them for that purpose with an identity card similar to the annexed model.

(5) Members of crews, including masters, pilots and apprentices, of the merchant marine and the crews of civil aircraft of the Parties to the conflict, who do not benefit by more favourable treatment under any other provisions of international law.

(6) Inhabitants of a non-occupied territory, who on the approach of the enemy spontaneously take up arms to resist the invading forces, without having had time to form themselves into regular armed units, provided they carry arms openly and respect the laws and customs of war.

B. The following shall likewise be treated as prisoners of war under the present Convention:

(1) Persons belonging, or having belonged, to the armed forces of the occupied country, if the occupying Power considers it necessary by reason of such allegiance to intern them, even though it has originally liberated them while hostilities were going on outside the territory it occupies, in particular where such persons have made an unsuccessful attempt to rejoin the armed forces to which they belong and which are engaged in combat, or where they fail to comply with a summons made to them with a view to internment.

(2) The persons belonging to one of the categories enumerated in the present Article, who have been received by neutral or non-belligerent Powers on their territory and whom these Powers are required to intern under international law, without prejudice to any more favourable treatment which these Powers may choose to give and with the exception of Articles 8, 10, 15, 30, fifth paragraph, 58-67, 92, 126 and, where diplomatic relations exist between the Parties to the conflict and the neutral or non-belligerent Power concerned, those Articles concerning the Protecting Power. Where such diplomatic relations exist, the Parties to a conflict on whom these persons depend shall be allowed to perform towards them the functions of a Protecting Power as provided in the present Convention, without prejudice to the functions which these Parties normally exercise in conformity with diplomatic and consular usage and treaties. . . .

ARTICLE 7

Prisoners of war may in no circumstances renounce in part or in entirety the rights secured to them by the present Convention, and by the special agreements referred to in the foregoing Article, if such there be. . . .

PART II
General Protection of Prisoners of War
ARTICLE 12

Prisoners of war are in the hands of the enemy Power, but not of the individuals or military units who have captured them. Irrespective of the individual responsibilities that may exist, the Detaining Power is responsible for the treatment given them.

Prisoners of war may only be transferred by the Detaining Power to a Power which is a party to the Convention and after the Detaining Power has satisfied itself of the willingness and ability of such transferee Power to apply the Convention. When prisoners of war are transferred under such circumstances, responsibility for the application of the Convention rests on the Power accepting them while they are in its custody.

Nevertheless, if that Power fails to carry out the provisions of the Convention in any important respect, the Power by whom the prisoners of war were transferred shall, upon being notified by the Protecting Power, take effective measures to correct the situation or shall request the return of the prisoners of war. Such requests must be complied with.

ARTICLE 13

Prisoners of war must at all times be humanely treated. Any unlawful act or omission by the Detaining Power causing death or seriously endangering the health of a prisoner of war in its custody is prohibited, and will be regarded as a serious breach of the present Convention. In particular, no prisoner of war may be subjected to physical mutilation or to medical or scientific experiments of any kind which are not justified by the medical, dental or hospital treatment of the prisoner concerned and carried out in his interest.

Likewise, prisoners of war must at all times be protected, particularly against acts of violence or intimidation and against insults and public curiosity.

Measures of reprisal against prisoners of war are prohibited.

ARTICLE 14

Prisoners of war are entitled in all circumstances to respect for their persons and their honour.

Women shall be treated with all the regard due to their sex and shall in all cases benefit by treatment as favourable as that granted to men.

Prisoners of war shall retain the full civil capacity which they enjoyed at the time of their capture. The Detaining Power may not restrict the exercise, either within or without its own territory, of the rights such capacity confers except in so far as the captivity requires.

ARTICLE 15

The Power detaining prisoners of war shall be bound to provide free of charge for their maintenance and for the medical attention required by their state of health.

ARTICLE 16

Taking into consideration the provisions of the present Convention relating to rank and sex, and subject to any privileged treatment which may be accorded to them by reason of their state of health, age or professional qualifications, all prisoners of war shall be treated alike by the Detaining Power, without any adverse distinction based on race, nationality, religious belief or political opinions, or any other distinction founded on similar criteria.

PART III
Captivity

Section I
Beginning of Captivity

ARTICLE 17

Every prisoner of war, when questioned on the subject, is bound to give only his surname, first names and rank, date of birth, and army, regimental, personal or serial number, or failing this, equivalent information.

If he wilfully infringes this rule, he may render himself liable to a restriction of the privileges accorded to his rank or status.

Each Party to a conflict is required to furnish the persons under its jurisdiction who are liable to become prisoners of war, with an identity card showing the owner's surname, first names, rank, army, regimental, personal or serial number or equivalent information, and date of birth. The identity card may, furthermore, bear the signature or the fingerprints, or both, of the owner, and may bear, as well, any other information the Party to the conflict may wish to add concerning persons belonging to its armed forces. As far as possible the card shall measure 6.5 x 10 cm. and shall be issued in duplicate. The identity card shall be shown by the prisoner of war upon demand, but may in no case be taken away from him.

No physical or mental torture, nor any other form of coercion, may be inflicted on prisoners of war to secure from them information of any kind whatever. Prisoners of war who refuse to answer may not be threatened, insulted, or exposed to unpleasant or disadvantageous treatment of any kind. Prisoners of war who, owing to their physical or mental condition, are unable to state their identity, shall be handed over to the medical service. The identity of such prisoners shall be established by all possible means, subject to the provisions of the preceding paragraph.

The questioning of prisoners of war shall be carried out in a language which they understand.

ARTICLE 18

All effects and articles of personal use, except arms, horses, military equipment and military documents, shall remain in the possession of prisoners of war, likewise their metal helmets and gas masks and like articles issued for personal protection. Effects and articles used for their clothing or feeding shall likewise remain in their possession, even if such effects and articles belong to their regulation military equipment.

At no time should prisoners of war be without identity documents. The Detaining Power shall supply such documents to prisoners of war who possess none.

Badges of rank and nationality, decorations and articles having above all a personal or sentimental value may not be taken from prisoners of war.

Sums of money carried by prisoners of war may not be taken away from them except by order of an officer, and after the amount and particulars of the owner have been recorded in a special register and an itemized receipt has been given, legibly inscribed with the name, rank and unit of the person issuing the said receipt. Sums in the currency of the Detaining Power, or which are changed into such currency at the prisoner's request, shall be placed to the credit of the prisoner's account as provided in Article 64.

The Detaining Power may withdraw articles of value from prisoners of war only for reasons of security; when such articles are withdrawn, the procedure laid down for sums of money impounded shall apply.

Such objects, likewise sums taken away in any currency other than that of the Detaining Power and the conversion of which has not been asked for by the owners, shall be kept in the custody of the Detaining Power and shall be returned in their initial shape to prisoners of war at the end of their captivity.

ARTICLE 19

Prisoners of war shall be evacuated, as soon as possible after their capture, to camps situated in an area far enough from the combat zone for them to be out of danger.

Only those prisoners of war who, owing to wounds or sickness, would run greater risks by being evacuated than by remaining where they are, may be temporarily kept back in a danger zone.

Prisoners of war shall not be unnecessarily exposed to danger while awaiting evacuation from a fighting zone.

ARTICLE 20

The evacuation of prisoners of war shall always be effected humanely and in conditions similar to those for the forces of the Detaining Power in their changes of station.

The Detaining Power shall supply prisoners of war who are being evacuated with sufficient food and potable water, and with the necessary clothing and medical attention. The Detaining Power shall take all suitable precautions to ensure their safety during evacuation, and shall establish as soon as possible a list of the prisoners of war who are evacuated.

If prisoners of war must, during evacuation, pass through transit camps, their stay in such camps shall be as brief as possible.

Section II
Internment of Prisoners of War

Chapter I
General Observations

ARTICLE 21

The Detaining Power may subject prisoners of war to internment. It may impose on them the obligation of not leaving, beyond certain limits, the camp where they are interned, or if the said camp is fenced in, of not going outside its perimeter. Subject to the provisions of the present Convention relative to penal and disciplinary sanctions, prisoners of war may not be held in close confinement except where necessary to safeguard their health and then only during the continuation of the circumstances which make such confinement necessary.

Prisoners of war may be partially or wholly released on parole or promise, in so far as is allowed by the laws of the Power on which they depend. Such measures shall be taken particularly in cases where this may contribute to the improvement of their state of health. No prisoner of war shall be compelled to accept liberty on parole or promise.

Upon the outbreak of hostilities, each Party to the conflict shall notify the adverse Party of the laws and regulations allowing or forbidding its own nationals to accept liberty on parole or promise. Prisoners of war who are paroled or who have given their promise in conformity with the laws and regulations so notified, are bound on their personal honour scrupulously to fulfil, both towards the Power on which they depend and towards the Power which has captured them, the engagements of their paroles or promises. In such cases, the Power on which they depend is bound neither to require nor to accept from them any service incompatible with the parole or promise given.

ARTICLE 22

Prisoners of war may be interned only in premises located on land and affording every guarantee of hygiene and healthfulness. Except in particular cases which are justified by the interest of the prisoners themselves, they shall not be interned in penitentiaries. Prisoners of war interned in unhealthy areas, or where the climate is injurious for them, shall be removed as soon as possible to a more favourable climate.

The Detaining Power shall assemble prisoners of war in camps or camp compounds according to their nationality, language and customs, provided that such prisoners shall not be separated from prisoners of war belonging to the armed forces with which they were serving at the time of their capture, except with their consent.

ARTICLE 23

No prisoner of war may at any time be sent to, or detained in areas where he may be exposed to the fire of the combat zone, nor may his presence be used to render certain points or areas immune from military operations.

Prisoners of war shall have shelters against air bombardment and other hazards of war, to the same extent as the local civilian population. With the exception of those engaged in the protection of their quarters against the aforesaid hazards, they may enter such shelters as soon as possible after the giving of the alarm. Any other protective measure taken in favour of the population shall also apply to them.

Detaining Powers shall give the Powers concerned, through the intermediary of the Protecting Powers, all useful information regarding the geographical location of prisoner of war camps.

Whenever military considerations permit, prisoner of war camps shall be indicated in the daytime by the letters PW or PG, placed so as to be clearly visible from the air. The Powers concerned may, however, agree upon any other system of marking. Only prisoner of war camps shall be marked as such.

ARTICLE 24

Transit or screening camps of a permanent kind shall be fitted out under conditions similar to those described in the present Section, and the prisoners therein shall have the same treatment as in other camps.

Chapter II
Quarters, Food and Clothing of Prisoners of War

ARTICLE 25

Prisoners of war shall be quartered under conditions as favourable as those for the forces of the Detaining Power who are billeted in the same area. The said conditions shall make allowance for the habits and customs of the prisoners and shall in no case be prejudicial to their health.

The foregoing provisions shall apply in particular to the dormitories of prisoners of war as regards both total surface and minimum cubic space, and the general installations, bedding and blankets.

The premises provided for the use of prisoners of war individually or collectively, shall be entirely protected from dampness and adequately heated and lighted, in particular between dusk and lights out. All precautions must be taken against the danger of fire.

In any camps in which women prisoners of war, as well as men, are accommodated, separate dormitories shall be provided for them.

ARTICLE 26

The basic daily food rations shall be sufficient in quantity, quality and variety to keep prisoners of war in good health and to prevent loss of weight or the development of nutritional deficiencies. Account shall also be taken of the habitual diet of the prisoners.

The Detaining Power shall supply prisoners of war who work with such additional rations as are necessary for the labour on which they are employed.

Sufficient drinking water shall be supplied to prisoners of war. The use of tobacco shall be permitted.

Prisoners of war shall, as far as possible, be associated with the preparation of their meals; they may be employed for that purpose in the kitchens. Furthermore, they shall be given the means of preparing, themselves, the additional food in their possession.

Adequate premises shall be provided for messing.

Collective disciplinary measures affecting food are prohibited.

ARTICLE 27

Clothing, underwear and footwear shall be supplied to prisoners of war in sufficient quantities by the Detaining Power, which shall make allowance for the climate of the region where the prisoners are detained. Uniforms of enemy armed forces captured by the Detaining Power should, if suitable for the climate, be made available to clothe prisoners of war.

The regular replacement and repair of the above articles shall be assured by the Detaining Power. In addition, prisoners of war who work shall receive appropriate clothing, wherever the nature of the work demands.

ARTICLE 28

Canteens shall be installed in all camps, where prisoners of war may procure foodstuffs, soap and tobacco and ordinary articles in daily use. The tariff shall never be in excess of local market prices.

The profits made by camp canteens shall be used for the benefit of the prisoners; a special fund shall be created for this purpose. The prisoners' representative shall have the right to collaborate in the management of the canteen and of this fund.

When a camp is closed down, the credit balance of the special fund shall be handed to an international welfare organization, to be employed for the benefit of prisoners of war of the same nationality as those who have contributed to the fund. In case of a general repatriation, such profits shall be kept by the Detaining Power, subject to any agreement to the contrary between the Powers concerned.

Chapter III
Hygiene and Medical Attention

ARTICLE 29

The Detaining Power shall be bound to take all sanitary measures necessary to ensure the cleanliness and healthfulness of camps and to prevent epidemics.

Prisoners of war shall have for their use, day and night, conveniences which conform to the rules of hygiene and are maintained in a constant state of cleanliness. In any camps in which women prisoners of war are accommodated, separate conveniences shall be provided for them.

Also, apart from the baths and showers with which the camps shall be furnished prisoners of war shall be provided with sufficient water and soap for their personal toilet and for washing their personal laundry; the necessary installations, facilities and time shall be granted them for that purpose.

ARTICLE 30

Every camp shall have an adequate infirmary where prisoners of war may have the attention they require, as well as appropriate diet. Isolation wards shall, if necessary, be set aside for cases of contagious or mental disease.

Prisoners of war suffering from serious disease, or whose condition necessitates special treatment, a surgical operation or hospital care, must be admitted to any military or civilian medical unit where such treatment can be given, even if their repatriation is contemplated in the near future. Special facilities shall be afforded for the care to be given to the disabled, in particular to the blind, and for their rehabilitation, pending repatriation.

Prisoners of war shall have the attention, preferably, of medical personnel of the Power on which they depend and, if possible, of their nationality.

Prisoners of war may not be prevented from presenting themselves to the medical authorities for examination. . . .

ARTICLE 32

Prisoners of war who, though not attached to the medical service of their armed forces, are physicians, surgeons, dentists, nurses or medical orderlies, may be required by the Detaining Power to exercise their medical functions in the interests of prisoners of war . . .

Chapter IV
Medical Personnel and Chaplains Retained to Assist Prisoners of War

ARTICLE 33

Members of the medical personnel and chaplains while retained by the Detaining Power with a view to assisting prisoners of war, shall not be considered as prisoners of war. They shall, however, receive as a minimum the benefits and protection of the present Convention, and shall also be granted all facilities necessary to provide for the medical care of, and religious ministration to prisoners of war.

They shall continue to exercise their medical and spiritual functions for the benefit of prisoners of war, preferably those belonging to the armed forces upon which they depend, within the scope of the military laws and regulations of the Detaining Power and under the control of its competent services, in accordance with their professional etiquette. . . .

Chapter V
Religious, Intellectual and Physical Activities

ARTICLE 34

Prisoners of war shall enjoy complete latitude in the exercise of their religious duties, including attendance at the service of their faith, on condition that they comply with the disciplinary routine prescribed by the military authorities.

Adequate premises shall be provided where religious services may be held.

ARTICLE 35

Chaplains who fall into the hands of the enemy Power and who remain or are retained with a view to assisting prisoners of war, shall be allowed to minister to them and to exercise freely their ministry amongst prisoners of war of the same religion, in accordance with their religious conscience. They shall be allocated among the various camps and labour detachments containing prisoners of war belonging to the same forces, speaking the same language or practising the same religion. They shall enjoy the necessary facilities, including the means of transport provided for in Article 33, for visiting the prisoners of war outside their camp. They shall be free to correspond, subject to censorship, on matters concerning their religious duties with the ecclesiastical authorities in the country of detention and with international religious organizations. Letters and cards which they may send for this purpose shall be in addition to the quota provided for in Article 71.

ARTICLE 36

Prisoners of war who are ministers of religion, without having officiated as chaplains to their own forces, shall be at liberty, whatever their denomination, to minister freely to the members of their community. For this purpose, they shall receive the same treatment as the chaplains retained by the Detaining Power. They shall not be obliged to do any other work.

ARTICLE 37

When prisoners of war have not the assistance of a retained chaplain or of a prisoner of war minister of their faith, a minister belonging to the prisoners' or a similar denomination, or in his absence a qualified layman, if such a course is feasible from a confessional point of view, shall be appointed, at the request of the prisoners concerned, to fill this office. This appointment, subject to the approval of the Detaining Power, shall take place with the agreement of the community of prisoners concerned and, wherever necessary, with the approval of the local religious authorities of the same faith. The person thus appointed shall comply with all regulations established by the Detaining Power in the interests of discipline and military security.

ARTICLE 38

While respecting the individual preferences of every prisoner, the Detaining Power shall encourage the practice of intellectual, educational, and recreational pursuits, sports and games amongst prisoners, and shall take the measures necessary to ensure the exercise thereof by providing them with adequate premises and necessary equipment.

Prisoners shall have opportunities for taking physical exercise, including sports and games, and for being out of doors. Sufficient open spaces shall be provided for this purpose in all camps.

Chapter VI
Discipline

ARTICLE 39

Every prisoner of war camp shall be put under the immediate authority of a responsible commissioned officer belonging to the regular armed forces of the Detaining Power. Such officer shall have in his possession a copy of the present Convention; he shall ensure that its provisions are known to the camp staff and the guard and shall be responsible, under the direction of his government, for its application.

Prisoners of war, with the exception of officers, must salute and show to all officers of the Detaining Power the external marks of respect provided for by the regulations applying in their own forces.

Officer prisoners of war are bound to salute only officers of a higher rank of the Detaining Power; they must, however, salute the camp commander regardless of his rank.

ARTICLE 40

The wearing of badges of rank and nationality, as well as of decorations, shall be permitted.

ARTICLE 41

In every camp the text of the present Convention and its Annexes and the contents of any special agreement provided for in Article 6, shall be posted, in the prisoners' own language, in places where all may read them. Copies shall be supplied, on request, to the prisoners who cannot have access to the copy which has been posted.

Regulations, orders, notices and publications of every kind relating to the conduct of prisoners of war shall be issued to them in a language which they understand. . . .

ARTICLE 42

The use of weapons against prisoners of war, especially against those who are escaping or attempting to escape, shall constitute an extreme measure, which shall always be preceded by warnings appropriate to the circumstances.

Chapter VII
Rank of Prisoners of War

ARTICLE 43

Upon the outbreak of hostilities, the Parties to the conflict shall communicate to one another the titles and ranks of all the persons mentioned in Article 4 of the present Convention, in order to ensure equality of treatment between prisoners of equivalent rank. . . .

ARTICLE 44

Officers and prisoners of equivalent status shall be treated with the regard due to their rank and age. . . .

Chapter VIII
Transfer of Prisoners of War After Their Arrival in Camp

ARTICLE 46

The Detaining Power, when deciding upon the transfer of prisoners of war, shall take into account the interests of the prisoners themselves, more especially so as not to increase the difficulty of their repatriation.

The transfer of prisoners of war shall always be effected humanely and in conditions not less favourable than those under which the forces of the Detaining Power are transferred. . . .

The Detaining Power shall supply prisoners of war during transfer with sufficient food and drinking water to keep them in good health, likewise with the necessary clothing, shelter and medical attention. . . .

ARTICLE 47

Sick or wounded prisoners of war shall not be transferred as long as their recovery may be endangered by the journey, unless their safety imperatively demands it.

ARTICLE 48

In the event of transfer, prisoners of war shall be officially advised of their departure and of their new postal address. Such notifications shall be given in time for them to pack their luggage and inform their next of kin. . . .

Section III
Labour of Prisoners of War

ARTICLE 49

The Detaining Power may utilize the labour of prisoners of war who are physically fit, taking into account their age, sex, rank and physical aptitude, and with a view particularly to maintaining them in a good state of physical and mental health.

Non-commissioned officers who are prisoners of war shall only be required to do supervisory work. Those not so required may ask for other suitable work which shall, so far as possible, be found for them.

If officers or persons of equivalent status ask for suitable work, it shall be found for them, so far as possible, but they may in no circumstances be compelled to work.

ARTICLE 50

Besides work connected with camp administration, installation or maintenance, prisoners of war may be compelled to do only such work as is included in the following classes:

(a) agriculture; (b) industries connected with the production or the extraction of raw materials, and manufacturing industries, with the exception of metallurgical, machinery and chemical industries; public works and building operations which have no military character or purpose; (c) transport and handling of stores which are not military in character or purpose; (d) commercial business, and arts and crafts; (e) domestic service; (f) public utility services having no military character or purpose.

Should the above provisions be infringed, prisoners of war shall be allowed to exercise their right of complaint, in conformity with Article 78.

ARTICLE 51

Prisoners of war must be granted suitable working conditions, especially as regards accommodation, food, clothing and equipment; such conditions shall not be inferior to those enjoyed by nationals of the Detaining Power employed in similar work; account shall also be taken of climatic conditions.

The Detaining Power, in utilizing the labour of prisoners of war, shall ensure that in areas in which such prisoners are employed, the national legislation concerning the protection of labour, and, more particularly, the regulations for the safety of workers, are duly applied. . . .

ARTICLE 52

Unless he be a volunteer, no prisoner of war may be employed on labour which is of an unhealthy or dangerous nature.

No prisoner of war shall be assigned to labour which would be looked upon as humiliating for a member of the Detaining Power's own forces.

The removal of mines or similar devices shall be considered as dangerous labour. . . .

Section IV
Financial Resources of Prisoners of War

ARTICLE 58

Upon the outbreak of hostilities, and pending an arrangement on this matter with the Protecting Power, the Detaining Power may determine the maximum amount of money in cash or in any similar form, that prisoners may have in their possession. Any amount in excess, which was properly in their possession and which has been taken or withheld from them, shall be placed to their account, together with any monies deposited by them, and shall not be converted into any other currency without their consent. . . .

ARTICLE 60

The Detaining Power shall grant all prisoners of war a monthly advance of pay, the amount of which shall be fixed by conversion, into the currency of the said Power, of the following amounts:

Category I: Prisoners ranking below sergeants: eight Swiss francs.

Category II: Sergeants and other non-commissioned officers, or prisoners of equivalent rank: twelve Swiss francs.

Category III: Warrant officers and commissioned officers below the rank of major or prisoners of equivalent rank: fifty Swiss francs.

Category IV: Majors, lieutenant-colonels, colonels or prisoners of equivalent rank: sixty Swiss francs.

Category V: General officers or prisoners of war of equivalent rank: seventy-five Swiss francs.

However, the Parties to the conflict concerned may by special agreement modify the amount of advances of pay due to prisoners of the preceding categories.

Furthermore, if the amounts indicated in the first paragraph above would be unduly high compared with the pay of the Detaining Power's armed forces or would, for any reason, seriously embarrass the Detaining Power, then, pending the conclusion of a special agreement with the Power on which the prisoners depend to vary the amounts indicated above, the Detaining Power:

(a) shall continue to credit the accounts of the prisoners with the amounts indicated in the first paragraph above; (b) may temporarily limit the amount made available from these advances of pay to prisoners of war for their own use, to sums which are reasonable, but which, for Category I, shall never be inferior to the amount that the Detaining Power gives to the members of its own armed forces.

The reasons for any limitations will be given without delay to the Protecting Power. . . .

ARTICLE 62

Prisoners of war shall be paid a fair working rate of pay by the detaining authorities direct. The rate shall be fixed by the said authorities, but shall at no time be less than one-fourth of one Swiss franc for a full working day. . . .

ARTICLE 66

On the termination of captivity, through the release of a prisoner of war or his repatriation, the Detaining Power shall give him a statement, signed by an authorized officer of that Power, showing the credit balance then due to him. . . .

Section V
Relations of Prisoners of War With the Exterior

. . .

ARTICLE 70

Immediately upon capture, or not more than one week after arrival at a camp, even if it is a transit camp, likewise in case of sickness or transfer to hospital or to another camp, every prisoner of war shall be enabled to write direct to his family, on the one hand, and to the Central Prisoners of War Agency . . .

ARTICLE 71

Prisoners of war shall be allowed to send and receive letters and cards. . . .

ARTICLE 72

Prisoners of war shall be allowed to receive by post or by any other means individual parcels or collective shipments containing, in particular, foodstuffs, clothing, medical supplies and articles of a religious, educational or recreational character which may meet their needs, including books, devotional articles, scientific equipment, examination papers, musical instruments, sports outfits and materials allowing prisoners of war to pursue their studies or their cultural activities. . . .

ARTICLE 76

The censoring of correspondence addressed to prisoners of war or despatched by them shall be done as quickly as possible. Mail shall be censored only by the despatching State and the receiving State, and once only by each. . . .

Section VI
Relations Between Prisoners of War
and the Authorities

Chapter I
Complaints of Prisoners of War
Respecting the Conditions of Captivity

ARTICLE 78

Prisoners of war shall have the right to make known to the military authorities in whose power they are, their requests regarding the conditions of captivity to which they are subjected.

They shall also have the unrestricted right to apply to the representatives of the Protecting Powers either through their prisoners' representative or, if they consider it necessary, direct, in order to draw their attention to any points on which they may have complaints to make regarding their conditions of captivity.

These requests and complaints shall not be limited nor considered to be a part of the correspondence quota referred to in Article 71. They must be transmitted immediately. Even if they are recognized to be unfounded, they may not give rise to any punishment.

Prisoners' representatives may send periodic reports on the situation in the camps and the needs of the prisoners of war to the representatives of the Protecting Powers.

Chapter II
Prisoner of War Representatives

ARTICLE 79
In all places where there are prisoners of war, except in those where there are officers, the prisoners shall freely elect by secret ballot, every six months, and also in case of vacancies, prisoners' representatives entrusted with representing them before the military authorities, the Protecting Powers, the International Committee of the Red Cross and any other organization which may assist them. These prisoners' representatives shall be eligible for re-election. . . .

Chapter III
Penal and Disciplinary Sanctions

I. General Provisions

ARTICLE 82
A prisoner of war shall be subject to the laws, regulations and orders in force in the armed forces of the Detaining Power; the Detaining Power shall be justified in taking judicial or disciplinary measures in respect of any offence committed by a prisoner of war against such laws, regulations or orders. However, no proceedings or punishments contrary to the provisions of this Chapter shall be allowed. . . .

ARTICLE 84
A prisoner of war shall be tried only by a military court, unless the existing laws of the Detaining Power expressly permit the civil courts to try a member of the armed forces of the Detaining Power in respect of the particular offence alleged to have been committed by the prisoner of war.

In no circumstances whatever shall a prisoner of war be tried by a court of any kind which does not offer the essential guarantees of independence and impartiality as generally recognized, and, in particular, the procedure of which does not afford the accused the rights and means of defence provided for in Article 105. . . .

ARTICLE 87
Prisoners of war may not be sentenced by the military authorities and courts of the Detaining Power to any penalties except those provided for in respect of members of the armed forces of the said Power who have committed the same acts. . . .

Collective punishment for individual acts, corporal punishment, imprisonment in premises without daylight and, in general, any form of torture or cruelty, are forbidden.

No prisoner of war may be deprived of his rank by the Detaining Power, or prevented from wearing his badges.

ARTICLE 88
Officers, non-commissioned officers and men who are prisoners of war undergoing a disciplinary or judicial punishment, shall not be subjected to more severe treatment than that applied in respect of the same punishment to members of the armed forces of the Detaining Power of equivalent rank.

A woman prisoner of war shall not be awarded or sentenced to a punishment more severe, or treated whilst undergoing punishment more severely, than a woman member of the armed forces of the Detaining Power dealt with for a similar offence.

In no case may a woman prisoner of war be awarded or sentenced to a punishment more severe, or treated whilst undergoing punishment more severely, than a male member of the armed forces of the Detaining Power dealt with for a similar offence.

Prisoners of war who have served disciplinary or judicial sentences may not be treated differently from other prisoners of war.

II. Disciplinary Sanctions

ARTICLE 89
The disciplinary punishments applicable to prisoners of war are the following:

(1) A fine which shall not exceed 50 per cent of the advances of pay and working pay which the prisoner of war would otherwise receive under the provisions of Articles 60 and 62 during a period of not more than thirty days.

(2) Discontinuance of privileges granted over and above the treatment provided for by the present Convention.

(3) Fatigue duties not exceeding two hours daily.

(4) Confinement.

The punishment referred to under (3) shall not be applied to officers.

In no case shall disciplinary punishments be inhuman, brutal or dangerous to the health of prisoners of war.

ARTICLE 90
The duration of any single punishment shall in no case exceed thirty days. . . .

ARTICLE 91
The escape of a prisoner of war shall be deemed to have succeeded when:

(1) he has joined the armed forces of the Power on which he depends, or those of an allied Power;

(2) he has left the territory under the control of the Detaining Power, or of an ally of the said Power;

(3) he has joined a ship flying the flag of the Power on which he depends, or of an allied Power, in the territorial waters of the Detaining Power, the said ship not being under the control of the last named Power.

Prisoners of war who have made good their escape in the sense of this Article and who are recaptured, shall not be liable to any punishment in respect of their previous escape.

ARTICLE 92
A prisoner of war who attempts to escape and is recaptured before having made good his escape in the sense of Article 91 shall be liable only to a disciplinary punishment in respect of this act, even if it is a repeated offence. . . .

ARTICLE 97
Prisoners of war shall not in any case be transferred to penitentiary establishments (prisons, penitentiaries, convict prisons, etc.) to undergo disciplinary punishment therein.

All premises in which disciplinary punishments are undergone shall conform to the sanitary requirements set forth in Article 25. A prisoner of war undergoing punishment shall be enabled to keep himself in a state of cleanliness, in conformity with Article 29.

Officers and persons of equivalent status shall not be lodged in the same quarters as non-commissioned officers or men.

Women prisoners of war undergoing disciplinary punishment shall be confined in separate quarters from male prisoners of war and shall be under the immediate supervision of women.

ARTICLE 98

A prisoner of war undergoing confinement as a disciplinary punishment, shall continue to enjoy the benefits of the provisions of this Convention except in so far as these are necessarily rendered inapplicable by the mere fact that he is confined. In no case may he be deprived of the benefits of the provisions of Articles 78 and 126.

A prisoner of war awarded disciplinary punishment may not be deprived of the prerogatives attached to his rank.

Prisoners of war awarded disciplinary punishment shall be allowed to exercise and to stay in the open air at least two hours daily.

They shall be allowed, on their request, to be present at the daily medical inspections. They shall receive the attention which their state of health requires and, if necessary, shall be removed to the camp infirmary or to a hospital.

They shall have permission to read and write, likewise to send and receive letters. Parcels and remittances of money however, may be withheld from them until the completion of the punishment; they shall meanwhile be entrusted to the prisoners' representative, who-will hand over to the infirmary the perishable goods contained in such parcels.

III. Judicial Proceedings

ARTICLE 99

No prisoner of war may be tried or sentenced for an act which is not forbidden by the law of the Detaining Power or by international law, in force at the time the said act was committed.

No moral or physical coercion may be exerted on a prisoner of war in order to induce him to admit himself guilty of the act of which he is accused.

No prisoner of war may be convicted without having had an opportunity to present his defence and the assistance of a qualified advocate or counsel.

ARTICLE 100

Prisoners of war and the Protecting Powers shall be informed as soon as possible of the offences which are punishable by the death sentence under the laws of the Detaining Power.

Other offences shall not thereafter be made punishable by the death penalty without the concurrence of the Power on which the prisoners of war depend.

The death sentence cannot be pronounced on a prisoner of war unless the attention of the court has, in accordance with Article 87, second paragraph, been particularly called to the fact that since the accused is not a national of the Detaining Power, he is not bound to it by any duty of allegiance, and that he is in its power as the result of circumstances independent of his own will.

ARTICLE 101

If the death penalty is pronounced on a prisoner of war, the sentence shall not be executed before the expiration of a period of at least six months from the date when the Protecting Power receives, at an indicated address, the detailed communication provided for in Article 107.

ARTICLE 102

A prisoner of war can be validly sentenced only if the sentence has been pronounced by the same courts according to the same procedure as in the case of members of the armed forces of the Detaining Power, and if, furthermore, the provisions of the present Chapter have been observed.

ARTICLE 103

Judicial investigations relating to a prisoner of war shall be conducted as rapidly as circumstances permit and so that his trial shall take place as soon as possible. . . .

ARTICLE 105

The prisoner of war shall be entitled to assistance by one of his prisoner comrades, to defence by a qualified advocate or counsel of his own choice, to the calling of witnesses and, if he deems necessary, to the services of a competent interpreter. He shall be advised of these rights by the Detaining Power in due time before the trial.

Failing a choice by the prisoner of war, the Protecting Power shall find him an advocate or counsel, and shall have at least one week at its disposal for the purpose. . . .

ARTICLE 106

Every prisoner of war shall have, in the same manner as the members of the armed forces of the Detaining Power, the right of appeal or petition from any sentence pronounced upon him, with a view to the quashing or revising of the sentence or the reopening of the trial. He shall be fully informed of his right to appeal or petition and of the time limit within which he may do so. . . .

ARTICLE 108

Sentences pronounced on prisoners of war after a conviction has become duly enforceable, shall be served in the same establishments and under the same conditions as in the case of members of the armed forces of the Detaining Power. These conditions shall in all cases conform to the requirements of health and humanity. . . .

PART IV
Termination of Captivity

Section I
Direct Repatriation and Accommodation in Neutral Countries

ARTICLE 109

Subject to the provisions of the third paragraph of this Article, Parties to the conflict are bound to send back to their own country, regardless of number or rank, seriously wounded and seriously sick prisoners of war, after having cared for them until they are fit to travel . . .

Section II
Release and Repatriation of Prisoners of War at the Close of Hostilities

ARTICLE 118

Prisoners of war shall be released and repatriated without delay after the cessation of active hostilities. . . .

Section III
Death of Prisoners of War

ARTICLE 120

Wills of prisoners of war shall be drawn up so as to satisfy the conditions of validity required by the legislation of their country of origin, which will take steps to inform the Detaining Power of its requirements in this respect. At the request of the prisoner of war and, in all cases, after death, the will shall be transmitted without delay to the Protecting Power; a certified copy shall be sent to the Central Agency.

Death certificates, in the form annexed to the present Convention, or lists certified by a responsible officer, of all persons who die as prisoners of war shall be forwarded as rapidly as possible to the Prisoner of War Information Bureau established in accordance with Article 122. The death certificates or certified lists shall show particulars of identity as set out in the third paragraph of Article 17, and also the date and place of death, the cause of death, the date and place of burial and all particulars necessary to identify the graves.

The burial or cremation of a prisoner of war shall be preceded by a medical examination of the body with a view to confirming death and enabling a report to be made and, where necessary, establishing identity.

The detaining authorities shall ensure that prisoners of war who have died in captivity are honourably buried, if possible according to the rites of the religion to which they belonged, and that their graves are respected, suitably maintained and marked so as to be found at any time. Wherever possible, deceased prisoners of war who depended on the same Power shall be interred in the same place.

Deceased prisoners of war shall be buried in individual graves unless unavoidable circumstances require the use of collective graves. Bodies may be cremated only for imperative reasons of hygiene, on account of the religion of the deceased or in accordance with his express wish to this effect. In case of cremation, the fact shall be stated and the reasons given in the death certificate of the deceased.

In order that graves may always be found, all particulars of burials and graves shall be recorded with a Graves Registration Service established by the Detaining Power. Lists of graves and particulars of the prisoners of war interred in cemeteries and elsewhere shall be transmitted to the Power on which such prisoners of war depended. Responsibility for the care of these graves and for records of any subsequent moves of the bodies shall rest on the Power controlling the territory, if a Party to the present Convention. These provisions shall also apply to the ashes, which shall be kept by the Graves Registration Service until proper disposal thereof in accordance with the wishes of the home country.

ARTICLE 121

Every death or serious injury of a prisoner of war caused or suspected to have been caused by a sentry, another prisoner of war, or any other person, as well as any death the cause of which is unknown, shall be immediately followed by an official enquiry by the Detaining Power. . . .

PART V
Information Bureaux and Relief Societies
for Prisoners of War

ARTICLE 122

Upon the outbreak of a conflict and in all cases of occupation, each of the Parties to the conflict shall institute an official Information Bureau for prisoners of war who are in its power. . . .

PART VI
Execution of the Convention

Section I. General Provisions

ARTICLE 126

Representatives or delegates of the Protecting Powers shall have permission to go to all places where prisoners of war may be,

particularly to places of internment, imprisonment and labour, and shall have access to all premises occupied by prisoners of war; they shall also be allowed to go to the places of departure, passage and arrival of prisoners who are being transferred. They shall be able to interview the prisoners, and in particular the prisoners' representatives, without witnesses, either personally or through an interpreter. . . .

ARTICLE 129

The High Contracting Parties undertake to enact any legislation necessary to provide effective penal sanctions for persons committing, or ordering to be committed, any of the grave breaches of the present Convention defined in the following Article. . . .

ARTICLE 130

Grave breaches to which the preceding Article relates shall be those involving any of the following acts, if committed against persons or property protected by the Convention: wilful killing, torture or inhuman treatment, including biological experiments, wilfully causing great suffering or serious injury to body or health, compelling a prisoner of war to serve in the forces of the hostile Power, or wilfully depriving a prisoner of war of the rights of fair and regular trial prescribed in this Convention.

ARTICLE 131

No High Contracting Party shall be allowed to absolve itself or any other High Contracting Party of any liability incurred by itself or by another High Contracting Party in respect of breaches referred to in the preceding Article.

ARTICLE 132

At the request of a Party to the conflict, an enquiry shall be instituted, in a manner to be decided between the interested Parties, concerning any alleged violation of the Convention. . . .

Consequences

The 1929 convention was used as the basis for many war crimes prosecutions, chiefly against German and Japanese military personnel, following World War II, even though Japan was not a signatory to the agreement. During that conflict, the Allied powers (except for the Soviet Union) generally adhered to the provisions of the convention. German and Italian authorities also observed it, although violations were frequent, and POW treatment often depended on the disposition or caprice of a particular prison commandant. Prisoners held in German POW camps administered by the Luftwaffe (air force) were generally better treated in accordance with the Geneva rules than those held by camps administered by the Wehrmacht (army), and prisoners from the Western nations almost always fared far better than those from the East, especially Russians. The Japanese generally did not accord any POWs even the most basic humane treatment and often deliberately abused prisoners. (Japan, it should be noted, while not a signatory to the 1929 convention, did sign that of 1949.)

Collectively, the Geneva Conventions have the force of international law and moral law, even over those few states that have not subscribed to them. The conventions are taken to represent the minimum standards that are to be regarded as universal in the treatment of POWs and in the other war-related issues addressed by the conventions. They provide a per se basis for war crimes prosecutions in cases of prisoner mistreatment and abuse.

The 1949 Geneva Convention Relative to the Treatment of Prisoners of War in particular became a problem for U.S. policymakers in the military actions they launched in response to terrorist attacks against New York City (the World Trade Center) and the Washington, D.C., area (the Pentagon and an apparent failed attack against the White House or the Capitol) of September 11, 2001. Following these attacks, the United States conducted military operations in Afghanistan and Iraq pursuant to an undeclared "war on terror." Many prisoners were captured and detained in the course of both campaigns. The vast majority of these were identified by U.S. military and/or civilian intelligence agents not as members of any national armed forces but as "terrorists" or "insurgents." As such, Secretary of Defense Donald Rumsfeld initially claimed that they were not subject to the protections of the 1949 Geneva Convention, but that they nevertheless would be treated humanely in the "spirit" of the convention. Under public pressure, this claim was somewhat and variously modified, but as of early 2005 the United States has not acknowledged the military combatant status of these detainees and has not agreed to be legally bound by the Geneva Conventions in regard to all aspects of their treatment.

Reports of the abuse of prisoners, including isolation, humiliation, sleep deprivation, threats, and even some forms of physical abuse (including outright tor-ture) steadily emerged from Camp X-Ray, the detention facility at the U.S. base at Guantánamo Bay, Cuba, and then from its successor there, Camp Delta. Even more notoriously, in 2004, photographs of grotesque prisoner abuse, including the apparent simulation of homosexual and other sex acts, sadomasochistic sexual scenarios, apparent attack by guard dogs, and electric shock torture, all perpetrated by U.S. military personnel at Abu Ghraib Prison, Iraq, came to widespread public attention through the media. Since then, more photographs, videos, and accounts of abuse have surfaced from Abu Ghraib and other facilities in Iraq and in Afghanistan. The U.S. military commenced an investigation, and legal proceedings were begun against a handful of enlisted soldiers directly involved in some of the abuse. Several members of the military, of the civilian U.S. government, and journalists have asserted that the abuse was actually an aspect of authorized policy set either by upper-level military commanders or, perhaps, even by the secretary of defense and his immediate subordinates. As of the beginning of 2005, these assertions have been neither conclusively substantiated nor conclusively disproved. What is undeniable are certain instances of abuse, both reported and visually recorded, which are clear violations of internationally accepted standards of prisoner treatment. Whether they are also violations of the 1949 Geneva POW convention in the strictest legal sense remains open to dispute and depends on the final determination of the military status of the detainees.

Source

Avalon Project at the Yale Law School, "Geneva Convention (III) Relative to the Treatment of Prisoners of War; August 12, 1949." Available online. URL: http://www.yale.edu/lawweb/avalon/lawofwar/geneva03.htm. Accessed May 16, 2005.

Diplomatic Treaties

AGREEMENT BETWEEN POLAND AND THE SOVIET UNION

TREATY AT A GLANCE

Completed
Ratified July 30, 1941, at London

Signatories
Poland and the Soviet Union

Overview
Stalin had concluded the Hitler-Stalin Pact with Germany on August 23, 1939, thereby opening Poland to German invasion and reserving a portion of Poland for the USSR. After Germany invaded the Soviet Union, however, the USSR and Poland reestablished diplomatic relations.

Historical Background

On August 23, 1939, Adolf Hitler and Joseph Stalin, representatives of the century's two irreconcilably opposed totalitarian ideologies, stunned the world by signing a nonaggression pact. The HITLER-STALIN PACT gave Hitler license to invade Poland, actively abetted by Soviet forces invading from the east, on September 1, 1939. Stalin also decided to increase Soviet influence in the West by invading Finland on November 30, 1939, which ignited a short but costly war that secured Finland's surrender on March 12, 1940.

Then, on June 22, 1941, Hitler, without warning, violated the nonaggression pact by invading the Soviet Union. Early resistance to the invasion was weak and poorly coordinated because Stalin was, in a word, stupefied, which may seem odd given the mutual distrust between him and Hitler. Perhaps it was the timing and scale of the invasion and the inability of Stalin's generals to check it quickly that led him to the days-long drinking binge described by Nikita Khrushchev and others, during which he was nearly comatose and certainly incapacitated. If so, he had only himself to blame, since his 1936–38 purges had stripped the Red Army of most of its senior officer corps.

Within a short time, however, the dictator shook off his panic and took personal command of the Red Army, mounting an increasingly effective defense. He moved with swift and strategic deliberation, evacuating vital war industries east, into Siberia and Central Asia, just ahead of the advancing German armies. As Winston Churchill had emboldened the British people, so Stalin rallied the Soviets, appealing to patriotism and, for the sake of morale, disbanding the Communist International while at the same time officially rehabilitating the Orthodox Church.

It was within this context of joining now the Allied camp that Stalin treated diplomatically with the exiled representatives of the free Poland he had stabbed in the back in 1939. He would do what was necessary—and only what was necessary—to fight effectively the first threat to his regime since the assassination of Leon Trotsky, once the second most powerful Bolshevik after Lenin, who had fled the Soviet Union come Stalin's rise and formed the so-called Fourth International in opposition.

Terms

The agreement of July 30, 1941, reestablished diplomatic relations between the Soviet Union and Poland, and Soviet premier Stalin agreed that the German-Soviet treaties of 1939 relating to the disposition of Polish territory had "lost their validity." The phrase, however, is highly significant, for Stalin refused to renounce his claim to Polish territory he had seized. Nevertheless, the Polish government in exile was eager to conclude the agreement, however imperfect, if only to obtain the release of Polish prisoners held in Soviet camps.

The Government of the Republic of Poland and the Government of the Union of Soviet Socialist Republics have concluded the present Agreement and decided as follows:

1. The Government of the Union of Soviet Socialist Republics recognizes that the Soviet-German treaties of 1939 relative to territorial changes in Poland have lost their validity. The Government of the Republic of Poland declares that Poland is not bound by any Agreement with any third State directed against the U.S.S.R.

2. Diplomatic relations will be restored between the two Governments upon the signature of this Agreement and an exchange of Ambassadors will follow immediately.

3. The two Governments mutually undertake to render one another aid and support of all kinds in the present war against Hitlerite Germany.

4. The Government of the Union of Soviet Socialist Republics expresses its consent to the formation on the territory of the Union of Soviet Socialist Republics of a Polish army under a commander appointed by the Government of the Republic of Poland, in agreement with the Government of the Union of Soviet Socialist Republics. The Polish army on the territory of the Union of Soviet Socialist Republics will be subordinated in operational matters to the Supreme Command of the U.S.S.R. on which there will be a representative of the Polish army. All details as to command, organization and employment of this force will be settled in a subsequent agreement.

5. This Agreement will come into force immediately upon its signature and without ratification. The present Agreement is drawn up in two copies, each of them in the Russian and Polish languages. Both texts have equal force.

Secret Protocol

1. Various claims both of public and private nature will be dealt with in the course of further negotiations between the two Governments.

2. This Protocol enters into force simultaneously with the Agreement of the 30th of July, 1941.

PROTOCOL

1. As soon as diplomatic relations are reestablished the Government of the Union of Soviet Socialist Republics will grant amnesty to all Polish citizens who are at present deprived of their freedom on the territory of the U.S.S.R. either as prisoners of war or on other adequate grounds.

2. The present Protocol comes into force simultaneously with the Agreement of July 30, 1941.

Consequences

The following month, on August 14, 1941, a Polish-Soviet Military Agreement was concluded, which provided for the organization of a Polish army within the Soviet Union. On December 4, 1941, a Polish-Soviet Declaration of Friendship and Mutual Assistance was signed by General Władysław Sikorski and Premier Stalin in Moscow. Despite this, the Soviet Union asserted that the Polish territory it had annexed before the outbreak of the war would remain forever Soviet, and the Poles continued to be distressed over treatment of Polish prisoners released from the camps.

The deteriorating relations came to a crisis point on April 13, 1943, when German radio announced the discovery of a mass grave of some 10,000 Polish army officers near Smolensk, in the Soviet Union. The Polish government in exile requested an International Red Cross investigation, to which the Soviets responded with a claim that the Germans had been responsible for the massacre. Accusing Poland and Great Britain of collusion with Hitler, the Soviets severed diplomatic relations with Poland on April 25, 1943.

After the war, Poland became a Soviet satellite state until the late 1980s, when the rise of the Polish labor union Solidarity and the reforms of the Soviet system by Mikhail Gorbachev presaged the end of the cold war, the collapse of the WARSAW PACT, and a newly independent Poland's petition to enter the North Atlantic Treaty Organization (NATO).

Source
J. A. S. Grenville, *The Major International Treaties, 1914–1973* (New York: Stein and Day, 1975), 214–215.

Proclamations and Declarations

ACT OF HAVANA

TREATY AT A GLANCE

Completed
July 30, 1940, at Havana, Cuba

Signatories
The "American Republics"

Overview
The act provided for the provisional administration of European colonies and possessions in the Americas during World War II.

Historical Background

When World War II commenced in Europe with the German invasion of Poland in September 1939, the United States—soon to be deeply implicated in the defense of Great Britain through the LEND-LEASE AGREEMENT and, a bit later, through an undeclared war with Germany at sea—sought to shore up its own defenses by boosting inter-American solidarity and cooperation. A meeting of the foreign ministers of the American republics was held in Panama from September 23 through October 3, 1939, to work on a joint declaration of neutrality, the establishment of a neutral zone extending to 300 miles off the shores of the American republics, and a resolution that if any region in the Americas belonging to a European state should change sovereignty, thereby jeopardizing the security of the Americas, a consultative meeting would be urgently called. As Germany conquered the Netherlands and France, alarm increased in the Americas, especially in the United States, and a second meeting was called, this time in Havana, Cuba, from July 21 to July 30, 1940. It adopted the Act of Havana.

Terms

The act stated that should a change of sovereignty pose a threat in European colonies and possessions in the Americas, the American republics would create a committee to administer the colony or possession. If the emergency developed before the committee could act, then one republic could take action alone. In practice, of course, this would be the United States, which, in effect, became the guarantor of the security of the Americas during World War II.

Convention on the Provisional Administration of European Colonies and Possessions in the Americas, Havana, 30 July 1940

The Governments represented at the Second Meeting of Ministers of Foreign Affairs of the American Republics,

Considering . . .

That as a result of the events which are taking place in the European continent situations may develop in the territories of the possessions which some of the belligerent nations have in the Americas which may extinguish or materially impair the sovereignty which they exercise over them, or leave their Government without a leader, thus creating a state of danger to the peace of the continent and a state of affairs in which the rule of law, order, and respect for life, liberty and the property of inhabitants may disappear . . .

That any transfer, or attempted transfer, of the sovereignty, jurisdiction, possession of any interest in or control over any such region to another non-American State, would be regarded by the American Republics as against American sentiments and principles and the rights of American States to maintain their security and political independence . . .

That the American Republics, through their respective Government agencies, reserve the right to judge whether any transfer or attempted transfer of sovereignty, jurisdiction, cession or incorporation of geographic regions in the Americas, possessed by European countries up to September 1, 1939, has the effect of impairing their political independence even though no formal transfer or change in the status of such region or regions shall have taken place; . . .

. . . Being desirous of protecting their peace and safety and of promoting the interests of any of the regions herein referred to which may fall within the purview of the foregoing recitations, have resolved to conclude the following convention:

ARTICLE I

If a non-American State shall directly or indirectly attempt to replace another non-American State in the sovereignty or control which it exercised over any territory located in the Americas, thus threatening the peace of the continent, such territory shall automatically come under the provisions of this Convention and shall be submitted to a provisional administrative régime.

ARTICLE II

The administration shall be exercised, as may be considered advisable in each case, by one or more American States, with their previous approval.

ARTICLE III

When the administration shall have been established for any region it shall be exercised in the interests of the security of the Americas and for the benefit of the region under administration, with a view to its welfare and progress, until such time as the region is in a position to govern itself or is restored to its former status, whenever the latter is compatible with the security of the American Republics. . . .

ARTICLE XVI

A Commission to be known as the "Inter-American Commission for Territorial Administration" is hereby established, to be composed of a representative from each one of the States which ratifies this Convention; it shall be the international organization to which this Convention refers. Once this Convention has become effective, any country which ratifies it may convoke the first meeting proposing the city in which it is to be held. The Commission shall elect its chairman, complete its organization and fix its definitive seat. Two-thirds of the members of the Commission shall constitute a quorum and two-thirds of the members present may adopt decisions.

ARTICLE XVII

The Commission is authorized to establish a provisional administration in the regions to which the present Convention refers; allow such administration to be exercised by the number of States which it may determine in each case, and supervise its exercise under the terms of the preceding Articles.

Consequences

The Act of Havana was in keeping with the MONROE DOCTRINE as it had come to be practiced during the late 19th and early 20th centuries, as the United States began its own version of European imperialism. Guaranteeing Latin American security during World War II reinforced the U.S. tendency to see itself as the policeman of the Western Hemisphere, and the policy of pushing countries south of the border toward ideological and security alliances beneficial to U.S. interests continued long into the cold war.

Source

J. A. S. Grenville, *The Major International Treaties, 1914–1973* (New York: Stein and Day, 1975), 324–325.

ATLANTIC CHARTER

TREATY AT A GLANCE

Completed
August 14, 1941, pursuant to a conference aboard the
USS *Augusta* off Newfoundland

Signatories
United States and Great Britain

Overview
Issued during the darkest days of Britain's involvement in World War II and five months before the United States entered the war, the Atlantic Charter was an Anglo-American statement of common principles.

Historical Background

From the time Adolf Hitler invaded Poland, the American president, Franklin Delano Roosevelt, began seeking ways to come to the aid of Great Britain in the face of an isolationist Congress hostile to U.S. involvement in the European war. As Germany marched over Europe and isolated the British, Roosevelt persisted, pushing the pace of U.S. rearmament from a mere $2 million in defense spending in January 1940 to some $10.5 million following the fall of France. Caught in a presidential election campaign against a strong Republican candidate, Wendell Willkie, Roosevelt paid close attention to opinion polls indicating that Americans favored a policy of "all aid short of war" to Britain. He promised voters he would not send American soldiers to fight in a foreign war but also urged increased support for British prime minister Winston Churchill's government. Voters ignored Willkie's absolutely valid argument that Roosevelt was hoping to provoke an attack, which would mean the war was no longer foreign, and sent FDR back to the White House for a third term. After the election, the public, including the defeated Willkie, supported Roosevelt's LEND-LEASE AGREEMENT, a scheme to help the besieged and nearly bankrupt Britain by lending, instead of selling, Churchill all the arms he needed.

What the public did not know was that Roosevelt had secretly authorized joint U.S.-British staff talks and collaborated with Churchill's government on how to meet the German U-boat threat. In April 1941 he gave the U.S. Navy license to attack German subs in the North Atlantic, reached an executive agreement with the exiled Danish government to place Greenland under American protection, and in July sent the U.S. Marines to occupy Iceland. By the time Germany invaded Russia, he was all but fighting an undeclared war with Hitler at sea, and now he extended lend-lease to the USSR. Finally, Roosevelt began pressing Congress for amendments to the Selective Service Act to raise the ceiling on the number of men in the armed forces, lift the ban on the use of troops outside the Western Hemisphere, and permit him to extend the tours of draftees.

The Republicans had had enough, and Roosevelt's proposed amendments sparked the last great congressional debate on isolationism versus intervention. It was during the middle of this debate that FDR and Churchill met secretly off the coast of Newfoundland to draft a manifesto of the common principles that bound the two nations, and a free people, together: the Atlantic Charter.

Terms

Roosevelt and Churchill met for four days (August 9–12) aboard the USS *Augusta*. Their unofficial manifesto set forth eight principles of American and British aims in war as well as peace, all of them reminiscent of Woodrow Wilson's Fourteen Points.

Joint Declaration of the President of the United States of America and the Prime Minister, Mr Churchill, representing His Majesty's Government in the United Kingdom, being met together, deem it right to make known certain common principles in the national policies of their respective countries on which they base their hopes for a better future for the world.

First, their countries seek no aggrandizement, territorial or other;

Second, they desire to see no territorial changes that do not accord with the freely expressed wishes of the peoples concerned;

Third, they respect the right of all peoples to choose the form of government under which they will live; and they wish to see sovereign rights and self-government restored to those who have been forcibly deprived of them;

Fourth, they will endeavour, with due respect for their existing obligations, to further the enjoyment by all States, great or small, victor or vanquished, of access, on equal terms, to the trade and to the raw materials of the world which are needed for their economic prosperity;

Fifth, they desire to bring about the fullest collaboration between all nations in the economic field with the object of securing, for all, improved labour standards, economic advancement and social security;

Sixth, after the final destruction of the Nazi tyranny, they hope to see established a peace which will afford to all nations the means of dwelling in safety within their own boundaries, and which will afford assurance that all the men in all the lands may live out their lives in freedom from fear and want;

Seventh, such a peace should enable all men to traverse the high seas and oceans without hindrance;

Eighth, they believe that all of the nations of the world, for realistic as well as spiritual reasons must come to the abandonment of the use of force. Since no future peace can be maintained if land, sea or air armaments continue to be employed by nations which threaten, or may threaten, aggression outside of their frontiers, they believe, pending the establishment of a wider and permanent system of general security, that the disarmament of such nations is essential. They will likewise aid and encourage all other practicable measures which will lighten for peace-loving peoples the crushing burden of armaments.

Consequences

Churchill later claimed that Roosevelt promised to "wage war but not declare it" and to look for some event, some incident, that would justify open hostilities by the United States. It was certainly true that Roosevelt pushed Congress to vote on November 7 for arming merchant ships and allowing them to sail into the war zone, which would indicate that he believed submarine warfare might become a casus belli for the United States, just as it had in World War I. Indeed, Admiral Dönitz's U-boats had already torpedoed two American destroyers, *Kearney* and *Reuben James*. As it turned out, in less than a month, the Japanese would give FDR more than enough to make his undeclared war official. Not surprisingly, Roosevelt immediately made the war in Europe the major emphasis of the American war effort, though most Americans supported the war as a means of seeking revenge against Japan. In any case, the Atlantic Charter continued to inform American war aims: the charter's principles were endorsed by 26 allied nations in the UNITED NATIONS DECLARATION on January 1, 1942.

Source

Avalon Project at the Yale Law School, "The Atlantic Conference—August 9–12, 1945." Available online. URL: http://www.yale.edu/lawweb/avalon/wwii/atlantic/atmenu.htm. Accessed May 16, 2005.

UNITED NATIONS DECLARATION

TREATY AT A GLANCE

Completed
January 1, 1942, at Washington, D.C.

Signatories
United States, Great Britain, the Soviet Union, and China,
plus 22 other nations allied against the Axis powers

Overview
In a meeting at Washington. D.C., the "Big Three" powers plus China, but not Free France, proclaimed their unity with other free world countries against the Axis powers in World War II. All 26 signatories pledged their resources to achieving complete victory and adopted the principles of the Atlantic Charter in a document that would become the seedbed of the postwar United Nations organization.

Historical Background

Franklin Delano Roosevelt, the president of the United States, and Winston Churchill, the British prime minister, met in secret off the Dutch coast in the summer of 1941 at a time when Roosevelt was engaged in the last great battle with an isolationist Congress over his LEND-LEASE AGREEMENT and Churchill was trying to keep up the spirits of a Britain that for almost a year had been holding out alone against the onslaught of the Axis powers. They issued a joint manifesto, the ATLANTIC CHARTER, outlining for the world—and for their new ally, the Soviet Union, which had only a month before been invaded by Nazi Germany—the principles upon which an anti-Axis alliance should be founded. There were eight of them: the renunciation of territorial aggression; the prohibition of territorial changes without consent of the peoples concerned; the restoration of sovereign rights and self-government; a guaranteed access to raw materials for all nations; world economic cooperation; freedom from fear and want; freedom of the seas; and disarmament of aggressors.

Since September 1940 Germany, Italy, and Japan had been united in their quest for world domination pursuant to the AXIS PACT, but on the day Roosevelt and Churchill issued their joint statement, August 14, 1941, the United States was not yet even a belligerent, although FDR was seeking to extend lend-lease to the Russians and was fighting an undeclared naval war in the Atlantic with the Nazis. Roosevelt clearly expected to be engaged in the war soon, believing it would come, as World War I had come, as the result of German U-boat attacks on U.S. ships. Instead, FDR found his day of infamy via the Japanese sneak attack on Pearl Harbor on December 7, 1941. On December 11, Germany and Italy declared war on the United States. The United States became an ally of both Britain and Russia in the war in Europe against Germany and Italy, but only Great Britain and the United States were allied in the Pacific war against Japan.

The first attempt to draft the terms of this grand alliance came when Churchill, immediately following Pearl Harbor, requested an emergency conference with Roosevelt, and the two met for three weeks following December 22 in Washington, D.C. Called the Arcadia Conference, the meeting saw the two leaders reaffirm a Europe-first policy, which meant that the United States would put its considerable resources toward defeating Nazi Germany rather than seeking instant revenge against Japan, which most Americans probably favored. At the conference, Roosevelt and Churchill also conceived of Gymnast, a plan for Anglo-American landings in North Africa. They created a Combined Chiefs of Staff Committee to prosecute the war. And on January 1, 1942, they issued—in the spirit, they pointed out, of the Atlantic Charter—the United Nations Declaration.

Terms

Roosevelt came up with the phrase "United Nations," and he envisioned the declaration not merely as a direct response to the Axis Pact but also as a vehicle to circumvent the right of the U.S. Senate to pass by a two-thirds majority treaties of alliance negotiated with foreign powers. As it turned out, the USSR signed on to the document, as did China and two dozen others, but not the Free French (in the midst of a struggle for leadership within the movement), despite a loophole that would have allowed "appropriate authorities which are not Governments" to adhere to its tenets:

> *The Governments signatory hereto,*
>
> *Having subscribed* to a common programme of purposes and principals embodied in the Joint Declaration of the President of the United States of America and the Prime Minister of the United Kingdom of Great Britain and Northern Ireland dated August 14, 1941 known as the Atlantic Charter,
>
> *Being convinced* that complete victory over their enemies is essential to defend life, liberty, independence and religious freedom, and to preserve human rights and justice in their own lands, and that they are now engaged in a common struggle against savage and brutal forces seeking to subjugate the world,
>
> *Declare:*
>
> (i) Each Government pledges itself to employ its full resources, military or economic, against those members of the Tripartite Pact and its adherents with which such Government is at war.
>
> (ii) Each Government pledges itself to cooperate with the Governments signatory hereto and not to make a separate armistice or peace with the enemies.
>
> The foregoing Declaration may be adhered to by other nations which are, or may be, rendering material assistance and contributions in the struggle for victory over Hitlerism.

Consequences

The joint declaration listed the Allied nations in alphabetical order except for the United States, Britain, the USSR, and China. These were placed at the head of the list, thus setting out their status as "great powers." The Atlantic Charter principles upon which the declaration was based indicated the vague Wilsonian war aims pursued by the United States, and these principles, including the privileged position of the great powers, became one of the bases for the postwar establishment of a permanent organization bearing the name the Allies adopted during the war: the United Nations (see UNITED NATIONS CHARTER).

Source

J. A. S. Grenville, *The Major International Treaties, 1914–1973* (New York: Stein and Day, 1975), 212.

CASABLANCA DECLARATION

TREATY AT A GLANCE

Completed
February 12, 1943, at Casablanca, Morocco

Signatories
United States and Great Britain

Overview
One of several conferences between the major Allied powers, Casablanca was noteworthy for its surprise declaration from Roosevelt and Churchill that the Allied goal in World War II was the "unconditional surrender" of the Axis powers.

Historical Background

After the American entry into World War II, U.S. president Franklin Delano Roosevelt and British prime minister Winston Churchill, who had already on occasion met in secret summits, began holding a series of well-publicized conferences on the conduct of the war. Although the Allied leaders always discussed matters of substance and came to major decisions at the conferences, not all of the statements, reports, or declarations they issued reflected their importance. Much of what was discussed of necessity remained secret. For example, one could hardly have expected the joint statement that followed the Quebec Conference in August 1943 to have announced the American decision to share with the British its results under the top secret Manhattan Project, which would produce the atomic bombs that ended the war in the Pacific. Some of the public announcements were significant, however, beyond the propaganda purposes their language was clearly meant to serve. The Casablanca Conference, one of the earliest such summits, in January 1943, produced just such a significant declaration.

Roosevelt and Churchill met in Casablanca in the wake of Operation Torch, the combined allied invasion of North Africa, to determine the strategy for the coming year. Roosevelt once again soothed Churchill's feelings by putting off the opening of a second front in France in favor of operations in Sicily. General George Marshall and Admiral Ernest King won approval at the conference for offensives in Burma and the southwest Pacific. The two leaders spent a lot of time trying to persuade the rival military leaders of Free France, Charles de Gaulle and Henri Giraud, to at least feign

unity. Then, as the conference was drawing to a close, Roosevelt made the parting pronouncement that peace could only come with the total elimination of Germany's and Japan's military and their "unconditional surrender."

With this declaration, which was not nearly so spontaneous as he would have those in attendance believe, Roosevelt was trying to send a signal to Joseph Stalin about American resolve in the war. He felt he needed to do so because his commander in Operation Torch, Dwight Eisenhower, had blundered politically in North Africa. The collaborationist Vichy government had severed diplomatic relations with Washington and ordered French forces to resist the Allied invasion. Looking for a French leader with enough prestige to rally French Africa against the Axis, the Allies had turned to Henri Giraud, a hero of the Free French who had escaped from a prison camp. The only trouble was that Giraud demanded command of the whole invasion force. Then Admiral François Darlan showed up suddenly in Algiers. A leading fascist, Darlan was, according to the Vichy government, the commander of the local French forces, and he promised Eisenhower he would make them stop fighting the Allies if the American commander recognized him as the political chief of North Africa. Eisenhower made the deal, and the Americans escaped utter humiliation only when a French royalist assassinated Darlan and de Gaulle outmaneuvered Giraud to become de facto leader of the Free French.

It all seemed sinister to Stalin, who had objected to the North African invasion from the start, suspecting his Western allies of delaying a direct invasion of the mainland as a way of bleeding the Red Army by letting it do the brunt of the fighting against the Nazis. Thus, Roosevelt's "unconditional surrender" was aimed as much at the ally who was absent from Casablanca as it was at the enemies whose future it was destined to dictate.

Terms

The declaration itself was couched in the tough-guy phrasing and casual punctuation of American wartime propaganda, as would be most such documents.

The decisions reached and the actual plans made at Casablanca were not confined to any one theater of war or to any one continent or ocean or sea. Before this year is out, it will be made known to the world—in actions rather than words—that the Casablanca Conference produced plenty of news; and it will be bad news for the Germans and Italians—and the Japanese.

We have lately concluded a long, hard battle in the Southwest Pacific and we have made notable gains. That battle started in the Solomons and New Guinea last summer. It has demonstrated our superior power in planes and, most importantly, in the fighting qualities of our individual soldiers and sailors.

American armed forces in the Southwest Pacific are receiving powerful aid from Australia and New Zealand and also directly from the British themselves.

We do not expect to spend the time it would take to bring Japan to final defeat merely by inching our way forward from island to island across the vast expanse of the Pacific.

Great and decisive actions against the Japanese will be taken to drive the invader from the soil of China. Important actions will be taken in the skies over China-and over Japan itself.

The discussions at Casablanca have been continued in Chungking with the Generalissimo by General Arnold and have resulted in definite plans for offensive operations.

There are many roads which lead right to Tokyo. We shall neglect none of them.

In an attempt to ward off the inevitable disaster, the Axis propagandists are trying all of their old tricks in order to divide the United Nations. They seek to create the idea that if we win this war, Russia, England, China, and the United States are going to get into a cat-and-dog fight.

This is their final effort to turn one nation against another, in the vain hope that they may settle with one or two at a time-that any of us may be so gullible and so forgetful as to be duped into making "deals" at the expense of our Allies.

To these panicky attempts to escape the consequences of their crimes we say-all the United Nations say-that the only terms on which we shall deal with an Axis government or any Axis factions are the terms proclaimed at Casablanca: "Unconditional Surrender." In our uncompromising policy we mean no harm to the common people of the Axis nations. But we do mean to impose punishment and retribution in full upon their guilty, barbaric leaders . . .

In the years of the American and French revolutions the fundamental principle guiding our democracies was established. The cornerstone of our whole democratic edifice was the principle that from the people and the people alone flows the authority of government.

It is one of our war aims, as expressed in the Atlantic Charter, that the conquered populations of today be again the masters of their destiny. There must be no doubt anywhere that it is the unalterable purpose of the United Nations to restore to conquered peoples their sacred rights.

Consequences

In many ways the Casablanca Declaration was a rash act. It committed the United States to a power vacuum in postwar Europe rather than a balance of power, which would vastly complicate the peace and give Stalin ample opportunity to fill the vacuum with puppet regimes. It may also have discouraged Germans from attempting to oust Adolf Hitler even when facing sure defeat. And it certainly underlay Japan's determination to fight on in Asia long after losing all realistic hope of anything but utter defeat.

Source

Avalon Project at the Yale Law School, "Casablanca Conference 1943." Available online. URL: http://www.yale.edu/lawweb/avalon/wwii/casablan.htm. Accessed May 16, 2005.

JOINT FOUR-NATION DECLARATION OF THE MOSCOW CONFERENCE

TREATY AT A GLANCE

Completed
October 30, 1943, at Moscow

Signatories
United States, Great Britain, the Soviet Union, and China

Overview
The Moscow Conference was held in part to reassure Stalin of the seriousness of Allied intentions to open a second front in Europe and in part to secure his acquiescence in the Anglo-American occupation of Italy. Joining the United States, Britain, and China in a joint declaration of Allied war aims, Stalin not only secured the help he needed to fight Germany but laid the groundwork for Soviet hegemony in postwar eastern Europe.

Historical Background

After the United States entered World War II, President Franklin Delano Roosevelt and British prime minister Winston Churchill began holding a series of war summits to discuss war aims and set Allied strategies. The Soviets would not attend any of these conferences until the winter of 1943, although Roosevelt in particular was aware of the need to make Joseph Stalin feel part of the Allied effort. In fact, his surprise announcement at the Casablanca Conference in January 1943 that the Allies would be seeking an "unconditional surrender" from Germany was aimed at reassuring the Soviet leader of the Allies' seriousness and resolve (see CASABLANCA DECLARATION).

For his part, Stalin had made clear his desire for an Allied invasion of the European mainland from the west as soon as possible, while Churchill continued to argue for an attack through northern Africa and up the Mediterranean into Europe's "soft underbelly." Following the Quebec Conference, at which Roosevelt and Churchill agreed on May 1944 as the deadline for an invasion of France, the British and Americans sent Anthony Eden and Cordell Hull to Moscow to reassure Comrade Stalin of their governments' intentions to open this Allied "second front" and to make sure that he was in tune with other Allied plans.

Terms

At the Moscow Conference, Eden and Hull first and foremost secured Stalin's blessing for the arrangements Roosevelt and Churchill had made concerning Italy. Anglo-American commanders on the spot would run the occupied country, while the interallied commission that Stalin had requested as a governing body would instead merely advise those commanders. Following their conference, the diplomats issued a joint declaration, including China, which at the Cairo Conference a month later would formally become one of the great powers of the alliance (see CAIRO DECLARATION).

***

The governments of the United States of America, United Kingdom, the Soviet Union, and China;

United in their determination, in accordance with the declaration by the United Nations of January, 1942, and subsequent declarations, to continue hostilities against those Axis powers with which they respectively are at war until such powers have laid down their arms on the basis of unconditional surrender;

Conscious of their responsibility to secure the liberation of themselves and the peoples allied with them from the menace of aggression;

Recognizing the necessity of insuring a rapid and orderly transition from war to peace and of establishing and maintaining international peace and security with the least diversion of the world's human and economic resources for armaments;

Jointly declare:

1. That their united action, pledged for the prosecution of the war against their respective enemies, will be continued for the organization and maintenance of peace and security.

2. That those of them at war with a common enemy will act together in all matters relating to the surrender and disarmament of that enemy.

3. That they will take all measures deemed by them to be necessary to provide against any violation of the terms imposed upon the enemy.

4. That they recognize the necessity of establishing at the earliest practicable date a general international organization, based on the principle of the sovereign equality of all peace-loving states, and open to membership by all such states, large and small, for the maintenance of international peace and security.

5. That for the purpose of maintaining international peace and security pending the re-establishment of law and order and the inauguration of a system of general security they will consult with one another and as occasion requires with other members of the United Nations, with a view to joint action on behalf of the community of nations.

6. That after the termination of hostilities they will not employ their military forces within the territories of other states except for the purposes envisaged in this declaration and after joint consultation.

7. That they will confer and cooperate with one another and with other members of the United Nations to bring about a practicable general agreement with respect to the regulation of armaments in the post-war period.

DECLARATION REGARDING ITALY

The Foreign Secretaries of the United States, the United Kingdom and the Soviet Union have established that their three governments are in complete agreement that Allied policy toward Italy must be based upon the fundamental principle that Fascism and all its evil influence and configuration shall be completely destroyed and that the Italian people shall be given every opportunity to establish governmental and other institutions based on democratic principles.

The Foreign Secretaries of the United States and the United Kingdom declare that the action of their governments form the inception of the invasion of Italian territory, in so far as paramount military requirements have permitted, has been based upon this policy.

In furtherance of this policy in the future the Foreign Secretaries of the three governments are agreed that the following measures are important and should be put into effect:

1. It is essential that the Italian Government should be made more democratic by inclusion of representatives of those sections of the Italian people who have always opposed Fascism.

2. Freedom of speech, of religious worship, of political belief, of press and of public meeting, shall be restored in full measure to the Italian people, who shall be entitled to form anti-Fascist political groups.

3. All institutions and organizations created by the Fascist regime shall be suppressed.

4. All Fascist or pro-Fascist elements shall be removed from the administration and from institutions and organizations of a public character.

5. All political prisoners of the Fascist regime shall be released and accorded full amnesty.

6. Democratic organs of local government shall be created.

7. Fascist chiefs and army generals known or suspected to be war criminals shall be arrested and handed over to justice.

In making this declaration the three Foreign Secretaries recognize that so long as active military operations continue in Italy the time at which it is possible to give full effect to the principles stated above will be determined by the Commander-in-Chief on the basis of instructions received through the combined chiefs of staff.

The three governments, parties to this declaration, will, at the request of any one of them, consult on this matter. It is further understood that nothing in this resolution is to operate against the right of the Italian people ultimately to choose their own form of government.

DECLARATION ON AUSTRIA

The governments of the United Kingdom, the Soviet Union and the United States of America are agreed that Austria, the first free country to fall a victim to Hitlerite aggression, shall be liberated from German domination.

They regard the annexation imposed on Austria by Germany on March 15, 1938, as null and void. They consider themselves as in no way bound by any charges effected in Austria since that date. They declare that they wish to see re-established a free and independent Austria and thereby to open the way for the Austrian people themselves, as well as those neighboring States which will be face with similar problems, to find that political and economic security which is the only basis for lasting peace. Austria is reminded, however that she has a responsibility, which she cannot evade, for participation in the war at the side of Hitlerite Germany, and that in the final settlement account will inevitably be taken of her own contribution to her liberation.

STATEMENT OF ATROCITIES

Signed by President Roosevelt, Prime Minister Churchill and Premier Stalin.

The United Kingdom, the United States and the Soviet Union have received from many quarters evidence of atrocities, massacres and cold-blooded mass executions which are being perpetrated by Hitlerite forces in many of the countries they have overrun and from which they are now being steadily expelled. The brutalities of Nazi domination are no new thing, and all peoples or territories in their grip have suffered from the worst form of government by terror. What is new is that many of the territories are now being redeemed by the the advancing armies of the liberating powers, and that in their desperation the recoiling Hitlerites and Huns are redoubling their ruthless cruelties. This is now evidenced with particular clearness by monstrous crimes on the territory of the Soviet Union which is being liberated from Hitlerites, and on French and Italian territory.

Accordingly, the aforesaid three Allied powers, speaking in the interest of the thirty-two United Nations, hereby solemnly declare and give full warning of their declaration as follows:

At the time of granting of any armistice to any government which may be set up in Germany, those German officers and men and members of the Nazi party who have been responsible for or have taken a consenting part in the above atrocities, massacres and executions will be sent back to the countries in which their abominable deeds were done in order that they may be judged and punished according to the laws of these liberated countries and of free governments which will be erected therein. Lists will be compiled in all possible detail from all these countries having regard especially to invaded parts of the Soviet Union, to Poland and Czechoslovakia, to Yugoslavia and Greece including Crete and other islands, to Norway, Denmark, Netherlands, Belgium, Luxemburg, France and Italy.

Thus, Germans who take part in wholesale shooting of Polish officers or in the execution of French, Dutch, Belgian or Norwegian hostages of Cretan peasants, or who have shared in slaughters inflicted on the people of Poland or in territories of the Soviet Union which are now being swept clear of the enemy, will know they will be brought back to the scene of their crimes and judged on the spot by the peoples whom they have outraged.

Let those who have hitherto not imbued their hands with innocent blood beware lest they join the ranks of the guilty, for most assuredly the three Allied powers will pursue them to the uttermost ends of the earth and will deliver them to their accusers in order that justice may be done.

The above declaration is without prejudice to the case of German criminals whose offenses have no particular geographical localization and who will be punished by joint decision of the government of the Allies.

Consequences

Stalin's cooperation at the conference was deceptive. Later, when the Red Army liberated the Axis-controlled states of eastern Europe, Stalin would point to the Italian precedent to justify his imposition of unilateral military control by the Soviet Union through long occupation of what became East Germany beginning in 1944, the installation of a puppet communist government in Poland immediately after the war, and the communist takeover of Czechoslovakia in 1948.

Source
Avalon Project at the Yale Law School, "The Moscow Conference, October 1943." Available online. URL: http://www.yale.edu/lawweb/avalon/wwii/moscow.htm. Accessed May 16, 2005.

CAIRO DECLARATION

TREATY AT A GLANCE

Completed
December 1, 1943, at Cairo, Egypt

Signatories
United States, Great Britain, and China

Overview
At the Cairo Conference in November 1943, the American, British, and Chinese leaders prescribed the Allied terms for ending World War II in the Pacific. It was at this conference that China joined the Allies as one of the great powers in the fight against the three Axis nations.

Historical Background

In 1943 Nationalist Chinese leader Generalissimo Chiang Kai-shek joined U.S. president Franklin Delano Roosevelt and British prime minister Winston Churchill at a war council held in Cairo between November 22 and 26, one of a series of such meetings among the Allies throughout the war. Churchill was not at all happy that Roosevelt had invited Chiang, whom Churchill viewed as not much better than a Chinese warlord.

Certainly, Chiang represented trouble for British colonial interest in China and East Asia, and, always a greedy man, he was proving more bothersome than helpful in Allied attempts to prosecute the war in the China-Burma-India theater. Nationalist Chinese generals under Chiang demanded an unlimited supply of weapons and goods but were totally unreliable on the battlefield, except for those troops trained and led by Chinese Communists, who were supposedly allied with Chiang's Nationalists in a United Front but whose participation Chiang subverted whenever possible. But Roosevelt, whose family also had financial roots in the Far East, was insistent, and Cairo established Chiang as the voice of a great power ally in the war.

Terms

At the Cairo Conference the three leaders discussed at length the war in Burma and issued a declaration setting goals for ending the war in the Pacific, which included, in addition to an "unconditional surrender," the retaking from Japan of Manchuria, Formosa, Taiwan, Korea, the Pescadores (P'eng-hu), and all the Pacific islands Japan had conquered or acquired since 1914.

The several military missions have agreed upon future military operations against Japan. The Three Great Allies expressed their resolve to bring unrelenting pressure against their brutal enemies by sea, land, and air. This pressure is already mounting.

The Three Great Allies are fighting this war to restrain and punish the aggression of Japan. They covet no gain for themselves and have no thought of territorial expansion.

It is their purpose that Japan shall be stripped of all the islands in the Pacific which she has seized or occupied since the beginning of the first World War in 1914, and that all the territories Japan has stolen from the Chinese, such as Manchuria, Formosa, and the Pescadores, shall be restored to the Republic of China.

Japan will also be expelled from all other territories which she has taken by violence and greed. The aforesaid three great powers, mindful of the enslavement of the people of Korea, are determined that in due course Korea shall become free and independent.

With these objects in view the three Allies, in harmony with those of the United Nations at war with Japan, will continue to persevere in the serious and prolonged operations necessary to procure the unconditional surrender of Japan.

THE WORLD AT WAR 681

Consequences

Chiang's inclusion among the Great Powers' leaders of World War II would turn out an embarrassment. Not only would he prove less than useful in fighting the Japanese in the Pacific, but the long-corrupted and immensely vain Chiang would find himself and his Nationalist government chased off the mainland soon after the war by the Chinese Communists under Mao Zedong to Taiwan, in 1949. There he set up shop as head of the "true [non-Communist] China" and continued to exploit the Western democracies in the name of a freedom he and the Nationalists had failed to deliver even when they did have nominal control of the mainland.

Source

Avalon Project at the Yale Law School, "Cairo Conference 1943." Available online. URL: http://www.yale.edu/lawweb/avalon/wwii/cairo.htm. Accessed May 16, 2005.

THREE-POWER DECLARATIONS OF
THE TEHRAN CONFERENCE

TREATY AT A GLANCE

Completed
December 1, 1943, at Tehran, Iran

Signatories
United States, Great Britain, and the Soviet Union

Overview
The first Big Three summit, the Tehran Conference covered the shape Europe would take in the postwar world. It was at this conference that President Franklin D. Roosevelt won an agreement in principle from Winston Churchill and Joseph Stalin to create a United Nations organization after the war.

Historical Background

The last of a series of diplomatic and strategic planning conferences held by the Allied powers in 1943, the Tehran Conference was also the first Big Three summit. Soviet premier Joseph Stalin had not attended the meetings in Casablanca, Quebec, or Cairo, and neither U.S. president Franklin Delano Roosevelt nor British prime minister Winston Churchill came to Moscow in October (see CASABLANCA DECLARATION and CAIRO DECLARATION). All were present at the November 25–December 1 conference, and for the first time the personal and ideological dynamics that would have such impact on the peace process following World War II came into operation.

From Stalin's point of view, the meeting probably only underscored the validity of marxist theory, as the inevitable conflict between national imperial powers predicted by communist ideology had certainly become evident. It was hardly surprising that Roosevelt, the product of a Puritan culture that just yesterday had clung to its moral isolation from the rest of a corrupt world, should have trouble with the contradictions inherent in the views of Winston Churchill, representing a colonial empire that had been protecting its assets and imposing its will on the world for two and a half centuries via a combination of sea power, free trade, and diplomatic chicanery. To Stalin both allies no doubt seemed self-serving, the one wishing to remake the world in its image, the other seeking to maintain a centuries-old policy of a balance of power in Europe.

As for the Soviet dictator himself, Churchill certainly had no illusions about the ruthlessness of this canny survivor of the treacherous political culture of the Bolsheviks, who clung to power by relentlessly destroying any who could even remotely pose a threat to his rule and who, as it turned out, engaged in mass murder as blithely as any Nazi. Roosevelt, on the other hand, chose to believe he could reason with the man if only he could get beyond Stalin's quite evident suspicions. So while Roosevelt openly, even buoyantly, criticized Churchill in "Uncle Joe's" presence and demanded that the prime minister come to terms with the need to end European colonizing, including British imperialism, after the war, Stalin steadfastly insisted on the strategies and policies that would allow the Soviet Union precisely to realize many of old imperial Russia's fondest dreams in eastern Europe.

Churchill—and others, even other Americans—brooded in silence. Churchill wanted to fight the Nazis to the last drop of Russian blood, and Stalin knew it; Stalin wanted to establish hegemony over eastern Europe, and Churchill knew it. Roosevelt wanted to end the war and build a new world order in which such wars could never recur, and neither Churchill nor Stalin believed it.

Stalin demanded the territories he had already gained with the acquiescence of the Nazis—the 1941 frontier in Poland at the Curzon Line (Poland could be compensated with German land to the west)—plus the

Baltic coast of East Prussia. Churchill advocated the breaking up of Germany and turning the Danube area—Austria, Hungary, Bavaria—into a "peaceful, cowlike confederation." He wanted similar confederations in eastern Europe, but Stalin, worried that his Allies were reviving the notion of a cordon sanitaire between the West and the Bolsheviks that the peacemakers at Versailles tried to establish in 1918, objected, especially since it would interfere with his plans to establish hegemony over the area, piece by piece if need be. No, Stalin said, the Allies should Balkanize eastern Europe, punish France for collaborating and strip away her colonies, and keep Poland and Italy as weak as they ever were. Stalin, as some at the conference, such as U.S. diplomat Charles Bolen, noted at the time, wanted the Soviet Union to be the only important military power and political force on the continent of Europe.

All this the Big Three discussed and debated, but that is not what they declared to the world public. Instead, they chose to emphasize the agreement Roosevelt wrung from the others to form an international organization that would become the forum for the globe's diplomacy in a postwar world—led, naturally enough, by the United States, Britain, the Soviet Union, and, Roosevelt insisted, China.

Terms

The Tehran declarations, then, fit the tone of the propaganda proclamations issued by the previous summit conferences, but for the first time the Allies floated the notion of a United Nations to arise from the ashes of the most destructive war in history.

Declaration of the Three Powers

We the President of the United States, the Prime Minister of Great Britain, and the Premier of the Soviet Union, have met these four days past, in this, the Capital of our Ally, Iran, and have shaped and confirmed our common policy.

We express our determination that our nations shall work together in war and in the peace that will follow..

As to war-our military staffs have joined in our round table discussions, and we have concerted our plans for the destruction of the German forces. We have reached complete agreement as to the scope and timing of the operations to be undertaken from the east, west and south.

The common understanding which we have here reached guarantees that victory will be ours.

And as to peace-we are sure that our concord will win an enduring Peace. We recognize fully the supreme responsibility resting upon us and all the United Nations to make a peace which will command the goodwill of the overwhelming mass of the peoples of the world and banish the scourge and terror of war for many generations.

With our Diplomatic advisors we have surveyed the problems of the future. We shall seek the cooperation and active participation of all nations, large and small, whose peoples in heart and mind are dedicated, as are our own peoples, to the elimination of tyranny and slavery, oppression and intolerance. We will welcome them, as they may choose to come, into a world family of Democratic Nations.

No power on earth can prevent our destroying the German armies by land, their U Boats by sea, and their war plants from the air.

Our attack will be relentless and increasing.

Emerging from these cordial conferences we look with confidence to the day when all peoples of the world may live free lives, untouched by tyranny, and according to their varying desires and their own consciences.

We came here with hope and determination. We leave here, friends in fact, in spirit and in purpose.

Signed at Tehran, December 1, 1943

FRANKLIN D. ROOSEVELT
WINSTON S. CHURCHILL
J. V. STALIN

Declaration of the Three Powers Regarding Iran

The President of the United States, the Premier of the U.S.S.R. and the Prime Minister of the United Kingdom, having consulted with each other and with the Prime Minister of Iran, desire to declare the mutual agreement of their three Governments regarding their relations with Iran.

The Governments of the United States, the U.S.S.R., and the United Kingdom recognize the assistance which Iran has given in the prosecution of the war against the common enemy, particularly by facilitating the transportation of supplies from overseas to the Soviet Union.

The Three Governments realize that the war has caused special economic difficulties for Iran, and they are agreed that they will continue to make available to the Government of Iran such economic assistance as may be possible, having regard to the heavy demands made upon them by their world-wide military operations, and to the world-wide shortage of transport, raw materials, and supplies for civilian consumption.

With respect to the post-war period, the Governments of the United States, the U.S.S.R., and the United Kingdom are in accord with the Government of Iran that any economic problems confronting Iran at the close of hostilities should receive full consideration, along with those of other members of the United Nations, by conferences or international agencies held or created to deal with international economic matters.

The Governments of the United States, the U.S.S.R., and the United Kingdom are at one with the Government of Iran in their desire for the maintenance of the independence, sovereignty and territorial integrity of Iran. They count upon the participation of Iran, together with all other peace-loving nations, in the establishment of international peace, security and prosperity after the war, in accordance with the principles of the

Atlantic Charter, to which all four Governments have subscribed.

WINSTON S. CHURCHILL
J. STALIN
FRANKLIN D. ROOSEVELT

The Big Three also noted the military conclusions of the conference in relation to the continuation of the war, including the deadline that Churchill and Roosevelt had already set for the opening of the second front in Europe that had all along been the diplomatic obsession of the Russians, which now had a code name: Operation Overlord.

Military Conclusions
of the Tehran Conference

The Conference:—

(1) Agreed that the Partisans in Yugoslavia should be supported by supplies and equipment to the greatest possible extent, and also by commando operations:

(2) Agreed that, from the military point of view, it was most desirable that Turkey should come into the war on the side of the Allies before the end of the year:

(3) Took note of Marshal Stalin's statement that if Turkey found herself at war with Germany, and as a result Bulgaria declared war on Turkey or attacked her, the Soviet Union would immediately be at war with Bulgaria. The Conference further took note that this fact could be explicitly stated in the forthcoming negotiations to bring Turkey into the war:

(4) Took note that Operation OVERLORD would be launched during May 1944, in conjunction with an operation against Southern France. The latter operation would be undertaken in as great a strength as availability of landing-craft permitted. The Conference further took note of Marshal Stalin's statement that the Soviet forces would launch an offensive at about the same time with the object of preventing the German forces from transferring from the Eastern to the Western Front:

(5) Agreed that the military staffs of the Three Powers should henceforward keep in close touch with each other in regard to the impending operations in Europe. In particular it was agreed that a cover plan to mystify and mislead the enemy as regards these operations should be concerted between the staffs concerned.

FRANKLIN D. ROOSEVELT
JOSEPH V. STALIN
WINSTON S. CHURCHILL

TEHRAN, December 1, 1943.

Consequences

At Tehran the Allies got a glimpse of Stalin's vision for postwar Europe, one Roosevelt chose to ignore and Churchill to brood over. Stalin got what he wanted most: a commitment to the opening of a second front on the Continent.

Source

Avalon Project at the Yale Law School, "Tehran Conference, November 28–December 1, 1943." Available online. URL: http://www.yale.edu/lawweb/avalon/wwii/tehran.html. Accessed May 16, 2005.

REPORT OF THE YALTA (CRIMEA) CONFERENCE

TREATY AT A GLANCE

Completed
February 11, 1945, at Yalta, Crimea, USSR (present-day Ukraine)

Signatories
Great Britain, United States, and the Soviet Union

Overview
The results of the Yalta Conference (February 4–11, 1945) between the Big Three Allied leaders were published in a report containing their consensus on the conduct of the closing months of World War II and on the organization of the postwar world. Since the strains among the Allies were becoming evident, the conference and report not only laid the groundwork for the establishment of the United Nations but also presaged the coming cold war.

Historical Background

During the summer of 1944, Churchill, who had early on cast a critical eye on the Bolsheviks and had no great love for his putative ally Joseph Stalin, lobbied for an Italian campaign in the European theater of the war in hopes that the Western powers among the Allies would reach the Danube before the Red Army. Representing a Britain that was the weakest of the Big Three powers in the alliance (the other two of course being the United States and the Soviet Union), Churchill was interested in restoring a balance of power in Europe that might keep England competitive with its old imperial rival Russia. Toward that end, he preempted President Franklin Delano Roosevelt by meeting with Stalin in October to make a deal on their respective nations' spheres of influence in the postwar world.

Roosevelt seemed hardly to mind. Not only was he ill and growing sicker, but American war aims in general were nebulous at best and pretty much nonexistent except for a reaffirmation of Woodrow Wilson's post–World War I internationalism. Stalin, for his part, was perfectly willing to barter. He planned ultimately only to honor those arrangements he was forced to honor. Like Churchill, Stalin realized Roosevelt's unwillingness to strain the alliance was helping the Soviet leader to undermine Churchill's ministers' diplomatic goals. In fact, Roosevelt's pliant attitude toward Stalin made the British prime minister gloomy about his country's postwar prospects. Heading for the last summit conference of the war, he warned colleagues that this world conflict might prove even more disappointing than the last one.

When a dying Roosevelt arrived at Yalta on the Crimean peninsula in February 1945, he was completely exhausted from the strenuous journey. If Churchill saw Yalta as the final opportunity for the British and Americans to take a firm stand against Soviet control of eastern Europe, Roosevelt probably viewed it as the last chance to forestall the disintegration of the alliance upon what everyone knew was the coming victory. Certainly, the U.S. position showed little evidence of economic motives. Indeed, Roosevelt seemed not even to have a contingency plan for the breakdown of relations with an increasingly assertive USSR. What he feared more than that, evidently, was a retreat at home into American isolationism, which would scuttle his Wilsonian vision of a great power postwar condominium housed in an effective United Nations organization.

Wishing for Soviet participation in a postwar United Nations, Roosevelt was prepared in both word (at the Yalta Conference) and deed (in the allied advance across Europe) to assure Stalin that the Anglo-Saxons were not ganging up on him. But Stalin, for all his former revolutionary zeal, proved as old-fashioned a European as Churchill: he sought postwar security through military and political control of eastern Europe, control that would create a buffer for Russia against the liberal democracies and the kind of ideas that might threaten even his iron control over the varied peoples of the USSR.

At length, the Big Three were able to maintain their unity at the Yalta Conference only by resorting to vague language or by postponing any attempt to resolve the more explosive issues that divided them.

Terms

The Yalta Conference, held February 4–11, 1945, and report reaffirmed earlier agreements to accept nothing less than unconditional surrender of the Axis powers (see CASABLANCA DECLARATION). Inviting the Free French to join them, the Big Three decided to divide the defeated Germany into zones of occupation, with the French zone carved out of lands held by the Americans and British, while the Soviet zone would extend to the Elbe. The German capital, Berlin, would also be divided into four zones, although it would be surrounded by Soviet-held territory. Overall, the occupation would be run by a joint European Advisory Commission.

Even though the Western powers rejected the extreme plans, discussed earlier at Quebec, to turn Germany into a pastoral nation and pushed for revitalized German industry under Allied control, Stalin continued to insist on reparations, on stripping the vanquished foe of some $20 billion in industrial machinery and raw materials. The conference meekly assigned the question to a reparations commission. Stalin also revived earlier talk about breaking up Germany into small states, but here at least the Americans heeded British warnings about further Balkanization in central Europe in the face of the newly powerful Soviet behemoth, and this too they left for additional study.

> For the past eight days Winston S. Churchill, Prime Minister of Great Britain, Franklin D. Roosevelt, President of the United States of America, and Marshal J.V. Stalin, Chairmen of the Council of People's Commissars of the Union of Soviet Socialist Republics, have met with the Foreign Secretaries, Chiefs of Staff and other advisers in the Crimea. . . .
>
> The following statement is made by the Prime Minister of Great Britain, the President of the United States of America, and the Chairman of the Council of People's Commissars of the Union of Soviet Socialist Republics, on the results of the Crimea Conference.

> ### I. THE DEFEAT OF GERMANY
> We have considered and determined the military plans of the three Allied Powers for the final defeat of the common enemy. The military staffs of the three Allied nations have met in daily meetings throughout the Conference. These meetings have been most satisfactory from every point of view and have resulted in closer coordination of the military effort of the three Allies than ever before. The fullest information has been interchanged. The timing, scope and coordination of new and even more powerful blows to be launched by our armies and air forces into the heart of Germany from the East, West, North, and South have been fully agreed and planned in detail.

> Our combined military plans will be made known only as we execute them, but we believe that the very close working partnership among the three staffs attained at this Conference will result in shortening the war. Meetings of the three staffs will be continued in the future whenever the need arises.

> Nazi Germany is doomed. The German people will only make the cost of their defeat heavier to themselves by attempting to continue a hopeless resistance.

> ### II. THE OCCUPATION AND CONTROL OF GERMANY
> We have agreed on common politics and plans for enforcing the unconditional surrender terms which we shall impose together on Nazi Germany after German armed resistance has been finally crushed. These terms will not be made known until the final defeat of Germany has been accomplished. Under the agreed plan, the forces of the Three Powers will each occupy a separate zone of Germany. Coordinated administration and control has been provided for under the plan through a central Control Commission consisting of the Supreme Commanders of the Three Powers with headquarters in Berlin. It has been agreed that France should be invited by the Three Powers, if she should so desire, to take over a zone of occupation, and to participate as a fourth member of the Control Commission. The limits of the French zone will be agreed by the four Governments concerned through their representatives on the European Advisory Commission.

> It is our inflexible purpose to destroy German militarism and Nazism and to ensure that Germany will never again be able to disturb the peace of the world. We are determined to disarm and disband all German armed forces; break up for all time the German General Staff that has repeatedly contrived the resurgence of German militarism; remove or destroy all German military equipment; eliminate or control all German industry that could be used for military production; bring all war criminals to just and swift punishment and exact reparation in kind for the destruction wrought by the Germans; wipe out the Nazi party, Nazi laws, organizations and institutions, remove all Nazi and militarist influences from public office and from the cultural and economic life of the German people; and take in harmony such other measures in Germany as may be necessary to the future peace and safety of the world. It is not our purpose to destroy the people of Germany, but only when Nazism and militarism have been extirpated, will there be hope for a decent life for Germans, and a place for them in the comity of nations.

III. REPARATION BY GERMANY

We have considered the question of the damage caused by Germany to the Allied nations in this war and recognized it as just that Germany be obliged to make compensation for this damage in kind to the greatest extent possible. A Commission for the Compensation of Damage will be established. The Commission will be instructed to consider the question of the extent and methods for compensating damage caused by Germany to the Allied countries. The Commission will work in Moscow.

Stalin was more conciliatory when the rest of the Allies wished to issue a call—pursuant to proposals made at the Dumbarton Oaks Conference back in August through October of 1944 —for a Conference of United Nations to be held in San Francisco on April 25, 1945. He nevertheless demanded that all 16 of the republics that made up the USSR be represented. Although the United States might have made a similar argument for its 48 individual states, it did not. Stalin's rationale again owed something to Russia's ages-long competition with the British Empire: he needed such representation, so he claimed, to balance all the nations of that empire, which would naturally vote with London. The Soviets also demanded that the permanent members of the Security Council, which of course included Russia, retain a veto on all issues instead of merely on questions involving sanctions and threats to the collective peace.

In light of concessions elsewhere, however, Stalin settled for three members in the General Assembly and a limited veto. A relieved Roosevelt declared, "The Russians have given in so much at the conference that I don't think we should let them down." Like Wilson, Roosevelt put much—and as it turned out—too much stock in international peacekeeping organizations.

IV. UNITED NATIONS CONFERENCE

We are resolved upon the earliest possible establishment with our Allies of a general international organization to maintain peace and security. We believe that this is essential, both to prevent aggression and to remove the political. economic and social causes of war through the close and continuing collaboration of all peace-loving peoples.

The foundations were laid at Dumbarton Oaks. On the important question of voting procedure, however, agreement was not there reached. The present Conference has been able to resolve this difficulty.

We have agreed that a Conference of United Nations should be called to meet at San Francisco in the United States on the 25th April 1945, to prepare the charter of such an organization, along the lines proposed in the informal conversations at Dumbarton Oaks.

The Government of China and the Provisional Government of France will be immediately consulted and invited to sponsor invitations to the Conference jointly with the Governments of the United States, Great Britain and the Union of Soviet Socialist Republics. As soon as the consultation with China and France has been completed, the text of the proposals on voting procedure will be made public.

The Americans also put great stock—and as it turned out, too much stock—in free elections. Roosevelt proposed a Declaration on Liberated Europe, by which the Big Three committed to help all liberated peoples to solve their pressing political and economic problems "by democratic means" and endorsed free elections of governments "responsive to the will of the people." To Bolshevik ears—for whom the lexicon of democracy meant something quite different from what it did for Americans—this may well have sounded like more Wilsonian rhetoric, perhaps meant by FDR for domestic consumption to keep his nation from once again isolating itself from European affairs. Since Roosevelt announced, much to Churchill's dismay, that the United States intended to withdraw its troops from Europe within two years, Stalin would feel perfectly comfortable that he could, if he wished, soon simply ignore the declaration.

V. DECLARATION ON LIBERATED EUROPE

We have drawn up and subscribed to a Declaration on Liberated Europe. This Declaration provides for concerting the policies of the Three Powers and for joint action by them in meeting the political and economic problems of liberated Europe in accordance with democratic principles. The text of the Declaration is as follows:

The Premier of the Union of Soviet Socialist Republics, the Prime Minister of the United Kingdom, and the President of the United States of America have consulted with each other in the common interests of the peoples of their countries and those of liberated Europe. They jointly declare their mutual agreement to concert during the temporary period of instability in liberated Europe the policies of their three Governments in assisting the peoples liberated from the domination of Nazi Germany and the peoples of the former Axis satellite States of Europe to solve by democratic means their pressing political and economic problems.

The establishment of order in Europe and the rebuilding of national economic life must be achieved by processes which will enable the liberated peoples to destroy the last vestiges of Nazism and Fascism and to create democratic institutions of their own choice. This is a principle of the Atlantic Charter—the right of all peoples to choose the form of government under which they will live—the restoration of sovereign rights and self-government to those peoples who have been forcibly deprived of them by the aggressor nations.

To foster the conditions in which the liberated peoples may exercise those rights, the three Governments will jointly assist the people in any European liberated State or former Axis satellite State in Europe where in their judgement conditions require: (a) to establish conditions of internal peace; (b) to carry out emergency measures for the relief of distressed peoples; (c) to form interim governmental authorities broadly representative of all democratic elements in the population and pledged to the earliest possible establishment through free elections of Governments responsive to the will of the people; and (d) to facilitate where necessary the holding of such elections.

The three Governments will consult the other United Nations and provisional authorities or other Governments in Europe when matters of direct interest to them are under consideration.

When, in the opinion of the three Governments, conditions in any European liberated State or any former Axis satellite State in Europe make such action necessary, they will immediately consult together on the measures necessary to discharge the joint responsibilities set forth in this Declaration.

By this Declaration we reaffirm our faith in the principles of the Atlantic Charter, our pledge in the Declaration by the United Nations, and our determination to build in cooperation with other peace-loving nations a world order under law, dedicated to peace, security, freedom and the general well-being of all mankind.

In issuing this Declaration, the Three Powers express the hope that the Provisional Government of the French Republic may be associated with them in the procedure suggested.

Poland, as always with the Soviets, proved the biggest sticking point at Yalta. The British and Americans wanted to keep the Curzon Line, agreed to in Tehran, as the Soviet-Polish border and even to modify that line slightly in Poland's favor. Churchill, however, objected to assigning 2.7 million Germans to Poland in the west, to—as he put it—stuffing "the Polish goose so full of Germans that it died of indigestion." So, once again the three leaders put off the question; it would be resolved, they declared, at a peace conference come war's end. Roosevelt, with Churchill's stout backing, secured a promise from Stalin to permit free elections among "non-Fascist elements" within a month of that peace. But it was a vague promise, and Stalin reserved for himself the sole right to determine who exactly was "Fascist" while at the same time rejecting international supervision of the elections.

VI. POLAND

We came to the Crimea Conference resolved to settle our differences about Poland. We discussed fully all aspects of the question. We reaffirm our common desire to see established a strong, free independent and democratic Poland. As a result of our discussions we have agreed on the conditions in which a new Polish Provisional Government of National Unity may be formed in such a manner as to command recognition by the three major Powers.

The agreement reached is as follows:

A new situation has been created in Poland as a result of her complete liberation by the Red Army. This calls for the establishment of a Polish Provisional Government which can be more broadly based than was possible before the recent liberation of western Poland. The Provisional Government which is now functioning in Poland should therefore be reorganized on a broader democratic basis with the inclusion of democratic leaders from Poland itself and from Poles abroad. This new Government should then be called the Polish Provisional Government of National Unity.

M. Molotov, Mr Harriman and Sir A. Clark Kerr are authorized as a Commission to consult in the first instance in Moscow with members of the present Provisional Government and with other Polish democratic leaders from within Poland and from abroad, with a view to the reorganization of the present Government along the above lines. This Polish Provisional Government of National Unity shall be pledged to the holding of free and unfettered elections as soon as possible on the basis of universal suffrage and secret ballot. In these elections all democratic and anti-Nazi parties shall have the right to take part and to put forward candidates.

When a Polish Provisional Government of National Unity has been properly formed in conformity with the above, the Government of the Union of Soviet Socialist Republics, which now maintains diplomatic relations with the present Provisional Government of Poland, and the Government of the United Kingdom and the Government of the United States will establish diplomatic relations with the new Polish Government of National Unity, and will exchange Ambassadors by whose report the respective Governments will be kept informed about the situation in Poland.

The three Heads of Government consider that the eastern frontier of Poland should follow the Curzon line with digressions from it in some regions of 5 to 8 kilometres in favour of Poland. They recognize that Poland must receive substantial accessions of territory in the north and west. They feel that the opinion of the new Polish Provisional Government of National Unity should be sought in due course on the extent of these accessions and that the final delimitation of the western frontier of Poland should thereafter await the Peace Conference.

The conference took up the question of Yugoslavia, once again trying to yoke the future interests of communists and democrats, and then arranged for the foreign secretaries of each power to keep in closer contact for the duration of the war.

VII. YUGOSLAVIA

We have agreed to recommend to Marshal Tito and Dr Subasić that the Agreement between them should be put into effect immediately, and that a new Government should be formed on the basis of that Agreement.

We also recommend that as soon as the new Government has been formed it should declare that:

(i) The Anti-Fascist Assembly of National Liberation (Avnoj) should be extended to include members of the last Yugoslav Parliament (Skupshtina) who have not compromised themselves by collaboration with the enemy, thus forming a body to be known as a temporary Parliament; and

(ii) Legislative acts passed by the Assembly of National Liberation will be subject to subsequent ratification by a Constituent Assembly.

There was also a general review of other Balkan questions.

VIII. MEETINGS OF FOREIGN SECRETARIES
Throughout the Conference, besides the daily meetings of the Heads of Governments, and the Foreign Secretaries, separate meetings of the three Foreign Secretaries, and their advisers, have also been held daily.

These meetings have proved of the utmost value and the Conference agreed that permanent machinery should be set up for regular consultation between the three Foreign Secretaries. They will, therefore, meet as often as may be necessary, probably about every three or four months. These meetings will be held in rotation in the three capitals, the first meeting being held in London, after the United Nations Conference on World Organization.

IX. UNITY FOR PEACE AS FOR WAR
Our meeting here in the Crimea has reaffirmed our common determination to maintain and strengthen in the peace to come that unity of purpose and of action which has made victory possible and certain for the United Nations in this war. We believe that this is a sacred obligation which our Governments owe to our peoples and to all the peoples of the world.

Only with continuing and growing cooperation and understanding among our three countries, and among all the peace-loving nations, can the highest aspiration of humanity be realized-a secure and lasting peace which will, in the words of the Atlantic Charter 'Afford assurance that all the men in all the lands may live out their lives in freedom from fear and want'.

Victory in this war and establishment of the proposed international organization will provide the greatest opportunity in all history to create in the years to come the essential conditions of such a peace.
[Signed]

WINSTON S. CHURCHILL
FRANKLIN D. ROOSEVELT
J.V. STALIN
11th February 1945

Finally, Roosevelt at Yalta obtained from the USSR a promise to declare war against Japan "two to three months" after the surrender of Germany, in return for U.S. support of the Soviet acquisition of territories lost in the Russo-Japanese War of 1904–05 and Soviet dominance in Outer Mongolia and Manchuria—all the objectives of the old imperial Russia in East Asia (see YALTA AGREEMENT).

Consequences

Within a month it became clear that Russia had no intention of meeting the expectations raised at Yalta. Molotov announced on March 23 that most of the London Poles, whom the United States and Great Britain had fought so hard to include in the provisional "unity" government, were being disqualified by the Russians from Polish elections. Similar news of general Soviet foot-dragging and bad faith had been reaching Roosevelt and Churchill from all the various commissions the conference had set up.

When he heard Molotov had disqualified the London Poles, Roosevelt banged his fist on the arm of his wheelchair and barked, "We can't do business with Stalin. He has broken every one of the promises he made at Yalta." Angry and disillusioned, FDR retreated to Warm Springs, Georgia, and died on April 12. In the coming years he would be attacked for attending the conference in the first place, for his eagerness to placate Stalin, and for including in his entourage Alger Hiss, who later was exposed as a communist agent.

Whether Roosevelt was duped at Yalta and sold out eastern Europe to the Bolsheviks, as his right-wing American critics charged, the conference would certainly have turned out differently if the United States had listened more carefully to Churchill's advice. The atmosphere of trust might well have been replaced with the hard-nosed Old World haggling more typical of European peace conferences in the past, but even then there would have been little Churchill and Roosevelt could have done to stop Stalin other than threatening Russia, whose Red Army was just then engaged in soundly defeating the common enemy, with a new world war. Short of that, Roosevelt would certainly have been expected to give up some of the recently liberated states in his (and Churchill's) haggling with Stalin, which he could hardly have done without turning his back on the very principles for which he claimed to be fighting the war and alienating millions of U.S. voters.

On the other hand, Roosevelt was facing a costly campaign against Japan in East Asia, so purchasing Soviet help was both realistic and, in terms of American lives saved, humane. FDR could no more have predicted that the atomic bomb would render Soviet aid useless than he could have known that the young, aristocratic Hiss was in reality a sinister spy. After all, the scientists of the Manhattan Project had their doubts about "the gadget" right up to the moment it exploded in the desert around Alamogordo at 0529:45 on July

16, 1945. And even after Richard Nixon exposed him, Hiss was only convicted of perjury, never of espionage. Millions of people continued to consider him not only innocent but a martyr to right-wing fanaticism until some 50 years later, when the fall of the Soviet Union and the opening of its state archives lent more credence to the charges.

The Yalta Report itself was a noble statement and set important goals. If it was rightly criticized for failing to establish any specific plan for achieving these goals, the report at least presented a facade of unity among the Allies, which was important at that moment. While it is true that the report's ultimate vagueness, most evident in the broad provision for the four-power occupation of Germany, resolved fewer issues than it left unresolved, only when the document is read in the full context of subsequent events does it seem clear that the sharp ideological differences unofficially motivating the Western Allies and the Soviet Union were narrowly overcome by their common need to defeat Nazi Germany.

Source

Avalon Project at the Yale Law School. "The Yalta Conference." Available online. URL: http://www.yale.edu/lawweb/avalon/wwii/yalta.htm. Accessed May 16, 2005.

SOVIET DENUNCIATION OF THE PACT WITH JAPAN

TREATY AT A GLANCE

Completed
April 5, 1945, at Moscow

Signatories
Unilateral declaration by the Soviet Union

Overview
Having entered into a neutrality agreement with the Japanese in the spring of 1941 to avoid the threat of a two-front war with the Axis powers, Stalin honored the agreement until the defeat of Nazi Germany left him free to renounce the Japanese pact. Even then he did not comply fully with the Yalta Agreement and declare war on Japan, waiting till the dropping of the atomic bomb on Hiroshima made Allied victory imminent and he had to do so to ensure the Soviets a share in the Allied spoils in east Asia

Historical Background

Soviet premier Joseph Stalin had signed a neutrality pact with Japan in April of 1941 (see PACT OF NEUTRALITY BETWEEN UNION OF SOVIET SOCIALIST REPUBLICS AND JAPAN), when he was still at least nominally friendly with Nazi Germany. The AXIS PACT of 1940 had given Stalin pause because of the clear threat of a two-front war should Hitler choose to ignore Stalin's scrupulous, even obsequious adherence to German-Soviet agreements and invade the Soviet Union.

On Japan's part, the agreement allowed that nation to pursue a southern strategy of expanding its empire into the French, Dutch, and British colonies of east Asia without threat from the north. Choosing to pass on Hitler's invitation to jointly attack Russia, a plan enjoying the support of the Japanese foreign minister, Emperor Hirohito's military strategists sought to reap the benefit of the Nazi invasion without sharing in the fighting. Japan's rear was secure, and it could blithely move on to establish its East Asia Co-Prosperity Zone at the expense of China and the West.

Stalin, too, had good reason to honor the neutrality. He had his hands full with the Germans, and if his Western Allies seemed content to fight the Nazis to the last drop of Russian blood, he was equally content to leave the dying in the Pacific to them alone.

Once Germany fell, however, the situation changed. Although he had no intention, despite the YALTA AGREEMENT, of opening the kind of second front against Japan that he had demanded Britain and the United States open against Germany, he nevertheless wanted a say in the peace that would follow a Japanese defeat.

Terms

On April 5, 1945, the American ambassador in Moscow transmitted to the U.S. secretary of state, via telegram, the following statement from the press section of the foreign office, regarding the Soviet's timely denunciation of the USSR-Japanese neutrality pact.

Today at 3 P.M. People's Commissar for Foreign Affairs of the USSR Mr. V. M. Molotov, received the Japanese Ambassador, Mr. N. Sato, and made the following statement to him in the name of the Soviet Government:

The neutrality pact between the Soviet Union and Japan was concluded on April 13, 1941, that is, before the attack of Germany on the USSR and before the outbreak of war between Japan on the one hand and England and the United States on the other. Since that time the situation has been basically altered. Germany has attacked the USSR, and Japan, ally of Germany, is aiding the latter in its war against the USSR. Furthermore Japan is waging a war with the USA and England, which are allies of the Soviet Union.

In these circumstances the neutrality pact between Japan and the USSR has lost its sense, and the prolongation of that pact has become impossible.

On the strength of the above and in accordance with Article Three of the above mentioned pact, which envisaged the right of denunciation one year before the lapse of the five year period of operation of the pact, the Soviet Government hereby makes known to the Government of Japan its wish to denounce the pact of April 13, 1941.

The Japanese Ambassador Mr. N. Sato, promised to inform the Japanese Government of the statement of the Soviet Government.

Consequences

Stalin did not immediately declare war on Japan, since he did not want to pay the costs of a joint invasion of the main islands by the Allies, which according to all estimates would be quite bloody. Instead, he planned to wait until victory was all but certain, then declare and move in quickly to share in the spoils. The new American president, Harry S. Truman, understood Stalin's game, and this might have been one of the factors leading him to the fateful and controversial decision to order history's only nuclear attack (see JAPANESE SURRENDER DOCUMENTS). Two days after the United States dropped the first atomic bomb on Hiroshima, August 8, 1945, the USSR declared war on Japan and invaded Manchuria.

Source

J. A. S. Grenville, *The Major International Treaties, 1914–1973* (New York: Stein and Day, 1975), 230.

POTSDAM PROTOCOL

TREATY AT A GLANCE

Completed
August 2, 1945, at Potsdam, Germany

Signatories
Soviet Union, the United States, and Great Britain

Overview
Product of the Potsdam Conference (July 17–August 2, 1945), the Potsdam Protocol created the mechanism for concluding peace treaties with Italy and the minor Axis powers, finalized plans for the military occupation of Germany, agreed upon German disarmament, and called for the trial and punishment of leading Nazis as war criminals.

Historical Background

The Potsdam Conference was the final Allied summit of World War II. It followed the defeat of Germany and came on the eve of Japan's surrender.

Following the earlier Yalta Conference, Franklin Roosevelt was exhausted and sought recuperation at his Warm Springs, Georgia, spa. He died there on April 12 of a cerebral hemorrhage, and thus Harry S. Truman represented the United States at Potsdam. Britain's Winston Churchill, having led his nation through the darkest days of the war, participated at Potsdam. When Churchill was ousted in the July general elections, however, he was replaced by the new prime minister, Clement Attlee, before the conference ended. Of the original "Big Three," only Stalin signed the protocol.

Terms

Article 1 of the Protocol established a Council of Foreign Ministers to attend to the work of concluding treaties with Italy and the lesser Axis powers:

I. ESTABLISHMENT OF A COUNCIL OF FOREIGN MINISTERS

A. The Conference reached the following agreement for the establishment of a Council of Foreign Ministers to do the necessary preparatory work for the peace settlements:

1. There shall be established a Council composed of the Foreign Ministers of the United Kingdom, the Union of Soviet Socialist Republics, China, France, and the United States.

2. (i) The Council shall normally meet in London, which shall be the permanent seat of the joint Secretariat which the Council will form. . . .

3. (i) As its immediate important task, the Council shall be authorized to draw up, with a view to their submission to the United Nations, treaties of peace with Italy, Rumania, Bulgaria, Hungary and Finland, and to propose settlements of territorial questions outstanding on the termination of the war in Europe. The Council shall be utilized for the preparation of a peace settlement for Germany to be accepted by the Government of Germany when a Government adequate for the purpose is established.

(ii) For the discharge of each of these tasks the Council will be composed of the Members representing those States which were signatory to the terms of surrender imposed upon the enemy State concerned. For the purposes of the peace settlement for Italy, France shall be regarded as a signatory to the terms of surrender for Italy. Other Members will be invited to participate when matters directly concerning them are under discussion.

(iii) Other matters may from time to time be referred to the Council by agreement between the Member Governments.

4. (i) Whenever the Council is considering a question of direct interest to a State not represented thereon, such a State should be invited to send representatives to participate in the discussion and study of that question.

(ii) The Council may adapt its procedure to the particular problems under consideration. In some cases it may hold its own preliminary discussions prior to the participation of other interested States. In other cases, the Council may convoke a formal conference of the States chiefly interested in seeking a solution of the particular problem.

B. It was agreed that the three Governments should each address an identical invitation to the Governments of China and France to adopt this text and to join in establishing the Council. . . .

Article 2 established the principles that would govern the military occupation of Germany and set forth a policy popularly called "denazification," the removal of prominent Nazis from public office. Moreover, in conjunction with Article 6 (calling for war crimes trials), Article 2 called for the arrest and punishment of war criminals and leading Nazis (in effect, de facto war criminals):

II. THE PRINCIPLES TO GOVERN THE TREATMENT OF GERMANY IN THE INITIAL CONTROL PERIOD

A. *Political Principles*

1. In accordance with the Agreement on Control Machinery in Germany, supreme authority in Germany is exercised, on instructions from their respective Governments, by the Commanders-in-Chief of the armed forces of the United States of America, the United Kingdom, the Union of Soviet Socialist Republics, and the French Republic, each in his own zone of occupation, and also jointly, in matters affecting Germany as a whole, in their capacity as members of the Control Council.

2. So far as is practicable, there shall be uniformity of treatment of the German population throughout Germany.

3. The purposes of the occupation of Germany by which the Control Council shall be guided are:

(i) The complete disarmament and demilitarization of Germany and the elimination or control of all German industry that could be used for military production. . . .

(ii) To convince the German people that they have suffered a total military defeat and that they cannot escape responsibility for what they have brought upon themselves, since their own ruthless warfare and the fanatical Nazi resistance have destroyed German economy and made chaos and suffering inevitable.

(iii) To destroy the National Socialist Party and its affiliated and supervised organizations, to dissolve all Nazi institutions, to ensure that they are not revived in any form, and to prevent all Nazi and militarist activity or propaganda.

(iv) To prepare for the eventual reconstruction of German political life on a democratic basis and for eventual peaceful cooperation in international life by Germany.

4. All Nazi laws which provided the basis of the Hitler régime or established discrimination on grounds of race, creed, or political opinion shall be abolished. No such discrimination, whether legal, administrative or otherwise, shall be tolerated.

5. War criminals and those who have participated in planning or carrying out Nazi enterprises involving or resulting in atrocities or war crimes shall be arrested and brought to judgement. Nazi leaders, influential Nazi supporters and high officials of Nazi organizations and institutions and other persons dangerous to the occupation or its objectives shall be arrested and interned.

6. All members of the Nazi Party who have been more than nominal participants in its activities and all other persons hostile to Allied purposes shall be removed from public and semi-public office, and from positions of responsibility in important private undertakings. Such persons shall be replaced by persons who, by their political and moral qualities, are deemed capable of assisting in developing genuine democratic institutions in Germany.

7. German education shall be so controlled as completely to eliminate Nazi and militarist doctrines and to make possible the successful development of democratic ideas.

8. The judicial system will be reorganized in accordance with the principles of democracy, of justice under law, and of equal rights for all citizens without distinction of race, nationality or religion.

9. The administration of Germany should be directed towards the decentralization of the political structure and the development of local responsibility. To this end:

(i) local self-government shall be restored throughout Germany on democratic principles and in particular through elective councils as rapidly as is consistent with military security and the purposes of military occupation;

(ii) all democratic political parties with rights of assembly and of public discussion shall be allowed and encouraged throughout Germany;

(iii) representative and elective principles shall be introduced into regional, provincial and State (*Land*) administration as rapidly as may be justified by the successful application of these principles in local self-government;

(iv) for the time being, no central German Government shall be established. Notwithstanding this, however, certain essential central German administrative departments, headed by State Secretaries, shall be established, particularly in the fields of finance, transport, communications, foreign trade and industry. Such departments will act under the direction of the Control Council.

10. Subject to the necessity for maintaining military security, freedom of speech, press and religion shall be permitted, and religious institutions shall be respected, Subject likewise to the maintenance of military security, the formation of free trade unions shall be permitted.

A second part of Article 2 established the economic principles of the occupation. These included prohibiting arms production, developing agriculture and "peaceful domestic industries," speedily repairing the essential infrastructure, and (in contrast to the spirit prevailing at the time of the Treaty of Versailles [1919] ending World War I) establishing reparations that would "leave enough resources to enable the German people to subsist without external assistance":

B. *Economic Principles*

11. In order to eliminate Germany's war potential, the production of arms, ammunition and implements of war as well as all types of aircraft and sea-going ships shall be prohibited and prevented. Production of metals, chemicals, machinery and other items that are directly necessary to a war economy shall be rigidly controlled and restricted to Germany's approved postwar peacetime needs to meet the objectives stated in paragraph 15. Productive capacity not needed for permitted production shall be removed in accordance with the reparations plan recommended by the Allied Commission on Reparations and approved by the Governments concerned or if not removed shall be destroyed.

12. At the earliest practicable date, the German economy shall be decentralized for the purpose of eliminating the present excessive concentration of economic power as exemplified in particular by cartels, syndicates, trusts and other monopolistic arrangements.

13. In organizing the German economy, primary emphasis shall be given to the development of agriculture and peaceful domestic industries.

14. During the period of occupation Germany shall be treated as a single economic unit. To this end common policies shall be established in regard to:

(a) mining and industrial production and its allocation;

(b) agriculture, forestry and fishing;

(c) wages, prices and rationing;

(d) import and export programmes for Germany as a whole;

(e) currency and banking, central taxation and customs;

(f) reparation and removal of industrial war potential;

(g) transportation and communications.

In applying these policies account shall be taken, where appropriate, of varying local conditions.

15. Allied controls shall be imposed upon the German economy but only to the extent necessary. . . .

16. In the imposition and maintenance of economic controls established by the Control Council, German administrative machinery shall be created and the German authorities shall be required to the fullest extent practicable to proclaim and assume administration of such controls. . . .

17. Measures shall be promptly taken:

(a) to effect essential repair of transport;

(b) to enlarge coal production;

(c) to maximize agricultural output;

and

(d) to effect emergency repair of housing and essential utilities.

18. Appropriate steps shall be taken by the Control Council to exercise control and the power of disposition over German-owned external assets not already under the control of United Nations which have taken part in the war against Germany.

19. Payment of reparations should leave enough resources to enable the German people to subsist without external assistance. In working out the economic balance of Germany the necessary means must be provided to pay for imports approved by the Control Council in Germany. The proceeds of exports from current production and stocks shall be available in the first place for payments for such imports. . . .

Article 3 went on to define the parameters of German reparations:

III. REPARATIONS FROM GERMANY

1. Reparation claims for the U.S.S.R. shall be met by removals from the zone of Germany occupied by the U.S.S.R., and from appropriate German external assets.

2. The U.S.S.R. undertakes to settle the reparation claims of Poland from its own share of reparations.

3. The reparation claims of the United States, the United Kingdom and other countries entitled to reparations shall be met from the Western zones and from appropriate German external assets.

4. In addition to the reparations to be taken by the U.S.S.R. from its own zone of occupation, the U.S.S.R. shall receive additionally from the Western zones:

(a) Fifteen per cent of such usable and complete industrial capital equipment, in the first place from the metallurgical, chemical and machine manufacturing industries as is unnecessary for the German peace economy and should be removed from the Western zones of Germany, in exchange for an equivalent value of food, coal, potash, zinc, timber, clay products, petroleum products, and such other commodities as may be agreed upon.

(b) Ten per cent of such industrial capital equipment as is unnecessary for the German peace economy and should be removed from the Western zones, to be transferred to the Soviet Government on reparations account without payment or exchange of any kind in return.

Removals of equipment as provided in (a) and (b) above shall be made simultaneously. . . .

8. The Soviet Government renounces all claims in respect of reparations to shares of German enterprises which are located in the Western zones of Germany as well as to German foreign assets in all countries except those specified in paragraph 9 below.

9. The Governments of the U.K. and U.S.A. renounce all claims in respect of reparations to shares of German enterprises which are located in the Eastern zone of occupation in Germany, as well as to German foreign assets in Bulgaria, Finland, Hungary, Rumania and Eastern Austria. . . .

Article 4 divided the vessels of the German navy and merchant marine between the three signatory powers. Article 5 addressed details of the proposed western frontier of the Soviet Union. Article 6 called for war crimes trials to begin at the earliest possible date. Articles 7 and 8 addressed the disposition of Austria and Poland:

VII. AUSTRIA

The Conference examined a proposal by the Soviet Government on the extension of the authority of the Austrian Provisional Government to all of Austria.

The three Governments agreed that they were prepared to examine this question after the entry of the British and American forces into the city of Vienna.

It was agreed that reparations should not be exacted from Austria.

VIII. POLAND

A. *Declaration*

We have taken note with pleasure of the agreement reached among representative Poles from Poland and abroad which has made possible the formation, in accordance with the decisions reached at the Crimea Conference, of a Polish Provisional Government of National Unity recognized by the Three Powers. The establishment by the British and the United States Governments of diplomatic relations with the Polish Provincial Government of National Unity has resulted in the withdrawal of their recognition from the former Polish Government in London, which no longer exists.

The British and United States Governments have taken measures to protect the interest of the Polish Provisional Government of National Unity as the recognized Government of the Polish State in the property belonging to the Polish State located in their territories and under their control, whatever the form of this property may be. They have further taken measures to prevent alienation to third parties of such property. All proper facilities will be given to the Polish Provisional Government of National Unity for the exercise of the ordinary legal remedies for the recovery of any property belonging to the Polish State which may have been wrongfully alienated.

The Three Powers are anxious to assist the Polish Provisional Government of National Unity in facilitating the return of Poland as soon as practicable of all Poles abroad who wish to go, including members of the Polish armed forces and the Merchant Marine. They expect that those Poles who return home shall be accorded personal and property rights on the same basis as all Polish citizens.

The Three Powers note that the Polish Provisional Government of National Unity, in accordance with the decisions of the Crimea Conference, has agreed to the holding of free and unfettered elections as soon as possible on the basis of universal suffrage and secret ballot in which all democratic and anti-Nazi parties shall have the right to take part and to put forward candidates, and that representatives of the Allied press shall enjoy full freedom to report to the world upon developments in Poland before and during the elections.

B. *Western Frontier of Poland*

In conformity with the agreement on Poland reached at the Crimea Conference the three Heads of Government have sought the opinion of the Polish Provisional Government of National Unity in regard to the accession of territory in the north and west which Poland should receive. The President of the National Council of Poland and members of the Polish Provisional Government of National Unity have been received at the Conference and have fully presented their views. The three Heads of Government reaffirm their opinion that the final delimitation of the western frontier of Poland should await the peace settlement.

The three Heads of Government agree that, pending the final determination of Poland's western frontier, the former German territories east of a line running from the Baltic Sea immediately west of Swinamunde, and thence along the Oder river to the confluence of the western Neisse river and along the western Neisse to the Czechoslovak frontier, including that portion of East Prussia not placed under the administration of the Union of Soviet Socialist Republics in accordance with the understanding reached at this Conference and including the area of the former Free City of Danzig, shall be under the administration of the Polish State and for such purposes should not be considered as part of the Soviet zone of occupation in Germany.

Article 9 called for the conclusion of treaties with Italy and minor Axis powers, as provided for in the REPORT OF THE YALTA (CRIMEA) CONFERENCE. It also proposed opening the "United Nations Organization" to "all . . . peace-loving States who accept the obligations contained in the present Charter." They opposed the membership of Spain, however, on the grounds that its present government had "been founded with the support of the Axis powers":

> In view of its origins, its nature, its record and its close association with the aggressor States, [it does not] possess the qualifications necessary to justify . . . membership.

The balance of the protocol dealt with questions of territorial trusteeship; revision of Allied Control Commission procedures in Romania, Bulgaria, and Hungary; the disposition of oil equipment in Romania; the withdrawal of Allied troops from Iran; a pledge to create an International Zone in Tangier; and a resolution to revise an agreement on the Black Sea Straits. The most important matter concerned the "orderly transfer of German populations":

The three Governments, having considered the question in all its aspects, recognize that the transfer to Germany of German populations, or elements thereof, remaining in Poland, Czechoslovakia and Hungary, will have to be undertaken. They agree that any transfers that take place should be effected in an orderly and humane manner.

Consequences

The protocol hardly began to suggest the scope of the enormous refugee and "displaced person" crisis created by World War II. As a whole, it barely hinted at the profound ideological differences motivating the Western and Eastern Allies at the end of the war. Still, with the USSR and the Western nations disagreeing on several major issues (the amount of German reparations, the ultimate boundaries and political unification of Germany, the future governments of eastern Europe, and Soviet demands in the Mediterranean region), the conference clearly foreshadowed the coming cold war.

Source

Avalon Project at the Yale Law School, "Potsdam Conference." Available online. URL: http://www.yale.edu/lawweb/avalon/decade/decade17.htm. Accessed May 16, 2005.

Part Thirteen

COLD WAR, PEACEFUL COEXISTENCE

INTRODUCTION

It had happened before, at the end of World War I, and it was happening again at the end of World War II: the next conflict began smoldering in the ashes of a world ruined by the near-total devastation of modern war. Among the powers occupying the ruins of Nazi Germany and Nazi-dominated eastern Europe, as suspicions of each other's postwar intentions flared, that conflict sometimes threatened to burst into flame. At the end of the World War I, a grand round of treaty making, dictated by the victors, which was intended to dampen the enmities created by the war by finding a "just" resolution to its causes and conduct, had only fanned the hatreds to burn brighter.

In contrast, after World War II, the victors simply moved into the burned-over area with their armed forces, set up camp, and began bickering with each other. At first their animosity was held in check by the sheer scale of the devastation from what had been the greatest conflict in the history of the planet. Europe looked as people imagined the surface of the Moon would look. All the great cities of central and eastern Europe, much of London, and western Russia were pitted remnants standing jagged against the horizon. Transportation networks had been ripped to shreds, farmland turned into scorched earth, industrial production brought to a complete standstill. Japan was just as blighted, its cities flattened by firebombing and two nuclear blasts, its industry and shipping vaporized. China, under occupation for 14 years, was facing a decade of civil war almost as destructive as the war itself.

In Europe 45 million people were homeless, half of them in places such as Poland, the Ukraine, and western Russia, which had been burned to the ground three times during the fighting. Indeed, the war loosed on the earth a vast army of refugees. Twenty-seven million had fled the Nazis or were forced out by them, and nearly 5 million more had been seized and made into slaves. Huge numbers, too, fled the coming of the Russians, many of them ethnic Germans or collaborators who feared, accurately, an especially brutal reprisal. All told, experts estimated, 60 million people from 27 countries and 55 ethnic groups were uprooted by the war. There were the prisoners of war: 7 million taken by the Allies during the war, and 8 million more liberated from Axis camps. Finally, there were the 670,000 survivors of the death camps, who left behind some 6 million Jews and 3 million Slavs, Gypsies (Rom), and other "social undesirables" whom the Nazis had exterminated.

Nobody wished to risk a renewed conflict that could wreak this kind of damage, but everybody feared that this kind of damage could be wreaked on them if they were not careful. There in the battle-spawned ruins of central and eastern Europe, the liberal democracies and Communist Russia, erstwhile Allies, became suspicious of each other, worried about the next step, eager to get a jump on the other. In one sense, what was happening was nothing new. In the past, long before either World War I or World War II, grand wartime coalitions had invariably broken up once the common fight gave way to diplomatic sparing over the division of the spoils. Indeed, the Versailles peace negotiations could be, and were, viewed as one huge debate about reparations and revenge, couched in the grandiose language of a hollow idealism. This time, however, the postwar diplomats became the midwives of something new. The result of their work would hardly be recognizable as a peace, but it would not quite appear to be a war, either.

This new condition gestated in diplomatic disputes over such matters as what to do with the utterly defeated Germany, who would exercise hegemony over eastern Europe, and how the world would handle the spectacular scientific revolution in weapons of mass destruction, showcased in the leveling of two Japanese cities. Some, maybe even most, of these disputes might have been avoided. The feuding victors after the wars of Louis XIV and Napoleon or World War I at least managed to negotiate treaties, and the rancor between them had been leavened by passage of time or the worry that the enemy they had so recently vanquished might yet rise again. That did not happen after 1945. No one called a grand peace conference. No one worried about a Germany or a Japan or, for that matter, an Italy rising anew to pose a threat. These defeated nations were bombed out, blasted almost to oblivion, and none of the old Axis powers held the ultimate postwar ace in the hole, the atomic bomb.

So, distrust and miscommunication and the incompatible goals of the Allies became not the mere squabbling between victors familiar from the past but swelled into unreconcilable diplomatic quarrels between countries, which developed year by year into ever more rigid political positions, which became so hidebound that they caused the world to split into two ideological and armed camps. This smoldering conflict that no one could put out but no one wanted to stir up into a third worldwide conflagration would be dubbed—by U.S. presidential adviser Bernard Baruch and press pundit Walter Lippmann—the cold war.

The Nature of the Conflict

The fact that every major industrial region of the world but North America had been laid waste by the war in many ways determined the nature of the conflict. On a stunned globe, the United States now accounted for nearly half the gross annual product. It enjoyed a technological lead lately symbolized by, but hardly limited to, its nuclear franchise. And yet, America mostly just wanted to go home after the war and get back to business.

Matters were otherwise in the Soviet Union, where Stalin—who had done no small amount of mass murder himself and who feared nothing so much as a personal loss of power—took heart in the fact that though his country too might be in ruins, his armies occupied much of Europe, and puppet Communist parties were agitating for control of the rest. When the war ended on the Continent, Stalin had been justified in feeling safe at last; it appeared as if the Allies were going to allow him to build a buffer zone around the new Soviet empire, which would keep both his borders and his people safe from Western encroachments. Then Harry S. Truman dropped the bomb on Hiroshima, and Stalin felt the need—as Winston Churchill would say in a Missouri speech—to drop an iron curtain in Europe.

Posing asymmetrical threats (meaning threats unsuited to the other's potential response) to each other, the United States and the Soviet Union began a postwar struggle in 1945 over treatment of occupied Germany and the composition of the Polish government. It spread in 1946 as Russia communized the lands under its occupation, and the former allies failed to finalize a plan for the control of atomic energy. From 1947 to 1950 Washington and Moscow reacted to threats, real or simply perceived, from each other, and the temporary division of Europe calcified into two blocs, followed by the same process in much of the rest of the world as this conflict became universalized, institutionalized, and militarized. The reason there was no TREATY OF VERSAILLES after World War II to set up a peace from which could grow the next conflict was that the next conflict was already under way. There was merely the end of combat proper and a series of treaties—some establishing defense alliances, like the TREATY OF BRUSSELS; some creating commercial unions, like the TREATY OF ROME; some that launched new states, like the AUSTRIAN STATE TREATY and the SOVIET DECLARATION ON THE SOVEREIGNTY OF THE GERMAN DEMOCRATIC REPUBLIC—that over time reconstructed the postwar world.

At the same time, the cold war magnified and distorted historical trends established or fed by the two world wars in the first half of the 20th century: Asian nationalism and the breakup of the old colonial empires; the continuation of the three-decades-long Chinese Revolution and its denouement in a Communist takeover; the movement in Western Europe toward diplomatic and economic integration; and the bursting forth of two superpowers on to the world's diplomatic stage. These trends led to a new round of alliances—the ANGLO-TRANSJORDAN ALLIANCE, the NORTH ATLANTIC TREATY Organization, the SINO-SOVIET TREATY OF FRIENDSHIP, ALLIANCE, AND MUTUAL ASSISTANCE, the BAGHDAD PACT, the WARSAW PACT—that reflected in one way or another the ideological rending of the world in twain. The irony was that for all this turmoil and the extreme danger of world annihilation a mere push of a button away, the cold war also gave birth to the closest thing to a world order since Otto von Bismarck's alliance system had immolated itself in 1914.

The Truman Doctrine

Hoping to avoid the mistakes of Versailles, America's first impulse toward postwar Europe was a generous one. George C. Marshall, secretary of state under President Truman and former army chief of staff during World War II, announced in his June 5, 1947, commencement address at Harvard University a bold plan of economic assistance to rebuild war-ravaged Europe. A brilliant military leader whose energies had so recently been focused on destroying the might of Germany and Japan, Marshall developed a sweeping plan for rebuilding what war had devastated. To a France, England, and central Europe economically crippled by the war, Marshall, fearing they might thus fall prey to the siren call of communism, promulgated a policy of economic aid on an unprecedented scale to restore "normal economic health in the world, without which there can be no political stability and no assured peace."

Great Britain and France spearheaded the formation of the Committee for European Economic Cooperation, made up of delegates from 16 nations, and the committee officially requested $22.4 billion from the United States. Congress appropriated more than $13 billion in funds to be disbursed through the Marshall Plan, and it also authorized a Displaced Persons Plan, through which nearly three hundred thousand Europeans, including many survivors of the Holocaust, became American citizens. As a direct result of the Marshall Plan, Western Europe was able to get back on its feet and over the coming years form new alliances under such agreements as the Treaty of Paris, the Treaty of Rome, and the EUROPEAN FREE TRADE ASSOCIATION CONVENTION , all of which (in part) were made feasible by the formation of a West German republic out of the western sector of divided Germany. Beginning in 1947, with the economic merger of the U.S. and British occupation zones into "Bizonia," through its official birth as the Federal Republic of Germany on May 23, 1949, and into the 1950s as the new European trading bloc was forming, West Germany experienced remarkable and rapid economic growth under the Marshall Plan. Well before that, however—in fact, from the very start, despite Marshall's pronouncement at Harvard that the policy of aid was not aimed "against any country or doctrine but against hunger, poverty, desperation, and chaos"—the Marshall Plan occasioned the drawing of the battlelines along which the long, tense, and debilitating cold war would be fought, dominating world politics for some four decades.

The reality of the communist threat was underscored in September 1947, when the Soviet Union tested its first atomic bomb, a weapon the United States had been smug enough to think it alone in the world had the capacity to develop and detonate. The communist provocations in eastern Europe and the Balkans continued, as Greece became embroiled in a civil war sparked by communists, and Turkey came under Russian pressure to provide bases and naval passage through the Dardanelles.

Suddenly, Truman announced a new get-tough doctrine to accompany the rehabbing of Europe under the Marshall Plan. Not truly understanding Stalin and his aggression (few did), Truman was basing his new policy on a "long memorandum" he had received from Moscow in 1946, written by young diplomat George Kennan. In 1947, writing under the pseudonym of "Mr. X," Kennan developed the ideas contained in his memo and published a highly influential article in the journal *Foreign Affairs*, presenting the idea of "containment" of Soviet communism "by the adroit and vigilant application of counter-force at a series of constantly shifting geographic points."

Following Kennan's lead, Truman called for combatting communism by containing its spread, using for this containment all means necessary, including military force. In effect, the Truman Doctrine meant that the United States was put on a footing of perpetual preparedness, and such a degree of preparedness required permanent and continual sources of information about foreign governments, hostile and potentially hostile, as well as the capability for "covert action," foreign policy initiatives to be kept hidden from the American public. In the chill climate of the cold war, the Central Intelligence Agency (CIA)—an outgrowth of America's World War II espionage organization, the Office of Strategic Services (OSS)—came into being. It expanded rapidly in size and power, to the point of becoming a kind of shadow government (similar if not quite on the scale or power of the Russian's own security apparatus, the KGB) and exploiting statutes granting the agency great leeway and ensuring the secrecy of its operations. In addition to the CIA, Truman's new "national security" measures included the establishment of a permanent Chiefs of Staff, making the air force independent of the army and beefing up its Strategic Air Command, under whose bailiwick would fall the responsibility for deployment of nuclear weapons, and the negotiating of a string of regional alliances on the borders of the Communist bloc that would serve as firewalls to Soviet mischief.

There was mischief enough to follow. In February 1948 communist partisans, backed by Stalin and the Red Army, overran Czechoslovakia, which led Britain, France, and the Benelux countries to speed up their mutual defense agreement, the Treaty of Brussels. In response, the Soviets, who occupied the eastern sector of Germany, withdrew from the Allied Control Council overseeing the occupation and blockaded the city of Berlin (squarely in the eastern sector but divided into western and eastern zones) in June 1948. During the blockade, the United States airlifted supplies for nearly a year to residents of West Berlin, and the Truman administration got busy implementing the containment policy. The North Atlantic Treaty Organization (NATO), formed in 1949, joined the United States to Canada and 10 Western European nations in a military alliance. An attack on any one member nation was deemed an attack on all of them. NATO became the model for the military alliances the United States organized with Mediterranean nations in the Central Treaty Organization (CENTO), and with the nations of Southeast Asia in SEATO under the SOUTH-EAST ASIA COLLECTIVE DEFENSE TREATY. By the 1950s the United States had a string of allies around the world that all but enclosed the Soviet Union and its satellite nations.

Of course, the Soviet Union countered. After Stalin's death in 1953, the Soviets at last recognized the German Democratic Republic as a sovereign state, officially ending its World War II occupation of East Germany while offering an entity to counterbalance a West Germany, which—truly sovereign since 1949—was being touted as the "economic miracle" of the Marshall Plan. When a now-rearmed West Germany joined NATO in 1955, Nikita Khrushchev, the Soviet Union's new leader, responded with the Warsaw Pact, an alliance of his East European satellites, including this newly "sovereign" East Germany. Alliances with India and other neutral nations followed.

However, when Soviet satellite states threatened to break away, as did Hungary and Poland in 1956, Khrushchev did not shy away from using tanks to keep them in line. In 1961 he built a wall—symbolic to all the world of the harshness and hopelessness of communist oppression—separating the Soviet sector of Berlin from the rest of the city. And when Fidel Castro gained power in Cuba, the Soviet Union placed its nuclear missiles a scant 90 miles away from America's shores. The Cuban Missile Crisis of October 1962, perhaps more than any other event in the cold war, made the American public realize that the world, divided into two camps, both armed to the teeth with weapons of unimaginable destruction, stayed ready through the postwar years to touch off a war not to "end all wars" but to end the world itself.

Indeed, by then the conflict had escalated almost beyond imagination. As far back as October 1949, the United States had commenced a program to step up production of uranium and plutonium, a necessary first step in the creation of the H-bomb. On November 1, 1952, the first hydrogen bomb, code-named Mike, was detonated at Eniwetok Atoll in the Pacific. The test was so secret that it wasn't reported to the public until February 2, 1954, when President Dwight David Eisenhower made a statement. On March 24 of that year, a hydrogen bomb test in the Marshall Islands exceeded all estimates of its power.

The U.S. monopoly on the hydrogen bomb was, however, even briefer than the one it had enjoyed on the atomic bomb. The Soviets tested an H-bomb on November 23, 1955. As the nuclear arms race turned into a thermonuclear arms race, it reached critical mass and became self-sustaining. With the U.S. and USSR matching one another "device" for "device," soon it was the delivery systems for these bombs—intercontinental missiles developed by former German scientists hijacked by both ideological camps—that took center stage.

The Third World

Not only had the cold war escalated, it had spread to every corner of the globe, directly connecting events in faraway Africa, Asia, and Latin America to events in Europe in ways that the Continent's old imperial nations of the 18th and 19th and even early 20th centuries would never have imagined.

Late in 1949, after forcing the Chinese Nationalist army under Chiang Kai-shek to flee to the small island of Taiwan, Mao Zedong and his fellow Communists declared China's vast mainland to be the People's Republic of China, an event viewed in the capitalist West as a major "defeat" in the rapidly developing cold war. When the United States rejected Mao's overtures to establish diplomatic relations, he allied his country with the Soviet Union under the Sino-Soviet Treaty of Friendship, Alliance, and Mutual Assistance, but it was an uneasy alliance. Mao, every bit the strongman in China that Stalin was in Russia, found it no easier to share the limelight with "Uncle Joe" than he had formerly with Generalissimo Chiang.

But the West, particularly the United States, was too busy blaming, then purging, the China experts in its State Department for the "loss" of the mainland to notice. First they signed the UNITED STATES–NATIONALIST CHINESE MUTUAL DEFENSE TREATY with a Chiang who was too corrupt and discredited to contribute anything to the "mutual" defense, as those purged old China hands knew all too well. As far as U.S. policy makers were concerned, China and Russia had formed a united front implacably opposed to what the United States and its European allies were now calling the free world, a view that led U.S. politicians to overestimate the cohesion of the so-called Communist bloc for some three decades and stubbornly to deny recognition of a government that for the first time since the fall of the ancient Qing dynasty at the beginning of the 20th century had truly united the massive Chinese population.

This misunderstanding greatly inflated the importance of the first of a series of brush wars—the communists called them "wars of national liberation"—in what would become known as the third world. On June 27, 1950, after Communist-backed forces crossed the 38th parallel dividing North from South Korea, President Truman, concluding—incorrectly—that the Soviet Union had directed the assault, committed

American military supplies to South Korea and moved the U.S. Seventh Fleet into the Formosa Strait, a show of force meant to intimidate a China Truman assumed to be a Soviet puppet. Truman acted with neither a declaration of war nor the advice and consent of the Senate. Instead, the United States called for United Nations sanctions against the North, an action that committed America to a war the U.S. government euphemistically dubbed a police action.

Before it was over, the war became immensely unpopular with the American public. The casualty list in and of itself had a great impact on the United States, still wearied from World War II, then only five years in the past. The Korean conflict also had a major effect on the U.S. armed forces, bringing a popular president, Truman, into direct conflict with a popular war hero, Douglas MacArthur, whom the president relieved of command after MacArthur proposed bombing bridges over the Yalu River, which would have meant attacking Red China directly. In addition, the war cost the Democratic Party the White House, and Eisenhower was elected in 1952 promising that he personally would go to Korea specifically to end the fighting, which he did, signing the KOREAN WAR ARMISTICE in 1953.

The Korean War heightened the anticommunist hysteria of the McCarthy era and reshaped international politics by prompting the United States to demand greater contributions from its European allies to NATO and to form SEATO. In the face of such U.S. demands, two European cabinets—in France and in Britain—fell from power, West Germany was let into NATO, and the Soviets responded by creating the Warsaw Pact. Finally, Korea occasioned the first U.S. military buildup in South Vietnam, another step in the American cold war policy of containing communism.

Even parts of the globe not obviously subject to direct communist influence were affected by the cold war. After World War II, the British, faced with continual conflict between Arabs and Jews in Palestine, which they had occupied since 1917, withdrew from the country and turned it, and the Jewish-Arab conflict, over to the United Nations, which responded by partitioning Palestine into Jewish and Arab sectors. Over Arab protests, the Jews established the state of Israel in 1948.

Not a decade later, on July 26, 1956, the new Egyptian president, Gamal Abdel Nasser, nationalized the Suez Canal, which touched off a crisis that changed Middle Eastern diplomacy forever. Great Britain and France, their influence already waning, could no longer serve as U.S. surrogates in the region, which put pressure on American diplomats to "solve" the Mideast's nigh unsolvable problems. Israel had—under a secret arrangement with Britain and France—

invaded Egypt to take back the canal and depose, if possible, Nasser. Israel was established as a power to be reckoned with in the region, even if it did meekly withdraw its troops at the demand of a very angry Dwight David Eisenhower. The Arab states, in response to what they considered British and French treachery, followed Nasser's lead in turning to the Soviets for aid and support. His success in nationalizing the Suez Canal and standing up to the old European colonial powers England and France made him a leader of the third world, which—like the Arab States—grew warmer toward the Soviet bloc.

Sometimes anticommunism served to mask economic colonialism in the third world, just as wars of national liberation sometimes masked Soviet influence peddling. Such was the case, for example, in Iran during 1953. Responding to a liberalized Iranian parliament's announcement that it intended to nationalize the country's vast oil deposits, the intelligence agencies of the British and American governments began plotting the ouster of Iran's highest elected official, Dr. Mohammad Mossadegh, via covert action, using the excuse that he was backed by communist elements. Operation Ajax restored the monarchy of Reza Shah Pahlavi, who was exceedingly "friendly" to the free world powers. It also set a precedent for a series of such cloak-and-dagger meddlings in the affairs of other countries, which undermined indigenous democratic movements, often influenced by marxist economic programs, in favor of repressive oligarchies—including many in Latin America, such as Guatemala, Chile, Argentina, Nicaragua, and El Salvador, to name a few. These covert actions, which came to characterize the CIA created by Allen Dulles, undermined the credibility of American foreign policy abroad and hurt its standing with such third world groups as the Organization of American States (see CHARTER OF THE ORGANIZATION OF AMERICAN STATES), in which it had played a founding role.

On the other hand, in Africa, marxist governments with Soviet-friendly policies often accompanied postwar decolonization. In 1960 British prime minister Harold Macmillan, who had come to office in the wake of a crisis that had resulted in Britain's granting Ghana its independence in 1957, spoke to the parliament of the white-ruled South Africa about the new realities in Africa, announcing that a "wind of change" was sweeping the continent. Macmillan's phrase was no mere political hyperbole, since by 1960, 17 new nations had emerged from the old African colonial states, and from 1960 to 1965 another 11 were to follow. This all led to the formation of the Organization of African Unity (see CHARTER OF THE ORGANIZATION OF AFRICAN UNITY) and in effect left only the white-settler nations in the south as the last outposts of Africa's

European-dominated past. None of these marxist-inspired liberations yet ignited brush wars in Africa on the scale of Korea or Vietnam, or important ideological standoffs such as those in Berlin or against Cuba, in part because major portions of the emerging third world remained vaguely defined in the East vs. West political geography of the cold war.

Counterinsurgency

In the late 1950s and the 1960s, there were indications that eastern Europe was itself not especially overjoyed to be a part of the Communist bloc. On October 24, 1956, Hungary's prime minister, Imre Nagy, defied the USSR by announcing an end to one-party rule, thereby igniting Hungary's movement to remove itself from the Soviet sphere of influence established in eastern Europe at the end of World War II, a movement the West came to call the Hungarian Revolution. Regardless of the United States's continued commitment to the Truman Doctrine, Eisenhower declined to intervene in the anti-Soviet revolution and, much to the shock of the Hungarians, announced that the United States would offer no aid to the new government. Accordingly, the Soviets attacked on November 4, and despite impassioned radio pleas to America, no help was forthcoming. Within weeks, the revolution was liquidated, and Hungary, barely recovered from the devastation of the world war, was in shambles. The Soviets had killed some tens of thousands and had imprisoned more. Almost a quarter-million Hungarians fled the country.

Eisenhower, a frugal and careful commander, had as an economy measure cut back spending on the U.S. armed forces and increased America's reliance on its airborne nuclear threat to deter communist aggression. Insisting on his right to reply with "massive retaliatory power" at places of his own choosing, he was apparently unwilling to risk thermonuclear war for a country already considered part of the Soviet sphere.

If the arrival of the missile age and its promise of instant destruction had made Eisenhower more cautious in his execution the cold war, it led his successor, John F. Kennedy, to be more vigorous in his responses to perceived communist aggression around the globe, and especially in the third world. Kennedy called his technique counterinsurgency. Overtly, Kennedy launched the Peace Corps, the Latin American ALLIANCE FOR PROGRESS, and National Aeronautics and Space Administration's (NASA) race to the Moon, to name a few new programs aimed at "paying any price" to compete successfully with the communists anywhere in the world and out of it. Covertly, Kennedy unleashed the CIA on such "trouble spots" as Cuba and

Southeast Asia, resulting in the Bay of Pigs fiasco and in the assassination of South Vietnamese president Diem. These in turn led, respectively, to the Cuban Missile Crisis and, after Kennedy's own assassination, to the war in Vietnam.

Cuba had of course been one of those third world countries that Eisenhower "lost" to the Soviets when Fidel Castro came to power in 1959, after overthrowing a typically corrupt U.S. "strongman" client named Fulgenico Batista. On October 22, 1962, Kennedy appeared on national television to make a startling announcement: the Soviet Union was building bomber and nuclear missile bases in Cuba, and he intended to stop them. When Khrushchev refused to back down, the world rushed right to the brink of nuclear war. Back-channel negotiations between Kennedy and Khrushchev ultimately resolved the crisis, but not before contradictions between official diplomatic responses and the secret talks threatened to make the situation spin out of control.

So close had the world come to Armaggedon that both Kennedy and Khrushchev immediately agreed to disarmament talks, during which they agreed on the special HOT LINE MEMORANDUM to establish a direct communications link between the White House and the Kremlin and avoid any misunderstandings in the future that might accidentally spark a nuclear conflagration. The very existence of the Hot Line underscored the failure of the cold war policy of diplomatic brinkmanship, and the very same meeting of the Disarmament Committee that created the Hot Line also produced the limited NUCLEAR TEST BAN TREATY. Clearly, some kind of major disarmament agreement was in the cards as John Kennedy, sobered by the experience, looked toward a second term as president.

Kennedy's assassination brought to the White House a Lyndon Johnson as determined to hold the line against communist influence in Vietnam as Kennedy himself had been in Cuba. Although Johnson would follow up on Kennedy's initiatives to sign the TREATY ON THE NON-PROLIFERATION OF NUCLEAR WEAPONS, his Vietnam policies would serve to heat up and prolong the cold war. On August 7, 1964, in response to an apparent attack on a U.S. destroyer conducting espionage activities in the Gulf of Tonkin, off the coast of North Vietnam, the U.S. Senate passed the Gulf of Tonkin Resolution, giving President Johnson a free hand to prevent further "aggression" by North Vietnam and providing broad congressional support for expanding the war in Southeast Asia. Even as the resolution was being passed, Johnson assured the American public that its sons would not die fighting an Asian war.

Scarcely was the 1964 presidential election over, though, when Johnson—faced with withdrawing from, or escalating, the conflict—chose to commit 22,000 fresh troops. By 1965, 75,000 Americans were fighting in Vietnam; by 1966, 375,000; by the next election, over half a million. Earlier in the conflict, both Kennedy and then Johnson had referred to the troops as military advisers. By 1966 there was no way to denominate them as anything other than combat troops. As draft calls increased by 100 percent in 1965, young men flooded into American colleges to avoid conscription and service in that "little green country." Starting in February of that year, the United States bombed the North, then stopped to watch Communist leader Ho Chi Minh's response, which was invariably to send yet more leaders, more weapons, and more troops to help the insurgent Vietcong. Over the next eight years, the American army in Vietnam would grow to a peak of 542,000, and the economic cost of the war would bleed Johnson's cherished domestic reforms—his Great Society—dry.

By then, too, opposition to the war was mounting in America, as some of its business leaders began to question the astronomical costs of the war, and many of its draft-age students its morality. An obsessed Johnson and military leaders, acting almost as if they were independent of the publicly stated American policy, no longer bothered to consult citizens or senators while they turned Vietnam into the fourth-bloodiest conflict in American history. Johnson's own secretary of defense, Robert McNamara, admitted in 1967 that the bombing had not stopped North Vietnam's infiltration. Then, in 1968, as if to prove McNamara's point, came the stunning massive and coordinated attack of the Vietcong in the January Tet Offensive. Whether the Vietcong "won" the Tet Offensive or not, it was certainly successful in putting the lie to Lyndon Johnson's public claims about the war. As 350,000 refugees abandoned their hamlets en masse and poured into the recently besieged towns, the United States began to strong-arm its puppet regime in South Vietnam toward the peace table. On May 10, 1968, talks with the North opened in Paris, which would years later lead to the PARIS PEACE ACCORDS.

Détente

The talks came too late, however, for the Johnson presidency. Widely criticized in the media, the focus of ever-growing campus protests, and challenged by prominent members of his own party, such as Eugene McCarthy and Robert Kennedy, Johnson declined to run for reelection. Robert Kennedy's assassination on June 6, 1968, following his sound victory in the California presidential primary, destroyed the potential for the election to become a public referendum on Vietnam. The murder turned a disorienting, violent, and chaotic year into a brutally incomprehensible one, vir-

tually ensuring that the United States would be politically incapable of avoiding profound, dangerous divisions in the body politic more serious than any since the Civil War. A politically revived Richard Nixon made plans to continue the grim policy, legalized by the Gulf of Tonkin Resolution, of bombing a small country into oblivion to satisfy the ideological needs of the cold war once he finally managed to take the Oval Office. After much domestic turmoil and a brutal escalation of the bombing over the next three years, Nixon, himself faced with reelection, engineered a peace that abandoned the corrupt leadership of South Vietnam and brought American involvement in the war to an inglorious close.

But Nixon, heading for a second term, had a broader agenda on his mind than the quagmire that, in retrospect, became a symbol of the lunatic quality of cold war foreign policy. As Vietnam had made evident, the Kennedy-Johnson counterinsurgency fervor of the 1960s, far from establishing U.S. hegemony, had instead wrought a diffusion of world power and an erosion of the rigid separation of the globe into superpower blocs. Western Europe and Japan, now recovered from World War II's devastation, had experienced dynamic growth that was leading to a certain independence in foreign as well as domestic policy. The Sino-Soviet split had become ever more evident behind the smoke screen of Vietnam. The third world was also showing itself more resistant to superpower coercion as the United States squandered its capital, its good name, and its domestic tranquility in Southeast Asia. The Russians, having achieved something close to parity with the United States in their nuclear arsenal, were increasingly obsessed with a potentially hostile China; the United States, exhausted and divided, wanted to scale back its global commitments. In these circumstances, Nixon became the first U.S president to visit both Beijing and Moscow, laying the groundwork for official recognition by the United States for Communist China and détente with the Soviet Union.

Détente, French for "release of tension," entered America's diplomatic vocabulary beginning in 1971 and was heard frequently in the spring of 1972. With some justification, cynics said Nixon's trip to Moscow on May 22, 1972, like his earlier trip to China, was an election-year political tactic to deflect criticism of his conservative domestic policies and his continued prosecution of the war in Vietnam. More kindly put, Nixon had realized that the war itself was an impediment to these broader international possibilities and used the ending of the conflict as a wedge into the triangulation of foreign affairs he was seeking to establish. Whatever his motivation, the results—especially of his meetings with Soviet premier Leonid Brezhnev, whose cold warrior credentials, like Nixon's, were well-established—

proved historic and profound. Seven agreements were signed, including the AGREEMENT ON THE PREVENTION OF NUCLEAR WAR, covering unprecedented cooperation in scientific research, particularly in space exploration, and expanded trade. When Brezhnev returned Nixon's visit in June 1973, coming to the United States for a second summit, the two signed the JOINT COMMUNIQUÉ BY THE UNITED STATES AND THE SOVIET UNION, defining the essence of their détente.

The Watergate scandal, itself a struggle over the "imperial" presidency created in no small measure by the developments of the cold war, would cut short Nixon's diplomatic efforts before they reached fruition. Détente did not end the cold war and hardly lasted beyond Nixon's removal from office, but it had raised the possibility of truly peaceful coexistence, which Khrushchev and Kennedy had first begun working toward in the wake of the Cuban Missile Crisis. The Nixon-Brezhnev détente was the first weak beacon of a new era in international relations. After much confusion, that era would come to witness the collapse of an ideological dispute plaguing diplomacy since the end of World War I and dividing the globe into two dangerously armed camps since the end of World War II.

TREATIES

Mutual Defense Treaties, Military Alliances, and Nonaggression Pacts

PACT OF RIO
(INTER-AMERICAN TREATY OF RECIPROCAL ASSISTANCE)

TREATY AT A GLANCE

Completed
September 2, 1947, at Rio de Janeiro, Brazil

Signatories
Argentina, Bolivia, Brazil, Chile, Colombia, Costa Rica, Cuba (withdrew in 1960), the Dominican Republic, El Salvador, Guatemala, Haiti, Honduras, Mexico, Panama, Paraguay, Peru, the United States, Uruguay, and Venezuela

Overview
Concluded in the early days of the cold war, the Pact of Rio set up an inter-American alliance against armed attack (pursuant to Article 51 of the United Nations Charter) and established procedures to be followed in the event of other acts of aggression.

Historical Background

In the wake of World War II, as relations between the Soviet Union and its European allies deteriorated and a crisis began brewing in Berlin, the United States was alarmed by what it assumed was Stalin's expansionist intentions in a postwar world. In 1946 during a speech in Fulton, Missouri, British prime minister Winston Churchill accused the Russians of lowering an iron curtain between communist East Europe and the liberal democracies of the West he called the free world. An influential U.S. State Department telegram from Russia by diplomat George Kennan had described the Kremlin's political philosophy as "a neurotic view of world affairs" and warned that the USSR would employ every means possible to subvert, divide, and undermine the West through the action of communists abroad and fellow travelers.

In response, President Harry S. Truman adopted a policy of what Kennan had labeled "containment" of communism and toward that end began constructing a national security state. He created a permanent Joint Chiefs of Staff; established the U.S. Air Force, with a prominent Strategic Air Command to deploy atomic bombs, as a separate branch of the armed services; and launched the Central Intelligence Agency. Diplomatically, the Truman Administration began negotiating a series of regional pacts that linked the United States to countries ringing the Soviet Union or where it felt Soviet-backed subversion might be employed in the future. The United States had traditionally worried about foreign influence on Latin America, so not only would the CIA become covertly active in the region, but Truman would include his southern neighbors in this initial run of cold war treaty making.

Terms

The Pact of Rio (the Inter-American Treaty of Reciprocal Assistance) was the product of the Ninth Inter-American Conference for the Maintenance of Continental Peace and Security, which met near Rio de Janeiro from August 15 through September 2, 1947. Although Canada was not a party to the treaty, the document's Article 4 defined the region covered as all of

North and South America, including Canada, Greenland, and a portion of Antarctica.

Although the pact mandated two-thirds majority agreement on cooperative defensive action, each signatory was explicitly permitted to act immediately on its own in its direct self-defense. The pact also defined "indirect aggression"—chiefly, the support of revolution in one state by another (in the cold war, this effectively meant communist subversion)—which called for a consensus among the signatories before action could be taken. Moreover, pursuant to Article 53 of the UNITED NATIONS CHARTER, any enforcement action decided upon would require authorization from the UN Security Council.

~≷⊚

In the name of their Peoples, the Governments represented at the Inter-American Conference for the Maintenance of Continental Peace and Security, desirous of consolidating and strengthening their relations of friendship and good neighborliness, and

Considering . . .

That the High Contracting Parties reiterate their will to remain united in an Inter-American System consistent with the purposes of the United Nations, and reaffirm the existence of the agreement which they have concluded concerning those matters relating to the maintenance of international peace and security which are appropriate for regional action;

The High Contracting Parties reaffirm their adherence to the principles of inter-American solidarity and cooperation, and especially to those set forth in the preamble and declarations of the Act of Chapultepec, all of which should be understood to be accepted as standards of their mutual relations and as the juridical basis of the Inter-American System . . .

That the obligation of mutual assistance and common defense of the American Republics is essentially related to their democratic ideals and their will to cooperate permanently in the fulfillment of the principles and purposes of a policy of peace . . .

Have resolved, in conformity with the objectives stated above, to conclude the following Treaty, in order to assure peace, through adequate means, to provide for effective reciprocal assistance to meet armed attacks against any American State, and in order to deal with threats of aggression against any of them:

ARTICLE 1

The High Contracting Parties formally condemn war and undertake in their international relations nor to resort to the threat or use of force in any manner inconsistent with the provisions of the Charter of the United Nations of this Treaty.

ARTICLE 2

As a consequence of the principle set forth in the preceding Article, the High Contracting Parties undertake to submit every controversy which may arise between them to methods of peaceful settlement and to endeavor to settle any such controversy among themselves by means of the procedures in force in the Inter-American System before referring it to the General Assembly or the Security Council of the United Nations.

ARTICLE 3

1. The High Contracting Parties agree that an armed attack by any State against an American State shall be considered as an attack against all the American States and, consequently, each one of the said Contracting Parties undertakes to assist in meeting the attack in the exercise of the inherent right of individual or collective self-defense recognized by Article 51 of the Charter of the United Nations.

2. On the request of the State or States directly attacked and until the decision of the Organ of Consultation of the Inter-American System, each one of the Contracting Parties may determine the immediate measures which it may individually take in fulfillment of the obligation contained in the preceding paragraph and in accordance with the principle of continental solidarity. The Organ of Consultation shall meet without delay for the purpose of examining those measures and agreeing upon the measures of a collective character that should be taken.

3. The provisions of this Article shall be applied in case of any armed attack which takes place within the region described in Article 4 or within the territory of an American State. When the attack takes place outside the said areas, the provision of Article 6 shall be applied.

4. Measures of self-defense provided for under this Article maybe taken until the Security Council of the United Nations has taken the measures necessary to maintain international peace and security.

ARTICLE 4

The regions to which this Treaty refers are the North and South American continents and Greenland and an area of Antarctica.

ARTICLE 5

The High Contracting Parties shall immediately send to the Security Council of the United Nations, in conformity with Articles 51 and 54 of the Charter of the United Nations, complete information concerning the activities undertaken or in contemplation in the exercise of the right of self-defense or for the purpose of maintaining inter-American peace and security.

ARTICLE 6

If the inviolability or the integrity of the territory or the sovereignty or political independence of any American State should be affected by an aggression which is not an armed attack or by an extra-continental or intra-continental conflict, or by any other fact or situation that might endanger the peace of America, the Organ of Consultation shall meet immediately in order to agree on measures which must be taken in case of aggression to assist the victim of aggression or, in any case, the measures which should be taken for the common defense and for the maintenance of the peace and security of the continent.

ARTICLE 7

In the case of a conflict between two or more American States, without prejudice to the right of self-defense in conformity with Article 51 of the Charter of the United Nations, the High Contracting Parties meeting in consultation shall call upon the contending States to suspend hostilities and restore matters to the *status quo ante bellum*, and shall take in addition all other necessary measures to re-establish or maintain inter-American peace and security and for the solution of the conflict by peaceful means. The rejection of the pacifying action will be considered in the determination of the aggressor and in the application of the measures which the consultative meeting may agree upon.

Article 8 listed the sanctions available to pact members, ranging from breaking off diplomatic relations to economic sanctions to the use of armed forces.

ARTICLE 9

In addition to other acts which the Organ of Consultation may characterize as aggression, the following shall be considered as such:

(a) Unprovoked armed attack by a State against the territory, the people, or the land, sea or air forces of another State;

(b) Invasion, by the armed forces of a State, of the territory of an American State, through the trespassing of boundaries demarcated in accordance with treaty, judicial decision, or arbitral award, or, in the absence of frontiers thus demarcated, invasion affecting a region which is under the effective jurisdiction of another State.

ARTICLE 10

None of the provisions of this Treaty shall be construed as impairing the rights and obligations of the High Contracting Parties under the Charter of the United Nations.

ARTICLE 11

The consultations to which this Treaty refers shall be carried out by means of the Meetings of Ministers of Foreign Affairs of the American Republics which have ratified the Treaty, or in the manner or by the organ which in the future may be agreed upon.

ARTICLE 12

The Governing Board of the Pan-American Union may act provisionally as an organ of consultation until the meeting of the Organ of Consultation referred to in the preceding Article takes place.

ARTICLE 13

The consultations shall be initiated at the request addressed to the Governing Board of the Pan-American Union by any of the signatory States which has ratified the Treaty.

ARTICLE 14

In the voting referred to in this Treaty only the representatives of the signatory States which have ratified the Treaty may take part.

ARTICLE 15

The Governing Board of the Pan-American Union shall act in all matters concerning this Treaty as an organ of liaison among the signatory States which have ratified this Treaty and between these States and the United Nations.

ARTICLE 16

The decisions of the Governing Board of the Pan-American Union referred to in Articles 13 and 15 above shall be taken by an absolute majority of the members entitled to a vote.

ARTICLE 17

The Organ of Consultation shall take its decisions by a vote of two-thirds of the signatory States which have ratified the Treaty.

ARTICLE 18

In the case of a situation or dispute between American States, the parties directly interested shall be excluded from the voting referred to in the two preceding Articles.

ARTICLE 19

To constitute a quorum in all the meetings referred to in the previous Articles, it shall be necessary that the number of States represented shall be at least equal to the number of votes necessary for the taking of the decision.

ARTICLE 20

Decisions which require the application of the measures specified in Article 8 shall be binding upon all the signatory States which have ratified this Treaty, with the sole exception that no State shall be required to use armed force without its consent.

ARTICLE 21

The measures agreed upon by the Organ of Consultation shall be executed through the procedures and agencies now existing or those which may in the future be established.

Articles 22 through 24 of the treaty dealt with registration and ratification, which required two-thirds of the signatories.

ARTICLE 25

This Treaty shall remain in force indefinitely, but may be denounced by any High Contracting Party by a notification in writing to the Pan-American Union, which shall inform all the other High Contracting Parties of each notification of denunciation received.

After the expiration of two years from the date of the receipt by the Pan-American Union of a notification of denunciation by any High Contracting Party, the present Treaty shall cease to be in force and with respect to such State, but shall remain in force and effect with respect to all other High Contracting Parties.

ARTICLE 26

The principles and fundamental provisions of this Treaty shall be incorporated in the Organic Pact of the Inter-American System.

Consequences

The Pact of Rio made hemispheric defense the joint responsibility of all the American republics, although it did not supersede the MONROE DOCTRINE, which since the early 19th century had asserted the United States's right to act unilaterally in the hemisphere in defense of what it declared its own vital interests. The Pact of Rio served as a model for the NORTH ATLANTIC TREATY, which established NATO, and for other regional defense agreements. The Organization of American States was established in 1948, in part to enforce the Pact of Rio (see CHARTER OF THE ORGANIZATION OF THE AMERICAN STATES).

Source

J. A. S. Grenville and Bernard Waserstein, eds., *The Major International Treaties Since 1945* (London and New York: Methuen, 1987), 88–89.

ANGLO-TRANSJORDAN ALLIANCE

TREATY AT A GLANCE

Completed
March 15, 1948

Signatories
Great Britain and Transjordan (present-day Jordan)

Overview
Great Britain, seeking to shore up its relations with the Arabs in the wake of the growing Zionist crisis in Palestine, allied itself with the Hashemite Kingdom of Transjordan. The alliance failed to inspire others to make similar arrangements, just as Britain's waning influence failed to prevent the creation of an Israeli state.

Historical Background

During World War II, there had been a hidden tension between U.S. president Franklin Delano Roosevelt and his ally and friend British prime minister Winston Churchill. Roosevelt disapproved of British and French colonialism and had little patience with Churchill's plans to shore up its waning colonial empire after the war, especially in the Middle East. This lack of patience would color the "special relationship" between the two powers after the war, a subtle if persistent irritant in the background of their diplomacy that came closest to breaking out into the open in the Suez Canal crisis of 1956.

Immediately after the war, however, the United States was generally content to let the British wield their influence in the Middle East to protect American cold war interests against the Soviet Union, so long as it was evident Britain continued to divest itself directly of its colonial holdings. In keeping with this subtle pressure, Britain conducted a gallant balancing act, favoring the growth of Arab unity in the region but striving to ensure that Arab governments friendly to Britain would dominate any such alliance. During the war, Britain supported an Arab unity conference that met in Alexandria, Egypt, in October 1944 and led to the formation of the PACT OF THE ARAB LEAGUE.

The league's founding members were Egypt, Iraq, Syria, Lebanon, Transjordan, Saudi Arabia, and Yemen. Rivalries and tensions between league members and clauses calling for unanimous votes weakened the body, headquartered in Cairo, and often made it impossible for the league to adopt common policies. Unable effectively to resist the growing Zionism in Palestine, the league came increasingly under the dominance of an Egypt struggling to free itself of its French and British colonial past and thus did not become the ally for which Great Britain had hoped. Instead, Egypt used the league to develop a common Arab front against the continued British and French military presence in the Middle East and against Zionism.

In Arab eyes, of course, the British had much to answer for when it came to the Zionist agitation for an Israeli state in the Middle East. It was Britain's World War I BALFOUR DECLARATION that first endorsed "a national home" for the Jewish people in Palestine, and the British had failed to control the Zionists under its Palestinian Mandate. When the arrival of large numbers of Holocaust survivors seeking homes in Palestine in the wake of World War II met with British resistance, renewed violence erupted, and a war-weary Britain—under U.S. pressure—at last caved in, turning the entire problem over to the United Nations in 1947, which in November voted to partition Palestine into Arab and Jewish states. Seeking to shore up its bona fides with the Arabs, Great Britain concluded a military alliance with neighboring Transjordan in 1948.

Terms

The two countries promised to come to each other's aid if engaged in war, and in fulfillment of this pledge, Transjordan made bases available for British forces and permitted the stationing of such forces in Transjordan.

ARTICLE 1

There shall be perpetual peace and friendship between His Britannic Majesty and His Majesty the King of the Hashimite Kingdom of Transjordan.

A close alliance shall continue between the High Contracting Parties in consecration of their friendship, their cordial understanding and their good relations.

Each of the High Contracting Parties undertakes not to adopt in regard to foreign countries an attitude which is inconsistent with the Alliance or might create difficulties for the other party thereto.

ARTICLE 2

Should any dispute between either High Contracting Party and a third State produce a situation which would involve the risk of a rupture with that State, the High Contracting Parties will concert together with a view to the settlement of the said dispute by peaceful means in accordance with the provisions of the Charter of the United Nations and of any other international obligations which may be applicable to the case.

ARTICLE 3

Should either High Contracting Party notwithstanding the provisions of Article 2 become engaged in war, the other High Contracting Party will, subject always to the provisions of Article 4, immediately come to his aid as a measure of collective defence.

In the event of an imminent menace of hostilities the High Contracting Parties will immediately concert together the necessary measures of defence.

ARTICLE 4

Nothing in the present Treaty is intended to, or shall in any way prejudice the rights and obligations which devolve, or may devolve, upon either of the High Contracting Parties under the Charter of the United Nations or under any other existing international agreements, conventions or treaties.

ARTICLE 5

The present Treaty of which the Annex is an integral part shall replace the Treaty of Alliance signed in London on 22nd March 1946, of the Christian Era, together with its Annex and all Letters and Notes, interpreting or otherwise exchanged in 1946 in connection therewith, provided however that Article 9 of the said Treaty shall remain in force in accordance with and as modified by the Notes exchanged on this day on this subject.

ARTICLE 6

Should any difference arise relative to the application or interpretation of the present Treaty and should the high Contracting Powers fail to settle such difference by direct negotiations, it shall be referred to the International Court of justice unless the parties agree to another mode of settlement.

ARTICLE 7

The present Treaty shall be ratified and shall come into force upon the exchange of instruments of ratification which shall take place at London as soon as possible. It shall remain in forcer for a period of twenty years from the date of its coming into force. At any time after fifteen years from the date of the coming into force of the present Treaty, the high Contracting Parties will, at the request of either of them, negotiate a revised Treaty which shall provide for the continued cooperation of the High Contracting Parties in the defence of their common interests. The period of fifteen years shall be reduced if a complete system of security agreements under Article 43 of the Charter of the United Nations is concluded before the expiry of this period. At the end of twenty years, if the present Treaty has not been revised it shall remain in force until the expiry of one year after notice of termination has been given by either High Contracting Party to the other through the diplomatic channel.

Annex

ARTICLE 1

(a) The High Contracting Parties recognize that, in the common in interests of both, each of them must be in a position to discharge his obligations under Article 3 of the Treaty.

(b) In the event of either High Contracting Party becoming engaged in war, of or a menace of hostilities, each high Contracting Party will invite the other to bring to his territory or territory controlled by him the necessary forces of all arms. Each will furnish to the other all the facilities and assistance in his power, including the use of all means and lines of communication, and on financial terms to be agreed upon,

(c) His Majesty the King of the Hashimite Kingdom of Transjordan will safeguard, maintain and develop as necessary the airfields, ports, roads and other means and lines of communication in and across the Hashimite Kingdom of Transjordan as may be required for the purposes of the present Treaty and its Annex, and will call upon his Britannic Majesty's assistance as may be required for this purpose.

(d) Until such time as the High Contracting Parties agree that the state of world security renders such measures unnecessary, His Majesty the King of the Hashimite Kingdom of Transjordan invites His Britannic Majesty to maintain units of the Royal Air Force at Amman and Mafrak airfields. His Majesty the King of the Hashimite Kingdom of Transjordan will provide all the necessary facilities for the accommodation and maintenance of the units mentioned in this paragraph, including facilities for the storage of their ammunition and supplies and the lease of any land required.

ARTICLE 2

In the common defence interests of the high Contracting Parties a permanent joint advisory body will be set up immediately on the coming into force of the present Treaty to coordinate defence matters between the Governments of the High Contracting parties within the scope of the present Treaty.

This body, which will be known as the Anglo-Transjordan Joint Defence Board, will be composed of competent military representatives of the Governments of the High Contracting Parties in equal numbers. . . .

Consequences

The treaty was to last 20 years, but it did not have much effect on other Arab states. Negotiations with

Egypt and Iraq in 1948 failed, thus denying the British the bases they sought in those countries. In 1948 the British withdrew from Palestine, and on the eve of their departure, on May 14, Palestine's Jews proclaimed the state of Israel.

The immediate result was the first of several Arab-Israeli wars, as armies from the Arab states invaded Palestine. Now the lack of unity and cooperation within the Arab League and its alienation from Great Britain and France (and thus the United States) took their toll, as the Israelis pushed back the invaders in 1949. As more Jews immigrated into Israel, some 700,000 Arab Palestinians fled the territory into Transjordan, whereupon the Israelis confiscated their property. The Middle East "problem" had been born, and it was not susceptible to such cold war solutions as the BAGHDAD PACT, formed to check the growing influence of the Soviet Union among Arabs disenchanted with the West and its backing of Israel.

Transjordan, soon to become simply Jordan, maintained its alliance with Britain, which helped to navigate a dangerous course in the coming years, as the Hashemite kingdom provided a home for anti-Israeli Palestinian terrorists but was careful to avoid the kind of overt hostility, often urged on it by other Arab states, that might provoke retaliation from the Israelis.

Source

J. A. S. Grenville, *The Major International Treaties, 1914–1973* (New York: Stein and Day, 1975), 495–498.

TREATY OF BRUSSELS

TREATY AT A GLANCE

Completed
March 17, 1948, at Brussels, Belgium

Signatories
Great Britain, France, the Netherlands, Belgium, and Luxembourg

Overview
When Great Britain, France, and the Benelux nations responded to the 1948 Communist coup in Czechoslovakia by signing a mutual defense alliance in Brussels, the Soviet Union responded by withdrawing from the Allied Control Council, which was overseeing the occupation of Berlin, and by blocking all access to that city with Soviet troops. The Allies responded in turn with the Berlin Airlift. The cold war had begun.

Historical Background

While the four powers occupying Germany after World War II were struggling for position in what was to become the cold war, the Western European states moved to take advantage of the newly introduced Marshall Plan by placing their military, political, and economic cooperation on a new footing. In general, the effect of the Marshall Plan was to harden the divisions developing in postwar Europe. While the effect of the plan in Germany would ultimately be to foster its division into East and West Germany, the former under Soviet domination, the latter the favored child of the United States, in Western Europe the Marshall plan pushed forward the movement for integration. In January 1948 Britain and France launched a plan to expand their wartime partnership into a more comprehensive Western European union, a plan that was lent urgency by the Communist takeover of Czechoslovakia in February. Negotiations in March between Britain, France, and the Benelux countries (the Netherlands, Belgium, and Luxembourg, formed together by a wartime treaty in September 1944) resulted in the signing of the Treaty of Brussels.

Terms

The treaty read in part as follows:

Resolved
To reaffirm their faith in fundamental human rights, in the dignity and worth of the human person and in the other ideals proclaimed in the Charter of the United Nations;

To fortify and preserve the principles of democracy, personal freedom and political liberty, the constitutional traditions and the rule of law, which are their common heritage;

To strengthen, with these aims in view, the economic, social and cultural ties by which they are already united;

To cooperate loyally and to coordinate their efforts to create in Western Europe a firm basis for European economic recovery;

To afford assistance to each other, in accordance with the Charter of the United Nations, in maintaining international peace and security and in resisting any policy of aggression;

To take such steps as may be held to be necessary in the event of a renewal by Germany of a policy of aggression;

To associate progressively in the pursuance of these aims other States inspired by the same ideals and animated by the like determination;

Desiring for these purposes to conclude a Treaty for collaboration in economic, social and cultural matters and for collective self-defence . . .

ARTICLE I
Convinced of the close community of their interests and of the necessity of uniting in order to promote the economic recovery of Europe, the High Contracting Parties will so organize and coordinate their economic activities as to produce the best possible results, by the elimination of conflict in their economic policies, the coordination of production and the development of commercial exchanges.

The cooperation provided for in the preceding paragraph, which will be effected through the Consultative Council referred to in Article VII as well as through other bodies, shall not involve any duplication of, or prejudice to, the work of other economic organizations in which the High Contracting Parties are or may be represented but shall on the contrary assist the work of those organizations.

ARTICLE II

The High Contracting Parties will make every effort in common, both by direct consultation and in specialized agencies, to promote the attainment of a higher standard of living by their peoples and to develop on corresponding lines the social and other related services of their countries.

The High Contracting Parties will consult with the object of achieving the earliest possible application of recommendations of immediate practical interest, relating to social matters, adopted with their approval in the specialized agencies.

They will endeavor to conclude as soon as possible conventions with each other in the sphere of social security.

ARTICLE III

The High Contracting Parties will make every effort in common to lead their peoples towards a better understanding of the principles which form the basis of their common civilization and to promote cultural exchanges by conventions between themselves or by other means.

ARTICLE IV

If any of the High Contracting Parties should be the object of an armed attack in Europe, the other High Contracting Parties will, in accordance with the provisions of Article 51 of the Charter of the United Nations, afford the Party so attacked all the military and other aid and assistance in their power.

ARTICLE V

All measures taken as a result of the preceding Article shall be immediately reported to the Security Council. They shall be terminated as soon as the Security Council has taken the measures necessary to maintain or restore international peace and security.

The present Treaty does not prejudice in any way the obligations of the High Contracting Parties under the provisions of the Charter of the United Nations. It shall not be interpreted as affecting in any way the authority and responsibility of the Security Council under the Charter to take at any time such action as it deems necessary in order to maintain or restore international peace and security.

ARTICLE VI

The High Contracting Parties declare, each so far as he is concerned, that none of the international engagements now in force between him and any other of the High Contracting Parties or any third State is in conflict with the provisions of the present Treaty.

None of the High Contracting Parties will conclude any alliance or participate in any coalition directed against any other of the High Contracting Parties.

ARTICLE VII

For the purpose of consulting together on all the questions dealt with in the present Treaty, the High Contracting Parties will create a Consultative Council, which shall be so organized as to be able to exercise its functions continuously. The Council shall meet at such times as it shall deem fit.

At the request of any of the High Contracting Parties, the Council shall be immediately convened in order to permit the High Contracting Parties to consult with regard to any situation which may constitute a threat to peace, in whatever area this threat should arise; with regard to the attitude to be adopted and the steps to be taken in case of a renewal by Germany of an aggressive policy; or with regard to any situation constituting a danger to economic stability.

ARTICLE VIII

[Settling disputes between signatories by peaceful means.]

ARTICLE IX

The High Contracting Parties may, by agreement, invite any other State to accede to the present Treaty on condition to be agreed between them and the State so invited. . . .

Consequences

The treaty redirected the military alliance between the signatories, from being directed solely at the potential for renewed German aggression, toward defense against any aggressor, which under the circumstances of course meant the growing Soviet bloc, and paved the way for further collaboration in economic, social, and cultural fields. Two months after its signing, the United States and Great Britain announced an economic merger of their zones of occupation, and in July the United States formally ended Germany's "punitive" period and announced its policy now to be making West Germany economically self-sufficient.

Meanwhile, when the western Europeans had not only signed the Brussels Treaty but also made clear their intentions of pressing ahead with the establishment of a West German currency and government, the Russians walked out of the Allied Control Council, which oversaw German occupation. In June the Soviets used their occupation forces to block Allied and rail access to the western zones of Berlin. This, the first Berlin Crisis, would lead to the Berlin Airlift and the first major East-West confrontation of the cold war.

Source

Avalon Project at the Yale Law School, "Treaty of Economic, Social, and Cultural Collaboration and Collective Self-defense (Brussels Treaty), March 17, 1948." Available online. URL: http://www.yale.edu/lawweb/avalon/intdip/westeu/we001.htm. Accessed December 28, 2004.

NORTH ATLANTIC TREATY

TREATY AT A GLANCE

Completed
April 4, 1949, at Washington, D.C.

Signatories
Belgium, Canada, Denmark, France, Iceland, Italy, Luxembourg,
the Netherlands, Norway, Portugal, United Kingdom, and
United States (Greece and Turkey joined in 1952;
the Federal Republic of Germany in 1955; Spain in 1982;
the reunited Germany in 1990; Poland, Hungary, and
the Czech Republic in 1999; Bulgaria, Estonia, Latvia,
Lithuania, Romania, Slovakia, and Slovenia in 2004)

Overview
The North Atlantic Treaty established the North Atlantic Treaty
Organization (NATO), which had as its purpose the deterrence of
potential Soviet aggression in Europe, one in a series of such
regional alliances aimed at "containing" the spread of communism.

Historical Background

One of the many effects of the Marshall Plan, America's scheme for revitalizing a war-torn Europe in the wake of the Nazi Armageddon, was a hardening of the division on the Continent created by a growing rift between the Soviets and the other great power Allies. Stalin had denounced the plan as a capitalist plot even as he himself was plotting to overthrow the fragile new republics of eastern Europe and partition Germany in order to ring his country with puppet states that could serve as military and cultural buffers against the West, whose influence he saw as a threat to his dictatorship. When the Western European states, Great Britain, and the United States responded to the Stalin-backed Communist coup in Czechoslovakia in March 1948 by pressing ahead with the unification of the West German zones of occupation and the establishment of a West German currency and government, the Russians stormed out of the Allied Control Council. Three months later, Soviet occupation forces in the eastern zone shut off Allied access by road or rail to the western zones of Berlin.

U.S. president Harry S. Truman was worried about the expansion of Soviet influence, particularly in Europe, and persuaded by the famous "Long Telegram" from Moscow by American diplomat George Kennan, suggesting that a policy of "containment" should be exercised toward Stalin. Truman had already begun to set up a national security apparatus, including a permanent Joint Chiefs of Staff, the Strategic Air Command, and the CIA. He had also signed the PACT OF RIO, which would serve as a model for a series of regional mutual defense agreements linking the United States to nations ringing the USSR and its new client states.

Announcing he was ready to "get tough" with the Soviets in what policy mavens such as presidential advisor Bernard Baruch and press pundit Walter Lippmann were calling the cold war, Truman was forced to test his new policy in response to this latest move by the Russians in Berlin. Made necessary by the anomaly of an American-British-French zone of interest stuck some 100 miles inside an eastern Germany occupied by Soviet troops, the Berlin Crisis became a defining moment in the history of this new cold war. Allied commander in Berlin Lucius Clay and Secretary of State Dean Acheson wanted to flex American muscle and send an armed convoy straight through the Russian zone to Berlin, but the Joint Chiefs and certainly the British and the French were unwilling to risk provoking a war. Instead, Truman responded with an immense and ultimately quite effective airlift to keep West Berlin supplied with food, fuel, and medicine.

Historians have often wondered what Stalin hoped to accomplish. Perhaps he feared the rearmament of a

West German state and hoped to block it. Perhaps he was trying to scare the American public to retreat into its traditional isolationist shell. The real result of the Berlin blockade was to frighten the Western powers into taking stronger measures than they might otherwise have taken to contain the Soviet "threat." On April 4, 1949, the foreign policy heads of the United States, Great Britain, France, Italy, the Netherlands, Belgium, Luxembourg, Portugal, Denmark, Iceland, Norway, and Canada met in Washington to found the North Atlantic Treaty Organization, NATO, the premier cold war multinational mutual alliance.

Terms

The preamble to the North Atlantic Treaty clearly established the signatories' purpose:

> The Parties to this Treaty reaffirm their faith in the purposes and principles of the Charter of the United Nations and their desire to live in peace with all peoples and all governments.
>
> They are determined to safeguard the freedom, common heritage and civilization of their peoples, founded on the principles of democracy, individual liberty and the rule of law.
>
> They seek to promote stability and well-being in the North Atlantic area.
>
> They are resolved to unite their efforts for collective defence and for the preservation of peace and security.
>
> They therefore agree to this North Atlantic Treaty
> . . .

But the crux of the North Atlantic Treaty was Article 5:

> The Parties agree that an armed attack against one or more of them in Europe or North America shall be considered an attack against them all, and consequently they agree that, if such an armed attack occurs, each of them, in exercise of the right of individual or collective self-defence recognized by Article 51 of the Charter of the United Nations, will assist the Party or Parties so attacked by taking forthwith, individually, and in concert with the other Parties, such action as it deems necessary, including the use of armed force, to restore and maintain the security of the North Atlantic area.
>
> Any such armed attack and all measures taken as a result thereof shall immediately be reported to the Security Council. Such measures shall be terminated when the Security Council has taken the measures necessary to restore and maintain international peace and security.

Clearly the idea here was to check Soviet aggression. If the USSR launched an assault on Western Europe, the United States, with the biggest military and the largest stockpile of nuclear weaponry, would respond as if America itself had been attacked. In the long run, of course, the cold war ended, and the dreaded Soviet invasion of Europe never materialized. Ironically enough, the only time in history the provision was invoked came after an assault on U.S. territory, not Western Europe—on September 12, 2001, in response to the terrorist attack against the World Trade Center in New York City and the Pentagon in Washington, D.C., the day before.

NATO conformed to Article 51 of the UNITED NATIONS CHARTER, which granted nations the right of collective defense, but NATO also promoted political, social, and economic ties among its the members:

ARTICLE 1
The Parties undertake, as set forth in the Charter of the United Nations, to settle any international dispute in which they may be involved by peaceful means in such a manner that international peace and security and justice are not endangered, and to refrain in their international relations from the threat or use of force in any manner inconsistent with the purposes of the United Nations.

ARTICLE 2
The Parties will contribute toward the further development of peaceful and friendly international relations by strengthening their free institutions, by bringing about a better understanding of the principles upon which these institutions are founded, and by promoting conditions of stability and well-being. They will seek to eliminate conflict in their international economic policies and will encourage economic collaboration between any or all of them.

Consequences

If the impetus for the treaty was the increasing intensity of the cold war, including the communist coup d'état in Prague in February 1948 and the Berlin Blockade, beginning in June 1948, NATO nevertheless began without an established military structure. It took the outbreak of the Korean War, in June 1950, to prompt the establishment of a NATO military force, the principal element of which was Allied Command Europe, headquartered in Brussels, Belgium (Supreme Headquarters Allied Powers in Europe [SHAPE]). Policy was made by the North Atlantic Council, which met in Brussels (it met in Paris until 1967, France having withdrawn from the military structure of NATO the year before). However, the alliance was first and foremost a military one, and the Military Committee, composed of senior military representatives from each country (except Iceland, which had no military forces but was represented by a civilian, and France), recommended defense measures it considered necessary.

With the end of the cold war and the disbanding of the WARSAW PACT Organization, which had been

720 ENCYCLOPEDIA OF HISTORICAL TREATIES AND ALLIANCES

formed by the Soviet bloc to counter NATO, some European leaders called for replacing NATO with some less exclusively military organization, especially as former Communist bloc countries now sought entry. In the early 1990s, the United States took steps to reduce its NATO presence, substituting for the large standing forces of NATO contingency plans relying on smaller "rapid deployment forces," with reinforcements available from the United States in time of need.

On March 24, 1999, NATO saw its first military engagement outside the context of the cold war in Kosovo. There, NATO waged an 11-week bombing campaign against Serbia and Montenegro, which ended on June 11 and played a key role in resolving the Kosovo War.

Six weeks after the coordinated al-Qaeda attacks of September 11, 2001, in New York City and Washington, D.C., NATO held a summit in Prague at which seven countries—Estonia, Latvia, Lithuania, Slovenia, Bulgaria, Slovakia, and Romania—were encouraged to apply for membership and two others—Albania and Macedonia—were discouraged from doing so because of their economic, political, and military woes. By the time these seven joined the alliance in March 2004, Croatia had also applied and was in the process of qualifying for membership.

Meanwhile, NATO faced a crisis after France and Belgium fought measures to protect Turkey should it join the United States and Great Britain in the war the Americans seemed increasingly determined to wage on Iraq. Germany refused to override the French and Belgian vetoes. NATO did, however, agree to take command of the International Security Assistance Force in Afghanistan in August 2003, the first ever for NATO outside the North Atlantic area. But the United States

launched its Iraq war isolated from all the major world powers (except for Great Britain) and resentful of its former European allies.

Thus, while NATO was willing to join the U.S. war on terror, it was not anxious to support the Bush administration's preemptive war on a country that had clearly not expressly attacked the United States or any other NATO member—despite repeated assertions (which turned out later to be incorrect) by U.S. secretary of state Colin Powell that Iraq's Saddam Hussein was hoarding "weapons of mass destruction." Indeed, the collapse of NATO's primary enemy in Eastern Europe and the crisis over the U.S.-led invasion of Iraq caused many in both North America and Europe to question whether the alliance was obsolete. While some imagined that the terrorist threat might give the organization new life, others believed the new enemy called for new means and methods whose assumptions were fundamentally different from those on which NATO had been built.

In that context, Norway's response to the reelection in November 2004 of George W. Bush as president of the United States was ominous indeed for NATO's future. Norwegian prime minister Kjell Magne Bondevik publicly questioned any benefit to Norway of better defense relations with the European Union through NATO. Norwegian political analysts considered NATO to be a politically dead organization—and their skepticism was spreading.

Source

J. A. S. Grenville and Bernard Waserstein, eds., *The Major International Treaties Since 1945* (London and New York: Methuen, 1987), 207–209.

SINO-SOVIET TREATY OF FRIENDSHIP, ALLIANCE, AND MUTUAL ASSISTANCE

TREATY AT A GLANCE

Completed
February 14, 1950, at Moscow

Signatories
People's Republic of China and the Soviet Union

Overview
This treaty, which supplanted alliance and friendship treaties with Nationalist China of 1945 and 1946, resulted from the 1949 victory of Mao Zedong's Communist regime in China and created a Euroasian Communist bloc greatly feared in the West. It turned out more feared than real, regardless of Russian claims about the unity of the communist world.

Historical Background

For decades an intermittent civil war had raged in China between the Communists and the National Party, founded by the revered Sun Yat-sen but now the personal property of Generalissimo Chiang Kai-shek. The war never completely ceased to rage even during the Japanese invasion and occupation of World War II, when U.S. president Franklin Delano Roosevelt was inviting Chiang to allied summits and insisting his China be included as one of the Great Powers. In 1945 the new president, Harry S. Truman, continuing the U.S. commitment to its illusion of a "strong, unified and democratic China," packed Secretary of State George Marshall off to East Asia to work out a truce and create a coalition government under Chiang. Stalin, too, who had blundered badly in China during the 1920s, backed Chiang, believing him too strong for the Chinese Communists, even with Soviet support, to defeat but not strong enough to challenge Russian interests in Manchuria, Mongolia, and Xinjiang Uigher (Sinkiang). At the same time, the Soviets painted Mao Zedong, leader of the Chinese communist insurgency, as little more than an agrarian reformer, and like Truman, Stalin called for a coalition government.

Neither Chiang Kai-shek in Chongqing (Chungking) nor Mao Zedong in Yan'an even considered compromising with the other, and the fighting resumed in earnest in October 1946. Chiang and his corrupt corps of warlord generals had made a habit during the war of grabbing all the money, goods, arms, and materiel they could from the Allies, then failing to show up (at least, to be willing to fight) on the battlefield. So the Nationalist leader may have been surprised when Truman, unhappy with the rejection of Marshall's mission, imposed an arms embargo on him. But, given the heating up of the ideological struggle in Europe policy wonks were calling the cold war, perhaps inevitably after May 1947, the Truman administration extended aid again to Chiang and called this new step "neutrality against the communists."

Many of the Old China Hands in the State Department loathed Chiang for his dissolute personal life and political corruption, and their influence reinforced the Europe-first bias of American policy, which stretched back to the beginning of the war. By the time Mao's forces had overrun the mainland and forced the Nationalists to flee to Formosa (Taiwan), not just the China lobby but Secretary of State and supreme cold warrior Dean Acheson himself had decided, as he said, to "wait for the dust to settle."

Stalin, as leader of the communist world, could afford no such luxury. The victory of the Communists led by Mao Zedong initiated a new chapter in Soviet-Chinese relations, expressed in the 1950 treaty.

Terms

The new agreement declared the alliance with the Nationalists null and void, but the Chinese still acknowledged the independence of Outer Mongolia.

The Soviets and the Chinese agreed to collaborate in meeting any future aggression from Japan or from any state allied with Japan; the latter part of this provision was an indirect means of forming a standing alliance against the United States, which had major military installations in Japan. The Soviet Union relinquished many of the rights it had acquired in northern China by virtue of the earlier treaty with the Nationalists, and it agreed to extend credit and economic aid to China.

The Central People's Government of the People's Republic of China and the Presidium of the Supreme Soviet of the Union of Soviet Socialist Republics, fully determined to prevent jointly, by strengthening friendship and cooperation between the People's Republic of China and the Union of Soviet Socialist Republics, the revival of Japanese imperialism and the resumption of aggression on the part of Japan or any other State that may collaborate in any way with Japan in acts of aggression; imbued with the desire to consolidate lasting peace and universal security in the Far East and throughout the world in conformity with the aims and principles of the United Nations; profoundly convinced that the consolidation of good neighborly relations and friendship between the People's Republic of China and the Union of Soviet Socialist Republics meets the vital interests of the peoples of China and the Soviet Union, have towards this end decided to conclude the present Treaty and have appointed as their plenipotentiary representatives: Chou En-lai, Premier of the Government Administration Council and Minister of Foreign Affairs, acting for the Central People's Government of the People's Republic of China; and Andrei Yanuaryevich Vyshinsky, Minister of Foreign Affairs of the U.S.S.R., acting for the Presidium of the Supreme Soviet of the Union of Soviet Socialist Republics. Both plenipotentiary representatives having communicated their full powers found them in good and due form, have agreed upon the following:

ARTICLE 1

Both Contracting Parties undertake jointly to adopt all necessary measures at their disposal for the purpose of preventing the resumption of aggression and violation of peace on the part of Japan or any other State that may collaborate with Japan directly or indirectly in acts of aggression. In the event of one of the Contracting Parties being attacked by Japan or any State allied with her and thus being involved in a state of war, the other Contracting Party shall immediately render military and other assistance by all means at its disposal.

The Contracting Parties also declare their readiness to participate in a spirit of sincere cooperation in all international actions aimed at ensuring peace and security throughout the world and to contribute their full share to the earliest implementation of these tasks.

ARTICLE 2

Both Contracting Parties undertake in a spirit of mutual agreement to bring about the earliest conclusion of a peace treaty with Japan jointly with other Powers which were allies in the Second World War.

ARTICLE 3

Each Contracting Party undertakes not to conclude any alliance directed against the other Contracting Party and not to take part in any coalition or in any actions or measures directed against the other Contracting Party.

ARTICLE 4

Both Contracting Parties, in the interests of consolidating peace and universal security, will consult with each other in regard to all important international problems affecting the common interests of China and the Soviet Union.

ARTICLE 5

Each Contracting Party undertakes, in a spirit of friendship and cooperation and in conformity with the principles of equality, mutual benefit and mutual respect for the national sovereignty and territorial integrity and noninterference in the internal affairs of the other Contracting Party, to develop and consolidate economic and cultural ties between China and the Soviet Union, to render the other all possible economic assistance and to carry out necessary economic cooperation.

ARTICLE 6

The present Treaty shall come into force immediately after its ratification; the exchange of instruments of ratification shall take place in Peking.

The present Treaty shall be valid for thirty years. If neither of the Contracting Parties gives notice a year before the expiration of this term of its intention to denounce the Treaty, it shall remain in force for another five years and shall be further extended in compliance with this provision.

Done in Moscow on 14 February 1950, in two copies, each in the Chinese and Russian languages, both texts being equally valid.

On the authorization of the Central People's Government of the People's Republic of China

CHOU EN-LAI

On the authorization of the Presidium of the Supreme Soviet of the Union of Soviet Socialist Republics

A. Y. VYSHINSKY

Consequences

The Communist revolution in China kicked off a foreign policy debate within the United States, fueled by right-wing Republican demands to find out "who lost China." Mao's takeover, the apparent solidarity with Moscow, the Berlin Blockade, and the first Soviet atomic bomb test struck a series of hammer blows one after the other on the credibility of the State Department and gave the Republicans a stick with which to beat Truman out of the running for reelection in 1952. When Alger Hiss, a high-ranking State Department official, president of the Carnegie Endowment for World Peace, and sometimes communist spy, was convicted of perjury in testimony before Congress, the

China lobby at the State Department was discredited and the Old China Hands were drummed from the foreign policy community by the likes of Joseph McCarthy.

Although McCarthy, who operated via innuendo and intimidation, failed to prove much in his witch-hunts, the recent opening of KGB files in Russia have provided hints that his charges were not quite as groundless as they have for the most part been considered to be since he was discredited in the mid-1950s. Be that as it may, with the China lobby vacant at State, America lost those who knew East Asia best, which meant that for much of the cold war, the United States was operating blindly in the Orient.

One of the great surprises for many when the Pentagon Papers were published, documenting the decision making that led to the war in Vietnam, was just how ignorant those responsible for the policy were of Vietnam itself and its relation to the Soviet Union and China. Vietnam then became an object lesson in its own right. A measure of the mess created when governments let ideology rather than fact dictate the basic information on which they base their foreign policies, Vietnam became the example of a failing that characterized much of the diplomacy on both sides of the cold war.

For much of the cold war decade of the 1950s, the Soviet Union and China appeared to act in very close collaboration as a formidable Communist bloc, a "fact" which the Soviets and the Chinese knew was untrue but never admitted so, and a "fact" which the West accepted blindly and acted upon, although there were hints of a potential rift between the two powers from the start. The problem was in part that the Chinese, hailed as the new communist vanguard by many in the West, were ideological purists, while the Soviets, since at least the Third (Communist) International of the First World War, had grown comfortable with glossing over the potential contradiction between leading a world revolution and simultaneously advancing the cause of a new Russian empire. The Chinese often bridled at this Russian arrogance, and by 1956 Mao Zedong had begun to bait the Soviets by sometimes openly challenging Russian preeminence in the communist world.

In 1958 and 1959, the Soviet Union declined to provide nuclear assistance to China on terms acceptable to the Chinese, and in 1960 the Soviets withdrew their nuclear technicians from China. Soviet premier Nikita Khrushchev's efforts to achieve "peaceful coexistence" with the United States widened the gulf between the USSR and China and, throughout the 1960s acrimonious disputes over border regions developed. Mao and the Chinese Communists now typically referred to the Russians as "revisionists" and were making a bid for leadership of the third world national liberation movements, which included, for example, Vietnam.

By the time Richard Nixon became president, he was able to get behind the thin gloss of cooperation between Russia and China over Vietnam. He entered into outright détente with the Soviet Union, established regular diplomatic relations with mainland China, and even contemplated playing one off the other.

Source

J. A. S. Grenville and Bernard Waserstein, eds., *The Major International Treaties Since 1945* (London and New York: Methuen, 1987), 168–170.

ANZUS TREATY

Historical Background

By 1951 Harry S. Truman was committed to the cold war. At home he had built a national security apparatus, which included a permanent Joint Chiefs of Staff, in many ways reminiscent in their status and function of the traditional German high command; a separate Air Force, with its A-bomb-toting Strategic Air Command; the Central Intelligence Agency and a commitment to the use of nuclear weapons rather than the building of a huge standing army in order to deter communist aggression at home and abroad.

As part of his cold war policy, built on George Kennan's notion of "containing" the communists as much as possible within their current territories all over the world, Truman had signed a number of regional pacts linking American defense with that of countries who bordered the communist bloc. One of this series of cold war mutual defense treaties, the ANZUS pact was formed to better defend the western Pacific, a need made apparent to the Truman administration two years earlier with the Communist revolution in China.

Terms

The preamble took into account other U.S. Pacific obligations as well as those obligations of Australia and New Zealand that were part of the British Commonwealth.

Security Treaty between Australia, New Zealand and the United States (ANZUS), San Francisco, 1 September 1951

The parties to this Treaty, Reaffirming their faith in the purposes and principles of the Charter of the United Nations and their desire to live in peace with all peoples and all Governments, and desiring to strengthen the fabric of peace in the Pacific area,

Noting that the United States already has arrangements pursuant to which its armed forces are stationed in the Philippines, and has armed forces and administrative responsibilities in the Ryukyus, and upon the coming into force of the Japanese Peace Treaty may also station armed forces in and about Japan to assist in the preservation of peace and security in the Japan area,

Recognizing that Australia and New Zealand as members of the British Commonwealth of Nations have military obligations outside as well as within the Pacific area,

Desiring to declare publicly and formally their sense of unity, so that no potential aggressor could be under the illusion that any of them stand alone in the Pacific area, and

Desiring further to coordinate their efforts for collective defense for the preservation of peace and security pending the development of a morecomprehensive system of regional security in the Pacific area,

Therefore declare and agree as follows:

ARTICLE I

The parties undertake, as set forth in the Charter of the United Nations, to settle any international disputes in which they may be involved by peaceful means in such a manner that international peace and security and justice are not endangered and to refrain in their international relations from the threat or use of force in any manner inconsistent with the purposes of the United Nations.

ARTICLE II

In order more effectively to achieve the objective of this Treaty the parties separately and jointly by means

COLD WAR, PEACEFUL COEXISTENCE 725

of continuous and effective self-help and mutual aid will maintain and develop their individual and collective capacity to resist armed attack.

ARTICLE III

The parties will consult together whenever in the opinion of any of them the territorial integrity, political independence or security of any of the parties is threatened in the Pacific.

The defense clause (Article 4) bound each signatory to act against armed attack on any other signatory in the Pacific, provided that such action was taken in conformity with each nation's "constitutional processes":

ARTICLE IV

Each party recognizes that an armed attack in the Pacific area on any of the parties would be dangerous to its own peace and safety and declares that it would act to meet the common danger in accordance with its constitutional processes.

Any such armed attack and all measures taken as a result thereof shall be immediately reported to the Security Council of the United Nations. Such measures shall be terminated when the Security Council has taken the measures necessary to restore and maintain international peace and security.

ARTICLE V

For the purpose of Article IV, an armed attack on any of the parties is deemed to include an armed attack on the metropolitan territory of any of the parties, or on the island territories under its jurisdiction in the Pacific or on its armed forces, public vessels or aircraft in the Pacific.

ARTICLE VI

This Treaty does not affect and shall not be interpreted as affecting in any way the rights and obligations of the parties under the Charter of the United Nations or the responsibility of the United Nations for the maintenance of international peace and security.

ARTICLE VII

The parties hereby establish a Council, consisting of their Foreign Ministers or their Deputies, to consider matters concerning the implementation of this Treaty.

The Council should be so organized as to be able to meet at any time.

ARTICLE VIII

Pending the development of a more comprehensive system of regional security in the Pacific area and the development by the United Nations of more effective means to maintain international peace and security, the Council, established by Article VII, is authorized to maintain a consultative relationship with States, Regional Organizations, Associations of States or other authorities in the Pacific area in a position to further the purposes of this Treaty and to contribute to the security of that area.

ARTICLE IX

This Treaty shall be ratified by the parties in accordance with their respective constitutional processes. . . .

ARTICLE X

This Treaty shall remain in force indefinitely. Any party may cease to be a member of the Council established by Article VII one year after notice has been given to the Government of Australia, which will inform the Governments of the other parties of the deposit of such notice.

Pursuant to Article II, the members' foreign ministers form the ANZUS Council, which meets annually to discuss issues related to defense in the Pacific area.

Consequences

The United States suspended its ANZUS obligations to New Zealand in 1986 when that country banned visits by nuclear-powered or nuclear-armed ships. Australia, however, remains within ANZUS and, maintains a defense link with New Zealand, albeit outside the ANZUS framework.

Source

Avalon Project at the Yale Law School, "Security Treaty Between the United States, Australia, and New Zealand (ANZUS), September 1, 1951." Available online. URL: http://www.yale.edu/lawweb/avalon/intdip/usmulti/usmu002.htm. Accessed May 16, 2005.

UNITED STATES–SOUTH KOREA MUTUAL DEFENSE TREATY

TREATY AT A GLANCE

Completed
October 10, 1953, at Washington, D.C.

Signatories
United States and South Korea

Overview
This treaty followed the signing of the armistice ending the Korean War (July 27, 1953) and served to reassure South Korea that the United States would preserve its sovereignty and defend the nation against any future aggression.

Historical Background

Korea was a Japanese possession from 1910 to 1945. Following World War II, the Soviet Union administered the surrender of Japanese forces north of the 38th parallel in Korea, and the United States supervised the surrender in the south. The two wartime allies established a joint commission to form a provisional Korean government, very soon falling into dispute over the legitimacy of political groups—communist versus democratic—vying for control of Korea. Finally, in 1947 the United States asked the United Nations to attempt to unify the northern and southern halves of the country; instead, the 38th parallel became a permanent international boundary in 1948, separating the Western-leaning Republic of Korea in the South from the Communist Democratic People's Republic of Korea in the North.

By 1949 both the Soviet Union and the United States had withdrawn most of the occupation troops, leaving behind small advisory teams. North Korea, however, was far better prepared for war than the South, and sporadic border clashes broke out during 1949 and 1950. On June 25, 1950, North Korean forces invaded the South. The UN Security Council voted to act in defense of South Korea, and U.S. president Harry S. Truman committed U.S. military action—without a congressional declaration of war. By October 1, 1950, U.S.-dominated United Nations forces had pushed the North Koreans back across the 38th parallel and out of South Korea. Although Truman's National Security Council advised against advancing north of the 38th parallel, President Truman followed the advice of his military advisers, which was to keep advancing to the

north in order to destroy the North Korean army. This action provoked Communist China to join the war, and the augmented forces pushed the United Nations troops back to the south. The South Korean capital of Seoul fell for a second time.

General Douglas MacArthur, leading the U.S.-UN forces, asked for more troops to broaden the war. President Truman and the United Nations wished instead to limit the war in order to avoid the possibility of ultimate nuclear confrontation with the Soviets. Truman undertook an initiative to bring about a cease-fire, which MacArthur deliberately undermined by broadcasting a bellicose ultimatum to the enemy commander. This ultimately led to Truman's dismissal of MacArthur as supreme commander of the U.S.-UN forces. There followed a stalemate at the 38th parallel, from which grew armistice negotiations and the war's end.

To compensate South Korea for having abandoned its policy of reunification by force, the United States offered the Mutual Defense Treaty.

Terms

The treaty read as follows:

ARTICLE I
The parties undertake to settle any international disputes in which they may be involved by peaceful means . . .

ARTICLE II
The parties will consult together whenever, in the opinion of either of them, the political independence or security of either of the parties is threatened by external

armed attack. Separately and jointly, by self-help and mutual aid, the parties will maintain and develop appropriate means to deter armed attack and will take suitable measures in consultation and agreement to implement this Treaty and to further its purposes.

ARTICLE III
Each party recognizes that an armed attack in the Pacific area on either of the parties in territories now under their respective administrative control, or hereafter recognized by one of the parties as lawfully brought under the administrative control of the other, would be dangerous to its own peace and safety and declares that it would act to meet the common danger in accordance with its constitutional processes.

ARTICLE IV
The Republic of Korea grants, and the United States of America accepts, the right to dispose United States land, air and sea forces in and about the territory of the Republic of Korea as determined by mutual agreement.

ARTICLE V
This Treaty shall be ratified by the United States of America and the Republic of Korea in accordance with their respective constitutional processes . . .

ARTICLE VI
This Treaty shall remain in force indefinitely. Either party may terminate it one year after notice has been given to the other party.

United States ratification of the treaty (on November 17, 1954) was subject to an additional understanding:

That neither party is obligated, under Article III . . . to come to the aid of the other except in case of an external attack against such party; nor shall anything in the present Treaty be construed as requiring the United States to give assistance to Korea except in the event of an armed attack against territory which has been recognized by the United States as lawfully brought under the administrative control of the Republic of Korea.

Consequences

The treaty allowed the United States to avoid the possibility of entanglement in a civil war within South Korea or in a war initiated by South Korean aggression against the North. North Korea, left to develop an insular, nominally communist totalitarian state, managed by the end of the 20th century to develop a nuclear weapons program. Consequently, U.S. president George W. Bush, early in the 21st century, branded the country part of an "axis of evil," which he declared the ultimate enemy in his ill-defined global war on terror.

Source
Avalon Project at the Yale Law School, "Mutual Defense Treaty Between the United States and the Republic of Korea; October 1, 1953." Available online. URL: http://www.yale.edu/lawweb/avalon/diplomacy/korea/kor001.htm. Accessed May 16, 2005.

SOUTHEAST ASIA COLLECTIVE DEFENSE TREATY

TREATY AT A GLANCE

Completed
September 8, 1954, at Manila, the Philippines

Signatories
Australia, France, Great Britain, New Zealand, Pakistan,
the Philippines, Thailand, and United States

Overview
This treaty created the Southeast Asia Treaty Organization as a collective defense umbrella to shelter the signatories from (presumably communist) aggression. Under a special protocol, Cambodia, Laos, and South Vietnam were also protected.

Historical Background

President Harry S. Truman had set up the basic alliance system of the cold war. First having beefed up the United States national security apparatus by establishing a permanent Joint Chiefs of Staff, separating the air force from the U.S. Army and creating with it the nuclear-armed Strategic Air Command, and creating the CIA, Truman then entered into a series of regional pacts aimed at "containing" the Communist bloc within its current spheres of influence and guarding against the spread of communist ideology outside that bloc: the PACT OF RIO with Latin American nations in 1947; the NATO alliance in 1949 (see NORTH ATLANTIC TREATY); the ANZUS TREATY with Australia and New Zealand in 1951; and a defense treaty with Japan, also in 1951 (see JAPANESE–UNITED STATES SECURITY TREATY). As a result of this ideological commitment to contain communist "aggression" anywhere it might appear in the world, Truman found himself dragged into an undeclared and limited war in Korea, during which he was forced to fire Douglas MacArthur for insubordination and wrangled with Congress over the conflict's legality.

Dwight Eisenhower came into office in 1953 determined to end the Korean conflict, and he did. The war itself and the new administration brought some changes in U.S. diplomatic strategy. Believing that the cold war would be a long struggle, fearing that the greater danger was therefore not defeat on the battlefield but the temptation to spend the country to death in brushfire wars that would exhaust the public's will to continue fighting, Eisenhower announced that henceforth America would reserve the right to respond to aggression with "massive retaliatory power" at any place she so chose. That way, he and his secretary of state, John Foster Dulles, reasoned, the United States could balance a healthy domestic economy with the barest essentials in military force: its airborne nuclear threat. Cutting defense by 30 percent but beefing up Strategic Air Command, Eisenhower then continued Truman's search for regional pacts that would link the U.S. nuclear deterrence to countries ringing the entire Soviet bloc.

One such agreement would be the 1955 BAGHDAD PACT, which created what would become the Central Treaty Organization. Even before that, Eisenhower and Dulles had expanded NATO to include Greece and Turkey and would expand it further still (the same year the Baghdad Pact Organization was created) by including West Germany. In between, the French had suffered disastrous defeat in Indochina at the hands of communist forces, and Foster Dulles advocated the creation of SEATO, the Asian equivalent of Europe's collective defense body, NATO. Accordingly, a treaty was concluded, which, along with the others, completed the alliance system begun by Truman in 1947.

Terms

The SEATO signatories pledged collective action in the event of external aggression or internal subversion against any one of them. Economic cooperation was also provided for, but the principal thrust of the treaty was military, and specifically military defense against the forces of communism.

The parties to this Treaty,

Recognizing the sovereign equality of all the parties,

Reiterating their faith in the purposes and principles set forth in the Charter of the United Nations and their desire to live in peace with all peoples and all Governments,

Reaffirming that, in accordance with the Charter of the United Nations, they uphold the principle of equal rights and self-determination of peoples, and declaring that they will earnestly strive by every peaceful means to promote self-government and to secure the independence of all countries whose peoples desire it and are able to undertake its responsibilities,

Desiring to strengthen the fabric of peace and freedom and to uphold the principles of democracy, individual liberty and the rule of law, and to promote the economic well-being and development of all peoples in the treaty area,

Intending to declare publicly and formally their sense of unity, so that any potential aggressor will appreciate that the parties stand together in the area, and

Desiring further to coordinate their efforts for collective defense for the preservation of peace and security,

Therefore agree as follows:

ARTICLE I

The parties undertake, as set forth in the Charter of the United Nations, to settle any international disputes in which they may be involved by peaceful means in such a manner that international peace and security and justice are not endangered, and to refrain in their international relations from the threat or use of force in any manner inconsistent with the purposes of the United Nations.

ARTICLE II

In order more effectively to achieve the objectives of this Treaty, the parties, separately and jointly, by means of continuous and effective self-help and mutual aid will maintain and develop their individual and collective capacity to resist armed attack and to prevent and counter subversive activities directed from without against their territorial integrity and political stability.

ARTICLE III

The parties undertake to strengthen their free institutions and to cooperate with one another in the further development of economic measures, including technical assistance, designed both to promote economic progress and social well-being and to further the individual and collective efforts of Governments toward these ends.

ARTICLE IV

1. Each party recognizes that aggression by means of armed attack in the treaty area against any of the parties or against any State or territory which the parties by unanimous agreement may hereafter designate, would endanger its own peace and safety, and agrees that it will in that event act to meet the common danger in accordance with its constitutional processes. Measures taken under this paragraph shall be immediately reported to the Security Council of the United Nations.

2. If, in the opinion of any of the parties, the inviolability or the integrity of the territory or the sovereignty or political independence of any party in the treaty area or of any other State or territory to which the provisions of paragraph I of this Article

from time to time apply is threatened in any way other than by armed attack or is affected or threatened by any fact or situation which might endanger the peace of the area, the parties shall consult immediately in order to agree on the measures which should be taken for the common defense.

3. It is understood that no action on the territory of any State designated by unanimous agreement under paragraph I of this Article or on any territory so designated shall be taken except at the invitation or with the consent of the Government concerned.

ARTICLE V

The parties hereby establish a Council, on which each of them shall be represented, to consider matters concerning the implementation of this Treaty. The Council shall provide for consultation with regard to military and any other planning as the situation obtaining in the treaty area may from time to time require. The Council shall be so organized as to be able to meet at any time.

ARTICLE VI

This Treaty does not affect and shall not be interpreted as affecting in any way the rights and obligations of any of the parties under the Charter of the United Nations or the responsibility of the United Nations for the maintenance of international peace and security. Each party declares that none of the international engagements now in force between it and any other of the parties or any third party is in conflict with the provisions of this Treaty, and undertakes not to enter into any international engagement in conflict with this Treaty.

ARTICLE VII

Any other State in a position to further the objectives of this Treaty and to contribute to the security of the area may, by unanimous agreement of the parties, be invited to accede to this Treaty. . . .

ARTICLE VIII

As used in this Treaty, the "treaty area" is the general area of southeast Asia, including also the entire territories of the Asian parties, and the general area of the south-west Pacific not including the Pacific area north of 21 degrees 30 minutes north latitude. The parties may, by unanimous agreement, amend this Article to include within the treaty area the territory of any State acceding to this Treaty in accordance with Article VII or otherwise to change the treaty.

A special protocol extended the provisions of Articles 3 and 4 to Cambodia, Laos, and Vietnam:

The parties to the South-east Asia Collective Defense Treaty unanimously designate for the purposes of Article IV of the Treaty the States of Cambodia and Laos and the free territory under the jurisdiction of the State of Vietnam.

The parties further agree that the above-mentioned States and territory shall be eligible in respect of the economic measures contemplated by Article III.

This Protocol shall enter into force simultaneously with the coming into force of the Treaty.

Consequences

In contrast to NATO, SEATO failed to secure long-term military commitments from its members. Moreover, and critically, SEATO members were highly reluctant to support American intervention in the Vietnam War. Pakistan withdrew from SEATO in 1972, after the Indo-Pakistani War. Five years later, in 1977, SEATO was dissolved.

Source

Avalon Project at the Yale Law School, "Southeast Asia Collective Defense Treaty (Manila Pact), September 8, 1954." Available online. URL: http://www.yale.edu/lawweb/avalon/intdip/usmulti/usmu003.htm. Accessed May 16, 2005.

UNITED STATES–NATIONALIST CHINA MUTUAL DEFENSE TREATY

TREATY AT A GLANCE

Completed
December 2, 1954, at Washington, D.C.

Signatories
United States and the Republic of China (Nationalist China)

Overview
Following the 1954 attack by Communist (Mainland) China on the Nationalist-held islands of Quemoy (Jinmen) and Matsu (Mazu), the United States committed itself by treaty to the defense of Nationalist-held Taiwan (Formosa).

Historical Background

In 1949 the island of Taiwan (also called Formosa) became the refuge for the government-in-exile of the Republic of China, led by Chiang Kai-shek and his Nationalist Party (Kuomintang), following the final Communist victory on the vast mainland and the proclamation of the People's Republic of China. Immediately (and ever since), both Nationalist and Communist China claimed Taiwan as a province of China and sought its reunification—on very different terms—with the mainland.

Taiwan, which had been vastly modernized and industrialized during the long Japanese occupation of 1895–1945, flourished in the looming shadow of mainland China. When the strategically important islands of Quemoy and Matsu, held by the Nationalists but close to the mainland coast, were attacked in 1954, the United States agreed by treaty to come to Taiwan's aid in the event of armed attack.

Terms

Fulfillment of the United States's pledge under the treaty was subject to each nation's "constitutional processes" (a proviso meant to preempt the possibility of military intervention without Congressional approval). Nor was the United States absolutely obligated to defend Quemoy and Matsu. Moreover, the U.S. Senate modified the treaty with three "understandings" before ratifying it: first, the treaty was to have no bearing on the ultimate legal title to Taiwan, a provision that allowed the United States to avoid commitment to either side's claims in what amounted to a civil war; second, the United States would intervene only if the Nationalists acted in self-defense; third, the treaty would not automatically apply to the protection of additional territory without the consent of the Senate. Finally, although the treaty was slated to remain in force indefinitely, either "party may terminate it one year after notice has been given to the other party."

The parties to this Treaty,

Reaffirming their faith in the purposes and principles of the Charter of the United Nations and their desire to live in peace with all peoples and all Governments, and desiring to strengthen the fabric of peace in the West Pacific area,

Recalling with mutual pride the relationship which brought their two peoples together in a common bond of sympathy and mutual ideals to fight side by side against imperialist aggression during the last war,

Desiring to declare publicly and formally their sense of unity and their common determination to defend themselves against external armed attack, so that no potential aggressor could be under the illusion that either of them stands alone in the West Pacific area, and

Desiring further to strengthen their present efforts for collective defense for the preservation of peace and security pending the development of a more comprehensive system of regional security in the West Pacific area,

Have agreed as follows:

ARTICLE I

The parties undertake, as set forth in the Charter of the United Nations, to settle any international dispute in which they may be involved by peaceful means in such a manner that international peace, security and justice are not endangered and to refrain in their international relations from the threat or use of force in any manner inconsistent with the purposes of the United Nations.

ARTICLE II

In order more effectively to achieve the objective of this Treaty, the parties separately and jointly by self-help and mutual aid will maintain and develop their individual and collective capacity to resist armed attack and communist subversive activities directed from without against their territorial integrity and political stability.

ARTICLE III

The parties undertake to strengthen their free institutions and to cooperate with each other in the development of economic progress and social well-being and to further their individual and collective efforts toward these ends.

ARTICLE IV

The parties, through their Foreign Ministers or their deputies, will consult together from time to time regarding the implementation of this Treaty.

ARTICLE V

Each party recognizes that an armed attack in the West Pacific area directed against the territories of either of the parties would be dangerous to its own peace and safety and declares that it would act to meet the common danger in accordance with its constitutional processes.

Any such armed attack and all measures taken as a result thereof shall be immediately reported to the Security Council of the United Nations. Such measures shall be terminated when the Security Council has taken the measures necessary to restore and maintain international peace and security.

ARTICLE VI

For the purposes of Articles 11 and V, the terms 'territorial' and 'territories' shall mean in respect of the Republic of China, Taiwan and the Pescadores; and in respect of the United States of America, the island territories in the West Pacific under its jurisdiction. The provisions of Articles II and V will be applicable to such other territories as may be determined by mutual agreement.

ARTICLE VII

The Government of the Republic of China grants, and the Government of the United States of America accepts, the right to dispose such United States land, air and sea forces in and about Taiwan and the Pescadores as may be required for their defense, as determined by mutual agreement.

ARTICLE VIII

This Treaty does not affect and shall not be interpreted as affecting in any way the rights and obligations of the parties under the Charter of the United Nations or the responsibility of the United Nations for the maintenance of international peace and security.

ARTICLE IX

This Treaty shall be ratified by the United States of America and the Republic of China in accordance with their respective constitutional processes . . .

ARTICLE X

This Treaty shall remain in force indefinitely. Either party may terminate it one year after notice has been given to the other party.

Consequences

For decades the Nationalist Chinese lobby and right-wing members of Congress prevented even the thought that the United States might recognize the Chinese Communist government, which controlled the mainland. When Richard Nixon became president of the United States, he used his superb credentials as a conservative cold warrior to engineer such diplomatic recognition, which created something of a crisis in U.S.-Taiwanese relations. Since the 1970s Congress has repeatedly rejected any suggestion that the United States "abandon" Taiwan diplomatically to the mainland and the Chinese Communist government has on several occasions threatened the use of force to "reunite" the island with China proper.

Source

Avalon Project at the Yale Law School, "Mutual Defense Treaty Between the United States and the Republic of China, December 2, 1954." Available online. URL: http://www.yale.edu/lawweb/avalon/diplomacy/china/chin001.htm. Accessed May 16, 2005.

BAGHDAD PACT

TREATY AT A GLANCE

Completed
February 24, 1955, at Baghdad, Iraq

Signatories
Originally Turkey and Iraq, followed by Great Britain, Pakistan, Iran (signatories under the Central Treaty Organization [CENTO] were the United States, Great Britain, Turkey, Pakistan, and Iran)

Overview
Pushed by U.S. secretary of state John Foster Dulles as part of the American cold war policy of "containment" of communism, the Baghdad Pact was one in a series of regional alliances around the world aimed at checking the expansion of the Soviet bloc. With Great Britain's influence waning in the Middle East and Iraq withdrawing from the pact under pressure from other Arab states, the United States signed on to the agreement with the remaining four nations, using it as the basis for the Central Treaty Organization (CENTO).

Historical Background

Early in the cold war, Harry S. Truman developed the strategy of "containing" communism with a series of regional pacts linking the United States to countries either ringing the Soviet bloc or willing to work jointly to prevent the spread of Soviet influence. The first of these was the Pact of Rio in 1947, followed in 1949 by the NORTH ATLANTIC TREATY (NATO) alliance, and the ANZUS PACT with Australia and New Zealand in 1951, and supplemented by the 1951 JAPANESE–UNITED STATES SECURITY TREATY. Under President Dwight David Eisenhower, Secretary of State John Foster Dulles continued to follow the Truman Doctrine by completing the alliance system, negotiating the SOUTH-EAST ASIA COLLECTIVE DEFENSE TREATY (SEATO) in 1954 and pressing for a similar alliance in the Middle East, whose vast oil reserves had long fueled the economies of the free world.

The rivalries of the Arab states, however, made any attempt to incorporate them into an alliance cordoning off the Soviet Union impossible. In 1953, as an alternative, Dulles pushed hard to establish a "northern tier" alliance for the defense of Turkey, Iran, Iraq, Afghanistan, and Pakistan, which had by 1954 only resulted in the signing of a treaty alliance between Pakistan and Turkey.

Meanwhile, revolutions in Egypt and Iran provided a sense of urgency to the U.S. strategy. With British backing, the American CIA managed covertly to depose the vaguely marxist president of Iran, Dr. Mohammad Mossadegh, and return their callow client Shah Reza Pahlavi to the Peacock Throne, but in Egypt strongman Gamal Abdel Nasser took control after the ouster of the sybaritic and British-backed King Farouk and began touting land reform and closer ties to the Soviets. On February 24, 1955, Turkey entered into a treaty alliance with Iraq, and the British—awakened to dangers of "communist influence" in the region—signed on to that agreement in April 1955. Britain was followed by Pakistan, which signed the agreement in September, and then by the newly restored Shah of Iran, who acceded in October 1955. This series of alliances became known as the Baghdad Pact.

Terms

The treaty between Turkey and Iraq, which served as the "text" of the pact read in part:

> Whereas the friendly and brotherly relations existing between Iraq and Turkey are in constant progress, and in order to complement the contents of the Treaty of Friendship and Good Neighborhood concluded between His Majesty the King of Iraq and His Excellency the President of the Turkish Republic signed in Ankara on the 29th of March 1946, which recognized

the fact that peace and security between the two countries is an integral part of the peace and security of all
the nations of the world and in particular the nations
of the Middle East, and that it is the basis for their foreign policies.

Whereas Article II of the Treaty of Joint Defence
and Economic cooperation between the Arab League
States provides that no provision of that treaty shall in
any way affect, or is designed to affect, any of the
rights and obligations accruing to the Contracting Parties from the United Nations charter;

And having realized the great responsibilities borne
by them in their capacity as members of the United
Nations concerned with the maintenance of peace and
security in the Middle east region which necessitate
taking the required measures in accordance with Article 51 of the United Nations Charter . . . have agreed
as follows:

ARTICLE 1

Consistent with Article 51 of the United Nations Charter the High Contracting Parties will cooperate for
their security and defence. Such measures as they
agree to take to give effect to this cooperation may
form the subject of special agreements with each other.

ARTICLE 2

In order to ensure the realization and effect application
of the cooperation provided for in Article 1 above, the
competent authorities of the High Contracting Parties
will determine the measures to be taken as soon as the
present Pact enters into force. These measures will
become operative as soon as they have been approved
by the Governments of the High Contracting Parties.

ARTICLE 3

The High Contracting parties undertake to refrain
from any interference whatsoever in each other's internal affairs. They will settle any dispute between themselves in a peaceful way in accordance with the United
Nations Charter.

ARTICLE 4

The High Contracting Parties declare that the dispositions of the present Pact are not in contradiction with
any of the international obligations contracted by
either of them with any third State or States. They do
not derogate from, and cannot be interpreted as derogating from, the said international obligations. The
High Contracting Parties undertake not to enter into
any international obligation incompatible with the
present Pact.

ARTICLE 5

This Pact shall be open for accession to any Member
State of the Arab League or any other State actively
concerned with the security and peace in this region
and which is fully recognized by both of the High Contracting Parties. Accession shall come into force from
the date on which the instrument of accession of the
State concerned is deposited with the Ministry of Foreign Affairs of Iraq.

Any acceding State party to the present Pact may
conclude special agreements in accordance with Article 1, with one or more States parties to the present
Pact. The competent authority of any acceding State
may determine measures in accordance with Article 2.
These measures will become operative as soon as they
have been approved by the Governments of the parties
concerned.

ARTICLE 6

A Permanent Council at ministerial level with be set
up to function within the framework of the purposes
of this Pact when at least four Powers become parties
to the Pact.

The Council will draw up its own rules of
procedure.

ARTICLE 7

This Pact remains in force for a period of five years,
renewable for other five-year periods. Any Contracting
Party may withdraw from the Pact by notifying the
other parties in writing of its desire to do so, six
months before the expiration of any of the above-mentioned periods, in which case the Pact remains valid
for the other parties.

ARTICLE 8

[Ratification.]

With Great Britain, Pakistan, and Iran endorsing
the pact, it had became, incrementally, a Five Power
alliance—with one Arab member.

Consequences

By joining the alliance, Iraq's Hashemite royal house
risked the enmity of the other Arab states, especially
Egypt. Jordan's king, who wished to join the alliance
with his Hashemite kin, was more circumspect because
of the nationalist Arab opposition in Jordan, inspired
by Nasser's example. The United States, which stood
ready as ever to aid with guns and money, had not
signed the pact, out of its awareness of Britain's sensitivity to the waning British presence in the region.
Instead, the United States was content to leave security
in the region to its English "cousins," as the CIA called
them.

All of that changed, however, with the Suez Canal
Crisis of 1956. From the start, Nasser had ambitions to
become the major leader in the Middle East. Seeking
rapid development for Egypt, he made plans to construct the massive Aswan High Dam on the Nile as a
vehicle of economic expansion. He tried negotiating
financial backing for the dam with Britain and the
United States, but they were uneasy about his ties to
the Soviet bloc. When he signed an arms deal with
Czechoslovakia in 1956, Britain, the United States, and
consequently the World Bank withdrew from the project. Undaunted, Nasser nationalized the Suez Canal,

whose proceeds had previously gone to European bondholders, and announced that use fees would be dedicated to constructing the new dam, predicting they would pay for it in five years.

Fearing that the unpredictable Nasser might close the canal and cut off oil to Western Europe, Britain and France began making secret plans with Israel to take back control of the canal by force and, if possible, depose Nasser. When diplomatic efforts appeared unlikely to settle the crisis, they struck. Shortly after 10 Israeli brigades invaded Egypt on October 29, 1956, and routed Nasser's army, the two European nations, according to plan, demanded that both Israel and Egypt withdraw from the canal zone. They then announced that they intended to intervene and enforce the cease-fire already called for by the United Nations.

When Soviet Russia threatened to put a stop to the nonsense, and Eisenhower, furious with England, France, and Israel, indicated that he would let the Russians bomb them to kingdom come, if it came to that, first the French and the British, then the Israelis, meekly abandoned their adventure. Nasser emerged from the crisis not merely a victor but a national hero and leader of the so-called third world of nonaligned nations.

Britain's position in the Middle East was gravely weakened, and her chief and longtime Arab ally, Iraq, shared in the fall from grace. The United States openly replaced Britain as the major Western power operating in the region as Eisenhower proclaimed a new policy: America would support the independence and integrity of Middle Eastern states as a vital national interest. He promised armed support to resist aggression from "any country controlled by international communism," provided the president regarded it as necessary and such armed support was requested.

Meanwhile, as Nasser's reputation soared, he proceeded with the construction of the Aswan Dam, aided now by the Soviet Union, and he set out to realize yet another goal: the unification of Arab countries. The crisis for the Western diplomatic alignment of the Baghdad Pact broke in 1958. That year the government of Syria merged with Egypt to form the United Arab Republic, and on July 14, a revolution ousted Iraq's royal dynasty and its pro-Western, conservative government under Nuri al-Said. Fearing a revolution in their own country, as well, the Lebanese asked for American protection, and the U.S. Sixth Fleet landed marines in the Levant. At the same time, Britain sent troops to Jordan in response to King Hussein's appeal for help. Two weeks after the Iraqi revolution, the United States linked itself formally to the pact by executive agreements, and in March 1959 Iraq formally withdrew from the alliance. Now renamed the Central Treaty Organization, CENTO set up new headquarters in Ankara.

Nasser's bid to recruit all of the other Arab countries into the fold of the UAR was short-lived. Not only did the other nations fail to join, but Syria withdrew in 1961. Nevertheless, Egypt did become a haven for Arab radicals and anticolonial revolutionaries, as Nasser welcomed political refugees from other Arab countries. Even as he embraced foreign radicals, he cracked down on civil freedom in his own country. The end seemed to come in 1967, when Nasser called for the withdrawal of United Nations Emergency Force troops from the Gaza Strip and instituted a blockade of Eilat, precipitating a brilliant preemptive war by Israel that destroyed Egypt's air force on the ground. On June 9, 1967, Gamal Abdel Nasser appeared on Egyptian television to announce his resignation. Hundreds of thousands of Egyptians took to the streets to demonstrate their demand that Nasser remain in power. While some of the demonstrations may have been engineered by Nasser himself, undeniably some were spontaneous. A hard-liner against Israel and the West, supremely repressive at home, Nasser—until his death from a heart attack on September 28, 1970—remained the most popular and influential Arab leader in the world.

As for CENTO, when the cold war began to thaw in the late 1970s, Soviet relations with two CENTO powers, Iran and Turkey, became more relaxed as the USSR also extended economic aid, although never on the scale of the United States, whose vital interest in the region declaimed by the Eisenhower Doctrine would continue to lead to turmoil.

Source

Avalon Project at the Yale Law School, "Baghdad Pact, February 4, 1955." Available online. URL: http://www.yale.edu/lawweb/avalon/mideast/baghdad.htm. Accessed May 16, 2005.

WARSAW PACT

TREATY AT A GLANCE

Completed
May 14, 1955, at Warsaw, Poland

Signatories
Albania, Bulgaria, Hungary, German Democratic Republic
(East Germany), Poland, Romania, the Soviet Union,
and Czechoslovakia

Overview
The "Treaty of Friendship, Cooperation and Mutual Assistance," or
Warsaw Pact, created the Warsaw Treaty Organization, a military
alliance between the USSR and its Eastern European satellites as a
Communist counterpart to NATO.

Historical Background

The Korean conflict, with MacArthur's nuclear brinkmanship and Mao Zedong's Communist invasion, spooked Western Europe, especially after the United States, bogged down in a "police action" of questionable legality in what easily could have been considered a civil war, requested a sizable increase in Europe's contribution to NATO. In 1951 both the French and British governments fell over the issue, before a committee worked out a compromise distribution that spread the costs more equitably, or at least more acceptably.

The real solution was obvious, though none of the members wanted to face it: rearm West Germany. The French, traditionally nervous about Germans armed to the teeth, refused, unless the German army was merged into some kind of larger, international force. Called the European Defense Community (EDC), such a force had disturbing implications for Great Britain, especially, but also for some in France. It meant a common defense ministry, a coordinated foreign policy, a joint defense budget, maybe even a common parliament to approve the budgets and the policies. It meant, in short, a United States of Europe, whether one called it that or not. West Germany immediately ratified the EDC, but it was simply more than the British could stomach. Still clinging to visions of an empire on which the sun never set, proud now of their "special relationship" with their bastard child, the United States, the British opted out.

The French response was more nuanced. France had a strong Stalinist Communist Party, which opposed the EDC almost by reflex, while the haughty and mili-tary-minded, mostly right-wing Gaulists shuddered at the notion of merging their crack troops with the dregs of Europe in a hodgepodge security service. The French, as was their wont, argued endlessly about the subject till Stalin had died, the Korean war had come to a whimpering close, and all sense of urgency had dissipated. Then, despite American secretary of state John Foster Dulles's threats to institute an "agonizing reappraisal" of his country's commitment to postwar Europe, the French took a pass and voted down the EDC on August 30, 1954.

Undaunted, the United States came up with an eloquently simple alternative: NATO admitted West Germany into its alliance and put Allied commanders in charge of the Bundeswehr, the German army. The unhappy Soviets responded with a military alliance of their own between the USSR and its satellites in Eastern Europe. A week after West Germany entered NATO, the Soviet Union and its satellites, Albania, Bulgaria, Czechoslovakia, the German Democratic Republic (East Germany), Hungary, Poland, and Romania, formed the Warsaw Treaty Organization, though the Warsaw Pact was more like an accurate description of current conditions than a bold new move in the deadly chess game of the cold war.

Terms

The pact organization was a military alliance under the unified high command of a Soviet marshal, with headquarters in Moscow. All important posts within the satellite forces were held by Soviet-trained, if not

Soviet-born, officers. Equipment was standardized according to Soviet specifications.

~~✦~~

The Contracting Parties,

Reaffirming their desire to create a system of collective security in Europe based on the participation of all European States, irrespective of their social and political structure, whereby the said States may be enabled to combine their efforts in the interests of ensuring peace in Europe;

Taking into consideration, at the same time, the situation that has come about in Europe as a result of the ratification of the Paris Agreements, which provide for the constitution of a new military group in the form of a "West European Union", with the participation of a remilitarized West Germany and its inclusion in the North Atlantic bloc, thereby increasing the danger of a new war and creating a threat to the national security of peaceloving States;

Being convinced that in these circumstances the peace-loving States of Europe must take the necessary steps to safeguard their security and to promote the maintenance of peace in Europe;

Being guided by the purposes and principles of the Charter of the United Nations;

In the interests of the further strengthening and development of friendship, cooperation and mutual assistance in accordance with the principles of respect for the independence and sovereignty of States and of non-intervention in their domestic affairs;

Have resolved to conclude the present Treaty of Friendship, Cooperation and Mutual Assistance and have appointed as their plenipotentiaries . . . who have agreed as follows:

ARTICLE 1

The Contracting Parties undertake, in accordance with the Charter of the United Nations, to refrain in their international relations from the threat or use of force and to settle their international disputes by peaceful means in such a manner that international peace and security are not endangered.

ARTICLE 2

The Contracting Parties declare that they are prepared to participate, in a spirit of sincere cooperation, in all international action for ensuring international peace and security and will devote their full efforts to the realization of these aims.

In this connection, the Contracting Parties shall endeavor to secure, in agreement with other States desiring to cooperate in this matter, the adoption of effective measures for the general reduction of armaments and the prohibition of atomic, hydrogen and other weapons of mass destruction.

ARTICLE 3

The Contracting Parties shall consult together on all important international questions involving their common interests, with a view to strengthening international peace and security.

Whenever any one of the Contracting Parties considers that a threat of armed attack on one or more of the States parties to the Treaty has arisen, they shall consult together immediately with a view to providing for their joint defence and maintaining peace and security.

ARTICLE 4

In the event of an armed attack in Europe on one or more of the States parties to the Treaty by any State or group of States, each State party to the Treaty shall, in the exercise of the right of individual or collective self-defence, in accordance with Article 51 of the United Nations Charter, afford the State or States so attacked immediate assistance, individually and in agreement with the other States parties to the Treaty, by all the means it considers necessary, including the use of armed force. The States parties to the Treaty shall consult together immediately concerning the joint measures necessary to restore and maintain international peace and security.

Measures taken under this Article shall be reported to the Security Council in accordance with the provisions of the United Nations Charter. These measures shall be discontinued as soon as the Security Council takes the necessary action to restore and maintain international peace and security.

ARTICLE 5

The Contracting Parties have agreed to establish a Unified Command, to which certain elements of their armed forces shall be allocated by agreement between the parties, and which shall act in accordance with jointly established principles. The parties shall likewise take such other concerted action as may be necessary to reinforce their defensive strength, in order to defend the peaceful labor of their peoples, guarantee the inviolability of their frontiers and territories and afford protection against possible aggression.

ARTICLE 6

For the purpose of carrying out the consultations provided for in the present Treaty between the States parties thereto, and for the consideration of matters arising in connection with the application of the present Treaty, a Political Consultative Committee shall be established, in which each State party to the Treaty shall be represented by a member of the Government or by some other specially appointed representative.

The Committee may establish such auxiliary organs as may prove to be necessary.

ARTICLE 7

The Contracting Parties undertake not to participate in any coalitions or alliances, and not to conclude any agreements, the purposes of which are incompatible with the purposes of the present Treaty.

The Contracting Parties declare that their obligations under international treaties at present in force are not incompatible with the provisions of the present Treaty.

ARTICLE 8

The Contracting Parties declare that they will act in a spirit of friendship and cooperation to promote the further development and strengthening of the economic and cultural ties among them, in accordance with the principles of respect for each other's independence and sovereignty and of non-intervention in each other's domestic affairs.

ARTICLE 9

The present Treaty shall be open for accession by other States, irrespective of their social and political structure, which express their readiness by participating in the present Treaty, to help in combining the efforts of the peaceloving States to ensure the peace and security of the peoples. Such accessions shall come into effect with the consent of the States parties to the Treaty after the instruments of accession have been deposited with the Government of the Polish People's Republic.

ARTICLE 10

The present Treaty shall be subject to ratification, and the instruments of ratification shall be deposited with the Government of the Polish People's Republic.

The Treaty shall come into force on the date of deposit of the last instrument of ratification. The Government of the Polish People's Republic shall inform the other States parties to the Treaty of the deposit of each instrument of ratification.

ARTICLE 11

The present Treaty shall remain in force for twenty years. For Contracting Parties which do not, one year before the expiration of that term, give notice of termination of the Treaty to the Government of the Polish People's Republic, the Treaty shall remain in force for a further ten years.

In the event of the establishment of a system of collective security in Europe and the conclusion for that purpose of a General European Treaty concerning collective security, a goal which the Contracting Parties shall steadfastly strive to achieve, the present Treaty shall cease to have effect as from the date on which the General European Treaty comes into force.

Done at Warsaw, this fourteenth day of May 1955, in one copy, in the Russian, Polish, Czech and German languages, all the texts being equally authentic. Certified copies of the present Treaty shall be transmitted by the Government of the Polish People's Republic to all the other parties to the Treaty.

Consequences

Hungary withdrew from the Warsaw Pact in 1956 but was compelled to return after the Soviets crushed the Hungarian revolt. Likewise, in 1968 Czechoslovakia withdrew but was forced back by an invasion by Soviet-led Warsaw Pact forces. Albania withdrew the same year, having concluded an alliance with China, which had drifted away from Soviet domination.

It was the end of the cold war and the concomitant creation of democratic governments throughout much of Eastern Europe that finally undid the Warsaw Treaty Organization. Hungary again withdrew in 1990, and the reunification of Germany put an end to East Germany's participation. Other former satellites agitated for withdrawal of Soviet forces from their territory, and the organization's military function officially ended on April 1, 1991. It continued to function briefly as a political entity but was formally dissolved at a meeting in Prague on July 1.

Source

Avalon Project at the Yale Law School, "The Warsaw Security Pact: May 14, 1955." Available online. URL: http://www.yale.edu/lawweb/avalon/intdip/soviet/warsaw.htm. Accessed May 16, 2005.

TREATY OF MUTUAL COOPERATION AND SECURITY BETWEEN THE UNITED STATES AND JAPAN

TREATY AT A GLANCE

Completed
January 19, 1960, at Washington, D.C.

Signatories
United States and Japan

Overview
This treaty supplanted the Japanese–United States Security Treaty of 1951, reducing the American military presence in Japan, removing derogations of Japanese sovereignty, and acknowledging that Japanese forces could be used only in self-defense.

Historical Background

As Japan recovered economically from World War II, Japanese politicians made passionate pleas for a revision of the JAPANESE–UNITED STATES SECURITY TREATY of 1951. Issues that motivated the call for revision included the desire to reestablish national sovereignty in full, to be treated by the nations of the world as an equal, and to obtain some gesture acknowledging that the Japanese people had been the victims of nuclear attack.

Terms

The new treaty substantially reduced the number of U.S. military personnel stationed in Japan, although the United States was assured of its continued right to operate bases for its naval, land, and air forces on Japanese soil. The new treaty affirmed Japan's sovereignty, removing any and all derogations of that sovereignty contained in or implied by the earlier treaty. Finally, the 1960 document acknowledged that Japanese forces could be used only in self-defense. The earlier treaty had left this issue vague by citing Japan's obligations under the UNITED NATIONS CHARTER. The implication was that Japan could be called upon to participate in a military action mandated by the United Nations, even if such action did not strictly involve self-defense.

The treaty, in part, read:

ARTICLE I

The parties undertake, as set forth in the Charter of the United Nations, to settle any international disputes in which they may be involved by peaceful means in such a manner that international peace and security and justice are not endangered and to refrain in their international relations from the threat or use of force against the territorial integrity or political independence of any State, or in any other manner inconsistent with the purposes of the United Nations.

The parties will endeavor in concert with other peace-loving countries to strengthen the United Nations so that its mission of maintaining international peace and security may be discharged more effectively.

ARTICLE II

The parties will contribute toward the further development of peaceful and friendly international relations by strengthening their free institutions, by bringing about a better understanding of the principles upon which these institutions are founded, and by promoting conditions of stability and well-being. They will seek to eliminate conflict in their international economic policies and will encourage economic collaboration between them.

ARTICLE III

The parties, individually and in cooperation with each other, by means of continuous and effective self-help and mutual aid, will maintain and develop, subject to their constitutional provisions, their capacities to resist armed attack.

ARTICLE IV

The parties will consult together from time to time regarding the implementation of this Treaty, and, at the request of either party, whenever the security of Japan or international peace and security in the Far East is threatened.

ARTICLE V

Each party recognizes that an armed attack against either party in the territories under the administration of Japan would be dangerous to its own peace and safety and declares that it would act to meet the common danger in accordance with its constitutional provisions and processes.

Any such armed attack and all measures taken as a result thereof shall be immediately reported to the Security Council of the United Nations in accordance with the provisions of Article 51 of the Charter. Such measures shall be terminated when the Security Council has taken the measures necessary to restore and maintain international peace and security.

ARTICLE VI

For the purpose of contributing to the security of Japan and the maintenance of international peace and security in the Far East, the United States of America is granted the use by its land, air and naval forces of facilities and areas in Japan.

The use of these facilities and areas as well as the status of the United States armed forces in Japan shall be governed by a separate agreement, replacing the Administrative Agreement under Article III of the Security Treaty between the United States of America and Japan, signed at Tokyo on February 28, 1952, as amended, and by such other arrangement as may be agreed upon.

This, the use of bases in Japan and its islands and the deployment of U.S. troops and equipment in Japan, was touchy enough to require an exchanges of notes clarifying each side's understanding of Article 6. Japan wrote concerning her understanding of the implementation of Article 6:

> Major changes in the deployment into Japan of United States armed forces, major changes in their equipment, and the use of facilities and areas in Japan as bases for military combat operations to be undertaken from Japan other than those conducted under Article V of [the] Treaty, shall be the subjects of prior consultation with the Government of Japan.

Further arrangements were then made under Article 6, touching not merely upon the implementation of Article 6 but upon the ultimate fate of those "facilities and areas," i.e., American bases in Japan under discussion. These read in part:

> 2. At the request of either Government, the Governments of the United States and Japan shall review such arrangements and may agree that such facilities and

areas shall be returned to Japan or that additional facilities and areas shall be returned to Japan or that additional facilities and areas may be provided.

> 3. The facilities and areas used by the United States armed forces shall be returned to Japan whenever they are no longer needed for purposes of this Agreement, and the United States agrees to keep the needs for facilities and areas under continual observation with a view toward such return. . . .

That settled, more or less, the rest of the original text read:

ARTICLE VII

This Treaty does not affect and shall not be interpreted as affecting in any way the rights and obligations of the parties under the CHarter of the United Nations or the responsibility of the United Nations for the maintenance of international peace and security.

ARTICLE VIII

This Treaty shall be ratified by the United States of America and Japan in accordance with their respective constitutional processes. . . .

ARTICLE IX

The Security Treaty between the United States and Japan signed at the city of San Francisco on September 8, 1851 shall expire upon the entering into force of this Treaty.

ARTICLE X

This Treaty shall remain in force until in the opinion of the Governments of the United States and Japan there shall have come into force such United Nations arrangements as will satisfactorily provide for the maintenance of peace and security in the Japan area.

However, after the Treaty has been in force for ten years, either party may give notice to the other party of its intention to terminate the Treaty, in which case the Treaty shall terminate one year after such notice has been given. . . .

Finally the two powers appended to the treaty the following:

Agreed Minute to the Treaty of Mutual Cooperation and Security

Japanese plenipotentiary:
While the question of the status of the islands administered by the United States under Article 3 of the Treaty of Peace with Japan has not been made a subject of discussion in the course of treaty negotiations, I would like to emphasize the strong concern of the Government of Japan for the safety of the people of these islands since Japan possesses residual sovereignty over these islands. If an armed attack occurs or is threatened against these islands, the two countries will of course consult together closely under Article IV of the Treaty of Mutual Cooperation and Security. In event of an armed attack, it is the intention of the Government of

Japan to explore with the United States measures which it might be able to take for the welfare of the islanders.

United States plenipotentiary:
In the event of an armed attack against these islands, the United States Government will consult at once with the Government of Japan and intends to take the necessary measures for the defense of these islands, and to do its utmost to secure the welfare of the islanders.

Consequences

Protected from worry of foreign intervention and from the necessity to invest capital, needed to rebuild its industrial base, in wasteful defense spending, Japan had created an economy that by the 1950s was ready to take off. And it did, making Japan an economic powerhouse and the Pacific Rim as a whole a region of economic expansion and growth. Although a slump late in the century slowed the overheated economies of eastern Asia considerably, they—Japan supreme among them—remained strong and potentially vibrant pieces of the increasingly internationalized world trade.

Source
American Information Web, "Treaty of Mutual Cooperation and Security between Japan and the United States of America." Available online. URL: http://usinfo.org/law/majorlaws/anpo.html. Accessed May 16, 2005.

Peace Treaties and Truces

KOREAN WAR ARMISTICE

TREATY AT A GLANCE

Completed
July 27, 1953, at Panmunjom, Korea (present-day North Korea)

Signatories
United Nations command and North Korea and China

Overview
Concluded between the United Nations Command and North Korea and China (without the participation of South Korea), the armistice ended the shooting in the Korean War, dividing North and South along the 38th parallel.

Historical Background

Negotiations toward an armistice in the Korean conflict began late in June 1951, when the Soviets proposed a conference between the belligerents. The countries participating in the United Nations forces wanted to end the fighting, then resolve political questions in a postwar international conference. The Communists, however, insisted that the political questions be resolved in the process of negotiating a cease-fire. The latter course was adopted, causing the armistice talks to drag on for two years.

When the talks formally began on July 10, 1951, Vice Admiral C. Turner Joy represented the UN command, and North Korean general Nam Il represented the Communists. Only after days of argument, on July 26, was agreement reached on a four-point agenda: establishing a demarcation line and demilitarized zone, supervising the truce, arranging for the exchange of prisoners of war, and making recommendations to the governments involved in the war. From that point on, the talks were beset by problems, delays, arguments, and suspensions.

After many months, only one obstacle to truce remained: the handling of prisoners of war. The United Nations insisted that prisoners be allowed to decide themselves whether or not they would return home, whereas the Communists wanted forced repatriation. At last, in April 1953 the deadlock was broken by a compromise that permitted prisoners to choose sides under supervision of a neutral commission.

At this point, however, South Korean president Syngman Rhee, outraged by the prospect of a settlement that did not bring about the reunification of Korea, attempted to torpedo the proceedings on June 18 by releasing some 25,000 North Korean prisoners who wanted to live in the South. To salve Rhee, the United States agreed to the UNITED STATES–SOUTH KOREA MUTUAL DEFENSE TREATY, long-term economic aid, and other concessions. The July 27, 1953, armistice was signed, however, without the participation of South Korea.

Terms

The major provisions of the armistice were:

ARTICLE I: MILITARY DEMARCATION LINE
AND DEMILITARIZED ZONE

1. A military demarcation line shall be fixed and both sides shall withdraw two (2) kilometers from this line so as to establish a militarized zone between the opposing forces. A demilitarized zone shall be established as a buffer zone to prevent the occurrence of incidents which might lead to a resumption of hostilities.

2. The military demarcation line is located on the attached map . . .

24. The general mission of the Military Armistice Commission shall be to supervise the implementation of this Armistice Agreement and to settle through negotiations any violations of this Armistice Agreement. . . .

742

Point 36 established the Neutral Nations Supervisory Commission to administer the truce. The document later continued:

ARTICLE III: ARRANGEMENTS
RELATING TO PRISONERS OF WAR.

51. The release and repatriation of prisoners of war held in the custody of each side at the time this Armistice Agreement becomes effective shall be effected in conformity with the following provisions agreed upon by both sides prior to the signing of this Agreement.

(a) Within sixty (60) days after this Armistice Agreement becomes effective, each side shall, without offering any hindrance, directly repatriate and hand over in groups all those prisoners of war in its custody who insist on repatriation to the side to which they belonged at the time of the capture. Repatriation shall be accomplished in accordance with the related provisions of this Article. In order to expedite the repatriation process of such personnel, each side shall, prior to the signing of the Armistice Agreement, exchange the total numbers, by nationalities, of personnel to be directly repatriated. Each group of prisoners of war delivered to the other side shall be accompanied by rosters, prepared by nationality, to include name, rank (if any) and internment or military serial number.

(b) Each side shall release all those remaining prisoners of war, who are not directly repatriated, from its military control and from its custody and hand them over to the Neutral Nations Repatriation Commission for disposition in accordance with the provisions in the Annex hereto "Terms of Reference for Neutral Nations Repatriation Commission" . . .

ARTICLE IV: RECOMMENDATION TO THE GOVERNMENTS CONCERNED ON BOTH SIDES.

60. In order to ensure the peaceful settlement of the Korean question, the Military Commanders of both sides hereby recommend to the Governments of the countries concerned on both sides that, within three (3) months after the Armistice Agreement is signed and becomes effective, a political conference of a higher level of both sides be held by representatives appointed respectively to settle through negotiation the questions of the withdrawal of all foreign forces from Korea, the peaceful settlement of the Korean question, etc.

Consequences

Discussions in Geneva, Switzerland, were set up to decide the political issues, but the two nations have yet to be reunified, and the military situation in North and South Korea remains potentially explosive.

Source

Korean War Web site, "The Armistice Agreement." Available online. URL: http://Koreanwar.com/ArmisticeAgreement.html. Accessed May 16, 2005.

GENEVA AGREEMENTS OF 1954

TREATY AT A GLANCE

Completed
July 15, 1954, at Geneva, Switzerland

Signatories
France, Great Britain, the United States, the Soviet Union, the People's Republic of China, the Democratic Republic of Vietnam (North Vietnam), the State of Vietnam (South Vietnam), Laos, and Cambodia

Overview
When the United States refused to rescue the French after their colonial war in Indochina turned sour and desperate in 1954, France agreed to meet in Geneva, where French Southeast Asia not only was partitioned but more or less became the responsibility of the Americans, thus setting the stage for the Vietnam War.

Historical Background

At the end of World War II, Europe's old colonial powers expelled the Japanese from South Asia only to find themselves faced with a wave of indigenous national liberation movements. In Malaya the British fought a successful counterinsurgency against communist guerrillas, but the Dutch were much less fortunate in Indonesia, where they were forced to grant the country independence in 1949. In Indochina the French waged a prolonged, painful, and ultimately failed war with the Communist Vietminh. When the French army found itself surrounded and desperate at Dien Bien Phu in 1954, Paris appealed to the United States for help, specifically for air support.

By that time the cold war colored every aspect of American foreign policy, and U.S. diplomats and policy makers certainly viewed the insurgency in French Indochina as part of the Moscow-backed, worldwide Communist campaign to undermine the West's liberal democracies and take control everywhere they could. Thus, for the first time, American leaders began talking about Indochina as a domino. If it fell, they reasoned, so would topple the rest of Southeast Asia into the Communist camp. Despite the one-day-to-be-infamous Domino Theory, U.S. president Dwight David Eisenhower was reluctant to send American troops into Asian jungles, to arrogate—as Truman had in Korea—war-making powers to the Oval Office, or to sacrifice such a cold war asset as the U.S. reputation for being basically an anti-imperialist nation on the altar of French desire. Besides, neither he nor the American public wanted another Korea.

Instead, then, the United States came out in support of partitioning Indochina as the best strategy to "contain" the Vietminh. A new French premier, promising peace, replaced de Gaulle, and Pierre Mendès-France, upon assuming office, agreed to meet in Geneva and work out some kind of accord.

Terms

In a kind of diplomatic farce, various states attending the Geneva Conference of 1954 did not recognize others: the United States, for example, did not recognize as legitimate the People's Republic of China, nor the French the Vietminh government. There they were, nevertheless, negotiating the 10 documents that went to make up three military agreements, six unilateral declarations, and a "Final Declaration" as follows:

Final Declaration of the Geneva Conference on the Problem of Restoring Peace in Indo-China

In Which the Representatives of Cambodia, the Democratic Republic of Viet Nam, France, Laos, the People's Republic of China, the State of Viet Nam, the Union of Soviet Socialist Republics, the United Kingdom and the United States of America Took Part

1. The Conference takes note of the agreements ending hostilities in Cambodia, Laos and Viet Nam and organizing international control and the supervision of the execution of the provisions of these agreements.

2. The Conference expresses satisfaction at the ending of hostilities in Cambodia, Laos and Viet Nam; the Conference expresses its conviction that the execution of the provisions set out in the present Declaration and in the agreements on the cessation of hostilities will permit Cambodia, Laos and Viet Nam henceforth to play their part, in full independence and sovereignty, in the peaceful community of nations.

3. The Conference takes note of the declarations made by the Governments of Cambodia and of Laos of their intention to adopt measures permitting all citizens to take their place in the national community, in particular by participating in the next general elections, which, in conformity with the constitution of each of these countries, shall take place in the course of the year 1955, by secret ballot and in conditions of respect for fundamental freedoms.

4. The Conference takes note of the clauses in the agreement on the cessation of hostilities in Viet Nam prohibiting the introduction into Viet Nam of foreign troops and military personnel as well as of all kinds of arms and munitions. The Conference also takes note of the declarations made by the Governments of Cambodia and Laos of their resolution not to quest foreign aid, whether in war material, in personnel or in instructors except for the purpose of the effective defence of their territory and, in the case Laos, to the extent defined by the agreements on the cessation of hostilities in Laos.

5. The Conference takes note of the causes in the agreement on the cessation hostilities in Viet Nam to the effect that no military base under the control of a foreign State may be established in the regrouping zones of the two parties, the latter having the obligation to see that the zones allotted to them shall not constitute part of any military alliance and shall be utilized for the resumption of hostilities or in the service of an aggressive policy. The Conference also takes note of the declarations of the Governments of Cambodia and Laos to the effect that they will not join in any agreement with other States if this agreement includes the obligation to participate in a military alliance not in conformity with the principles of the Charter of the United Nations or, in the case of Laos, with the principles of the agreement on the cessation of hostilities in Laos or, so long as their security is not threatened, the obligation to establish bases on Cambodian-Laotian territory for the military of foreign Powers.

6. The Conference recognizes that the essential purpose of the agreement relating to Viet Nam is to settle military questions with a view to ending hostilities and that the military demarcation line is provisional and should not in any way be interpreted as constituting a political or territorial boundary. The Conference expresses its conviction that the execution of the provisions set out in the present Declaration and in the agreement on the cessation of hostilities creates the necessary basis for the achievement in the near future of a political settlement in Viet Nam.

7. The Conference declares that, so far as Viet Nam is concerned, the settlement of political problems, effected on the basis of respect for the principles of independence, unity and territorial integrity, shall permit the Vietnamese people to enjoy the fundamental freedoms, guaranteed by democratic institutions established as a result of free general elections by secret ballot. In order to ensure that sufficient progress in the restoration of peace has been made, and that all the necessary conditions obtain for free expression of the national will, general elections shall be held in July 1956, under the supervision of an international commission composed of representatives of the Member States of the International Supervisory Commission, referred to in the agreement on the cessation of hostilities. Consultations will be held on this subject between the competent representative authorities of the two zones from July 20, 1955, onwards.

8. The provisions of the agreements on the cessation of hostilities intended to ensure the protection of individuals and of property must be most strictly applied and must, in particular, allow everyone in Viet Nam to decide freely in which zone he wishes to live.

9. The competent representative authorities of the Northern and Southern zones of Viet Nam, as well as the authorities of Laos and Cambodia, must not permit any individual or collective reprisals against persons who have collaborated in any way with one of the parties during the war, or against members of such persons' families.

10. The Conference takes note of the declaration of the Government of the French Republic to the effect that it is ready to withdraw its troops from the territory of Cambodia, Laos and Viet Nam, at the request of the Governments concerned and within periods which shall be fixed by agreement between the parties except in the cases where, by agreement between the two parties, a certain number of French troops shall remain at specified points and for a specified time.

11. The Conference takes note of the declaration of the French Government to the effect that for the settlement of all the problems connected with the re-establishment and consolidation of peace in Cambodia, Laos and Viet Nam, the French Government will proceed from the principle of respect for the independence and sovereignty, unity and territorial integrity of Cambodia, Laos and Viet Nam.

12. In their relations with Cambodia, Laos and Viet Nam, each member of the Geneva Conference undertakes to respect the sovereignty, the independence, the unity and the territorial integrity of the above-mentioned States, and to refrain from any interference in their internal affairs.

13. The members of the Conference agree to consult one another on any question which may be referred to them by the International Supervisory Commission, in order to study such measures as may prove necessary to ensure that the agreements on the cessation of hostilities in Cambodia, Laos and Viet Nam are respected.

Document No. 3: AGREEMENT ON THE CESSATION OF HOSTILITIES IN CAMBODIA, 20 JULY 1954

Chapter I: Principles and Conditions Governing Execution of the Ceasefire

ARTICLE 1
As from twenty-third July, 1954, at 0800 hours (Peking mean time) complete cessation of all hostilities throughout Cambodia shall be ordered and enforced by the Commanders of the Armed Forces of the two parties for all troops and personnel of the land, naval and air forces under their control.

ARTICLE 2
In conformity with the principle of a simultaneous ceasefire throughout Indo-China, there shall be a simultaneous cessation of hostilities throughout Cambodia, in all the combat areas and for all the forces of the two parties.

To obviate any mistake or misunderstanding and to ensure that both the end of hostilities and all other operations arising from cessation of hostilities are in fact simultaneous . . .

NHIEK TIOULONG,
General

For the Commander-in-Chief of the Units of the Khmer Resistance Forces and for the Commander-in-Chief of the Vietnamese Military Units:

TA-QUANG-BUU,
Vice-Minister of National Defence
of the Democratic Republic of Viet Nam

Document No. 4: AGREEMENT ON THE CESSATION OF HOSTILITIES IN LAOS, 20 JULY 1954

For the Commander-in-Chief of the forces of the French Union Forces in Indo-China:

DELTEIL,
Brigadier-General

For the Commander-in-Chief of the fighting units of "Pathet-Laos" and for the Commander-in-Chief of the People's Army of Viet Nam

TA-QUANG-BUU,
Vice-Minister of National Defence
of the Democratic Republic of Viet Nam

Document No. 5: AGREEMENT ON THE CESSATION OF HOSTILITIES IN VIET NAM, 20 JULY 1954

Chapter I: Provisional Military Demarcation Line and Demilitarized Zone

ARTICLE 1

A provisional military demarcation line shall be fixed, on either side of which the forces of the two parties shall be regrouped after their withdrawal, the forces of the People's Army of Viet Nam to the north of the line and the forces of the French Union to the south.

The provisional military demarcation line is fixed as shown on the map attached . . .

It is also agreed that a demilitarized zone shall be established on either side of the demarcation line, to a width of not more than 5 km from it, to act as a buffer zone and avoid any incidents which might result in the resumption of hostilities.

ARTICLE 2

The period within which the movement of all forces of either party into the regrouping zone on either side of the provisional military demarcation line shall be completed shall not exceed three hundred (300) days from the date of the present Agreement's entry into force. . . .

Chapter III: Ban on the Introduction of Fresh Troops, Military Personnel, Arms and Munitions. Military Bases . . .

ARTICLE 16

With effect from the date of entry into force of the present Agreement, the introduction into Viet Nam of any troop reinforcements and additional military personnel is prohibited. . .

ARTICLE 18

With effect from the date of entry into force of the present Agreement, the establishment of new military bases is prohibited throughout Viet Nam territory.

ARTICLE 19

With effect from the date of entry into force of the present Agreement, no military base under the control of a foreign State may be established in the regrouping zone of either party; the two parties shall ensure that the zones assigned to them do not adhere to any military alliance and are not used for the resumption of hostilities or to further an aggressive policy . . .

ARTICLE 25

The Commanders of the Forces of the two parties shall afford full protection and all possible assistance and cooperation to the Joint Commission and its joint groups and to the International Commission and its inspection teams in the performance of the functions and tasks assigned to them by the present Agreement . . .

ARTICLE 27

The signatories of the present Agreement and their successors in their functions shall be responsible for ensuring the observance and enforcement of the terms and provisions thereof. The Commanders of the Forces of the two parties shall, within their respective commands, take all steps and make all arrangements necessary to ensure full compliance with all the provisions of the present Agreement by all elements and military personnel under their command.

The procedures laid down in the present Agreement shall, whenever necessary, be studied by the Commanders of the two parties and, if necessary, defined more specifically by the Joint Commission.

Chapter VI: Joint Commission and International Commission for Supervision and Control in Viet Nam . . .

ARTICLE 28

Responsibility for the execution of the agreement on the cessation of hostilities shall rest with the parties.

ARTICLE 29

An International Commission shall ensure the control and supervision of this execution.

ARTICLE 30

In order to facilitate, under the condition shown below, the execution of provisions concerning joint actions by die two parties, a Joint Commission shall be set up in Viet Nam.

For the Commander-in-Chief of the French Union Forces in Indo-China:

DELTEIL,
Brigadier-General

For the Commander-in-Chief of the People's Army of Viet Nam:
TA-QUANG-BUU,
Vice-Minister of National Defence

Document No. 6: DECLARATION BY THE ROYAL GOVERNMENT OF CAMBODIA, 21 JULY 1954

(Reference: Article 3 of the Final Declaration)
The Royal Government of Cambodia.

In the desire to ensure harmony and agreement among the peoples of the Kingdom,

Declares itself resolved to take the necessary measures to integrate all citizens, without discrimination, into the national community and to guarantee them the enjoyment of the rights and freedoms for which the Constitution of the Kingdom provides. . . .

Document No. 7: DECLARATION BY THE ROYAL GOVERNMENT OF LAOS, 21 JULY 1954

(Reference: Article 3 of the Final Declaration)
The Royal Government of Laos,

In the desire to ensure harmony and agreement among the peoples of the Kingdom,

Declares itself resolved to take the necessary measures to integrate all citizens, without discrimination, into the national community and to guarantee them the enjoyment of the rights and freedoms for which the Constitution of the Kingdom provides;

Affirms that all Laotian citizens may freely participate as electors or candidates in general elections by secret ballot. . . .

Document No. 8: DECLARATION BY THE ROYAL GOVERNMENT OF CAMBODIA, 21 JULY 1954

(Reference: Articles 4 and 5 of the Final Declaration)
The Royal Government of Cambodia is resolved never to take part in an aggressive policy and never to permit the territory of Cambodia to be utilized, in the service of such a policy.

The Royal Government of Cambodia will not join in any agreement with other States, if this agreement carries for Cambodia the obligation to enter into military alliance not in conformity with the principles of the Charter of the United Nations, or, as long as its security is not threatened, the obligation to establish bases on Cambodian territory for the military forces of foreign Powers.

The Royal Government of Cambodia is resolved to settle its international disputes by peaceful means, in such a manner as not to endanger peace, international security and justice.

During the period which will elapse between the date of the cessation of hostilities in Viet Nam and that of the final settlement of political problems in this country, the Royal Government of Cambodia will not solicit foreign aid in war material, personnel or instructors except for the purpose of the effective defence of the territory.

Document No. 9: DECLARATION BY THE ROYAL GOVERNMENT OF LAOS, 21 JULY 1954

(Reference: Articles 4 and 5 of the Final Declaration)
The Royal Government of Laos is resolved never to pursue a policy of aggression and will never permit the territory of Laos to be used in furtherance of such a policy.

The Royal Government of Laos will never join in any agreement with other States if this agreement includes the obligation for the Royal Government of Laos to participate in a military alliance not in conformity with the principles of the Charter of the United Nations or with the principles of the agreement on the cessation of hostilities or, unless its security is threatened, the obligation to establish bases on Laotian territory for military forces of foreign Powers.

The Royal Government of Laos is resolved to settle its international disputes by peaceful means so that international peace and security and justice are not endangered.

During the period between the cessation of hostilities in Viet Nam and the final settlement of that country's political problems, the Royal Government of Laos will not request foreign aid, whether in war material, in personnel or in instructors, except for the purpose of its effective territorial defence and to the extent defined by the agreement on the cessation of hostilities.

Document No. 10: DECLARATION BY THE GOVERNMENT OF THE FRENCH REPUBLIC, 21 JULY 1954

(Reference: Article 10 of the Final Declaration)
The Government of the French Republic declares that it is ready to withdraw its troops from the territory of Cambodia, Laos and Viet Nam, at the request of the Governments concerned and within a period which shall be fixed by agreement between the parties, except in the cases where, by agreement between the two parties, a certain number of French troops shall remain at specified points and for a specified time.

Document No. 11: DECLARATION BY THE GOVERNMENT OF THE FRENCH REPUBLIC, 21 JULY 1954

(Reference: Article 11 of the Final Declaration)
For the settlement of all the problems connected with the reestablishment and consolidation of peace in Cambodia, Laos and Viet Nam, the French Government will proceed from the principle of respect for the independence and sovereignty, the unity and territorial integrity of Cambodia, Laos and Viet Nam.

Consequences

The United States, in unilateral declarations, repudiated important sections of these accords and refused to sign any of the agreements to the Final Declaration. The Geneva Agreements, as a collection of documents, in fact contained no actual treaty binding on all participants, and certainly no political treaties as such were signed at all. This makes the agreements unusual by treaty standards and probably unique in modern times.

In any case, the military agreements imposed by the accords divided Vietnam into two parts, a Democratic Republic controlling de facto the north and recognized only by the Soviet Union and China, and the State of Vietnam housed uneasily in the south. Elections were set for 1956. They never took place, aborted by the United States, which had assumed France's former role as South Vietnam's sponsor. And thereby hangs the tale of the United States being dragged into a war less popular and much longer and deadlier than the Korean conflict, which it was seeking to avoid repeating.

Source

Avalon Project at the Yale Law School, "Indochina—Agreement on the Cessation of Hostilities in Viet-Nam, July 20, 1954." Available online. URL: http://www.yale.edu/lawweb/avalon/intdip/indoch/inch001.htm. Accessed May 16, 2005.

AUSTRIAN STATE TREATY

TREATY AT A GLANCE

Completed
May 15, 1955

Signatories
United States, the Soviet Union, Great Britain, and France

Overview
The Austrian State Treaty provided for the first Soviet military withdrawal in Europe since World War II and brought into being a neutral Austrian nation.

Historical Background

Although the United States and the Soviet Union in the JOINT FOUR-NATION DECLARATION OF THE MOSCOW CONFERENCE of 1943 had expressed their wish "to see re-established a free and independent Austria," come the end of the war, Austria was placed under military occupation in July 1945 and, like Germany, divided into four zones of occupation, French, American, Soviet, and British. Like Berlin, Vienna was placed under joint administration. In April the Soviets gave their stamp of approval to the formation of a provisional government under Dr. Karl Renner as chancellor, and full Allied recognition followed in October. Elections were held in November making Renner president and Leopold Figl chancellor.

The negotiations reestablishing Austrian sovereignty stalled, however, and the country remained under four-power occupation. At the start, there were three specific differences between the Soviets and the Western democracies that held up postwar settlement over Austria. First, the Soviet Union and Yugoslavia wanted to transfer "German" assets in Austria sufficient to meet their demands for reparations, although the POTSDAM PROTOCOL had stated that Austria was to pay no such reparations. Second, the Yugoslavs, backed by the Russians, laid claim to Austrian territory that the Allies were not willing to allow. And third, the four powers fell to bickering about just what constituted "democracy." Before these differences could be hammered out, Austria's fate became caught up in the great-power machinations of the cold war. For a time, the Soviets hoped to link concessions over Austria with a German settlement more favorable to their interests, but after that, Austria became merely yet another pawn on the cold war chessboard.

Soviet dictator Joseph Stalin's death on March 5, 1953, sparked hopes for a thaw in the cold war. A collective leadership sprang up in its wake, which, while somewhat ephemeral, nevertheless managed to execute the dreaded chief of Russia's secret police, Lavrentry Beria, and to free thousands from Soviet prison camps. Riots in East Germany and Poland led Moscow to scale back its exploitation of Eastern bloc satellites and reduce its reparation demands on East Germany. The Soviets even sent a delegation to Belgrade in 1955 to attempt a reconciliation with Tito. As part of this turmoil preceding Nikita Khrushchev's emergence, the Russians finally signed on to the Austrian State Treaty, some 10 years after the negotiations had begun.

Terms

Austria had not been obliged to sign a "peace treaty" at the close of World War II because the Allies had declared it a victim of German aggression under the 1938 Anschluss (see "GENTLEMEN'S AGREEMENT" BETWEEN AUSTRIA AND GERMANY). Thus, the treaty returning its sovereignty was called a "state treaty":

> Whereas on 13th March 1938, Hitlerite Germany annexed Austria by force and incorporated its territory in the German Reich;
>
> Whereas in the Moscow Declaration published on 1st November 1943 the Governments of the Union of Soviet Socialist Republics, the United Kingdom and the United States of America declared that they regarded the annexation of Austria by Germany on 13th March 1938 as null and void and affirmed their wish to see Austria re-established as a free and independent State, and the French Committee of National Liberation made a similar declaration on 16th November 1943 . . .

Part I Political and Territorial Clauses

ARTICLE 1. RE-ESTABLISHMENT OF AUSTRIA
AS A FREE AND INDEPENDENT STATE
The Allied and Associated Powers recognize that Austria is re-established as a sovereign, independent and democratic State.

ARTICLE 2. MAINTENANCE OF
AUSTRIA'S INDEPENDENCE
The Allied and Associated Powers declare that they will respect the independence and territorial integrity of Austria as established under the present Treaty.

Article 3 required that Germany recognize Austrian independence and renounce all territorial claims to Austria, which were to be codified in a German peace treaty. Article 4 forbade the two to reunite, asserting that Austria was not to promote such a union by any means:

ARTICLE 4. PROHIBITION OF ANSCHLUSS
I. The Allied and Associated Powers declare that political or economic union between Austria and Germany is prohibited. Austria fully recognizes its responsibilities in this matter and shall not enter into political or economic union with Germany in any form whatsoever . . .

Article 5 returned Austria's borders to pre-Anschluss days:

ARTICLE 5. FRONTIERS OF AUSTRIA
The frontiers of Austria shall be those existing on 1st January 1938.

Article 6 guaranteed human rights within Austria, while Article 7 protected the minority rights of Slovenes and Croats. Article 8 settled the old disputes over the nature of Austrian democracy:

ARTICLE 8. DEMOCRATIC INSTITUTIONS
Austria shall have a democratic Government based on elections by secret ballot and shall guarantee to all citizens free, equal and universal suffrage as well as the right to be elected to public office without discrimination as to race, sex, language, religion or political opinion.

In support of these institutions, Article 9 provided for the dissolution of Nazi organizations, and Article 10 called for the liquidation of the remnants of the Nazi regime and the reestablishment of "a democratic system." Article 11 required Austria to recognize all peace treaties between other belligerents of the Second World War.

Part 2 of the treaty dealt with military and weapons matters, with Articles 12–16 preventing Austria from acquiring special weapons, such as the atomic bomb and German and Japanese aircraft; placing restrictions on former Nazis serving in the armed services; and calling on Austria to cooperate in preventing Germany from rearming. Article 17 set the time limit on these limitations:

ARTICLE 17. DURATION OF LIMITATIONS
Each of the military and air clauses of the present Treaty shall remain in force until modified in whole or in part by agreement between the Allied and Associated Powers and Austria or, after Austria becomes a member of the United Nations, by agreement between the Security Council and Austria.

Article 18 dealt with the repatriation of prisoners of war, and article 19 with the maintenance of war graves.

Part 3 set the terms for ending Allied occupation:

ARTICLE 20. WITHDRAWAL OF ALLIED FORCES
. . . The forces of the Allied and Associated Powers and members of the Allied Commission for Austria shall be withdrawn from Austria within ninety days from the coming into force of the present Treaty, and in so far as possible not later that 31st December 1955. . . .

And Part 4 dealt with claims arising out of the war:

ARTICLE 21. REPARATION
No reparation shall be exacted from Austria arising out of the existence of a state of war in Europe after 1st September 1939.

ARTICLE 22. GERMAN ASSETS IN AUSTRIA
The Soviet Union, the United Kingdom, the United States of American and France have the right to dispose of all German assets in Austria in accordance with the Protocol of the Berlin Conference of 2nd August 1945.
1. The Soviet Union shall receive for a period of validity of thirty years concessions to oilfields equivalent to 60 percent of the extraction of oil in Austria for 1947, as well as property rights to all buildings, construction, equipment, and other property belonging to these oilfields, in accordance with list No. 1 and map No. 1 annexed to the Treaty . . .
2. The United Kingdom, the United States of America and France hereby transfer to Austria all property, rights and interests held or claimed by her on behalf of any of them in Austria as former German assets or war booty.

Consequences

By signing the Austrian State Treaty, the Soviet Union would have lost its right to station troops in Hungary and Romania in accordance with earlier agreements it had signed in 1947, but the WARSAW PACT, concluded the day before Russia signed the treaty, permitted the Soviets to keep their garrisons in those countries. Austria's neutrality was not written into the state treaty but was established as a constitutional law by the new Austrian parliament on October 26, 1955. Understanding that to create a lasting independence square in the

750 ENCYCLOPEDIA OF HISTORICAL TREATIES AND ALLIANCES

face of the Soviet Union, they would need to be neutral, the Austrians declared of their "own free will" their perpetual neutrality, which they proclaimed they would defend by all means at their disposal. The Austrian constitution forbade the joining of any military alliance or the permitting of any foreign bases in Austrian territory. In effect, the Soviets had secured Austrian neutrality and its nonparticipation in NATO in return for agreeing to withdraw its occupation forces and shut down the administration of the Russian zone, which constituted the first withdrawal of the Soviet military from European soil since the war and allowed Austria to escape the fate of its East European neighbors.

Source
J. A. S. Grenville, *The Major International Treaties, 1914–1973* (New York: Stein and Day, 1975), 281–283.

PARIS PEACE ACCORDS

TREATY AT A GLANCE

Completed
January 27, 1973, at Paris

Signatories
United States, Republic of Vietnam (South Vietnam), Democratic Republic of Vietnam (North Vietnam), Provisional Revolutionary Government of the Republic of South Vietnam

Overview
The product of a long series of peace conferences held in Paris, the agreement of January 27, 1973, brought a cease-fire to one of the longest, costliest, and most divisive wars in American history.

Historical Background

Following World War II, the Vietnamese, led by the communist-inspired Ho Chi Minh, defeated the armies of the French colonizers, resulting in a 1954 peace conference held in Geneva, Switzerland (see GENEVA AGREEMENTS OF 1954), which divided Vietnam into a Communist North and a democratically aligned South pending the outcome of free elections slated to be held in 1956. Learning that those elections would likely result in a unified Vietnam under a Communist leadership, the United States covertly backed South Vietnamese president Ngo Dinh Diem when he aborted the elections and launched a military campaign to suppress communist opposition. The result was a nation that remained divided and was now mired in a guerrilla-style civil war.

Fearing that the loss of South Vietnam to communism would bring about the "fall" of the entire Southeast Asian region to communist domination (dubbed the "domino theory": if one "domino" falls, the others will surely follow), President John F. Kennedy committed some 16,000 so-called U.S. advisers to aid Diem in combat. During Kennedy's administration, the American CIA plotted the assassination of Diem (who, they all agreed, had grown too corrupt to support), ushering in a military coup and a dozen unstable governments, all incapable of standing without U.S. support.

On August 7, 1964, the United States Senate passed the Gulf of Tonkin Resolution following reports that a navy destroyer, the USS *Maddox*, had been fired on by North Vietnamese torpedo boats. The resolution gave President Lyndon B. Johnson broad powers in expanding American involvement in Vietnam. By 1965, 75,000 Americans were fighting; in 1966, 375,00; 1968, more than half a million. As the involvement deepened, popular opinion in the United States first became divided over the war and then overwhelmingly opposed to it.

When President Richard Nixon took office in 1969, he began turning more of the fighting over to the less-than-enthusiastic Army of the Republic of Vietnam, while he ordered massive (and illegal) bombings of nearby Cambodia to cover the American withdrawal. The bombings provoked widespread protests throughout the United States, especially on college campuses (at Kent State University in Ohio, National Guard troops killed four students during a demonstration). Even middle-class suburbanites, businesspeople, and civic leaders took note and turned against the war when the publishing of the Pentagon Papers (a secret government study leaked to the *New York Times* in 1971) revealed a pattern of confusion and deliberate deception, beginning with Harry S. Truman and culminating with Lyndon Johnson, in the nation's ever-growing involvement in Southeast Asia. It seemed to support what many had considered the outlandish claims of the protesters. Responding to popular pressure, President Nixon sent his negotiator Henry Kissinger to peace talks held in Paris. The result was an agreement with the Communists to end the war.

Terms

The agreement read as follows:

Agreement to End the Vietnam War, Paris, 27 January 1973

The parties participating in the Paris Conference on Vietnam, with a view to ending the war and restoring peace in Vietnam on the basis of respect for the Vietnamese people's fundamental national rights and the South Vietnamese people's right to self-determination, and to contributing to the consolidation of peace in Asia and the world, have agreed on the following provisions and undertake to respect and to implement them:

Chapter I: The Vietnamese People's Fundamental National Rights

ARTICLE 1

The United States and all other countries respect the independence, sovereignty, unity and territorial integrity of Vietnam as recognized by the 1954 Geneva Agreements on Vietnam.

Chapter II: Cessation of Hostilities— Withdrawal of Troops

ARTICLE 2

A ceasefire shall be observed throughout South Vietnam as of 24.00 hours GMT, on January 27, 1973.

At the same hour, the United States will stop all its military activities against the territory of the Democratic Republic of Vietnam by ground, air and naval forces, wherever they may be based, and end the mining of the territorial waters, ports, harbors, and waterways of the Democratic Republic of Vietnam.

The United States will remove, permanently deactivate or destroy all the mines in the territorial waters, ports, harbors, and waterways of North Vietnam as soon as this Agreement goes into effect.

The complete cessation of hostilities mentioned in this Article shall be durable and without limit of time.

ARTICLE 3

The parties undertake to maintain the ceasefire and to ensure a lasting and stable peace.

As soon as the ceasefire goes into effect:

(a) The United States forces and those of the other foreign countries allied with the United States and the Republic of Vietnam shall remain in place pending the implementation of the plan of troop withdrawal. The Four Party Joint Military Commission described in Article 16 shall determine the modalities.

(b) The armed forces of the two South Vietnamese parties shall remain in place. The Two-Party Joint Military Commission described in Article 17 shall determine the areas controlled by each party and the modalities of stationing.

(c) The regular forces of all services and arms and the irregular forces of the parties in South Vietnam shall stop all offensive activities against each other and shall strictly abide by the following stipulations:

All acts of force on the ground, in the air, and on the sea shall be prohibited;

All hostile acts, terrorism and reprisals by both sides will be banned.

ARTICLE 4

The United States will not continue its military involvement or intervene in the internal affairs of South Vietnam.

ARTICLE 5

Within sixty days of the signing of this Agreement, there will be a total withdrawal from South Vietnam of troops, military advisers, and military personnel, including technical military personnel and military personnel associated with the pacification programs, armaments, munitions and war material of the United States and those of the other foreign countries mentioned in Article 3 (a). Advisers from the above-mentioned countries to all paramilitary organizations and the police force will also be withdrawn within the same period of time.

ARTICLE 6

The dismantlement of all military bases in South Vietnam of the United States and of the other foreign countries mentioned in Article 3 (a) shall be completed within sixty days of the signing of this Agreement.

ARTICLE 7

From the enforcement of the ceasefire to the formation of the Government provided for in Articles 9 (b) and 14 of this Agreement, the two South Vietnamese parties shall not accept the introduction of troops, military advisers, and military personnel including technical military personnel, armaments, munitions, and war material into South Vietnam.

The two South Vietnamese parties shall be permitted to make periodic replacement of armaments, munitions and war material which have been destroyed, damaged, worn out or used up after the ceasefire, on the basis of piece-for-piece, of the same characteristics and properties, under the supervision of the Joint Military Commission of the two South Vietnamese parties and of the International Commission of Control and Supervision.

Chapter III: The Return of Captured Military Personnel and Foreign Civilians, and Captured and Detained Vietnamese Civilian Personnel

ARTICLE 8

(a) The return of captured military personnel and foreign civilians of the parties shall be carried out simultaneously with and completed not later than the same day as the troop withdrawal mentioned in Article 5. The parties shall exchange complete lists of the above-mentioned captured military personnel and foreign civilians on the day of the signing of this Agreement.

(b) The parties shall help each other to get information about those military personnel and foreign civilians of the parties missing in action, to determine the location and take care of the graves of the dead so as to facilitate the exhumation and repatriation of the remains, and to take any such other measures as may be required to get information about those still considered missing in action.

(c) The question of the return of Vietnamese civilian personnel captured and detained in South Vietnam will be resolved by the two South Vietnamese parties on the basis of the principles of Article 21 (b) of the Agreement on the cessation of hostilities in Vietnam of July 20, 1954.

The two South Vietnamese parties will do so in a spirit of national reconciliation and accord, with a view to ending hatred and enmity, in order to ease suffering and to reunite families. The two South Vietnamese parties will do their utmost to resolve this question within ninety days after the ceasefire comes into effect.

Chapter IV: The Exercise of the South Vietnamese People's Right of Self-Determination

ARTICLE 9
The Government of the United States of America and the Government of the Democratic Republic of Vietnam undertake to respect the following principles for the exercise of the South-Vietnamese people's right to self-determination:

(a) The South Vietnamese people's right to self-determination is sacred, inalienable, and shall be respected by all countries.

(b) The South Vietnamese people shall decide themselves the political future of South Vietnam through genuinely free and democratic elections under international supervision.

(c) Foreign countries shall not impose any political tendency or personality on the South Vietnamese people.

ARTICLE 10
The two South Vietnamese parties undertake to respect the ceasefire and maintain peace in South Vietnam, settle all matters of contention through negotiations, and avoid all armed conflict.

ARTICLE 11
Immediately after the ceasefire, the two South Vietnamese parties will:

Achieve national reconciliation and concord, end hatred and enmity, prohibit all acts of reprisal and discrimination against individuals or organizations that have collaborated with one side or the other;

Ensure the democratic liberties of the people: personal freedom, freedom of speech, freedom of the press, freedom of meeting, freedom of organization, freedom of political activities, freedom of belief, freedom of movement, freedom of residence, freedom of work, right to property ownership and right to free enterprise.

ARTICLE 12
(a) Immediately after the ceasefire, the two South Vietnamese parties shall hold consultations in a spirit of national reconciliation and concord, mutual respect and mutual nonelimination to set up a National Council of National Reconciliation and Concord of three equal segments.

The Council shall operate on the principle of unanimity. After the National Council of National Reconciliation and Concord has assumed its functions, the two South Vietnamese parties will consult about the formation of councils at lower levels.

The two South Vietnamese parties shall sign an agreement on the internal matters of South Vietnam as soon as possible and do their utmost to accomplish this within ninety days after the ceasefire comes into effect, in keeping with the South Vietnamese people's aspirations for peace, independence and democracy.

(b) The National Council of National Reconciliation and Concord shall have the task of promoting the two South Vietnamese parties' implementation of this Agreement, achievement of national reconciliation and concord and ensurance of democratic liberties.

The National Council of National Reconciliation and Concord will organize the free and democratic general elections provided for in Article 9 (b) and decide the procedures and modalities of these general elections.

The institutions for which the general elections are to be held will be agreed upon through consultations between the two South Vietnamese parties. The National Council of National Reconciliation and Concord will also decide the procedures and modalities of such local elections as the two South Vietnamese parties agree upon.

ARTICLE 13
The question of Vietnamese armed forces in South Vietnam shall be settled by the two South Vietnamese parties in a spirit of national reconciliation and concord, equality and mutual respect, without foreign interference, in accordance with the post-war situation.

Among the questions to be discussed by the two South Vietnamese parties are steps to reduce their military effectives and to demobilize the troops being reduced. The two South Vietnamese parties will accomplish this as soon as possible.

ARTICLE 14
South Vietnam will pursue a foreign policy of peace and independence. It will be prepared to establish relations with all countries irrespective of their political and social systems on the basis of mutual respect for independence and sovereignty, and accept economic and technical aid from any country with no political conditions attached.

The acceptance of military aid by South Vietnam in the future shall come under the authority of the Government set up after the general elections in South Vietnam provided for in Article g (b).

Chapter V: The Reunification of Vietnam and the Relationship between North and South Vietnam

ARTICLE 15
The reunification of Vietnam shall be carried out step by step through peaceful means on the basis of discussion and agreements between North and South Vietnam, without coercion or annexation by either party and without foreign interference. The time for reunification will be agreed upon by North and South Vietnam.

Pending the reunification:

(a) The military demarcation line between the two zones at the seventeenth parallel is only provisional and not a political or territorial boundary, as provided for in paragraph 6 of the Final Declaration of the 1954 Geneva Conference.

(b) North and South Vietnam shall respect the demilitarized zone on either side of the provisional military demarcation line.

(c) North and South Vietnam shall promptly start negotiations with a view to re-establishing normal relations in various fields. Among the questions to be negotiated are the modalities of civilian movement across the provisional military demarcation line.

(d) North and South Vietnam shall not join any military alliance or military block and shall not allow foreign Powers to maintain military bases, troops, military advisers, and military personnel on their respective territories, as stipulated in the 1954 Geneva Agreements on Vietnam.

Chapter VI: The Joint Military Commissions, the International Commission of Controls and Supervision, the International Conference

ARTICLE 16

(a) The parties participating in the Paris Conference on Vietnam shall immediately designate representatives to form a Four Party Joint Military Commission with the task of ensuring joint action by the parties in implementing the following provisions of this Agreement:

The first paragraph of Article 2, regarding the enforcement of the ceasefire throughout South Vietnam:

Article 3 (a), regarding the ceasefire by United States forces and those of the other foreign countries referred to in that Article;

Article 3 (c), regarding the ceasefire between all parties in South Vietnam;

Article 5, regarding the withdrawal from South Vietnam of United States troops and those of the other foreign countries mentioned in Article 3 (a);

Article 6, regarding the dismantlement of military bases in South Vietnam of the United States and those of the other foreign countries mentioned in Article 3 (a);

Article 8 (a), regarding the return of captured military personnel and foreign civilians of the parties;

Article 8 (b), regarding the mutual assistance of the parties in getting information about those military personnel and foreign civilians of the parties missing in action.

(b) The Four Party Joint Military Commission shall operate in accordance with the principle of consultations and unanimity. Disagreements shall be referred to the International Commission of Control and Supervision.

(c) The Four Party Joint Military Commission shall begin operating immediately after the signing of this Agreement and end its activities in sixty days, after the completion of the withdrawal of United States troops and those of the other foreign countries mentioned in Article 3 (a) and the completion of the return of captured military personnel and foreign civilians of the parties.

(d) The four parties shall agree immediately on the organization, the working procedure, means of activity, and expenditures of the Four Party Joint Military Commission.

ARTICLE 17

(a) The two South Vietnamese parties shall immediately designate representatives to form a Two Party Joint Military Commission with the task of ensuring joint action by the two South Vietnamese parties in implementing the following provisions of this Agreement:

The first paragraph of Article 2, regarding the enforcement of the ceasefire throughout South Vietnam, when the Four Party Joint Military Commission has ended its activities;

Article 3 (b), regarding the ceasefire between the two South Vietnamese parties;

Article 3 (c), regarding the ceasefire between all parties in South Vietnam, when the Four Party Joint Military Commission has ended its activities;

Article 7, regarding the prohibition of the introduction of troops into South Vietnam and all other provisions of this Article;

Article 8 (c) regarding the question of the return of Vietnamese civilian personnel captured and detained in South Vietnam;

Article 13, regarding the reduction of the military effectives of the two South Vietnamese parties and the demobilization of the troops being reduced.

(b) Disagreements shall be referred to the International Commission of Control and Supervision.

(c) After the signing of this Agreement the Two Party Joint Military Commission shall agree immediately on the measures and organization aimed at enforcing the ceasefire and preserving peace in South Vietnam.

ARTICLE 18

(a) After the signing of this Agreement, an International Commission of Control and Supervision shall be established immediately.

(b) Until the International Conference provided for in Article 19 makes definitive arrangements, the International Commission of Control and Supervision will report to the four parties on matters concerning the control and supervision of the implementation of the following provisions of this Agreement:

The first paragraph of Article 2, regarding the enforcement of the ceasefire through South Vietnam;

Article 3 (a), regarding the ceasefire by United States forces and those of the other foreign countries referred to in that Article;

Article 3 (c), regarding the ceasefire between all the parties in South Vietnam;

Article 5, regarding the withdrawal from South Vietnam of United States troops and those of the other foreign countries mentioned in Article 3 (a);

Article 6, regarding the dismantlement of military bases in South Vietnam of the United States and those of the other foreign countries mentioned in Article 3 (a);

Article 8 (a), regarding the return of captured military personnel and foreign civilians of the parties.

The International Commission of Control and Supervision shall form control teams for carrying out its tasks. The four parties shall agree immediately on the location and operation of these teams. The parties will facilitate their operation.

(c) Until the International Conference makes definitive arrangements, the International Commission of Control and Supervision will report to the two South Vietnamese parties on matters concerning the control and supervision of the implementation of the following provisions of this Agreement:

The first paragraph of Article 2, regarding the enforcement of the ceasefire throughout South Vietnam, when the Four Party Joint Military Commission has ended its activities;

Article 3 (b), regarding the ceasefire between the two South Vietnamese parties;

Article 3 (c), regarding the ceasefire between all parties in South Vietnam, when the Four Party Joint Military Commission has ended its activities;

Article 7, regarding the prohibition of the introduction of troops into South Vietnam and all other provisions of this Article;

Article 8 (c), regarding the question of the return of Vietnamese civilian personnel captured and detained in South Vietnam;

Article 9 (b), regarding the free and democratic general elections in South Vietnam;

Article 13, regarding the reduction of the military effectives of the two South Vietnamese parties and the demobilization of the troops being reduced.

The International Commission of Control and Supervision shall form control teams for carrying out its tasks. The two South Vietnamese parties shall agree immediately on the location and operation of these teams. The two South Vietnamese parties will facilitate their operations.

(d) The International Commission of Control and Supervision shall be composed of representatives of four countries: Canada, Hungary, Indonesia and Poland. The chairmanship of this commission will rotate among the members for specific periods to be determined by the commission.

(e) The International Commission of Control and Supervision shall carry out its tasks in accordance with the principle of respect for the sovereignty of South Vietnam.

(f) The International Commission of Control and Supervision shall operate in accordance with the principle of consultations and unanimity.

(g) The International Commission of Control and Supervision shall begin operating when a ceasefire comes into force in Vietnam. As regards the provisions in Article 18 (b) concerning the four parties, the International Commission of Control and Supervision shall end its activities when the commission's tasks of control and supervision regarding these provisions have been fulfilled.

As regards the provisions in Article 18 (c) concerning the two South Vietnamese parties, the International Commission of Control and Supervision shall end its activities on the request of the Government formed after the general elections in South Vietnam provided for in Article 9 (b).

(h) The four parties shall agree immediately on the organization, means of activity, and expenditures of the International Commission of Control and Supervision. The relationship between the International Commission and the International Conference will be agreed upon by the International Commission and the International Conference.

ARTICLE 19

The parties agree on the convening of an International Conference within thirty days of the signing of this Agreement to acknowledge the signed agreements; to guarantee the ending of the war, the maintenance of peace in Vietnam, the respect of the Vietnamese people's fundamental national rights, and the South Vietnamese people's right to self-determination; and to contribute to and guarantee peace in Indo-China.

The United States and the Democratic Republic of Vietnam, on behalf of the parties participating in the Paris Conference on Vietnam, will propose to the following parties that they participate in this International Conference: the People's Republic of China, the Republic of France, the Union of Soviet Socialist Republics, the United Kingdom, the four countries of the International Commission of Control and Supervision, and the Secretary-General of the United Nations, together with the parties participating in the Paris Conference on Vietnam.

Chapter VII: Regarding Cambodia and Laos

ARTICLE 20

(a) The parties participating in the Paris Conference on Vietnam shall strictly respect the 1954 Geneva Agreements on Cambodia and the 1962 Geneva Agreements on Laos, which recognized the Cambodian and the Laos people's fundamental national rights, i.e. the independence, sovereignty, unity and territorial integrity of these countries. The parties shall respect the neutrality of Cambodia and Laos.

The parties participating in the Paris Conference on Vietnam undertake to refrain from using the territory of Cambodia and the territory of Laos to encroach on the sovereignty and security of one another and of other countries.

(b) Foreign countries shall put an end to all military activities in Cambodia and Laos, totally withdraw from and refrain from reintroducing into these two countries troops, military advisers and military personnel, armaments, munitions and war material.

(c) The internal affairs of Cambodia and Laos shall be settled by the people of each of these countries without foreign interference.

(d) The problems existing between the Indo-Chinese countries shall be settled by the Indo-Chinese parties on the basis of respect for each other's independence, sovereignty and territorial integrity and non-interference in each other's internal affairs.

Chapter VIII: The Relationship between the United States and the Democratic Republic of Vietnam

ARTICLE 21

The United States anticipates that this Agreement will usher in an era of reconciliation with the Democratic Republic of Vietnam as with all the peoples of Indo-China. In pursuance of its traditional policy, the United States will contribute to healing the wounds of war and to post-war reconstruction of the Democratic Republic of Vietnam and throughout Indo-China.

ARTICLE 22

The ending of the war, the restoration of peace in Vietnam, and the strict implementation of this Agreement will create conditions for establishing a new, equal and mutually beneficial relationship between the United States and the Democratic Republic of Vietnam on the basis of respect for each other's independence and sovereignty, and noninterference in each other's internal affairs. At the same time, this will ensure stable peace in Vietnam and contribute to the preservation of lasting peace in Indo-China and Southeast Asia.

Chapter IX: Other Provisions

ARTICLE 23

This Agreement shall enter into force upon signature by plenipotentiary representatives of the parties participating in the Paris Conference on Vietnam. All the parties concerned shall strictly implement this Agreement and its Protocols.

Done in Paris this twenty-seventh day of January, one thousand nine hundred and seventy-three, in Vietnamese and English. The Vietnamese and English texts are officially and equally authentic.

For the Government of the United States of America:
WILLIAM P. ROGERS,
Secretary of State

For the Government of the Republic of Vietnam:
TRAN VAN LAM,
Minister for Foreign Affairs

For the Government of the Democratic Republic of Vietnam:
NGUYEN DUY TRINH,
Minister for Foreign Affairs.

For the Provisional Revolutionary Government of
the Republic of South Vietnam:
NGUYEN THI BINH,
Minister for Foreign Affairs

Consequences

The Paris accords brought U.S. withdrawal and the return of the POWs. A four-party Joint Military Commission was set up to prevent the resumption of hostilities, and the four-power (Canada, Poland, Hungary, and Indonesia) International Commission of Control and Supervision supervised the cease-fire.

Yet, both the Communists and the South Vietnamese (backed by American aid) repeatedly violated the accords. For its part, the United States continued to bomb Cambodia and resumed reconnaissance flights over North Vietnam. However, President Nixon's own position at home was rapidly eroding as the Watergate scandal emerged. While the President was preoccupied, Congress approved an amendment requiring the cessation of military operations in and over Indochina by August 15. Then, in November 1973 Congress passed the War Powers Act, requiring the president to inform Congress within 48 hours of deployment of U.S. military forces abroad, withdrawing them within 60 days in the absence of explicit congressional endorsement. Combined, these two measures ensured an absolute end to American involvement in Indochina.

The South still planned new offensives, misplacing its confidence in continued U.S. aid. Congress, however, was intent on abandoning Vietnam, and soon the North turned victory after victory into a rout. South Vietnamese president Nguyen Van Thieu resigned office and fled, leaving Duong Van Minh to become president long enough to surrender unconditionally to the North on April 30, 1975, the day Saigon fell, South Vietnam ceased to exist, and North and South were reunited as the Republic of Vietnam.

Source

J. A. S. Grenville and Bernard Waserstein, eds., *The Major International Treaties Since 1945* (London and New York: Methuen, 1987), 284–293.

Trade Agreements and Commercial Treaties

TREATY OF PARIS (1951)

TREATY AT A GLANCE

Completed
April 18, 1951, at Paris; entered into force July 23, 1952

Signatories
France, Federal Republic of Germany (West Germany), Italy,
Belgium, Luxembourg, and the Netherlands

Overview
Amid the confusion and cross-purposes of the growing cold war,
the French abandoned their traditional diplomacy of demanding
reparations, which would obstruct German economic revival, to
come up with a plan, enthusiastically embraced by the new West
Germany, that served as an initial step toward a general European
union.

Historical Background

In the early wrangling over the occupation of Germany, France often sided with the Soviet Union in an almost knee-jerk French reaction to keep Germany weak and to secure reparations, much like the French attitude that after World War I drove the Allies to distraction and, ultimately, the world toward a second world war. But the Communist takeover of Czechoslovakia and the Berlin Crisis of 1948 opened French eyes to the dangers of Stalinism, and French leaders saw the need to reconcile German recovery with their own security. What was more, the French devised a solution. French technocrat Jean Monnet and Foreign Minister Robert Schuman came up with a plan in 1950 that called for a merger of West European coal and steel industries to hasten recovery, cut down competition, and make future wars between France and Germany undesirable.

Meanwhile, the new chancellor of West Germany, Konrad Adenauer, was well on his way to creating the conditions for what would soon be called the Wirtschaftswunder, the German "economic miracle" of the 1950s. He had made economic and political rehabilitation the primary goal of his foreign policy, and he not only had successfully seen to the founding of the Federal Republic of Germany on May 23, 1949, and the drafting of a solid democratic constitution, but also had embraced a dynamic free-market economic policy that benefited immensely from the Marshall Plan.

Yet, Adenauer still faced the challenge of achieving security while obtaining full sovereignty for West Germany. As it turned out, the cold war helped him do both at once. Although Adenauer knew the resolute Soviets had pretty much destroyed any real possibility of reuniting his republic with East Germany, politically he could not avoid the emotional pull the idea of reunification had on all Germans. He refused to recognize either the East German regime or Polish claims to former German territory east of the Oder and Neisse Rivers, and he extended the diplomatic snub to any country that did recognize the German Democratic Republic (GDR) in the East.

By 1950 the Soviets were also playing off the German longing to be one nation again, suggesting in the Prague Proposal in October a united, demilitarized German state. The idea was attractive to American diplomat George Kennan, author of the famous "Long Memorandum," which had served as the basis of the Truman Doctrine. Kennan saw in such a neutral zone as the Soviets were proposing to make of Germany a good buffer state in central Europe, separating the major cold war rivals in Europe. The only trouble was that Russia also insisted on a Constituent Council to run the country, with equal representation from the

East and the West, although West Germany had double the population of the GDR.

When the Schuman Plan was suggested, Adenauer embraced the offer at once, before the Americans could sell them down the river with a neutered state where the East German Communists would be at best obstructive and more likely subversive, dragging a disarmed united Germany into alignment with Moscow. Through the Schuman Plan, Adenauer made German one of "the Six," the founding nations of the European Coal and Steel Community.

Terms

The ECSC treaty called for pooling the resources and coordinating the industrial policies of the six founding nations—France, West Germany, Italy, Belgium, Luxembourg, and the Netherlands—and created a customs union and a free trade area free from national regulations or restrictions.

. . . Considering that world peace may be safeguarded only by creative efforts equal to the dangers which menace it;

Convinced that the contribution which an organized and vital Europe can bring to civilization is indispensable to the maintenance of peaceful relations;

Conscious of the fact that Europe can be built by concrete actions which create a real solidarity and by establishment of common bases for economic development;

Desirous of assisting through the expansion of their basic production in raising the standards of living and in furthering the works of peace;

Resolved to substitute for historical rivalries a fusion of their essential interests; to establish, by creating an economic community, and the foundation of a broad and independent community among peoples long divided by bloody conflicts; and to lay the bases of institutions capable of giving direction to their future common destiny;

[The High Contracting Parties] Have decided to create a European Coal and Steel Community. . . .

TITLE ONE: THE EUROPEAN COAL AND STEEL COMMUNITY

ARTICLE 1

By the present Treaty the HIGH CONTRACTING PARTIES institute among themselves a EUROPEAN COAL AND STEEL COMMUNITY, based on a common market, common objectives, and common institutions.

ARTICLE 2

The mission of the European Coal and Steel Community is to contribute to economic expansion, the development of employment and the improvement of the standard of living in the participating countries through the institution, in harmony with the general economy of the Member States, of a common market as defined in Article 4.

The Community must progressively establish conditions which will in themselves assure the most rational distribution of production at the highest possible level of productivity, while safeguarding the continuity of employment and avoiding the creation of fundamental and persistent disturbances in the economies of the Member States.

ARTICLE 3

Within the framework of their respective powers and responsibilities in the common interest, the institution shall:

(a) see that the common market is regularly supplied, taking account of the needs of third countries;

(b) assure all consumers in comparative positions within the common market equal access to the sources of production;

(c) seek the establishment of the lowest prices which are possible without requiring any corresponding rise either in the prices charged by the same enterprises in other transactions or in the price level as a whole in another period, while at the same time permitting necessary amortization and providing normal possibilities of remunerations for capital invested;

(d) see that conditions are maintained which will encourage enterprises to expand and improve their ability to produce and to promote a policy of rational development of natural resources, avoiding inconsiderate exhaustion of such resources;

(e) promote the improvement of the living and working conditions of the labor force in each of the industries under its jurisdiction so as to make possible the equalization of such conditions in an upward direction;

(f) further the development of international trade and see that equitable limits are observed in prices charged on external markets;

(g) promote the regular expansion of production and the modernization of production as well as the improvement of its quality, under conditions which preclude any protection against competing industries except where justified by illegitimate action on the part of such industries or in their favor.

ARTICLE 4

The following are recognized to be incompatible with the common market for coal and steel, and are, therefore, abolished and prohibited within the Community in the manner set forth in the present Treaty:

(a) import and export duties, or charges with an equivalent effect, and quantitative restrictions on the movement of coal and steel;

(b) measures or practices discriminating among producers, specifically as concerns prices, delivery terms and transportation rates, as well as measures or practices which hamper the buyer in the free choice of his supplier;

(c) subsidies or State assistance, or special charges imposed by the State, in any form whatsoever;

(d) restrictive practices tending toward division of markets or the exploitation of the consumer.

ARTICLE 5

The Community shall accomplish its mission, under the conditions provided for in the present Treaty, with limited direct intervention.

To this end the Community will:

enlighten and facilitate the action of interested parties by collecting information, organizing consultations and defining general objectives;

place financial means at the disposal of enterprises for their investments and participate the in the expense of readaptation;

assure the establishment, the maintenance and the observance of normal conditions of competition and take direct action with respect to production and the operation of the market only when circumstances make it absolutely necessary;

publish the justifications for its action and take the necessary measures to ensure observance of the rules set forth in the present Treaty,

The institutions of the Community shall carry out these activities with as little administrative machinery as possible and in close cooperation with interested parties.

ARTICLE 6

The Community shall have juridical personality . . .

TITLE TWO: THE INSTITUTIONS OF THE COMMUNITY

ARTICLE 7

The institutions of the Community shall be as follows:

a HIGH AUTHORITY, assisted by a Consultative Committee;

a COMMON ASSEMBLY, hereafter referred to as "the Assembly";

a SPECIAL COUNCIL, composed of MINISTERS, hereafter referred to as "the Council";

a COURT OF JUSTICE, hereafter referred to as "the Court."

Chapter I: The High Authority

ARTICLE 8

The High Authority shall be responsible for assuring the fulfillment of the purposes stated in the present Treaty under the terms thereof.

ARTICLE 9

The High Authority shall be composed of nine members designated for six years and chosen for their general competence.

A member shall be eligible for reappointment. The number of members of the High Authority may be reduced by unanimous decision of the Council.

Only nationals of the Member States may be members of the High Authority.

The High Authority may not include more than two members of the same nationality.

The members of the High Authority shall exercise their functions in complete independence, in the general interest of the Community. In the fulfillment of their duties, they shall neither solicit nor accept instructions from any Government or from any organization. They will abstain from all conduct incompatible with the supranational character of their functions.

Each Member State agrees to respect this supranational character and to make no effort to influence the members of the High Authority in the execution of their duties.

The members of the High Authority may not exercise any business or professional activities, paid or unpaid, nor acquire or hold, directly or indirectly, any interest in any business related to coal and steel during their term in office or for a period of three years thereafter.

ARTICLE 10

The Governments of the Member States shall designate eight members of the High Authority by agreement among themselves. These eight members will elect a ninth member, who shall be deemed elected if he receives at least five votes.

The members thus designated will remain in office for six years following the date of the establishment of the common market.

In case a vacancy should occur during this first period for one of the reasons set forth in Article 12, it will be filled under the provisions of the third paragraph of that Article, by common agreement among the Governments of Member States . . .

ARTICLE 11

The President and the Vice President of the High Authority shall be designated from among the membership of the High Authority for two years, in accordance with the procedure provided for the designation of members of the High Authority by the Governments of the Member States. They may be reelected.

Except in the case of a complete redesignation of the membership of the High Authority, the designation of the President and Vice President shall be made with the consultation of the High Authority.

ARTICLE 12

In addition to the provisions for regular redesignation, the terms of office of a member of the High Authority may be terminated by death or resignation . . .

ARTICLE 13

The High Authority shall act by vote of a majority of its membership.

Its quorum shall be fixed by its rules of procedure. However, this quorum must be greater than one-half of its membership.

ARTICLE 14

The execution of its responsibilities under the present Treaty and in accordance with the provisions thereof, the High Authority shall issue decisions, recommendations and opinions.

Decisions shall be binding in all their details.

Recommendations shall be binding with respect to the objectives which they specify but shall leave to those whom they are directed the choice of appropriate means for attaining these objectives.

Opinions shall not be binding.

When the High Authority is empowered to issue a decision, it may limit itself to making a recommendation.

ARTICLE 15

The Decisions, recommendations and opinions of the High Authority shall state the reasons therefor, and shall take note of the opinions which the High Authority is required to obtain.

When such decisions and recommendations are individual in character, they shall be binding on the interested party upon their notification to him.

In other cases, they shall take effect automatically upon publication.

The High Authority shall determine the manner in which the provisions of the present Article are to be carried out.

ARTICLE 16

The High Authority shall take all appropriate measures of an internal nature to assure the functioning of its services . . .

ARTICLE 17

The High Authority shall publish annually, at least a month before the meeting of the Assembly, a general report on the activities of the Community and on its administrative expenditures.

ARTICLE 18

There shall be created a Consultative Committee, attached to the High Authority. It shall consist of not less than thirty and not more than fifty-one members, and shall include producers, workers and consumers and dealers in equal numbers.

The members of the Consultative Committee shall be appointed by the Council.

As concerns producers and workers, the Council shall designate the representative organizations among which it shall allocate the seats to be filled. Each organization shall be asked to draw up a list comprising twice the number of seats to allocated to it. Designations shall be made from this list.

The members of the Consultative Committee shall be designated in their individual capacity. They shall not be bound by any mandate or instruction from the organizations which proposed them as candidates.

A President and officers shall be elected for one-year terms by the Consultative Committee from its own membership. The Committee shall fix its own rules of procedure.

The allowances of members of the Consultative Committee shall be determined by the Council on proposal by the High Authority.

ARTICLE 19

The High Authority may consult the Consultative Committee in any case it deems proper. It shall be required to do so whenever such consultation is prescribed by the present Treaty.

The High Authority shall submit to the Consultative Committee the general objectives and programme established under the terms of Article 46, and shall keep the Committee informed of the broad lines of its action under the terms of Articles 54, 65 and 66.

If the High Authority deems it necessary, it shall give the Consultative Committee a period in which to present its opinion of not less than ten days from the date of the notification to the effect addressed to the President of the Committee.

The Consultative Committee shall be convoked by its President, either at the request of the High Authority or at the request of a majority of its members, for the purpose of discussing a given question.

The minutes of the meetings shall be convoked by its President, either at the request of the High Authority or at the request of a majority of its members, for the purpose of discussing a given question.

The minutes of the meetings shall be transmitted to the High Authority and to the Council at the same time as the opinions of the Committee.

Chapter II: The Assembly

ARTICLE 20

The Assembly shall be composed of delegates whom the Parliaments of each of the Member States shall be called upon to designate once a year from among their own membership, or who shall be elected by direct universal suffrage, according to the procedure determined by each High Contracting Party.

The number of delegates is fixed as follows:

Germany 18
Belgium 10
France 18
Italy 18
Luxemburg 4
Netherlands 10

The representatives of the people of the Saar are included in the number of delegates attributed to France.

ARTICLE 22

The Assembly shall hold an annual session. It shall convene regularly on the second Tuesday in May. Its session may not last beyond the end of the current fiscal year.

The Assembly may be convoked in extraordinary sessions on the request of the Council in order to state its opinion on such questions as may be put to it by the Council.

It may also meet in extraordinary sessions on the request of a majority of its members or of the High Authority.

ARTICLE 23

The Assembly shall designate its President and officers from among its membership.

The members of the High Authority may attend all meetings. The President of the High Authority or such of its members as it may designate shall be heard at their request.

The High Authority shall reply orally or in writing to all questions put to it by the Assembly or its members.

The members of the Council may attend all meetings and shall be heard at their request.

ARTICLE 24

The Assembly shall discuss in open session the general report submitted to it by the High Authority.

If a motion of censure on the report is presented to the Assembly, a vote may be taken thereon only after a period of not less than three days following its introduction, and such vote shall be by open ballot.

If the motion of censure is adopted by two-thirds of the members present and voting, representing a majority of the total membership, the members of the High Authority must resign in a body. They shall continue to carry out current business until their replacement in accordance with Article 10.

ARTICLE 25

The Assembly shall fix its own rules of procedure, by a vote of a majority of its total membership.

The acts of the Assembly shall be published in a manner to be prescribed in such rules of procedure.

Chapter III: The Council

ARTICLE 26

The Council shall exercise its functions in the events and in the manner provided in the present Treaty in particular with a view to harmonizing the action of the High Authority and that of the Governments, which are responsible for the general economic policy of their countries.

To this end, the Council and the High Authority shall consult together and exchange information.

The Council may request the High Authority to examine all proposals and measures which it may deem necessary or appropriate for the realization of the common objectives.

ARTICLE 27

The Council shall be composed of representatives of the Member States. Each State shall designate thereto one of the members of its Government.

The Presidency of the Council shall be exercised for a term of three months by each member of the Council in rotation in the alphabetical order of the Member States.

ARTICLE 28

Meetings of the Council shall be called by its President on the request of a State or of the High Authority.

When the Council is consulted by the High Authority, it may deliberate without necessarily proceeding to a vote. The minutes of its meetings shall be forwarded to the High Authority.

Whenever the present Treaty requires concurrence of the Council, this concurrence shall be deemed to have been granted if the proposal submitted by the High Authority is approved:

—by an absolute majority of the representatives of the Member States, including the vote of the representatives of one of the States which produces at least 20 per cent of the total value of coal and steel produced in the Community;

—or, in case of an equal division of votes, and if the High Authority maintains its proposal after a second reading, by the representatives of the two Member States, each of which produces at least 20 per cent of the total value of coal and steel in the Community.

Wherever the present Treaty requires a unanimous decision or unanimous concurrence, such decision or concurrence will be adopted if supported by the votes of all of the members of the Council.

The decisions of the Council, other than those which require a qualified majority or a unanimous vote, will be taken by a vote of the majority of the total membership. This majority shall be deemed to exist if it includes the absolute majority of the representatives of the Member States including the vote of the representative of one of the States which produces at least 20 per cent of the total value of coal and steel produced in the Community.

In case of a vote, any member of the Council may act as a proxy for not more than one other member.

The Council shall communicate with the Member States through the intermediary of its President.

The acts of the Council shall be published under a procedure which it shall establish.

ARTICLE 29

The Council shall fix the salaries, allowances and pensions of the President of the High Authority, and of the President, the Judges, the Court Advocates and the Clerk of the Court.

ARTICLE 30

The Council shall establish its own rules of procedure.

Chapter IV: The Court

ARTICLE 31

The function of the Court is to ensure the rule of law in the interpretation and application of the present Treaty and of its implementing regulations.

ARTICLE 32

The Court shall be composed of seven Judges, appointed for six years and by agreement among the Governments of the Member States from among persons of recognized independence and competence.

A partial change in the membership of the Court shall occur every three years, affecting alternatively three members and four members. The three members whose terms expire at the end of the first period of three years shall be designated by lot.

Judges shall be eligible for reappointment.

The number of Judges may be increased by unanimous vote of the Council or proposal by the Court.

Consequences

The establishment of the ECSC was an important initial step on the road toward full European union. The process would continue in fits and starts over the coming decades, affected now by this political development, now by this international crisis, creating new treaties, such as the TREATY OF ROME, the EUROPEAN FREE TRADE ASSOCIATION CONVENTION, the Merger Treaty, the European Single Act, and the MAASTRICHT TREATY, each incorporating the terms of the previous treaty, as the bonds of the disparate countries weathered the times and grew tighter.

Source

Nicholas Rengger, ed., *Treaties and Alliances of the World,* 5th ed. (London: Longman Current Events, 1990), 306–308.

TREATY OF ROME

TREATY AT A GLANCE

Completed
March 25, 1957, at Rome; entered into force January 1, 1958

Signatories
Belgium, Federal Republic of Germany (West Germany), France, Italy, Luxembourg, and the Netherlands

Overview
The seminal treaty in the creation of the European Community (EC), the Treaty of Rome established the European Atomic Energy Community (EURATOM) and the European Economic Community (EEC, better known as the Common Market).

Historical Background

Shortly after the conclusion of World War II, the French statesman Jean Monnet had proposed a plan for a united Europe, which inspired French foreign minister Robert Schuman to propose a 1950 plan that became the basis of the European Coal and Steel Community (ECSC), created by the Treaty of Paris (April 18, 1951; effective January 1, 1952). The earliest forerunner of what eventually became the European Community, or EC (known as the European Union [EU] since November 1, 1993), the ECSC pooled resources and coordinated industrial policies and enterprise related to the production and distribution of coal, iron ore, and steel in France, the Federal Republic of Germany, Italy, Belgium, the Netherlands, and Luxembourg. For these commodities among these nations, a single economic market—encompassing a customs union and a free trade area—was created under the management of the "High Authority."

Further steps toward European unity came in fits and starts, with long periods of inaction, such as that following the establishment of the ECSC. In the wake of the Hungarian Revolt and the Suez Canal Crisis of October 1956, the movement to integrate the European community gained renewed vigor. The crushing of the first truly meaningful protest against the Soviets' postwar hegemony in Eastern Europe since Stalin had begun launching his satellite governments immediately after the war reminded the Europeans just how close the Russians were and how brutal they could be. The Suez crisis reinforced their growing resentment against America's patronizing attitude.

Inspired by Monnet and Belgian economist Paul-Henri Spaak, the Treaty of Rome (concluded on March 25, 1957; effective January 1, 1958) brought the six ECSC nations together in the creation of the European Atomic Energy Community (EURATOM) and the so-called Common Market, officially known as the European Economic Community (EEC).

Terms

The Treaty of Rome begins by establishing the philosophical and political principles of the EEC:

ARTICLE 1
By this Treaty, the High Contracting Parties establish among themselves a European Economic Community.

ARTICLE 2
The Community shall have as its task, by establishing a common market and progressively approximating the economic policies of Member States, to promote throughout the Community a harmonious development of economic activities, a continuous balanced expansion, an increase in stability, an accelerated raising of the standard of living and closer relations between the States belonging to it.

ARTICLE 3
For the purposes set out in Article 2, the activities of the Community shall include, as provided in this Treaty and in accordance with the timetable set out therein:

(a) the elimination, as between Member States, of customs duties and of quantitative restrictions on the import and export of goods, and of all other measures having equivalent effect;

(b) the establishment of a common customs tariff and of a common commercial policy towards third countries;

(c) the abolition, as between Member States, of obstacles to freedom of movement for persons, services and capital;

(d) the adoption of a common policy in the sphere of agriculture;

(e) the adoption of a common policy in the sphere of transport;

(f) the institution of a system ensuring that competition in the common market is not discord;

(g) the application of procedures by which the economic policies of Member States can be coordinated and disequilibria in their balances of payments remedied;

(h) the approximation of laws of Member States to the extent required for the proper functioning of the common market;

(i) the creation of a European Social Fund in order to improve the employment opportunities for workers and to contribute to the raising of their standard of living;

(j) the establishment of a European Investment Bank to facilitate the economic expansion of the Community by opening up fresh resources;

(k) the association of the overseas countries and territories in order to increase trade and to promote economic and social development.

The central basis of the EEC was the free movement of goods between member nations, which was accomplished through the creation of the Customs Union:

Chapter 1: The Customs Union

Section 1. Elimination of Customs Duties between Member States

ARTICLE 12

Member States shall refrain from introducing between themselves any new customs duties on imports or exports or any charges having equivalent effect, and from increasing those which they already apply in their trade with each other.

ARTICLE 13

Customs duties on imports in force between the Member States shall be progressively abolished by them during the transitional period in accordance with Articles 14 and 15. . . .

The principle of free movement was extended to labor as well:

TITLE III: FREE MOVEMENT OF PERSONS, SERVICES AND CAPITAL

Chapter 1: Workers

ARTICLE 48

1. Freedom of movement for workers shall be secured within the Community by the end of the transitional period at the latest.

2. Such freedom of movement shall entail the abolition of any discrimination based on nationality between workers of the Member States as regards employment, remuneration and other conditions of work and employment.

3. It shall entail the right, subject to limitations justified on grounds of public policy, public security or public health:

(a) to accept offers of employment actually made;

(b) to move freely within the territory of Member States for this purpose;

(c) to stay in a Member State for the purpose of employment in accordance with the provisions governing the employment of nationals of that State laid down by law, regulation or administrative action;

(d) to remain in the territory of a Member State after having been employed in that State, subject to the conditions which shall be embodied in implementing regulations to be drawn up by the Commission.

4. The provisions of this Article shall not apply to employment in the public service.

ARTICLE 49

As soon as this Treaty enters into force, the Council shall, acting on a proposal from the Commission and after consulting the Economic and Social Committee, issue directives or make regulations setting out measures required to bring about, by progressive stages, freedom of movement for workers, as defined in Article 48, in particular:

(a) by ensuring close cooperation between national employment services;

(b) by systematically and progressively abolishing those administrative procedures and practices and those qualifying periods in respect of eligibility for available employment, whether resulting from national legislation, or from agreements previously concluded between Member States, the maintenance of which would form an obstacle to liberalization of the movement of workers;

(c) by systematically and progressively abolishing all such qualifying periods and other restrictions provided for either under national legislation or under agreements previously concluded between Member States as imposed on workers of other Member States conditions regarding the free choice of employment other than those imposed on workers of the State concerned;

(d) by setting up appropriate machinery to bring offers of employment into touch with applications for employment and to facilitate the achievement of a balance between supply and demand in the employment market in such a way as to avoid serious threats to the standard of living and level of employment in the various regions and industries.

Pursuant to the policy on labor, Title 3 of the treaty provided for "Social Policy":

TITLE III: SOCIAL POLICY

Chapter 1: Social Provisions

ARTICLE 117

Member States agree upon the need to promote improved working conditions and an improved standard of living for workers, so as to make possible their harmonization while the improvement is being maintained.

They believe that such a development will ensue not only from the functioning of the common market, which will favor the harmonization of social systems, but also from the procedures provided for in this Treaty and from the approximation of provisions laid down by law, regulation and administrative action.

ARTICLE 118

Without prejudice to the other provisions of this Treaty and in conformity with its general objectives, the Commission shall have the task of promoting close cooperation between Member States in the social field. . . .

ARTICLE 119

Each Member State shall during the first stage ensure and subsequently maintain the application of the principle that men and women should receive equal pay for equal work. . . .

Chapter 2: The European Social Fund

ARTICLE 123

In order to improve employment opportunities for workers in the common market and to contribute thereby to raising the standard of living, a European Social Fund is thereby established in accordance with the provisions set out below; it shall have the task of rendering the employment of workers easier and of increasing their geographical and occupational mobility within the Community.

ARTICLE 124

The Fund shall be administered by the Commission.

The Commission shall be assisted in this task by a Committee presided over by a member of the Commission and composed of representatives of Governments, trade unions and employers' organizations.

Consequences

On April 8, 1965, the Merger Treaty was concluded (effective July 1, 1967), establishing among the signatory nations a common Council of Ministers, a European Commission, a European Parliament, a Court of Justice, and a European Council. Twenty-one years later, the European Single Act (ESA)—signed on February 26, 1986; effective July 1, 1987—augmented the authority of the European Parliament and laid the foundation for the so-called 1992 Program, a bold plan to tear down all remaining barriers to the completion of a unified European market. While EURATOM accelerated the European development of atomic energy and nuclear research, the EEC greatly broadened the scope of what had been established by the ECSC, extending common market and free trade principles to most economic sectors.

Throughout the 1960s, France resolutely opposed British participation in the Common Market because it was felt that Britain's ties to its Commonwealth and its close relationship with the United States presented a conflict with the interests of the EEC. Britain finally joined the European Community (along with Ireland and Denmark) in 1973. Greece joined in 1981, followed by Spain and Portugal in 1986. When East and West Germany were unified in 1990 as the expanded Federal Republic of Germany, membership in the EC was automatically extended to cover the former East German territories.

The Treaty of Rome, though much amended, remained in force even as the European Community became the European Union in 1993 under the terms of the MAASTRICHT TREATY, creating what is today a supranational organization of 25 nations (the original EU 12—Belgium, Denmark, France, Germany, Greece, Ireland, Italy, Luxembourg, Netherlands, Portugal, Spain, and Great Britain—were joined by Austria, Finland, and Sweden in 1995 and by Greek Cyprus, the Czech Republic, Estonia, Hungary, Latvia, Lithuania, Malta, Poland, Slovakia, and Slovenia in 2004–05) sharing not only a vibrant common market but an increasingly strong international currency, the Euro.

Source

Nicholas Rengger, ed., *Treaties and Alliances of the World*, 5th ed. (London: Longman Current Events, 1990), 308–310.

EUROPEAN FREE TRADE ASSOCIATION CONVENTION

TREATY AT A GLANCE

Completed
January 4, 1960, at Stockholm, Sweden;
entered into force May 3, 1960

Signatories
Austria, Denmark, Norway, Portugal, Sweden, Switzerland,
and the United Kingdom

Overview
This convention established Europe's "other" Common Market, a
trade alliance with deliberately more limited scope than the ECC.

Historical Background

Called the Outer Seven (in contrast to the Inner Six nations of the ECC, or Common Market), Austria, Denmark, Norway, Portugal, Sweden, Switzerland, and the United Kingdom created EFTA as a free trade area in industrial products. Unlike the TREATY OF ROME, which established the Common Market, the EFTA convention did not call for a common external tariff on agricultural and industrial goods, thereby allowing the signatory nations more latitude in trading with such nations as the United States. For Sweden, Switzerland, and Austria—as well as Finland, which joined EFTA as an associate member in 1961—the alternative organization provided an opportunity to enjoy the benefits of free trade without compromising political neutrality by a close alliance with a politically unified group of Western nations.

Terms

The essence of EFTA was described in the 1960 Convention:

ARTICLE 1: THE ASSOCIATION
1. An international organization to be known as the European Free Trade Association, hereinafter referred to as "the Association," is hereby established.

2. The Members of the Association, hereinafter referred to as "Member States," shall be the States which ratify this Convention and such other States as may accede to it.

3. The Area of the Association shall be the territories to which this Convention applies.

4. The Institutions of the Association shall be a Council and such other organs as the Council may set up.

ARTICLE 2: OBJECTIVES
The objectives of the Association shall be

(a) to promote in the Area of the Association and in each Member State a sustained expansion of economic activity, full employment, increased productivity and the rational use of resources, financial stability and continuous improvement in living standards,

(b) to secure that trade between Member States takes place in conditions of fair competition,

(c) to avoid significant disparity between Member States in the conditions of supply of raw materials produced within the Area of the Association, and

(d) to contribute to the harmonious development and expansion of world trade and to the progressive removal of barriers to it.

ARTICLE 3: IMPORT DUTIES
1. Member States shall reduce and ultimately eliminate, in accordance with this Article, customs duties and any other charges with equivalent effect, except duties notified in accordance with Article 6 and other charges which fall within that Article, imposed on or in connection with the importation of goods which are eligible for Area tariff treatment in accordance with Article 4. Any such duty or other charge is hereinafter referred to as an "import duty."

2. (a) On and after each of the following dates, Member States shall not apply an import duty on any product at a level exceeding the percentage of the basic duty specified against that date [reducing from 80 per cent on 1 July 1960 to 10 per cent on 1 January 1969].

(b) On and after 1st January 1970, Member States shall not apply any import duties . . .

ARTICLE 30: ECONOMIC AND FINANCIAL POLICIES
Member States recognize that the economic and financial policies of each of them affect the economies of other Member States and intend to pursue those policies

in a manner which serves to promote the objectives of the Association. They shall periodically exchange views on all aspects of those policies. In so doing, they shall take into account the corresponding activities within the Organization for European Economic Cooperation and other international organizations. The Council may make recommendations to Member States on matters relating to those policies to the extent necessary to ensure the attainment of the objectives and the smooth operation of the Association.

ARTICLE 31: GENERAL CONSULTATIONS AND COMPLAINTS PROCEDURES

1. If any Member considers that any benefit conferred upon it by this Convention or any objective of the Association is being or may be frustrated and if no satisfactory settlement is reached between the Member States concerned, any of those Member States may refer the matter to the Council.

2. The Council shall promptly, by majority vote, make arrangements for examining the matter. Such arrangements may include a reference to an examining committee constituted in accordance with Article 33. Before taking action under paragraph 3 of this Article, the Council shall so refer the matter at the request of any Member State concerned. Member States shall furnish all information which they can make available and shall lend their assistance to establish the facts.

3. When considering the matter, the Council shall have regard to whether it has been established that an obligation under the Convention has not been fulfilled, and whether and to what extent any benefit conferred by the Convention or any objective of the Association is being or may be frustrated. In the light of this consideration and of the report of any examining committee which may have been appointed, the Council may, by majority vote, make to any Member State such recommendations as it considers appropriate.

4. If a Member State does not or is unable to comply with a recommendation made in accordance with paragraph 3 of this Article and the Council finds, by majority vote, that an obligation under this Convention has not been fulfilled, the Council may, by majority decision, authorize any Member State to suspend to the Member State which has not complied with the recommendation the application of such obligations under this Convention as the Council considers appropriate.

5. Any Member State may, at any time while the matter is under consideration, request the Council to authorize, as a matter of urgency, interim measures to safeguard its position. If it appears to the Council that the circumstances are sufficiently serious to justify interim action, and without prejudice to any action which it may subsequently take in accordance with the preceding paragraphs of this Article, the Council may, by majority decision, authorize a Member State to suspend its obligations under this Convention to such an extent and for such a period as the Council considers appropriate.

Consequences

Headquartered in Geneva, Switzerland, EFTA traded extensively with the European Community, and it conducted many cooperative research and development programs with the EC. Thus, both EFTA and the EC, which have promoted European unification in and of themselves, achieved a further degree of integration by their cooperation with one another. Britain and Denmark withdrew from the EFTA when they joined the EC in 1973. Portugal withdrew in 1986, when it joined the EC. Iceland joined EFTA in 1970, and associate member Finland became a full member in 1986. In 1995 Austria and Sweden also made their plans to leave EFTA and applied for membership in the EC.

Then, in 1993, under the terms of the MASSTRICHT TREATY, the European Community (EC) became the European Union (EU), which originally included Belgium, Denmark, France, Germany, Greece, Ireland, Italy, Luxembourg, Netherlands, Portugal, Spain, and Great Britain, but not Austria, Finland, and Sweden. These three soon joined, however, in 1995. The EU established its own currency, the Euro. By the time the EU added to its roll those countries formerly dominated by the Soviet Union—the Czech Republic, Estonia, Hungary, Latvia, Lithuania, Malta, Poland, Slovakia, Slovenia—as well as Greek Cyprus, in 2004–05)—it was no longer merely a common market; it was well on its way to becoming a world trading power.

Source

Nicholas Rengger, ed., *Treaties and Alliances of the World,* 5th ed. (London: Longman Current Events, 1990), 344–345.

ALLIANCE FOR PROGRESS
(DECLARATION OF PUNTA DEL ESTE)

TREATY AT A GLANCE

Completed
August 17, 1961, at Punta del Este, Uruguay

Signatories
United States and 22 Latin American countries

Overview
The Charter of Punta del Este, Uruguay, formally established a $100 billion program for the economic and social development of Latin America, originally proposed by President John F. Kennedy as a means of maintaining the nations of Latin America in the U.S. sphere of influence and keeping them out of the communist camp.

Historical Background

With the coming of John F. Kennedy to the White House in 1960, the cold war heated up. Whereas the cautious spendthrift Dwight D. Eisenhower sought to avoid conflict and keep a lid on defense funding, choosing his showdowns carefully for maximum political payoff with minimum bloodshed, Kennedy and his select cadre of advisers, called by the media at the time and since the "best and the brightest," imagined themselves as modern warriors and "tough guys": clear-eyed, realistic, unsentimental optimists who were intent on saving the world for democracy. Convinced that the United States could be doing more to demonstrate its technological and moral superiority to the Soviet Union, Kennedy set out to win the "hearts and minds" of the third world and accelerate social progress at home. "Let every nation know," he said in his inaugural speech on January 20, 1961, "whether it wishes us well or wishes us ill, that we shall pay any price, bear any burden, support any friend, oppose any foe, to assure the survival and success of liberty."

Nowhere was this new attitude toward the third world more evident than in Latin America, where it amounted to almost a clean break in American diplomacy. One of the best and the brightest, W. W. Rostow, had described in what he called a "non-Communist manifesto," the stages of economic development in third world countries. Following that text Kennedy increased foreign aid to these "developing nations," whether or not they were aligned with the United States through the series of regional pacts by which Harry S. Truman and Eisenhower had drawn the ideological battle lines of the cold war. Created in March 1961 and targeted specifically at Latin America, the Alliance for Progress was a vehicle for deploying such aid in this reinvigorated and stylishly new foreign policy.

Terms

The Declaration to the Peoples of America, which preceded the charter proper, set out the goals of the Alliance for Progress.

Declaration to the Peoples of America

Assembled in Punta del Este, inspired by the principles consecrated in the Charter of the Organizations of American States, in Operation Pan America and in the Act of Bogota, the representatives of the American Republics hereby agree to establish an Alliance for Progress: a vast effort to bring a better life to all the peoples of the continent.

This Alliance is established on the basic principle that free men working through the institution of representative democracy can best satisfy man's aspirations, including those for work, home and land, health and schools. No system can guarantee true progress unless it affirms the dignity of the individual which is the foundation of our civilization.

Therefore the countries signing this Declaration in the exercise of their sovereignty have agreed to work toward the following goals during the coming years:

To improve and strengthen democratic institutions through the application of the principle of self-determination by the people.

To accelerate economic and social development, thus rapidly bringing about a substantial and steady increase in the average income in order to narrow the gap between the standard of living in Latin American countries and that enjoyed in the industrialized countries.

To encourage, in accordance with the characteristics of each country, programs of comprehensive agrarian reform, leading to the effective transformation, where required, of unjust structures and systems of land tenure and use; with a view to replacing latifundia and dwarf holdings by an equitable system of property so that, supplemented by timely and adequate credit, technical assistance and improved marketing arrangements, the land will become for the man who works it the basis of his economic stability, the foundation of his increasing welfare, and the guarantee of his freedom and dignity.

To assure fair wages and satisfactory working conditions to all our workers; to establish effective systems of labor-management relations and procedures for consultation and cooperation among government authorities, employers' associations, and trade unions in the interests of social and economic development.

To wipe out illiteracy; to extend, as quickly as possible, the benefits of primary education to all Latin Americans; and to provide broader facilities, on a vast scale, for secondary and technical training and for higher education.

To press forward with programs of health and sanitation in order to prevent sickness, combat contagious disease, and strengthen our human potential.

To reform tax laws, demanding more from those who have most, to punish tax evasion severely, and to redistribute the national income in order to benefit those who are most in need, while, at the same time, promoting savings and investment and reinvestment of capital.

To maintain monetary and fiscal policies which, while avoiding the disastrous effects of inflation or deflation, will protect the purchasing power of the many, guarantee the greatest possible price stability, and form an adequate basis for economic development.

To stimulate private enterprise in order to encourage the development of Latin American countries at a rate which will help them to provide jobs for their growing populations, to eliminate unemployment, and to take their place among the modern industrialized nations of the world.

To find a quick and lasting solution to the grave problem created by excessive price fluctuations in the basic exports of Latin American countries on which their prosperity so heavily depends.

To accelerate the integration of Latin America so as to stimulate the economic and social development of the continent. This process has already begun through the General Treaty of Economic Integration of Central America and, in other countries, through the Latin American Free Trade Association.

This Declaration expresses the conviction of the nations of Latin America that these profound economic, social, and cultural changes can come about only through the self-help efforts of each country. Nonetheless, in order to achieve the goals which have been established with the necessary speed, domestic efforts must be reinforced by essential contributions of external assistance.

The United States, for its part, pledges its efforts to supply financial and technical cooperation in order to achieve the aims of the Alliance for Progress. To this end, the United States will provide a major part of the minimum of twenty billion dollars, principally in public funds, which Latin America will require over the next ten years from all external sources in order to supplement its own efforts.

The United States will provide from public funds, as an immediate contribution to the economic and social progress of Latin America, more than one billion dollars during the twelve months which began on March 13, 1961, when the Alliance for Progress was announced.

The United States intends to furnish development loans on a long-term basis, where appropriate running up to fifty years and in general at very low or zero rates of interest.

For their part, the countries of Latin America agree to devote a steadily increasing share of their own resources to economic and social development, and to make reforms necessary to assure that all share fully in the fruits of the Alliance for Progress.

Further, as a contribution to the Alliance for Progress, each of the countries of Latin America will formulate a comprehensive and well-conceived national program for the development of its own economy.

Independent and highly qualified experts will be made available to Latin American countries in order to assist in formulating and examining national development plans.

Conscious of the overriding importance of this Declaration, the signatory countries declare that the inter-American community is now beginning a new era when it will supplement its institutional, legal, cultural and social accomplishments with immediate and concrete actions to secure a better life, under freedom and democracy, for the present and future generations.

By addressing the chronic poverty and oppression that plagued the peoples of Latin America, the United States hoped not only to improve the quality of life in the hemisphere but to maintain the Latin American nations in the U.S. sphere of influence without resorting to overtly imperialist measures. The Alliance for Progress was an ambitious attempt to use large-scale economic "weapons" to fight the ongoing cold war in the Americas. The Declaration and the Preamble that followed it inextricably linked economic aid to a political philosophy of "personal dignity and political liberty":

Preamble

We, the American Republics, hereby proclaim our decision to unite in a common effort to bring our people accelerated economic progress and broader social justice within the framework of personal dignity and political liberty.

Almost two hundred years ago we began in this hemisphere the long struggle for freedom which now inspires people in all parts of the world. Today, in ancient lands, men moved to hope by revolutions of our young nations search for liberty. Now we must give a new meaning to that revolutionary heritage. For America stands at a turning point in history. The men and women of our hemisphere are reaching for the better life which today's skills have placed within their grasp. They are determined for themselves and for their children to have decent and ever more abundant lives, to gain access to knowledge and equal opportunity for all, to end those conditions which benefit the few at the expense of the needs and dignity of the many. It is our inescapable task to fulfill these just desires-to demonstrate to the poor and forsaken of our countries, and of all our lands, that the creative powers of free men hold the key to their progress and to the progress of future generations. And our certainty of ultimate success rests not alone on our faith in ourselves and in our nations but on the indomitable spirit of free man which has been the heritage of American civilization.

Inspired by these principles, and by the principles of Operation Pan-America and the Act of Bogotá, the American Republics hereby resolve to adopt the following program of action to establish and carry forward an Alliance for Progress.

Chapter 4 of Title 2 of the charter set out the broad parameters of "external assistance in support of national development programs":

1. The economic and social development of Latin America will require a large amount of additional public and private financial assistance on the part of capital-exporting countries, including the members of the Development Assistance Group and international lending agencies. The measures provided for in the Act of Bogotá and the new measures provided for in this Charter, are designed to create a framework within which such additional assistance can be provided and effectively utilized.

2. The United States will assist those participating countries whose development programs establish self-help measures and economic and social policies consistent with the principles of this Charter. To supplement the domestic efforts of such countries, the United States is prepared to allocate resources which, along with those anticipated from other external sources, will be of a scope and magnitude adequate to realize the goals envisaged in this Charter. Such assistance will be allocated to both social and economic development and, where appropriate, will take the form of grants or loans on flexible terms and conditions. The participating countries will request the support of other capital-exporting countries and appropriate institutions so that they may provide assistance for the attainment of these objectives.

3. The United States will help in the financing of technical assistance projects proposed by participating country or by the General Secretariat of the Organization of American States for the purpose of:

(a) Providing experts contracted in agreement with the Governments to work under their direction and to assist them in the preparation of specific investment projects and the strengthening of national mechanisms for preparing projects, using specialized engineering firms where appropriate;

(b) Carrying out, pursuant to existing agreements for cooperation among the General Secretariat of the Organization of American States, the Economic Commission for Latin America, and the Inter-American Development Bank, field investigations and studies, including those relating to development problems, the organization of national agencies for the preparation of development programs, agrarian reform and rural development, health, cooperatives, housing, education and professional training, and taxation and tax administration; and

(c) Covening meetings of experts and officials on development and related problems.

The Governments or above-mentioned organizations should, when appropriate, seek the cooperation of the United Nations and its specialized agencies in the execution of these activities.

4. The participating Latin American countries recognize that each has in varying degree a capacity to assist fellow Republics by providing technical and financial assistance. They recognize that this capacity will increase as their economies grow. They therefore affirm their intention to assist fellow Republics increasingly as their individual circumstances permit.

Consequences

The original 10-year treaty was extended indefinitely in 1965, but the Alliance for Progress effectively ended in 1974, when the United States discontinued funding. To be sure, some advances were made in the areas of health, education, housing, and economic growth, but the program failed to meet most of its ambitious and idealistic expectations.

Source

Avalon Project at the Yale Law School, "Declaration of Punta del Este, August 17, 1961." Available online. URL: http://www.yale.edu/lawweb/avalon/intdip/interam/intam15.htm. Accessed May 16, 2005.

Multinational Conventions and Agreements

CHARTER OF THE ORGANIZATION OF AMERICAN STATES

TREATY AT A GLANCE

Completed
April 30, 1948, at Bogotá, Colombia

Signatories
Antigua and Barbuda, Argentina, Bahamas, Barbados (joined 1967),
Bolivia, Brazil, Chile, Colombia, Costa Rica, Cuba (expelled 1962),
Dominica, the Dominican Republic, Ecuador, El Salvador, Grenada,
Guatemala, Haiti, Honduras, Jamaica, Mexico, Nicaragua, Panama,
Paraguay, Peru, Saint Kitts–Nevis, Saint Lucia, Saint Vincent and
the Grenadines, Suriname, Trinidad and Tobago (joined 1967),
the United States, Uruguay, and Venezuela

Overview
This pact created the Organization of American States, the principal regional political body of the Americas.

Historical Background

The origin of the Organization of American States (OAS) may be traced to the First International Conference of American States, held in Washington, D.C., in 1889 and 1890. That conference established the International Union of American Republics, which in 1910 became the Pan-American Union. This organization was fairly limited in scope, concerned mainly with operating as a system for the exchange of information and for consultation on issues of common interest. However, in the course of the following decades, the organization's scope widened. World War II brought an increased spirit of solidarity among the republics of the Americas (see ACT OF HAVANA), and in 1948, as a result of the Ninth International Conference of American States, held in Bogotá, Colombia, the OAS was established.

Terms

The 1948 charter began with an idealistic preamble, far closer in spirit and tone to the UNITED NATIONS CHARTER than to the earlier, more legalistic COVENANT OF THE LEAGUE OF NATIONS:

> IN THE NAME OF THEIR PEOPLES, THE STATES REPRESENTED AT THE NINTH INTERNATIONAL CONFERENCE OF AMERICAN STATES,

Convinced that the historic mission of America is to offer to man a land of liberty, and a favorable environment for the development of his personality and the realization of his just aspirations;

Conscious that that mission has already inspired numerous agreements, whose essential value lies in the desire of the American peoples to live together in peace, and, through their mutual understanding and respect for the sovereignty of each one, to provide for the betterment of all, in independence, in equality and under law;

Confident that the true significance of American solidarity and good neighborliness can only mean the consolidation on this continent, within the framework of democratic institutions, of a system of individual liberty and social justice based on respect for the essential rights of man;

Persuaded that their welfare and their contribution to the progress and the civilization of the world will increasingly require intensive continental cooperation;

Resolved to persevere in the noble undertaking that humanity has conferred upon the United Nations, whose principles and purposes they solemnly reaffirm;

Convinced that juridical organization is a necessary condition for security and peace founded on moral order and on justice; and

In accordance with Resolution IX of the Inter-American Conference on Problems of War and Peace, held at Mexico City,

Have agreed upon the following CHARTER OF THE ORGANIZATION OF AMERICAN STATES.

The Charter comprised 112 articles. The most important follow:

PART ONE

Chapter I: Nature and Purposes

ARTICLE 1

The American States establish by this Charter the international organization that they have developed to achieve an order of peace and justice, to promote their solidarity, to strengthen their collaboration, and to defend their sovereignty, their territorial integrity and their independence. Within the United Nations, the Organization of American States is a regional agency. . . .

ARTICLE 4

The Organization of American States, in order to put into practice the principles on which it is founded and to fulfill its regional obligations under the Charter of the United Nations, proclaims the following essential purposes:

a) To strengthen the peace and security of the continent;

b) To prevent possible causes of difficulties and to ensure the pacific settlement of disputes that may arise among the Member States;

c) To provide for common action on the part of those States in the event of aggression;

d) To seek the solution of political, juridical and economic problems that may arise among them; and

e) to promote, by cooperative action, their economic, social and cultural development. . . .

Chapter III: Fundamental Rights and Duties of States

ARTICLE 6

States are juridically equal, enjoy equal rights and equal capacity to exercise these rights, and have equal duties. The rights of each State depend not upon its power to ensure the exercise thereof, but upon the mere fact of its existence as a person under international law. . . .

ARTICLE 15

No State or group of States has the right to intervene, directly or indirectly, for any reason whatever, in the internal or external affairs of any other State. The foregoing principle prohibits not only armed force but also any other form of interference or attempted threat against the personality of the State or against its political, economic and cultural elements.

ARTICLE 16

No State may use or encourage the use of coercive measures of an economic or political character in order to force the sovereign will of another State and obtain from it advantages of any kind.

ARTICLE 17

The territory of a State is inviolable; it may not be the object, even temporarily, of military occupation or of other measures of force taken by another State, directly or indirectly, on any grounds whatever. No territorial acquisitions or special advantages obtained either by force or by other means of coercion shall be recognized.

ARTICLE 18

The American States bind themselves in their international relations not to have recourse to the use of force, except in the case of self-defense in accordance with existing treaties or in fulfillment thereof.

ARTICLE 19

Measures adopted for the maintenance of peace and security in accordance with existing treaties do not constitute a violation of the principles set forth in Articles 15 and 17.

Chapter IV: Pacific Settlement of Disputes

ARTICLE 20

All international disputes that may arise between American States shall be submitted to the peaceful procedures set forth in this Charter, before being referred to the Security Council of the United Nations. . . .

Chapter V: Collective Security

ARTICLE 24

Every act of aggression by a State against the territorial integrity or the inviolability of the territory or against the sovereignty or political independence of an American State shall be considered an act of aggression against the other American States.

ARTICLE 25

If the inviolability or the integrity of the territory or the sovereignty or political independence of any American State should be affected by an armed attack or by an act of aggression that is not an armed attack, or by an extra-continental conflict, or by a conflict between two or more American States, or by any other fact or situation that might endanger the peace of America, the American States, in furtherance of the principles of continental solidarity or collective self defense, shall apply the measures and procedures established in the special treaties on the subject. . . .

Consequences

Mainly concerned with political matters, particularly the maintenance of peace in the Western Hemisphere and the settlement of disputes within the framework of the inter-American system, the OAS also implemented the mutual security PACT OF RIO. By the 1960s, as Latin America became identified with the nations of the so-called third world, rather than with the first, or "free," world, as imagined by the ALLIANCE FOR PROGRESS, economic cooperation—instead of simply U.S. aid—had become an increasingly important aspect of the OAS.

Source

Avalon Project at the Yale Law School, "Bogota Conference of American States, Charter of the Organization of American States, March 30–May 2, 1948." Available online. URL: http://www.yale.edu/lawweb/avalon/decade/decad062.htm. Accessed May 16, 2005.

CHARTER OF THE ORGANIZATION OF AFRICAN UNITY

TREATY AT A GLANCE

Completed
May 25, 1963, at Addis Ababa, Ethiopia

Signatories
African and Malagasy states and governments

Overview
A development of early-20th-century Pan-Africa movements, the OAU was chartered to defend the independence, sovereignty, and territorial integrity of member states and to promote unity and cooperative mutual development.

Historical Background

British prime minister Harold Macmillan was elected in the wake of a crisis that led Britain to grant Ghana its independence in 1957. Shortly after taking office, he spoke before the parliament of white-ruled South Africa on the topic of the new political realities in Africa. A "wind of change," he said, was sweeping the continent. This was no mere political hyperbole. By the time of Macmillan's speech, 17 new nations had formed out of Europe's old colonies in Africa; from 1960 to 1965 another 11 would become independent. The white-settler nations in the south were virtually the last outposts of Africa's European-dominated past.

The change that Macmillan referred to had its most immediate origins in a conference of black politicians held in Manchester, England, in October 1945. There a 36-year-old activist from the West African colony of the Gold Coast named Kwame Nkrumah declared that "we affirm the rights of all colonial peoples to control their destiny" and warned Europe that "the long, long night is over." Another speaker, Nigeria's Nnamdi Azikiwe, set a deadline for independence in British-held Africa: 15 years. And the conference targeted not only Britain's African empire but demanded independence for all the other European colonies: the French territories, which comprised most of the west and center of the continent; the Belgian Congo; Portuguese Guinea, Mozambique, and Angola; the independent white-settler state of South Africa, with its black majority; and South Africa's own virtual colony, South-West Africa.

Few outside Britain ever heard of the Manchester declaration, and few British officials took the words of Nkrumah, Azikiwe, and the others there seriously. Less than a century before, most Europeans had regarded Africa—or at least Africa south of the Sahara—as the Dark Continent, and only a generation or two before, a Europe then at the apex of centuries of imperial expansion around the world had divided the subcontinent between the Western world's great powers. Now all of a sudden, a few radicals, who many simply assumed to be communists, were talking about independence.

But the African nationalists were appealing to principles long accepted in the West, and their words would prove prophetic. The Great Powers themselves had affirmed the right to national self-determination in the 1918 peace settlements at Versailles (see TREATY OF VERSAILLES), plagued as most of them saw it by an American president named Woodrow Wilson determined to make all the slaughter mean something, and what he wanted it to mean was that the Great War had made the world safe for democracy, for national governments ruled for and by their peoples. Again in 1945 the United States insisted that the right to national self-determination become a cornerstone of the UNITED NATIONS CHARTER. Already by then, India was well on the way to independence from British rule, and in the Far East, new nations were emerging from the chaos World War II had made of the area's Dutch and French colonial past. Little wonder, then, that Africa's black leaders should also be seeking nationhood for their peoples or that some of them should be turning to the revolution-minded marxist government in Russia, whose propaganda constantly emphasized Bolshevik hatred of colonialism.

Conditions in post–World War II Africa seemed ripe for revolution. Both the world wars had exposed the vulnerability of the colonial rulers, and in 1945 the winners and losers in World War II were crippled by its almost mindless destructiveness, saddled with massive war debts, and faced with the awesome task of reconstructing homelands scarred by bombed-out ruins and widespread social dislocations. The economy of the African colonies was more complex but also conducive to change. The war had ushered in a period of booming commodity prices that would last throughout the 1940s and 1950s, raising hopes for, and expectations of, widespread prosperity in those countries geared to exporting raw materials.

But especially in those colonies with large white-settler populations, such as Kenya, the immigrants had taken advantage of the European distractions provided by the war to increase their own power locally, and as European-dominated businesses like mining and large-scale farming grew, it was they—and not the indigenous natives—who benefited. Even in West Africa, where independent peasant farmers had prospered because of the booms, Britain organized schemes for monopolies to buy up the land, which soon led West African natives to join in the social resentment spreading across the continent. Most provocative, perhaps, was a fresh wave of settlers who descended on postwar Africa at the behest of the colonial governments, technical experts coming for the best of reasons—to work on veterinary medicine, crop development, road building, improvements in health care, welfare programs—but who in the long run only appeared to make white colonial "oppression" more pervasive than ever.

The growing tinderbox first exploded in the Gold Coast, in Britain's richest and best-educated colony. Britain's always small white colony there had long depended on a system of government dominated by traditional tribal chiefs, and in 1946 a new constitution drafted by the whites granted Africans a majority on the ruling legislative council. But political and economic discontent continued to smolder, flaring up especially after the return of Nkrumah in 1947. By 1948 Africans were rioting and looting in the major townships, and Britain tried to appease them by appointing a new, all-African committee to rewrite the constitution. The Africans called for a general strike in 1950 after Nkrumah demanded immediate self-rule, and though he was jailed for his efforts, the new constitution was more radical than Britain had planned for, placing political power firmly in African hands.

In the ensuing national elections, Nkrumah's Convention People's Party won hands down, and Nkrumah himself was released from jail to form a government. Under his guidance, the resource rich Gold Coast was set on the path to self-government, emerging in 1957 as the first newly independent country south of the Sahara and taking the name of a medieval West African kingdom, Ghana.

In more ways than one, Ghana was to prove a model for the continent as a whole. And as Harold Macmillan tacitly admitted in his 1960 parliamentary address to South Africa, independence could hardly be confined any longer to the relatively rich colonies of West Africa, but, would inexorably spread to central and East Africa, as well.

The French by then certainly thought the British prime minister's conclusions were accurate. At first they had tried to co-opt the winds of change on the continent. In 1944 Charles de Gaulle's Free French government-in-exile had met in Brazzaville in the French Congo to draft a blueprint for French Africa's future, and without consulting the Africans, it declared that they all should be partners in a French union, with their own seats in France's National Assembly in Paris, as long as they realized that the establishment of self-government in the colonies, however far off, could not even be contemplated.

After the war, one of the Africans who had attended that Constituent Assembly, Felix Houphouët, who added to his surname the sobriquet Boigny, meaning "immovable" object, won election to the newly restored National Assembly and traveled to Paris, where within a decade he had become a member of the French cabinet and dominated the drafting of a law that gave the vote to all Africans in France's African holdings. By then France had been forced, after a long and bloody war for independence, to withdraw from Indochina and was deeply mired in its struggle to hang onto Algeria. At the height of the Algerian crisis, General de Gaulle came to power and offered France's 12 colonies in sub-Sahara African the choice between independence and membership in a new French Community, which would grant each member internal autonomy.

Only Guinea, led by Ahmed Sekou Touré, refused to join, opting for full independence. De Gaulle's response was immediate and draconian: he ordered the instant withdrawal of the French colonial government and everything connected with it. French doctors, teachers, lawyers, and civil servants left en masse, taking with them all records and equipment, including unplugged generators and telephones literally ripped from the walls, nearly destroying Guinea's infrastructure and its economy. But Touré had become an African hero, and Ghana offered a substantial loan to avert immediate economic ruin, while the Soviet Union promised long-term aid.

Like Ghana, Guinea was quickly accepted into the United Nations, and its sudden prestige emboldened other French-speaking African nations to request formal independence. By 1960 all of the former French colonial holdings in Africa but Somaliland, a small enclave on the Horn, were at least technically independent, and the notion of a unified French Community was history.

As was British East Africa. Kenya's powerful white community had firmly resisted any form of majority rule, and in 1945 it had even sought to build up its settler population, centered around Nairobi, the capital, located in what they called the White Highlands of the farm-rich Rift Valley. Although the settlers made a feint toward appeasing native Africans by bringing a few into Kenya's Legislative Council, the tokenism fooled no one, much less satisfied them, and native discontent began to find a voice in Jomo Kenyatta. A tall, gregarious Kikuyu, Kenyatta had spent 17 years in England, where he married an English wife, whom he abandoned after returning to Kenya in 1946.

The following year he became president of the Kenya African Union, the voice of the country's now rabid nationalism. In the early 1950s, Kenya's colonial authorities charged Kenyatta with masterminding the Mau Mau uprising, a bloody terrorist campaign aimed at Kenya's white settlers. Though he vehemently denied being involved, the white government jailed Kenyatta for eight years, spent both in prison and under house arrest, succeeding only in making his popularity with the country's black population reach legendary proportions. The continuing Mau Mau troubles, the revolution in West Africa, the winning of independence by three other East African colonies (Tanganyika, Zanzibar, and Uganda), all persuaded the British-backed colonials of the impossibility of staying on. Kenyatta, now called *mzee* (grand old man) by his fellow Africans, was released from house arrest to lead his country to independence in 1963.

In the rush to independence, few Africans considered the implications of a continent suddenly awash in sovereign new nations. Kwame Nkrumah promoted a continent united by the ideals of socialist internationalism and its own black identity, and some leaders were sufficiently attracted to experiment with linkages into larger economic units. Mali teamed up with Senegal in 1959, and in 1963 Kenya, Tanganyika, and Uganda tried to establish a common customs union, but neither plan worked very well. Africa's new national leaders were more enthusiastic about creating political blocs, one school of a half dozen following Nkrumah's hard-line rejection of any contact with the former colonial powers and his dedication to radical socialism. A much larger group came together under the banner of moderation, seeking both economic and political stability through collaboration with the erstwhile colonial West. Two years later the schism was resolved when 39 nations joined the Organization of African Unity in Addis Ababa.

Terms

The Charter of the OAU read as follows:

We, the Heads of African and Malagasy States and Governments assembled in the City of Addis Ababa, Ethiopia;

Convinced that it is the inalienable right of all people to control their own destiny;

Conscious of the fact that freedom, equality, justice and dignity are essential objectives for the achievement of the legitimate aspirations of the African peoples;

Conscious of our responsibility to harness the natural and human resources of our continent for the total advancement of our peoples in spheres of human endeavor;

Inspired by a common determination to promote understanding among our peoples and cooperation among our States in response to the aspirations of our peoples for brotherhood and solidarity, in a larger unity transcending ethnic and national differences;

Convinced that, in order to translate this determination into a dynamic force in the cause of human progress, conditions for peace and security must be established and maintained;

Determined to safeguard and consolidate the hard-won independence as well as the sovereignty and territorial integrity of our States, and to resist neocolonialism in all its forms;

Dedicated to the general progress of Africa;

Persuaded that the Charter of the United Nations and the Universal Declaration of Human Rights, to the principles of which we reaffirm our adherence, provide a solid foundation for peaceful and positive cooperation among States;

Desirous that all African States should henceforth unite so that the welfare and well-being of their peoples can be assured;

Resolved to reinforce the links between our States by establishing and strengthening common institutions;

Have agreed to the present Charter.

Establishment

ARTICLE I

1. The High Contracting Parties do by the present Charter establish an Organization to be known as the "*Organization of African Unity*."

2. The Organization shall include the Continental African States, Madagascar and other Islands surrounding Africa.

Purposes

ARTICLE II

1. The Organization shall have the following purposes:

(a) To promote the unity and solidarity of the African States;

(b) To coordinate and intensify their collaboration and efforts to achieve a better life for the peoples of Africa;

(c) To defend their sovereignty, their territorial integrity and independence;

(d) To eradicate all forms of colonialism from Africa; and

(e) To promote international cooperation, having due regard to the Charter of the United Nations and the Universal Declaration of Human Rights.

2. To these ends, the Member States shall coordinate and harmonize their general policies, especially in the following fields:

(a) Political and diplomatic cooperation;

(b) Economic cooperation, including transport and communications;

(c) Educational and cultural cooperation;

(d) Health, sanitation, and nutritional cooperation;

(e) Scientific and technical cooperation; and

(f) Cooperation for defence and security.

Principles

ARTICLE III

The Member States, in pursuit of the purposes stated in Article II, solemnly affirm and declare their adherence to the following principles:

1. The sovereign equality of all Member States;

2. Non-interference in the internal affairs of States;

3. Respect for the sovereignty and territorial integrity of each State and for its inalienable right to independent existence;

4. Peaceful settlement of disputes by negotiation, mediation, conciliation or arbitration;

5. Unreserved condemnation, in all its forms, of political assassination as well as of subversive activities on the part of neighboring States or any other States;

6. Absolute dedication to the total emancipation of the African territories which are still dependent;

7. Affirmation of a policy of non-alignment with regard to all blocs.

Membership

ARTICLE IV

Each independent sovereign African State shall be entitled to become a Member of the Organization.

Rights and Duties of Member States

ARTICLE V

All Member States shall enjoy equal rights and have equal duties.

ARTICLE VI

The Member States ledge themselves to observe scrupulously the principles enumerated in Article III of the present Charter.

Institutions

ARTICLE VII

The Organization shall accomplish its purposes through the following principal institutions:

1. The Assembly of Heads of State and Government;

2. The Council of Ministers;

3. The General Secretariat;

4. The Commission of Mediation, Conciliation and Arbitration.

The Assembly of Heads of State and Government

ARTICLE VIII

The Assembly of Heads of State and Government shall be the supreme organ of the Organization. It shall, subject to the provisions of this Charter, discuss matters of common concern to Africa with a view to coordinating and harmonizing the general policy of the Organization. It may in addition review the structure, functions and acts of all the organs and any specialized agencies which may be created in accordance with the present Charter.

ARTICLE IX

The Assembly shall be composed of the Heads of State and Government or their duly accredited representatives and it shall meet at least once a year. At the request of any Member State and on approval by a two-thirds majority of the Member States, the Assembly shall meet in extraordinary session.

ARTICLE X

1. Each Member State shall have one vote.

2. All resolutions shall be determined by a two-thirds majority of the Members of the Organization.

3. Questions of procedure shall require a simple majority. Whether or not a question is one of procedure shall be determined by a simple majority of all Member States of the Organization.

4. Two-thirds of the total membership of the Organization shall form a quorum at any meeting of the Assembly.

Article XI. The Assembly shall have the power to determine its own rules of procedure.

The Council of Ministers

ARTICLE XII

1. The Council of Ministers shall consist of Foreign Ministers or such other Ministers as are designated by the Governments of Member States.

2. The Council of Ministers shall meet at least twice a year. When requested by any Member State and approved by two-thirds of all Member States, it shall meet in extraordinary session.

ARTICLE XIII

1. The Council of Ministers shall be responsible to the Assembly of Heads of State and Government. It shall be entrusted with the responsibility of preparing conferences of the Assembly.

2. It shall take cognisance of any matter referred to it by the Assembly. It shall be entrusted with the implementation of the decisions of the Assembly of Heads of State and Government. It shall coordinate inter-African cooperation in accordance with the instructions of the Assembly and in conformity with Article II (2) of the present Charter.

ARTICLE XI

1. Each Member State shall have one vote.

2. All resolutions shall be determined by a simple majority of the members of the Council of Ministers.

3. Two-thirds of the total membership of the Council of Ministers shall form a quorum for any meeting of the Council.

ARTICLE XV

The Council shall have the power to determine its own rules of procedure.

General Secretariat

ARTICLE XVI

There shall be an Administrative Secretary-General of the Organization, who shall be appointed by the Assembly of Heads of State and Government. The Administrative Secretary-General shall direct the affairs of the Secretariat.

ARTICLE XVII

There shall be one or more Assistant Secretaries-General of the Organization, who shall be appointed by the Assembly of Heads of State and Government.

ARTICLE XVIII

The functions and conditions of services of the Secretary-General, of the Assistant Secretaries-General and other employees of the Secretariat shall be governed by the provisions of this Charter and the regulations approved by the Assembly of Heads of State and Government.

1. In the performance of their duties the Administrative Secretary-General and his staff shall not seek or receive instructions from any Government or from any other authority external to the Organization. They shall refrain from any action which might reflect on their position as international officials responsible only to the Organization.

2. Each Member of the Organization undertakes to respect the exclusive character of the responsibilities of the Administrative Secretary-General and the Staff and not seek to influence them in the discharge of their responsibilities.

Commission of Mediation, Conciliation and Arbitration

ARTICLE XIX

Member States pledge to settle any disputes among themselves by peaceful means and, to this end, decide to establish a Commission of Mediation, Conciliation and Arbitration, the composition of which and conditions of service shall be defined by a separate Protocol to be approved by the Assembly of Heads of State and Government. Said Protocol shall be regarded as forming an integral part of the present Charter.

Specialized Commissions

ARTICLE XX

The Assembly shall establish such Specialized Commissions as it may deem necessary, including the following:
1. Economic and Social Commission;
2. Educational and Cultural Commission;
3. Health, Sanitation, and Nutrition Commission;
4. Defence Commission;
5. Scientific, Technical and Research Commission.

ARTICLE XXI

Each Specialized Commission referred to in Article XX shall be composed of the Ministers concerned or other Ministers or plenipotentiaries designated by the Governments of the Member States.

ARTICLE XXII

The functions of the Specialized Commissions shall be carried out in accordance with the provisions of the present Charter and of the regulations approved by the Council of Ministers.

The Budget

ARTICLE XXIII

The budget of the Organization prepared by the Administrative Secretary-General shall be approved by the Council of Ministers. The budget shall be provided by contributions from Member States in accordance with the scale of assessment of the United Nations; provided, however, that no Member State shall be assessed an amount exceeding 20 per cent of the yearly regular budget of the Organization. The Member States agree to pay their respective contributions regularly.

Signature and Ratification of the Charter

ARTICLE XXIV

1. This Charter shall be open for signature to all independent sovereign African States and shall be ratified by the signatory States in accordance with their respective constitutional processes.

2. The original instrument, done if possible in African languages, in English and French, all texts being equally authentic, shall be deposited with the Government of Ethiopia which shall transmit certified copies thereof to all independent sovereign African States.

3. Instruments of ratification shall be deposited with the Government of Ethiopia, which shall notify all signatories of each such deposit.

Entry into Force

ARTICLE XXV

This Charter shall enter into force immediately upon receipt by the Government of Ethiopia of the instruments of ratification from two-thirds of the signatory States.

Registration of the Charter

ARTICLE XXVI

This Charter shall, after due ratification, be registered with the Secretariat of the United Nations through the Government of Ethiopia in conformity with Article 102 of the Charter of the United Nations.

Interpretation of the Charter

ARTICLE XXVII

Any question which may arise concerning the interpretation of this Charter shall be decided by a vote of two-thirds of the Assembly of Heads of State and Government of the Organization.

Adhesion and Accession

ARTICLE XXVIII

1. Any independent sovereign African State may at any time notify the Administrative Secretary-General of its intention to adhere or accede to this Charter.

2. The Administrative Secretary-General shall, on receipt of such notification, communicate a copy of it to all the Member States. Admission shall be decided by a simple majority of the Member States. The decision of each Member State shall be transmitted to the Administrative Secretary-General, who shall, upon receipt of the required number of votes, communicate the decision to the State concerned.

Miscellaneous

ARTICLE XXIX

The working languages of the Organization and all its institutions shall be, if possible, African languages, English and French.

ARTICLE XXX

The Administrative Secretary-General may accept on behalf of the Organization gifts, bequests and other donations made to the Organization, provided that this is approved by the Council of Ministers.

ARTICLE XXXI

The Council of Ministers shall decide on the privileges and immunities to be accorded to the personnel of the Secretariat in the respective territories of the Member States.

Cessation of Membership

ARTICLE XXXII

Any State which desires to renounce its membership shall forward a written notification to the Administrative Secretary-General. At the end of one year from the date of such notification, if not withdrawn, the Charter shall cease to apply with respect to the renouncing State, which shall thereby cease to belong to the Organization.

Amendment to the Charter

ARTICLE XXXIII

This Charter may be amended or revised if any Member State makes a written request to the Administrative Secretary-General to that effect; provided, however, that the proposed amendment is not submitted to the Assembly for consideration until all the Member States have been duly notified of it and a period of one year has elapsed. Such an amendment shall not be effective unless approved by at least two-thirds of all the Member States.

IN FAITH WHEREOF, We, the Heads of African State and Government, have signed this Charter.

Consequences

Despite this display of Pan-Africanism, most of the African nations were too wedded to their borders and too committed to the concept of nationhood to give up even a little of their hard-won new sovereignty. What they saw happening in the former Belgian Congo only made them more adamantine about national sovereignty. The Congo, a huge country twice the size of any other black African state, had suffered from a particularly brutal colonial heritage, stemming from its days as the personal fiefdom of King Leopold of Belgium. The postwar Belgian Congo was flooded with white immigrants flocking to the mineral-rich Katanga province (now Shaba) and tripling the settler population. As black unrest rose in the 1950s on the heels of unemployment and white contempt, the Belgians showed no sign of relinquishing power, and the long-oppressed, mostly illiterate native population lacked even a nascent black elite to organize and promote the cause of nationhood. Only one man had more than a local following, a former postal worker and now the leader of the radical Congolese National Movement, Patrice Lumumba, and even his influence was dissipated by the hostility of regional leaders.

When the Belgian government suddenly abandoned the Congo following rioting in Leopoldville in January 1959, the country collapsed into political chaos. Congolese army officers mutinied against their white superiors, paralyzing the newly independent national government and creating a state of anarchy in which local loyalties overwhelmed national sentiment. Katanga declared independence from the Congo, and Lumumba appealed to the United Nations to come in and restore order. Dag Hammarskjöld sent troops under his personal direction, and confusion reigned in the ruling circles. Lumumba was arrested by his former aide, army chief Joseph-Désiré Mobutu, just as the parliament in Leopoldville was voting Lumumba "special powers." Though the United Nations continued to recognize Lumumba as the Congo's legitimate ruler, he was spirited away to Katanga and shot in 1961, possibly on the orders of the man he had himself placed in the office of president, Joseph Kasavubu.

Kasavubu had Moise Tshombe, Katanga's strongman, arrested for treason, then released. Dag Hammarskjöld, flying into Katanga to negotiate with Tshombe, was killed in a mysterious plane crash. The United Nations marched in, overturned Katanga, and exiled Tshombe, who returned after the United Nations had pulled out at the head of a band of white mercenary thugs, once more leading Katanga into secession. The country dissolved into civil war, Kasavubu was overthrown in a bloodless coup by Mobutu, and Tshombe fled to Spain, where he was sentenced to death in absentia. Hijacking a plane to Algeria, he arrived only to be arrested and held, awaiting extradition, until he was murdered in 1969. Meanwhile, the military had enforced a precarious peace on the Congo, which it renamed Zaire (the country has since reverted to its name of the Congo).

Two other African countries suffered similar fates. Nigeria, after attaining independence in 1960, fell prey almost instantly to a civil war between the Muslim north and the more developed, primarily Christian south and east. It turned into a bloodbath, leading to the exposure and starvation of the civilian population in the region called Biafra, which became an international scandal.

In Uganda, a nation, like many of the new African countries, with no natural political unity, having been created by the British out of a patchwork of rival kingdoms and tribes, the first president, Milton Obote, launched a war on the Baganda people that ultimately led to escalating violence, brutal repression, and economic collapse, ushering into power a corrupt former heavyweight boxing champion named Idi Amin. One of only two army officers in the Ugandan army at the time of independence, Amin had gained a reputation for brutality while serving with the King's Rifles in

Kenya in the wake of the Mau Mau uprising, a reputation which once in power he more than lived up to. By the time Amin was finally deposed by Tanzanian troops in 1979, he had become world famous as the very definition of a bloody tyrant, having murdered in a number of especially horrifying ways some 150,000 people.

The chaotic sequence of events in the Congo, Nigeria, and Uganda forced the newly linked countries in the Organization of African Unity to assert the primacy of the nation-state over the secessionist demands of various regions, since no nation wanted to risk suffering such brutal excesses. The organization mediated the Algerian-Moroccan crisis of 1965 and settled the border disputes between Somalia and Ethiopia and between Somalia and Kenya from 1965 to 1967. However, OAU efforts to mediate the Nigerian-Biafran civil war of 1968–70 and the Chad civil war during the 1980s failed, and its influence continued to dwindle as the United Nations became increasingly active in peacekeeping and mediation missions in later ethnic and tribal conflicts in Somalia, Kenya, Botswana, and other regions during the 1990s.

The marginalization of the OAU had to do with the fact that the British, French, and Portuguese empires had dissolved as differently as they had formed, and the varying geopolitical patterns that emerged in the east, west, and center of the continent produced largely artificial frontiers inherited from the colonial past. The emerging nations had to struggle to unite disparate peoples, languages, and traditions in a search for genuine nationhood made even more complicated by the frustrations of their assumption that eventually all of black Africa would be free.

Instead, in the south, the intransigent white settlers of Rhodesia and the Republic of South Africa, defining themselves as every bit as native to Africa as the blacks, held onto their minority-controlled governments, affecting the politics of all the emerging nations and dominating the development of the whole southern half of Africa, although both countries ultimately came under native African rule. The meddling of the cold war superpowers in such countries as Angola and Mozambique added another twist to the complex crosscurrents that had created seemingly intractable problems, many of which remained unresolved throughout Africa in the early years of the 21st century, and all of which undermined the potential of the OAU.

Source

University of Minnesota Human Rights Library, "Charter of the Organization of African Unity." Available online. URL: http://ww1.umn.edu/humanrts/africa/OAU-Charter_1993.html.

Weapons Treaties

NUCLEAR TEST BAN TREATY

TREATY AT A GLANCE

Completed
August 5, 1963, at Moscow; entered into force October 10, 1963

Signatories
United States, the United Kingdom, the Soviet Union

Overview
The so-called Test Ban Treaty forbade nuclear weapons testing in the atmosphere, in outer space, and underwater, while still permitting underground testing.

Historical Background

In the years following World War II, the United States, the Soviet Union, and China, as each developed their weapons, had regularly detonated nuclear and thermonuclear devices. Although the tests were carried out in remote locations, radioactive fallout in measurable amounts was carried into populated regions and was found in water, in the atmosphere, and in the food chain (in the United States and Great Britain, milk was routinely monitored for radioactivity).

As early as January 1946, less than half a year after the bombing of Hiroshima and Nagasaki, the United Nations General Assembly created the Atomic Energy Commission, which was charged, in part, with promoting nuclear disarmament. By June the commission had devised a plan to outlaw all atomic weapons, but debate over the scheme ended with a Soviet veto. The USSR categorically refused to allow UN–mandated inspectors inside its borders and likewise declined to relinquish its veto power over atomic matters in the Security Council by entrusting the regulation of such matters to the Atomic Energy Commission.

After the failure of the Atomic Energy Commission, a 10-power Disarmament Committee, consisting of five Eastern-bloc and five Western-bloc nations, was set up in Geneva, Switzerland, independently of the United Nations in September 1959. It broke down by June 1960. On December 20, 1961, the United States and the Soviet Union issued a joint resolution in the UN General Assembly to form a new, 18-nation Disarmament Committee. Consisting of five NATO countries, five Warsaw Pact countries, and eight nonaligned nations (Brazil, Burma, Ethiopia, India, Mexico, Nigeria, Egypt, and Sweden), it met in almost continuous session in Geneva and was later enlarged to 26 members. (France, although it was a member from the beginning, boycotted the entire process because it was in the process of developing its own nuclear arsenal and had no desire to compromise its program.) The first fruit of the Disarmament Committee was the Nuclear Test-Ban Treaty, which was signed in Moscow on August 5, 1963, by the Soviet Union, the United States, and the United Kingdom.

Terms

The treaty, banning all nuclear tests except those underground, was of considerable environmental importance. Even more important, however, was its symbolic significance as a first, albeit very small, step toward disarmament. The original signatories announced their hope that other states would subscribe to the treaty, and beginning August 8, 1963, it was held open for signature in all three capitals: Washington, Moscow, and London. By the date on which the treaty entered into force, October 10, 1963, 105 nations had signed. The significant exceptions were the People's Republic of China and France, both of which had nuclear arsenals; Albania, Cuba, Guinea, Kampuchea (now Cambodia), North Korea, and Saudi Arabia, all at that point non-nuclear nations, also declined to subscribe.

The Governments of the United States of America, the United Kingdom of Great Britain and Northern Ireland, and the Union of Soviet Socialist Republics, hereinafter referred to as the "original parties,"

Proclaiming as their principal aim the speediest possible achievement of an agreement on general and complete disarmament under strict international control in accordance with the objectives of the United Nations which would put an end to the armaments race and eliminate the incentive to the production and testing of all kinds of weapons, including nuclear weapons,

Seeking to achieve the discontinuance of all test explosions of nuclear weapons for all time, determined to continue negotiations to this end, and desiring to put an end to the contamination of man's environment by radioactive substances,

Have agreed as follows:

ARTICLE I

1. Each of the parties to this Treaty undertakes to prohibit, to prevent, and not to carry out any nuclear weapon test explosion, or any other nuclear explosion, at any place under its jurisdiction or control:

(a) in the atmosphere; beyond its limits, including outer space; or under water, including territorial waters or high seas; or

(b) in any other environment if such explosion causes radioactive debris to be present outside the territorial limits of the State under whose jurisdiction or control such explosion is conducted. It is understood in this connection that the provisions of this sub-paragraph are without prejudice to the conclusion of a treaty resulting in the permanent banning of all nuclear test explosions, including all such explosions underground, the conclusion of which, as the parties have stated in the Preamble to this Treaty, they seek to achieve.

2. Each of the parties to this Treaty undertakes furthermore to refrain from causing, encouraging, or in any way participating in, the carrying out of any nuclear weapon test explosion, or any other nuclear explosion, anywhere which would take place in any of the environments described, or have the effect referred to, in paragraph I of this Article. . . .

ARTICLE III

This Treaty shall be open to all States for signature . . .

ARTICLE IV

This Treaty shall be of unlimited duration.

Each party shall in exercising its national sovereignty have the right to withdraw from the Treaty if it decides that extraordinary events, related to the subject matter of this Treaty, have jeopardized the supreme interest of its country. It shall give notice of such withdrawal to all other parties to the Treaty three months in advance. . .

[signed]
RUSK, HOME, GROMYKO

Consequences

France continued its program, often in the face of direct protest from international antinuclear and peace organizations, such as Greenpeace, and so did mainland China. As new countries—Israel, South Africa, India, Pakistan—joined the nuclear "club," they too tested their weapons.

Efforts to develop a comprehensive ban on testing, even underground, bore fruit during the administration of U.S. president Bill Clinton, who after frustrating, delayed, and tough negotiations, presented such a treaty to the Senate in 1999. There Republicans, bent on embarrassing a president they had just spent a year vainly trying to remove from office via impeachment proceedings, refused to ratify the document for what appeared to be the petty motive of denying Clinton a "positive legacy." Nevertheless, Russia signed on to the new treaty, as did 51 other nations, excluding India and Pakistan, raising the potential for U.S. involvement once the political winds had changed sufficiently.

Source

Federation of American Scientists, "Limited Test Ban Treaty." Available online. URL: http://www.fas.org/nuke/control/ltbt/text/ltbt2.htm. Accessed December 29, 2004.

TREATY ON THE NON-PROLIFERATION OF NUCLEAR WEAPONS

TREATY AT A GLANCE

Completed
July 1, 1968, at London, Moscow, and Washington, D.C.;
entered into force March 5, 1970

Signatories
As of spring 2005, 130 nations had subscribed to the treaty

Overview
Administered by the International Atomic Energy Commission, the nonproliferation treaty (TNP) requires the signatories—countries that did not possess nuclear weapons prior to 1967—to agree to certain safeguards against their developing weapons in order to receive assistance in planning and developing their own nuclear industries.

Historical Background

The United States came out of World War II the globe's only major nuclear power, with a much-depleted Great Britain serving as something of a junior partner. Many took outsized comfort in this monopoly until the Soviet Union tested its first atomic bomb in 1949. The cold war, already under way, had grown deadly, since the two emerging superpowers would soon have a stockpile of nuclear weapons capable of destroying the world many times over. The United States responded to the news of a Russian bomb by ferreting out and executing the "atomic spies" Julius and Ethel Rosenberg, as its domestic politics turned paranoid. This was followed by an extensive civil defense program and fast-tract hydrogen bomb program.

Hardly had the United States begun testing its thermonuclear devices, when so did the Russians. Both France and Communist China joined the club in the 1950s, and by the 1960s there were rumors that Israel had developed nuclear weapons. The Cuban Missile Crisis brought the world as close as it has probably ever come to nuclear war, and in its wake the macho posturing of both Nikita Khrushchev, the USSR's premier, and U.S. president John Kennedy, so evident at their 1960 "summit" in Paris, gave way to sober reflection on how best to halt the madness of nuclear proliferation.

Terms

Largely the result of negotiations between the United States and the Soviet Union, the world's two major nuclear superpowers, TNP was aimed at preventing the spread of the development of nuclear weapons to other states. It entered into force on March 5, 1970, and by spring 2005 had been signed by 130 states, of which 98 agreed to full safeguard inspections. The spirit of the treaty is expressed in its preamble:

> The States concluding this Treaty, hereinafter referred to as the "Parties to the Treaty,"
>
> Considering the devastation that would be visited upon all mankind by a nuclear war and the consequent need to make every effort to avert the danger of such a war and to take measures to safeguard the security of peoples;
>
> Believing that the proliferation of nuclear weapons would seriously enhance the danger of nuclear war,
>
> In conformity with resolutions of the United Nations General Assembly calling for the conclusion of an agreement on the prevention of wider dissemination of nuclear weapons;
>
> Undertaking to cooperate in facilitating the application of International Atomic Energy Agency safeguards on peaceful nuclear activities;
>
> Expressing their support for research, development and other efforts to further the application, within the framework of the International Atomic Energy Agency safeguards system, of the principle of safeguarding

effectively the flow of source and special fissionable materials by use of instruments and other techniques at certain strategic points;

Affirming the principle that the benefits of peaceful applications of nuclear technology, including any technological by-products which may be derived by nuclear-weapon States from the development of nuclear explosive devices, should be available for peaceful purposes to all Parties to the Treaty, whether nuclear-weapon or non-nuclear-weapon States;

Convinced that, in furtherance of this principle, all Parties to the Treaty are entitled to participate in the fullest possible exchange of scientific information for, and to contribute alone or in cooperation with other States to, the further development of the applications of atomic energy for peaceful purposes;

Declaring their intention to achieve at the earliest possible date the cessation of the nuclear arms race and to undertake effective measures in the direction of nuclear disarmament;

Urging the cooperation of all States in the attainment of this objective;

Recalling the determination expressed by the Parties to the 1963 Treaty banning nuclear weapon tests in the atmosphere, in outer space and under water in its Preamble to seek to achieve the discontinuance of all test explosions of nuclear weapons for all time and to continue negotiations to this end;

Desiring to further the easing of international tension and the strengthening of trust between States in order to facilitate the cessation of the manufacture of nuclear weapons, the liquidation of all their existing stockpiles, and the elimination from national arsenals of nuclear weapons and the means of their delivery pursuant to a Treaty on general and complete disarmament under strict and effective international control;

Recalling that, in accordance with the Charter of the United Nations, States must refrain in their international relations from the threat or use of force against the territorial integrity or political independence of any State, or in any other manner inconsistent with the purposes of the United Nations, and that the establishment and maintenance of international peace and security are to be promoted with the least diversion for armaments of the world's human and economic resources;

Have agreed as follows . . .

The signatories agreed not "to transfer to any recipient whatsoever nuclear weapons or other nuclear explosive devices or control over such weapons or explosive devices directly, or indirectly; and not in any way to assist, encourage, or induce any non-nuclear-weapon State to manufacture or otherwise acquire nuclear weapons or other nuclear explosive devices, or control over such weapons or explosive devices." They agreed "not to . . . acquire . . . nuclear weapons" from any other state nor to manufacture such weapons. Moreover, in accordance with Article 3:

1. Each non-nuclear-weapon State Party to the Treaty undertakes to accept safeguards, as set forth in an agreement to be negotiated and concluded with the International Atomic Energy Agency in accordance with the Statute of the International Atomic Energy Agency and the Agency's safeguards system, for the exclusive purpose of verification of the fulfillment of its obligations assumed under this Treaty with a view to preventing diversion of nuclear energy from peaceful uses to nuclear weapons or other nuclear explosive devices. Procedures for the safeguards required by this Article shall be followed with respect to source or special fissionable material whether it is being produced, processed or used in any principal nuclear facility or is outside any such facility. The safeguards required by this Article shall be applied on all source or special fissionable material in all peaceful nuclear activities within the territory of such State, under its jurisdiction, or carried out under its control anywhere. . . .

3. The safeguards required by this Article shall be implemented in a manner designed to comply with Article IV of this Treaty, and to avoid hampering the economic or technological development of the Parties or international cooperation in the field of peaceful nuclear activities, including the international exchange of nuclear material and equipment for the processing, use or production of nuclear material for peaceful purposes in accordance with the provisions of this Article and the principle of safeguarding set forth in the Preamble of the Treaty. . . .

ARTICLE IV

1. Nothing in this Treaty shall be interpreted as affecting the inalienable right of all the Parties to the Treaty to develop research, production and use of nuclear energy for peaceful purposes without discrimination and in conformity with Articles I and II of this Treaty.

In addition to pledging neither to acquire nor develop nuclear weapons, the signatories also agreed, in Article 6, "to pursue negotiations in good faith on effective measures relating to cessation of the nuclear arms race at an early date and to nuclear disarmament, and on a treaty on general and complete disarmament under strict and effective international control." The treaty was held open, and continues so, to all nations for signature.

In accordance with Article 10, calling for "a conference [25 years after the treaty enters into force] . . . to decide whether the Treaty shall continue in force indefinitely, or shall be extended for an additional fixed period or periods," the United Nations reviewed TNP in 1995.

Consequences

In the meantime, others had joined the nuclear club or soon would—Israel now for certain, South Africa,

India, and Pakistan. The potential for local disputes—in the Middle East, say, or on the Indian subcontinent—to escalate into atomic warfare had grown, and with plutonium and the other ingredients necessary for building a bomb becoming at least available with enough money and effort, the potential for nuclear terrorism entered the picture. The Israeli Air Force staged a preemptive strike on one of Iraq's supposedly benign nuclear power plants before its construction could be completed, and diplomats worldwide felt a catch in their chests when it appeared that the international-rogue state of North Korea had developed a bomb.

Nevertheless, in 1999 the United States Senate in a political brawl with President Bill Clinton dealt a blow to efforts at containing the nuclear threat by refusing to ratify—in an apparent pique of personal animosity—the latest treaty banning the spread and testing of nuclear weapons. The collapse of the Soviet Union led to renewed worries about proliferation, since the centralized control once exercised by Moscow could no longer be relied upon to prevent the sale of nuclear technology, equipment, and fissionable materials by former Soviet republics, or even individual Soviet generals, on the growing black market in all kinds of weapons supplied by international and sometimes shady arms dealers. Despite many rumors to just that effect, no such sales or transfers had yet come to light before the end of the 20th century. Such sales or transfers or their imminent likelihood, however, became something of a working assumption for the U.S.-led "war on terror" in the first decade of the 21st century. In 2002, President George W. Bush cited the nefarious activities of Abdul Qadeer Khan, a Pakistani nuclear scientist and adviser who sold nuclear technology, components, and equipment to Iran, Libya, and North Korea. President Bush regarded Khan's dealings as evidence of the ongoing dangers of the illicit transfer of nuclear weapons technologies.

Source

Federation of American Scientists, "Treaty on the Non-Proliferation of Nuclear Weapons." Available online. URL: http://www.fas.org/nuke/control/npt/text/npt2.htm. Accessed December 28, 2004.

AGREEMENT ON THE PREVENTION OF NUCLEAR WAR

TREATY AT A GLANCE

Completed
June 22, 1973, at Washington, D.C.

Signatories
United States and the Soviet Union

Overview
The Agreement on the Prevention of Nuclear War repudiated the nuclear policies that had guided both nations since the beginning of the cold war.

Historical Background

During the early 1970s, U.S. president Richard Nixon and Soviet premier Leonid Brezhnev, both known as ideological hard-liners and confirmed cold warriors, surprised the world by opening a dialogue aimed at achieving détente. Using that reputation to provide considerable diplomatic flexibility, Nixon—whose presidency was marred by the Watergate scandal, which led to his resignation—had a major impact on American foreign policy. In four years, from 1969 to 1972, the United States abandoned cold war attitudes once believed unshakable while still adhering to the long-standing policy dating back to President Harry S. Truman of "containing" the spread of communism. Not only recognizing but actually visiting the People's Republic of China, Nixon managed subtly to exploit the Sino-Soviet split to facilitate his withdrawal from the Vietnam conflict and to push the Russians step by step toward a general détente agreement. Some understanding about defusing the threat posed by both nations' nuclear arsenals was one of those steps.

Terms

Nixon and Brezhnev concluded the Strategic Arms Limitation Treaty (SALT I) and followed this with an agreement to adopt policies to prevent nuclear war.

The United States of America and the Union of Soviet Socialist Republics, hereinafter referred to as the parties:

Guided by the objectives of strengthening world peace and international security;

Conscious that nuclear war would have devastating consequences for mankind;

Proceeding from the desire to bring about conditions in which the danger of an outbreak of nuclear war anywhere in the world would be reduced and ultimately eliminated;

Proceeding from their obligations under the Charter of the United Nations regarding the maintenance of peace, refraining from the threat or use of force, and the avoidance of war, and in conformity with the agreements to which either party has subscribed;

Proceeding from the basic principle of relations between the United States of America and the Union of Soviet Socialist Republics signed in Moscow on May 29, 1972;

Reaffirming that the development of relations between the U.S.A. and the U.S.S.R. is not directed against other countries and their interests, have agreed as follows:

ARTICLE I

The United States and the Soviet Union agree that an objective of their policies is to remove the danger of nuclear war and of the use of nuclear weapons.

Accordingly, the parties agree that they will act in such a manner as to prevent the development of situations capable of causing a dangerous exacerbation of their relations, as to avoid military confrontations, and as to exclude the outbreak of nuclear war between them and between either of the parties and other countries.

ARTICLE II

The parties agree, in accordance with Article I and to realize the objective stated in that Article, to proceed from the premise that each party will refrain from the threat or use of force against the other party, against the allies of the other party and against other countries, in circumstances which may endanger international peace and security. The parties agree that they will be guided by these considerations in the formulation of their foreign policies and in their actions in the field of international relations.

ARTICLE III

The parties undertake to develop their relations with each other and with other countries in a way consistent with the purposes of this Agreement.

ARTICLE IV

If at any time relations between the parties or between either party and other countries appear to involve the risk of a nuclear conflict, or if relations between countries not parties to this Agreement appear to involve the risk of nuclear war between the U.S.A. and the U.S.S.R. or between either party and other countries, the United States and the Soviet Union, acting in accordance with the provisions of this Agreement, shall immediately enter into urgent consultations with each other and make every effort to avert this risk.

ARTICLE V

Each party shall be free to inform the Security Council of the United Nations, the Secretary-General of the United Nations and the Governments of allied or other countries of the progress and outcome of consultations initiated in accordance with Article IV of this Agreement.

ARTICLE VI

Nothing in this Agreement shall affect or impair:

(a) The inherent right of individual or collective self-defense as envisaged by Article 51 of the Charter of the United Nations;

(b) The provisions of the Charter of the United Nations, including those relating to the maintenance or restoration of international peace and security; and

(c) The obligations undertaken by either party towards its allies or other countries in treaties, agreements and other appropriate documents.

ARTICLE VII

This Agreement shall be of unlimited duration.

ARTICLE VIII

This Agreement shall enter into force upon signature.

Done at the City of Washington, D.C., on June 22, 1973, in two copies, each in the English and in the Russian languages, both texts being equally authentic.

For the United States of America: Richard Nixon, President of the United States of America; for the Union of Soviet Socialist Republics: Leonid Brezhnev, General Secretary of the Central Committee of the C.P.S.U.

Consequences

The agreement contained little of a practical or detailed nature. There was no prescription or mechanism for averting nuclear war. Yet the agreement was an act of communication and a public repudiation of the nuclear policies—and nuclear assumptions—that had guided both nations since the commencement of the cold war.

Source

J. A. S. Grenville, *The Major International Treaties, 1914–1973* (New York: Stein and Day, 1975), 541–549.

Diplomatic Treaties

HOT LINE MEMORANDUM

TREATY AT A GLANCE

Completed
June 20, 1963, at Geneva, Switzerland

Signatories
United States and the Soviet Union

Overview
Near-disastrous miscommunications during the Cuban Missile Crisis between U.S. president John F. Kennedy and Soviet premier Nikita Khrushchev via third parties brought the world to the brink of a nuclear holocaust. Persuaded of the need for a direct line of communications in case of a similar crisis in the future, both leaders signed on to a memorandum at the 1963 Geneva disarmament conference establishing what became called in the popular press the nuclear hot line.

Historical Background

When Fidel Castro came to power in 1959, he embraced the revolutionary tenets of Marxist-Leninism and nationalized Cuba's industries and sugar plantations. In response the U.S. launched in effect a trade war against the tiny island, by imposing a full-scale economic boycott, and launched a plan to overthrow the Cuban leader that resulted in the fiasco called the Bay of Pigs. The failed invasion only drove Castro deeper into the Soviet camp, and in retrospect, it is not so hard to understand that he would agree to permit the Soviet Union to construct missile bases on his island. The surprise is that he almost pulled it off.

His hopes of keeping the construction of the bases a secret long enough for the Russians to deploy their missiles were dashed in October 1962, when an American spy plane photographed the nearly completed bases. President Kennedy, still reeling from the domestic criticism of his handling of the Bay of Pigs, demanded the immediate withdrawal of the Soviet missiles and the closing of the bases, ordering a naval blockade of the island on October 24. When the Soviet premier Nikita Khrushchev, proved just as determined to complete the bases, the world seemed on the brink of a nuclear Armageddon, as the two superpowers squared off in what became known as the Cuban Mis-

sile Crisis. The world held its breath as each passing day apparently brought two thermonuclear superpowers closer and closer to a shooting war.

Kennedy stood his ground, and on October 28, Nikita Khrushchev offered to remove the missiles under United Nations supervision in exchange for a promise that the United States would never again attempt an invasion of the island. On the following day President Kennedy suspended the blockade, and by November 2 the missile bases were being dismantled. Since, as both Kennedy and Khrushchev understood, the United States was hardly going to mount another attack on Cuba after the abject failure of the last one, the showdown over the missiles was a triumph for the young American president. The negotiations between the two leaders that led them to this ultimately sensible solution were conducted outside normal diplomatic channels, because both leaders tried to avoid losing face before those critical of their performance in their respective governments. When Kennedy and his advisers became confused by the contradictions between Khrushchev's diplomatic communiqués and his back-channel messages, they came very close to taking more aggressive measures that could easily have led to nuclear war.

The notion of some kind of safeguards against the danger of "accidental" nuclear war had been broached by the Soviets as far back as 1954, and Kennedy himself had discussed measures to reduce the risk of war before the United Nations General Assembly in September 1961. Sobered by this recent and direct experience of the dangers, Kennedy and Khrushchev both began talk about summits and peace and ending the arms race, as the former looked toward a second term in the White House.

As early as they could, in the summer of 1963, they agreed to a multinational conference on disarmament in Geneva, where they quickly moved to at least reduce the risk of accidentally provoking Armageddon by the simple expedient of setting up a direct telephone link between the leaders in the Kremlin and the White House.

Terms

The memorandum read as follows:

⁓⊚

Memorandum of Understanding between the United States of America and the Union of Soviet Socialist Republics Regarding the Establishment of a Direct Communications Link

For use in time of emergency the Government of the United States of America and the Government of the Union of Soviet Socialist Republics have agreed to establish as son as technically feasible a direct communications link between the two Governments.

Each Government shall be responsible for the arrangements for the link of its own territory. Each Government shall take the necessary steps to ensure continuous functioning of the link and prompt delivery to its head of government of any communications received by means of the link from the head of government of the other party.

Arrangements for establishing the link are set forth in the Annex which is attached hereto and forms an integral part hereof.

DONE in duplicate in the English and Russian languages at Geneva, Switzerland, this 20th day of June, 1963.

For the Government of the United States of America:
CHARLES C. STELLE
Acting Representative of the United States of America at the Eighteen-Country Committee on Disarmament.

For the Government of the Soviet Socialist Republics:
SEMYON K. CSARAPIN
Acting Representative of the Union of Soviet Socialist Republics to the Eighteen-Nation Committee on Disarmament

Annex
To the Memorandum of Understanding Between the United States of America and the Union of Soviet

Socialist Republics Regarding the Establishment of a Direct Communications Link

The direct communications link between Washington and Moscow established in accordance with the Memorandum, and the operation of such link, shall be governed by the following provisions:

1. The direct communications link shall consist of:

a. Two terminal points with telegraph-teleprinter equipment between which communications shall be directly exchanged;

b. One full-time duplex telegraph circuit, routed Washington-London-Copenhagen-Stockholm-Helsinki-Moscow, which shall be used for the transmission of messages;

c. One full-time duplex radiotelegraph circuit, routed Washington-Tangier-Moscow, which shall be used for service and for coordinating of operations between the two terminal points.

If experience in operating the direct communications link should demonstrate that the establishment of an additional wire telegraph circuit is advisable, such circuit may be established by mutual agreement between authorized representatives of both Governments.

2. In case of interruption of the wire circuit, transmission of messages shall be effected via the radio circuit, and for this purpose provision shall be made at the terminal points for the capability of prompt switching of all necessary equipment from one circuit to another.

3. The terminal points of the link shall be so equipped as to provide for the transmission and reception of messages from Moscow to Washington in the Russian language and from Washington to Moscow in the English language. In this connection, the USSR shall furnish the United States four sets of telegraph terminal equipment, including pages printers, transmitters, and reperforators, with one year's supply of spare parts and all necessary special tools, test equipment, operating instructions, and other technical literature, to provide for transmission and reception of messages in the Russian language.

The United States shall furnish the Soviet Union four sets of telegraph terminal equipment, including pages printers, transmitters, and reperforators, with one year's supply of spare parts and all necessary special tools, test equipment, operating instructions, and other technical literature, to provide for transmission and reception of messages in the English language.

The equipment described in this paragraph shall be exchanged directly between the parties without any payment being required therefor.

4. The terminal points of the direct communications link shall be provided with encoding equipment. For the terminal point in the USSR, four sets of such equipment (each capable of simplex operation), with one year's supply of spare parts, with all the necessary special tools, test equipment, operating instructions and other technical literature, and with all necessary blank tape, shall be furnished by the United States to the USSR against payment cost thereof by the USSR.

The USSR shall provide for preparation and delivery of keying tapes to the terminal point of the link in the United States for reception of messages from the USSR. The United States shall provide for preparation and delivery of keying tapes to the terminal point of the link in the USSR for reception of messages from the United States. Delivery of prepared keying tapes to the

789 COLD WAR, PEACEFUL COEXISTENCE

terminal points of the link shall be effected through the Embassy of the USSR in Washington (for the terminal of the link in the USSR) and through the Embassy of the United States in Moscow (for the terminal link in the United States).

5. The United States and the USSR shall designate the agencies responsible for the arrangements regarding the direct communications link, for its technical maintenance, continuity and reliability, and for the timely transmission of messages.

Such agencies may, by mutual agreement, decide matters and develop instructions relating to the technical maintenance and operation of the direct communications link and effect arrangements to improve the operation of the link.

6. Technical parameters of the telegraph circuits of the link and of the terminal equipment, shall be in accordance with CCITT and CCIR recommendations.

Transmission and reception of messages over the direct communications link shall be effected in accordance with applicable recommendations of international telegraph and radio communications regulations, as well as with mutually agreed instructions.

7. The costs of the direct communications link shall be borne as follows:

a. The USSR shall pay the full cost of leasing the portion of the telegraph circuit from Moscow to Helsinki and 50 percent of the cost of leasing the portion of the telegraph circuit from Helsinki to London. The United states shall pay the full cost of leasing the portion of the telegraph circuit from Washington to London and 50 percent of the cost of leasing the portion of the telegraph circuit from London to Helsinki.

b. Payment of the cost of leasing the radio telegraph circuit between Washington and Moscow shall be effected without any transfer of payments between the parties. The USSR shall bear the expenses relating to the transmission of messages from Moscow to Washington. The United States shall bear the expenses relating to the transmission of messages from Washington to Moscow.

Consequences

John Kennedy never realized his hopes of coming to terms with the Russians on nuclear arms, to make, as he put it, "this small planet" safer, since his assassination cut short his presidency. Nikita Khrushchev, too, was soon removed from his position with one finger on the button and one hand on the telephone by a dour and more determined cold warrior named Leonid Brezhnev. As the awful potential for destruction continued to loom over the world in the lingering cold war, the Hot Line, as the direct communication link was soon dubbed, became a virtual icon of the times, an image of a world grown so dangerous that destruction lay a missed phone call away.

Source

J. A. S. Grenville and Bernard Waserstein, eds., *The Major International Treaties Since 1945* (London and New York: Methuen, 1987), 441–446.

Proclamations and Declarations

SOVIET DECLARATION ON THE SOVEREIGNTY OF THE GERMAN DEMOCRATIC REPUBLIC

TREATY AT A GLANCE

Completed
March 24, 1954

Signatories
Declaration by the Soviet Union
(a similar declaration was issued by East Germany)

Overview
In the wake of Stalin's death and the subsequent turmoil inside the Communist bloc, the Soviet Union—worried its hold on East Germany was slipping—declared the region it had carved out of a defeated Germany after World War II a fully sovereign country, shortly before including it into a mutual alliance with the Soviets' other East European satellites called the Warsaw Pact.

Historical Background

When the United States, bogged down in the Korean War, requested a sizable increase in Europe's contribution to the NORTH ATLANTIC TREATY Organization (NATO), it sparked another round in the integration of Europe, which had been proceeding in fits and starts since the end of World War II. In 1951 both the French and British governments fell out of power over the costly issue of rearmament before a NATO committee could come up with an acceptable distribution of the common defense burden, and the obvious solution was to rearm West Germany. This the French simply refused to do unless the future German army was merged into a larger European Defense Community.

As talk of the EDC raced about the capitals of Western Europe, the aging Soviet autocrat Joseph Stalin died, and a group of highly placed party members moved quickly to dispose of his hated and feared secret police chief, Lavrenty Beria. From March 1953 until Nikita Khrushchev's ascent to power in 1956, the Soviet Union lost some of its stranglehold on Eastern Europe just as the West was talking about the real possibility of a United States of Europe.

Anti-Soviet riots broke out in both East Germany and Poland, and Moscow was forced to scale back its exploitation of its Eastern bloc satellites and reduce its reparation demands on East Germany. To head off further trouble and to make sure the West understood it was continuing its commitment to communism in East Germany, the Soviets formally declared the German Democratic Republic's "return" to full postwar sovereignty.

Terms

The declaration read as follows:

⁓◎

The Government of the Union of the Soviet Socialist Republics continues undeviatingly to strive to go on regulating the German problem in conformity with the interests of strengthening peace and of safeguarding the national reunion of Germany on the basis of democracy.

These aims are served by practical steps to bring closer East and West Germany by the holding of free elections throughout Germany and the conclusion of a peace treaty with Germany.

Regardless of the efforts of the Union of Soviet Socialist Republic, no steps were taken at the recent Berlin Conference of the Foreign Ministers of the Four Powers towards the restoration of German unity and towards the conclusion of a peace treaty.

In view of this situation and in consequence of negotiations between the Soviet Government and the Government of the German Democratic Republic, the Government of the Soviet Union considers it necessary, at this time, before Germany is unified and before the peace treaty, to take further steps which are in the interests of the German people, namely:

1. The Union of Soviet Socialist Republics will take up relations with the German Democratic Republic on the same basis as with other sovereign nations. The German Democratic Republic will have the freedom to decide in accordance with its own judgement on domestic and foreign questions including relations with West Germany.

2. The Union of Soviet Socialist Republics retains in the German Democratic Republic those functions which are related to guaranteeing security and which result from the obligations of the Soviet Union arising from Four Power agreements. The Government of the Soviet Union takes note of the declaration of the Government of the German Democratic Republic that it will fulfil the obligations arising for the German Democratic Republic from the Potsdam Agreements concerning the development of Germany as a democratic and peace-loving State, as well as the obligations which are related to the present (*zeitweiligen*) stay of Soviet troops in the German Democratic Republic.

3. The supervision of the activities of the State organs of the German Democratic Republic, which hitherto has been exercised by the High Commissioner of the Soviet Union, will be given up. In conformity with the foregoing, the function of the High Commissioner of the Soviet Union in Germany will be restricted to the range of questions which are related to the above-mentioned guarantee of security, and the maintenance of the relevant agreements concluded with the representatives of the occupation authorities of the United States, Great Britain and France in all German questions as well as to obligations which arise from the negotiated agreements of the Four Powers concerning Germany. . . .

Consequences

As a kind of diplomatic preemptive strike, the treaty did what it was supposed to do. The EDC never came to pass after all, because in the long run, neither the French nor the British could countenance merging their armies with the Germans, even the West Germans. The French debated the issue up until the time Stalin's death and the Korean armistice eroded the sense of emergency, then withdrew into haughty Gaulist disdain for mingling Charles de Gaulle's proud veterans in with some European potpourri. The British, still clinging to vestiges of empire and anxious to maintain their "special relationship" with the United States, decided—in the words of Anthony Eden—that a European federation was "something which we know, in our bones, we cannot do."

An angry John Foster Dulles threatened that if the EDC failed, the United States just might have to go through an "agonizing reappraisal" of its commitment to European security. The Europeans quickly came up with a new solution: admitting West Germany and its armed forces into NATO. In response, the Soviet Union formed the WARSAW PACT and dragged the East Germany it had just declared sovereign into a military alliance of its satellites.

Source
J. A. S. Grenville, *The Major International Treaties, 1914–1973* (New York: Stein and Day, 1975), 292–293.

JOINT COMMUNIQUÉ BY THE UNITED STATES AND THE SOVIET UNION (DÉTENTE)

TREATY AT A GLANCE

Completed
June 25, 1973, at San Clemente, California

Signatories
United States and the Soviet Union

Overview
In the summer of 1973, the leaders of the two superpowers long caught up in a cold war—Leonid Brezhnev and Richard Nixon—retired from their second summit meeting to Nixon's beachside residence in San Clemente, California, and issued a joint communiqué that captured the essence of the recently achieved détente at its high point.

Historical Background

On May 22, 1972, Richard M. Nixon became the first U.S. president to visit Moscow. Putting his long-established anticommunist credentials to good use, he there proposed to the secretary-general of the Communist Party, Leonid I. Brezhnev, a policy of détente. When Brezhnev proved receptive, the two made history, producing seven agreements that covered issues ranging from the prevention of accidental nuclear attack to expanded trade.

Brezhnev returned Nixon's initiative with a second summit meeting in Washington in June 1973. With the Soviet Union now squabbling with a China increasingly aggressive in its bid for a leadership role in the worldwide communist movement, Brezhnev seemed in no mood for flogging the old, familiar ideological differences separating communism from capitalism. When Nikita Khrushchev had arrived in New York in 1959 blustering to the American press that "We will bury you," he had announced he wanted to visit Disneyland. Brezhnev instead quietly withdrew with Nixon to his West Coast retreat at San Clemente to issue a joint communiqué on détente. The difference was telling.

Terms

The substance of the communiqué read as follows:

I. THE GENERAL STATE OF UNITED STATES–SOVIET RELATIONS

Both sides expressed their mutual satisfaction with the fact that the American-Soviet summit meeting in Moscow in May 1972 and the joint decisions taken there have resulted in a substantial advance in the strengthening of peaceful relations between the United States and the Soviet Union and have created the basis for the further development of broad and mutually beneficial cooperation in various fields of mutual interest to the peoples of both countries and in the interests of all mankind. They noted their satisfaction with the mutual effort to implement strictly and fully the treaties and agreements concluded between the United States and the Soviet Union and to expand areas of cooperation.

They agreed that the process of reshaping relations between the United States and the Soviet Union on the basis of peaceful coexistence and equal security, as set forth in the basic principles of relations between the United States and the Soviet Union signed in Moscow on May 29, 1972, is progressing in an encouraging manner. They emphasized the great importance that each side attaches to these basic principles. They reaffirmed their commitment to the continued scrupulous implementation and to the enhancement of the effectiveness of each of the provisions of that document

Both sides noted with satisfaction that the outcome of the American-Soviet meeting in Moscow in May 1972 was welcomed by other States and by world opinion as an important contribution to strengthening peace and international security, to curbing the arms race and to developing businesslike cooperation among States with different social systems.

Both sides viewed the return visit to the United States of the General Secretary of the Central Committee of the C.P.S.U., L. I. Brezhnev, and the talks held during the visit as an expression of their mutual determination to continue the course towards a major improvement in American-Soviet relations.

Both sides are convinced that the discussions they have just held represent a further milestone in the constructive development of their relations.

Convinced that such a development of American-Soviet relations serves the interests of both of their peoples and all of mankind, it was decided to take further major steps to give these relations maximum stability and to turn the development of friendship and cooperation between their peoples into a permanent factor for worldwide peace.

II. THE PREVENTION OF NUCLEAR WAR AND THE LIMITATION OF STRATEGIC ARMAMENTS

Issues related to the maintenance and strengthening of international peace were a central point of the talks between President Nixon and General Secretary Brezhnev.

Conscious of the exceptional importance for all mankind of taking effective measures to that end, they discussed ways in which both sides could work toward removing the danger of war, and especially nuclear war, between the United States and the Soviet Union, and between either party and other countries.

Consequently, in accordance with the Charter of the United Nations and the basic principles of relations of May 29, 1972, it was decided to conclude an agreement between the United States and the Soviet Union on the prevention of nuclear war. That agreement was signed by the President and the General Secretary on June 22, 1973. The text has been published separately.

The President and the General Secretary, in appraising this agreement, believe that it constitutes a historical landmark in Soviet-American relations and substantially strengthens the foundations of international security as a whole. The United States and the Soviet Union state their readiness to "consider additional ways of strengthening peace and removing for ever the danger of war, and particularly nuclear war."

In the course of the meetings, intensive discussions were held on questions of strategic arms limitation. In this connection both sides emphasized the fundamental importance of the treaty on the limitation of anti-ballistic missile systems and the interim agreement on certain measures with respect to the limitation of strategic offensive arms, signed between the United States and the Soviet Union in May 1972, which, for the first time in history placed actual limits on the most modern and most formidable types of armaments.

Having exchanged views on the progress in the implementation of these agreements, both sides reaffirmed their intention to carry them out and their readiness to move ahead jointly towards an agreement on the further limitation of strategic arms.

Both sides noted that progress has been made in the negotiations that resumed in November 1972, and that the prospects for reaching a permanent agreement on more complete measures limiting strategic offensive armaments are favorable.

Both sides agreed that the progress made in the limitation of strategic armaments is an exceedingly important contribution to the strengthening of American-Soviet relations and to world peace.

On the basis of their discussions, the President and the General Secretary signed on June 21, 1973, basic principles of negotiations on the further limitation of strategic offensive arms. The text has been published separately.

The United States and the Soviet Union attach great importance to joining with all States in the cause of strengthening peace, reducing the burden of armaments and reaching agreements on arms limitation and disarmament measures.

Considering the important role which an effective international agreement with respect to chemical weapons would play, the two sides agreed to continue their efforts to conclude such an agreement in cooperation with other countries.

The two sides agree to make every effort to facilitate the work of the committee on disarmament which has been meeting in Geneva. They will actively participate in negotiations aimed at working out new measures to curb and end the arms race.

They reaffirm that the ultimate objective is general and complete disarmament, including nuclear disarmament, under strict international control. A world disarmament conference could play a role in this process at an appropriate time.

III. INTERNATIONAL QUESTIONS: THE REDUCTION OF TENSIONS AND STRENGTHENING OF INTERNATIONAL SECURITY

President Nixon and General Secretary Brezhnev reviewed the major questions of the current international situation. They gave special attention to the developments which have occurred since the time of the United States-Soviet summit meeting in Moscow.

It was noted with satisfaction that positive trends are developing in international relations towards the further relaxation of tensions and the strengthening of cooperative relations in the interests of peace. In the opinion of both sides, the current process of improvement in the international situation creates new and favorable opportunities for reducing tensions, settling outstanding international issues and creating a permanent structure of peace.

The two sides expressed their deep satisfaction at the conclusion of the agreement on ending the war and restoring peace in Vietnam, and also at the results of the international conference on Vietnam, which approved and supported that agreement.

The two sides are convinced that the conclusion of the agreement on ending the war and restoring peace in Vietnam, and the subsequent signing of the agreement on restoring peace and achieving national concord in Laos, meet the fundamental interests and aspirations of the peoples of Vietnam and Laos and open up a possibility for establishing a lasting peace in Indo-China based on respect for the independence, sovereignty, unity and territorial integrity of the countries of that area. Both sides emphasized that these agreements must be strictly implemented.

They further stressed the need to bring an early end to the military conflict in Cambodia in order to bring peace to the entire area of Indo-China. They also reaffirmed their stand that the political futures of Vietnam, Laos and Cambodia should be left to the respective peoples to determine, free from outside interference.

In the course of the talks both sides noted with satisfaction that in Europe the process of relaxing tensions and developing cooperation is actively continuing and thereby contributing to international stability.

The two sides expressed satisfaction with the further normalization of relations among European countries resulting from treaties and agreements signed in recent years, particularly between the Soviet Union and the Federal Republic of Germany.

They also welcome the coming into force of the quadripartite agreement of September 3, 1971. They share the conviction that strict observance of the treaties and agreements that have been concluded will contribute to the security and well-being of all parties concerned.

They also welcome the prospect of United Nations membership this year for the Federal Republic of Germany and the German Democratic Republic and recall, in this connection, that the United States, the Soviet Union, United Kingdom and France have signed the quadripartite declaration of November 9, 1972, on this subject.

The United States and the Soviet Union reaffirm their desire, guided by the appropriate provisions of the joint American-Soviet Union communiqué adopted in Moscow in May 1972, to continue their separate and joint contributions to strengthening peaceful relations in Europe. Both sides affirm that ensuring a lasting peace in Europe is a paramount goal of their policies.

In this connection satisfaction was expressed with the fact that as a result of common efforts by many States, including the United States and the Soviet Union, the preparatory work has been successfully completed for the conference on security and cooperation in Europe, which will be convened on July 3, 1973. The United States and the Soviet Union hold the view that the conference will enhance the possibilities for strengthening European security and developing cooperation among the participating States. The United States and the Soviet Union will conduct their policies so as to realize the goals of the conference and bring about a new era of good relations in this part of the world.

Reflecting their continued positive attitude towards the conference, both sides will make efforts to bring the conference to a successful conclusion at the earliest possible time. Both sides proceed from the assumption that progress in the work of the conference will produce possibilities for completing it at the highest level.

The United States and the Soviet Union believe that the goal of strengthening stability and security in Europe would be further advanced if the relaxation of political tensions were accompanied by a reduction of military tensions in Central Europe. In this respect they attach great importance to the negotiations on the mutual reduction of forces and armaments and associated measures in Central Europe, which will begin on October 30, 1973.

Both sides state their readiness to make, along with other States, their contribution to the achievement of mutually acceptable decisions on the substance of this problem, based on the strict observance of the principle of the undiminished security of any of the parties.

The Middle East
The parties expressed their deep concern with the situation in the Middle East and exchanged opinions regarding ways of reaching a Middle East settlement.

Each of the parties set forth its position on this problem.

Both parties agreed to continue to exert their efforts to promote the quickest possible settlement in the Middle East. This settlement should be in accordance with the interests of all States in the area, be consistent with their independence and sovereignty and should take into due account the legitimate interests of the Palestinian people.

Consequences

Unfortunately, the millennium that seemed at hand did not come to pass. Summit III, held in June 1974, was cool to chilly, and ongoing arms talks came to a grinding halt. In the meantime, Congress blocked several of the commercial agreements concluded with the USSR because of human rights violations against Soviet Jews, and President Nixon, beleaguered by Watergate, had neither the attention span nor the energy to fight for the preservation of détente.

President Jimmy Carter tried to pick up the pieces with SALT II, but Brezhnev balked at the depth of missile cutbacks demanded, even while Carter pressed forward with a military buildup and a well-intentioned but morally superior human rights campaign. Cooling U.S.-Soviet relations were plunged into the deep freeze by Carter's successor, Ronald Reagan, who adopted a bellicose military stance and referred to the Soviet Union as the "evil empire."

What if Nixon had not sabotaged his presidency with Watergate? Perhaps the cold war would have ended a decade earlier, or even sooner.

Source
J. A. S. Grenville, *The Major International Treaties, 1914–1973* (New York: Stein and Day, 1975), 542.

Part Fourteen
A NEW WORLD ORDER

INTRODUCTION

By the mid-1970s détente was dead, and the thaw in the cold war seemed at an end. At the same time, the longest wave of economic expansion the world had yet experienced came crashing to an end when the Organization of Petroleum Exporting Countries (OPEC), dominated by Middle East Arabs unhappy with the West's support of Israel, suddenly hiked the price of oil. The spiraling inflation that resulted undercut, for a while, the growing international economy that had been helping decolonizing third world countries, especially in Africa, to develop and grow their young nations. The Watergate scandal had derailed Richard Nixon's presidency and with it his apparent special rapport with fellow cold warrior Leonid Brezhnev. Not long after the United States extricated itself from the Vietnam quagmire, the Soviets would find themselves bogged down in their own version of that conflict in Afghanistan, and American diplomats, reflexively anti-Soviet, pushed for support of the Afghani rebels. Peaceful coexistence, the goal of 1960s diplomacy seemed now a chimera.

High inflation and the end of détente also destabilized an already volatile Middle East. With the fall of the shah in Iran, a fundamentalist Islamic regime came to power and took American diplomats, covert agents, press reporters, and businesspeople hostage. American policy makers suddenly discovered there was nobody in Iran willing to talk to them, much less negotiate the release of the hostages, and the resulting diplomatic crisis doomed the presidency of Jimmy Carter and undermined American prestige and foreign policy. Even before then, the outbreak of the Yom Kippur War between Egypt and Israel had emphasized the apparently intractable problems of the region. Meanwhile, unrest in Africa (such as a Soviet- and Cuban-supported military junta's overthrow of Haile Selassie in Ethiopia) and in Latin America (such as the U.S.-backed military coup in Chile against left-wing president Salvador Allende and the rise of the avowedly marxist Sandinistas in Nicaragua) gave proof that, certainly in the third world, the cold war not only was still active but was intensifying.

Adding to the sense of general malaise was the marked increase in ideologically fueled terrorism. The new danger first gained widespread attention in America and Europe—just as had the American morass in Vietnam: through television—when a group of terrorists calling themselves Black September and affiliated with the Palestine Liberation Organization took Israel's Olympic team hostage at the games in Munich in 1972 (11 Israeli athletes were murdered). The Israelis struck back with the determination for which they were becoming noted, and often in the West admired, with air raids on guerrilla bases and naval installations in Lebanon and Syria. Part of the terrorists' complaint was that their situation, and the third world in general, never came to the attention of an international community fixated on the East-West struggle that had dominated world affairs since World War II. As it became clearer that the Soviets were funding terrorist training camps, however, even random terror seemed a part of the cycle of violence in a time when war had no fronts, made no distinctions between soldiers or civilians, and recognized no one as innocent.

By the early 1980s, even the staid English had become more bellicose, as Prime Minister Margaret Thatcher ordered the once-vaunted British navy to invade the hapless Falklands. The decade or so stretching from the early 1970s to the early 1980s certainly belied any notion that the "global village," which media pundits and diplomats alike began talking about in the 1960s, was a friendly place.

End of the Cold War

Then something like a miracle occurred. In the Middle East, Israel and Egypt suddenly appeared ready to give peace a chance, and they began by meeting on American soil and signing the CAMP DAVID ACCORDS in 1978. In Europe popular uprisings in the Soviet bloc—always brutally suppressed in the past—not only went unchallenged but also seemed to be encouraged by new leadership in the Kremlin. Czechoslovakians freely demonstrated against the Communist regime on the anniversary of the 1968 Soviet invasion. In Poland a workers' union called Solidarity demanded democratic reforms, and the Sejim, the parliament, legalized the return of confiscated property to the Catholic Church. Soviet-puppet president Wojciech Jaruzelski, to the shock of all, approved free elections for June 1989, the first in 40 years, during which Solidarity won all the available seats. Meanwhile, on May 2, 1989, Hungary unraveled the barbed wire along its borders with Austria, the first real breach in the Iron Curtain. In the fall, the citizens of Berlin began to tear down the Berlin Wall, consummate symbol of the cold war. Within three months the unthinkable had happened: all of eastern Europe had broken free of Soviet domination, and East and West Germany were talking about reuniting. The changes were not only limited to Europe and the Mideast. Almost as unthinkable as the fall of the Berlin Wall was the fact that the United States had given back the Panama Canal to the Panamanians in a new PANAMA CANAL TREATY. And in China the repressive Maoist "Gang of Four" had been re-placed by leaders who talked of economic reforms and joining the world market.

Late in 1989 the Conference on Security and Cooperation in Europe met with NATO and the Soviets to proclaim in the CHARTER OF PARIS FOR A NEW EUROPE that the cold war had ended. As if to prove the point, the various Soviet republics began declaring themselves sovereign or independent, and two years after the Paris conference, an aborted military coup in Russia by conservative Communists led to the dissolution of the Communist Party and the collapse of the Soviet Union. Suddenly, the reckless international security system engendered by cold war diplomacy—in which two superpowers, armed with weapons capable of destroying the planet many times over, divided the world into hostile camps, vied for influence over unaligned third world countries, and held each other in check at tremendous costs to their own people in dollars and freedom—seemed superfluous. In the wake of the cold war, an America that felt it had "won" was in fact no longer quite sure of its place in a world in which the threat of massive retaliation was a hollow boast, and its foreign policy began to drift.

Many wished to take credit for ending the cold war, which had come as a surprise to most if not all the world's leading powers. American historians staked out claims for the effect that the hard-line anti-Soviet ascendancy of Ronald Reagan and George Herbert Walker Bush may have had. The last of a breed formed by the experiences of World War II and its aftermath, they came into office talking about the "evil empire" of the USSR, invaded two woefully outgunned third world countries, Grenada and Panama, and following the defeat of Saddam Hussein in the 1991 Persian Gulf War, left speaking vaguely about a "New World Order." But the cold war belligerence of the Reagan-Bush administrations had more to do with American frustration over the recent course of foreign affairs than with a clear-eyed plan to end the madness of threatening nuclear war at any moment in order to maintain a general peace.

Some later claimed the last American cold war administration spent the Soviets into the ground; this indeed describes what happened, but not intentionally. Instead, the newly aggressive American policy was a response to the helpless feeling U.S. voters experienced after the country lost a war in Southeast Asia to a relatively tiny nation and American policy makers failed to deal decisively with the Iranian fundamentalists during the 1979 hostage crisis. Determined not to fall prey to the "Vietnam Syndrome" or to Jimmy Carter's fate, Reagan and Bush both acted vigorously to restore American pride, but their hostility toward international agreements in general and the United Nations in particular presaged the rise of a neo-isolationism in the Republican Party rather than a desire to pursue a lasting international peace.

Internal developments in the USSR, not a new direction in American foreign policy, changed the political and diplomatic landscape of the Soviet Union and Eastern Europe. After the death of Leonid Brezhnev, the USSR was run by a string of aging and ailing Communist Party members, one a former director of the KGB, before Mikhail Gorbachev took the helm. When he came to power, the country was mired in a seemingly endless and costly conflict in Afghanistan, the Communist Party had long ago atrophied into a cautious bureaucratic institution aimed at protecting the status quo at almost any cost, and the Soviet economy was saddled with a huge, entrenched defense establishment and a system of political satellites and trading partners whose wealth had been depleted by years of Soviet plunder. Gorbachev's subsequent attempts to reform both the Russian economy and the political culture of the Communist Party led him to divest the Soviets of their European "empire" and garnered for him a Nobel Peace Prize. They also led directly to the end of the cold war.

There were others who played a role in easing the tense and dangerous conditions of a world divided into nuclear-armed bunkers. Certainly among them were Anwar Sadat and Menachem Begin, who also won Nobel Prizes for their efforts to find a way out of the impasse in the Middle East and who paid a price—Sadat was assassinated as a result—at home for doing so.

But even these men, Gorbachev included, were surprised by the swiftness of the fall of the old world order and the rise of the new. One moment, it seemed the Russians were walking out of the START talks because Ronald Reagan had fantasies about a space-deployed nuclear shield; the next, he and Gorbachev were urging their reluctant, even horrified, generals to get rid of all their missiles at once. Perhaps the cold war system, like Otto von Bismarck's interlocking alliances before World War I, had been pushed to its limits, and its collapse was inevitable. If so, it is all the more remarkable that its collapse, unlike the collapse of Bismarck's world, did not lead to the war everyone had for so long feared.

New World Order

By the time of the Gulf War, George H. W. Bush could hardly afford any longer to act unilaterally, as his predecessor, Ronald Reagan, had been wont to do, and without the scrim of United Nations backing, his own Congress would have derailed his Middle Eastern strategy. Indeed, the New World Order of which he talked was evolving not from high-handed American diplomacy exercised in a world now free of any Soviet check. American diplomacy appeared to lack focus. At home, the neo-isolationism of a few outspoken Republicans made American presidents, Democrat or Republican, Bush or his successor, Bill Clinton, cautious, even ditheringly so, when it came time to dealing with such post–cold war problems as the ethnic violence in Africa and Bosnia. The DAYTON ACCORDS, bringing the genocide in the former Yugoslavia to a close, was a testament not so much to American sway in the world but, surprisingly, to the combined pressure of Europe and Russia through the increasingly confident United Nations. Neither did the United States seem particularly adept at dealing with the persistent problem of terrorism by Islamic fundamentalists such as HAMAS (see HAMAS COVENANT), which continued to threaten the on-again, off-again Middle East peace process. Ultimately, Islamic extremists would destabilize the entire region.

In the meantime, the New World Order seemed to be forming more out of the kinds of human rights and environmentalist policies whose roots lay in late 19th-century peace movements and which first took institutional hold after the incredible devastation of World War II gave birth to the United Nations. U.S. president Jimmy Carter had endorsed such policies—in fact had made human rights the touchstone of American diplomacy—before his presidency had been derailed by the Iran hostage crisis. Such documents as the VIENNA DECLARATION ON HUMAN RIGHTS; CONVENTION ON PROHIBITIONS OR RESTRICTIONS ON THE USE OF CERTAIN CONVENTIONAL WEAPONS; CONVENTION AGAINST TORTURE AND OTHER CRUEL, INHUMAN OR DEGRADING TREATMENT OR PUNISHMENT; THE CONVENTION ON THE RIGHTS OF THE CHILD; THE MONTREAL PROTOCOL ON THE OZONE LAYER; or the agreements produced by the "Earth Summit" in Rio de Janeiro, among them the RIO DECLARATION, CONVENTION ON CLIMATE CHANGE, and CONVENTION ON BIODIVERSITY, would have been created regardless of American foreign policy and were in fact sometimes passed despite active resistance from Reagan's or the first President Bush's administration, but they were in a tradition first given international airing, if not international legitimacy, by Woodrow Wilson at Versailles.

Thus, rather than providing the world's only remaining superpower with a clear legacy, the cold war in its passing had left the United States strapped to a defense establishment (with a huge budget) it did not need, a powerful national security apparatus it did not know what to do with, and an American foreign policy community ambivalent at best about the direction world diplomacy had taken. In retrospect, the cold war seemed to have been cyclical, with both the United States and the USSR alternating between periods of assertion and relaxation. In the long run, it was not this or that individual leader who engineered its close but the tremendous costs for both sides in energy and money and, more importantly, the rise of other players in an increasingly global marketplace.

By the time the first President Bush left office, policy wags were joking that the cold war was over, and Japan had won. Certainly, the rise of Japan and the Pacific Rim countries as a trading bloc was essential to new directions in diplomacy, but as the United States learned, these directions were resistant even to old-style bilateral trade agreements. To the contrary, it was the success of the European Common Market in unifying Europe commercially and culturally, as represented by the MAASTRICHT TREATY, that became the model for American free traders in shaping the NORTH AMERICAN FREE TRADE AGREEMENT (NAFTA) and a subsequent U.S.–Central America Free Trade Agreement (CAFTA) drawn up along the lines of NAFTA. Signed into law by President George W. Bush on August 2, 2005, CAFTA liberalizes trade between the United States and five Central American countries: Costa Rica, El Salvador, Guatemala, Honduras, and Nicaragua. Together, NAFTA and CAFTA are seen as steps toward an eventual Free Trade Area of the Americas, which would encompass 34 economies of the western Hemisphere. It was not so much that the arrival of a global village put an end to the cold war and its hostilities but that the end of the cold war cleared the way for the emergence of a truly global market, soon to be symbolized by the birth of of a new currency, the Euro.

As the 20th century came to a close, it was difficult to predict with any assurance which of the treaties concluded in its last 25 years would prove to have the kind of historical significance and impact that, say, the now totally irrelevant TREATY OF VERSAILLES (1919) had on the world after the Great War. Most (such as the KYOTO PROTOCOL ON CLIMATE CHANGE; PROTOCOL ON THE INVOLVEMENT OF CHILDREN IN ARMED CONFLICT; THE PROTOCOL ON THE SALE OF CHILDREN; CHILD PROSTITUTION, AND CHILD PORNOGRAPHY, AND THE ROME STATUTE) involved more than bilateral agreements, although certainly nuclear weapons understandings between the United States and the former USSR, such as the INF TREATY, which Reagan skillfully negotiated, were judged essential to understanding the era, as were the documents in the ongoing Middle East peace process. These treaties dealt with the unfinished business of the cold war, but even those that did not often showed the footprint of U.S. diplomacy. The BELFAST AGREEMENT, for example, which promised to bring an end to the long-standing troubles between the British and the Irish in Northern Ireland, was made possible by the quasi-official efforts of former U.S. senator–cum–special adviser to the president George Mitchell (who later similarly promoted a Middle East peace settlement) to bring the two sides together. Still, most of the seminal documents continued to have some element of multinational negotiation, if not always the outright imprint of the United Nations. So long had the world been divided into nation-states competing for markets, territory, and dominance and making treaties that in many ways calculated the success of that competition, it was hard to fathom that such treaty making might, in fact, have become passé.

As the 20th century came to a close, there certainly were those surveying the turmoil in the poorer nations of the world and the growing ethnic divisions in even some of the richest, who argued that the global village remained a dream of fools and that the future would look more like the chaotic world after the collapse of the Roman and Byzantine Empires. To some it seemed that the world was in one of those periods of history following a long period of diplomatic consensus— Europe, say, under the CONGRESS OF VIENNA—that would yield to another round of great wars and the rise of new powers. The nature of such wide-ranging diplomatic "settlements" as the cold war makes those living under them blind to other arrangements, which is why its close came as such a shock to so many.

Nevertheless, by the end of the 20th century, there was much talk in the United States of the "peace dividend," the cutback in the size of military budgets allowed by the end of the cold war that policymakers believed would boost the world economy to new heights. And certainly the Clinton administration witnessed a long period of economic growth that included the scaling back of American defense spending and the expansion of worldwide trade. But under vicious attack domestically from his political enemies in Congress, Clinton followed a cautious foreign policy quietly dedicated to international consensus building.

His successor, George W. Bush, however, came from the isolationist-minded wing of the Republican Party and ran on a platform expressly opposed to "nation building," a right-wing code word for opposition to foreign interventions, even those urged by our allies and sponsored by the United Nations. Still, Bush had barely squeaked into office over Clinton's vice president, Al Gore, who was a staunch advocate of multilateralism, which was popular with voters; there was every reason to believe that in general U.S. diplomacy would continue on the same basic, if ill-tempered, post–cold war course of Ronald Reagan and the first President Bush.

All that changed on September 11, 2001, with the terrorist attacks on the World Trade Center in New York City and the Pentagon in Washington, D.C. In response, the administration of President George W. Bush came to favor unilateral and even preemptive military action, as in the overthrow of Iraq's Saddam Hussein in Operation Iraqi Freedom (2003–   ).

TREATIES

Mutual Defense Treaties, Military Alliances, and Nonaggression Pacts

CHARTER OF PARIS FOR A NEW EUROPE (PARIS CHARTER)

TREATY AT A GLANCE

Completed
November 21, 1990, at Paris

Signatories
The member states of NATO and the former Warsaw Pact, plus
13 other formerly "nonaligned" European nations

Overview
In the wake of Mikhail Gorbachev's reforms in the USSR and the liberation of Eastern Europe from Soviet dominance, the nations of Europe, east and west, formed the Conference on Security and Cooperation in Europe (CSCE). With the fall of the Berlin Wall and the reunification of Germany, the CSCE met in Paris in 1990 to proclaim in the Paris Charter the end of the cold war.

Historical Background

At the end of World War II, the Allied powers agreed to divide Germany and its capital, Berlin, into four sectors each in order to weaken forever the nation that had started two world wars. In both nation and city, one sector each would be controlled by the United States, Great Britain, France, and the Soviet Union. For those living in West Berlin, located deep within Soviet-occupied East Germany, life was psychologically trying, for they were separated from the developments in the liberal democratic sectors of Germany, to which they were linked politically, while being surrounded by the more oppressive Russian sector, where the hand of occupation was demonstrably heavier. The Soviets took every opportunity to heighten the anxious fatalism that many observers at the time noted as a characteristic of West Berliners.

The divided city presented problems for the communists, as well, since residents of East Berlin were slipping across to West Berlin at every opportunity. The draconian economic system imposed by the Soviets, the elaborate secret police measures they employed to

keep tabs on East Germans, and the sheer lack of opportunity for East Germans to make a decent life compared to their fellow Germans in the West caused many East Germans to opt for what the liberal democratic Allies never hesitated to proclaim as freedom. The Soviets and East Germany's Communist Party were embarrassed by the hemorrhaging, and party leader Walter Ulbricht did all he could to put an end to the situation. First he gave border patrols the order to shoot to kill defecting East Berliners. When the flow of refugees failed to stop, he directed the construction of a concrete and barbed wire wall through the city in 1961.

Of course, the Berlin Wall served a much larger purpose than containing the citizens of East Berlin. For Ulbricht and his Soviet masters, it was an act of defiance directed against the West. For most of the rest of the world, it was a symbol of oppression, of the antithesis of freedom.

By 1989, with Soviet premier Mikhail Gorbachev making overtures of reconciliation with the West, the Berlin Wall had outlived its usefulness. Of late it had been poorly maintained and generally allowed to crumble. Now, in the fall of 1989, East Germans eagerly dismantled it, brick by brick, before turning to chase the Communists out of their government. Even before they did the latter, however, they began to "unify" their country again with their feet: 133,000 people picked up, walked across the rubble, and took up residence in the West during the month after the fall of the Berlin Wall.

Such an influx put tremendous strain on West German resources, but it also forced Chancellor Helmut Kohl to face up to the reality and begin planning for reunification in order to stem the tide. On November 28, 1989, he announced a 10-point plan under which the East and the West would expand cooperation until full political unity was achieved. He made it clear to the Soviets and Western Europeans alike, who after all might have some concerns about the reunification of a country that in this century had led the globe into two world wars, that the process must occur under the Conference on Security and Cooperation in Europe (CSCE), the European Community, and the East-West disarmament regimes initiated by the 1988 INF TREATY.

The CSCE was a summit held during the détente years of 1973 and 1975 in Helsinki, Finland, and attended by WARSAW PACT countries as well as the nations of the NORTH ATLANTIC TREATY ORGANIZATION and 13 "neutral" and nonaligned European states (see VIENNA DECLARATION ON HUMAN RIGHTS). In the wake of Gorbachev's reforms and the liberation of the rest of Eastern Europe from Communist domination, the CSCE was gearing up for another summit. The Warsaw Pact and NATO nations held a meeting in Ottawa, Canada, on German reunification in 1990, and as bilateral talks between the Federal (West) German Republic and the (East) German Democratic Republic proceeded at an emergency pace, the CSCE set the site for its second meeting in Paris. Within a year, on October 2, 1990, the two Germanies had been politically rejoined, faster than anyone had imagined. A month later, on November 19, 1990, the CSCE opened its Paris summit and proclaimed the cold war at an end.

Terms

At the conference, the member states agreed in the Conventional Forces in Europe Treaty to various arms limitations, equal in number, for both NATO and the Soviets. In the Paris Charter, moreover, the Soviets, the Americans, and Europeans both east and west announced to the world that Europe was henceforth united, that all blocs—military and economic—had ceased to exist, and that all those signing the agreement stood for democracy, freedom, and human rights.

Charter of Paris for a New Europe: A New Era of Democracy, Peace, and Unity

We, the Heads of State or Government of the States participating in the Conference on Security and Cooperation in Europe, have assembled in Paris at a time of profound change and historic expectations. The era of confrontation and division of Europe has ended. We declare that henceforth our relations will be founded on respect and co-operation.

Europe is liberating itself from the legacy of the past. The courage of men and women, the strength of the will of the peoples and the power of the ideas of the Helsinki Final Act have opened a new era of democracy, peace and unity in Europe.

Ours is a time for fulfilling the hopes and expectations our peoples have cherished for decades: steadfast commitment to democracy based on human rights and fundamental freedoms; prosperity through economic liberty and social justice; and equal security for all our countries.

The Ten Principles of the Final Act will guide us towards this ambitious future, just as they have lighted our way towards better relations for the past fifteen years. Full implementation of all CSCE commitments must form the basis for the initiatives we are now taking to enable our nations to live in accordance with their aspirations.

HUMAN RIGHTS, DEMOCRACY AND RULE OF LAW
We undertake to build, consolidate and strengthen democracy as the only system of government of our nations. In this endeavor, we will abide by the following:

Human rights and fundamental freedoms are the birthright of all human beings, are inalienable and are guaranteed by law. Their protection and promotion is the first responsibility of government. Respect for them is an essential safeguard against an over-mighty State. Their observance and full exercise are the foundation of freedom, justice and peace.

Democratic government is based on the will of the people, expressed regularly through free and fair elections. Democracy has as its foundation respect for the human person and the rule of law. Democracy is the best safeguard of freedom of expression, tolerance of all groups of society, and equality of opportunity for each person.

Democracy, with its representative and pluralist character, entails accountability to the electorate, the obligation of public authorities to comply with the law and justice administered impartially. No one will be above the law.

We affirm that, without discrimination, every individual has the right to:
freedom of thought, conscience and religion or belief,
freedom of expression,
freedom of association and peaceful assembly,
freedom of movement;
No one will be:
subject to arbitrary arrest or detention,
subject to torture or other cruel, inhuman or degrading treatment or punishment;
everyone also has the right:
to know and act upon his rights,

to participate in free and fair elections,
to fair and public trial if charged with an offense,
to own property alone or in association and to exercise
    individual enterprise,
to enjoy his economic, social and cultural rights.

We affirm that the ethnic, cultural, linguistic and religious identity of national minorities will be protected and that persons belonging to national minorities have the right freely to express, preserve, and develop that identity without any discrimination and in full equality before the law.

We will ensure that everyone will enjoy recourse to effective remedies, national or international, against any violation of his rights. Full respect for these precepts is the bedrock on which we will seek to construct the new Europe. Our States will cooperate and support each other with the aim of making democratic gains irreversible.

ECONOMIC LIBERTY AND RESPONSIBILITY

Economic liberty, social justice and environmental responsibility are indispensable for prosperity.

The free will of the individual, exercised in democracy and protected by the rule of law, forms the necessary basis for successful economic and social development. We will promote economic activity which respects and upholds human dignity.

Freedom and political pluralism are necessary elements in our common objective of developing market economies towards sustainable economic growth, prosperity, social justice, expanding employment and efficient use of economic resources. The success of the transition to market economy by countries making efforts to this effect is important and in the interest of us all. It will enable us to share a higher level of prosperity which is our common objective.

We will cooperate to this end.

Preservation of the environment is a shared responsibility of all our nations. While supporting national and regional efforts in this field, we must also look to the pressing need for joint action on a wider scale.

FRIENDLY RELATIONS AMONG PARTICIPATING STATES

Now that a new era is dawning in Europe, we are determined to expand and strengthen friendly relations and cooperation among the States of Europe, the United States of America and Canada, and to promote friendship among our peoples.

To uphold and promote democracy, peace and unity in Europe, we solemnly pledge our full commitment to the Ten Principles of the Helsinki Final Act. We affirm the continuing validity of the Ten Principles and our determination to put them into practice. All the Principles apply equally and unreservedly, each of them being interpreted taking into account the others. They form the basis for our relations.

In accordance with our obligations under the Charter of the United Nations and commitments under the Helsinki Final Act, we renew our pledge to refrain from the threat or use of force against the territorial integrity or political independence of any State, or from acting in any other manner inconsistent with the principles or purposes of those documents.

We recall that non-compliance with obligations under the Charter of the United Nations constitutes a violation of international law.

We reaffirm or commitment to settle disputes by peaceful means. We decide to develop mechanisms for the prevention and resolution of conflicts among the participating States.

With the ending of the division of Europe, we will strive for a new quality in our security relations while fully respecting each other's freedom of choice in that respect. Security is indivisible and the security of every participating State is inseparably linked to that of all the others. We therefore pledge to cooperate in strengthening confidence and security among us and in promoting arms control and disarmament.

We welcome the joint Declaration of Twenty-Two States on the improvement of their relations.

Our relations will rest on our common adherence to democratic values and to human rights and fundamental freedoms. We are convinced that in order to strengthen peace and security among our States, the advancement of democracy, and respect for and effective exercise of human rights, are indispensable. We reaffirm the equal rights of peoples and their right to self-determination in conformity with the Charter of the United Nations and with the relevant norms of international law, including those relating to territorial integrity of States.

We are determined to enhance political consultation and to widen cooperation to solve economic, social, environmental, cultural and humanitarian problems. This common resolve and our growing interdependence will help to overcome the mistrust of decades, to increase stability and to build a united Europe.

We want Europe to be a source of peace, open to dialogue and to cooperation with other countries, welcoming exchanges and involved in the search for common responses to the challenges of the future.

SECURITY

Friendly relations among us will benefit from the consolidation of democracy and improved security.

We welcome the signature of the Treaty on Conventional Armed Forces in Europe by twenty-two participating States, which will lead to lower levels of armed forces. We endorse the adoption of a substantial new set of Confidence-and Security-building Measures which will lead to increased transparency and confidence among all participating States. These are important steps towards enhanced stability and security in Europe.

The unprecedented reduction in armed forces resulting from the Treaty on Conventional Armed Forces in Europe, together with new approaches to security and cooperation within the CSCE process, will lead to a new perception of security in Europe and a new dimension in our relations. In this context we fully recognize the freedom of States to choose their own security arrangements.

UNITY

Europe whole and free is calling for a new beginning. We invite our peoples to join in this great endeavor.

We note with great satisfaction the Treaty on the Final Settlement with respect to Germany signed in Moscow on 12 September 1990 and sincerely welcome the fact that the German people have united to become one State in accordance with the principles of the Final Act of the Conference on Security and Cooperation in Europe and in full accord with their neighbors. The establishment of the national unity of Germany is an important contribution to a just and lasting order of peace for a united, democratic Europe aware of its responsibility for stability, peace and cooperation.

The participation of both North American and European States is a fundamental characteristic of the CSCE; it underlies its past achievements and is essential to the future of the CSCE process. An abiding adherence to shared values and our common heritage are the ties which bind us together. With all the rich diversity of our nations, we are united in our commitment to expand our cooperation in all fields. The challenges confronting us can only be met by common action, cooperation and solidarity.

THE CSCE AND THE WORLD

The destiny of our nations is linked to that of all other nations. We support fully the United Nations and the enhancement of its role in promoting international peace, security and justice.

We reaffirm our commitment to the principles and purposes of the United Nations as enshrined in the Charter and condemn all violations of these principles. We recognize with satisfaction the growing role of the United Nations in world affairs and its increasing effectiveness, fostered by the improvement in relations among our States.

Aware of the dire needs of a great part of the world, we commit ourselves to solidarity with all other countries. Therefore, we issue a call from Paris today to all the nations of the world. We stand ready to join with any and all States in common efforts to protect and advance the community of fundamental human values.

GUIDELINES FOR THE FUTURE

Proceeding from our firm commitment to the full implementation of all CSCE principles and provisions, we now resolve to give a new impetus to a balanced and comprehensive development of our cooperation in order to address the needs and aspirations of our peoples.

HUMAN DIMENSION

We declare our respect for human rights and fundamental freedoms to be irrevocable. We will fully implement and build upon the provisions relating to the human dimension of the CSCE.

Proceeding from the Document of the Copenhagen Meeting of the Conference on the Human Dimension, we will cooperate to strengthen democratic institutions and to promote the application of the rule of law. To that end, we decide to convene a seminar of experts in Oslo from 4 to 15 November 1991.

Determined to foster the rich contribution of national minorities to the life of our societies, we undertake further to improve their situation. We reaffirm our deep conviction that friendly relations among our peoples, as well as peace, justice, stability and democracy, require that the ethnic, cultural, linguistic and religious identity of national minorities be protected and conditions for the promotion of that identity be created. We declare that questions related to national minorities can only be satisfactorily resolved in a democratic political framework. We further acknowledge that the rights of persons belonging to national minorities must be fully respected as part of universal human rights. Being aware of the urgent need for increased cooperation on, as well as better protection of, national minorities, we decide to convene a meeting of experts on national minorities to be held in Geneva from 1 to 19 July 1991.

We express our determination to combat all forms of racial and ethnic hatred, anti-semitism, xenophobia and discrimination against anyone as well as persecution on religious and ideological grounds.

In accordance with our CSCE commitments, we stress that free movement and contacts among our citizens as well as the free flow of information and ideas are crucial for the maintenance and development of free societies and flourishing cultures. We welcome increased tourism and visits among our countries.

The human dimension mechanism has proved its usefulness, and we are consequently determined to expand it to include new procedures involving, inter alia, the services of experts or a roster of eminent persons experienced in human rights issues which could be raised under the mechanism. We shall provide, in the context of the mechanism, for individuals to be involved in the protection of their rights. Therefore, we undertake to develop further our commitments in this respect, in particular at the Moscow Meeting of the Conference on the Human Dimension, without prejudice to obligations under existing international instruments to which our States may be parties.

We recognize the important contribution of the Council of Europe to the promotion of human rights and the principles of democracy and the rule of law as well as to the development of cultural co-operation. We welcome moves by several participating States to join the Council of Europe and adhere to its European Convention on Human Rights. We welcome as well the readiness of the Council of Europe to make its experience available to the CSCE.

SECURITY

The changing political and military environment in Europe opens new possibilities for common efforts in the field of military security. We will build on the important achievements attained in the Treaty on Conventional Armed Forces in Europe and in the Negotiations on Confidence- and Security-Building Measures. We undertake to continue the CSBM negotiations under the same mandate, and to seek to conclude them no later than the Follow-up Meeting of the CSCE to be held in Helsinki in 1992. We also welcome the decision of the participating States concerned to continue the CFE negotiation under the same mandate and to seek to conclude it no later than the Helsinki Follow-up Meeting. Following a period for national preparations, we look forward to a more structured co-operation among all participating States on security matters, and to discussions and consultations among the thirty-four participating States aimed at establishing by 1992, from the conclusion of the Helsinki Follow-up Meeting, new negotiations on disarmament and confidence and security building open to all participating States.

We call for the earliest possible conclusion of the Convention on an effectively verifiable, global and comprehensive ban on chemical weapons, and we intend to be original signatories to it.

We reaffirm the importance of the Open Skies initiative and call for the successful conclusion of the negotiations as soon as possible.

Although the threat of conflict in Europe has diminished, other dangers threaten the stability of our societies. We are determined to cooperate in defending democratic institutions against activities which violate the independence, sovereign equality or territorial integrity of the participating States. These include illegal activities involving outside pressure, coercion and subversion.

We unreservedly condemn, as criminal, all acts, methods and practices of terrorism and express our determination to work for its eradication both bilaterally and through multilateral cooperation. We will also join together in combating illicit trafficking in drugs. Being aware that an essential complement to the duty of States to refrain from the threat or use of force is the peaceful settlement of disputes, both being essential factors for the maintenance and consolidation of international peace and security, we will not only seek effective ways of preventing, through political means, conflicts which may yet emerge, but also define, in conformity with international law, appropriate mechanisms for the peaceful resolution of any disputes which may arise. Accordingly, we undertake to seek new forms of cooperation in this area, in particular a range of methods for the peaceful settlement of disputes, including mandatory third-party involvement. We stress that full use should be made in this context of the opportunity of the meeting on the peaceful settlement of disputes which will be convened in Valletta at the beginning of 1991. The Council of Ministers for Foreign Affairs will take into account the Report of the Valletta Meeting.

ECONOMIC CO-OPERATION

We stress that economic cooperation based on market economy constitutes an essential element of our relations and will be instrumental in the construction of a prosperous and united Europe. Democratic institutions and economic liberty foster economic and social progress, as recognized in the Document of the Bonn Conference on Economic Cooperation, the results of which we strongly support.

We underline that cooperation in the economic field, science and technology is now an important pillar of the CSCE. The participating States should periodically review progress and give new impulses in these fields.

We are convinced that our overall economic cooperation should be expanded, free enterprise encouraged and trade increased and diversified according to GATT rules.

We will promote social justice and progress and further the welfare of our peoples. We recognize in this context the importance of effective policies to address the problem of unemployment.

We reaffirm the need to continue to support democratic countries in transition towards the establishment of market economy and the creation of the basis for self-sustained economic and social growth, as already undertaken by the Group of twenty-four countries. We further underline the necessity of their increased integration, involving the acceptance of disciplines as well as benefits, into the international economic and financial system.

We consider that increased emphasis on economic cooperation within the CSCE process should take into account the interests of developing participating States.

We recall the link between respect for and promotion of human rights and fundamental freedoms and scientific progress. Cooperation in the field of science and technology will play an essential role in economic and social development. Therefore, it must evolve towards a greater sharing of appropriate scientific and technological information and knowledge with a view to overcoming the technological gap which exists among the participating States. We further encourage the participating States to work together in order to develop human potential and the spirit of free enterprise.

We are determined to give the necessary impetus to cooperation among our States in the fields of energy, transport and tourism for economic and social development. We welcome, in particular, practical steps to create optimal conditions for the economic and rational development of energy resources, with due regard for environmental considerations.

We recognize the important role of the European Community in the political and economic development of Europe. International economic organizations such as the Economic Commission for Europe of the United Nations (ECE/UN), the Bretton Woods Institutions, the Organization for Economic Cooperation and Development (OECD), the European Free Trade Association (EFTA) and the International Chamber of Commerce (ICC) also have a significant task in promoting economic cooperation, which will be further enhanced by the establishment of the European Bank for Reconstruction and Development (EBRD). In order to pursue our objectives, we stress the necessity for effective coordination of the activities of these organizations and emphasize the need to find methods for all our States to take part in these activities.

ENVIRONMENT

We recognize the urgent need to tackle the problems of the environment and the importance of individual and co-operative efforts in this area. We pledge to intensify our endeavors to protect and improve our environment in order to restore and maintain a sound ecological balance in air, water and soil. Therefore, we are determined to make full use of the CSCE as a framework for the formulation of common environmental commitments and objectives, and thus to pursue the work reflected in the Report of the Sofia Meeting on the Protection of the Environment.

We emphasize the significant role of a well-informed society in enabling the public and individuals to take initiatives to improve the environment. To this end, we commit ourselves to promote public awareness and education on the environment as well as the public reporting of the environmental impact of policies, projects and programs.

We attach priority to the introduction of clean and low-waste technology, being aware of the need to support countries which do not yet have their own means for appropriate measures.

We underline that environmental policies should be supported by appropriate legislative measures and administrative structures to ensure their effective implementation.

We stress the need for new measures providing for the systematic evaluation of compliance with the existing commitments and, moreover, for the development of more ambitious commitments with regard to notification and exchange of information about the state of the environment and potential environmental hazards. We also welcome the creation of the European Environment Agency (EEA).

We welcome the operational activities, problem-oriented studies and policy reviews in various existing international organizations engaged in the protection of the environment, such as the United Nations Environment Program (UNEP), the

Economic Commission for Europe of the United Nations (ECE/UN) and the Organization for Economic Cooperation and Development (OECD). We emphasize the need for strengthening their cooperation and for their efficient coordination.

CULTURE

We recognize the essential contribution of our common European culture and our shared values in overcoming the division of the continent. Therefore, we underline our attachment to creative freedom and to the protection and promotion of our cultural and spiritual heritage, in all its richness and diversity.

In view of the recent changes in Europe, we stress the increased importance of the Cracow Symposium and we look forward to its consideration of guidelines for intensified cooperation in the field of culture. We invite the Council of Europe to contribute to this Symposium.

In order to promote greater familiarity amongst our peoples, we favor the establishment of cultural centers in cities of other participating States as well as increased cooperation in the audio-visual field and wider exchange in music, theater, literature and the arts.

We resolve to make special efforts in our national policies to promote better understanding, in particular among young people, through cultural exchanges, cooperation in all fields of education and, more specifically, through teaching and training in the languages of other participating States. We intend to consider first results of this action at the Helsinki Follow-up Meeting in 1992.

MIGRANT WORKERS

We recognize that the issues of migrant workers and their families legally residing in host countries have economic, cultural and social aspects as well as their human dimension. We reaffirm that the protection and and promotion of their rights, as well as the implementation of relevant international obligations, is our common concern.

MEDITERRANEAN

We consider that the fundamental political changes that have occurred in Europe have a positive relevance to the Mediterranean region. Thus, we will continue efforts to strengthen security and cooperation in the Mediterranean as an important factor for stability in Europe. We welcome the Report of the Palma de Mallorca Meeting on the Mediterranean, the results of which we all support.

We are concerned with the continuing tensions in the region, and renew our determination to intensify efforts towards finding just, viable and lasting solutions, through peaceful means, to outstanding crucial problems, based on respect for the principles of the Final Act.

We wish to promote favorable conditions for a harmonious development and diversification of relations with the non-participating Mediterranean States. Enhanced cooperation with these States will be pursued with the aim of promoting economic and social development and thereby enhancing stability in the region. To this end, we will strive together with these countries towards a substantial narrowing of the prosperity gap between Europe and its Mediterranean neighbors.

NON-GOVERNMENTAL ORGANIZATIONS

We recall the major role that non-governmental organizations, religious and other groups and individuals have played in the achievement of the objectives of the CSCE and will further facilitate their activities for the implementation of the CSCE commitments by the participating States. These organizations, groups and individuals must be involved in an appropriate way in the activities and new structures of the CSCE in order to fulfill their important tasks.

NEW STRUCTURES AND INSTITUTIONS OF THE CSCE PROCESS

Our common efforts to consolidate respect for human rights, democracy and the rule of law, to strengthen peace and to promote unity in Europe require a new quality of political dialogue and cooperation and thus development of the structures of the CSCE.

The intensification of our consultations at all levels is of prime importance in shaping our future relations. To this end, we decide on the following:

We, the Heads of State or Government, shall meet next time in Helsinki on the occasion of the CSCE Follow-up Meeting 1992. Thereafter, we will meet on the occasion of subsequent follow-up meetings.

Our Ministers for Foreign Affairs will meet, as a Council, regularly and at least once a year. These meetings will provide the central forum for political consultations within the CSCE process. The Council will consider issues relevant to the Conference on Security and Cooperation in Europe and take appropriate decisions.

The first meeting of the Council will take place in Berlin. A Committee of Senior Officials will prepare the meetings of the Council and carry out its decisions. The Committee will review current issues and may take appropriate decisions, including in the form of recommendations to the Council.

Additional meetings of the representatives of the participating States may be agreed upon to discuss questions of urgent concern.

The Council will examine the development of provisions for convening meetings of the Committee of Senior Officials in emergency situations. Meetings of other Ministers may also be agreed by the participating States. In order to provide administrative support for these consultations we establish a Secretariat in Prague.

Follow-up meetings of the participating States will be held, as a rule, every two years to allow the participating States to take stock of developments, review the implementation of their commitments and consider further steps in the CSCE process.

We decide to create a Conflict Prevention Center in Vienna to assist the Council in reducing the risk of conflict.

We decide to establish an Office for Free Elections in Warsaw to facilitate contacts and the exchange of information on elections within participating States.

Recognizing the important role parliamentarians can play in the CSCE process, we call for greater parliamentary involvement in the CSCE, in particular through the creation of a CSCE parliamentary assembly, involving members of parliaments from all participating States. To this end, we urge that contacts be pursued at parliamentary level to discuss the field of activities, working methods and rules of procedure of such a CSCE parliamentary structure, drawing on existing experience and work already undertaken in this field.

We ask our Ministers for Foreign Affairs to review this matter on the occasion of their first meeting as a Council.

Procedural and organizational modalities relating to certain provisions contained in the Charter of Paris for a New Europe are set out in the Supplementary Document which is adopted together with the Charter of Paris.

We entrust to the Council the further steps which may be required to ensure the implementation of decisions contained in the present document, as well as in the Supplementary Document, and to consider further efforts for the strengthening of security and cooperation in Europe. The Council may adopt any amendment to the Supplementary Document which it may deem appropriate.

The original of the Charter of Paris for a New Europe, drawn up in English, French, German, Italian, Russian and Spanish, will be transmitted to the Government of the French Republic, which will retain it in its archives. Each of the participating States will receive from the Government of the French Republic a true copy of the Charter of Paris.

The text of the Charter of Paris will be published in each participating State, which will disseminate it and make it known as widely as possible.

The Government of the French Republic is requested to transmit to the Secretary-General of the United Nations the text of the Charter of Paris for a New Europe, which is not eligible for registration under Article 102 of the Charter of the United Nations, with a view to its circulation to all the members of the Organization as an official document of the United Nations.

The Government of the French Republic is also requested to transmit the text of the Charter of Paris to all the other international organizations mentioned in the text.

Wherefore, we, the undersigned High Representatives of the participating States, mindful of the high political significance we attach to the results of the Summit Meeting, and declaring our determination to act in accordance with the provisions we have adopted, have subscribed our signatures below:

Done at Paris,
on 21 November 1990

There followed a supplementary document to put into effect provisions of the charter creating a Council, a Committee of Senior Officials, the CSCE Secretariat, a Conflict Prevention Center, and an Office for Free Elections.

Consequences

No less than did the destruction of the Berlin Wall, the Paris Charter marked the joyous phase of the cold war's end. Gone were the reckless diplomatic networks of a national security system in which two superpowers, armed with weapons capable of destroying the planet many times over, had divided the world as surely as the wall had Berlin. Gone, too, for the most part, were the two hostile worlds that had struggled for influence over an unaligned third world, even as they poured tremendous resources into holding one another at bay.

Yet the end of the cold war hardly brought unalloyed rejoicing. In its wake, the cold war left a somehow murkier world, with one superpower in a state of virtual disintegration and the other, America, no longer quite sure of its place in the new international order being born. The cold war destroyed the Soviet economy and put the United States deeply into debt, leaving it with troubled inner cities, unserved by the social programs that might have been, and now burdened with a massive and unwieldy international security apparatus it did not know precisely how to employ.

Source

Federation of American Scientists, "Charter of Paris for a New Europe." Available online. URL: http://www.fas.org/nuke/control/paris/. Accessed December 30, 2004.

Peace Treaties and Truces

CAMP DAVID ACCORDS

TREATY AT A GLANCE

Completed
September 17, 1978, at Camp David, Maryland

Signatories
Egypt and Israel (United States as witness)

Overview
On September 17, 1978, Israeli prime minister Menachem Begin and Egyptian president Anwar Sadat, after holding talks hosted by U.S. president Jimmy Carter at Camp David, concluded agreements paving the way for a peace treaty between Israel and Egypt and a broader plan for peace in the Middle East. The Camp David Accords and the peace process that grew out of them won for both Sadat and Begin the Nobel Peace Prize.

Historical Background

Even in a century of tremendous, rapid, and continual change, there are certain conditions of existence that are taken as given and unalterable. One such was the implacable enmity between Israel and Egypt, rooted in Old Testament times but in the modern world a direct result of the United Nations having carved Israel out of Arab lands in 1948. Since that year, Egypt and Israel had been in a continual state of war.

It took the foresight and courage of Egypt's president, Anwar Sadat, a former army officer who had served at a high level under no less a figure than Gamal Abdel Nasser, to make the first steps to alter the unalterable. During November 19 through 21, 1977, in a daring—almost breathtaking—political move, he became the first Egyptian head of state to visit Israel, coming to Jerusalem to address the Knesset (Israeli parliament). This visit gave rise to a series of negotiations between Sadat and Begin, which reached a deadlock in 1978.

At that point, United States president Jimmy Carter invited both heads of state to the rural Maryland retreat established by Franklin Roosevelt in 1942. Called back then Shangri-La, it had been renamed Camp David in 1953 by President Dwight D. Eisenhower, after his grandson. At Camp David, Carter mediated negotiations between Sadat and Begin, and following 12 days of talks, the three emerged with two documents: a framework for a peace treaty between Israel and Egypt, and an outline of a program for peace throughout the Middle East.

Terms

The first document called for a phased withdrawal of Israeli troops from the Sinai, occupied since the Six-Day War of 1967. In return, Egypt pledged the safe and unrestricted passage of Israeli shipping through the Suez Canal. The second document called for Israel to phase in self-government for the Palestinians in the Israeli-occupied West Bank and Gaza Strip. On March 26, 1979, Israel and Egypt concluded a definitive treaty that embodied the Camp David Accords.

The Camp David Accords

THE FRAMEWORK FOR PEACE IN THE MIDDLE EAST

Muhammad Anwar al-Sadat, President of the Arab Republic of Egypt, and Menachem Begin, Prime Minister of Israel, met with Jimmy Carter, President of the United States of America, at Camp David from September 5 to September 17, 1978, and have agreed on the following framework for peace in the Middle East. They invite other parties to the Arab-Israel conflict to adhere to it.

Preamble

The search for peace in the Middle East must be guided by the following:

*The agreed basis for a peaceful settlement of the conflict between Israel and its neighbors is United Nations Security Council Resolution 242, in all its parts.

*After four wars during 30 years, despite intensive human efforts, the Middle East, which is the cradle of civilization and the birthplace of three great religions, does not enjoy the blessings of peace. The people of the Middle East yearn for peace so that the vast human and natural resources of the region can be turned to the pursuits of peace and so that this area can become a model for coexistence and cooperation among nations.

*The historic initiative of President Sadat in visiting Jerusalem and the reception accorded to him by the parliament, government and people of Israel, and the reciprocal visit of Prime Minister Begin to Ismailia, the peace proposals made by both leaders, as well as the warm reception of these missions by the peoples of both countries, have created an unprecedented opportunity for peace which must not be lost if this generation and future generations are to be spared the tragedies of war.

*The provisions of the Charter of the United Nations and the other accepted norms of international law and legitimacy now provide accepted standards for the conduct of relations among all states.

*To achieve a relationship of peace, in the spirit of Article 2 of the United Nations Charter, future negotiations between Israel and any neighbor prepared to negotiate peace and security with it are necessary for the purpose of carrying out all the provisions and principles of Resolutions 242 and 338.

*Peace requires respect for the sovereignty, territorial integrity and political independence of every state in the area and their right to live in peace within secure and recognized boundaries free from threats or acts of force. Progress toward that goal can accelerate movement toward a new era of reconciliation in the Middle East marked by cooperation in promoting economic development, in maintaining stability and in assuring security.

*Security is enhanced by a relationship of peace and by cooperation between nations which enjoy normal relations. In addition, under the terms of peace treaties, the parties can, on the basis of reciprocity, agree to special security arrangements such as demilitarized zones, limited armaments areas, early warning stations, the presence of international forces, liaison, agreed measures for monitoring and other arrangements that they agree are useful.

Framework

Taking these factors into account, the parties are determined to reach a just, comprehensive, and durable settlement of the Middle East conflict through the conclusion of peace treaties based on Security Council resolutions 242 and 338 in all their parts. Their purpose is to achieve peace and good neighborly relations. They recognize that for peace to endure, it must involve all those who have been most deeply affected by the conflict. They therefore agree that this framework, as appropriate, is intended by them to constitute a basis for peace not only between Egypt and Israel, but also between Israel and each of its other neighbors which is prepared to negotiate peace with Israel on this basis. With that objective in mind, they have agreed to proceed as follows:

1. West Bank and Gaza

1. Egypt, Israel, Jordan and the representatives of the Palestinian people should participate in negotiations on the resolution of the Palestinian problem in all its aspects. To achieve that objective, negotiations relating to the West Bank and Gaza should proceed in three stages:

1. Egypt and Israel agree that, in order to ensure a peaceful and orderly transfer of authority, and taking into account the security concerns of all the parties, there should be transitional arrangements for the West Bank and Gaza for a period not exceeding five years. In order to provide full autonomy to the inhabitants, under these arrangements the Israeli military government and its civilian administration will be withdrawn as soon as a self-governing authority has been freely elected by the inhabitants of these areas to replace the existing military government. To negotiate the details of a transitional arrangement, Jordan will be invited to join the negotiations on the basis of this framework. These new arrangements should give due consideration both to the principle of self-government by the inhabitants of these territories and to the legitimate security concerns of the parties involved.

2. Egypt, Israel, and Jordan will agree on the modalities for establishing elected self-governing authority in the West Bank and Gaza. The delegations of Egypt and Jordan may include Palestinians from the West Bank and Gaza or other Palestinians as mutually agreed. The parties will negotiate an agreement which will define the powers and responsibilities of the self-governing authority to be exercised in the West Bank and Gaza. A withdrawal of Israeli armed forces will take place and there will be a redeployment of the remaining Israeli forces into specified security locations. The agreement will also include arrangements for assuring internal and external security and public order. A strong local police force will be established, which may include Jordanian citizens. In addition, Israeli and Jordanian forces will participate in joint patrols and in the manning of control posts to assure the security of the borders.

3. When the self-governing authority (administrative council) in the West Bank and Gaza is established and inaugurated, the transitional period of five years will begin. As soon as possible, but not later than the third year after the beginning of the transitional period, negotiations will take place to determine the final status of the West Bank and Gaza and its relationship with its neighbors and to conclude a

peace treaty between Israel and Jordan by the end of the transitional period. These negotiations will be conducted among Egypt, Israel, Jordan and the elected representatives of the inhabitants of the West Bank and Gaza. Two separate but related committees will be convened, one committee, consisting of representatives of the four parties which will negotiate and agree on the final status of the West Bank and Gaza, and its relationship with its neighbors, and the second committee, consisting of representatives of Israel and representatives of Jordan to be joined by the elected representatives of the inhabitants of the West Bank and Gaza, to negotiate the peace treaty between Israel and Jordan, taking into account the agreement reached in the final status of the West Bank and Gaza. The negotiations shall be based on all the provisions and principles of UN Security Council Resolution 242. The negotiations will resolve, among other matters, the location of the boundaries and the nature of the security arrangements. The solution from the negotiations must also recognize the legitimate right of the Palestinian peoples and their just requirements. In this way, the Palestinians will participate in the determination of their own future through:

1. The negotiations among Egypt, Israel, Jordan and the representatives of the inhabitants of the West Bank and Gaza to agree on the final status of the West Bank and Gaza and other outstanding issues by the end of the transitional period.

2. Submitting their agreements to a vote by the elected representatives of the inhabitants of the West Bank and Gaza.

3. Providing for the elected representatives of the inhabitants of the West Bank and Gaza to decide how they shall govern themselves consistent with the provisions of their agreement.

4. Participating as stated above in the work of the committee negotiating the peace treaty between Israel and Jordan.

4. All necessary measures will be taken and provisions made to assure the security of Israel and its neighbors during the transitional period and beyond. To assist in providing such security, a strong local police force will be constituted by the self-governing authority. It will be composed of inhabitants of the West Bank and Gaza. The police will maintain liaison on internal security matters with the designated Israeli, Jordanian, and Egyptian officers.

5. During the transitional period, representatives of Egypt, Israel, Jordan, and the self-governing authority will constitute a continuing committee to decide by agreement on the modalities of admission of persons displaced from the West Bank and Gaza in 1967, together with necessary measures to prevent disruption and disorder. Other matters of common concern may also be dealt with by this committee.

6. Egypt and Israel will work with each other and with other interested parties to establish agreed procedures for a prompt, just and permanent implementation of the resolution of the refugee problem.

2. Egypt-Israel

1. Egypt-Israel undertake not to resort to the threat or the use of force to settle disputes. Any disputes shall be settled by peaceful means in accordance with the provisions of Article 33 of the U.N. Charter.

2. In order to achieve peace between them, the parties agree to negotiate in good faith with a goal of concluding within three months from the signing of the Framework a peace treaty between them while inviting the other parties to the conflict to proceed simultaneously to negotiate and conclude similar peace treaties with a view to achieving a comprehensive peace in the area. The Framework for the Conclusion of a Peace Treaty between Egypt and Israel will govern the peace negotiations between them. The parties will agree on the modalities and the timetable for the implementation of their obligations under the treaty.

3. Associated Principles

1. Egypt and Israel state that the principles and provisions described below should apply to peace treaties between Israel and each of its neighbors—Egypt, Jordan, Syria and Lebanon.

2. Signatories shall establish among themselves relationships normal to states at peace with one another. To this end, they should undertake to abide by all the provisions of the U.N. Charter. Steps to be taken in this respect include:

1. full recognition;

2. abolishing economic boycotts;

3. guaranteeing that under their jurisdiction the citizens of the other parties shall enjoy the protection of the due process of law.

3. Signatories should explore possibilities for economic development in the context of final peace treaties, with the objective of contributing to the atmosphere of peace, cooperation and friendship which is their common goal.

4. Claims commissions may be established for the mutual settlement of all financial claims.

5. The United States shall be invited to participate in the talks on matters related to the modalities of the implementation of the agreements and working out the timetable for the carrying out of the obligations of the parties.

6. The United Nations Security Council shall be requested to endorse the peace treaties and ensure that their provisions shall not be violated. The permanent members of the Security Council shall be requested to underwrite the peace treaties and ensure respect for the provisions. They shall be requested to conform their policies and actions with the undertaking contained in this Framework.

For the Government of Israel:
MENACHEM BEGIN

For the Government of
the Arab Republic of Egypt
MUHAMMED ANWAR AL-SADAT

Witnessed by
JIMMY CARTER,
President of the United States of America

FRAMEWORK FOR THE CONCLUSION OF A PEACE TREATY BETWEEN EGYPT AND ISRAEL

In order to achieve peace between them, Israel and Egypt agree to negotiate in good faith with a goal of concluding within three months of the signing of this framework a peace treaty between them:

It is agreed that:

*The site of the negotiations will be under a United Nations flag at a location or locations to be mutually agreed.

*All of the principles of U.N. Resolution 242 will apply in this resolution of the dispute between Israel and Egypt.

*Unless otherwise mutually agreed, terms of the peace treaty will be implemented between two and three years after the peace treaty is signed.

The following matters are agreed between the parties:

1. the full exercise of Egyptian sovereignty up to the internationally recognized border between Egypt and mandated Palestine;

2. the withdrawal of Israeli armed forces from the Sinai;

3. the use of airfields left by the Israelis near al-Arish, Rafah, Ras en-Naqb, and Sharm el-Sheikh for civilian purposes only, including possible commercial use only by all nations;

4. the right of free passage by ships of Israel through the Gulf of Suez and the Suez Canal on the basis of the Constantinople Convention of 1888 applying to all nations; the Strait of Tiran and Gulf of Aqaba are international waterways to be open to all nations for unimpeded and nonsuspendable freedom of navigation and overflight;

5. the construction of a highway between the Sinai and Jordan near Eilat with guaranteed free and peaceful passage by Egypt and Jordan; and

6. the stationing of military forces listed below.

STATIONING OF FORCES

No more than one division (mechanized or infantry) of Egyptian armed forces will be stationed within an area lying approximately 50 km. (30 miles) east of the Gulf of Suez and the Suez Canal.

Only United Nations forces and civil police equipped with light weapons to perform normal police functions will be stationed within an area lying west of the international border and the Gulf of Aqaba, varying in width from 20 km. (12 miles) to 40 km. (24 miles).

In the area within 3 km. (1.8 miles) east of the international border there will be Israeli limited military forces not to exceed four infantry battalions and United Nations observers.

Border patrol units not to exceed three battalions will supplement the civil police in maintaining order in the area not included above.

The exact demarcation of the above areas will be as decided during the peace negotiations.

Early warning stations may exist to insure compliance with the terms of the agreement.

United Nations forces will be stationed:

1. in part of the area in the Sinai lying within about 20 km. of the Mediterranean Sea and adjacent to the international border, and

2. in the Sharm el-Sheikh area to insure freedom of passage through the Strait of Tiran; and these forces will not be removed unless such removal is approved by the Security Council of the United Nations with a unanimous vote of the five permanent members.

After a peace treaty is signed, and after the interim withdrawal is complete, normal relations will be established between Egypt and Israel, including full recognition, including diplomatic, economic and cultural relations; termination of economic boycotts and barriers to the free movement of goods and people; and mutual protection of citizens by the due process of law.

INTERIM WITHDRAWAL

Between three months and nine months after the signing of the peace treaty, all Israeli forces will withdraw east of a line extending from a point east of El-Arish to Ras Muhammad, the exact location of this line to be determined by mutual agreement.

For the Government of
the Arab Republic of Egypt:
MUHAMMED ANWAR AL-SADAT

For the Government of Israel:
MENACHEM BEGIN

Witnessed by:
JIMMY CARTER,
President of the United States of America

Consequences

Peace remained an uncertain commodity in the Middle East. On October 6, 1981, as Sadat was reviewing a military parade commemorating the Arab-Israeli War of 1973, he was assassinated by Muslim extremists for his role in bringing about the accords.

Nevertheless, all provisions except for Palestinian self-rule were fulfilled on schedule. After a historic White House meeting between Israeli foreign minister Yitzhak Rabin and PLO president Yasser Arafat, mediated by President Bill Clinton in 1993, the process of returning the West Bank and the Gaza Strip to the Palestinians got under way in 1994, although violence continued to plague the long-disputed areas even as they were being granted self-rule.

In July 2000, President Bill Clinton hosted a Middle East peace summit at Camp David between Israeli prime minister Ehud Barak and Palestinian Authority chairman Yasser Arafat. It began on July 11 and ended on July 25 without an agreement. Arafat held that the Palestinians were not being offered enough in terms of territory, the status of Jerusalem, and the Temple Mount, nor on the issue of Palestinian refugees. Barak countered that Israel had offered all that it could. In the absence of an agreement, a second Palestinian intifada, a violent uprising to end the Israeli occupation of Palestine, began on September 28, 2000, and as of summer 2005, sporadically continues.

In April 2003, the administration of President George W. Bush issued its "Roadmap to Peace," in which a coalition consisting of Israel, Palestine, the United States, Russia, and the European Union would cooperate to bring a permanent two-state solution to the Israeli-Palestinian conflict. Two phases were outlined for the resolution. Phase I would include measures to end terror and violence, to normalize Palestinian life, and to build Palestinian institutions of government. Phase II would focus on creating an independent, constitutionally based Palestinian state with provisional borders and the attributes of full sovereignty as an intermediate step toward a permanent settlement of Palestinian status.

The U.S. "war on terror" following the September 11, 2001, terrorist attacks on the country and the subsequent U.S. invasion of Afghanistan and Iraq impeded the Middle East peace process by prompting the Palestinians and their allies to doubt American willingness to serve as a good-faith broker of peace in a conflict involving Islamic interests.

See also ISRAEL–PALESTINE LIBERATION ORGANIZATION PEACE AGREEMENTS.

Source

Avalon Project at the Yale Law School. "Camp David Accords; September 17, 1978." Available online. URL: http://www.yale. edu/lawweb/avalon/mideast/campdav.htm. Accessed December 30, 2004.

ISRAEL–PALESTINE LIBERATION ORGANIZATION PEACE AGREEMENTS

TREATIES AT A GLANCE

Completed
September 9, 1993; September 13, 1993; and October 23, 1998

Signatories
Israel and the Palestine Liberation Organization

Overview
In the wake of the Gulf War, the Middle East peace process, as begun at Camp David but stalled after 1979 and limited to Egypt and Israel, got under way again in 1991 with agreements between Israel and the PLO to recognize each other's right to exist and to follow the Camp David Accords framework of swapping occupied land for regional peace.

Historical Background

In the late 1970s, the Middle East remained prone to crisis despite the peace achieved between Egypt and Israel that had begun with the CAMP DAVID ACCORDS. In 1978 an Arab summit in Baghdad pledged four hundred million dollars to the Palestine Liberation Organization over the next decade, and any comprehensive peace was blocked by the Arab states—outside of Egypt, of course—with their refusal to negotiate without bringing in the PLO and the refusal of Israel, backed by the United States, to negotiate with the PLO. Given the deadlock, Prime Minister Menachem Begin and Defense Minister Ariel Sharon, a hero of the 1973 Yom Kippur War, steeled themselves to put an end to terrorist raids by forcibly clearing PLO strongholds inside Lebanon. In a kind of thinking typical of Israeli foreign policy since the Jews had first secured a homeland in Palestine back in 1948, Begin and Sharon reasoned that if they invaded Lebanon and eliminated of the PLO, they would force the selection of a new Lebanese president who would willing to sign a peace treaty with Israel along the lines of the Egyptian-Israeli agreements completed in 1979.

They struck on June 7, 1982, and as it turned out, the Israelis advanced all the way to Beirut. It was a savage campaign, one that entrenched Syrian occupation of parts of Lebanon, intensified what was in effect a civil war already under way between Palestinians, Muslims of various sects (and allegiances), and Christian militiamen; and produced one of the bitterest ironies in history: a summary slaughter by troops operating under Israeli auspices reminiscent of Nazi SS actions in the ghettos of World War II. When Israeli forces and their Christian Phalangist Lebanese allies encircled West Beirut, trapped PLO people and Syrians were forced to evacuate. The assassination of the pro-Israeli Lebanese president-elect, Bashir Gemayel, provoked Israeli troops to move into West Beirut, where the Phalangists summarily massacred more than a thousand Palestinian civilians in two refugee camps while the Israelis did nothing to stop them. The bloodshed provoked the United States to send in the marines to evacuate the PLO, while American diplomats tried in vain to stitch together a coalition Lebanese government and somehow persuade both the Israelis and the Syrians to withdraw.

As resentment of the U.S. presence in Lebanon mounted on all sides, outbursts of terrorism increased, and the peace process begun by Henry Kissinger and carried forward by Jimmy Carter at Camp David seemed to be unraveling. Fundamentalist Islamic radicals took American hostages in Beirut, and despite Ronald Reagan's resolve to follow the Israeli example and refuse to negotiate with kidnappers, concern for the victims and fear of future reprisals damaged his credibility with Congress and other nations alike. Even as traffic barricades went up outside the White House, Arab terrorists launched a suicide car-bomb attack on the marine barracks in Beirut, which killed hundreds of

U.S. soldiers. There was little the United States could do but withdraw, which it did by February 1984. Meanwhile, Israel and Phalangist troops themselves began a slow withdrawal, having done about as much damage to the Israeli cause and the cause for peace as they could. Lebanon slid even further into chaos, while Israel kept control of the extreme southern part of Lebanon.

Then, as often happened with Israel, the violence seemed to produce results, albeit in unexpected ways. In the mid-1980s a shell-shocked PLO and Jordan advanced a plan for a peace process calling for direct talks between Israel and a joint Palestinian-Jordanian negotiating team under a United Nations–sponsored international conference. The Israelis, their reputation outside the Middle East sullied by Lebanon, expressed an interest. Negotiations in which Washington served as the intermediary between Israel and Jordan continued for about a year, but they finally collapsed, mainly because Israel continued to refuse to negotiate directly with the PLO, and PLO leader Yasser Arafat refused to accept unconditionally UN Security Council Resolutions 242 and 338, which recognized Israel's right to exist. Raids and counterraids continued, and in October 1985 the Israeli Air Force bombed PLO headquarters in Tunis, to which the Palestine Nationalist Front responded a week later with the infamous terrorist hijacking of the cruise ship *Achille Lauro*.

By 1987 Israel was facing a major Palestinian uprising closer to home, in the so-called occupied territories. This intifada (Arabic for "shaking"), sparked in part by a sharp rise in Palestinian unemployment, came on the 20th anniversary of Israeli's occupation of the Jordan River's West Bank and the Gaza Strip, and it took a number of different forms: boycotts of Israeli goods, attacks against Israeli civilians and settlers, demonstrations to show public support for Palestinian nationhood, and rock throwing by youths against Israeli soldiers. Israel reacted with brutal suppression whose severity was condemned not only by the Palestinians but also by many Israelis.

Despite their political gridlock over the peace proposals and many other issues, Israel's Labour and Likud Parties did agree that the intifada had to be suppressed before any change could take place in the status of the occupied territories. King Hussein of Jordan, his situation always unsettled, was more impatient. Refusing to await the outcome of the intifada, he announced on July 31, 1988, that Jordan was renouncing its official claims to the West Bank and East Jerusalem. In response, the PLO National Council endorsed UN Resolutions 242 and 338 on November 14, recognizing Israel as a legitimate state, while declaring on the next day, November 15, the establishment of "a Palestinian state with Jerusalem as its capital," despite Israeli con-

trol of the area. In December Arafat explicitly recognized Israel's right to exist, further undermining Israeli truculence in refusing to deal with the PLO. By 1989, while the Israelis could suppress the intifada, they could not eliminate it, and it spread to involve Palestinian violence against politically rival Palestinians. Although the negative impact of the uprising on the economy was lessened, the measures needed to cope with the Palestinians, combined with the budgetary cutbacks needed to reduce inflation, led to substantial unemployment in Jerusalem.

The region grew even more unstable with the onset of the Persian Gulf War, sparked by Iraq's invasion of Kuwait in August 1990, which upset the balance of power within the Middle East, already upset by the collapse of the Soviet Union. Worried that the Israelis might destroy the delicate coalition fighting against Saddam Hussein, the United States persuaded Israel not to react when Iraq linked its withdrawal from Kuwait to an Israeli withdrawal from the occupied territories and began SCUD missile attacks on Israeli cities. In the wake of the war, which demonstrated, if nothing else, the might and sophistication of the U.S. military, a new round of Mideast peace talks was set in motion in 1991.

After an initial general meeting that included the United States and the Soviet Union, Israel and various Arab nations met for bilateral talks, but negotiations seemed to be ending in deadlock. Then suddenly, thanks to behind-the-scenes efforts of U.S. president Bill Clinton, among others, on September 13, 1993, Israel and the PLO signed the Declaration of Principles on Interim Self-Government Arrangements in the occupied territories, which included a clear schedule for Israel's disengagement from the area. The signing of this agreement, which signaled mutual recognition of the PLO and Israel, provided for a transitional period of self-rule to begin in the Gaza Strip and the Jericho area of the West Bank in May 1994. As an amazed world watched the spectacle of Israeli prime minister Yitzhak Rabin and Yasser Arafat, long mortal enemies, awkwardly shake hands on the White House lawn for the world's television cameras, a comprehensive peace seemed unexpectedly possible.

Terms

The Israeli-PLO rapprochement began with a series of letters establishing the mutual recognition of Israel and the PLO on September 9, 1993, and continued with the Declaration of Principles on September 13, 1993. These ultimately led, also, after many twists and turns and not a few major setbacks, to the 1998 Wye River Memorandum.

1. Letter from Yasser Arafat to Prime Minister Rabin

September 9, 1993
YITZHAK RABIN
Prime Minister of Israel

Mr. Prime Minister,
The signing of the Declaration of Principles marks a new era in the history of the Middle East. In firm conviction thereof, I would like to confirm the following PLO commitments:

The PLO recognizes the right of the State of Israel to exist in peace and security.

The PLO accepts United Nations Security Council Resolutions 242 and 338.

The PLO commits itself to the Middle East peace process, and to a peaceful resolution of the conflict between the two sides and declares that all outstanding issues relating to permanent status will be resolved through negotiations.

The PLO considers that the signing of the Declaration of Principles constitutes a historic event, inaugurating a new epoch of peaceful coexistence, free from violence and all other acts which endanger peace and stability. Accordingly, the PLO renounces the use of terrorism and other acts of violence and will assume responsibility over all PLO elements and personnel in order to assure their compliance, prevent violations and discipline violators

In view of the promise of a new era and the signing of the Declaration of Principles and based on Palestinian acceptance of Security Council Resolutions 242 and 338, the PLO affirms that those articles of the Palestinian Covenant which deny Israel's right to exist, and the provisions of the Covenant which are inconsistent with the commitments of this letter are now inoperative and no longer valid. Consequently, the PLO undertakes to submit to the Palestinian National Council for formal approval the necessary changes in regard to the Palestinian Covenant.

Sincerely,
YASSER ARAFAT
Chairman
The Palestine Liberation Organization

2. Letter from Yasser Arafat to Norwegian Prime Minister Holst

September 9, 1993
His Excellency
JOHAN JORGEN HOLST
Foreign Minister of Norway

Dear Minister Holst,
I would like to confirm to you that, upon the signing of the Declaration of Principles, the PLO encourages and calls upon the Palestinian people in the West Bank and Gaza Strip to take part in the steps leading to the normalization of life, rejecting violence and terrorism, contributing to peace and stability and participating actively in shaping reconstruction, economic development and cooperation.

Sincerely,
YASSER ARAFAT
Chairman
The Palestine Liberation Organization

3. Letter from Prime Minister Rabin to Yasser Arafat

September 9, 1993
YASSER ARAFAT
Chairman
The Palestinian Liberation Organization

Mr. Chairman,
In response to your letter of September 9, 1993, I wish to confirm to you that, in light of the PLO commitments included in your letter, the Government of Israel has decided to recognize the PLO as the representative of the Palestinian people and commence negotiations with the PLO within the Middle East peace process.

YITZHAK RABIN
Prime Minister of Israel

Declaration of Principles on Interim Self-Government Arrangements

September 13, 1993
The Government of the State of Israel and the P.L.O. team (in the Jordanian-Palestinian delegation to the Middle East Peace Conference) (the "Palestinian Delegation"), representing the Palestinian people, agree that it is time to put an end to decades of confrontation and conflict, recognize their mutual legitimate and political rights, and strive to live in peaceful coexistence and mutual dignity and security and achieve a just, lasting and comprehensive peace settlement and historic reconciliation through the agreed political process. Accordingly, the, two sides agree to the following principles:

ARTICLE I
AIM OF THE NEGOTIATIONS
The aim of the Israeli-Palestinian negotiations within the current Middle East peace process is, among other things, to establish a Palestinian Interim Self-Government Authority, the elected Council (the "Council"), for the Palestinian people in the West Bank and the Gaza Strip, for a transitional period not exceeding five years, leading to a permanent settlement based on Security Council Resolutions 242 and 338.

It is understood that the interim arrangements are an integral part of the whole peace process and that the negotiations on the permanent status will lead to the implementation of Security Council Resolutions 242 and 338.

ARTICLE II
FRAMEWORK FOR THE INTERIM PERIOD
The agreed framework for the interim period is set forth in this Declaration of Principles.

ARTICLE III
ELECTIONS
1. In order that the Palestinian people in the West Bank and Gaza Strip may govern themselves according to democratic principles, direct, free and general political elections will be held for the Council under agreed supervision and international observation, while the Palestinian police will ensure public order.

2. An agreement will be concluded on the exact mode and conditions of the elections in accordance with the protocol

attached as Annex I, with the goal of holding the elections not later than nine months after the entry into force of this Declaration of Principles.

3. These elections will constitute a significant interim preparatory step toward the realization of the legitimate rights of the Palestinian people and their just requirements.

ARTICLE IV
JURISDICTION

Jurisdiction of the Council will cover West Bank and Gaza Strip territory, except for issues that will be negotiated in the permanent status negotiations. The two sides view the West Bank and the Gaza Strip as a single territorial unit, whose integrity will be preserved during the interim period.

ARTICLE V
TRANSITIONAL PERIOD AND PERMANENT STATUS NEGOTIATIONS

1. The five-year transitional period will begin upon the withdrawal from the Gaza Strip and Jericho area.

2. Permanent status negotiations will commence as soon as possible, but not later than the beginning of the third year of the interim period, between the Government of Israel and the Palestinian people's representatives.

3. It is understood that these negotiations shall cover remaining issues, including: Jerusalem, refugees, settlements, security arrangements, borders, relations and cooperation with other neighbors, and other issues of common interest.

4. The two parties agree that the outcome of the permanent status negotiations should not be prejudiced or preempted by agreements reached for the interim period.

ARTICLE VI
PREPARATORY TRANSFER OF POWERS AND RESPONSIBILITIES

1. Upon the entry into force of this Declaration of Principles and the withdrawal from the Gaza Strip and the Jericho area, a transfer of authority from the Israeli military government and its Civil Administration to the authorised Palestinians for this task, as detailed herein, will commence. This transfer of authority will be of a preparatory nature until the inauguration of the Council.

2. Immediately after the entry into force of this Declaration of Principles and the withdrawal from the Gaza Strip and Jericho area, with the view to promoting economic development in the West Bank and Gaza Strip, authority will be transferred to the Palestinians on the following spheres: education and culture, health, social welfare, direct taxation, and tourism. The Palestinian side will commence in building the Palestinian police force, as agreed upon. Pending the inauguration of the Council, the two parties may negotiate the transfer of additional powers and responsibilities, as agreed upon.

ARTICLE VII
INTERIM AGREEMENT

1. The Israeli and Palestinian delegations will negotiate an agreement on the interim period (the "Interim Agreement").

2. The Interim Agreement shall specify, among other things, the structure of the Council, the number of its members, and the transfer of powers and responsibilities from the Israeli military government and its Civil Administration to the Council. The Interim Agreement shall also specify the Council's executive authority, legislative authority in accordance with Article IX below, and the independent Palestinian judicial organs.

3. The Interim Agreement shall include arrangements, to be implemented upon the inauguration of the Council, for the assumption by the Council of all of the powers and responsibilities transferred previously in accordance with Article VI above.

4. In order to enable the Council to promote economic growth, upon its inauguration, the Council will establish, among other things, a Palestinian Electricity Authority, a Gaza Sea Port Authority, a Palestinian Development Bank, a Palestinian Export Promotion Board, a Palestinian Environmental Authority, a Palestinian Land Authority and a Palestinian Water Administration Authority, and any other Authorities agreed upon, in accordance with the Interim Agreement that will specify their powers and responsibilities.

5. After the inauguration of the Council, the Civil Administration will be dissolved, and the Israeli military government will be withdrawn.

ARTICLE VIII
PUBLIC ORDER AND SECURITY

In order to guarantee public order and internal security for the Palestinians of the West Bank and the Gaza Strip, the Council will establish a strong police force, while Israel will continue to carry the responsibility for defending against external threats, as well as the responsibility for overall security of Israelis for the purpose of safeguarding their internal security and public order.

ARTICLE IX
LAWS AND MILITARY ORDERS

1. The Council will be empowered to legislate, in accordance with the Interim Agreement, within all authorities transferred to it.

2. Both parties will review jointly laws and military orders presently in force in remaining spheres.

ARTICLE X
JOINT ISRAELI-PALESTINIAN LIAISON COMMITTEE

In order to provide for a smooth implementation of this Declaration of Principles and any subsequent agreements pertaining to the interim period, upon the entry into force of this Declaration of Principles, a Joint Israeli-Palestinian Liaison Committee will be established in order to deal with issues requiring coordination, other issues of common interest, and disputes.

ARTICLE XI
ISRAELI-PALESTINIAN COOPERATION IN ECONOMIC FIELDS

Recognizing the mutual benefit of cooperation in promoting the development of the West Bank, the Gaza Strip and Israel, upon the entry into force of this Declaration of Principles, an Israeli-Palestinian Economic Cooperation Committee will be established in order to develop and implement in a cooperative manner the programs identified in the protocols attached as Annex III and Annex IV.

ARTICLE XII
LIAISON AND COOPERATION WITH JORDAN AND EGYPT

The two parties will invite the Governments of Jordan and Egypt to participate in establishing further liaison and cooperation arrangements between the Government of Israel and the Palestinian representatives, on the one hand, and the Governments of Jordan and Egypt, on the other hand, to promote cooperation between them. These arrangements will include the constitution of a Continuing Committee that will decide by agreement on the modalities of admission of persons displaced from the West Bank and Gaza Strip in 1967, together with necessary measures to prevent disruption and disorder. Other matters of common concern will be dealt with by this Committee.

ARTICLE XIII
REDEPLOYMENT OF ISRAELI FORCES

1. After the entry into force of this Declaration of Principles, and not later than the eve of elections for the Council, a redeployment of Israeli military forces in the West Bank and the Gaza Strip will take place, in addition to withdrawal of Israeli forces carried out in accordance with Article XIV.

2. In redeploying its military forces, Israel will be guided by the principle that its military forces should be redeployed outside populated areas.

3. Further redeployments to specified locations will be gradually implemented commensurate with the assumption of responsibility for public order and internal security by the Palestinian police force pursuant to Article VIII above.

ARTICLE XIV
ISRAELI WITHDRAWAL FROM
THE GAZA STRIP AND JERICHO AREA

Israel will withdraw from the Gaza Strip and Jericho area, as detailed in the protocol attached as Annex II.

ARTICLE XV
RESOLUTION OF DISPUTES

1. Disputes arising out of the application or interpretation of this Declaration of Principles. or any subsequent agreements pertaining to the interim period, shall be resolved by negotiations through the Joint Liaison Committee to be established pursuant to Article X above.

2. Disputes which cannot be settled by negotiations may be resolved by a mechanism of conciliation to be agreed upon by the parties.

3. The parties may agree to submit to arbitration disputes relating to the interim period, which cannot be settled through conciliation. To this end, upon the agreement of both parties, the parties will establish an Arbitration Committee.

ARTICLE XVI
ISRAELI-PALESTINIAN COOPERATION
CONCERNING REGIONAL PROGRAMS

Both parties view the multilateral working groups as an appropriate instrument for promoting a "Marshall Plan", the regional programs and other programs, including special programs for the West Bank and Gaza Strip, as indicated in the protocol attached as Annex IV.

ARTICLE XVII
MISCELLANEOUS PROVISIONS

1. This Declaration of Principles will enter into force one month after its signing.

2. All protocols annexed to this Declaration of Principles and Agreed Minutes pertaining thereto shall be regarded as an integral part hereof.

Done at Washington, D.C., this thirteenth day of September, 1993.

For the Government of Israel
For the P.L.O.
Witnessed By:
The United States of America
The Russian Federation

Annex I
PROTOCOL ON THE MODE AND
CONDITIONS OF ELECTIONS

1. Palestinians of Jerusalem who live there will have the right to participate in the election process, according to an agreement between the two sides.

2. In addition, the election agreement should cover, among other things, the following issues:

  1. the system of elections;

  2. the mode of the agreed supervision and international observation and their personal composition; and

  3. rules and regulations regarding election campaign, including agreed arrangements for the organizing of mass media, and the possibility of licensing a broadcasting and TV station.

3. The future status of displaced Palestinians who were registered on 4th June 1967 will not be prejudiced because they are unable to participate in the election process due to practical reasons.

Annex II
PROTOCOL ON WITHDRAWAL OF ISRAELI FORCES
FROM THE GAZA STRIP AND JERICHO AREA

1. The two sides will conclude and sign within two months from the date of entry into force of this Declaration of Principles, an agreement on the withdrawal of Israeli military forces from the Gaza Strip and Jericho area. This agreement will include comprehensive arrangements to apply in the Gaza Strip and the Jericho area subsequent to the Israeli withdrawal.

2. Israel will implement an accelerated and scheduled withdrawal of Israeli military forces from the Gaza Strip and Jericho area, beginning immediately with the signing of the agreement on the Gaza Strip and Jericho area and to be completed within a period not exceeding four months after the signing of this agreement.

3. The above agreement will include, among other things:

  1. Arrangements for a smooth and peaceful transfer of authority from the Israeli military government and its Civil Administration to the Palestinian representatives.

  2. Structure, powers and responsibilities of the Palestinian authority in these areas, except: external security, settlements, Israelis, foreign relations, and other mutually agreed matters.

  3. Arrangements for the assumption of internal security and public order by the Palestinian police force consisting of police officers recruited locally and from abroad holding Jordanian passports and Palestinian documents issued by Egypt. Those who will participate in the Palestinian police force coming from abroad should be trained as police and police officers.

4. A temporary international or foreign presence, as agreed upon.

5. Establishment of a joint Palestinian-Israeli Coordination and Cooperation Committee for mutual security purposes.

6. An economic development and stabilization program, including the establishment of an Emergency Fund, to encourage foreign investment, and financial and economic support. Both sides will coordinate and cooperate jointly and unilaterally with regional and international parties to support these aims.

7. Arrangements for a safe passage for persons and transportation between the Gaza Strip and Jericho area.

4. The above agreement will include arrangements for coordination between both parties regarding passages:

1. Gaza - Egypt; and

2. Jericho - Jordan.

5. The offices responsible for carrying out the powers and responsibilities of the Palestinian authority under this Annex II and Article VI of the Declaration of Principles will be located in the Gaza Strip and in the Jericho area pending the inauguration of the Council.

6. Other than these agreed arrangements, the status of the Gaza Strip and Jericho area will continue to be an integral part of the West Bank and Gaza Strip, and will not be changed in the interim period.

Annex III
PROTOCOL ON ISRAELI-PALESTINIAN COOPERATION IN ECONOMIC AND DEVELOPMENT PROGRAMS

The two sides agree to establish an Israeli-Palestinian continuing Committee for Economic Cooperation, focusing, among other things, on the following:

1. Cooperation in the field of water, including a Water Development Program prepared by experts from both sides, which will also specify the mode of cooperation in the management of water resources in the West Bank and Gaza Strip, and will include proposals for studies and plans on water rights of each party, as well as on the equitable utilization of joint water resources for implementation in and beyond the interim period.

2. Cooperation in the field of electricity, including an Electricity Development Program, which will also specify the mode of cooperation for the production, maintenance, purchase and sale of electricity resources.

3. Cooperation in the field of energy, including an Energy Development Program, which will provide for the exploitation of oil and gas for industrial purposes, particularly in the Gaza Strip and in the Negev, and will encourage further joint exploitation of other energy resources. This Program may also provide for the construction of a Petrochemical industrial complex in the Gaza Strip and the construction of oil and gas pipelines.

4. Cooperation in the field of finance, including a Financial Development and Action Program for the encouragement of international investment in the West Bank and the Gaza Strip, and in Israel, as well as the establishment of a Palestinian Development Bank.

5. Cooperation in the field of transport and communications, including a Program, which will define guidelines for the establishment of a Gaza Sea Port Area, and will provide for the establishing of transport and communications lines to and from

the West Bank and the Gaza Strip to Israel and to other countries. In addition, this Program will provide for carrying out the necessary construction of roads, railways, communications lines, etc.

6. Cooperation in the field of trade, including studies, and Trade Promotion Programs, which will encourage local, regional and inter-regional trade, as well as a feasibility study of creating free trade zones in the Gaza Strip and in Israel, mutual access to these zones, and cooperation in other areas related to trade and commerce.

7. Cooperation in the field of industry, including Industrial Development Programs, which will provide for the establishment of joint Israeli- Palestinian Industrial Research and Development Centers, will promote Palestinian-Israeli joint ventures, and provide guidelines for cooperation in the textile, food, pharmaceutical, electronics, diamonds, computer and science-based industries.

8. A program for cooperation in, and regulation of, labor relations and cooperation in social welfare issues.

9. A Human Resources Development and Cooperation Plan, providing for joint Israeli-Palestinian workshops and seminars, and for the establishment of joint vocational training centers, research institutes and data banks.

10. An Environmental Protection Plan, providing for joint and/or coordinated measures in this sphere.

11. A program for developing coordination and cooperation in the field of communication and media.

12. Any other programs of mutual interest.

Annex IV
PROTOCOL ON ISRAELI-PALESTINIAN COOPERATION CONCERNING REGIONAL DEVELOPMENT PROGRAMS

1. The two sides will cooperate in the context of the multilateral peace efforts in promoting a Development Program for the region, including the West Bank and the Gaza Strip, to be initiated by the G-7. The parties will request the G-7 to seek the participation in this program of other interested states, such as members of the Organisation for Economic Cooperation and Development, regional Arab states and institutions, as well as members of the private sector.

2. The Development Program will consist of two elements:

1. an Economic Development Program for the West Bank and the Gaza Strip.

2. a Regional Economic Development Program.

3. The Economic Development Program for the West Bank and the Gaza strip will consist of the following elements:

1. A Social Rehabilitation Program, including a Housing and Construction Program.

2. A Small and Medium Business Development Plan.

3. An Infrastructure Development Program (water, electricity, transportation and communications, etc.).

4. A Human Resources Plan.

5. Other programs.

4. The Regional Economic Development Program may consist of the following elements:

1. The establishment of a Middle East Development Fund, as a first step, and a Middle East Development Bank, as a second step.

2. The development of a joint Israeli-Palestinian-Jordanian Plan for coordinated exploitation of the Dead Sea area.

3. The Mediterranean Sea (Gaza)—Dead Sea Canal.

4. Regional Desalinization and other water development projects.

5. A regional plan for agricultural development, including a coordinated regional effort for the prevention of desertification.

6. Interconnection of electricity grids.

7. Regional cooperation for the transfer, distribution and industrial exploitation of gas, oil and other energy resources.

8. A Regional Tourism, Transportation and Telecommunications Development Plan.

9. Regional cooperation in other spheres.

3. The two sides will encourage the multilateral working groups, and will coordinate towards their success. The two parties will encourage intersessional activities, as well as pre-feasibility and feasibility studies, within the various multilateral working groups.

AGREED MINUTES TO THE DECLARATION OF PRINCIPLES ON INTERIM SELF-GOVERNMENT ARRANGEMENTS

A. General Understandings and Agreements

Any powers and responsibilities transferred to the Palestinians pursuant to the Declaration of Principles prior to the inauguration of the Council will be subject to the same principles pertaining to Article IV, as set out in these Agreed Minutes below.

B. Specific Understandings and Agreements

ARTICLE IV

It is understood that:

1. Jurisdiction of the Council will cover West Bank and Gaza Strip territory, except for issues that will be negotiated in the permanent status negotiations: Jerusalem, settlements, military locations, and Israelis.

2. The Council's jurisdiction will apply with regard to the agreed powers, responsibilities, spheres and authorities transferred to it.

ARTICLE VI (2)

It is agreed that the transfer of authority will be as follows:

1. The Palestinian side will inform the Israeli side of the names of the authorised Palestinians who will assume the powers, authorities and responsibilities that will be transferred to the Palestinians according to the Declaration of Principles in the following fields: education and culture, health, social welfare, direct taxation, tourism, and any other authorities agreed upon.

2. It is understood that the rights and obligations of these offices will not be affected.

3. Each of the spheres described above will continue to enjoy existing budgetary allocations in accordance with arrangements to be mutually agreed upon. These arrangements also will provide for the necessary adjustments required in order to take into account the taxes collected by the direct taxation office.

4. Upon the execution of the Declaration of Principles, the Israeli and Palestinian delegations will immediately commence negotiations on a detailed plan for the transfer of authority on the above offices in accordance with the above understandings.

ARTICLE VII (2)

The Interim Agreement will also include arrangements for coordination and cooperation.

ARTICLE VII (5)

The withdrawal of the military government will not prevent Israel from exercising the powers and responsibilities not transferred to the Council.

ARTICLE VIII

It is understood that the Interim Agreement will include arrangements for cooperation and coordination between the two parties in this regard. It is also agreed that the transfer of powers and responsibilities to the Palestinian police will be accomplished in a phased manner, as agreed in the Interim Agreement.

ARTICLE X

It is agreed that, upon the entry into force of the Declaration of Principles, the Israeli and Palestinian delegations will exchange the names of the individuals designated by them as members of the Joint Israeli-Palestinian Liaison Committee.

It is further agreed that each side will have an equal number of members in the Joint Committee. The Joint Committee will reach decisions by agreement. The Joint Committee may add other technicians and experts, as necessary. The Joint Committee will decide on the frequency and place or places of its meetings.

Annex II

It is understood that, subsequent to the Israeli withdrawal, Israel will continue to be responsible for external security, and for internal security and public order of settlements and Israelis. Israeli military forces and civilians may continue to use roads freely within the Gaza Strip and the Jericho area.

Done at Washington, D.C., this thirteenth day of September, 1993.

For the Government of Israel
For the P.L.O.

Witnessed By:
The United States of America
The Russian Federation

The Wye River Memorandum

October 23, 1998

The following are steps to facilitate implementation of the Interim Agreement on the West Bank and Gaza Strip of September 28, 1995 (the "Interim Agreement") and other related agreements including the Note for the Record of January 17, 1997 (hereinafter referred to as "the prior agreements") so that the Israeli and Palestinian sides can more effectively carry out their reciprocal responsibilities, including those relating to further redeployments and security respectively. These steps are to be carried out in a parallel phased approach in accordance with this Memorandum and the attached time line. They are subject to the relevant terms and conditions of the prior agreements and do not supersede their other agreements.

I. FURTHER REDEPLOYMENTS

A. Phase One and Two Further Redeployments

1. Pursuant to the Interim Agreement and subsequent agreements, the Israeli side's implementation of the first and sec-

A NEW WORLD ORDER 821

ond F.R.D. will consist of the transfer to the Palestinian side of 13% from Area C as follows:

    1% to Area (A)

    12% to Area (B)

The Palestinian side has informed that it will allocate an area/areas amounting to 3% from the above Area (B) to be designated as Green Areas and/or Nature Reserves. The Palestinian side has further informed that they will act according to the established scientific standards, and that therefore there will be no changes in the status of these areas, without prejudice to the rights of the existing inhabitants in these areas including Bedouins; while these standards do not allow new construction in these areas, existing roads and buildings may be maintained.

The Israeli side will retain in these Green Areas/Nature Reserves the overriding security responsibility for the purpose of protecting Israelis and confronting the threat of terrorism. Activities and movements of the Palestinian Police forces may be carried out after coordination and confirmation; the Israeli side will respond to such requests expeditiously.

2. As part of the foregoing implementation of the first and second F.R.D., 14.2% from Area (B) will become Area (A).

B. Third Phase of Further Redeployments

With regard to the terms of the Interim Agreement and of Secretary Christopher's letters to the two sides of January 17, 1997 relating to the further redeployment process, there will be a committee to address this question. The United States will be briefed regularly.

II. SECURITY

In the provisions on security arrangements of the Interim Agreement, the Palestinian side agreed to take all measures necessary in order to prevent acts of terrorism, crime and hostilities directed against the Israeli side, against individuals falling under the Israeli side's authority and against their property, just as the Israeli side agreed to take all measures necessary in order to prevent acts of terrorism, crime and hostilities directed against the Palestinian side, against individuals falling under the Palestinian side's authority and against their property. The two sides also agreed to take legal measures against offenders within their jurisdiction and to prevent incitement against each other by any organizations, groups or individuals within their jurisdiction.

Both sides recognize that it is in their vital interests to combat terrorism and fight violence in accordance with Annex I of the Interim Agreement and the Note for the Record. They also recognize that the struggle against terror and violence must be comprehensive in that it deals with terrorists, the terror support structure, and the environment conducive to the support of terror. It must be continuous and constant over a long term, in that there can be no pauses in the work against terrorists and their structure. It must be cooperative in that no effort can be fully effective without Israeli-Palestinian cooperation and the continuous exchange of information, concepts, and actions.

Pursuant to the prior agreements, the Palestinian side's implementation of its responsibilities for security, security cooperation, and other issues will be as detailed below during the time periods specified in the attached time line:

A. Security Actions

1. Outlawing and Combating Terrorist Organizations

    1. The Palestinian side will make known its policy of zero tolerance for terror and violence against both sides.

    2. A work plan developed by the Palestinian side will be shared with the U.S. and thereafter implementation will begin immediately to ensure the systematic and effective combat of terrorist organizations and their infrastructure.

    3. In addition to the bilateral Israeli-Palestinian security cooperation, a U.S.-Palestinian committee will meet biweekly to review the steps being taken to eliminate terrorist cells and the support structure that plans, finances, supplies and abets terror. In these meetings, the Palestinian side will inform the U.S. fully of the actions it has taken to outlaw all organizations (or wings of organizations, as appropriate) of a military, terrorist or violent character and their support structure and to prevent them from operating in areas under its jurisdiction.

    4. The Palestinian side will apprehend the specific individuals suspected of perpetrating acts of violence and terror for the purpose of further investigation, and prosecution and punishment of all persons involved in acts of violence and terror.

    5. A U.S.-Palestinian committee will meet to review and evaluate information pertinent to the decisions on prosecution, punishment or other legal measures which affect the status of individuals suspected of abetting or perpetrating acts of violence and terror.

2. Prohibiting Illegal Weapons

    1. The Palestinian side will ensure an effective legal framework is in place to criminalize, in conformity with the prior agreements, any importation, manufacturing or unlicensed sale, acquisition or possession of firearms, ammunition or weapons in areas under Palestinian jurisdiction.

    2. In addition, the Palestinian side will establish and vigorously and continuously implement a systematic program for the collection and appropriate handling of all such illegal items in accordance with the prior agreements. The U.S. has agreed to assist in carrying out this program.

    3. A U.S.-Palestinian-Israeli committee will be established to assist and enhance cooperation in preventing the smuggling or other unauthorized introduction of weapons or explosive materials into areas under Palestinian jurisdiction.

3. Preventing Incitement

    1. Drawing on relevant international practice and pursuant to Article XXII (1) of the Interim Agreement and the Note for the Record, the Palestinian side will issue a decree prohibiting all forms of incitement to violence or terror, and establishing mechanisms for acting systematically against all expressions or threats of violence or terror. This decree will be comparable to the existing Israeli legislation which deals with the same subject.

    2. A U.S.-Palestinian-Israeli committee will meet on a regular basis to monitor cases of possible incitement to violence or terror and to make recommendations and reports on how to prevent such incitement. The Israeli, Palestinian and U.S. sides will each appoint a media specialist, a law enforcement representative, an educational specialist and a current or former elected official to the committee.

B. Security Cooperation

The two sides agree that their security cooperation will be based on a spirit of partnership and will include, among other things, the following steps:

1. Bilateral Cooperation

There will be full bilateral security cooperation between the two sides which will be continuous, intensive and comprehensive.

2. Forensic Cooperation

There will be an exchange of forensic expertise, training, and other assistance.

3. Trilateral Committee

In addition to the bilateral Israeli-Palestinian security cooperation, a high-ranking U.S.-Palestinian-Israeli committee will meet as required and not less than biweekly to assess current threats, deal with any impediments to effective security cooperation and coordination and address the steps being taken to combat terror and terrorist organizations. The committee will also serve as a forum to address the issue of external support for terror. In these meetings, the Palestinian side will fully inform the members of the committee of the results of its investigations concerning terrorist suspects already in custody and the participants will exchange additional relevant information. The committee will report regularly to the leaders of the two sides on the status of cooperation, the results of the meetings and its recommendations.

C. Other Issues

1. Palestinian Police Force

1. The Palestinian side will provide a list of its policemen to the Israeli side in conformity with the prior agreements.

2. Should the Palestinian side request technical assistance, the U.S. has indicated its willingness to help meet their needs in cooperation with other donors.

3. The Monitoring and Steering Committee will, as part of its functions, monitor the implementation of this provision and brief the U.S.

2. PLO Charter

The Executive Committee of the Palestine Liberation Organization and the Palestinian Central Council will reaffirm the letter of 22 January 1998 from PLO Chairman Yasir Arafat to President Clinton concerning the nullification of the Palestinian National Charter provisions that are inconsistent with the letters exchanged between the PLO and the Government of Israel on 9/10 September 1993. PLO Chairman Arafat, the Speaker of the Palestine National Council, and the Speaker of the Palestinian Council will invite the members of the PNC, as well as the members of the Central Council, the Council, and the Palestinian Heads of Ministries to a meeting to be addressed by President Clinton to reaffirm their support for the peace process and the aforementioned decisions of the Executive Committee and the Central Council.

3. Legal Assistance in Criminal Matters

Among other forms of legal assistance in criminal matters, the requests for arrest and transfer of suspects and defendants pursuant to Article II (7) of Annex IV of the Interim Agreement will be submitted (or resubmitted) through the mechanism of the Joint Israeli-Palestinian Legal Committee and will be responded to in conformity with Article II (7) (f) of Annex IV of the Interim Agreement within the twelve week period. Requests submitted after the eighth week will be responded to in conformity with Article II (7) (f) within four weeks of their submission. The U.S. has been requested by the sides to report on a regular basis on the steps being taken to respond to the above requests.

4. Human Rights and the Rule of Law

Pursuant to Article XI (1) of Annex I of the Interim Agreement, and without derogating from the above, the Palestinian Police will exercise powers and responsibilities to implement this Memorandum with due regard to internationally accepted norms of human rights and the rule of law, and will be guided by the need to protect the public, respect human dignity, and avoid harassment.

III. INTERIM COMMITTEES AND ECONOMIC ISSUES

1. The Israeli and Palestinian sides reaffirm their commitment to enhancing their relationship and agree on the need to actively promote economic development in the West Bank and Gaza. In this regard, the parties agree to continue or to reactivate all standing committees established by the Interim Agreement, including the Monitoring and Steering Committee, the Joint Economic Committee (JEC), the Civil Affairs Committee (CAC), the Legal Committee, and the Standing Cooperation Committee.

2. The Israeli and Palestinian sides have agreed on arrangements which will permit the timely opening of the Gaza Industrial Estate. They also have concluded a "Protocol Regarding the Establishment and Operation of the International Airport in the Gaza Strip During the Interim Period."

3. Both sides will renew negotiations on Safe Passage immediately. As regards the southern route, the sides will make best efforts to conclude the agreement within a week of the entry into force of this Memorandum. Operation of the southern route will start as soon as possible thereafter. As regards the northern route, negotiations will continue with the goal of reaching agreement as soon as possible. Implementation will take place expeditiously thereafter.

4. The Israeli and Palestinian sides acknowledge the great importance of the Port of Gaza for the development of the Palestinian economy, and the expansion of Palestinian trade. They commit themselves to proceeding without delay to conclude an agreement to allow the construction and operation of the port in accordance with the prior agreements. The Israeli-Palestinian Committee will reactivate its work immediately with a goal of concluding the protocol within sixty days, which will allow commencement of the construction of the port.

5. The two sides recognize that unresolved legal issues adversely affect the relationship between the two peoples. They therefore will accelerate efforts through the Legal Committee to address outstanding legal issues and to implement solutions to these issues in the shortest possible period. The Palestinian side will provide to the Israeli side copies of all of its laws in effect.

6. The Israeli and Palestinian sides also will launch a strategic economic dialogue to enhance their economic relationship. They will establish within the framework of the JEC an Ad Hoc Committee for this purpose. The committee will review the following four issues: (1) Israeli purchase taxes; (2) cooperation in combating vehicle theft; (3) dealing with unpaid Palestinian debts; and (4) the impact of Israeli standards as barriers to trade and the expansion of the A1 and A2 lists. The committee will submit an interim report within three weeks of the entry into force of this Memorandum, and within six weeks will submit its conclusions and recommendations to be implemented.

7. The two sides agree on the importance of continued international donor assistance to facilitate implementation by

both sides of agreements reached. They also recognize the need for enhanced donor support for economic development in the West Bank and Gaza. They agree to jointly approach the donor community to organize a Ministerial Conference before the end of 1998 to seek pledges for enhanced levels of assistance.

IV. PERMANENT STATUS NEGOTIATIONS

The two sides will immediately resume permanent status negotiations on an accelerated basis and will make a determined effort to achieve the mutual goal of reaching an agreement by May 4, 1999. The negotiations will be continuous and without interruption. The U.S. has expressed its willingness to facilitate these negotiations.

V. UNILATERAL ACTIONS

Recognizing the necessity to create a positive environment for the negotiations, neither side shall initiate or take any step that will change the status of the West Bank and the Gaza Strip in accordance with the Interim Agreement.

ATTACHMENT: TIME LINE

This Memorandum will enter into force ten days from the date of signature

Done at Washington, D.C., this 23d day of October 1998.

For the Government of the State of Israel:
BENJAMIN NETANYAHU
For the PLO:
YASSER ARAFAT
Witnessed by:
WILLIAM J. CLINTON
The United States of America

Consequences

The Middle East peace between Israel and the region's Arab states was and is an ongoing process, and much happened between those initial talks of 1991 and the 1998 memorandum. Rabin and Arafat were jointly awarded the Nobel Peace Prize for their 1993 efforts, just as Anwar Sadat and Begin had been awarded the prize for their efforts at Camp David. And just as Sadat had paid the price for his boldness when his life ended in a hail of bullets fired by assassins among his own bodyguards, Rabin was assassinated in 1994 by a Jew enraged by his giving away of God's land in exchange for earthly peace. The negotiations involved a separate peace signed between Israel and the Hashemite kingdom of Jordan, also in 1994.

The coming to office of conservative prime minister Benjamin Netanyahu stalled the process, as he tried to tread his way through Israel's political minefield, made increasingly treacherous by the influx of conservative Sephardic Jews from the former Soviet empire. There were acts of terror and increasing, if sporadic, violence between the two sides, as the new Palestinian government took control of the old occupied territories. But by the end of the 20th century, it appeared that the once intractable Middle East "problem," conceived in World War I, carried to term in the second, and born in the cold war, might ultimately find a solution.

These hopes were later dashed, especially by the U.S. "war on terror" that followed the terrorist attacks in Washington, D.C., and New York City in 2001. When the United States invaded Iraq in 2003, Islamist extremists succeeded in coupling the Israeli conflict with the American as anti-Arab. However, the death of longtime PLO leader Yasser Arafat in late 2004 created credible hope that Israel and Palestine would reach an accord, pursuant to a U.S.-endorsed "road map to peace."

Sources

Israel Ministry of Foreign Affairs, "Israel-PLO Recognition: Exchange of Letters between PM Rabin and Chairman Arafat." Available online. URL: http://www.mfa.gov.il/MFA/Peace%20 Process/Guide%20to%20the%20Peace%20Process/Israel-PLO%20Recognition%20-%20Exchange%20of%20Letters %20betwe. Accessed April 20, 2005.

United States Institute of Peace, "Declaration of Principles on Interim Self-Government Arrangements," United States Institute of Peace Library. Available online. URL: http://www.usip.org/library/pa/israel_plo/oslo_09131993.html. Accessed December 30, 2004.

———, "The Wye River Memorandum," United States Institute of Peace Library. Available online. URL: http://www.usip.org/library/pa/israel_plo/wye_10231998.html. Accessed December 30, 2004.

DAYTON ACCORDS

TREATY AT A GLANCE

Completed
November 21, 1995, at Dayton, Ohio

Signatories
Republic of Bosnia and Herzegovina, the Republic of Croatia,
and the Federal Republic of Yugoslavia

Overview
After the collapse of Soviet Russia and the end of the cold war,
Yugoslavia, once the most independent of Soviet-allied nations,
began to break apart in a bloody storm of nationalism and ethnic
hatred. A diplomatic world shocked by the return of genocide
on a scale similar to the Nazi-spawned Holocaust began once
again, under the Dayton Accords, to hunt for, arrest, and try war
criminals.

Historical Background

With a blindness born of arrogant faith in rational ideology, the nations of the 20th century repeatedly ignored the ethnic identifications and enmities that, with primal savagery, often motivate political life today just as surely as these forces drove it in the ancient tribal past. The modern nation of Yugoslavia came into being following the dissolution of the Austro-Hungarian Empire at the end of World War I. But until World War II, Yugoslavia was not so much a single nation as it was a collection of strongly nationalistic and ethnically diverse factions. They were briefly united in opposition to the German-Italian invasion of World War II, an opposition led by Josip Broz—known as Tito—a Communist who, after expelling the invaders, instituted a marxist regime by the end of the war. Tito's government was unique in Eastern Europe in that it was maintained independently of Soviet military and economic support and even provoked Joseph Stalin to expel Yugoslavia from the Communist bloc in 1948.

Remaining true to his vision of communism, Tito opened up reasonably cordial relations with the West and forged Yugoslavia into a genuinely unified nation. Yet, that all ended with Tito's death in 1980, as if to prove that Yugoslavia had been held together by the force of its remarkable leader's personality. The Croatians and Slovenes, the largest nationalist groups in the country, developed separatist movements. In January 1990 the Communist Party voted to relinquish its constitutional monopoly on power in Yugoslavia and open the political process to others, but this power sharing did not satisfy the Slovenes, who walked out of the conference. Later in the year, both Slovenia and Croatia unilaterally declared their independence from Yugoslavia and proposed a new, decentralized union. Slobodan Milošević, Communist leader of Serbia, another Yugoslav republic, opposed the plan, and Croatia's Serbian minority rose up against the Croatian government. At this point, the Serbian-led Yugoslav army moved in to support the Croatian Serbs.

The civil war soon lost all pretense of being a political struggle and emerged as ethnic warfare among three groups, the Serbs, the Croats, and the Muslims (Bosniaks). The United Nations imposed a truce in January 1992, but it proved short-lived, as Bosnia seceded in March 1992, and the Serb population of that republic rebelled. Bosnia was soon reduced to anarchy, and the capital city of Sarajevo was under continual siege and bombardment while the United Nations and the European Community made repeated attempts to negotiate a settlement but for the most part stood by, deliberating action in what seemed a hopelessly murky eruption of human passion.

Atrocities and the deliberate targeting of civilian populations were carried out under the command of Radovan Karadžić in the name of "ethnic cleansing," the Serbs' systematic expulsion of Muslims and Croatians from Serb-controlled areas in Bosnia. It seemed an agenda worthy of Adolf Hitler, and by late 1993, ethnic cleansing had created some 700,000 refugees, who clogged western Europe.

Karadžić was born on June 19, 1945, in a mountain village in the Yugoslav republic of Montenegro. His father had been member of the Chetniks, the Serbs who fought both the Nazis (along with their Croatian collaborators) and the Partisans, the communist guerrillas led by Tito. At age 15, Karadžić moved to Sarajevo, where he studied medicine, became a physician and psychiatrist, and wrote poetry and children's books. Imprisoned for nearly a year in the mid-1980s for embezzling state funds, he was one of the founders of the Serbian Democratic Party, of which he became president in 1990. Two years later, when the Bosnian Serbs declared their independence, he became president of "Srpska" as well and allied himself with Yugoslavia.

Backed by Milošević and with the support of General Ratko Mladić—the Bosnian Serb military leader who, like Karadžić, would be indicted for war crimes—Karadžić took control of parts of Bosnia and began his purges. From 1992 to 1995, he swung back and forth, depending on the pressure exerted by the United States and western Europe, between blood-chillingly ruthless military action and public expressions of an interest in peace initiatives being advanced by hand-wringing Western leaders. Late in 1995 Milošević closed the borders with Bosnia and appeared to be abandoning the Bosnian Serbs. Worried by the desertion of his ethnic ally and fearful of repercussions, Karadžić gave in to Western demands and signed accords reached in talks near Dayton, Ohio, that provided for a division of the country into Bosniak-Croat and Serb sections but with a unified presidency.

Terms

The accords read as follows:

Dayton Peace Accords

General Framework Agreement for Peace in Bosnia and Herzegovina

The Republic of Bosnia and Herzegovina, the Republic of Croatia and the Federal Republic of Yugoslavia (the "Parties"),

Recognizing the need for a comprehensive settlement to bring an end to the tragic conflict in the region,

Desiring to contribute toward that end and to promote an enduring peace and stability,

Affirming their commitment to the Agreed Basic Principles issued on September 8, 1995, the Further Agreed Basic Principles issued on September 26, 1995, and the cease-fire agreements of September 14 and October 5, 1995,

Noting the agreement of August 29, 1995, which authorized the delegation of the Federal Republic of Yugoslavia to sign, on behalf of the Republika Srpska, the parts of the peace plan

concerning it, with the obligation to implement the agreement that is reached strictly and consequently,

Have agreed as follows:

ARTICLE I
The Parties shall conduct their relations in accordance with the principles set forth in the United Nations Charter, as well as the Helsinki Final Act and other documents of the Organization for Security and Cooperation in Europe. In particular, the Parties shall fully respect the sovereign equality of one another, shall settle disputes by peaceful means, and shall refrain from any action, by threat or use of force or otherwise, against the territorial integrity or political independence of Bosnia and Herzegovina or any other State.

ARTICLE II
The Parties welcome and endorse the arrangements that have been made concerning the military aspects of the peace settlement and aspects of regional stabilization, as set forth in the Agreements at Annex 1-A and Annex 1-B. The Parties shall fully respect and promote fulfillment of the commitments made in Annex 1-A, and shall comply fully with their commitments as set forth in Annex 1-B.

ARTICLE III
The Parties welcome and endorse the arrangements that have been made concerning the boundary demarcation between the two Entities, the Federation of Bosnia and Herzegovina and Republika Srpska, as set forth in the Agreement at Annex 2. The Parties shall fully respect and promote fulfillment of the commitments made therein.

ARTICLE IV
The Parties welcome and endorse the elections program for Bosnia and Herzegovina as set forth in Annex 3. The Parties shall fully respect and promote fulfillment of that program.

ARTICLE V
The Parties welcome and endorse the arrangements that have been made concerning the Constitution of Bosnia and Herzegovina, as set forth in Annex 4. The Parties shall fully respect and promote fulfillment of the commitments made therein.

ARTICLE VI
The Parties welcome and endorse the arrangements that have been made concerning the establishment of an arbitration tribunal, a Commission on Human Rights, a Commission on Refugees and Displaced Persons, a Commission to Preserve National Monuments, and Bosnia and Herzegovina Public Corporations, as set forth in the Agreements at Annexes 5-9. The Parties shall fully respect and promote fulfillment of the commitments made therein.

ARTICLE VII
Recognizing that the observance of human rights and the protection of refugees and displaced persons are of vital importance in achieving a lasting peace, the Parties agree to and shall comply fully with the provisions concerning human rights set forth in Chapter One of the Agreement at Annex 6, as well as the provisions concerning refugees and displaced persons set forth in Chapter One of the Agreement at Annex 7.

ARTICLE VIII
The Parties welcome and endorse the arrangements that have been made concerning the implementation of this peace settlement,

including in particular those pertaining to the civilian (non-military) implementation, as set forth in the Agreement at Annex 10, and the international police task force, as set forth in the Agreement at Annex 11. The Parties shall fully respect and promote fulfillment of the commitments made therein.

ARTICLE IX

The Parties shall cooperate fully with all entities involved in implementation of this peace settlement, as described in the Annexes to this Agreement, or which are otherwise authorized by the United Nations Security Council, pursuant to the obligation of all Parties to cooperate in the investigation and prosecution of war crimes and other violations of international humanitarian law.

ARTICLE X

The Federal Republic of Yugoslavia and the Republic of Bosnia and Herzegovina recognize each other as sovereign independent States within their international borders. Further aspects of their mutual recognition will be subject to subsequent discussions.

ARTICLE XI

This Agreement shall enter into force upon signature.

DONE at Paris, this [21st] day of [November], 1995, in the Bosnian, Croatian, English and Serbian languages, each text being equally authentic.

For the Republic of Bosnia and Herzegovina
For the Republic of Croatia
For the Federal Republic of Yugoslavia
Witnessed by:
European Union Special Negotiator
For the French Republic
For the Federal Republic of Germany
For the Russian Federation
For the United Kingdom of Great Britain and Northern Ireland
For the United States of America

Consequences

On July 25, and again on November 16, 1995, the United Nations International Criminal Tribunal for the Former Yugoslavia, held in The Hague, had indicted Karadžić for war crimes, including among others genocide, murder, and rape of civilians. Since the accords disallowed anyone indicted for war crimes from participating in the elections set for September 14, 1996, Karadžić had to relinquish both his government role and his place in his party. On July 19, 1996, he announced he would step down as president of the self-proclaimed Republika Srpska and as head of the Serbian Democratic Party of Bosnia and Herzegovina. But men who shared his political views replaced him, and no one could be quite sure—even though he was forbidden from appearing in public or in the media—whether he was truly deposed. The NATO troops who arrived in Bosnia to enforce the Dayton Accords had orders to

arrest him, but they did not do so, either because they could not get to him or they were fearful of reprisals—the story varied. In any case, Karadžić continued to live openly enough in Pale, the Bosnian Serb headquarters.

The war in Bosnia and Herzegovina ceased with the signing of the Dayton Accords, and some 250,000 people had by mid-1997 resettled in their former homeland, most of them from Germany. The return of these ethnic minorities, however, created problems. The United Nations attempted to meet the challenge presented by the repopulation of the so-called minority areas by launching the Open Cities program. Under the program towns could declare their readiness to accept former Yugoslavians, regardless of whether they were from Bosnia or Herzegovina, whether they were Serb, Croat, or Muslim, but significant progress was slow. Few returned to Croatia despite commitments of support from Croatia and the United Nations. Given the trouble Milošević was yet to wreak on the region, they seemed prescient.

The United Nations' effort to hold Karadžić, as the leader of the Bosnian Serbs, responsible for the "ethnic cleansing" of Serb-dominated areas in Bosnia was valiant, but from the historical perspective the struggle in what had been Yugoslavia demonstrated the folly of thinking the world could be structured according to cold war oppositions equated with good and evil, communism and democracy. The death of communism did not bring a millennium of bliss but ushered in a world of greater complexity than ever before, challenging all nations to decide just how to align themselves.

American foreign policy following World War II had been motivated chiefly by the strategic doctrine of containing communism. Hot spots like Bosnia, the African country of Somalia, and Haiti, however, presented no clear-cut ideological "good guys" to aid in fighting the "bad," who seemed to be plentiful on all sides. As the horribly familiar pictures of detention camps in eastern Europe began appearing on television, two U.S. presidents, George H. W. Bush and Bill Clinton, dithered while a neo-isolationist Congress snapped at their heels. With the implosion of communism, American foreign policy, and indeed the foreign policy of much of the world, appeared adrift and rudderless. When it did snap back into focus during the presidency of Bush's son, George W., the world was no longer split East and West, but between Islamic jihadists and a far from united world of "developed" nations.

Source

University of Minnesota Human Rights Center, "General Framework Agreement for Peace in Bosnia and Herzegovina," University of Minnesota Human Rights Library. Available online. URL: http://www1.umn.edu/humanrts/icty/dayton/daytonframework.html. Accessed December 30, 2004.

BELFAST AGREEMENT (GOOD FRIDAY AGREEMENT)

TREATY AT A GLANCE

Completed
April 10, 1998 (Good Friday);
entered into force December 2, 1999

Signatories
Great Britain, Northern Ireland, and Ireland

Overview
The Belfast Agreement set out a plan for fully representative self-government (home rule) in Northern Ireland in an effort to bring peace to the long-troubled region. After voters in both Ireland and Northern Ireland ratified the agreement, governing power was devolved on December 2, 1999, to an elected assembly headed by a Protestant first minister, David Trimble of the mainstream Ulster Unionist Party, and his Roman Catholic deputy, Seamus Mallon of the moderate Roman Catholic Social Democratic and Labour Party. In addition, the agreement provided for the establishment of Human Rights and Equality Commissions, the early release of terrorist prisoners from both the Protestant and Catholic sides of the community, the decommissioning (disarming) of paramilitary forces, and extensive reforms of criminal justice and policing in Northern Ireland.

Historical Background

The IRISH PEACE TREATY of 1921, which created the Irish Free State, a political entity short of a sovereign republic but almost entirely independent of Great Britain, stipulated the right of the six northern counties of Ireland, which had a Protestant majority, to remain within the British fold. Northern Ireland was thereby constituted in an arrangement that was satisfactory to approximately 1 million Protestants but that provided virtually no protection for some half-million Roman Catholic nationalists living within the six counties. The result was increasing instability in Northern Ireland, which reached a level of grave crisis by the mid-1960s, when many Catholics organized a militant civil rights movement. Civil disorder and violence became epidemic and endemic as Northern Ireland was thrust into a state of low-level civil war—known popularly, with grim understatement, as "the Troubles"—which brought British forces into the counties by the early 1970s. The Roman Catholics initially welcomed these soldiers as protectors but soon resented them as an invading force, and during 1972, the Irish Republican Army (IRA), born in the Irish Revolution of 1916–22,

was revived, along with another paramilitary group, known as the Provisionals. Protestant unionists—those who favored British government—responded by forming their own paramilitary forces.

The 1970s saw major, chronic violence, which devastated Northern Ireland's already weak economy. Conditions became so chaotic that in March 1972, Conservative British prime minister Edward Heath suspended Home Rule in Northern Ireland, which thereby reverted to direct control by London, and the British army remained a major presence in the six counties, enforcing a significant degree of martial law.

During the 1980s, the level of violence subsided somewhat, and various attempts were made to resolve the situation once and for all, including the Anglo-Irish Agreement of 1985, which gave the republic of Ireland an official consultative role in the affairs of Northern Ireland. During the 1990s, talks were held among all of Northern Ireland's constitutional parties except for Sinn Féin, the political wing of the Provisional IRA, which was excluded because, like the Protestant unionist paramilitary groups, it was deemed a terrorist organization. At last in 1994, with former U.S. senator George Mitchell moderating a sit-down, both the IRA and the unionist paramilitary organizations announced that they had agreed to end the violence. This was a major breakthrough, but the issue of "decommissioning" (i.e., disarmament) remained a thorny one. Nevertheless, continued negotiation led to the Belfast Agreement of 1998.

Terms

In addition to creating Northern Ireland's new devolved government, the agreement establishes an interconnected group of institutions that form three so-called strands of relationships.

Strand One, dealing with relationships within Northern Ireland, creates the Northern Ireland Assembly, its Executive, and a consultative Civic Forum. Members of the assembly are elected by proportional representation. Ministers in the Northern Ireland Executive are subsequently appointed according to party strengths in the assembly. All important decisions must have the support of both sides of the community: Protestant and Catholic.

Strand Two addresses relationships between Northern Ireland and the Republic of Ireland. The agreement creates a North-South Ministerial Council, which brings together members of the Northern Ireland Executive and the Irish government. The council oversees the work of six cross-border Implementation Bodies.

Strand Three deals with East-West relationships within the British Isles. The agreement creates a British-Irish Inter-Governmental Conference to promote bilateral cooperation between the United Kingdom and Ireland. This conference replaces the Anglo-Irish Inter-Governmental Council and Conference set up under the Anglo-Irish Agreement of 1985. Also, a new British-Irish Council incorporates members of all the devolved administrations within the United Kingdom and representatives of the Isle of Man and the Channel Islands as well as the British and Irish governments.

In addition to the three Strands, the agreement includes such measures as the establishment of an Equality Commission and a Human Rights Commission, a reform review of criminal justice and policing agencies and practices, and funding for victims of violence.

Belfast Agreement ("Good Friday Agreement")

Declaration of Support

1. We, the participants in the multi-party negotiations, believe that the agreement we have negotiated offers a truly historic opportunity for a new beginning.

2. The tragedies of the past have left a deep and profoundly regrettable legacy of suffering. We must never forget those who have died or been injured, and their families. But we can best honour them through a fresh start, in which we firmly dedicate ourselves to the achievement of reconciliation, tolerance, and mutual trust, and to the protection and vindication of the human rights of all.

3. We are committed to partnership, equality and mutual respect as the basis of relationships within Northern Ireland, between North and South, and between these islands.

4. We reaffirm our total and absolute commitment to exclusively democratic and peaceful means of resolving differences on political issues, and our opposition to any use or threat of force by others for any political purpose, whether in regard to this agreement or otherwise.

5. We acknowledge the substantial differences between our continuing, and equally legitimate, political aspirations. However, we will endeavour to strive in every practical way towards reconciliation and rapprochement within the framework of democratic and agreed arrangements. We pledge that we will, in good faith, work to ensure the success of each and every one of the arrangements to be established under this agreement. It is accepted that all of the institutional and constitutional arrangements—an Assembly in Northern Ireland, a North/South Ministerial Council, implementation bodies, a British-Irish Council and a British-Irish Intergovernmental Conference and any amendments to British Acts of Parliament and the Constitution of Ireland—are interlocking and interdependent and that in particular the functioning of the Assembly and the North/South Council are so closely inter-related that the success of each depends on that of the other.

6. Accordingly, in a spirit of concord, we strongly commend this agreement to the people, North and South, for their approval.

Constitutional Issues

1. The participants endorse the commitment made by the British and Irish Governments that, in a new British-Irish Agreement replacing the Anglo-Irish Agreement, they will:

(i) recognise the legitimacy of whatever choice is freely exercised by a majority of the people of Northern Ireland with regard to its status, whether they prefer to continue to support the Union with Great Britain or a sovereign united Ireland;

(ii) recognise that it is for the people of the island of Ireland alone, by agreement between the two parts respectively and without external impediment, to exercise their right of self-determination on the basis of consent, freely and concurrently given, North and South, to bring about a united Ireland, if that is their wish, accepting that this right must be achieved and exercised with and subject to the agreement and consent of a majority of the people of Northern Ireland;

(iii) acknowledge that while a substantial section of the people in Northern Ireland share the legitimate wish of a majority of the people of the island of Ireland for a united Ireland, the present wish of a majority of the people of Northern Ireland, freely exercised and legitimate, is to maintain the Union and, accordingly, that Northern Ireland's status as part of the United

Kingdom reflects and relies upon that wish; and that it would be wrong to make any change in the status of Northern Ireland save with the consent of a majority of its people;

(iv) affirm that if, in the future, the people of the island of Ireland exercise their right of self-determination on the basis set out in sections (i) and (ii) above to bring about a united Ireland, it will be a binding obligation on both Governments to introduce and support in their respective Parliaments legislation to give effect to that wish;

(v) affirm that whatever choice is freely exercised by a majority of the people of Northern Ireland, the power of the sovereign government with jurisdiction there shall be exercised with rigorous impartiality on behalf of all the people in the diversity of their identities and traditions and shall be founded on the principles of full respect for, and equality of, civil, political, social and cultural rights, of freedom from discrimination for all citizens, and of parity of esteem and of just and equal treatment for the identity, ethos, and aspirations of both communities;

(vi) recognise the birthright of all the people of Northern Ireland to identify themselves and be accepted as Irish or British, or both, as they may so choose, and accordingly confirm that their right to hold both British and Irish citizenship is accepted by both Governments and would not be affected by any future change in the status of Northern Ireland.

2. The participants also note that the two Governments have accordingly undertaken in the context of this comprehensive political agreement, to propose and support changes in, respectively, the Constitution of Ireland and in British legislation relating to the constitutional status of Northern Ireland. . . .

STRAND ONE
Democratic Institutions in Northern Ireland

1. This agreement provides for a democratically elected Assembly in Northern Ireland which is inclusive in its membership, capable of exercising executive and legislative authority, and subject to safeguards to protect the rights and interests of all sides of the community.

The Assembly

2. A 108-member Assembly will be elected by PR(STV) from existing Westminster constituencies.

3. The Assembly will exercise full legislative and executive authority in respect of those matters currently within the responsibility of the six Northern Ireland Government Departments, with the possibility of taking on responsibility for other matters as detailed elsewhere in this agreement.

4. The Assembly—operating where appropriate on a cross-community basis—will be the prime source of authority in respect of all devolved responsibilities.

Safeguards

5. There will be safeguards to ensure that all sections of the community can participate and work together successfully in the operation of these institutions and that all sections of the community are protected, including:

(a) allocations of Committee Chairs, Ministers and Committee membership in proportion to party strengths;

(b) the European Convention on Human Rights (ECHR) and any Bill of Rights for Northern Ireland supplementing it, which neither the Assembly nor public bodies can infringe, together with a Human Rights Commission;

(c) arrangements to provide that key decisions and legislation are proofed to ensure that they do not infringe the ECHR and any Bill of Rights for Northern Ireland;

(d) arrangements to ensure key decisions are taken on a cross-community basis;

(i) either parallel consent, i.e. a majority of those members present and voting, including a majority of the unionist and nationalist designations present and voting;

(ii) or a weighted majority (60%) of members present and voting, including at least 40% of each of the nationalist and unionist designations present and voting.

Key decisions requiring cross-community support will be designated in advance, including election of the Chair of the Assembly, the First Minister and Deputy First Minister, standing orders and budget allocations. In other cases such decisions could be triggered by a petition of concern brought by a significant minority of Assembly members (30/108).

(e) an Equality Commission to monitor a statutory obligation to promote equality of opportunity in specified areas and parity of esteem between the two main communities, and to investigate individual complaints against public bodies.

Operation of the Assembly

6. At their first meeting, members of the Assembly will register a designation of identity—nationalist, unionist or other—for the purposes of measuring cross-community support in Assembly votes under the relevant provisions above.

7. The Chair and Deputy Chair of the Assembly will be elected on a cross-community basis, as set out in paragraph 5(d) above.

8. There will be a Committee for each of the main executive functions of the Northern Ireland Administration. The Chairs and Deputy Chairs of the Assembly Committees will be allocated proportionally, using the d'Hondt system. Membership of the Committees will be in broad proportion to party strengths in the Assembly to ensure that the opportunity of Committee places is available to all members.

9. The Committees will have a scrutiny, policy development and consultation role with respect to the Department with which each is associated, and will have a role in initiation of legislation. They will have the power to:

consider and advise on Departmental budgets and Annual Plans in the context of the overall budget allocation;

approve relevant secondary legislation and take the Committee stage of relevant primary legislation;

call for persons and papers;

initiate enquiries and make reports;

consider and advise on matters brought to the Committee by its Minister. . . .

Executive Authority

14. Executive authority to be discharged on behalf of the Assembly by a First Minister and Deputy First Minister and up to ten Ministers with Departmental responsibilities.

15. The First Minister and Deputy First Minister shall be jointly elected into office by the Assembly voting on a cross-community basis, according to 5(d)(i) above.

16. Following the election of the First Minister and Deputy First Minister, the posts of Ministers will be allocated to parties on the basis of the d'Hondt system by reference to the number of seats each party has in the Assembly.

17. The Ministers will constitute an Executive Committee, which will be convened, and presided over, by the First Minister and Deputy First Minister.

18. The duties of the First Minister and Deputy First Minister will include, inter alia, dealing with and co-ordinating the work of the Executive Committee and the response of the Northern Ireland administration to external relationships.

19. The Executive Committee will provide a forum for the discussion of, and agreement on, issues which cut across the responsibilities of two or more Ministers, for prioritising executive and legislative proposals and for recommending a common position where necessary (e.g. in dealing with external relationships).

20. The Executive Committee will seek to agree each year, and review as necessary, a programme incorporating an agreed budget linked to policies and programmes, subject to approval by the Assembly, after scrutiny in Assembly Committees, on a cross-community basis.

21. A party may decline the opportunity to nominate a person to serve as a Minister or may subsequently change its nominee.

22. All the Northern Ireland Departments will be headed by a Minister. All Ministers will liaise regularly with their respective Committee.

23. As a condition of appointment, Ministers, including the First Minister and Deputy First Minister, will affirm the terms of a Pledge of Office (Annex A) undertaking to discharge effectively and in good faith all the responsibilities attaching to their office.

24. Ministers will have full executive authority in their respective areas of responsibility, within any broad programme agreed by the Executive Committee and endorsed by the Assembly as a whole.

25. An individual may be removed from office following a decision of the Assembly taken on a cross-community basis, if (s)he loses the confidence of the Assembly, voting on a cross-community basis, for failure to meet his or her responsibilities including, inter alia, those set out in the Pledge of Office. Those who hold office should use only democratic, non-violent means, and those who do not should be excluded or removed from office under these provisions.

Legislation

26. The Assembly will have authority to pass primary legislation for Northern Ireland in devolved areas, subject to:

(a) the ECHR and any Bill of Rights for Northern Ireland supplementing it which, if the courts found to be breached, would render the relevant legislation null and void;

(b) decisions by simple majority of members voting, except when decision on a cross-community basis is required;

(c) detailed scrutiny and approval in the relevant Departmental Committee;

(d) mechanisms, based on arrangements proposed for the Scottish Parliament, to ensure suitable co-ordination, and avoid disputes, between the Assembly and the Westminster Parliament;

(e) option of the Assembly seeking to include Northern Ireland provisions in United Kingdom-wide legislation in the Westminster Parliament, especially on devolved issues where parity is normally maintained (e.g. social security, company law).

27. The Assembly will have authority to legislate in reserved areas with the approval of the Secretary of State and subject to Parliamentary control.

28. Disputes over legislative competence will be decided by the Courts.

29. Legislation could be initiated by an individual, a Committee or a Minister. . . .

32. Role of Secretary of State:

(a) to remain responsible for NIO matters not devolved to the Assembly, subject to regular consultation with the Assembly and Ministers;

(b) to approve and lay before the Westminster Parliament any Assembly legislation on reserved matters;

(c) to represent Northern Ireland interests in the United Kingdom Cabinet;

(d) to have the right to attend the Assembly at their invitation.

33. The Westminster Parliament (whose power to make legislation for Northern Ireland would remain unaffected) will:

(a) legislate for non-devolved issues, other than where the Assembly legislates with the approval of the Secretary of State and subject to the control of Parliament;

(b) to legislate as necessary to ensure the United Kingdom's international obligations are met in respect of Northern Ireland;

(c) scrutinise, including through the Northern Ireland Grand and Select Committees, the responsibilities of the Secretary of State.

34. A consultative Civic Forum will be established. It will comprise representatives of the business, trade union and voluntary sectors, and such other sectors as agreed by the First Minister and the Deputy First Minister. It will act as a consultative mechanism on social, economic and cultural issues. The First Minister and the Deputy First Minister will by agreement provide administrative support for the Civic Forum and establish guidelines for the selection of representatives to the Civic Forum. . . .

Annex A
Pledge of Office

To pledge:

(a) to discharge in good faith all the duties of office;

(b) commitment to non-violence and exclusively peaceful and democratic means;

(c) to serve all the people of Northern Ireland equally, and to act in accordance with the general obligations on government to promote equality and prevent discrimination;

(d) to participate with colleagues in the preparation of a programme for government;

(e) to operate within the framework of that programme when agreed within the Executive Committee and endorsed by the Assembly;

(f) to support, and to act in accordance with, all decisions of the Executive Committee and Assembly;

(g) to comply with the Ministerial Code of Conduct. . . .

STRAND TWO
North/South Ministerial Council

1. Under a new British/Irish Agreement dealing with the totality of relationships, and related legislation at Westminster and in the Oireachtas, a North/South Ministerial Council to be established to bring together those with executive responsibilities in Northern Ireland and the Irish Government, to develop consultation, co-operation and action within the island of Ireland—including through implementation on an all-island and cross-border basis—on matters of mutual interest within the competence of the Administrations, North and South.

2. All Council decisions to be by agreement between the two sides. Northern Ireland to be represented by the First Minister, Deputy First Minister and any relevant Ministers, the Irish Government by the Taoiseach and relevant Ministers, all operating in accordance with the rules for democratic authority and accountability in force in the Northern Ireland Assembly and the Oireachtas respectively. Participation in the Council to be one of the essential responsibilities attaching to relevant posts in the two Administrations. If a holder of a relevant post will not participate normally in the Council, the Taoiseach in the case of the Irish Government and the First and Deputy First Minister in the case of the Northern Ireland Administration to be able to make alternative arrangements. . . .

5. The Council:

(i) to exchange information, discuss and consult with a view to co-operating on matters of mutual interest within the competence of both Administrations, North and South;

(ii) to use best endeavours to reach agreement on the adoption of common policies, in areas where there is a mutual cross-border and all-island benefit, and which are within the competence of both Administrations, North and South, making determined efforts to overcome any disagreements;

(iii) to take decisions by agreement on policies for implementation separately in each jurisdiction, in relevant meaningful areas within the competence of both Administrations, North and South;

(iv) to take decisions by agreement on policies and action at an all-island and cross-border level to be implemented by the bodies to be established as set out in paragraphs 8 and 9 below. . . .

STRAND THREE
British-Irish Council

1. A British-Irish Council (BIC) will be established under a new British-Irish Agreement to promote the harmonious and mutu-

ally beneficial development of the totality of relationships among the peoples of these islands.

2. Membership of the BIC will comprise representatives of the British and Irish Governments, devolved institutions in Northern Ireland, Scotland and Wales, when established, and, if appropriate, elsewhere in the United Kingdom, together with representatives of the Isle of Man and the Channel Islands.

3. The BIC will meet in different formats: at summit level, twice per year; in specific sectoral formats on a regular basis, with each side represented by the appropriate Minister; in an appropriate format to consider cross-sectoral matters.

4. Representatives of members will operate in accordance with whatever procedures for democratic authority and accountability are in force in their respective elected institutions.

5. The BIC will exchange information, discuss, consult and use best endeavours to reach agreement on co-operation on matters of mutual interest within the competence of the relevant Administrations. Suitable issues for early discussion in the BIC could include transport links, agricultural issues, environmental issues, cultural issues, health issues, education issues and approaches to EU issues. Suitable arrangements to be made for practical co-operation on agreed policies.

6. It will be open to the BIC to agree common policies or common actions. Individual members may opt not to participate in such common policies and common action.

7. The BIC normally will operate by consensus. In relation to decisions on common policies or common actions, including their means of implementation, it will operate by agreement of all members participating in such policies or actions. . . .

British-Irish Intergovernmental Conference

1. There will be a new British-Irish Agreement dealing with the totality of relationships. It will establish a standing British-Irish Intergovernmental Conference, which will subsume both the Anglo-Irish Intergovernmental Council and the Intergovernmental Conference established under the 1985 Agreement.

2. The Conference will bring together the British and Irish Governments to promote bilateral co-operation at all levels on all matters of mutual interest within the competence of both Governments.

3. The Conference will meet as required at Summit level (Prime Minister and Taoiseach). Otherwise, Governments will be represented by appropriate Ministers. Advisers, including police and security advisers, will attend as appropriate.

4. All decisions will be by agreement between both Governments. The Governments will make determined efforts to resolve disagreements between them. There will be no derogation from the sovereignty of either Government.

5. In recognition of the Irish Government's special interest in Northern Ireland and of the extent to which issues of mutual concern arise in relation to Northern Ireland, there will be regular and frequent meetings of the Conference concerned with non-devolved Northern Ireland matters, on which the Irish Government may put forward views and proposals. These meetings, to be co-chaired by the Minister for Foreign Affairs and the Secretary of State for Northern Ireland, would also deal with all-island and cross-border co-operation on non-devolved issues.

6. Co-operation within the framework of the Conference will include facilitation of co-operation in security matters. The Conference also will address, in particular, the areas of rights, justice, prisons and policing in Northern Ireland (unless and

until responsibility is devolved to a Northern Ireland administration) and will intensify co-operation between the two Governments on the all-island or cross-border aspects of these matters. . . .

Rights, Safeguards and Equality of Opportunity

Human Rights

1. The parties affirm their commitment to the mutual respect, the civil rights and the religious liberties of everyone in the community. Against the background of the recent history of communal conflict, the parties affirm in particular:

- the right of free political thought;
- the right to freedom and expression of religion;
- the right to pursue democratically national and political aspirations;
- the right to seek constitutional change by peaceful and legitimate means;
- the right to freely choose one's place of residence;
- the right to equal opportunity in all social and economic activity, regardless of class, creed, disability, gender or ethnicity;
- the right to freedom from sectarian harassment; and
- the right of women to full and equal political participation.

United Kingdom Legislation

2. The British Government will complete incorporation into Northern Ireland law of the European Convention on Human Rights (ECHR), with direct access to the courts, and remedies for breach of the Convention, including power for the courts to overrule Assembly legislation on grounds of inconsistency.

3. Subject to the outcome of public consultation underway, the British Government intends, as a particular priority, to create a statutory obligation on public authorities in Northern Ireland to carry out all their functions with due regard to the need to promote equality of opportunity in relation to religion and political opinion; gender; race; disability; age; marital status; dependants; and sexual orientation. Public bodies would be required to draw up statutory schemes showing how they would implement this obligation. Such schemes would cover arrangements for policy appraisal, including an assessment of impact on relevant categories, public consultation, public access to information and services, monitoring and timetables.

4. The new Northern Ireland Human Rights Commission (see paragraph 5 below) will be invited to consult and to advise on the scope for defining, in Westminster legislation, rights supplementary to those in the European Convention on Human Rights, to reflect the particular circumstances of Northern Ireland, drawing as appropriate on international instruments and experience. These additional rights to reflect the principles of mutual respect for the identity and ethos of both communities and parity of esteem, and—taken together with the ECHR—to constitute a Bill of Rights for Northern Ireland. Among the issues for consideration by the Commission will be:

- the formulation of a general obligation on government and public bodies fully to respect, on the basis of equality of treatment, the identity and ethos of both communities in Northern Ireland; and
- a clear formulation of the rights not to be discriminated against and to equality of opportunity in both the public and private sectors.

New Institutions in Northern Ireland

5. A new Northern Ireland Human Rights Commission, with membership from Northern Ireland reflecting the community balance, will be established by Westminster legislation, independent of Government, with an extended and enhanced role beyond that currently exercised by the Standing Advisory Commission on Human Rights, to include keeping under review the adequacy and effectiveness of laws and practices, making recommendations to Government as necessary; providing information and promoting awareness of human rights; considering draft legislation referred to them by the new Assembly; and, in appropriate cases, bringing court proceedings or providing assistance to individuals doing so.

6. Subject to the outcome of public consultation currently underway, the British Government intends a new statutory Equality Commission to replace the Fair Employment Commission, the Equal Opportunities Commission (NI), the Commission for Racial Equality (NI) and the Disability Council. Such a unified Commission will advise on, validate and monitor the statutory obligation and will investigate complaints of default.

7. It would be open to a new Northern Ireland Assembly to consider bringing together its responsibilities for these matters into a dedicated Department of Equality.

8. These improvements will build on existing protections in Westminster legislation in respect of the judiciary, the system of justice and policing.

Comparable Steps by the Irish Government

9. The Irish Government will also take steps to further strengthen the protection of human rights in its jurisdiction. The Government will, taking account of the work of the All-Party Oireachtas Committee on the Constitution and the Report of the Constitution Review Group, bring forward measures to strengthen and underpin the constitutional protection of human rights. These proposals will draw on the European Convention on Human Rights and other international legal instruments in the field of human rights and the question of the incorporation of the ECHR will be further examined in this context. The measures brought forward would ensure at least an equivalent level of protection of human rights as will pertain in Northern Ireland. In addition, the Irish Government will:

- establish a Human Rights Commission with a mandate and remit equivalent to that within Northern Ireland;
- proceed with arrangements as quickly as possible to ratify the Council of Europe Framework Convention on National Minorities (already ratified by the UK);
- implement enhanced employment equality legislation;
- introduce equal status legislation; and
- continue to take further active steps to demonstrate its respect for the different traditions in the island of Ireland.

A Joint Committee

10. It is envisaged that there would be a joint committee of representatives of the two Human Rights Commissions, North and South, as a forum for consideration of human rights issues in the island of Ireland. The joint committee will consider, among other matters, the possibility of establishing a charter, open to signature by all democratic political parties, reflecting and endorsing agreed measures for the protection of the fundamental rights of everyone living in the island of Ireland.

Reconciliation and Victims of Violence

11. The participants believe that it is essential to acknowledge and address the suffering of the victims of violence as a necessary element of reconciliation. They look forward to the results of the work of the Northern Ireland Victims Commission.

12. It is recognised that victims have a right to remember as well as to contribute to a changed society. The achievement of a peaceful and just society would be the true memorial to the victims of violence. The participants particularly recognise that young people from areas affected by the troubles face particular difficulties and will support the development of special community-based initiatives based on international best practice. The provision of services that are supportive and sensitive to the needs of victims will also be a critical element and that support will need to be channelled through both statutory and community-based voluntary organisations facilitating locally-based self-help and support networks. This will require the allocation of sufficient resources, including statutory funding as necessary, to meet the needs of victims and to provide for community-based support programmes.

13. The participants recognise and value the work being done by many organisations to develop reconciliation and mutual understanding and respect between and within communities and traditions, in Northern Ireland and between North and South, and they see such work as having a vital role in consolidating peace and political agreement. Accordingly, they pledge their continuing support to such organisations and will positively examine the case for enhanced financial assistance for the work of reconciliation. An essential aspect of the reconciliation process is the promotion of a culture of tolerance at every level of society, including initiatives to facilitate and encourage integrated education and mixed housing.

Rights, Safeguards and Equality of Opportunity

Economic, Social and Cultural Issues

1. Pending the devolution of powers to a new Northern Ireland Assembly, the British Government will pursue broad policies for sustained economic growth and stability in Northern Ireland and for promoting social inclusion, including in particular community development and the advancement of women in public life.

2. Subject to the public consultation currently under way, the British Government will make rapid progress with:

(i) a new regional development strategy for Northern Ireland, for consideration in due course by a the Assembly, tackling the problems of a divided society and social cohesion in urban, rural and border areas, protecting and enhancing the environment, producing new approaches to transport issues, strengthening the physical infrastructure of the region, developing the advantages and resources of rural areas and rejuvenating major urban centres;

(ii) a new economic development strategy for Northern Ireland, for consideration in due course by a the Assembly, which would provide for short and medium term economic planning linked as appropriate to the regional development strategy; and

(iii) measures on employment equality included in the recent White Paper ("Partnership for Equality") and covering the extension and strengthening of anti-discrimination legislation, a review of the national security aspects of the present fair employment legislation at the earliest possible time, a new more focused Targeting Social Need initiative and a range of measures aimed at combating unemployment and progressively eliminating the differential in unemployment rates between the two communities by targeting objective need.

3. All participants recognise the importance of respect, understanding and tolerance in relation to linguistic diversity, including in Northern Ireland, the Irish language, Ulster-Scots and the languages of the various ethnic communities, all of which are part of the cultural wealth of the island of Ireland.

4. In the context of active consideration currently being given to the UK signing the Council of Europe Charter for Regional or Minority Languages, the British Government will in particular in relation to the Irish language, where appropriate and where people so desire it:

- take resolute action to promote the language;
- facilitate and encourage the use of the language in speech and writing in public and private life where there is appropriate demand;
- seek to remove, where possible, restrictions which would discourage or work against the maintenance or development of the language;
- make provision for liaising with the Irish language community, representing their views to public authorities and investigating complaints;
- place a statutory duty on the Department of Education to encourage and facilitate Irish medium education in line with current provision for integrated education;
- explore urgently with the relevant British authorities, and in co-operation with the Irish broadcasting authorities, the scope for achieving more widespread availability of Teilifís na Gaeilge in Northern Ireland;
- seek more effective ways to encourage and provide financial support for Irish language film and television production in Northern Ireland; and
- encourage the parties to secure agreement that this commitment will be sustained by a new Assembly in a way which takes account of the desires and sensitivities of the community.

5. All participants acknowledge the sensitivity of the use of symbols and emblems for public purposes, and the need in particular in creating the new institutions to ensure that such symbols and emblems are used in a manner which promotes mutual respect rather than division. Arrangements will be made to monitor this issue and consider what action might be required.

Decommissioning

1. Participants recall their agreement in the Procedural Motion adopted on 24 September 1997 "that the resolution of the decommissioning issue is an indispensable part of the process of negotiation", and also recall the provisions of paragraph 25 of Strand 1 above.

2. They note the progress made by the Independent International Commission on Decommissioning and the Governments in developing schemes which can represent a workable basis for achieving the decommissioning of illegally-held arms in the possession of paramilitary groups.

3. All participants accordingly reaffirm their commitment to the total disarmament of all paramilitary organisations. They also confirm their intention to continue to work constructively and in good faith with the Independent Commission, and to use any influence they may have, to achieve the decommissioning of all paramilitary arms within two years following endorsement in referendums North and South of the agreement and in the context of the implementation of the overall settlement.

4. The Independent Commission will monitor, review and verify progress on decommissioning of illegal arms, and will report to both Governments at regular intervals.

6. Both Governments will take all necessary steps to facilitate the decommissioning process to include bringing the relevant schemes into force by the end of June.

Security

1. The participants note that the development of a peaceful environment on the basis of this agreement can and should mean a normalisation of security arrangements and practices.

2. The British Government will make progress towards the objective of as early a return as possible to normal security arrangements in Northern Ireland, consistent with the level of threat and with a published overall strategy, dealing with:

(i) the reduction of the numbers and role of the Armed Forces deployed in Northern Ireland to levels compatible with a normal peaceful society;

(ii) the removal of security installations;

(iii) the removal of emergency powers in Northern Ireland; and

(iv) other measures appropriate to and compatible with a normal peaceful society.

3. The Secretary of State will consult regularly on progress, and the response to any continuing paramilitary activity, with the Irish Government and the political parties, as appropriate.

4. The British Government will continue its consultation on firearms regulation and control on the basis of the document published on 2 April 1998.

5. The Irish Government will initiate a wide-ranging review of the Offences Against the State Acts 1939–85 with a view to both reform and dispensing with those elements no longer required as circumstances permit.

Policing and Justice

1. The participants recognise that policing is a central issue in any society. They equally recognise that Northern Ireland's history of deep divisions has made it highly emotive, with great hurt suffered and sacrifices made by many individuals and their families, including those in the RUC and other public servants. They believe that the agreement provides the opportunity for a new beginning to policing in Northern Ireland with a police service capable of attracting and sustaining support from the community as a whole. They also believe that this agreement offers a unique opportunity to bring about a new political dispensation which will recognise the full and equal legitimacy and worth of the identities, senses of allegiance and ethos of all sections of the community in Northern Ireland. They consider that this opportunity should inform and underpin the development of a police service representative in terms of the make-up of the community as a whole and which, in a peaceful environment, should be routinely unarmed.

2. The participants believe it essential that policing structures and arrangements are such that the police service is professional, effective and efficient, fair and impartial, free from partisan political control; accountable, both under the law for its actions and to the community it serves; representative of the society it polices, and operates within a coherent and co-operative criminal justice system, which conforms with human rights norms. The participants also believe that those structures and arrangements must be capable of maintaining law and order including responding effectively to crime and to any terrorist threat and to public order problems. A police service which cannot do so will fail to win public confidence and acceptance. They believe that any such structures and arrangements should be capable of delivering a policing service, in constructive and inclusive partnerships with the community at all levels, and with the maximum delegation of authority and responsibility, consistent with the foregoing principles. These arrangements should be based on principles of protection of human rights and professional integrity and should be unambiguously accepted and actively supported by the entire community.

3. An independent Commission will be established to make recommendations for future policing arrangements in Northern Ireland including means of encouraging widespread community support for these arrangements within the agreed framework of principles reflected in the paragraphs above and in accordance with the terms of reference at Annex A. The Commission will be broadly representative with expert and international representation among its membership and will be asked to consult widely and to report no later than Summer 1999.

4. The participants believe that the aims of the criminal justice system are to:

- deliver a fair and impartial system of justice to the community;
- be responsive to the community's concerns, and encouraging community involvement where appropriate;
- have the confidence of all parts of the community; and
- deliver justice efficiently and effectively.

5. There will be a parallel wide-ranging review of criminal justice (other than policing and those aspects of the system relating to the emergency legislation) to be carried out by the British Government through a mechanism with an independent element, in consultation with the political parties and others. . . .

ANNEX A
Commission on Policing for Northern Ireland
Terms of Reference

Taking account of the principles on policing as set out in the agreement, the Commission will inquire into policing in Northern Ireland and, on the basis of its findings, bring forward proposals for future policing structures and arrangements, including means of encouraging widespread community support for those arrangements.

Its proposals on policing should be designed to ensure that policing arrangements, including composition, recruitment, training, culture, ethos and symbols, are such that in a new approach Northern Ireland has a police service that can enjoy widespread support from, and is seen as an integral part of, the community as a whole.

Its proposals should include recommendations covering any issues such as re-training, job placement and educational and professional development required in the transition to policing in a peaceful society. . . .

ANNEX B
Review of the Criminal Justice System
Terms of Reference

Taking account of the aims of the criminal justice system as set out in the Agreement, the review will address the structure, management and resourcing of publicly funded elements of the criminal justice system and will bring forward proposals for future criminal justice arrangements (other than policing and those aspects of the system relating to emergency legislation, which the Government is considering separately) covering such issues as:

the arrangements for making appointments to the judiciary and magistracy, and safeguards for protecting their independence;

the arrangements for the organisation and supervision of the prosecution process, and for safeguarding its independence;

measures to improve the responsiveness and accountability of, and any lay participation in the criminal justice system;

mechanisms for addressing law reform;

the scope for structured co-operation between the criminal justice agencies on both parts of the island; and

the structure and organisation of criminal justice functions that might be devolved to an Assembly, including the possibility of establishing a Department of Justice, while safeguarding the essential independence of many of the key functions in this area. . . .

Prisoners

1. Both Governments will put in place mechanisms to provide for an accelerated programme for the release of prisoners, including transferred prisoners, convicted of scheduled offences in Northern Ireland or, in the case of those sentenced outside Northern Ireland, similar offences (referred to hereafter as qualifying prisoners). Any such arrangements will protect the rights of individual prisoners under national and international law.

2. Prisoners affiliated to organisations which have not established or are not maintaining a complete and unequivocal ceasefire will not benefit from the arrangements. The situation in this regard will be kept under review. . . .

Agreement between the Government of the United Kingdom of Great Britain and Northern Ireland and the Government of Ireland

The British and Irish Governments:

Welcoming the strong commitment to the Agreement reached on 10th April 1998 by themselves and other participants in the multi-party talks and set out in Annex 1 to this Agreement (hereinafter "the Multi-Party Agreement");

Considering that the Multi-Party Agreement offers an opportunity for a new beginning in relationships within Northern Ireland, within the island of Ireland and between the peoples of these islands;

Wishing to develop still further the unique relationship between their peoples and the close co-operation between their countries as friendly neighbours and as partners in the European Union;

Reaffirming their total commitment to the principles of democracy and non-violence which have been fundamental to the multi-party talks;

Reaffirming their commitment to the principles of partnership, equality and mutual respect and to the protection of civil, political, social, economic and cultural rights in their respective jurisdictions;

Have agreed as follows:

ARTICLE 1

The two Governments:

(i) recognise the legitimacy of whatever choice is freely exercised by a majority of the people of Northern Ireland with regard to its status, whether they prefer to continue to support the Union with Great Britain or a sovereign united Ireland;

(ii) recognise that it is for the people of the island of Ireland alone, by agreement between the two parts respectively and without external impediment, to exercise their right of self-determination on the basis of consent, freely and concurrently given, North and South, to bring about a united Ireland, if that is their wish, accepting that this right must be achieved and exercised with and subject to the agreement and consent of a majority of the people of Northern Ireland;

(iii) acknowledge that while a substantial section of the people in Northern Ireland share the legitimate wish of a majority of the people of the island of Ireland for a united Ireland, the present wish of a majority of the people of Northern Ireland, freely exercised and legitimate, is to maintain the Union and accordingly, that Northern Ireland's status as part of the United Kingdom reflects and relies upon that wish; and that it would be wrong to make any change in the status of Northern Ireland save with the consent of a majority of its people;

(iv) affirm that, if in the future, the people of the island of Ireland exercise their right of self-determination on the basis set out in sections (i) and (ii) above to bring about a united Ireland, it will be a binding obligation on both Governments to introduce and support in their respective Parliaments legislation to give effect to that wish;

(v) affirm that whatever choice is freely exercised by a majority of the people of Northern Ireland, the power of the sovereign government with jurisdiction there shall be exercised with rigorous impartiality on behalf of all the people in the diversity of their identities and traditions and shall be founded on the principles of full respect for, and equality of, civil, political, social and cultural rights, of freedom from discrimination for all citizens, and of parity of esteem and of just and equal treatment for the identity, ethos and aspirations of both communities;

(vi) recognise the birthright of all the people of Northern Ireland to identify themselves and be accepted as Irish or British, or both, as they may so choose, and accordingly confirm that their right to hold both British and Irish citizenship is accepted by both Governments and would not be affected by any future change in the status of Northern Ireland.

ARTICLE 2

The two Governments affirm their solemn commitment to support, and where appropriate implement, the provisions of the Multi-Party Agreement. In particular there shall be established in accordance with the provisions of the Multi-Party Agreement immediately on the entry into force of this Agreement, the following institutions:

(i) a North/South Ministerial Council;

(ii) the implementation bodies referred to in paragraph 9

(ii) of the section entitled "Strand Two" of the Multi-Party Agreement;

(iii) a British-Irish Council;

(iv) a British-Irish Intergovernmental Conference.

ARTICLE 3

(1) This Agreement shall replace the Agreement between the British and Irish Governments done at Hillsborough on 15th November 1985 which shall cease to have effect on entry into force of this Agreement. . . .

Consequences

Ratification of the Belfast Agreement on December 2, 1999, officially devolved the government of Northern Ireland upon an elected assembly headed by a first minister and his or her deputy. Unfortunately, the issue of the "decommissioning" of paramilitary groups proved troublesome and threatened to undermine the agreement. Less than three months after devolution, London was forced to restore direct rule on an emergency basis. The Northern Ireland Assembly was recalled again in May 2000, but in 2001, Trimble resigned over continued IRA resistance to decommissioning. As of summer 2005, Northern Ireland's elected assembly is functioning, and the peace process is proceeding, albeit tenuously. On July 28, 2005, the IRA formally ordered an end to its armed campaign. Still, the outcome of the Belfast Agreement must be classified as a work in progress.

Source

Northern Ireland Office of the First Minister and Deputy Minister, "The Belfast Agreement." Available online. URL: http://www.ofmdfmni.gov.uk/publications/ba.htm. Accessed December 30, 2004.

Trade Agreements and Commercial Treaties

PANAMA CANAL TREATY (1977)
(AND THE U.S.-PANAMA NEUTRALITY ACT)

TREATY AT A GLANCE

Completed
September 7, 1977, at Washington, D.C.; ratified by U.S. Senate
June 1978; implemented under the Panama Canal Act of 1979

Signatories
United States and the Republic of Panama

Overview
After nearly a century of uneasy relations over the Panama Canal,
the Republic of Panama (which had come into existence shortly before negotiating the first Panama Canal Treaty [Hay–Bunau-
Varilla Treaty] in effect to allow the building of the canal) and the
United States (which had run the Panama Canal Zone as its virtual
colony) reached an agreement that in 1999 returned sovereignty
over the canal to Panama.

Historical Background

The first PANAMA CANAL TREATY (Hay–Bunau-Varilla
Treaty) in 1904 was the political result of efforts by
U.S. president Theodore Roosevelt and those, like Senator Mark Hanna, who backed him in Congress, not
only to create an American-controlled canal in Central
American connecting the Atlantic and Pacific Oceans
but also to create a country that would allow them to
build such a canal. Although they more or less carved
Panama out of Colombia (then called New Granada),
the newly independent Panamanians themselves found
much to irritate them in the treaty from the moment it
was signed.

The treaty was negotiated by a French citizen,
Phillipe-Jean Bunau-Varilla, who had not set foot in
New Granada in 18 years and thus never in Panama
itself. Bunau-Varilla later admitted that he was willing
for Panama to pay any price and fight any battle to
ensure acceptance of the treaty by the United States
Senate. From the Panamanian point of view, the most
onerous clause of the treaty granted the United States
the right to the entire 10-mile, ocean-to-ocean Canal
Zone as "if it were sovereign," and it did so for almost

a century. In effect, the Canal Zone was a foreign
colony running through the center of Panama, despite
Roosevelt's protests in 1906 that he had intended no
such result.

Over the years new negotiations, especially in
1936 and 1955, dampened some of the more inflam-
matory effects of the treaty, but Panama continued to
press for more radical changes. Years of wrangling
between the two governments finally produced an
agreement in 1977.

Terms

The 1977 treaty terminated all previous agreements. It
abolished the Canal Zone. It recognized Panama as territorial sovereign in the zone. But it did not get the
United States out of Panama's business. Until it expired
in 1999, the treaty gave the United States the right to
manage, operate, and maintain the canal and to use
whatever lands and waters it felt necessary to those
ends. In addition, it provided for a joint feasibility study
for a sea level canal and gave the United States the
option to add a third lane of locks to the existing canal.

Panama Canal Treaty

The United States of America and the Republic of Panama, Acting in the spirit of the Joint Declaration of April 3, 1964, by the Representatives of the Governments of the United States of America and the Republic of Panama, and of the Joint Statement of Principles of February 7, 1974, initialed by the Secretary of State of the United States of America and the Foreign Minister of the Republic of Panama, and Acknowledging the Republic of Panama's sovereignty over its territory, Have decided to terminate the prior Treaties pertaining to the Panama Canal and to conclude a new Treaty to serve as the basis for a new relationship between them and, accordingly, have agreed upon the following:

ARTICLE I
ABROGATION OF PRIOR TREATIES AND ESTABLISHMENT OF A NEW RELATIONSHIP

1. Upon its entry into force, this Treaty terminates and supersedes:

(a) The Isthmian Canal Convention between the United States of America and the Republic of Panama, signed at Washington, November 18, 1903;

(b) The Treaty of Friendship and Cooperation signed at Washington, March 2, 1936, and the Treaty of Mutual Understanding and Cooperation and the related Memorandum of Understandings Reached, signed at Panama, January 25, 1955, between the United States of America and the Republic of Panama;

(c) All other treaties, conventions, agreements, and exchanges of notes between the United States of America and the Republic of Panama concerning the Panama Canal, which were in force prior to the entry into force of this Treaty; and

(d) Provisions concerning the Panama Canal, which appear in other treaties, conventions, agreements, and exchanges of notes between the United States of America and the Republic of Panama, which were in force prior to the entry into force of this Treaty.

2. In accordance with the terms of this Treaty and related agreements, the Republic of Panama, as territorial sovereign, grants to the United States of America, for the duration of this Treaty, the rights necessary to regulate the transit of ships through the Panama Canal, and to manage, operate, maintain, improve, protect and defend the Canal. The Republic of Panama guarantees to the United States of America the peaceful use of the land and water areas which it has been granted the rights to use for such purposes pursuant to this Treaty and related agreements.

3. The Republic of Panama shall participate increasingly in the management and protection and defense of the Canal, as provided in this Treaty.

4. In view of the special relationship established by this Treaty, the United States of America and the Republic of Panama shall cooperate to assure the uninterrupted and efficient operation of the Panama Canal.

ARTICLE II
RATIFICATION, ENTRY INTO FORCE, AND TERMINATION

1. The Treaty shall be subject to ratification in accordance with the constitutional procedures of the two Parties. The instruments of ratification of this Treaty shall be exchanged at Panama at the same time as the instruments of ratification of the Treaty Concerning the Permanent Neutrality and Operation of the Panama Canal, signed this date, are exchanged. This Treaty shall enter into force, simultaneously with the Treaty Concerning the Permanent Neutrality and Operation of the Panama Canal, six calendar months from the date of the exchange of the instruments of ratification.

2. This Treaty shall terminate at noon, Panama time, December 31, 1999.

ARTICLE III
CANAL OPERATION AND MANAGEMENT

1. The Republic of Panama, as territorial sovereign, grants to the United States of America the rights to manage, operate, and maintain the Panama Canal, its complementary works, installations, and equipment and to provide for the orderly transit of vessels through the Panama Canal. The United States of America accepts the grant of such rights and undertakes to exercise them in accordance with this Treaty and related agreements.

2. In carrying out the foregoing responsibilities, the United States of America may:

(a) Use for the aforementioned purposes, without cost except as provided in this Treaty, the various installations and areas (including the Panama Canal) and waters, described in the Agreement in Implementation of this Article, signed this date, as well as such other areas and installations as are made available to the United States of America under this Treaty and related agreements, and take the measures necessary to ensure sanitation of such areas;

(b) Make such improvements and alterations to the aforesaid installations and areas as it deems appropriate, consistent with the terms of this Treaty;

(c) Make and enforce all rules pertaining to the passage of vessels through the Canal and other rules with respect to navigation and maritime matters, in accordance with this Treaty and related agreements. The Republic of Panama will lend its cooperation, when necessary, in the enforcement of such rules;

(d) Establish, modify, collect and retain tolls for the use of the Panama Canal, and other charges, and establish and modify methods of their assessment;

(e) Regulate relations with employees of the United States Government;

(f) Provide supporting services to facilitate the performance of its responsibilities under this Article;

(g) Issue and enforce regulations for the exercise of the rights and responsibilities of the United States of America under this Treaty and related agreements. The Republic of Panama will lend its cooperation, when necessary, in the enforcement of such rules; and

(h) Exercise any other right granted under this Treaty, or otherwise agreed upon between the two Parties.

3. Pursuant to the foregoing grant of rights, the United States of America shall, in accordance with the terms of this Treaty and the provisions of United States law, carry out its responsibilities by means of a United States Government agency called the Panama Canal Commission, which shall be constituted by and be in conformity with the laws of the United States of America.

(a) The Panama Canal Commission shall be supervised by a Board composed of nine members, five of whom shall be nationals of the United States of America, and four of whom shall be Panamanian nationals proposed by the Republic of Panama for appointment to such positions by the United States of America in a timely manner.

(b) Should the Republic of Panama request the United States of America to remove a Panamanian national from membership on the Board, the United States of America shall agree to such request. In that event, the Republic of Panama shall propose another Panamanian national for appointment by the United States of America to such position in a timely manner. In case of removal of a Panamanian member of the Board on the initiative of the United States of America, both Parties will consult in advance in order to reach agreement concerning such removal, and the Republic of Panama shall propose another Panamanian national for appointment by the United States of America in his stead.

(c) The United States of America shall employ a national of the United States of America as Administrator of the Panama Canal Commission, and a Panamanian national as Deputy Administrator, through December 31, 1989. Beginning January 1, 1990, a Panamanian national shall be employed as the Administrator and a national of the United States of America shall occupy the position of Deputy Administrator. Such Panamanian nationals shall be proposed to the United States of America by the Republic of Panama for appointment to such positions by the United States of America.

(d) Should the United States of America remove the Panamanian national from his position as Deputy Administrator, or Administrator, the Republic of Panama shall propose another Panamanian national for appointment to such position by the United States of America.

4. An illustrative description of the activities the Panama Canal Commission will perform in carrying out the responsibilities and rights of the United States of America under this Article is set forth at the Annex. Also set forth in the Annex are procedures for the discontinuance or transfer of those activities performed prior to the entry into force of this Treaty by the Panama Canal Company or the Canal Zone Government which are not to be carried out by the Panama Canal Commission.

5. The Panama Canal Commission shall reimburse the Republic of Panama for the costs incurred by the Republic of Panama in providing the following public services in the Canal operation areas and in housing areas set forth in the Agreement in Implementation of Article III of this Treaty and occupied by both United States and Panamanian citizen employees of the Panama Canal Commission: police, fire protection, street maintenance, street lighting, street cleaning, traffic management and garbage collection. The Panama Canal Commission shall pay the Republic of Panama the sum of ten million United States dollars (US$10,000,000) per annum for the foregoing services. It is agreed that every three years from the date that this Treaty enters into force, the costs involved in furnishing said services shall be reexamined to determine whether adjustment of the annual payment should be made because of inflation and other relevant factors affecting the cost of such services.

6. The Republic of Panama shall be responsible for providing, in all areas comprising the former Canal Zone, services of a general jurisdictional nature such as customs and immigration, postal services, courts and licensing, in accordance with this Treaty and related agreements.

7. The United States of America and the Republic of Panama shall establish a Panama Canal Consultative Committee, composed of an equal number of high-level representatives of the United States of America and the Republic of Panama, and which may appoint such subcommittees as it may deem appropriate. This Committee shall advise the United States of America and the Republic of Panama on matters of policy affecting the Canal's operation. In view of both Parties' special interest in the continuity and efficiency of the Canal operation in the future, the Committee shall advise on matters such as general tolls policy, employment and training policies to increase the participation of Panamanian nationals in the operation of the Canal, and international policies on matters concerning the Canal. The Committee's recommendations shall be transmitted to the two Governments, which shall give such recommendations full consideration in the formulation of such policy decisions.

8. In addition to the participation of Panamanian nationals at high management levels of the Panama Canal Commission, as provided for in paragraph 3 of this Article, there shall be growing participation of Panamanian nationals at all other levels and areas of employment in the aforesaid commission, with the objective of preparing, in an orderly and efficient fashion, for the assumption by the Republic of Panama of full responsibility for the management, operation and maintenance of the Canal upon the termination of this Treaty.

9. The use of the areas, waters and installations with respect to which the United States of America is granted rights pursuant to this Article, and the rights and legal status of United States Government agencies and employees operating in the Republic of Panama pursuant to this Article, shall be governed by Agreement in Implementation of this Article, signed this date.

10. Upon entry into force of this Treaty, the United States Government agencies known as the Panama Canal Company and the Canal Zone Government shall cease to operate within the territory of the Republic of Panama that formerly constituted the Canal Zone.

ARTICLE IV
PROTECTION AND DEFENSE

1. The United States of America and the Republic of Panama commit themselves to protect and defend the Panama Canal. Each Party shall act, in accordance with its constitutional processes, to meet the danger resulting from an armed attack or other actions which threaten the security of the Panama Canal or of ships transiting it.

2. For the duration of this Treaty, the United States of America shall have primary responsibility to protect and defend the Canal. The rights of the United States of America to station, train, and move military forces within the Republic of Panama are described in the Agreement in Implementation of this Article, signed this date. The use of areas and installations and the legal status of the armed forces of the United States of America in the Republic of Panama shall be governed by the aforesaid Agreement.

3. In order to facilitate the participation and cooperation of the armed forces of both Parties in the protection and defense of the Canal, the United States of America and the Republic of Panama shall establish a Combined Board comprised of an equal number of senior military representatives of each Party. These

representatives shall be charged by their respective governments with consulting and cooperating on all matters pertaining to the protection and defense of the Canal, and with planning for actions to be taken in concert for that purpose. Such combined protection and defense arrangements shall not inhibit the identity or lines of authority of the armed forces of the United States of America or the Republic of Panama. The Combined Board shall provide for coordination and cooperation concerning such matters as:

(a) The preparation of contingency plans for the protection and defense of the Canal based upon the cooperative efforts of the armed forces of both Parties;

(b) The planning and conduct of combined military exercises; and

(c) The conduct of United States and Panamanian military operations with respect to the protection and defense of the Canal.

4. The Combined Board shall, at five-year intervals throughout the duration of this Treaty, review the resources being made available by the two Parties for the protection and defense of the Canal. Also, the Combined Board shall make appropriate recommendations to the two Governments respecting projected requirements, the efficient utilization of available resources of the two Parties, and other matters of mutual interest with respect to the protection and defense of the Canal.

5. To the extent possible consistent with its primary responsibility for the protection and defense of the Panama Canal, the United States of America will endeavor to maintain its armed forces in the Republic of Panama in normal times at a level not in excess of that of the armed forces of the United States of America in the territory of the former Canal Zone immediately prior to the entry into force of this Treaty.

ARTICLE V
PRINCIPLE OF NON-INTERVENTION

Employees of the Panama Canal Commission, their dependents and designated contractors of the Panama Canal Commission, who are nationals of the United States of America, shall respect the laws of the Republic of Panama and shall abstain from any activity incompatible with the spirit of this Treaty. Accordingly, they shall abstain from any political activity in the Republic of Panama as well as from any intervention in the internal affairs of the Republic of Panama. The United States of America shall take all measures within its authority to ensure that the provisions of this Article are fulfilled.

ARTICLE VI
PROTECTION OF THE ENVIRONMENT

1. The United States of America and the Republic of Panama commit themselves to implement this Treaty in a manner consistent with the protection of the natural environment of the Republic of Panama. To this end, they shall consult and cooperate with each other in all appropriate ways to ensure that they shall give due regard to the protection and conservation of the environment.

2. A Joint Commission on the Environment shall be established with equal representation from the United States and the Republic of Panama, which shall periodically review the implementation of this Treaty and shall recommend as appropriate to the two Governments ways to avoid or, should this not be possible, to mitigate the adverse environmental impacts which

might result from their respective actions pursuant to the Treaty.

3. The United States of America and the Republic of Panama shall furnish the Joint Commission on the Environment complete information on any action taken in accordance with this Treaty which, in the judgment of both, might have a significant effect on the environment. Such information shall be made available to the Commission as far in advance of the contemplated action as possible to facilitate the study by the Commission of any potential environmental problems and to allow for consideration of the recommendation of the Commission before the contemplated action is carried out.

ARTICLE VII
FLAGS

1. The entire territory of the Republic of Panama, including the areas the use of which the Republic of Panama makes available to the United States of America pursuant to this Treaty and related agreements, shall be under the flag of the Republic of Panama, and consequently such flag always shall occupy the position of honor.

2. The flag of the United States of America may be displayed, together with the flag of the Republic of Panama, at the headquarters of the Panama Canal Commission, at the site of the Combined Board, and as provided in the Agreement in Implementation of Article IV of this Treaty.

3. The flag of the United States of America also may be displayed at other places and on some occasions, as agreed by both Parties.

ARTICLE VIII
PRIVILEGES AND IMMUNITIES

1. The installations owned or used by the agencies or instrumentalities of the United States of America operating in the Republic of Panama pursuant to this Treaty and related agreements, and their official archives and documents, shall be inviolable. The two Parties shall agree on procedures to be followed in the conduct of any criminal investigation at such locations by the Republic of Panama.

2. Agencies and instrumentalities of the Government of the United States of America operating in the Republic of Panama pursuant to this Treaty and related agreements shall be immune from the jurisdiction of the Republic of Panama.

3. In addition to such other privileges and immunities as are afforded to employees of the United States Government and their dependents pursuant to this Treaty, the United States of America may designate up to twenty officials of the Panama Canal Commission who, along with their dependents, shall enjoy the privileges and immunities accorded to diplomatic agents and their dependents under international law and practice. The United States of America shall furnish to the Republic of Panama a list of the names of said officials and their dependents, identifying the positions they occupy in the Government of the United States of America, and shall keep such list current at all times.

ARTICLE IX
APPLICABLE LAWS AND LAW ENFORCEMENT

1. In accordance with the provisions of this Treaty and related agreements, the law of the Republic of Panama shall apply in the areas made available for the use of the United States of America pursuant to this Treaty. The law of the Republic of Panama shall

be applied to matters or events which occurred in the former Canal Zone prior to the entry into force of this Treaty only to the extent specifically provided in prior treaties and agreements.

2. Natural or juridical persons who, on the date of entry into force of this Treaty, are engaged in business or non-profit activities at locations in the former Canal Zone may continue such business or activities at those locations under the same terms and conditions prevailing prior to the entry into force of this Treaty for a thirty-month transition period from its entry into force. The Republic of Panama shall maintain the same operating conditions as those applicable to the aforementioned enterprises prior to the entry into force of this Treaty in order that they may receive licenses to do business in the Republic of Panama subject to their compliance with the requirements of its law. Thereafter, such persons shall receive the same treatment under the law of the Republic of Panama as similar enterprises already established in the rest of the territory of the Republic of Panama without discrimination.

3. The rights of ownership, as recognized by the United States of America, enjoyed by natural or juridical private persons in buildings and other improvements to real property located in the former Canal Zone shall be recognized by the Republic of Panama in conformity with its laws.

4. With respect to buildings and other improvements to real property located in the Canal operating areas, housing areas or other areas subject to the licensing procedure established in Article IV of the Agreement in Implementation of Article III of this Treaty, the owners shall be authorized to continue using the land upon which their property is located in accordance with the procedures established in that Article.

5. With respect to buildings and other improvements to real property located in areas of the former Canal Zone to which the aforesaid licensing procedure is not applicable, or may cease to be applicable during the lifetime or upon termination of this Treaty, the owners may continue to use the land upon which their property is located, subject to the payment of a reasonable charge to the Republic of Panama. Should the Republic of Panama decide to sell such land, the owners of the buildings or other improvements located thereon shall be offered a first option to purchase such land at a reasonable cost. In the case of non-profit enterprises, such as churches and fraternal organizations, the cost of purchase will be nominal in accordance with the prevailing practice in the rest of the territory of the Republic of Panama.

6. If any of the aforementioned persons are required by the Republic of Panama to discontinue their activities or vacate their property for public purposes, they shall be compensated at fair market value by the Republic of Panama.

7. The provisions of paragraphs 2-6 above shall apply to natural or juridical persons who have been engaged in business or non- profit activities at locations in the former Canal Zone for at least six months prior to the date of signature of this Treaty.

8. The Republic of Panama shall not issue, adopt or enforce any law, decree, regulation, or international agreement or take any other action which purports to regulate or would otherwise interfere with the exercise on the part of the United States of America of any right granted under this Treaty or related agreements.

9. Vessels transiting the Canal, and cargo, passengers and crews carried on such vessels shall be exempt from any taxes, fees, or other charges by the Republic of Panama. However, in the event such vessels call at a Panamanian port, they may be assessed charges thereto, such as charges for services provided to the vessel. The Republic of Panama may also require the passengers and crew disembarking from such vessels to pay such taxes, fees and charges as are established under Panamanian law for persons entering its territory. Such taxes, fees and charges shall be assessed on a nondiscriminatory basis.

10. The United States of America and the Republic of Panama will cooperate in taking such steps as may from time to time be necessary to guarantee the security of the Panama Canal Commission, its property, its employees and their dependents, and their property, the Forces of the United States of America and the members thereof, the civilian component of the United States Forces, the dependents of members of the Forces and civilian component, and their property, and the contractors of the Panama Canal Commission and of the United States Forces, their dependents, and their property. The Republic of Panama will seek from its Legislative Branch such legislation as may be needed to carry out the foregoing purposes and to punish any offenders.

11. The Parties shall conclude an agreement whereby nationals of either State, who are sentenced by the courts of the other State, and who are not domiciled therein, may elect to serve their sentences in their State of nationality.

ARTICLE X
EMPLOYMENT WITH
THE PANAMA CANAL COMMISSION

1. In exercising its rights and fulfilling its responsibilities as the employer, the United States of America shall establish employment and labor regulations which shall contain the terms, conditions and prerequisites for all categories of employees of the Panama Canal Commission. These regulations shall be provided to the Republic of Panama prior to their entry into force.

2. (a) The regulations shall establish a system of preference when hiring employees, for Panamanian applicants possessing the skills and qualifications required for employment by the Panama Canal Commission. The United States of America shall endeavor to ensure that the number of Panamanian nationals employed by the Panama Canal Commission in relation to the total number of its employees will conform to the proportion established for foreign enterprises under the law of the Republic of Panama.

(b) The terms and conditions of employment to be established will in general be no less favorable to persons already employed by the Panama Canal Company or Canal Zone Government prior to the entry into force of this Treaty, than those in effect immediately prior to that date.

3. (a) The United States of America shall establish an employment policy for the Panama Canal Commission that shall generally limit the recruitment of personnel outside the Republic of Panama to persons possessing requisite skills and qualifications which are not available in the Republic of Panama.

(b) The United States of America will establish training programs for Panamanian employees and apprentices in order to increase the number of Panamanian nationals qualified to assume positions with the Panama Canal Commission, as positions become available.

(c) Within five years from the entry into force of this Treaty, the number of United States nationals employed by the Panama Canal Commission who were previously employed by the Panama Canal Company shall be at least twenty percent less than the total number of United States nationals working for the Panama Canal Company immediately prior to the entry into force of this Treaty.

(d) The United States of America shall periodically inform the Republic of Panama, through the Coordinating Committee, established pursuant to the Agreement in Implementation of Article III of this Treaty, of available positions within the Panama Canal Commission. The Republic of Panama shall similarly provide the United States of America any information it may have as to the availability of Panamanian nationals claiming to have skills and qualifications that might be required by the Panama Canal Commission, in order that the United States of America may take this information into account.

4. The United States of America will establish qualification standards for skills, training, and experience required by the Panama Canal Commission. In establishing such standards, to the extent they include a requirement for a professional license, the United States of America, without prejudice to its right to require additional professional skills and qualifications, shall recognize the professional licenses issued by the Republic of Panama.

5. The United States of America shall establish a policy for the periodic rotation, at a maximum of every five years, of United States citizen employees and other non-Panamanian employees, hired after the entry into force of this Treaty. It is recognized that certain exceptions to the said policy of rotation may be made for sound administrative reasons, such as in the case of employees holding positions requiring certain non-transferable or non-recruitable skills.

6. With regard to wages and fringe benefits, there shall be no discrimination on the basis of nationality, sex, or race. Payments by the Panama Canal Commission of additional remuneration, or the provision of other benefits, such as home leave benefits, to United States nationals employed prior to entry into force of this Treaty, or to persons of any nationality, including Panamanian nationals who are thereafter recruited outside of the Republic of Panama and who change their place of residence, shall not be considered to be discrimination for the purpose of this paragraph.

7. Persons employed by the Panama Canal Commission or Canal Zone Government prior to the entry into force of this Treaty, who are displaced from their employment as a result of the discontinuance by the United States of America of certain activities pursuant to this Treaty, will be placed by the United States of America, to the maximum extent feasible, in other appropriate jobs with the Government of the United States in accordance with United States Civil Service regulations. For such persons who are not United States nationals, placement efforts will be confined to United States Government activities located within the Republic of Panama.

Likewise, persons previously employed in activities for which the Republic of Panama assumes responsibility as a result of this Treaty will be continued in their employment to the maximum extent feasible by the Republic of Panama. The Republic of Panama shall, to the maximum extent feasible, ensure that the terms and conditions of employment applicable to personnel employed in the activities for which it assumed responsibility are not less favorable than those in effect immediately prior to the entry into force of this Treaty. Non-United States nationals employed by the Panama Canal Company or Canal Zone Gov-

ernment prior to the entry into force of this Treaty who are involuntarily separated from their positions because of the discontinuance of an activity by reason of this Treaty, who are not entitled to an immediate annuity under the United States Civil Service Retirement System, and for whom continued employment in the Republic of Panama by the Government of the United States of America is not practicable, will be provided special job placement assistance by the Republic of Panama for employment in positions for which they may be qualified by experience and training.

8. The Parties agree to establish a system whereby the Panama Canal Commission may, if deemed mutually convenient or desirable by the two Parties, assign certain employees of the Panama Canal Commission, for a limited period of time, to assist in the operation of activities transferred to the responsibility of the Republic of Panama as a result of this Treaty or related agreements. The salaries and other costs of employment of any such persons assigned to provide such assistance shall be reimbursed to the United States of America by the Republic of Panama.

9. (a) The right of employees to negotiate collective contracts with the Panama Canal Commission is recognized. Labor relations with employees of the Panama Canal Commission shall be conducted in accordance with forms of collective bargaining established by the United States of America after consultation with employee unions.

(b) Employee unions shall have the right to affiliate with international labor organizations.

10. The United States of America will provide an appropriate early optional retirement program for all persons employed by the Panama Canal Company or Canal Zone Government immediately prior to the entry into force of this Treaty. In this regard, taking into account the unique circumstances created by the provisions of this Treaty, including its duration, and their effect upon such employees, the United States of America shall, with respect to them:

(a) determine that conditions exist which invoke applicable United States law permitting early retirement annuities and apply such law for a substantial period of the duration of the treaty;

(b) seek special legislation to provide more liberal entitlement to, and calculation of, retirement annuities than is currently provided for by law.

ARTICLE XI
PROVISIONS FOR THE TRANSITION PERIOD

1. The Republic of Panama shall reassume plenary jurisdiction over the former Canal Zone upon entry into force of this Treaty and in accordance with its terms. In order to provide for an orderly transition to the full application of the jurisdictional arrangements established by this Treaty and related agreements, the provisions of this Article shall become applicable upon the date this Treaty enters into force, and shall remain in effect for thirty calendar months. The authority granted in this Article to the United States of America for this transition period shall supplement, and is not intended to limit, the full application and effect of the rights and authority granted to the United States of America elsewhere in this Treaty and in related agreements.

2. During this transition period, the criminal and civil laws of the United States of America shall apply concurrently with

those of the Republic of Panama in certain of the areas and installations made available for the use of the United States of America pursuant to this Treaty, in accordance with the following provisions:

(a) The Republic of Panama permits the authorities of the United States of America to have the primary right to exercise criminal jurisdiction over United States citizen employees of the Panama Canal Commission and their dependents, and members of the United States Forces and civilian component and their dependents, in the following cases:

(i) for any offense committed during the transition period within such areas and installations, and

(ii) for any offense committed prior to that period in the former Canal Zone.

The Republic of Panama shall have the primary right to exercise jurisdiction over all other offenses committed by such persons, except as otherwise agreed.

(b) Either Party may waive its primary right to exercise jurisdiction in a specific case or category of cases.

3. The United States of America shall retain the right to exercise jurisdiction in criminal cases relating to offenses committed prior to the entry into force of this Treaty in violation of the laws applicable in the former Canal Zone.

4. For the transition period, the United States of America shall retain police authority and maintain a police force in the aforementioned areas and installations. In such areas, the police authorities of the United States of America may take into custody any person not subject to their primary jurisdiction if such person is believed to have committed or to be committing an offense against applicable laws or regulations, and shall promptly transfer custody to the police authorities of the Republic of Panama. The United States of America and the Republic of Panama shall establish joint police patrols in agreed areas. Any arrests conducted by a joint patrol shall be the responsibility of the patrol member or members representing the Party having primary jurisdiction over the person or persons arrested.

5. The courts of the United States of America and related personnel, functioning in the former Canal Zone immediately prior to the entry into force of this Treaty, may continue to function during the transition period for the judicial enforcement of the jurisdiction to be exercised by the United States of America in accordance with this Article.

6. In civil cases, the civilian courts of the United States of America in the Republic of Panama shall have no jurisdiction over new cases of a private civil nature, but shall retain full jurisdiction during the transition period to dispose of any civil cases, including admiralty cases, already instituted and pending before the courts prior to the entry into force of this Treaty.

7. The laws, regulations, and administrative authority of the United States of America applicable in the former Canal Zone immediately prior to the entry into force of this Treaty shall, to the extent not inconsistent with this Treaty and related agreements, continue in force for the purpose of the exercise by the United States of America of law enforcement and judicial jurisdiction only during the transition period. The United States of America may amend, repeal or otherwise change such laws, regulations and administrative authority. The two Parties shall consult concerning procedural and substantive matters relative to the implementation of this Article, including the disposition of cases pending at the end of the transition period and, in this respect, may enter into appropriate agreements by an exchange of notes or other instrument.

8. During this transition period, the United States of America may continue to incarcerate individuals in the areas and installations made available for the use of the United States of America by the Republic of Panama pursuant to this Treaty and related agreements, or to transfer them to penal facilities in the United States of America to serve their sentences.

ARTICLE XII
A SEA-LEVEL CANAL OR A THIRD LANE OF LOCKS

1. The United States of America and the Republic of Panama recognize that a sea-level canal may be important for international navigation in the future. Consequently, during the duration of this Treaty, both Parties commit themselves to study jointly the feasibility of a sea-level canal in the Republic of Panama, and in the event they determine that such a waterway is necessary, they shall negotiate terms, agreeable to both Parties, for its construction.

2. The United States of America and the Republic of Panama agree on the following:

(a) No new interoceanic canal shall be constructed in the territory of the Republic of Panama during the duration of this Treaty, except in accordance with the provisions of this Treaty, or as the two Parties may otherwise agree; and

(b) During the duration of this Treaty, the United States of America shall not negotiate with third States for the right to construct an interoceanic canal on any other route in the Western Hemisphere, except as the two Parties may otherwise agree.

3. The Republic of Panama grants to the United States of America the right to add a third lane of locks to the existing Panama Canal. This right may be exercised at any time during the duration of this Treaty, provided that the United States of America has delivered to the Republic of Panama copies of the plans for such construction.

4. In the event the United States of America exercises the right granted in paragraph 3 above, it may use for that purpose, in addition to the areas otherwise made available to the United States of America pursuant to this Treaty, such other areas as the two Parties may agree upon. The terms and conditions applicable to Canal operating areas made available by the Republic of Panama for the use of the United States of America pursuant to Article III of this Treaty shall apply in a similar manner to such additional areas.

5. In the construction of the aforesaid works, the United States of America shall not use nuclear excavation techniques without the previous consent of the Republic of Panama.

ARTICLE XIII
PROPERTY TRANSFER AND ECONOMIC PARTICIPATION BY THE REPUBLIC OF PANAMA

1. Upon termination of this Treaty, the Republic of Panama shall assume total responsibility for the management, operation, and maintenance of the Panama Canal, which shall be turned over in operating condition and free of liens and debts, except as the two Parties may otherwise agree.

2. The United States of America transfers, without charge, to the Republic of Panama all right, title and interest the United States of America may have with respect to all real property, including non-removable improvements thereon, as set forth below:

(a) Upon the entry into force of this Treaty, the Panama Railroad and such property that was located in the former Canal Zone but that is not within the land and water areas the use of which is made available to the United States of America pursuant to this Treaty. However, it is agreed that the transfer on such date shall not include buildings and other facilities, except housing, the use of which is retained by the United States of America pursuant to this Treaty and related agreements, outside such areas;

(b) Such property located in an area or a portion thereof at such time as the use by the United States of America of such area or portion thereof ceases pursuant to agreement between the two Parties.

(c) Housing units made available for occupancy by members of the Armed Forces of the Republic of Panama in accordance with paragraph 5(b) of Annex B to the Agreement in Implementation of Article IV of this Treaty at such time as such units are made available to the Republic of Panama.

(d) Upon termination of this Treaty, all real property and non-removable improvements that were used by the United States of America for the purposes of this Treaty and related agreements and equipment related to the management, operation and maintenance of the Canal remaining in the Republic of Panama.

3. The Republic of Panama agrees to hold the United States of America harmless with respect to any claims which may be made by third parties relating to rights, title and interest in such property.

4. The Republic of Panama shall receive, in addition, from the Panama Canal Commission a just and equitable return on the national resources which it has dedicated to the efficient management, operation, maintenance, protection and defense of the Panama Canal, in accordance with the following:

(a) An annual amount to be paid out of Canal operating revenues computed at a rate of thirty hundredths of a United States dollar (US$0.30) per Panama Canal net ton, or its equivalency, for each vessel transiting the Canal after the entry into force of this Treaty, for which tolls are charged. The rate of thirty hundredths of a United States dollar (US$0.30) per Panama Canal net ton, or its equivalency, will be adjusted to reflect changes in the United States wholesale price index for total manufactured goods during biennial periods. The first adjustment shall take place five years after entry into force of this Treaty, taking into account the changes that occurred in such price index during the preceding two years. Thereafter, successive adjustments shall take place at the end of each biennial period. If the United States of America should decide that another indexing method is preferable, such method shall be proposed to the Republic of Panama and applied if mutually agreed.

(b) A fixed annuity of ten million United States dollars (US$10,000,000) to be paid out of Canal operating revenues. This amount shall constitute a fixed expense of the Panama Canal Commission.

(c) An annual amount of up to ten million United States dollars (US$10,000,000) per year, to be paid out of Canal operating revenues to the extent that such revenues exceed expenditures of the Panama Canal Commission including amounts paid pursuant to this Treaty. In the event Canal operating revenues in any year do not produce a surplus sufficient to cover this pay-

ment, the unpaid balance shall be paid from operating surpluses in future years in a manner to be mutually agreed.

ARTICLE XIV
SETTLEMENT OF DISPUTES

In the event that any question should arise between the Parties concerning the interpretation of this Treaty or related agreements, they shall make every effort to resolve the matter through consultation in the appropriate committees established pursuant to this Treaty and related agreements, or, if appropriate, through diplomatic channels. In the event the Parties are unable to resolve a particular matter through such means, they may, in appropriate cases, agree to submit the matter to conciliation, mediation, arbitration, or such other procedure for the peaceful settlement of the dispute as they may mutually deem appropriate.

DONE at Washington, this 7th day of September, 1977, in duplicate, in the English and Spanish languages, both texts being equally authentic.

Annex
Procedures for the Cessation or Transfer of Activities Carried Out by the Panama Canal Company and the Canal Zone Government and Illustrative List of the Functions That May Be Performed by the Panama Canal Commission

1. The laws of the Republic of Panama shall regulate the exercise of private economic activities within the areas made available by the Republic of Panama for the use of the United States of America pursuant to this Treaty. Natural or juridical persons who, at least six months prior to the date of signature of this Treaty, were legally established and engaged in the exercise of economic activities in accordance with the provisions of paragraphs 2-7 of Article IX of this Treaty.

2. The Panama Canal Commission shall not perform governmental or commercial functions as stipulated in paragraph 4 of this Annex, provided, however, that this shall not be deemed to limit in any way the right of the United States of America to perform those functions that may be necessary for the efficient management, operation and maintenance of the Canal.

3. It is understood that the Panama Canal Commission, in the exercise of the rights of the United States of America with respect to the management, operation and maintenance of the Canal, may perform functions such as are set forth below by way of illustration:

a. Management of the Canal enterprise.

b. Aids to navigation in Canal waters and in proximity thereto.

c. Control of vessel movement.

d. Operation and maintenance of the locks.

e. Tug service for the transit of vessels and dredging for the piers and docks of the Panama Canal Commission.

f. Control of the water levels in Gatun, Alajuela (Madden), and Miraflores Lakes.

g. Non-commercial transportation services in Canal waters.

h. Meteorological and hydrographic services.

i. Admeasurement.

j. Non-commercial motor transport and maintenance.

k. Industrial security through the use of watchmen.

l. Procurement and warehousing.

m. Telecommunications.

n. Protection of the environment by preventing and controlling the spillage of oil and substances harmful to human or animal life and of the ecological equilibrium in areas used in operation of the Canal and the anchorages.

o. Non-commercial vessel repair.

p. Air conditioning services in Canal installations.

q. Industrial sanitation and health services.

r. Engineering design, construction and maintenance of Panama Canal Commission installations.

s. Dredging of the Canal channel, terminal ports and adjacent waters.

t. Control of the banks and stabilizing of the slopes of the Canal.

u. Non-commercial handling of cargo on the piers and docks of the Panama Canal Commission.

v. Maintenance of public areas of the Panama Canal Commission, such as parks and gardens.

w. Generation of electric power.

x. Purification and supply of water.

y. Marine salvage in Canal waters.

z. Such other functions as may be necessary or appropriate to carry out, in conformity with this Treaty and related agreements, the rights and responsibilities of the United States of America with respect to the management, operation and maintenance of the Panama Canal.

4. The following activities and operations carried out by the Panama Canal Company and the Canal Zone Government shall not be carried out by the Panama Canal Commission, effective upon the dates indicated herein:

(a) Upon the date of entry into force of this Treaty:

(i) Wholesale and retail sales, including those through commissaries, food stores, department stores, optical shops and pastry shops;

(ii) The production of food and drink, including milk products and bakery products;

(iii) The operation of public restaurants and cafeterias and the sale of articles through vending machines;

(iv) The operation of movie theaters, bowling alleys, pool rooms and other recreational and amusement facilities for the use of which a charge is payable;

(v) The operation of laundry and dry cleaning plants other than those operated for official use;

(vi) The repair and service of privately owned automobiles or the sale of petroleum or lubricants thereto, including the operation of gasoline stations, repair garages and tire repair and recapping facilities, and the repair and service of other privately owned property, including appliances, electronic devices, boats, motors, and furniture;

(vii) The operation of cold storage and freezer plants other than those operated for official use;

(viii) The operation of freight houses other than those operated for official use;

(ix) The operation of commercial services to and supply of privately owned and operated vessels, including the constitution of vessels, the sale of petroleum and lubricants and the provision of water, tug services not related to the Canal or other United States Government operations, and repair of such vessels, except in situations where repairs may be necessary to remove disabled vessels from the Canal;

(x) Printing services other than for official use;

(xi) Maritime transportation for the use of the general public;

(xii) Health and medical services provided to individuals, including hospitals, leprosariums, veterinary, mortuary and cemetery services;

(xiii) Educational services not for professional training, including schools and libraries;

(xiv) Postal services;

(xv) Immigration, customs and quarantine controls, except those measures necessary to ensure the sanitation of the Canal;

(xvi) Commercial pier and dock services, such as the handling of cargo and passengers; and

(xvii) Any other commercial activity of a similar nature, not related to the management, operation or maintenance of the Canal.

(b) Within thirty calendar months from the date of entry into force of this Treaty, governmental services such as:

(i) Police;

(ii) Courts; and

(iii) Prison system.

5. (a) With respect to those activities or functions described in paragraph 4 above, or otherwise agreed upon by the two Parties, which are to be assumed by the Government of the Republic of Panama or by private persons subject to its authority, the two Parties shall consult prior to the discontinuance of such activities or functions by the Panama Canal Commission to develop appropriate arrangements for the orderly transfer and continued efficient operation or conduct thereof.

(b) In the event that appropriate arrangements cannot be arrived at to ensure the continued performance of a particular activity or function described in paragraph 4 above which is necessary to the efficient management, operation or maintenance of the Canal, the Panama Canal Commission may, to the extent consistent with the other provisions of this Treaty and related agreements, continue to perform such activity or function until such arrangements can be made.

The United States Senate ratified the treaty in 1978 after one of the more heated, and certainly one of the longest, debates in American history. The Senate added these caveats:

(a) RESERVATIONS:

(1) Pursuant to its adherence to the principle of non-intervention, any action taken by the United States of America in the exercise of its rights to assure that the Panama Canal shall remain open, neutral, secure, and accessible, pursuant to the provisions of the Panama Canal Treaty, the Treaty Concerning the Permanent Neutrality and Operation of the Panama Canal, and the resolutions of ratification thereto, shall be only for the purpose of assuring that the Canal shall remain open, neutral, secure, and accessible, and shall not have as its purpose or be interpreted as a right of intervention in the internal affairs of the Republic of

Panama or interference with its political independence or sovereign integrity.

(2) The instruments of ratification of the Panama Canal Treaty to be exchanged by the United States of America and the Republic of Panama shall each include provisions whereby each Party agrees to waive its rights and release the other Party from its obligations under paragraph 2 of Article XII of the Treaty.

(3) Notwithstanding any provision of the Treaty, no funds may be drawn from the Treasury of the United States of America for payments under paragraph 4 of Article XIII without statutory authorization.

(4) Any accumulated unpaid balance under paragraph 4(c) of Article XIII of the Treaty at the date of termination of the Treaty shall be payable only to the extent of any operating surplus in the last year of the duration of the Treaty, and nothing in such paragraph may be constructed as obligating the United States of America to pay, after the date of the termination of the Treaty, any such unpaid balance which shall have accrued before such date.

(5) Exchange of the instruments of ratification of the Panama Canal Treaty and of the Treaty Concerning the Permanent Neutrality and Operation of the Panama Canal shall not be effective earlier than March 31, 1979, and such Treaties shall not enter into force prior to October 1, 1979, unless legislation necessary to implement the provisions of the Panama Canal Treaty shall have been enacted by the Congress of the United States of America before March 31, 1979.

(6) After the date of entry into force of the Treaty, the Panama Canal Commission shall, unless otherwise provided by legislation enacted by the Congress of the United States of America, be obligated to reimburse the Treasury of the United States of America, as nearly as possible, for the interest cost of the funds or other assets directly invested in the Commission by the Government of the United States of America and for the interest cost of the funds or other assets directly invested in the predecessor Panama Canal Company by the Government of the United States of America and not reimbursed before the date of entry into force of the Treaty. Such reimbursement for such interest costs shall be made at a rate determined by the Secretary of the Treasury of the United States of America and at annual intervals to the extent earned, and if not earned, shall be made from subsequent earnings. For purposes of this reservation, the phrase "funds or other assets directly invested" shall have the same meaning as the phrase "net direct investment" has under section 62 of title 2 of the Canal Zone Code.

(b) UNDERSTANDINGS:

(1) Before the first day of the three-year period beginning on the date of entry into force of the Treaty and before each three-year period following thereafter, the two Parties shall agree upon the specific levels and quality of services, as are referred to in paragraph 5 of Article III of the Treaty, to be provided during the following three-year period and, except for the first three-year period, on the reimbursement to be made for the costs of such services, such services to be limited to such as are essential to the effective functioning of the Canal operating areas and the housing areas referred to in paragraph 5 of Article III. If payments made under paragraph 5 of Article III for the preceding three-year period, including the initial three-year period, exceed or are less than the actual costs to the Republic of Panama for supplying, during such period, the specific levels and quality of services agreed upon, then the Panama Canal Commission shall deduct from or add to the payment required to be made to the Republic of Panama for each of the following three years one-third of such excess or deficit, as the case may be. There shall be an independent and binding audit, conducted by an auditor mutually selected by both Parties, of any costs of services disputed by the two Parties pursuant to the reexamination of such costs provided for in this understanding.

(2) Nothing in paragraph 3, 4, or 5 of Article IV of the Treaty may be construed to limit either the provisions of the first paragraph of Article IV providing that each Party shall act, in accordance with its constitutional processes, to meet danger threatening the security of the Panama Canal, or the provisions of paragraph 2 of Article IV providing that the United States of America shall have primary responsibility to protect and defend the Canal for the duration of the Treaty.

(3) Nothing in paragraph 4(c) of Article XIII of the Treaty shall be construed to limit the authority of the United States of America, through the United States Government agency called the Panama Canal Commission, to make such financial decisions and incur such expenses as are reasonable and necessary for the management, operation, and maintenance of the Panama Canal. In addition, toll rates established pursuant to paragraph 2(d) of Article III need not be set at levels designed to produce revenues to cover the payment to the Republic of Panama described in paragraph 4(c) of Article XIII.

(4) Any agreement concluded pursuant to paragraph II of Article IX of the Treaty with respect to the transfer of prisoners shall be concluded in accordance with the constitutional processes of both Parties.

(5) Nothing in the Treaty, in the Annex or Agreed Minute relating to the Treaty, or in any other agreement relating to the Treaty obligates the United States of America to provide any economic assistance, military grant assistance, security supporting assistance, foreign military sales credits, or international military education and training to the Republic of Panama.

(6) The President shall include all reservations and understandings incorporated by the Senate in this resolution of ratification in the instrument of ratification to be exchanged with the Government of the Republic of Panama.

The 1977 treaty was supplemented by a separate, but closely related, neutrality treaty, which—unlike the main treaty—had no termination date. Under the neutrality treaty, both countries guaranteed the permanent neutrality of the canal, with nondiscriminatory tolls and complete access for all nations. U.S. warships—and Panamanian warships, too, should Panama ever need them—were entitled to first call on the use of the canal.

Treaty Concerning the Permanent Neutrality and Operation of the Panama Canal

The United States of America and the Republic of Panama have agreed upon the following:

ARTICLE I

The Republic of Panama declares that the Canal, as an international transit waterway, shall be permanently neutral in accordance with the regime established in this Treaty. The same regime of neutrality shall apply to any other international waterway that may be built either partially or wholly in the territory of the Republic of Panama.

ARTICLE II

The Republic of Panama declares the neutrality of the Canal in order that both in time of peace and in time of war it shall remain secure and open to peaceful transit by the vessels of all nations on terms of entire equality, so that there will be no discrimination against any nation, or its citizens or subjects, concerning the conditions or charges of transit, or for any other reason, and so that the Canal, and therefore the Isthmus of Panama, shall not be the target of reprisals in any armed conflict between other nations of the world. The foregoing shall be subject to the following requirements:

(a) Payment of tolls and other charges for transit and ancillary services, provided they have been fixed in conformity with the provisions of Article III (c);

(b) Compliance with applicable rules and regulations, provided such rules and regulations are applied in conformity with the provisions of Article III;

(c) The requirement that transiting vessels commit no acts of hostility while in the Canal; and

(d) Such other conditions and restrictions as are established by this Treaty.

ARTICLE III

1. For purposes of the security, efficiency and proper maintenance of the Canal the following rules shall apply:

(a) The Canal shall be operated efficiently in accordance with conditions of transit through the Canal, and rules and regulations that shall be just, equitable and reasonable, and limited to those necessary for safe navigation and efficient, sanitary operation of the Canal;

(b) Ancillary services necessary for transit through the Canal shall be provided;

(c) Tolls and other charges for transit and ancillary services shall be just, reasonable, equitable and consistent with the principles of international law;

(d) As a pre-condition of transit, vessels may be required to establish clearly the financial responsibility and guarantees for payment of reasonable and adequate indemnification, consistent with international practice and standards, for damages resulting from acts or omissions of such vessels when passing through the Canal. In the case of vessels owned or operated by a State or for which it has acknowledged responsibility, a certification by that State that it shall observe its obligations under international law to pay for damages resulting from the act or omission of such vessels when passing through the Canal shall be deemed sufficient to establish such financial responsibility;

(e) Vessels of war and auxiliary vessels of all nations shall at all times be entitled to transit the Canal, irrespective of their internal operation, means of propulsion, origin, destination or armament, without being subjected, as a condition of transit, to inspection, search for surveillance. However, such vessels may be required to certify that they have complied with all applicable health, sanitation and quarantine regulations. In addition, such vessels shall be entitled to refuse to disclose their internal operation, origin, armament, cargo or destination. However, auxiliary vessels may be required to present written assurances, certified by an official at a high level of the government of the State requesting the exemption, that they are owned or operated by that government and in this case are being used only on government non-commercial service.

2. For the purposes of this Treaty, the terms "Canal," "vessel of war," "auxiliary vessel," "internal operation," "armament" and "inspection" shall have the meanings assigned them in Annex A to this Treaty.

ARTICLE IV

The United States of America and the Republic of Panama agree to maintain the regime of neutrality established in this Treaty, which shall be maintained in order that the Canal shall remain permanently neutral, notwithstanding the termination of any other treaties entered into by the two Contracting Parties.

ARTICLE V

After the termination of the Panama Canal Treaty, only the Republic of Panama shall operate the Canal and maintain military forces, defense sites and military installations within its national territory.

ARTICLE VI

1. In recognition of the important contributions of the United States of America and of the Republic of Panama to the construction, operation, maintenance, and protection and defense of the Canal, vessels of war

and auxiliary vessels of those nations shall, notwithstanding any other provisions of this Treaty, be entitled to transit the Canal irrespective of their internal operation, means of propulsion, origin, destination, armament or cargo carried. Such vessels of war and auxiliary vessels will be entitled to transit the Canal expeditiously.

2. The United States of America, so long as it has responsibility for the operation of the Canal, may continue to provide the Republic of Colombia toll-free transit through the Canal for its troops, vessels and materials of war. Thereafter, the Republic of Panama may provide the Republic of Colombia and the Republic of Costa Rica with the right of toll-free transit.

ARTICLE VII

1. The United States of America and the Republic of Panama shall jointly sponsor a resolution in the Organization of American States opening to accession by all nations of the world the Protocol to this Treaty whereby all the signatories will adhere to the objective of this Treaty, agreeing to respect the regime of neutrality set forth herein.

2. The Organization of American States shall act as the depositary for this Treaty and related instruments.

ARTICLE VIII

This Treaty shall be subject to ratification in accordance with the constitutional procedures of the two Parties. The instruments of ratification of this Treaty shall be exchanged at Panama at the same time as the instruments of ratification of the Panama Canal Treaty, signed this date, are exchanged. This Treaty shall enter into force, simultaneously with the Panama Canal Treaty, six calendar months from the date of the exchange of the instruments of ratification.

DONE at Washington, this 7th day of September, 1977, in the English and Spanish languages, both texts being equally authentic.

Annex A

1. "Canal" includes the existing Panama Canal, the entrances thereto and the territorial seas of the Republic of Panama adjacent thereto, as defined on the map annexed hereto (Annex B), and any other interoceanic waterway in which the United States of America is a participant or in which the United States of America has participated in connection with the construction or financing, that may be operated wholly or partially within the territory of the Republic of Panama, the entrances thereto and the territorial seas adjacent thereto.

2. "Vessel of war" means a ship belonging to the naval forces of a State, and bearing the external marks distinguishing warships of its nationality, under the command of an officer duly commissioned by the government and whose name appears in the Navy List, and manned by a crew which is under regular naval discipline.

3. "Auxiliary vessel" means any ship, not a vessel of war, that is owned or operated by a State and used, for the time being, exclusively on government non-commercial service.

4. "Internal operation" encompasses all machinery and propulsion systems, as well as the management and control of the vessel, including its crew. It does not include the measures necessary to transit vessels under the control of pilots while such vessels are in the Canal.

5. "Armament" means arms, ammunition, implements of war and other equipment of a vessel which possesses characteristics appropriate for use for warlike purposes.

6. "Inspection" includes on-board examination of vessel structure, cargo, armament and internal operation. It does not include those measures strictly necessary for admeasurement, nor those measures strictly necessary to assure safe, sanitary transit and navigation, including examination of deck and visual navigation equipment, nor in the case of live cargoes, such as cattle or other livestock, that may carry communicable diseases, those measures necessary to assure that health and sanitation requirements are satisfied.

The neutrality treaty was debated in the U.S. Senate along with the Panama Canal Treaty and was ratified with the latter. As with the main treaty, however, the Senate added caveats:

United States Senate Modifications (Incorporated into the June 1978 Instruments of Ratification)

(A) AMENDMENTS

(1) At the end of Article IV, insert the following:

"A correct and authoritative statement of certain rights and duties of the Parties under the foregoing is contained in the Statement of Understanding issued by the Government of the United States of America on October 14, 1977, and by the Government of the Republic of Panama on October 18, 1977, which is hereby incorporated as an integral part of this Treaty, as follows:

"'Under the Treaty Concerning the Permanent Neutrality and Operation of the Panama Canal (the Neutrality Treaty), Panama and the United States have the responsibility to assure that the Panama Canal will remain open and secure to ships of all nations. The correct interpretation of this principle is that each of the two countries shall, in accordance with their respective constitutional processes, defend the Canal against any threat to the regime of neutrality, and consequently shall have the right to act against any aggression or threat directed against the Canal or against the peaceful transit of vessels through the Canal.

"This does not mean, nor shall it be interpreted as, a right of intervention of the United States in the internal affairs of Panama. Any United States action will be directed at insuring that the Canal will remain open, secure, and accessible, and it shall never be directed against the territorial integrity or political independence of Panama.'"

(2) At the end of the first paragraph of Article VI, insert the following:

"In accordance with the Statement of Understanding mentioned in Article IV above: The Neutrality Treaty provides that the vessels of war and auxiliary vessels of the United States and Panama will be entitled to transit the Canal expeditiously. This is intended, and it shall so be interpreted, to assure the transit of such vessels through the Canal as quickly as possible, without any impediment, with expedited treatment, and in case of need or emergency, to go to the head of the line of vessels in order to transit the Canal rapidly.'"

(B) CONDITIONS:

(1) Notwithstanding the provisions of Article V or any other provision of the Treaty, if the Canal is closed, or its operations are interfered with, the United States of America and the Republic of Panama shall each independently have the right to take such steps as each deems necessary, in accordance with its constitutional processes, including the use of military force in the Republic of Panama, to reopen the Canal or restore the operations of the Canal, as the case may be.

(2) The instruments of ratification of the Treaty shall be exchanged only upon the conclusion of a Protocol of Exchange, to be signed by authorized representatives of both Governments, which shall constitute an integral part of the Treaty documents and which shall include the following:

"Nothing in the Treaty shall preclude the Republic of Panama and the United States of America from making, in accordance with their respective constitutional processes, any agreement or arrangement between the two countries to facilitate performance at any time after December 31, 1999, of their responsibilities to maintain the regime of neutrality established in the Treaty, including agreements or arrangements for the stationing of any United States military forces or the maintenance of defense sites after that date in the Republic of Panama that the Republic of Panama and the United States of America may deem necessary or appropriate."

(C) RESERVATIONS:

(1) Before the date of entry into force of the Treaty, the two Parties shall begin to negotiate for an agreement under which the American Battle Monuments Commission would, upon the date of entry into force of such agreement and thereafter, administer, free of all taxes and other charges and without compensation to the Republic of Panama and in accordance with the practices, privileges, and immunities associated with the administration of cemeteries outside the United States of America by the American Battle Monuments Commission, including the display of the flag of the United States of America, such part of Corozal Cemetery in the former Canal Zone as encompasses the remains of citizens of the United States of America.

(2) The flag of the United States of America may be displayed, pursuant to the provisions of paragraph 3 of Article VII of the Panama Canal Treaty, at such part of Corozal Cemetery in the former Canal Zone as encompasses the remains of citizens of the United States of America.

(3) The President—

(a) shall have announced, before the date of entry into force of the Treaty, his intention to transfer, consistent with an agreement with the Republic of Panama, and before the date of termination of the Panama Canal Treaty, to the American Battle Monuments Commission the administration of such part of Corozal Cemetery as encompasses the remains of citizens of the United States of America; and

(b) shall have announced, immediately after the date of exchange of instruments of ratification, plans, to be carried out at the expense of the Government of the United States of America, for—

(i) removing, before the date of entry into force of the Treaty, the remains of citizens of the United States of America from Mount Hope Cemetery to such part of Corozal Cemetery as encompasses such remains, except that the remains of any citizen whose next of kin objects in writing to the Secretary of the Army not later than three months after the date of exchange of the instruments of ratification of the Treaty shall not be removed; and

(ii) transporting to the United States of America for reinterment, if the next of kin so requests, not later than thirty months after the date of entry into force of the Treaty, any such remains encompassed by Corozal Cemetery and, before the date of entry into force of the Treaty, any remains removed from Mount Hope Cemetery pursuant to subclause (i); and

(c) shall have fully advised, before the date of entry into force of the Treaty, the next of kin objecting under clause (b) (i) of all available options and their implications.

(4) To carry out the purposes of Article III of the Treaty of assuring the security, efficiency, and proper maintenance of the Panama Canal, the United States of America and the Republic of Panama, during their respective periods of responsibility for Canal operation and maintenance, shall, unless the amount of the operating revenues of the Canal exceeds the amount needed to carry out the purposes of such Article, use such revenues of the Canal only for purposes consistent with the purposes of Article III.

(D) UNDERSTANDING:

(1) Paragraph 1 (c) of Article III of the Treaty shall be construed as requiring, before any adjustment in tolls for use of the Canal, that the effects of any such toll adjustment on the trade patterns of the two Parties shall be given full consideration, including consideration of the following factors in a manner consistent with the regime of neutrality:

(a) the costs of operating and maintaining the Panama Canal;

(b) the competitive position of the use of the Canal in relation to other means of transportation;

(c) the interests of both Parties in maintaining their domestic fleets;

(d) the impact of such an adjustment on the various geographic areas of each of the two Parties; and

(e) the interests of both Parties in maximizing their international commerce. The United States of America and the Republic of Panama shall cooperate in exchanging information necessary for the consideration of such factors.

(2) The agreement 'to maintain the regime of neutrality established in this Treaty' in Article IV of the Treaty means that either of the two Parties to the Treaty may, in accordance with its constitutional processes, take unilateral action to defend the Panama Canal against any threat, as determined by the Party taking such action.

(3) The determination of 'need or emergency' for the purpose of any vessel of war or auxiliary vessel of the United States of America or the Republic of Panama going to the head of the line of vessels in order to transit the Panama Canal rapidly shall be made by the nation operating such vessel.

(4) Nothing in the Treaty, in Annex A or B thereto, in the Protocol relating to the Treaty, or in any other agreement relating to the Treaty, obligates the United States of America to provide any economic assistance, military grant assistance, security supporting assistance, foreign military sales credits, or international military education and training to the Republic of Panama.

(5) The President shall include all amendments, conditions, reservations, and understandings incorporated by the Senate in this resolution of ratification in the instrument of ratification to be exchanged with the Government of the Republic of Panama.

Following Senate ratification, the Panama Canal Treaty and the neutrality treaty were implemented under the Panama Canal Act of 1979. The international status of the Panama Canal continued to be affected by older agreements. Under the Hay-Pauncefote Treaty of 1904, which immediately preceded the first Panama Canal Treaty, Great Britain continued to benefit from an arrangement it had first made in the CLAYTON-BULWER TREATY of 1850. In short, in order to clear the diplomatic decks for building and controlling the canal, the United States had agreed that there would always be "entire equity" in the treatment of ships of all nations with the respect to "conditions and charges of traffic" in exchange for Britain's agreement to give up its interest in the Isthmus of Panama. And in 1914 the United States had in effect compensated Colombia for backing Panama's independence by exempting Colombia from paying tolls. These arrangements remained in place.

Consequences

Even while agreeing to turn the canal over to Panama after the Panama Canal Treaty expired in 1999, the United States reserved the right to use military force, when and if necessary, to keep the canal open. President George Herbert Walker Bush used this right as a rationale to thinly veil his "intervention" in Panama in 1989 through 1990.

What really occurred, of course, was that Bush invaded Panama in order to arrest its leader, Manuel Noriega, one of a number of Latin American strongmen whom the United States during the cold war had covertly helped to power. Since then Noriega had supported his regime with trafficking in narcotics, which had become a hot social issue in America in the mid-1980s. Noriega was hunted down, arrested, extradited, tried, and convicted by the United States, but the Panamanians did not accept Bush's ruse for legitimizing the attack and shut down the canal in December 1989—for a day or so.

In 1999, with much ill humor, and a lot of ominous grumbling in the U.S. Senate, sovereignty over the Panama Canal reverted to the Republic of Panama.

Source

U.S. Department of State, "Panama Canal Treaty of 1977." Available online. URL: http://www.state.gov/p/wha/rlnks/11936.htm. Accessed December 30, 2004.

MAASTRICHT TREATY
(CONSOLIDATED TREATY ON EUROPEAN UNITY)

TREATY AT A GLANCE

Completed
February 7, 1992, at Maastricht, the Netherlands;
entered into force January 1, 1993

Signatories
Belgium, Denmark, Germany, Greece, Spain, France, Ireland, Italy,
Luxembourg, the Netherlands, Portugal, and Great Britain

Overview
Beginning with the creation of the European Coal and Steel Community, a series of cold war agreements led to the establishment of a Common Market and a growing community among the states of Europe. In 1986 the European Single Act increased the powers of the existing European Parliament and paved the way for an epoch-making plan to eliminate all trade barriers among participating European nations, effectively transforming Europe into a single, unified market. These agreements were consolidated under the Maastricht Treaty.

Historical Background

The European continent is big, but throughout its long and troubled history, it has never proved quite big enough to contain, peacefully, its diversity of peoples, languages, national laws, and ambitions. Limited by geographical realities, the Continent obviously could not be enlarged. Therefore, in the years following the second all-consuming war of the century, many European leaders began to look for ways in which to create out of a jarring and fractious welter a harmonious European community, that, nevertheless respected individual national identities.

The result was the European Community (EC), formerly called the European Economic Community (EEC) and also known as the Common Market. It was an intergovernmental organization of 12 Western European nations (Belgium, Denmark, France, Germany, Greece, Ireland, Italy, Luxembourg, the Netherlands, Portugal, Spain, and the United Kingdom) aimed at creating a united Europe through peaceful means in order to promote economic growth and social cohesion among the European peoples and general cooperation among governments.

A plan for a united Europe was first proposed after World War II by Jean Monnet, a French statesman.

Another French official, Foreign Minister Robert Schuman, proposed a plan that resulted in the creation of the European Coal and Steel Community (ECSC) in 1952, which pooled resources and coordinated industrial policies and activities in the coal, iron ore, and steel industries of France, West Germany, Italy, Belgium, the Netherlands, and Luxembourg. A customs union and a free trade area were created for these economic sectors, which operated free from national regulations or restrictions.

The establishment of the ECSC required a treaty, the TREATY OF PARIS (April 18, 1951), which led to another, the TREATY OF ROME (March 25, 1957), which established the European Atomic Energy Community (EURATOM) and the European Economic Community (EEC, or Common Market). EURATOM pooled research and regulation of atomic energy, while the EEC broadened the common market concept to most of the nations' other industries and economic sectors. The Merger Treaty (April 8, 1965) created common governing institutions for the Common Market: the Council of Ministers, the European Commission, the European Parliament, the Court of Justice, and the European Council.

The European Single Act (ESA) of February 26, 1986 (entering into force on July 1, 1987) greatly extended the powers of the European Parliament and prepared the way for a grand plan designed to create a true, barrier-free European community—for economic purposes, in effect, a single, unified Europe. In December 1991 the Maastricht Treaty was drawn up, providing for the eventual creation of a single European currency, the European Central Bank, and Community-wide citizenship.

Terms

The Maastricht agreement incorporated the Treaty of Paris, the Treaty of Rome, the Merger Treaty, and the European Single Act into its text. The treaty provides a blueprint for modern Europe.

HIS MAJESTY THE KING OF THE BELGIANS,
HER MAJESTY THE QUEEN OF DENMARK,
THE PRESIDENT OF THE FEDERAL REPUBLIC OF GERMANY,
THE PRESIDENT OF THE HELLENIC REPUBLIC,
HIS MAJESTY THE KING OF SPAIN,
THE PRESIDENT OF THE FRENCH REPUBLIC,
THE PRESIDENT OF IRELAND,
THE PRESIDENT OF THE ITALIAN REPUBLIC,
HIS ROYAL HIGHNESS THE GRAND DUKE OF LUXEMBOURG,
HER MAJESTY THE QUEEN OF THE NETHERLANDS,
THE PRESIDENT OF THE PORTUGUESE REPUBLIC,
HER MAJESTY THE QUEEN OF THE UNITED KINGDOM OF GREAT BRITAIN AND NORTHERN IRELAND,

RESOLVED to mark a new stage in the process of European integration undertaken with the establishment of the European Communities,

RECALLING the historic importance of the ending of the division of the European continent and the need to create firm bases for the construction of the future Europe,

CONFIRMING their attachment to the principles of liberty, democracy and respect for human rights and fundamental freedoms and of the rule of law,

CONFIRMING their attachment to fundamental social rights as defined in the European Social Charter signed at Turin on 18 October 1961 and in the 1989 Community Charter of the Fundamental Social Rights of Workers,

DESIRING to deepen the solidarity between their peoples while respecting their history, their culture and their traditions,

DESIRING to enhance further the democratic and efficient functioning of the institutions so as to enable them better to carry out, within a single institutional framework, the tasks entrusted to them,

RESOLVED to achieve the strengthening and the convergence of their economies and to establish an economic and monetary union including, in accordance with the provisions of this Treaty, a single and stable currency,

DETERMINED to promote economic and social progress for their peoples, taking into account the principle of sustainable development and within the context of the accomplishment of the internal market and of reinforced cohesion and environmental protection, and to implement policies ensuring that advances in economic integration are accompanied by parallel progress in other fields,

RESOLVED to establish a citizenship common to nationals of their countries,

RESOLVED to implement a common foreign and security policy including the progressive framing of a common defence policy, which might lead to a common defence in accordance with the provisions of Article 17, thereby reinforcing the European identity and its independence in order to promote peace, security and progress in Europe and in the world,

RESOLVED to facilitate the free movement of persons, while ensuring the safety and security of their peoples, by establishing an area of freedom, security and justice, in accordance with the provisions of this Treaty,

RESOLVED to continue the process of creating an ever closer union among the peoples of Europe, in which decisions are taken as closely as possible to the citizen in accordance with the principle of subsidiarity,

IN VIEW of further steps to be taken in order to advance European integration,

HAVE DECIDED to establish a European Union and to this end have designated as their Plenipotentiaries . . .

WHO, having exchanged their full powers, found in good and due form, have agreed as follows.

Title I
Common Provisions

ARTICLE 1 (EX ARTICLE A)
By this Treaty, the HIGH CONTRACTING PARTIES establish among themselves a EUROPEAN UNION, hereinafter called "the Union."

This Treaty marks a new stage in the process of creating an ever closer union among the peoples of Europe, in which decisions are taken as openly as possible and as closely as possible to the citizen.

The Union shall be founded on the European Communities, supplemented by the policies and forms of cooperation established by this Treaty. Its task shall be to organize, in a manner demonstrating consistency and solidarity, relations between the Member States and between their peoples.

ARTICLE 2 (EX ARTICLE B)
The Union shall set itself the following objectives:

—to promote economic and social progress and a high level of employment and to achieve balanced and sustainable development, in particular through the creation of an area without internal frontiers, through the strengthening of economic and social cohesion and through the establishment of economic and monetary union, ultimately including a single currency in accordance with the provisions of this Treaty;

—to assert its identity on the international scene, in particular through the implementation of a common foreign and security policy including the progressive framing of a common defence policy, which might lead to a common defence, in accordance with the provisions of Article 17;

—to strengthen the protection of the rights and interests of the nationals of its Member States through the introduction of a citizenship of the Union;

—to maintain and develop the Union as an area of freedom, security and justice, in which the free movement of persons is assured in conjunction with appropriate measures with respect to external border controls, asylum, immigration and the prevention and combating of crime;

—to maintain in full the *acquis communautaire* and build on it with a view to considering to what extent the policies and forms of cooperation introduced by this Treaty may need to be revised with the aim of ensuring the effectiveness of the mechanisms and the institutions of the Community.

The objectives of the Union shall be achieved as provided in this Treaty and in accordance with the conditions and the timetable set out therein while respecting the principle of subsidiarity as defined in Article 5 of the Treaty establishing the European Community.

ARTICLE 3 (EX ARTICLE C)

The Union shall be served by a single institutional framework which shall ensure the consistency and the continuity of the activities carried out in order to attain its objectives while respecting and building upon the *acquis communautaire*.

The Union shall in particular ensure the consistency of its external activities as a whole in the context of its external relations, security, economic and development policies. The Council and the Commission shall be responsible for ensuring such consistency and shall cooperate to this end. They shall ensure the implementation of these policies, each in accordance with its respective powers.

ARTICLE 4 (EX ARTICLE D)

The European Council shall provide the Union with the necessary impetus for its development and shall define the general political guidelines thereof.

The European Council shall bring together the Heads of State or Government of the Member States and the President of the Commission. They shall be assisted by the Ministers for Foreign Affairs of the Member States and by a Member of the Commission.

The European Council shall meet at least twice a year, under the chairmanship of the Head of State or Government of the Member State which holds the Presidency of the Council.

The European Council shall submit to the European Parliament a report after each of its meetings and a yearly written report on the progress achieved by the Union.

ARTICLE 5 (EX ARTICLE E)

The European Parliament, the Council, the Commission, the Court of Justice and the Court of Auditors shall exercise their powers under the conditions and for the purposes provided for, on the one hand, by the provisions of the Treaties establishing the European Communities and of the subsequent Treaties and Acts modifying and supplementing them and, on the other hand, by the other provisions of this Treaty.

ARTICLE 6 (EX ARTICLE F)

1. The Union is founded on the principles of liberty, democracy, respect for human rights and fundamental freedoms, and the rule of law, principles which are common to the Member States.

2. The Union shall respect fundamental rights, as guaranteed by the European Convention for the Protection of Human Rights and Fundamental Freedoms signed in Rome on 4 November 1950 and as they result from the constitutional traditions common to the Member States, as general principles of Community law.

3. The Union shall respect the national identities of its Member States.

4. The Union shall provide itself with the means necessary to attain its objectives and carry through its policies.

ARTICLE 7 (EX ARTICLE F.1)

1. The Council, meeting in the composition of the Heads of State or Government and acting by unanimity on a proposal by one-third of the Member States or by the Commission and after obtaining the assent of the European Parliament, may determine the existence of a serious and persistent breach by a Member State of principles mentioned in Article 6(1), after inviting the government of the Member State in question to submit its observations.

2. Where such a determination has been made, the Council, acting by a qualified majority, may decide to suspend certain of the rights deriving from the application of this Treaty to the Member State in question, including the voting rights of the representative of the government of that Member State in the Council. In doing so, the Council shall take into account the possible consequences of such a suspension on the rights and obligations of natural and legal persons. The obligations of the Member State in question under this Treaty shall in any case continue to be binding on that State.

3. The Council, acting by a qualified majority, may decide subsequently to vary or revoke measures taken under paragraph 2 in response to changes in the situation which led to their being imposed.

4. For the purposes of this Article, the Council shall act without taking into account the vote of the representative of the government of the Member State in question. Abstentions by members present in person or represented shall not prevent the adoption of decisions referred to in paragraph 1. A qualified majority shall be defined as the same proportion of the weighted votes of the members of the Council concerned as laid down in Article 205(2) of the Treaty establishing the European Community. This paragraph shall also apply in the event of voting rights being suspended pursuant to paragraph 2.

5. For the purposes of this Article, the European Parliament shall act by a two-thirds majority of the votes cast, representing a majority of its members.

Title II
Provisions Amending the Treaty Establishing the European Economic Community with a View to Establishing the European Community . . .

Title III
Provisions Amending the Treaty Establishing the European Coal and Steel Community . . .

Title IV
Provisions Amending the Treaty Establishing the European Atomic Energy Community . . .

Title V
Provisions on a Common Foreign and Security Policy

ARTICLE 11 (EX ARTICLE J.1)

1. The Union shall define and implement a common foreign and security policy covering all areas of foreign and security policy, the objectives of which shall be:

—to safeguard the common values, fundamental interests, independence and integrity of the Union in conformity with the principles of the United Nations Charter;

—to strengthen the security of the Union in all ways;

—to preserve peace and strengthen international security, in accordance with the principles of the United Nations Charter, as well as the principles of the Helsinki Final Act and the objectives of the Paris Charter, including those on external borders;

—to promote international cooperation;

—to develop and consolidate democracy and the rule of law, and respect for human rights and fundamental freedoms.

2. The Member States shall support the Union's external and security policy actively and unreservedly in a spirit of loyalty and mutual solidarity. The Member States shall work together to enhance and develop their mutual political solidarity. They shall refrain from any action which is contrary to the interests of the Union or likely to impair its effectiveness as a cohesive force in international relations. The Council shall ensure that these principles are complied with.

ARTICLE 12 (EX ARTICLE J.2)

The Union shall pursue the objectives set out in Article 11 by:

—defining the principles of and general guidelines for the common foreign and security policy;

—deciding on common strategies;

—adopting joint actions;

—adopting common positions;

—strengthening systematic cooperation between Member States in the conduct of policy.

ARTICLE 13 (EX ARTICLE J.3)

1. The European Council shall define the principles of and general guidelines for the common foreign and security policy, including for matters with defence implications.

2. The European Council shall decide on common strategies to be implemented by the Union in areas where the Member States have important interests in common. Common strategies shall set out their objectives, duration and the means to be made available by the Union and the Member States.

3. The Council shall take the decisions necessary for defining and implementing the common foreign and security policy on the basis of the general guidelines defined by the European Council. The Council shall recommend common strategies to the European Council and shall implement them, in particular by adopting joint actions and common positions. The Council shall ensure the unity, consistency and effectiveness of action by the Union.

ARTICLE 14 (EX ARTICLE J.4)

1. The Council shall adopt joint actions. Joint actions shall address specific situations where operational action by the Union is deemed to be required. They shall lay down their objectives, scope, the means to be made available to the Union, if necessary their duration, and the conditions for their implementation.

2. If there is a change in circumstances having a substantial effect on a question subject to joint action, the Council shall review the principles and objectives of that action and take the necessary decisions. As long as the Council has not acted, the joint action shall stand.

3. Joint actions shall commit the Member States in the positions they adopt and in the conduct of their activity.

4. The Council may request the Commission to submit to it any appropriate proposals relating to the common foreign and security policy to ensure the implementation of a joint action.

5. Whenever there is any plan to adopt a national position or take national action pursuant to a joint action, information shall be provided in time to allow, if necessary, for prior consultations within the Council. The obligation to provide prior information shall not apply to measures which are merely a national transposition of Council decisions.

6. In cases of imperative need arising from changes in the situation and failing a Council decision, Member States may take the necessary measures as a matter of urgency having regard to the general objectives of the joint action. The Member State concerned shall inform the Council immediately of any such measures.

7. Should there be any major difficulties in implementing a joint action, a Member State shall refer them to the Council which shall discuss them and seek appropriate solutions. Such solutions shall not run counter to the objectives of the joint action or impair its effectiveness.

ARTICLE 15 (EX ARTICLE J.5)

The Council shall adopt common positions. Common positions shall define the approach of the Union to a particular matter of a geographical or thematic nature. Member States shall ensure that their national policies conform to the common positions.

ARTICLE 16 (EX ARTICLE J.6)

Member States shall inform and consult one another within the Council on any matter of foreign and security policy of general interest in order to ensure that the Union's influence is exerted as effectively as possible by means of concerted and convergent action.

ARTICLE 17 (EX ARTICLE J.7)

1. The common foreign and security policy shall include all questions relating to the security of the Union, including the progressive framing of a common defence policy, in accordance with the second subparagraph, which might lead to a common defence, should the European Council so decide. It shall in that case recommend to the Member States the adoption of such a decision in accordance with their respective constitutional requirements.

The Western European Union (WEU) is an integral part of the development of the Union providing the Union with access to an operational capability notably in the context of paragraph

2. It supports the Union in framing the defence aspects of the common foreign and security policy as set out in this Article.

The Union shall accordingly foster closer institutional relations with the WEU with a view to the possibility of the integration of the WEU into the Union, should the European Council so decide. It shall in that case recommend to the Member States the adoption of such a decision in accordance with their respective constitutional requirements.

The policy of the Union in accordance with this Article shall not prejudice the specific character of the security and defence policy of certain Member States and shall respect the obligations of certain Member States, which see their common defence realized in the North Atlantic Treaty Organization (NATO), under the North Atlantic Treaty and be compatible with the common security and defence policy established within that framework.

The progressive framing of a common defence policy will be supported, as Member States consider appropriate, by cooperation between them in the field of armaments.

2. Questions referred to in this Article shall include humanitarian and rescue tasks, peace-keeping tasks and tasks of combat forces in crisis management, including peacemaking.

3. The Union will avail itself of the WEU to elaborate and implement decisions and actions of the Union which have defence implications. The competence of the European Council to establish guidelines in accordance with Article 13 shall also obtain in respect of the WEU for those matters for which the Union avails itself of the WEU.

When the Union avails itself of the WEU to elaborate and implement decisions of the Union on the tasks referred to in paragraph 2 all Member States of the Union shall be entitled to participate fully in the tasks in question. The Council, in agreement with the institutions of the WEU, shall adopt the necessary practical arrangements to allow all Member States contributing to the tasks in question to participate fully and on an equal footing in planning and decision taking in the WEU. Decisions having defence implications dealt with under this paragraph shall be taken without prejudice to the policies and obligations referred to in paragraph 1, third subparagraph.

4. The provisions of this Article shall not prevent the development of closer cooperation between two or more Member States on a bilateral level, in the framework of the WEU and the Atlantic Alliance, provided such cooperation does not run counter to or impede that provided for in this Title.

5. With a view to furthering the objectives of this Article, the provisions of this Article will be reviewed in accordance with Article 48.

ARTICLE 18 (EX ARTICLE J.8)

1. The Presidency shall represent the Union in matters coming within the common foreign and security policy.

2. The Presidency shall be responsible for the implementation of decisions taken under this Title; in that capacity it shall in principle express the position of the Union in international organizations and international conferences.

3. The Presidency shall be assisted by the Secretary-General of the Council who shall exercise the function of High Representative for the common foreign and security policy.

4. The Commission shall be fully associated in the tasks referred to in paragraphs 1 and 2.

The Presidency shall be assisted in those tasks if need be by the next Member State to hold the Presidency.

5. The Council may, whenever it deems it necessary, appoint a special representative with a mandate in relation to particular policy issues.

ARTICLE 19 (EX ARTICLE J.9)

1. Member States shall coordinate their action in international organizations and at international conferences. They shall uphold the common positions in such form.

In international organizations and at international conferences where not all the Member States participate, those which do take part shall uphold the common positions.

2. Without prejudice to paragraph 1 and Article 14(3), Member States represented in international organizations or international conferences where not all the Member States participate shall keep the latter informed of any matter of common interest.

Member States which are also members of the United Nations Security Council will concert and keep the other Member States fully informed. Member States which are permanent members of the Security Council will, in the execution of their functions, ensure the defence of the positions and the interests of the Union, without prejudice to their responsibilities under the provisions of the United Nations Charter.

ARTICLE 20 (EX ARTICLE J.10)

The diplomatic and consular missions of the Member States and the Commission Delegations in third countries and international conferences, and their representations to international organizations, shall cooperate in ensuring that the common positions and joint actions adopted by the Council are complied with and implemented. They shall step up cooperation by exchanging information, carrying out joint assessments and contributing to the implementation of the provisions referred to in Article 20 of the Treaty establishing the European Community.

ARTICLE 21 (EX ARTICLE J.11)

The Presidency shall consult the European Parliament on the main aspects and the basic choices of the common foreign and security policy and shall ensure that the views of the European Parliament are duly taken into consideration. The European Parliament shall be kept regularly informed by the Presidency and the Commission of the development of the Union's foreign and security policy. The European Parliament may ask questions of the Council or make recommendations to it. It shall hold an annual debate on progress in implementing the common foreign and security Policy.

ARTICLE 22 (EX ARTICLE J.12)

1. Any Member State or the Commission may refer to the Council any question relating to the common foreign and security policy and may submit proposals to the Council.

2. In cases requiring a rapid decision, the Presidency, of its own motion, or at the request of the Commission or a Member State, shall convene an extraordinary Council meeting within forty-eight hours or, in an emergency, within a shorter period.

ARTICLE 23 (EX ARTICLE J.13)

1. Decisions under this Title shall be taken by the Council acting unanimously. Abstentions by members present in person or represented shall not prevent the adoption of such decisions. When abstaining in a vote, any member of the Council may qualify its abstention by making a formal declaration under the present subparagraph. In that case, it shall not be obliged to apply the decision, but shall accept that the decision commits the Union.

In a spirit of mutual solidarity, the Member State concerned shall refrain from any action likely to conflict with or impede Union action based on that decision and the other Member States shall respect its position. If the members of the Council qualifying their abstention in this way represent more than one-third of the votes weighted in accordance with Article 205(2) of the Treaty establishing the European Community, the decision shall not be adopted.

2. By derogation from the provisions of paragraph 1, the Council shall act by qualified majority:

—when adopting joint actions, common positions or taking any other decision on the basis of a common strategy;

—when adopting any decision implementing a joint action or a common position.

If a member of the Council declares that, for important and stated reasons of national policy, it intends to oppose the adoption of a decision to be taken by qualified majority, a vote shall not be taken. The Council may, acting by a qualified majority, request that the matter be referred to the European Council for decision by unanimity.

The votes of the members of the Council shall be weighted in accordance with Article 205(2) of the Treaty establishing the European Community. For their adoption, decisions shall require at least 62 votes in favor, cast by at least 10 members.

This paragraph shall not apply to decisions having military or defence implications.

3. For procedural questions, the Council shall act by a majority of its members.

ARTICLE 24 (EX ARTICLE J.14)

When it is necessary to conclude an agreement with one or more States or international organizations in implementation of this Title, the Council, acting unanimously, may authorize the Presidency, assisted by the Commission as appropriate, to open negotiations to that effect.

Such agreements shall be concluded by the Council acting unanimously on a recommendation from the Presidency.

No agreement shall be binding on a Member State whose representative in the Council states that it has to comply with the requirements of its own constitutional procedure; the other members of the Council may agree that the agreement shall apply provisionally to them.

The provisions of this Article shall also apply to matters falling under Title VI.

ARTICLE 25 (EX ARTICLE J.15)

Without prejudice to Article 207 of the Treaty establishing the European Community, a Political Committee shall monitor the international situation in the areas covered by the common foreign and security policy and contribute to the definition of policies by delivering opinions to the Council at the request of the Council or on its own initiative. It shall also monitor the implementation of agreed policies, without prejudice to the responsibility of the Presidency and the Commission.

ARTICLE 26 (EX ARTICLE J.16)

The Secretary General of the Council, High Representative for the common foreign and security policy, shall assist the Council in matters coming within the scope of the common foreign and security policy, in particular through contributing to the formulation, preparation and implementation of policy decisions, and, when appropriate and acting on behalf of the Council at the request of the Presidency, through conducting political dialogue with third parties.

ARTICLE 27 (EX ARTICLE J.17)

The Commission shall be fully associated with the work carried out in the common foreign and security policy field.

ARTICLE 28 (EX ARTICLE J.18)

1. Articles 189, 190, 196 to 199, 203, 204, 206 to 209, 213 to 219, 255 and 290 of the Treaty establishing the European Community shall apply to the provisions relating to the areas referred to in this Title.

2. Administrative expenditure which the provisions relating to the areas referred to in this Title entail for the institutions shall be charged to the budget of the European Communities.

3. Operational expenditure to which the implementation of those provisions gives rise shall also be charged to the budget of the European Communities, except for such expenditure arising from operations having military or defence implications and cases where the Council acting unanimously decides otherwise. In cases where expenditure is not charged to the budget of the European Communities it shall be charged to the Member States in accordance with the gross national product scale, unless the Council acting unanimously decides otherwise. As for expenditure arising from operations having military or defence implications, Member States whose representatives in the Council have made a formal declaration under Article 23(1), second subparagraph, shall not be obliged to contribute to the financing thereof.

4. The budgetary procedure laid down in the Treaty establishing the European Community shall apply to the expenditure charged to the budget of the European Communities.

Title VI
Provisions on Police and Judicial Cooperation in Criminal Matters

ARTICLE 29 (EX ARTICLE K.1)

Without prejudice to the powers of the European Community, the Union's objective shall be to provide citizens with a high level of safety within an area of freedom, security and justice by developing common action among the Member States in the fields of police and judicial cooperation in criminal matters and by preventing and combating racism and xenophobia. That objective shall be achieved by preventing and combating crime, organized or otherwise, in particular terrorism, trafficking in persons and offenses against children, illicit drug trafficking and illicit arms trafficking, corruption and fraud, through:

—closer cooperation between police forces, customs authorities and other competent authorities in the Member States, both directly and through the European Police Office (Europol), in accordance with the provisions of Articles 30 and 32;

—closer cooperation between judicial and other competent authorities of the Member States in accordance with the provisions of Articles 31(a) to (d) and 32;

—approximation, where necessary, of rules on criminal matters in the Member States, in accordance with the provisions of Article 31(e).

ARTICLE 30 (EX ARTICLE K.2)

1. Common action in the field of police cooperation shall include:

(a) operational cooperation between the competent authorities, including the police, customs and other specialized law enforcement services of the Member States in relation to the prevention, detection and investigation of criminal offenses;

(b) the collection, storage, processing, analysis and exchange of relevant information, including information held by law enforcement services on reports on suspicious financial transactions, in particular through Europol, subject to appropriate provisions on the protection of personal data;

(c) cooperation and joint initiatives in training, the exchange of liaison officers, secondments, the use of equipment, and forensic research;

(d) the common evaluation of particular investigative techniques in relation to the detection of serious forms of organized crime.

2. The Council shall promote cooperation through Europol and shall in particular, within a period of five years after the date of entry into force of the Treaty of Amsterdam:

(a) enable Europol to facilitate and support the preparation, and to encourage the coordination and carrying out, of specific investigative actions by the competent authorities of the Member States, including operational actions of joint teams comprising representatives of Europol in a support capacity;

(b) adopt measures allowing Europol to ask the competent authorities of the Member States to conduct and coordinate their investigations in specific cases and to develop specific expertise which may be put at the disposal of Member States to assist them in investigating cases of organized crime;

(c) promote liaison arrangements between prosecuting/investigating officials specializing in the fight against organized crime in close cooperation with Europol;

(d) establish a research, documentation and statistical network on cross-border crime.

ARTICLE 31 (EX ARTICLE K.3)

Common action on judicial cooperation in criminal matters shall include:

(a) facilitating and accelerating cooperation between competent ministries and judicial or equivalent authorities of the Member States in relation to proceedings and the enforcement of decisions;

(b) facilitating extradition between Member States;

(c) ensuring compatibility in rules applicable in the Member States, as may be necessary to improve such cooperation;

(d) preventing conflicts of jurisdiction between Member States;

(e) progressively adopting measures establishing minimum rules relating to the constituent elements of criminal acts and to penalties in the fields of organized crime, terrorism and illicit drug trafficking.

ARTICLE 32 (EX ARTICLE K.4)

The Council shall lay down the conditions and limitations under which the competent authorities referred to in Articles 30 and 31 may operate in the territory of another Member State in liaison and in agreement with the authorities of that State.

ARTICLE 33 (EX ARTICLE K.5)

This Title shall not affect the exercise of the responsibilities incumbent upon Member States with regard to the maintenance of law and order and the safeguarding of internal security.

ARTICLE 34 (EX ARTICLE K.6)

1. In the areas referred to in this Title, Member States shall inform and consult one another within the Council with a view to coordinating their action. To that end, they shall establish collaboration between the relevant departments of their administrations.

2. The Council shall take measures and promote cooperation, using the appropriate form and procedures as set out in this Title, contributing to the pursuit of the objectives of the Union. To that end, acting unanimously on the initiative of any Member State or of the Commission, the Council may:

(a) adopt common positions defining the approach of the Union to a particular matter;

(b) adopt framework decisions for the purpose of approximation of the laws and regulations of the Member States. Framework decisions shall be binding upon the Member States as to the result to be achieved but shall leave to the national authorities the choice of form and methods. They shall not entail direct effect;

(c) adopt decisions for any other purpose consistent with the objectives of this Title, excluding any approximation of the laws and regulations of the Member States. These decisions shall be binding and shall not entail direct effect; the Council, acting by a qualified majority, shall adopt measures necessary to implement those decisions at the level of the Union;

(d) establish conventions which it shall recommend to the Member States for adoption in accordance with their respective constitutional requirements. Member States shall begin the procedures applicable within a time limit to be set by the Council. Unless they provide otherwise, conventions shall, once adopted by at least half of the Member States, enter into force for those Member States. Measures implementing conventions shall be adopted within the Council by a majority of two-thirds of the Contracting Parties.

3. Where the Council is required to act by a qualified majority, the votes of its members shall be weighted as laid down in Article 205(2) of the Treaty establishing the European Community, and for their adoption acts of the Council shall require at least 62 votes in favor, cast by at least 10 members.

4. For procedural questions, the Council shall act by a majority of its members.

ARTICLE 35 (EX ARTICLE K.7)

1. The Court of Justice of the European Communities shall have jurisdiction, subject to the conditions laid down in this Article, to give preliminary rulings on the validity and interpretation of framework decisions and decisions, on the interpretation of conventions established under this Title and on the validity and interpretation of the measures implementing them.

2. By a declaration made at the time of signature of the Treaty of Amsterdam or at any time thereafter, any Member State shall be able to accept the jurisdiction of the Court of Justice to give preliminary rulings as specified in paragraph 1.

3. A Member State making a declaration pursuant to paragraph 2 shall specify that either:

(a) any court or tribunal of that State against whose decisions there is no judicial remedy under national law may request the Court of Justice to give a preliminary ruling on a question raised in a case pending before it and concerning the validity or interpretation of an act referred to in paragraph 1 if that court or tribunal considers that a decision on the question is necessary to enable it to give judgment, or

(b) any court or tribunal of that State may request the Court of Justice to give a preliminary ruling on a question raised in a case pending before it and concerning the validity or interpretation of an act referred to in paragraph 1 if that court or tribunal considers that a decision on the question is necessary to enable it to give judgment.

4. Any Member State, whether or not it has made a declaration pursuant to paragraph 2, shall be entitled to submit statements of case or written observations to the Court in cases which arise under paragraph 1.

5. The Court of Justice shall have no jurisdiction to review the validity or proportionality of operations carried out by the police or other law enforcement services of a Member State or the exercise of the responsibilities incumbent upon Member States with regard to the maintenance of law and order and the safeguarding of internal security.

6. The Court of Justice shall have jurisdiction to review the legality of framework decisions and decisions in actions brought by a Member State or the Commission on grounds of lack of competence, infringement of an essential procedural requirement, infringement of this Treaty or of any rule of law relating to its application, or misuse of powers. The proceedings provided for in this paragraph shall be instituted within two months of the publication of the measure.

7. The Court of Justice shall have jurisdiction to rule on any dispute between Member States regarding the interpretation or the application of acts adopted under Article 34(2) whenever such dispute cannot be settled by the Council within six months of its being referred to the Council by one of its members. The Court shall also have jurisdiction to rule on any dispute between Member States and the Commission regarding the interpretation or the application of conventions established under Article 34(2)(d).

ARTICLE 36 (EX ARTICLE K.8)

1. A Coordinating Committee shall be set up consisting of senior officials. In addition to its coordinating role, it shall be the task of the Committee to:

—give opinions for the attention of the Council, either at the Council's request or on its own initiative;

—contribute, without prejudice to Article 207 of the Treaty establishing the European Community, to the preparation of the Council's discussions in the areas referred to in Article 29.

2. The Commission shall be fully associated with the work in the areas referred to in this Title.

ARTICLE 37 (EX ARTICLE K.9)

Within international organizations and at international conferences in which they take part, Member States shall defend the common positions adopted under the provisions of this Title. Articles 18 and 19 shall apply as appropriate to matters falling under this Title.

ARTICLE 38 (EX ARTICLE K.10)

Agreements referred to in Article 24 may cover matters falling under this Title.

ARTICLE 39 (EX ARTICLE K.11)

1. The Council shall consult the European Parliament before adopting any measure referred to in Article 34(2)(b), (c) and (d). The European Parliament shall deliver its opinion within a time-limit which the Council may lay down, which shall not be less than three months. In the absence of an opinion within that time-limit, the Council may act.

2. The Presidency and the Commission shall regularly inform the European Parliament of discussions in the areas covered by this Title.

3. The European Parliament may ask questions of the Council or make recommendations to it. Each year, it shall hold a debate on the progress made in the areas referred to in this Title.

ARTICLE 40 (EX ARTICLE K.12)

1. Member States which intend to establish closer cooperation between themselves may be authorized, subject to Articles 43 and 44, to make use of the institutions, procedures and mechanisms laid down by the Treaties provided that the cooperation proposed:

(a) respects the powers of the European Community, and the objectives laid down by this Title;

(b) has the aim of enabling the Union to develop more rapidly into an area of freedom, security and justice.

2. The authorization referred to in paragraph 1 shall be granted by the Council, acting by a qualified majority at the request of the Member States concerned and after inviting the Commission to present its opinion; the request shall also be forwarded to the European Parliament.

If a member of the Council declares that, for important and stated reasons of national policy, it intends to oppose the granting of an authorization by qualified majority, a vote shall not be taken. The Council may, acting by a qualified majority, request that the matter be referred to the European Council for decision by unanimity.

The votes of the members of the Council shall be weighted in accordance with Article 205(2) of the Treaty establishing the European Community.

For their adoption, decisions shall require at least 62 votes in favor, cast by at least 10 members.

3. Any Member State which wishes to become a party to cooperation set up in accordance with this Article shall notify its intention to the Council and to the Commission, which shall give an opinion to the Council within three months of receipt of that notification, possibly accompanied by a recommendation for such specific arrangements as it may deem necessary for that Member State to become a party to the cooperation in question.

Within four months of the date of that notification, the Council shall decide on the request and on such specific arrangements as it may deem necessary.

The decision shall be deemed to be taken unless the Council, acting by a qualified majority, decides to hold it in abeyance; in this case, the Council shall state the reasons for its decision and set a deadline for reexamining it.

For the purposes of this paragraph, the Council shall act under the conditions set out in Article 44.

4. The provisions of Articles 29 to 41 shall apply to the closer cooperation provided for by this Article, save as otherwise provided for in this Article and in Articles 43 and 44.

The provisions of the Treaty establishing the European Community concerning the powers of the Court of Justice of the European Communities and the exercise of those powers shall apply to paragraphs 1, 2 and 3.

5. This Article is without prejudice to the provisions of the Protocol integrating the Schengen acquis into the framework of the European Union.

ARTICLE 41 (EX ARTICLE K.13)

1. Articles 189, 190, 195, 196 to 199, 203, 204, 205(3), 206 to 209, 213 to 219, 255 and 290 of the Treaty establishing the European Community shall apply to the provisions relating to the areas referred to in this Title.

2. Administrative expenditure which the provisions relating to the areas referred to in this Title entail for the institutions shall be charged to the budget of the European Communities.

3. Operational expenditure to which the implementation of those provisions gives rise shall also be charged to the budget of the European Communities, except where the Council acting unanimously decides otherwise. In cases where expenditure is not charged to the budget of the European Communities it shall be charged to the Member States in accordance with the gross national product scale, unless the Council acting unanimously decides otherwise.

4. The budgetary procedure laid down in the Treaty establishing the European Community shall apply to the expenditure charged to the budget of the European Communities.

ARTICLE 42 (EX ARTICLE K.14)

The Council, acting unanimously on the initiative of the Commission or a Member State, and after consulting the European Parliament, may decide that action in areas referred to in Article 29 shall fall under Title IV of the Treaty establishing the European Community, and at the same time determine the relevant voting conditions relating to it. It shall recommend the Member States to adopt that decision in accordance with their respective constitutional requirements.

Title VII (ex Title VIa)
Provisions on Closer Cooperation

ARTICLE 43 (EX ARTICLE K.15)

1. Member States which intend to establish closer cooperation between themselves may make use of the institutions, procedures and mechanisms laid down by this Treaty and the Treaty establishing the European Community provided that the cooperation:

(a) is aimed at furthering the objectives of the Union and at protecting and serving its interests;

(b) respects the principles of the said Treaties and the single institutional framework of the Union;

(c) is only used as a last resort, where the objectives of the said Treaties could not be attained by applying the relevant procedures laid down therein;

(d) concerns at least a majority of Member States;

(e) does not affect the "acquis communautaire" and the measures adopted under the other provisions of the said Treaties;

(f) does not affect the competences, rights, obligations and interests of those Member States which do not participate therein;

(g) is open to all Member States and allows them to become parties to the cooperation at any time, provided that they comply with the basic decision and with the decisions taken within that framework;

(h) complies with the specific additional criteria laid down in Article 11 of the Treaty establishing the European Community and Article 40 of this Treaty, depending on the area concerned, and is authorized by the Council in accordance with the procedures laid down therein.

2. Member States shall apply, as far as they are concerned, the acts and decisions adopted for the implementation of the cooperation in which they participate. Member States not participating in such cooperation shall not impede the implementation thereof by the participating Member States.

ARTICLE 44 (EX ARTICLE K.16)

1. For the purposes of the adoption of the acts and decisions necessary for the implementation of the cooperation referred to in Article 43, the relevant institutional provisions of this Treaty and of the Treaty establishing the European Community shall apply. However, while all members of the Council shall be able to take part in the deliberations, only those representing participating Member States shall take part in the adoption of decisions. The qualified majority shall be defined as the same proportion of the weighted votes of the members of the Council concerned as laid down in Article 205(2) of the Treaty establishing the European Community. Unanimity shall be constituted by only those Council members concerned.

2. Expenditure resulting from implementation of the cooperation, other than administrative costs entailed for the institutions, shall be borne by the participating Member States, unless the Council, acting unanimously, decides otherwise.

ARTICLE 45 (EX ARTICLE K.17)

The Council and the Commission shall regularly inform the European Parliament of the development of closer cooperation established on the basis of this Title.

Title VIII (ex Title VII)
Final Provisions

ARTICLE 46 (EX ARTICLE L)

The provisions of the Treaty establishing the European Community, the Treaty establishing the European Coal and Steel Community and the Treaty establishing the European Atomic Energy Community concerning the powers of the Court of Justice of the European Communities and the exercise of those powers shall apply only to the following provisions of this Treaty:

(a) provisions amending the Treaty establishing the European Economic Community with a view to establishing the European Community, the Treaty establishing the European Coal and Steel Community and the Treaty establishing the European Atomic Energy Community;

(b) provisions of Title VI, under the conditions provided for by Article 35;

(c) provisions of Title VII, under the conditions provided for by Article 11 of the Treaty establishing the European Community and Article 40 of this Treaty;

(d) Article 6(2) with regard to action of the institutions, insofar as the Court has jurisdiction under the Treaties establishing the European Communities and under this Treaty;

(e) Articles 46 to 53.

ARTICLE 47 (EX ARTICLE M)

Subject to the provisions amending the Treaty establishing the European Economic Community with a view to establishing the

European Community, the Treaty establishing the European Coal and Steel Community and the Treaty establishing the European Atomic Energy Community, and to these final provisions, nothing in this Treaty shall affect the Treaties establishing the European Communities or the subsequent Treaties and Acts modifying or supplementing them.

ARTICLE 48 (EX ARTICLE N)

The government of any Member State or the Commission may submit to the Council proposals for the amendment of the Treaties on which the Union is founded.

If the Council, after consulting the European Parliament and, where appropriate, the Commission, delivers an opinion in favor of calling a conference of representatives of the governments of the Member States, the conference shall be convened by the President of the Council for the purpose of determining by common accord the amendments to be made to those Treaties. The European Central Bank shall also be consulted in the case of institutional changes in the monetary area.

The amendments shall enter into force after being ratified by all the Member States in accordance with their respective constitutional requirements.

ARTICLE 49 (EX ARTICLE O)

Any European State which respects the principles set out in Article 6(1) may apply to become a member of the Union. It shall address its application to the Council, which shall act unanimously after consulting the Commission and after receiving the assent of the European Parliament, which shall act by an absolute majority of its component members.

The conditions of admission and the adjustments to the Treaties on which the Union is founded which such admission entails shall be the subject of an agreement between the Member States and the applicant State. This agreement shall be submitted for ratification by all the contracting States in accordance with their respective constitutional requirements.

ARTICLE 50 (EX ARTICLE P)

1. Articles 2 to 7 and 10 to 19 of the Treaty establishing a Single Council and a Single Commission of the European Communities, signed in Brussels on 8 April 1965, are hereby repealed.

2. Article 2, Article 3(2) and Title III of the Single European Act signed in Luxembourg on 17 February 1986 and in The Hague on 28 February 1986 are hereby repealed.

ARTICLE 51 (EX ARTICLE Q)

This Treaty is concluded for an unlimited period.

ARTICLE 52 (EX ARTICLE R)

1. This Treaty shall be ratified by the High Contracting Parties in accordance with their respective constitutional requirements. The instruments of ratification shall be deposited with the Government of the Italian Republic.

2. This Treaty shall enter into force on 1 January 1993, provided that all the instruments of ratification have been deposited, or, failing that, on the first day of the month following the deposit of the instrument of ratification by the last signatory State to take this step.

ARTICLE 53 (EX ARTICLE S)

This Treaty, drawn up in a single original in the Danish, Dutch, English, French, German, Greek, Irish, Italian, Portuguese and Spanish languages, the texts in each of these languages being equally authentic, shall be deposited in the archives of the government of the Italian Republic, which will transmit a certified copy to each of the governments of the other signatory States.

Pursuant to the Accession Treaty of 1994, the Finnish and Swedish versions of this Treaty shall also be authentic.

In witness whereof the undersigned Plenipotentiaries have signed this Treaty.

Done at Maastricht on the seventh day of February in the year one thousand nine hundred and ninety-two.

MARK EYSKENS
UFFE ELLEMANN-JENSEN
HANS-DIETRICH GENSCHER
ANTONIOS SAMARAS
FRANCISCO FERNÁNDEZ ORDÓÑEZ
ROLAND DUMAS
GERARD COLLINS
GIANNI DE MICHELIS
JACQUES F. POOS
HANS VAN DEN BROEK
JOÃO DE DEUS PINHEIRO
DOUGLAS HURD
PHILIPPE MAYSTADT
ANDERS FOGH RASMUSSEN
THEODOR WAIGEL
EFTHYMIOS CHRISTODOULOU
CARLOS SOLCHAGA CATALÁN
PIERRE BARAGOVOY
BERTIE AHERN
GUIDO CARLI
JEAN-CLAUDE JUNCKER
WILLEM KOK
JORGE BRAGA DE MACEDO
FRANCIS MAUDE

Consequences

Put to a popular referendum vote, Denmark rejected the treaty in June 1992, but it approved it in 1993 after engineering certain exemptions from some of its provisions. Another holdout, Britain, after much debate—a debate that ultimately led to the downfall of England's disputatious premier Margaret Thatcher, an adamantine foe of full unity with Europe—approved the treaty in August 1993.

Delay in final approval upset the program's schedule, and planners found the creation of a single currency to be fraught with more problems than anticipated, principally because the German mark was so much stronger than other European currencies. Nevertheless, faced with economic competition from the United States, Japan, and other Asian nations, the European Union, as the EC was renamed in late 1993, was determined by the mid-1990s to enact the provisions of the Maastricht Treaty, creating a Europe more unified than at any time since the height of the ancient Roman Empire.

By the early 21st century, the European Union (EU) seemed a healthy and thriving political entity. Its quite strong new currency, the euro, proved more than a match for the German mark and the American dollar. However, a treaty establishing a European Constitution, signed by 25 member nations of the EU, failed to achieve ratification by France (May 29, 2005) and the Netherlands (June 1, 2005). This prompted other member nations to postpone their ratification procedures, thereby casting doubt on the future of the constitution.

Source

European Union, "Treaty on European Union," Europa: Gateway to the European Union. Available online. URL: http://europa.eu.int/en/record/mt/top.html. Accessed December 30, 2004.

NORTH AMERICAN FREE TRADE AGREEMENT (NAFTA)

TREATY AT A GLANCE

Completed
December 17, 1992; entered into force January 1, 1994

Signatories
United States, Mexico, and Canada

Overview
NAFTA was a trade pact signed in 1992 that would gradually eliminate most tariffs and other trade barriers on products and services passing between the United States, Canada, and Mexico and create a powerful trading bloc comprised of the three largest countries in North America.

Historical Background

In the wake of World War II, the nations of Western Europe, from time immemorial bellicose competitors and territorial rivals, managed through a series of trade agreements, including the TREATY OF PARIS (1951), the TREATY OF ROME, the EUROPEAN FREE TRADE ASSOCIATION CONVENTION, and the MAASTRICHT TREATY, not only to eliminate tariffs and stimulate trade, the traditional goal of such treaties, but also to create a Common Market and European Community that wielded considerable clout in the world market and in international diplomacy.

The North American Free Trade Agreement was inspired by that success, as the United States, Mexico, and Canada tried to duplicate both the economic and the political windfalls Europe had garnered as the result initially of the cold war. As they envisioned it, the pact would effectively create a free trade bloc among the three largest countries of North America. President Ronald Reagan had taken the initiative and negotiated a free trade agreement between Canada and the United States in 1988.

NAFTA, which would basically extend this agreement's provisions to Mexico, was negotiated by President George H. W. Bush, with Canadian prime minister Brian Mulroney and Mexican president Carlos Salinas de Gortari. Preliminary agreement on the pact was reached in August 1992, and it was signed by the three nations on December 17, 1992.

Terms

Seeking to forge a common market among Canada, Mexico, and the United States, NAFTA's major provisions in general called for a reduction of tariffs, customs duties, and other trade barriers among the three signatory nations. NAFTA removed some of those barriers immediately, but others, in fact, most of them, were to be removed over periods sometimes as long as 15 years. The treaty would eventually establish duty-free access for a vast range of manufactured goods and commodities traded between the partners. Some provisions were designed to give both U.S. and Canadian enterprises greater access to Mexican markets in banking, insurance, advertising, telecommunications, and trucking.

The NAFTA is a long, book-length document whose provisions—as is in the nature of such treaties—will necessarily change from time to time. Its comprehensiveness is apparent in the Table of Contents.

The Preamble makes clear NAFTA's purpose, Chapter 1 defines the area, objectives, and some special concerns of the agreement, Chapter 2 provides general definitions, and Chapter 3 will provide a feel for the complex detail of the treaty.

NAFTA TABLE OF CONTENTS

Preamble

The Government of Canada, the Government of the United Mexican States and the Government of the United States of America, resolved to:

STRENGTHEN the special bonds of friendship and cooperation among their nations;

CONTRIBUTE to the harmonious development and expansion of world trade and provide a catalyst to broader international cooperation;

CREATE an expanded and secure market for the goods and services produced in their territories;

REDUCE distortions to trade;

ESTABLISH clear and mutually advantageous rules governing their trade;

ENSURE a predictable commercial framework for business planning and investment;

BUILD on their respective rights and obligations under the General Agreement on Tariffs and Trade and other multilateral and bilateral instruments of cooperation;

ENHANCE the competitiveness of their firms in global markets;

FOSTER creativity and innovation, and promote trade in goods and services that are the subject of intellectual property rights;

CREATE new employment opportunities and improve working conditions and living standards in their respective territories;

UNDERTAKE each of the preceding in a manner consistent with environmental protection and conservation;

PRESERVE their flexibility to safeguard the public welfare;

PROMOTE sustainable development;

STRENGTHEN the development and enforcement of environmental laws and regulations; and

PROTECT, enhance and enforce basic workers' rights;

HAVE AGREED as follows:

PART ONE
GENERAL PART

Chapter One
Objectives

ARTICLE 101: ESTABLISHMENT OF THE FREE TRADE AREA

The Parties to this Agreement, consistent with Article XXIV of the General Agreement on Tariffs and Trade, hereby establish a free trade area.

ARTICLE 102: OBJECTIVES

1. The objectives of this Agreement, as elaborated more specifically through its principles and rules, including national treatment, most-favored-nation treatment and transparency are to:

(a) eliminate barriers to trade in, and facilitate the cross border movement of, goods and services between the territories of the Parties;

(b) promote conditions of fair competition in the free trade area;

(c) increase substantially investment opportunities in their territories;

(d) provide adequate and effective protection and enforcement of intellectual property rights in each Party's territory;

(e) create effective procedures for the implementation and application of this Agreement, and for its joint administration and the resolution of disputes; and

(f) establish a framework for further trilateral, regional and multilateral cooperation to expand and enhance the benefits of this Agreement.

2. The Parties shall interpret and apply the provisions of this Agreement in the light of its objectives set out in paragraph 1 and in accordance with applicable rules of international law.

ARTICLE 103: RELATION TO OTHER AGREEMENTS

1. The Parties affirm their existing rights and obligations with respect to each other under the General Agreement on Tariffs and Trade and other agreements to which such Parties are party.

2. In the event of any inconsistency between the provisions of this Agreement and such other agreements, the provisions of this Agreement shall prevail to the extent of the inconsistency, except as otherwise provided in this Agreement.

ARTICLE 104: RELATION TO ENVIRONMENTAL AND CONSERVATION AGREEMENTS

1. In the event of any inconsistency between this Agreement and the specific trade obligations set out in:

(a) Convention on the International Trade in Endangered Species of Wild Fauna and Flora, done at Washington, March 3, 1973;

(b) the Montreal Protocol on Substances that Deplete the Ozone Layer, done at Montreal, September 16, 1987, as amended June 29, 1990;

(c) Basel Convention on the Control of Transboundary Movements of Hazardous Wastes and Their Disposal, done at Basel, March 22, 1989, upon its entry into force for Canada, Mexico and the United States; or

(d) the agreements set out in Annex 104.1,

such obligations shall prevail to the extent of the inconsistency, provided that where a Party has a choice among equally effective and reasonably available means of complying with such obligations, the Party chooses the alternative that is the least inconsistent with the other provisions of this Agreement.

2. The Parties may agree in writing to modify Annex 104.1 to include any amendment to the agreements listed in paragraph 1, and any other environmental or conservation agreement.

ARTICLE 105: EXTENT OF OBLIGATIONS

The Parties shall ensure that all necessary measures are taken in order to give effect to the provisions of this Agreement, including their observance, except as otherwise provided in this Agreement, by state and provincial governments.

Annex 104

BILATERAL AND OTHER ENVIRONMENTAL AND CONSERVATION AGREEMENTS

1. The Agreement Between the Government of Canada and the Government of the United States of America Concerning the Transboundary Movement of Hazardous Waste, signed at Ottawa, October 28, 1986.

2. The Agreement between the United States of America and the United Mexican States on Cooperation for the Protection and Improvement of the Environment in the Border Area, signed at La Paz, Baja California Sur, August 14, 1983.

Chapter Two
General Definitions

ARTICLE 201: DEFINITIONS OF GENERAL APPLICATION

1. For purposes of this Agreement, unless otherwise specified:

Commission means the Free Trade Commission established under Article 2001;

Customs Valuation Code means the Agreement on Implementation of Article VII of the General Agreement on Tariffs and Trade, including its interpretative notes;

days means calendar days, including weekends and holidays;

enterprise means any entity constituted or organized under applicable law, whether or not for profit, and whether privately-owned or governmentally-owned, including any corporation, trust, partnership, sole proprietorship, joint venture or other association;

enterprise of a Party means an enterprise constituted or organized under the laws of, or principally carrying on its business in the territory of, a Party;

existing means in effect at the time of entry into force of this Agreement;

Generally Accepted Accounting Principles means the recognized consensus or substantial authoritative support in the territory of a Party with respect to the recording of revenues, expenses, costs, assets and liabilities, disclosure of information and preparation of financial statements. These standards may be broad guidelines of general application as well as detailed standards, practices and procedures;

Harmonized System means the Harmonized Commodity Description and Coding System, and its legal notes, as adopted and implemented by the Parties in their respective tariff laws;

measure includes any law, regulation, procedure, requirement or practice;

national means a natural person who is a citizen or permanent resident of a Party and any other natural person referred to in Annex 201.1;

originating means qualifying under the rules of origin set out in Chapter Four (Rules of Origin);

person means a natural person or an enterprise;

person of a Party means a national, or an enterprise of a Party;

state enterprise means an enterprise that is owned, or controlled through ownership interests, by a Party; and

territory means for a Party the territory of that Party as set out in Annex 201.1.

2. For purposes of this Agreement, unless otherwise specified, a reference to province or state includes local governments.

Annex 201.1

COUNTRY-SPECIFIC DEFINITIONS

For purposes of this Agreement, unless otherwise specified:

national also includes:

(a) for Mexico, a national or a citizen according to Articles 30 and 34, respectively, of the Mexican Constitution; and

(b) for the United States, "national of the United States" as defined in the existing provisions of the United States Immigration and Nationality Act;

territory means:

(a) with respect to Canada, the territory to which its customs laws apply, including any areas beyond the territorial seas of Canada within which, in accordance with international law and its domestic laws, Canada may exercise rights with respect to the seabed and subsoil and their natural resources;

(b) with respect to Mexico,

(i) the states of the Federation and the Federal District,

(ii) the islands, including the reefs and keys, in adjacent seas,

(iii) the islands of Guadalupe and Revillagigedo situated in the Pacific Ocean,

(iv) the continental shelf and the submarine shelf of such islands, keys and reefs,

(v) the waters of the territorial seas, in accordance with international law and its interior maritime waters,

(vi) the space located above the national territory, in accordance with international law,

(vii) any areas beyond the territorial seas of Mexico within which, in accordance with international law, including the United Nations Convention on the Law of the Sea, and its domestic laws, Mexico may exercise rights with respect to the seabed and subsoil and their natural resources; and

(c) with respect to the United States,

(i) the customs territory of the United States, which includes the 50 states, the District of Columbia and Puerto Rico,

(ii) the foreign trade zones located in the United States and Puerto Rico, and

(iii) any areas beyond the territorial seas of the United States within which, in accordance with international law and its domestic laws, the United States may exercise rights with respect to the seabed and subsoil and their natural resources.

PART TWO
TRADE IN GOODS

Chapter Three
National Treatment and Market Access for Goods

Subchapter A—National Treatment

ARTICLE 301: NATIONAL TREATMENT

1. Each Party shall accord national treatment to the goods of another Party in accordance with Article III of the General Agreement on Tariffs and Trade (GATT), including its interpretative notes, and to this end Article III of the GATT and its interpretative notes, or any equivalent provision of a successor agreement to which all Parties are party, are incorporated into and made part of this Agreement.

2. The provisions of paragraph 1 regarding national treatment shall mean, with respect to a province or state, treatment no less favorable than the most favorable treatment accorded by such province or state to any like, directly competitive or substitutable goods, as the case may be, of the Party of which it forms a part.

3. Paragraphs 1 and 2 shall not apply to the measures set out in Annex 301.3.

Subchapter B—Tariffs

ARTICLE 302: TARIFF ELIMINATION

1. Except as otherwise provided in this Agreement, no Party may increase any existing customs duty, or adopt any customs duty, on an originating good.

2. Except as otherwise provided in this Agreement, each Party shall progressively eliminate its customs duties on originating goods in accordance with its Schedule set out in Annex 302.2 or as otherwise indicated in Annex 300-B.

3. At the request of any Party, the Parties shall consult to consider accelerating the elimination of customs duties set out in their Schedules. An agreement between any two or more Parties to accelerate the elimination of a customs duty on a good shall supersede any prior inconsistent duty rate or staging category in their Schedules for such good when approved by each such Party in accordance with Article 2202(2) (Amendments).

ARTICLE 303: RESTRICTION ON DRAWBACK
AND DUTY DEFERRAL PROGRAMS

1. Except as otherwise provided in this Article, no Party may refund the amount of customs duties paid, or waive or reduce the amount of customs duties owed, on a good imported into its territory that is:

(a) subsequently exported to the territory of another Party,

(b) used as a material in the production of another good that is subsequently exported to the territory of another Party, or

(c) substituted by an identical or similar good used as a material in the production of another good that is subsequently exported to the territory of another Party, in an amount that exceeds the lesser of the total amount of customs duties paid or owed on the good on importation into its territory, or the total amount of customs duties paid to another Party on the good that has been subsequently exported to the territory of that other Party.

2. No Party may, by reason of an exportation described in paragraph 1, refund, waive or reduce:

(a) an antidumping or countervailing duty that is applied pursuant to a Party's domestic law and that is not applied inconsistently with Chapter Nineteen (Review and Dispute Settlement in Antidumping and Countervailing Duty Matters);

(b) a premium offered or collected on an imported good arising out of any tendering system in respect of the administration of quantitative import restrictions, tariff rate quotas or tariff preference levels;

(c) a fee applied pursuant to section 22 of the U.S. Agricultural Adjustment Act, subject to Chapter Seven (Agriculture); or

(d) customs duties paid or owed on a good imported into its territory and substituted by an identical or similar good that is subsequently exported to the territory of another Party.

3. Where a good is imported into the territory of a Party pursuant to a duty deferral program and is subsequently exported to the territory of another Party, or is used as a material in the production of another good that is subsequently exported to the territory of another Party, or is substituted by an identical or similar good used as a material in the production of another good that is subsequently exported to the territory of another Party, the Party from whose territory the good is exported:

(a) shall assess the customs duties as if the exported good had been withdrawn for domestic consumption; and

(b) may waive or reduce such customs duties to the extent permitted under paragraph 1.

4. In determining the amount of customs duties that may be refunded, waived or reduced pursuant to paragraph 1 on a good imported into its territory, each Party shall require presentation of satisfactory evidence of the amount of customs duties paid to another Party on the good that has been subsequently exported to the territory of that other Party.

5. Where satisfactory evidence of the customs duties paid to the Party to which a good is subsequently exported under a duty deferral program described in paragraph 3 is not presented within 60 days after the date of exportation, the Party from whose territory the good was exported:

(a) shall collect customs duties as if the exported good had been withdrawn for domestic consumption; and

(b) may refund such customs duties to the extent permitted under paragraph 1 upon the timely presentation of such evidence under the laws and regulations of the Party.

6. This Article shall not apply to:

(a) a good entered under bond for transportation and exportation to the territory of another Party;

(b) a good exported to the territory of another Party in the same condition as when imported into the territory of the Party from which the good was exported (processes such as testing, cleaning, repacking or inspecting the good, or preserving it in its same condition, shall not be considered to change a good's condition). Where originating and non-originating fungible goods are commingled and exported in the same form, the origin of the good may be determined on the basis of the inventory methods provided for in the Uniform Regulations

(c) a good imported into the territory of the Party that is deemed to be exported from the territory of a Party, or used as a material in the production of another good that is deemed to be exported to the territory of another Party, or is substituted by an identical or similar good used as a material in the production of another good that is deemed to be exported to the territory of another Party, by reason of

(i) delivery to a duty-free shop,

(ii) delivery for ship's stores or supplies for ships or aircraft, or

(iii) delivery for use in joint undertakings of two more of the Parties and that will subsequently become the property of the Party into whose territory the good was imported;

(d) a refund of customs duties by a Party on a particular good imported into its territory and subsequently exported to the territory of another Party, where that refund is granted by reason of the failure of such good to conform to sample or specification, or by reason of the shipment of such good without the consent of the consignee;

(e) a dutiable originating good that is imported into the territory of a Party and is subsequently exported to the territory of another Party, or used as a material in the production of another good that is subsequently exported to the territory of another Party, or is substituted by an identical or similar good used as a material in the production of another good that is subsequently exported to the territory of another Party; or

(f) a good set out in Annex 303.6.

7. This Article shall apply as of the date set out in each Party's section of Annex 303.7.

8. Notwithstanding any other provision of this Article and except as specifically provided in Annex 303.8, no Party may refund the amount of customs duties paid, or waive or reduce the amount of customs duties owed, on a non-originating good provided for under tariff provision 8540.xx (cathode-ray color television picture tubes, including video monitor tubes, with a diagonal exceeding 14") that is imported into the Party's territory and subsequently exported to the territory of another Party, or is used as a material in the production of another good that is subsequently exported to the territory of another Party, or is substituted by an identical or similar good used as a material in the production of another good that is subsequently exported to the territory of another Party.

ARTICLE 304: WAIVER OF CUSTOMS DUTIES

1. Except as set out in Annex 304.1, no Party may adopt any new waiver of customs duties, or expand with respect to existing recipients or extend to any new recipient the application of an existing waiver of customs duties, where the waiver is conditioned, explicitly or implicitly, upon the fulfillment of a performance requirement.

2. Except as set out in Annex 304.2, no Party may, explicitly or implicitly, condition on the fulfillment of a performance requirement the continuation of any existing waiver of customs duties.

3. If a waiver or a combination of waivers of customs duties granted by a Party with respect to goods for commercial use by a designated person, and thus not generally available to all importers, can be shown by another Party to have an adverse impact on the commercial interests of a person of that Party, or of a person owned or controlled by a person of that Party that is located in the territory of the Party granting the waiver, or on the other Party's economy, the Party granting the waiver shall either cease to grant it or make it generally available to any importer.

4. This Article shall not apply to measures covered by Article 303 (Restriction on Drawback and Duty Deferral).

ARTICLE 305: TEMPORARY ADMISSION OF GOODS

1. Each Party shall grant duty-free temporary admission for:

(a) professional equipment necessary for carrying out the business activity, trade or profession of a business person who qualifies for temporary entry pursuant to Chapter 16 (Temporary Entry for Business Persons),

(b) equipment for the press or for sound or television broadcasting and cinematographic equipment,

(c) goods imported for sports purposes and goods intended for display and demonstration, and

(d) commercial samples and advertising films, imported from the territory of another Party, regardless of their origin and regardless of whether like, directly competitive or substitutable goods are available in the territory of the Party.

2. Except as otherwise provided in this Agreement, no Party may condition the duty-free temporary admission of a good referred to in subparagraph 1(a), (b), or (c), other than to require that such good:

(a) be imported by a national or resident of another Party who seeks temporary entry;

(b) be used solely by or under the personal supervision of such person in the exercise of the business activity, trade or profession of that person;

(c) not be sold or leased while in its territory;

(d) be accompanied by a bond in an amount no greater than 110 percent of the charges that would otherwise be owed upon entry or final importation, or by another form of security, releasable upon exportation of the good, except that a bond for customs duties shall not be required for an originating good;

(e) be capable of identification when exported;

(f) be exported upon the departure of that person or within such other period of time as is reasonably related to the purpose of the temporary admission; and

(g) be imported in no greater quantity than is reasonable for its intended use.

3. Except as otherwise provided in this Agreement, no Party may condition the duty-free temporary admission of a good referred to in subparagraph 1(d), other than to require that such good:

(a) be imported solely for the solicitation of orders for goods, or services provided from the territory, of another Party or non-Party;

(b) not be sold, leased, or put to any use other than exhibition or demonstration while in its territory;

(c) be capable of identification when exported;

(d) be exported within such period as is reasonably related to the purpose of the temporary admission; and

(e) be imported in no greater quantity than is reasonable for its intended use.

4. A Party may impose the customs duty and any other charge on a good temporarily admitted duty-free under paragraph 1 that would be owed upon entry or final importation of such good if any condition that the Party imposes under paragraph 2 or 3 has not been fulfilled.

5. Subject to Chapters Eleven (Investment) and Twelve (Cross-Border Trade in Services):

(a) each Party shall allow a locomotive, truck, truck tractor, or tractor trailer unit, railway car, other railroad equipment, trailer ("vehicle") or container, used in international traffic, that enters its territory from the territory of another Party to exit its territory on any route that is reasonably related to the economic and prompt departure of such vehicle or container;

(b) no Party may require any bond or impose any penalty or charge solely by reason of any difference between the port of entry and the port of departure of a vehicle or container;

(c) no Party may condition the release of any obligation, including any bond, that it imposes in respect of the entry of a vehicle or container into its territory on its exit through any particular port of departure; and

(d) no Party may require that the vehicle or carrier bringing a container from the territory of another Party into its territory be the same vehicle or carrier that takes such container to the territory of another Party.

ARTICLE 306: DUTY-FREE ENTRY OF CERTAIN COMMERCIAL SAMPLES AND PRINTED ADVERTISING MATERIALS

Each Party shall grant duty-free entry to commercial samples of negligible value, and to printed advertising materials, imported from the territory of another Party, regardless of their origin, but may require that:

(a) such samples be imported solely for the solicitation of orders for goods of, or services provided from, the territory of another Party or non-Party; or

(b) such advertising materials be imported in packets that each contain no more than one copy of each such material and that neither such materials nor packets form part of a larger consignment.

ARTICLE 307: GOODS RE-ENTERED AFTER REPAIR OR ALTERATION

1. Except as set out in Annex 307.1, no Party may apply a customs duty on a good, regardless of its origin, that re-enters its territory after that good has been exported from its territory to the terri-tory of another Party for repair or alteration, regardless of whether such repair or alteration could be performed in its territory.

2. Notwithstanding Article 303 (Duty Drawback), no Party shall apply a customs duty to a good, regardless of its origin, imported temporarily from the territory of another Party for repair or alteration.

3. Each Party shall act in accordance with Annex 307.3 respecting the repair and rebuilding of vessels.

ARTICLE 308: MOST-FAVORED-NATION RATES OF DUTY ON CERTAIN GOODS

1. Each Party shall act in accordance with Annex 308.1 respecting certain automatic data processing goods and their parts.

2. Each Party shall act in accordance with Annex 308.2 respecting certain color television tubes.

3. Each Party shall accord most-favored-nation duty-free treatment to Local Area Network (LAN) apparatus imported into its territory as set out in each Party's section of Annex 308.3.

Subchapter C—Non-Tariff Measures

ARTICLE 309: IMPORT AND EXPORT RESTRICTIONS

1. Except as otherwise provided in this Agreement, no Party shall adopt or maintain any prohibition or restriction on the importation of any good of another Party or on the exportation or sale for export of any good destined for the territory of another Party, except in accordance with Article XI of the GATT, including its interpretative notes, and to this end Article XI of the GATT and its interpretative notes, or any equivalent provision of a successor agreement to which all Parties are party, are incorporated into and made part of this Agreement.

2. The Parties understand that the GATT rights and obligations incorporated by paragraph 1 prohibit, in any circumstances in which any other form of restriction is prohibited, export price requirements and, except as permitted in enforcement of countervailing and antidumping orders and undertakings, import price requirements.

3. In the event that a Party adopts or maintains a prohibition or restriction on the importation from or exportation to a non-Party of a good, nothing in this Agreement shall be construed to prevent the Party from:

(a) limiting or prohibiting the importation from the territory of another Party of such good of that non- Party; or

(b) requiring as a condition of export of such good of the Party to the territory of another Party, that the good not be re-exported to that non-Party, directly or indirectly, without having been increased in value and improved in condition [subject to review].

4. In the event that a Party adopts or maintains a prohibition or restriction on the importation of a good from a non-Party, the Parties, upon request of any Party, shall consult with a view to avoiding undue interference with or distortion of pricing, marketing and distribution arrangements in another Party.

5. Paragraphs 1 through 4 shall:

(a) not apply to the measures set out in Annex 301.3;

(b) apply to automotive goods as modified in Annex 300-A (Trade and Investment in the Automotive Sector); and

(c) apply to trade in textile and apparel goods, as modified in Annex 300-B (Textile and Apparel Goods).

6. For purposes of this Article, goods of another Party shall mean [under review].

ARTICLE 310: NON-DISCRIMINATORY ADMINISTRATION OF RESTRICTIONS (GATT ARTICLE XIII)

[need for this Article is under review]

ARTICLE 311: CUSTOMS USER FEES

1. No Party may adopt any customs user fee of the type referred to in Annex 311 for originating goods.

2. Each Party may maintain existing such fees only in accordance with Annex 311.2.

ARTICLE 312: COUNTRY OF ORIGIN MARKING

Each Party shall comply with Annex 312 with respect to its measures relating to country of origin marking.

ARTICLE 313: BLENDING REQUIREMENTS

No Party may adopt or maintain any measure requiring that distilled spirits imported from the territory of another Party for bottling be blended with any distilled spirits of the Party.

ARTICLE 314: DISTINCTIVE PRODUCTS

Each Party shall comply with Annex 314 respecting standards and labelling of the distinctive products set out therein.

ARTICLE 315: EXPORT TAXES

Except as set out in Annex 315 or Article 604 (Energy-Export Taxes), no Party may adopt or maintain any duty, tax, or other charge on the export of any good to the territory of another Party, unless such duty, tax, or charge is adopted or maintained on:

(a) exports of any such good to the territory of all other Parties; and

(b) any such good when destined for domestic consumption.

ARTICLE 316: OTHER EXPORT MEASURES

1. Except as set out in Annex 316, a Party may adopt or maintain a restriction otherwise justified under the provisions of Articles XI:2(a) or XX(g), (i) or (j) of the GATT with respect to the export of a good of the Party to the territory of another Party, only if:

(a) the restriction does not reduce the proportion of the total export shipments of the specific good made available to that other Party relative to the total supply of that good of the Party maintaining the restriction as compared to the proportion prevailing in the most recent 36-month period for which data are available prior to the imposition of the measure, or in such other representative period on which the Parties may agree;

(b) the Party does not adopt any measure, such as a license, fee, tax or minimum price requirement, that has the effect of raising the price for exports of a good to that other Party above the price charged for such good when consumed domestically, except that a measure taken pursuant to subparagraph (a) that only restricts the volume of exports shall not be considered to have such effect; and

(c) the restriction does not require the disruption of normal channels of supply to that other Party or normal proportions among specific goods or categories of goods supplied to that other Party.

2. The Parties shall cooperate in the maintenance and development of effective controls on the export of each other's goods to a non-Party in implementing this Article.

Subchapter D—Consultations

ARTICLE 317: COMMITTEE ON TRADE IN GOODS

1. The Parties hereby establish a Committee on Trade in Goods, comprising representatives of each Party.

2. The Committee shall meet at the request of any Party or the Commission to consider any matter arising under this Chapter.

ARTICLE 318: THIRD-COUNTRY DUMPING

1. The Parties affirm the importance of cooperation with respect to actions under Article 12 of the Agreement on Implementation of Article VI of the General Agreement on Tariffs and Trade.

2. Where a Party presents an application to another Party requesting anti-dumping action on its behalf, those Parties shall consult within 30 days respecting the factual basis of the request, and the requested Party shall give full consideration to the request.

Subchapter E—Definitions

ARTICLE 319: DEFINITIONS

For purposes of this Chapter:

advertising films means recorded visual media, with or without sound-tracks, consisting essentially of images showing the nature or operation of goods or services offered for sale or lease by a person established or resident in the territory of any Party, provided that the films are of a kind suitable for exhibition to prospective customers but not for broadcast to the general public, and provided that they are imported in packets that each contain no more than one copy of each film and that do not form part of a larger consignment;

commercial samples of negligible value means commercial samples having a value (individually or in the aggregate as shipped) of not more than one U.S. dollar, or the equivalent amount in the currency of another Party, or so marked, torn, perforated or otherwise treated that they are unsuitable for sale or for use except as commercial samples;

customs duty includes any customs or import duty and a charge of any kind imposed in connection with the importation of a good, including any form of surtax or surcharge in connection with such importation, but does not include any:

(a) charge equivalent to an internal tax imposed consistently with Article III:2 of the GATT, or any equivalent provision of a successor agreement to which all Parties are party, in respect of like, directly competitive or substitutable goods of the Party, or in respect of goods from which the imported good has been manufactured or produced in whole or in part;

(b) antidumping or countervailing duty that is applied pursuant to a Party's domestic law and not applied inconsistently with Chapter Nineteen (Review and Dispute Settlement in Antidumping and Countervailing Duty Matters);

(c) fee or other charge in connection with importation commensurate with the cost of services rendered;

(d) premium offered or collected on an imported good arising out of any tendering system in respect of the administration of quantitative import restrictions or tariff rate quotas or tariff preference levels; and

(e) fee applied pursuant to section 22 of the U.S. Agricultural Adjustment Act, subject to Chapter Seven (Agriculture);

distilled spirits include distilled spirits and distilled spirit-containing beverages;

duty deferral program includes measures such as those governing foreign-trade zones, temporary importations under bond, bonded warehouses, "maquiladoras", and inward processing programs;

duty-free means free of customs duty;

goods imported for sports purposes means sports requisites for use in sports contests, demonstrations or training in the territory of the Party into whose territory such goods are imported;

goods intended for display or demonstration includes their component parts, ancillary apparatus and accessories;

item means a tariff classification item at the eight- or ten-digit level set out in a Party's tariff schedule;

material means "material" as defined in Chapter Four (Rules of Origin);

most-favored-nation rate of duty does not include any other concessionary rate of duty;

performance requirement means a requirement that:

(a) a given level or percentage of goods or services be exported;

(b) domestic goods or services of the Party granting a waiver of customs duties be substituted for imported goods or services;

(c) a person benefitting from a waiver of customs duties purchase other goods or services in the territory of the Party granting the waiver or accord a preference to domestically produced goods or services; or

(d) a person benefitting from a waiver of customs duties produce goods or provide services, in the territory of the Party granting the waiver, with a given level or percentage of domestic content; or

(e) relates in any way the volume or value of imports to the volume or value of exports or to the amount of foreign exchange inflows;

printed advertising materials means those goods classified in Chapter 49 of the Harmonized System, including brochures, pamphlets, leaflets, trade catalogues, yearbooks published by trade associations, tourist promotional materials and posters, that are used to promote, publicize or advertise a good or service, are essentially intended to advertise a good or service, and are supplied free of charge;

repair or alteration does not include an operation or process that either destroys the essential characteristics of a good or creates a new or commercially different good;

satisfactory evidence means:

(a) a receipt, or a copy of a receipt, evidencing payment of customs duties on a particular entry;

(b) a copy of the entry document with evidence that it was received by a customs administration;

(c) a copy of a final customs duty determination by a customs administration respecting the relevant entry; or

(d) any other evidence of payment of customs duties acceptable under the Uniform Regulations developed in accordance with Chapter Five (Customs Procedures);

total export shipments means all shipments from total supply to users located in the territory of another Party;

total supply means all shipments, whether intended for domestic or foreign users, from:

(a) domestic production;

(b) domestic inventory; and

(c) other imports as appropriate; and

waiver of customs duties means a measure that waives otherwise applicable customs duties on any good imported from any country, including the territory of another Party.

Consequences

While the first Bush administration signed a preliminary agreement, it was left to the incoming U.S. president, Bill Clinton, to finish the negotiations and to have the completed treaty ratified. As befitting a president who had run on a campaign centered around economic issues, Clinton stood out as the strongest proponent of free trade in decades. But NAFTA was threatened with derailment from its "fast track" to ratification because of American partisan politics. Many Democrats, whose large labor constituency was traditionally protectionist, opposed the president from their own party, especially on free trade, which had been historically the political currency of the Republicans.

At the same time, the Republican majority in Congress intensely disliked Clinton and would spend much of his first term in office investigating his personal life in an attempt to find grounds for impeachment. With a Republican majority in Congress for the first time in 40 years and a Democrat in the White House, the U.S. government basically ground to a halt. Not since the Civil War had American partisanship been so bitter, and it was threatening not just NAFTA but American diplomacy across the board: in the U.S. response to the human rights crises in Africa and eastern Europe; in its policies toward nuclear disarmament and test bans; and in its trade policies, including those toward Europe, China, and Southeast Asia, as well as toward Mexico and Latin America.

NAFTA survived because the traditional free trade policy of the Republican Party prevailed over its growing isolationist and nativist protectionist wings, and Congress approved the treaty despite its animosity toward a president it would soon impeach. NAFTA, on the other hand, contributed to the tremendous economic boom the United States was enjoying under Bill Clinton, which saved his presidency. The reason this is important is that it allowed Clinton to reassure those who had worried about the effect NAFTA would have on U.S. jobs. While some jobs did migrate to Mexico under the relaxed import provisions of the treaty because U.S. firms moved some operations there to take advantage of cheaper labor, the increase in U.S. exports and the growing demand for U.S. services to its new trading partners also created many new jobs.

Fears about the spreading global market and the formation of competitive trading blocs failed, for these reasons, to fix on NAFTA itself but instead surfaced at the meetings of the World Trade Organization in Seattle, Washington, and Washington, D.C., in 1999 and 2000, respectively. There a motley crew of protesters ranging from right-wing nativists to labor union protectionists to environmentalists to youthful anarchists, some of them violent, filled the streets and engaged in a kind of civil unrest the United States had not seen since the demonstrations against the Vietnam War. The protesters had no coherent program—some decried the influence of foreigners on U.S. policy; others the degradation of the environment encouraged by free trade policies that failed to insist on ecologically sound business practices among the partners; still others the Big Brother quality of multinational financial institutions. In the long run, however, such demonstrations failed to ignite a retreat into American isolationism, whose strong current runs throughout American history.

A decade after NAFTA went into force, President George W. Bush signed int law, on August 2, 2005, a U.S.–Central America Free Trade Agreement (CAFTA) that liberalizes trade between the United States and five Central American countries: Costa Rica, El Salvador, Guatemala, Honduras, and Nicaragua. Together, NAFTA and CAFTA are seen as steps toward an eventual Free Trade Area of the Americas (FTAA), which would encompass 34 economies in the Western Hemisphere. The new world order—which began ever so haltingly to develop after World War II with the establishment of the United Nations, GATT, the World Bank, et al.—for the time being has held its course.

Source

NAFTA Secretariat, "North American Free Trade Agreement." Available online. URL: http://www.nafta-sec-alean.org./Default Site/index_e.aspx?DetailID=78. Accessed April 20, 2005.

Multinational Conventions and Agreements

CONVENTION ON PROHIBITIONS OR RESTRICTIONS ON THE USE OF CERTAIN CONVENTIONAL WEAPONS WHICH MAY BE DEEMED TO BE EXCESSIVELY INJURIOUS OR TO HAVE INDISCRIMINATE EFFECTS

TREATY AT A GLANCE

Completed
April 10, 1981; entered into force December 2, 1983

Signatories
As of summer 2005, 50 signatories, 99 parties

Overview
As adopted and opened for signature, the convention included three protocols. The aim of the convention and its three original protocols is to provide new rules for the protection of military personnel and, particularly, civilians and civilian objects from attack or injury by conventional weapons whose effects are indiscriminately destructive. The protocols specifically address limitations on weapons that produce fragments that cannot readily be detected in the human body by X-rays (Protocol I), limitations on land mines and booby traps (Protocol II), and limitations on incendiary weapons (Protocol III). In subsequent years, additional protocols have been added, and the convention allows for others to be added as the General Assembly and United Nations members deem necessary.

Historical Background

In 1899, Czar Nicholas II of Russia called for an international conference, to be convened at The Hague, Netherlands, with the object of instituting arms limitations as a first step toward eventual international disarmament. The resulting HAGUE CONVENTION OF 1899 fell far short of the czar's idealistic ambitions in that it did not ultimately address the broadest issues of arms limitation, let alone move toward disarmament; nevertheless, it did set forth provisions for arbitration as an alternative to war and also included declarations against the use of asphyxiating gases and expanding bullets as inhumane weapons. A second conference produced another HAGUE CONVENTION (1907), which failed to renew the declarations against gas warfare and expanding bullets but did more fully define the procedure, institutions, and apparatus for peaceful international arbitration and also produced a *Convention on Prisoners of War,* codifying rules of prisoner of war (POW) treatment already generally accepted and in practice.

The strongest agreement against certain inhumane weapons came in the post–World War I Protocol for the Prohibition of the Use in War of Asphyxiating, Poisonous or Other Gases, and of Bacteriological Methods of Warfare (1925), which constituted an international ban on poison gas and biological warfare. The broader issue of arms limitation had been addressed in the 1922 WASHINGTON NAVAL TREATY, which set limits to the naval strength of the five signatories, the United States, British Empire, France, Italy, and Japan. The 1930 London Naval Treaty amplified the Washington Naval Treaty by further attempting to create a balance of naval strength among the world's major powers.

In 1929, many of the world's nations adopted a series of so-called Geneva Conventions on warfare, most important of which were, the GENEVA CONVENTION RELATIVE TO THE TREATMENT OF PRISONERS OF WAR and the CONVENTION FOR THE AMELIORATION OF THE CONDITION OF THE WOUNDED AND SICK IN ARMIES IN THE FIELD. (Both of these conventions were renewed and expanded in 1949.) During this period, there were even attempts to renounce war altogether, as in the KELLOGG-BRIAND PACT of 1928 and the Saavedra Lamas Treaty of 1933, a Pan-American treaty that condemned and disavowed warfare.

Clearly, the fact and scope of World War II demonstrated the ineffectiveness of most attempts to limit and rationalize warfare, let alone avoid it. However, the enormity of atrocities perpetrated during World War II, including the Holocaust and other programs of genocide, stimulated new attempts at curbing war and humanizing the practices of warfare. While most of the early postwar treaties and conventions addressed the potentially apocalyptic issue of nuclear and thermonuclear weapons, later agreements focused on certain "conventional" (that is, non-nuclear) devices. The Convention on Prohibitions or Restrictions on the Use of Certain Conventional Weapons Which May Be Deemed to Be Excessively Injurious or to Have Indiscriminate Effects, which entered into force in 1983, is among the most important of these.

Terms

The convention proper is nothing more than an umbrella for a set of protocols dealing with limitations on specific weapons and weapons types. As originally adopted and opened for signature, the convention included three protocols:

> Protocol I on Non-Detectable Fragments prohibits the use of any weapon the primary effect of which is to injure by fragments that, in the human body, escape detection by X-rays.
>
> Protocol II on Prohibitions or Restrictions on the Use of Mines, Booby-Traps, and Other Devices prohibits the use of non-detectable anti-personnel mines and their transfer; prohibits the use of non-self-destructing and non-self-deactivating mines outside of fenced, monitored, and marked areas; broadens obligations of protection in favor of peacekeeping and other missions of the United Nations and its agencies; requires states parties to enforce compliance with its provisions within their jurisdiction; and calls for penal sanctions in case of violation. As amended on May 3, 1996, the scope of the protocol's application was extended to cover both international and internal armed conflicts.
>
> Protocol III on Prohibitions or Restrictions on the Use of Incendiary Weapons prohibits, in all circumstances, making the civilian population, individual civilians, or civilian objects the target of attack by any weapon or munition primarily designed to set fire to objects or to cause burn injury.

In subsequent years, two additional protocols have been added. These are treated in separate entries in this book: PROTOCOL ON BLINDING LASER WEAPONS TO THE CONVENTION ON PROHIBITIONS OR RESTRICTIONS ON THE USE OF CERTAIN CONVENTIONAL WEAPONS WHICH MAY BE DEEMED TO BE EXCESSIVELY INJURIOUS OR TO HAVE INDISCRIMINATE EFFECTS and PROTOCOL ON EXPLOSIVE REMNANTS OF WAR TO THE CONVENTION ON PROHIBITIONS OR RESTRICTIONS ON THE USE OF CERTAIN CONVENTIONAL WEAPONS WHICH MAY BE DEEMED TO BE EXCESSIVELY INJURIOUS OR TO HAVE INDISCRIMINATE EFFECTS.

Convention on Prohibitions or Restrictions on the Use of Certain Conventional Which May Be Deemed to Be Excessively Injurious Or to Have Indiscriminate Effects

The High Contracting Parties,

Recalling that every State has the duty, in conformity with the Charter of the United Nations, to refrain in its international relations from the threat or use of force against the sovereignty, territorial integrity or political independence of any State, or in any other manner inconsistent with the purposes of the United Nations,

Further recalling the general principle of the protection of the civilian population against the effects of hostilities,

Basing themselves on the principle of international law that the right of the parties to an armed conflict to choose methods or means of warfare is not unlimited, and on the principle that prohibits the employment in armed conflicts of weapons, projectiles and material and methods of warfare of a nature to cause superfluous injury or unnecessary suffering,

Also recalling that it is prohibited to employ methods or means of warfare which are intended, or may be expected, to cause widespread, long-term and severe damage to the natural environment,

Confirming their determination that in cases not covered by this Convention and its annexed Protocols or by other international agreements, the civilian population and the combatants shall at all times remain under the protection and authority of the principles of international law derived from established custom, from the principles of humanity and from the dictates of public conscience,

Desiring to contribute to international détente, the ending of the arms race and the building of confidence among States, and hence to the realization of the aspiration of all peoples to live in peace,

Recognizing the importance of pursuing every effort which may contribute to progress towards general and complete disarmament under strict and effective international control,

Reaffirming the need to continue the codification and progressive development of the rules of international law applicable in armed conflict,

Wishing to prohibit or restrict further the use of certain conventional weapons and believing that the positive results achieved in this area may facilitate the main talks on disarmament with a view to putting an end to the production, stockpiling and proliferation of such weapons,

Emphasizing the desirability that all States become parties to this Convention and its annexed Protocols, especially the militarily significant States,

Bearing in mind that the General Assembly of the United Nations and the United Nations Disarmament Commission may decide to examine the question of a possible broadening of the scope of the prohibitions and restrictions contained in this Convention and its annexed Protocols,

Further bearing in mind that the Committee on Disarmament may decide to consider the question of adopting further measures to prohibit or restrict the use of certain conventional weapons,

Have agreed as follows:

ARTICLE 1
SCOPE OF APPLICATION
This Convention and its annexed Protocols shall apply in the situations referred to in Article 2 common to the Geneva Conventions of 12 August 1949 for the Protection of War Victims, including any situation described in paragraph 4 of Article 1 of Additional Protocol 1 to these Conventions.

ARTICLE 2
RELATIONS WITH OTHER INTERNATIONAL AGREEMENTS
Nothing in this Convention or its annexed Protocols shall be interpreted as detracting from other obligations imposed upon the High Contracting Parties by international humanitarian law applicable in armed conflict. . . .

ARTICLE 5
ENTRY INTO FORCE
1. This Convention shall enter into force six months after the date of deposit of the twentieth instrument of ratification, acceptance, approval or accession.

2. For any State which deposits its instrument of ratification, acceptance, approval or accession after the date of the deposit of the twentieth instrument of ratification, acceptance, approval or accession, this Convention shall enter into force six months after the date on which that State has deposited its instrument of ratification, acceptance, approval or accession.

3. Each of the Protocols annexed to this Convention shall enter into force six months after the date by which twenty States have notified their consent to be bound by it in accordance with paragraph 3 or 4 of Article 4 of this Convention.

4. For any State which notifies its consent to be bound by a Protocol annexed te, this Convention after the date by which twenty States have notified their consent to be bound by it, the Protocol shall enter into force six months after the date on which that State has notified its consent so to be bound.

ARTICLE 6
DISSEMINATION
The High Contracting Parties undertake, in time of peace as in time of armed conflict, to disseminate this Convention and those of its annexed Protocols by which they are bound as widely as possible in their respective countries and, in particular, to include the study thereof in their programmes of military instruction, so that those instruments may become known to their armed forces. . . .

Protocol on Non-Detectable Fragments (Protocol I)
It is prohibited to use any weapon the primary effect of which is to injure by fragments which in the human body escape detection by X-rays.

Protocol on Prohibitions or Restrictions on the Use of Mines, Booby-Traps and Other Devices

ARTICLE 1
MATERIAL SCOPE OF APPLICATION
This Protocol relates to the use on land of the mines, booby-traps and other devices defined herein, including mines laid to interdict beaches, waterway crossings or river crossings, but does not apply to the use of anti-ship mines at sea or in inland waterways.

ARTICLE 2
DEFINITIONS
For the purpose of this Protocol:
1. "Mine" means any munition placed under, on or near the ground or other surface area and designed to be detonated or exploded by the presence, proximity or contact of a person or vehicle, and "remotely delivered mine" means any mine so defined delivered by artillery, rocket, mortar or similar means or dropped from an aircraft.

2. "Booby-trap" means any device or material which is designed, constructed or adapted to kill or injure and which functions unexpectedly when a person disturbs or approaches an apparently harmless object or performs an apparently safe act.

3. "Other devices" means manually-emplaced munitions and devices designed to kill, injure or damage and which are actuated by remote control or automatically after a lapse of time.

4. "Military objective" means, so far as objects are concerned, any object which by its nature, location, purpose or use makes an effective contribution to military action and whose total or partial destruction, capture or neutralization, in the circumstances ruling at the time, offers a definite military advantage.

5. "Civilian objects" are all objects which are not military objectives as defined in paragraph 4.

6. "Recording" means a physical, administrative and technical operation designed to obtain, for the purpose of registration in the official records, all available information facilitating the location of minefields, mines and booby-traps.

ARTICLE 3
GENERAL RESTRICTIONS ON THE USE OF MINES, BOOBY-TRAPS AND OTHER DEVICES
1. This Article applies to:
   (a) Mines;
   (b) Booby-traps; and
   (c) Other devices.

2. It is prohibited in all circumstances to direct weapons to which this Article applies, either in offence, defence or by way of reprisals, against the civilian population as such or against individual civilians.

3. The indiscriminate use of weapons to which this Article applies is prohibited. Indiscriminate use is any placement of such weapons:

(a) Which is not on, or directed against, a military objective; or

(b) Which employs a method or means of delivery which cannot bc directed at a specific military objective; or

(c) Which may be expected to cause incidental loss of civilian life, injury to civilians, damage to civilian objects, or a combination thereof, which would be excessive in relation to the concrete and direct military advantage anticipated.

4. All feasible precautions shall be taken to protect civilians from the effects of weapons to which this Article applies. Feasible precautions are those precautions which are practicable or practically possible taking into account all circumstances ruling at the time, including humanitarian and military considerations.

ARTICLE 4
RESTRICTIONS ON THE USE OF MINES OTHER THAN REMOTELY DELIVERED MINES, BOOBY-TRAPS AND OTHER DEVICES IN POPULATED AREAS

1. This Article applies to:
(a) Mines other than remotely delivered mines;
(b) Booby-traps; and
(c) Other devices.

2. It is prohibited to use weapons to which this Article applies in any city, town, village or other area containing a similar concentration of civilians in which combat between ground forces is not taking place or does not appear to be imminent, unless either:

(a) They are placed on or in the close vicinity of a military objective belonging to or under the control of an adverse party; or

(b) Measures are taken to protect civilians from their effects, for example, the posting of warning signs, the posting of sentries, the issue of warnings or the provision of fences.

ARTICLE 5
RESTRICTIONS ON THE USE OF REMOTELY DELIVERED MINES

1. The use of remotely delivered mines is prohibited unless such mines are only used within an area which is itself a military objective or which contains military objectives, and unless:

(a) Their location can be accurately recorded in accordance with Article 7 (1) (a); or

(b) An effective neutralizing mechanism is used on each such mine, that is to say, a self-actuating mechanism which is designed to render a mine harmless or cause it to destroy itself when it is anticipated that the mine will no longer serve the military purpose for which it was placed in position, or a remotely-controlled mechanism which is designed to render harmless or destroy a mine when the mine no longer serves the military purpose for which it was placed in position.

2. Effective advance warning shall be given of any delivery or dropping of remotely delivered mines which may affect the civilian population, unless circumstances do not permit.

ARTICLE 6
PROHIBITION ON THE USE OF CERTAIN BOOBY-TRAPS

1. Without prejudice to the rules of international law applicable in armed conflict relating to treachery and perfidy, it is prohibited in all circumstances to use:

(a) Any booby-trap in the form of an apparently harmless portable object which is specifically designed and constructed to contain explosive material and tc, detonate when it is disturbed or approached, or

(b) Booby-traps which are in any way attached to or associated with:

(i) Internationally recognized protective emblems, signs or signals;

(ii) Sick, wounded or dead persons;

(iii) Burial or cremation sites or graves;

(iv) Medical facilities, medical equipment, medical supplies or medical transportations;

(v) Children's toys or other portable objects or products specially designed for the feeding, health, hygiene, clothing or education of children;

(vi) Food or drink;

(vii) Kitchen utensils or appliances except in military establishments, military locations or military supply depots;

(viii) Objects clearly of a religious nature;

(ix) Historic monuments, works of art or places of worship which constitute the cultural or spiritual heritage of peoples;

(x) Animals or their carcasses.

2. It is prohibited in all circumstances to use any booby-trap which is assigned to cause superfluous injury or unnecessary suffering.

ARTICLE 7
RECORDING AND PUBLICATION OF THE LOCATION OF MINE-FIELDS, MINES AND BOOBY-TRAPS

1. The parties to a conflict shall record the location of:
(a) All pre-planned minefields laid by them; and
(b) All areas in which they have made large-scale and pre-planned use of booby-traps.

2. The parties shall endeavour to ensure the recording of the location of all other minefields, mines and booby-traps which they have laid or placed in position.

3. All such records shall be retained by the parties who shall:

(a) Immediately after the cessation of active hostilities:

(i) Take all necessary and appropriate measures, including the use of such records, to protect civilians from the effects of minefields, mines and booby-traps; and either

(ii) In cases where the forces of neither party are in the territory of the adverse party, make available to, each other and to the Secretary-General of the United Nations all information in their possession concerning the location of minefields, mines and booby-traps in the territory of the adverse party; or

(iii) Once complete withdrawal of the forces of the parties from the territory of the adverse party has taken place, make available to the adverse party and to the Secretary-General of the United Nations all information in their possession concerning the location of minefields, mines and booby-traps in the territory of the adverse party;

(b) When a United Nations force or mission performs functions in any area, make available to the authority mentioned in Article 8 such information as is required by that Article;

(c) Whenever possible, by mutual agreement, provide for the release of information concerning the location of minefields, mines and booby-traps, particularly in agreements governing the cessation of hostilities.

ARTICLE 8
PROTECTION OF UNITED NATIONS FORCES AND MISSIONS FROM THE EFFECTS OF MINEFIELDS, MINES AND BOOBY-TRAPS

1. When a United Nations force or mission performs functions of peace-keeping, observation or similar functions in any area, each party to the conflict shall, if requested by the head of the United Nations force or mission in that area, as far as it is able:

(a) Remove or render harmless all mines or booby-traps in that area;

(b) Take such measures as may be necessary to protect the force or mission from the effects of minefields, mines and booby-traps while carrying out its duties; and

(c) Make available to the head of the United Nations force or mission in that area, all information in the party's possession concerning the location of minefields, mines and booby-traps in that area.

2. When a United Nations fact-finding mission performs functions in any area, any party to the conflict concerned shall provide protection to that mission except where, because of the size of such mission, it cannot adequately provide such protection. In that case it shall make available to the head of the mission the information in its possession concerning the location of minefields, mines and booby-traps in that area.

ARTICLE 9
INTERNATIONAL CO-OPERATION IN THE REMOVAL OF MINEFIELDS, MINES AND BOOBY-TRAPS

After the cessation of active hostilities, the parties shall endeavour to reach agreement, both among themselves and, where appropriate, with other States and with international organizations, on the provision of information and technical and material assistance—including, in appropriate circumstances, joint operations—necessary to remove or otherwise render ineffective minefields, mines and booby-traps placed in position during the conflict.

TECHNICAL ANNEX TO THE PROTOCOL ON PROHIBITIONS OR RESTRICTIONS ON THE USE OF MINES, BOOBY-TRAPS AND OTHER DEVICES (PROTOCOL II)

GUIDELINES ON RECORDING

Whenever an obligation for the recording of the location of minefields, mines and booby-traps arises under the Protocol, the following guidelines shall be taken into account.

1. With regard to pre-planned minefields and large-scale and pre-planned use of booby-traps:

(a) Maps, diagrams or other records should be made in such a way as to indicate the extent of the minefield or booby-trapped area; and

(b) The location of the minefield or booby-trapped area should be specified by relation to the co-ordinates of a single reference point and by the estimated dimensions of the area containing mines and booby-traps in relation to that single reference point.

2. With regard to other minefields, mines and booby-traps laid or placed in position:

In so far as possible, the relevant information specified in paragraph 1 above should be recorded so as to enable the areas containing minefields, mines and booby-traps to be identified.

Protocol on Prohibitions or Restrictions on the Use of Incendiary Weapons (Protocol III)

ARTICLE 1
DEFINITIONS

For the purpose of this Protocol:

1. "Incendiary weapon" means any weapon or munition which is primarily designed to set fire to objects or to cause burn injury to persons through the action of flame, heat, or a combination thereof, produced by a chemical reaction of a substance delivered on the target.

(a) Incendiary weapons can take the form of, for example, flame throwers, fougasses, shells, rockets, grenades, mines, bombs and other containers of incendiary substances.

(b) Incendiary weapons do not include:

(i) Munitions which may have incidental incendiary effects, such as illuminants, tracers, smoke or signalling systems;

(a) Munitions designed to combine penetration, blast or fragmentation effects with an additional incendiary effect, such as armour-piercing projectiles, fragmentation shells, explosive bombs and similar combined-effects munitions in which the incendiary effect is not specifically designed to cause burn injury to persons, but to be used against military objectives, such as armoured vehicles, aircraft and installations or facilities.

2. "Concentration of civilians" means any concentration of civilians, be it permanent or temporary, such as in inhabited parts of cities, or inhabited towns or villages, or as in camps or columns of refugees or evacuees, or groups of nomads.

3. "Military objective" means, so far as objects are concerned, any object which by its nature, location, purpose or use makes an effective contribution to military action and whose total or partial destruction, capture or neutralization, in the circumstances ruling at the time, offers, a definite military advantage.

4. "Civilian objects" are all objects which are not military objectives as defined in paragraph 3.

5. "Feasible precautions" are those precautions which are practicable or practically possible taking into account all circumstances ruling at the time, including humanitarian and military considerations.

ARTICLE 2
PROTECTION OF CIVILIANS AND CIVILIAN OBJECTS

1. It is prohibited in all circumstances to make the civilian pop-

ulation as such, individual civilians or civilian objects the object of attack by incendiary weapons.

2. It is prohibited in all circumstances to make any military objective located within a concentration of civilians the object of attack by air-delivered incendiary weapons.

3. It is further prohibited to make any military objective located within a concentration of civilians the object of attack by means of incendiary weapons other than air-delivered incendiary weapons, except when such military objective is clearly separated from the concentration of civilians and all feasible precautions are taken with a view to limiting the incendiary effects to the military objective and to avoiding, and in any event to minimizing, incidental loss of civilian life, injury to civilians and damage to civilian objects.

4. It is prohibited to make forests or other kinds of plant cover the object of attack by incendiary weapons except when such natural elements are used to cover, conceal or camouflage combatants or other military objectives, or are themselves military objectives.

Consequences

Of the weapons restricted here, the only class that remains an especially serious threat is that of the land mine. (See CONVENTION ON THE PROHIBITION OF THE USE, STOCKPILING, PRODUCTION AND TRANSFER OF ANTI-PERSONNEL MINES AND ON THEIR DESTRUCTION for a discussion of this issue and of the United States's refusal to agree to the ban.)

In recent years, a further limitation of the convention and its protocols has become increasingly apparent. As covenants among sovereign states, these agreements have no force or effect on terrorists, terrorist organizations, or on the military arm of states without territory and/or full international recognition (such as Palestine, for example). All of these groups make use of booby traps and other weapons, often improvised, that are indiscriminately destructive.

Source

United Nations, "Convention on Prohibitions or Restrictions on the Use of Certain Conventional Weapons Which May Be Deemed to Be Excessively Injurious or to Have Indiscriminate Effects," Millennium Assembly of the United Nations. Available online. URL: http://www.un.org/millennium/law/xxvi-18–19.htm Accessed December 30, 2004.

CONVENTION AGAINST TORTURE AND OTHER CRUEL, INHUMAN OR DEGRADING TREATMENT OR PUNISHMENT

<hr>

TREATY AT A GLANCE

Completed
December 10, 1984; entered into force June 26, 1987

Signatories
As of summer 2005, 74 signatories, 140 parties

Overview
Pursuant to the desire "to make more effective the struggle against torture and other cruel, inhuman or degrading treatment or punishment throughout the world," the convention defines torture broadly in both physical and mental terms and prohibits it absolutely.

<hr>

Historical Background

Torture and other cruel, inhuman, or degrading treatment or punishment have long been regarded by most of the world's nations as immoral and, when practiced as state policy, as violations of so-called customary international law (the international equivalent of common law, which comes into being when states follow certain practices generally and consistently out of a sense of legal obligation). In addition to being prohibited by customary international law, torture is also disallowed in most major legal systems. In practice, codified international law is the product of customary international law, law common to major national legal systems, or a combination of both of these. Thus torture is, in effect, prohibited by international law, even without the present convention. Furthermore, all comprehensive international instruments that in any way relate to legal punishment or to the treatment of prisoners of war explicitly prohibit torture. The preponderance of such prohibitions in major international instruments also reinforces the prohibition of torture as part of the accepted body of international law. On the basis, then, of long tradition and a generally accepted perception of law and morality in this matter, and in harmony with the United Nations Universal Declaration of Human Rights (1948), Article 5, which states that "No one shall be subject to torture or to cruel, inhuman or degrading treatment or punishment," the United Nations General Assembly adopted a formal Convention against Torture and Other Cruel, Inhuman or Degrading Treatment or Punishment on December 10, 1984.

A significant group of the parties to the convention asserted reservations with regard to Articles 20 and 21, which give a 10-person UN Committee against Torture the authority to investigate and report on alleged instances of torture in any signatory nation. The reservations withheld recognition of the committee's "competence" or "authority" to conduct such investigations. Some signatories, most notably China and the United States, declined to accede to paragraph 1 of article 30:

> Any dispute between two or more States Parties concerning the interpretation or application of this Convention which cannot be settled through negotiation shall, at the request of one of them, be submitted to arbitration. If within six months from the date of the request for arbitration the Parties are unable to agree on the organization of the arbitration, any one of those Parties may refer the dispute to the International Court of Justice by request in conformity with the Statute of the Court.

In addition to disallowing Article 30, paragraph 1, the United States ratified the treaty with a number of other significant reservations, including the stipulation that "the United States considers itself bound by the obligation under article 16 to prevent 'cruel, inhuman or degrading treatment or punishment', only insofar as the term 'cruel, inhuman or degrading treatment or punishment' means the cruel, unusual and inhumane treatment or punishment prohibited by the Fifth, Eighth, and/or Fourteenth Amendments to the Constitution of the United States." The U.S. reservations also include the stipulation that "the United States understands that international law does not prohibit the death penalty, and does not consider this Convention to restrict or prohibit the United States from applying the death penalty consistent with the Fifth, Eighth and/or Fourteenth Amendments to the Constitution of the United States, including any constitutional period of confinement prior to the imposition of the death penalty." To preserve federalism, the United States stipulates its understanding that "this Convention shall be implemented by the United States Government to the extent that it exercises legislative and judicial jurisdiction over the matters covered by the Convention and otherwise by the state and local governments."

Terms

The convention defines torture as the infliction of pain or suffering, "whether physical or mental," and prohibits the practice absolutely. Each state party is bound to "take effective . . . measures to prevent acts of torture in any territory under its jurisdiction." Moreover, "no exceptional circumstances whatsoever" may be used to justify torture, nor can an "order from a superior officer or public authority" be used to justify torture.

Part II of the convention establishes a UN Committee against Torture, consisting of 10 expert authorities in the field of human rights, elected by the member states of the United Nations. The committee is charged with investigating incidents of reported torture and reporting on programs instituted by states parties to eliminate torture. The convention also stipulates that states parties submit reports every four years on the status of national programs to eliminate and prohibit the use of torture.

Convention against Torture and Other Cruel, Inhuman or Degrading Treatment or Punishment

The States Parties to this Convention,

Considering that, in accordance with the principles proclaimed in the Charter of the United Nations, recognition of the equal and inalienable rights of all members of the human family is the foundation of freedom, justice and peace in the world,

Recognizing that those rights derive from the inherent dignity of the human person,

Considering the obligation of States under the Charter, in particular Article 55, to promote universal respect for, and observance of, human rights and fundamental freedoms,

Having regard to article 5 of the Universal Declaration of Human Rights and article 7 of the International Covenant on Civil and Political Rights, both of which provide that no one shall be subjected to torture or to cruel, inhuman or degrading treatment or punishment,

Having regard also to the Declaration on the Protection of All Persons from Being Subjected to Torture and Other Cruel, Inhuman or Degrading Treatment or Punishment, adopted by the General Assembly on 9 December 1975,

Desiring to make more effective the struggle against torture and other cruel, inhuman or degrading treatment or punishment throughout the world,

Have agreed as follows:

PART I

ARTICLE 1

1. For the purposes of this Convention, the term "torture" means any act by which severe pain or suffering, whether physical or mental, is intentionally inflicted on a person for such purposes as obtaining from him or a third person information or a confession, punishing him for an act he or a third person has committed or is suspected of having committed, or intimidating or coercing him or a third person, or for any reason based on discrimination of any kind, when such pain or suffering is inflicted by or at the instigation of or with the consent or acquiescence of a public official or other person acting in an official capacity. It does not include pain or suffering arising only from, inherent in or incidental to lawful sanctions.

2. This article is without prejudice to any international instrument or national legislation which does or may contain provisions of wider application.

ARTICLE 2

1. Each State Party shall take effective legislative, administrative, judicial or other measures to prevent acts of torture in any territory under its jurisdiction.

2. No exceptional circumstances whatsoever, whether a state of war or a threat of war, internal political in stability or any other public emergency, may be invoked as a justification of torture.

3. An order from a superior officer or a public authority may not be invoked as a justification of torture.

ARTICLE 3
GENERAL COMMENT ON ITS IMPLEMENTATION

1. No State Party shall expel, return ("refouler") or extradite a person to another State where there are substantial grounds for believing that he would be in danger of being subjected to torture.

2. For the purpose of determining whether there are such grounds, the competent authorities shall take into account all relevant considerations including, where applicable, the existence in the State concerned of a consistent pattern of gross, flagrant or mass violations of human rights.

ARTICLE 4

1. Each State Party shall ensure that all acts of torture are offences under its criminal law. The same shall apply to an attempt to commit torture and to an act by any person which constitutes complicity or participation in torture.

2. Each State Party shall make these offences punishable by appropriate penalties which take into account their grave nature.

ARTICLE 5

1. Each State Party shall take such measures as may be necessary to establish its jurisdiction over the offences referred to in article 4 in the following cases:

(a) When the offences are committed in any territory under its jurisdiction or on board a ship or aircraft registered in that State;

(b) When the alleged offender is a national of that State;

(c) When the victim is a national of that State if that State considers it appropriate.

2. Each State Party shall likewise take such measures as may be necessary to establish its jurisdiction over such offences in cases where the alleged offender is present in any territory under its jurisdiction and it does not extradite him pursuant to article 8 to any of the States mentioned in paragraph I of this article.

3. This Convention does not exclude any criminal jurisdiction exercised in accordance with internal law.

ARTICLE 6

1. Upon being satisfied, after an examination of information available to it, that the circumstances so warrant, any State Party in whose territory a person alleged to have committed any offence referred to in article 4 is present shall take him into custody or take other legal measures to ensure his presence. The custody and other legal measures shall be as provided in the law of that State but may be continued only for such time as is necessary to enable any criminal or extradition proceedings to be instituted.

2. Such State shall immediately make a preliminary inquiry into the facts.

3. Any person in custody pursuant to paragraph I of this article shall be assisted in communicating immediately with the nearest appropriate representative of the State of which he is a national, or, if he is a stateless person, with the representative of the State where he usually resides.

4. When a State, pursuant to this article, has taken a person into custody, it shall immediately notify the States referred to in article 5, paragraph 1, of the fact that such person is in custody and of the circumstances which warrant his detention. The State which makes the preliminary inquiry contemplated in paragraph 2 of this article shall promptly report its findings to the said States and shall indicate whether it intends to exercise jurisdiction.

ARTICLE 7

1. The State Party in the territory under whose jurisdiction a person alleged to have committed any offence referred to in article 4 is found shall in the cases contemplated in article 5, if it does not extradite him, submit the case to its competent authorities for the purpose of prosecution.

2. These authorities shall take their decision in the same manner as in the case of any ordinary offence of a serious nature under the law of that State. In the cases referred to in article 5, paragraph 2, the standards of evidence required for prosecution and conviction shall in no way be less stringent than those which apply in the cases referred to in article 5, paragraph 1.

3. Any person regarding whom proceedings are brought in connection with any of the offences referred to in article 4 shall be guaranteed fair treatment at all stages of the proceedings.

ARTICLE 8

1. The offences referred to in article 4 shall be deemed to be included as extraditable offences in any extradition treaty existing between States Parties. States Parties undertake to include such offences as extraditable offences in every extradition treaty to be concluded between them.

2. If a State Party which makes extradition conditional on the existence of a treaty receives a request for extradition from another State Party with which it has no extradition treaty, it may consider this Convention as the legal basis for extradition in respect of such offences. Extradition shall be subject to the other conditions provided by the law of the requested State.

3. States Parties which do not make extradition conditional on the existence of a treaty shall recognize such offences as extraditable offences between themselves subject to the conditions provided by the law of the requested State.

4. Such offences shall be treated, for the purpose of extradition between States Parties, as if they had been committed not only in the place in which they occurred but also in the territories of the States required to establish their jurisdiction in accordance with article 5, paragraph 1.

ARTICLE 9

1. States Parties shall afford one another the greatest measure of assistance in connection with criminal proceedings brought in respect of any of the offences referred to in article 4, including the supply of all evidence at their disposal necessary for the proceedings.

2. States Parties shall carry out their obligations under paragraph I of this article in conformity with any treaties on mutual judicial assistance that may exist between them.

ARTICLE 10

1. Each State Party shall ensure that education and information regarding the prohibition against torture are fully included in the training of law enforcement personnel, civil or military, medical personnel, public officials and other persons who may be involved in the custody, interrogation or treatment of any individual subjected to any form of arrest, detention or imprisonment.

2. Each State Party shall include this prohibition in the rules or instructions issued in regard to the duties and functions of any such person.

ARTICLE 11

Each State Party shall keep under systematic review interrogation rules, instructions, methods and practices as well as arrangements for the custody and treatment of persons subjected to any form of arrest, detention or imprisonment in any territory under its jurisdiction, with a view to preventing any cases of torture.

ARTICLE 12

Each State Party shall ensure that its competent authorities proceed to a prompt and impartial investigation, wherever there is reasonable ground to believe that an act of torture has been committed in any territory under its jurisdiction.

ARTICLE 13

Each State Party shall ensure that any individual who alleges he has been subjected to torture in any territory under its jurisdiction has the right to complain to, and to have his case promptly and impartially examined by, its competent authorities. Steps shall be taken to ensure that the complainant and witnesses are protected against all ill-treatment or intimidation as a consequence of his complaint or any evidence given.

ARTICLE 14

1. Each State Party shall ensure in its legal system that the victim of an act of torture obtains redress and has an enforceable right to fair and adequate compensation, including the means for as full rehabilitation as possible. In the event of the death of the victim as a result of an act of torture, his dependants shall be entitled to compensation.

2. Nothing in this article shall affect any right of the victim or other persons to compensation which may exist under national law.

ARTICLE 15

Each State Party shall ensure that any statement which is established to have been made as a result of torture shall not be invoked as evidence in any proceedings, except against a person accused of torture as evidence that the statement was made.

ARTICLE 16

1. Each State Party shall undertake to prevent in any territory under its jurisdiction other acts of cruel, inhuman or degrading treatment or punishment which do not amount to torture as defined in article I, when such acts are committed by or at the instigation of or with the consent or acquiescence of a public official or other person acting in an official capacity. In particular, the obligations contained in articles 10, 11, 12 and 13 shall apply with the substitution for references to torture of references to other forms of cruel, inhuman or degrading treatment or punishment.

2. The provisions of this Convention are without prejudice to the provisions of any other international instrument or national law which prohibits cruel, inhuman or degrading treatment or punishment or which relates to extradition or expulsion.

PART II

ARTICLE 17

1. There shall be established a Committee against Torture (hereinafter referred to as the Committee) which shall carry out the functions hereinafter provided. The Committee shall consist of ten experts of high moral standing and recognized competence in the field of human rights, who shall serve in their personal capacity. The experts shall be elected by the States Parties, consideration being given to equitable geographical distribution and to the usefulness of the participation of some persons having legal experience.

2. The members of the Committee shall be elected by secret ballot from a list of persons nominated by States Parties. Each State Party may nominate one person from among its own nationals. States Parties shall bear in mind the usefulness of nominating persons who are also members of the Human Rights Committee established under the International Covenant on Civil and Political Rights and who are willing to serve on the Committee against Torture.

3. Elections of the members of the Committee shall be held at biennial meetings of States Parties convened by the Secretary-General of the United Nations. At those meetings, for which two thirds of the States Parties shall constitute a quorum, the persons elected to the Committee shall be those who obtain the largest number of votes and an absolute majority of the votes of the representatives of States Parties present and voting.

4. The initial election shall be held no later than six months after the date of the entry into force of this Convention. At least four months before the date of each election, the Secretary-General of the United Nations shall address a letter to the States Parties inviting them to submit their nominations within three months. The Secretary-General shall prepare a list in alphabetical order of all persons thus nominated, indicating the States Parties which have nominated them, and shall submit it to the States Parties.

5. The members of the Committee shall be elected for a term of four years. They shall be eligible for re-election if renominated. However, the term of five of the members elected at the first election shall expire at the end of two years; immediately after the first election the names of these five members shall be chosen by lot by the chairman of the meeting referred to in paragraph 3 of this article.

6. If a member of the Committee dies or resigns or for any other cause can no longer perform his Committee duties, the State Party which nominated him shall appoint another expert from among its nationals to serve for the remainder of his term, subject to the approval of the majority of the States Parties. The approval shall be considered given unless half or more of the States Parties respond negatively within six weeks after having been informed by the Secretary-General of the United Nations of the proposed appointment.

7. States Parties shall be responsible for the expenses of the members of the Committee while they are in performance of Committee duties. (amendment (see General Assembly resolution 47/111 of 16 December 1992); status of ratification)

ARTICLE 18

1. The Committee shall elect its officers for a term of two years. They may be re-elected.

2. The Committee shall establish its own rules of procedure, but these rules shall provide, inter alia, that:

(a) Six members shall constitute a quorum;

(b) Decisions of the Committee shall be made by a majority vote of the members present.

3. The Secretary-General of the United Nations shall provide the necessary staff and facilities for the effective performance of the functions of the Committee under this Convention.

4. The Secretary-General of the United Nations shall convene the initial meeting of the Committee. After its initial meeting, the Committee shall meet at such times as shall be provided in its rules of procedure.

5. The States Parties shall be responsible for expenses incurred in connection with the holding of meetings of the States Parties and of the Committee, including reimbursement to the United Nations for any expenses, such as the cost of staff and facilities, incurred by the United Nations pursuant to paragraph 3 of this article.

ARTICLE 19

1. The States Parties shall submit to the Committee, through the Secretary-General of the United Nations, reports on the measures they have taken to give effect to their undertakings under this Convention, within one year after the entry into force of the Convention for the State Party concerned. Thereafter the States

Parties shall submit supplementary reports every four years on any new measures taken and such other reports as the Committee may request.

2. The Secretary-General of the United Nations shall transmit the reports to all States Parties.

3. Each report shall be considered by the Committee which may make such general comments on the report as it may consider appropriate and shall forward these to the State Party concerned. That State Party may respond with any observations it chooses to the Committee.

4. The Committee may, at its discretion, decide to include any comments made by it in accordance with paragraph 3 of this article, together with the observations thereon received from the State Party concerned, in its annual report made in accordance with article 24. If so requested by the State Party concerned, the Committee may also include a copy of the report submitted under paragraph I of this article.

ARTICLE 20

1. If the Committee receives reliable information which appears to it to contain well-founded indications that torture is being systematically practised in the territory of a State Party, the Committee shall invite that State Party to co-operate in the examination of the information and to this end to submit observations with regard to the information concerned.

2. Taking into account any observations which may have been submitted by the State Party concerned, as well as any other relevant information available to it, the Committee may, if it decides that this is warranted, designate one or more of its members to make a confidential inquiry and to report to the Committee urgently.

3. If an inquiry is made in accordance with paragraph 2 of this article, the Committee shall seek the co-operation of the State Party concerned. In agreement with that State Party, such an inquiry may include a visit to its territory.

4. After examining the findings of its member or members submitted in accordance with paragraph 2 of this article, the Commission shall transmit these findings to the State Party concerned together with any comments or suggestions which seem appropriate in view of the situation.

5. All the proceedings of the Committee referred to in paragraphs 1 to 4 of this article shall be confidential, and at all stages of the proceedings the co-operation of the State Party shall be sought. After such proceedings have been completed with regard to an inquiry made in accordance with paragraph 2, the Committee may, after consultations with the State Party concerned, decide to include a summary account of the results of the proceedings in its annual report made in accordance with article 24.

ARTICLE 21

1. A State Party to this Convention may at any time declare under this article that it recognizes the competence of the Committee to receive and consider communications to the effect that a State Party claims that another State Party is not fulfilling its obligations under this Convention. Such communications may be received and considered according to the procedures laid down in this article only if submitted by a State Party which has made a declaration recognizing in regard to itself the competence of the Committee. No communication shall be dealt with by the Committee under this article if it concerns a State Party which has not made such a declaration. Communications received under this article shall be dealt with in accordance with the following procedure;

(a) If a State Party considers that another State Party is not giving effect to the provisions of this Convention, it may, by written communication, bring the matter to the attention of that State Party. Within three months after the receipt of the communication the receiving State shall afford the State which sent the communication an explanation or any other statement in writing clarifying the matter, which should include, to the extent possible and pertinent, reference to domestic procedures and remedies taken, pending or available in the matter;

(b) If the matter is not adjusted to the satisfaction of both States Parties concerned within six months after the receipt by the receiving State of the initial communication, either State shall have the right to refer the matter to the Committee, by notice given to the Committee and to the other State;

(c) The Committee shall deal with a matter referred to it under this article only after it has ascertained that all domestic remedies have been invoked and exhausted in the matter, in conformity with the generally recognized principles of international law. This shall not be the rule where the application of the remedies is unreasonably prolonged or is unlikely to bring effective relief to the person who is the victim of the violation of this Convention;

(d) The Committee shall hold closed meetings when examining communications under this article;

(e) Subject to the provisions of subparagraph (c), the Committee shall make available its good offices to the States Parties concerned with a view to a friendly solution of the matter on the basis of respect for the obligations provided for in this Convention. For this purpose, the Committee may, when appropriate, set up an ad hoc conciliation commission;

(f) In any matter referred to it under this article, the Committee may call upon the States Parties concerned, referred to in subparagraph (b), to supply any relevant information;

(g) The States Parties concerned, referred to in subparagraph (b), shall have the right to be represented when the matter is being considered by the Committee and to make submissions orally and/or in writing;

(h) The Committee shall, within twelve months after the date of receipt of notice under subparagraph (b), submit a report:

(i) If a solution within the terms of subparagraph (e) is reached, the Committee shall confine its report to a brief statement of the facts and of the solution reached;

(ii) If a solution within the terms of subparagraph (e) is not reached, the Committee shall confine its report to a brief statement of the facts; the written submissions and record of the oral submissions made by the States Parties concerned shall be attached to the report.

In every matter, the report shall be communicated to the States Parties concerned.

2. The provisions of this article shall come into force when five States Parties to this Convention have made declarations under paragraph 1 of this article. Such declarations shall be deposited by the States Parties with the Secretary-General of the United Nations, who shall transmit copies thereof to the other States Parties. A declaration may be withdrawn at any time by notification to the Secretary-General. Such a withdrawal shall not prejudice the consideration of any matter which is the subject of a communication already transmitted under this article; no further communication by any State Party shall be received under this article after the notification of withdrawal of the declaration has been received by the Secretary-General, unless the State Party concerned has made a new declaration.

ARTICLE 22

1. A State Party to this Convention may at any time declare under this article that it recognizes the competence of the Committee to receive and consider communications from or on behalf of individuals subject to its jurisdiction who claim to be victims of a violation by a State Party of the provisions of the Convention. No communication shall be received by the Committee if it concerns a State Party which has not made such a declaration.

2. The Committee shall consider inadmissible any communication under this article which is anonymous or which it considers to be an abuse of the right of submission of such communications or to be incompatible with the provisions of this Convention.

3. Subject to the provisions of paragraph 2, the Committee shall bring any communications submitted to it under this article to the attention of the State Party to this Convention which has made a declaration under paragraph I and is alleged to be violating any provisions of the Convention. Within six months, the receiving State shall submit to the Committee written explanations or statements clarifying the matter and the remedy, if any, that may have been taken by that State.

4. The Committee shall consider communications received under this article in the light of all information made available to it by or on behalf of the individual and by the State Party concerned.

5. The Committee shall not consider any communications from an individual under this article unless it has ascertained that:

(a) The same matter has not been, and is not being, examined under another procedure of international investigation or settlement;

(b) The individual has exhausted all available domestic remedies; this shall not be the rule where the application of the remedies is unreasonably prolonged or is unlikely to bring effective relief to the person who is the victim of the violation of this Convention.

6. The Committee shall hold closed meetings when examining communications under this article.

7. The Committee shall forward its views to the State Party concerned and to the individual.

8. The provisions of this article shall come into force when five States Parties to this Convention have made declarations under paragraph 1 of this article. Such declarations shall be deposited by the States Parties with the Secretary-General of the United Nations, who shall transmit copies thereof to the other States Parties. A declaration may be withdrawn at any time by notification to the Secretary-General. Such a withdrawal shall not prejudice the consideration of any matter which is the subject of a communication already transmitted under this article; no further communication by or on behalf of an individual shall be received under this article after the notification of withdrawal of the declaration has been received by the Secretary-General, unless the State Party has made a new declaration.

ARTICLE 23

The members of the Committee and of the ad hoc conciliation commissions which may be appointed under article 21, paragraph I (e), shall be entitled to the facilities, privileges and immunities of experts on mission for the United Nations as laid down in the relevant sections of the Convention on the Privileges and Immunities of the United Nations.

ARTICLE 24

The Committee shall submit an annual report on its activities under this Convention to the States Parties and to the General Assembly of the United Nations.

PART III

ARTICLE 25

1. This Convention is open for signature by all States. 2. This Convention is subject to ratification. Instruments of ratification shall be deposited with the Secretary-General of the United Nations.

ARTICLE 26

This Convention is open to accession by all States. Accession shall be effected by the deposit of an instrument of accession with the Secretary-General of the United Nations.

ARTICLE 27

1. This Convention shall enter into force on the thirtieth day after the date of the deposit with the Secretary-General of the United Nations of the twentieth instrument of ratification or accession.

2. For each State ratifying this Convention or acceding to it after the deposit of the twentieth instrument of ratification or accession, the Convention shall enter into force on the thirtieth day after the date of the deposit of its own instrument of ratification or accession.

ARTICLE 28

1. Each State may, at the time of signature or ratification of this Convention or accession thereto, declare that it does not recognize the competence of the Committee provided for in article 20.

2. Any State Party having made a reservation in accordance with paragraph I of this article may, at any time, withdraw this reservation by notification to the Secretary-General of the United Nations.

ARTICLE 29

1. Any State Party to this Convention may propose an amendment and file it with the Secretary-General of the United Nations. The Secretary-General shall thereupon communicate the proposed amendment to the States Parties with a request that they notify him whether they favour a conference of States Parties for the purpose of considering and voting upon the proposal. In the event that within four months from the date of such communication at least one third of the States Parties favours such a conference, the Secretary-General shall convene the con-

ference under the auspices of the United Nations. Any amendment adopted by a majority of the States Parties present and voting at the conference shall be submitted by the Secretary-General to all the States Parties for acceptance.

2. An amendment adopted in accordance with paragraph I of this article shall enter into force when two thirds of the States Parties to this Convention have notified the Secretary-General of the United Nations that they have accepted it in accordance with their respective constitutional processes.

3. When amendments enter into force, they shall be binding on those States Parties which have accepted them, other States Parties still being bound by the provisions of this Convention and any earlier amendments which they have accepted.

ARTICLE 30

1. Any dispute between two or more States Parties concerning the interpretation or application of this Convention which cannot be settled through negotiation shall, at the request of one of them, be submitted to arbitration. If within six months from the date of the request for arbitration the Parties are unable to agree on the organization of the arbitration, any one of those Parties may refer the dispute to the International Court of Justice by request in conformity with the Statute of the Court.

2. Each State may, at the time of signature or ratification of this Convention or accession thereto, declare that it does not consider itself bound by paragraph I of this article. The other States Parties shall not be bound by paragraph I of this article with respect to any State Party having made such a reservation.

3. Any State Party having made a reservation in accordance with paragraph 2 of this article may at any time withdraw this reservation by notification to the Secretary-General of the United Nations.

ARTICLE 31

1. A State Party may denounce this Convention by written notification to the Secretary-General of the United Nations. Denunciation becomes effective one year after the date of receipt of the notification by the Secretary-General.

2. Such a denunciation shall not have the effect of releasing the State Party from its obligations under this Convention in regard to any act or omission which occurs prior to the date at which the denunciation becomes effective, nor shall denunciation prejudice in any way the continued consideration of any matter which is already under consideration by the Committee prior to the date at which the denunciation becomes effective.

3. Following the date at which the denunciation of a State Party becomes effective, the Committee shall not commence consideration of any new matter regarding that State.

ARTICLE 32

The Secretary-General of the United Nations shall inform all States Members of the United Nations and all States which have signed this Convention or acceded to it of the following:

(a) Signatures, ratifications and accessions under articles 25 and 26;

(b) The date of entry into force of this Convention under article 27 and the date of the entry into force of any amendments under article 29;

(c) Denunciations under article 31.

ARTICLE 33

1. This Convention, of which the Arabic, Chinese, English, French, Russian and Spanish texts are equally authentic, shall be deposited with the Secretary-General of the United Nations.

2. The Secretary-General of the United Nations shall transmit certified copies of this Convention to all States.

Consequences

As it was adopted and entered into force, the convention lacked a mechanism for practical enforcement; therefore, on December 18, 2002, the General Assembly adopted the OPTIONAL PROTOCOL TO THE CONVENTION AGAINST TORTURE AND OTHER CRUEL, INHUMAN OR DEGRADING TREATMENT OR PUNISHMENT, which provides such a mechanism. As of spring 2005, the Optional Protocol had yet to enter into force. Until this protocol does enter into force, it is impossible to gauge the effect of the convention proper.

Sources

Office of the United Nations High Commissioner for Human Rights, "Convention against Torture and Other Cruel, Inhuman or Degrading Treatment or Punishment." Available online. URL: http://www.unhchr.ch/html/menu3/b/h_cat39.htm. Accessed December 30, 2004.

———. "Declarations and Reservations." Available online. URL: http://www.unhchr.ch/html/menu2/6/cat/treaties/convention-reserv.htm. Accessed December 30, 2004.

MONTREAL PROTOCOL ON SUBSTANCES THAT DEPLETE THE OZONE LAYER

TREATY AT A GLANCE

Completed
September 16, 1987, at Montreal, Quebec;
entered into force January 1, 1989

Signatories
Initially, the 24 nations attending the conference; as of summer 2005, 46 nations are signatories and 189 are party to the protocol

Overview
In September 1987 representatives of 24 nations gathered at an unsponsored international conference in Montreal, Canada, and agreed in principle to a treaty calling for limiting the production of chlorofluorocarbons (CFCs), used widely in such modern conveniences as aerosol sprays and air-conditioning equipment and which damage Earth's ozone layer.

Historical Background

Before the late 1970s, few people knew about the layer of ozone that envelops the earth at the level of its troposphere. Then scientists began to detect decreases in ozone concentrations in the envelope, a fact that received much attention in the press. High-altitude flights by U2 "spy planes," modified as ER-2 research aircraft, confirmed the decreases, especially over Antarctica, where ozone concentrations decline naturally each spring. The scientific community's growing concern led the United Nations Environment Programme (UNEP) to begin addressing the issue of ozone depletion in 1977.

Ozone (O_3) is created when oxygen (O_2) molecules are bombarded by solar ultraviolet rays and some of the free oxygen atoms recombine with O_2 to form O_3. Unlike the two-atom oxygen, the three-atom ozone absorbs ultraviolet light and therefore protects the oxygen beneath it in the atmosphere, also absorbing most of the harmful, high-radiation ultraviolet rays before they reach the earth. Depletion of the ozone layer is dangerous because it allows oxygen to be lost and admits higher levels of ultraviolet radiation, which could cause eye damage and skin cancer in human beings and animals.

Of even greater concern, however, was the so-called greenhouse effect. Some of the naturally occurring gases of the lower atmosphere—water vapor, carbon dioxide, and methane (CH_4)—keep ground temperatures at a global average of about 60 degrees Fahrenheit by trapping solar radiation reflected from the heated surface of the earth much as the glass roof of a greenhouse admits sunlight but does not allow the lower-frequency infrared radiation to escape, thereby maintaining a higher temperature within the greenhouse. Insofar as the ozone layer is compromised, more high-energy ultraviolet radiation reaches the earth and warms its surface, producing higher than normal amounts of infrared radiation. This radiation is being trapped not only by naturally occurring atmospheric gases but by a host of human-generated pollutant gases. The result may be a rise in average surface temperatures, which could lead to a partial melting of the polar icecaps and a major rise in sea level, which would bring cataclysmic floods along with other severe environmental disturbances.

Scientists have long known that the Earth's stratosphere turns over very slowly, since, for one thing, debris from the testing of nuclear bombs in the late 1950s and early 1960s were readily detectable a decade later. When airlines announced in the early 1970s plans to develop a commercial fleet of supersonic aircraft, it seemed to many scientists and a growing number of those calling themselves environmentalists that since the planes would cruise so high, it was inevitable their exhaust would accumulate in the stratosphere, the nitric oxide in that exhaust depleting the ozone layer. A huge debate ensued, which led the U.S. Department of Transportation to conduct a vast research program that played a major role in the federal government's decision to suspend funds for a large supersonic transport (SST). The French went ahead to develop a smaller SST, the Concorde, which, as it turned out, had a negligible effect on the stratosphere's ozone layer.

The vitriolic debate, however, had spawned a new interdisciplinary and international cadre of chemists, physicists, and biologists, seeking to understand the stratosphere and, in concert with environmental activists, to prevent damage to the earth's atmosphere. Their cause was immensely strengthened in 1985 when Joseph C. Garman and his associates at the British Antarctic Survey reported that the level of ozone over Antarctica had dropped precipitously every October since 1982, with the first such drop occurring apparently as early as 1978. Something more than nature, claimed the scientists and environmentalists, was affecting the ozone. A "hole" seemed to have appeared, they said, in the ozone layer, and its size was measurably increasing. A similar hole also appeared to be developing over the Arctic. Studies concluded that chlorofluorocarbons—CFCs, which were used widely as aerosol propellants and refrigerants—were directly responsible for damaging the ozone layer.

Technological advances that had greatly eased life on earth were threatening perhaps to destroy it, causing not merely a rip in the atmosphere but also in international relations. Countries most addicted to the scientifically spawned gadgetry of the 20th century were the most culpable for the era's environmental degradation, and third world nations were loath to give up the potential improvements in their standards of living to help correct the excesses of the economically advanced.

With the debate heating up, the governments of the world met at the Vienna Convention on the Protection of the Ozone Layer in 1985, where the parties attending committed themselves to protect the ozone and cooperate with each other in scientific research to improve understanding of atmospheric processes. Such tepid promises to "study the problem" did not sit well with the more active environmentalists present, however, and an unsponsored conference was scheduled for two years later at Montreal.

Terms

The conference produced the Montreal Protocol on Substances That Deplete the Ozone Layer, which was adopted by UNEP later that year. UNEP strengthened its control provisions through four "adjustments" to the protocol, which has been modified five times since: in London in 1990, Copenhagen in 1992, Vienna in 1995, Montreal in 1997, and Beijing in 1999.

The 1987 Montreal Protocol on Substances that Deplete the Ozone Layer

As adjusted and amended by the second Meeting of the Parties (London, 27–29 June 1990) and by the fourth Meeting of the Parties (Copenhagen, 23–25 November 1992) and further adjusted by the seventh Meeting of the Parties (Vienna, 5–7 December 1995) and further adjusted and amended by the ninth Meeting of the Parties (Montreal, 15–17 September 1997)

Preamble

The Parties to this Protocol,

Being Parties to the Vienna Convention for the Protection of the Ozone Layer,

Mindful of their obligation under that Convention to take appropriate measures to protect human health and the environment against adverse effects resulting or likely to result from human activities which modify or are likely to modify the ozone layer,

Recognizing that world-wide emissions of certain substances can significantly deplete and otherwise modify the ozone layer in a manner that is likely to result in adverse effects on human health and the environment,

Conscious of the potential climatic effects of emissions of these substances,

Aware that measures taken to protect the ozone layer from depletion should be based on relevant scientific knowledge, taking into account technical and economic considerations,

Determined to protect the ozone layer by taking precautionary measures to control equitably total global emissions of substances that deplete it, with the ultimate objective of their elimination on the basis of developments in scientific knowledge, taking into account technical and economic considerations and bearing in mind the developmental needs of developing countries,

Acknowledging that special provision is required to meet the needs of developing countries, including the provision of additional financial resources and access to relevant technologies, bearing in mind that the magnitude of funds necessary is predictable, and the funds can be expected to make a substantial difference in the world's ability to address the scientifically established problem of ozone depletion and its harmful effects,

Noting the precautionary measures for controlling emissions of certain chlorofluorocarbons that have already been taken at national and regional levels,

Considering the importance of promoting international co-operation in the research, development and transfer of alternative technologies relating to the control and reduction of emissions of substances that deplete the ozone layer, bearing in mind in particular the needs of developing countries,

HAVE AGREED AS FOLLOWS:

In general, the parties agree to control the annual production of such substances as CFC, halons and other halogenated CFCs, carbon tetrachloride, methyl chloroform, hydrochlorofluorocarbons, hydrobromo-fluorocarbons, methyl bromide either at 1986 annual levels, commencing 7 months or 36 months after the protocol enters into force, or at 50 percent of the 1986 level beginning July 1, 1988, depending on the potential for damage to the ozone calculated for each substance. Article 2A, covering CFCs, is an example of the "control measure" provisions in the treaty, many of which simply duplicate its language for each named substance:

ARTICLE 2A: CFCS

1. Each Party shall ensure that for the twelve-month period commencing on the first day of the seventh month following the date of entry into force of this Protocol, and in each twelve-month period thereafter, its calculated level of consumption of the controlled substances in Group I of Annex A does not exceed its calculated level of consumption in 1986. By the end of the same period, each Party producing one or more of these substances shall ensure that its calculated level of production of the substances does not exceed its calculated level of production in 1986, except that such level may have increased by no more than ten per cent based on the 1986 level. Such increase shall be permitted only so as to satisfy the basic domestic needs of the Parties operating under Article 5 and for the purposes of industrial rationalization between Parties.

2. Each Party shall ensure that for the period from 1 July 1991 to 31 December 1992 its calculated levels of consumption and production of the controlled substances in Group I of Annex A do not exceed 150 per cent of its calculated levels of production and consumption of those substances in 1986; with effect from 1 January 1993, the twelve-month control period for these controlled substances shall run from 1 January to 31 December each year.

3. Each Party shall ensure that for the twelve-month period commencing on 1 January 1994, and in each twelve-month period thereafter, its calculated level of consumption of the controlled substances in Group I of Annex A does not exceed, annually, twenty-five per cent of its calculated level of consumption in 1986. Each Party producing one or more of these substances shall, for the same periods, ensure that its calculated level of production of the substances does not exceed, annually, twenty-five per cent of its calculated level of production in 1986. However, in order to satisfy the basic domestic needs of the Parties operating under paragraph 1 of Article 5, its calculated level of production may exceed that limit by up to ten per cent of its calculated level of production in 1986.

4. Each Party shall ensure that for the twelve-month period commencing on 1 January 1996, and in each twelve-month period thereafter, its calculated level of consumption of the controlled substances in Group I of Annex A does not exceed zero. Each Party producing one or more of these substances shall, for the same periods, ensure that its calculated level of production of the substances does not exceed zero. However, in order to satisfy the basic domestic needs of the Parties operating under paragraph 1 of Article 5, its calculated level of production may exceed that limit by up to fifteen per cent of its calculated level of production in 1986. This paragraph will apply save to the extent that the Parties decide to permit the level of production or consumption that is necessary to satisfy uses agreed by them to be essential.

Article 3 provided the formula for calculating the control levels in Article 2 for each substance listed in a series of indexes. Article 4 covered the control of trade with nations, depending on whether or not they were party to the protocol:

ARTICLE 4: CONTROL OF TRADE WITH NON-PARTIES

1. As of 1 January 1990, each party shall ban the import of the controlled substances in Annex A from any State not party to this Protocol.

1 bis. Within one year of the date of the entry into force of this paragraph, each Party shall ban the import of the controlled substances in Annex B from any State not party to this Protocol.

1 ter. Within one year of the date of entry into force of this paragraph, each Party shall ban the import of any controlled substances in Group II of Annex C from any State not party to this Protocol.

1 qua. Within one year of the date of entry into force of this paragraph, each Party shall ban the import of the controlled substance in Annex E from any State not party to this Protocol.

2. As of 1 January 1993, each Party shall ban the export of any controlled substances in Annex A to any State not party to this Protocol.

2 bis. Commencing one year after the date of entry into force of this paragraph, each Party shall ban the export of any controlled substances in Annex B to any State not party to this Protocol.

2 ter. Commencing one year after the date of entry into force of this paragraph, each Party shall ban the export of any controlled substances in Group II of Annex C to any State not party to this Protocol.

2 qua. Commencing one year of the date of entry into force of this paragraph, each Party shall ban the export of the controlled substance in Annex E to any State not party to this Protocol.

3. By 1 January 1992, the Parties shall, following the procedures in Article 10 of the Convention, elaborate in an annex a list of products containing controlled substances in Annex A. Parties that have not objected to the annex in accordance with those procedures shall ban, within one year of the annex having become effective, the import of those products from any State not party to this Protocol.

3 bis. Within three years of the date of the entry into force of this paragraph, the Parties shall, following the procedures in Article 10 of the Convention, elabo-

rate in an annex a list of products containing controlled substances in Annex B. Parties that have not objected to the annex in accordance with those procedures shall ban, within one year of the annex having become effective, the import of those products from any State not party to this Protocol.

3 ter. Within three years of the date of entry into force of this paragraph, the Parties shall, following the procedures in Article 10 of the Convention, elaborate in an annex a list of products containing controlled substances in Group II of Annex C. Parties that have not objected to the annex in accordance with those procedures shall ban, within one year of the annex having become effective, the import of those products from any State not party to this Protocol.

4. By 1 January 1994, the Parties shall determine the feasibility of banning or restricting, from States not party to this Protocol, the import of products produced with, but not containing, controlled substances in Annex A. If determined feasible, the Parties shall, following the procedures in Article 10 of the Convention, elaborate in an annex a list of such products. Parties that have not objected to the annex in accordance with those procedures shall ban, within one year of the annex having become effective, the import of those products from any State not party to this Protocol.

4 bis. Within five years of the date of the entry into force of this paragraph, the Parties shall determine the feasibility of banning or restricting, from States not party to this Protocol, the import of products produced with, but not containing, controlled substances in Annex B. If determined feasible, the Parties shall, following the procedures in Article 10 of the Convention, elaborate in an annex a list of such products. Parties that have not objected to the annex in accordance with those procedures shall ban or restrict, within one year of the annex having become effective, the import of those products from any State not party to this Protocol.

4 ter. Within five years of the date of entry into force of this paragraph, the Parties shall determine the feasibility of banning or restricting, from States not party to this Protocol, the import of products produced with, but not containing, controlled substances in Group II of Annex C. If determined feasible, the Parties shall, following the procedures in Article 10 of the Convention, elaborate in an annex a list of such products. Parties that have not objected to the annex in accordance with those procedures shall ban or restrict, within one year of the annex having become effective, the import of those products from any State not party to this Protocol.

5. Each Party undertakes to the fullest practicable extent to discourage the export to any State not party to this Protocol of technology for producing and for utilizing controlled substances in Annexes A and B, Group II of Annex C and Annex E.

6. Each Party shall refrain from providing new subsidies, aid, credits, guarantees or insurance programmes for the export to States not party to this Pro-

tocol of products, equipment, plants or technology that would facilitate the production of controlled substances in Annexes A and B, Group II of Annex C and Annex E.

7. Paragraphs 5 and 6 shall not apply to products, equipment, plants or technology that improve the containment, recovery, recycling or destruction of controlled substances, promote the development of alternative substances, or otherwise contribute to the reduction of emissions of controlled substances in Annexes A and B, Group II of Annex C and Annex E.

8. Notwithstanding the provisions of this Article, imports and exports referred to in paragraphs 1 to 4 ter of this Article may be permitted from, or to, any State not party to this Protocol, if that State is determined, by a meeting of the Parties, to be in full compliance with Article 2, Articles 2A to 2E, Articles 2G and 2H and this Article, and have submitted data to that effect as specified in Article 7.

9. For the purposes of this Article, the term "State not party to this Protocol" shall include, with respect to a particular controlled substance, a State or regional economic integration organization that has not agreed to be bound by the control measures in effect for that substance.

10. By 1 January 1996, the Parties shall consider whether to amend this Protocol in order to extend the measures in this Article to trade in controlled substances in Group I of Annex C and in Annex E with States not party to the Protocol.

ARTICLE 4A: CONTROL OF TRADE WITH PARTIES

1. Where, after the phase-out date applicable to it for a controlled substance, a Party is unable, despite having taken all practicable steps to comply with its obligation under the Protocol, to cease production of that substance for domestic consumption, other than for uses agreed by the Parties to be essential, it shall ban the export of used, recycled and reclaimed quantities of that substance, other than for the purpose of destruction.

2. Paragraph 1 of this Article shall apply without prejudice to the operation of Article 11 of the Convention and the non-compliance procedure developed under Article 8 of the Protocol.

ARTICLE 4B: LICENSING

1. Each Party shall, by 1 January 2000 or within three months of the date of entry into force of this Article for it, whichever is the later, establish and implement a system for licensing the import and export of new, used, recycled and reclaimed controlled substances in Annexes A, B, C and E.

2. Notwithstanding paragraph 1 of this Article, any Party operating under paragraph 1 of Article 5 which decides it is not in a position to establish and implement a system for licensing the import and export of controlled substances in Annexes C and E, may delay taking those actions until 1 January 2005 and 1 January 2002, respectively.

3. Each Party shall, within three months of the date of introducing its licensing system, report to the Secretariat on the establishment and operation of that system.

4. The Secretariat shall periodically prepare and circulate to all Parties a list of the Parties that have reported to it on their licensing systems and shall forward this information to the Implementation Committee for consideration and appropriate recommendations to the Parties.

Exceptions were made for developing countries. Essentially, developing countries, unless they were excessive in their use of ozone-damaging substances, could delay compliance until 1993.

ARTICLE 5: SPECIAL SITUATION OF DEVELOPING COUNTRIES

1. Any Party that is a developing country and whose annual calculated level of consumption of the controlled substances in Annex A is less than 0.3 kilograms per capita on the date of the entry into force of the Protocol for it, or any time thereafter until 1 January 1999, shall, in order to meet its basic domestic needs, be entitled to delay for ten years its compliance with the control measures set out in Articles 2A to 2E, provided that any further amendments to the adjustments or Amendment adopted at the Second Meeting of the Parties in London, 29 June 1990, shall apply to the Parties operating under this paragraph after the review provided for in paragraph 8 of this Article has taken place and shall be based on the conclusions of that review.

1 bis. The Parties shall, taking into account the review referred to in paragraph 8 of this Article, the assessments made pursuant to Article 6 and any other relevant information, decide by 1 January 1996, through the procedure set forth in paragraph 9 of Article 2:

(a) With respect to paragraphs 1 to 6 of Article 2F, what base year, initial levels, control schedules and phase-out date for consumption of the controlled substances in Group I of Annex C will apply to Parties operating under paragraph 1 of this Article;

(b) With respect to Article 2G, what phase-out date for production and consumption of the controlled substances in Group II of Annex C will apply to Parties operating under paragraph 1 of this Article; and

(c) With respect to Article 2H, what base year, initial levels and control schedules for consumption and production of the controlled substance in Annex E will apply to Parties operating under paragraph 1 of this Article.

2. However, any Party operating under paragraph 1 of this Article shall exceed neither an annual calculated level of consumption of the controlled substances in Annex A of 0.3 kilograms per capita nor an annual calculated level of consumption of controlled substances of Annex B of 0.2 kilograms per capita.

3. When implementing the control measures set out in Articles 2A to 2E, any Party operating under paragraph 1 of this Article shall be entitled to use:

(a) For controlled substances under Annex A, either the average of its annual calculated level of consumption for the period 1995 to 1997 inclusive or a calculated level of consumption of 0.3 kilograms per capita, whichever is the lower, as the basis for determining its compliance with the control measures relating to consumption.

(b) For controlled substances under Annex B, the average of its annual calculated level of consumption for the period 1998 to 2000 inclusive or a calculated level of consumption of 0.2 kilograms per capita, whichever is the lower, as the basis for determining its compliance with the control measures relating to consumption.

(c) For controlled substances under Annex A, either the average of its annual calculated level of production for the period 1995 to 1997 inclusive or a calculated level of production of 0.3 kilograms per capita, whichever is the lower, as the basis for determining its compliance with the control measures relating to production.

(d) For controlled substances under Annex B, either the average of its annual calculated level of production for the period 1998 to 2000 inclusive or a calculated level of production of 0.2 kilograms per capita, whichever is the lower, as the basis for determining its compliance with the control measures relating to production.

4. If a Party operating under paragraph 1 of this Article, at any time before the control measures obligations in Articles 2A to 2H become applicable to it, finds itself unable to obtain an adequate supply of controlled substances, it may notify this to the Secretariat. The Secretariat shall forthwith transmit a copy of such notification to the Parties, which shall consider the matter at their next Meeting, and decide upon appropriate action to be taken.

5. Developing the capacity to fulfil the obligations of the Parties operating under paragraph 1 of this Article to comply with the control measures set out in Articles 2A to 2E, and any control measures in Articles 2F to 2H that are decided pursuant to paragraph 1 bis of this Article, and their implementation by those same Parties will depend upon the effective implementation of the financial co-operation as provided by Article 10 and the transfer of technology as provided by Article 10A.

6. Any Party operating under paragraph 1 of this Article may, at any time, notify the Secretariat in writing that, having taken all practicable steps it is unable to implement any or all of the obligations laid down in Articles 2A to 2E, or any or all obligations in Articles 2F to 2H that are decided pursuant to paragraph 1 bis of this Article, due to the inadequate implementation of Articles 10 and 10A. The Secretariat shall forthwith

transmit a copy of the notification to the Parties, which shall consider the matter at their next Meeting, giving due recognition to paragraph 5 of this Article and shall decide upon appropriate action to be taken.

7. During the period between notification and the Meeting of the Parties at which the appropriate action referred to in paragraph 6 above is to be decided, or for a further period if the Meeting of the Parties so decides, the non-compliance procedures referred to in Article 8 shall not be invoked against the notifying Party.

8. A Meeting of the Parties shall review, not later than 1995, the situation of the Parties operating under paragraph 1 of this Article, including the effective implementation of financial co-operation and transfer of technology to them, and adopt such revisions that may be deemed necessary regarding the schedule of control measures applicable to those Parties.

8 bis. Based on the conclusions of the review referred to in paragraph 8 above:

(a) With respect to the controlled substances in Annex A, a Party operating under paragraph 1 of this Article shall, in order to meet its basic domestic needs, be entitled to delay for ten years its compliance with the control measures adopted by the Second Meeting of the Parties in London, 29 June 1990, and reference by the Protocol to Articles 2A and 2B shall be read accordingly;

(b) With respect to the controlled substances in Annex B, a Party operating under paragraph 1 of this Article shall, in order to meet its basic domestic needs, be entitled to delay for ten years its compliance with the control measures adopted by the Second Meeting of the Parties in London, 29 June 1990, and reference by the Protocol to Articles 2C to 2E shall be read accordingly . . .

Subsequent articles provided for assessment and review of the progress made under the control measures, for reporting data on the production and import and export of the substances covered by the treaty, on research, development, and on educating the public about the issues. Decisions about institutional actions to be taken by those signatory parties not complying with the treaty were postponed. The treaty called for a "financial mechanism," the Multilateral Fund, to provide financial assistance and technical cooperation, including the transfer of technologies, which was covered in Article 10A:

ARTICLE 10A: TRANSFER OF TECHNOLOGY
Each Party shall take every practicable step, consistent with the programmes supported by the financial mechanism, to ensure:

(a) that the best available, environmentally safe substitutes and related technologies are expeditiously transferred to Parties operating under paragraph 1 of Article 5; and

(b) that the transfers referred to in subparagraph (a) occur under fair and most favourable conditions.

Annexes (A through E, at the current writing) were attached to the Protocol listing the controlled substances covered by the document by their chemical composition and a calibration of their "ozone-depleting quotient."

Consequences

In its context, the Montreal resolution was a remarkable instance of international cooperation directed toward averting ecological disaster. Manufacturers of such substances as Freon quickly began to develop alternatives that would not harm the atmosphere. Most major Western industrial nations also pledged to stabilize or reduce the emission of carbon dioxide, a gas that greatly increases the greenhouse effect. While the United States, without a well-developed public transportation system and hooked on the internal combustion engine, did promise to reduce CFC manufacture and use, it made no promises regarding carbon dioxide production.

The Montreal Conference was one of the earliest and perhaps the most successful international conference to deal specifically with "green" issues. Much of its success could no doubt be traced to the narrowness and clear definition of its purpose and to the general agreement among the participants about the facts surrounding fluorocarbons. Nevertheless, the conference did inspire other meetings, the most significant of which could well have been the 1992 "Earth Summit" held in Rio de Janeiro, which produced both the Rio Declaration and the Convention on Biodiversity.

Source
Secretariat for the Vienna Convention for the Protection of the Ozone Layer and the Montreal Protocol on Substances That Deplete the Ozone Layer, "The Montreal Protocol on Substances that Deplete the Ozone Layer as adjusted and/or amended in London 1990, Copenhagen 1992, Vienna 1995, Montreal 1997, Beijing 1999," United Nations Environment Programme. Available online. URL: http://www.unep.org/ozone/Montreal-Protocol/Montreal-Protocol2000.shtml. Accessed January 3, 2005.

CONVENTION ON THE RIGHTS OF THE CHILD

TREATY AT A GLANCE

Completed
Adopted November 20, 1989; entered into force September 2, 1990

Signatories
As of summer 2005, 194 member states of the United Nations,
of which all but two, Somalia and the United States,
have ratified or acceded to the convention

Overview
The Convention on the Rights of the Child enumerates universally agreed standards and obligations that establish the basic human rights of children everywhere. This document is the most universally accepted human rights instrument in history, having been signed by every country in the world and (as of summer 2005) ratified by all except for Somalia and the United States.

Historical Background

Early national legislation concerning the welfare of children focused on regulating or eliminating child labor. The first multilateral conventions in this area to which the United States was party had a similar focus. In 1936, for instance, Belgium, Brazil, France, Norway, Sweden, and the United States concluded the Convention Fixing the Minimum Age for the Admission of Children to Employment at Sea. This document, severely limited in scope and application, was the only agreement on the rights of the child to which the United States was a party until 1973, when the United States ratified a much more general multilateral child labor agreement, the Convention Concerning Minimum Age for Admission to Employment.

Although the 1936 child labor at sea convention was the first multilateral children's rights agreement to which the United States subscribed, it was not the first international instrument relating to the rights of children. A Declaration of the Rights of the Child was endorsed in 1924 by the League of Nations, and the Universal Declaration of Human Rights, adopted by the UN General Assembly in 1948, stipulated that "motherhood and childhood are entitled to special care and protection." Later in the year, the General Assembly adopted its own Declaration of the Rights of the Child, a brief statement founded on the 1924 document. The United Nations adopted a third Declaration of the Rights of the Child in 1959. However, to ensure that issues relating to child rights carry the full weight of international law, a "Convention" or "Covenant," not merely a "Declaration," is required. In 1978, therefore, on the eve of the UN-sponsored International Year of the Child, Poland proposed a draft text for the Convention on the Rights of the Child. While no nation ever goes on record opposing the rights of children, the formulation of broadly based multilateral agreements in this area is not as simple a matter as it may seem. Nations are subject to a wide variety of cultural, family, and economic conditions. Beginning in 1979, this document was revised and expanded by the United Nations Commission on Human Rights. The formidable task of the commission was to establish an exhaustive set of minimum human rights standards applicable to children universally and without exception or modification. Ultimately, the commission formulated the 41 articles of the present convention.

The UN General Assembly unanimously adopted the Convention on the Rights of the Child on November 20, 1989. The United States signed the convention shortly after it was adopted by the General Assembly, but, as of spring 2005, has yet to ratify it. The stumbling block had been the prohibition of capital punishment for juveniles. Because a number of U.S. states allow the execution of minors, serious issues of states' rights and federalism arise, which threaten to make the convention unenforceable in this country. However, on March 1, 2005, the U.S. Supreme Court found the execution of minors under age 18 unconstitutional. This may clear the way for U.S. ratification of the convention.

Terms

The convention sets out the human rights that all children have. These are the right to survival; to develop to the fullest; to be protected from harmful influences, abuse, and exploitation; and to participate fully in family, cultural, and social life. The convention sets standards for national policies relating to health care, education, law, and civil and social services in order to safeguard these basic, nonnegotiable rights. States that are party to the convention agree to create and undertake actions and policies intended to promote the best interests of the child.

The convention establishes legal as well as moral obligations, requiring states to bring their national legislation into line with convention provisions (except where national standards are already higher). The parties are also accountable for their policies and actions, and they agree to monitoring by the UN-sponsored Committee on the Rights of the Child.

In its first 41 substantive articles, the convention outlines the human rights to be respected and protected for every child under the age of 18 years. Of particular interest is the prohibition of capital punishment for those under age 18. Articles 42–45 cover the obligation of parties to disseminate the convention's principles and provisions to adults and children, to monitor progress toward the realization of child rights, and to report national progress to the international community. Articles 46–54 address the processes of accession, ratification, and entry into force. In May 2000, two optional protocols to the convention were adopted by the General Assembly; these are the PROTOCOL TO THE CONVENTION ON THE RIGHTS OF THE CHILD ON THE INVOLVEMENT OF CHILDREN IN ARMED CONFLICT and the PROTOCOL TO THE CONVENTION ON THE RIGHTS OF THE CHILD ON THE SALE OF CHILDREN, CHILD PROSTITUTION AND CHILD PORNOGRAPHY.

Convention on the Rights of the Child

Preamble

The States Parties to the present Convention,

Considering that, in accordance with the principles proclaimed in the Charter of the United Nations, recognition of the inherent dignity and of the equal and inalienable rights of all members of the human family is the foundation of freedom, justice and peace in the world,

Bearing in mind that the peoples of the United Nations have, in the Charter, reaffirmed their faith in fundamental human rights and in the dignity and worth of the human person, and have determined to promote social progress and better standards of life in larger freedom,

Recognizing that the United Nations has, in the Universal Declaration of Human Rights and in the International Covenants on Human Rights, proclaimed and agreed that everyone is entitled to all the rights and freedoms set forth therein, without distinction of any kind, such as race, colour, sex, language, religion, political or other opinion, national or social origin, property, birth or other status,

Recalling that, in the Universal Declaration of Human Rights, the United Nations has proclaimed that childhood is entitled to special care and assistance,

Convinced that the family, as the fundamental group of society and the natural environment for the growth and well-being of all its members and particularly children, should be afforded the necessary protection and assistance so that it can fully assume its responsibilities within the community,

Recognizing that the child, for the full and harmonious development of his or her personality, should grow up in a family environment, in an atmosphere of happiness, love and understanding,

Considering that the child should be fully prepared to live an individual life in society, and brought up in the spirit of the ideals proclaimed in the Charter of the United Nations, and in particular in the spirit of peace, dignity, tolerance, freedom, equality and solidarity,

Bearing in mind that the need to extend particular care to the child has been stated in the Geneva Declaration of the Rights of the Child of 1924 and in the Declaration of the Rights of the Child adopted by the General Assembly on 20 November 1959 and recognized in the Universal Declaration of Human Rights, in the International Covenant on Civil and Political Rights (in particular in articles 23 and 24), in the International Covenant on Economic, Social and Cultural Rights (in particular in article 10) and in the statutes and relevant instruments of specialized agencies and international organizations concerned with the welfare of children,

Bearing in mind that, as indicated in the Declaration of the Rights of the Child, "the child, by reason of his physical and mental immaturity, needs special safeguards and care, including appropriate legal protection, before as well as after birth,"

Recalling the provisions of the Declaration on Social and Legal Principles relating to the Protection and Welfare of Children, with Special Reference to Foster Placement and Adoption Nationally and Internationally; the United Nations Standard Minimum Rules for the Administration of Juvenile Justice (The Beijing Rules); and the Declaration on the Protection of Women and Children in Emergency and Armed Conflict,

Recognizing that, in all countries in the world, there are children living in exceptionally difficult conditions, and that such children need special consideration,

Taking due account of the importance of the traditions and cultural values of each people for the protection and harmonious development of the child,

Recognizing the importance of international co-operation for improving the living conditions of children in every country, in particular in the developing countries,

Have agreed as follows:

PART I

ARTICLE 1

For the purposes of the present Convention, a child means every human being below the age of eighteen years unless under the law applicable to the child, majority is attained earlier.

ARTICLE 2

1. States Parties shall respect and ensure the rights set forth in the present Convention to each child within their jurisdiction without discrimination of any kind, irrespective of the child's or his or her parent's or legal guardian's race, colour, sex, language, religion, political or other opinion, national, ethnic or social origin, property, disability, birth or other status.

2. States Parties shall take all appropriate measures to ensure that the child is protected against all forms of discrimination or punishment on the basis of the status, activities, expressed opinions, or beliefs of the child's parents, legal guardians, or family members.

ARTICLE 3

1. In all actions concerning children, whether undertaken by public or private social welfare institutions, courts of law, administrative authorities or legislative bodies, the best interests of the child shall be a primary consideration.

2. States Parties undertake to ensure the child such protection and care as is necessary for his or her well-being, taking into account the rights and duties of his or her parents, legal guardians, or other individuals legally responsible for him or her, and, to this end, shall take all appropriate legislative and administrative measures.

3. States Parties shall ensure that the institutions, services and facilities responsible for the care or protection of children shall conform with the standards established by competent authorities, particularly in the areas of safety, health, in the number and suitability of their staff, as well as competent supervision.

ARTICLE 4

States Parties shall undertake all appropriate legislative, administrative, and other measures for the implementation of the rights recognized in the present Convention. With regard to economic, social and cultural rights, States Parties shall undertake such measures to the maximum extent of their available resources and, where needed, within the framework of international co-operation.

ARTICLE 5

States Parties shall respect the responsibilities, rights and duties of parents or, where applicable, the members of the extended family or community as provided for by local custom, legal guardians or other persons legally responsible for the child, to provide, in a manner consistent with the evolving capacities of the child, appropriate direction and guidance in the exercise by the child of the rights recognized in the present Convention.

ARTICLE 6

1. States Parties recognize that every child has the inherent right to life.

2. States Parties shall ensure to the maximum extent possible the survival and development of the child.

ARTICLE 7

1. The child shall be registered immediately after birth and shall have the right from birth to a name, the right to acquire a nationality and, as far as possible, the right to know and be cared for by his or her parents.

2. States Parties shall ensure the implementation of these rights in accordance with their national law and their obliga-tions under the relevant international instruments in this field, in particular where the child would otherwise be stateless.

ARTICLE 8

1. States Parties undertake to respect the right of the child to preserve his or her identity, including nationality, name and family relations as recognized by law without unlawful interference.

2. Where a child is illegally deprived of some or all of the elements of his or her identity, States Parties shall provide appropriate assistance and protection, with a view to re-establishing speedily his or her identity.

ARTICLE 9

1. States Parties shall ensure that a child shall not be separated from his or her parents against their will, except when competent authorities subject to judicial review determine, in accordance with applicable law and procedures, that such separation is necessary for the best interests of the child. Such determination may be necessary in a particular case such as one involving abuse or neglect of the child by the parents, or one where the parents are living separately and a decision must be made as to the child's place of residence.

2. In any proceedings pursuant to paragraph 1 of the present article, all interested parties shall be given an opportunity to participate in the proceedings and make their views known.

3. States Parties shall respect the right of the child who is separated from one or both parents to maintain personal relations and direct contact with both parents on a regular basis, except if it is contrary to the child's best interests. 4. Where such separation results from any action initiated by a State Party, such as the detention, imprisonment, exile, deportation or death (including death arising from any cause while the person is in the custody of the State) of one or both parents or of the child, that State Party shall, upon request, provide the parents, the child or, if appropriate, another member of the family with the essential information concerning the whereabouts of the absent member(s) of the family unless the provision of the information would be detrimental to the well-being of the child. States Parties shall further ensure that the submission of such a request shall of itself entail no adverse consequences for the person(s) concerned.

ARTICLE 10

1. In accordance with the obligation of States Parties under article 9, paragraph 1, applications by a child or his or her parents to enter or leave a State Party for the purpose of family reunification shall be dealt with by States Parties in a positive, humane and expeditious manner. States Parties shall further ensure that the submission of such a request shall entail no adverse consequences for the applicants and for the members of their family.

2. A child whose parents reside in different States shall have the right to maintain on a regular basis, save in exceptional circumstances personal relations and direct contacts with both parents. Towards that end and in accordance with the obligation of States Parties under article 9, paragraph 1, States Parties shall respect the right of the child and his or her parents to leave any country, including their own, and to enter their own country. The right to leave any country shall be subject only to such restrictions as are prescribed by law and which are necessary to protect the national security, public order (ordre public), public health or morals or the rights and freedoms of others and are consistent with the other rights recognized in the present Convention.

ARTICLE 11

1. States Parties shall take measures to combat the illicit transfer and non-return of children abroad.

2. To this end, States Parties shall promote the conclusion of bilateral or multilateral agreements or accession to existing agreements.

ARTICLE 12

1. States Parties shall assure to the child who is capable of forming his or her own views the right to express those views freely in all matters affecting the child, the views of the child being given due weight in accordance with the age and maturity of the child.

2. For this purpose, the child shall in particular be provided the opportunity to be heard in any judicial and administrative proceedings affecting the child, either directly, or through a representative or an appropriate body, in a manner consistent with the procedural rules of national law.

ARTICLE 13

1. The child shall have the right to freedom of expression; this right shall include freedom to seek, receive and impart information and ideas of all kinds, regardless of frontiers, either orally, in writing or in print, in the form of art, or through any other media of the child's choice.

2. The exercise of this right may be subject to certain restrictions, but these shall only be such as are provided by law and are necessary:

(a) For respect of the rights or reputations of others; or

(b) For the protection of national security or of public order (ordre public), or of public health or morals.

ARTICLE 14

1. States Parties shall respect the right of the child to freedom of thought, conscience and religion.

2. States Parties shall respect the rights and duties of the parents and, when applicable, legal guardians, to provide direction to the child in the exercise of his or her right in a manner consistent with the evolving capacities of the child.

3. Freedom to manifest one's religion or beliefs may be subject only to such limitations as are prescribed by law and are necessary to protect public safety, order, health or morals, or the fundamental rights and freedoms of others.

ARTICLE 15

1. States Parties recognize the rights of the child to freedom of association and to freedom of peaceful assembly.

2. No restrictions may be placed on the exercise of these rights other than those imposed in conformity with the law and which are necessary in a democratic society in the interests of national security or public safety, public order (ordre public), the protection of public health or morals or the protection of the rights and freedoms of others.

ARTICLE 16

1. No child shall be subjected to arbitrary or unlawful interference with his or her privacy, family, home or correspondence, nor to unlawful attacks on his or her honour and reputation.

2. The child has the right to the protection of the law against such interference or attacks.

ARTICLE 17

States Parties recognize the important function performed by the mass media and shall ensure that the child has access to information and material from a diversity of national and international sources, especially those aimed at the promotion of his or her social, spiritual and moral well-being and physical and mental health. To this end, States Parties shall:

(a) Encourage the mass media to disseminate information and material of social and cultural benefit to the child and in accordance with the spirit of article 29;

(b) Encourage international co-operation in the production, exchange and dissemination of such information and material from a diversity of cultural, national and international sources;

(c) Encourage the production and dissemination of children's books;

(d) Encourage the mass media to have particular regard to the linguistic needs of the child who belongs to a minority group or who is indigenous;

(e) Encourage the development of appropriate guidelines for the protection of the child from information and material injurious to his or her well-being, bearing in mind the provisions of articles 13 and 18.

ARTICLE 18

1. States Parties shall use their best efforts to ensure recognition of the principle that both parents have common responsibilities for the upbringing and development of the child. Parents or, as the case may be, legal guardians, have the primary responsibility for the upbringing and development of the child. The best interests of the child will be their basic concern.

2. For the purpose of guaranteeing and promoting the rights set forth in the present Convention, States Parties shall render appropriate assistance to parents and legal guardians in the performance of their child-rearing responsibilities and shall ensure the development of institutions, facilities and services for the care of children.

3. States Parties shall take all appropriate measures to ensure that children of working parents have the right to benefit from child-care services and facilities for which they are eligible.

ARTICLE 19

1. States Parties shall take all appropriate legislative, administrative, social and educational measures to protect the child from all forms of physical or mental violence, injury or abuse, neglect or negligent treatment, maltreatment or exploitation, including sexual abuse, while in the care of parent(s), legal guardian(s) or any other person who has the care of the child.

2. Such protective measures should, as appropriate, include effective procedures for the establishment of social programmes to provide necessary support for the child and for those who have the care of the child, as well as for other forms of prevention and for identification, reporting, referral, investigation, treatment and follow-up of instances of child maltreatment described heretofore, and, as appropriate, for judicial involvement.

ARTICLE 20

1. A child temporarily or permanently deprived of his or her family environment, or in whose own best interests cannot be allowed to remain in that environment, shall be entitled to special protection and assistance provided by the State.

2. States Parties shall in accordance with their national laws ensure alternative care for such a child.

3. Such care could include, inter alia, foster placement, kafalah of Islamic law, adoption or if necessary placement in suitable institutions for the care of children. When considering solutions, due regard shall be paid to the desirability of continuity in a child's upbringing and to the child's ethnic, religious, cultural and linguistic background.

ARTICLE 21

States Parties that recognize and/or permit the system of adoption shall ensure that the best interests of the child shall be the paramount consideration and they shall:

(a) Ensure that the adoption of a child is authorized only by competent authorities who determine, in accordance with applicable law and procedures and on the basis of all pertinent and reliable information, that the adoption is permissible in view of the child's status concerning parents, relatives and legal guardians and that, if required, the persons concerned have given their informed consent to the adoption on the basis of such counselling as may be necessary;

(b) Recognize that inter-country adoption may be considered as an alternative means of child's care, if the child cannot be placed in a foster or an adoptive family or cannot in any suitable manner be cared for in the child's country of origin;

(c) Ensure that the child concerned by inter-country adoption enjoys safeguards and standards equivalent to those existing in the case of national adoption;

(d) Take all appropriate measures to ensure that, in inter-country adoption, the placement does not result in improper financial gain for those involved in it;

(e) Promote, where appropriate, the objectives of the present article by concluding bilateral or multilateral arrangements or agreements, and endeavour, within this framework, to ensure that the placement of the child in another country is carried out by competent authorities or organs.

ARTICLE 22

1. States Parties shall take appropriate measures to ensure that a child who is seeking refugee status or who is considered a refugee in accordance with applicable international or domestic law and procedures shall, whether unaccompanied or accompanied by his or her parents or by any other person, receive appropriate protection and humanitarian assistance in the enjoyment of applicable rights set forth in the present Convention and in other international human rights or humanitarian instruments to which the said States are Parties.

2. For this purpose, States Parties shall provide, as they consider appropriate, co-operation in any efforts by the United Nations and other competent intergovernmental organizations or non-governmental organizations co-operating with the United Nations to protect and assist such a child and to trace the parents or other members of the family of any refugee child in order to obtain information necessary for reunification with his or her family. In cases where no parents or other members of the family can be found, the child shall be accorded the same protection as any other child permanently or temporarily deprived of his or her family environment for any reason , as set forth in the present Convention.

ARTICLE 23

1. States Parties recognize that a mentally or physically disabled child should enjoy a full and decent life, in conditions which ensure dignity, promote self-reliance and facilitate the child's active participation in the community.

2. States Parties recognize the right of the disabled child to special care and shall encourage and ensure the extension, subject to available resources, to the eligible child and those responsible for his or her care, of assistance for which application is made and which is appropriate to the child's condition and to the circumstances of the parents or others caring for the child.

3. Recognizing the special needs of a disabled child, assistance extended in accordance with paragraph 2 of the present article shall be provided free of charge, whenever possible, taking into account the financial resources of the parents or others caring for the child, and shall be designed to ensure that the disabled child has effective access to and receives education, training, health care services, rehabilitation services, preparation for employment and recreation opportunities in a manner conducive to the child's achieving the fullest possible social integration and individual development, including his or her cultural and spiritual development

4. States Parties shall promote, in the spirit of international cooperation, the exchange of appropriate information in the field of preventive health care and of medical, psychological and functional treatment of disabled children, including dissemination of and access to information concerning methods of rehabilitation, education and vocational services, with the aim of enabling States Parties to improve their capabilities and skills and to widen their experience in these areas. In this regard, particular account shall be taken of the needs of developing countries.

ARTICLE 24

1. States Parties recognize the right of the child to the enjoyment of the highest attainable standard of health and to facilities for the treatment of illness and rehabilitation of health. States Parties shall strive to ensure that no child is deprived of his or her right of access to such health care services.

2. States Parties shall pursue full implementation of this right and, in particular, shall take appropriate measures:

(a) To diminish infant and child mortality;

(b) To ensure the provision of necessary medical assistance and health care to all children with emphasis on the development of primary health care;

(c) To combat disease and malnutrition, including within the framework of primary health care, through, inter alia, the application of readily available technology and through the provision of adequate nutritious foods and clean drinking-water, taking into consideration the dangers and risks of environmental pollution;

(d) To ensure appropriate pre-natal and post-natal health care for mothers;

(e) To ensure that all segments of society, in particular parents and children, are informed, have access to education and are supported in the use of basic knowledge of child health and nutrition, the advantages of breastfeeding, hygiene and environmental sanitation and the prevention of accidents;

(f) To develop preventive health care, guidance for parents and family planning education and services.

3. States Parties shall take all effective and appropriate measures with a view to abolishing traditional practices prejudicial to the health of children.

4. States Parties undertake to promote and encourage international co-operation with a view to achieving progressively the full realization of the right recognized in the present article. In this regard, particular account shall be taken of the needs of developing countries.

ARTICLE 25

States Parties recognize the right of a child who has been placed by the competent authorities for the purposes of care, protection or treatment of his or her physical or mental health, to a periodic review of the treatment provided to the child and all other circumstances relevant to his or her placement.

ARTICLE 26

1. States Parties shall recognize for every child the right to benefit from social security, including social insurance, and shall take the necessary measures to achieve the full realization of this right in accordance with their national law.

2. The benefits should, where appropriate, be granted, taking into account the resources and the circumstances of the child and persons having responsibility for the maintenance of the child, as well as any other consideration relevant to an application for benefits made by or on behalf of the child.

ARTICLE 27

1. States Parties recognize the right of every child to a standard of living adequate for the child's physical, mental, spiritual, moral and social development.

2. The parent(s) or others responsible for the child have the primary responsibility to secure, within their abilities and financial capacities, the conditions of living necessary for the child's development.

3. States Parties, in accordance with national conditions and within their means, shall take appropriate measures to assist parents and others responsible for the child to implement this right and shall in case of need provide material assistance and support programmes, particularly with regard to nutrition, clothing and housing.

4. States Parties shall take all appropriate measures to secure the recovery of maintenance for the child from the parents or other persons having financial responsibility for the child, both within the State Party and from abroad. In particular, where the person having financial responsibility for the child lives in a State different from that of the child, States Parties shall promote the accession to international agreements or the conclusion of such agreements, as well as the making of other appropriate arrangements.

ARTICLE 28

1. States Parties recognize the right of the child to education, and with a view to achieving this right progressively and on the basis of equal opportunity, they shall, in particular:

(a) Make primary education compulsory and available free to all;

(b) Encourage the development of different forms of secondary education, including general and vocational education, make them available and accessible to every child, and take appropriate measures such as

the introduction of free education and offering financial assistance in case of need;

(c) Make higher education accessible to all on the basis of capacity by every appropriate means;

(d) Make educational and vocational information and guidance available and accessible to all children;

(e) Take measures to encourage regular attendance at schools and the reduction of drop-out rates.

2. States Parties shall take all appropriate measures to ensure that school discipline is administered in a manner consistent with the child's human dignity and in conformity with the present Convention.

3. States Parties shall promote and encourage international cooperation in matters relating to education, in particular with a view to contributing to the elimination of ignorance and illiteracy throughout the world and facilitating access to scientific and technical knowledge and modern teaching methods. In this regard, particular account shall be taken of the needs of developing countries.

ARTICLE 29

General comment on its implementation

1. States Parties agree that the education of the child shall be directed to:

(a) The development of the child's personality, talents and mental and physical abilities to their fullest potential;

(b) The development of respect for human rights and fundamental freedoms, and for the principles enshrined in the Charter of the United Nations;

(c) The development of respect for the child's parents, his or her own cultural identity, language and values, for the national values of the country in which the child is living, the country from which he or she may originate, and for civilizations different from his or her own;

(d) The preparation of the child for responsible life in a free society, in the spirit of understanding, peace, tolerance, equality of sexes, and friendship among all peoples, ethnic, national and religious groups and persons of indigenous origin;

(e) The development of respect for the natural environment.

2. No part of the present article or article 28 shall be construed so as to interfere with the liberty of individuals and bodies to establish and direct educational institutions, subject always to the observance of the principle set forth in paragraph 1 of the present article and to the requirements that the education given in such institutions shall conform to such minimum standards as may be laid down by the State.

ARTICLE 30

In those States in which ethnic, religious or linguistic minorities or persons of indigenous origin exist, a child belonging to such a minority or who is indigenous shall not be denied the right, in community with other members of his or her group, to enjoy his or her own culture, to profess and practise his or her own religion, or to use his or her own language.

ARTICLE 31

1. States Parties recognize the right of the child to rest and leisure, to engage in play and recreational activities appropriate

to the age of the child and to participate freely in cultural life and the arts.

2. States Parties shall respect and promote the right of the child to participate fully in cultural and artistic life and shall encourage the provision of appropriate and equal opportunities for cultural, artistic, recreational and leisure activity.

ARTICLE 32

1. States Parties recognize the right of the child to be protected from economic exploitation and from performing any work that is likely to be hazardous or to interfere with the child's education, or to be harmful to the child's health or physical, mental, spiritual, moral or social development.

2. States Parties shall take legislative, administrative, social and educational measures to ensure the implementation of the present article. To this end, and having regard to the relevant provisions of other international instruments, States Parties shall in particular:

(a) Provide for a minimum age or minimum ages for admission to employment;

(b) Provide for appropriate regulation of the hours and conditions of employment;

(c) Provide for appropriate penalties or other sanctions to ensure the effective enforcement of the present article.

ARTICLE 33

States Parties shall take all appropriate measures, including legislative, administrative, social and educational measures, to protect children from the illicit use of narcotic drugs and psychotropic substances as defined in the relevant international treaties, and to prevent the use of children in the illicit production and trafficking of such substances.

ARTICLE 34

States Parties undertake to protect the child from all forms of sexual exploitation and sexual abuse. For these purposes, States Parties shall in particular take all appropriate national, bilateral and multilateral measures to prevent:

(a) The inducement or coercion of a child to engage in any unlawful sexual activity;

(b) The exploitative use of children in prostitution or other unlawful sexual practices;

(c) The exploitative use of children in pornographic performances and materials.

ARTICLE 35

States Parties shall take all appropriate national, bilateral and multilateral measures to prevent the abduction of, the sale of or traffic in children for any purpose or in any form.

ARTICLE 36

States Parties shall protect the child against all other forms of exploitation prejudicial to any aspects of the child's welfare.

ARTICLE 37

States Parties shall ensure that:

(a) No child shall be subjected to torture or other cruel, inhuman or degrading treatment or punishment. Neither capital punishment nor life imprisonment without possibility of release shall be imposed for offences committed by persons below eighteen years of age;

(b) No child shall be deprived of his or her liberty unlawfully or arbitrarily. The arrest, detention or imprisonment of a child shall be in conformity with the law and shall be used only as a measure of last resort and for the shortest appropriate period of time;

(c) Every child deprived of liberty shall be treated with humanity and respect for the inherent dignity of the human person, and in a manner which takes into account the needs of persons of his or her age. In particular, every child deprived of liberty shall be separated from adults unless it is considered in the child's best interest not to do so and shall have the right to maintain contact with his or her family through correspondence and visits, save in exceptional circumstances;

(d) Every child deprived of his or her liberty shall have the right to prompt access to legal and other appropriate assistance, as well as the right to challenge the legality of the deprivation of his or her liberty before a court or other competent, independent and impartial authority, and to a prompt decision on any such action.

ARTICLE 38

1. States Parties undertake to respect and to ensure respect for rules of international humanitarian law applicable to them in armed conflicts which are relevant to the child.

2. States Parties shall take all feasible measures to ensure that persons who have not attained the age of fifteen years do not take a direct part in hostilities.

3. States Parties shall refrain from recruiting any person who has not attained the age of fifteen years into their armed forces. In recruiting among those persons who have attained the age of fifteen years but who have not attained the age of eighteen years, States Parties shall endeavour to give priority to those who are oldest.

4. In accordance with their obligations under international humanitarian law to protect the civilian population in armed conflicts, States Parties shall take all feasible measures to ensure protection and care of children who are affected by an armed conflict.

ARTICLE 39

States Parties shall take all appropriate measures to promote physical and psychological recovery and social reintegration of a child victim of: any form of neglect, exploitation, or abuse; torture or any other form of cruel, inhuman or degrading treatment or punishment; or armed conflicts. Such recovery and reintegration shall take place in an environment which fosters the health, self-respect and dignity of the child.

ARTICLE 40

1. States Parties recognize the right of every child alleged as, accused of, or recognized as having infringed the penal law to be treated in a manner consistent with the promotion of the child's sense of dignity and worth, which reinforces the child's respect for the human rights and fundamental freedoms of others and which takes into account the child's age and the desirability of promoting the child's reintegration and the child's assuming a constructive role in society.

2. To this end, and having regard to the relevant provisions of international instruments, States Parties shall, in particular, ensure that:

(a) No child shall be alleged as, be accused of, or recognized as having infringed the penal law by reason of acts or omissions that were not prohibited by national or international law at the time they were committed;

(b) Every child alleged as or accused of having infringed the penal law has at least the following guarantees:

(i) To be presumed innocent until proven guilty according to law;

(ii) To be informed promptly and directly of the charges against him or her, and, if appropriate, through his or her parents or legal guardians, and to have legal or other appropriate assistance in the preparation and presentation of his or her defence;

(iii) To have the matter determined without delay by a competent, independent and impartial authority or judicial body in a fair hearing according to law, in the presence of legal or other appropriate assistance and, unless it is considered not to be in the best interest of the child, in particular, taking into account his or her age or situation, his or her parents or legal guardians;

(iv) Not to be compelled to give testimony or to confess guilt; to examine or have examined adverse witnesses and to obtain the participation and examination of witnesses on his or her behalf under conditions of equality;

(v) If considered to have infringed the penal law, to have this decision and any measures imposed in consequence thereof reviewed by a higher competent, independent and impartial authority or judicial body according to law;

(vi) To have the free assistance of an interpreter if the child cannot understand or speak the language used;

(vii) To have his or her privacy fully respected at all stages of the proceedings.

3. States Parties shall seek to promote the establishment of laws, procedures, authorities and institutions specifically applicable to children alleged as, accused of, or recognized as having infringed the penal law, and, in particular:

(a) The establishment of a minimum age below which children shall be presumed not to have the capacity to infringe the penal law;

(b) Whenever appropriate and desirable, measures for dealing with such children without resorting to judicial proceedings, providing that human rights and legal safeguards are fully respected.

4. A variety of dispositions, such as care, guidance and supervision orders; counselling; probation; foster care; education and vocational training programmes and other alternatives to institutional care shall be available to ensure that children are dealt with in a manner appropriate to their well-being and proportionate both to their circumstances and the offence.

ARTICLE 41

Nothing in the present Convention shall affect any provisions which are more conducive to the realization of the rights of the child and which may be contained in:

(a) The law of a State party; or

(b) International law in force for that State.

PART II

ARTICLE 42

States Parties undertake to make the principles and provisions of the Convention widely known, by appropriate and active means, to adults and children alike.

ARTICLE 43

1. For the purpose of examining the progress made by States Parties in achieving the realization of the obligations undertaken in the present Convention, there shall be established a Committee on the Rights of the Child, which shall carry out the functions hereinafter provided.

2. The Committee shall consist of ten experts of high moral standing and recognized competence in the field covered by this Convention. The members of the Committee shall be elected by States Parties from among their nationals and shall serve in their personal capacity, consideration being given to equitable geographical distribution, as well as to the principal legal systems. . . .

ARTICLE 44

1. States Parties undertake to submit to the Committee, through the Secretary-General of the United Nations, reports on the measures they have adopted which give effect to the rights recognized herein and on the progress made on the enjoyment of those rights:

(a) Within two years of the entry into force of the Convention for the State Party concerned;

(b) Thereafter every five years. . . .

ARTICLE 45

In order to foster the effective implementation of the Convention and to encourage international co-operation in the field covered by the Convention:

(a) The specialized agencies, the United Nations Children's Fund, and other United Nations organs shall be entitled to be represented at the consideration of the implementation of such provisions of the present Convention as fall within the scope of their mandate. The Committee may invite the specialized agencies, the United Nations Children's Fund and other competent bodies as it may consider appropriate to provide expert advice on the implementation of the Convention in areas falling within the scope of their respective mandates. The Committee may invite the specialized agencies, the United Nations Children's Fund, and other United Nations organs to submit reports on the implementation of the Convention in areas falling within the scope of their activities;

(b) The Committee shall transmit, as it may consider appropriate, to the specialized agencies, the United Nations Children's Fund and other competent bodies, any reports from States Parties that contain a request, or indicate a need, for technical advice or assistance, along with the Committee's observations and suggestions, if any, on these requests or indications;

(c) The Committee may recommend to the General Assembly to request the Secretary-General to undertake on its behalf studies on specific issues relating to the rights of the child;

(d) The Committee may make suggestions and general recommendations based on information received pursuant to articles 44 and 45 of the present Convention. Such suggestions and general recommendations shall be transmitted to any State Party concerned and reported to the General Assembly, together with comments, if any, from States Parties. . . .

Consequences

Although the convention is legally binding under international law, its major effect is moral. It has served to raise the consciousness of the world community concerning the rights of children and has also helped to focus and coordinate the efforts of governmental, United Nations, and nongovernmental agencies active in children's welfare. Finally, as the most universally accepted convention on human rights, the Convention on the Rights of the Child has established a precedent for even more comprehensive legally binding covenants on human rights. That the United States has so far failed to ratify a convention on the rights of children that is so universally accepted is widely perceived as, at the very least, a national embarrassment, especially because the major bar to ratification has been failure to reconcile the prohibition against capital punishment of minors with the laws of various states. The March 1, 2005, decision by the U.S. Supreme Court that declared the execution of minors under age 18 unconstitutional, may clear the way for ratification, which had not occurred as of summer 2005.

Source

United Nations Children's Fund, "Convention on the Rights of the Child." Available online. URL: http://www.unicef.org/crc/crc.htm. Accessed January 3, 2005.

CONVENTION ON CLIMATE CHANGE

TREATY AT A GLANCE

Completed
Adopted May 9, 1992; entered into force March 21, 1994

Signatories
As of summer 2005, 165 United Nations
member states had signed and 189 were party to it

Overview
This international convention is intended to guide nations in regulating levels of greenhouse gas concentration in the atmosphere to avoid the occurrence of climate change, especially global warming, on a level that would impede sustainable economic development or compromise initiatives in food production. This is a "framework" convention, meant to serve as a first step and foundation in global environmental regulation but not itself legally binding on the signatories. Within this framework, the signatories intend to set the protocols that are legally binding instruments.

Historical Background

Most agricultural and industrial activities are based on combustion processes. The many gases these processes release, chief among them carbon dioxide (CO_2), amplify the natural greenhouse effect in the Earth's atmosphere. CO_2 and a host of so-called minor greenhouse gases form a layer of the atmosphere that allows relatively short wavelength constituents of sunlight to reach the surface of the Earth but tends to prevent passage away from the Earth of the relatively long infrared wavelengths that are radiated back. In effect, the greenhouse gases create a kind of insulating blanket around the planet, much as the glass of a greenhouse admits sunlight but seals within the greenhouse structure the radiated heat the sunlight produces. Whether in an actual greenhouse or on Earth blanketed by greenhouse gases, the net effect is that the temperature inside the greenhouse is warmer than outside. Without the natural greenhouse gases, the Earth's surface would be some 30 degrees Celsius (54 degrees Fahrenheit) colder than it is today.

Scientists theorize, however, that the ambient temperature of the planet has steadily risen since the late 19th century due directly to human causes, principally increased emissions of carbon dioxide. Burning such fuels as coal, oil, and natural gas emits huge amounts of carbon dioxide into the air. The destruction of forests (for building materials and other products) also liberates large amounts of carbon into the atmosphere and diminishes a natural control for greenhouse gas emissions—the process of photosynthesis, which converts atmospheric CO_2 to oxygen (O_2) and is conducted on a massive scale in the world's forests. Even such nonindustrial activities as raising cattle and planting rice emit methane, nitrous oxide, and other "minor" greenhouse gases. The international scientific consensus is that if emissions continue to grow at current rates, atmospheric levels of carbon dioxide will double during the 21st century from their preindustrial levels. By 2100, some predict a tripling of emissions. According to most scientists, such an accumulation of greenhouse gases is likely to bring a global warming of 1.5 to 4.5 degrees Celsius (2.7 to 8.1 degrees Fahrenheit) over the next 100 years. It is difficult to predict how such warming will affect life on Earth; such prediction is the most controversial aspect of global warming theory. It is possible, for example, that long-established wind and rainfall patterns will change, perhaps altering population and development patterns. The rise of sea levels, caused by the melting of the polar ice caps, may threaten islands and low-lying coastal areas. Moreover, a reduction in the salinity concentration of seawater as ice melts may drastically impact the ocean environment and also alter the temperature of established ocean currents, which may in turn create profound climate change, including an increase in major storm activity.

Although most of the excess greenhouse gases are produced by industrialized nations, they circulate throughout the atmosphere and affect the planet as a whole. Certain regions are especially vulnerable to global warming. These include low-lying and small islands, low-lying coastlines and flood-prone areas, areas liable to drought and desertification, and mountain ecosystems.

By the late 1980s and early 1990s, international scientific consensus on global warming had become sufficiently compelling to move the United Nations to action. Within the international political community, as represented in the United Nations, a consensus developed that states had a responsibility to protect the world's climate system for the benefit of present as well as future generations. While the extent and effects of global warming are not fully known and are often hotly disputed, the prevailing scientific consensus is that the phenomenon presents a potentially catastrophic danger, which, through international cooperation and regulation, can be averted or at least ameliorated. Because the phenomenon is global, respecting no political boundaries, concerted and coordinated worldwide action is warranted and required. The issue of global warming therefore presented a problem ideally suited to UN action.

Terms

The ultimate goal of the Convention on Climate Change is to stabilize greenhouse gases in the atmosphere at levels that will not dangerously upset the global climate system. The convention attempts to provide for this stabilization within a time frame that allows ecosystems to adapt naturally to climate change, ensures that food production is not threatened, and enables economic development (especially in developing nations) to proceed in a sustainable manner. The convention assumes as self-evident that most of the world's greenhouse gas emissions come from developed countries, which, therefore, must take the lead in combating climate change by adopting national policies that incorporate measures to limit emissions of greenhouse gases. Next in line behind developed nations are those whose economies are in transition, most notably the recently independent states of eastern Europe. The industrial infrastructure of these transitional countries is typically old and outdated and therefore creates inordinate amounts of pollution, especially as industrial production in these new market economies increases. The convention attempts to balance the need to modernize this infrastructure with the need for short-term economic development. Finally, in less developed nations, the convention attempts even more vigorously to recognize the immediate need for development and

adjusts greenhouse gas standards to accommodate it. For these countries, the first and overriding priorities are economic and social development and the eradication of poverty. The convention is designed to guide the developing nations to cope with their share of global emissions as their economies expand and they use more energy.

Overall, the aim of the convention is to ensure that developed nations reduce their emissions of carbon dioxide and other greenhouse gases to 1990 levels. These developed nations are also enjoined to help developing nations deal with the requirements of the convention and the effects of climate change. The convention calls for industrialized nations to provide funds and technological assistance to help developing nations measure flows of greenhouse gases and to assist countries that are particularly vulnerable to harmful effects of climate change to meet the costs of adaptation.

The convention requires all nations to provide information on quantities of greenhouse gases they release and how much is absorbed by their sinks (plants, forests, and oceans, for example); to publish regular updates on programs to control emissions and to adapt to climate change; to promote the sound management and conservation of such greenhouse gas sinks; to cooperate in planning for the impact of climate change on coastal zones, water resources, and agriculture; and to cooperate in the protection of areas prone to floods or drought, particularly in Africa.

The convention seeks to ensure that measures taken to combat climate change will not be used arbitrarily to restrict international trade, and it establishes a specific group to help in the transfer of funds and technology to assist nations in controlling greenhouse gases and in dealing with climate change.

The convention begins by defining key terms, then states the principal objective of the convention that states parties undertake to protect the climate system for present and future generations. The mechanism of this protection is outlined in major provisions that address the following key points:

- The principle that developing countries should be given assistance to enable them to fulfill the terms of the convention
- The principle of international cooperation, necessary to obtain maximum benefit from initiatives in the control of the climate system
- The agreement of states parties to prepare national inventories on greenhouse gas emissions and on actions taken to remove them
- The agreement of states parties to formulate and implement programs for the control of climate change
- The agreement of states parties to undertake cooperation in technology for the control of change in the climate system

- The agreement of states parties to incorporate suitable policies for the control of climate change in their national plans
- The agreement of states parties to undertake education and training policies to enhance public awareness of climate change

State parties that are developed nations (these are enumerated in Annex I of the convention) agree to take special measures to limit their emissions of greenhouse gases and to enhance the capacity of their sinks and reservoirs for the stabilization of such gases. The developed nations (and other parties listed in Annex II) also undertake to provide financial support to the developing nations to enable them to comply with the terms of the convention.

The convention provides for the establishment and promotion of networks and cooperative programs of research into and systematic observation of climate change and the establishment of a Conference of Parties to function as the supreme body of the convention responsible for overseeing its implementation. The convention also includes provisions for a financial mechanism to provide, as appropriate, resources and to settle disputes.

United Nations Framework Convention on Climate Change

The Parties to this Convention,

Acknowledging that change in the Earth's climate and its adverse effects are a common concern of humankind,

Concerned that human activities have been substantially increasing the atmospheric concentrations of greenhouse gases, that these increases enhance the natural greenhouse effect, and that this will result on average in an additional warming of the Earth's surface and atmosphere and may adversely affect natural ecosystems and humankind,

Noting that the largest share of historical and current global emissions of greenhouse gases has originated in developed countries, that per capita emissions in developing countries are still relatively low and that the share of global emissions originating in developing countries will grow to meet their social and development needs,

Aware of the role and importance in terrestrial and marine ecosystems of sinks and reservoirs of greenhouse gases,

Noting that there are many uncertainties in predictions of climate change, particularly with regard to the timing, magnitude and regional patterns thereof,

Acknowledging that the global nature of climate change calls for the widest possible cooperation by all countries and their participation in an effective and appropriate international response, in accordance with their common but differentiated responsibilities and respective capabilities and their social and economic conditions,

Recalling the pertinent provisions of the Declaration of the United Nations Conference on the Human Environment, adopted at Stockholm on 16 June 1972,

Recalling also that States have, in accordance with the Charter of the United Nations and the principles of international law, the sovereign right to exploit their own resources pursuant to their own environmental and developmental policies, and the responsibility to ensure that activities within their jurisdiction or control do not cause damage to the environment of other States or of areas beyond the limits of national jurisdiction,

Reaffirming the principle of sovereignty of States in international cooperation to address climate change,

Recognizing that States should enact effective environmental legislation, that environmental standards, management objectives and priorities should reflect the environmental and developmental context to which they apply, and that standards applied by some countries may be inappropriate and of unwarranted economic and social cost to other countries, in particular developing countries,

Recalling the provisions of General Assembly resolution 44/228 of 22 December 1989 on the United Nations Conference on Environment and Development, and resolutions 43/53 of 6 December 1988, 44/207 of 22 December 1989, 45/212 of 21 December 1990 and 46/169 of 19 December 1991 on protection of global climate for present and future generations of mankind,

Recalling also the provisions of General Assembly resolution 44/206 of 22 December 1989 on the possible adverse effects of sea-level rise on islands and coastal areas, particularly low-lying coastal areas and the pertinent provisions of General Assembly resolution 44/172 of 19 December 1989 on the implementation of the Plan of Action to Combat Desertification,

Recalling further the Vienna Convention for the Protection of the Ozone Layer, 1985, and the Montreal Protocol on Substances that Deplete the Ozone Layer, 1987, as adjusted and amended on 29 June 1990,

Noting the Ministerial Declaration of the Second World Climate Conference adopted on 7 November 1990,

Conscious of the valuable analytical work being conducted by many States on climate change and of the important contributions of the World Meteorological Organization, the United Nations Environment Programme and other organs, organizations and bodies of the United Nations system, as well as other international and intergovernmental bodies, to the exchange of results of scientific research and the coordination of research,

Recognizing that steps required to understand and address climate change will be environmentally, socially and economically most effective if they are based on relevant scientific, technical and economic considerations and continually re-evaluated in the light of new findings in these areas,

Recognizing that various actions to address climate change can be justified economically in their own right and can also help in solving other environmental problems,

Recognizing also the need for developed countries to take immediate action in a flexible manner on the basis of clear priorities, as a first step towards comprehensive response strategies at the global, national and, where agreed, regional levels that take into account all greenhouse gases, with due consideration of their relative contributions to the enhancement of the greenhouse effect,

Recognizing further that low-lying and other small island countries, countries with low-lying coastal, arid and semi-arid areas or areas liable to floods, drought and desertification, and developing countries with fragile mountainous ecosystems are particularly vulnerable to the adverse effects of climate change,

Recognizing the special difficulties of those countries, especially developing countries, whose economies are particularly dependent on fossil fuel production, use and exportation, as a consequence of action taken on limiting greenhouse gas emissions,

Affirming that responses to climate change should be coordinated with social and economic development in an integrated manner with a view to avoiding adverse impacts on the latter, taking into full account the legitimate priority needs of developing countries for the achievement of sustained economic growth and the eradication of poverty,

Recognizing that all countries, especially developing countries, need access to resources required to achieve sustainable social and economic development and that, in order for developing countries to progress towards that goal, their energy consumption will need to grow taking into account the possibilities for achieving greater energy efficiency and for controlling greenhouse gas emissions in general, including through the application of new technologies on terms which make such an application economically and socially beneficial,

Determined to protect the climate system for present and future generations,

Have agreed as follows:

ARTICLE 1
DEFINITIONS

For the purposes of this Convention:

1. "Adverse effects of climate change" means changes in the physical environment or biota resulting from climate change which have significant deleterious effects on the composition, resilience or productivity of natural and managed ecosystems or on the operation of socio-economic systems or on human health and welfare.

2. "Climate change" means a change of climate which is attributed directly or indirectly to human activity that alters the composition of the global atmosphere and which is in addition to natural climate variability observed over comparable time periods.

3. "Climate system" means the totality of the atmosphere, hydrosphere, biosphere and geosphere and their interactions.

4. "Emissions" means the release of greenhouse gases and/or their precursors into the atmosphere over a specified area and period of time.

5. "Greenhouse gases" means those gaseous constituents of the atmosphere, both natural and anthropogenic, that absorb and re-emit infrared radiation.

6. "Regional economic integration organization" means an organization constituted by sovereign States of a given region which has competence in respect of matters governed by this Convention or its protocols and has been duly authorized, in accordance with its internal procedures, to sign, ratify, accept, approve or accede to the instruments concerned.

7. "Reservoir" means a component or components of the climate system where a greenhouse gas or a precursor of a greenhouse gas is stored.

8. "Sink" means any process, activity or mechanism which removes a greenhouse gas, an aerosol or a precursor of a greenhouse gas from the atmosphere.

9. "Source" means any process or activity which releases a greenhouse gas, an aerosol or a precursor of a greenhouse gas into the atmosphere.

ARTICLE 2
OBJECTIVE

The ultimate objective of this Convention and any related legal instruments that the Conference of the Parties may adopt is to achieve, in accordance with the relevant provisions of the Convention, stabilization of greenhouse gas concentrations in the atmosphere at a level that would prevent dangerous anthropogenic interference with the climate system. Such a level should be achieved within a time-frame sufficient to allow ecosystems to adapt naturally to climate change, to ensure that food production is not threatened and to enable economic development to proceed in a sustainable manner.

ARTICLE 3
PRINCIPLES

In their actions to achieve the objective of the Convention and to implement its provisions, the Parties shall be guided, INTER ALIA, by the following:

1. The Parties should protect the climate system for the benefit of present and future generations of humankind, on the basis of equity and in accordance with their common but differentiated responsibilities and respective capabilities. Accordingly, the developed country Parties should take the lead in combating climate change and the adverse effects thereof.

2. The specific needs and special circumstances of developing country Parties, especially those that are particularly vulnerable to the adverse effects of climate change, and of those Parties, especially developing country Parties, that would have to bear a disproportionate or abnormal burden under the Convention, should be given full consideration.

3. The Parties should take precautionary measures to anticipate, prevent or minimize the causes of climate change and mitigate its adverse effects. Where there are threats of serious or irreversible damage, lack of full scientific certainty should not be used as a reason for postponing such measures, taking into account that policies and measures to deal with climate change should be cost-effective so as to ensure global benefits at the lowest possible cost. To achieve this, such policies and measures should take into account different socio-economic contexts, be comprehensive, cover all relevant sources, sinks and reservoirs of greenhouse gases and adaptation, and comprise all economic sectors. Efforts to address climate change may be carried out cooperatively by interested Parties.

4. The Parties have a right to, and should, promote sustainable development. Policies and measures to protect the climate system against human-induced change should be appropriate for the specific conditions of each Party and should be integrated with national development programmes, taking into account that economic development is essential for adopting measures to address climate change.

5. The Parties should cooperate to promote a supportive and open international economic system that would lead to sustainable economic growth and development in all Parties, particularly developing country Parties, thus enabling them better to address the problems of climate change. Measures taken to combat climate change, including unilateral ones, should not constitute a means of arbitrary or unjustifiable discrimination or a disguised restriction on international trade.

ARTICLE 4
COMMITMENTS

1. All Parties, taking into account their common but differentiated responsibilities and their specific national and regional development priorities, objectives and circumstances, shall:

(a) Develop, periodically update, publish and make available to the Conference of the Parties, in accordance with Article 12, national inventories of anthropogenic emissions by sources and removals by sinks of all greenhouse gases not controlled by the Montreal Protocol, using comparable methodologies to be agreed upon by the Conference of the Parties;

(b) Formulate, implement, publish and regularly update national and, where appropriate, regional programmes containing measures to mitigate climate change by addressing anthropogenic emissions by sources and removals by sinks of all greenhouse gases not controlled by the Montreal Protocol, and measures to facilitate adequate adaptation to climate change;

(c) Promote and cooperate in the development, application and diffusion, including transfer, of technologies, practices and processes that control, reduce or prevent anthropogenic emissions of greenhouse gases not controlled by the Montreal Protocol in all relevant sectors, including the energy, transport, industry, agriculture, forestry and waste management sectors;

(d) Promote sustainable management, and promote and cooperate in the conservation and enhancement, as appropriate, of sinks and reservoirs of all greenhouse gases not controlled by the Montreal Protocol, including biomass, forests and oceans as well as other terrestrial, coastal and marine ecosystems;

(e) Cooperate in preparing for adaptation to the impacts of climate change; develop and elaborate appropriate and integrated plans for coastal zone management, water resources and agriculture, and for the protection and rehabilitation of areas, particularly in Africa, affected by drought and desertification, as well as floods;

(f) Take climate change considerations into account, to the extent feasible, in their relevant social, economic and environmental policies and actions, and employ appropriate methods, for example impact assessments, formulated and determined nationally, with a view to minimizing adverse effects on the economy, on public health and on the quality of the environment, of projects or measures undertaken by them to mitigate or adapt to climate change;

(g) Promote and cooperate in scientific, technological, technical, socio-economic and other research, systematic observation and development of data archives related to the climate system and intended to further the understanding and to reduce or eliminate the remaining uncertainties regarding the causes, effects, magnitude and timing of climate change and the economic and social consequences of various response strategies;

(h) Promote and cooperate in the full, open and prompt exchange of relevant scientific, technological, technical, socio-economic and legal information related to the climate system and climate change, and to the economic and social consequences of various response strategies;

(i) Promote and cooperate in education, training and public awareness related to climate change and encourage the widest participation in this process, including that of non-governmental organizations; and

(j) Communicate to the Conference of the Parties information related to implementation, in accordance with Article 12.

2. The developed country Parties and other Parties included in Annex I commit themselves specifically as provided for in the following:

(a) Each of these Parties shall adopt national policies and take corresponding measures on the mitigation of climate change, by limiting its anthropogenic emissions of greenhouse gases and protecting and enhancing its greenhouse gas sinks and reservoirs. These policies and measures will demonstrate that developed countries are taking the lead in modifying longer-term trends in anthropogenic emissions consistent with the objective of the Convention, recognizing that the return by the end of the present decade to earlier levels of anthropogenic emissions of carbon dioxide and other greenhouse gases not controlled by the Montreal Protocol would contribute to such modification, and taking into account the differences in these Parties' starting points and approaches, economic structures and resource bases, the need to maintain strong and sustainable economic growth, available technologies and other individual circumstances, as well as the need for equitable and appropriate contributions by each of these Parties to the global effort regarding that objective. These Parties may implement such policies and measures jointly with other Parties and may assist other Parties in contributing to the achievement of the objective of the Convention and, in particular, that of this subparagraph;

(b) In order to promote progress to this end, each of these Parties shall communicate, within six months of the entry into force of the Convention for it and periodically thereafter, and in accordance with Article 12, detailed information on its policies and measures referred to in subparagraph (a) above, as well as on its resulting projected anthropogenic emissions by sources and removals by sinks of greenhouse gases not controlled by the Montreal Protocol for the period referred to in subparagraph (a), with the aim of returning individually or jointly to their 1990 levels these anthropogenic emissions of carbon dioxide and other greenhouse gases not controlled by the Montreal Protocol. This information will be reviewed by the Conference of the Parties, at its first session and periodically thereafter, in accordance with Article 7;

(c) Calculations of emissions by sources and removals by sinks of greenhouse gases for the purposes of subparagraph (b) above should take into account the best available scientific knowledge, including of the effective capacity of sinks and the respective contributions of such gases to climate change. The Conference of the Parties shall consider and agree on methodologies for these calculations at its first session and review them regularly thereafter;

(d) The Conference of the Parties shall, at its first session, review the adequacy of subparagraphs (a) and (b) above. Such review shall be carried out in the light of the best available scientific information and assessment on climate change and its impacts, as well as relevant technical, social and economic information. Based on this review, the Conference of the Parties shall take appropriate action, which may include the adoption of amendments to the commitments in subparagraphs (a) and (b) above. The Conference of the Parties, at its first session, shall also take decisions regarding criteria for joint implementation as indicated in subparagraph (a) above. A second review of subparagraphs (a) and (b) shall take place not later than 31 December 1998, and thereafter at regular intervals determined by the Conference of the Parties, until the objective of the Convention is met;

(e) Each of these Parties shall:

(i) Coordinate as appropriate with other such Parties, relevant economic and administrative instruments developed to achieve the objective of the Convention; and

(ii) Identify and periodically review its own policies and practices which encourage activities that lead to greater levels of anthropogenic emissions of greenhouse gases not controlled by the Montreal Protocol than would otherwise occur;

(f) The Conference of the Parties shall review, not later than 31 December 1998, available information with a view to taking decisions regarding such amendments to the lists in Annexes I and II as may be appropriate, with the approval of the Party concerned;

(g) Any Party not included in Annex I may, in its instrument of ratification, acceptance, approval or accession, or at any time thereafter, notify the Depositary that it intends to be bound by subparagraphs (a) and (b) above. The Depositary shall inform the other signatories and Parties of any such notification.

3. The developed country Parties and other developed Parties included in Annex II shall provide new and additional financial resources to meet the agreed full costs incurred by developing country Parties in complying with their obligations under Article 12, paragraph 1. They shall also provide such financial resources, including for the transfer of technology, needed by the developing country Parties to meet the agreed full incremental costs of implementing measures that are covered by paragraph 1 of this Article and that are agreed between a developing country Party and the international entity or entities referred to in Article 11, in accordance with that Article. The implementation of these commitments shall take into account the need for adequacy and predictability in the flow of funds and the importance of appropriate burden sharing among the developed country Parties.

4. The developed country Parties and other developed Parties included in Annex II shall also assist the developing country Parties that are particularly vulnerable to the adverse effects of climate change in meeting costs of adaptation to those adverse effects.

5. The developed country Parties and other developed Parties included in Annex II shall take all practicable steps to pro-

mote, facilitate and finance, as appropriate, the transfer of, or access to, environmentally sound technologies and know-how to other Parties, particularly developing country Parties, to enable them to implement the provisions of the Convention. In this process, the developed country Parties shall support the development and enhancement of endogenous capacities and technologies of developing country Parties. Other Parties and organizations in a position to do so may also assist in facilitating the transfer of such technologies.

6. In the implementation of their commitments under paragraph 2 above, a certain degree of flexibility shall be allowed by the Conference of the Parties to the Parties included in Annex I undergoing the process of transition to a market economy, in order to enhance the ability of these Parties to address climate change, including with regard to the historical level of anthropogenic emissions of greenhouse gases not controlled by the Montreal Protocol chosen as a reference.

7. The extent to which developing country Parties will effectively implement their commitments under the Convention will depend on the effective implementation by developed country Parties of their commitments under the Convention related to financial resources and transfer of technology and will take fully into account that economic and social development and poverty eradication are the first and overriding priorities of the developing country Parties.

8. In the implementation of the commitments in this Article, the Parties shall give full consideration to what actions are necessary under the Convention, including actions related to funding, insurance and the transfer of technology, to meet the specific needs and concerns of developing country Parties arising from the adverse effects of climate change and/or the impact of the implementation of response measures, especially on:

(a) Small island countries;

(b) Countries with low-lying coastal areas;

(c) Countries with arid and semi-arid areas, forested areas and areas liable to forest decay;

(d) Countries with areas prone to natural disasters;

(e) Countries with areas liable to drought and desertification;

(f) Countries with areas of high urban atmospheric pollution;

(g) Countries with areas with fragile ecosystems, including mountainous ecosystems;

(h) Countries whose economies are highly dependent on income generated from the production, processing and export, and/or on consumption of fossil fuels and associated energy-intensive products; and

(i) Land-locked and transit countries.

Further, the Conference of the Parties may take actions, as appropriate, with respect to this paragraph.

9. The Parties shall take full account of the specific needs and special situations of the least developed countries in their actions with regard to funding and transfer of technology.

10. The Parties shall, in accordance with Article 10, take into consideration in the implementation of the commitments of the Convention the situation of Parties, particularly developing country Parties, with economies that are vulnerable to the adverse effects of the implementation of measures to respond to climate change. This applies notably to Parties with economies that are highly dependent on income generated from the pro-

duction, processing and export, and/or consumption of fossil fuels and associated energy-intensive products and/or the use of fossil fuels for which such Parties have serious difficulties in switching to alternatives.

ARTICLE 5
RESEARCH AND SYSTEMATIC OBSERVATION
In carrying out their commitments under Article 4, paragraph 1(g), the Parties shall:

(a) Support and further develop, as appropriate, international and intergovernmental programmes and networks or organizations aimed at defining, conducting, assessing and financing research, data collection and systematic observation, taking into account the need to minimize duplication of effort;

(b) Support international and intergovernmental efforts to strengthen systematic observation and national scientific and technical research capacities and capabilities, particularly in developing countries, and to promote access to, and the exchange of, data and analyses thereof obtained from areas beyond national jurisdiction; and

(c) Take into account the particular concerns and needs of developing countries and cooperate in improving their endogenous capacities and capabilities to participate in the efforts referred to in subparagraphs (a) and (b) above.

ARTICLE 6
EDUCATION, TRAINING AND PUBLIC AWARENESS
In carrying out their commitments under Article 4, paragraph 1(i), the Parties shall:

(a) Promote and facilitate at the national and, as appropriate, subregional and regional levels, and in accordance with national laws and regulations, and within their respective capacities:

(i) The development and implementation of educational and public awareness programmes on climate change and its effects;

(ii) Public access to information on climate change and its effects;

(iii) Public participation in addressing climate change and its effects and developing adequate responses; and

(iv) Training of scientific, technical and managerial personnel.

(b) Cooperate in and promote, at the international level, and, where appropriate, using existing bodies:

(i) The development and exchange of educational and public awareness material on climate change and its effects; and

(ii) The development and implementation of education and training programmes, including the strengthening of national institutions and the exchange or secondment of personnel to train experts in this field, in particular for developing countries.

ARTICLE 7
CONFERENCE OF THE PARTIES
1. A Conference of the Parties is hereby established.

2. The Conference of the Parties, as the supreme body of this Convention, shall keep under regular review the implementation of the Convention and any related legal instruments that the Conference of the Parties may adopt, and shall make, within its mandate, the decisions necessary to promote the effective implementation of the Convention. To this end, it shall:

(a) Periodically examine the obligations of the Parties and the institutional arrangements under the Convention, in the light of the objective of the Convention, the experience gained in its implementation and the evolution of scientific and technological knowledge;

(b) Promote and facilitate the exchange of information on measures adopted by the Parties to address climate change and its effects, taking into account the differing circumstances, responsibilities and capabilities of the Parties and their respective commitments under the Convention;

(c) Facilitate, at the request of two or more Parties, the coordination of measures adopted by them to address climate change and its effects, taking into account the differing circumstances, responsibilities and capabilities of the Parties and their respective commitments under the Convention;

(d) Promote and guide, in accordance with the objective and provisions of the Convention, the development and periodic refinement of comparable methodologies, to be agreed on by the Conference of the Parties, inter alia, for preparing inventories of greenhouse gas emissions by sources and removals by sinks, and for evaluating the effectiveness of measures to limit the emissions and enhance the removals of these gases;

(e) Assess, on the basis of all information made available to it in accordance with the provisions of the Convention, the implementation of the Convention by the Parties, the overall effects of the measures taken pursuant to the Convention, in particular environmental, economic and social effects as well as their cumulative impacts and the extent to which progress towards the objective of the Convention is being achieved;

(f) Consider and adopt regular reports on the implementation of the Convention and ensure their publication;

(g) Make recommendations on any matters necessary for the implementation of the Convention;

(h) Seek to mobilize financial resources in accordance with Article 4, paragraphs 3, 4 and 5, and Article 11;

(i) Establish such subsidiary bodies as are deemed necessary for the implementation of the Convention;

(j) Review reports submitted by its subsidiary bodies and provide guidance to them;

(k) Agree upon and adopt, by consensus, rules of procedure and financial rules for itself and for any subsidiary bodies;

(l) Seek and utilize, where appropriate, the services and cooperation of, and information provided by, competent international organizations and intergovernmental and non-governmental bodies; and

(m) Exercise such other functions as are required for the achievement of the objective of the Convention as well as all other functions assigned to it under the Convention.

3. The Conference of the Parties shall, at its first session, adopt its own rules of procedure as well as those of the subsidiary bodies established by the Convention, which shall include decision-making procedures for matters not already covered by decision-making procedures stipulated in the Convention. Such procedures may include specified majorities required for the adoption of particular decisions.

4. The first session of the Conference of the Parties shall be convened by the interim secretariat referred to in Article 21 and shall take place not later than one year after the date of entry into force of the Convention. Thereafter, ordinary sessions of the Conference of the Parties shall be held every year unless otherwise decided by the Conference of the Parties.

5. Extraordinary sessions of the Conference of the Parties shall be held at such other times as may be deemed necessary by the Conference, or at the written request of any Party, provided that, within six months of the request being communicated to the Parties by the secretariat, it is supported by at least one third of the Parties.

6. The United Nations, its specialized agencies and the International Atomic Energy Agency, as well as any State member thereof or observers thereto not Party to the Convention, may be represented at sessions of the Conference of the Parties as observers. Any body or agency, whether national or international, governmental or non-governmental, which is qualified in matters covered by the Convention, and which has informed the secretariat of its wish to be represented at a session of the Conference of the Parties as an observer, may be so admitted unless at least one third of the Parties present object. The admission and participation of observers shall be subject to the rules of procedure adopted by the Conference of the Parties.

ARTICLE 8
SECRETARIAT

1. A secretariat is hereby established.

2. The functions of the secretariat shall be:

(a) To make arrangements for sessions of the Conference of the Parties and its subsidiary bodies established under the Convention and to provide them with services as required;

(b) To compile and transmit reports submitted to it;

(c) To facilitate assistance to the Parties, particularly developing country Parties, on request, in the compilation and communication of information required in accordance with the provisions of the Convention;

(d) To prepare reports on its activities and present them to the Conference of the Parties;

(e) To ensure the necessary coordination with the secretariats of other relevant international bodies;

(f) To enter, under the overall guidance of the Conference of the Parties, into such administrative and contractual arrangements as may be required for the effective discharge of its functions; and

(g) To perform the other secretariat functions specified in the Convention and in any of its protocols and such other functions as may be determined by the Conference of the Parties.

3. The Conference of the Parties, at its first session, shall designate a permanent secretariat and make arrangements for its functioning.

ARTICLE 9
SUBSIDIARY BODY FOR SCIENTIFIC AND TECHNOLOGICAL ADVICE

1. A subsidiary body for scientific and technological advice is hereby established to provide the Conference of the Parties and, as appropriate, its other subsidiary bodies with timely information and advice on scientific and technological matters relating to the Convention. This body shall be open to participation by all Parties and shall be multidisciplinary. It shall comprise government representatives competent in the relevant field of expertise. It shall report regularly to the Conference of the Parties on all aspects of its work.

2. Under the guidance of the Conference of the Parties, and drawing upon existing competent international bodies, this body shall:

(a) Provide assessments of the state of scientific knowledge relating to climate change and its effects;

(b) Prepare scientific assessments on the effects of measures taken in the implementation of the Convention;

(c) Identify innovative, efficient and state-of-the-art technologies and know-how and advise on the ways and means of promoting development and/or transferring such technologies;

(d) Provide advice on scientific programmes, international cooperation in research and development related to climate change, as well as on ways and means of supporting endogenous capacity-building in developing countries; and

(e) Respond to scientific, technological and methodological questions that the Conference of the Parties and its subsidiary bodies may put to the body.

3. The functions and terms of reference of this body may be further elaborated by the Conference of the Parties.

ARTICLE 10
SUBSIDIARY BODY FOR IMPLEMENTATION

1. A subsidiary body for implementation is hereby established to assist the Conference of the Parties in the assessment and review of the effective implementation of the Convention. This body shall be open to participation by all Parties and comprise government representatives who are experts on matters related to climate change. It shall report regularly to the Conference of the Parties on all aspects of its work.

2. Under the guidance of the Conference of the Parties, this body shall:

(a) Consider the information communicated in accordance with Article 12, paragraph 1, to assess the overall aggregated effect of the steps taken by the Parties in the light of the latest scientific assessments concerning climate change;

(b) Consider the information communicated in accordance with Article 12, paragraph 2, in order to assist the Conference of the Parties in carrying out the reviews required by Article 4, paragraph 2(d); and

(c) Assist the Conference of the Parties, as appropriate, in the preparation and implementation of its decisions.

ARTICLE 11
FINANCIAL MECHANISM

1. A mechanism for the provision of financial resources on a grant or concessional basis, including for the transfer of technology, is hereby defined. It shall function under the guidance of and be accountable to the Conference of the Parties, which shall decide on its policies, programme priorities and eligibility criteria related to this Convention. Its operation shall be entrusted to one or more existing international entities.

2. The financial mechanism shall have an equitable and balanced representation of all Parties within a transparent system of governance.

3. The Conference of the Parties and the entity or entities entrusted with the operation of the financial mechanism shall agree upon arrangements to give effect to the above paragraphs, which shall include the following:

(a) Modalities to ensure that the funded projects to address climate change are in conformity with the policies, programme priorities and eligibility criteria established by the Conference of the Parties;

(b) Modalities by which a particular funding decision may be reconsidered in light of these policies, programme priorities and eligibility criteria;

(c) Provision by the entity or entities of regular reports to the Conference of the Parties on its funding operations, which is consistent with the requirement for accountability set out in paragraph 1 above; and

(d) Determination in a predictable and identifiable manner of the amount of funding necessary and available for the implementation of this Convention and the conditions under which that amount shall be periodically reviewed. . . .

ARTICLE 17
PROTOCOLS

1. The Conference of the Parties may, at any ordinary session, adopt protocols to the Convention.

Consequences

As originally framed, the Convention on Climate Change sets no mandatory limits on greenhouse gas emissions for individual nations, nor does it contain any enforcement provisions; therefore, it is legally nonbinding. What the convention does allow for is the inclusion of subsequent protocols that will set mandatory emission limits. The most important of these is the KYOTO PROTOCOL ON CLIMATE CHANGE, which became the object of far more intense attention, controversy, and contention than the original convention itself.

There is no question that the Convention on Climate Change demonstrates worldwide awareness of and concern about global warming, and in part as a result of the agreement, many states have introduced measures to curb the emissions of greenhouse gases. The effects and effectiveness of these measures will require decades to evaluate, and given the exigencies of national and global economies, it is by no means certain to what degree nations will remain committed to the convention. In an encouraging development, the lower house of the Russian parliament enacted legislation on September 30, 2004, to enable its delayed ratification of the Kyoto Protocol, which would provide legally binding enforcement of convention provisions. The United States has subscribed to the nonbinding framework. As of summer 2005, however, the United States, a leading producer of greenhouse gases, still has not signed the Kyoto Protocol, and the administration of President George W. Bush had announced its intention not to sign the protocol.

Source

United Nations, "United Nations Framework Convention on Climate Change," Secretariat of the United Nations Framework Convention on Climate Change. Available online. URL: http://unfccc.int/files/essential_background/background_pu blications_htmlpdf/application/pdf/c onveng.pdf. Accessed January 3, 2005.

CONVENTION ON BIODIVERSITY

TREATY AT A GLANCE

Completed
June 1992 at Rio de Janeiro, Brazil;
entered into force December 29, 1993

Signatories
As of summer 2005, 168 United Nations member states
had signed and 188 were party to it

Overview
When 178 countries met in Rio de Janeiro during June 1992 to map out strategies and policies for cleaning up the world's environment and encouraging environmentally sound economic development, the conference was dubbed by the international press the first Earth Summit. Perhaps the most important agreement reached at the summit was the Convention on Biodiversity, which the United States steadfastly refused to sign.

Historical Background

Awareness of the Earth's dwindling biotic richness had been growing during the years leading up to the 1992 Earth Summit in Rio de Janeiro. Early in the year, the World Resources Institute, in collaboration with the United Nations Environment Programme (UNEP) and other organizations, released *Global Biodiversity Strategy: Guidelines for Action to Save, Study, and Use Earth's Biotic Wealth Sustainably and Equitably*. A detailed strategy for conserving the Earth's biodiversity, the report represented the culmination of three years of intense research and review involving 45 corporations, foundations, and government agencies and about 500 concerned scientists, environmentalists, and other individuals from all parts of the globe. It became the text from which the attendees at the Earth Summit worked.

There were some 10,000 delegates from 178 nations who gathered in Rio, under the auspices of the United Nations, in a historic attempt to overcome political differences and economic self-interest to develop planetary policies for the environment. The delegates produced an 800-page blueprint for the environmentally responsible development of third world countries, a nonbinding declaration of "ecoprinciples" called the RIO DECLARATION, and international legislation to preserve ecological diversity and to combat global warming.

Terms

Under the Convention on Biodiversity, governments agreed to accept responsibility for safeguarding the profuse species, genetic materials, and ecosystems that make up the natural world of the planet. The treaty bound the signatories to protect the biological species within their borders. The conference took note of the fact that the planet loses 50–100 species each day, many of them in third world nations, which destroy their resources, especially the rain forests, at a rapid rate in an effort to meet the economic needs of their people. The convention secured third world pledges that biodiversity would be preserved in exchange for the payment of royalties and property rights, to be paid by corporations that harvest third world resources. In addition, many of the developed nations agreed to render direct environmental financial assistance to the third world.

Convention on Biological Diversity

Preamble
The Contracting Parties,

Conscious of the intrinsic value of biological diversity and of the ecological, genetic, social, economic, scientific, educational, cultural, recreational and aesthetic values of biological diversity and its components,

Conscious also of the importance of biological diversity for evolution and for maintaining life-sustaining systems of the biosphere,

Affirming that the conservation of biological diversity is a common concern of humankind,

Reaffirming that States have sovereign rights over their own biological resources,

Reaffirming also that States are responsible for conserving their biological diversity and for using their biological resources in a sustainable manner,

Concerned that biological diversity is being significantly reduced by certain human activities,

Aware of the general lack of information and knowledge regarding biological diversity and of the urgent need to develop scientific, technical and institutional capacities to provide the basic understanding upon which to plan and implement appropriate measures,

Noting that it is vital to anticipate, prevent and attack the causes of significant reduction or loss of biological diversity at source,

Noting also that where there is a threat of significant reduction or loss of biological diversity, lack of full scientific certainty should not be used as a reason for postponing measures to avoid or minimize such a threat,

Noting further that the fundamental requirement for the conservation of biological diversity is the in-situ conservation of ecosystems and natural habitats and the maintenance and recovery of viable populations of species in their natural surroundings,

Noting further that ex-situ measures, preferably in the country of origin, also have an important role to play,

Recognizing the close and traditional dependence of many indigenous and local communities embodying traditional lifestyles on biological resources, and the desirability of sharing equitably benefits arising from the use of traditional knowledge, innovations and practices relevant to the conservation of biological diversity and the sustainable use of its components,

Recognizing also the vital role that women play in the conservation and sustainable use of biological diversity and affirming the need for the full participation of women at all levels of policy-making and implementation for biological diversity conservation,

Stressing the importance of, and the need to promote, international, regional and global cooperation among States and intergovernmental organizations and the non-governmental sector for the conservation of biological diversity and the sustainable use of its components,

Acknowledging that the provision of new and additional financial resources and appropriate access to relevant technologies can be expected to make a substantial difference in the world's ability to address the loss of biological diversity,

Acknowledging further that special provision is required to meet the needs of developing countries, including the provision of new and additional financial resources and appropriate access to relevant technologies,

Noting in this regard the special conditions of the least developed countries and small island States,

Acknowledging that substantial investments are required to conserve biological diversity and that there is the expectation of a broad range of environmental, economic and social benefits from those investments,

Recognizing that economic and social development and poverty eradication are the first and overriding priorities of developing countries,

Aware that conservation and sustainable use of biological diversity is of critical importance for meeting the food, health and other needs of the growing world population, for which purpose access to and sharing of both genetic resources and technologies are essential,

Noting that, ultimately, the conservation and sustainable use of biological diversity will strengthen friendly relations among States and contribute to peace for humankind,

Desiring to enhance and complement existing international arrangements for the conservation of biological diversity and sustainable use of its components, and

Determined to conserve and sustainably use biological diversity for the benefit of present and future generations,

ARTICLE 1. OBJECTIVES

The objectives of this Convention, to be pursued in accordance with its relevant provisions, are the conservation of biological diversity, the sustainable use of its components and the fair and equitable sharing of the benefits arising out of the utilization of genetic resources, including by appropriate access to genetic resources and by appropriate transfer of relevant technologies, taking into account all rights over those resources and to technologies, and by appropriate funding.

Article 2 defined terms used in the treaty, ranging from "biotechnology" to "sustainable use," new to many at the time, but since quite familiar.

ARTICLE 3. PRINCIPLE

States have, in accordance with the Charter of the United Nations and the principles of international law, the sovereign right to exploit their own resources pursuant to their own environmental policies, and the responsibility to ensure that activities within their jurisdiction or control do not cause damage to the environment of other States or of areas beyond the limits of national jurisdiction.

ARTICLE 4. JURISDICTIONAL SCOPE

Subject to the rights of other States, and except as otherwise expressly provided in this Convention, the provisions of this Convention apply, in relation to each Contracting Party:

(a) In the case of components of biological diversity, in areas within the limits of its national jurisdiction; and

(b) In the case of processes and activities, regardless of where their effects occur, carried out under its jurisdiction or control, within the area of its national jurisdiction or beyond the limits of national jurisdiction.

ARTICLE 5. COOPERATION

Each Contracting Party shall, as far as possible and as appropriate, cooperate with other Contracting Parties, directly or, where appropriate, through competent international organizations, in respect of areas beyond national jurisdiction and on other matters of mutual interest, for the conservation and sustainable use of biological diversity.

ARTICLE 6. GENERAL MEASURES FOR CONSERVATION AND SUSTAINABLE USE

Each Contracting Party shall, in accordance with its particular conditions and capabilities:

(a) Develop national strategies, plans or programmes for the conservation and sustainable use of biological diversity or adapt for this purpose existing strategies, plans or programmes which shall reflect, inter alia, the measures set out in this Convention relevant to the Contracting Party concerned; and

(b) Integrate, as far as possible and as appropriate, the conservation and sustainable use of biological diversity into relevant sectoral or cross-sectoral plans, programmes and policies.

ARTICLE 7. IDENTIFICATION AND MONITORING

Each Contracting Party shall, as far as possible and as appropriate, in particular for the purposes of Articles 8 to 10:

(a) Identify components of biological diversity important for its conservation and sustainable use having regard to the indicative list of categories set down in Annex I;

(b) Monitor, through sampling and other techniques, the components of biological diversity identified pursuant to subparagraph (a) above, paying particular attention to those requiring urgent conservation measures and those which offer the greatest potential for sustainable use;

(c) Identify processes and categories of activities which have or are likely to have significant adverse impacts on the conservation and sustainable use of biological diversity, and monitor their effects through sampling and other techniques; and

(d) Maintain and organize, by any mechanism data, derived from identification and monitoring activities pursuant to subparagraphs (a), (b) and (c) above.

ARTICLE 8. IN-SITU CONSERVATION

Each Contracting Party shall, as far as possible and as appropriate:

(a) Establish a system of protected areas or areas where special measures need to be taken to conserve biological diversity;

(b) Develop, where necessary, guidelines for the selection, establishment and management of protected areas or areas where special measures need to be taken to conserve biological diversity;

(c) Regulate or manage biological resources important for the conservation of biological diversity whether within or outside protected areas, with a view to ensuring their conservation and sustainable use;

(d) Promote the protection of ecosystems, natural habitats and the maintenance of viable populations of species in natural surroundings;

(e) Promote environmentally sound and sustainable development in areas adjacent to protected areas with a view to furthering protection of these areas;

(f) Rehabilitate and restore degraded ecosystems and promote the recovery of threatened species, inter alia, through the development and implementation of plans or other management strategies;

(g) Establish or maintain means to regulate, manage or control the risks associated with the use and release of living modified organisms resulting from biotechnology which are likely to have adverse environmental impacts that could affect the conservation and sustainable use of biological diversity, taking also into account the risks to human health;

(h) Prevent the introduction of, control or eradicate those alien species which threaten ecosystems, habitats or species;

(i) Endeavour to provide the conditions needed for compatibility between present uses and the conservation of biological diversity and the sustainable use of its components;

(j) Subject to its national legislation, respect, preserve and maintain knowledge, innovations and practices of indigenous and local communities embodying traditional lifestyles relevant for the conservation and sustainable use of biological diversity and promote their wider application with the approval and involvement of the holders of such knowledge, innovations and practices and encourage the equitable sharing of the benefits arising from the utilization of such knowledge, innovations and practices;

(k) Develop or maintain necessary legislation and/or other regulatory provisions for the protection of threatened species and populations;

(l) Where a significant adverse effect on biological diversity has been determined pursuant to Article 7, regulate or manage the relevant processes and categories of activities; and

(m) Cooperate in providing financial and other support for in-situ conservation outlined in subparagraphs (a) to (l) above, particularly to developing countries.

ARTICLE 9. EX-SITU CONSERVATION

Each Contracting Party shall, as far as possible and as appropriate, and predominantly for the purpose of complementing in-situ measures:

(a) Adopt measures for the ex-situ conservation of components of biological diversity, preferably in the country of origin of such components;

(b) Establish and maintain facilities for ex-situ conservation of and research on plants, animals and micro-organisms, preferably in the country of origin of genetic resources;

(c) Adopt measures for the recovery and rehabilitation of threatened species and for their reintroduction into their natural habitats under appropriate conditions;

(d) Regulate and manage collection of biological resources from natural habitats for ex-situ conservation purposes so as not to threaten ecosystems and in-situ populations of species, except where special temporary ex-situ measures are required under sub-paragraph (c) above; and

(e) Cooperate in providing financial and other support for ex-situ conservation outlined in subparagraphs (a) to (d) above and in the establishment and maintenance of ex-situ conservation facilities in developing countries.

ARTICLE 10. SUSTAINABLE USE OF COMPONENTS OF BIOLOGICAL DIVERSITY

Each Contracting Party shall, as far as possible and as appropriate:

(a) Integrate consideration of the conservation and sustainable use of biological resources into national decision-making;

(b) Adopt measures relating to the use of biological resources to avoid or minimize adverse impacts on biological diversity;

(c) Protect and encourage customary use of biological resources in accordance with traditional cultural practices that are compatible with conservation or sustainable use requirements;

(d) Support local populations to develop and implement remedial action in degraded areas where biological diversity has been reduced; and

(e) Encourage cooperation between its governmental authorities and its private sector in developing methods for sustainable use of biological resources.

ARTICLE 11. INCENTIVE MEASURES

Each Contracting Party shall, as far as possible and as appropriate, adopt economically and socially sound measures that act as incentives for the conservation and sustainable use of components of biological diversity.

ARTICLE 12. RESEARCH AND TRAINING

The Contracting Parties, taking into account the special needs of developing countries, shall:

(a) Establish and maintain programmes for scientific and technical education and training in measures for the identification, conservation and sustainable use of biological diversity and its components and provide support for such education and training for the specific needs of developing countries;

(b) Promote and encourage research which contributes to the conservation and sustainable use of biological diversity, particularly in developing countries, inter alia, in accordance with decisions of the Conference of the Parties taken in consequence of recommendations of the Subsidiary Body on Scientific, Technical and Technological Advice; and

(c) In keeping with the provisions of Articles 16, 18 and 20, promote and cooperate in the use of scientific advances in biological diversity research in developing methods for conservation and sustainable use of biological resources.

ARTICLE 13. PUBLIC EDUCATION AND AWARENESS

The Contracting Parties shall:

(a) Promote and encourage understanding of the importance of, and the measures required for, the conservation of biological diversity, as well as its propagation through media, and the inclusion of these topics in educational programmes; and

(b) Cooperate, as appropriate, with other States and international organizations in developing educational and public awareness programmes, with respect to conservation and sustainable use of biological diversity.

ARTICLE 14. IMPACT ASSESSMENT AND MINIMIZING ADVERSE IMPACTS

1. Each Contracting Party, as far as possible and as appropriate, shall:

(a) Introduce appropriate procedures requiring environmental impact assessment of its proposed projects that are likely to have significant adverse effects on biological diversity with a view to avoiding or minimizing such effects and, where appropriate, allow for public participation in such procedures;

(b) Introduce appropriate arrangements to ensure that the environmental consequences of its programmes and policies that are likely to have significant adverse impacts on biological diversity are duly taken into account;

(c) Promote, on the basis of reciprocity, notification, exchange of information and consultation on activities under their jurisdiction or control which are likely to significantly affect adversely the biological diversity of other States or areas beyond the limits of national jurisdiction, by encouraging the conclusion of bilateral, regional or multilateral arrangements, as appropriate;

(d) In the case of imminent or grave danger or damage, originating under its jurisdiction or control, to biological diversity within the area under jurisdiction of other States or in areas beyond the limits of national jurisdiction, notify immediately the potentially affected States of such danger or damage, as well as initiate action to prevent or minimize such danger or damage; and

(e) Promote national arrangements for emergency responses to activities or events, whether caused naturally or otherwise, which present a grave and imminent danger to biological diversity and encourage international cooperation to supplement such national efforts and, where appropriate and agreed by the States or regional economic integration organizations concerned, to establish joint contingency plans.

(f) The Conference of the Parties shall examine, on the basis of studies to be carried out, the issue of liability and redress, including restoration and compensation, for damage to biological diversity, except where such liability is a purely internal matter.

ARTICLE 15. ACCESS TO GENETIC RESOURCES

1. Recognizing the sovereign rights of States over their natural resources, the authority to determine access to

genetic resources rests with the national governments and is subject to national legislation.

2. Each Contracting Party shall endeavour to create conditions to facilitate access to genetic resources for environmentally sound uses by other Contracting Parties and not to impose restrictions that run counter to the objectives of this Convention.

3. For the purpose of this Convention, the genetic resources being provided by a Contracting Party, as referred to in this Article and Articles 16 and 19, are only those that are provided by Contracting Parties that are countries of origin of such resources or by the Parties that have acquired the genetic resources in accordance with this Convention.

4. Access, where granted, shall be on mutually agreed terms and subject to the provisions of this Article.

5. Access to genetic resources shall be subject to prior informed consent of the Contracting Party providing such resources, unless otherwise determined by that Party.

6. Each Contracting Party shall endeavour to develop and carry out scientific research based on genetic resources provided by other Contracting Parties with the full participation of, and where possible in, such Contracting Parties.

7. Each Contracting Party shall take legislative, administrative or policy measures, as appropriate, and in accordance with Articles 16 and 19 and, where necessary, through the financial mechanism established by Articles 20 and 21 with the aim of sharing in a fair and equitable way the results of research and development and the benefits arising from the commercial and other utilization of genetic resources with the Contracting Party providing such resources. Such sharing shall be upon mutually agreed terms.

ARTICLE 16. ACCESS TO AND TRANSFER OF TECHNOLOGY

1. Each Contracting Party, recognizing that technology includes biotechnology, and that both access to and transfer of technology among Contracting Parties are essential elements for the attainment of the objectives of this Convention, undertakes subject to the provisions of this Article to provide and/or facilitate access for and transfer to other Contracting Parties of technologies that are relevant to the conservation and sustainable use of biological diversity or make use of genetic resources and do not cause significant damage to the environment.

2. Access to and transfer of technology referred to in paragraph 1 above to developing countries shall be provided and/or facilitated under fair and most favourable terms, including on concessional and preferential terms where mutually agreed, and, where necessary, in accordance with the financial mechanism established by Articles 20 and 21. In the case of technology subject to patents and other intellectual property rights, such access and transfer shall be provided on terms which recognize and are consistent with the adequate and effective protection of intellectual property rights. The application of this paragraph shall be consistent with paragraphs 3, 4 and 5 below.

3. Each Contracting Party shall take legislative, administrative or policy measures, as appropriate, with the aim that Contracting Parties, in particular those that are developing countries, which provide genetic resources are provided access to and transfer of technology which makes use of those resources, on mutually agreed terms, including technology protected by patents and other intellectual property rights, where necessary, through the provisions of Articles 20 and 21 and in accordance with international law and consistent with paragraphs 4 and 5 below.

4. Each Contracting Party shall take legislative, administrative or policy measures, as appropriate, with the aim that the private sector facilitates access to, joint development and transfer of technology referred to in paragraph 1 above for the benefit of both governmental institutions and the private sector of developing countries and in this regard shall abide by the obligations included in paragraphs 1, 2 and 3 above.

5. The Contracting Parties, recognizing that patents and other intellectual property rights may have an influence on the implementation of this Convention, shall cooperate in this regard subject to national legislation and international law in order to ensure that such rights are supportive of and do not run counter to its objectives.

ARTICLE 17. EXCHANGE OF INFORMATION

1. The Contracting Parties shall facilitate the exchange of information, from all publicly available sources, relevant to the conservation and sustainable use of biological diversity, taking into account the special needs of developing countries.

2. Such exchange of information shall include exchange of results of technical, scientific and socioeconomic research, as well as information on training and surveying programmes, specialized knowledge, indigenous and traditional knowledge as such and in combination with the technologies referred to in Article 16, paragraph 1. It shall also, where feasible, include repatriation of information.

ARTICLE 18. TECHNICAL AND SCIENTIFIC COOPERATION

1. The Contracting Parties shall promote international technical and scientific cooperation in the field of conservation and sustainable use of biological diversity, where necessary, through the appropriate international and national institutions.

2. Each Contracting Party shall promote technical and scientific cooperation with other Contracting Parties, in particular developing countries, in implementing this Convention, inter alia, through the development and implementation of national policies. In promoting such cooperation, special attention should be given to the development and strengthening of national capabilities, by means of human resources development and institution building.

3. The Conference of the Parties, at its first meeting, shall determine how to establish a clearing-house mechanism to promote and facilitate technical and scientific cooperation.

4. The Contracting Parties shall, in accordance with national legislation and policies, encourage and develop methods of cooperation for the development and use of technologies, including indigenous and traditional technologies, in pursuance of the objectives of this Convention. For this purpose, the Contracting Parties shall also promote cooperation in the training of personnel and exchange of experts.

5. The Contracting Parties shall, subject to mutual agreement, promote the establishment of joint research programmes and joint ventures for the development of technologies relevant to the objectives of this Convention.

ARTICLE 19. HANDLING OF BIOTECHNOLOGY AND DISTRIBUTION OF ITS BENEFITS

1. Each Contracting Party shall take legislative, administrative or policy measures, as appropriate, to provide for the effective participation in biotechnological research activities by those Contracting Parties, especially developing countries, which provide the genetic resources for such research, and where feasible in such Contracting Parties.

2. Each Contracting Party shall take all practicable measures to promote and advance priority access on a fair and equitable basis by Contracting Parties, especially developing countries, to the results and benefits arising from biotechnologies based upon genetic resources provided by those Contracting Parties. Such access shall be on mutually agreed terms.

3. The Parties shall consider the need for and modalities of a protocol setting out appropriate procedures, including, in particular, advance informed agreement, in the field of the safe transfer, handling and use of any living modified organism resulting from biotechnology that may have adverse effect on the conservation and sustainable use of biological diversity.

4. Each Contracting Party shall, directly or by requiring any natural or legal person under its jurisdiction providing the organisms referred to in paragraph 3 above, provide any available information about the use and safety regulations required by that Contracting Party in handling such organisms, as well as any available information on the potential adverse impact of the specific organisms concerned to the Contracting Party into which those organisms are to be introduced.

ARTICLE 20. FINANCIAL RESOURCES

1. Each Contracting Party undertakes to provide, in accordance with its capabilities, financial support and incentives in respect of those national activities which are intended to achieve the objectives of this Convention, in accordance with its national plans, priorities and programmes.

2. The developed country Parties shall provide new and additional financial resources to enable developing country Parties to meet the agreed full incremental costs to them of implementing measures which fulfil the obligations of this Convention and to benefit from its provisions and which costs are agreed between a developing country Party and the institutional structure referred to in Article 21, in accordance with policy, strategy, programme priorities and eligibility criteria and an indicative list of incremental costs established by the Conference of the Parties. Other Parties, including countries undergoing the process of transition to a market economy, may voluntarily assume the obligations of the developed country Parties. For the purpose of this Article, the Conference of the Parties, shall at its first meeting establish a list of developed country Parties and other Parties which voluntarily assume the obligations of the developed country Parties. The Conference of the Parties shall periodically review and if necessary amend the list. Contributions from other countries and sources on a voluntary basis would also be encouraged. The implementation of these commitments shall take into account the need for adequacy, predictability and timely flow of funds and the importance of burden-sharing among the contributing Parties included in the list.

3. The developed country Parties may also provide, and developing country Parties avail themselves of, financial resources related to the implementation of this Convention through bilateral, regional and other multilateral channels.

4. The extent to which developing country Parties will effectively implement their commitments under this Convention will depend on the effective implementation by developed country Parties of their commitments under this Convention related to financial resources and transfer of technology and will take fully into account the fact that economic and social development and eradication of poverty are the first and overriding priorities of the developing country Parties.

5. The Parties shall take full account of the specific needs and special situation of least developed countries in their actions with regard to funding and transfer of technology.

6. The Contracting Parties shall also take into consideration the special conditions resulting from the dependence on, distribution and location of, biological diversity within developing country Parties, in particular small island States.

7. Consideration shall also be given to the special situation of developing countries, including those that are most environmentally vulnerable, such as those with arid and semi- arid zones, coastal and mountainous areas.

ARTICLE 21. FINANCIAL MECHANISM

1. There shall be a mechanism for the provision of financial resources to developing country Parties for purposes of this Convention on a grant or concessional basis the essential elements of which are described in this Article. The mechanism shall function under the

authority and guidance of, and be accountable to, the Conference of the Parties for purposes of this Convention. The operations of the mechanism shall be carried out by such institutional structure as may be decided upon by the Conference of the Parties at its first meeting. For purposes of this Convention, the Conference of the Parties shall determine the policy, strategy, programme priorities and eligibility criteria relating to the access to and utilization of such resources. The contributions shall be such as to take into account the need for predictability, adequacy and timely flow of funds referred to in Article 20 in accordance with the amount of resources needed to be decided periodically by the Conference of the Parties and the importance of burden-sharing among the contributing Parties included in the list referred to in Article 20, paragraph 2. Voluntary contributions may also be made by the developed country Parties and by other countries and sources. The mechanism shall operate within a democratic and transparent system of governance.

2. Pursuant to the objectives of this Convention, the Conference of the Parties shall at its first meeting determine the policy, strategy and programme priorities, as well as detailed criteria and guidelines for eligibility for access to and utilization of the financial resources including monitoring and evaluation on a regular basis of such utilization. The Conference of the Parties shall decide on the arrangements to give effect to paragraph 1 above after consultation with the institutional structure entrusted with the operation of the financial mechanism.

3. The Conference of the Parties shall review the effectiveness of the mechanism established under this Article, including the criteria and guidelines referred to in paragraph 2 above, not less than two years after the entry into force of this Convention and thereafter on a regular basis. Based on such review, it shall take appropriate action to improve the effectiveness of the mechanism if necessary.

4. The Contracting Parties shall consider strengthening existing financial institutions to provide financial resources for the conservation and sustainable use of biological diversity.

Articles 22 through 26 dealt with the convention's relationship to other international conventions, the nature of the conference in the future, the establishment of a secretariat and subsidiary bodies, and called for reports on the implementation of the convention's provisions by the signatory parties. Then the document turned to settling disputes:

ARTICLE 27. SETTLEMENT OF DISPUTES

1. In the event of a dispute between Contracting Parties concerning the interpretation or application of this Convention, the parties concerned shall seek solution by negotiation.

2. If the parties concerned cannot reach agreement by negotiation, they may jointly seek the good offices of, or request mediation by, a third party.

3. When ratifying, accepting, approving or acceding to this Convention, or at any time thereafter, a State or regional economic integration organization may declare in writing to the Depositary that for a dispute not resolved in accordance with paragraph 1 or paragraph 2 above, it accepts one or both of the following means of dispute settlement as compulsory:

(a) Arbitration in accordance with the procedure laid down in Part 1 of Annex II;

(b) Submission of the dispute to the International Court of Justice.

4. If the parties to the dispute have not, in accordance with paragraph 3 above, accepted the same or any procedure, the dispute shall be submitted to conciliation in accordance with Part 2 of Annex II unless the parties otherwise agree.

5. The provisions of this Article shall apply with respect to any protocol except as otherwise provided in the protocol concerned.

The rest of the convention dealt with diplomatic technicalities, such as adopting protocols, annexes, and amendments, voting procedures, and the like. An important annex was adopted covering arbitration and conciliation:

Annex II

Part 1. Arbitration

ARTICLE 1

The claimant party shall notify the secretariat that the parties are referring a dispute to arbitration pursuant to Article 27. The notification shall state the subject-matter of arbitration and include, in particular, the articles of the Convention or the protocol, the interpretation or application of which are at issue. If the parties do not agree on the subject matter of the dispute before the President of the tribunal is designated, the arbitral tribunal shall determine the subject matter. The secretariat shall forward the information thus received to all Contracting Parties to this Convention or to the protocol concerned.

ARTICLE 2

1. In disputes between two parties, the arbitral tribunal shall consist of three members. Each of the parties to the dispute shall appoint an arbitrator and the two arbitrators so appointed shall designate by common agreement the third arbitrator who shall be the President of the tribunal. The latter shall not be a national of one of the parties to the dispute, nor have his or her usual place of residence in the territory of one of these parties, nor be employed by any of them, nor have dealt with the case in any other capacity.

2. In disputes between more than two parties, parties in the same interest shall appoint one arbitrator jointly by agreement.

3. Any vacancy shall be filled in the manner prescribed for the initial appointment.

ARTICLE 3

1. If the President of the arbitral tribunal has not been designated within two months of the appointment of the second arbitrator, the Secretary-General of the United Nations shall, at the request of a party, designate the President within a further two-month period.

2. If one of the parties to the dispute does not appoint an arbitrator within two months of receipt of the request, the other party may inform the Secretary-General who shall make the designation within a further two-month period.

ARTICLE 4

The arbitral tribunal shall render its decisions in accordance with the provisions of this Convention, any protocols concerned, and international law.

ARTICLE 5

Unless the parties to the dispute otherwise agree, the arbitral tribunal shall determine its own rules of procedure.

ARTICLE 6

The arbitral tribunal may, at the request of one of the parties, recommend essential interim measures of protection.

ARTICLE 7

The parties to the dispute shall facilitate the work of the arbitral tribunal and, in particular, using all means at their disposal, shall:

(a) Provide it with all relevant documents, information and facilities; and

(b) Enable it, when necessary, to call witnesses or experts and receive their evidence.

ARTICLE 8

The parties and the arbitrators are under an obligation to protect the confidentiality of any information they receive in confidence during the proceedings of the arbitral tribunal.

ARTICLE 9

Unless the arbitral tribunal determines otherwise because of the particular circumstances of the case, the costs of the tribunal shall be borne by the parties to the dispute in equal shares. The tribunal shall keep a record of all its costs, and shall furnish a final statement thereof to the parties.

ARTICLE 10

Any Contracting Party that has an interest of a legal nature in the subject-matter of the dispute which may be affected by the decision in the case, may intervene in the proceedings with the consent of the tribunal.

ARTICLE 11

The tribunal may hear and determine counterclaims arising directly out of the subject-matter of the dispute.

ARTICLE 12

Decisions both on procedure and substance of the arbitral tribunal shall be taken by a majority vote of its members.

ARTICLE 13

If one of the parties to the dispute does not appear before the arbitral tribunal or fails to defend its case, the other party may request the tribunal to continue the proceedings and to make its award. Absence of a party or a failure of a party to defend its case shall not constitute a bar to the proceedings. Before rendering its final decision, the arbitral tribunal must satisfy itself that the claim is well founded in fact and law.

ARTICLE 14

The tribunal shall render its final decision within five months of the date on which it is fully constituted unless it finds it necessary to extend the time-limit for a period which should not exceed five more months.

ARTICLE 15

The final decision of the arbitral tribunal shall be confined to the subject-matter of the dispute and shall state the reasons on which it is based. It shall contain the names of the members who have participated and the date of the final decision. Any member of the tribunal may attach a separate or dissenting opinion to the final decision.

ARTICLE 16

The award shall be binding on the parties to the dispute. It shall be without appeal unless the parties to the dispute have agreed in advance to an appellate procedure.

ARTICLE 17

Any controversy which may arise between the parties to the dispute as regards the interpretation or manner of implementation of the final decision may be submitted by either party for decision to the arbitral tribunal which rendered it.

Part 2. Conciliation

ARTICLE 1

A conciliation commission shall be created upon the request of one of the parties to the dispute. The commission shall, unless the parties otherwise agree, be composed of five members, two appointed by each Party concerned and a President chosen jointly by those members.

ARTICLE 2

In disputes between more than two parties, parties in the same interest shall appoint their members of the commission jointly by agreement. Where two or more parties have separate interests or there is a disagreement as to whether they are of the same interest, they shall appoint their members separately.

ARTICLE 3

If any appointments by the parties are not made within two months of the date of the request to create a conciliation commission, the Secretary-General of the United Nations shall, if asked to do so by the party that made the request, make those appointments within a further two-month period.

ARTICLE 4

If a President of the conciliation commission has not been chosen within two months of the last of the members of the commission being appointed, the Secretary-General of the United Nations shall, if asked to do so by a party, designate a President within a further two-month period.

ARTICLE 5

The conciliation commission shall take its decisions by majority vote of its members. It shall, unless the parties to the dispute otherwise agree, determine its own procedure. It shall render a proposal for resolution of the dispute, which the parties shall consider in good faith.

ARTICLE 6

A disagreement as to whether the conciliation commission has competence shall be decided by the commission.

Consequences

The Convention on Biodiversity was probably the most important accomplishment of the summit. However, the international press, especially the U.S. press, was more interested in global warming. Summit participants developed an accord whereby nations would abstain from using substances that harm the ozone layer and would act to reduce the production of so-called greenhouse gases. Since these were essentially the products of combustion created by industry and automobiles, this accord was politically controversial in the auto-addicted United States, which worried President George H. W. Bush. Much attention was paid to the rift between the Bush administration and the delegates the United States had sent to Rio. At odds officially with his own government, he declined to sign the biodiversity treaty, which was subscribed to by some 120 other nations. In addition, he watered down the pact concerning global warming by agreeing to restrict the use of chlorofluorocarbons (CFCs) and other chemicals that harm the ozone layer but refusing to be bound by agreements on the abatement of greenhouse gases. Approaching reelection, his popularity foundering in a stubborn economic recession, Bush was loath to take any action that might appear to cost American jobs or limit their lifestyles.

After Rio, other nations continued to sign the convention, but the United States remained leery of what it perceived to be the treaty's North-South ideological backdrop and its potential challenge to U.S. development abroad as well as its sovereignty at home. In 1994, despite the fact that the convention's ratification was approved by the Senate Foreign Relations Committee, opposition to its passage forced then majority leader George Mitchell to withdraw it from the calendar in a stunning defeat for the administration of Bill Clinton and the army of environmentalist organizations that had carefully orchestrated what they all, including President Clinton and Vice President Al Gore, had assumed was certain ratification.

Source

Secretariat of the Convention on Biological Diversity, "Convention on Biodiversity," United Nations Environment Programme. Available online. URL: http://www.biodiv.org/convention/articles.asp. Accessed on January 3, 2005.

PROTOCOL ON BLINDING LASER WEAPONS (PROTOCOL IV) TO THE CONVENTION ON PROHIBITIONS OR RESTRICTIONS ON THE USE OF CERTAIN CONVENTIONAL WEAPONS WHICH MAY BE DEEMED TO BE EXCESSIVELY INJURIOUS OR TO HAVE INDISCRIMINATE EFFECTS

TREATY AT A GLANCE

Completed
October 13, 1995; entered into force July 30, 1998

Signatories
As of summer 2005, 80 United Nations members
had signed and become party to it

Overview
The Convention on Prohibitions or Restrictions on the Use of Certain Conventional Weapons Which May Be Deemed to Be Excessively Injurious or to Have Indiscriminate Effects came into force as an umbrella document for three conventional arms limitation protocols originally organic to it. Since that time, two additional protocols have been drafted, including the Protocol on Blinding Laser Weapons, which prohibits the use of "laser weapons specifically designed . . . to cause permanent blindness."

Historical Background

For a discussion of the historical background of this protocol, see CONVENTION ON PROHIBITIONS OR RESTRICTIONS ON THE USE OF CERTAIN CONVENTIONAL WHICH MAY BE DEEMED TO BE EXCESSIVELY INJURIOUS OR TO HAVE INDISCRIMINATE EFFECTS.

At the time that this protocol was completed, several nations had been working on tactical laser weapons for some two decades; however, no such weapons had (or, as of mid-2005, have) been fielded. The protocol was developed to prohibit only "laser weapons specifically designed, as their sole combat function or as one of their combat functions, to cause permanent blindness to unenhanced vision." This left open the development of other laser weapons, including some currently (as of spring 2005) under development by the United States. For example, contractors Lockheed Martin and Raytheon are developing "directed energy weapons," enormously powerful 100-kilowatt infrared lasers for use on the F-35 Joint Strike Fighter (JSF). These laser weapons are intended to destroy communication lines, power grids, and fuel dumps or to precisely focus on targets—for instance, the engine of a vehicle. As precise as these weapons could be, there is fear that their high intensity may cause collateral damage, including blindness from refracted or reflected energy, which may spread unpredictably and over a wide area. The protocol does not address weapons that may produce such collateral damage. As of spring 2005, it was predicted that the infrared laser weapon for the JSF would be operational by 2010.

The Committee on Conventional Weapons (CCW) of the U.S. Department of Defense pointed out that the protocol fails to extend the prohibition beyond the limits of the overall weapons convention itself; that is, like the convention, the protocol applies only to international armed conflicts and to internal conflicts for "national liberation." It does not apply to other internal conflicts. Nevertheless, in 1996, the CCW concluded that the protocol was fully consistent with U.S. military interests, Department of Defense policy, and humanitarian concerns generally and therefore recommended ratification at an early date. Despite the CCW recommendation, as of spring 2005, the United States has not signed this protocol, although officials hold that, as a matter of policy, the United States will in any case refrain from the use of laser weapons prohibited by it.

Terms

The protocol has a single substantive provision: it prohibits the use of laser weapons expressly designed to cause permanent blindness in enemy personnel.

Protocol on Blinding Laser Weapons (Protocol IV) to the Convention on Prohibitions or Restrictions on the Use of Certain Conventional Weapons Which May Be Deemed to Be Excessively Injurious or to Have Indiscriminate Effects

ARTICLE 1
It is prohibited to employ laser weapons specifically designed, as their sole combat function or as one of their combat functions, to cause permanent blindness to unenhanced vision, that is to the naked eye or to the eye with corrective eyesight devices. The High Contracting Parties shall not transfer such weapons to any State or non-State entity.

ARTICLE 2
In the employment of laser systems, the High Contracting Parties shall take all feasible precautions to avoid the incidence of permanent blindness to unenhanced vision. Such precautions shall include training of their armed forces and other practical measures.

ARTICLE 3
Blinding as an incidental or collateral effect of the legitimate military employment of laser systems, including laser systems used against optical equipment, is not covered by the prohibition of this Protocol.

ARTICLE 4
For the purpose of this protocol "permanent blindness" means irreversible and uncorrectable loss of vision which is seriously disabling with no prospect of recovery. Serious disability is equivalent to visual acuity of less than 20/200 Snellen measured using both eyes.

Consequences

To date, blinding laser weapons have not been employed in any known armed conflict. To what extent, if any, this is due to the protocol cannot be determined.

Source
Office of the Undersecretary of Defense for Acquisition, Technology, and Logistics, "Arms Control Implementation and Compliance: CCW: Protocol on Blinding Laser Weapons (Protocol IV)." Available online. URL: http://www.defenselink.mil/acq/acic/treaties/ccwapl/ccwapl_laser.htm. Accessed January 3, 2005.

CONVENTION ON THE PROHIBITION OF THE USE, STOCKPILING, PRODUCTION, AND TRANSFER OF ANTI-PERSONNEL MINES AND ON THEIR DESTRUCTION (LAND MINE BAN TREATY)

TREATY AT A GLANCE

Completed
September 18, 1997, at Oslo, Norway (and December 3, 1997, at Ottawa, Canada); entered into force March 1, 1999

Signatories
As of summer 2005, 145 member states of the United Nations but not including the United States, China, and Russia

Overview
With high-profile support from the likes of Diana, the Princess of Wales, the long campaign to ban deadly antipersonnel land mines reached fruition in 1997, garnering for its proponents that year's Nobel Peace Prize.

Historical Background

Land mines are inexpensive to manufacture, costing about $5 apiece, but they are costly to detect and defuse: destroying one mine in 2001 ran about $1,000. Antipersonnel mines, which are more compact and more common than antitank mines, are popular with many belligerents because they are cheap, easy to place, and since they are indiscriminate in their destructiveness, useful instruments of psychological terror. Experts estimate that by the early 1990s, there were more than 100 million antipersonnel land mines planted about the current and former battlefields of the world, which were killing some 25,000 people a year, most of them civilians, many of them children. What was more, land mines remained deadly hazards long after a conflict had ended or a war had moved to other locations.

Because they are cheap, easy to plant, and expensive to remove, unexploded land mines are more likely to be found in poor and developing nations than in the lands of major powers, who, if nothing else, can afford the costs of getting rid of them once a conflict has ended. And because these less-developed nations, say Cambodia, Angola, or even Bosnia and Herzegovina, are likely to have health services that are overcrowded and underfunded by national budgets bled dry by war,

they tend to turn their backs on the deaths and injuries resulting from land mines, which would only place additional strains on dwindling resources.

Egypt has more unexploded mines than any other country, some 23 million of them buried in the sand. Many of them date from World War II, but they also came to be planted in the string of Arab-Israeli conflicts in 1948, 1956, 1967, and 1973. In 2001, Bosnia and Herzegovina was the most densely mined, with an average of 152 mines per square mile. It took the newly reunified Germany three years and $175 million to clear the last 1,100 mines along the old border between the former East and West Germany, all that was left of the 1.5 million planted there during the cold war. The United Nations tried to help out where it could, operating mine-removal programs in Afghanistan, Angola, Bosnia and Herzegovina, Cambodia, Croatia, El Salvador, Mozambique, Nicaragua, and Somalia. The Organization of American States, too, came up with a scheme to get rid of the 170,000 land mines it estimated lay beneath the soil of Central America—in Nicaragua, Honduras, Guatemala, and Costa Rica—by the turn of the millennium.

Such was the situation in November 1991, when American activist Jody Williams helped found the International Campaign to Ban Landmines (ICBL). The

Vietnam Veterans of America Foundation (VVAF), along with the German-based group Medico International, provided the institutional base for the formation of ICBL, with Williams as campaign coordinator. In part, Williams's campaign was a belated response to long-simmering frustrations and disappointments stretching back a decade, when, despite high hopes, the 1980 Geneva Convention on Inhumane Weapons failed to ban outright antipersonnel land mines (although attending nations, reconvening later in the mid-1990s, agreed to standardize some specifications for producing the weapons). Under Williams, ICBL expanded into a coalition of about 1,000 nongovernmental humanitarian, medical, and developmental groups from more than 50 nations.

By the mid-1990s, Williams had managed to get land mines back on the international agenda. In 1994 U.S. president Bill Clinton addressed the United Nations General Assembly on the subject, calling for the eventual elimination of antipersonnel land mines. He would repeat the appeal in September 1996, after the United States had announced in March a unilateral ban on the use of "dumb" antipersonnel mines and pledged to destroy its stockpile of such weapons by the end of 1999.

But Clinton's appeals were deceptive. The United States did not want the new policy to apply to Korea, where it planned to continue using "dumb" mines in the Demilitarized Zone. And the United States was not alone. Both China and Finland advocated "reasonable limits" rather than an outright ban and pointed to the defensive nature of mines along a border. Chile employed mines to combat drug merchants crossing the mountains. So, despite UN secretary-general Boutros Boutros-Ghali's harsh criticism that his organization's Conference on Disarmament (CD) had ignored the "groundswell" in public opinion against mines and his warning that by the time of the next review conference, in 2001, an additional 50,000 human beings would have been killed and a further 80,000 injured by land mines, the CD dragged its heels on negotiating a ban on antipersonnel land mines.

At first Williams and her compatriots turned to unilateral and regional actions by governments, which they hoped might be more successful than the global approach of the Convention on Inhumane Weapons and the CD. In March 1995 Belgium became the first country to enact a law completely banning the manufacture, trade, use, and stockpiling of antipersonnel mines. That same year South Africa announced a permanent ban on the export of antipersonnel mines, while France established a moratorium on their production. In April 1996 Germany renounced the use of antipersonnel mines by its armed forces and said that it planned to destroy the remaining mines of that kind. In

September, Italy, one of the largest producers of land mines, pledged to renounce the production and export of these weapons and thus became the 33rd nation with a moratorium on the export of antipersonnel mines.

Eventually, buoyed by these successes, the ICBL returned to the international road to a ban with the so-called Ottawa Process, named after the site of an October 1996 conference sponsored by Canada, with the express aim of achieving a global ban at the earliest possible date. In addition to nations, the process included a number of nongovernmental organizations. A treaty text was adopted at a follow-up conference in Oslo in September.

Terms

The treaty mandated an absolute ban on land mine production, export, and use as well as the destruction of existing stockpiles and the removal of active mines.

Convention on the Prohibition of the Use, Stockpiling, Production and Transfer of Anti-Personnel Mines and on Their Destruction, September 18, 1997

Preamble

The States Parties,

Determined to put an end to the suffering and casualties caused by anti-personnel mines, that kill or maim hundreds of people every week, mostly innocent and defenseless civilians and especially children, obstruct economic development and reconstruction, inhibit the repatriation of refugees and internally displaced persons, and have other severe consequences for years after emplacement,

Believing it necessary to do their utmost to contribute in an efficient and coordinated manner to face the challenge of removing anti-personnel mines placed throughout the world, and to assure their destruction,

Wishing to do their utmost in providing assistance for the care and rehabilitation, including the social and economic reintegration of mine victims,

Recognizing that a total ban of anti-personnel mines would also be an important confidence-building measure,

Welcoming the adoption of the Protocol on Prohibitions or Restrictions on the Use of Mines, Booby-Traps and Other Devices, as amended on 3 May 1996, annexed to the Convention on Prohibitions or Restrictions on the Use of Certain Conventional Weapons Which May Be Deemed to Be Excessively Injurious or to Have Indiscriminate Effects, and calling for the early ratification of this Protocol by all States which have not yet done so,

Welcoming also United Nations General Assembly Resolution 51/45 S of 10 December 1996 urging all States to pursue vigorously an effective, legally-binding international agreement to ban the use, stockpiling, production and transfer of anti-personnel landmines,

Welcoming furthermore the measures taken over the past years, both unilaterally and multilaterally, aiming at prohibiting, restricting or suspending the use, stockpiling, production and transfer of anti-personnel mines,

Stressing the role of public conscience in furthering the principles of humanity as evidenced by the call for a total ban of anti- personnel mines and recognizing the efforts to that end undertaken by the International Red Cross and Red Crescent Movement, the International Campaign to Ban Landmines and numerous other non-governmental organizations around the world,

Recalling the Ottawa Declaration of 5 October 1996 and the Brussels Declaration of 27 June 1997 urging the international community to negotiate an international and legally binding agreement prohibiting the use, stockpiling, production and transfer of anti-personnel mines,

Emphasizing the desirability of attracting the adherence of all States to this Convention, and determined to work strenuously towards the promotion of its universalization in all relevant fora including, inter alia, the United Nations, the Conference on Disarmament, regional organizations, and groupings, and review conferences of the Convention on Prohibitions or Restrictions on the Use of Certain Conventional Weapons Which May Be Deemed to Be Excessively Injurious or to Have Indiscriminate Effects,

Basing themselves on the principle of international humanitarian law that the right of the parties to an armed conflict to choose methods or means of warfare is not unlimited, on the principle that prohibits the employment in armed conflicts of weapons, projectiles and materials and methods of warfare of a nature to cause superfluous injury or unnecessary suffering and on the principle that a distinction must be made between civilians and combatants,

Have agreed as follows:

ARTICLE 1. GENERAL OBLIGATIONS

1. Each State Party undertakes never under any circumstances:

a) To use anti-personnel mines;

b) To develop, produce, otherwise acquire, stockpile, retain or transfer to anyone, directly or indirectly, anti-personnel mines;

c) To assist, encourage or induce, in any way, anyone to engage in any activity prohibited to a State Party under this Convention.

2. Each State Party undertakes to destroy or ensure the destruction of all anti-personnel mines in accordance with the provisions of this Convention.

ARTICLE 2. DEFINITIONS

1. "Anti-personnel mine" means a mine designed to be exploded by the presence, proximity or contact of a person and that will incapacitate, injure or kill one or more persons. Mines designed to be detonated by the presence, proximity or contact of a vehicle as opposed to a person, that are equipped with anti-handling devices, are not considered anti-personnel mines as a result of being so equipped.

2. "Mine" means a munition designed to be placed under, on or near the ground or other surface area and to be exploded by the presence, proximity or contact of a person or a vehicle.

3. "Anti-handling device" means a device intended to protect a mine and which is part of, linked to, attached to or placed under the mine and which activates when an attempt is made to tamper with or otherwise intentionally disturb the mine.

4. "Transfer" involves, in addition to the physical movement of anti-personnel mines into or from national territory, the transfer of title to and control over the mines, but does not involve the transfer of territory containing emplaced anti-personnel mines.

5. "Mined area" means an area which is dangerous due to the presence or suspected presence of mines.

ARTICLE 3. EXCEPTIONS

1. Notwithstanding the general obligations under Article 1, the retention or transfer of a number of anti-personnel mines for the development of and training in mine detection, mine clearance, or mine destruction techniques is permitted. The amount of such mines shall not exceed the minimum number absolutely necessary for the above-mentioned purposes.

2. The transfer of anti-personnel mines for the purpose of destruction is permitted.

ARTICLE 4. DESTRUCTION OF STOCKPILED ANTI-PERSONNEL MINES

Except as provided for in Article 3, each State Party undertakes to destroy or ensure the destruction of all stockpiled anti-personnel mines it owns or possesses, or that are under its jurisdiction or control, as soon as possible but not later than four years after the entry into force of this Convention for that State Party.

ARTICLE 5. DESTRUCTION OF ANTI-PERSONNEL MINES IN MINED AREAS

1. Each State Party undertakes to destroy or ensure the destruction of all anti-personnel mines in mined areas under its jurisdiction or control, as soon as possible but not later than ten years after the entry into force of this Convention for that State Party.

2. Each State Party shall make every effort to identify all areas under its jurisdiction or control in which anti-personnel mines are known or suspected to be emplaced and shall ensure as soon as possible that all anti-personnel mines in mined areas under its jurisdiction or control are perimeter-marked, monitored and protected by fencing or other means, to ensure the effective exclusion of civilians, until all anti-personnel mines contained therein have been destroyed. The marking shall at least be to the standards set out in the Protocol on Prohibitions or Restrictions on the Use of Mines, Booby-Traps and Other Devices, as amended on 3 May 1996, annexed to the Convention on Prohibitions or Restrictions on the Use of Certain Conventional Weapons Which May Be Deemed to Be Excessively Injurious or to Have Indiscriminate Effects.

3. If a State Party believes that it will be unable to destroy or ensure the destruction of all anti-personnel mines referred to in paragraph 1 within that time period, it may submit a request to a Meeting of the States Parties or a Review Conference for an extension of the deadline for completing the destruction of such anti-personnel mines, for a period of up to ten years.

4. Each request shall contain:

a) The duration of the proposed extension;

b) A detailed explanation of the reasons for the proposed extension, including:

(i) The preparation and status of work conducted under national demining programs;

(ii) The financial and technical means available to the State Party for the destruction of all the anti-personnel mines; and

(iii) Circumstances which impede the ability of the State Party to destroy all the anti-personnel mines in mined areas;

c) The humanitarian, social, economic, and environmental implications of the extension; and

d) Any other information relevant to the request for the proposed extension.

5. The Meeting of the States Parties or the Review Conference shall, taking into consideration the factors contained in paragraph 4, assess the request and decide by a majority of votes of States Parties present and voting whether to grant the request for an extension period.

6. Such an extension may be renewed upon the submission of a new request in accordance with paragraphs 3, 4 and 5 of this Article. In requesting a further extension period a State Party shall submit relevant additional information on what has been undertaken in the previous extension period pursuant to this Article.

ARTICLE 6. INTERNATIONAL COOPERATION AND ASSISTANCE

1. In fulfilling its obligations under this Convention each State Party has the right to seek and receive assistance, where feasible, from other States Parties to the extent possible.

2. Each State Party undertakes to facilitate and shall have the right to participate in the fullest possible exchange of equipment, material and scientific and technological information concerning the implementation of this Convention. The States Parties shall not impose undue restrictions on the provision of mine clearance equipment and related technological information for humanitarian purposes.

3. Each State Party in a position to do so shall provide assistance for the care and rehabilitation, and social and economic reintegration, of mine victims and for mine awareness programs. Such assistance may be provided, inter alia, through the United Nations system, international, regional or national organizations or institutions, the International Committee of the Red Cross, national Red Cross and Red Crescent societies and their International Federation, non-governmental organizations, or on a bilateral basis.

4. Each State Party in a position to do so shall provide assistance for mine clearance and related activities. Such assistance may be provided, inter alia, through the United Nations system, international or regional organizations or institutions, non-governmental organizations or institutions, or on a bilateral basis, or by contributing to the United Nations Voluntary Trust Fund for Assistance in Mine Clearance, or other regional funds that deal with demining.

5. Each State Party in a position to do so shall provide assistance for the destruction of stockpiled anti-personnel mines.

6. Each State Party undertakes to provide information to the database on mine clearance established within the United Nations system, especially information concerning various means and technologies of mine clearance, and lists of experts, expert agencies or national points of contact on mine clearance.

7. States Parties may request the United Nations, regional organizations, other States Parties or other competent intergov-

ernmental or non-governmental fora to assist its authorities in the elaboration of a national demining program to determine, inter alia:

a) The extent and scope of the anti-personnel mine problem;

b) The financial, technological and human resources that are required for the implementation of the program;

c) The estimated number of years necessary to destroy all anti-personnel mines in mined areas under the jurisdiction or control of the concerned State Party;

d) Mine awareness activities to reduce the incidence of mine-related injuries or deaths;

e) Assistance to mine victims;

f) The relationship between the Government of the concerned State Party and the relevant governmental, inter-governmental or non-governmental entities that will work in the implementation of the program.

8. Each State Party giving and receiving assistance under the provisions of this Article shall cooperate with a view to ensuring the full and prompt implementation of agreed assistance programs.

ARTICLE 7. TRANSPARENCY MEASURES

1. Each State Party shall report to the Secretary-General of the United Nations as soon as practicable, and in any event not later than 180 days after the entry into force of this Convention for that State Party on:

a) The national implementation measures referred to in Article 9;

b) The total of all stockpiled anti-personnel mines owned or possessed by it, or under its jurisdiction or control, to include a breakdown of the type, quantity and, if possible, lot numbers of each type of anti-personnel mine stockpiled;

c) To the extent possible, the location of all mined areas that contain, or are suspected to contain, anti-personnel mines under its jurisdiction or control, to include as much detail as possible regarding the type and quantity of each type of anti-personnel mine in each mined area and when they were emplaced;

d) The types, quantities and, if possible, lot numbers of all anti-personnel mines retained or transferred for the development of and training in mine detection, mine clearance or mine destruction techniques, or transferred for the purpose of destruction, as well as the institutions authorized by a State Party to retain or transfer anti-personnel mines, in accordance with Article 3;

e) The status of programs for the conversion or de-commissioning of anti-personnel mine production facilities;

f) The status of programs for the destruction of anti-personnel mines in accordance with Articles 4 and 5, including details of the methods which will be used in destruction, the location of all destruction sites and the applicable safety and environmental standards to be observed;

g) The types and quantities of all anti-personnel mines destroyed after the entry into force of this Convention for that State Party, to include a breakdown of the quantity of each type of anti-personnel mine destroyed, in accordance with Articles 4 and 5, respectively, along with, if possible, the lot numbers of each type of anti-personnel mine in the case of destruction in accordance with Article 4;

h) The technical characteristics of each type of anti-personnel mine produced, to the extent known, and those currently owned or possessed by a State Party, giving, where reasonably possible, such categories of information as may facilitate identification and clearance of anti-personnel mines; at a minimum, this information shall include the dimensions, fusing, explosive content, metallic content, color photographs and other information which may facilitate mine clearance; and

i) The measures taken to provide an immediate and effective warning to the population in relation to all areas identified under paragraph 2 of Article 5.

2. The information provided in accordance with this Article shall be updated by the States Parties annually, covering the last calendar year, and reported to the Secretary-General of the United Nations not later than 30 April of each year.

3. The Secretary-General of the United Nations shall transmit all such reports received to the States Parties.

ARTICLE 8. FACILITATION AND CLARIFICATION OF COMPLIANCE

1. The States Parties agree to consult and cooperate with each other regarding the implementation of the provisions of this Convention, and to work together in a spirit of cooperation to facilitate compliance by States Parties with their obligations under this Convention.

2. If one or more States Parties wish to clarify and seek to resolve questions relating to compliance with the provisions of this Convention by another State Party, it may submit, through the Secretary-General of the United Nations, a Request for Clarification of that matter to that State Party. Such a request shall be accompanied by all appropriate information. Each State Party shall refrain from unfounded Requests for Clarification, care being taken to avoid abuse. A State Party that receives a Request for Clarification shall provide, through the Secretary-General of the United Nations, within 28 days to the requesting State Party all information which would assist in clarifying this matter.

3. If the requesting State Party does not receive a response through the Secretary-General of the United Nations within that time period, or deems the response to the Request for Clarification to be unsatisfactory, it may submit the matter through the Secretary-General of the United Nations to the next Meeting of the States Parties. The Secretary-General of the United Nations shall transmit the submission, accompanied by all appropriate information pertaining to the Request for Clarification, to all States Parties. All such information shall be presented to the requested State Party which shall have the right to respond.

4. Pending the convening of any meeting of the States Parties, any of the States Parties concerned may request the Secretary- General of the United Nations to exercise his or her good offices to facilitate the clarification requested.

5. The requesting State Party may propose through the Secretary-General of the United Nations the convening of a Special Meeting of the States Parties to consider the matter. The Secretary-General of the United Nations shall thereupon communicate this proposal and all information submitted by the States Parties concerned, to all States Parties with a request that they indicate whether they favor a Special Meeting of the States Parties, for the purpose of considering the matter. In the event that within 14 days from the date of such communication, at least one-third of the States Parties favors such a Special Meeting, the Secretary-General of the United Nations shall convene this Special Meeting of the States Parties within a further 14 days. A quorum for this Meeting shall consist of a majority of States Parties.

6. The Meeting of the States Parties or the Special Meeting of the States Parties, as the case may be, shall first determine whether to consider the matter further, taking into account all information submitted by the States Parties concerned. The Meeting of the States Parties or the Special Meeting of the States Parties shall make every effort to reach a decision by consensus. If despite all efforts to that end no agreement has been reached, it shall take this decision by a majority of States Parties present and voting.

7. All States Parties shall cooperate fully with the Meeting of the States Parties or the Special Meeting of the States Parties in the fulfillment of its review of the matter, including any fact-finding missions that are authorized in accordance with paragraph 8.

8. If further clarification is required, the Meeting of the States Parties or the Special Meeting of the States Parties shall authorize a fact-finding mission and decide on its mandate by a majority of States Parties present and voting. At any time the requested State Party may invite a fact-finding mission to its territory. Such a mission shall take place without a decision by a Meeting of the States Parties or a Special Meeting of the States Parties to authorize such a mission. The mission, consisting of up to 9 experts, designated and approved in accordance with paragraphs 9 and 10, may collect additional information on the spot or in other places directly related to the alleged compliance issue under the jurisdiction or control of the requested State Party.

9. The Secretary-General of the United Nations shall prepare and update a list of the names, nationalities and other relevant data of qualified experts provided by States Parties and communicate it to all States Parties. Any expert included on this list shall be regarded as designated for all fact-finding missions unless a State Party declares its non-acceptance in writing. In the event of non-acceptance, the expert shall not participate in fact-finding missions on the territory or any other place under the jurisdiction or control of the objecting State Party, if the non-acceptance was declared prior to the appointment of the expert to such missions.

10. Upon receiving a request from the Meeting of the States Parties or a Special Meeting of the States Parties, the Secretary-General of the United Nations shall, after consultations with the requested State Party, appoint the members of the mission, including its leader. Nationals of States Parties requesting the fact-finding mission or directly affected by it shall not be appointed to the mission. The members of the fact-finding mission shall enjoy privileges and immunities under Article VI of the Convention on the Privileges and Immunities of the United Nations, adopted on 13 February 1946.

11. Upon at least 72 hours notice, the members of the fact-finding mission shall arrive in the territory of the requested State Party at the earliest opportunity. The requested State Party shall take the necessary administrative measures to receive, transport and accommodate the mission, and shall be responsible for ensuring the security of the mission to the maximum extent possible while they are on territory under its control.

12. Without prejudice to the sovereignty of the requested State Party, the fact-finding mission may bring into the territory of the requested State Party the necessary equipment which shall be used exclusively for gathering information on the alleged compliance issue. Prior to its arrival, the mission will advise the

requested State Party of the equipment that it intends to utilize in the course of its fact-finding mission.

13. The requested State Party shall make all efforts to ensure that the fact-finding mission is given the opportunity to speak with all relevant persons who may be able to provide information related to the alleged compliance issue.

14. The requested State Party shall grant access for the fact-finding mission to all areas and installations under its control where facts relevant to the compliance issue could be expected to be collected. This shall be subject to any arrangements that the requested State Party considers necessary for:

a) The protection of sensitive equipment, information and areas;

b) The protection of any constitutional obligations the requested State Party may have with regard to proprietary rights, searches and seizures, or other constitutional rights; or

c) The physical protection and safety of the members of the fact-finding mission.

In the event that the requested State Party makes such arrangements, it shall make every reasonable effort to demonstrate through alternative means its compliance with this Convention.

15. The fact-finding mission may remain in the territory of the State Party concerned for no more than 14 days, and at any particular site no more than 7 days, unless otherwise agreed.

16. All information provided in confidence and not related to the subject matter of the fact-finding mission shall be treated on a confidential basis.

17. The fact-finding mission shall report, through the Secretary-General of the United Nations, to the Meeting of the States Parties or the Special Meeting of the States Parties the results of its findings.

18. The Meeting of the States Parties or the Special Meeting of the States Parties shall consider all relevant information, including the report submitted by the fact-finding mission, and may request the requested State Party to take measures to address the compliance issue within a specified period of time. The requested State Party shall report on all measures taken in response to this request.

19. The Meeting of the States Parties or the Special Meeting of the States Parties may suggest to the States Parties concerned ways and means to further clarify or resolve the matter under consideration, including the initiation of appropriate procedures in conformity with international law. In circumstances where the issue at hand is determined to be due to circumstances beyond the control of the requested State Party, the Meeting of the States Parties or the Special Meeting of the States Parties may recommend appropriate measures, including the use of cooperative measures referred to in Article 6.

20. The Meeting of the States Parties or the Special Meeting of the States Parties shall make every effort to reach its decisions referred to in paragraphs 18 and 19 by consensus, otherwise by a two-thirds majority of States Parties present and voting.

ARTICLE 9. NATIONAL IMPLEMENTATION MEASURES

Each State Party shall take all appropriate legal, administrative and other measures, including the imposition of penal sanctions, to prevent and suppress any activity prohibited to a State Party under this Convention undertaken by persons or on territory under its jurisdiction or control.

ARTICLE 10. SETTLEMENT OF DISPUTES

1. The States Parties shall consult and cooperate with each other to settle any dispute that may arise with regard to the application or the interpretation of this Convention. Each State Party may bring any such dispute before the Meeting of the States Parties.

2. The Meeting of the States Parties may contribute to the settlement of the dispute by whatever means it deems appropriate, including offering its good offices, calling upon the States parties to a dispute to start the settlement procedure of their choice and recommending a time-limit for any agreed procedure.

3. This Article is without prejudice to the provisions of this Convention on facilitation and clarification of compliance.

ARTICLE 11. MEETINGS OF THE STATES PARTIES

1. The States Parties shall meet regularly in order to consider any matter with regard to the application or implementation of this Convention, including:

a) The operation and status of this Convention;

b) Matters arising from the reports submitted under the provisions of this Convention;

c) International cooperation and assistance in accordance with Article 6;

d) The development of technologies to clear anti-personnel mines;

e) Submissions of States Parties under Article 8; and

f) Decisions relating to submissions of States Parties as provided for in Article 5.

2. The First Meeting of the States Parties shall be convened by the Secretary-General of the United Nations within one year after the entry into force of this Convention. The subsequent meetings shall be convened by the Secretary-General of the United Nations annually until the first Review Conference.

3. Under the conditions set out in Article 8, the Secretary-General of the United Nations shall convene a Special Meeting of the States Parties.

4. States not parties to this Convention, as well as the United Nations, other relevant international organizations or institutions, regional organizations, the International Committee of the Red Cross and relevant non-governmental organizations may be invited to attend these meetings as observers in accordance with the agreed Rules of Procedure.

ARTICLE 12. REVIEW CONFERENCES

1. A Review Conference shall be convened by the Secretary-General of the United Nations five years after the entry into force of this Convention. Further Review Conferences shall be convened by the Secretary-General of the United Nations if so requested by one or more States Parties, provided that the interval between Review Conferences shall in no case be less than five years. All States Parties to this Convention shall be invited to each Review Conference.

2. The purpose of the Review Conference shall be:

a) To review the operation and status of this Convention;

b) To consider the need for and the interval between further Meetings of the States Parties referred to in paragraph 2 of Article 11;

c) To take decisions on submissions of States Parties as provided for in Article 5; and

d) To adopt, if necessary, in its final report conclusions related to the implementation of this Convention.

3. States not parties to this Convention, as well as the United Nations, other relevant international organizations or institutions, regional organizations, the International Committee of the Red Cross and relevant non-governmental organizations may be invited to attend each Review Conference as observers in accordance with the agreed Rules of Procedure.

ARTICLE 13. AMENDMENTS

1. At any time after the entry into force of this Convention any State Party may propose amendments to this Convention. Any proposal for an amendment shall be communicated to the Depositary, who shall circulate it to all States Parties and shall seek their views on whether an Amendment Conference should be convened to consider the proposal. If a majority of the States Parties notify the Depositary no later than 30 days after its circulation that they support further consideration of the proposal, the Depositary shall convene an Amendment Conference to which all States Parties shall be invited.

2. States not parties to this Convention, as well as the United Nations, other relevant international organizations or institutions, regional organizations, the International Committee of the Red Cross and relevant non-governmental organizations may be invited to attend each Amendment Conference as observers in accordance with the agreed Rules of Procedure.

3. The Amendment Conference shall be held immediately following a Meeting of the States Parties or a Review Conference unless a majority of the States Parties request that it be held earlier.

4. Any amendment to this Convention shall be adopted by a majority of two-thirds of the States Parties present and voting at the Amendment Conference. The Depositary shall communicate any amendment so adopted to the States Parties.

5. An amendment to this Convention shall enter into force for all States Parties to this Convention which have accepted it, upon the deposit with the Depositary of instruments of acceptance by a majority of States Parties. Thereafter it shall enter into force for any remaining State Party on the date of deposit of its instrument of acceptance.

ARTICLE 14. COSTS

1. The costs of the Meetings of the States Parties, the Special Meetings of the States Parties, the Review Conferences and the Amendment Conferences shall be borne by the States Parties and States not parties to this Convention participating therein, in accordance with the United Nations scale of assessment adjusted appropriately.

2. The costs incurred by the Secretary-General of the United Nations under Articles 7 and 8 and the costs of any fact-finding mission shall be borne by the States Parties in accordance with the United Nations scale of assessment adjusted appropriately.

ARTICLE 15. SIGNATURE

This Convention, done at Oslo, Norway, on 18 September 1997, shall be open for signature at Ottawa, Canada, by all States from 3 December 1997 until 4 December 1997, and at the United Nations Headquarters in New York from 5 December 1997 until its entry into force.

ARTICLE 16. RATIFICATION, ACCEPTANCE, APPROVAL OR ACCESSION

1. This Convention is subject to ratification, acceptance or approval of the Signatories.

2. It shall be open for accession by any State which has not signed the Convention.

3. The instruments of ratification, acceptance, approval or accession shall be deposited with the Depositary.

ARTICLE 17. ENTRY INTO FORCE

1. This Convention shall enter into force on the first day of the sixth month after the month in which the 40th instrument of ratification, acceptance, approval or accession has been deposited.

2. For any State which deposits its instrument of ratification, acceptance, approval or accession after the date of the deposit of the 40th instrument of ratification, acceptance, approval or accession, this Convention shall enter into force on the first day of the sixth month after the date on which that State has deposited its instrument of ratification, acceptance, approval or accession.

ARTICLE 18. PROVISIONAL APPLICATION

Any State may at the time of its ratification, acceptance, approval or accession, declare that it will apply provisionally paragraph 1 of Article 1 of this Convention pending its entry into force.

ARTICLE 19. RESERVATIONS

The Articles of this Convention shall not be subject to reservations.

ARTICLE 20. DURATION AND WITHDRAWAL

1. This Convention shall be of unlimited duration.

2. Each State Party shall, in exercising its national sovereignty, have the right to withdraw from this Convention. It shall give notice of such withdrawal to all other States Parties, to the Depositary and to the United Nations Security Council. Such instrument of withdrawal shall include a full explanation of the reasons motivating this withdrawal.

3. Such withdrawal shall only take effect six months after the receipt of the instrument of withdrawal by the Depositary. If, however, on the expiry of that six-month period, the withdrawing State Party is engaged in an armed conflict, the withdrawal shall not take effect before the end of the armed conflict.

4. The withdrawal of a State Party from this Convention shall not in any way affect the duty of States to continue fulfilling the obligations assumed under any relevant rules of international law.

ARTICLE 21. DEPOSITARY

The Secretary-General of the United Nations is hereby designated as the Depositary of this Convention.

ARTICLE 22. AUTHENTIC TEXTS

The original of this Convention, of which the Arabic, Chinese, English, French, Russian and Spanish texts are equally authentic, shall be deposited with the Secretary-General of the United Nations.

Consequences

The United States, which much preferred the CD as the forum for regulating land mines, only reluctantly joined the Oslo conference. American efforts to amend the draft treaty to allow several exceptions—like the use of land mines in Korea—failed, and President Clinton announced that the United States would not sign the treaty. He did nevertheless launch an initiative to raise $1 billion each year for mine-clearing operations, with the goal of eradicating by 2010 all land mines threatening civilian populations. A number of countries with large stockpiles of land mines, such as Russia and China, did not even bother to attend the Oslo meeting.

Despite these rejections, the campaign to ban land mines received worldwide support. Diana, Princess of Wales, who had been the world's most visible advocate of a land mine ban, was scheduled to address the Oslo conference before she was killed in an automobile accident on August 31. U.S. senator Patrick Leahy and Canadian foreign minister Lloyd Axworthy also backed the treaty. In December 1997, 131 nations met in Ot-

tawa, and 123 signed or indicated that they would sign the Oslo document. On December 10, six days after the closing of the latest Ottawa conference, Williams and ICBL were awarded the Nobel Peace Prize. Accepting the Nobel Prize on behalf of ICBL was Cambodian Tun Channareth, who had lost his legs to a land mine in 1982. After Williams received the prize, Boris Yeltsin announced that Russia would support the treaty, leaving the United States and China as the major signatory holdouts. See also PROTOCOL ON EXPLOSIVE REMNANTS OF WAR.

Source

International Campaign to Ban Landmines. "Convention on the Prohibition of the Use, Stockpiling, Production and Transfer of Anti-Personnel Mines and on Their Destruction." Available online. URL: http://www.icbl.org/treaty/text/english. Accessed on January 3, 2005.

KYOTO PROTOCOL ON CLIMATE CHANGE

TREATY AT A GLANCE

Completed
December 11, 1997; entered into force February 16, 2005

Signatories
Ratified or acceded to by 151 United Nations member states
as of summer 2005; United States has signed but not ratified it

Overview
The United Nations framework Convention on Climate Change is a nonbonding agreement among the parties to limit greenhouse gas emissions to combat global warming. An amendment to the framework convention, the Kyoto Protocol is a legally binding agreement under which industrialized countries agree to reduce their collective emissions of some greenhouse gases by 5.2 percent compared to the year 1990. (Compared to the emissions levels that would be expected by 2010 without the protocol, this target actually represents a 29 percent reduction.)

Historical Background

For general historical background of global warming and other environmental issues see the entry on CONVENTION ON CLIMATE CHANGE.

Because it quantifies emissions reduction targets and financial commitments, the Kyoto Protocol has been highly controversial. Advocates, including the European Union and many environmentalist organizations, claim that the protocol is critical in reducing greenhouse gas. Some critics, including U.S. president George W. Bush, argue that the protocol will prevent or damage economic growth, while others argue that the protocol does not go far enough to curb greenhouse emissions. These latter individuals, including a minority of environmental scientists, believe that the Kyoto standards will be ineffective in altering climate change. Some scientists have attacked the protocol's provisions regarding carbon credits, whereby states would be allowed to exceed prescribed emissions in return for planting "Kyoto forests," or tree farms, which are calculated to reduce total carbon dioxide (CO_2) output. Critics point to recent evidence suggesting that this arrangement may actually increase CO_2 emissions for the first 10 years because of the growth pattern of young forests and the effect it has on soil-trapped CO_2. Moreover, a number of industrial countries have seized on carbon credits as a key part of their strategies for reducing their net greenhouse gas outputs, a fact that casts serious doubt on the effectiveness of the protocol.

Supporters of the protocol claim that it is necessary to compare global warming with and without the agreement. While even some advocates concede that the effect of the protocol on global warming will be very small—a reduction of 0.15 degrees Celsius (0.27 degrees Fahrenheit) by 2100, out of a projected total change of 1.4 to 5.8 degrees Celsius (2.52 to 10.44 degrees Fahrenheit)—they point out that it is nevertheless a critical first step, which has more political than immediately practical importance. The protocol, they argue, creates conditions that may, in the future, bring emissions reductions of as much as 70 percent. Critics counter that speculative future gains do not justify the expense of small immediate gains. They assert that the Kyoto Protocol is more expensive than the global warming it avoids.

Finally, a number of critics theorize that if the world's industrial nations reduce their greenhouse emissions, it is highly likely that there will be no net change in emissions worldwide. If industrialized countries reduce their demand for fossil fuels, these commodities will fall in price, thereby making them attractive to poorer, less developed nations, which will increase their consumption of such fuels.

Despite serious reservations, on September 30, 2004, the lower house of the Russian parliament enacted legislation to enable the government's delayed ratification of the Kyoto Protocol. The Russian senate assented on October 26, Russian president Vladimir Putin signed the legislation, and it was ratified on November 18. Russia's was the 55th ratification—all that was necessary to put the protocol into force.

The United States is a signatory to the protocol but, as of summer 2005, had neither ratified nor withdrawn from the protocol; therefore, the protocol was nonbinding on the United States. On June 25, 1997, even before the Kyoto Protocol was negotiated, the U.S. Senate had passed by a 95-0 vote the Byrd-Hagel Resolution (S. Res. 98), which conveyed the sense of the Senate that the United States should not become a signatory to any protocol that lacked binding targets and timetables for developing as well as industrialized nations. Pointedly turning his back on the resolution, Vice President Al Gore signed the Kyoto Protocol on November 12, 1998, but the Clinton administration did not submit it to the Senate for ratification, assuming that it would simply be rejected. President Clinton's successor, George W. Bush, repeatedly indicated that he would not submit the treaty to the Senate because of various regulatory details. Meanwhile, 39 of the countries listed in Annex B have signed the protocol.

Terms

The states parties to the protocol, all signatories of the United Nations Convention on Climate Change, agree to "implement and/or further elaborate policies and measures [to limit greenhouse gas emissions] in accordance with . . . national circumstances." Their agreement is legally binding because the protocol, in contrast to the convention itself, is a legally binding instrument. The industrialized countries that are party to the protocol agree to reduce their collective emissions of some greenhouse gases by 5.2 percent compared to the year 1990. (Compared to the emissions levels that would be expected by 2010 without the protocol, this target actually represents a 29 percent reduction.) The goal of the protocol is to lower overall emissions of six greenhouse gases—CO_2, methane, nitrous oxide, sulphur hexafluoride, hydrofluorocarbons, and perfluorocarbons—calculated as an average over the five-year period of 2008 to 2012. Individual national targets range from 8 percent reductions for the European Union and some others to 7 percent for the United States, 6 percent for Japan, and 0 percent for Russia, whereas Australia is permitted an increase of 8 percent and Iceland 10 percent.

The protocol also reaffirms the principle that developed countries have to pay and supply technology to less-developed nations for climate-related studies and projects. While each of the industrialized states parties

agrees to limit emissions to the levels described in the protocol, many countries have limits that are set above their current production. These extra amounts are "emission credits," which can be purchased by other countries. Russia, for example, enters the protocol with many emissions credits, which it can sell off at great profit to countries that exceed their emissions targets. Credits are also earned by countries that institute "clean energy" programs and that plant forests to serve as "carbon sinks."

Other specific policies and measures set out in the Kyoto Protocol include the following:

- Enhancement of energy efficiency in relevant sectors of the national economy
- Protection and enhancement of sinks and reservoirs of greenhouse gases not controlled by the MONTREAL PROTOCOL ON THE OZONE LAYER (taking into account its commitments under relevant international environmental agreements)
- Promotion of sustainable forest management practices, afforestation, and reforestation
- Promotion of sustainable forms of agriculture in light of climate change considerations
- Research on and promotion, development, and increased use of new and renewable forms of energy, of carbon dioxide sequestration technologies, and of advanced and innovative environmentally sound technologies
- Progressive reduction or phasing out of market imperfections, fiscal incentives, and tax and duty exemptions and subsidies in all greenhouse gas–emitting sectors that run counter to the objective of the convention and application of market instruments
- Encouragement of appropriate reforms in relevant sectors aimed at promoting policies and measures that limit or reduce emissions of greenhouse gases not controlled by the Montreal Protocol
- Measures to limit and/or reduce emissions of greenhouse gases not controlled by the Montreal Protocol in the transport sector
- Limitation and/or reduction of methane emissions through recovery and use in waste management, as well as in the production, transport, and distribution of energy

There are two annexes to the Kyoto Protocol. Annex A lists the greenhouse gases and their chief sources, and Annex B lists the greenhouse gas reduction commitment for each state party.

Kyoto Protocol to the United Nations Framework Convention on Climate Change

. . .

ARTICLE 2

1. Each Party included in Annex I, in achieving its quantified emission limitation and reduction commitments under Article 3, in order to promote sustainable development, shall:

(a) Implement and/or further elaborate policies and measures in accordance with its national circumstances, such as:

(i) Enhancement of energy efficiency in relevant sectors of the national economy;

(ii) Protection and enhancement of sinks and reservoirs of greenhouse gases not controlled by the Montreal Protocol, taking into account its commitments under relevant international environmental agreements; promotion of sustainable forest management practices, afforestation and reforestation;

(iii) Promotion of sustainable forms of agriculture in light of climate change considerations;

(iv) Research on, and promotion, development and increased use of, new and renewable forms of energy, of carbon dioxide sequestration technologies and of advanced and innovative environmentally sound technologies;

(v) Progressive reduction or phasing out of market imperfections, fiscal incentives, tax and duty exemptions and subsidies in all greenhouse gas emitting sectors that run counter to the objective of the Convention and application of market instruments;

(vi) Encouragement of appropriate reforms in relevant sectors aimed at promoting policies and measures which limit or reduce emissions of greenhouse gases not controlled by the Montreal Protocol;

(vii) Measures to limit and/or reduce emissions of greenhouse gases not controlled by the Montreal Protocol in the transport sector;

(viii) Limitation and/or reduction of methane emissions through recovery and use in waste management, as well as in the production, transport and distribution of energy;

(b) Cooperate with other such Parties to enhance the individual and combined effectiveness of their policies and measures adopted under this Article, pursuant to Article 4, paragraph 2 (e) (i), of the Convention. To this end, these Parties shall take steps to share their experience and exchange information on such policies and measures, including developing ways of improving their comparability, transparency and effectiveness. The Conference of the Parties serving as the meeting of the Parties to this Protocol shall, at its first session or as soon as practicable thereafter, consider ways to facilitate such cooperation, taking into account all relevant information.

2. The Parties included in Annex I shall pursue limitation or reduction of emissions of greenhouse gases not controlled by the Montreal Protocol from aviation and marine bunker fuels, working through the International Civil Aviation Organization and the International Maritime Organization, respectively.

3. The Parties included in Annex I shall strive to implement policies and measures under this Article in such a way as to minimize adverse effects, including the adverse effects of climate change, effects on international trade, and social, environmental and economic impacts on other Parties, especially developing country Parties and in particular those identified in Article 4, paragraphs 8 and 9, of the Convention, taking into account Article 3 of the Convention. The Conference of the Parties serving as the meeting of the Parties to this Protocol may take further action, as appropriate, to promote the implementation of the provisions of this paragraph.

4. The Conference of the Parties serving as the meeting of the Parties to this Protocol, if it decides that it would be beneficial to coordinate any of the policies and measures in paragraph 1 (a) above, taking into account different national circumstances and potential effects, shall consider ways and means to elaborate the coordination of such policies and measures.

ARTICLE 3

1. The Parties included in Annex I shall, individually or jointly, ensure that their aggregate anthropogenic carbon dioxide equivalent emissions of the greenhouse gases listed in Annex A do not exceed their assigned amounts, calculated pursuant to their quantified emission limitation and reduction commitments inscribed in Annex B and in accordance with the provisions of this Article, with a view to reducing their overall emissions of such gases by at least 5 per cent below 1990 levels in the commitment period 2008 to 2012.

2. Each Party included in Annex I shall, by 2005, have made demonstrable progress in achieving its commitments under this Protocol.

3. The net changes in greenhouse gas emissions by sources and removals by sinks resulting from direct human-induced land-use change and forestry activities, limited to afforestation, reforestation and deforestation since 1990, measured as verifiable changes in carbon stocks in each commitment period, shall be used to meet the commitments under this Article of each Party included in Annex I. The greenhouse gas emissions by sources and removals by sinks associated with those activities shall be reported in a transparent and verifiable manner and reviewed in accordance with Articles 7 and 8.

4. Prior to the first session of the Conference of the Parties serving as the meeting of the Parties to this Protocol, each Party included in Annex I shall provide, for consideration by the Subsidiary Body for Scientific and Technological Advice, data to establish its level of carbon stocks in 1990 and to enable an estimate to be made of its changes in carbon stocks in subsequent years. The Conference of the Parties serving as the meeting of the Parties to this Protocol shall, at its first session or as soon as practicable thereafter, decide upon modalities, rules and guidelines as to how, and which, additional human-induced activities related to changes in greenhouse gas emissions by sources and removals by sinks in the agricultural soils and the land-use change and forestry categories shall be added to, or subtracted from, the assigned amounts for Parties included in Annex I, taking into account uncertainties, transparency in reporting, verifiability, the methodological work of the Intergovernmental Panel on Climate Change, the advice provided by the Subsidiary Body for Scientific and Technological Advice in accordance with Article 5 and the decisions of the Conference of the Parties. Such a decision shall apply in the second and subsequent commitment periods. A Party may choose to apply such a decision on these

additional human-induced activities for its first commitment period, provided that these activities have taken place since 1990.

5. The Parties included in Annex I undergoing the process of transition to a market economy whose base year or period was established pursuant to decision 9/CP.2 of the Conference of the Parties at its second session shall use that base year or period for the implementation of their commitments under this Article. Any other Party included in Annex I undergoing the process of transition to a market economy which has not yet submitted its first national communication under Article 12 of the Convention may also notify the Conference of the Parties serving as the meeting of the Parties to this Protocol that it intends to use an historical base year or period other than 1990 for the implementation of its commitments under this Article. The Conference of the Parties serving as the meeting of the Parties to this Protocol shall decide on the acceptance of such notification.

6. Taking into account Article 4, paragraph 6, of the Convention, in the implementation of their commitments under this Protocol other than those under this Article, a certain degree of flexibility shall be allowed by the Conference of the Parties serving as the meeting of the Parties to this Protocol to the Parties included in Annex I undergoing the process of transition to a market economy.

7. In the first quantified emission limitation and reduction commitment period, from 2008 to 2012, the assigned amount for each Party included in Annex I shall be equal to the percentage inscribed for it in Annex B of its aggregate anthropogenic carbon dioxide equivalent emissions of the greenhouse gases listed in Annex A in 1990, or the base year or period determined in accordance with paragraph 5 above, multiplied by five. Those Parties included in Annex I for whom land-use change and forestry constituted a net source of greenhouse gas emissions in 1990 shall include in their 1990 emissions base year or period the aggregate anthropogenic carbon dioxide equivalent emissions by sources minus removals by sinks in 1990 from land-use change for the purposes of calculating their assigned amount.

8. Any Party included in Annex I may use 1995 as its base year for hydrofluorocarbons, perfluorocarbons and sulphur hexafluoride, for the purposes of the calculation referred to in paragraph 7 above.

9. Commitments for subsequent periods for Parties included in Annex I shall be established in amendments to Annex B to this Protocol, which shall be adopted in accordance with the provisions of Article 21, paragraph 7. The Conference of the Parties serving as the meeting of the Parties to this Protocol shall initiate the consideration of such commitments at least seven years before the end of the first commitment period referred to in paragraph 1 above.

10. Any emission reduction units, or any part of an assigned amount, which a Party acquires from another Party in accordance with the provisions of Article 6 or of Article 17 shall be added to the assigned amount for the acquiring Party.

11. Any emission reduction units, or any part of an assigned amount, which a Party transfers to another Party in accordance with the provisions of Article 6 or of Article 17 shall be subtracted from the assigned amount for the transferring Party.

12. Any certified emission reductions which a Party acquires from another Party in accordance with the provisions of Article 12 shall be added to the assigned amount for the acquiring Party.

13. If the emissions of a Party included in Annex I in a commitment period are less than its assigned amount under this Article, this difference shall, on request of that Party, be added to the assigned amount for that Party for subsequent commitment periods.

14. Each Party included in Annex I shall strive to implement the commitments mentioned in paragraph 1 above in such a way as to minimize adverse social, environmental and economic impacts on developing country Parties, particularly those identified in Article 4, paragraphs 8 and 9, of the Convention. In line with relevant decisions of the Conference of the Parties on the implementation of those paragraphs, the Conference of the Parties serving as the meeting of the Parties to this Protocol shall, at its first session, consider what actions are necessary to minimize the adverse effects of climate change and/or the impacts of response measures on Parties referred to in those paragraphs. Among the issues to be considered shall be the establishment of funding, insurance and transfer of technology.

ARTICLE 4

1. Any Parties included in Annex I that have reached an agreement to fulfil their commitments under Article 3 jointly, shall be deemed to have met those commitments provided that their total combined aggregate anthropogenic carbon dioxide equivalent emissions of the greenhouse gases listed in Annex A do not exceed their assigned amounts calculated pursuant to their quantified emission limitation and reduction commitments inscribed in Annex B and in accordance with the provisions of Article 3. The respective emission level allocated to each of the Parties to the agreement shall be set out in that agreement.

2. The Parties to any such agreement shall notify the secretariat of the terms of the agreement on the date of deposit of their instruments of ratification, acceptance or approval of this Protocol, or accession thereto. The secretariat shall in turn inform the Parties and signatories to the Convention of the terms of the agreement.

3. Any such agreement shall remain in operation for the duration of the commitment period specified in Article 3, paragraph 7.

4. If Parties acting jointly do so in the framework of, and together with, a regional economic integration organization, any alteration in the composition of the organization after adoption of this Protocol shall not affect existing commitments under this Protocol. Any alteration in the composition of the organization shall only apply for the purposes of those commitments under Article 3 that are adopted subsequent to that alteration.

5. In the event of failure by the Parties to such an agreement to achieve their total combined level of emission reductions, each Party to that agreement shall be responsible for its own level of emissions set out in the agreement.

6. If Parties acting jointly do so in the framework of, and together with, a regional economic integration organization which is itself a Party to this Protocol, each member State of that regional economic integration organization individually, and together with the regional economic integration organization

acting in accordance with Article 24, shall, in the event of failure to achieve the total combined level of emission reductions, be responsible for its level of emissions as notified in accordance with this Article.

ARTICLE 5

1. Each Party included in Annex I shall have in place, no later than one year prior to the start of the first commitment period, a national system for the estimation of anthropogenic emissions by sources and removals by sinks of all greenhouse gases not controlled by the Montreal Protocol. Guidelines for such national systems, which shall incorporate the methodologies specified in paragraph 2 below, shall be decided upon by the Conference of the Parties serving as the meeting of the Parties to this Protocol at its first session.

2. Methodologies for estimating anthropogenic emissions by sources and removals by sinks of all greenhouse gases not controlled by the Montreal Protocol shall be those accepted by the Intergovernmental Panel on Climate Change and agreed upon by the Conference of the Parties at its third session. Where such methodologies are not used, appropriate adjustments shall be applied according to methodologies agreed upon by the Conference of the Parties serving as the meeting of the Parties to this Protocol at its first session. Based on the work of, *inter alia,* the Intergovernmental Panel on Climate Change and advice provided by the Subsidiary Body for Scientific and Technological Advice, the Conference of the Parties serving as the meeting of the Parties to this Protocol shall regularly review and, as appropriate, revise such methodologies and adjustments, taking fully into account any relevant decisions by the Conference of the Parties. Any revision to methodologies or adjustments shall be used only for the purposes of ascertaining compliance with commitments under Article 3 in respect of any commitment period adopted subsequent to that revision.

3. The global warming potentials used to calculate the carbon dioxide equivalence of anthropogenic emissions by sources and removals by sinks of greenhouse gases listed in Annex A shall be those accepted by the Intergovernmental Panel on Climate Change and agreed upon by the Conference of the Parties at its third session. Based on the work of, *inter alia,* the Intergovernmental Panel on Climate Change and advice provided by the Subsidiary Body for Scientific and Technological Advice, the Conference of the Parties serving as the meeting of the Parties to this Protocol shall regularly review and, as appropriate, revise the global warming potential of each such greenhouse gas, taking fully into account any relevant decisions by the Conference of the Parties. Any revision to a global warming potential shall apply only to commitments under Article 3 in respect of any commitment period adopted subsequent to that revision.

ARTICLE 6

1. For the purpose of meeting its commitments under Article 3, any Party included in Annex I may transfer to, or acquire from, any other such Party emission reduction units resulting from projects aimed at reducing anthropogenic emissions by sources or enhancing anthropogenic removals by sinks of greenhouse gases in any sector of the economy, provided that:

(a) Any such project has the approval of the Parties involved;

(b) Any such project provides a reduction in emissions by sources, or an enhancement of removals by sinks, that is additional to any that would otherwise occur;

(c) It does not acquire any emission reduction units if it is not in compliance with its obligations under Articles 5 and 7; and

(d) The acquisition of emission reduction units shall be supplemental to domestic actions for the purposes of meeting commitments under Article 3.

2. The Conference of the Parties serving as the meeting of the Parties to this Protocol may, at its first session or as soon as practicable thereafter, further elaborate guidelines for the implementation of this Article, including for verification and reporting.

3. A Party included in Annex I may authorize legal entities to participate, under its responsibility, in actions leading to the generation, transfer or acquisition under this Article of emission reduction units.

4. If a question of implementation by a Party included in Annex I of the requirements referred to in this Article is identified in accordance with the relevant provisions of Article 8, transfers and acquisitions of emission reduction units may continue to be made after the question has been identified, provided that any such units may not be used by a Party to meet its commitments under Article 3 until any issue of compliance is resolved.

ARTICLE 7

1. Each Party included in Annex I shall incorporate in its annual inventory of anthropogenic emissions by sources and removals by sinks of greenhouse gases not controlled by the Montreal Protocol, submitted in accordance with the relevant decisions of the Conference of the Parties, the necessary supplementary information for the purposes of ensuring compliance with Article 3, to be determined in accordance with paragraph 4 below.

2. Each Party included in Annex I shall incorporate in its national communication, submitted under Article 12 of the Convention, the supplementary information necessary to demonstrate compliance with its commitments under this Protocol, to be determined in accordance with paragraph 4 below.

3. Each Party included in Annex I shall submit the information required under paragraph 1 above annually, beginning with the first inventory due under the Convention for the first year of the commitment period after this Protocol has entered into force for that Party. Each such Party shall submit the information required under paragraph 2 above as part of the first national communication due under the Convention after this Protocol has entered into force for it and after the adoption of guidelines as provided for in paragraph 4 below. The frequency of subsequent submission of information required under this Article shall be determined by the Conference of the Parties serving as the meeting of the Parties to this Protocol, taking into account any timetable for the submission of national communications decided upon by the Conference of the Parties.

4. The Conference of the Parties serving as the meeting of the Parties to this Protocol shall adopt at its first session, and review periodically thereafter, guidelines for the preparation of the information required under this Article, taking into account guidelines for the preparation of national communications by Parties included in Annex I adopted by the Conference of the

Parties. The Conference of the Parties serving as the meeting of the Parties to this Protocol shall also, prior to the first commitment period, decide upon modalities for the accounting of assigned amounts. . . .

ARTICLE 10

All Parties, taking into account their common but differentiated responsibilities and their specific national and regional development priorities, objectives and circumstances, without introducing any new commitments for Parties not included in Annex I, but reaffirming existing commitments under Article 4, paragraph 1, of the Convention, and continuing to advance the implementation of these commitments in order to achieve sustainable development, taking into account Article 4, paragraphs 3, 5 and 7, of the Convention, shall:

(a) Formulate, where relevant and to the extent possible, cost-effective national and, where appropriate, regional programmes to improve the quality of local emission factors, activity data and/or models which reflect the socio-economic conditions of each Party for the preparation and periodic updating of national inventories of anthropogenic emissions by sources and removals by sinks of all greenhouse gases not controlled by the Montreal Protocol, using comparable methodologies to be agreed upon by the Conference of the Parties, and consistent with the guidelines for the preparation of national communications adopted by the Conference of the Parties;

(b) Formulate, implement, publish and regularly update national and, where appropriate, regional programmes containing measures to mitigate climate change and measures to facilitate adequate adaptation to climate change:

(i) Such programmes would, *inter alia,* concern the energy, transport and industry sectors as well as agriculture, forestry and waste management. Furthermore, adaptation technologies and methods for improving spatial planning would improve adaptation to climate change; and

(ii) Parties included in Annex I shall submit information on action under this Protocol, including national programmes, in accordance with Article 7; and other Parties shall seek to include in their national communications, as appropriate, information on programmes which contain measures that the Party believes contribute to addressing climate change and its adverse impacts, including the abatement of increases in greenhouse gas emissions, and enhancement of and removals by sinks, capacity building and adaptation measures;

(c) Cooperate in the promotion of effective modalities for the development, application and diffusion of, and take all practicable steps to promote, facilitate and finance, as appropriate, the transfer of, or access to, environmentally sound technologies, know-how, practices and processes pertinent to climate change, in particular to developing countries, including the formulation of policies and programmes for the effective transfer of environmentally sound technologies that are publicly owned or in the public domain and the creation of an enabling environment for the private sector, to promote and enhance the transfer of, and access to, environmentally sound technologies;

(d) Cooperate in scientific and technical research and promote the maintenance and the development of systematic observation systems and development of data archives to reduce uncertainties related to the climate system, the adverse impacts of climate change and the economic and social consequences of various response strategies, and promote the development and strengthening of endogenous capacities and capabilities to participate in international and intergovernmental efforts, programmes and networks on research and systematic observation, taking into account Article 5 of the Convention;

(e) Cooperate in and promote at the international level, and, where appropriate, using existing bodies, the development and implementation of education and training programmes, including the strengthening of national capacity building, in particular human and institutional capacities and the exchange or secondment of personnel to train experts in this field, in particular for developing countries, and facilitate at the national level public awareness of, and public access to information on, climate change. Suitable modalities should be developed to implement these activities through the relevant bodies of the Convention, taking into account Article 6 of the Convention;

(f) Include in their national communications information on programmes and activities undertaken pursuant to this Article in accordance with relevant decisions of the Conference of the Parties; and

(g) Give full consideration, in implementing the commitments under this Article, to Article 4, paragraph 8, of the Convention.

ARTICLE 11

. . .

2. In the context of the implementation of Article 4, paragraph 1, of the Convention, in accordance with the provisions of Article 4, paragraph 3, and Article 11 of the Convention, and through the entity or entities entrusted with the operation of the financial mechanism of the Convention, the developed country Parties and other developed Parties included in Annex II to the Convention shall:

(a) Provide new and additional financial resources to meet the agreed full costs incurred by developing country Parties in advancing the implementation of existing commitments under Article 4, paragraph 1 (a), of the Convention that are covered in Article 10, subparagraph (a); and

(b) Also provide such financial resources, including for the transfer of technology, needed by the developing country Parties to meet the agreed full incremental costs of advancing the implementation of existing commitments under Article 4, paragraph 1, of the Convention that are covered by Article 10 and that are agreed between a developing country Party and the international entity or entities referred to in Article 11 of the Convention, in accordance with that Article.

The implementation of these existing commitments shall take into account the need for adequacy and predictability in the flow of funds and the importance of appropriate burden sharing among developed country Parties. The guidance to the entity or entities entrusted with the operation of the financial mechanism of the Convention in relevant decisions of the Conference of the Parties, including those agreed before the adoption of this Protocol, shall apply *mutatis mutandis* to the provisions of this paragraph.

3. The developed country Parties and other developed Parties in Annex II to the Convention may also provide, and developing country Parties avail themselves of, financial resources for the implementation of Article 10, through bilateral, regional and other multilateral channels.

ARTICLE 12

1. A clean development mechanism is hereby defined.

2. The purpose of the clean development mechanism shall be to assist Parties not included in Annex I in achieving sustainable development and in contributing to the ultimate objective of the Convention, and to assist Parties included in Annex I in achieving compliance with their quantified emission limitation and reduction commitments under Article 3.

3. Under the clean development mechanism:

(a) Parties not included in Annex I will benefit from project activities resulting in certified emission reductions; and

(b) Parties included in Annex I may use the certified emission reductions accruing from such project activities to contribute to compliance with part of their quantified emission limitation and reduction commitments under Article 3, as determined by the Conference of the Parties serving as the meeting of the Parties to this Protocol.

4. The clean development mechanism shall be subject to the authority and guidance of the Conference of the Parties serving as the meeting of the Parties to this Protocol and be supervised by an executive board of the clean development mechanism.

5. Emission reductions resulting from each project activity shall be certified by operational entities to be designated by the Conference of the Parties serving as the meeting of the Parties to this Protocol, on the basis of:

(a) Voluntary participation approved by each Party involved;

(b) Real, measurable, and long-term benefits related to the mitigation of climate change; and

(c) Reductions in emissions that are additional to any that would occur in the absence of the certified project activity.

6. The clean development mechanism shall assist in arranging funding of certified project activities as necessary.

7. The Conference of the Parties serving as the meeting of the Parties to this Protocol shall, at its first session, elaborate modalities and procedures with the objective of ensuring transparency, efficiency and accountability through independent auditing and verification of project activities.

8. The Conference of the Parties serving as the meeting of the Parties to this Protocol shall ensure that a share of the proceeds from certified project activities is used to cover administrative expenses as well as to assist developing country Parties that are particularly vulnerable to the adverse effects of climate change to meet the costs of adaptation.

9. Participation under the clean development mechanism, including in activities mentioned in paragraph 3 (a) above and in the acquisition of certified emission reductions, may involve private and/or public entities, and is to be subject to whatever guidance may be provided by the executive board of the clean development mechanism.

10. Certified emission reductions obtained during the period from the year 2000 up to the beginning of the first commitment period can be used to assist in achieving compliance in the first commitment period. . . .

Annex A

Greenhouse Gases

Carbon dioxide (CO_2)
Methane (CH_4)
Nitrous oxide (N_2O)
Hydrofluorocarbons (HFCs)
Perfluorocarbons (PFCs)
Sulphur hexafluoride (SF_6)

Sectors/Source Categories

Energy
    Fuel combustion
    Energy industries
        Manufacturing industries and construction
        Transport
        Other sectors
        Other
    Fugitive emissions from fuels
        Solid fuels
        Oil and natural gas
        Other

Industrial processes
    Mineral products
    Chemical industry
    Metal production
    Other production
    Production of halocarbons and sulphur hexafluoride
    Consumption of halocarbons and sulphur hexafluoride
    Other

Solvent and other product use
    Agriculture
        Enteric fermentation
        Manure management
        Rice cultivation
        Agricultural soils
        Prescribed burning of savannas
        Field burning of agricultural residues
        Other
    Waste
        Solid waste disposal on land
        Wastewater handling
        Waste incineration
        Other

Annex B	
Party	Quantified Emission Limitation or Reduction Commitment (percentage of base year or period)
Australia	108
Austria	92
Belgium	92
Bulgaria**	92
Canada	94
Croatia**	95
Czech Republic**	92
Denmark	92
Estonia**	92
European Community	92
Finland	92
France	92
Germany	92
Greece	92
Hungary**	94
Iceland	110
Ireland	92
Italy	92
Japan	94
Latvia**	92
Liechtenstein	92
Lithuania**	92
Luxembourg	92
Monaco	92
Netherlands	92
New Zealand	100
Norway	101
Poland**	94
Portugal	92
Romania**	92
Russian Federation**	100
Slovakia**	92
Slovenia**	92
Spain	92
Sweden	92
Switzerland	92
Ukraine**	100
United Kingdom of Great Britain and Northern Ireland	92
United States of America	93

** Denotes countries that are undergoing the process of transition to a market economy.

Consequences

After Russian president Putin authorized ratification in late 2004, the Kyoto Protocol was cleared to enter into force. Some 10 years will have to pass before a meaningful initial assessment can be made of the substantive impact of the protocol on global warming.

Source

United Nations, "Kyoto Protocol to the United Nations Framework Convention on Climate Change," Secretariat of the United Nations Framework Convention on Climate Change. Available online. URL: http://unfccc.int/resource/docs/convkp/kpeng.pdf. Accessed January 3, 2005.

OPTIONAL PROTOCOL TO THE CONVENTION ON THE RIGHTS OF THE CHILD ON THE SALE OF CHILDREN, CHILD PROSTITUTION AND CHILD PORNOGRAPHY

TREATY AT A GLANCE

Completed
May 25, 2000; entered into force January 18, 2002

Signatories
As of summer 2005, 111 member states of the United Nations,
of which 97 have ratified it

Overview
With the optional Protocol to the Convention on the Rights of the Child on the Involvement of Children in Armed Conflict, this protocol, also optional, was adopted by United Nations resolution and subjoined to the landmark Convention on the Rights of the Child as the first instrument of international law to define and combat the international sale of children, child prostitution, and child pornography.

Historical Background

The precise number of children in the world who are victimized in the multibillion-dollar commercial sex trade is unknown, but it is estimated that about 1 million children (persons under age 18) are currently trafficked for coerced sexual exploitation or labor. International authorities also believe that online (Internet) stalkers and international pornography rings, as well sex tourism (adult travel to nations in which underage sexual partners are available for sale), are on the rise.

Beginning in the late 1980s and early 1990s, law enforcement personnel worldwide, including Interpol, recognized that the sexual abuse of children by adults had become a problem of global scope. Sexual exploitation of children is certainly not a new phenomenon, but modern methods of travel and communication have allowed sexual predators to locate and reach vulnerable children worldwide. The explosive growth of the Internet has spawned networks on which child pornography and other information are exchanged in vast quantities, over a wide range, and in very short periods of time. The United Nations CONVENTION ON THE RIGHTS OF THE CHILD, introduced in 1989, mandates the protection of children from all forms of abuse, including sexual abuse. This optional protocol amplifies this mandate, focusing specifically on international sexual exploitation and predation.

In addition to the United Nations Convention on the Rights of the Child and the present protocol, the global community has adopted two important measures to protect children from sexual exploitation. International Labor Organization Convention 182, adopted in 1999, binds states parties to take immediate and effective measures to prohibit and eliminate the worst forms of child labor, specifically including child prostitution and pornography. The PROTOCOL TO PREVENT, SUPPRESS AND PUNISH TRAFFICKING IN PERSONS, ESPECIALLY WOMEN AND CHILDREN, which supplements the UN CONVENTION AGAINST TRANSNATIONAL ORGANIZED CRIME, was adopted by the General Assembly in November 2000.

Terms

The protocol protects children up to age 18 by treating the actions of exploiters as criminal acts that merit serious criminal punishment. The protocol emphasizes the criminalization of the most serious violations of children's rights, including the sale of children, illegal adoption, and child prostitution and pornography. The protocol also stresses the necessity and great value of

936 ENCYCLOPEDIA OF HISTORICAL TREATIES AND ALLIANCES

international cooperation to combat these transnational activities. It further calls for programs of public awareness and informational and educational campaigns in the area of the sexual exploitation of children.

In addition to requiring states parties to criminalize the sexual exploitation and abuse of children under the age of 18 and to cooperate with other states parties in combating such exploitation and abuse, the protocol requires states parties to provide victims with counseling and rehabilitation. The protocol includes provisions that address such diverse issues as jurisdiction and extradition, mutual legal assistance, and asset confiscation. Finally, the protocol requires states parties to report at regular intervals on the status of sexual exploitation of children with the state and the ongoing efforts to combat it.

※◎

Optional Protocol to the Convention on the Rights of the Child on the Sale of Children, Child Prostitution and Child Pornography

The States Parties to the present Protocol,

Considering that, in order further to achieve the purposes of the Convention on the Rights of the Child and the implementation of its provisions, especially articles 1, 11, 21, 32, 33, 34, 35 and 36, it would be appropriate to extend the measures that States Parties should undertake in order to guarantee the protection of the child from the sale of children, child prostitution and child pornography,

Considering also that the Convention on the Rights of the Child recognizes the right of the child to be protected from economic exploitation and from performing any work that is likely to be hazardous or to interfere with the child's education, or to be harmful to the child's health or physical, mental, spiritual, moral or social development,

Gravely concerned at the significant and increasing international traffic of children for the purpose of the sale of children, child prostitution and child pornography,

Deeply concerned at the widespread and continuing practice of sex tourism, to which children are especially vulnerable, as it directly promotes the sale of children, child prostitution and child pornography,

Recognizing that a number of particularly vulnerable groups, including girl children, are at greater risk of sexual exploitation, and that girl children are disproportionately represented among the sexually exploited,

Concerned about the growing availability of child pornography on the Internet and other evolving technologies, and recalling the International Conference on Combating Child Pornography on the Internet (Vienna, 1999) and, in particular, its conclusion calling for the worldwide criminalization of the production, distribution, exportation, transmission, importation, intentional possession and advertising of child pornography, and stressing the importance of closer cooperation and

partnership between Governments and the Internet industry,

Believing that the elimination of the sale of children, child prostitution and child pornography will be facilitated by adopting a holistic approach, addressing the contributing factors, including underdevelopment, poverty, economic disparities, inequitable socio-economic structure, dysfunctioning families, lack of education, urban-rural migration, gender discrimination, irresponsible adult sexual behaviour, harmful traditional practices, armed conflicts and trafficking of children,

Believing that efforts to raise public awareness are needed to reduce consumer demand for the sale of children, child prostitution and child pornography, and also believing in the importance of strengthening global partnership among all actors and of improving law enforcement at the national level,

Noting the provisions of international legal instruments relevant to the protection of children, including the Hague Convention on the Protection of Children and Cooperation with Respect to Inter-Country Adoption, the Hague Convention on the Civil Aspects of International Child Abduction, the Hague Convention on Jurisdiction, Applicable Law, Recognition, Enforcement and Cooperation in Respect of Parental Responsibility and Measures for the Protection of Children, and International Labour Organization Convention No. 182 on the Prohibition and Immediate Action for the Elimination of the Worst Forms of Child Labour,

Encouraged by the overwhelming support for the Convention on the Rights of the Child, demonstrating the widespread commitment that exists for the promotion and protection of the rights of the child,

Recognizing the importance of the implementation of the provisions of the Programme of Action for the Prevention of the Sale of Children, Child Prostitution and Child Pornography and the Declaration and Agenda for Action adopted at the World Congress against Commercial Sexual Exploitation of Children, held at Stockholm from 27 to 31 August 1996, and the other relevant decisions and recommendations of pertinent international bodies,

Taking due account of the importance of the traditions and cultural values of each people for the protection and harmonious development of the child,

Have agreed as follows:

ARTICLE 1
States Parties shall prohibit the sale of children, child prostitution and child pornography as provided for by the present Protocol.

ARTICLE 2
For the purpose of the present Protocol:

(a) Sale of children means any act or transaction whereby a child is transferred by any person or group of persons to another for remuneration or any other consideration;

(b) Child prostitution means the use of a child in sexual activities for remuneration or any other form of consideration;

(c) Child pornography means any representation, by whatever means, of a child engaged in real or simulated explicit sexual activities or any representation of the sexual parts of a child for primarily sexual purposes.

ARTICLE 3
1. Each State Party shall ensure that, as a minimum, the following acts and activities are fully covered under its criminal or

penal law, whether these offences are committed domestically or transnationally or on an individual or organized basis:

(a) In the context of sale of children as defined in article 2:

(i) The offering, delivering or accepting, by whatever means, a child for the purpose of:

a. Sexual exploitation of the child;

b. Transfer of organs of the child for profit;

c. Engagement of the child in forced labour;

(ii) Improperly inducing consent, as an intermediary, for the adoption of a child in violation of applicable international legal instruments on adoption;

(b) Offering, obtaining, procuring or providing a child for child prostitution, as defined in article 2;

(c) Producing, distributing, disseminating, importing, exporting, offering, selling or possessing for the above purposes child pornography as defined in article 2.

2. Subject to the provisions of a State Party's national law, the same shall apply to an attempt to commit any of these acts and to complicity or participation in any of these acts.

3. Each State Party shall make these offences punishable by appropriate penalties that take into account their grave nature.

4. Subject to the provisions of its national law, each State Party shall take measures, where appropriate, to establish the liability of legal persons for offences established in paragraph 1 of the present article. Subject to the legal principles of the State Party, this liability of legal persons may be criminal, civil or administrative.

5. States Parties shall take all appropriate legal and administrative measures to ensure that all persons involved in the adoption of a child act in conformity with applicable international legal instruments.

ARTICLE 4

1. Each State Party shall take such measures as may be necessary to establish its jurisdiction over the offences referred to in article 3, paragraph 1, when the offences are committed in its territory or on board a ship or aircraft registered in that State.

2. Each State Party may take such measures as may be necessary to establish its jurisdiction over the offences referred to in article 3, paragraph 1, in the following cases:

(a) When the alleged offender is a national of that State or a person who has his habitual residence in its territory;

(b) When the victim is a national of that State.

3. Each State Party shall also take such measures as may be necessary to establish its jurisdiction over the above-mentioned offences when the alleged offender is present in its territory and it does not extradite him or her to another State Party on the ground that the offence has been committed by one of its nationals.

4. This Protocol does not exclude any criminal jurisdiction exercised in accordance with internal law.

ARTICLE 5

1. The offences referred to in article 3, paragraph 1, shall be deemed to be included as extraditable offences in any extradition treaty existing between States Parties and shall be included as extraditable offences in every extradition treaty subsequently concluded between them, in accordance with the conditions set forth in those treaties.

2. If a State Party that makes extradition conditional on the existence of a treaty receives a request for extradition from another State Party with which it has no extradition treaty, it may consider this Protocol as a legal basis for extradition in respect of such offences. Extradition shall be subject to the conditions provided by the law of the requested State.

3. States Parties that do not make extradition conditional on the existence of a treaty shall recognize such offences as extraditable offences between themselves subject to the conditions provided by the law of the requested State.

4. Such offences shall be treated, for the purpose of extradition between States Parties, as if they had been committed not only in the place in which they occurred but also in the territories of the States required to establish their jurisdiction in accordance with article 4.

5. If an extradition request is made with respect to an offence described in article 3, paragraph 1, and if the requested State Party does not or will not extradite on the basis of the nationality of the offender, that State shall take suitable measures to submit the case to its competent authorities for the purpose of prosecution.

ARTICLE 6

1. States Parties shall afford one another the greatest measure of assistance in connection with investigations or criminal or extradition proceedings brought in respect of the offences set forth in article 3, paragraph 1, including assistance in obtaining evidence at their disposal necessary for the proceedings.

2. States Parties shall carry out their obligations under paragraph 1 of the present article in conformity with any treaties or other arrangements on mutual legal assistance that may exist between them. In the absence of such treaties or arrangements, States Parties shall afford one another assistance in accordance with their domestic law.

ARTICLE 7

States Parties shall, subject to the provisions of their national law:

(a) Take measures to provide for the seizure and confiscation, as appropriate, of:

(i) Goods such as materials, assets and other instrumentalities used to commit or facilitate offences under the present Protocol;

(ii) Proceeds derived from such offences;

(b) Execute requests from another State Party for seizure or confiscation of goods or proceeds referred to in subparagraph (a) (i);

(c) Take measures aimed at closing, on a temporary or definitive basis, premises used to commit such offences.

ARTICLE 8

1. States Parties shall adopt appropriate measures to protect the rights and interests of child victims of the practices prohibited under the present Protocol at all stages of the criminal justice process, in particular by:

(a) Recognizing the vulnerability of child victims and adapting procedures to recognize their special needs, including their special needs as witnesses;

(b) Informing child victims of their rights, their role and the scope, timing and progress of the proceedings and of the disposition of their cases;

(c) Allowing the views, needs and concerns of child victims to be presented and considered in proceedings where their personal interests are affected, in a manner consistent with the procedural rules of national law;

(d) Providing appropriate support services to child victims throughout the legal process;

(e) Protecting, as appropriate, the privacy and identity of child victims and taking measures in accordance with national law to avoid the inappropriate dissemination of information that could lead to the identification of child victims;

(f) Providing, in appropriate cases, for the safety of child victims, as well as that of their families and witnesses on their behalf, from intimidation and retaliation;

(g) Avoiding unnecessary delay in the disposition of cases and the execution of orders or decrees granting compensation to child victims.

2. States Parties shall ensure that uncertainty as to the actual age of the victim shall not prevent the initiation of criminal investigations, including investigations aimed at establishing the age of the victim.

3. States Parties shall ensure that, in the treatment by the criminal justice system of children who are victims of the offences described in the present Protocol, the best interest of the child shall be a primary consideration.

4. States Parties shall take measures to ensure appropriate training, in particular legal and psychological training, for the persons who work with victims of the offences prohibited under the present Protocol.

5. States Parties shall, in appropriate cases, adopt measures in order to protect the safety and integrity of those persons and/or organizations involved in the prevention and/or protection and rehabilitation of victims of such offences.

6. Nothing in the present article shall be construed as prejudicial to or inconsistent with the rights of the accused to a fair and impartial trial.

ARTICLE 9

1. States Parties shall adopt or strengthen, implement and disseminate laws, administrative measures, social policies and programmes to prevent the offences referred to in the present Protocol. Particular attention shall be given to protect children who are especially vulnerable to these practices.

2. States Parties shall promote awareness in the public at large, including children, through information by all appropriate means, education and training, about the preventive measures and harmful effects of the offences referred to in the present Protocol. In fulfilling their obligations under this article, States Parties shall encourage the participation of the community and, in particular, children and child victims, in such information and education and training programmes, including at the international level.

3. States Parties shall take all feasible measures with the aim of ensuring all appropriate assistance to victims of such offences, including their full social reintegration and their full physical and psychological recovery.

4. States Parties shall ensure that all child victims of the offences described in the present Protocol have access to adequate procedures to seek, without discrimination, compensation for damages from those legally responsible.

5. States Parties shall take appropriate measures aimed at effectively prohibiting the production and dissemination of material advertising the offences described in the present Protocol.

ARTICLE 10

1. States Parties shall take all necessary steps to strengthen international cooperation by multilateral, regional and bilateral arrangements for the prevention, detection, investigation, prosecution and punishment of those responsible for acts involving the sale of children, child prostitution, child pornography and child sex tourism. States Parties shall also promote international cooperation and coordination between their authorities, national and international non-governmental organizations and international organizations.

2. States Parties shall promote international cooperation to assist child victims in their physical and psychological recovery, social reintegration and repatriation.

3. States Parties shall promote the strengthening of international cooperation in order to address the root causes, such as poverty and underdevelopment, contributing to the vulnerability of children to the sale of children, child prostitution, child pornography and child sex tourism.

4. States Parties in a position to do so shall provide financial, technical or other assistance through existing multilateral, regional, bilateral or other programmes.

ARTICLE 11

Nothing in the present Protocol shall affect any provisions that are more conducive to the realization of the rights of the child and that may be contained in:

(a) The law of a State Party;

(b) International law in force for that State.

ARTICLE 12

1. Each State Party shall submit, within two years following the entry into force of the Protocol for that State Party, a report to the Committee on the Rights of the Child providing comprehensive information on the measures it has taken to implement the provisions of the Protocol.

2. Following the submission of the comprehensive report, each State Party shall include in the reports they submit to the Committee on the Rights of the Child, in accordance with article 44 of the Convention, any further information with respect to the implementation of the Protocol. Other States Parties to the Protocol shall submit a report every five years.

3. The Committee on the Rights of the Child may request from States Parties further information relevant to the implementation of this Protocol. . . .

Consequences

There is no hard measure of the impact of this optional protocol on the sexual exploitation of children through prostitution and child pornography; however, it is clear that many nations have enacted laws and have instituted law enforcement programs subsequent to and pursuant to the protocol.

Source

Office of the High Commissioner for Human Rights, "Optional Protocol to the Convention on the Rights of the Child on the Sale of Children, Child Prostitution and Child Pornography." Available online. URL: http://www.unhchr.ch/html/menu2/dopchild.htm. Accessed January 4, 2005.

ROME STATUTE OF THE INTERNATIONAL CRIMINAL COURT

TREATY AT A GLANCE

Completed
Adopted July 17, 1998; entered into force July 1, 2002

Signatories
As of summer 2005, 139 member states of the United Nations;
99 have become full parties; United States has signed
but declined to become a party

Overview
This international statute established the International Criminal Court, located at The Hague, Netherlands, with the authority and power to try those accused of genocide, war crimes, and crimes against humanity in cases where national courts are either unable or unwilling to do so. This permanent international court is the first in world history. Although a signatory to the statute, the United States informed the UN secretary-general on May 6, 2002, that it "does not intend to become a party to the treaty . . . [and therefore] has no legal obligations arising from its signature on December 31, 2000."

Historical Background

On December 9, 1948, the United Nations General Assembly passed Resolution 260, "Recognizing that at all periods of history genocide has inflicted great losses on humanity" and, further, "that, in order to liberate mankind from such an odious scourge, international co-operation is required." By this resolution, the General Assembly adopted the GENEVA CONVENTION ON THE PREVENTION AND PUNISHMENT OF THE CRIME OF GENOCIDE, in which genocide was defined as "a crime under international law." Article VI of the convention provides that persons charged with genocide "shall be tried by a competent tribunal of the State in the territory of which the act was committed or by such international penal tribunal as may have jurisdiction." Article VI also authorized the International Law Commission "to study the desirability and possibility of establishing an international judicial organ for the trial of persons charged with genocide." Accordingly, the General Assembly established a committee to prepare proposals relating to the establishment of such a court. The committee prepared a draft statute in 1951 and a revised draft statute in 1953, but both drafts were tabled pending the adoption of a definition of a key term: *aggression.*

After 1953, the United Nations periodically took up the question of the establishment of an international criminal court, but it was not until December 1989 that the General Assembly formally asked the International Law Commission to resume work on an international criminal court with jurisdiction to include drug trafficking. In 1993, when the conflict in the former Yugoslavia erupted, and war crimes, crimes against humanity, and genocide reemerged dramatically into world consciousness, the United Nations Security Council established an ad hoc International Criminal Tribunal for the Former Yugoslavia, to hold individuals accountable for war crimes and other atrocities. Soon after this, the International Law Commission successfully completed its work on the draft statute for an international criminal court, which it submitted to the General Assembly in 1994. The General Assembly formed the Ad Hoc Committee on the Establishment of an International Criminal Court, which met twice in 1995. Based on the report of the Ad Hoc Committee, the General Assembly created the Preparatory Committee on the Establishment of an International Criminal Court, which met from 1996 to 1998 and completed the drafting of the text in April 1998. The United Nations Diplomatic Conference of Plenipotentiaries on the Establishment of an International Criminal Court, meeting in Rome, Italy, from June 15 to July 17, 1998, at last finalized and adopted the convention, bringing to culmination a 50-year process.

The Rome Statute has created significant controversy. The most notable objections to the agreement have come from Israel, China, and the United States. Israel took exception to the clause defining a war crime as "the transfer of parts of the civilian population of an occupying power into occupied territory," because this seemed to imply that any settlement activity in occupied territories is a war crime. Since much of Israeli settlement is in territory claimed by others, primarily Palestinians, Israel anticipated the possibility of the international prosecution of Israeli settlers or even of Israeli government officials. Despite these severe misgivings, however, Israel finally signed the Rome Statute.

More intractable and basic is the continuing objection of the People's Republic of China, which asserts that the Rome Statute interferes with the domestic affairs of sovereign states. Not only has China refused to sign the statute, it has urged other states to refrain from doing so on the grounds of protecting the principle of national sovereignty.

The United States, during the administration of President George W. Bush, has declined to become a party to the statute, which was signed during the administration of Bush's predecessor, President Bill Clinton. In a November 14, 2002, speech to the Federalist Society in Washington, D.C., Undersecretary for Arms Control and International Security John R. Bolton explained the Bush administration's reasons for opposing the statute. He said that the International Criminal Court (ICC), created by the statute, "is an organization whose precepts go against fundamental American notions of sovereignty, checks and balances, and national independence." Of most immediate concern was legal protection for "U.S. military forces and civilian personnel and private citizens . . . currently active in peacekeeping and humanitarian missions in almost 100 countries at any given time." Bolton quoted President Bush: "'The United States cooperates with many other nations to keep the peace, but we will not submit American troops to prosecutors and judges whose jurisdiction we do not accept. . . . Every person who serves under the American flag will answer to his or her own superiors and to military law, not to the rulings of an unaccountable International Criminal Court.'"

Bolton conceded that "In the eyes of its supporters, the ICC is simply an overdue addition to the family of international organizations, an evolutionary step ahead of the Nuremberg tribunal, and the next logical institutional development over the ad hoc war crimes courts for the Former Yugoslavia and Rwanda," but he argued that the "ICC's authority is vague and excessively elastic, and the Court's discretion ranges far beyond normal or acceptable judicial responsibilities, giving it broad and unacceptable powers of interpretation that are essentially political and legislative in nature." Bolton also argued that the "ICC does not, and cannot, fit into a coherent, international structural 'constitutional' design that delineates clearly how laws are made, adjudicated or enforced, subject to popular accountability and structured to protect liberty." The prosecutor has "unchecked judicial power," which is "clearly inconsistent with American standards of constitutionalism." (Bolton's remarks are reproduced on the U.S. State Department Web site, at http://www.state.gov/t/us/rm/15158.htm.)

The United States has also raised a strictly legal objection to the Rome Statute, arguing that it gives the ICC jurisdiction over nationals of non–state parties (that is, nonparticipants in the treaty) for crimes they may commit on the territory of a state that is a party to the treaty. This, the United States argues, effectively makes the treaty binding on non–states parties and is therefore a violation of international law. Those who support the Rome Statute counter that international law already gives states the right to try foreign nationals for crimes committed on their territory, and, if a state has such a basic right of jurisdiction, it must of necessity also have the right to pass its jurisdiction to an international organization acting on its behalf. Others, both in the United States and elsewhere, have countered this position by asserting that *territorial* jurisdiction can never be delegated. This objection notwithstanding, supporters of the statute also assert that the crimes over which the ICC has jurisdiction are already recognized under international law as "crimes of universal jurisdiction," that is, crimes any state may try, even if they are committed by *foreign* nationals on *foreign* territory. Thus, states parties are entitled to authorize the court to exercise this already established universal jurisdiction on their behalf. Again, the United States and others have objected that by no means are all the crimes for which the Rome Statute provides the ICC with jurisdiction clearly or even generally accepted as subject to universal jurisdiction as defined by customary international law.

That the Roman Statute entered into force in 2002 over U.S. objections did not render those objections moot. The very same year, Congress passed the American Servicemen's Protection Act, which prohibited furnishing U.S. military aid to any country (except for NATO allies and a few others) that had ratified the Rome Statute unless that country concluded a bilateral agreement with the United States agreeing not to hand over U.S. nationals to ICC jurisdiction. In accordance with the act, military aid to 35 nations was stopped, pending the conclusion of bilateral agreements. By July 2003, approximately 50 states had signed the required documents. The exact number is not known, since at least seven countries, possibly more, have concluded the agreements secretly.

On perhaps an even more belligerent note, the American Servicemen's Protection Act also prohibited the United States from cooperating with the ICC, and it authorized the president to use military force to free any U.S. military personnel held by the court. (Later, the act was modified to allow cooperation when dealing with enemies of the United States.) In the United Nations, in July 2002, the United States threatened to exercise its Security Council veto to block renewal of the mandates of various United Nations peacekeeping operations unless the Security Council agreed to exempt U.S. nationals permanently from the jurisdiction of the International Criminal Court. Under much pressure, the Security Council compromised by allowing an exemption for one year, subject to annual reconsideration and renewal.

Terms

The convention created, at The Hague, Netherlands, an international criminal court that puts into place what many jurists have called the missing link in the international legal system. Whereas the International Court of Justice (also headquartered at the Hague) handles only cases between states, the International Criminal Court addresses *individual* responsibility in acts of genocide and other egregious violations of human rights.

The purpose of the court is to address crimes that national courts are either unwilling or unable to address. Jurisdiction is limited to genocide, war crimes, and crimes against humanity; eventually, the court's purview will also encompass the crime of aggression. The court's authority is further limited to crimes committed after July 1, 2002, when the statute entered into force. It cannot try persons for crimes committed before this date.

The statute defines *genocide* according to a list of prohibited acts, the most important of which include killing or causing serious harm with intent to destroy, a national, ethnic, racial, or religious group, whether in whole or in part. The statute defines *crimes against humanity* to include (among others) the extermination of civilians, enslavement, torture, rape, forced pregnancy, persecution on political, racial, national, ethnic, cultural, religious or gender grounds, and enforced disappearances; an important proviso is that such acts must be shown to be part of a widespread or systematic attack directed against a civilian population. The statute is very specific on the stipulation that the crimes against humanity be "widespread or systematic," because the framers of the statute wanted to ensure that this class of crimes would have to be of significant magnitude and

scope to fall under the court's jurisdiction. The provision was intended to address the sovereignty concerns of states parties, fearful that their nationals would be arrested and tried at will by an international body. The statute is at pains to exclude from jurisdiction such more or less random acts of violence as rape, murder, or even torture, even when these are carried out, in isolated incidents, by soldiers in uniform.

In the statute, war crimes include grave breaches of the Geneva Conventions and other major violations of accepted international laws and customs. Again, the crimes in question must be shown to have been committed as part of a plan or policy or on a large scale.

The issue of aggression is specified in the statute as a crime within the court's jurisdiction; however, implementation of this area of jurisdiction currently awaits agreement by the states parties on a definition of aggression and the precise conditions under which the court may exercise its jurisdiction. As of spring 2005, agreement on these two broad areas seems distant.

Significantly, the Rome Statute does not include terrorism in the mandate of the court. It was the consensus of the framers that an array of current treaties already prohibit specific acts of terrorism, and it is planned that a comprehensive convention against terrorism will be drafted. The issue has not been foreclosed; however, the door has been left open to the future addition of terrorism to the court's jurisdiction.

Another significant area left out of the Rome Statute is drug trafficking. Due to the magnitude of the problem, the delegates decided that it would be impractical to include it in the mandate of the court. The volume of crime and the concomitant volume of required investigations would overwhelm the court's resources, preventing it from fulfilling its other mandates. As with the terrorism issue, however, the area of drug trafficking has by no means been foreclosed and may, in the future, be reconsidered.

The international court, as established by the convention, exists to try individuals only in times of conflict, whether internal or international, when normal national courts are unwilling or unable to act, either as a result of a lack of political will to prosecute their own citizens or because the national institutions have simply collapsed.

Finally, the convention contemplates not merely a punitive function for the international court, but a purpose to deter future outrages. The fact is that most perpetrators of war crimes and crimes against humanity throughout history have gone unpunished; therefore, it is reasonable to conclude that most perpetrators of atrocity have believed that they would enjoy impunity. The convention seeks to end this attitude and thereby contribute to the deterrence of genocide, war crimes, and crimes against humanity.

Rome Statute of the International Criminal Court

Preamble

Conscious that all peoples are united by common bonds, their cultures pieced together in a shared heritage, and concerned that this delicate mosaic may be shattered at any time,

Mindful that during this century millions of children, women and men have been victims of unimaginable atrocities that deeply shock the conscience of humanity,

Recognizing that such grave crimes threaten the peace, security and well-being of the world,

Affirming that the most serious crimes of concern to the international community as a whole must not go unpunished and that their effective prosecution must be ensured by taking measures at the national level and by enhancing international cooperation,

Determined to put an end to impunity for the perpetrators of these crimes and thus to contribute to the prevention of such crimes,

Recalling that it is the duty of every State to exercise its criminal jurisdiction over those responsible for international crimes,

Reaffirming the Purposes and Principles of the Charter of the United Nations, and in particular that all States shall refrain from the threat or use of force against the territorial integrity or political independence of any State, or in any other manner inconsistent with the Purposes of the United Nations,

Emphasizing in this connection that nothing in this Statute shall be taken as authorizing any State Party to intervene in an armed conflict in the internal affairs of any State,

Determined to these ends and for the sake of present and future generations, to establish an independent permanent International Criminal Court in relationship with the United Nations system, with jurisdiction over the most serious crimes of concern to the international community as a whole,

Emphasizing that the International Criminal Court established under this Statute shall be complementary to national criminal jurisdictions,

Resolved to guarantee lasting respect for the enforcement of international justice,

Have agreed as follows:

PART 1.
Establishment of the Court

ARTICLE 1
THE COURT

An International Criminal Court ("the Court") is hereby established. It shall be a permanent institution and shall have the power to exercise its jurisdiction over persons for the most serious crimes of international concern, as referred to in this Statute, and shall be complementary to national criminal jurisdictions. The jurisdiction and functioning of the Court shall be governed by the provisions of this Statute. . . .

ARTICLE 3
SEAT OF THE COURT

1. The seat of the Court shall be established at The Hague in the Netherlands ("the host State"). . . .

ARTICLE 4
LEGAL STATUS AND POWERS OF THE COURT

1. The Court shall have international legal personality. It shall also have such legal capacity as may be necessary for the exercise of its functions and the fulfilment of its purposes.

2. The Court may exercise its functions and powers, as provided in this Statute, on the territory of any State Party and, by special agreement, on the territory of any other State.

PART 2.
Jurisdiction, Admissibility and Applicable Law

ARTICLE 5
CRIMES WITHIN THE JURISDICTION OF THE COURT

1. The jurisdiction of the Court shall be limited to the most serious crimes of concern to the international community as a whole. The Court has jurisdiction in accordance with this Statute with respect to the following crimes:

(a) The crime of genocide;
(b) Crimes against humanity;
(c) War crimes;
(d) The crime of aggression. . . .

ARTICLE 6
GENOCIDE

For the purpose of this Statute, "genocide" means any of the following acts committed with intent to destroy, in whole or in part, a national, ethnical, racial or religious group, as such:

(a) Killing members of the group;
(b) Causing serious bodily or mental harm to members of the group;
(c) Deliberately inflicting on the group conditions of life calculated to bring about its physical destruction in whole or in part;
(d) Imposing measures intended to prevent births within the group;
(e) Forcibly transferring children of the group to another group.

ARTICLE 7
CRIMES AGAINST HUMANITY

1. For the purpose of this Statute, "crime against humanity" means any of the following acts when committed as part of a widespread or systematic attack directed against any civilian population, with knowledge of the attack:

(a) Murder;
(b) Extermination;
(c) Enslavement;
(d) Deportation or forcible transfer of population;
(e) Imprisonment or other severe deprivation of physical liberty in violation of fundamental rules of international law;
(f) Torture;
(g) Rape, sexual slavery, enforced prostitution, forced pregnancy, enforced sterilization, or any other form of sexual violence of comparable gravity;
(h) Persecution against any identifiable group or collectivity on political, racial, national, ethnic, cultural, religious, gender as defined in paragraph 3, or other grounds that are universally recognized as impermissible under international law, in connection with any act referred to in this paragraph or any crime within the jurisdiction of the Court;

(i) Enforced disappearance of persons;

(j) The crime of apartheid;

(k) Other inhumane acts of a similar character intentionally causing great suffering, or serious injury to body or to mental or physical health.

2. For the purpose of paragraph 1:

(a) "Attack directed against any civilian population" means a course of conduct involving the multiple commission of acts referred to in paragraph 1 against any civilian population, pursuant to or in furtherance of a State or organizational policy to commit such attack;

(b) "Extermination" includes the intentional infliction of conditions of life, *inter alia* the deprivation of access to food and medicine, calculated to bring about the destruction of part of a population;

(c) "Enslavement" means the exercise of any or all of the powers attaching to the right of ownership over a person and includes the exercise of such power in the course of trafficking in persons, in particular women and children;

(d) "Deportation or forcible transfer of population" means forced displacement of the persons concerned by expulsion or other coercive acts from the area in which they are lawfully present, without grounds permitted under international law;

(e) "Torture" means the intentional infliction of severe pain or suffering, whether physical or mental, upon a person in the custody or under the control of the accused; except that torture shall not include pain or suffering arising only from, inherent in or incidental to, lawful sanctions;

(f) "Forced pregnancy" means the unlawful confinement, of a woman forcibly made pregnant, with the intent of affecting the ethnic composition of any population or carrying out other grave violations of international law. This definition shall not in any way be interpreted as affecting national laws relating to pregnancy;

(g) "Persecution" means the intentional and severe deprivation of fundamental rights contrary to international law by reason of the identity of the group or collectivity;

(h) "The crime of apartheid" means inhumane acts of a character similar to those referred to in paragraph 1, committed in the context of an institutionalized regime of systematic oppression and domination by one racial group over any other racial group or groups and committed with the intention of maintaining that regime;

(i) "Enforced disappearance of persons" means the arrest, detention or abduction of persons by, or with the authorization, support or acquiescence of, a State or a political organization, followed by a refusal to acknowledge that deprivation of freedom or to give information on the fate or whereabouts of those persons, with the intention of removing them from the protection of the law for a prolonged period of time.

3. For the purpose of this Statute, it is understood that the term "gender" refers to the two sexes, male and female, within the context of society. The term "gender" does not indicate any meaning different from the above.

ARTICLE 8
WAR CRIMES

1. The Court shall have jurisdiction in respect of war crimes in particular when committed as a part of a plan or policy or as part of a large-scale commission of such crimes.

2. For the purpose of this Statute, "war crimes" means:

(a) Grave breaches of the Geneva Conventions of 12 August 1949, namely, any of the following acts against persons or property protected under the provisions of the relevant Geneva Convention:

(i) Willful killing;

(ii) Torture or inhuman treatment, including biological experiments;

(iii) Willfully causing great suffering, or serious injury to body or health;

(iv) Extensive destruction and appropriation of property, not justified by military necessity and carried out unlawfully and wantonly;

(v) Compelling a prisoner of war or other protected person to serve in the forces of a hostile Power;

(vi) Wilfully depriving a prisoner of war or other protected person of the rights of fair and regular trial;

(vii) Unlawful deportation or transfer or unlawful confinement;

(viii) Taking of hostages.

(b) Other serious violations of the laws and customs applicable in international armed conflict, within the established framework of international law, namely, any of the following acts:

(i) Intentionally directing attacks against the civilian population as such or against individual civilians not taking direct part in hostilities;

(ii) Intentionally directing attacks against civilian objects, that is, objects which are not military objectives;

(iii) Intentionally directing attacks against personnel, installations, material, units or vehicles involved in a humanitarian assistance or peacekeeping mission in accordance with the Charter of the United Nations, as long as they are entitled to the protection given to civilians or civilian objects under the international law of armed conflict;

(iv) Intentionally launching an attack in the knowledge that such attack will cause incidental loss of life or injury to civilians or damage to civilian objects or widespread, long-term and severe damage to the natural environment which would be clearly excessive in relation to the concrete and direct overall military advantage anticipated;

(v) Attacking or bombarding, by whatever means, towns, villages, dwellings or buildings which are undefended and which are not military objectives;

(vi) Killing or wounding a combatant who, having laid down his arms or having no longer means of defence, has surrendered at discretion;

(vii) Making improper use of a flag of truce, of the flag or of the military insignia and uniform of the enemy or of the United Nations, as well as of the distinctive emblems of the Geneva Conventions, resulting in death or serious personal injury;

(viii) The transfer, directly or indirectly, by the Occupying Power of parts of its own civilian population into the territory it occupies, or the deportation or transfer of all or parts of the population of the occupied territory within or outside this territory;

(ix) Intentionally directing attacks against buildings dedicated to religion, education, art, science or charitable purposes, historic monuments, hospitals and places where the sick and wounded are collected, provided they are not military objectives;

(x) Subjecting persons who are in the power of an adverse party to physical mutilation or to medical or scientific experiments of any kind which are neither justified by the medical, dental or hospital treatment of the person concerned nor carried out in his or her interest, and which cause death to or seriously endanger the health of such person or persons;

(xi) Killing or wounding treacherously individuals belonging to the hostile nation or army;

(xii) Declaring that no quarter will be given;

(xiii) Destroying or seizing the enemy's property unless such destruction or seizure be imperatively demanded by the necessities of war;

(xiv) Declaring abolished, suspended or inadmissible in a court of law the rights and actions of the nationals of the hostile party;

(xv) Compelling the nationals of the hostile party to take part in the operations of war directed against their own country, even if they were in the belligerent's service before the commencement of the war;

(xvi) Pillaging a town or place, even when taken by assault;

(xvii) Employing poison or poisoned weapons;

(xviii) Employing asphyxiating, poisonous or other gases, and all analogous liquids, materials or devices;

(xix) Employing bullets which expand or flatten easily in the human body, such as bullets with a hard envelope which does not entirely cover the core or is pierced with incisions;

(xx) Employing weapons, projectiles and material and methods of warfare which are of a nature to cause superfluous injury or unnecessary suffering or which are inherently indiscriminate in violation of the international law of armed conflict, provided that such weapons, projectiles and material and methods of warfare are the subject of a comprehensive prohibition and are included in an annex to this Statute, by an amendment in accordance with the relevant provisions set forth in articles 121 and 123;

(xxi) Committing outrages upon personal dignity, in particular humiliating and degrading treatment;

(xxii) Committing rape, sexual slavery, enforced prostitution, forced pregnancy, as defined in article 7, paragraph 2 (f), enforced sterilization, or any other form of sexual violence also constituting a grave breach of the Geneva Conventions;

(xxiii) Utilizing the presence of a civilian or other protected person to render certain points, areas or military forces immune from military operations;

(xxiv) Intentionally directing attacks against buildings, material, medical units and transport, and personnel using the distinctive emblems of the Geneva Conventions in conformity with international law;

(xxv) Intentionally using starvation of civilians as a method of warfare by depriving them of objects indispensable to their survival, including wilfully impeding relief supplies as provided for under the Geneva Conventions;

(xxvi) Conscripting or enlisting children under the age of fifteen years into the national armed forces or using them to participate actively in hostilities.

(c) In the case of an armed conflict not of an international character, serious violations of article 3 common to the four Geneva Conventions of 12 August 1949, namely, any of the following acts committed against persons taking no active part in the hostilities, including members of armed forces who have laid down their arms and those placed *hors de combat* by sickness, wounds, detention or any other cause:

(i) Violence to life and person, in particular murder of all kinds, mutilation, cruel treatment and torture;

(ii) Committing outrages upon personal dignity, in particular humiliating and degrading treatment;

(iii) Taking of hostages;

(iv) The passing of sentences and the carrying out of executions without previous judgement pronounced by a regularly constituted court, affording all judicial guarantees which are generally recognized as indispensable.

(d) Paragraph 2 (c) applies to armed conflicts not of an international character and thus does not apply to situations of internal disturbances and tensions, such as riots, isolated and sporadic acts of violence or other acts of a similar nature.

(e) Other serious violations of the laws and customs applicable in armed conflicts not of an international character, within the established framework of international law, namely, any of the following acts:

(i) Intentionally directing attacks against the civilian population as such or against individual civilians not taking direct part in hostilities;

(ii) Intentionally directing attacks against buildings, material, medical units and transport, and personnel using the distinctive emblems of the Geneva Conventions in conformity with international law;

(iii) Intentionally directing attacks against personnel, installations, material, units or vehicles involved in a humanitarian assistance or peacekeeping mission in accordance with the Charter of the United Nations, as long as they are entitled to the protection given to civilians or civilian objects under the law of armed conflict;

(iv) Intentionally directing attacks against buildings dedicated to religion, education, art, science or charitable purposes, historic monuments, hospitals and places where the sick and wounded are collected, provided they are not military objectives;

(v) Pillaging a town or place, even when taken by assault;

(vi) Committing rape, sexual slavery, enforced prostitution, forced pregnancy, as defined in article 7, paragraph 2 (f), enforced sterilization, and any other form of sexual violence also constituting a serious violation of article 3 common to the four Geneva Conventions;

(vii) Conscripting or enlisting children under the age of fifteen years into armed forces or groups or using them to participate actively in hostilities;

(viii) Ordering the displacement of the civilian population for reasons related to the conflict, unless the security of the civilians involved or imperative military reasons so demand;

(ix) Killing or wounding treacherously a combatant adversary;

(x) Declaring that no quarter will be given;

(xi) Subjecting persons who are in the power of another party to the conflict to physical mutilation or to medical or scientific experiments of any kind which are neither justified by the medical, dental or hospital treatment of the person concerned nor carried out in his or her interest, and which cause death to or seriously endanger the health of such person or persons;

(xii) Destroying or seizing the property of an adversary unless such destruction or seizure be imperatively demanded by the necessities of the conflict;

(f) Paragraph 2 (e) applies to armed conflicts not of an international character and thus does not apply to situations of internal disturbances and tensions, such as riots, isolated and sporadic acts of violence or other acts of a similar nature. It applies to armed conflicts that take place in the territory of a State when there is protracted armed conflict between governmental authorities and organized armed groups or between such groups.

3. Nothing in paragraphs 2 (c) and (d) shall affect the responsibility of a Government to maintain or re-establish law and order in the State or to defend the unity and territorial integrity of the State, by all legitimate means. . . .

ARTICLE 11
JURISDICTION *RATIONE TEMPORIS*

1. The Court has jurisdiction only with respect to crimes committed after the entry into force of this Statute.

2. If a State becomes a Party to this Statute after its entry into force, the Court may exercise its jurisdiction only with respect to crimes committed after the entry into force of this Statute for that State, unless that State has made a declaration under article 12, paragraph 3.

ARTICLE 12
PRECONDITIONS TO THE EXERCISE OF JURISDICTION

1. A State which becomes a Party to this Statute thereby accepts the jurisdiction of the Court with respect to the crimes referred to in article 5.

2. In the case of article 13, paragraph (a) or (c), the Court may exercise its jurisdiction if one or more of the following States are Parties to this Statute or have accepted the jurisdiction of the Court in accordance with paragraph 3:

(a) The State on the territory of which the conduct in question occurred or, if the crime was committed on board a vessel or aircraft, the State of registration of that vessel or aircraft;

(b) The State of which the person accused of the crime is a national.

3. If the acceptance of a State which is not a Party to this Statute is required under paragraph 2, that State may, by declaration lodged with the Registrar, accept the exercise of jurisdiction by the Court with respect to the crime in question. The accepting State shall cooperate with the Court without any delay or exception in accordance with Part 9.

ARTICLE 13
EXERCISE OF JURISDICTION

The Court may exercise its jurisdiction with respect to a crime referred to in article 5 in accordance with the provisions of this Statute if:

(a) A situation in which one or more of such crimes appears to have been committed is referred to the Prosecutor by a State Party in accordance with article 14;

(b) A situation in which one or more of such crimes appears to have been committed is referred to the Prosecutor by the Security Council acting under Chapter VII of the Charter of the United Nations; or

(c) The Prosecutor has initiated an investigation in respect of such a crime in accordance with article 15. . . .

ARTICLE 15
PROSECUTOR

1. The Prosecutor may initiate investigations *proprio motu* on the basis of information on crimes within the jurisdiction of the Court.

2. The Prosecutor shall analyse the seriousness of the information received. For this purpose, he or she may seek additional information from States, organs of the United Nations, intergovernmental or non-governmental organizations, or other reliable sources that he or she deems appropriate, and may receive written or oral testimony at the seat of the Court.

3. If the Prosecutor concludes that there is a reasonable basis to proceed with an investigation, he or she shall submit to the Pre-Trial Chamber a request for authorization of an investigation, together with any supporting material collected. Victims may make representations to the Pre-Trial Chamber, in accordance with the Rules of Procedure and Evidence.

4. If the Pre-Trial Chamber, upon examination of the request and the supporting material, considers that there is a reasonable basis to proceed with an investigation, and that the case appears to fall within the jurisdiction of the Court, it shall authorize the commencement of the investigation, without prejudice to subsequent determinations by the Court with regard to the jurisdiction and admissibility of a case.

5. The refusal of the Pre-Trial Chamber to authorize the investigation shall not preclude the presentation of a subsequent request by the Prosecutor based on new facts or evidence regarding the same situation.

6. If, after the preliminary examination referred to in paragraphs 1 and 2, the Prosecutor concludes that the information provided does not constitute a reasonable basis for an investigation, he or she shall inform those who provided the information. This shall not preclude the Prosecutor from considering further information submitted to him or her regarding the same situation in the light of new facts or evidence. . . .

ARTICLE 17
ISSUES OF ADMISSIBILITY

1. Having regard to paragraph 10 of the Preamble and article 1, the Court shall determine that a case is inadmissible where:

(a) The case is being investigated or prosecuted by a State which has jurisdiction over it, unless the State is unwilling or unable genuinely to carry out the investigation or prosecution;

(b) The case has been investigated by a State which has jurisdiction over it and the State has decided not to prosecute the person concerned, unless the decision resulted from the unwillingness or inability of the State genuinely to prosecute;

(c) The person concerned has already been tried for conduct which is the subject of the complaint, and a trial by the Court is not permitted under article 20, paragraph 3;

(d) The case is not of sufficient gravity to justify further action by the Court. . . .

ARTICLE 21
APPLICABLE LAW

1. The Court shall apply:

(a) In the first place, this Statute, Elements of Crimes and its Rules of Procedure and Evidence;

(b) In the second place, where appropriate, applicable treaties and the principles and rules of international law, including the established principles of the international law of armed conflict;

(c) Failing that, general principles of law derived by the Court from national laws of legal systems of the world including, as appropriate, the national laws of States that would normally exercise jurisdiction over the crime, provided that those principles are not inconsistent with this Statute and with international law and internationally recognized norms and standards.

2. The Court may apply principles and rules of law as interpreted in its previous decisions.

3. The application and interpretation of law pursuant to this article must be consistent with internationally recognized human rights, and be without any adverse distinction founded on grounds such as gender, as defined in article 7, paragraph 3, age, race, colour, language, religion or belief, political or other opinion, national, ethnic or social origin, wealth, birth or other status.

PART 3.
General Principles of Criminal Law

ARTICLE 22
NULLUM CRIMEN SINE LEGE

1. A person shall not be criminally responsible under this Statute unless the conduct in question constitutes, at the time it takes place, a crime within the jurisdiction of the Court.

2. The definition of a crime shall be strictly construed and shall not be extended by analogy. In case of ambiguity, the definition shall be interpreted in favour of the person being investigated, prosecuted or convicted.

3. This article shall not affect the characterization of any conduct as criminal under international law independently of this Statute.

ARTICLE 23
NULLA POENA SINE LEGE

A person convicted by the Court may be punished only in accordance with this Statute.

ARTICLE 24
NON-RETROACTIVITY RATIONE PERSONAE

1. No person shall be criminally responsible under this Statute for conduct prior to the entry into force of the Statute.

2. In the event of a change in the law applicable to a given case prior to a final judgement, the law more favourable to the person being investigated, prosecuted or convicted shall apply.

ARTICLE 25
INDIVIDUAL CRIMINAL RESPONSIBILITY

1. The Court shall have jurisdiction over natural persons pursuant to this Statute.

2. A person who commits a crime within the jurisdiction of the Court shall be individually responsible and liable for punishment in accordance with this Statute. . . .

ARTICLE 26
EXCLUSION OF JURISDICTION OVER PERSONS UNDER EIGHTEEN

The Court shall have no jurisdiction over any person who was under the age of 18 at the time of the alleged commission of a crime.

ARTICLE 27
IRRELEVANCE OF OFFICIAL CAPACITY

1. This Statute shall apply equally to all persons without any distinction based on official capacity. In particular, official capacity as a Head of State or Government, a member of a Government or parliament, an elected representative or a government official shall in no case exempt a person from criminal responsibility under this Statute, nor shall it, in and of itself, constitute a ground for reduction of sentence. . . .

ARTICLE 28
RESPONSIBILITY OF COMMANDERS AND OTHER SUPERIORS

In addition to other grounds of criminal responsibility under this Statute for crimes within the jurisdiction of the Court:

1. A military commander or person effectively acting as a military commander shall be criminally responsible for crimes within the jurisdiction of the Court committed by forces under his or her effective command and control, or effective authority and control as the case may be, as a result of his or her failure to exercise control properly over such forces, where:

(a) That military commander or person either knew or, owing to the circumstances at the time, should have known that the forces were committing or about to commit such crimes; and

(b) That military commander or person failed to take all necessary and reasonable measures within his or her power to prevent or repress their commission or to submit the matter to the competent authorities for investigation and prosecution.

2. With respect to superior and subordinate relationships not described in paragraph 1, a superior shall be criminally responsible for crimes within the jurisdiction of the Court committed by subordinates under his or her effective authority and control, as a result of his or her failure to exercise control properly over such subordinates, where:

(a) The superior either knew, or consciously disregarded information which clearly indicated, that the subordinates were committing or about to commit such crimes;

(b) The crimes concerned activities that were within the effective responsibility and control of the superior; and

(c) The superior failed to take all necessary and reasonable measures within his or her power to prevent or repress their commission or to submit the matter to the competent authorities for investigation and prosecution.

ARTICLE 29
NON-APPLICABILITY OF STATUTE OF LIMITATIONS

The crimes within the jurisdiction of the Court shall not be subject to any statute of limitations.

ARTICLE 30
MENTAL ELEMENT

1. Unless otherwise provided, a person shall be criminally responsible and liable for punishment for a crime within the jurisdiction of the Court only if the material elements are committed with intent and knowledge. . . .

ARTICLE 31
GROUNDS FOR EXCLUDING CRIMINAL RESPONSIBILITY

1. In addition to other grounds for excluding criminal responsibility provided for in this Statute, a person shall not be criminally responsible if, at the time of that person's conduct:

(a) The person suffers from a mental disease or defect that destroys that person's capacity to appreciate the unlawfulness or nature of his or her conduct, or capacity to control his or her conduct to conform to the requirements of law;

(b) The person is in a state of intoxication that destroys that person's capacity to appreciate the unlawfulness or nature of his or her conduct, or capacity to control his or her conduct to conform to the requirements of law, unless the person has become voluntarily intoxicated under such circumstances that the person knew, or disregarded the risk, that, as a result of the intoxication, he or she was likely to engage in conduct constituting a crime within the jurisdiction of the Court;

(c) The person acts reasonably to defend himself or herself or another person or, in the case of war crimes, property which is essential for the survival of the person or another person or property which is essential for accomplishing a military mission, against an imminent and unlawful use of force in a manner proportionate to the degree of danger to the person or the other person or property protected. The fact that the person was involved in a defensive operation conducted by forces shall not in itself constitute a ground for excluding criminal responsibility under this subparagraph;

(d) The conduct which is alleged to constitute a crime within the jurisdiction of the Court has been caused by duress resulting from a threat of imminent death or of continuing or imminent serious bodily harm against that person or another person, and the person acts necessarily and reasonably to avoid this threat, provided that the person does not intend to cause a greater harm than the one sought to be avoided. . . .

ARTICLE 33
SUPERIOR ORDERS AND PRESCRIPTION OF LAW

1. The fact that a crime within the jurisdiction of the Court has been committed by a person pursuant to an order of a Government or of a superior, whether military or civilian, shall not relieve that person of criminal responsibility unless:

(a) The person was under a legal obligation to obey orders of the Government or the superior in question;

(b) The person did not know that the order was unlawful; and

(c) The order was not manifestly unlawful.

2. For the purposes of this article, orders to commit genocide or crimes against humanity are manifestly unlawful.

PART 4.
Composition and Administration of the Court

ARTICLE 34
ORGANS OF THE COURT

The Court shall be composed of the following organs:

(a) The Presidency;

(b) An Appeals Division, a Trial Division and a Pre-Trial Division;

(c) The Office of the Prosecutor;

(d) The Registry.

ARTICLE 35
SERVICE OF JUDGES

1. All judges shall be elected as full-time members of the Court and shall be available to serve on that basis from the commencement of their terms of office. . . .

ARTICLE 36
QUALIFICATIONS, NOMINATION AND ELECTION OF JUDGES

1. Subject to the provisions of paragraph 2, there shall be 18 judges of the Court. . . .

3. (a) The judges shall be chosen from among persons of high moral character, impartiality and integrity who possess the qualifications required in their respective States for appointment to the highest judicial offices. . . .

ARTICLE 38
THE PRESIDENCY

1. The President and the First and Second Vice-Presidents shall be elected by an absolute majority of the judges. They shall each serve for a term of three years or until the end of their respective terms of office as judges, whichever expires earlier. They shall be eligible for re-election once.

2. The First Vice-President shall act in place of the President in the event that the President is unavailable or disqualified. The Second Vice-President shall act in place of the President in the event that both the President and the First Vice-President are unavailable or disqualified.

3. The President, together with the First and Second Vice-Presidents, shall constitute the Presidency, which shall be responsible for:

(a) The proper administration of the Court, with the exception of the Office of the Prosecutor; and

(b) The other functions conferred upon it in accordance with this Statute.

4. In discharging its responsibility under paragraph 3 (a), the Presidency shall coordinate with and seek the concurrence of the Prosecutor on all matters of mutual concern.

ARTICLE 39
CHAMBERS

1. As soon as possible after the election of the judges, the Court shall organize itself into the divisions specified in article 34, paragraph (b). The Appeals Division shall be composed of the President and four other judges, the Trial Division of not less than six judges and the Pre-Trial Division of not less than six judges. . . .

ARTICLE 40
INDEPENDENCE OF THE JUDGES

1. The judges shall be independent in the performance of their functions.

2. Judges shall not engage in any activity which is likely to interfere with their judicial functions or to affect confidence in their independence. . . .

ARTICLE 42
THE OFFICE OF THE PROSECUTOR

1. The Office of the Prosecutor shall act independently as a separate organ of the Court. It shall be responsible for receiving referrals and any substantiated information on crimes within the jurisdiction of the Court, for examining them and for conducting investigations and prosecutions before the Court. A member of the Office shall not seek or act on instructions from any external source.

2. The Office shall be headed by the Prosecutor. The Prosecutor shall have full authority over the management and administration of the Office, including the staff, facilities and other resources thereof. The Prosecutor shall be assisted by one or more Deputy Prosecutors, who shall be entitled to carry out any of the acts required of the Prosecutor under this Statute. The Prosecutor and the Deputy Prosecutors shall be of different nationalities. They shall serve on a full-time basis. . . .

ARTICLE 43
THE REGISTRY

1. The Registry shall be responsible for the non-judicial aspects of the administration and servicing of the Court, without prejudice to the functions and powers of the Prosecutor in accordance with article 42. . . .

ARTICLE 44
STAFF

1. The Prosecutor and the Registrar shall appoint such qualified staff as may be required to their respective offices. In the case of the Prosecutor, this shall include the appointment of investigators. . . .

PART 5.
Investigation and Prosecution

ARTICLE 53
INITIATION OF AN INVESTIGATION

1. The Prosecutor shall, having evaluated the information made available to him or her, initiate an investigation unless he or she determines that there is no reasonable basis to proceed under this Statute. In deciding whether to initiate an investigation, the Prosecutor shall consider whether:

(a) The information available to the Prosecutor provides a reasonable basis to believe that a crime within the jurisdiction of the Court has been or is being committed;

(b) The case is or would be admissible under article 17; and

(c) Taking into account the gravity of the crime and the interests of victims, there are nonetheless substantial reasons to believe that an investigation would not serve the interests of justice. . . .

ARTICLE 54
DUTIES AND POWERS OF THE PROSECUTOR WITH RESPECT TO INVESTIGATIONS

1. The Prosecutor shall:

(a) In order to establish the truth, extend the investigation to cover all facts and evidence relevant to an assessment of whether there is criminal responsibility under this Statute, and, in doing so, investigate incriminating and exonerating circumstances equally;

(b) Take appropriate measures to ensure the effective investigation and prosecution of crimes within the jurisdiction of the Court, and in doing so, respect the interests and personal circumstances of victims and witnesses, including age, gender as defined in article 7, paragraph 3, and health, and take into account the nature of the crime, in particular where it involves sexual violence, gender violence or violence against children; and

(c) Fully respect the rights of persons arising under this Statute.

2. The Prosecutor may conduct investigations on the territory of a State:

(a) In accordance with the provisions of Part 9; or

(b) As authorized by the Pre-Trial Chamber under article 57, paragraph 3 (d).

3. The Prosecutor may:

(a) Collect and examine evidence;

(b) Request the presence of and question persons being investigated, victims and witnesses;

(c) Seek the cooperation of any State or intergovernmental organization or arrangement in accordance with its respective competence and/or mandate;

(d) Enter into such arrangements or agreements, not inconsistent with this Statute, as may be necessary to facilitate the cooperation of a State, intergovernmental organization or person;

(e) Agree not to disclose, at any stage of the proceedings, documents or information that the Prosecutor obtains on the condition of confidentiality and solely for the purpose of generating new evidence, unless the provider of the information consents; and

(f) Take necessary measures, or request that necessary measures be taken, to ensure the confidentiality of information, the protection of any person or the preservation of evidence. . . .

ARTICLE 57
FUNCTIONS AND POWERS OF THE PRE-TRIAL CHAMBER

. . .

3. In addition to its other functions under this Statute, the Pre-Trial Chamber may:

(a) At the request of the Prosecutor, issue such orders and warrants as may be required for the purposes of an investigation;

(b) Upon the request of a person who has been arrested or has appeared pursuant to a summons under article 58, issue such orders, including measures such as those described in article 56, or seek such cooperation pursuant to Part 9 as may be necessary to assist the person in the preparation of his or her defence;

(c) Where necessary, provide for the protection and privacy of victims and witnesses, the preservation of evidence, the protection of persons who have been arrested or appeared in response to a summons, and the protection of national security information;

(d) Authorize the Prosecutor to take specific investigative steps within the territory of a State Party without having secured the cooperation of that State under Part 9 if, whenever possible having regard to the views of the State concerned, the Pre-Trial Chamber has determined in that case that the State is clearly unable to execute a request for cooperation due to the unavailability of any authority or any component of its judicial system competent to execute the request for cooperation under Part 9.

(e) Where a warrant of arrest or a summons has been issued under article 58, and having due regard to the strength of the evidence and the rights of the parties concerned, as provided for in this Statute and the Rules of Procedure and Evidence, seek the cooperation of States pursuant to article 93, paragraph 1 (j), to take protective measures for the purpose of forfeiture in particular for the ultimate benefit of victims. . . .

PART 6.
The Trial

. . .

ARTICLE 63
TRIAL IN THE PRESENCE OF THE ACCUSED

1. The accused shall be present during the trial. . . .

ARTICLE 64
FUNCTIONS AND POWERS OF THE TRIAL CHAMBER

1. The functions and powers of the Trial Chamber set out in this article shall be exercised in accordance with this Statute and the Rules of Procedure and Evidence.

2. The Trial Chamber shall ensure that a trial is fair and expeditious and is conducted with full respect for the rights of the accused and due regard for the protection of victims and witnesses.

3. Upon assignment of a case for trial in accordance with this Statute, the Trial Chamber assigned to deal with the case shall:

(a) Confer with the parties and adopt such procedures as are necessary to facilitate the fair and expeditious conduct of the proceedings;

(b) Determine the language or languages to be used at trial; and

(c) Subject to any other relevant provisions of this Statute, provide for disclosure of documents or information not previously disclosed, sufficiently in advance of the commencement of the trial to enable adequate preparation for trial. . . .

8. (a) At the commencement of the trial, the Trial Chamber shall have read to the accused the charges previously confirmed by the Pre-Trial Chamber. The Trial Chamber shall satisfy itself that the accused understands the nature of the charges. It shall afford him or her the opportunity to make an admission of guilt in accordance with article 65 or to plead not guilty. . . .

9. The Trial Chamber shall have, *inter alia,* the power on application of a party or on its own motion to:

(a) Rule on the admissibility or relevance of evidence; and

(b) Take all necessary steps to maintain order in the course of a hearing.

10. The Trial Chamber shall ensure that a complete record of the trial, which accurately reflects the proceedings, is made and that it is maintained and preserved by the Registrar.

ARTICLE 66
PRESUMPTION OF INNOCENCE

1. Everyone shall be presumed innocent until proved guilty before the Court in accordance with the applicable law.

2. The onus is on the Prosecutor to prove the guilt of the accused.

3. In order to convict the accused, the Court must be convinced of the guilt of the accused beyond reasonable doubt.

ARTICLE 67
RIGHTS OF THE ACCUSED

1. In the determination of any charge, the accused shall be entitled to a public hearing, having regard to the provisions of this Statute, to a fair hearing conducted impartially, and to the following minimum guarantees, in full equality:

(a) To be informed promptly and in detail of the nature, cause and content of the charge, in a language which the accused fully understands and speaks;

(b) To have adequate time and facilities for the preparation of the defence and to communicate freely with counsel of the accused's choosing in confidence;

(c) To be tried without undue delay;

(d) Subject to article 63, paragraph 2, to be present at the trial, to conduct the defence in person or through legal assistance of the accused's choosing, to be informed, if the accused does not have legal assistance, of this right and to have legal assistance assigned by the Court in any case where the interests of justice so require, and without payment if the accused lacks sufficient means to pay for it;

(e) To examine, or have examined, the witnesses against him or her and to obtain the attendance and examination of witnesses on his or her behalf under the same conditions as witnesses against him or her. The accused shall also be entitled to raise defences and to present other evidence admissible under this Statute;

(f) To have, free of any cost, the assistance of a competent interpreter and such translations as are necessary to meet the requirements of fairness, if any of the proceedings of or documents presented to the Court are not in a language which the accused fully understands and speaks;

(g) Not to be compelled to testify or to confess guilt and to remain silent, without such silence being a consideration in the determination of guilt or innocence;

(h) To make an unsworn oral or written statement in his or her defence; and

(i) Not to have imposed on him or her any reversal of the burden of proof or any onus of rebuttal. . . .

ARTICLE 68
PROTECTION OF THE VICTIMS AND WITNESSES AND THEIR PARTICIPATION IN THE PROCEEDINGS

1. The Court shall take appropriate measures to protect the safety, physical and psychological well-being, dignity and privacy of victims and witnesses. . . .

ARTICLE 69
EVIDENCE

1. Before testifying, each witness shall, in accordance with the Rules of Procedure and Evidence, give an undertaking as to the truthfulness of the evidence to be given by that witness. . . .

ARTICLE 72
PROTECTION OF
NATIONAL SECURITY INFORMATION

. . .

4. If a State learns that information or documents of the State are being, or are likely to be, disclosed at any stage of the proceedings, and it is of the opinion that disclosure would prejudice its national security interests, that State shall have the right to intervene in order to obtain resolution of the issue in accordance with this article. . . .

ARTICLE 74
REQUIREMENTS FOR THE DECISION

. . .

2. The Trial Chamber's decision shall be based on its evaluation of the evidence and the entire proceedings. The decision shall not exceed the facts and circumstances described in the charges and any amendments to the charges. The Court may base its decision only on evidence submitted and discussed before it at the trial.

3. The judges shall attempt to achieve unanimity in their decision, failing which the decision shall be taken by a majority of the judges.

4. The deliberations of the Trial Chamber shall remain secret.

5. The decision shall be in writing and shall contain a full and reasoned statement of the Trial Chamber's findings on the evidence and conclusions. The Trial Chamber shall issue one decision. When there is no unanimity, the Trial Chamber's decision shall contain the views of the majority and the minority. The decision or a summary thereof shall be delivered in open court.

ARTICLE 75
REPARATIONS TO VICTIMS

1. The Court shall establish principles relating to reparations to, or in respect of, victims, including restitution, compensation and rehabilitation. . . .

ARTICLE 76
SENTENCING

1. In the event of a conviction, the Trial Chamber shall consider the appropriate sentence to be imposed and shall take into account the evidence presented and submissions made during the trial that are relevant to the sentence. . . .

PART 7.
Penalties

ARTICLE 77
APPLICABLE PENALTIES

1. Subject to article 110, the Court may impose one of the following penalties on a person convicted of a crime under article 5 of this Statute:

(a) Imprisonment for a specified number of years, which may not exceed a maximum of 30 years; or

(b) A term of life imprisonment when justified by the extreme gravity of the crime and the individual circumstances of the convicted person.

2. In addition to imprisonment, the Court may order:

(a) A fine under the criteria provided for in the Rules of Procedure and Evidence;

(b) A forfeiture of proceeds, property and assets derived directly or indirectly from that crime, without prejudice to the rights of bona fide third parties. . . .

ARTICLE 79
TRUST FUND

1. A Trust Fund shall be established by decision of the Assembly of States Parties for the benefit of victims of crimes within the jurisdiction of the Court, and of the families of such victims. . . .

PART 8.
Appeal and Revision

ARTICLE 81
APPEAL AGAINST DECISION OF ACQUITTAL OR CONVICTION OR AGAINST SENTENCE

1. A decision under article 74 may be appealed in accordance with the Rules of Procedure and Evidence as follows:

(a) The Prosecutor may make an appeal on any of the following grounds:

(i) Procedural error,

(ii) Error of fact, or

(iii) Error of law;

(b) The convicted person or the Prosecutor on that person's behalf may make an appeal on any of the following grounds:

(i) Procedural error,

(ii) Error of fact,

(iii) Error of law, or

(iv) Any other ground that affects the fairness or reliability of the proceedings or decision.

2. (a) A sentence may be appealed, in accordance with the Rules of Procedure and Evidence, by the Prosecutor or the convicted person on the ground of disproportion between the crime and the sentence;

(b) If on an appeal against sentence the Court considers that there are grounds on which the conviction might be set aside, wholly or in part, it may invite the Prosecutor and the convicted person to submit grounds under article 81, paragraph 1 (a) or (b), and may render a decision on conviction in accordance with article 83;

(c) The same procedure applies when the Court, on an appeal against conviction only, considers that there are grounds to reduce the sentence under paragraph 2 (a). . . .

PART 9.
International Cooperation and Judicial Assistance

ARTICLE 86
GENERAL OBLIGATION TO COOPERATE

States Parties shall, in accordance with the provisions of this Statute, cooperate fully with the Court in its investigation and prosecution of crimes within the jurisdiction of the Court. . . .

PART 10.
Enforcement

ARTICLE 103
ROLE OF STATES IN ENFORCEMENT OF SENTENCES OF IMPRISONMENT

1. (a) A sentence of imprisonment shall be served in a State designated by the Court from a list of States which have indicated to the Court their willingness to accept sentenced persons. . . .

ARTICLE 105
ENFORCEMENT OF THE SENTENCE

1. Subject to conditions which a State may have specified in accordance with article 103, paragraph 1 (b), the sentence of imprisonment shall be binding on the States Parties, which shall in no case modify it. . . .

PART 11.
Assembly of States Parties

ARTICLE 112
ASSEMBLY OF STATES PARTIES

1. An Assembly of States Parties to this Statute is hereby established. Each State Party shall have one representative in the Assembly who may be accompanied by alternates and advisers. Other States which have signed the Statute or the Final Act may be observers in the Assembly.

2. The Assembly shall:

(a) Consider and adopt, as appropriate, recommendations of the Preparatory Commission;

(b) Provide management oversight to the Presidency, the Prosecutor and the Registrar regarding the administration of the Court;

(c) Consider the reports and activities of the Bureau established under paragraph 3 and take appropriate action in regard thereto;

(d) Consider and decide the budget for the Court;

(e) Decide whether to alter, in accordance with article 36, the number of judges;

(f) Consider pursuant to article 87, paragraphs 5 and 7, any question relating to non-cooperation;

(g) Perform any other function consistent with this Statute or the Rules of Procedure and Evidence. . . .

ARTICLE 123
REVIEW OF THE STATUTE

1. Seven years after the entry into force of this Statute the Secretary-General of the United Nations shall convene a Review Conference to consider any amendments to this Statute. Such review may include, but is not limited to, the list of crimes contained in article 5. The Conference shall be open to those participating in the Assembly of States Parties and on the same conditions.

2. At any time thereafter, at the request of a State Party and for the purposes set out in paragraph 1, the Secretary-General of the United Nations shall, upon approval by a majority of States Parties, convene a Review Conference. . . .

ARTICLE 126
ENTRY INTO FORCE

1. This Statute shall enter into force on the first day of the month after the 60th day following the date of the deposit of the 60th instrument of ratification, acceptance, approval or accession with the Secretary-General of the United Nations.

Consequences

The statute entered into force on July 1, 2002, whereupon the International Criminal Court was formally created. During the rest of 2002 and most of 2003, the administration and mechanics of the court were set up. In December 2003, President Yoweri Museveni of Uganda referred the activities of a guerrilla group within his nation, the Lord's Resistance Army, to the prosecutor of the International Criminal Court. In January 2004, the prosecutor determined that a sufficient basis existed to start planning for the first investigation of the International Criminal Court. In April 2004, the ICC began to investigate crimes in the Democratic Republic of Congo and in January 2005 opened an inquiry into the situation in the Central African Republic. As of summer 2005, all of these investigations were ongoing.

Source

United Nations, "Rome Statute of the International Criminal Court," International Criminal Court Web Site. Available online. URL: http://www.icc-cpi.int/library/about/officialjournal/Rome_Statute_120704-EN.pdf. Accessed January 3, 2005.

OPTIONAL PROTOCOL TO THE CONVENTION ON THE RIGHTS OF THE CHILD ON THE INVOLVEMENT OF CHILDREN IN ARMED CONFLICT

TREATY AT A GLANCE

Completed
Adopted May 25, 2000, entered into force February 12, 2002

Signatories
As of summer 2005, 117 member states of the United Nations,
of which 98 had either ratified or become party to it

Overview
The Optional Protocol seeks to reduce the "harmful and wide-spread impact of armed conflict on children"—that is, persons under age 18—by outlawing the targeting of children and facilities and institutions associated with them during armed conflict and by barring the conscription of children under the age of 18 ("unless, under the law applicable to the child, majority is attained earlier," but in no case under the age of 15).

Historical Background

From its inception at the end of World War II, the United Nations has recognized a special responsibility to safeguard the rights and welfare of the world's children and took the first major step toward carrying out this responsibility with the founding of UNICEF, the United Nations Children's Fund, in 1946. Since then, various United Nations–sponsored resolutions and multilateral conventions have defined children's rights and have sought to provide guarantees for them. The most important multilateral agreement is the CONVENTION ON THE RIGHTS OF THE CHILD, which was adopted by General Assembly Resolution 44/25 on November 20, 1989, and entered into force on September 2, 1990. Over the years, this document has been amplified by several protocols, of which this Optional Protocol on the Involvement of Children in Armed Conflict is among the most significant.

It has been estimated that (as of spring 2005) more than 500,000 children under age 18 serve in government armed forces, paramilitaries, civil militias, and various nonstate armed groups in more than 85 countries. It is further estimated, according to the Coalition to Stop the Use of Child Soldiers, that, at any one time, more than 300,000 of these children are actively fighting as sol-diers. In addition, armed conflicts throughout the world inflict particular hardship and harm on children, physically, emotionally, culturally, and economically. Children sometimes find themselves not merely the innocent victims of armed conflict, but, as the rising generation, the chosen targets of programs of aggression, vengeance, and ethnic cleansing. Responding to this international crisis and tragedy, most of the member states of the United Nations have signed the Optional Protocol.

The United States added its ratification on December 24, 2002, after intensive study by the Department of State and the Department of Defense. Because voluntary enlistment in the United States armed forces may be made at age 17, the Department of Defense needed to ensure that the protocol could not be interpreted to limit this practice. As for conscription, existing U.S. law already prohibits the compulsory recruitment of persons under age 18 and also prohibits voluntary enlistment by children under age 17. Seventeen-year-olds may enlist only with parental consent.

Terms

The states parties to Optional Protocol to the Convention on the Rights of the Child on the Involvement of

Children in Armed Conflict agree to "take all measures to ensure that members of their armed forces who have not attained the age of 18 years do not take a direct part in hostilities" and that those under 18 "are not compulsorily recruited into their armed forces." Voluntary enlistment of those under 18 is permitted with the "informed consent" of parents or guardians. Each state party also agrees to cooperate in United Nations–sponsored efforts to effect the "social reintegration" of victims of "acts contrary to this Protocol," to monitor compliance within its own jurisdiction, and to report to the UN's Committee on the Rights of the Child on "the measures it has taken to implement the provisions of the Protocol."

Optional Protocol to the Convention on the Rights of the Child on the Involvement of Children in Armed Conflict

The States Parties to the present Protocol,

Encouraged by the overwhelming support for the Convention on the Rights of the Child, demonstrating the widespread commitment that exists to strive for the promotion and protection of the rights of the child,

Reaffirming that the rights of children require special protection, and calling for continuous improvement of the situation of children without distinction, as well as for their development and education in conditions of peace and security,

Disturbed by the harmful and widespread impact of armed conflict on children and the long-term consequences this has for durable peace, security and development,

Condemning the targeting of children in situations of armed conflict and direct attacks on objects protected under international law, including places generally having a significant presence of children, such as schools and hospitals,

Noting the adoption of the Statute of the International Criminal Court and, in particular, its inclusion as a war crime of conscripting or enlisting children under the age of 15 years or using them to participate actively in hostilities in both international and non-international armed conflicts,

Considering, therefore, that to strengthen further the implementation of rights recognized in the Convention on the Rights of the Child there is a need to increase the protection of children from involvement in armed conflict,

Noting that article 1 of the Convention on the Rights of the Child specifies that, for the purposes of that Convention, a child means every human being below the age of 18 years unless, under the law applicable to the child, majority is attained earlier,

Convinced that an optional protocol to the Convention raising the age of possible recruitment of persons into armed forces and their participation in hostilities will contribute effectively to the implementation of the principle that the best interests of the child are to be a primary consideration in all actions concerning children,

Noting that the twenty-sixth international Conference of the Red Cross and Red Crescent in December 1995 recom-

mended, *inter alia,* that parties to conflict take every feasible step to ensure that children under the age of 18 years do not take part in hostilities,

Welcoming the unanimous adoption, in June 1999, of International Labour Organization Convention No. 182 on the Prohibition and Immediate Action for the Elimination of the Worst Forms of Child Labour, which prohibits, *inter alia,* forced or compulsory recruitment of children for use in armed conflict,

Condemning with the gravest concern the recruitment, training and use within and across national borders of children in hostilities by armed groups distinct from the armed forces of a State, and recognizing the responsibility of those who recruit, train and use children in this regard,

Recalling the obligation of each party to an armed conflict to abide by the provisions of international humanitarian law,

Stressing that this Protocol is without prejudice to the purposes and principles contained in the Charter of the United Nations, including Article 51, and relevant norms of humanitarian law,

Bearing in mind that conditions of peace and security based on full respect of the purposes and principles contained in the Charter and observance of applicable human rights instruments are indispensable for the full protection of children, in particular during armed conflicts and foreign occupation,

Recognizing the special needs of those children who are particularly vulnerable to recruitment or use in hostilities contrary to this Protocol owing to their economic or social status or gender,

Mindful of the necessity of taking into consideration the economic, social and political root causes of the involvement of children in armed conflicts,

Convinced of the need to strengthen international cooperation in the implementation of this Protocol, as well as the physical and psychosocial rehabilitation and social reintegration of children who are victims of armed conflict,

Encouraging the participation of the community and, in particular, children and child victims in the dissemination of informational and educational programmes concerning the implementation of the Protocol,

Have agreed as follows:

ARTICLE 1

States Parties shall take all feasible measures to ensure that members of their armed forces who have not attained the age of 18 years do not take a direct part in hostilities.

ARTICLE 2

States Parties shall ensure that persons who have not attained the age of 18 years are not compulsorily recruited into their armed forces.

ARTICLE 3

1. States Parties shall raise the minimum age for the voluntary recruitment of persons into their national armed forces from that set out in article 38, paragraph 3, of the Convention on the Rights of the Child, taking account of the principles contained in that article and recognizing that under the Convention persons under 18 are entitled to special protection.

2. Each State Party shall deposit a binding declaration upon ratification of or accession to this Protocol that sets forth the minimum age at which it will permit voluntary recruitment into its national armed forces and a description of the safeguards that

it has adopted to ensure that such recruitment is not forced or coerced.

3. States Parties that permit voluntary recruitment into their national armed forces under the age of 18 shall maintain safeguards to ensure, as a minimum, that:

(a) Such recruitment is genuinely voluntary;

(b) Such recruitment is done with the informed consent of the person=s parents or legal guardians;

(c) Such persons are fully informed of the duties involved in such military service;

(d) Such persons provide reliable proof of age prior to acceptance into national military service.

4. Each State Party may strengthen its declaration at any time by notification to that effect addressed to the Secretary-General of the United Nations, who shall inform all States Parties. Such notification shall take effect on the date on which it is received by the Secretary-General.

5. The requirement to raise the age in paragraph 1 of the present article does not apply to schools operated by or under the control of the armed forces of the States Parties, in keeping with articles 28 and 29 of the Convention on the Rights of the Child.

ARTICLE 4

1. Armed groups that are distinct from the armed forces of a State should not, under any circumstances, recruit or use in hostilities persons under the age of 18 years.

2. States Parties shall take all feasible measures to prevent such recruitment and use, including the adoption of legal measures necessary to prohibit and criminalize such practices.

3. The application of the present article under this Protocol shall not affect the legal status of any party to an armed conflict.

ARTICLE 5

Nothing in the present Protocol shall be construed as precluding provisions in the law of a State Party or in international instruments and international humanitarian law that are more conducive to the realization of the rights of the child.

ARTICLE 6

1. Each State Party shall take all necessary legal, administrative and other measures to ensure the effective implementation and enforcement of the provisions of this Protocol within its jurisdiction.

2. States Parties undertake to make the principles and provisions of the present Protocol widely known and promoted by appropriate means, to adults and children alike.

3. States Parties shall take all feasible measures to ensure that persons within their jurisdiction recruited or used in hostilities contrary to this Protocol are demobilized or otherwise released from service. States Parties shall, when necessary, accord to these persons all appropriate assistance for their physical and psychological recovery and their social reintegration.

ARTICLE 7

1. States Parties shall cooperate in the implementation of the present Protocol, including in the prevention of any activity contrary to the Protocol and in the rehabilitation and social reintegration of persons who are victims of acts contrary to this Protocol, including through technical cooperation and financial assistance. Such assistance and cooperation will be undertaken in consultation with concerned States Parties and relevant international organizations.

2. States Parties in a position to do so shall provide such assistance through existing multilateral, bilateral or other programmes, or, *inter alia*, through a voluntary fund established in accordance with the rules of the General Assembly.

ARTICLE 8

1. Each State Party shall submit, within two years following the entry into force of the Protocol for that State Party, a report to the Committee on the Rights of the Child providing comprehensive information on the measures it has taken to implement the provisions of the Protocol, including the measures taken to implement the provisions on participation and recruitment.

2. Following the submission of the comprehensive report, each State Party shall include in the reports they submit to the Committee on the Rights of the Child, in accordance with article 44 of the Convention, any further information with respect to the implementation of the Protocol. Other States Parties to the Protocol shall submit a report every five years.

3. The Committee on the Rights of the Child may request from States Parties further information relevant to the implementation of this Protocol. . . .

Consequences

As of mid-2005, it is difficult to assess the impact of the protocol, and it may be several years before statistically meaningful data can be accumulated on the numbers of underage combatants throughout the world. At present, however, according to such nongovernmental agencies (NGOs) as the Coalition to Stop the Use of Child Soldiers, and the United Nations itself, underage combatants remain very much on the battlefield, particularly as members of insurgent groups and various unorganized militia forces, entities that have no formal connection to any legally constituted government. At the very least, the protocol promises to keep the issue of child soldiers in the public eye and on the international diplomatic agenda.

Source

Office of the High Commissioner for Human Rights, "Optional Protocol to the Convention on the Rights of the Child on the Involvement of Children in Armed Conflict." Available online. URL: http://www.unhchr.ch/html/menu2/6/protocol-child.htm. Accessed January 4, 2005.

Weapons Treaties

INF TREATY
(INTERMEDIATE-RANGE NUCLEAR FORCE TREATY)

TREATY AT A GLANCE

Completed
Signed December 8, 1987, at Washington, D.C.;
entered into force June 1, 1988

Signatories
United States and the Soviet Union

Overview
With the entry of two new players into the arena of nuclear arms limitation talks, U.S. president Ronald Reagan and Soviet premier Mikhail Gorbachev, negotiations—basically stalled since the collapse of détente—resumed. The result was the INF Treaty, which greatly reduced the world's nuclear arsenals and helped to end the cold war.

Historical Background

By the mid-1970s the Soviet Union achieved a rough nuclear strategic parity with the United States, which led to a turning point in the cold war, albeit a surprising one. In the late 1970s, the Soviet Union began replacing its aging intermediate-range SS-4 and SS-5 missiles with a newer model, the SS-20. The SS-20s carried three warheads, each capable of hitting targets independently of the others, which made them more dangerous than the SS-4s and SS-5s, each of which had only a single warhead. The new intermediate-range missiles also had a range of 3,000 miles (5,000 kilometers), which meant they could hit targets all over Western Europe, in North Africa, and anywhere in the Middle East. If they were fired from Soviet bases in the east of Russia, they could strike most of Asia, Southeast Asia, and Alaska.

The Soviet deployment of the SS-20s sent the European diplomatic community into a panic; it occasioned some saber rattling in the American defense establishment; along with the Soviet invasion of Afghanistan, it led President Jimmy Carter to denounce his naïveté in believing he could deal "honestly" with the Russians; and it ended any hope that the Nixon-Brezhnev détente could be salvaged. It also prompted

the NORTH ATLANTIC TREATY Organization to order, in late 1977, a study of its Intermediate-range Nuclear Force (INF), with an eye toward upgrading that force in keeping with the doctrine, first promulgated by U.S. president Dwight David Eisenhower, of a "flexible response"—meaning the United States and the alliance was free to respond to Soviet aggression whenever they chose, wherever in the world they chose, even if this involved a nuclear attack.

In the spring of 1979, NATO's Nuclear Planning Group established the Special Consultative Group to come up with recommendations regarding the INF based on such study. That group produced the Integrated Decision Document, formulating the basic aims and guiding principles of NATO's INF policy, calling for upgrading the missiles and seeking to engage the Russians in arms control talks. In November NATO's ministers voted unanimously to adopt this "dual track" strategy to counter Soviet SS-20 deployments—seeking through negotiations between the United States and the Soviet Union to reduce INF forces to the lowest possible level while deploying 464 single-warhead U.S. ground-launched cruise (GLCM) missiles and 108 Pershing II ballistic missiles, and to start doing so in December 1983.

At first, the Soviet Union refused to talk at all, even to engage in "preliminary" talks, unless NATO called off the deployment of its INF missiles. But by July 1980, with the Soviets now bogged down in the increasingly costly war in Afghanistan, an aging Brezhnev losing his grip on power inside the Kremlin, and a new American presidential candidate, Ronald Reagan, who was clearly willing to spend any amount of money on missile defense, doing well in the election polls, the Russians changed their position. Preliminary discussions began in Geneva in the fall of 1980. The Americans had come up with a string of musts for the talks: any agreement must provide for equality both in limits and rights between the United States and the Soviet Union, it must be strictly bilateral and thus exclude British and French systems, it had to limit systems on a global basis, it could not adversely affect NATO's conventional defense capability, and it needed to be easily and readily verifiable.

Agreement to begin formal talks was reached on September 23, 1981, after Reagan had been in office for half a year, denounced the Soviets as an "evil empire," and begun rapidly beefing up the U.S. defense budget. On November 18 Reagan announced a negotiating proposal in which the United States would agree to eliminate its Pershing IIs and GLCMs if the Soviet Union would dismantle all of its SS-20s, SS-4s, and SS-5s. This proposal became known as the "zero-zero offer," and few took it as anything more than Reaganite rhetoric. At the beginning of the talks, the Soviet Union opposed the deployment of any U.S. INF missiles in Europe and proposed a ceiling of 300 "medium-range" missiles and nuclear-capable aircraft for both sides, with British and French nuclear forces counting toward the ceiling for the West. But the United States continued to emphasize Reagan's "zero option," while introducing the notion of an interim agreement aimed at voters in Reagan's upcoming reelection campaign. After two years of talks, the Soviets walked out.

During 1984, the year of Reagan's second campaign for office, there were no INF negotiations. The United States carried out its deployments as planned in West Germany, Italy, and the United Kingdom, while making preparations for deployment in Belgium.

In January 1985 the situation changed again. Mikhail Gorbachev came into power that year and began to shake up the Soviet Union. He wanted to reform its economy and the political culture of the Communist Party, he wanted out of Afghanistan, and he hit it off with Ronald Reagan. Secretary of State George Shultz and Soviet foreign minister Andrey Gromyko agreed to separate but parallel negotiations on INF, strategic arms (START), and defense and space issues as part of a new bilateral forum called the Nuclear and Space Talks (NST). The United States and the Soviet Union agreed that all questions regarding these three areas would be considered in their interrelationship. Negotiations would be conducted by a single delegation from each side, divided into three groups, one for defense and space, one for START, and one for INF. Formal talks resumed in March 1985 in all three areas.

In November 1985 President Reagan and General Secretary Gorbachev met in Geneva, where they issued a joint statement calling for an "interim accord on intermediate-range nuclear forces." The two leaders were consciously pushing their foreign ministers and defense officers faster than any of them wanted to go. For another year the talks continued, seesawing back and forth, as the bewildering and arcane process of nuclear arms negotiations moved ahead. On January 15, 1986, a frustrated Gorbachev announced a Soviet proposal for a three-stage program to ban nuclear weapons by the year 2000, which included elimination of all U.S. and Soviet INF missiles in Europe. A series of high-level discussions took place in August and September 1986, followed by another meeting between Reagan and Gorbachev, this one in Reykjavík, Iceland, in October 1986.

Several months later, on February 28, 1987, the Soviet Union announced that it was prepared to reach a separate INF agreement. On March 4, 1987, the United States tabled a draft INF Treaty text, which reflected the agreement Reagan and Gorbachev reached at Reykjavík, and submitted a comprehensive verification regime. In April the Soviet Union presented its own draft treaty, and by July it had agreed in principle to some of the provisions in the U.S. comprehensive verification program.

On June 15 Reagan proposed the elimination of all U.S. and Soviet shorter-range missile systems. On July 22, 1987, Gorbachev agreed to a "double global zero" treaty to eliminate intermediate-range and shorter-range missiles. In September the two sides reached agreement in principle to complete the treaty before the end of the year. On December 8, 1987, the treaty was signed by President Reagan and General Secretary Gorbachev at a summit meeting in Washington.

Terms

When it was signed, the INF Treaty's verification clauses were the most detailed and stringent in the history of nuclear arms control, designed both to eliminate all declared INF systems entirely within three years and to ensure compliance with a total ban on such missiles. One of the landmark nuclear weapons treaties, it read in full as follows:

Treaty between the United States of America and the Union of Soviet Socialist Republics on the Elimination of Their Intermediate Range and Shorter Range Missiles

The United States of America and the Union of Soviet Socialist Republics, hereinafter referred to as the Parties,

Conscious that nuclear war would have devastating consequences for all mankind,

Guided by the objective of strengthening strategic stability,

Convinced that the measures set forth in this Treaty will help to reduce the risk of outbreak of war and strengthen international peace and security, and

Mindful of their obligations under Article VI of the Treaty on the Non-Proliferation of Nuclear Weapons,

Have agreed as follows:

ARTICLE I

In accordance with the provisions of this Treaty which includes the Memorandum of Understanding and Protocols which form an integral part thereof, each Party shall eliminate its intermediate-range and shorter-range missiles, not have such systems thereafter, and carry out the other obligations set forth in this Treaty.

ARTICLE II

For the purposes of this Treaty:

1. The term "ballistic missile" means a missile that has a ballistic trajectory over most of its flight path. The term "ground-launched ballistic missile (GLBM)" means a ground-launched ballistic missile that is a weapon-delivery vehicle.

2. The term "cruise missile" means an unmanned, self-propelled vehicle that sustains flight through the use of aerodynamic lift over most of its flight path. The term "ground-launched cruise missile (GLCM)" means a ground-launched cruise missile that is a weapon-delivery vehicle.

3. The term "GLBM launcher" means a fixed launcher or a mobile land-based transporter-erector-launcher mechanism for launching a GLBM.

4. The term "GLCM launcher" means a fixed launcher or a mobile land-based transporter-erector-launcher mechanism for launching a GLCM.

5. The term "intermediate-range missile" means a GLBM or a GLCM having a range capability in excess of 1000 kilometers but not in excess of 5500 kilometers.

6. The term "shorter-range missile" means a GLBM or a GLCM having a range capability equal to or in excess of 500 kilometers but not in excess of 1000 kilometers.

7. The term "deployment area" means a designated area within which intermediate-range missiles and launchers of such missiles may operate and within which one or more missile operating bases are located.

8. The term "missile operating base" means:

(a) in the case of intermediate-range missiles, a complex of facilities, located within a deployment area, at which intermediate-range missiles and launchers of such missiles normally operate, in which support structures associated with such missiles and launchers are also located and in which support equipment associated with such missiles and launchers is normally located; and

(b) in the case of shorter-range missiles, a complex of facilities, located any place, at which shorter-range missiles and launchers of such missiles normally operate and in which support equipment associated with such missiles and launchers is normally located.

9. The term "missile support facility," as regards intermediate-range or shorter-range missiles and launchers of such missiles, means a missile production facility or a launcher production facility, a missile repair facility or a launcher repair facility, a training facility, a missile storage facility or a launcher storage facility, a test range, or an elimination facility as those terms are defined in the Memorandum of Understanding.

10. The term "transit" means movement, notified in accordance with paragraph 5(f) of Article IX of this Treaty, of an intermediate-range missile or a launcher of such a missile between missile support facilities, between such a facility and a deployment area or between deployment areas, or of a shorter-range missile or a launcher of such a missile from a missile support facility or a missile operating base to an elimination facility.

11. The term "deployed missile" means an intermediate-range missile located within a deployment area or a shorter-range missile located at a missile operating base.

12. The term "non-deployed missile" means an intermediate-range missile located outside a deployment area or a shorter-range missile located outside a missile operating base.

13. The term "deployed launcher" means a launcher of an intermediate-range missile located within a deployment area or a launcher of a shorter-range missile located at a missile operating base.

14. The term "non-deployed launcher" means a launcher of an intermediate-range missile located outside a deployment area or a launcher of a shorter-range missile located outside a missile operating base.

15. The term "basing country" means a country other than the United States of America or the Union of Soviet Socialist Republics on whose territory intermediate-range or shorter-range missiles of the Parties, launchers of such missiles or support structures associated with such missiles and launchers were located at any time after November 1, 1987. Missiles or launchers in transit are not considered to be "located."

ARTICLE III

1. For the purposes of this Treaty, existing types of intermediate-range missiles are:

(a) for the United States of America, missiles of the types designated by the United States of America as the Pershing II and the BGM-109G, which are known to the Union of Soviet Socialist Republics by the same designations; and

(b) for the Union of Soviet Socialist Republics, missiles of the types designated by the Union of Soviet Socialist Republics as the RSD-10, the R-12 and the R-14, which are known to the United States of America as the SS-20, the SS-4 and the SS-5, respectively.

2. For the purposes of this Treaty, existing types of shorter-range missiles are:

(a) for the United States of America, missiles of the type designated by the United States of America as the Pershing IA, which is known to the Union of Soviet Socialist Republics by the same designation; and

(b) for the Union of Soviet Socialist Republics, missiles of the types designated by the Union of Soviet Socialist Republics as the OTR-22 and the OTR-23, which are known to the United States of America as the SS-12 and the SS-23, respectively.

ARTICLE IV

1. Each Party shall eliminate all its intermediate-range missiles and launchers of such missiles, and all support structures and support equipment of the categories listed in the Memorandum of Understanding associated with such missiles and launchers, so that no later than three years after entry into force of this Treaty and thereafter no such missiles, launchers, support structures or support equipment shall be possessed by either Party.

2. To implement paragraph 1 of this Article, upon entry into force of this Treaty, both Parties shall begin and continue throughout the duration of each phase, the reduction of all types of their deployed and non-deployed intermediate-range missiles and deployed and non-deployed launchers of such missiles and support structures and support equipment associated with such missiles and launchers in accordance with the provisions of this Treaty. These reductions shall be implemented in two phases so that:

(a) by the end of the first phase, that is, no later than 29 months after entry into force of this Treaty:

(i) the number of deployed launchers of intermediate-range missiles for each Party shall not exceed the number of launchers that are capable of carrying or containing at one time missiles considered by the Parties to carry 171 warheads;

(ii) the number of deployed intermediate-range missiles for each Party shall not exceed the number of such missiles considered by the Parties to carry 180 warheads;

(iii) the aggregate number of deployed and non-deployed launchers of intermediate-range missiles for each Party shall not exceed the number of launchers that are capable of carrying or containing at one time missiles considered by the Parties to carry 200 warheads;

(iv) the aggregate number of deployed and non-deployed intermediate-range missiles for each Party shall not exceed the number of such missiles considered by the Parties to carry 200 warheads; and

(v) the ratio of the aggregate number of deployed and non-deployed intermediate-range GLBMs of existing types for each Party to the aggregate number of deployed and non-deployed intermediate-range missiles of existing types possessed by that Party shall not exceed the ratio of such intermediate-range GLBMs to such intermediate-range missiles for that Party as of November 1, 1987, as set forth in the Memorandum of Understanding; and

(b) by the end of the second phase, that is, no later than three years after entry into force of this Treaty, all intermediate-range missiles of each Party, launchers of such missiles and all support structures and support equipment of the categories listed in the Memorandum of Understanding associated with such missiles and launchers, shall be eliminated.

ARTICLE V

1. Each Party shall eliminate all its shorter-range missiles and launchers of such missiles, and all support equipment of the categories listed in the Memorandum of Understanding associated with such missiles and launchers, so that no later than 18 months after entry into force of this Treaty and thereafter no such missiles, launchers or support equipment shall be possessed by either Party.

2. No later than 90 days after entry into force of this Treaty, each Party shall complete the removal of all its deployed shorter-range missiles and deployed and non-deployed launchers of such missiles to elimination facilities and shall retain them at those locations until they are eliminated in accordance with the procedures set forth in the Protocol on Elimination. No later than 12 months after entry into force of this Treaty, each Party shall complete the removal of all its non-deployed shorter-range missiles to elimination facilities and shall retain them at those locations until they are eliminated in accordance with the procedures set forth in the Protocol on Elimination.

3. Shorter-range missiles and launchers of such missiles shall not be located at the same elimination facility. Such facilities shall be separated by no less than 1000 kilometers.

ARTICLE VI

1. Upon entry into force of this Treaty and thereafter, neither Party shall:

(a) produce or flight-test any intermediate-range missiles or produce any stages of such missiles or any launchers of such missiles; or

(b) produce, flight-test or launch any shorter-range missiles or produce any stages of such missiles or any launchers of such missiles.

2. Notwithstanding paragraph 1 of this Article, each Party shall have the right to produce a type of GLBM not limited by this Treaty which uses a stage which is outwardly similar to, but not interchangeable with, a stage of an existing type of intermediate-range GLBM having more than one stage, providing that that Party does not produce any other stage which is outwardly similar to, but not interchangeable with, any other stage of an existing type of intermediate-range GLBM.

ARTICLE VII

For the purposes of this Treaty:

1. If a ballistic missile or a cruise missile has been flight-tested or deployed for weapon delivery, all missiles of that type shall be considered to be weapon-delivery vehicles.

2. If a GLBM or GLCM is an intermediate-range missile, all GLBMs or GLCMs of that type shall be considered to be intermediate-range missiles. If a GLBM or GLCM is a shorter-range missile, all GLBMs or GLCMs of that type shall be considered to be shorter-range missiles.

3. If a GLBM is of a type developed and tested solely to intercept and counter objects not located on the surface of the earth, it shall not be considered to be a missile to which the limitations of this Treaty apply.

4. The range capability of a GLBM not listed in Article III of this Treaty shall be considered to be the maximum range to which it has been tested. The range capability of a GLCM not listed in Article III of this Treaty shall be considered to be the maximum distance which can be covered by the missile in its standard design mode flying until fuel exhaustion, determined by projecting its flight path onto the earths sphere from the point of launch to the point of impact. GLBMs or GLCMs that have a range capability equal to or in excess of 500 kilometers but not in excess of 1000 kilometers shall be considered to be shorter-range missiles. GLBMs or GLCMs that have a range capability in excess of 1000 kilometers but not in excess of 5500

kilometers shall be considered to be intermediate-range missiles.

5. The maximum number of warheads an existing type of intermediate-range missile or shorter-range missile carries shall be considered to be the number listed for missiles of that type in the Memorandum of Understanding.

6. Each GLBM or GLCM shall be considered to carry the maximum number of warheads listed for a GLBM or GLCM of the type in the Memorandum of Understanding.

7. If a launcher has been tested for launching a GLBM or a GLCM, all launchers of that type shall be considered to have been tested for launching GLBMs or GLCMs.

8. If a launcher has contained or launched a particular type of GLBM or GLCM, all launchers of that type shall be considered to be launchers of that type of GLBM or GLCM.

9. The number of missiles each launcher of an existing type of intermediate-range missile or shorter-range missile shall be considered to be capable of carrying or containing at one time is the number listed for launchers of missiles of that type in the Memorandum of Understanding.

10. Except in the case of elimination in accordance with the procedures set forth in the Protocol on Elimination, the following shall apply:

(a) for GLBMs which are stored or moved in separate stages, the longest stage of an intermediate-range or shorter-range GLBM shall be counted as a complete missile;

(b) for GLBMs which are not stored or moved in separate stages, a canister of the type used in the launch of an intermediate-range GLBM, unless a Party proves to the satisfaction of the other Party that it does not contain such a missile, or an assembled intermediate-range or shorter-range GLBM, shall be counted as a complete missile; and

(c) for GLCMs, the airframe of an intermediate-range or shorter-range GLCM shall be counted as a complete missile.

11. A ballistic missile which is not a missile to be used in a ground-based mode shall not be considered to be a GLBM if it is test-launched at a test site from a fixed land-based launcher which is used solely for test purposes and which is distinguishable from GLBM launchers. A cruise missile which is not a missile to be used in a ground-based mode shall not be considered to be a GLCM if it is test-launched at a test site from a fixed land-based launcher which is used solely for test purposes and which is distinguishable from GLCM launchers.

12. Each Party shall have the right to produce and use for booster systems, which might otherwise be considered to be intermediate-range or shorter-range missiles, only existing types of booster stages for such booster systems. Launches of such booster systems shall not be considered to be flight-testing of intermediate-range or shorter-range missiles provided that:

(a) stages used in such booster systems are different from stages used in those missiles listed as existing types of intermediate-range or shorter-range missiles in Article III of this Treaty;

(b) such booster systems are used only for research and development purposes to test objects other than the booster systems themselves;

(c) the aggregate number of launchers for such booster systems shall not exceed 35 for each Party at any one time; and

(d) the launchers for such booster systems are fixed, emplaced above ground and located only at research and development launch sites which are specified in the Memorandum of Understanding.

Research and development launch sites shall not be subject to inspection pursuant to Article XI of this Treaty.

ARTICLE VIII

1. All intermediate-range missiles and launchers of such missiles shall be located in deployment areas, at missile support facilities or shall be in transit. Intermediate-range missiles or launchers of such missiles shall not be located elsewhere.

2. Stages of intermediate-range missiles shall be located in deployment areas, at missile support facilities or moving between deployment areas, between missile support facilities or between missile support facilities and deployment areas.

3. Until their removal to elimination facilities as required by paragraph 2 of Article V of this Treaty, all shorter-range missiles and launchers of such missiles shall be located at missile operating bases, at missile support facilities or shall be in transit. Shorter-range missiles or launchers of such missiles shall not be located elsewhere.

4. Transit of a missile or launcher subject to the provisions of this Treaty shall be completed within 25 days.

5. All deployment areas, missile operating bases and missile support facilities are specified in the Memorandum of Understanding or in subsequent updates of data pursuant to paragraphs 3, 5(a) or 5(b) of Article IX of this Treaty. Neither Party shall increase the number of, or change the location or boundaries of, deployment areas, missile operating bases or missile support facilities, except for elimination facilities, from those set forth in the Memorandum of Understanding. A missile support facility shall not be considered to be part of a deployment area even though it may be located within the geographic boundaries of a deployment area.

6. Beginning 30 days after entry into force of this Treaty, neither Party shall locate intermediate-range or shorter-range missiles, including stages of such missiles, or launchers of such missiles at missile production facilities, launcher production facilities or test ranges listed in the Memorandum of Understanding.

7. Neither Party shall locate any intermediate-range or shorter-range missiles at training facilities.

8. A non-deployed intermediate-range or shorter-range missile shall not be carried on or contained within a launcher of such a type of missile, except as required for maintenance conducted at repair facilities or for elimination by means of launching conducted at elimination facilities.

9. Training missiles and training launchers for intermediate-range or shorter-range missiles shall be subject to the same locational restrictions as are set forth for intermediate-range and shorter-range missiles and launchers of such missiles in paragraphs 1 and 3 of this Article.

ARTICLE IX

1. The Memorandum of Understanding contains categories of data relevant to obligations undertaken with regard to this Treaty and lists all intermediate-range and shorter-range missiles, launchers of such missiles, and support structures and support equipment associated with such missiles and launchers, possessed by the Parties as of November 1, 1987. Updates of that data and notifications required by this Article shall be provided according to the categories of data contained in the Memorandum of Understanding.

2. The Parties shall update that data and provide the notifications required by this Treaty through the Nuclear Risk Reduction Centers, established pursuant to the Agreement Between the United States of America and the Union of Soviet Socialist Republics on the Establishment of Nuclear Risk Reduction Centers of September 15, 1987.

3. No later than 30 days after entry into force of this Treaty, each Party shall provide the other Party with updated data, as of the date of entry into force of this Treaty, for all categories of data contained in the Memorandum of Understanding.

4. No later than 30 days after the end of each six-month interval following the entry into force of this Treaty, each Party shall provide updated data for all categories of data contained in the Memorandum of Understanding by informing the other Party of all changes, completed and in process, in that data, which have occurred during the six-month interval since the preceding data exchange, and the net effect of those changes.

5. Upon entry into force of this Treaty and thereafter, each Party shall provide the following notifications to the other Party:

(a) notification, no less than 30 days in advance, of the scheduled date of the elimination of a specific deployment area, missile operating base or missile support facility;

(b) notification, no less than 30 days in advance, of changes in the number or location of elimination facilities, including the location and scheduled date of each change;

(c) notification, except with respect to launches of intermediate-range missiles for the purpose of their elimination, no less than 30 days in advance, of the scheduled date of the initiation of the elimination of intermediate-range and shorter-range missiles, and stages of such missiles, and launchers of such missiles and support structures and support equipment associated with such missiles and launchers, including:

(i) the number and type of items of missile systems to be eliminated;

(ii) the elimination site;

(iii) for intermediate-range missiles, the location from which such missiles, launchers of such missiles and support equipment associated with such missiles and launchers are moved to the elimination facility; and

(iv) except in the case of support structures, the point of entry to be used by an inspection team conducting an inspection pursuant to paragraph 7 of Article XI of this Treaty and the estimated time of departure of an inspection team from the point of entry to the elimination facility;

(d) notification, no less than ten days in advance, of the scheduled date of the launch, or the scheduled date of the initiation of a series of launches, of intermediate-range missiles for the purpose of their elimination, including:

(i) the type of missiles to be eliminated;

(ii) the location of the launch, or, if elimination is by a series of launches, the location of such launches and the number of launches in the series;

(iii) the point of entry to be used by an inspection team conducting an inspection pursuant to paragraph 7 of Article XI of this Treaty; and

(iv) the estimated time of departure of an inspection team from the point of entry to the elimination facility;

(e) notification, no later than 48 hours after they occur, of changes in the number of intermediate-range and shorter-range missiles, launchers of such missiles and support structures and support equipment associated with such missiles and launchers resulting from elimination as described in the Protocol on Elimination, including:

(i) the number and type of items of a missile system which were eliminated; and

(ii) the date and location of such elimination; and

(f) notification of transit of intermediate-range or shorter-range missiles or launchers of such missiles, or the movement of training missiles or training launchers for such intermediate-range and shorter-range missiles, no later than 48 hours after it has been completed, including:

(i) the number of missiles or launchers;

(ii) the points, dates, and times of departure and arrival;

(iii) the mode of transport; and

(iv) the location and time at that location at least once every four days during the period of transit.

6. Upon entry into force of this Treaty and thereafter, each Party shall notify the other Party, no less than ten days in advance, of the scheduled date and location of the launch of a research and development booster system as described in paragraph 12 of Article VII of this Treaty.

ARTICLE X

1. Each Party shall eliminate its intermediate-range and shorter-range missiles and launchers of such missiles and support structures and support equipment associated with such missiles and launchers in accordance with the procedures set forth in the Protocol on Elimination.

2. Verification by on-site inspection of the elimination of items of missile systems specified in the Protocol on Elimination shall be carried out in accordance with Article XI of this Treaty, the Protocol on Elimination and the Protocol on Inspection.

3. When a Party removes its intermediate-range missiles, launchers of such missiles and support equipment associated with such missiles and launchers from deployment areas to elimination facilities for the purpose of their elimination, it shall do so in complete deployed organizational units. For the United States of America, these units shall be Pershing II batteries and BGM-109G flights. For the Union of Soviet Socialist Republics, these units shall be SS-20 regiments composed of two or three battalions.

4. Elimination of intermediate-range and shorter-range missiles and launchers of such missiles and support equipment associated with such missiles and launchers shall be carried out at the facilities that are specified in the Memorandum of Understanding or notified in accordance with paragraph 5(b) of Article IX of this Treaty, unless eliminated in accordance with Sections IV or V of the Protocol on Elimination. Support structures, associated with the missiles and launchers subject to this Treaty, that are subject to elimination shall be eliminated in situ.

5. Each Party shall have the right, during the first six months after entry into force of this Treaty, to eliminate by means of launching no more than 100 of its intermediate-range missiles.

6. Intermediate-range and shorter-range missiles which have been tested prior to entry into force of this Treaty, but never deployed, and which are not existing types of intermediate-range or shorter-range missiles listed in Article III of this Treaty,

and launchers of such missiles, shall be eliminated within six months after entry into force of this Treaty in accordance with the procedures set forth in the Protocol on Elimination. Such missiles are:

(a) for the United States of America, missiles of the type designated by the United States of America as the Pershing IB, which is known to the Union of Soviet Socialist Republics by the same designation; and

(b) for the Union of Soviet Socialist Republics, missiles of the type designated by the Union of Soviet Socialist Republics as the RK-55, which is known to the United States of America as the SSC-X-4.

7. Intermediate-range and shorter-range missiles and launchers of such missiles and support structures and support equipment associated with such missiles and launchers shall be considered to be eliminated after completion of the procedures set forth in the Protocol on Elimination and upon the notification provided for in paragraph 5(e) of Article IX of this Treaty.

8. Each Party shall eliminate its deployment areas, missile operating bases and missile support facilities. A Party shall notify the other Party pursuant to paragraph 5(a) of Article IX of this Treaty once the conditions set forth below are fulfilled:

(a) all intermediate-range and shorter-range missiles, launchers of such missiles and support equipment associated with such missiles and launchers located there have been removed;

(b) all support structures associated with such missiles and launchers located there have been eliminated; and

(c) all activity related to production, flight-testing, training, repair, storage or deployment of such missiles and launchers has ceased there.

Such deployment areas, missile operating bases and missile support facilities shall be considered to be eliminated either when they have been inspected pursuant to paragraph 4 of Article XI of this Treaty or when 60 days have elapsed since the date of the scheduled elimination which was notified pursuant to paragraph 5(a) of Article IX of this Treaty. A deployment area, missile operating base or missile support facility listed in the Memorandum of Understanding that met the above conditions prior to entry into force of this Treaty, and is not included in the initial data exchange pursuant to paragraph 3 of Article IX of this Treaty, shall be considered to be eliminated.

9. If a Party intends to convert a missile operating base listed in the Memorandum of Understanding for use as a base associated with GLBM or GLCM systems not subject to this Treaty, then that Party shall notify the other Party, no less than 30 days in advance of the scheduled date of the initiation of the conversion, of the scheduled date and the purpose for which the base will be converted.

ARTICLE XI

1. For the purpose of ensuring verification of compliance with the provisions of this Treaty, each Party shall have the right to conduct on-site inspections. The Parties shall implement on-site inspections in accordance with this Article, the Protocol on Inspection and the Protocol on Elimination.

2. Each Party shall have the right to conduct inspections provided for by this Article both within the territory of the other Party and within the territories of basing countries.

3. Beginning 30 days after entry into force of this Treaty, each Party shall have the right to conduct inspections at all missile operating bases and missile support facilities specified in the Memorandum of Understanding other than missile production facilities, and at all elimination facilities included in the initial data update required by paragraph 3 of Article IX of this Treaty. These inspections shall be completed no later than 90 days after entry into force of this Treaty. The purpose of these inspections shall be to verify the number of missiles, launchers, support structures and support equipment and other data, as of the date of entry into force of this Treaty, provided pursuant to paragraph 3 of Article IX of this Treaty.

4. Each Party shall have the right to conduct inspections to verify the elimination, notified pursuant to paragraph 5(a) of Article IX of this Treaty, of missile operating bases and missile support facilities other than missile production facilities, which are thus no longer subject to inspections pursuant to paragraph 5(a) of this Article. Such an inspection shall be carried out within 60 days after the scheduled date of the elimination of that facility. If a Party conducts an inspection at a particular facility pursuant to paragraph 3 of this Article after the scheduled date of the elimination of that facility, then no additional inspection of that facility pursuant to this paragraph shall be permitted.

5. Each Party shall have the right to conduct inspections pursuant to this paragraph for 13 years after entry into force of this Treaty. Each Party shall have the right to conduct 20 such inspections per calendar year during the first three years after entry into force of this Treaty, 15 such inspections per calendar year during the subsequent five years, and ten such inspections per calendar year during the last five years. Neither Party shall use more than half of its total number of these inspections per calendar year within the territory of any one basing country. Each Party shall have the right to conduct:

(a) inspections, beginning 90 days after entry into force of this Treaty, of missile operating bases and missile support facilities other than elimination facilities and missile production facilities, to ascertain, according to the categories of data specified in the Memorandum of Understanding, the numbers of missiles, launchers, support structures and support equipment located at each missile operating base or missile support facility at the time of the inspection; and

(b) inspections of former missile operating bases and former missile support facilities eliminated pursuant to paragraph 8 of Article X of this Treaty other than former missile production facilities.

6. Beginning 30 days after entry into force of this Treaty, each Party shall have the right, for 13 years after entry into force of this Treaty, to inspect by means of continuous monitoring:

(a) the portals of any facility of the other Party at which the final assembly of a GLBM using stages, any of which is outwardly similar to a stage of a solid-propellant GLBM listed in Article III of this Treaty, is accomplished; or

(b) if a Party has no such facility, the portals of an agreed former missile production facility at which existing types of intermediate-range or shorter-range GLBMs were produced.

The Party whose facility is to be inspected pursuant to this paragraph shall ensure that the other Party is able to establish a permanent continuous monitoring system at that facility within six months after entry into force of this Treaty or within six months of initiation of the process of final assembly described in subparagraph (a). If, after the end of the second year after entry into force of this Treaty, neither Party conducts the process of final assembly described in subparagraph (a) for a period of 12 consecutive months, then neither Party shall have the right to inspect by means of continuous monitoring any missile production facility of the other Party unless the process of final assembly as described in subparagraph (a) is initiated again. Upon entry into force of this Treaty, the facilities to be inspected by continuous monitoring shall be: in accordance with subparagraph (b), for the United States of America, Hercules Plant Number 1, at Magna, Utah; in accordance with subparagraph (a), for the Union of Soviet Socialist Republics, the Votkinsk Machine Building Plant, Udmurt Autonomous Soviet Socialist Republic, Russian Soviet Federative Socialist Republic.

7. Each Party shall conduct inspections of the process of elimination, including elimination of intermediate-range missiles by means of launching, of intermediate-range and shorter-range missiles and launchers of such missiles and support equipment associated with such missiles and launchers carried out at elimination facilities in accordance with Article X of this Treaty and the Protocol on Elimination. Inspectors conducting inspections provided for in this paragraph shall determine that the processes specified for the elimination of the missiles, launchers and support equipment have been completed.

8. Each Party shall have the right to conduct inspections to confirm the completion of the process of elimination of intermediate-range and shorter-range missiles and launchers of such missiles and support equipment associated with such missiles and launchers eliminated pursuant to Section V of the Protocol on Elimination, and of training missiles, training missile stages, training launch canisters and training launchers eliminated pursuant to Sections II, IV and V of the Protocol on Elimination.

ARTICLE XII

1. For the purpose of ensuring verification of compliance with the provisions of this Treaty, each Party shall use national technical means of verification at its disposal in a manner consistent with generally recognized principles of international law.

2. Neither Party shall:

(a) interfere with national technical means of verification of the other Party operating in accordance with paragraph 1 of this Article; or

(b) use concealment measures which impede verification of compliance with the provisions of this Treaty by national technical means of verification carried out in accordance with paragraph 1 of this Article. This obligation does not apply to cover or concealment practices, within a deployment area, associated with normal training, maintenance and operations, including the use of environmental shelters to protect missiles and launchers.

3. To enhance observation by national technical means of verification, each Party shall have the right until a Treaty between the Parties reducing and limiting strategic offensive arms enters into force, but in any event for no more than three years after entry into force of this Treaty, to request the implementation of cooperative measures at deployment bases for road-mobile GLBMs with a range capability in excess of 5500 kilometers, which are not former missile operating bases eliminated pursuant to paragraph 8 of Article X of this Treaty. The Party making such a request shall inform the other Party of the deployment base at which cooperative measures shall be implemented. The Party whose base is to be observed shall carry out the following cooperative measures:

(a) no later than six hours after such a request, the Party shall have opened the roofs of all fixed structures for launchers located at the base, removed completely all missiles on launchers from such fixed structures for launchers and displayed such missiles on launchers in the open without using concealment measures; and

(b) the Party shall leave the roofs open and the missiles on launchers in place until twelve hours have elapsed from the time of the receipt of a request for such an observation.

Each Party shall have the right to make six such requests per calendar year. Only one deployment base shall be subject to these cooperative measures at any one time.

ARTICLE XIII

1. To promote the objectives and implementation of the provisions of this Treaty, the Parties hereby establish the Special Verification Commission. The Parties agree that, if either Party so requests, they shall meet within the framework of the Special Verification Commission to:

(a) resolve questions relating to compliance with the obligations assumed; and

(b) agree upon such measures as may be necessary to improve the viability and effectiveness of this Treaty.

2. The Parties shall use the Nuclear Risk Reduction Centers, which provide for continuous communication between the Parties, to:

(a) exchange data and provide notifications as required by paragraphs 3, 4, 5 and 6 of Article IX of this Treaty and the Protocol on Elimination;

(b) provide and receive the information required by paragraph 9 of Article X of this Treaty;

(c) provide and receive notifications of inspections as required by Article XI of this Treaty and the Protocol on Inspection; and

(d) provide and receive requests for cooperative measures as provided for in paragraph 3 of Article XII of this Treaty.

ARTICLE XIV

The Parties shall comply with this Treaty and shall not assume any international obligations or undertakings which would conflict with its provisions.

ARTICLE XV

1. This Treaty shall be of unlimited duration.

2. Each Party shall, in exercising its national sovereignty, have the right to withdraw from this Treaty if it decides that extraordinary events related to the subject matter of this Treaty have jeopardized its supreme interests. It shall give notice of its decision to withdraw to the other Party six months prior to withdrawal from this Treaty. Such notice shall include a statement of the extraordinary events the notifying Party regards as having jeopardized its supreme interests.

ARTICLE XVI

Each Party may propose amendments to this Treaty. Agreed amendments shall enter into force in accordance with the procedures set forth in Article XVII governing the entry into force of this Treaty.

ARTICLE XVII

1. This Treaty, including the Memorandum of Understanding and Protocols, which form an integral part thereof, shall be subject to ratification in accordance with the constitutional procedures of each Party. This Treaty shall enter into force on the date of the exchange of instruments of ratification.

2. This Treaty shall be registered pursuant to Article 102 of the Charter of the United Nations.

DONE at Washington on December 8, 1987, in two copies, each in the English and Russian languages, both texts being equally authentic.

For the United States of America:
RONALD REAGAN
President of the United States of America
For the Union of Soviet Socialist Republics:
MIKHAIL GORBACHEV
General Secretary of the Central Committee of the CPSU

Consequences

There continued to be some tugs-of-war between the two sides even after the treaty went into effect, but many of these were worked out by the Special Verification Commission (SVC) set up under Article 13. The U.S. On-Site Inspection Agency (OSIA) was established January 15, 1988, to coordinate and implement the inspection provisions of the treaty, and both sides conducted inspections in 1988 to verify that each side had the number of INF systems, facilities, and locations they claimed to have during the negotiations. In late April and early May 1991, the United States eliminated its last ground-launched cruise missile and ground-launched ballistic missile covered under the INF Treaty. The last declared Soviet SS-20 was eliminated on May 11, 1991. A total of 2,692 missiles were destroyed under the treaty.

The next year after signing the treaty, Gorbachev formally renounced the Brezhnev Doctrine, under which the Soviet Union had claimed the right to intervene militarily anywhere in the Warsaw Pact countries, not unlike the right Dwight Eisenhower had claimed in the 1950s to respond to Soviet aggression anywhere in the free world he chose. The Soviet system of maintaining buffer satellite states in eastern Europe was essentially dismantled, resulting in a rapid thaw of Soviet-American relations and, ultimately, an end to the cold war. Gorbachev was awarded the Nobel Peace Prize in 1990, a year before a coup by hard-line Communist members of the military failed to depose him, thus beginning the final dissolution of the Communist Party itself and of the entire Soviet Union.

Following the collapse of the Soviet Union in December 25, 1991, the United States sought to keep the INF Treaty in force and spread the agreement to the 12 former Soviet republics, which the United States considered successor states of the USSR, and thus party to the original agreement. Of those 12, six—Belarus, Kazakhstan, Russia, Turkmenistan, Ukraine, and Uzbekistan—have sites subject to the INF agreement inspections. Of those six, four—Belarus, Kazakhstan, Russia, and Ukraine—readily agreed to accept the terms of the treaty and become active in implementing it within their territories. With the acquiescence of all the parties involved, Turkmenistan and Uzbekistan—each with only one such site on its territory—while accepting the terms of the treaty, do not take an active role in the process, such as attending sessions of the SVC or participating in inspections.

Source

Federation of American Scientists. "Intermediate-Range Nuclear Forces [INF] Texts." Available online. URL: http:// www.fas.org/nuke/control/inf/text/index.html. Accessed January 4, 2005.

Proclamations and Declarations

HAMAS COVENANT

TREATY AT A GLANCE

Completed
August 18, 1988

Signatories
Unilateral declaration by an Islamic terrorist group, although the principles were adhered to by the Muslim Brotherhood and the Palestine Liberation Organization (PLO)

Overview
In the wake of the Israeli occupation of the West Bank and the Gaza Strip, militants in the PLO and fundamentalists in the Muslim Brotherhood, both calling for a holy war against the Jews, founded the radical terrorist society HAMAS.

Historical Background

Founded in 1928 in Egypt by Hasan al-Banna, the Muslim Brotherhood began as a fundamentalist religious organization that advocated a return to the Koran and the Hadith as guidelines for a healthy, modern Islamic society. The brotherhood spread rapidly throughout Egypt, the Sudan, Syria, Palestine, Lebanon, and North Africa and after 1938 grew increasingly political, demanding purity of the Islamic world and rejecting Westernization, secularization, and modernization. The brotherhood created a terrorist arm, which in the mid-1940s posed a threat to the Egyptian monarchy and the ruling Wafd Party. When Gamal Abdel Nasser came to power in the wake of the Egyptian revolution, the brotherhood attempted to assassinate him in October 1954. Nasser responded with brutal repression, executing six of its leaders for treason, imprisoning dozens of others, and driving the organization underground.

Throughout the 1960s and 1970s, the brotherhood remained clandestine, but with the rise of Islamic fundamentalism across the Middle East beginning in the late 1970s, it experienced a public rebirth. The brotherhood's new acolytes aimed to reorganize society and government according to Islamic doctrines, and they were vehemently anti-Western. Syrian strongman Hafiz al-Assad was forced to crush an uprising by the Muslim Brotherhood in Hamah in February 1982. About the same time, the Muslim Brotherhood reappeared in Egypt and Jordan, where by the late 1980s it was competing openly in elections.

Islamic activists connected with the pan-Arab Muslim Brotherhood had established a network of charities, clinics, and schools in Gaza and were active in many mosques, but they limited their agitation in the West Bank mostly to the universities. Those activities were generally nonviolent, but a number of small groups in the territories occupied by Israel began to call for jihad, or holy war, against the Jews. In December 1987, at the beginning of the Palestinian intifada (uprising), HAMAS—an acronym of Harakat-al-Muqawma al-Islamiyya, or the "Islamic resistance movement," which also means in Arabic "zeal"—was established by members of the Muslim Brotherhood and religious factions of the Palestine Liberation Organization (PLO).

Terms

In its 1988 charter, HAMAS maintained that Palestine was an Islamic homeland that could never be surrendered to non-Muslims and that waging jihad to liberate Palestine was the duty of all Palestinians. Part anti-Israeli screed, part religious manifesto, part historical essay, part political agenda, the covenant captures the intensity of the Arab terrorists' sense of mission.

The Covenant of the Islamic Resistance Movement

In The Name Of The Most Merciful Allah

"Ye are the best nation that hath been raised up unto mankind: ye command that which is just, and ye forbid that which is unjust, and ye believe in Allah. And if they who have received the scriptures had believed, it had surely been the better for them: there are believers among them, but the greater part of them are transgressors. They shall not hurt you, unless with a slight hurt; and if they fight against you, they shall turn their backs to you, and they shall not be helped. They are smitten with vileness wheresoever they are found; unless they obtain security by entering into a treaty with Allah, and a treaty with men; and they draw on themselves indignation from Allah, and they are afflicted with poverty. This they suffer, because they disbelieved the signs of Allah, and slew the prophets unjustly; this, because they were rebellious, and transgressed." (Al-Imran—verses 109–111)

"Israel will exist and will continue to exist until Islam will obliterate it, just as it obliterated others before it" (The Martyr, Imam Hassan al-Banna, of blessed memory).

"The Islamic world is on fire. Each of us should pour some water, no matter how little, to extinguish whatever one can without waiting for the others." (Sheikh Amjad al-Zahawi, of blessed memory).

In The Name Of The Most Merciful Allah

INTRODUCTION

Praise be unto Allah, to whom we resort for help, and whose forgiveness, guidance and support we seek; Allah bless the Prophet and grant him salvation, his companions and supporters, and to those who carried out his message and adopted his laws - everlasting prayers and salvation as long as the earth and heaven will last. Hereafter:

O People:

Out of the midst of troubles and the sea of suffering, out of the palpitations of faithful hearts and cleansed arms; out of the sense of duty, and in response to Allah's command, the call has gone out rallying people together and making them follow the ways of Allah, leading them to have determined will in order to fulfill their role in life, to overcome all obstacles, and surmount the difficulties on the way. Constant preparation has continued and so has the readiness to sacrifice life and all that is precious for the sake of Allah.

Thus it was that the nucleus (of the movement) was formed and started to pave its way through the tempestuous sea of hopes and expectations, of wishes and yearnings, of troubles and obstacles, of pain and challenges, both inside and outside.

When the idea was ripe, the seed grew and the plant struck root in the soil of reality, away from passing emotions, and hateful haste. The Islamic Resistance Movement emerged to carry out its role through striving for the sake of its Creator, its arms intertwined with those of all the fighters for the liberation of Palestine. The spirits of its fighters meet with the spirits of all the fighters who have sacrificed their lives on the soil of Palestine, ever since it was conquered by the companions of the Prophet, Allah bless him and grant him salvation, and until this day.

This Covenant of the Islamic Resistance Movement (HAMAS), clarifies its picture, reveals its identity, outlines its stand, explains its aims, speaks about its hopes, and calls for its support, adoption and joining its ranks. Our struggle against the Jews is very great and very serious. It needs all sincere efforts. It is a step that inevitably should be followed by other steps. The Movement is but one squadron that should be supported by more and more squadrons from this vast Arab and Islamic world, until the enemy is vanquished and Allah's victory is realised.

Thus we see them coming on the horizon "and you shall learn about it hereafter" "Allah hath written, Verily I will prevail, and my apostles: for Allah is strong and mighty." (The Dispute—verse 21).

"Say to them, This is my way: I invite you to Allah, by an evident demonstration; both I and he who followeth me; and, praise be unto Allah! I am not an idolator." (Joseph—verse 107).

Hamas (means) strength and bravery—(according to) Al-Mua'jam al-Wasit: c1.

DEFINITION OF THE MOVEMENT
Ideological Starting-Points

ARTICLE ONE

The Islamic Resistance Movement: The Movement's programme is Islam. From it, it draws its ideas, ways of thinking and understanding of the universe, life and man. It resorts to it for judgement in all its conduct, and it is inspired by it for guidance of its steps.

The Islamic Resistance Movement's Relation with the Moslem Brotherhood Group

ARTICLE TWO

The Islamic Resistance Movement is one of the wings of Moslem Brotherhood in Palestine. Moslem Brotherhood Movement is a universal organization which constitutes the largest Islamic movement in modern times. It is characterised by its deep understanding, accurate comprehension and its complete embrace of all Islamic concepts of all aspects of life, culture, creed, politics, economics, education, society, justice and judgement, the spreading of Islam, education, art, information, science of the occult and conversion to Islam.

Structure and Formation

ARTICLE THREE

The basic structure of the Islamic Resistance Movement consists of Moslems who have given their allegiance to Allah whom they truly worship, - "I have created the jinn and humans only for the purpose of worshipping" - who know their duty towards themselves, their families and country. In all that, they fear Allah and raise the banner of Jihad in the face of the oppressors, so that they would rid the land and the people of their uncleanliness, vileness and evils.

"But we will oppose truth to vanity, and it shall confound the same; and behold, it shall vanish away." (Prophets—verse 18)

ARTICLE FOUR

The Islamic Resistance Movement welcomes every Moslem who embraces its faith, ideology, follows its programme, keeps its secrets, and wants to belong to its ranks and carry out the duty. Allah will certainly reward such one.

Time and Place Extent of the Islamic Resistance Movement

ARTICLE FIVE

Time extent of the Islamic Resistance Movement: By adopting Islam as its way of life, the Movement goes back to the time of the birth of the Islamic message, of the righteous ancestor, for Allah is its target, the Prophet is its example and the Koran is its constitution. Its extent in place is anywhere that there are Moslems who embrace Islam as their way of life everywhere in the globe. This being so, it extends to the depth of the earth and reaches out to the heaven.

"Dost thou not see how Allah putteth forth a parable; representing a good word, as a good tree, whose root is firmly fixed in the earth, and whose branches reach unto heaven; which bringeth forth its fruit in all seasons, by the will of its Lord? Allah propoundeth parables unto men, that they may be instructed." (Abraham—verses 24-25)

Characteristics and Independence

ARTICLE SIX

The Islamic Resistance Movement is a distinguished Palestinian movement, whose allegiance is to Allah, and whose way of life is Islam. It strives to raise the banner of Allah over every inch of Palestine, for under the wing of Islam followers of all religions can coexist in security and safety where their lives, possessions and rights are concerned. In the absence of Islam, strife will be rife, oppression spreads, evil prevails and schisms and wars will break out.

How excellent was the Moslem poet, Mohamed Ikbal, when he wrote:

"If faith is lost, there is no security and there is no life for him who does not adhere to religion. He who accepts life without religion, has taken annihilation as his companion for life."

The Universality of the Islamic Resistance Movement

ARTICLE SEVEN

As a result of the fact that those Moslems who adhere to the ways of the Islamic Resistance Movement spread all over the world, rally support for it and its stands, strive towards enhancing its struggle, the Movement is a universal one. It is well-equipped for that because of the clarity of its ideology, the nobility of its aim and the loftiness of its objectives.

On this basis, the Movement should be viewed and evaluated, and its role be recognised. He who denies its right, evades supporting it and turns a blind eye to facts, whether intentionally or unintentionally, would awaken to see that events have overtaken him and with no logic to justify his attitude. One should certainly learn from past examples.

The injustice of next-of-kin is harder to bear than the smite of the Indian sword.

"We have also sent down unto thee the book of the Koran with truth, confirming that scripture which was revealed before it; and preserving the same safe from corruption. Judge therefore between them according to that which Allah hath revealed; and follow not their desires, by swerving from the truth which hath come unto thee. Unto every of you have we given a law, and an open path; and if Allah had pleased, he had surely made you one people; but he hath thought it fit to give you different laws, that he might try you in that which he hath given you

respectively. Therefore strive to excel each other in good works; unto Allah shall ye all return, and then will he declare unto you that concerning which ye have disagreed." (The Table, verse 48).

The Islamic Resistance Movement is one of the links in the chain of the struggle against the Zionist invaders. It goes back to 1939, to the emergence of the martyr Izz al-Din al Kissam and his brethren the fighters, members of Moslem Brotherhood. It goes on to reach out and become one with another chain that includes the struggle of the Palestinians and Moslem Brotherhood in the 1948 war and the Jihad operations of the Moslem Brotherhood in 1968 and after.

Moreover, if the links have been distant from each other and if obstacles, placed by those who are the lackeys of Zionism in the way of the fighters obstructed the continuation of the struggle, the Islamic Resistance Movement aspires to the realisation of Allah's promise, no matter how long that should take. The Prophet, Allah bless him and grant him salvation, has said:

"The Day of Judgement will not come about until Moslems fight the Jews (killing the Jews), when the Jew will hide behind stones and trees. The stones and trees will say O Moslems, O Abdulla, there is a Jew behind me, come and kill him. Only the Gharkad tree, (evidently a certain kind of tree) would not do that because it is one of the trees of the Jews." (related by al-Bukhari and Moslem).

The Slogan of the Islamic Resistance Movement

ARTICLE EIGHT

Allah is its target, the Prophet is its model, the Koran its constitution: Jihad is its path and death for the sake of Allah is the loftiest of its wishes.

OBJECTIVES
Incentives and Objectives

ARTICLE NINE

The Islamic Resistance Movement found itself at a time when Islam has disappeared from life. Thus rules shook, concepts were upset, values changed and evil people took control, oppression and darkness prevailed, cowards became like tigers: homelands were usurped, people were scattered and were caused to wander all over the world, the state of justice disappeared and the state of falsehood replaced it. Nothing remained in its right place. Thus, when Islam is absent from the arena, everything changes. From this state of affairs the incentives are drawn.

As for the objectives: They are the fighting against the false, defeating it and vanquishing it so that justice could prevail, homelands be retrieved and from its mosques would the voice of the mu'azen emerge declaring the establishment of the state of Islam, so that people and things would return each to their right places and Allah is our helper.

"And if Allah had not prevented men, the one by the other, verily the earth had been corrupted: but Allah is beneficient towards his creatures." (The Cow—verse 251).

ARTICLE TEN

As the Islamic Resistance Movement paves its way, it will back the oppressed and support the wronged with all its might. It will spare no effort to bring about justice and defeat injustice, in word and deed, in this place and everywhere it can reach and have influence therein.

969 A NEW WORLD ORDER

STRATEGIES AND METHODS
Strategies of the Islamic Resistance Movement: Palestine Is Islamic Waqf

ARTICLE ELEVEN

The Islamic Resistance Movement believes that the land of Palestine is an Islamic Waqf consecrated for future Moslem generations until Judgement Day. It, or any part of it, should not be squandered: it, or any part of it, should not be given up. Neither a single Arab country nor all Arab countries, neither any king or president, nor all the kings and presidents, neither any organization nor all of them, be they Palestinian or Arab, possess the right to do that. Palestine is an Islamic Waqf land consecrated for Moslem generations until Judgement Day. This being so, who could claim to have the right to represent Moslem generations till Judgement Day?

This is the law governing the land of Palestine in the Islamic Sharia (law) and the same goes for any land the Moslems have conquered by force, because during the times of (Islamic) conquests, the Moslems consecrated these lands to Moslem generations till the Day of Judgement.

It happened like this: When the leaders of the Islamic armies conquered Syria and Iraq, they sent to the Caliph of the Moslems, Umar bin-el-Khatab, asking for his advice concerning the conquered land - whether they should divide it among the soldiers, or leave it for its owners, or what? After consultations and discussions between the Caliph of the Moslems, Omar bin-el-Khatab and companions of the Prophet, Allah bless him and grant him salvation, it was decided that the land should be left with its owners who could benefit by its fruit. As for the real ownership of the land and the land itself, it should be consecrated for Moslem generations till Judgement Day. Those who are on the land, are there only to benefit from its fruit. This Waqf remains as long as earth and heaven remain. Any procedure in contradiction to Islamic Sharia, where Palestine is concerned, is null and void.

"Verily, this is a certain truth. Wherefore praise the name of thy Lord, the great Allah." (The Inevitable—verse 95).

Homeland and Nationalism from the Point of View of the Islamic Resistance Movement in Palestine

ARTICLE TWELVE

Nationalism, from the point of view of the Islamic Resistance Movement, is part of the religious creed. Nothing in nationalism is more significant or deeper than in the case when an enemy should tread Moslem land. Resisting and quelling the enemy become the individual duty of every Moslem, male or female. A woman can go out to fight the enemy without her husband's permission, and so does the slave: without his master's permission.

Nothing of the sort is to be found in any other regime. This is an undisputed fact. If other nationalist movements are connected with materialistic, human or regional causes, nationalism of the Islamic Resistance Movement has all these elements as well as the more important elements that give it soul and life. It is connected to the source of spirit and the granter of life, hoisting in the sky of the homeland the heavenly banner that joins earth and heaven with a strong bond.

If Moses comes and throws his staff, both witch and magic are annulled.

"Now is the right direction manifestly distinguished from deceit: whoever therefore shall deny Tagut, and believe in Allah, he shall surely take hold with a strong handle, which shall not be broken; Allah is he who heareth and seeth." (The Cow—Verse 256)

Peaceful Solutions, Initiatives and International Conferences

ARTICLE THIRTEEN

Initiatives, and so-called peaceful solutions and international conferences, are in contradiction to the principles of the Islamic Resistance Movement. Abusing any part of Palestine is abuse directed against part of religion. Nationalism of the Islamic Resistance Movement is part of its religion. Its members have been fed on that. For the sake of hoisting the banner of Allah over their homeland they fight. "Allah will be prominent, but most people do not know."

Now and then the call goes out for the convening of an international conference to look for ways of solving the (Palestinian) question. Some accept, others reject the idea, for this or other reason, with one stipulation or more for consent to convening the conference and participating in it. Knowing the parties constituting the conference, their past and present attitudes towards Moslem problems, the Islamic Resistance Movement does not consider these conferences capable of realising the demands, restoring the rights or doing justice to the oppressed. These conferences are only ways of setting the infidels in the land of the Moslems as arbitraters. When did the infidels do justice to the believers?

"But the Jews will not be pleased with thee, neither the Christians, until thou follow their religion; say, The direction of Allah is the true direction. And verily if thou follow their desires, after the knowledge which hath been given thee, thou shalt find no patron or protector against Allah." (The Cow—verse 120)

There is no solution for the Palestinian question except through Jihad. Initiatives, proposals and international conferences are all a waste of time and vain endeavors. The Palestinian people know better than to consent to having their future, rights and fate toyed with. As is said in the honourable Hadith:

"The people of Syria are Allah's lash in His land. He wreaks His vengeance through them against whomsoever He wishes among His slaves It is unthinkable that those who are double-faced among them should prosper over the faithful. They will certainly die out of grief and desperation."

The Three Circles

ARTICLE FOURTEEN

The question of the liberation of Palestine is bound to three circles: the Palestinian circle, the Arab circle and the Islamic circle. Each of these circles has its role in the struggle against Zionism. Each has its duties, and it is a horrible mistake and a sign of deep ignorance to overlook any of these circles. Palestine is an Islamic land which has the first of the two kiblahs (direction to which Moslems turn in praying), the third of the holy (Islamic) sanctuaries, and the point of departure for Mohamed's midnight journey to the seven heavens (i.e., Jerusalem).

"Praise be unto him who transported his servant by night, from the sacred temple of Mecca to the farther temple of Jerusalem, the circuit of which we have blessed, that we might show him some of our signs; for Allah is he who heareth, and seeth." (The Night-Journey—verse 1)

Since this is the case, liberation of Palestine is then an individual duty for very Moslem wherever he may be. On this basis, the problem should be viewed. This should be realised by every Moslem.

The day the problem is dealt with on this basis, when the three circles mobilize their capabilities, the present state of affairs will change and the day of liberation will come nearer.

"Verily ye are stronger than they, by reason of the terror cast into their breasts from Allah. This, because they are not people of prudence." (The Emigration—verse 13)

The Jihad for the Liberation of Palestine Is an Individual Duty

ARTICLE FIFTEEN

The day that enemies usurp part of Moslem land, Jihad becomes the individual duty of every Moslem. In face of the Jews' usurpation of Palestine, it is compulsory that the banner of Jihad be raised. To do this requires the diffusion of Islamic consciousness among the masses, both on the regional, Arab and Islamic levels. It is necessary to instill the spirit of Jihad in the heart of the nation so that they would confront the enemies and join the ranks of the fighters.

It is necessary that scientists, educators and teachers, information and media people, as well as the educated masses, especially the youth and sheikhs of the Islamic movements, should take part in the operation of awakening (the masses). It is important that basic changes be made in the school curriculum, to cleanse it of the traces of ideological invasion that affected it as a result of the orientalists and missionaries who infiltrated the region following the defeat of the Crusaders at the hands of Salah el-Din (Saladin). The Crusaders realised that it was impossible to defeat the Moslems without first having ideological invasion pave the way by upsetting their thoughts, disfiguring their heritage and violating their ideals. Only then could they invade with soldiers. This, in its turn, paved the way for the imperialistic invasion that made Allenby declare on entering Jerusalem: "Only now have the Crusades ended." General Guru stood at Salah el-Din's grave and said: "We have returned, O Salah el-Din." Imperialism has helped towards the strengthening of ideological invasion, deepening, and still does, its roots. All this has paved the way towards the loss of Palestine.

It is necessary to instill in the minds of the Moslem generations that the Palestinian problem is a religious problem, and should be dealt with on this basis. Palestine contains Islamic holy sites. In it there is al- Aqsa Mosque which is bound to the great Mosque in Mecca in an inseparable bond as long as heaven and earth speak of Isra' (Mohammed's midnight journey to the seven heavens) and Mi'raj (Mohammed's ascension to the seven heavens from Jerusalem).

"The bond of one day for the sake of Allah is better than the world and whatever there is on it. The place of one's whip in Paradise is far better than the world and whatever there is on it. A worshipper's going and coming in the service of Allah is better than the world and whatever there is on it." (As related by al-Bukhari, Moslem, al-Tarmdhi and Ibn Maja.)

"I swear by the holder of Mohammed's soul that I would like to invade and be killed for the sake of Allah, then invade and be killed, and then invade again and be killed." (As related by al-Bukhari and Moslem.)

The Education of the Generations

ARTICLE SIXTEEN

It is necessary to follow Islamic orientation in educating the Islamic generations in our region by teaching the religious duties, comprehensive study of the Koran, the study of the Prophet's Sunna (his sayings and doings), and learning about Islamic history and heritage from their authentic sources. This should be done by specialised and learned people, using a curriculum that would healthily form the thoughts and faith of the Moslem student. Side by side with this, a comprehensive study of the enemy, his human and financial capabilities, learning about his points of weakness and strength, and getting to know the forces supporting and helping him, should also be included. Also, it is important to be acquainted with the current events, to follow what is new and to study the analysis and commentaries made of these events. Planning for the present and future, studying every trend appearing, is a must so that the fighting Moslem would live knowing his aim, objective and his way in the midst of what is going on around him.

"O my son, verily every matter, whether good or bad, though it be the weight of a grain of mustard-seed, and be hidden in a rock, or in the heavens, or in the earth, Allah will bring the same to light; for Allah is clear-sighted and knowing. O my son, be constant at prayer, and command that which is just, and forbid that which is evil: and be patient under the afflictions which shall befall thee; for this is a duty absolutely incumbent on all men. Distort not thy face out of contempt to men, neither walk in the earth with insolence; for Allah loveth no arrogant, vain-glorious person." (Lokman—verses 16-18)

The Role of the Moslem Woman

ARTICLE SEVENTEEN

The Moslem woman has a role no less important than that of the moslem man in the battle of liberation. She is the maker of men. Her role in guiding and educating the new generations is great. The enemies have realised the importance of her role. They consider that if they are able to direct and bring her up the way they wish, far from Islam, they would have won the battle. That is why you find them giving these attempts constant attention through information campaigns, films, and the school curriculum, using for that purpose their lackeys who are infiltrated through Zionist organizations under various names and shapes, such as Freemasons, Rotary Clubs, espionage groups and others, which are all nothing more than cells of subversion and saboteurs. These organizations have ample resources that enable them to play their role in societies for the purpose of achieving the Zionist targets and to deepen the concepts that would serve the enemy. These organizations operate in the absence of Islam and its estrangement among its people. The Islamic peoples should perform their role in confronting the conspiracies of these saboteurs. The day Islam is in control of guiding the affairs of life, these organizations, hostile to humanity and Islam, will be obliterated.

ARTICLE EIGHTEEN

Woman in the home of the fighting family, whether she is a mother or a sister, plays the most important role in looking after the family, rearing the children and embuing them with moral values and thoughts derived from Islam. She has to teach them to perform the religious duties in preparation for the role of fighting awaiting them. That is why it is necessary to pay great attention to schools and the curriculum followed in educating Moslem girls, so that they would grow up to be good mothers, aware of their role in the battle of liberation.

She has to be of sufficient knowledge and understanding where the performance of housekeeping matters are concerned, because economy and avoidance of waste of the family budget, is one of the requirements for the ability to continue moving forward in the difficult conditions surrounding us. She should put before her eyes the fact that the money available to her is just like blood which should never flow except through the veins so that both children and grown-ups could continue to live.

"Verily, the Moslems of either sex, and the true believers of either sex, and the devout men, and the devout women, and the men of veracity, and the women of veracity, and the patient men, and the patient women, and the humble men, and the humble women, and the alms-givers of either sex who remember Allah frequently; for them hath Allah prepared forgiveness and a great reward." (The Confederates—verse 25)

The Role of Islamic Art in the Battle of Liberation
ARTICLE NINETEEN
Art has regulations and measures by which it can be determined whether it is Islamic or pre-Islamic (Jahili) art. The issues of Islamic liberation are in need of Islamic art that would take the spirit high, without raising one side of human nature above the other, but rather raise all of them harmoniously an in equilibrium.

Man is a unique and wonderful creature, made out of a handful of clay and a breath from Allah. Islamic art addresses man on this basis, while pre-Islamic art addresses the body giving preference to the clay component in it.

The book, the article, the bulletin, the sermon, the thesis, the popular poem, the poetic ode, the song, the play and others, contain the characteristics of Islamic art, then these are among the requirements of ideological mobilization, renewed food for the journey and recreation for the soul. The road is long and suffering is plenty. The soul will be bored, but Islamic art renews the energies, resurrects the movement, arousing in them lofty meanings and proper conduct. "Nothing can improve the self if it is in retreat except shifting from one mood to another."

All this is utterly serious and no jest, for those who are fighters do not jest.

Social Mutual Responsibility
ARTICLE TWENTY
Moslem society is a mutually responsible society. The Prophet, prayers and greetings be unto him, said: "Blessed are the generous, whether they were in town or on a journey, who have collected all that they had and shared it equally among themselves."

The Islamic spirit is what should prevail in every Moslem society. The society that confronts a vicious enemy which acts in a way similar to Nazism, making no differentiation between man and woman, between children and old people—such a society is entitled to this Islamic spirit. Our enemy relies on the methods of collective punishment. He has deprived people of their homeland and properties, pursued them in their places of exile and

gathering, breaking bones, shooting at women, children and old people, with or without a reason. The enemy has opened detention camps where thousands and thousands of people are thrown and kept under sub-human conditions. Added to this, are the demolition of houses, rendering children orphans, meting cruel sentences against thousands of young people, and causing them to spend the best years of their lives in the dungeons of prisons.

In their Nazi treatment, the Jews made no exception for women or children. Their policy of striking fear in the heart is meant for all. They attack people where their breadwinning is concerned, extorting their money and threatening their honour. They deal with people as if they were the worst war criminals. Deportation from the homeland is a kind of murder.

To counter these deeds, it is necessary that social mutual responsibility should prevail among the people. The enemy should be faced by the people as a single body which if one member of it should complain, the rest of the body would respond by feeling the same pains.

ARTICLE TWENTY-ONE
Mutual social responsibility means extending assistance, financial or moral, to all those who are in need and joining in the execution of some of the work. Members of the Islamic Resistance Movement should consider the interests of the masses as their own personal interests. They must spare no effort in achieving and preserving them. They must prevent any foul play with the future of the upcoming generations and anything that could cause loss to society. The masses are part of them and they are part of the masses. Their strength is theirs, and their future is theirs. Members of the Islamic Resistance Movement should share the people's joy and grief, adopt the demands of the public and whatever means by which they could be realised. The day that such a spirit prevails, brotherliness would deepen, cooperation, sympathy and unity will be enhanced and the ranks will be solidified to confront the enemies.

Supportive Forces Behind the Enemy
ARTICLE TWENTY-TWO
For a long time, the enemies have been planning, skillfully and with precision, for the achievement of what they have attained. They took into consideration the causes affecting the current of events. They strived to amass great and substantive material wealth which they devoted to the realisation of their dream. With their money, they took control of the world media, news agencies, the press, publishing houses, broadcasting stations, and others. With their money they stirred revolutions in various parts of the world with the purpose of achieving their interests and reaping the fruit therein. They were behind the French Revolution, the Communist revolution and most of the revolutions we heard and hear about, here and there. With their money they formed secret societies, such as Freemasons, Rotary Clubs, the Lions and others in different parts of the world for the purpose of sabotaging societies and achieving Zionist interests. With their money they were able to control imperialistic countries and instigate them to colonize many countries in order to enable them to exploit their resources and spread corruption there.

You may speak as much as you want about regional and world wars. They were behind World War I, when they were able to destroy the Islamic Caliphate, making financial gains and controlling resources. They obtained the Balfour Declaration, formed the League of Nations through which they could rule the world. They were behind World War II, through which they made huge financial gains by trading in armaments, and paved the way for the establishment of their state. It was they who instigated the replacement of the League of Nations with the United Nations and the Security Council to enable them to rule the world through them. There is no war going on anywhere, without having their finger in it.

"So often as they shall kindle a fire for war, Allah shall extinguish it; and they shall set their minds to act corruptly in the earth, but Allah loveth not the corrupt doers." (The Table—verse 64)

The imperialistic forces in the Capitalist West and Communist East, support the enemy with all their might, in money and in men. These forces take turns in doing that. The day Islam appears, the forces of infidelity would unite to challenge it, for the infidels are of one nation.

"O true believers, contract not an intimate friendship with any besides yourselves: they will not fail to corrupt you. They wish for that which may cause you to perish: their hatred hath already appeared from out of their mouths; but what their breasts conceal is yet more inveterate. We have already shown you signs of their ill will towards you, if ye understand." (The Family of Imran—verse 118)

It is not in vain that the verse is ended with Allah's words "if ye understand."

OUR ATTITUDES TOWARDS

A. Islamic Movements

ARTICLE TWENTY-THREE

The Islamic Resistance Movement views other Islamic movements with respect and appreciation. If it were at variance with them on one point or opinion, it is in agreement with them on other points and understandings. It considers these movements, if they reveal good intentions and dedication to Allah, that they fall into the category of those who are trying hard since they act within the Islamic circle. Each active person has his share.

The Islamic Resistance Movement considers all these movements as a fund for itself. It prays to Allah for guidance and directions for all and it spares no effort to keep the banner of unity raised, ever striving for its realisation in accordance with the Koran and the Prophet's directives.

"And cleave all of you unto the covenant of Allah, and depart not from it, and remember the favour of Allah towards you: since ye were enemies, and he reconciled your hearts, and ye became companions and brethren by his favour: and ye were on the brink of a pit of fire, and he delivered you thence. Allah declareth unto you his signs, that ye may be directed." (The Family of Imran— Verse 102)

ARTICLE TWENTY-FOUR

The Islamic Resistance Movement does not allow slandering or speaking ill of individuals or groups, for the believer does not indulge in such malpractices. It is necessary to differentiate between this behaviour and the stands taken by certain individuals and groups. Whenever those stands are erroneous, the Islamic Resistance Movement preserves the right to expound the error and to warn against it. It will strive to show the right path

and to judge the case in question with objectivity. Wise conduct is indeed the target of the believer who follows it wherever he discerns it.

"Allah loveth not the speaking ill of anyone in public, unless he who is injured call for assistance; and Allah heareth and knoweth: whether ye publish a good action, or conceal it, or forgive evil, verily Allah is gracious and powerful." (Women — verses 147-148)

B. Nationalist Movements in the Palestinian Arena

ARTICLE TWENTY-FIVE

The Islamic Resistance Movement respects these movements and appreciates their circumstances and the conditions surrounding and affecting them. It encourages them as long as they do not give their allegiance to the Communist East or the Crusading West. It confirms to all those who are integrated in it, or sympathetic towards it, that the Islamic Resistance Movement is a fighting movement that has a moral and enlightened look of life and the way it should cooperate with the other (movements). It detests opportunism and desires only the good of people, individuals and groups alike. It does not seek material gains, personal fame, nor does it look for a reward from others. It works with its own resources and whatever is at its disposal "and prepare for them whatever force you can", for the fulfilment of the duty, and the earning of Allah's favour. It has no other desire than that.

The Movement assures all the nationalist trends operating in the Palestinian arena for the liberation of Palestine, that it is there for their support and assistance. It will never be more than that, both in words and deeds, now and in the future. It is there to bring together and not to divide, to preserve and not to squander, to unify and not to throw asunder. It evaluates every good word, sincere effort and good offices. It closes the door in the face of side disagreements and does not lend an ear to rumours and slanders, while at the same time fully realising the right for self-defence.

Anything contrary or contradictory to these trends, is a lie disseminated by enemies or their lackeys for the purpose of sowing confusion, disrupting the ranks and occupy them with side issues.

"O true believers, if a wicked man come unto you with a tale, inquire strictly into the truth thereof; lest ye hurt people through ignorance, and afterwards repent of what ye have done." (The Inner Apartments—verse 6)

ARTICLE TWENTY-SIX

In viewing the Palestinian nationalist movements that give allegiance neither to the East nor the West, in this positive way, the Islamic Resistance Movement does not refrain from discussing new situations on the regional or international levels where the Palestinian question is concerned. It does that in such an objective manner revealing the extent of how much it is in harmony or contradiction with the national interests in the light of the Islamic point of view.

C. The Palestinian Liberation Organization

ARTICLE TWENTY-SEVEN

The Palestinian Liberation Organization is the closest to the heart of the Islamic Resistance Movement. It contains the father and the brother, the next of kin and the friend. The Moslem does not estrange himself from his father, brother, next of kin or friend. Our homeland is one, our situation is one, our fate is one and the enemy is a joint enemy to all of us.

Because of the situations surrounding the formation of the Organization, of the ideological confusion prevailing in the Arab world as a result of the ideological invasion under whose influence the Arab world has fallen since the defeat of the Crusaders and which was, and still is, intensified through orientalists, missionaries and imperialists, the Organization adopted the idea of the secular state. And that it how we view it.

Secularism completely contradicts religious ideology. Attitudes, conduct and decisions stem from ideologies.

That is why, with all our appreciation for The Palestinian Liberation Organization—and what it can develop into—and without belittling its role in the Arab-Israeli conflict, we are unable to exchange the present or future Islamic Palestine with the secular idea. The Islamic nature of Palestine is part of our religion and whoever takes his religion lightly is a loser.

"Who will be adverse to the religion of Abraham, but he whose mind is infatuated? (The Cow—verse 130)

The day the Palestinian Liberation Organization adopts Islam as its way of life, we will become its soldiers, and fuel for its fire that will burn the enemies.

Until such a day, and we pray to Allah that it will be soon, the Islamic Resistance Movement's stand towards the PLO is that of the son towards his father, the brother towards his brother, and the relative to relative, suffers his pain and supports him in confronting the enemies, wishing him to be wise and well-guided.

"Stand by your brother, for he who is brotherless is like the fighter who goes to battle without arms. One's cousin is the wing one flies with—could the bird fly without wings?"

D. Arab and Islamic Countries

ARTICLE TWENTY-EIGHT

The Zionist invasion is a vicious invasion. It does not refrain from resorting to all methods, using all evil and contemptible ways to achieve its end. It relies greatly in its infiltration and espionage operations on the secret organizations it gave rise to, such as the Freemasons, The Rotary and Lions clubs, and other sabotage groups. All these organizations, whether secret or open, work in the interest of Zionism and according to its instructions. They aim at undermining societies, destroying values, corrupting consciences, deteriorating character and annihilating Islam. It is behind the drug trade and alcoholism in all its kinds so as to facilitate its control and expansion.

Arab countries surrounding Israel are asked to open their borders before the fighters from among the Arab and Islamic nations so that they could consolidate their efforts with those of their Moslem brethren in Palestine.

As for the other Arab and Islamic countries, they are asked to facilitate the movement of the fighters from and to it, and this is the least thing they could do.

We should not forget to remind every Moslem that when the Jews conquered the Holy City in 1967, they stood on the threshold of the Aqsa Mosque and proclaimed that "Mohammed is dead, and his descendants are all women."

Israel, Judaism and Jews challenge Islam and the Moslem people. "May the cowards never sleep."

E. Nationalist and Religious Groupings, Institutions, Intellectuals, The Arab and Islamic World

The Islamic Resistance Movement hopes that all these groupings will side with it in all spheres, would support it, adopt its stand and solidify its activities and moves, work towards rallying support for it so that the Islamic people will be a base and a stay for it, supplying it with strategic depth and all human material and informative spheres, in time and in place. This should be done through the convening of solidarity conferences, the issuing of explanatory bulletins, favourable articles and booklets, enlightening the masses regarding the Palestinian issue, clarifying what confronts it and the conspiracies woven around it. They should mobilize the Islamic nations, ideologically, educationally and culturally, so that these peoples would be equipped to perform their role in the decisive battle of liberation, just as they did when they vanquished the Crusaders and the Tatars and saved human civilization. Indeed, that is not difficult for Allah.

"Allah hath written, Verily I will prevail, and my apostles: for Allah is strong and mighty." (The Dispute—verse 21)

ARTICLE THIRTY

Writers, intellectuals, media people, orators, educaters and teachers, and all the various sectors in the Arab and Islamic world—all of them are called upon to perform their role, and to fulfill their duty, because of the ferocity of the Zionist offensive and the Zionist influence in many countries exercised through financial and media control, as well as the consequences that all this leads to in the greater part of the world.

Jihad is not confined to the carrying of arms and the confrontation of the enemy. The effective word, the good article, the useful book, support and solidarity—together with the presence of sincere purpose for the hoisting of Allah's banner higher and higher—all these are elements of the Jihad for Allah's sake.

"Whosoever mobilises a fighter for the sake of Allah is himself a fighter. Whosoever supports the relatives of a fighter, he himself is a fighter." (Related by al-Bukhari, Moslem, Abu-Dawood and al-Tarmadhi).

F. Followers of Other Religions: The Islamic Resistance Movement Is a Humanistic Movement

ARTICLE THIRTY-ONE

The Islamic Resistance Movement is a humanistic movement. It takes care of human rights and is guided by Islamic tolerance when dealing with the followers of other religions. It does not antagonize anyone of them except if it is antagonized by it or stands in its way to hamper its moves and waste its efforts.

Under the wing of Islam, it is possible for the followers of the three religions—Islam, Christianity and Judaism—to coexist in peace and quiet with each other. Peace and quiet would not be possible except under the wing of Islam. Past and present history are the best witness to that.

It is the duty of the followers of other religions to stop disputing the sovereignty of Islam in this region, because the day these followers should take over there will be nothing but carnage, displacement and terror. Everyone of them is at variance with his fellow-religionists, not to speak about followers of other religionists. Past and present history are full of examples to prove this fact.

"They will not fight against you in a body, except in fenced towns, or from behind walls. Their strength in war among themselves is great: thou thinkest them to be united; but their hearts are divided. This, because they are people who do not understand." (The Emigration—verse 14)

Islam confers upon everyone his legitimate rights. Islam prevents the incursion on other people's rights. The Zionist Nazi activities against our people will not last for long. "For the state of injustice lasts but one day, while the state of justice lasts till Doomsday."

"As to those who have not borne arms against you on account of religion, nor turned you out of your dwellings, Allah forbiddeth you not to deal kindly with them, and to behave justly towards them; for Allah loveth those who act justly." (The Tried—verse 8)

The Attempt to Isolate the Palestinian People

ARTICLE THIRTY-TWO

World Zionism, together with imperialistic powers, try through a studied plan and an intelligent strategy to remove one Arab state after another from the circle of struggle against Zionism, in order to have it finally face the Palestinian people only. Egypt was, to a great extent, removed from the circle of the struggle, through the treacherous Camp David Agreement. They are trying to draw other Arab countries into similar agreements and to bring them outside the circle of struggle.

The Islamic Resistance Movement calls on Arab and Islamic nations to take up the line of serious and persevering action to prevent the success of this horrendous plan, to warn the people of the danger emanating from leaving the circle of struggle against Zionism. Today it is Palestine, tomorrow it will be one country or another. The Zionist plan is limitless. After Palestine, the Zionists aspire to expand from the Nile to the Euphrates. When they will have digested the region they overtook, they will aspire to further expansion, and so on. Their plan is embodied in the "Protocols of the Elders of Zion", and their present conduct is the best proof of what we are saying.

Leaving the circle of struggle with Zionism is high treason, and cursed be he who does that. "for whoso shall turn his back unto them on that day, unless he turneth aside to fight, or retreateth to another party of the faithful, shall draw on himself the indignation of Allah, and his abode shall be hell; an ill journey shall it be thither." (The Spoils—verse 16). There is no way out except by concentrating all powers and energies to face this Nazi, vicious Tatar invasion. The alternative is loss of one's country, the dispersion of citizens, the spread of vice on earth and the destruction of religious values. Let every person know that he is responsible before Allah, for "the doer of the slightest good deed is rewarded in like, and the doer of the slightest evil deed is also rewarded in like."

The Islamic Resistance Movement considers itself to be the spearhead of the circle of struggle with world Sionism and a step on the road. The Movement adds its efforts to the efforts of all those who are active in the Palestinian arena. Arab and Islamic Peoples should augment by further steps on their part; Islamic groupings all over the Arab world should also do the same, since all of these are the best-equipped for the future role in the fight with the warmongering Jews.

"And we have put enmity and hatred between them, until the day of resurrection. So often as they shall kindle a fire of war, Allah shall extinguish it; and they shall set their minds to act corruptly in the earth, but Allah loveth not the corrupt doers." (The Table—verse 64)

ARTICLE THIRTY-THREE

The Islamic Resistance Movement, being based on the common coordinated and interdependent conceptions of the laws of the universe, and flowing in the stream of destiny in confronting and fighting the enemies in defence of the Moslems and Islamic civilization and sacred sites, the first among which is the Aqsa Mosque, urges the Arab and Islamic peoples, their governments, popular and official groupings, to fear Allah where their view of the Islamic Resistance Movement and their dealings with it are concerned. They should back and support it, as Allah wants them to, extending to it more and more funds till Allah's purpose is achieved when ranks will close up, fighters join other fighters and masses everywhere in the Islamic world will come forward in response to the call of duty while loudly proclaiming: Hail to Jihad. Their cry will reach the heavens and will go on being resounded until liberation is achieved, the invaders vanquished and Allah's victory comes about.

"And Allah will certainly assist him who shall be on his side: for Allah is strong and mighty." (The Pilgrimage—verse 40)

THE TESTIMONY OF HISTORY
Across History in Confronting the Invaders

ARTICLE THIRTY-FOUR

Palestine is the navel of the globe and the crossroad of the continents. Since the dawn of history, it has been the target of expansionists. The Prophet, Allah bless him and grant him salvation, had himself pointed to this fact in the noble Hadith in which he called on his honourable companion, Ma'adh ben-Jabal, saying: O Ma'ath, Allah throw open before you, when I am gone, Syria, from Al-Arish to the Euphrates. Its men, women and slaves will stay firmly there till the Day of Judgement. Whoever of you should choose one of the Syrian shores, or the Holy Land, he will be in constant struggle till the Day of Judgement."

Expansionists have more than once put their eye on Palestine which they attacked with their armies to fulfill their designs on it. Thus it was that the Crusaders came with their armies, bringing with them their creed and carrying their Cross. They were able to defeat the Moslems for a while, but the Moslems were able to retrieve the land only when they stood under the wing of their religious banner, united their word, hallowed the name of Allah and surged out fighting under the leadership of Salah el-Din al-Ayyubi. They fought for almost twenty years and at the end the Crusaders were defeated and Palestine was liberated.

"Say unto those who believe not, Ye shall be overcome, and thrown together into hell; an unhappy couch it shall be." (The Family of Imran—verse 12)

This is the only way to liberate Palestine. There is no doubt about the testimony of history. It is one of the laws of the universe and one of the rules of existence. Nothing can overcome iron except iron. Their false futile creed can only be defeated by the righteous Islamic creed. A creed could not be fought except by a creed, and in the last analysis, victory is for the just, for justice is certainly victorious.

"Our word hath formerly been given unto our servants the apostles; that they should certainly be assisted against the infidels, and that our armies should surely be the conquerors." (Those Who Rank Themselves—verses 171–172)

ARTICLE THIRTY-FIVE

The Islamic Resistance Movement views seriously the defeat of the Crusaders at the hands of Salah el-Din al-Ayyubi and the rescuing of Palestine from their hands, as well as the defeat of the Tatars at Ein Galot, breaking their power at the hands of Qataz and Al-Dhaher Bivers and saving the Arab world from the Tatar onslaught which aimed at the destruction of every meaning of human civilization. The Movement draws lessons and examples from all this. The present Zionist onslaught has also been preceded by Crusading raids from the West and other Tatar raids from the East. Just as the Moslems faced those raids and planned fighting and defeating them, they should be able to confront the Zionist invasion and defeat it. This is indeed no problem for the Almighty Allah, provided that the intentions are pure, the determination is true and that Moslems have benefited from past experiences, rid themselves of the effects of ideological invasion and followed the customs of their ancestors.

The Islamic Resistance Movement Is Composed of Soldiers

ARTICLE THIRTY-SIX

While paving its way, the Islamic Resistance Movement emphasizes time and again to all the sons of our people, to the Arab and Islamic nations, that it does not seek personal fame, material gain, or social prominence. It does not aim to compete against any one from among our people, or take his place. Nothing of the sort at all. It will not act against any of the sons of Moslems or those who are peaceful towards it from among non-Moslems, be they here or anywhere else. It will only serve as a support for all groupings and organizations operating against the Zionist enemy and its lackeys.

The Islamic Resistance Movement adopts Islam as its way of life. Islam is its creed and religion. Whoever takes Islam as his way of life, be it an organization, a grouping, a country or any other body, the Islamic Resistance Movement considers itself as their soldiers and nothing more.

We ask Allah to show us the right course, to make us an example to others and to judge between us and our people with truth. "O Lord, do thou judge between us and our nation with truth; for thou art the best judge." (Al Araf—Verse 89)

The last of our prayers will be praise to Allah, the Master of the Universe.

Consequences

Dedicated to the destruction of Israel and the creation of an Islamic state in Palestine, the new organization quickly acquired a broad following among Arabs. Its hard-line position eventually brought it into conflict with one of its founding organizations, the PLO, which in 1988 recognized Israel's right to exist. HAMAS's armed wing, the Izz al-Din al-Qassam forces, launched a campaign of terrorism against Israel, which quickly imprisoned the founder of HAMAS, Sheikh Ahmad Yasin, in 1991 and arrested hundreds of HAMAS activists.

HAMAS renounced the 1993 peace agreement between Israel and the PLO and, along with the Islamic Jihad group, subsequently stepped up its terror by using suicide bombers. The PLO and Israel responded with harsh security and punitive measures, although PLO chairman Yasser Arafat sought to include HAMAS in the political process, appointing some of its members to leadership positions in the Palestinian Authority.

In March 2005, HAMAS announced its readiness to join the PLO. As of July 2005, there was no word as to the status of this proposed union.

Source

Avalon Project at the Yale Law School. "Hamas Covenant 1988." Available online. URL: http://www.yale.edu/lawweb/avalon/mideast/hamas.htm. Accessed August 8, 2005.

RIO DECLARATION

TREATY AT A GLANCE

Completed
June 14, 1992, at Rio de Janeiro, Brazil

Signatories
Member nations of the United Nations
attending the Earth Summit

Overview
During June 1992, 178 countries met to map out strategies and policies for cleaning up the world's environment and encouraging environmentally sound economic development. At the so-called Earth Summit, the attending countries issued the Rio Declaration, a call to arms for the world's environmentalists, and produced a number of other documents, including the important Convention on Biodiversity.

Historical Background

Under the auspices of the United Nations, ten thousand delegates from 178 nations converged on Rio de Janeiro in an attempt to overcome political differences and economic self-interest so that planetary policies for the environment could be developed. The result of the summit was historic, hopeful, and disappointing at the same time. The delegates produced an 800-page blueprint for the environmentally responsible development of third world countries, international legislation to preserve ecological diversity and to combat global warming, and a nonbinding declaration of "ecoprinciples," the Rio Declaration.

Terms

The Declaration read:

The Rio Declaration on Environment and Development (1992)

Preamble

The United Nations Conference on Environment and Development,

Having met at Rio de Janeiro from 3 to 14 June 1992,

Reaffirming the Declaration of the United Nations Conference on the Human Environment, adopted at Stockholm on 16 June 1972, and seeking to build upon it,

With the goal of establishing a new and equitable global partnership through the creation of new levels of cooperation among States, key sectors of societies and people,

Working towards international agreements which respect the interests of all and protect the integrity of the global environmental and developmental system,

Recognizing the integral and interdependent nature of the Earth, our home,

Proclaims that:

PRINCIPLE 1

Human beings are at the centre of concerns for sustainable development.

They are entitled to a healthy and productive life in harmony with nature.

PRINCIPLE 2

States have, in accordance with the Charter of the United Nations and the principles of international law, the sovereign right to exploit their own resources pursuant to their own environmental and developmental policies, and the responsibility to ensure that activities within their jurisdiction or control do not cause damage to the environment of other States or of areas beyond the limits of national jurisdiction.

PRINCIPLE 3

The right to development must be fulfilled so as to equitably meet developmental and environmental needs of present and future generations.

PRINCIPLE 4

In order to achieve sustainable development, environmental protection shall constitute an integral part of the development process and cannot be considered in isolation from it.

PRINCIPLE 5

All States and all people shall cooperate in the essential task of eradicating poverty as an indispensable requirement for sustainable development, in order to decrease the disparities in standards of living and better meet the needs of the majority of the people of the world.

PRINCIPLE 6

The special situation and needs of developing countries, particularly the least developed and those most environmentally vulnerable, shall be given special priority. International actions in the field of environment and development should also address the interests and needs of all countries.

PRINCIPLE 7

States shall cooperate in a spirit of global partnership to conserve, protect and restore the health and integrity of the Earth's ecosystem. In view of the different contributions to global environmental degradation, States have common but differentiated responsibilities. The developed countries acknowledge the responsibility that they bear in the international pursuit of sustainable development in view of the pressures their societies place on the global environment and of the technologies and financial resources they command.

PRINCIPLE 8

To achieve sustainable development and a higher quality of life for all people, States should reduce and eliminate unsustainable patterns of production and consumption and promote appropriate demographic policies.

PRINCIPLE 9

States should cooperate to strengthen endogenous capacity-building for sustainable development by improving scientific understanding through exchanges of scientific and technological knowledge, and by enhancing the development, adaptation, diffusion and transfer of technologies, including new and innovative technologies.

PRINCIPLE 10

Environmental issues are best handled with the participation of all concerned citizens, at the relevant level. At the national level, each individual shall have appropriate access to information concerning the environment that is held by public authorities, including information on hazardous materials and activities in their communities, and the opportunity to participate in decision-making processes. States shall facilitate and encourage public awareness and participation by making information widely available. Effective access to judicial and administrative proceedings, including redress and remedy, shall be provided.

PRINCIPLE 11

States shall enact effective environmental legislation. Environmental standards, management objectives and priorities should reflect the environmental and developmental context to which they apply. Standards applied by some countries may be inappropriate and of unwarranted economic and social cost to other countries, in particular developing countries.

PRINCIPLE 12

States should cooperate to promote a supportive and open international economic system that would lead to economic growth and sustainable development in all countries, to better address the problems of environmental degradation. Trade policy measures for environmental purposes should not constitute a means of arbitrary or unjustifiable discrimination or a disguised restriction on international trade. Unilateral actions to deal with environmental challenges outside the jurisdiction of the importing country should be avoided. Environmental measures addressing transboundary or global environmental problems should, as far as possible, be based on an international consensus.

PRINCIPLE 13

States shall develop national law regarding liability and compensation for the victims of pollution and other environmental damage. States shall also cooperate in an expeditious and more determined manner to develop further international law regarding liability and compensation for adverse effects of environmental damage caused by activities within their jurisdiction or control to areas beyond their jurisdiction.

PRINCIPLE 14

States should effectively cooperate to discourage or prevent the relocation and transfer to other States of any activities and substances that cause severe environmental degradation or are found to be harmful to human health.

PRINCIPLE 15

In order to protect the environment, the precautionary approach shall be widely applied by States according to their capabilities. Where there are threats of serious or irreversible damage, lack of full scientific certainty shall not be used as a reason for postponing cost-effective measures to prevent environmental degradation.

PRINCIPLE 16

National authorities should endeavour to promote the internalization of environmental costs and the use of economic instruments, taking into account the approach that the polluter should, in principle, bear the cost of pollution, with due regard to the public interest and without distorting international trade and investment.

PRINCIPLE 17

Environmental impact assessment, as a national instrument, shall be undertaken for proposed activities that are likely to have a significant adverse impact on the environment and are subject to a decision of a competent national authority.

PRINCIPLE 18

States shall immediately notify other States of any natural disasters or other emergencies that are likely to produce sudden harmful effects on the environment of those States. Every effort shall be made by the international community to help States so afflicted.

PRINCIPLE 19

States shall provide prior and timely notification and relevant information to potentially affected States on activities that may have a significant adverse transboundary environmental effect and shall consult with those States at an early stage and in good faith.

PRINCIPLE 20

Women have a vital role in environmental management and development. Their full participation is therefore essential to achieve sustainable development.

PRINCIPLE 21

The creativity, ideals and courage of the youth of the world should be mobilized to forge a global partnership in order to achieve sustainable development and ensure a better future for all.

PRINCIPLE 22

Indigenous people and their communities, and other local communities, have a vital role in environmental management and development because of their knowledge and traditional practices. States should recognize and duly support their identity, culture and interests and enable their effective participation in the achievement of sustainable development.

PRINCIPLE 23

The environment and natural resources of people under oppression, domination and occupation shall be protected.

PRINCIPLE 24

Warfare is inherently destructive of sustainable development. States shall therefore respect international law providing protection for the environment in times of armed conflict and cooperate in its further development, as necessary.

PRINCIPLE 25

Peace, development and environmental protection are interdependent and indivisible.

PRINCIPLE 26

States shall resolve all their environmental disputes peacefully and by appropriate means in accordance with the Charter of the United Nations.

PRINCIPLE 27

States and people shall cooperate in good faith and in a spirit of partnership in the fulfilment of the principles embodied in this Declaration and in the further development of international law in the field of sustainable development.

Consequences

While the Convention on Biodiversity was arguably the most important accomplishment of the summit, the press was more interested in global warming. Summit participants developed an accord whereby nations would abstain from using substances that harm the ozone layer and would act to reduce the production of so-called greenhouse gases, essentially the products of combustion created by industry and automobiles, which act to insulate the surface of the earth, preventing the escape of infrared radiation and therefore tending to warm the earth's surface. This would lead to ecological damage, including flooding caused by the partial melting of the polar ice caps.

In spirit, the Earth Summit was epoch making. For the first time, the nations of the world assembled in the belief that despite the exclusivity of their political borders, they all shared the same planet and therefore had a profound common cause. However, most of the resolutions arrived at were voluntary, nonbinding, and so vague as to be open to a wide range of interpretation. Most disappointing was the role of the United States, which—operating under a president, George Herbert Walker Bush, at odds even with the delegates his government sent to the conference—seemed to participate in the summit grudgingly and abrogated much of its traditional leadership role in environmental matters.

Still, the historical thrust of the summit was significant: for the first time ever, most of the nations of the world pledged to take into account global environmental concerns when creating internal economic policy.

The FRAMEWORK CONVENTION ON CLIMATE CHANGE, the CONVENTION ON BIOLOGICAL DIVERSITY, and a nonbinding "Statement on Forest Principles" all flowed from the Rio Declaration.

Source

United Nations Environment Programme, "Rio Declaration on Environment and Development." Available online. URL: http://www.unep.org/Documents/Default.asp?DocumentID=78&ArticleID=1163. Accessed January 4, 2005.

VIENNA DECLARATION ON HUMAN RIGHTS

TREATY AT A GLANCE

Completed
June 25, 1993, at Vienna

Signatories
Member states of the United Nations

Overview
The World Conference on Human Rights produced a declaration that sought to sum up the progress made on this issue in the nearly 50 years since the end of World War II.

Historical Background

The horrible human rights abuses of the Nazis during World War II created a real legacy of concern in the postwar world for the protection of such rights. In addition to producing the GENEVA CONVENTION ON THE PREVENTION AND PUNISHMENT OF THE CRIME OF GENOCIDE in 1948, the United Nations also that year set out a catalog of protections in the Universal Declaration of Human Rights, which was adopted without dissent on December 10. Representing scarcely less than the sum of all the traditional political and civil rights of national constitutions and legal systems, the declaration was not a treaty in any sense. Rather than establishing enforceable legal obligations, it meant to reiterate and proclaim a common standard of dignity and respect for all nations and all peoples. Some measure of the difficulty of dealing with what the American Declaration of Independence had called "self-evident" truths, it took 18 years from the time the document was adopted and completed for signature to its ratification by the United Nations, and in those two decades the Universal Declaration acquired more judicial status than the framers had intended: it became widely used, even by national courts, as a means of judging compliance with human rights obligations by U.N. member states.

The postwar concern with human rights was evident at a global level even outside the United Nations, most notably in the proceedings of the Conference on Security and Cooperation in Europe. A summit of the WARSAW PACT countries, the NORTH ATLANTIC TREATY Organization nations, and 13 nonaligned European states held in Helsinki during the détente years of 1973 and 1975, the conference produced a mutually satisfactory definition of peace and stability between East and West that would have been impossible at the height of the Cold War. At the summit, the Soviet Union was especially interested in securing recognition for its western frontiers, established at the close of World War II. The NATO countries, with no realistic claims to territory in return, pressed for concessions from the Soviets on human rights and their attendant freedoms. The Helsinki Final Act, like the Universal Declaration of Human Rights, was not a treaty and was not intended to be a legally binding instrument. Nevertheless, as with the Universal Declaration, its human rights provisions came to serve as yardsticks for external scrutiny of violations of those rights and for the appropriate responses to those violations.

Human rights continued to be both an important focus of international relations and a problem for diplomacy, especially during the administration of U.S. president Jimmy Carter, who made them the touchstone of American foreign policy—and paid the price for doing so. Even through the administrations of hardliners such as Ronald Reagan and George Bush, U.S. diplomats continued to pay lip service to human rights when dealing with other nations. Trade relations with China, for example, which the United States generally considered a major violator of such rights, were often complicated by these concerns. Despite the damage done to America's claim to any moral high ground by the Vietnam War, the United States nevertheless managed in general to establish itself as one of the world's champions of such rights.

So much emphasis had come to be placed on the issue that by 1993 it was perhaps inevitable that a World Conference on Human Rights should be convened to attempt to consolidate the gains of the four decades since World War II.

Terms

Held in Vienna, the United Nations–sponsored conference issued a declaration that attempted to describe the basic human rights of a new international era. In doing so, it produced a document that summarizes four decades of human rights and humanitarian treaties and conventions. It is quoted here in full:

୬

The World Conference on Human Rights,

Considering that the promotion and protection of human rights is a matter of priority for the international community, and that the Conference affords a unique opportunity to carry out a comprehensive analysis of the international human rights system and of the machinery for the protection of human rights, in order to enhance and thus promote a fuller observance of those rights, in a just and balanced manner,

Recognizing and affirming that all human rights derive from the dignity and worth inherent in the human person, and that the human person is the central subject of human rights and fundamental freedoms, and consequently should be the principal beneficiary and should participate actively in the realization of these rights and freedoms,

Reaffirming their commitment to the purposes and principles contained in the Charter of the United Nations and the Universal Declaration of Human Rights,

Reaffirming the commitment contained in Article 56 of the Charter of the United Nations to take joint and separate action, placing proper emphasis on developing effective international cooperation for the realization of the purposes set out in Article 55, including universal respect for, and observance of, human rights and fundamental freedoms for all,

Emphasizing the responsibilities of all States, in conformity with the Charter of the United Nations, to develop and encourage respect for human rights and fundamental freedoms for all, without distinction as to race, sex, language or religion,

Recalling the Preamble to the Charter of the United Nations, in particular the determination to reaffirm faith in fundamental human rights, in the dignity and worth of the human person, and in the equal rights of men and women and of nations large and small,

Recalling also the determination expressed in the Preamble of the Charter of the United Nations to save succeeding generations from the scourge of war, to establish conditions under which justice and respect for obligations arising from treaties and other sources of international law can be maintained, to promote social progress and better standards of life in larger freedom, to practice tolerance and good neighbourliness, and to employ international machinery for the promotion of the economic and social advancement of all peoples,

Emphasizing that the Universal Declaration of Human Rights, which constitutes a common standard of achievement for all peoples and all nations, is the source of inspiration and has been the basis for the United Nations in making advances in standard setting as contained in the existing international human rights instruments, in particular the International Covenant on Civil and Political Rights and the International Covenant on Economic, Social and Cultural Rights,

Considering the major changes taking place on the international scene and the aspirations of all the peoples for an international order based on the principles enshrined in the Charter of the United Nations, including promoting and encouraging respect for human rights and fundamental freedoms for all and respect for the principle of equal rights and self-determination of peoples, peace, democracy, justice, equality, rule of law, pluralism, development, better standards of living and solidarity,

Deeply concerned by various forms of discrimination and violence, to which women continue to be exposed all over the world,

Recognizing that the activities of the United Nations in the field of human rights should be rationalized and enhanced in order to strengthen the United Nations machinery in this field and to further the objectives of universal respect for observance of international human rights standards,

Having taken into account the Declarations adopted by the three regional meetings at Tunis, San José and Bangkok and the contributions made by Governments, and bearing in mind the suggestions made by intergovernmental and non-governmental organizations, as well as the studies prepared by independent experts during the preparatory process leading to the World Conference on Human Rights,

Welcoming the International Year of the World's Indigenous People 1993 as a reaffirmation of the commitment of the international community to ensure their enjoyment of all human rights and fundamental freedoms and to respect the value and diversity of their cultures and identities,

Recognizing also that the international community should devise ways and means to remove the current obstacles and meet challenges to the full realization of all human rights and to prevent the continuation of human rights violations resulting thereof throughout the world,

Invoking the spirit of our age and the realities of our time which call upon the peoples of the world and all States Members of the United Nations to rededicate themselves to the global task of promoting and protecting all human rights and fundamental freedoms so as to secure full and universal enjoyment of these rights,

Determined to take new steps forward in the commitment of the international community with a view to achieving substantial progress in human rights endeavours by an increased and sustained effort of international cooperation and solidarity,

Solemnly adopts the Vienna Declaration and Programme of Action.

I

1. The World Conference on Human Rights reaffirms the solemn commitment of all States to fulfil their obligations to promote universal respect for, and observance and protection of, all human rights and fundamental freedoms for all in accordance with the Charter of the United Nations, other instruments relating to human rights, and international law. The universal nature of these rights and freedoms is beyond question.

In this framework, enhancement of international cooperation in the field of human rights is essential for the full achievement of the purposes of the United Nations.

Human rights and fundamental freedoms are the birthright of all human beings; their protection and promotion is the first responsibility of Governments.

2. All peoples have the right of self-determination. By virtue of that right they freely determine their political status, and freely pursue their economic, social and cultural development.

Taking into account the particular situation of peoples under colonial or other forms of alien domination or foreign occupation, the World Conference on Human Rights recognizes the right of peoples to take any legitimate action, in accordance with the Charter of the United Nations, to realize their inalienable right of self-determination. The World Conference on Human Rights considers the denial of the right of self- determination as a violation of human rights and underlines the importance of the effective realization of this right.

In accordance with the Declaration on Principles of International Law concerning Friendly Relations and Cooperation Among States in accordance with the Charter of the United Nations, this shall not be construed as authorizing or encouraging any action which would dismember or impair, totally or in part, the territorial integrity or political unity of sovereign and independent States conducting themselves in compliance with the principle of equal rights and self- determination of peoples and thus possessed of a Government representing the whole people belonging to the territory without distinction of any kind.

3. Effective international measures to guarantee and monitor the implementation of human rights standards should be taken in respect of people under foreign occupation, and effective legal protection against the violation of their human rights should be provided, in accordance with human rights norms and international law, particularly the Geneva Convention relative to the Protection of Civilian Persons in Time of War, of 14 August 1949, and other applicable norms of humanitarian law.

4. The promotion and protection of all human rights and fundamental freedoms must be considered as a priority objective of the United Nations in accordance with its purposes and principles, in particular the purpose of international cooperation. In the framework of these purposes and principles, the promotion and protection of all human rights is a legitimate concern of the international community. The organs and specialized agencies related to human rights should therefore further enhance the coordination of their activities based on the consistent and objective application of international human rights instruments.

5. All human rights are universal, indivisible and interdependent and interrelated. The international community must treat human rights globally in a fair and equal manner, on the same footing, and with the same emphasis. While the significance of national and regional particularities and various historical, cultural and religious backgrounds must be borne in mind, it is the duty of States, regardless of their political, economic and cultural systems, to promote and protect all human rights and fundamental freedoms.

6. The efforts of the United Nations system towards the universal respect for, and observance of, human rights and fundamental freedoms for all, contribute to the stability and well-being necessary for peaceful and friendly relations among nations, and to improved conditions for peace and security as well as social and economic development, in conformity with the Charter of the United Nations.

7. The processes of promoting and protecting human rights should be conducted in conformity with the purposes and principles of the Charter of the United Nations, and international law.

8. Democracy, development and respect for human rights and fundamental freedoms are interdependent and mutually reinforcing. Democracy is based on the freely expressed will of the people to determine their own political, economic, social and cultural systems and their full participation in all aspects of their lives. In the context of the above, the promotion and protection of human rights and fundamental freedoms at the national and international levels should be universal and conducted without conditions attached. The international community should support the strengthening and promoting of democracy, development and respect for human rights and fundamental freedoms in the entire world.

9. The World Conference on Human Rights reaffirms that least developed countries committed to the process of democratization and economic reforms, many of which are in Africa, should be supported by the international community in order to succeed in their transition to democracy and economic development.

10. The World Conference on Human Rights reaffirms the right to development, as established in the Declaration on the Right to Development, as a universal and inalienable right and an integral part of fundamental human rights.

As stated in the Declaration on the Right to Development, the human person is the central subject of development.

While development facilitates the enjoyment of all human rights, the lack of development may not be invoked to justify the abridgement of internationally recognized human rights.

States should cooperate with each other in ensuring development and eliminating obstacles to development. The international community should promote an effective international cooperation for the realization of the right to development and the elimination of obstacles to development.

Lasting progress towards the implementation of the right to development requires effective development policies at the national level, as well as equitable economic relations and a favourable economic environment at the international level.

11. The right to development should be fulfilled so as to meet equitably the developmental and environmental needs of present and future generations. The World Conference on Human Rights recognizes that illicit dumping of toxic and dangerous substances and waste potentially constitutes a serious threat to the human rights to life and health of everyone.

Consequently, the World Conference on Human Rights calls on all States to adopt and vigorously implement existing conventions relating to the dumping of toxic and dangerous products and waste and to cooperate in the prevention of illicit dumping.

Everyone has the right to enjoy the benefits of scientific progress and its applications. The World Conference on Human Rights notes that certain advances, notably in the biomedical and life sciences as well as in information technology, may have potentially adverse consequences for the integrity, dignity and human rights of the individual, and calls for international cooperation to ensure that human rights and dignity are fully respected in this area of universal concern.

12. The World Conference on Human Rights calls upon the international community to make all efforts to help alleviate the external debt burden of developing countries, in order to supplement the efforts of the Governments of such countries to

attain the full realization of the economic, social and cultural rights of their people.

13. There is a need for States and international organizations, in cooperation with non-governmental organizations, to create favourable conditions at the national, regional and international levels to ensure the full and effective enjoyment of human rights. States should eliminate all violations of human rights and their causes, as well as obstacles to the enjoyment of these rights.

14. The existence of widespread extreme poverty inhibits the full and effective enjoyment of human rights; its immediate alleviation and eventual elimination must remain a high priority for the international community.

15. Respect for human rights and for fundamental freedoms without distinction of any kind is a fundamental rule of international human rights law. The speedy and comprehensive elimination of all forms of racism and racial discrimination, xenophobia and related intolerance is a priority task for the international community. Governments should take effective measures to prevent and combat them. Groups, institutions, intergovernmental and non-governmental organizations and individuals are urged to intensify their efforts in cooperating and coordinating their activities against these evils.

16. The World Conference on Human Rights welcomes the progress made in dismantling apartheid and calls upon the international community and the United Nations system to assist in this process.

The World Conference on Human Rights also deplores the continuing acts of violence aimed at undermining the quest for a peaceful dismantling of apartheid.

17. The acts, methods and practices of terrorism in all its forms and manifestations as well as linkage in some countries to drug trafficking are activities aimed at the destruction of human rights, fundamental freedoms and democracy, threatening territorial integrity, security of States and destabilizing legitimately constituted Governments. The international community should take the necessary steps to enhance cooperation to prevent and combat terrorism.

18. The human rights of women and of the girl-child are an inalienable, integral and indivisible part of universal human rights. The full and equal participation of women in political, civil, economic, social and cultural life, at the national, regional and international levels, and the eradication of all forms of discrimination on grounds of sex are priority objectives of the international community.

Gender-based violence and all forms of sexual harassment and exploitation, including those resulting from cultural prejudice and international trafficking, are incompatible with the dignity and worth of the human person, and must be eliminated. This can be achieved by legal measures and through national action and international cooperation in such fields as economic and social development, education, safe maternity and health care, and social support.

The human rights of women should form an integral part of the United Nations human rights activities, including the promotion of all human rights instruments relating to women.

The World Conference on Human Rights urges Governments, institutions, intergovernmental and non-governmental organizations to intensify their efforts for the protection and promotion of human rights of women and the girl-child.

19. Considering the importance of the promotion and protection of the rights of persons belonging to minorities and the contribution of such promotion and protection to the political and social stability of the States in which such persons live,

The World Conference on Human Rights reaffirms the obligation of States to ensure that persons belonging to minorities may exercise fully and effectively all human rights and fundamental freedoms without any discrimination and in full equality before the law in accordance with the Declaration on the Rights of Persons Belonging to National or Ethnic, Religious and Linguistic Minorities.

The persons belonging to minorities have the right to enjoy their own culture, to profess and practise their own religion and to use their own language in private and in public, freely and without interference or any form of discrimination.

20. The World Conference on Human Rights recognizes the inherent dignity and the unique contribution of indigenous people to the development and plurality of society and strongly reaffirms the commitment of the international community to their economic, social and cultural well-being and their enjoyment of the fruits of sustainable development. States should ensure the full and free participation of indigenous people in all aspects of society, in particular in matters of concern to them. Considering the importance of the promotion and protection of the rights of indigenous people, and the contribution of such promotion and protection to the political and social stability of the States in which such people live, States should, in accordance with international law, take concerted positive steps to ensure respect for all human rights and fundamental freedoms of indigenous people, on the basis of equality and non-discrimination, and recognize the value and diversity of their distinct identities, cultures and social organization.

21. The World Conference on Human Rights, welcoming the early ratification of the Convention on the Rights of the Child by a large number of States and noting the recognition of the human rights of children in the World Declaration on the Survival, Protection and Development of Children and Plan of Action adopted by the World Summit for Children, urges universal ratification of the Convention by 1995 and its effective implementation by States parties through the adoption of all the necessary legislative, administrative and other measures and the allocation to the maximum extent of the available resources. In all actions concerning children, non-discrimination and the best interest of the child should be primary considerations and the views of the child given due weight. National and international mechanisms and programmes should be strengthened for the defence and protection of children, in particular, the girl-child, abandoned children, street children, economically and sexually exploited children, including through child pornography, child prostitution or sale of organs, children victims of diseases including acquired immunodeficiency syndrome, refugee and displaced children, children in detention, children in armed conflict, as well as children victims of famine and drought and other emergencies. International cooperation and solidarity should be promoted to support the implementation of the Convention and the rights of the child should be a priority in the United Nations system-wide action on human rights.

The World Conference on Human Rights also stresses that the child for the full and harmonious development of his or her personality should grow up in a family environment which accordingly merits broader protection.

22. Special attention needs to be paid to ensuring non-discrimination, and the equal enjoyment of all human rights and fundamental freedoms by disabled persons, including their active participation in all aspects of society.

23. The World Conference on Human Rights reaffirms that everyone, without distinction of any kind, is entitled to the right to seek and to enjoy in other countries asylum from persecution, as well as the right to return to one's own country. In this respect it stresses the importance of the Universal Declaration of Human Rights, the 1951 Convention relating to the Status of Refugees, its 1967 Protocol and regional instruments. It expresses its appreciation to States that continue to admit and host large numbers of refugees in their territories, and to the Office of the United Nations High Commissioner for Refugees for its dedication to its task. It also expresses its appreciation to the United Nations Relief and Works Agency for Palestine Refugees in the Near East.

The World Conference on Human Rights recognizes that gross violations of human rights, including in armed conflicts, are among the multiple and complex factors leading to displacement of people.

The World Conference on Human Rights recognizes that, in view of the complexities of the global refugee crisis and in accordance with the Charter of the United Nations, relevant international instruments and international solidarity and in the spirit of burden-sharing, a comprehensive approach by the international community is needed in coordination and cooperation with the countries concerned and relevant organizations, bearing in mind the mandate of the United Nations High Commissioner for Refugees. This should include the development of strategies to address the root causes and effects of movements of refugees and other displaced persons, the strengthening of emergency preparedness and response mechanisms, the provision of effective protection and assistance, bearing in mind the special needs of women and children, as well as the achievement of durable solutions, primarily through the preferred solution of dignified and safe voluntary repatriation, including solutions such as those adopted by the international refugee conferences. The World Conference on Human Rights underlines the responsibilities of States, particularly as they relate to the countries of origin.

In the light of the comprehensive approach, the World Conference on Human Rights emphasizes the importance of giving special attention including through intergovernmental and humanitarian organizations and finding lasting solutions to questions related to internally displaced persons including their voluntary and safe return and rehabilitation.

In accordance with the Charter of the United Nations and the principles of humanitarian law, the World Conference on Human Rights further emphasizes the importance of and the need for humanitarian assistance to victims of all natural and man-made disasters.

24. Great importance must be given to the promotion and protection of the human rights of persons belonging to groups which have been rendered vulnerable, including migrant workers, the elimination of all forms of discrimination against them, and the strengthening and more effective implementation of existing human rights instruments. States have an obligation to create and maintain adequate measures at the national level, in particular in the fields of education, health and social support, for the promotion and protection of the rights of persons in vulnerable sectors of their populations and to ensure the participation of those among them who are interested in finding a solution to their own problems.

25. The World Conference on Human Rights affirms that extreme poverty and social exclusion constitute a violation of human dignity and that urgent steps are necessary to achieve better knowledge of extreme poverty and its causes, including those related to the problem of development, in order to promote the human rights of the poorest, and to put an end to extreme poverty and social exclusion and to promote the enjoyment of the fruits of social progress. It is essential for States to foster participation by the poorest people in the decision-making process by the community in which they live, the promotion of human rights and efforts to combat extreme poverty.

26. The World Conference on Human Rights welcomes the progress made in the codification of human rights instruments, which is a dynamic and evolving process, and urges the universal ratification of human rights treaties. All States are encouraged to accede to these international instruments; all States are encouraged to avoid, as far as possible, the resort to reservations.

27. Every State should provide an effective framework of remedies to redress human rights grievances or violations. The administration of justice, including law enforcement and prosecutorial agencies and, especially, an independent judiciary and legal profession in full conformity with applicable standards contained in international human rights instruments, are essential to the full and non-discriminatory realization of human rights and indispensable to the processes of democracy and sustainable development. In this context, institutions concerned with the administration of justice should be properly funded, and an increased level of both technical and financial assistance should be provided by the international community. It is incumbent upon the United Nations to make use of special programmes of advisory services on a priority basis for the achievement of a strong and independent administration of justice.

28. The World Conference on Human Rights expresses its dismay at massive violations of human rights especially in the form of genocide, "ethnic cleansing" and systematic rape of women in war situations, creating mass exodus of refugees and displaced persons. While strongly condemning such abhorrent practices it reiterates the call that perpetrators of such crimes be punished and such practices immediately stopped.

29. The World Conference on Human Rights expresses grave concern about continuing human rights violations in all parts of the world in disregard of standards as contained in international human rights instruments and international humanitarian law and about the lack of sufficient and effective remedies for the victims.

The World Conference on Human Rights is deeply concerned about violations of human rights during armed conflicts, affecting the civilian population, especially women, children, the elderly and the disabled. The Conference therefore calls upon States and all parties to armed conflicts strictly to observe international humanitarian law, as set forth in the Geneva Conventions of 1949 and other rules and principles of international law, as well as minimum standards for protection of human rights, as laid down in international conventions.

The World Conference on Human Rights reaffirms the right of the victims to be assisted by humanitarian organizations, as set forth in the Geneva Conventions of 1949 and other relevant instruments of international humanitarian law, and calls for the safe and timely access for such assistance.

30. The World Conference on Human Rights also expresses its dismay and condemnation that gross and systematic violations and situations that constitute serious obstacles to the full enjoyment of all human rights continue to occur in different parts of the world. Such violations and obstacles include, as well as torture and cruel, inhuman and degrading treatment or punishment, summary and arbitrary executions, disappearances, arbitrary detentions, all forms of racism, racial discrimination and apartheid, foreign occupation and alien domination, xenophobia, poverty, hunger and other denials of economic, social and cultural rights, religious intolerance, terrorism, discrimination against women and lack of the rule of law.

31. The World Conference on Human Rights calls upon States to refrain from any unilateral measure not in accordance with international law and the Charter of the United Nations that creates obstacles to trade relations among States and impedes the full realization of the human rights set forth in the Universal Declaration of Human Rights and international human rights instruments, in particular the rights of everyone to a standard of living adequate for their health and well-being, including food and medical care, housing and the necessary social services. The World Conference on Human Rights affirms that food should not be used as a tool for political pressure.

32. The World Conference on Human Rights reaffirms the importance of ensuring the universality, objectivity and non-selectivity of the consideration of human rights issues.

33. The World Conference on Human Rights reaffirms that States are duty-bound, as stipulated in the Universal Declaration of Human Rights and the International Covenant on Economic, Social and Cultural Rights and in other international human rights instruments, to ensure that education is aimed at strengthening the respect of human rights and fundamental freedoms. The World Conference on Human Rights emphasizes the importance of incorporating the subject of human rights education programmes and calls upon States to do so. Education should promote understanding, tolerance, peace and friendly relations between the nations and all racial or religious groups and encourage the development of United Nations activities in pursuance of these objectives. Therefore, education on human rights and the dissemination of proper information, both theoretical and practical, play an important role in the promotion and respect of human rights with regard to all individuals without distinction of any kind such as race, sex, language or religion, and this should be integrated in the education policies at the national as well as international levels. The World Conference on Human Rights notes that resource constraints and institutional inadequacies may impede the immediate realization of these objectives.

34. Increased efforts should be made to assist countries which so request to create the conditions whereby each individual can enjoy universal human rights and fundamental freedoms. Governments, the United Nations system as well as other multilateral organizations are urged to increase considerably the resources allocated to programmes aiming at the establishment and strengthening of national legislation, national institutions

and related infrastructures which uphold the rule of law and democracy, electoral assistance, human rights awareness through training, teaching and education, popular participation and civil society.

The programmes of advisory services and technical cooperation under the Centre for Human Rights should be strengthened as well as made more efficient and transparent and thus become a major contribution to improving respect for human rights. States are called upon to increase their contributions to these programmes, both through promoting a larger allocation from the United Nations regular budget, and through voluntary contributions.

35. The full and effective implementation of United Nations activities to promote and protect human rights must reflect the high importance accorded to human rights by the Charter of the United Nations and the demands of the United Nations human rights activities, as mandated by Member States. To this end, United Nations human rights activities should be provided with increased resources.

36. The World Conference on Human Rights reaffirms the important and constructive role played by national institutions for the promotion and protection of human rights, in particular in their advisory capacity to the competent authorities, their role in remedying human rights violations, in the dissemination of human rights information, and education in human rights.

The World Conference on Human Rights encourages the establishment and strengthening of national institutions, having regard to the "Principles relating to the status of national institutions" and recognizing that it is the right of each State to choose the framework which is best suited to its particular needs at the national level.

37. Regional arrangements play a fundamental role in promoting and protecting human rights. They should reinforce universal human rights standards, as contained in international human rights instruments, and their protection. The World Conference on Human Rights endorses efforts under way to strengthen these arrangements and to increase their effectiveness, while at the same time stressing the importance of cooperation with the United Nations human rights activities.

The World Conference on Human Rights reiterates the need to consider the possibility of establishing regional and sub-regional arrangements for the promotion and protection of human rights where they do not already exist.

38. The World Conference on Human Rights recognizes the important role of non-governmental organizations in the promotion of all human rights and in humanitarian activities at national, regional and international levels. The World Conference on Human Rights appreciates their contribution to increasing public awareness of human rights issues, to the conduct of education, training and research in this field, and to the promotion and protection of all human rights and fundamental freedoms. While recognizing that the primary responsibility for standard-setting lies with States, the conference also appreciates the contribution of non-governmental organizations to this process. In this respect, the World Conference on Human Rights emphasizes the importance of continued dialogue and cooperation between Governments and non-governmental organizations. Non-governmental organizations and their members genuinely involved in the field of human rights should enjoy the rights and freedoms recognized in the Universal Dec-

laration of Human Rights, and the protection of the national law. These rights and freedoms may not be exercised contrary to the purposes and principles of the United Nations. Non-governmental organizations should be free to carry out their human rights activities, without interference, within the framework of national law and the Universal Declaration of Human Rights.

39. Underlining the importance of objective, responsible and impartial information about human rights and humanitarian issues, the World Conference on Human Rights encourages the increased involvement of the media, for whom freedom and protection should be guaranteed within the framework of national law.

II

A. Increased Coordination on Human Rights within the United Nations System

1. The World Conference on Human Rights recommends increased coordination in support of human rights and fundamental freedoms within the United Nations system. To this end, the World Conference on Human Rights urges all United Nations organs, bodies and the specialized agencies whose activities deal with human rights to cooperate in order to strengthen, rationalize and streamline their activities, taking into account the need to avoid unnecessary duplication. The World Conference on Human Rights also recommends to the Secretary-General that high-level officials of relevant United Nations bodies and specialized agencies at their annual meeting, besides coordinating their activities, also assess the impact of their strategies and policies on the enjoyment of all human rights.

2. Furthermore, the World Conference on Human Rights calls on regional organizations and prominent international and regional finance and development institutions to assess also the impact of their policies and programmes on the enjoyment of human rights.

3. The World Conference on Human Rights recognizes that relevant specialized agencies and bodies and institutions of the United Nations system as well as other relevant intergovernmental organizations whose activities deal with human rights play a vital role in the formulation, promotion and implementation of human rights standards, within their respective mandates, and should take into account the outcome of the World Conference on Human Rights within their fields of competence.

4. The World Conference on Human Rights strongly recommends that a concerted effort be made to encourage and facilitate the ratification of and accession or succession to international human rights treaties and protocols adopted within the framework of the United Nations system with the aim of universal acceptance. The Secretary-General, in consultation with treaty bodies, should consider opening a dialogue with States not having acceded to these human rights treaties, in order to identify obstacles and to seek ways of overcoming them.

5. The World Conference on Human Rights encourages States to consider limiting the extent of any reservations they lodge to international human rights instruments, formulate any reservations as precisely and narrowly as possible, ensure that none is incompatible with the object and purpose of the relevant treaty and regularly review any reservations with a view to withdrawing them.

6. The World Conference on Human Rights, recognizing the need to maintain consistency with the high quality of exist-

ing international standards and to avoid proliferation of human rights instruments, reaffirms the guidelines relating to the elaboration of new international instruments contained in General Assembly resolution 41/120 of 4 December 1986 and calls on the United Nations human rights bodies, when considering the elaboration of new international standards, to keep those guidelines in mind, to consult with human rights treaty bodies on the necessity for drafting new standards and to request the Secretariat to carry out technical reviews of proposed new instruments.

7. The World Conference on Human Rights recommends that human rights officers be assigned if and when necessary to regional offices of the United Nations Organization with the purpose of disseminating information and offering training and other technical assistance in the field of human rights upon the request of concerned Member States. Human rights training for international civil servants who are assigned to work relating to human rights should be organized.

8. The World Conference on Human Rights welcomes the convening of emergency sessions of the Commission on Human Rights as a positive initiative and that other ways of responding to acute violations of human rights be considered by the relevant organs of the United Nations system.

RESOURCES

9. The World Conference on Human Rights, concerned by the growing disparity between the activities of the Centre for Human Rights and the human, financial and other resources available to carry them out, and bearing in mind the resources needed for other important United Nations programmes, requests the Secretary-General and the General Assembly to take immediate steps to increase substantially the resources for the human rights programme from within the existing and future regular budgets of the United Nations, and to take urgent steps to seek increased extrabudgetary resources.

10. Within this framework, an increased proportion of the regular budget should be allocated directly to the Centre for Human Rights to cover its costs and all other costs borne by the Centre for Human Rights, including those related to the United Nations human rights bodies. Voluntary funding of the Centre's technical cooperation activities should reinforce this enhanced budget; the World Conference on Human Rights calls for generous contributions to the existing trust funds.

11. The World Conference on Human Rights requests the Secretary-General and the General Assembly to provide sufficient human, financial and other resources to the Centre for Human Rights to enable it effectively, efficiently and expeditiously to carry out its activities.

12. The World Conference on Human Rights, noting the need to ensure that human and financial resources are available to carry out the human rights activities, as mandated by intergovernmental bodies, urges the Secretary-General, in accordance with Article 101 of the Charter of the United Nations, and Member States to adopt a coherent approach aimed at securing that resources commensurate to the increased mandates are allocated to the Secretariat. The World Conference on Human Rights invites the Secretary-General to consider whether adjustments to procedures in the programme budget cycle would be necessary or helpful to ensure the timely and effective implementation of human rights activities as mandated by Member States.

CENTRE FOR HUMAN RIGHTS

13. The World Conference on Human Rights stresses the importance of strengthening the United Nations Centre for Human Rights.

14. The Centre for Human Rights should play an important role in coordinating system-wide attention for human rights. The focal role of the Centre can best be realized if it is enabled to cooperate fully with other United Nations bodies and organs. The coordinating role of the Centre for Human Rights also implies that the office of the Centre for Human Rights in New York is strengthened.

15. The Centre for Human Rights should be assured adequate means for the system of thematic and country rapporteurs, experts, working groups and treaty bodies. Follow-up on recommendations should become a priority matter for consideration by the Commission on Human Rights.

16. The Centre for Human Rights should assume a larger role in the promotion of human rights. This role could be given shape through cooperation with Member States and by an enhanced programme of advisory services and technical assistance. The existing voluntary funds will have to be expanded substantially for these purposes and should be managed in a more efficient and coordinated way. All activities should follow strict and transparent project management rules and regular programme and project evaluations should be held periodically. To this end, the results of such evaluation exercises and other relevant information should be made available regularly. The Centre should, in particular, organize at least once a year information meetings open to all Member States and organizations directly involved in these projects and programmes.

ADAPTATION AND STRENGTHENING OF THE UNITED NATIONS MACHINERY FOR HUMAN RIGHTS, INCLUDING THE QUESTION OF THE ESTABLISHMENT OF A UNITED NATIONS HIGH COMMISSIONER FOR HUMAN RIGHTS

17. The World Conference on Human Rights recognizes the necessity for a continuing adaptation of the United Nations human rights machinery to the current and future needs in the promotion and protection of human rights, as reflected in the present Declaration and within the framework of a balanced and sustainable development for all people. In particular, the United Nations human rights organs should improve their coordination, efficiency and effectiveness.

18. The World Conference on Human Rights recommends to the General Assembly that when examining the report of the Conference at its forty-eighth session, it begin, as a matter of priority, consideration of the question of the establishment of a High Commissioner for Human Rights for the promotion and protection of all human rights.

B. Equality, Dignity and Tolerance

1. RACISM, RACIAL DISCRIMINATION, XENOPHOBIA AND OTHER FORMS OF INTOLERANCE

19. The World Conference on Human Rights considers the elimination of racism and racial discrimination, in particular in their institutionalized forms such as apartheid or resulting from doctrines of racial superiority or exclusivity or contemporary forms and manifestations of racism, as a primary objective for the international community and a worldwide promotion programme in the field of human rights. United Nations organs and

agencies should strengthen their efforts to implement such a programme of action related to the third decade to combat racism and racial discrimination as well as subsequent mandates to the same end. The World Conference on Human Rights strongly appeals to the international community to contribute generously to the Trust Fund for the Programme for the Decade for Action to Combat Racism and Racial Discrimination.

20. The World Conference on Human Rights urges all Governments to take immediate measures and to develop strong policies to prevent and combat all forms and manifestations of racism, xenophobia or related intolerance, where necessary by enactment of appropriate legislation, including penal measures, and by the establishment of national institutions to combat such phenomena.

21. The World Conference on Human Rights welcomes the decision of the Commission on Human Rights to appoint a Special Rapporteur on contemporary forms of racism, racial discrimination, xenophobia and related intolerance. The World Conference on Human Rights also appeals to all States parties to the International Convention on the Elimination of All Forms of Racial Discrimination to consider making the declaration under article 14 of the Convention.

22. The World Conference on Human Rights calls upon all Governments to take all appropriate measures in compliance with their international obligations and with due regard to their respective legal systems to counter intolerance and related violence based on religion or belief, including practices of discrimination against women and including the desecration of religious sites, recognizing that every individual has the right to freedom of thought, conscience, expression and religion. The Conference also invites all States to put into practice the provisions of the Declaration on the Elimination of All Forms of Intolerance and of Discrimination Based on Religion or Belief.

23. The World Conference on Human Rights stresses that all persons who perpetrate or authorize criminal acts associated with ethnic cleansing are individually responsible and accountable for such human rights violations, and that the international community should exert every effort to bring those legally responsible for such violations to justice.

24. The World Conference on Human Rights calls on all States to take immediate measures, individually and collectively, to combat the practice of ethnic cleansing to bring it quickly to an end. Victims of the abhorrent practice of ethnic cleansing are entitled to appropriate and effective remedies.

2. PERSONS BELONGING TO NATIONAL OR ETHNIC, RELIGIOUS AND LINGUISTIC MINORITIES

25. The World Conference on Human Rights calls on the Commission on Human Rights to examine ways and means to promote and protect effectively the rights of persons belonging to minorities as set out in the Declaration on the Rights of Persons belonging to National or Ethnic, Religious and Linguistic Minorities. In this context, the World Conference on Human Rights calls upon the Centre for Human Rights to provide, at the request of Governments concerned and as part of its programme of advisory services and technical assistance, qualified expertise on minority issues and human rights, as well as on the prevention and resolution of disputes, to assist in existing or potential situations involving minorities.

26. The World Conference on Human Rights urges States and the international community to promote and protect the

rights of persons belonging to national or ethnic, religious and linguistic minorities in accordance with the Declaration on the Rights of Persons belonging to National or Ethnic, Religious and Linguistic Minorities.

27. Measures to be taken, where appropriate, should include facilitation of their full participation in all aspects of the political, economic, social, religious and cultural life of society and in the economic progress and development in their country.

INDIGENOUS PEOPLE

28. The World Conference on Human Rights calls on the Working Group on Indigenous Populations of the Sub-Commission on Prevention of Discrimination and Protection of Minorities to complete the drafting of a declaration on the rights of indigenous people at its eleventh session.

29. The World Conference on Human Rights recommends that the Commission on Human Rights consider the renewal and updating of the mandate of the Working Group on Indigenous Populations upon completion of the drafting of a declaration on the rights of indigenous people.

30. The World Conference on Human Rights also recommends that advisory services and technical assistance programmes within the United Nations system respond positively to requests by States for assistance which would be of direct benefit to indigenous people. The World Conference on Human Rights further recommends that adequate human and financial resources be made available to the Centre for Human Rights within the overall framework of strengthening the Centre's activities as envisaged by this document.

31. The World Conference on Human Rights urges States to ensure the full and free participation of indigenous people in all aspects of society, in particular in matters of concern to them.

32. The World Conference on Human Rights recommends that the General Assembly proclaim an international decade of the world's indigenous people, to begin from January 1994, including action-orientated programmes, to be decided upon in partnership with indigenous people. An appropriate voluntary trust fund should be set up for this purpose. In the framework of such a decade, the establishment of a permanent forum for indigenous people in the United Nations system should be considered.

MIGRANT WORKERS

33. The World Conference on Human Rights urges all States to guarantee the protection of the human rights of all migrant workers and their families.

34. The World Conference on Human Rights considers that the creation of conditions to foster greater harmony and tolerance between migrant workers and the rest of the society of the State in which they reside is, of particular importance.

35. The World Conference on Human Rights invites States to consider the possibility of signing and ratifying, at the earliest possible time, the International Convention on the Rights of All Migrant Workers and Members of Their Families.

3. THE EQUAL STATUS AND HUMAN RIGHTS OF WOMEN

36. The World Conference on Human Rights urges the full and equal enjoyment by women of all human rights and that this be a priority for Governments and for the United Nations. The World Conference on Human Rights also underlines the importance of the integration and full participation of women as both agents and beneficiaries in the development process, and reiterates the objectives established on global action for women towards sustainable and equitable development set forth in the Rio Declaration on Environment and Development and chapter 24 of Agenda 21, adopted by the United Nations Conference on Environment and Development (Rio de Janeiro, Brazil, 3-14 June 1992).

37. The equal status of women and the human rights of women should be integrated into the mainstream of United Nations system-wide activity. These issues should be regularly and systematically addressed throughout relevant United Nations bodies and mechanisms. In particular, steps should be taken to increase cooperation and promote further integration of objectives and goals between the Commission on the Status of Women, the Commission on Human Rights, the Committee for the Elimination of Discrimination against Women, the United Nations Development Fund for Women, the United Nations Development Programme and other United Nations agencies. In this context, cooperation and coordination should be strengthened between the Centre for Human Rights and the Division for the Advancement of Women.

38. In particular, the World Conference on Human Rights stresses the importance of working towards the elimination of violence against women in public and private life, the elimination of all forms of sexual harassment, exploitation and trafficking in women, the elimination of gender bias in the administration of justice and the eradication of any conflicts which may arise between the rights of women and the harmful effects of certain traditional or customary practices, cultural prejudices and religious extremism. The World Conference on Human Rights calls upon the General Assembly to adopt the draft declaration on violence against women and urges States to combat violence against women in accordance with its provisions. Violations of the human rights of women in situations of armed conflict are violations of the fundamental principles of international human rights and humanitarian law. All violations of this kind, including in particular murder, systematic rape, sexual slavery, and forced pregnancy, require a particularly effective response.

39. The World Conference on Human Rights urges the eradication of all forms of discrimination against women, both hidden and overt. The United Nations should encourage the goal of universal ratification by all States of the Convention on the Elimination of All Forms of Discrimination against Women by the year 2000. Ways and means of addressing the particularly large number of reservations to the Convention should be encouraged. Inter alia, the Committee on the Elimination of Discrimination against Women should continue its review of reservations to the Convention. States are urged to withdraw reservations that are contrary to the object and purpose of the Convention or which are otherwise incompatible with international treaty law.

40. Treaty monitoring bodies should disseminate necessary information to enable women to make more effective use of existing implementation procedures in their pursuits of full and equal enjoyment of human rights and non-discrimination. New procedures should also be adopted to strengthen

implementation of the commitment to women's equality and the human rights of women. The Commission on the Status of Women and the Committee on the Elimination of Discrimination against Women should quickly examine the possibility of introducing the right of petition through the preparation of an optional protocol to the Convention on the Elimination of All Forms of Discrimination against Women. The World Conference on Human Rights welcomes the decision of the Commission on Human Rights to consider the appointment of a special rapporteur on violence against women at its fiftieth session.

41. The World Conference on Human Rights recognizes the importance of the enjoyment by women of the highest standard of physical and mental health throughout their life span. In the context of the World Conference on Women and the Convention on the Elimination of All Forms of Discrimination against Women, as well as the Proclamation of Tehran of 1968, the World Conference on Human Rights reaffirms, on the basis of equality between women and men, a woman's right to accessible and adequate health care and the widest range of family planning services, as well as equal access to education at all levels.

42. Treaty monitoring bodies should include the status of women and the human rights of women in their deliberations and findings, making use of gender-specific data. States should be encouraged to supply information on the situation of women de jure and de facto in their reports to treaty monitoring bodies. The World Conference on Human Rights notes with satisfaction that the Commission on Human Rights adopted at its forty-ninth session resolution 1993/46 of 8 March 1993 stating that rapporteurs and working groups in the field of human rights should also be encouraged to do so. Steps should also be taken by the Division for the Advancement of Women in cooperation with other United Nations bodies, specifically the Centre for Human Rights, to ensure that the human rights activities of the United Nations regularly address violations of women's human rights, including gender-specific abuses. Training for United Nations human rights and humanitarian relief personnel to assist them to recognize and deal with human rights abuses particular to women and to carry out their work without gender bias should be encouraged.

43. The World Conference on Human Rights urges Governments and regional and international organizations to facilitate the access of women to decision-making posts and their greater participation in the decision-making process. It encourages further steps within the United Nations Secretariat to appoint and promote women staff members in accordance with the Charter of the United Nations, and encourages other principal and subsidiary organs of the United Nations to guarantee the participation of women under conditions of equality.

44. The World Conference on Human Rights welcomes the World Conference on Women to be held in Beijing in 1995 and urges that human rights of women should play an important role in its deliberations, in accordance with the priority themes of the World Conference on Women of equality, development and peace.

4. THE RIGHTS OF THE CHILD

45. The World Conference on Human Rights reiterates the principle of "First Call for Children" and, in this respect, underlines the importance of major national and international efforts, especially those of the United Nations Children's Fund, for promoting respect for the rights of the child to survival, protection, development and participation.

46. Measures should be taken to achieve universal ratification of the Convention on the Rights of the Child by 1995 and the universal signing of the World Declaration on the Survival, Protection and Development of Children and Plan of Action adopted by the World Summit for Children, as well as their effective implementation. The World Conference on Human Rights urges States to withdraw reservations to the Convention on the Rights of the Child contrary to the object and purpose of the Convention or otherwise contrary to international treaty law.

47. The World Conference on Human Rights urges all nations to undertake measures to the maximum extent of their available resources, with the support of international cooperation, to achieve the goals in the World Summit Plan of Action. The Conference calls on States to integrate the Convention on the Rights of the Child into their national action plans. By means of these national action plans and through international efforts, particular priority should be placed on reducing infant and maternal mortality rates, reducing malnutrition and illiteracy rates and providing access to safe drinking water and to basic education. Whenever so called for, national plans of action should be devised to combat devastating emergencies resulting from natural disasters and armed conflicts and the equally grave problem of children in extreme poverty.

48. The World Conference on Human Rights urges all States, with the support of international cooperation, to address the acute problem of children under especially difficult circumstances. Exploitation and abuse of children should be actively combated, including by addressing their root causes. Effective measures are required against female infanticide, harmful child labour, sale of children and organs, child prostitution, child pornography, as well as other forms of sexual abuse.

49. The World Conference on Human Rights supports all measures by the United Nations and its specialized agencies to ensure the effective protection and promotion of human rights of the girl child. The World Conference on Human Rights urges States to repeal existing laws and regulations and remove customs and practices which discriminate against and cause harm to the girl child.

50. The World Conference on Human Rights strongly supports the proposal that the Secretary-General initiate a study into means of improving the protection of children in armed conflicts. Humanitarian norms should be implemented and measures taken in order to protect and facilitate assistance to children in war zones. Measures should include protection for children against indiscriminate use of all weapons of war, especially anti-personnel mines. The need for aftercare and rehabilitation of children traumatized by war must be addressed urgently. The Conference calls on the Committee on the Rights of the Child to study the question of raising the minimum age of recruitment into armed forces.

51. The World Conference on Human Rights recommends that matters relating to human rights and the situation of children be regularly reviewed and monitored by all relevant organs and mechanisms of the United Nations system and by the supervisory bodies of the specialized agencies in accordance with their mandates.

52. The World Conference on Human Rights recognizes the important role played by non-governmental organizations in the effective implementation of all human rights instruments and, in particular, the Convention on the Rights of the Child.

53. The World Conference on Human Rights recommends that the Committee on the Rights of the Child, with the assistance of the Centre for Human Rights, be enabled expeditiously and effectively to meet its mandate, especially in view of the unprecedented extent of ratification and subsequent submission of country reports.

5. FREEDOM FROM TORTURE

54. The World Conference on Human Rights welcomes the ratification by many Member States of the Convention against Torture and Other Cruel, Inhuman or Degrading Treatment or Punishment and encourages its speedy ratification by all other Member States.

55. The World Conference on Human Rights emphasizes that one of the most atrocious violations against human dignity is the act of torture, the result of which destroys the dignity and impairs the capability of victims to continue their lives and their activities.

56. The World Conference on Human Rights reaffirms that under human rights law and international humanitarian law, freedom from torture is a right which must be protected under all circumstances, including in times of internal or international disturbance or armed conflicts.

57. The World Conference on Human Rights therefore urges all States to put an immediate end to the practice of torture and eradicate this evil forever through full implementation of the Universal Declaration of Human Rights as well as the relevant conventions and, where necessary, strengthening of existing mechanisms. The World Conference on Human Rights calls on all States to cooperate fully with the Special Rapporteur on the question of torture in the fulfilment of his mandate.

58. Special attention should be given to ensure universal respect for, and effective implementation of, the Principles of Medical Ethics relevant to the Role of Health Personnel, particularly Physicians, in the Protection of Prisoners and Detainees against Torture and other Cruel, Inhuman or Degrading Treatment or Punishment adopted by the General Assembly of the United Nations.

59. The World Conference on Human Rights stresses the importance of further concrete action within the framework of the United Nations with the view to providing assistance to victims of torture and ensure more effective remedies for their physical, psychological and social rehabilitation. Providing the necessary resources for this purpose should be given high priority, inter alia, by additional contributions to the United Nations Voluntary Fund for the Victims of Torture.

60. States should abrogate legislation leading to impunity for those responsible for grave violations of human rights such as torture and prosecute such violations, thereby providing a firm basis for the rule of law.

61. The World Conference on Human Rights reaffirms that efforts to eradicate torture should, first and foremost, be concentrated on prevention and, therefore, calls for the early adoption of an optional protocol to the Convention against Torture and Other Cruel, Inhuman and Degrading Treatment or Punishment, which is intended to establish a preventive system of regular visits to places of detention.

ENFORCED DISAPPEARANCES

62. The World Conference on Human Rights, welcoming the adoption by the General Assembly of the Declaration on the Protection of All Persons from Enforced Disappearance, calls upon all States to take effective legislative, administrative, judicial or other measures to prevent, terminate and punish acts of enforced disappearances. The World Conference on Human Rights reaffirms that it is the duty of all States, under any circumstances, to make investigations whenever there is reason to believe that an enforced disappearance has taken place on a territory under their jurisdiction and, if allegations are confirmed, to prosecute its perpetrators.

6. THE RIGHTS OF THE DISABLED PERSON

63. The World Conference on Human Rights reaffirms that all human rights and fundamental freedoms are universal and thus unreservedly include persons with disabilities. Every person is born equal and has the same rights to life and welfare, education and work, living independently and active participation in all aspects of society. Any direct discrimination or other negative discriminatory treatment of a disabled person is therefore a violation of his or her rights. The World Conference on Human Rights calls on Governments, where necessary, to adopt or adjust legislation to assure access to these and other rights for disabled persons.

64. The place of disabled persons is everywhere. Persons with disabilities should be guaranteed equal opportunity through the elimination of all socially determined barriers, be they physical, financial, social or psychological, which exclude or restrict full participation in society.

65. Recalling the World Programme of Action concerning Disabled Persons, adopted by the General Assembly at its thirty-seventh session, the World Conference on Human Rights calls upon the General Assembly and the Economic and Social Council to adopt the draft standard rules on the equalization of opportunities for persons with disabilities, at their meetings in 1993.

C. Cooperation, Development and Strengthening of Human Rights

66. The World Conference on Human Rights recommends that priority be given to national and international action to promote democracy, development and human rights.

67. Special emphasis should be given to measures to assist in the strengthening and building of institutions relating to human rights, strengthening of a pluralistic civil society and the protection of groups which have been rendered vulnerable. In this context, assistance provided upon the request of Governments for the conduct of free and fair elections, including assistance in the human rights aspects of elections and public information about elections, is of particular importance. Equally important is the assistance to be given to the strengthening of the rule of law, the promotion of freedom of expression and the administration of justice, and to the real and effective participation of the people in the decision-making processes.

68. The World Conference on Human Rights stresses the need for the implementation of strengthened advisory services and technical assistance activities by the Centre for Human Rights. The Centre should make available to States upon request assistance on specific human rights issues, including the preparation of reports under human rights treaties as well as for the

implementation of coherent and comprehensive plans of action for the promotion and protection of human rights. Strengthening the institutions of human rights and democracy, the legal protection of human rights, training of officials and others, broad-based education and public information aimed at promoting respect for human rights should all be available as components of these programmes.

69. The World Conference on Human Rights strongly recommends that a comprehensive programme be established within the United Nations in order to help States in the task of building and strengthening adequate national structures which have a direct impact on the overall observance of human rights and the maintenance of the rule of law. Such a programme, to be coordinated by the Centre for Human Rights, should be able to provide, upon the request of the interested Government, technical and financial assistance to national projects in reforming penal and correctional establishments, education and training of lawyers, judges and security forces in human rights, and any other sphere of activity relevant to the good functioning of the rule of law. That programme should make available to States assistance for the implementation of plans of action for the promotion and protection of human rights.

70. The World Conference on Human Rights requests the Secretary-General of the United Nations to submit proposals to the United Nations General Assembly, containing alternatives for the establishment, structure, operational modalities and funding of the proposed programme.

71. The World Conference on Human Rights recommends that each State consider the desirability of drawing up a national action plan identifying steps whereby that State would improve the promotion and protection of human rights.

72. The World Conference on Human Rights on Human Rights reaffirms that the universal and inalienable right to development, as established in the Declaration on the Right to Development, must be implemented and realized. In this context, the World Conference on Human Rights welcomes the appointment by the Commission on Human Rights of a thematic working group on the right to development and urges that the Working Group, in consultation and cooperation with other organs and agencies of the United Nations system, promptly formulate, for early consideration by the United Nations General Assembly, comprehensive and effective measures to eliminate obstacles to the implementation and realization of the Declaration on the Right to Development and recommending ways and means towards the realization of the right to development by all States.

73. The World Conference on Human Rights recommends that non-governmental and other grass-roots organizations active in development and/or human rights should be enabled to play a major role on the national and international levels in the debate, activities and implementation relating to the right to development and, in cooperation with Governments, in all relevant aspects of development cooperation.

74. The World Conference on Human Rights appeals to Governments, competent agencies and institutions to increase considerably the resources devoted to building well-functioning legal systems able to protect human rights, and to national institutions working in this area. Actors in the field of development cooperation should bear in mind the mutually reinforcing interrelationship between development, democracy and human rights. Cooperation should be based on dialogue and trans-

parency. The World Conference on Human Rights also calls for the establishment of comprehensive programmes, including resource banks of information and personnel with expertise relating to the strengthening of the rule of law and of democratic institutions.

75. The World Conference on Human Rights encourages the Commission on Human Rights, in cooperation with the Committee on Economic, Social and Cultural Rights, to continue the examination of optional protocols to the International Covenant on Economic, Social and Cultural Rights.

76. The World Conference on Human Rights recommends that more resources be made available for the strengthening or the establishment of regional arrangements for the promotion and protection of human rights under the programmes of advisory services and technical assistance of the Centre for Human Rights. States are encouraged to request assistance for such purposes as regional and subregional workshops, seminars and information exchanges designed to strengthen regional arrangements for the promotion and protection of human rights in accord with universal human rights standards as contained in international human rights instruments.

77. The World Conference on Human Rights supports all measures by the United Nations and its relevant specialized agencies to ensure the effective promotion and protection of trade union rights, as stipulated in the International Covenant on Economic, Social and Cultural Rights and other relevant international instruments. It calls on all States to abide fully by their obligations in this regard contained in international instruments.

D. Human Rights Education

78. The World Conference on Human Rights considers human rights education, training and public information essential for the promotion and achievement of stable and harmonious relations among communities and for fostering mutual understanding, tolerance and peace.

79. States should strive to eradicate illiteracy and should direct education towards the full development of the human personality and to the strengthening of respect for human rights and fundamental freedoms. The World Conference on Human Rights calls on all States and institutions to include human rights, humanitarian law, democracy and rule of law as subjects in the curricula of all learning institutions in formal and non-formal settings.

80. Human rights education should include peace, democracy, development and social justice, as set forth in international and regional human rights instruments, in order to achieve common understanding and awareness with a view to strengthening universal commitment to human rights.

81. Taking into account the World Plan of Action on Education for Human Rights and Democracy, adopted in March 1993 by the International Congress on Education for Human Rights and Democracy of the United Nations Educational, Scientific and Cultural Organization, and other human rights instruments, the World Conference on Human Rights recommends that States develop specific programmes and strategies for ensuring the widest human rights education and the dissemination of public information, taking particular account of the human rights needs of women.

82. Governments, with the assistance of intergovernmental organizations, national institutions and non-governmental organizations, should promote an increased awareness of hu-

man rights and mutual tolerance. The World Conference on Human Rights underlines the importance of strengthening the World Public Information Campaign for Human Rights carried out by the United Nations. They should initiate and support education in human rights and undertake effective dissemination of public information in this field. The advisory services and technical assistance programmes of the United Nations system should be able to respond immediately to requests from States for educational and training activities in the field of human rights as well as for special education concerning standards as contained in international human rights instruments and in humanitarian law and their application to special groups such as military forces, law enforcement personnel, police and the health profession. The proclamation of a United Nations decade for human rights education in order to promote, encourage and focus these educational activities should be considered.

E. Implementation and Monitoring Methods

83. The World Conference on Human Rights urges Governments to incorporate standards as contained in international human rights instruments in domestic legislation and to strengthen national structures, institutions and organs of society which play a role in promoting and safeguarding human rights.

84. The World Conference on Human Rights recommends the strengthening of United Nations activities and programmes to meet requests for assistance by States which want to establish or strengthen their own national institutions for the promotion and protection of human rights.

85. The World Conference on Human Rights also encourages the strengthening of cooperation between national institutions for the promotion and protection of human rights, particularly through exchanges of information and experience, as well as cooperation with regional organizations and the United Nations.

86. The World Conference on Human Rights strongly recommends in this regard that representatives of national institutions for the promotion and protection of human rights convene periodic meetings under the auspices of the Centre for Human Rights to examine ways and means of improving their mechanisms and sharing experiences.

87. The World Conference on Human Rights recommends to the human rights treaty bodies, to the meetings of chairpersons of the treaty bodies and to the meetings of States parties that they continue to take steps aimed at coordinating the multiple reporting requirements and guidelines for preparing State reports under the respective human rights conventions and study the suggestion that the submission of one overall report on treaty obligations undertaken by each State would make these procedures more effective and increase their impact.

88. The World Conference on Human Rights recommends that the States parties to international human rights instruments, the General Assembly and the Economic and Social Council should consider studying the existing human rights treaty bodies and the various thematic mechanisms and procedures with a view to promoting greater efficiency and effectiveness through better coordination of the various bodies, mechanisms and procedures, taking into account the need to avoid unnecessary duplication and overlapping of their mandates and tasks.

89. The World Conference on Human Rights recommends continued work on the improvement of the functioning, including the monitoring tasks, of the treaty bodies, taking into account multiple proposals made in this respect, in particular those made by the treaty bodies themselves and by the meetings of the chairpersons of the treaty bodies. The comprehensive national approach taken by the Committee on the Rights of the Child should also be encouraged.

90. The World Conference on Human Rights recommends that States parties to human rights treaties consider accepting all the available optional communication procedures.

91. The World Conference on Human Rights views with concern the issue of impunity of perpetrators of human rights violations, and supports the efforts of the Commission on Human Rights and the Sub-Commission on Prevention of Discrimination and Protection of Minorities to examine all aspects of the issue.

92. The World Conference on Human Rights recommends that the Commission on Human Rights examine the possibility for better implementation of existing human rights instruments at the international and regional levels and encourages the International Law Commission to continue its work on an international criminal court.

93. The World Conference on Human Rights appeals to States which have not yet done so to accede to the Geneva Conventions of 12 August 1949 and the Protocols thereto, and to take all appropriate national measures, including legislative ones, for their full implementation.

94. The World Conference on Human Rights recommends the speedy completion and adoption of the draft declaration on the right and responsibility of individuals, groups and organs of society to promote and protect universally recognized human rights and fundamental freedoms.

95. The World Conference on Human Rights underlines the importance of preserving and strengthening the system of special procedures, rapporteurs, representatives, experts and working groups of the Commission on Human Rights and the Sub-Commission on the Prevention of Discrimination and Protection of Minorities, in order to enable them to carry out their mandates in all countries throughout the world, providing them with the necessary human and financial resources. The procedures and mechanisms should be enabled to harmonize and rationalize their work through periodic meetings. All States are asked to cooperate fully with these procedures and mechanisms.

96. The World Conference on Human Rights recommends that the United Nations assume a more active role in the promotion and protection of human rights in ensuring full respect for international humanitarian law in all situations of armed conflict, in accordance with the purposes and principles of the Charter of the United Nations.

97. The World Conference on Human Rights, recognizing the important role of human rights components in specific arrangements concerning some peace-keeping operations by the United Nations, recommends that the Secretary-General take into account the reporting, experience and capabilities of the Centre for Human Rights and human rights mechanisms, in conformity with the Charter of the United Nations.

98. To strengthen the enjoyment of economic, social and cultural rights, additional approaches should be examined, such as a system of indicators to measure progress in the realization

of the rights set forth in the International Covenant on Economic, Social and Cultural Rights. There must be a concerted effort to ensure recognition of economic, social and cultural rights at the national, regional and international levels.

F. Follow-up to the World Conference on Human Rights

99. The World Conference on Human Rights on Human Rights recommends that the General Assembly, the Commission on Human Rights and other organs and agencies of the United Nations system related to human rights consider ways and means for the full implementation, without delay, of the recommendations contained in the present Declaration, including the possibility of proclaiming a United Nations decade for human rights. The World Conference on Human Rights further recommends that the Commission on Human Rights annually review the progress towards this end.

100. The World Conference on Human Rights requests the Secretary-General of the United Nations to invite on the occasion of the fiftieth anniversary of the Universal Declaration of Human Rights all States, all organs and agencies of the United Nations system related to human rights, to report to him on the progress made in the implementation of the present Declaration and to submit a report to the General Assembly at its fifty-third session, through the Commission on Human Rights and the Economic and Social Council. Likewise, regional and, as appropriate, national human rights institutions, as well as non-governmental organizations, may present their views to the Secretary-General on the progress made in the implementation of the present Dec-

laration. Special attention should be paid to assessing the progress towards the goal of universal ratification of international human rights treaties and protocols adopted within the framework of the United Nations system.

Consequences

Whether the Vienna Declaration would be as important a document as earlier 20th-century human rights declarations was still unclear as the millennium drew to a close. The conference itself, however, had proved a disappointment. Not only had it failed to reach agreement on such matters as the appointment of a United Nations commissioner for human rights, more ominously, it exposed the serious and growing divergences of view on human rights between the "developed" nations and the "less-developed" nations, which were UN euphemisms for the rich and poor of the world.

Source

United Nations, "Vienna Declaration and Programme of Action." Available online. URL: http://www.unhchr.ch/huridocda/ huridoca.nsf/(Symbol)/A.CONF.157.23.En?OpenDocument. Accessed January 4, 2005.

Epilogue
INTERNATIONAL THREATS, GLOBAL OPPORTUNITIES

INTRODUCTION

Broadcast news caught much of the event as folks, first in America, then throughout the world, gathered in private and public round the television sets that had become ubiquitous in modern times. They saw a Boeing 767 passenger jetliner (later identified as American Airlines flight 11 out of Boston) crash into the north tower of the World Trade Center in New York City's Lower Manhattan. This first attack had come at 8:45 A.M. (EDT), September 11, 2001. Minutes later, at 9:03, cameras were still rolling everywhere when a second 767, United Airlines flight 175, also out of Boston, hit the as-yet undamaged south tower. At 9:40, the Federal Aviation Administration shut down all U.S. airports, but, three minutes later, American Airlines flight 77, a Boeing 757, originating in Washington, D.C., crashed into the Pentagon, U.S. military headquarters. At 10:05 in New York, the south 110-story tower of the World Trade Center collapsed. At 10:10, a portion of the Pentagon collapsed. At almost precisely the same time, United Airlines flight 93, another 757, flying out of Newark, New Jersey, crashed in rural Somerset County, Pennsylvania, outside Pittsburgh. At 10:28, the north tower of the World Trade Center collapsed.

As endless replays of the crashes and collapses flickered across the screens, the truth of what had happened sank in: Before the watching eyes of the whole world, the United States had been attacked by terrorists. Four small groups of Middle Eastern men, most Saudis, apparently members of a terrorist organization called al-Qaeda (meaning "the base") and trained in the rudiments of flight, hijacked four U.S. commercial jetliners. They used them as suicide missiles, directing them to the World Trade Center and the Pentagon. The hijackers on the fourth aircraft that crashed in Pennsylvania were overpowered by passengers, who had heard via cell phone conversations of the attack on the World Trade Center. Tragically, a crash could not be averted, but the plane was most likely headed for the Capitol or some other high-profile Washington, D.C.–area target. The attacks were the first time the mainland had been significantly struck by a foreign power since the War of 1812 and the first assault against U.S. territory since the attack on Pearl Harbor, December 7, 1941, that launched U.S. participation in World War II. The death toll would be nearly 3,000.

The War on Terror

At first no one was calling it a war. Instead the assaults were treated similarly to those in the past, such as the 1993 bombing of the World Trade Center or even the 1995 bombing of the Alfred P. Murrah Federal Building in Oklahoma City. They were acts of criminal atrocity whose perpetrators could be brought to justice, or so promised U.S. president George W. Bush. Then, at the joint session of Congress on September 20, Bush described his plans to avenge the attacks as a new kind of war, one "unlike any we had ever seen," a war of "covert operations, secret even in success," a "War on Terrorism." As later became clear, in those nine days, a cabal of neoconservatives—who had long been burrowing into the foreign policy establishment and were now ensconced in the Departments of State and Defense—had captured the second President Bush's attention. They now persuaded him to use 9/11, as the fateful day came to be known, as an opportunity to promulgate actions against all America's foreign policy enemies, especially Saddam Hussein's Iraq.

That the so-called war on terror had no more a specific sovereign foe than, say, the War on Poverty or the War on Drugs was precisely the point. Not coincidentally, the war in some respects very much resembled such domestic programs with its establishment of a new Department of Homeland Security and grants of money to city and state governments to beef up their security operations. But the vagueness may also be the

996 ENCYCLOPEDIA OF HISTORICAL TREATIES AND ALLIANCES

nature of this new brand of asymmetric war, or so the Bush administration claimed. It is a warfare, said U.S. vice president Dick Cheney (whom many thought the true driving force behind the responses to 9/11), intended to be fought in the shadows, a "mean, nasty, dangerous, dirty business." This "fourth generation" warfare, dispersed and ill-defined, blurs the distinction between war and peace, between civilian and military participants. America's "foes" become targets that must be destroyed (or at least captured and punished) rather than sovereign political entities that can merely be defeated (or with which the United States might negotiate).

Thus, the Bush administration was not planning the invasion of Afghanistan, though its action might resemble such on the ground. Instead, it was launching an expedition to destroy al-Qaeda, the terrorist organization that apparently sponsored the attacks, and eliminate its mastermind and financier, Osama bin Laden, a middle-aged multimillionaire, Saudi by birth and now living in Afghanistan, where he enjoyed the protection of the radical Islamic Taliban government. He was implicated in earlier terrorist attacks, including the bombings of two U.S. embassies in 1998 and an attack on the U.S. guided-missile destroyer *Cole*, in a port at Yemen, on October 12, 2000. His al-Qaeda served as a center for the indoctrination, training, coordination, and financing of Muslim terrorists dedicated to carrying out jihad (holy war) against Israel, the West, and especially the United States.

Following September 11, then, the United States deployed its military in its undeclared war against terrorism, beginning with a campaign to capture or kill bin Laden, destroy al-Qaeda, and overthrow the Taliban government of Afghanistan. A rapid diplomatic effort forged a loose coalition of key world nations that pledged to support the war against terrorism. Pakistan, which shares a border with Afghanistan and had been a supporter of the Taliban regime, cooperated closely with the U.S.-led coalition, and even Iran, hostile to the United States since the fall of the shah and the hostage crisis of 1979–81, agreed to allow flyovers and to accept emergency landings. Only Iraq, clearly the war's next "target," refused cooperation.

The first attack against the Taliban government of Afghanistan was launched on October 7, 2001, nighttime in Kabul. Supported by some British air units, the United States attacked with B-1 bombers, B-2 "stealth" bombers, and the venerable B-52, as well as ship-launched cruise missiles. After less than a week of bombardment, the United States had achieved "air supremacy," and daylight raids were added to those at night. High-altitude bombers were replaced by lower-altitude strike aircraft, capable of close ground support. Simultaneously with the air raids, U.S. cargo transports dropped food packages intended for Afghan civilians. The U.S. air strikes were coordinated with action on the ground by anti-Taliban Afghan forces, primarily the Northern Alliance, which fielded about 15,000 men against the 40,000-man Taliban army. On October 20, the Northern Alliance ground forces were joined by about 100 U.S. Special Forces commandos, who staged the first U.S. raid on the ground, destroying some Taliban facilities and obtaining Taliban documents.

By November 2001, the pace of the Afghan war had rapidly accelerated. Combined U.S. and Northern Alliance attacks resulted in the fall of Mazar-e Sharif, gateway between Afghanistan and Taliban sympathizers in Pakistan, on November 12. The following day, the Afghan capital city of Kabul was occupied by Northern Alliance troops. By the end of the month, Kunduz, a northern Taliban stronghold, fell. Kandahar, the only major Taliban-held city, reeled under siege and seemed, by early December, about to fall to the Northern Alliance, which it did in the general routing of Afghan forces that followed, during which Osama bin Laden and much of al-Qaeda's senior leadership vanished. Throughout 2002, as U.S. Special Forces continued to hunt for bin Laden and other al-Qaeda leaders, President Bush repeatedly observed that the war against terrorism had not ended with the fall of the Taliban and would not end even with the capture of bin Laden (if he was still alive) and his associates. In late 2002, the speculation that had been running high all year as to the next battleground proved true when the Bush administration began stridently to argue the case for making Saddam Hussein's regime in Iraq the next target of the U.S.-led war on terror.

Although there was no evidence implicating Hussein or his nation in the terrorist attacks on the United States, President Bush and his administration argued that the regime supported anti-Western and, in particular, anti-American terrorism and that Hussein possessed weapons of mass destruction (perhaps nuclear, but certainly chemical and biological) with which he planned either to attack U.S. interests or aid others in doing so. On September 12, 2002, President Bush addressed the United Nations General Assembly, declaring that Iraq presented a threat to the United States and other nations and that the Iraqi regime was also a threat to the authority of the United Nations.

Bush secured congressional resolutions authorizing the use of U.S. military forces against Iraq (the final vote came on October 11, 2002), and on November 8, 2002, the United Nations approved Resolution 1441, pressuring Iraq to comply with its disarmament obligations and/or to prove that it had divested itself of all weapons of mass destruction. UN inspectors were dispatched to Iraq, which did submit an apparently evasive disclosure report. When the inspectors found nothing of significance in Iraq, the Bush administration persisted in its assertions that Iraq possessed the weapons, and on February 5, 2003, U.S. secretary of state Colin Powell presented the Bush administration's case to the UN Security Council. Despite this presentation, most of the international community was reluctant to support a war against Iraq. Some nations, most notably France and Germany, actively opposed such a war. Others did not directly oppose the war but declined to commit any substantive support to it, and still others, notably Spain, voiced support and pledged logistical and humanitarian assistance but likewise withheld active military forces. Only Great Britain enthusiastically endorsed the position of the Bush administration and resolved to participate in military action. (Italy and Poland also committed small military forces, and Japan sent a handful of logistical troops.)

While international and highly divisive domestic debate continued, the Bush administration suddenly shifted its definition of what constituted an appropriate cause for war. Whereas previously the president had proposed war as a consequence of Iraq's failure to produce what, despite an absence of evidence, he asserted to be a stockpile of weapons of mass destruction, on March 16, 2003, the president issued an ultimatum to Hussein demanding that he and his immediate cohorts (including his sons, Uday and Qusay) permanently leave Iraq within 48 hours. When this deadline passed, on March 19, President Bush authorized a "decapitation" attack on the Iraqi leadership, an aerial bombardment of a bunker in Baghdad believed to shelter Saddam Hussein. This attack was the commencement of the undeclared war that the United States dubbed Operation Iraqi Freedom. Hussein was apparently uninjured in the attack.

By April 14, 2003, U.S. and British forces had overrun Iraq, and the Pentagon announced that while some fighting continued, the major combat phase of Operation Iraqi Freedom was ended. All over the country, Iraqi officials were being taken into custody, and on April 20, the U.S. Marines left Baghdad, turning it over to U.S. Army occupying forces. Lieutenant General Jay Garner arrived in the capital to lead U.S. reconstruction efforts in Iraq and arrange for an interim civil authority in Baghdad. However, these efforts got off to a slow and unsteady start, and on May 11, Garner was replaced by a new administrator, diplomat L. Paul Bremer. Meanwhile, on May 2, President Bush had personally announced from the deck of the aircraft carrier *Abraham Lincoln* that major combat in Iraq had been concluded. At this point, Hussein and his sons were still at large. The latter two, Uday and Qusay, would be killed in a July 22 raid, leaving their father somewhere in hiding. Saddam was himself captured and imprisoned later in 2003.

Despite President Bush's announcement of victory, combat continued. U.S., British, and (in very small number) Polish military forces struggled variously to impose, restore, or maintain order throughout Iraq, which was chronically subjected to suicide bombings and other guerrilla-style attacks. The violence would continue to escalate, especially as news (and videos) of U.S. torture of Iraqi prisoners at Abu Ghraib prison and in facilities at Guantánamo, Cuba, reached the world. As of July 6, 2005, 1,750 U.S. troops had been killed, 1,163 of them since President Bush announced the end of major combat.

Diplomacy's Place in the Remade World Order

President Bush won reelection in 2004 by invoking support for his war on terror. But in the last week of the political campaign, when he spoke at the United Nations in a show of support for his candidate for the leadership of postwar Afghanistan, he was greeted by a decidedly chilly, if not hostile, complete silence of the General Assembly. Even before he began his second term, the U.S. occupation of Iraq and Afghanistan, despite the much touted national elections in both countries, had clearly undermined the initial military successes of the war. Most of the world, sympathetic to the United States after the 9/11 attacks, was opposed to U.S. foreign policy in a way unprecedented since World War II. Bush's "War on Terrorism" had pretty much destroyed any hope of an Arab-Israeli peace in the Middle East, despite the death of Yasser Arafat in late 2004. U.S. foreign policy in the rest of the world, even where diplomacy was much needed, as with a North Korea successfully arming itself with nuclear weaponry, was neglected. Thus, when the Bush administration signed a STRATEGIC OFFENSIVE REDUCTIONS TREATY (TREATY OF MOSCOW) with the president of the Russian Federation, Vladimir Putin, to reduce the number of strategic warheads in both country's arsenals, the irony was that the threat of a nuclear attack on the United States no longer lay with the Russians.

Indeed, the foreign policy pursued by the Bush administration after 9/11, one of preemptive war and the aggressive promotion (and, if necessary, installation) of friendly democratic governments was something of a shock for those who had listened to the presidential candidate George W. Bush talking against foreign adventures and what conservative Republicans then called "nation building." As it turns out, they meant nation building by the United Nations and former president Bill Clinton in the Balkans and Africa, not cultural neoimperialism in the Middle East.

This latter course was the one being urged by the disciples of Leo Strauss, longtime professor of philosophy at the University of Chicago, who were the foreign policy mavens of Bush's administration—Richard Perle; Paul Wolfowitz; the Kristols, father Irving and son William; Richard Pipes; Michael Ledeen; Donald Rumsfeld; and Dick Cheney. Members of the intellectual wing of the Republican Party, these men were initially brought together by neoconservative icon Norman Podhoretz, and their current bible may well be Samuel P. Huntington's *Clash of Civilizations: The Remaking of the World Order,* which argues that there is a new international struggle under way between the modern Western and Islamic worlds.

Entering the scene during the Ford administration in the 1970s, these "neocon" true believers stridently opposed the pragmatically minded Henry Kissinger and the détente he advocated. They pushed the Reagan administration to destroy the "evil empire" of his day, Soviet Russia, who (they argued back then) financed and armed worldwide terrorism. And they have made the younger President Bush their St. George to fight against those dragons that National Security staffer Richard Pipes labeled in the *New York Times* as "Islamic extremists bent on destroying non-Islamic civilizations," which meant, he wrote, "As such, America's war with Al-Qaeda is non-negotiable."

Since they want to prosecute Osama bin Laden and his ilk under U.S. law as it relates to organized crime, it is little wonder that many of the treaties of the Bush administration are directly related to the CONVENTION AGAINST TRANSNATIONAL ORGANIZED CRIME, such as the CONVENTION AGAINST CORRUPTION; PROTOCOL AGAINST THE SMUGGLING OF MIGRANTS BY LAND, SEA AND AIR; PRO-TOCOL AGAINST THE ILLICIT MANUFACTURING OF AND TRAFFICKING IN FIREARMS, THEIR PARTS AND COMPONENTS AND AMMUNITION; PROTOCOL TO PREVENT, SUPPRESS AND PUNISH TRAFFICKING IN PERSONS, ESPECIALLY WOMEN AND CHILDREN; or those aimed at terrorism itself, such as CONVENTION FOR THE SUPPRESSION OF THE FINANCING OF TERRORISM. Traditionally, however, the neocons have been hostile toward multilateral international agreements and even the United Nations as an organization, which they see as a threat to American foreign policy interests. They instinctively react against any measure that might limit U.S. power, hence the Bush administration's lack of enthusiasm for such agreements as the CONVENTION AGAINST TORTURE AND OTHER CRUEL, INHUMAN OR DEGRADING TREATMENT OR PUNISHMENT, the CONVENTION ON PROHIBITIONS OR RESTRICTIONS ON THE USE OF CERTAIN CONVENTIONAL WEAPONS WHICH MAY BE DEEMED TO BE EXCESSIVELY INJURIOUS OR TO HAVE INDISCRIMINATE EFFECTS, and their subsequent protocols. Even some of the treaties initially supported by the administration have yet to be ratified (as of 2005) because of reservations regarding issues of sovereignty.

Whether, as the neoconservatives argue, the biggest threat to world peace is the enemy they call variously Islamofacism, Islamic extremism, or global jihad, or whether the neocons' own "holy war" is seriously destabilizing the international order, as their critics argue, certainly the war on terror has thus far failed to locate, capture, or kill enough of the bad guys around the globe to justify its expense. Those costs include not only America's huge military budgets but the dangerous isolation of the world's only superpower from those nations that have been its friends and allies since at least the end of World War II.

TREATIES

Multinational Conventions and Agreements

INTERNATIONAL CONVENTION FOR THE SUPPRESSION OF THE FINANCING OF TERRORISM

TREATY AT A GLANCE

Completed
December 9, 1999; entered into force April 10, 2002

Signatories
As of summer 2005, 138 United Nations members
have become parties to the treaty

Overview
The International Convention for the Suppression of the Financing of Terrorism defines the legal framework for international cooperation in the investigation, arrest, prosecution, and extradition of persons who engage in terrorist financing.

Historical Background

Over the years, a number of multilateral treaties have been concluded to promote international cooperation in fighting terrorism, which is typically international in its scope. Important treaties and conventions (to which the United States is a party) include the 1963 Tokyo Convention on Offenses and Certain Other Acts Committed on Board Aircraft; the 1970 Hague Convention for the Unlawful Seizure of Aircraft; the 1971 Montreal Convention for the Suppression of Unlawful Acts against the Safety of Civil Aviation; the 1973 Convention on the Prevention and Punishment of Crimes against Internationally Protected Persons, Including Diplomatic Agents; the 1979 Convention against the Taking of Hostages; the 1979 Convention on the Physical Protection of Nuclear Material; the 1988 Protocol for the Suppression of Unlawful Acts of Violence at Airports Serving International Civil Aviation (which supplements the 1971 Montreal Convention); the 1988 Rome Convention for the Suppression of Unlawful Acts against the Safety of Maritime Navigation; the 1988 Protocol for the Suppression of Unlawful Acts against the Safety of Fixed Platforms Located on the Continental Shelf (which supplements the Rome Convention); the 1991 Convention on the Marking of Plastic Explosives for the Purpose of Detection; and the 1997 Convention for the Suppression of Terrorist Bombings. What is unique about the International Convention for the Suppression of the Financing of Terrorism is that it avoids issues of ideology and military force and instead addresses the lifeblood of organized terrorist activity: finance.

The convention derives its definition of *terrorism* from existing international treaties on terrorism: "Any . . . act intended to cause death or serious bodily injury to a civilian, or to any other person not taking an active part in the hostilities in a situation of armed conflict, when the purpose of such act, by its nature or context, is to intimidate a population, or to compel a government or international organization to do or to abstain from doing any act." Based on this foundation and a growing precedent of international cooperation in combating terrorism, the convention approaches this common menace from the standpoint of finance. Recognizing that terrorist action requires funding, the convention defines areas and means of international cooperation through which nations might cut off the flow of money to terrorist individuals, organizations, states, and activities.

It is of significance that the number of ratifications of the convention increased markedly following the September 11, 2001, terrorist attacks against the United States. This increase was due in part to Security

Council Resolution 1373, passed on September 28, 2001, which (among other things) called on all member states "to become parties as soon as possible to the relevant international conventions and protocols relating to terrorism, including the International Convention on the Suppression of the Financing of Terrorism of 9 December 1999." This was the first time in UN history that the Security Council had made such a request.

Terms

The major provisions of the International Convention for the Suppression of the Financing of Terrorism require each state party to criminalize the funding of terrorist activities under its domestic laws and to identify, detect, and seize or freeze funds identified as being used or allocated for terrorist purposes. In addition, states parties are required to prosecute or extradite individuals suspected of unlawful and willful involvement, direct or indirect, in the financing of terrorism and to cooperate with other states parties in the investigation and prosecution of such suspects. Each state party also agrees to ensure that its domestic laws require financial institutions to implement measures to identify, impede, and prevent the flow of terrorist funds.

National sovereignty is strictly protected by the convention, which applies only to acts committed transnationally. Domestic terrorism, in which the act and financing are confined to a single state, is to be prosecuted strictly under the laws of that state.

International Convention for the Suppression of the Financing of Terrorism

The States Parties to this Convention,

Bearing in mind the purposes and principles of the Charter of the United Nations concerning the maintenance of international peace and security and the promotion of good-neighbourliness and friendly relations and cooperation among States,

Deeply concerned about the worldwide escalation of acts of terrorism in all its forms and manifestations,

Recalling the Declaration on the Occasion of the Fiftieth Anniversary of the United Nations, contained in General Assembly resolution 50/6 of 24 October 1995,

Recalling also all the relevant General Assembly resolutions on the matter, including resolution 49/60 of 9 December 1994 and its annex on the Declaration on Measures to Eliminate International Terrorism, in which the States Members of the United Nations solemnly reaffirmed their unequivocal condemnation of all acts, methods and practices of terrorism as criminal and unjustifiable, wherever and by whomever committed, including those which jeopardize the friendly relations among States and peoples and threaten the territorial integrity and security of States,

Noting that the Declaration on Measures to Eliminate International Terrorism also encouraged States to review urgently the scope of the existing international legal provisions on the prevention, repression and elimination of terrorism in all its forms and manifestations, with the aim of ensuring that there is a comprehensive legal framework covering all aspects of the matter,

Recalling General Assembly resolution 51/210 of 17 December 1996, paragraph 3, subparagraph (f), in which the Assembly called upon all States to take steps to prevent and counteract, through appropriate domestic measures, the financing of terrorists and terrorist organizations, whether such financing is direct or indirect through organizations which also have or claim to have charitable, social or cultural goals or which are also engaged in unlawful activities such as illicit arms trafficking, drug dealing and racketeering, including the exploitation of persons for purposes of funding terrorist activities, and in particular to consider, where appropriate, adopting regulatory measures to prevent and counteract movements of funds suspected to be intended for terrorist purposes without impeding in any way the freedom of legitimate capital movements and to intensify the exchange of information concerning international movements of such funds,

Recalling also General Assembly resolution 52/165 of 15 December 1997, in which the Assembly called upon States to consider, in particular, the implementation of the measures set out in paragraphs 3 (a) to (f) of its resolution 51/210 of 17 December 1996,

Recalling further General Assembly resolution 53/108 of 8 December 1998, in which the Assembly decided that the Ad Hoc Committee established by General Assembly resolution 51/210 of 17 December 1996 should elaborate a draft international convention for the suppression of terrorist financing to supplement related existing international instruments,

Considering that the financing of terrorism is a matter of grave concern to the international community as a whole,

Noting that the number and seriousness of acts of international terrorism depend on the financing that terrorists may obtain,

Noting also that existing multilateral legal instruments do not expressly address such financing,

Being convinced of the urgent need to enhance international cooperation among States in devising and adopting effective measures for the prevention of the financing of terrorism, as well as for its suppression through the prosecution and punishment of its perpetrators,

Have agreed as follows:

ARTICLE 1
FOR THE PURPOSES OF THIS CONVENTION:

1. "Funds" means assets of every kind, whether tangible or intangible, movable or immovable, however acquired, and legal documents or instruments in any form, including electronic or digital, evidencing title to, or interest in, such assets, including, but not limited to, bank credits, travellers cheques, bank cheques, money orders, shares, securities, bonds, drafts, letters of credit.

2. "State or governmental facility" means any permanent or temporary facility or conveyance that is used or occupied by representatives of a State, members of Government, the legislature or the judiciary or by officials or employees of a State or any other public authority or entity or by employees or officials of an

intergovernmental organization in connection with their official duties.

3. "Proceeds" means any funds derived from or obtained, directly or indirectly, through the commission of an offence set forth in article 2.

ARTICLE 2

1. Any person commits an offence within the meaning of this Convention if that person by any means, directly or indirectly, unlawfully and wilfully, provides or collects funds with the intention that they should be used or in the knowledge that they are to be used, in full or in part, in order to carry out:

(a) An act which constitutes an offence within the scope of and as defined in one of the treaties listed in the annex; or

(b) Any other act intended to cause death or serious bodily injury to a civilian, or to any other person not taking an active part in the hostilities in a situation of armed conflict, when the purpose of such act, by its nature or context, is to intimidate a population, or to compel a government or an international organization to do or to abstain from doing any act. . . .

3. For an act to constitute an offence set forth in paragraph 1, it shall not be necessary that the funds were actually used to carry out an offence referred to in paragraph 1, subparagraphs (a) or (b).

4. Any person also commits an offence if that person attempts to commit an offence as set forth in paragraph 1 of this article.

5. Any person also commits an offence if that person:

(a) Participates as an accomplice in an offence as set forth in paragraph 1 or 4 of this article;

(b) Organizes or directs others to commit an offence as set forth in paragraph 1 or 4 of this article;

(c) Contributes to the commission of one or more offences as set forth in paragraphs 1 or 4 of this article by a group of persons acting with a common purpose. Such contribution shall be intentional and shall either:

(i) Be made with the aim of furthering the criminal activity or criminal purpose of the group, where such activity or purpose involves the commission of an offence as set forth in paragraph 1 of this article; or

(ii) Be made in the knowledge of the intention of the group to commit an offence as set forth in paragraph 1 of this article.

ARTICLE 3

This Convention shall not apply where the offence is committed within a single State, the alleged offender is a national of that State and is present in the territory of that State and no other State has a basis under article 7, paragraph 1, or article 7, paragraph 2, to exercise jurisdiction, except that the provisions of articles 12 to 18 shall, as appropriate, apply in those cases.

ARTICLE 4

Each State Party shall adopt such measures as may be necessary:

a) To establish as criminal offences under its domestic law the offences set forth in article 2;

(b) To make those offences punishable by appropriate penalties which take into account the grave nature of the offences.

ARTICLE 5

1. Each State Party, in accordance with its domestic legal principles, shall take the necessary measures to enable a legal entity located in its territory or organized under its laws to be held liable when a person responsible for the management or control of that legal entity has, in that capacity, committed an offence set forth in article 2. Such liability may be criminal, civil or administrative.

2. Such liability is incurred without prejudice to the criminal liability of individuals having committed the offences.

3. Each State Party shall ensure, in particular, that legal entities liable in accordance with paragraph 1 above are subject to effective, proportionate and dissuasive criminal, civil or administrative sanctions. Such sanctions may include monetary sanctions.

ARTICLE 6

Each State Party shall adopt such measures as may be necessary, including, where appropriate, domestic legislation, to ensure that criminal acts within the scope of this Convention are under no circumstances justifiable by considerations of a political, philosophical, ideological, racial, ethnic, religious or other similar nature.

ARTICLE 7

1. Each State Party shall take such measures as may be necessary to establish its jurisdiction over the offences set forth in article 2 when:

(a) The offence is committed in the territory of that State;

(b) The offence is committed on board a vessel flying the flag of that State or an aircraft registered under the laws of that State at the time the offence is committed;

(c) The offence is committed by a national of that State.

2. A State Party may also establish its jurisdiction over any such offence when:

(a) The offence was directed towards or resulted in the carrying out of an offence referred to in article 2, paragraph 1, subparagraph (a) or (b), in the territory of or against a national of that State;

(b) The offence was directed towards or resulted in the carrying out of an offence referred to in article 2, paragraph 1, subparagraph (a) or (b), against a State or government facility of that State abroad, including diplomatic or consular premises of that State;

(c) The offence was directed towards or resulted in an offence referred to in article 2, paragraph 1, subparagraph (a) or (b), committed in an attempt to compel that State to do or abstain from doing any act;

(d) The offence is committed by a stateless person who has his or her habitual residence in the territory of that State;

(e) The offence is committed on board an aircraft which is operated by the Government of that State.

3. Upon ratifying, accepting, approving or acceding to this Convention, each State Party shall notify the Secretary-General of the United Nations of the jurisdiction it has established in accordance with paragraph 2. Should any change take place, the State Party concerned shall immediately notify the Secretary-General.

4. Each State Party shall likewise take such measures as may be necessary to establish its jurisdiction over the offences set forth in article 2 in cases where the alleged offender is present in its territory and it does not extradite that person to any of the States Parties that have established their jurisdiction in accordance with paragraphs 1 or 2.

5. When more than one State Party claims jurisdiction over the offences set forth in article 2, the relevant States Parties shall strive to coordinate their actions appropriately, in particular concerning the conditions for prosecution and the modalities for mutual legal assistance.

6. Without prejudice to the norms of general international law, this Convention does not exclude the exercise of any criminal jurisdiction established by a State Party in accordance with its domestic law.

ARTICLE 8

1. Each State Party shall take appropriate measures, in accordance with its domestic legal principles, for the identification, detection and freezing or seizure of any funds used or allocated for the purpose of committing the offences set forth in article 2 as well as the proceeds derived from such offences, for purposes of possible forfeiture.

2. Each State Party shall take appropriate measures, in accordance with its domestic legal principles, for the forfeiture of funds used or allocated for the purpose of committing the offences set forth in article 2 and the proceeds derived from such offences.

3. Each State Party concerned may give consideration to concluding agreements on the sharing with other States Parties, on a regular or case-by-case basis, of the funds derived from the forfeitures referred to in this article.

4. Each State Party shall consider establishing mechanisms whereby the funds derived from the forfeitures referred to in this article are utilized to compensate the victims of offences referred to in article 2, paragraph 1, subparagraph (a) or (b), or their families.

5. The provisions of this article shall be implemented without prejudice to the rights of third parties acting in good faith.

ARTICLE 9

1. Upon receiving information that a person who has committed or who is alleged to have committed an offence set forth in article 2 may be present in its territory, the State Party concerned shall take such measures as may be necessary under its domestic law to investigate the facts contained in the information.

2. Upon being satisfied that the circumstances so warrant, the State Party in whose territory the offender or alleged offender is present shall take the appropriate measures under its domestic law so as to ensure that person' presence for the purpose of prosecution or extradition.

3. Any person regarding whom the measures referred to in paragraph 2 are being taken shall be entitled to:

(a) Communicate without delay with the nearest appropriate representative of the State of which that person is a national or which is otherwise entitled to protect that person's rights or, if that person is a stateless person, the State in the territory of which that person habitually resides;

(b) Be visited by a representative of that State;

(c) Be informed of that person's rights under subparagraphs (a) and (b).

4. The rights referred to in paragraph 3 shall be exercised in conformity with the laws and regulations of the State in the territory of which the offender or alleged offender is present, subject to the provision that the said laws and regulations must enable full effect to be given to the purposes for which the rights accorded under paragraph 3 are intended.

5. The provisions of paragraphs 3 and 4 shall be without prejudice to the right of any State Party having a claim to jurisdiction in accordance with article 7, paragraph 1, subparagraph (b), or paragraph 2, subparagraph (b), to invite the International Committee of the Red Cross to communicate with and visit the alleged offender.

6. When a State Party, pursuant to the present article, has taken a person into custody, it shall immediately notify, directly or through the Secretary-General of the United Nations, the States Parties which have established jurisdiction in accordance with article 7, paragraph 1 or 2, and, if it considers it advisable, any other interested States Parties, of the fact that such person is in custody and of the circumstances which warrant that person' detention. The State which makes the investigation contemplated in paragraph 1 shall promptly inform the said States Parties of its findings and shall indicate whether it intends to exercise jurisdiction.

ARTICLE 10

1. The State Party in the territory of which the alleged offender is present shall, in cases to which article 7 applies, if it does not extradite that person, be obliged, without exception whatsoever and whether or not the offence was committed in its territory, to submit the case without undue delay to its competent authorities for the purpose of prosecution, through proceedings in accordance with the laws of that State. Those authorities shall take their decision in the same manner as in the case of any other offence of a grave nature under the law of that State.

2. Whenever a State Party is permitted under its domestic law to extradite or otherwise surrender one of its nationals only upon the condition that the person will be returned to that State to serve the sentence imposed as a result of the trial or proceeding for which the extradition or surrender of the person was sought, and this State and the State seeking the extradition of the person agree with this option and other terms they may deem appropriate, such a conditional extradition or surrender shall be sufficient to discharge the obligation set forth in paragraph 1.

ARTICLE 11

1. The offences set forth in article 2 shall be deemed to be included as extraditable offences in any extradition treaty existing between any of the States Parties before the entry into force of this Convention. States Parties undertake to include such offences as extraditable offences in every extradition treaty to be subsequently concluded between them.

2. When a State Party which makes extradition conditional on the existence of a treaty receives a request for extradition from another State Party with which it has no extradition treaty, the requested State Party may, at its option, consider this Convention as a legal basis for extradition in respect of the offences set forth in article 2. Extradition shall be subject to the other conditions provided by the law of the requested State. . . .

ARTICLE 12

1. States Parties shall afford one another the greatest measure of assistance in connection with criminal investigations or criminal or extradition proceedings in respect of the offences set forth in article 2, including assistance in obtaining evidence in their possession necessary for the proceedings.

2. States Parties may not refuse a request for mutual legal assistance on the ground of bank secrecy.

3. The requesting Party shall not transmit nor use information or evidence furnished by the requested Party for investigations, prosecutions or proceedings other than those stated in the request without the prior consent of the requested Party. . . .

ARTICLE 13

None of the offences set forth in article 2 shall be regarded, for the purposes of extradition or mutual legal assistance, as a fiscal offence. Accordingly, States Parties may not refuse a request for extradition or for mutual legal assistance on the sole ground that it concerns a fiscal offence.

ARTICLE 14

None of the offences set forth in article 2 shall be regarded for the purposes of extradition or mutual legal assistance as a political offence or as an offence connected with a political offence or as an offence inspired by political motives. Accordingly, a request for extradition or for mutual legal assistance based on such an offence may not be refused on the sole ground that it concerns a political offence or an offence connected with a political offence or an offence inspired by political motives.

ARTICLE 15

Nothing in this Convention shall be interpreted as imposing an obligation to extradite or to afford mutual legal assistance, if the requested State Party has substantial grounds for believing that the request for extradition for offences set forth in article 2 or for mutual legal assistance with respect to such offences has been made for the purpose of prosecuting or punishing a person on account of that person's race, religion, nationality, ethnic origin or political opinion or that compliance with the request would cause prejudice to that person's position for any of these reasons. . . .

ARTICLE 18

1. States Parties shall cooperate in the prevention of the offences set forth in article 2 by taking all practicable measures, inter alia, by adapting their domestic legislation, if necessary, to prevent and counter preparations in their respective territories for the commission of those offences within or outside their territories, including:

(a) Measures to prohibit in their territories illegal activities of persons and organizations that knowingly encourage, instigate, organize or engage in the commission of offences set forth in article 2;

(b) Measures requiring financial institutions and other professions involved in financial transactions to utilize the most efficient measures available for the identification of their usual or occasional customers, as well as customers in whose interest accounts are opened, and to pay special attention to unusual or suspicious transactions and report transactions suspected of stemming from a criminal activity. For this purpose, States Parties shall consider:

(i) Adopting regulations prohibiting the opening of accounts the holders or beneficiaries of which are unidentified or unidentifiable, and measures to ensure that such institutions verify the identity of the real owners of such transactions;

(ii) With respect to the identification of legal entities, requiring financial institutions, when necessary, to take measures to verify the legal existence and the structure of the customer by obtaining, either from a public register or from the customer or both, proof of incorporation, including information concerning the customer's name, legal form, address, directors and provisions regulating the power to bind the entity;

(iii) Adopting regulations imposing on financial institutions the obligation to report promptly to the competent authorities all complex, unusual large transactions and unusual patterns of transactions, which have no apparent economic or obviously lawful purpose, without fear of assuming criminal or civil liability for breach of any restriction on disclosure of information if they report their suspicions in good faith;

(iv) Requiring financial institutions to maintain, for at least five years, all necessary records on transactions, both domestic or international.

2. States Parties shall further cooperate in the prevention of offences set forth in article 2 by considering:

(a) Measures for the supervision, including, for example, the licensing, of all money-transmission agencies;

(b) Feasible measures to detect or monitor the physical cross-border transportation of cash and bearer negotiable instruments, subject to strict safeguards to ensure proper use of information and without impeding in any way the freedom of capital movements.

3. States Parties shall further cooperate in the prevention of the offences set forth in article 2 by exchanging accurate and verified information in accordance with their domestic law and coordinating administrative and other measures taken, as appropriate, to prevent the commission of offences set forth in article 2, in particular by:

(a) Establishing and maintaining channels of communication between their competent agencies and services to facilitate the secure and rapid exchange of information concerning all aspects of offences set forth in article 2;

(b) Cooperating with one another in conducting inquiries, with respect to the offences set forth in article 2, concerning:

(i) The identity, whereabouts and activities of persons in respect of whom reasonable suspicion exists that they are involved in such offences;

(ii) The movement of funds relating to the commission of such offences.

4. States Parties may exchange information through the International Criminal Police Organization (Interpol). . . .

Consequences

Such financial measures as seizing or freezing assets are relatively easy steps for nations to take in cases of terrorism, and the degree of cooperation in this field and under this convention has been extensive, especially since the terrorist attacks against the United States on September 11, 2001. Clearly, international cooperation has increased, as Alan P. Larson, U.S. undersecretary for economic, business, and agricultural affairs, made clear in his testimony before the Senate Finance Committee on October 9, 2002, citing numerous instances of antiterrorism resulting directly from the convention, including cooperation with various Middle Eastern nations to prevent money laundering, cooperation with Saudi Arabia to cut off private Saudi funding to al-Qaeda, and the conclusion of cooperative agreements with South America and Asian nations to monitor and interdict funding of terrorists.

Source
United Nations, "International Convention for the Suppression of the Financing of Terrorism." Available online. URL: http://www.un.org/law/cod/finterr.htm. Accessed January 4, 2005.

CONVENTION AGAINST TRANSNATIONAL ORGANIZED CRIME

TREATY AT A GLANCE

Completed
November 15, 2000; entered
into force September 29, 2003

Signatories
As of summer 2005, 147 United Nations member states;
106 have become full parties

Overview
In an age of easy and rapid global travel, communications, and data exchange, the members of the United Nations have recognized that transnational crime is a very serious and growing problem that can be effectively addressed only through close international cooperation. The convention legally binds states parties to take specified measures against transnational organized crime, the most important of which include the creation of domestic criminal offenses to combat the problem and the adoption of comprehensive frameworks for mutual legal assistance, extradition, law-enforcement cooperation, and technical assistance and training. The object of the convention is to ensure that states parties will be able to rely on one another in investigating, prosecuting, and punishing crimes committed by organized criminal groups in cases where either the crimes or the groups that commit them have some element of transnational involvement.

Historical Background

In 1923, Johann Schober, commissioner of Vienna's police department, called for an international meeting of police agencies for the purpose of creating a network to promote cooperation among enforcement officials across borders. The result was the International Criminal Police Organization, better known as Interpol. Aside from a welter of individual extradition treaties concluded among nations, Interpol was the first major step toward international cooperation in investigating, preventing, fighting, and prosecuting crime. Interpol is not itself a police agency, but a worldwide network, a means of communication and coordination. Because policing involves many complex issues of sovereignty—often even within a given country, since most nations have a variety of more or less local police jurisdictions, sometimes in addition to a national police agency—international cooperation has often been very difficult. However, extraordinary technological developments in transportation, communication, and data transfer, together with the globalization of the econ-

omy, have taken transnational crime far beyond the issues of international fugitive flight, which traditionally motivated extradition treaties. Today, the commission of crime, especially organized crime, recognizes no borders; therefore, international cooperation and coordination have become essential.

The text of the convention was developed over 11 sessions by the Ad Hoc Committee established by the United Nations General Assembly and meeting in Vienna between January 1999 and October 2000. The committee also developed three important protocols supplementing the convention: the PROTOCOL TO PREVENT, SUPPRESS AND PUNISH TRAFFICKING IN PERSONS, ESPECIALLY WOMEN AND CHILDREN, SUPPLEMENTING THE UNITED NATIONS CONVENTION AGAINST TRANSNATIONAL ORGANIZED CRIME; the PROTOCOL AGAINST THE SMUGGLING OF MIGRANTS BY LAND, SEA AND AIR, SUPPLEMENTING THE UNITED NATIONS CONVENTION AGAINST TRANSNATIONAL ORGANIZED CRIME; and the PROTOCOL AGAINST THE ILLICIT MANUFACTURING OF AND TRAFFICKING IN FIREARMS, THEIR PARTS AND COMPONENTS AND AMMUNITION, SUPPLEMENT-

ING THE UNITED NATIONS CONVENTION AGAINST TRANSNATIONAL ORGANIZED CRIME.

Terms

The purpose of the convention is to promote cooperation in order to prevent and combat transnational organized crime more effectively. For purposes of the convention, *organized crime* is defined very broadly as "a structured group of three or more persons, existing for a period of time and acting in concert with the aim of committing one or more serious crimes or offences established in accordance with this Convention, in order to obtain, directly or indirectly, a financial or other material benefit."

The provisions of the convention are intended to make it more difficult for offenders and organized criminal groups to take advantage of gaps in national law, jurisdictional problems, or a lack of accurate information about the full scope of their activities. Provisions deal generally with the fight against organized crime and also specifically target some of the major activities in which transnational organized crime is commonly involved. These include money laundering, corruption, and the obstruction of investigations or prosecutions.

While the convention respects and protects national sovereignty, it provides the basis for stronger common action against money laundering, greater ease of extradition, and measures on the protection of witnesses and enhanced judicial cooperation. Key to implementing the provisions of the convention is finance, and this document includes a mechanism to provide funding to aid countries in implementing the convention.

Finally, the states parties to the convention each agree to criminalize an enumerated set of violations so that the criminal statutes of all signatories will be, in effect, synchronized and harmonized in order to avoid uncertainty as to whether a crime in one country also constitutes a crime in another.

United Nations Convention against Transnational Organized Crime

ARTICLE 1
STATEMENT OF PURPOSE

The purpose of this Convention is to promote cooperation to prevent and combat transnational organized crime more effectively.

ARTICLE 2
USE OF TERMS

For the purposes of this Convention:

(a) "Organized criminal group" shall mean a structured group of three or more persons, existing for a period of time and acting in concert with the aim of committing one or more serious crimes or offences established in accordance with this Convention, in order to obtain, directly or indirectly, a financial or other material benefit;

(b) "Serious crime" shall mean conduct constituting an offence punishable by a maximum deprivation of liberty of at least four years or a more serious penalty;

(c) "Structured group" shall mean a group that is not randomly formed for the immediate commission of an offence and that does not need to have formally defined roles for its members, continuity of its membership or a developed structure;

(d) "Property" shall mean assets of every kind, whether corporeal or incorporeal, movable or immovable, tangible or intangible, and legal documents or instruments evidencing title to, or interest in, such assets;

(e) "Proceeds of crime" shall mean any property derived from or obtained, directly or indirectly, through the commission of an offence;

(f) "Freezing" or "seizure" shall mean temporarily prohibiting the transfer, conversion, disposition or movement of property or temporarily assuming custody or control of property on the basis of an order issued by a court or other competent authority;

(g) "Confiscation", which includes forfeiture where applicable, shall mean the permanent deprivation of property by order of a court or other competent authority;

(h) "Predicate offence" shall mean any offence as a result of which proceeds have been generated that may become the subject of an offence as defined in article 6 of this Convention;

(i) "Controlled delivery" shall mean the technique of allowing illicit or suspect consignments to pass out of, through or into the territory of one or more States, with the knowledge and under the supervision of their competent authorities, with a view to the investigation of an offence and the identification of persons involved in the commission of the offence;

(j) "Regional economic integration organization" shall mean an organization constituted by sovereign States of a given region, to which its member States have transferred competence in respect of matters governed by this Convention and which has been duly authorized, in accordance with its internal procedures, to sign, ratify, accept, approve or accede to it; references to "States Parties" under this Convention shall apply to such organizations within the limits of their competence. . . .

ARTICLE 4
PROTECTION OF SOVEREIGNTY

1. States Parties shall carry out their obligations under this Convention in a manner consistent with the principles of sovereign equality and territorial integrity of States and that of non-intervention in the domestic affairs of other States. . . .

ARTICLE 5
CRIMINALIZATION OF PARTICIPATION IN
AN ORGANIZED CRIMINAL GROUP

1. Each State Party shall adopt such legislative and other measures as may be necessary to establish as criminal offences, when committed intentionally:

(a) Either or both of the following as criminal offences distinct from those involving the attempt or completion of the criminal activity:

(i) Agreeing with one or more other persons to commit a serious crime for a purpose relating directly or indirectly to the obtaining of a financial or other material benefit and, where required by domestic law, involving an act undertaken by one of the participants in furtherance of the agreement or involving an organized criminal group;

(ii) Conduct by a person who, with knowledge of either the aim and general criminal activity of an organized criminal group or its intention to commit the crimes in question, takes an active part in:

a. Criminal activities of the organized criminal group;

b. Other activities of the organized criminal group in the knowledge that his or her participation will contribute to the achievement of the above-described criminal aim;

(b) Organizing, directing, aiding, abetting, facilitating or counselling the commission of serious crime involving an organized criminal group.

2. The knowledge, intent, aim, purpose or agreement referred to in paragraph 1 of this article may be inferred from objective factual circumstances.

3. States Parties whose domestic law requires involvement of an organized criminal group for purposes of the offences established in accordance with paragraph 1 (a) (i) of this article shall ensure that their domestic law covers all serious crimes involving organized criminal groups. Such States Parties, as well as States Parties whose domestic law requires an act in furtherance of the agreement for purposes of the offences established in accordance with paragraph 1 (a) (i) of this article, shall so inform the Secretary-General of the United Nations at the time of their signature or of deposit of their instrument of ratification, acceptance or approval of or accession to this Convention.

ARTICLE 6
CRIMINALIZATION OF
THE LAUNDERING OF PROCEEDS OF CRIME

1. Each State Party shall adopt, in accordance with fundamental principles of its domestic law, such legislative and other measures as may be necessary to establish as criminal offences, when committed intentionally:

(a) (i) The conversion or transfer of property, knowing that such property is the proceeds of crime, for the purpose of concealing or disguising the illicit origin of the property or of helping any person who is involved in the commission of the predicate offence to evade the legal consequences of his or her action;

(ii) The concealment or disguise of the true nature, source, location, disposition, movement or ownership of or rights with respect to property, knowing that such property is the proceeds of crime;

(b) Subject to the basic concepts of its legal system:

(i) The acquisition, possession or use of property, knowing, at the time of receipt, that such property is the proceeds of crime;

(ii) Participation in, association with or conspiracy to commit, attempts to commit and aiding, abetting, facilitating and counselling the commission of any of the offences established in accordance with this article. . . .

ARTICLE 7
MEASURES TO COMBAT MONEY-LAUNDERING

1. Each State Party:

(a) Shall institute a comprehensive domestic regulatory and supervisory regime for banks and non-bank financial institutions and, where appropriate, other bodies particularly susceptible to money-laundering, within its competence, in order to deter and detect all forms of money-laundering, which regime shall emphasize requirements for customer identification, record-keeping and the reporting of suspicious transactions;

(b) Shall, without prejudice to articles 18 and 27 of this Convention, ensure that administrative, regulatory, law enforcement and other authorities dedicated to combating money-laundering (including, where appropriate under domestic law, judicial authorities) have the ability to cooperate and exchange information at the national and international levels within the conditions prescribed by its domestic law and, to that end, shall consider the establishment of a financial intelligence unit to serve as a national centre for the collection, analysis and dissemination of information regarding potential money-laundering.

2. States Parties shall consider implementing feasible measures to detect and monitor the movement of cash and appropriate negotiable instruments across their borders, subject to safeguards to ensure proper use of information and without impeding in any way the movement of legitimate capital. Such measures may include a requirement that individuals and businesses report the cross-border transfer of substantial quantities of cash and appropriate negotiable instruments.

3. In establishing a domestic regulatory and supervisory regime under the terms of this article, and without prejudice to any other article of this Convention, States Parties are called upon to use as a guideline the relevant initiatives of regional, interregional and multilateral organizations against money-laundering.

4. States Parties shall endeavour to develop and promote global, regional, subregional and bilateral cooperation among judicial, law enforcement and financial regulatory authorities in order to combat money-laundering.

ARTICLE 8
CRIMINALIZATION OF CORRUPTION

1. Each State Party shall adopt such legislative and other measures as may be necessary to establish as criminal offences, when committed intentionally:

(a) The promise, offering or giving to a public official, directly or indirectly, of an undue advantage, for the official himself or herself or another person or entity, in order that the official act or refrain from acting in the exercise of his or her official duties;

(b) The solicitation or acceptance by a public official, directly or indirectly, of an undue advantage, for the official himself or herself or another person or entity, in order that the official act or refrain from acting in the exercise of his or her official duties. . . .

ARTICLE 9
MEASURES AGAINST CORRUPTION

1. In addition to the measures set forth in article 8 of this Convention, each State Party shall, to the extent appropriate and consistent with its legal system, adopt legislative, administrative or other effective measures to promote integrity and to prevent, detect and punish the corruption of public officials. . . .

ARTICLE 10
LIABILITY OF LEGAL PERSONS

1. Each State Party shall adopt such measures as may be necessary, consistent with its legal principles, to establish the liability of legal persons for participation in serious crimes involving an organized criminal group and for the offences established in accordance with articles 5, 6, 8 and 23 of this Convention. . . .

ARTICLE 11
PROSECUTION, ADJUDICATION AND SANCTIONS

1. Each State Party shall make the commission of an offence established in accordance with articles 5, 6, 8 and 23 of this Convention liable to sanctions that take into account the gravity of that offence. . . .

ARTICLE 12
CONFISCATION AND SEIZURE

1. States Parties shall adopt, to the greatest extent possible within their domestic legal systems, such measures as may be necessary to enable confiscation of:

(a) Proceeds of crime derived from offences covered by this Convention or property the value of which corresponds to that of such proceeds;

(b) Property, equipment or other instrumentalities used in or destined for use in offences covered by this Convention.

2. States Parties shall adopt such measures as may be necessary to enable the identification, tracing, freezing or seizure of any item referred to in paragraph 1 of this article for the purpose of eventual confiscation.

3. If proceeds of crime have been transformed or converted, in part or in full, into other property, such property shall be liable to the measures referred to in this article instead of the proceeds.

4. If proceeds of crime have been intermingled with property acquired from legitimate sources, such property shall, without prejudice to any powers relating to freezing or seizure, be liable to confiscation up to the assessed value of the intermingled proceeds.

5. Income or other benefits derived from proceeds of crime, from property into which proceeds of crime have been transformed or converted or from property with which proceeds of crime have been intermingled shall also be liable to the measures referred to in this article, in the same manner and to the same extent as proceeds of crime.

6. For the purposes of this article and article 13 of this Convention, each State Party shall empower its courts or other competent authorities to order that bank, financial or commercial records be made available or be seized. States Parties shall not decline to act under the provisions of this paragraph on the ground of bank secrecy.

7. States Parties may consider the possibility of requiring that an offender demonstrate the lawful origin of alleged proceeds of crime or other property liable to confiscation, to the extent that such a requirement is consistent with the principles of their domestic law and with the nature of the judicial and other proceedings. . . .

ARTICLE 13
INTERNATIONAL COOPERATION
FOR PURPOSES OF CONFISCATION

. . .

2. Following a request made by another State Party having jurisdiction over an offence covered by this Convention, the requested State Party shall take measures to identify, trace and freeze or seize proceeds of crime, property, equipment or other instrumentalities referred to in article 12, paragraph 1, of this Convention for the purpose of eventual confiscation to be ordered either by the requesting State Party or, pursuant to a request under paragraph 1 of this article, by the requested State Party. . . .

ARTICLE 14
DISPOSAL OF CONFISCATED PROCEEDS
OF CRIME OR PROPERTY

1. Proceeds of crime or property confiscated by a State Party pursuant to articles 12 or 13, paragraph 1, of this Convention shall be disposed of by that State Party in accordance with its domestic law and administrative procedures. . . .

ARTICLE 15
JURISDICTION

1. Each State Party shall adopt such measures as may be necessary to establish its jurisdiction over the offences established in accordance with articles 5, 6, 8 and 23 of this Convention when:

(a) The offence is committed in the territory of that State Party; or

(b) The offence is committed on board a vessel that is flying the flag of that State Party or an aircraft that is registered under the laws of that State Party at the time that the offence is committed.

2. Subject to article 4 of this Convention, a State Party may also establish its jurisdiction over any such offence when:

(a) The offence is committed against a national of that State Party;

(b) The offence is committed by a national of that State Party or a stateless person who has his or her habitual residence in its territory; or

(c) The offence is:

(i) One of those established in accordance with article 5, paragraph 1, of this Convention and is committed outside its territory with a view to the commission of a serious crime within its territory;

(ii) One of those established in accordance with article 6, paragraph 1 (b) (ii), of this Convention and is committed outside its territory with a view to the commission of an offence established in accordance with article 6, paragraph 1 (a) (i) or (ii) or (b) (i), of this Convention within its territory. . . .

ARTICLE 16
EXTRADITION

. . .

3. Each of the offences to which this article applies shall be deemed to be included as an extraditable offence in any extradition treaty existing between States Parties. States Parties undertake to include such offences as extraditable offences in every extradition treaty to be concluded between them.

4. If a State Party that makes extradition conditional on the existence of a treaty receives a request for extradition from another State Party with which it has no extradition treaty, it may consider this Convention the legal basis for extradition in respect of any offence to which this article applies. . . .

ARTICLE 18
MUTUAL LEGAL ASSISTANCE

1. States Parties shall afford one another the widest measure of mutual legal assistance in investigations, prosecutions and judicial proceedings in relation to the offences covered by this Convention. . . .

ARTICLE 19
JOINT INVESTIGATIONS

States Parties shall consider concluding bilateral or multilateral agreements or arrangements whereby, in relation to matters that are the subject of investigations, prosecutions or judicial proceedings in one or more States, the competent authorities concerned may establish joint investigative bodies. In the absence of such agreements or arrangements, joint investigations may be undertaken by agreement on a case-by-case basis. The States Parties involved shall ensure that the sovereignty of the State Party in whose territory such investigation is to take place is fully respected.

ARTICLE 20
SPECIAL INVESTIGATIVE TECHNIQUES

1. If permitted by the basic principles of its domestic legal system, each State Party shall, within its possibilities and under the conditions prescribed by its domestic law, take the necessary measures to allow for the appropriate use of controlled delivery and, where it deems appropriate, for the use of other special investigative techniques, such as electronic or other forms of surveillance and undercover operations, by its competent authorities in its territory for the purpose of effectively combating organized crime. . . .

ARTICLE 23
CRIMINALIZATION OF OBSTRUCTION OF JUSTICE

Each State Party shall adopt such legislative and other measures as may be necessary to establish as criminal offences, when committed intentionally:

(a) The use of physical force, threats or intimidation or the promise, offering or giving of an undue advantage to induce false testimony or to interfere in the giving of testimony or the production of evidence in a proceeding in relation to the commission of offences covered by this Convention;

(b) The use of physical force, threats or intimidation to interfere with the exercise of official duties by a justice or law enforcement official in relation to the commission of offences covered by this Convention. Nothing in this subparagraph shall prejudice the right of States Parties to have legislation that protects other categories of public officials.

ARTICLE 24
PROTECTION OF WITNESSES

1. Each State Party shall take appropriate measures within its means to provide effective protection from potential retaliation or intimidation for witnesses in criminal proceedings who give testimony concerning offences covered by this Convention and, as appropriate, for their relatives and other persons close to them. . . .

ARTICLE 25
ASSISTANCE TO AND PROTECTION OF VICTIMS

1. Each State Party shall take appropriate measures within its means to provide assistance and protection to victims of offences covered by this Convention, in particular in cases of threat of retaliation or intimidation.

2. Each State Party shall establish appropriate procedures to provide access to compensation and restitution for victims of offences covered by this Convention.

3. Each State Party shall, subject to its domestic law, enable views and concerns of victims to be presented and considered at appropriate stages of criminal proceedings against offenders in a manner not prejudicial to the rights of the defence.

ARTICLE 26
MEASURES TO ENHANCE COOPERATION WITH LAW ENFORCEMENT AUTHORITIES

1. Each State Party shall take appropriate measures to encourage persons who participate or who have participated in organized criminal groups:

(a) To supply information useful to competent authorities for investigative and evidentiary purposes on such matters as:

(i)The identity, nature, composition, structure, location or activities of organized criminal groups;

(ii) Links, including international links, with other organized criminal groups;

(iii) Offences that organized criminal groups have committed or may commit;

(b) To provide factual, concrete help to competent authorities that may contribute to depriving organized criminal groups of their resources or of the proceeds of crime.

2. Each State Party shall consider providing for the possibility, in appropriate cases, of mitigating punishment of an accused person who provides substantial cooperation in the investigation or prosecution of an offence covered by this Convention.

3. Each State Party shall consider providing for the possibility, in accordance with fundamental principles of its domestic law, of granting immunity from prosecution to a person who provides substantial cooperation in the investigation or prosecution of an offence covered by this Convention.

4. Protection of such persons shall be as provided for in article 24 of this Convention. . . .

ARTICLE 27
LAW ENFORCEMENT COOPERATION

1. States Parties shall cooperate closely with one another, consistent with their respective domestic legal and administrative systems, to enhance the effectiveness of law enforcement action to combat the offences covered by this Convention. Each State Party shall, in particular, adopt effective measures:

(a) To enhance and, where necessary, to establish channels of communication between their competent authorities, agencies and services in order to facilitate the secure and rapid exchange of information concerning all aspects of the offences covered by this Convention, including, if the States Parties concerned deem it appropriate, links with other criminal activities;

(b) To cooperate with other States Parties in conducting inquiries with respect to offences covered by this Convention concerning:

(i) The identity, whereabouts and activities of persons suspected of involvement in such offences or the location of other persons concerned;

(ii) The movement of proceeds of crime or property derived from the commission of such offences;

(iii) The movement of property, equipment or other instrumentalities used or intended for use in the commission of such offences;

(c) To provide, when appropriate, necessary items or quantities of substances for analytical or investigative purposes;

(d) To facilitate effective coordination between their competent authorities, agencies and services and to promote the exchange of personnel and other experts, including, subject to bilateral agreements or arrangements between the States Parties concerned, the posting of liaison officers;

(e) To exchange information with other States Parties on specific means and methods used by organized criminal groups, including, where applicable, routes and conveyances and the use of false identities, altered or false documents or other means of concealing their activities;

(f) To exchange information and coordinate administrative and other measures taken as appropriate for the purpose of early identification of the offences covered by this Convention.

2. With a view to giving effect to this Convention, States Parties shall consider entering into bilateral or multilateral agreements or arrangements on direct cooperation between their law enforcement agencies ...

ARTICLE 28
COLLECTION, EXCHANGE AND ANALYSIS OF INFORMATION ON THE NATURE OF ORGANIZED CRIME

1. Each State Party shall consider analysing, in consultation with the scientific and academic communities, trends in organized crime in its territory, the circumstances in which organized crime operates, as well as the professional groups and technologies involved.

2. States Parties shall consider developing and sharing analytical expertise concerning organized criminal activities with each other and through international and regional organizations. . . .

ARTICLE 29
TRAINING AND TECHNICAL ASSISTANCE

1. Each State Party shall, to the extent necessary, initiate, develop or improve specific training programmes for its law enforcement personnel, including prosecutors, investigating magistrates and customs personnel, and other personnel charged with the prevention, detection and control of the offences covered by this Convention. Such programmes may include secondments and exchanges of staff. Such programmes shall deal, in particular and to the extent permitted by domestic law, with the following:

(a) Methods used in the prevention, detection and control of the offences covered by this Convention;

(b) Routes and techniques used by persons suspected of involvement in offences covered by this Convention, including in transit States, and appropriate countermeasures;

(c) Monitoring of the movement of contraband;

(d) Detection and monitoring of the movements of proceeds of crime, property, equipment or other instrumentalities and methods used for the transfer, concealment or disguise of such proceeds, property, equipment or other instrumentalities, as well as methods used in combating money-laundering and other financial crimes;

(e) Collection of evidence;

(f) Control techniques in free trade zones and free ports;

(g) Modern law enforcement equipment and techniques, including electronic surveillance, controlled deliveries and undercover operations;

(h) Methods used in combating transnational organized crime committed through the use of computers, telecommunications networks or other forms of modern technology; and

(i) Methods used in the protection of victims and witnesses.

2. States Parties shall assist one another in planning and implementing research and training programmes designed to share expertise in the areas referred to in paragraph 1 of this article and to that end shall also, when appropriate, use regional and international conferences and seminars to promote cooperation and to stimulate discussion on problems of mutual concern, including the special problems and needs of transit States.

3. States Parties shall promote training and technical assistance that will facilitate extradition and mutual legal assistance. Such training and technical assistance may include language training, secondments and exchanges between personnel in central authorities or agencies with relevant responsibilities. . . .

ARTICLE 30
OTHER MEASURES: IMPLEMENTATION OF THE CONVENTION THROUGH ECONOMIC DEVELOPMENT AND TECHNICAL ASSISTANCE

1. States Parties shall take measures conducive to the optimal implementation of this Convention to the extent possible, through international cooperation, taking into account the negative effects of organized crime on society in general, in particular on sustainable development.

2. States Parties shall make concrete efforts to the extent possible and in coordination with each other, as well as with international and regional organizations:

(a) To enhance their cooperation at various levels with developing countries, with a view to strengthening the capacity of the latter to prevent and combat transnational organized crime;

(b) To enhance financial and material assistance to support the efforts of developing countries to fight transnational organized crime effectively and to help them implement this Convention successfully;

(c) To provide technical assistance to developing countries and countries with economies in transition to assist them in meeting their needs for the implementation of this Convention. To that end, States Parties shall endeavour to make adequate and regular voluntary contributions to an account specifically designated for that purpose in a United Nations funding mechanism. States Parties may also give special consideration, in accordance with their domestic law and the provisions of this Convention, to contributing to the aforementioned account a percentage of the money or of the corresponding value of proceeds of crime or property confiscated in accordance with the provisions of this Convention;

(d) To encourage and persuade other States and financial institutions as appropriate to join them in efforts in accordance with this article, in particular by providing more training programmes and modern equipment to developing countries in order to assist them in achieving the objectives of this Convention. . . .

ARTICLE 31
PREVENTION

1. States Parties shall endeavour to develop and evaluate national projects and to establish and promote best practices and policies aimed at the prevention of transnational organized crime.

2. States Parties shall endeavour, in accordance with fundamental principles of their domestic law, to reduce existing or future opportunities for organized criminal groups to participate in lawful markets with proceeds of crime, through appropriate legislative, administrative or other measures. These measures should focus on:

(a) The strengthening of cooperation between law enforcement agencies or prosecutors and relevant private entities, including industry;

(b) The promotion of the development of standards and procedures designed to safeguard the integrity of public and relevant private entities, as well as codes of conduct for relevant professions, in particular lawyers, notaries public, tax consultants and accountants;

(c) The prevention of the misuse by organized criminal groups of tender procedures conducted by public authorities and of subsidies and licences granted by public authorities for commercial activity;

(d) The prevention of the misuse of legal persons by organized criminal groups; such measures could include:

(i) The establishment of public records on legal and natural persons involved in the establishment, management and funding of legal persons;

(ii) The introduction of the possibility of disqualifying by court order or any appropriate means for a reasonable period of time persons

convicted of offences covered by this Convention from acting as directors of legal persons incorporated within their jurisdiction;

(iii) The establishment of national records of persons disqualified from acting as directors of legal persons; and

(iv) The exchange of information contained in the records referred to in subparagraphs (d) (i) and (iii) of this paragraph with the competent authorities of other States Parties.

3. States Parties shall endeavour to promote the reintegration into society of persons convicted of offences covered by this Convention.

4. States Parties shall endeavour to evaluate periodically existing relevant legal instruments and administrative practices with a view to detecting their vulnerability to misuse by organized criminal groups.

5. States Parties shall endeavour to promote public awareness regarding the existence, causes and gravity of and the threat posed by transnational organized crime. Information may be disseminated where appropriate through the mass media and shall include measures to promote public participation in preventing and combating such crime.

6. Each State Party shall inform the Secretary-General of the United Nations of the name and address of the authority or authorities that can assist other States Parties in developing measures to prevent transnational organized crime.

7. States Parties shall, as appropriate, collaborate with each other and relevant international and regional organizations in promoting and developing the measures referred to in this article. This includes participation in international projects aimed at the prevention of transnational organized crime, for example by alleviating the circumstances that render socially marginalized groups vulnerable to the action of transnational organized crime.

ARTICLE 32
CONFERENCE OF THE PARTIES TO THE CONVENTION

1. A Conference of the Parties to the Convention is hereby established to improve the capacity of States Parties to combat transnational organized crime and to promote and review the implementation of this Convention. . . .

ARTICLE 34
IMPLEMENTATION OF THE CONVENTION

1. Each State Party shall take the necessary measures, including legislative and administrative measures, in accordance with fundamental principles of its domestic law, to ensure the implementation of its obligations under this Convention. . . .

Consequences

As of mid-2005, it is premature to attempt an assessment of the effectiveness of the convention; however, its virtually universal acceptance by the international community suggests a genuine appreciation of the borderless nature of modern organized crime and its implications for the economic well-being of the world. Whatever else the convention may accomplish, it compels nations to come to terms with issues of corruption by forcing them either to define domestic policies in opposition to many modes of transnational crime or suffer the moral, diplomatic, and possibly economic censure of the world as countenancing and contributing to corruption. The convention makes it more difficult for corrupt regimes to operate or to endure.

Source

United Nations Office on Drugs and Crime, "United Nations Convention Against Transnational Organized Crime." Available online. URL: http://www.unodc.org/pdf/crime/a_res_ 55/res5525e.pdf. Accessed January 4, 2005.

PROTOCOL AGAINST THE SMUGGLING OF MIGRANTS BY LAND, SEA AND AIR, SUPPLEMENTING THE UNITED NATIONS CONVENTION AGAINST TRANSNATIONAL ORGANIZED CRIME

TREATY AT A GLANCE

Completed
November 15, 2000;
entered into force January 28, 2004

Signatories
As of summer 2005, 112 member states of the United Nations,
of which 76 are full parties

Overview
A protocol annexed to the Convention against Transnational Organized Crime, this document provides for an international approach, encompassing cooperation, the exchange of information, and other appropriate measures, including socioeconomic measures, to combat the smuggling of migrants by land, sea and air.

Historical Background

For the overall historical background of international cooperation against transnational organized crime, see the entry on the United Nations CONVENTION AGAINST TRANSNATIONAL ORGANIZED CRIME. The immediate background of the resolution was a worldwide rise in the illegal, exploitative, and hazardous smuggling of migrants. This activity was not only a hazard to collective national security, because the migrants were entirely undocumented, but an even greater hazard to the migrants themselves. Typically, they were transported in deplorable conditions, with inadequate supplies of water, food, and other necessities. Many died. Others were abused by the smugglers or employers.

The origin of the Protocol against the Smuggling of Migrants by Land, Sea and Air is found in United Nations Resolution 53/111 of December 9, 1998, in which the General Assembly resolved to establish an open-ended intergovernmental ad-hoc committee to draw up a convention against transnational organized crime, together with protocols to prevent, suppress, and punish trafficking in persons, especially women and children (PROTOCOL TO PREVENT, SUPPRESS AND PUNISH TRAFFICKING IN PERSONS, ESPECIALLY WOMEN AND CHILDREN, SUPPLEMENTING THE UNITED NATIONS CONVENTION AGAINST TRANSNATIONAL ORGANIZED CRIME) and against the smuggling of migrants by land, air and sea.

As of summer 2005, the United States, a signatory, had not yet ratified the protocol to become a full party to it; however, on February 23, 2004, President George W. Bush requested the consent of the Senate in ratifying the protocol. On February 10, 2005, the consenting resolution was referred to the Committee on Foreign Relations. As of summer 2005, the measure was still in committee.

Terms

This protocol is intended to ensure the universal criminalization of the smuggling of migrants, while recognizing that migration itself is not a crime. The protocol requires states parties

- To make migrant smuggling a criminal offense under their national laws;
- To adopt special measures to detect, interdict, and prevent migrant smuggling by sea;
- Generally to increase international cooperation to prevent migrant smuggling; and
- To increase international cooperative efforts to seek out and prosecute traffickers and smugglers.

The convention also creates a global criminal law standard for the offense of smuggling migrants, and it provides mechanisms for rendering assistance to and protecting victims of smuggling. Importantly, the protocol applies to the smuggling of migrants only as the product of transnational organized crime.

Protocol against the Smuggling of Migrants by Land, Sea and Air, Supplementing the United Nations Convention against Transnational Organized Crime

Preamble

The States Parties to this Protocol,

Declaring that effective action to prevent and combat the smuggling of migrants by land, sea and air requires a comprehensive international approach, including cooperation, the exchange of information and other appropriate measures, including socio-economic measures, at the national, regional and international levels,

Recalling General Assembly resolution 54/212 of 22 December 1999, in which the Assembly urged Member States and the United Nations system to strengthen international cooperation in the area of international migration and development in order to address the root causes of migration, especially those related to poverty, and to maximize the benefits of international migration to those concerned, and encouraged, where relevant, interregional, regional and subregional mechanisms to continue to address the question of migration and development,

Convinced of the need to provide migrants with humane treatment and full protection of their rights,

Taking into account the fact that, despite work undertaken in other international forums, there is no universal instrument that addresses all aspects of smuggling of migrants and other related issues,

Concerned at the significant increase in the activities of organized criminal groups in smuggling of migrants and other related criminal activities set forth in this Protocol, which bring great harm to the States concerned,

Also concerned that the smuggling of migrants can endanger the lives or security of the migrants involved,

Recalling General Assembly resolution 53/111 of 9 December 1998, in which the Assembly decided to establish an open-ended intergovernmental ad hoc committee for the purpose of elaborating a comprehensive international convention against transnational organized crime and of discussing the elaboration of, inter alia, an international instrument addressing illegal trafficking in and transporting of migrants, including by sea,

Convinced that supplementing the United Nations Convention against Transnational Organized Crime with an international instrument against the smuggling of migrants by land, sea and air will be useful in preventing and combating that crime,

Have agreed as follows:

I
General Provisions
ARTICLE 1
RELATION WITH THE UNITED NATIONS CONVENTION AGAINST TRANSNATIONAL ORGANIZED CRIME

1. This Protocol supplements the United Nations Convention against Transnational Organized Crime. It shall be interpreted together with the Convention. . . .

ARTICLE 2
STATEMENT OF PURPOSE

The purpose of this Protocol is to prevent and combat the smuggling of migrants, as well as to promote cooperation among States Parties to that end, while protecting the rights of smuggled migrants. . . .

ARTICLE 4
SCOPE OF APPLICATION

This Protocol shall apply, except as otherwise stated herein, to the prevention, investigation and prosecution of the offences established in accordance with article 6 of this Protocol, where the offences are transnational in nature and involve an organized criminal group, as well as to the protection of the rights of persons who have been the object of such offences. . . .

ARTICLE 5
CRIMINAL LIABILITY OF MIGRANTS

Migrants shall not become liable to criminal prosecution under this Protocol for the fact of having been the object of conduct set forth in article 6 of this Protocol.

ARTICLE 6
CRIMINALIZATION

1. Each State Party shall adopt such legislative and other measures as may be necessary to establish as criminal offences, when committed intentionally and in order to obtain, directly or indirectly, a financial or other material benefit:

(a) The smuggling of migrants;

(b) When committed for the purpose of enabling the smuggling of migrants:

(i) Producing a fraudulent travel or identity document;

(ii) Procuring, providing or possessing such a document;

(c) Enabling a person who is not a national or a permanent resident to remain in the State concerned without complying with the necessary requirements for legally remaining in the State by the means mentioned in subparagraph (b) of this paragraph or any other illegal means.

2. Each State Party shall also adopt such legislative and other measures as may be necessary to establish as criminal offences:

(a) Subject to the basic concepts of its legal system, attempting to commit an offence established in accordance with paragraph 1 of this article;

(b) Participating as an accomplice in an offence established in accordance with paragraph 1 (a), (b) (i) or (c) of this article and, subject to the basic concepts of its legal system, participating as an accomplice in an offence established in accordance with paragraph 1 (b) (ii) of this article;

(c) Organizing or directing other persons to commit an offence established in accordance with paragraph 1 of this article.

3. Each State Party shall adopt such legislative and other measures as may be necessary to establish as aggravating circumstances to the offences established in accordance with paragraph 1 (a), (b) (i) and (c) of this article and, subject to the basic concepts of its legal system, to the offences established in accordance with paragraph 2 (b) and (c) of this article, circumstances:

(a) That endanger, or are likely to endanger, the lives or safety of the migrants concerned; or

(b) That entail inhuman or degrading treatment, including for exploitation, of such migrants.

4. Nothing in this Protocol shall prevent a State Party from taking measures against a person whose conduct constitutes an offence under its domestic law.

II
Smuggling of Migrants by Sea

ARTICLE 7
COOPERATION

States Parties shall cooperate to the fullest extent possible to prevent and suppress the smuggling of migrants by sea, in accordance with the international law of the sea.

ARTICLE 8
MEASURES AGAINST THE SMUGGLING
OF MIGRANTS BY SEA

1. A State Party that has reasonable grounds to suspect that a vessel that is flying its flag or claiming its registry, that is without nationality or that, though flying a foreign flag or refusing to show a flag, is in reality of the nationality of the State Party concerned is engaged in the smuggling of migrants by sea may request the assistance of other States Parties in suppressing the use of the vessel for that purpose. The States Parties so requested shall render such assistance to the extent possible within their means.

2. A State Party that has reasonable grounds to suspect that a vessel exercising freedom of navigation in accordance with international law and flying the flag or displaying the marks of registry of another State Party is engaged in the smuggling of migrants by sea may so notify the flag State, request confirmation of registry and, if confirmed, request authorization from the flag State to take appropriate measures with regard to that vessel. The flag State may authorize the requesting State, inter alia:

(a) To board the vessel;

(b) To search the vessel; and

(c) If evidence is found that the vessel is engaged in the smuggling of migrants by sea, to take appropriate measures with respect to the vessel and persons and cargo on board, as authorized by the flag State.

3. A State Party that has taken any measure in accordance with paragraph 2 of this article shall promptly inform the flag State concerned of the results of that measure.

4. A State Party shall respond expeditiously to a request from another State Party to determine whether a vessel that is claiming its registry or flying its flag is entitled to do so and to a request for authorization made in accordance with paragraph 2 of this article.

5. A flag State may, consistent with article 7 of this Protocol, subject its authorization to conditions to be agreed by it and the requesting State, including conditions relating to responsibility and the extent of effective measures to be taken. A State Party shall take no additional measures without the express authorization of the flag State, except those necessary to relieve imminent danger to the lives of persons or those which derive from relevant bilateral or multilateral agreements.

6. Each State Party shall designate an authority or, where necessary, authorities to receive and respond to requests for assistance, for confirmation of registry or of the right of a vessel to fly its flag and for authorization to take appropriate measures. Such designation shall be notified through the Secretary-General to all other States Parties within one month of the designation.

7. A State Party that has reasonable grounds to suspect that a vessel is engaged in the smuggling of migrants by sea and is without nationality or may be assimilated to a vessel without nationality may board and search the vessel. If evidence confirming the suspicion is found, that State Party shall take appropriate measures in accordance with relevant domestic and international law. . . .

III
Prevention, Cooperation and Other Measures

ARTICLE 10
INFORMATION

1. Without prejudice to articles 27 and 28 of the Convention, States Parties, in particular those with common borders or located on routes along which migrants are smuggled, shall, for the purpose of achieving the objectives of this Protocol, exchange among themselves, consistent with their respective domestic legal and administrative systems, relevant information on matters such as:

(a) Embarkation and destination points, as well as routes, carriers and means of transportation, known to be or suspected of being used by an organized criminal group engaged in conduct set forth in article 6 of this Protocol;

(b) The identity and methods of organizations or organized criminal groups known to be or suspected of being engaged in conduct set forth in article 6 of this Protocol;

(c) The authenticity and proper form of travel documents issued by a State Party and the theft or related misuse of blank travel or identity documents;

(d) Means and methods of concealment and transportation of persons, the unlawful alteration, reproduction or acquisition or other misuse of travel or identity documents used in conduct set forth in article 6 of this Protocol and ways of detecting them;

(e) Legislative experiences and practices and measures to prevent and combat the conduct set forth in article 6 of this Protocol; and

(f) Scientific and technological information useful to law enforcement, so as to enhance each other's ability to prevent, detect and investigate the conduct set forth in article 6 of this Protocol and to prosecute those involved.

2. A State Party that receives information shall comply with any request by the State Party that transmitted the information that places restrictions on its use.

ARTICLE 11
BORDER MEASURES

1. Without prejudice to international commitments in relation to the free movement of people, States Parties shall strengthen, to the extent possible, such border controls as may be necessary to prevent and detect the smuggling of migrants.

2. Each State Party shall adopt legislative or other appropriate measures to prevent, to the extent possible, means of transport operated by commercial carriers from being used in the commission of the offence established in accordance with article 6, paragraph 1 (a), of this Protocol.

3. Where appropriate, and without prejudice to applicable international conventions, such measures shall include establishing the obligation of commercial carriers, including any transportation company or the owner or operator of any means of transport, to ascertain that all passengers are in possession of the travel documents required for entry into the receiving State.

4. Each State Party shall take the necessary measures, in accordance with its domestic law, to provide for sanctions in cases of violation of the obligation set forth in paragraph 3 of this article.

5. Each State Party shall consider taking measures that permit, in accordance with its domestic law, the denial of entry or revocation of visas of persons implicated in the commission of offences established in accordance with this Protocol.

6. Without prejudice to article 27 of the Convention, States Parties shall consider strengthening cooperation among border control agencies by, inter alia, establishing and maintaining direct channels of communication. . . .

ARTICLE 14
TRAINING AND TECHNICAL COOPERATION

1. States Parties shall provide or strengthen specialized training for immigration and other relevant officials in preventing the conduct set forth in article 6 of this Protocol and in the humane treatment of migrants who have been the object of such conduct, while respecting their rights as set forth in this Protocol.

2. States Parties shall cooperate with each other and with competent international organizations, non-governmental organizations, other relevant organizations and other elements of civil society as appropriate to ensure that there is adequate personnel training in their territories to prevent, combat and eradicate the conduct set forth in article 6 of this Protocol and to protect the rights of migrants who have been the object of such conduct. Such training shall include:

    (a) Improving the security and quality of travel documents;

    (b) Recognizing and detecting fraudulent travel or identity documents;

    (c) Gathering criminal intelligence, relating in particular to the identification of organized criminal groups known to be or suspected of being engaged in conduct set forth in article 6 of this Protocol, the methods used to transport smuggled migrants, the misuse of travel or identity documents for purposes of conduct set forth in article 6 and the means of concealment used in the smuggling of migrants;

    (d) Improving procedures for detecting smuggled persons at conventional and non-conventional points of entry and exit; and

    (e) The humane treatment of migrants and the protection of their rights as set forth in this Protocol.

3. States Parties with relevant expertise shall consider providing technical assistance to States that are frequently countries of origin or transit for persons who have been the object of conduct set forth in article 6 of this Protocol. States Parties shall make every effort to provide the necessary resources, such as vehicles, computer systems and document readers, to combat the conduct set forth in article 6.

ARTICLE 15
OTHER PREVENTION MEASURES

1. Each State Party shall take measures to ensure that it provides or strengthens information programmes to increase public awareness of the fact that the conduct set forth in article 6 of this Protocol is a criminal activity frequently perpetrated by organized criminal groups for profit and that it poses serious risks to the migrants concerned.

2. In accordance with article 31 of the Convention, States Parties shall cooperate in the field of public information for the purpose of preventing potential migrants from falling victim to organized criminal groups.

3. Each State Party shall promote or strengthen, as appropriate, development programmes and cooperation at the national, regional and international levels, taking into account the socio-economic realities of migration and paying special attention to economically and socially depressed areas, in order to combat the root socio-economic causes of the smuggling of migrants, such as poverty and underdevelopment.

ARTICLE 16
PROTECTION AND ASSISTANCE MEASURES

1. In implementing this Protocol, each State Party shall take, consistent with its obligations under international law, all appropriate measures, including legislation if necessary, to preserve and protect the rights of persons who have been the object of conduct set forth in article 6 of this Protocol as accorded under applicable international law, in particular the right to life and the right not to be subjected to torture or other cruel, inhuman or degrading treatment or punishment.

2. Each State Party shall take appropriate measures to afford migrants appropriate protection against violence that may be inflicted upon them, whether by individuals or groups, by reason of being the object of conduct set forth in article 6 of this Protocol.

3. Each State Party shall afford appropriate assistance to migrants whose lives or safety are endangered by reason of being the object of conduct set forth in article 6 of this Protocol.

4. In applying the provisions of this article, States Parties shall take into account the special needs of women and children.

5. In the case of the detention of a person who has been the object of conduct set forth in article 6 of this Protocol, each State Party shall comply with its obligations under the Vienna Convention on Consular Relations, where applicable, including that of informing the person concerned without delay about the provisions concerning notification to and communication with consular officers.

ARTICLE 17
AGREEMENTS AND ARRANGEMENTS

States Parties shall consider the conclusion of bilateral or regional agreements or operational arrangements or understandings aimed at:

(a) Establishing the most appropriate and effective measures to prevent and combat the conduct set forth in article 6 of this Protocol; or

(b) Enhancing the provisions of this Protocol among themselves.

ARTICLE 18
RETURN OF SMUGGLED MIGRANTS

1. Each State Party agrees to facilitate and accept, without undue or unreasonable delay, the return of a person who has been the object of conduct set forth in article 6 of this Protocol and who is its national or who has the right of permanent residence in its territory at the time of return. . . .

Consequences

As of mid-2005, the protocol has not been in force long enough to assess its effectiveness.

Source

University of Minnesota Human Rights Library, "Protocol Against the Smuggling of Migrants by Land, Sea and Air, Supplementing the United Nations Convention Against Transnational Crime." Available online. URL: http://www1.umn.edu/humanrts/instree/smuggling.html. Accessed January 4, 2005.

PROTOCOL TO PREVENT, SUPPRESS AND PUNISH TRAFFICKING IN PERSONS, ESPECIALLY WOMEN AND CHILDREN, SUPPLEMENTING THE UNITED NATIONS CONVENTION AGAINST TRANSNATIONAL ORGANIZED CRIME

TREATY AT A GLANCE

Completed
November 15, 2000; entered into force December 25, 2003

Signatories
As of summer 2005, 117 member states of the United Nations,
of which 85 are full parties

Overview
A protocol annexed to the Convention against Transnational Organized Crime, this document provides for an international approach to combating transnational trafficking in human beings, especially women and children. The approach includes international cooperation, the exchange of information, and such other appropriate measures as socioeconomic sanctions.

Historical Background

For the overall historical background of international cooperation against transnational organized crime, see the entry on the United Nations CONVENTION AGAINST TRANSNATIONAL ORGANIZED CRIME. The protocol was motivated by an estimate of some 600,000 to 800,000 persons, mostly women and children, who are trafficked across borders each years, generally for sexual or labor exploitation.

The origin of the Protocol to Prevent, Suppress and Punish Trafficking in Persons, Especially Women and Children is found in United Nations Resolution 53/111 of December 9, 1998, in which the General Assembly resolved to establish an open-ended intergovernmental ad-hoc committee to draw up a convention against transnational organized crime, together with protocols to prevent, suppress and punish trafficking in persons, especially women and children, and against the smuggling of migrants by land, air and sea (PROTOCOL AGAINST THE SMUGGLING OF MIGRANTS BY LAND, SEA AND AIR, SUPPLEMENTING THE UNITED NATIONS CONVENTION AGAINST TRANSNATIONAL ORGANIZED CRIME).

The protocol is by no means the first international attempt to suppress trafficking in women and children.

Previous agreements of varying scope include the International Agreement of May 18, 1904, for the Suppression of the White Slave Traffic, as amended by the Protocol of 1948; the International Convention of the Suppression of the White Slave Traffic (1910), as amended by the Protocol of 1948; the International Convention for the Suppression of the Traffic in Women and Children (1921), as amended by the Protocol of 1947; and the International Convention for the Suppression of the Traffic in Women of Full Age (1933). More recently, on March 21, 1951, Brazil, Denmark, Ecuador, Finland, Honduras, India, Iran, Israel, Liberia, Luxembourg, Ceylon (Myanmar), Pakistan, Philippines, South Africa, and the former Yugoslavia concluded the Convention for the Suppression of the Traffic in Persons and of the Exploitation of the Prostitution of Others (a convention to which the United States has never been a party). What is new and innovative about the 2000 protocol is the criminalization of such trafficking as an international organized crime. This elevates transnational cooperation in suppressing such crime to the level of international law and ensures that domestic law will enhance rather than conflict with international law.

On February 23, 2004, President George W. Bush requested the consent of the Senate in ratifying the protocol, and the House of Representatives passed a resolution (H.R. 541) on February 26 urging the Senate to give its consent. As of summer 2005, however, the Senate had referred a consenting resolution to the Committee on Foreign Relations, and it has yet to emerge from the committee.

Terms

This protocol requires states parties to criminalize trafficking in persons. For the first time in an international instrument, a standard definition of the offense is provided, namely "the recruitment, transportation, transfer, harbouring, or receipt of persons, by means of the threat or use of force or other forms of coercion, of abduction, of fraud, of deception, of the abuse of power or of a position of vulnerability or of the giving or receiving of payments or benefits to achieve the consent of a person having control over another person, for the purpose of exploitation." States parties to the protocol agree to accept this definition and to criminalize the offense accordingly.

The protocol stipulates that exploitation includes, at minimum, "exploitation of the prostitution of others or other forms of sexual exploitation, forced labour or services, slavery or practices similar to slavery, servitude, or the removal of organs." States parties bind themselves to prosecute traffickers and to assist and protect the victims of trafficking in persons. The protocol incorporates the provisions of the Convention against Transnational Organized Crime, including those on extradition, mutual legal assistance, and law-enforcement cooperation, and further encourages states parties to establish domestic measures to protect both victims and witnesses. The protocol also implements a set of training programs for law-enforcement officials, prosecutors, and judges who deal with the offenses covered by the protocol.

Importantly, the protocol applies to the offense of trafficking only as a product of transnational organized crime, as defined in the convention.

Protocol to Prevent, Suppress and Punish Trafficking in Persons, Especially Women and Children, Supplementing the United Nations Convention against Transnational Organized Crime

Preamble

The States Parties to this Protocol,

Declaring that effective action to prevent and combat trafficking in persons, especially women and children, requires a comprehensive international approach in the countries of origin, transit and destination that includes measures to prevent such trafficking, to punish the traffickers and to protect the victims of such trafficking, including by protecting their internationally recognized human rights,

Taking into account the fact that, despite the existence of a variety of international instruments containing rules and practical measures to combat the exploitation of persons, especially women and children, there is no universal instrument that addresses all aspects of trafficking in persons,

Concerned that, in the absence of such an instrument, persons who are vulnerable to trafficking will not be sufficiently protected,

Recalling General Assembly resolution 53/111 of 9 December 1998, in which the Assembly decided to establish an open-ended intergovernmental ad hoc committee for the purpose of elaborating a comprehensive international convention against transnational organized crime and of discussing the elaboration of, inter alia, an international instrument addressing trafficking in women and children,

Convinced that supplementing the United Nations Convention against Transnational Organized Crime with an international instrument for the prevention, suppression and punishment of trafficking in persons, especially women and children, will be useful in preventing and combating that crime,

Have agreed as follows:

I
General Provisions

ARTICLE 1
RELATION WITH THE UNITED NATIONS CONVENTION AGAINST TRANSNATIONAL ORGANIZED CRIME

1. This Protocol supplements the United Nations Convention against Transnational Organized Crime. It shall be interpreted together with the Convention. . . .

ARTICLE 2
STATEMENT OF PURPOSE

The purposes of this Protocol are:

(a) To prevent and combat trafficking in persons, paying particular attention to women and children;

(b) To protect and assist the victims of such trafficking, with full respect for their human rights; and

(c) To promote cooperation among States Parties in order to meet those objectives.

ARTICLE 3
USE OF TERMS

For the purposes of this Protocol:

(a) "Trafficking in persons" shall mean the recruitment, transportation, transfer, harbouring or receipt of persons, by means of the threat or use of force or other forms of coercion, of abduction, of fraud, of deception, of the abuse of power or of a position of vulnerability or of the giving or receiving of payments or benefits to achieve the consent of a person having control over another person, for the purpose of exploitation. Exploitation shall include, at a minimum, the exploitation of the prostitution of others or other forms of sexual exploitation, forced labour or services, slavery or practices similar to slavery, servitude or the removal of organs;

(b) The consent of a victim of trafficking in persons to the intended exploitation set forth in subparagraph

(a) of this article shall be irrelevant where any of the means set forth in subparagraph (a) have been used;

(c) The recruitment, transportation, transfer, harbouring or receipt of a child for the purpose of exploitation shall be considered "trafficking in persons" even if this does not involve any of the means set forth in subparagraph (a) of this article;

(d) "Child" shall mean any person under eighteen years of age.

ARTICLE 4
SCOPE OF APPLICATION

This Protocol shall apply, except as otherwise stated herein, to the prevention, investigation and prosecution of the offences established in accordance with article 5 of this Protocol, where those offences are transnational in nature and involve an organized criminal group, as well as to the protection of victims of such offences.

ARTICLE 5
CRIMINALIZATION

1. Each State Party shall adopt such legislative and other measures as may be necessary to establish as criminal offences the conduct set forth in article 3 of this Protocol, when committed intentionally.

2. Each State Party shall also adopt such legislative and other measures as may be necessary to establish as criminal offences:

(a) Subject to the basic concepts of its legal system, attempting to commit an offence established in accordance with paragraph 1 of this article;

(b) Participating as an accomplice in an offence established in accordance with paragraph 1 of this article; and

(c) Organizing or directing other persons to commit an offence established in accordance with paragraph 1 of this article.

II
Protection of Victims of Trafficking in Persons

ARTICLE 6
ASSISTANCE TO AND PROTECTION OF
VICTIMS OF TRAFFICKING IN PERSONS

1. In appropriate cases and to the extent possible under its domestic law, each State Party shall protect the privacy and identity of victims of trafficking in persons, including, inter alia, by making legal proceedings relating to such trafficking confidential.

2. Each State Party shall ensure that its domestic legal or administrative system contains measures that provide to victims of trafficking in persons, in appropriate cases:

(a) Information on relevant court and administrative proceedings;

(b) Assistance to enable their views and concerns to be presented and considered at appropriate stages of criminal proceedings against offenders, in a manner not prejudicial to the rights of the defence.

3. Each State Party shall consider implementing measures to provide for the physical, psychological and social recovery of victims of trafficking in persons, including, in appropriate cases, in cooperation with non-governmental organizations, other relevant organizations and other elements of civil society, and, in particular, the provision of:

(a) Appropriate housing;

(b) Counselling and information, in particular as regards their legal rights, in a language that the victims of trafficking in persons can understand;

(c) Medical, psychological and material assistance; and

(d) Employment, educational and training opportunities.

4. Each State Party shall take into account, in applying the provisions of this article, the age, gender and special needs of victims of trafficking in persons, in particular the special needs of children, including appropriate housing, education and care.

5. Each State Party shall endeavour to provide for the physical safety of victims of trafficking in persons while they are within its territory.

6. Each State Party shall ensure that its domestic legal system contains measures that offer victims of trafficking in persons the possibility of obtaining compensation for damage suffered.

ARTICLE 7
STATUS OF VICTIMS OF TRAFFICKING
IN PERSONS IN RECEIVING STATES

1. In addition to taking measures pursuant to article 6 of this Protocol, each State Party shall consider adopting legislative or other appropriate measures that permit victims of trafficking in persons to remain in its territory, temporarily or permanently, in appropriate cases. . . .

ARTICLE 8
REPATRIATION OF VICTIMS OF
TRAFFICKING IN PERSONS

1. The State Party of which a victim of trafficking in persons is a national or in which the person had the right of permanent residence at the time of entry into the territory of the receiving State Party shall facilitate and accept, with due regard for the safety of that person, the return of that person without undue or unreasonable delay. . . .

III
Prevention, Cooperation and Other Measures

ARTICLE 9
PREVENTION OF TRAFFICKING IN PERSONS

1. States Parties shall establish comprehensive policies, programmes and other measures:

(a) To prevent and combat trafficking in persons; and

(b) To protect victims of trafficking in persons, especially women and children, from revictimization.

2. States Parties shall endeavour to undertake measures such as research, information and mass media campaigns and social and economic initiatives to prevent and combat trafficking in persons.

3. Policies, programmes and other measures established in accordance with this article shall, as appropriate, include cooperation with non-governmental organizations, other relevant organizations and other elements of civil society.

4. States Parties shall take or strengthen measures, including through bilateral or multilateral cooperation, to alleviate the factors that make persons, especially women and children, vulnerable to trafficking, such as poverty, underdevelopment and lack of equal opportunity.

5. States Parties shall adopt or strengthen legislative or other measures, such as educational, social or cultural measures, including through bilateral and multilateral cooperation, to discourage the demand that fosters all forms of exploitation of persons, especially women and children, that leads to trafficking.

ARTICLE 10
INFORMATION EXCHANGE AND TRAINING

1. Law enforcement, immigration or other relevant authorities of States Parties shall, as appropriate, cooperate with one another by exchanging information, in accordance with their domestic law, to enable them to determine:

(a) Whether individuals crossing or attempting to cross an international border with travel documents belonging to other persons or without travel documents are perpetrators or victims of trafficking in persons;

(b) The types of travel document that individuals have used or attempted to use to cross an international border for the purpose of trafficking in persons; and

(c) The means and methods used by organized criminal groups for the purpose of trafficking in persons, including the recruitment and transportation of victims, routes and links between and among individuals and groups engaged in such trafficking, and possible measures for detecting them.

2. States Parties shall provide or strengthen training for law enforcement, immigration and other relevant officials in the prevention of trafficking in persons. The training should focus on methods used in preventing such trafficking, prosecuting the traffickers and protecting the rights of the victims, including protecting the victims from the traffickers. The training should also take into account the need to consider human rights and child- and gender-sensitive issues and it should encourage cooperation with non-governmental organizations, other relevant organizations and other elements of civil society.

3. A State Party that receives information shall comply with any request by the State Party that transmitted the information that places restrictions on its use.

ARTICLE 11
BORDER MEASURES

1. Without prejudice to international commitments in relation to the free movement of people, States Parties shall strengthen, to the extent possible, such border controls as may be necessary to prevent and detect trafficking in persons.

2. Each State Party shall adopt legislative or other appropriate measures to prevent, to the extent possible, means of transport operated by commercial carriers from being used in the commission of offences established in accordance with article 5 of this Protocol.

3. Where appropriate, and without prejudice to applicable international conventions, such measures shall include establishing the obligation of commercial carriers, including any transportation company or the owner or operator of any means of transport, to ascertain that all passengers are in possession of the travel documents required for entry into the receiving State. . . .

Consequences

As of mid-2005, the protocol has not been in force long enough to assess its effectiveness.

Source

United Nations Crime and Justice Information Network, "Protocol to Prevent, Suppress and Punish Trafficking in Persons." Available online. URL: http://www.uncjin.org/Documents/conventions/dcatoc/final_documents_2/. Accessed April 20, 2005.

PROTOCOL AGAINST THE ILLICIT MANUFACTURING OF AND TRAFFICKING IN FIREARMS, THEIR PARTS AND COMPONENTS AND AMMUNITION, SUPPLEMENTING THE UNITED NATIONS CONVENTION AGAINST TRANSNATIONAL ORGANIZED CRIME

TREATY AT A GLANCE

Completed
May 31, 2001; entered into force July 3, 2005

Signatories
As of summer 2005, 52 member states of the United Nations,
of which 42 have become full parties

Overview
A protocol annexed to the Convention against Transnational Organized Crime, this document provides for an international approach to combating transnational trafficking in human beings, especially women and children. The approach includes international cooperation, the exchange of information, and such other appropriate measures as socioeconomic sanctions.

Historical Background

For an overview of the historical background of international cooperation in combating transnational organized crime, see the entry on the United Nations CONVENTION AGAINST TRANSNATIONAL ORGANIZED CRIME. The Protocol was motivated by the recognition that small arms have proliferated worldwide and are sold in greatest quantity to people in the least stable portions of the globe, especially in Africa.

Meeting in Lyon, France, in 1998, representatives of the G8 countries (France, United States, Britain, Germany, Japan, Italy, Canada, and Russia) formed a firearms subgroup, which proposed an international firearms protocol. Early in 1999, the United Nations General Assembly resolved to begin negotiation of the Convention on Transnational Organized Crime, as well as this supplementary protocol to deal with illicit firearms trafficking. By March 2001, the protocol had been drafted, and it was adopted by UN resolution in May.

Although the administrations of both President Bill Clinton and President George W. Bush have repeatedly voiced their endorsement of the protocol in principle, as of summer 2005, the United States has neither signed nor become a party to this protocol. The United States was instrumental in concluding with the other members of the Organization of American States (OAS) an Inter-American Convention against the Illicit Manufacturing of and Trafficking in Firearms, the first international agreement designed to prevent, combat, and eradicate illicit trafficking in firearms, ammunition, and explosives; however, Department of State officials and legislators continue to study the United Nations protocol, partly in an effort to ensure that it harmonizes with what the U.S. government considers the precedent-setting OAS convention. Of particular concern is how the protocol might impact existing international trade agreements, including the NORTH AMERICAN FREE TRADE AGREEMENT (NAFTA).

Terms

The Protocol against the Illicit Manufacturing of and Trafficking in Firearms, Their Parts and Components and Ammunitions contains practical measures to assist law-enforcement communities worldwide by enhancing international cooperation and promoting greater transparency in legal transfers of firearms. To accomplish this, the protocol sets out comprehensive procedures for the import, export, and transit of firearms as well as their parts, components, and ammunition. The protocol establishes a reciprocal system by which states parties are required to provide authorizations to one another before permitting shipments of firearms to leave, arrive, or transit through their territory. It is anticipated that this will not only curb and definitively criminalize illicit trafficking, it will also enable law-enforcement agencies to track the *legal* movement of shipments so that theft and diversion can be more readily prevented.

States parties to the protocol agree to enact new laws aimed at ending the illegal manufacture of firearms and at tracking down existing illicit weapons as well as prosecuting offenders. The parties will also cooperate to prevent, combat, and eradicate the illegal manufacturing and trafficking of firearms. They agree on international standards that tighten controls on the export and import of firearms. They further agree to exchange information about illicit firearms.

Central to the protocol is the criminalization of the manufacturing and trafficking of illegal firearms. Additionally, the states parties to the protocol will cooperate to confiscate all firearms that have been illegally manufactured or trafficked. The protocol provides for states parties to gather and hold for 10 years any information needed to trace and identify illegal firearms. This information includes the manufacturer's markings, country and date of issuance, date of expiration, and countries of export or import. Acting on an international standard set by the protocol, the parties agree to register and approve legal brokers for the manufacture, export, import, or transfer of firearms and to mark each firearm, when manufactured, with a serial number as well as the manufacturer's name and location.

The protocol provides measures to control the international flow of firearms. These measures include internationally standardized controls on import and export. Parties are required to set up a universal system for the export, import, and international transit licensing of firearms and to refuse the transit, reexport, retransfer or transshipment of firearms to any destination without written approval from the exporting country and licenses from receiving nations.

The protocol also encourages parties to conclude bilateral, regional, and international agreements to prevent, combat and eradicate the illegal manufacture and trafficking of firearms.

Protocol against the Illicit Manufacturing of and Trafficking in Firearms,

Their Parts and Components and Ammunition, Supplementing the United Nations Convention against Transnational Organized Crime

Preamble

The States Parties to this Protocol,

Aware of the urgent need to prevent, combat and eradicate the illicit manufacturing of and trafficking in firearms, their parts and components and ammunition, owing to the harmful effects of those activities on the security of each State, region and the world as a whole, endangering the well-being of peoples, their social and economic development and their right to live in peace,

Convinced, therefore, of the necessity for all States to take all appropriate measures to this end, including international cooperation and other measures at the regional and global levels,

Recalling General Assembly resolution 53/111 of 9 December 1998, in which the Assembly decided to establish an open-ended intergovernmental ad hoc committee for the purpose of elaborating a comprehensive international convention against transnational organized crime and of discussing the elaboration of, inter alia, an international instrument combating the illicit manufacturing of and trafficking in firearms, their parts and components and ammunition,

Bearing in mind the principle of equal rights and self-determination of peoples, as enshrined in the Charter of the United Nations and the Declaration on Principles of International Law concerning Friendly Relations and Cooperation among States in accordance with the Charter of the United Nations,

Convinced that supplementing the United Nations Convention against Transnational Organized Crime with an international instrument against the illicit manufacturing of and trafficking in firearms, their parts and components and ammunition will be useful in preventing and combating those crimes,

Have agreed as follows:

I
General Provisions

ARTICLE 1
RELATION WITH THE UNITED NATIONS CONVENTION AGAINST TRANSNATIONAL ORGANIZED CRIME

1. This Protocol supplements the United Nations Convention against Transnational Organized Crime. It shall be interpreted together with the Convention. . . .

ARTICLE 2
STATEMENT OF PURPOSE

The purpose of this Protocol is to promote, facilitate and strengthen cooperation among States Parties in order to prevent, combat and eradicate the illicit manufacturing of and trafficking in firearms, their parts and components and ammunition.

ARTICLE 3
USE OF TERMS

For the purposes of this Protocol:

(a) "Firearm" shall mean any portable barrelled weapon that expels, is designed to expel or may be readily converted to expel a shot, bullet or projectile by the action of an explosive, excluding antique firearms or their replicas. Antique firearms and their replicas shall be defined in accordance with domestic law. In no case, however, shall antique firearms include firearms manufactured after 1899;

(b) "Parts and components" shall mean any element or replacement element specifically designed for a firearm and essential to its operation, including a barrel, frame or receiver, slide or cylinder, bolt or breech block, and any device designed or adapted to diminish the sound caused by firing a firearm;

(c) "Ammunition" shall mean the complete round or its components, including cartridge cases, primers, propellant powder, bullets or projectiles, that are used in a firearm, provided that those components are themselves subject to authorization in the respective State Party;

(d) "Illicit manufacturing" shall mean the manufacturing or assembly of firearms, their parts and components or ammunition:

(i) From parts and components illicitly trafficked;

(ii) Without a licence or authorization from a competent authority of the State Party where the manufacture or assembly takes place; or

(iii) Without marking the firearms at the time of manufacture, in accordance with article 8 of this Protocol; Licensing or authorization of the manufacture of parts and components shall be in accordance with domestic law;

(e) "Illicit trafficking" shall mean the import, export, acquisition, sale, delivery, movement or transfer of firearms, their parts and components and ammunition from or across the territory of one State Party to that of another State Party if any one of the States Parties concerned does not authorize it in accordance with the terms of this Protocol or if the firearms are not marked in accordance with article 8 of this Protocol;

(f) "Tracing" shall mean the systematic tracking of firearms and, where possible, their parts and components and ammunition from manufacturer to purchaser for the purpose of assisting the competent authorities of States Parties in detecting, investigating and analysing illicit manufacturing and illicit trafficking.

ARTICLE 4
SCOPE OF APPLICATION

1. This Protocol shall apply, except as otherwise stated herein, to the prevention of illicit manufacturing of and trafficking in firearms, their parts and components and ammunition and to the investigation and prosecution of offences established in accordance with article 5 of this Protocol where those offences are transnational in nature and involve an organized criminal group.

2. This Protocol shall not apply to state-to-state transactions or to state transfers in cases where the application of the Protocol would prejudice the right of a State Party to take action in the interest of national security consistent with the Charter of the United Nations.

ARTICLE 5
CRIMINALIZATION

1. Each State Party shall adopt such legislative and other measures as may be necessary to establish as criminal offences the following conduct, when committed intentionally:

(a) Illicit manufacturing of firearms, their parts and components and ammunition;

(b) Illicit trafficking in firearms, their parts and components and ammunition;

(c) Falsifying or illicitly obliterating, removing or altering the marking(s) on firearms required by article 8 of this Protocol.

2. Each State Party shall also adopt such legislative and other measures as may be necessary to establish as criminal offences the following conduct:

(a) Subject to the basic concepts of its legal system, attempting to commit or participating as an accomplice in an offence established in accordance with paragraph 1 of this article; and

(b) Organizing, directing, aiding, abetting, facilitating or counselling the commission of an offence established in accordance with paragraph 1 of this article.

ARTICLE 6
CONFISCATION, SEIZURE AND DISPOSAL

1. Without prejudice to article 12 of the Convention, States Parties shall adopt, to the greatest extent possible within their domestic legal systems, such measures as may be necessary to enable confiscation of firearms, their parts and components and ammunition that have been illicitly manufactured or trafficked.

2. States Parties shall adopt, within their domestic legal systems, such measures as may be necessary to prevent illicitly manufactured and trafficked firearms, parts and components and ammunition from falling into the hands of unauthorized persons by seizing and destroying such firearms, their parts and components and ammunition unless other disposal has been officially authorized, provided that the firearms have been marked and the methods of disposal of those firearms and ammunition have been recorded.

II
Prevention

ARTICLE 7
RECORD-KEEPING

Each State Party shall ensure the maintenance, for not less than ten years, of information in relation to firearms and, where appropriate and feasible, their parts and components and ammunition that is necessary to trace and identify those firearms and, where appropriate and feasible, their parts and components and ammunition which are illicitly manufactured or trafficked and to prevent and detect such activities. Such information shall include:

(a) The appropriate markings required by article 8 of this Protocol;

(b) In cases involving international transactions in firearms, their parts and components and ammunition, the issuance and expiration dates of the appropriate licences or authorizations, the country of export, the country of import, the transit countries, where appropriate, and the final recipient and the description and quantity of the articles.

ARTICLE 8
MARKING OF FIREARMS

1. For the purpose of identifying and tracing each firearm, States Parties shall:

(a) At the time of manufacture of each firearm, either require unique marking providing the name of the manufacturer, the country or place of manufacture and the serial number, or maintain any alternative unique user-friendly marking with simple geometric symbols in combination with a numeric and/or alphanumeric code, permitting ready identification by all States of the country of manufacture;

(b) Require appropriate simple marking on each imported firearm, permitting identification of the country of import and, where possible, the year of import and enabling the competent authorities of that country to trace the firearm, and a unique marking, if the firearm does not bear such a marking. The requirements of this subparagraph need not be applied to temporary imports of firearms for verifiable lawful purposes;

(c) Ensure, at the time of transfer of a firearm from government stocks to permanent civilian use, the appropriate unique marking permitting identification by all States Parties of the transferring country.

2. States Parties shall encourage the firearms manufacturing industry to develop measures against the removal or alteration of markings. . . .

ARTICLE 10
GENERAL REQUIREMENTS FOR EXPORT, IMPORT AND TRANSIT LICENSING OR AUTHORIZATION SYSTEMS

1. Each State Party shall establish or maintain an effective system of export and import licensing or authorization, as well as of measures on international transit, for the transfer of firearms, their parts and components and ammunition. . . .

ARTICLE 11
SECURITY AND PREVENTIVE MEASURES

In an effort to detect, prevent and eliminate the theft, loss or diversion of, as well as the illicit manufacturing of and trafficking in, firearms, their parts and components and ammunition, each State Party shall take appropriate measures:

(a) To require the security of firearms, their parts and components and ammunition at the time of manufacture, import, export and transit through its territory; and

(b) To increase the effectiveness of import, export and transit controls, including, where appropriate, border controls, and of police and customs transborder cooperation.

ARTICLE 12
INFORMATION

1. Without prejudice to articles 27 and 28 of the Convention, States Parties shall exchange among themselves, consistent with their respective domestic legal and administrative systems, relevant case-specific information on matters such as authorized producers, dealers, importers, exporters and, whenever possible, carriers of firearms, their parts and components and ammunition.

2. Without prejudice to articles 27 and 28 of the Convention, States Parties shall exchange among themselves, consistent with their respective domestic legal and administrative systems, relevant information on matters such as:

(a) Organized criminal groups known to take part or suspected of taking part in the illicit manufacturing of or trafficking in firearms, their parts and components and ammunition;

(b) The means of concealment used in the illicit manufacturing of or trafficking in firearms, their parts and components and ammunition and ways of detecting them;

(c) Methods and means, points of dispatch and destination and routes customarily used by organized criminal groups engaged in illicit trafficking in firearms, their parts and components and ammunition; and

(d) Legislative experiences and practices and measures to prevent, combat and eradicate the illicit manufacturing of and trafficking in firearms, their parts and components and ammunition.

3. States Parties shall provide to or share with each other, as appropriate, relevant scientific and technological information useful to law enforcement authorities in order to enhance each other's abilities to prevent, detect and investigate the illicit manufacturing of and trafficking in firearms, their parts and components and ammunition and to prosecute the persons involved in those illicit activities.

4. States Parties shall cooperate in the tracing of firearms, their parts and components and ammunition that may have been illicitly manufactured or trafficked. Such cooperation shall include the provision of prompt responses to requests for assistance in tracing such firearms, their parts and components and ammunition, within available means.

5. Subject to the basic concepts of its legal system or any international agreements, each State Party shall guarantee the confidentiality of and comply with any restrictions on the use of information that it receives from another State Party pursuant to this article, including proprietary information pertaining to commercial transactions, if requested to do so by the State Party providing the information. If such confidentiality cannot be maintained, the State Party that provided the information shall be notified prior to its disclosure.

ARTICLE 13
COOPERATION

1. States Parties shall cooperate at the bilateral, regional and international levels to prevent, combat and eradicate the illicit manufacturing of and trafficking in firearms, their parts and components and ammunition. . . .

ARTICLE 14
TRAINING AND TECHNICAL ASSISTANCE

States Parties shall cooperate with each other and with relevant international organizations, as appropriate, so that States Parties may receive, upon request, the training and technical assistance necessary to enhance their ability to prevent, combat and eradicate the illicit manufacturing of and trafficking in firearms, their parts and components and ammunition, including technical, financial and material assistance in those matters identified in articles 29 and 30 of the Convention.

ARTICLE 15
BROKERS AND BROKERING

1. With a view to preventing and combating illicit manufacturing of and trafficking in firearms, their parts and components and ammunition, States Parties that have not yet done so shall consider establishing a system for regulating the activities of those who engage in brokering. . . .

Consequences

The protocol entered into force in July 2005. so its impact remains to be seen.

Source

United Nations Office on Drugs and Crime, "Protocol against the Illicit Manufacturing of and Trafficking in Firearms, Their Parts and Components and Ammunition, supplementing the United Nations Convention against Transnational Organized Crime." Available online. URL: http://www.unodc.org/pdf/crime/a_res_55/255e.pdf. Accessed January 4, 2005.

OPTIONAL PROTOCOL TO THE CONVENTION AGAINST TORTURE AND OTHER CRUEL, INHUMAN OR DEGRADING TREATMENT OR PUNISHMENT

TREATY AT A GLANCE

Completed
December 18, 2002 (not yet entered into force)

Signatories
As of summer 2005, 37 member states of the United Nations,
of which 10 are full parties

Overview
Because the Convention against Torture and Other Cruel, Inhuman or Degrading Treatment or Punishment, which entered into force on June 26, 1987, lacks a practical enforcement mechanism, the United Nations General Assembly adopted this optional protocol, which provides for "a system of regular visits undertaken by independent international and national bodies to places where people are deprived of their liberty, in order to prevent torture and other cruel, inhuman or degrading treatment or punishment" and other monitoring and enforcement measures.

Historical Background

For the historical background of the convention proper, see the entry on CONVENTION AGAINST TORTURE AND OTHER CRUEL, INHUMAN OR DEGRADING TREATMENT OR PUNISHMENT. While the underlying convention met with widespread acceptance and ratification, this optional protocol has encountered considerable resistance, especially from the United States, over issues of sovereignty and jurisdiction. The protocol is set to enter into force 30 days after completion of the 20th instrument of ratification or accession. As of summer 2005, only three nations have acceded to the protocol, and seven have ratified it; 30 other nations have so far signed the protocol but have yet to accede to or ratify it. As of summer 2005, the United States has neither signed nor ratified.

Terms

The protocol seeks to strengthen enforcement of the Convention against Torture and Other Cruel, Inhuman or Degrading Treatment or Punishment by allowing independent international experts to conduct regular visits to places of detention within states that have accepted the protocol by ratifying or acceding to it. The purpose of such visits will be to assess the condition of detention and the treatment of those detained and, where necessary, to make recommendations for improvements. Additionally, the protocol requires states to set up national mechanisms to visit and monitor places of detention and to cooperate with the international experts chosen under the protocol.

Optional Protocol to the Convention Against Torture and Other Cruel, Inhuman or Degrading Treatment or Punishment

Preamble
The States Parties to the present Protocol,
   Reaffirming that torture and other cruel, inhuman or degrading treatment or punishment are prohibited and constitute serious violations of human rights,

Convinced that further measures are necessary to achieve the purposes of the Convention against Torture and Other Cruel, Inhuman or Degrading Treatment or Punishment (hereinafter referred to as the Convention) and to strengthen the protection of persons deprived of their liberty against torture and other cruel, inhuman or degrading treatment or punishment,

Recalling that articles 2 and 16 of the Convention oblige each State Party to take effective measures to prevent acts of torture and other cruel, inhuman or degrading treatment or punishment in any territory under its jurisdiction,

Recognizing that States have the primary responsibility for implementing those articles, that strengthening the protection of people deprived of their liberty and the full respect for their human rights is a common responsibility shared by all and that international implementing bodies complement and strengthen national measures,

Recalling that the effective prevention of torture and other cruel, inhuman or degrading treatment or punishment requires education and a combination of various legislative, administrative, judicial and other measures,

Recalling also that the World Conference on Human Rights firmly declared that efforts to eradicate torture should first and foremost be concentrated on prevention and called for the adoption of an optional protocol to the Convention, intended to establish a preventive system of regular visits to places of detention,

Convinced that the protection of persons deprived of their liberty against torture and other cruel, inhuman or degrading treatment or punishment can be strengthened by non-judicial means of a preventive nature, based on regular visits to places of detention,

Have agreed as follows:

PART I

General principles

ARTICLE 1

The objective of the present Protocol is to establish a system of regular visits undertaken by independent international and national bodies to places where people are deprived of their liberty, in order to prevent torture and other cruel, inhuman or degrading treatment or punishment.

ARTICLE 2

1. A Subcommittee on Prevention of Torture and Other Cruel, Inhuman or Degrading Treatment or Punishment of the Committee against Torture (hereinafter referred to as the Subcommittee on Prevention) shall be established and shall carry out the functions laid down in the present Protocol.

2. The Subcommittee on Prevention shall carry out its work within the framework of the Charter of the United Nations and shall be guided by the purposes and principles thereof, as well as the norms of the United Nations concerning the treatment of people deprived of their liberty.

3. Equally, the Subcommittee on Prevention shall be guided by the principles of confidentiality, impartiality, non-selectivity, universality and objectivity.

4. The Subcommittee on Prevention and the States Parties shall cooperate in the implementation of the present Protocol.

ARTICLE 3

Each State Party shall set up, designate or maintain at the domestic level one or several visiting bodies for the prevention of torture and other cruel, inhuman or degrading treatment or punishment (hereinafter referred to as the national preventive mechanism).

ARTICLE 4

1. Each State Party shall allow visits, in accordance with the present Protocol, by the mechanisms referred to in articles 2 and 3 to any place under its jurisdiction and control where persons are or may be deprived of their liberty, either by virtue of an order given by a public authority or at its instigation or with its consent or acquiescence (hereinafter referred to as places of detention). These visits shall be undertaken with a view to strengthening, if necessary, the protection of these persons against torture and other cruel, inhuman or degrading treatment or punishment.

2. For the purposes of the present Protocol, deprivation of liberty means any form of detention or imprisonment or the placement of a person in a public or private custodial setting which that person is not permitted to leave at will by order of any judicial, administrative or other authority.

PART II

Subcommittee on Prevention

ARTICLE 5

1. The Subcommittee on Prevention shall consist of ten members. After the fiftieth ratification of or accession to the present Protocol, the number of the members of the Subcommittee on Prevention shall increase to twenty-five.

2. The members of the Subcommittee on Prevention shall be chosen from among persons of high moral character, having proven professional experience in the field of the administration of justice, in particular criminal law, prison or police administration, or in the various fields relevant to the treatment of persons deprived of their liberty.

3. In the composition of the Subcommittee on Prevention due consideration shall be given to equitable geographic distribution and to the representation of different forms of civilization and legal systems of the States Parties.

4. In this composition consideration shall also be given to balanced gender representation on the basis of the principles of equality and non-discrimination.

5. No two members of the Subcommittee on Prevention may be nationals of the same State.

6. The members of the Subcommittee on Prevention shall serve in their individual capacity, shall be independent and impartial and shall be available to serve the Subcommittee on Prevention efficiently.

ARTICLE 6

1. Each State Party may nominate, in accordance with paragraph 2 of the present article, up to two candidates possessing the qualifications and meeting the requirements set out in article 5, and in doing so shall provide detailed information on the qualifications of the nominees.

2. (a) The nominees shall have the nationality of a State Party to the present Protocol;

(b) At least one of the two candidates shall have the nationality of the nominating State Party;

(c) No more than two nationals of a State Party shall be nominated;

(d) Before a State Party nominates a national of another State Party, it shall seek and obtain the consent of that State Party.

3. At least five months before the date of the meeting of the States Parties during which the elections will be held, the Secretary-General of the United Nations shall address a letter to the States Parties inviting them to submit their nominations within three months. The Secretary-General shall submit a list, in alphabetical order, of all persons thus nominated, indicating the States Parties that have nominated them.

ARTICLE 7

1. The members of the Subcommittee on Prevention shall be elected in the following manner:

(a) Primary consideration shall be given to the fulfilment of the requirements and criteria of article 5 of the present Protocol;

(b) The initial election shall be held no later than six months after the entry into force of the present Protocol;

(c) The States Parties shall elect the members of the Subcommittee on Prevention by secret ballot;

(d) Elections of the members of the Subcommittee on Prevention shall be held at biennial meetings of the States Parties convened by the Secretary-General of the United Nations. At those meetings, for which two thirds of the States Parties shall constitute a quorum, the persons elected to the Subcommittee on Prevention shall be those who obtain the largest number of votes and an absolute majority of the votes of the representatives of the States Parties present and voting.

2. If during the election process two nationals of a State Party have become eligible to serve as members of the Subcommittee on Prevention, the candidate receiving the higher number of votes shall serve as the member of the Subcommittee on Prevention. Where nationals have received the same number of votes, the following procedure applies:

(a) Where only one has been nominated by the State Party of which he or she is a national, that national shall serve as the member of the Subcommittee on Prevention;

(b) Where both candidates have been nominated by the State Party of which they are nationals, a separate vote by secret ballot shall be held to determine which national shall become the member;

(c) Where neither candidate has been nominated by the State Party of which he or she is a national, a separate vote by secret ballot shall be held to determine which candidate shall be the member.

ARTICLE 8

If a member of the Subcommittee on Prevention dies or resigns, or for any cause can no longer perform his or her duties, the State Party that nominated the member shall nominate another eligible person possessing the qualifications and meeting the requirements set out in article 5, taking into account the need for a proper balance among the various fields of competence, to serve until the next meeting of the States Parties, subject to the approval of the majority of the States Parties. The approval shall be considered given unless half or more of the States Parties

respond negatively within six weeks after having been informed by the Secretary-General of the United Nations of the proposed appointment.

ARTICLE 9

The members of the Subcommittee on Prevention shall be elected for a term of four years. They shall be eligible for re-election once if renominated. The term of half the members elected at the first election shall expire at the end of two years; immediately after the first election the names of those members shall be chosen by lot by the Chairman of the meeting referred to in article 7, paragraph 1 (d).

ARTICLE 10

1. The Subcommittee on Prevention shall elect its officers for a term of two years. They may be re-elected.

2. The Subcommittee on Prevention shall establish its own rules of procedure. These rules shall provide, inter alia, that:

(a) Half the members plus one shall constitute a quorum;

(b) Decisions of the Subcommittee on Prevention shall be made by a majority vote of the members present;

(c) The Subcommittee on Prevention shall meet in camera.

3. The Secretary-General of the United Nations shall convene the initial meeting of the Subcommittee on Prevention. After its initial meeting, the Subcommittee on Prevention shall meet at such times as shall be provided by its rules of procedure. The Subcommittee on Prevention and the Committee against Torture shall hold their sessions simultaneously at least once a year.

PART III

Mandate of the Subcommittee on Prevention

ARTICLE 11

The Subcommittee on Prevention shall:

(a) Visit the places referred to in article 4 and make recommendations to States Parties concerning the protection of persons deprived of their liberty against torture and other cruel, inhuman or degrading treatment or punishment;

(b) In regard to the national preventive mechanisms:

(i) Advise and assist States Parties, when necessary, in their establishment;

(ii) Maintain direct, and if necessary confidential, contact with the national preventive mechanisms and offer them training and technical assistance with a view to strengthening their capacities;

(iii) Advise and assist them in the evaluation of the needs and the means necessary to strengthen the protection of persons deprived of their liberty against torture and other cruel, inhuman or degrading treatment or punishment;

(iv) Make recommendations and observations to the States Parties with a view to strengthening the capacity and the mandate of the national preventive mechanisms for the prevention of torture and other cruel, inhuman or degrading treatment or punishment;

(c) Cooperate, for the prevention of torture in general, with the relevant United Nations organs and mechanisms as well as with the international, regional and national institutions or organizations working towards the strengthening of the protection of all persons against torture and other cruel, inhuman or degrading treatment or punishment.

ARTICLE 12

In order to enable the Subcommittee on Prevention to comply with its mandate as laid down in article 11, the States Parties undertake:

(a) To receive the Subcommittee on Prevention in their territory and grant it access to the places of detention as defined in article 4 of the present Protocol;

(b) To provide all relevant information the Subcommittee on Prevention may request to evaluate the needs and measures that should be adopted to strengthen the protection of persons deprived of their liberty against torture and other cruel, inhuman or degrading treatment or punishment;

(c) To encourage and facilitate contacts between the Subcommittee on Prevention and the national preventive mechanisms;

(d) To examine the recommendations of the Subcommittee on Prevention and enter into dialogue with it on possible implementation measures.

ARTICLE 13

1. The Subcommittee on Prevention shall establish, at first by lot, a programme of regular visits to the States Parties in order to fulfil its mandate as established in article 11.

2. After consultations, the Subcommittee on Prevention shall notify the States Parties of its programme in order that they may, without delay, make the necessary practical arrangements for the visits to be conducted.

3. The visits shall be conducted by at least two members of the Subcommittee on Prevention. These members may be accompanied, if needed, by experts of demonstrated professional experience and knowledge in the fields covered by the present Protocol who shall be selected from a roster of experts prepared on the basis of proposals made by the States Parties, the Office of the United Nations High Commissioner for Human Rights and the United Nations Centre for International Crime Prevention. In preparing the roster, the States Parties concerned shall propose no more than five national experts. The State Party concerned may oppose the inclusion of a specific expert in the visit, whereupon the Subcommittee on Prevention shall propose another expert.

4. If the Subcommittee on Prevention considers it appropriate, it may propose a short follow-up visit after a regular visit.

ARTICLE 14

1. In order to enable the Subcommittee on Prevention to fulfil its mandate, the States Parties to the present Protocol undertake to grant it:

(a) Unrestricted access to all information concerning the number of persons deprived of their liberty in places of detention as defined in article 4, as well as the number of places and their location;

(b) Unrestricted access to all information referring to the treatment of those persons as well as their conditions of detention;

(c) Subject to paragraph 2 below, unrestricted access to all places of detention and their installations and facilities;

(d) The opportunity to have private interviews with the persons deprived of their liberty without witnesses, either personally or with a translator if deemed necessary, as well as with any other person who the Subcommittee on Prevention believes may supply relevant information;

(e) The liberty to choose the places it wants to visit and the persons it wants to interview.

2. Objection to a visit to a particular place of detention may be made only on urgent and compelling grounds of national defence, public safety, natural disaster or serious disorder in the place to be visited that temporarily prevent the carrying out of such a visit. The existence of a declared state of emergency as such shall not be invoked by a State Party as a reason to object to a visit.

ARTICLE 15

No authority or official shall order, apply, permit or tolerate any sanction against any person or organization for having communicated to the Subcommittee on Prevention or to its delegates any information, whether true or false, and no such person or organization shall be otherwise prejudiced in any way.

ARTICLE 16

1. The Subcommittee on Prevention shall communicate its recommendations and observations confidentially to the State Party and, if relevant, to the national preventive mechanism.

2. The Subcommittee on Prevention shall publish its report, together with any comments of the State Party concerned, whenever requested to do so by that State Party. If the State Party makes part of the report public, the Subcommittee on Prevention may publish the report in whole or in part. However, no personal data shall be published without the express consent of the person concerned.

3. The Subcommittee on Prevention shall present a public annual report on its activities to the Committee against Torture.

4. If the State Party refuses to cooperate with the Subcommittee on Prevention according to articles 12 and 14, or to take steps to improve the situation in the light of the recommendations of the Subcommittee on Prevention, the Committee against Torture may, at the request of the Subcommittee on Prevention, decide, by a majority of its members, after the State Party has had an opportunity to make its views known, to make a public statement on the matter or to publish the report of the Subcommittee on Prevention.

PART IV

National Preventive Mechanisms

ARTICLE 17

Each State Party shall maintain, designate or establish, at the latest one year after the entry into force of the present Protocol or of its ratification or accession, one or several independent national preventive mechanisms for the prevention of torture at the domestic level. Mechanisms established by decentralized units may be designated as national preventive mechanisms for the purposes of the present Protocol if they are in conformity with its provisions.

ARTICLE 18

1. The States Parties shall guarantee the functional independence of the national preventive mechanisms as well as the independence of their personnel.

2. The States Parties shall take the necessary measures to ensure that the experts of the national preventive mechanism have the required capabilities and professional knowledge. They shall strive for a gender balance and the adequate representation of ethnic and minority groups in the country.

3. The States Parties undertake to make available the necessary resources for the functioning of the national preventive mechanisms.

4. When establishing national preventive mechanisms, States Parties shall give due consideration to the Principles relating to the status of national institutions for the promotion and protection of human rights.

ARTICLE 19

The national preventive mechanisms shall be granted at a minimum the power:

(a) To regularly examine the treatment of the persons deprived of their liberty in places of detention as defined in article 4, with a view to strengthening, if necessary, their protection against torture and other cruel, inhuman or degrading treatment or punishment;

(b) To make recommendations to the relevant authorities with the aim of improving the treatment and the conditions of the persons deprived of their liberty and to prevent torture and other cruel, inhuman or degrading treatment or punishment, taking into consideration the relevant norms of the United Nations;

(c) To submit proposals and observations concerning existing or draft legislation.

ARTICLE 20

In order to enable the national preventive mechanisms to fulfil their mandate, the States Parties to the present Protocol undertake to grant them:

(a) Access to all information concerning the number of persons deprived of their liberty in places of detention as defined in article 4, as well as the number of places and their location;

(b) Access to all information referring to the treatment of those persons as well as their conditions of detention;

(c) Access to all places of detention and their installations and facilities;

(d) The opportunity to have private interviews with the persons deprived of their liberty without witnesses, either personally or with a translator if deemed necessary, as well as with any other person who the national preventive mechanism believes may supply relevant information;

(e) The liberty to choose the places they want to visit and the persons they want to interview;

(f) The right to have contacts with the Subcommittee on Prevention, to send it information and to meet with it.

ARTICLE 21

1. No authority or official shall order, apply, permit or tolerate any sanction against any person or organization for having communicated to the national preventive mechanism any information, whether true or false, and no such person or organization shall be otherwise prejudiced in any way.

2. Confidential information collected by the national preventive mechanism shall be privileged. No personal data shall be published without the express consent of the person concerned.

ARTICLE 22

The competent authorities of the State Party concerned shall examine the recommendations of the national preventive mechanism and enter into a dialogue with it on possible implementation measures.

ARTICLE 23

The States Parties to the present Protocol undertake to publish and disseminate the annual reports of the national preventive mechanisms.

PART V

Declaration

ARTICLE 24

1. Upon ratification, States Parties may make a declaration postponing the implementation of their obligations under either part III or part IV of the present Protocol.

2. This postponement shall be valid for a maximum of three years. After due representations made by the State Party and after consultation with the Subcommittee on Prevention, the Committee against Torture may extend that period for an additional two years.

PART VI

Financial Provisions

ARTICLE 25

1. The expenditure incurred by the Subcommittee on Prevention in the implementation of the present Protocol shall be borne by the United Nations.

2. The Secretary-General of the United Nations shall provide the necessary staff and facilities for the effective performance of the functions of the Subcommittee on Prevention under the present Protocol.

ARTICLE 26

1. A Special Fund shall be set up in accordance with the relevant procedures of the General Assembly, to be administered in accordance with the financial regulations and rules of the United Nations, to help finance the implementation of the recommendations made by the Subcommittee on Prevention after a visit to a State Party, as well as education programmes of the national preventive mechanisms.

2. The Special Fund may be financed through voluntary contributions made by Governments, intergovernmental and

non-governmental organizations and other private or public entities.

PART VII

Final Provisions

ARTICLE 27

1. The present Protocol is open for signature by any State that has signed the Convention.

2. The present Protocol is subject to ratification by any State that has ratified or acceded to the Convention. Instruments of ratification shall be deposited with the Secretary-General of the United Nations.

3. The present Protocol shall be open to accession by any State that has ratified or acceded to the Convention.

4. Accession shall be effected by the deposit of an instrument of accession with the Secretary-General of the United Nations.

5. The Secretary-General of the United Nations shall inform all States that have signed the present Protocol or acceded to it of the deposit of each instrument of ratification or accession.

ARTICLE 28

1. The present Protocol shall enter into force on the thirtieth day after the date of deposit with the Secretary-General of the United Nations of the twentieth instrument of ratification or accession.

2. For each State ratifying the present Protocol or acceding to it after the deposit with the Secretary-General of the United Nations of the twentieth instrument of ratification or accession, the present Protocol shall enter into force on the thirtieth day after the date of deposit of its own instrument of ratification or accession.

ARTICLE 29

The provisions of the present Protocol shall extend to all parts of federal States without any limitations or exceptions.

ARTICLE 30

No reservations shall be made to the present Protocol.

ARTICLE 31

The provisions of the present Protocol shall not affect the obligations of States Parties under any regional convention instituting a system of visits to places of detention. The Subcommittee on Prevention and the bodies established under such regional conventions are encouraged to consult and cooperate with a view to avoiding duplication and promoting effectively the objectives of the present Protocol.

ARTICLE 32

The provisions of the present Protocol shall not affect the obligations of States Parties to the four Geneva Conventions of 12 August 1949 and the Additional Protocols thereto of 8 June 1977, nor the opportunity available to any State Party to authorize the International Committee of the Red Cross to visit places of detention in situations not covered by international humanitarian law.

ARTICLE 33

1. Any State Party may denounce the present Protocol at any time by written notification addressed to the Secretary-General of the United Nations, who shall thereafter inform the other States Parties to the present Protocol and the Convention.

Denunciation shall take effect one year after the date of receipt of the notification by the Secretary-General.

2. Such a denunciation shall not have the effect of releasing the State Party from its obligations under the present Protocol in regard to any act or situation that may occur prior to the date on which the denunciation becomes effective, or to the actions that the Subcommittee on Prevention has decided or may decide to take with respect to the State Party concerned, nor shall denunciation prejudice in any way the continued consideration of any matter already under consideration by the Subcommittee on Prevention prior to the date on which the denunciation becomes effective.

3. Following the date on which the denunciation of the State Party becomes effective, the Subcommittee on Prevention shall not commence consideration of any new matter regarding that State.

ARTICLE 34

1. Any State Party to the present Protocol may propose an amendment and file it with the Secretary-General of the United Nations. The Secretary-General shall thereupon communicate the proposed amendment to the States Parties to the present Protocol with a request that they notify him whether they favour a conference of States Parties for the purpose of considering and voting upon the proposal. In the event that within four months from the date of such communication at least one third of the States Parties favour such a conference, the Secretary-General shall convene the conference under the auspices of the United Nations. Any amendment adopted by a majority of two thirds of the States Parties present and voting at the conference shall be submitted by the Secretary-General of the United Nations to all States Parties for acceptance.

2. An amendment adopted in accordance with paragraph 1 of the present article shall come into force when it has been accepted by a two-thirds majority of the States Parties to the present Protocol in accordance with their respective constitutional processes.

3. When amendments come into force, they shall be binding on those States Parties that have accepted them, other States Parties still being bound by the provisions of the present Protocol and any earlier amendment that they have accepted.

ARTICLE 35

Members of the Subcommittee on Prevention and of the national preventive mechanisms shall be accorded such privileges and immunities as are necessary for the independent exercise of their functions. Members of the Subcommittee on Prevention shall be accorded the privileges and immunities specified in section 22 of the Convention on the Privileges and Immunities of the United Nations of 13 February 1946, subject to the provisions of section 23 of that Convention.

ARTICLE 36

When visiting a State Party, the members of the Subcommittee on Prevention shall, without prejudice to the provisions and purposes of the present Protocol and such privileges and immunities as they may enjoy:

(a) Respect the laws and regulations of the visited State;

(b) Refrain from any action or activity incompatible with the impartial and international nature of their duties.

ARTICLE 37

1. The present Protocol, of which the Arabic, Chinese, English, French, Russian and Spanish texts are equally authentic, shall be deposited with the Secretary-General of the United Nations.

2. The Secretary-General of the United Nations shall transmit certified copies of the present Protocol to all States.

Consequences

As of mid-2005, the optional protocol had not yet entered into force.

Source

Office of the United Nations High Commissioner of Human Rights. "Optional Protocol to the Convention Against Torture and Other Cruel, Inhuman or Degrading." Available online. URL: http://www.unhchr.ch/html/menu2/6/cat/treaties/opcat.htm. Accessed January 4, 2005.

CONVENTION AGAINST CORRUPTION

TREATY AT A GLANCE

Completed
October 31, 2003 (not yet entered into force)

Signatories
As of summer 2005, 123 member states of the United Nations,
of which 28 have become full parties

Overview
The Convention against Corruption is intended as an effective international legal instrument, in addition to and independent of the Convention against Transnational Organized Crime, designed specifically to combat corruption. The convention addresses four major issues with regard to corruption: prevention, criminalization, international cooperation, and asset recovery.

Historical Background

In its Resolution 55/61 of December 4, 2000, the General Assembly established an ad hoc committee to draft a Convention against Corruption. The criminalization of corruption under international law is unprecedented, and, indeed, relatively few nations have strong domestic laws against all aspects of international corruption. Thus the committee was assigned to embark on a bold venture into unknown legal and diplomatic territory. The committee met in the Vienna headquarters of the Centre for International Crime Prevention, Office for Drug Control and Crime Prevention in seven sessions held between January 21, 2002, and October 1, 2003, to produce a comprehensive convention, the first to treat corruption not as a domestic issue but as an international issue and, what is more, one with profound social, diplomatic, and political ramifications.

Member nations concluded that corruption is especially harmful to poor nations and to the poorest people within nations because it diverts funds intended for development and undermines a government's ability to provide basic services. The result is not only suffering, but economic, political, and social instability—always a threat to world peace. This global view of corruption, as a problem that directly affects the world community, represents a landmark in multilateral treaty making.

Terms

The convention addresses prevention, criminalization, international cooperation in preventing and fighting corruption, and recovery of assets lost through corruption. The convention addresses both public-sector and private-sector corruption.

Although the convention provides for prosecution of corruption after the fact, it recognizes as more important the more effective strategy against corruption of preventing it in the first place. For this reason, an entire chapter of the document is devoted to the subject of prevention and provides measures directed at both the public and private sectors. Included among these measures are model preventive policies, which states parties may adopt and adapt. In the models, emphasis is placed on the establishment of anticorruption bodies and enhanced transparency in the financing of election campaigns and political parties. The convention holds that measures must be taken to ensure that a state's public services are subject to safeguards that promote efficiency and transparency as well as recruitment based on merit.

The convention establishes the common principles that all public servants should be subject to codes of conduct, requirements for financial and other disclosures, and appropriate disciplinary measures. The document specifies transparency and accountability measures in matters of public finance, including specific legal requirements for the prevention of corruption in such areas of the public sector as the judiciary and public procurement.

Beyond setting out model policies, the convention calls for states parties to promote the involvement of nongovernmental and community-based organizations, as well as other elements of civil society in fighting corruption.

The convention requires states parties to establish criminal and other offenses to cover the entire spectrum of corruption. In some cases, states parties are required to establish offenses, while, in other cases, they are encouraged to consider doing so. The convention thereby takes into account issues of national sovereignty and a permissible range of legal standards; nevertheless, the document goes far beyond previous instruments to criminalize not only basic forms of corruption, such as bribery and the embezzlement of public funds, but also such practices as trading in influence and the concealment and laundering of the proceeds of corruption.

The convention mandates international cooperation in fighting against corruption, including prevention, investigation, and the prosecution of offenders. States parties are bound to render specified forms of mutual legal assistance in gathering and transferring evidence for use in court and to extradite offenders. States also agree to undertake measures to support the tracing, freezing, seizure, and confiscation of the proceeds of corruption.

One of the most important and innovative features of the convention is asset recovery. Convention provisions specify the nature and extent of cooperation and assistance, especially in the case of embezzlement of public funds. Confiscated property is to be returned to the state requesting it. The convention also provides guidelines for compensation to legitimate asset owners and other individual and corporate victims.

United Nations Convention against Corruption

Preamble

The States Parties to this Convention,

Concerned about the seriousness of problems and threats posed by corruption to the stability and security of societies, undermining the institutions and values of democracy, ethical values and justice and jeopardizing sustainable development and the rule of law,

Concerned also about the links between corruption and other forms of crime, in particular organized crime and economic crime, including money-laundering,

Concerned further about cases of corruption that involve vast quantities of assets, which may constitute a substantial proportion of the resources of States, and that threaten the political stability and sustainable development of those States,

Convinced that corruption is no longer a local matter but a transnational phenomenon that affects all societies and economies, making international cooperation to prevent and control it essential,

Convinced also that a comprehensive and multidisciplinary approach is required to prevent and combat corruption effectively,

Convinced further that the availability of technical assistance can play an important role in enhancing the ability of States, including by strengthening capacity and by institution-building, to prevent and combat corruption effectively,

Convinced that the illicit acquisition of personal wealth can be particularly damaging to democratic institutions, national economies and the rule of law,

Determined to prevent, detect and deter in a more effective manner international transfers of illicitly acquired assets and to strengthen international cooperation in asset recovery,

Acknowledging the fundamental principles of due process of law in criminal proceedings and in civil or administrative proceedings to adjudicate property rights,

Bearing in mind that the prevention and eradication of corruption is a responsibility of all States and that they must cooperate with one another, with the support and involvement of individuals and groups outside the public sector, such as civil society, non-governmental organizations and community-based organizations, if their efforts in this area are to be effective,

Bearing also in mind the principles of proper management of public affairs and public property, fairness, responsibility and equality before the law and the need to safeguard integrity and to foster a culture of rejection of corruption,

Commending the work of the Commission on Crime Prevention and Criminal Justice and the United Nations Office on Drugs and Crime in preventing and combating corruption,

Recalling the work carried out by other international and regional organizations in this field, including the activities of the African Union, the Council of Europe, the Customs Cooperation Council (also known as the World Customs Organization), the European Union, the League of Arab States, the Organisation for Economic Cooperation and Development and the Organization of American States,

Taking note with appreciation of multilateral instruments to prevent and combat corruption, including, inter alia, the Inter-American Convention against Corruption, adopted by the Organization of American States on 29 March 1996, the Convention on the Fight against Corruption involving Officials of the European Communities or Officials of Member States of the European Union, adopted by the Council of the European Union on 26 May 1997, the Convention on Combating Bribery of Foreign Public Officials in International Business Transactions, adopted by the Organisation for Economic Cooperation and Development on 21 November 1997, the Criminal Law Convention on Corruption, adopted by the Committee of Ministers of the Council of Europe on 27 January 1999, the Civil Law Convention on Corruption, adopted by the Committee of Ministers of the Council of Europe on 4 November 1999, and the African Union Convention on Preventing and Combating Corruption, adopted by the Heads of State and Government of the African Union on 12 July 2003,

Welcoming the entry into force on 29 September 2003 of the United Nations Convention against Transnational Organized Crime,

Have agreed as follows:

Chapter I

General Provisions

ARTICLE 1

STATEMENT OF PURPOSE

The purposes of this Convention are:

(a) To promote and strengthen measures to prevent and combat corruption more efficiently and effectively;

(b) To promote, facilitate and support international cooperation and technical assistance in the prevention of and fight against corruption, including in asset recovery;

(c) To promote integrity, accountability and proper management of public affairs and public property.

ARTICLE 2
USE OF TERMS

For the purposes of this Convention:

(a)"Public official" shall mean: (i) any person holding a legislative, executive, administrative or judicial office of a State Party, whether appointed or elected, whether permanent or temporary, whether paid or unpaid, irrespective of that person's seniority; (ii) any other person who performs a public function, including for a public agency or public enterprise, or provides a public service, as defined in the domestic law of the State Party and as applied in the pertinent area of law of that State Party; (iii) any other person defined as a "public official" in the domestic law of a State Party. However, for the purpose of some specific measures contained in chapter II of this Convention, "public official" may mean any person who performs a public function or provides a public service as defined in the domestic law of the State Party and as applied in the pertinent area of law of that State Party;

(b) "Foreign public official" shall mean any person holding a legislative, executive, administrative or judicial office of a foreign country, whether appointed or elected; and any person exercising a public function for a foreign country, including for a public agency or public enterprise;

(c) "Official of a public international organization" shall mean an international civil servant or any person who is authorized by such an organization to act on behalf of that organization;

(d) "Property" shall mean assets of every kind, whether corporeal or incorporeal, movable or immovable, tangible or intangible, and legal documents or instruments evidencing title to or interest in such assets;

(e) "Proceeds of crime" shall mean any property derived from or obtained, directly or indirectly, through the commission of an offence;

(f) "Freezing" or "seizure" shall mean temporarily prohibiting the transfer, conversion, disposition or movement of property or temporarily assuming custody or control of property on the basis of an order issued by a court or other competent authority;

(g) "Confiscation", which includes forfeiture where applicable, shall mean the permanent deprivation of property by order of a court or other competent authority;

(h) "Predicate offence" shall mean any offence as a result of which proceeds have been generated that may become the subject of an offence as defined in article 23 of this Convention;

(i) "Controlled delivery" shall mean the technique of allowing illicit or suspect consignments to pass out of, through or into the territory of one or more States, with the knowledge and under the supervision of their competent authorities, with a view to the investigation of an offence and the identification of persons involved in the commission of the offence.

ARTICLE 3
SCOPE OF APPLICATION

1. This Convention shall apply, in accordance with its terms, to the prevention, investigation and prosecution of corruption and to the freezing, seizure, confiscation and return of the proceeds of offences established in accordance with this Convention.

2. For the purposes of implementing this Convention, it shall not be necessary, except as otherwise stated herein, for the offences set forth in it to result in damage or harm to state property.

ARTICLE 4
PROTECTION OF SOVEREIGNTY

1. States Parties shall carry out their obligations under this Convention in a manner consistent with the principles of sovereign equality and territorial integrity of States and that of non-intervention in the domestic affairs of other States. . . .

Chapter II

Preventive Measures

ARTICLE 5
PREVENTIVE ANTI-CORRUPTION POLICIES AND PRACTICES

1. Each State Party shall, in accordance with the fundamental principles of its legal system, develop and implement or maintain effective, coordinated anti-corruption policies that promote the participation of society and reflect the principles of the rule of law, proper management of public affairs and public property, integrity, transparency and accountability.

2. Each State Party shall endeavour to establish and promote effective practices aimed at the prevention of corruption.

3. Each State Party shall endeavour to periodically evaluate relevant legal instruments and administrative measures with a view to determining their adequacy to prevent and fight corruption.

4. States Parties shall, as appropriate and in accordance with the fundamental principles of their legal system, collaborate with each other and with relevant international and regional organizations in promoting and developing the measures referred to in this article. That collaboration may include participation in international programmes and projects aimed at the prevention of corruption.

ARTICLE 6
PREVENTIVE ANTI-CORRUPTION BODY OR BODIES

1. Each State Party shall, in accordance with the fundamental principles of its legal system, ensure the existence of a body or bodies, as appropriate, that prevent corruption by such means as:

(a) Implementing the policies referred to in article 5 of this Convention and, where appropriate, overseeing and coordinating the implementation of those policies;

(b) Increasing and disseminating knowledge about the prevention of corruption.

2. Each State Party shall grant the body or bodies referred to in paragraph 1 of this article the necessary independence, in

accordance with the fundamental principles of its legal system, to enable the body or bodies to carry out its or their functions effectively and free from any undue influence. The necessary material resources and specialized staff, as well as the training that such staff may require to carry out their functions, should be provided.

3. Each State Party shall inform the Secretary-General of the United Nations of the name and address of the authority or authorities that may assist other States Parties in developing and implementing specific measures for the prevention of corruption.

ARTICLE 7
PUBLIC SECTOR

1. Each State Party shall, where appropriate and in accordance with the fundamental principles of its legal system, endeavour to adopt, maintain and strengthen systems for the recruitment, hiring, retention, promotion and retirement of civil servants and, where appropriate, other non-elected public officials:

(a) That are based on principles of efficiency, transparency and objective criteria such as merit, equity and aptitude;

(b) That include adequate procedures for the selection and training of individuals for public positions considered especially vulnerable to corruption and the rotation, where appropriate, of such individuals to other positions;

(c) That promote adequate remuneration and equitable pay scales, taking into account the level of economic development of the State Party;

(d) That promote education and training programmes to enable them to meet the requirements for the correct, honourable and proper performance of public functions and that provide them with specialized and appropriate training to enhance their awareness of the risks of corruption inherent in the performance of their functions. Such programmes may make reference to codes or standards of conduct in applicable areas.

2. Each State Party shall also consider adopting appropriate legislative and administrative measures, consistent with the objectives of this Convention and in accordance with the fundamental principles of its domestic law, to prescribe criteria concerning candidature for and election to public office.

3. Each State Party shall also consider taking appropriate legislative and administrative measures, consistent with the objectives of this Convention and in accordance with the fundamental principles of its domestic law, to enhance transparency in the funding of candidatures for elected public office and, where applicable, the funding of political parties.

4. Each State Party shall, in accordance with the fundamental principles of its domestic law, endeavour to adopt, maintain and strengthen systems that promote transparency and prevent conflicts of interest.

ARTICLE 8
CODES OF CONDUCT FOR PUBLIC OFFICIALS

1. In order to fight corruption, each State Party shall promote, inter alia, integrity, honesty and responsibility among its public officials, in accordance with the fundamental principles of its legal system.

2. In particular, each State Party shall endeavour to apply, within its own institutional and legal systems, codes or standards of conduct for the correct, honourable and proper performance of public functions.

3. For the purposes of implementing the provisions of this article, each State Party shall, where appropriate and in accordance with the fundamental principles of its legal system, take note of the relevant initiatives of regional, interregional and multilateral organizations, such as the International Code of Conduct for Public Officials contained in the annex to General Assembly resolution 51/59 of 12 December 1996.

4. Each State Party shall also consider, in accordance with the fundamental principles of its domestic law, establishing measures and systems to facilitate the reporting by public officials of acts of corruption to appropriate authorities, when such acts come to their notice in the performance of their functions.

5. Each State Party shall endeavour, where appropriate and in accordance with the fundamental principles of its domestic law, to establish measures and systems requiring public officials to make declarations to appropriate authorities regarding, inter alia, their outside activities, employment, investments, assets and substantial gifts or benefits from which a conflict of interest may result with respect to their functions as public officials.

6. Each State Party shall consider taking, in accordance with the fundamental principles of its domestic law, disciplinary or other measures against public officials who violate the codes or standards established in accordance with this article.

ARTICLE 9
PUBLIC PROCUREMENT AND MANAGEMENT OF PUBLIC FINANCES

1. Each State Party shall, in accordance with the fundamental principles of its legal system, take the necessary steps to establish appropriate systems of procurement, based on transparency, competition and objective criteria in decision-making, that are effective, inter alia, in preventing corruption. Such systems, which may take into account appropriate threshold values in their application, shall address, inter alia:

(a) The public distribution of information relating to procurement procedures and contracts, including information on invitations to tender and relevant or pertinent information on the award of contracts, allowing potential tenderers sufficient time to prepare and submit their tenders;

(b) The establishment, in advance, of conditions for participation, including selection and award criteria and tendering rules, and their publication;

(c) The use of objective and predetermined criteria for public procurement decisions, in order to facilitate the subsequent verification of the correct application of the rules or procedures;

(d) An effective system of domestic review, including an effective system of appeal, to ensure legal recourse and remedies in the event that the rules or procedures established pursuant to this paragraph are not followed;

(e) Where appropriate, measures to regulate matters regarding personnel responsible for procurement, such as declaration of interest in particular public procurements, screening procedures and training requirements.

2. Each State Party shall, in accordance with the fundamental principles of its legal system, take appropriate measures to promote transparency and accountability in the management of public finances. Such measures shall encompass, inter alia:

(a) Procedures for the adoption of the national budget;

(b) Timely reporting on revenue and expenditure;

(c) A system of accounting and auditing standards and related oversight;

(d) Effective and efficient systems of risk management and internal control; and

(e) Where appropriate, corrective action in the case of failure to comply with the requirements established in this paragraph.

3. Each State Party shall take such civil and administrative measures as may be necessary, in accordance with the fundamental principles of its domestic law, to preserve the integrity of accounting books, records, financial statements or other documents related to public expenditure and revenue and to prevent the falsification of such documents.

ARTICLE 10
PUBLIC REPORTING

Taking into account the need to combat corruption, each State Party shall, in accordance with the fundamental principles of its domestic law, take such measures as may be necessary to enhance transparency in its public administration, including with regard to its organization, functioning and decision-making processes, where appropriate. Such measures may include, inter alia:

(a) Adopting procedures or regulations allowing members of the general public to obtain, where appropriate, information on the organization, functioning and decision-making processes of its public administration and, with due regard for the protection of privacy and personal data, on decisions and legal acts that concern members of the public;

(b) Simplifying administrative procedures, where appropriate, in order to facilitate public access to the competent decision-making authorities; and

(c) Publishing information, which may include periodic reports on the risks of corruption in its public administration.

ARTICLE 11
MEASURES RELATING TO THE JUDICIARY
AND PROSECUTION SERVICES

1. Bearing in mind the independence of the judiciary and its crucial role in combating corruption, each State Party shall, in accordance with the fundamental principles of its legal system and without prejudice to judicial independence, take measures to strengthen integrity and to prevent opportunities for corruption among members of the judiciary. Such measures may include rules with respect to the conduct of members of the judiciary.

2. Measures to the same effect as those taken pursuant to paragraph 1 of this article may be introduced and applied within the prosecution service in those States Parties where it does not form part of the judiciary but enjoys independence similar to that of the judicial service.

ARTICLE 12
PRIVATE SECTOR

1. Each State Party shall take measures, in accordance with the fundamental principles of its domestic law, to prevent corruption involving the private sector, enhance accounting and auditing standards in the private sector and, where appropriate, provide effective, proportionate and dissuasive civil, administrative or criminal penalties for failure to comply with such measures.

2. Measures to achieve these ends may include, inter alia:

(a) Promoting cooperation between law enforcement agencies and relevant private entities;

(b) Promoting the development of standards and procedures designed to safeguard the integrity of relevant private entities, including codes of conduct for the correct, honourable and proper performance of the activities of business and all relevant professions and the prevention of conflicts of interest, and for the promotion of the use of good commercial practices among businesses and in the contractual relations of businesses with the State;

(c) Promoting transparency among private entities, including, where appropriate, measures regarding the identity of legal and natural persons involved in the establishment and management of corporate entities;

(d) Preventing the misuse of procedures regulating private entities, including procedures regarding subsidies and licences granted by public authorities for commercial activities;

(e) Preventing conflicts of interest by imposing restrictions, as appropriate and for a reasonable period of time, on the professional activities of former public officials or on the employment of public officials by the private sector after their resignation or retirement, where such activities or employment relate directly to the functions held or supervised by those public officials during their tenure;

(f) Ensuring that private enterprises, taking into account their structure and size, have sufficient internal auditing controls to assist in preventing and detecting acts of corruption and that the accounts and required financial statements of such private enterprises are subject to appropriate auditing and certification procedures.

3. In order to prevent corruption, each State Party shall take such measures as may be necessary, in accordance with its domestic laws and regulations regarding the maintenance of books and records, financial statement disclosures and accounting and auditing standards, to prohibit the following acts carried out for the purpose of committing any of the offences established in accordance with this Convention:

(a) The establishment of off-the-books accounts;

(b) The making of off-the-books or inadequately identified transactions;

(c) The recording of non-existent expenditure;

(d) The entry of liabilities with incorrect identification of their objects;

(e) The use of false documents; and

(f) The intentional destruction of bookkeeping documents earlier than foreseen by the law.

4. Each State Party shall disallow the tax deductibility of expenses that constitute bribes, the latter being one of the constituent elements of the offences established in accordance with articles 15 and 16 of this Convention and, where appropriate, other expenses incurred in furtherance of corrupt conduct.

ARTICLE 13
PARTICIPATION OF SOCIETY

1. Each State Party shall take appropriate measures, within its means and in accordance with fundamental principles of its domestic law, to promote the active participation of individuals and groups outside the public sector, such as civil society, non-governmental organizations and community-based organizations, in the prevention of and the fight against corruption and to raise public awareness regarding the existence, causes and gravity of and the threat posed by corruption. . . .

ARTICLE 14
MEASURES TO PREVENT MONEY-LAUNDERING

1. Each State Party shall:

(a) Institute a comprehensive domestic regulatory and supervisory regime for banks and non-bank financial institutions, including natural or legal persons that provide formal or informal services for the transmission of money or value and, where appropriate, other bodies particularly susceptible to money-laundering, within its competence, in order to deter and detect all forms of money-laundering . . .

Chapter III

Criminalization and Law Enforcement

ARTICLE 15
BRIBERY OF NATIONAL PUBLIC OFFICIALS

Each State Party shall adopt such legislative and other measures as may be necessary to establish as criminal offences, when committed intentionally:

(a) The promise, offering or giving, to a public official, directly or indirectly, of an undue advantage, for the official himself or herself or another person or entity, in order that the official act or refrain from acting in the exercise of his or her official duties;

(b) The solicitation or acceptance by a public official, directly or indirectly, of an undue advantage, for the official himself or herself or another person or entity, in order that the official act or refrain from acting in the exercise of his or her official duties.

ARTICLE 16
BRIBERY OF FOREIGN PUBLIC OFFICIALS AND OFFICIALS OF PUBLIC INTERNATIONAL ORGANIZATIONS

1. Each State Party shall adopt such legislative and other measures as may be necessary to establish as a criminal offence, when committed intentionally, the promise, offering or giving to a foreign public official or an official of a public international organization, directly or indirectly, of an undue advantage, for the official himself or herself or another person or entity, in order that the official act or refrain from acting in the exercise of his or her official duties, in order to obtain or retain business or other undue advantage in relation to the conduct of international business.

2. Each State Party shall consider adopting such legislative and other measures as may be necessary to establish as a criminal offence, when committed intentionally, the solicitation or acceptance by a foreign public official or an official of a public international organization, directly or indirectly, of an undue advantage, for the official himself or herself or another person or entity, in order that the official act or refrain from acting in the exercise of his or her official duties.

ARTICLE 17
EMBEZZLEMENT, MISAPPROPRIATION OR OTHER DIVERSION OF PROPERTY BY A PUBLIC OFFICIAL

Each State Party shall adopt such legislative and other measures as may be necessary to establish as criminal offences, when committed intentionally, the embezzlement, misappropriation or other diversion by a public official for his or her benefit or for the benefit of another person or entity, of any property, public or private funds or securities or any other thing of value entrusted to the public official by virtue of his or her position.

ARTICLE 18
TRADING IN INFLUENCE

Each State Party shall consider adopting such legislative and other measures as may be necessary to establish as criminal offences, when committed intentionally:

(a) The promise, offering or giving to a public official or any other person, directly or indirectly, of an undue advantage in order that the public official or the person abuse his or her real or supposed influence with a view to obtaining from an administration or public authority of the State Party an undue advantage for the original instigator of the act or for any other person;

(b) The solicitation or acceptance by a public official or any other person, directly or indirectly, of an undue advantage for himself or herself or for another person in order that the public official or the person abuse his or her real or supposed influence with a view to obtaining from an administration or public authority of the State Party an undue advantage.

ARTICLE 19
ABUSE OF FUNCTIONS

Each State Party shall consider adopting such legislative and other measures as may be necessary to establish as a criminal offence, when committed intentionally, the abuse of functions or position, that is, the performance of or failure to perform an act, in violation of laws, by a public official in the discharge of his or her functions, for the purpose of obtaining an undue advantage for himself or herself or for another person or entity.

ARTICLE 20
ILLICIT ENRICHMENT

Subject to its constitution and the fundamental principles of its legal system, each State Party shall consider adopting such legislative and other measures as may be necessary to establish as a criminal offence, when committed intentionally, illicit enrichment, that is, a significant increase in the assets of a public official that he or she cannot reasonably explain in relation to his or her lawful income.

ARTICLE 21
BRIBERY IN THE PRIVATE SECTOR

Each State Party shall consider adopting such legislative and other measures as may be necessary to establish as criminal offences, when committed intentionally in the course of economic, financial or commercial activities:

(a) The promise, offering or giving, directly or indirectly, of an undue advantage to any person who directs or works, in any capacity, for a private sector entity, for the person himself or herself or for another person, in order that he or she, in breach of his or her duties, act or refrain from acting;

(b) The solicitation or acceptance, directly or indirectly, of an undue advantage by any person who directs or works, in any capacity, for a private sector entity, for the person himself or herself or for another person, in order that he or she, in breach of his or her duties, act or refrain from acting.

ARTICLE 22
EMBEZZLEMENT OF PROPERTY
IN THE PRIVATE SECTOR

Each State Party shall consider adopting such legislative and other measures as may be necessary to establish as a criminal offence, when committed intentionally in the course of economic, financial or commercial activities, embezzlement by a person who directs or works, in any capacity, in a private sector entity of any property, private funds or securities or any other thing of value entrusted to him or her by virtue of his or her position.

ARTICLE 23
LAUNDERING OF PROCEEDS OF CRIME

1. Each State Party shall adopt, in accordance with fundamental principles of its domestic law, such legislative and other measures as may be necessary to establish as criminal offences, when committed intentionally:

(a) (i) The conversion or transfer of property, knowing that such property is the proceeds of crime, for the purpose of concealing or disguising the illicit origin of the property or of helping any person who is involved in the commission of the predicate offence to evade the legal consequences of his or her action;

(ii) The concealment or disguise of the true nature, source, location, disposition, movement or ownership of or rights with respect to property, knowing that such property is the proceeds of crime;

(b) Subject to the basic concepts of its legal system:

(i) The acquisition, possession or use of property, knowing, at the time of receipt, that such property is the proceeds of crime;

(ii) Participation in, association with or conspiracy to commit, attempts to commit and aiding, abetting, facilitating and counselling the commission of any of the offences established in accordance with this article. . . .

ARTICLE 24
CONCEALMENT

Without prejudice to the provisions of article 23 of this Convention, each State Party shall consider adopting such legislative and other measures as may be necessary to establish as a criminal offence, when committed intentionally after the commission of any of the offences established in accordance with this Convention without having participated in such offences, the concealment or continued retention of property when the person involved knows that such property is the result of any of the offences established in accordance with this Convention.

ARTICLE 25
OBSTRUCTION OF JUSTICE

Each State Party shall adopt such legislative and other measures as may be necessary to establish as criminal offences, when committed intentionally:

(a) The use of physical force, threats or intimidation or the promise, offering or giving of an undue advantage to induce false testimony or to interfere in the giving of testimony or the production of evidence in a proceeding in relation to the commission of offences established in accordance with this Convention;

(b) The use of physical force, threats or intimidation to interfere with the exercise of official duties by a justice or law enforcement official in relation to the commission of offences established in accordance with this Convention. Nothing in this subparagraph shall prejudice the right of States Parties to have legislation that protects other categories of public official.

ARTICLE 26
LIABILITY OF LEGAL PERSONS

1. Each State Party shall adopt such measures as may be necessary, consistent with its legal principles, to establish the liability of legal persons for participation in the offences established in accordance with this Convention. . . .

ARTICLE 27
PARTICIPATION AND ATTEMPT

1. Each State Party shall adopt such legislative and other measures as may be necessary to establish as a criminal offence, in accordance with its domestic law, participation in any capacity such as an accomplice, assistant or instigator in an offence established in accordance with this Convention. . . .

ARTICLE 28
KNOWLEDGE, INTENT AND PURPOSE
AS ELEMENTS OF AN OFFENCE

Knowledge, intent or purpose required as an element of an offence established in accordance with this Convention may be inferred from objective factual circumstances.

ARTICLE 29
STATUTE OF LIMITATIONS

Each State Party shall, where appropriate, establish under its domestic law a long statute of limitations period in which to commence proceedings for any offence established in accordance with this Convention and establish a longer statute of limitations period or provide for the suspension of the statute of limitations where the alleged offender has evaded the administration of justice.

ARTICLE 30
PROSECUTION, ADJUDICATION AND SANCTIONS

1. Each State Party shall make the commission of an offence established in accordance with this Convention liable to sanctions that take into account the gravity of that offence. . . .

ARTICLE 31
FREEZING, SEIZURE AND CONFISCATION
1. Each State Party shall take, to the greatest extent possible within its domestic legal system, such measures as may be necessary to enable confiscation of:

(a) Proceeds of crime derived from offences established in accordance with this Convention or property the value of which corresponds to that of such proceeds;

(b) Property, equipment or other instrumentalities used in or destined for use in offences established in accordance with this Convention.

2. Each State Party shall take such measures as may be necessary to enable the identification, tracing, freezing or seizure of any item referred to in paragraph 1 of this article for the purpose of eventual confiscation. . . .

ARTICLE 32
PROTECTION OF WITNESSES, EXPERTS AND VICTIMS
1. Each State Party shall take appropriate measures in accordance with its domestic legal system and within its means to provide effective protection from potential retaliation or intimidation for witnesses and experts who give testimony concerning offences established in accordance with this Convention and, as appropriate, for their relatives and other persons close to them. . . .

ARTICLE 33
PROTECTION OF REPORTING PERSONS
Each State Party shall consider incorporating into its domestic legal system appropriate measures to provide protection against any unjustified treatment for any person who reports in good faith and on reasonable grounds to the competent authorities any facts concerning offences established in accordance with this Convention.

ARTICLE 34
CONSEQUENCES OF ACTS OF CORRUPTION
With due regard to the rights of third parties acquired in good faith, each State Party shall take measures, in accordance with the fundamental principles of its domestic law, to address consequences of corruption. In this context, States Parties may consider corruption a relevant factor in legal proceedings to annul or rescind a contract, withdraw a concession or other similar instrument or take any other remedial action.

ARTICLE 35
COMPENSATION FOR DAMAGE
Each State Party shall take such measures as may be necessary, in accordance with principles of its domestic law, to ensure that entities or persons who have suffered damage as a result of an act of corruption have the right to initiate legal proceedings against those responsible for that damage in order to obtain compensation.

ARTICLE 36
SPECIALIZED AUTHORITIES
Each State Party shall, in accordance with the fundamental principles of its legal system, ensure the existence of a body or bodies or persons specialized in combating corruption through law enforcement. Such body or bodies or persons shall be granted the necessary independence, in accordance with the fundamental principles of the legal system of the State Party, to be able to carry out their functions effectively and without any undue

influence. Such persons or staff of such body or bodies should have the appropriate training and resources to carry out their tasks.

ARTICLE 37
COOPERATION WITH LAW ENFORCEMENT AUTHORITIES
1. Each State Party shall take appropriate measures to encourage persons who participate or who have participated in the commission of an offence established in accordance with this Convention to supply information useful to competent authorities for investigative and evidentiary purposes and to provide factual, specific help to competent authorities that may contribute to depriving offenders of the proceeds of crime and to recovering such proceeds.

2. Each State Party shall consider providing for the possibility, in appropriate cases, of mitigating punishment of an accused person who provides substantial cooperation in the investigation or prosecution of an offence established in accordance with this Convention.

3. Each State Party shall consider providing for the possibility, in accordance with fundamental principles of its domestic law, of granting immunity from prosecution to a person who provides substantial cooperation in the investigation or prosecution of an offence established in accordance with this Convention. . . .

ARTICLE 38
COOPERATION BETWEEN NATIONAL AUTHORITIES
Each State Party shall take such measures as may be necessary to encourage, in accordance with its domestic law, cooperation between, on the one hand, its public authorities, as well as its public officials, and, on the other hand, its authorities responsible for investigating and prosecuting criminal offences. . . .

ARTICLE 39
COOPERATION BETWEEN
NATIONAL AUTHORITIES AND THE PRIVATE SECTOR
1. Each State Party shall take such measures as may be necessary to encourage, in accordance with its domestic law, cooperation between national investigating and prosecuting authorities and entities of the private sector, in particular financial institutions, relating to matters involving the commission of offences established in accordance with this Convention. . . .

ARTICLE 40
BANK SECRECY
Each State Party shall ensure that, in the case of domestic criminal investigations of offences established in accordance with this Convention, there are appropriate mechanisms available within its domestic legal system to overcome obstacles that may arise out of the application of bank secrecy laws. . . .

Chapter IV

International Cooperation

ARTICLE 43
INTERNATIONAL COOPERATION
1. States Parties shall cooperate in criminal matters in accordance with articles 44 to 50 of this Convention. Where appropriate and consistent with their domestic legal system, States Parties shall consider assisting each other in investigations of and proceedings in civil and administrative matters relating to corruption. . . .

ARTICLE 46
MUTUAL LEGAL ASSISTANCE

1. States Parties shall afford one another the widest measure of mutual legal assistance in investigations, prosecutions and judicial proceedings in relation to the offences covered by this Convention. . . .

ARTICLE 48
LAW ENFORCEMENT COOPERATION

1. States Parties shall cooperate closely with one another, consistent with their respective domestic legal and administrative systems, to enhance the effectiveness of law enforcement action to combat the offences covered by this Convention. . . .

ARTICLE 49
JOINT INVESTIGATIONS

States Parties shall consider concluding bilateral or multilateral agreements or arrangements whereby, in relation to matters that are the subject of investigations, prosecutions or judicial proceedings in one or more States, the competent authorities concerned may establish joint investigative bodies. In the absence of such agreements or arrangements, joint investigations may be undertaken by agreement on a case-by-case basis. The States Parties involved shall ensure that the sovereignty of the State Party in whose territory such investigation is to take place is fully respected.

ARTICLE 50
SPECIAL INVESTIGATIVE TECHNIQUES

1. In order to combat corruption effectively, each State Party shall, to the extent permitted by the basic principles of its domestic legal system and in accordance with the conditions prescribed by its domestic law, take such measures as may be necessary, within its means, to allow for the appropriate use by its competent authorities of controlled delivery and, where it deems appropriate, other special investigative techniques, such as electronic or other forms of surveillance and undercover operations, within its territory, and to allow for the admissibility in court of evidence derived therefrom. . . .

Chapter V

Asset Recovery

ARTICLE 51
GENERAL PROVISION

The return of assets pursuant to this chapter is a fundamental principle of this Convention, and States Parties shall afford one another the widest measure of cooperation and assistance in this regard.

ARTICLE 52
PREVENTION AND DETECTION OF TRANSFERS OF PROCEEDS OF CRIME

1. Without prejudice to article 14 of this Convention, each State Party shall take such measures as may be necessary, in accordance with its domestic law, to require financial institutions within its jurisdiction to verify the identity of customers, to take reasonable steps to determine the identity of beneficial owners of funds deposited into high-value accounts and to conduct enhanced scrutiny of accounts sought or maintained by or on behalf of individuals who are, or have been, entrusted with prominent public functions and their family members and close associates. Such enhanced scrutiny shall be reasonably designed to detect suspicious transactions for the purpose of reporting to competent authorities and should not be so construed as to discourage or prohibit financial institutions from doing business with any legitimate customer.

2. In order to facilitate implementation of the measures provided for in paragraph 1 of this article, each State Party, in accordance with its domestic law and inspired by relevant initiatives of regional, interregional and multilateral organizations against money-laundering, shall:

   (a) Issue advisories regarding the types of natural or legal person to whose accounts financial institutions within its jurisdiction will be expected to apply enhanced scrutiny, the types of accounts and transactions to which to pay particular attention and appropriate account-opening, maintenance and record-keeping measures to take concerning such accounts; and

   (b) Where appropriate, notify financial institutions within its jurisdiction, at the request of another State Party or on its own initiative, of the identity of particular natural or legal persons to whose accounts such institutions will be expected to apply enhanced scrutiny, in addition to those whom the financial institutions may otherwise identify.

3. In the context of paragraph 2 (a) of this article, each State Party shall implement measures to ensure that its financial institutions maintain adequate records, over an appropriate period of time, of accounts and transactions involving the persons mentioned in paragraph 1 of this article, which should, as a minimum, contain information relating to the identity of the customer as well as, as far as possible, of the beneficial owner.

4. With the aim of preventing and detecting transfers of proceeds of offences established in accordance with this Convention, each State Party shall implement appropriate and effective measures to prevent, with the help of its regulatory and oversight bodies, the establishment of banks that have no physical presence and that are not affiliated with a regulated financial group. Moreover, States Parties may consider requiring their financial institutions to refuse to enter into or continue a correspondent banking relationship with such institutions and to guard against establishing relations with foreign financial institutions that permit their accounts to be used by banks that have no physical presence and that are not affiliated with a regulated financial group.

5. Each State Party shall consider establishing, in accordance with its domestic law, effective financial disclosure systems for appropriate public officials and shall provide for appropriate sanctions for non-compliance. Each State Party shall also consider taking such measures as may be necessary to permit its competent authorities to share that information with the competent authorities in other States Parties when necessary to investigate, claim and recover proceeds of offences established in accordance with this Convention.

6. Each State Party shall consider taking such measures as may be necessary, in accordance with its domestic law, to require appropriate public officials having an interest in or signature or other authority over a financial account in a foreign country to report that relationship to appropriate authorities and to maintain appropriate records related to such accounts.

Such measures shall also provide for appropriate sanctions for non-compliance.

ARTICLE 53
MEASURES FOR DIRECT RECOVERY OF PROPERTY

Each State Party shall, in accordance with its domestic law:

(a) Take such measures as may be necessary to permit another State Party to initiate civil action in its courts to establish title to or ownership of property acquired through the commission of an offence established in accordance with this Convention;

(b) Take such measures as may be necessary to permit its courts to order those who have committed offences established in accordance with this Convention to pay compensation or damages to another State Party that has been harmed by such offences; and

(c) Take such measures as may be necessary to permit its courts or competent authorities, when having to decide on confiscation, to recognize another State Party's claim as a legitimate owner of property acquired through the commission of an offence established in accordance with this Convention.

ARTICLE 54
MECHANISMS FOR RECOVERY OF PROPERTY THROUGH INTERNATIONAL COOPERATION IN CONFISCATION

1. Each State Party, in order to provide mutual legal assistance pursuant to article 55 of this Convention with respect to property acquired through or involved in the commission of an offence established in accordance with this Convention, shall, in accordance with its domestic law:

(a) Take such measures as may be necessary to permit its competent authorities to give effect to an order of confiscation issued by a court of another State Party;

(b) Take such measures as may be necessary to permit its competent authorities, where they have jurisdiction, to order the confiscation of such property of foreign origin by adjudication of an offence of money-laundering or such other offence as may be within its jurisdiction or by other procedures authorized under its domestic law; and

(c) Consider taking such measures as may be necessary to allow confiscation of such property without a criminal conviction in cases in which the offender cannot be prosecuted by reason of death, flight or absence or in other appropriate cases.

2. Each State Party, in order to provide mutual legal assistance upon a request made pursuant to paragraph 2 of article 55 of this Convention, shall, in accordance with its domestic law:

(a) Take such measures as may be necessary to permit its competent authorities to freeze or seize property upon a freezing or seizure order issued by a court or competent authority of a requesting State Party that provides a reasonable basis for the requested State Party to believe that there are sufficient grounds for taking such actions and that the property would eventually be subject to an order of confiscation for purposes of paragraph 1 (a) of this article;

(b) Take such measures as may be necessary to permit its competent authorities to freeze or seize property upon a request that provides a reasonable basis for the requested State Party to believe that there are sufficient grounds for taking such actions and that the property would eventually be subject to an order of confiscation for purposes of paragraph 1 (a) of this article; and

(c) Consider taking additional measures to permit its competent authorities to preserve property for confiscation, such as on the basis of a foreign arrest or criminal charge related to the acquisition of such property.

ARTICLE 55
INTERNATIONAL COOPERATION FOR PURPOSES OF CONFISCATION

1. A State Party that has received a request from another State Party having jurisdiction over an offence established in accordance with this Convention for confiscation of proceeds of crime, property, equipment or other instrumentalities referred to in article 31, paragraph 1, of this Convention situated in its territory shall, to the greatest extent possible within its domestic legal system:

(a) Submit the request to its competent authorities for the purpose of obtaining an order of confiscation and, if such an order is granted, give effect to it; or

(b) Submit to its competent authorities, with a view to giving effect to it to the extent requested, an order of confiscation issued by a court in the territory of the requesting State Party in accordance with articles 31, paragraph 1, and 54, paragraph 1 (a), of this Convention insofar as it relates to proceeds of crime, property, equipment or other instrumentalities referred to in article 31, paragraph 1, situated in the territory of the requested State Party.

2. Following a request made by another State Party having jurisdiction over an offence established in accordance with this Convention, the requested State Party shall take measures to identify, trace and freeze or seize proceeds of crime, property, equipment or other instrumentalities referred to in article 31, paragraph 1, of this Convention for the purpose of eventual confiscation to be ordered either by the requesting State Party or, pursuant to a request under paragraph 1 of this article, by the requested State Party. . . .

ARTICLE 56
SPECIAL COOPERATION

Without prejudice to its domestic law, each State Party shall endeavour to take measures to permit it to forward, without prejudice to its own investigations, prosecutions or judicial proceedings, information on proceeds of offences established in accordance with this Convention to another State Party without prior request, when it considers that the disclosure of such information might assist the receiving State Party in initiating or carrying out investigations, prosecutions or judicial proceedings or might lead to a request by that State Party under this chapter of the Convention.

ARTICLE 57
RETURN AND DISPOSAL OF ASSETS

1. Property confiscated by a State Party pursuant to article 31 or 55 of this Convention shall be disposed of, including by return

to its prior legitimate owners, pursuant to paragraph 3 of this article, by that State Party in accordance with the provisions of this Convention and its domestic law. . . .

ARTICLE 58
FINANCIAL INTELLIGENCE UNIT

States Parties shall cooperate with one another for the purpose of preventing and combating the transfer of proceeds of offences established in accordance with this Convention and of promoting ways and means of recovering such proceeds and, to that end, shall consider establishing a financial intelligence unit to be responsible for receiving, analysing and disseminating to the competent authorities reports of suspicious financial transactions.

ARTICLE 59
BILATERAL AND MULTILATERAL AGREEMENTS AND ARRANGEMENTS

States Parties shall consider concluding bilateral or multilateral agreements or arrangements to enhance the effectiveness of international cooperation undertaken pursuant to this chapter of the Convention.

Chapter VI

Technical Assistance and Information Exchange

ARTICLE 60
TRAINING AND TECHNICAL ASSISTANCE

1. Each State Party shall, to the extent necessary, initiate, develop or improve specific training programmes for its personnel responsible for preventing and combating corruption. Such training programmes could deal, inter alia, with the following areas:

(a) Effective measures to prevent, detect, investigate, punish and control corruption, including the use of evidence-gathering and investigative methods;

(b) Building capacity in the development and planning of strategic anti-corruption policy;

(c) Training competent authorities in the preparation of requests for mutual legal assistance that meet the requirements of this Convention;

(d) Evaluation and strengthening of institutions, public service management and the management of public finances, including public procurement, and the private sector;

(e) Preventing and combating the transfer of proceeds of offences established in accordance with this Convention and recovering such proceeds;

(f) Detecting and freezing of the transfer of proceeds of offences established in accordance with this Convention;

(g) Surveillance of the movement of proceeds of offences established in accordance with this Convention and of the methods used to transfer, conceal or disguise such proceeds;

(h) Appropriate and efficient legal and administrative mechanisms and methods for facilitating the return of proceeds of offences established in accordance with this Convention;

(i) Methods used in protecting victims and witnesses who cooperate with judicial authorities; and

(j) Training in national and international regulations and in languages. . . .

ARTICLE 61
COLLECTION, EXCHANGE AND ANALYSIS OF INFORMATION ON CORRUPTION

1. Each State Party shall consider analysing, in consultation with experts, trends in corruption in its territory, as well as the circumstances in which corruption offences are committed.

2. States Parties shall consider developing and sharing with each other and through international and regional organizations statistics, analytical expertise concerning corruption and information with a view to developing, insofar as possible, common definitions, standards and methodologies, as well as information on best practices to prevent and combat corruption.

3. Each State Party shall consider monitoring its policies and actual measures to combat corruption and making assessments of their effectiveness and efficiency.

ARTICLE 62
OTHER MEASURES: IMPLEMENTATION OF THE CONVENTION THROUGH ECONOMIC DEVELOPMENT AND TECHNICAL ASSISTANCE

1. States Parties shall take measures conducive to the optimal implementation of this Convention to the extent possible, through international cooperation, taking into account the negative effects of corruption on society in general, in particular on sustainable development.

2. States Parties shall make concrete efforts to the extent possible and in coordination with each other, as well as with international and regional organizations:

(a) To enhance their cooperation at various levels with developing countries, with a view to strengthening the capacity of the latter to prevent and combat corruption;

(b) To enhance financial and material assistance to support the efforts of developing countries to prevent and fight corruption effectively and to help them implement this Convention successfully;

(c) To provide technical assistance to developing countries and countries with economies in transition to assist them in meeting their needs for the implementation of this Convention. To that end, States Parties shall endeavour to make adequate and regular voluntary contributions to an account specifically designated for that purpose in a United Nations funding mechanism. States Parties may also give special consideration, in accordance with their domestic law and the provisions of this Convention, to contributing to that account a percentage of the money or of the corresponding value of proceeds of crime or property confiscated in accordance with the provisions of this Convention;

(d) To encourage and persuade other States and financial institutions as appropriate to join them in efforts in accordance with this article, in particular by providing more training programmes and modern equipment to developing countries in order to assist them in achieving the objectives of this Convention. . . .

Chapter VII

Mechanisms for Implementation

ARTICLE 63
CONFERENCE OF THE STATES PARTIES
TO THE CONVENTION

1. A Conference of the States Parties to the Convention is hereby established to improve the capacity of and cooperation between States Parties to achieve the objectives set forth in this Convention and to promote and review its implementation. . . .

ARTICLE 68
ENTRY INTO FORCE

1. This Convention shall enter into force on the ninetieth day after the date of deposit of the thirtieth instrument of ratification, acceptance, approval or accession. . . .

Consequences

That 123 United Nations member states have signed the convention, as of mid-2005, testifies to the international enthusiasm for it in principle. (The United States has signed but not yet ratified it.) The document is complex, however, and doubtless will require close study by most signatories before ratification. As of summer 2005, the convention had been ratified by 28 signatories and therefore requires two more before coming into force. It is anticipated that the convention will significantly reduce corruption and thereby particularly benefit poorer and developing nations.

Source

United Nations Office on Drugs and Crime, "United Nations Convention Against Corruption." Available online. URL: http://www.unodc.org/pdf/crime/convention_corruption/signing/Convention-e.pdf. Accessed January 5, 2005.

PROTOCOL ON EXPLOSIVE REMNANTS OF WAR TO THE CONVENTION ON PROHIBITIONS OR RESTRICTIONS ON THE USE OF CERTAIN CONVENTIONAL WEAPONS WHICH MAY BE DEEMED TO BE EXCESSIVELY INJURIOUS OR TO HAVE INDISCRIMINATE EFFECTS

TREATY AT A GLANCE

Completed
November 28, 2003 (not yet entered into force)

Signatories
As of summer 2005, nine states have signed and become parties to the protocol. The ratification of 20 states is required for the protocol to come into force

Overview
This protocol was adopted and opened for signature as Protocol V to Convention on Prohibitions or Restrictions on the Use of Certain Conventional Weapons Which May Be Deemed to Be Excessively Injurious or to Have Indiscriminate Effects and calls for "post-conflict remedial measures . . . to minimise the risks and effects of explosive remnants of war" and a willingness "to address generic preventive measures . . . for improving the reliability of munitions, and therefore minimising the occurrence of explosive remnants of war." In layman's terms, the protocol addresses the problem of ordnance, which, having failed to detonate when used in combat, may explode at some later time, even after the conclusion of a conflict or war.

Historical Background

For a full discussion of the historical background of this protocol, see CONVENTION ON PROHIBITIONS OR RESTRICTIONS ON THE USE OF CERTAIN CONVENTIONAL WEAPONS WHICH MAY BE DEEMED TO BE EXCESSIVELY INJURIOUS OR TO HAVE INDISCRIMINATE EFFECTS.

This protocol is not the first agreement addressing the problems caused by unexploded ordnance. Unexploded remnants of cluster submunitions in Vietnam and elsewhere in Indochina were the subject of a proposal by Sweden to the Conference of Governmental Experts in Lucerne in 1974. Subsequent to this, Sweden and 13 other states called for the prohibition of antipersonnel cluster warheads. Other states, however, resisted, claiming that antipersonnel cluster weapons were neither indiscriminate nor cruel. In 1983, the United Nations General Assembly proposed cooperation between states in the collection, classification, and dissemination of information on remnants of war and also called for international cooperation in the clearing of such remnants. The General Assembly also called for designing high-explosive munitions with built-in mechanisms that render the munitions harmless after a time. Finally, there was also a call to address the issues of responsibility, including an obligation for compensation to injured parties.

Because the issue of responsibility, in particular, was expected to prove a stumbling block to ultimate ratification of the protocol, the protocol is silent on this topic. The framers of the protocol believed that it was more important to address the issues of prevention and cleanup as expeditiously as possible because the scale of the humanitarian problems of explosive remnants of war is likely to increase in the future as cluster bombs and land-based delivery systems for submunitions become more readily available and proliferate beyond the few countries that currently use them. The United States, as of mid-2005, had not signed the protocol.

See also CONVENTION ON THE PROHIBITION OF THE USE, STOCKPILING, PRODUCTION, AND TRANSFER OF ANTI-PERSONNEL MINES AND ON THEIR DESTRUCTION (LAND MINE BAN TREATY).

Terms

The purpose of the protocol is to reduce the hazards posed primarily by unexploded munitions that endanger civilian populations in former war zones. Two major steps are called for by the protocol: a program of "post-conflict remedial measures" to detect and to recover, destroy, dispose of, or otherwise render harmless the explosive remnants of war, and a commitment among states parties to research and adopt munition types that are less prone to initial failure and that therefore do not create a postconflict explosive hazard. Significantly, the issue of liability of a state for death or injury caused by unexploded ordnance is not addressed in the protocol.

The most important categories of munitions the protocol addresses include antivehicle mines (usually buried or otherwise concealed, and therefore especially dangerous), submunitions (bomblets delivered by a cluster bomb or artillery shell and dispersed in large numbers—as much as 600–700 per bomb), and unexploded ordnance ("dud" bombs and artillery shells). Note that the protocol applies to antivehicle mines; antipersonnel mines are addressed by the Land Mine Ban Treaty.

Protocol on Explosive Remnants of War

The High Contracting Parties,

Recognising the serious post-conflict humanitarian problems caused by explosive remnants of war,

Conscious of the need to conclude a Protocol on post-conflict remedial measures of a generic nature in order to minimise the risks and effects of explosive remnants of war,

And willing to address generic preventive measures, through voluntary best practices specified in a Technical Annex for improving the reliability of munitions, and therefore minimising the occurrence of explosive remnants of war,

Have agreed as follows:

ARTICLE 1
GENERAL PROVISION AND SCOPE OF APPLICATION

1. In conformity with the Charter of the United Nations and of the rules of the international law of armed conflict applicable to them, High Contracting Parties agree to comply with the obligations specified in this Protocol, both individually and in co-operation with other High Contracting Parties, to minimise the risks and effects of explosive remnants of war in post-conflict situations.

2. This Protocol shall apply to explosive remnants of war on the land territory including internal waters of High Contracting Parties.

3. This Protocol shall apply to situations resulting from conflicts referred to in Article 1, paragraphs 1 to 6, of the Convention, as amended on 21 December 2001.

4. Articles 3, 4, 5 and 8 of this Protocol apply to explosive remnants of war other than existing explosive remnants of war as defined in Article 2, paragraph 5 of this Protocol.

ARTICLE 2
DEFINITIONS

For the purpose of this Protocol,

1. *Explosive ordnance* means conventional munitions containing explosives, with the exception of mines, booby traps and other devices as defined in Protocol II of this Convention as amended on 3 May 1996.

2. *Unexploded ordnance* means explosive ordnance that has been primed, fused, armed, or otherwise prepared for use and used in an armed conflict. It may have been fired, dropped, launched or projected and should have exploded but failed to do so.

3. *Abandoned explosive ordnance* means explosive ordnance that has not been used during an armed conflict, that has been left behind or dumped by a party to an armed conflict, and which is no longer under control of the party that left it behind or dumped it. Abandoned explosive ordnance may or may not have been primed, fused, armed or otherwise prepared for use.

4. *Explosive remnants of war* means unexploded ordnance and abandoned explosive ordnance.

5. *Existing explosive remnants of war* means unexploded ordnance and abandoned explosive ordnance that existed prior to the entry into force of this Protocol for the High Contracting Party on whose territory it exists.

ARTICLE 3
CLEARANCE, REMOVAL OR DESTRUCTION
OF EXPLOSIVE REMNANTS OF WAR

1. Each High Contracting Party and party to an armed conflict shall bear the responsibilities set out in this Article with respect to all explosive remnants of war in territory under its control. In cases where a user of explosive ordnance which has become explosive remnants of war, does not exercise control of the territory, the user shall, after the cessation of active hostilities, provide where feasible, inter alia technical, financial, material or human resources assistance, bilaterally or through a mutually agreed third party, including inter alia through the United Nations system or other relevant organisations, to facilitate the marking and clearance, removal or destruction of such explosive remnants of war.

2. After the cessation of active hostilities and as soon as feasible, each High Contracting Party and party to an armed conflict shall mark and clear, remove or destroy explosive remnants of war in affected territories under its control. Areas affected by explosive remnants of war which are assessed pursuant to paragraph 3 of this Article as posing a serious human-

itarian risk shall be accorded priority status for clearance, removal or destruction.

3. After the cessation of active hostilities and as soon as feasible, each High Contracting Party and party to an armed conflict shall take the following measures in affected territories under its control, to reduce the risks posed by explosive remnants of war:

(a) survey and assess the threat posed by explosive remnants of war;

(b) assess and prioritise needs and practicability in terms of marking and clearance, removal or destruction;

(c) mark and clear, remove or destroy explosive remnants of war;

(d) take steps to mobilise resources to carry out these activities.

4. In conducting the above activities High Contracting Parties and parties to an armed conflict shall take into account international standards, including the International Mine Action Standards.

5. High Contracting Parties shall co-operate, where appropriate, both among themselves and with other states, relevant regional and international organisations and non-governmental organisations on the provision of inter alia technical, financial, material and human resources assistance including, in appropriate circumstances, the undertaking of joint operations necessary to fulfil the provisions of this Article.

ARTICLE 4
RECORDING, RETAINING AND TRANSMISSION OF INFORMATION

1. High Contracting Parties and parties to an armed conflict shall to the maximum extent possible and as far as practicable record and retain information on the use of explosive ordnance or abandonment of explosive ordnance, to facilitate the rapid marking and clearance, removal or destruction of explosive remnants of war, risk education and the provision of relevant information to the party in control of the territory and to civilian populations in that territory.

2. High Contracting Parties and parties to an armed conflict which have used or abandoned explosive ordnance which may have become explosive remnants of war shall, without delay after the cessation of active hostilities and as far as practicable, subject to these parties' legitimate security interests, make available such information to the party or parties in control of the affected area, bilaterally or through a mutually agreed third party including inter alia the United Nations or, upon request, to other relevant organisations which the party providing the information is satisfied are or will be undertaking risk education and the marking and clearance, removal or destruction of explosive remnants of war in the affected area.

3. In recording, retaining and transmitting such information, the High Contracting Parties should have regard to Part 1 of the Technical Annex.

ARTICLE 5
OTHER PRECAUTIONS FOR THE PROTECTION OF THE CIVILIAN POPULATION, INDIVIDUAL CIVILIANS AND CIVILIAN OBJECTS FROM THE RISKS AND EFFECTS OF EXPLOSIVE REMNANTS OF WAR

1. High Contracting Parties and parties to an armed conflict shall take all feasible precautions in the territory under their control affected by explosive remnants of war to protect the civilian population, individual civilians and civilian objects from the risks and effects of explosive remnants of war. Feasible precautions are those precautions which are practicable or practicably possible, taking into account all circumstances ruling at the time, including humanitarian and military considerations. These precautions may include warnings, risk education to the civilian population, marking, fencing and monitoring of territory affected by explosive remnants of war, as set out in Part 2 of the Technical Annex.

ARTICLE 6
PROVISIONS FOR THE PROTECTION OF HUMANITARIAN MISSIONS AND ORGANISATIONS FROM THE EFFECTS OF EXPLOSIVE REMNANTS OF WAR

1. Each High Contracting Party and party to an armed conflict shall:

(a) Protect, as far as feasible, from the effects of explosive remnants of war, humanitarian missions and organisations that are or will be operating in the area under the control of the High Contracting Party or party to an armed conflict and with that party's consent.

(b) Upon request by such a humanitarian mission or organisation, provide, as far as feasible, information on the location of all explosive remnants of war that it is aware of in territory where the requesting humanitarian mission or organisation will operate or is operating.

2. The provisions of this Article are without prejudice to existing International Humanitarian Law or other international instruments as applicable or decisions by the Security Council of the United Nations which provide for a higher level of protection.

ARTICLE 7
ASSISTANCE WITH RESPECT TO EXISTING EXPLOSIVE REMNANTS OF WAR

4. Each High Contracting Party has the right to seek and receive assistance, where appropriate, from other High Contracting Parties, from states non-party and relevant international organisations and institutions in dealing with the problems posed by existing explosive remnants of war.

5. Each High Contracting Party in a position to do so shall provide assistance in dealing with the problems posed by existing explosive remnants of war, as necessary and feasible. In so doing, High Contracting Parties shall also take into account the humanitarian objectives of this Protocol, as well as international standards including the International Mine Action Standards.

ARTICLE 8
CO-OPERATION AND ASSISTANCE

1. Each High Contracting Party in a position to do so shall provide assistance for the marking and clearance, removal or destruction of explosive remnants of war, and for risk education to civilian populations and related activities inter alia through the United Nations system, other relevant international, regional or national organisations or institutions, the International Committee of the Red Cross, national Red Cross and Red Crescent societies and their International Federation, non-governmental organisations, or on a bilateral basis.

2. Each High Contracting Party in a position to do so shall provide assistance for the care and rehabilitation and social and economic reintegration of victims of explosive remnants of war. Such assistance may be provided inter alia through the United Nations system, relevant international, regional or national organisations or institutions, the International Committee of the Red Cross, national Red Cross and Red Crescent societies and their International Federation, non-governmental organisations, or on a bilateral basis.

3. Each High Contracting Party in a position to do so shall contribute to trust funds within the United Nations system, as well as other relevant trust funds, to facilitate the provision of assistance under this Protocol.

4. Each High Contracting Party shall have the right to participate in the fullest possible exchange of equipment, material and scientific and technological information other than weapons related technology, necessary for the implementation of this Protocol. High Contracting Parties undertake to facilitate such exchanges in accordance with national legislation and shall not impose undue restrictions on the provision of clearance equipment and related technological information for humanitarian purposes.

5. Each High Contracting Party undertakes to provide information to the relevant databases on mine action established within the United Nations system, especially information concerning various means and technologies of clearance of explosive remnants of war, lists of experts, expert agencies or national points of contact on clearance of explosive remnants of war and, on a voluntary basis, technical information on relevant types of explosive ordnance.

6. High Contracting Parties may submit requests for assistance substantiated by relevant information to the United Nations, to other appropriate bodies or to other states. These requests may be submitted to the Secretary-General of the United Nations, who shall transmit them to all High Contracting Parties and to relevant international organisations and non-governmental organisations.

7. In the case of requests to the United Nations, the Secretary-General of the United Nations, within the resources available to the Secretary-General of the United Nations, may take appropriate steps to assess the situation and in co-operation with the requesting High Contracting Party and other High Contracting Parties with responsibility as set out in Article 3 above, recommend the appropriate provision of assistance. The Secretary-General may also report to High Contracting Parties on any such assessment as well as on the type and scope of assistance required, including possible contributions from the trust funds established within the United Nations system.

ARTICLE 9
GENERIC PREVENTIVE MEASURES

1. Bearing in mind the different situations and capacities, each High Contracting Party is encouraged to take generic preventive measures aimed at minimising the occurrence of explosive remnants of war, including, but not limited to, those referred to in part 3 of the Technical Annex.

2. Each High Contracting Party may, on a voluntary basis, exchange information related to efforts to promote and establish best practices in respect of paragraph 1 of this Article.

ARTICLE 10
CONSULTATIONS OF HIGH CONTRACTING PARTIES

1. The High Contracting Parties undertake to consult and co-operate with each other on all issues related to the operation of this Protocol. For this purpose, a Conference of High Contracting Parties shall be held as agreed to by a majority, but no less than eighteen High Contracting Parties.

2. The work of the conferences of High Contracting Parties shall include:

(a) review of the status and operation of this Protocol;

(b) consideration of matters pertaining to national implementation of this Protocol, including national reporting or updating on an annual basis.

(c) preparation for review conferences.

3. The costs of the Conference of High Contracting Parties shall be borne by the High Contracting Parties and States not parties participating in the Conference, in accordance with the United Nations scale of assessment adjusted appropriately.

ARTICLE 11
COMPLIANCE

1. Each High Contracting Party shall require that its armed forces and relevant agencies or departments issue appropriate instructions and operating procedures and that its personnel receive training consistent with the relevant provisions of this Protocol.

2. The High Contracting Parties undertake to consult each other and to co-operate with each other bilaterally, through the Secretary-General of the United Nations or through other appropriate international procedures, to resolve any problems that may arise with regard to the interpretation and application of the provisions of this Protocol.

Technical Annex

This Technical Annex contains suggested best practice for achieving the objectives contained in Articles 4, 5 and 9 of this Protocol. This Technical Annex will be implemented by High Contracting Parties on a voluntary basis.

1. Recording, storage and release of information for Unexploded Ordnance (UXO) and Abandoned Explosive Ordnance (AXO)

(a) Recording of information: Regarding explosive ordnance which may have become UXO a State should endeavour to record the following information as accurately as possible:

(i) the location of areas targeted using explosive ordnance;

(ii) the approximate number of explosive ordnance used in the areas under (i);

(iii) the type and nature of explosive ordnance used in areas under (i);

(iv) the general location of known and probable UXO;

Where a State has been obliged to abandon explosive ordnance in the course of operations, it should endeavour to leave AXO in a safe and secure manner and record information on this ordnance as follows:

(v) the location of AXO;

(vi) the approximate amount of AXO at each specific site;

(vii) the types of AXO at each specific site.

(b) Storage of information: Where a State has recorded information in accordance with paragraph (a), it should be stored in such a manner as to allow for its retrieval and subsequent release in accordance with paragraph (c).

(c) Release of information: Information recorded and stored by a State in accordance with paragraphs (a) and (b) should, taking into account the security interests and other obligations of the State providing the information, be released in accordance with the following provisions:

(i) Content:

On UXO the released information should contain details on:

(1) the general location of known and probable UXO;

(2) the types and approximate number of explosive ordnance used in the targeted areas;

(3) the method of identifying the explosive ordnance including colour, size and shape and other relevant markings;

(4) the method for safe disposal of the explosive ordnance.

On AXO the released information should contain details on:

(5) the location of the AXO;

(6) the approximate number of AXO at each specific site;

(7) the types of AXO at each specific site;

(8) the method of identifying the AXO, including colour, size and shape;

(9) information on type and methods of packing for AXO;

(10) state of readiness;

(11) the location and nature of any booby traps known to be present in the area of AXO. . . .

2. Warnings, risk education, marking, fencing and monitoring

KEY TERMS

(a) Warnings are the punctual provision of cautionary information to the civilian population, intended to minimise risks caused by explosive remnants of war in affected territories.

(b) Risk education to the civilian population should consist of risk education programmes to facilitate information exchange between affected communities, government authorities and humanitarian organisations so that affected communities are informed about the threat from explosive remnants of war. Risk education programmes are usually a long term activity.

BEST PRACTICE ELEMENTS OF WARNINGS AND RISK EDUCATION

. . .

(e) Warnings should be given, as soon as possible, depending on the context and the information available. A risk education programme should replace a warnings programme as soon as possible. Warnings and risk education always should be provided to the affected communities at the earliest possible time. . . .

MARKING, FENCING, AND MONITORING OF AN EXPLOSIVE REMNANTS OF WAR AFFECTED AREA

(h) When possible, at any time during the course of a conflict and thereafter, where explosive remnants of war exist the parties to a conflict should, at the earliest possible time and to the maximum extent possible, ensure that areas containing explosive remnants of war are marked, fenced and monitored so as to ensure the effective exclusion of civilians . . .

3. Generic preventive measures

States producing or procuring explosive ordnance should to the extent possible and as appropriate endeavour to ensure that the following measures are implemented and respected during the life-cycle of explosive ordnance.

(a) Munitions manufacturing management

(i) Production processes should be designed to achieve the greatest reliability of munitions. . . .

(b) Munitions management

In order to ensure the best possible long-term reliability of explosive ordnance, States are encouraged to apply best practice norms and operating procedures with respect to its storage, transport, field storage, and handling in accordance with the following guidance. . . .

(c) Training

The proper training of all personnel involved in the handling, transporting and use of explosive ordnance is an important factor in seeking to ensure its reliable operation as intended. . . .

(d) Transfer

A State planning to transfer explosive ordnance to another State that did not previously possess that type of explosive ordnance should endeavour to ensure that the receiving State has the capability to store, maintain and use that explosive ordnance correctly.

(e) Future production

A State should examine ways and means of improving the reliability of explosive ordnance that it intends to produce or procure, with a view to achieving the highest possible reliability.

Consequences

As of summer 2005, the protocol awaits signature and ratification by 11 states before it enters into force.

Source

United Nations, "Protocol on Explosive Remnants of War (Protocol V to the 1980 Convention), 28 November 2003," International Committee of the Red Cross: International Humanitarian Law. Available online. URL: http://www.icrc.org/ihl.nsf/0/c110d2926d08a892c1256e280056b275?OpenDocument. Accessed January 5, 2005.

Weapons Treaties

STRATEGIC OFFENSIVE REDUCTIONS TREATY (TREATY OF MOSCOW)

TREATY AT A GLANCE

Completed
May 24, 2002; ratified March 10, 2003

Signatories
United States and the Russian Federation

Overview
The Strategic Offensive Reductions Treaty (SORT), familiarly known as the Treaty of Moscow, is an agreement between the United States and the Russian Federation to reduce their strategic nuclear warheads to a level of between 1,700 and 2,200 units by December 31, 2012. This level is almost two-thirds below levels at the time of signature.

Historical Background

The introduction of nuclear weapons at the end of World War II was followed by a rapid proliferation of nuclear and thermonuclear weapons in the postwar period. Most of the weapons were stockpiled in the arsenals of the two great cold war antagonists, the United States and the Soviet Union. Despite the great distrust that existed between the two nations, they concluded a series of treaties intended to control, limit, or reduce the proliferation of nuclear and thermonuclear weapons. These included (among others) the NUCLEAR TEST BAN TREATY of 1963, the TREATY ON THE NON-PROLIFERATION OF NUCLEAR WEAPONS of 1968 (a multilateral treaty, eventually signed by more than 130 nations), the Strategic Arms Limitation Treaty (SALT I) of 1972, an AGREEMENT ON THE PREVENTION OF NUCLEAR WAR of 1973, the SALT II treaty of 1979, the INF (INTERMEDIATE-RANGE NUCLEAR FORCE) TREATY of 1987, the Strategic Arms Reduction Treaty (START I) of 1991, the Strategic Arms Reduction Treaty (START II) of 1993, and the Comprehensive Nuclear Test Ban Treaty of 1996. The Treaty of Moscow does not supercede the previous landmark agreements. Indeed, the comprehensive verification regime of START I—an agreement among Belarus, Kazakhstan, Russia, Ukraine, and the United States—

serves as the basis of the transparency and predictability that are vital principles of implementation for the new treaty.

The collapse of the Soviet Union in 1991 brought an end to the cold war, reducing both the level of mutual distrust as well as the perceived need for large stockpiles of strategic nuclear and thermonuclear weapons. Amid these new circumstances, President George W. Bush of the United States and President Vladimir Putin of the Russian Federation (a successor state to the Soviet Union) concluded the Strategic Offensive Reductions Treaty. The treaty codified deep strategic arms reductions announced by President Bush following a November 2001 summit with President Putin.

Terms

The treaty requires each signatory to reduce and limit its strategic nuclear warheads to between 1,700 and 2,200 warheads by December 31, 2012. Each side remains free to determine for itself the composition and structure of its strategic forces consistent within this limit. Twice annually, on an ongoing basis, the Bilateral Implementation Commission is to meet to discuss issues related to the treaty.

Strategic Offensive Reductions Treaty

The United States of America and the Russian Federation, hereinafter referred to as the Parties,

Embarking upon the path of new relations for a new century and committed to the goal of strengthening their relationship through cooperation and friendship,

Believing that new global challenges and threats require the building of a qualitatively new foundation for strategic relations between the Parties,

Desiring to establish a genuine partnership based on the principles of mutual security, cooperation, trust, openness, and predictability,

Committed to implementing significant reductions in strategic offensive arms,

Proceeding from the Joint Statements by the President of the United States of America and the President of the Russian Federation on Strategic Issues of July 22, 2001 in Genoa and on a New Relationship between the United States and Russia of November 13, 2001 in Washington,

Mindful of their obligations under the Treaty Between the United States of America and the Union of Soviet Socialist Republics on the Reduction and Limitation of Strategic Offensive Arms of July 31, 1991, hereinafter referred to as the START Treaty,

Mindful of their obligations under Article VI of the Treaty on the Non-Proliferation of Nuclear Weapons of July 1, 1968, and

Convinced that this Treaty will help to establish more favorable conditions for actively promoting security and cooperation, and enhancing international stability,

Have agreed as follows:

ARTICLE I

Each Party shall reduce and limit strategic nuclear warheads, as stated by the President of the United States of America on November 13, 2001 and as stated by the President of the Russian Federation on November 13, 2001 and December 13, 2001 respectively, so that by December 31, 2012 the aggregate number of such warheads does not exceed 1700-2200 for each Party. Each Party shall determine for itself the composition and structure of its strategic offensive arms, based on the established aggregate limit for the number of such warheads.

ARTICLE II

The Parties agree that the START Treaty remains in force in accordance with its terms.

ARTICLE III

For purposes of implementing this Treaty, the Parties shall hold meetings at least twice a year of a Bilateral Implementation Commission.

ARTICLE IV

1. This Treaty shall be subject to ratification in accordance with the constitutional procedures of each Party. This Treaty shall enter into force on the date of the exchange of instruments of ratification.

2. This Treaty shall remain in force until December 31, 2012 and may be extended by agreement of the Parties or superseded earlier by a subsequent agreement.

3. Each Party, in exercising its national sovereignty, may withdraw from this Treaty upon three months written notice to the other Party.

ARTICLE V

This Treaty shall be registered pursuant to Article 102 of the Charter of the United Nations.

Done at Moscow on May 24, 2002, in two copies, each in the English and Russian languages, both texts being equally authentic.

Consequences

Pursuant to the treaty, the United States resolved to retire all 50 of its 10-warhead Peacekeeper ICBMs (intercontinental ballistic missiles) and convert four Trident submarines from strategic service as nuclear weapons platforms to conventional service for the underwater deployment of U.S. Navy SEAL teams. The Trident missiles are to be removed from these ships. As of summer 2005, the Pentagon and other officials were still deciding on what additional steps to take in order to achieve the level of reduction specified by the treaty. It is expected that these steps will be announced and/or implemented throughout the reduction period specified by the treaty, that is, through December 31, 2012. As for the decommissioned warheads, some will be retained as spares, and some will be retired to long-term storage, while others will be destroyed outright. Although the number of warheads will be significantly reduced, the United States announced plans to continue to deploy full strategic (that is, nuclear-armed) forces in all three modes, on land, at sea, and in the air.

Source

White House, "Text of the Strategic Offensive Reductions Treaty." Available online. URL: http://www.whitehouse.gov/news/releases/2002/05/20020524-3.html. Accessed January 5, 2005.

CHRONOLOGICAL LIST
OF TREATIES

ca. 3100 B.C.E.
Inscription Fixing Boundaries between Lagash and Umma

40 B.C.E.
Treaty of Brundisium

811 C.E.
Treaty between Charlemagne and Michael I Rangabe

1192
Treaty between Richard the Lionhearted and Saladin

1215
Magna Carta

1360
Treaty of Brétigny

1620
Mayflower Compact

1648
Peace of Westphalia

1659
Treaty of the Pyrenees

1671
Taunton Agreement

1678–1679
Peace of Nijmegen

1697
Treaty of Ryswick

1713
Treaty of Utrecht

1714
Treaty of Rastadt (and Baden)

1748
Treaty of Aix-la-Chapelle

1763
Treaty of Paris (February 10)
Treaty of Hubertsburg (February 15)
Proclamation of 1763 (October 7)

1772–1776
First Partition of Poland

1776
Declaration of Independence

1778
Delaware Indian Treaty

1783
Treaty of Paris

1784
Second Treaty of Fort Stanwix (Treaty with the Six Nations)

1787
Northwest Ordinance

1789
Treaty of Fort Harmar (Treaty with the Six Nations)

1793
Second Partition of Poland

1794
Treaty of Canandaigua (Treaty with the Six Nations) (November 11)

1896

Treaty of Addis Ababa

1897

Treaty of Annexation of Hawaii

1898

Treaty of Paris

1899

Hague Convention of 1899

1901

Boxer Protocol

1902

Treaty of Vereeniging

1903

United States–Cuba Military Lease Agreement (February 23)

United States– Cuba Military Lease Agreement (May 22)

1904

Panama Canal Treaty (Hay–Bunau-Varilla Treaty) (February 26)

Entente Cordiale (April 8)

1905

Treaty of Portsmouth

1906

Algeciras Convention

1907

Hague Convention

1912

Treaty of Lausanne (Treaty of Ouchy)

1913

Treaty of London (May 30)

Treaty of Bucharest (August 10)

Treaty of Constantinople (September 29)

1914

Secret Treaty between Germany and the Ottoman Empire

1915

Treaty of London

1916

Sykes-Picot Agreement

1917

Balfour Declaration

1918

Treaty of Brest-Litovsk

1919

Covenant of the League of Nations (June 28)

Treaty between the Allied and Associated Powers and Poland on the Protection of Minorities (June 28)

Treaty of Guarantee (June 28)

Treaty of Versailles (June 28)

Treaty of St. Germain (September 10)

Treaty of Neuilly (November 27)

1920

Treaty of Trianon (June 4)

Treaty of Sèvres (August 10)

1920–1930

Little Entente Treaties

1921

Political Agreement between France and Poland (February 19)

Trade Agreement between Great Britain and Soviet Russia (March 16)

Treaty of Friendship between Russia and Turkey (March 16)

Treaty of Riga (March 18)

United States and Austria Treaty of Peace (August 24)

United States and Germany Treaty of Peace (August 25)

United States and Hungary Treaty of Peace (August 29)

Irish Peace Treaty (December 6)

Four Power Treaty (December 13)

1922

Nine Power Treaty Concerning China (February 6)

Washington Naval Treaty (February 6)

Treaty of Rapallo (April 16)

1923

Treaty of Lausanne

1924

Franco-Czech Alliance

1925

Locarno Treaties (October 16)

Treaty of Mutual Guarantee between France and Poland (October 16)

1927

Treaty of Understanding between France and Yugoslavia

1928

Kellogg-Briand Pact

1932

Soviet-Finnish Non-Aggression Treaty (January 21)

Franco-Soviet Non-Aggression Pact (November 19)

1933

Four Power Pact

1934

German-Polish Nonaggression Declaration

1935

Anglo-German Naval Agreement

1936

"Gentlemen's Agreement" between Austria and
    Germany (July 11)
Anti-Comintern Pact (November 25)

1937

Anti-Comintern Pact

1938

Munich Pact

1939

"Pact of Steel" (Alliance between Germany and
    Italy; May 22)
Trade Agreements between the Soviet Union
    and Germany (August 19, 1939, and
    February 11, 1940)
Hitler-Stalin Pact (German-Soviet Non-Aggression
    Treaty) (August 23)
Agreement of Mutual Assistance between United
    Kingdom and Poland (August 25)
Agreement of Mutual Assistance between Poland
    and France (September 4)
German-Soviet Boundary and Friendship Treaty
    (September 28)

1940

Act of Havana (July 30)
Axis Pact (September 27)

1941

Pact of Neutrality between the Soviet Union and
    Japan (April 13)
Agreement between Poland and the Soviet Union
    (July 30)
Atlantic Charter (August 14)
Agreement among Germany, Italy, and Japan
    on the Joint Prosecution of the War
    (December 11)

1942

United Nations Declaration (January 1)
Lend-Lease Agreement (February 23)
Treaty of Alliance between Great Britain and the
    Soviet Union (May 26)

1943

Casablanca Declaration (February 12)
Joint Four-Nation Declaration of the Moscow
    Conference (October 30)
Cairo Declaration (December 1)
Three-Power Declarations of the Tehran Conference
    (December 1)

Treaty of Friendship and Mutual Assistance and
    Post-war Cooperation between the Soviet Union
    and Czechoslovakia (December 12)

1944

Treaty of Friendship and Mutual Assistance between
    the Soviet Union and the French Republic

1945

Report of the Yalta (Crimea) Conference
    (February 11)
Yalta Agreement (February 11)
Act of Chapultepec (March 3)
Pact of the Arab League (March 22)
Soviet Denunciation of Pact with Japan (April 5)
German Act of Military Surrender (May 8)
Allied Statements on the Occupation of Germany
    (June 5, November 30)
United Nations Charter (June 25)
Potsdam Protocol (August 2)
Treaty of Friendship and Alliance between China and
    the Soviet Union (August 14)
Japanese Surrender Documents (September 2,
    3, and 12)
Articles of Agreement of the International Bank for
    Reconstruction and Development
    (December 27)

1947

Peace Treaty between the Allies and Italy
    (February 10)
Pact of Rio (Inter-American Treaty of Reciprocal
    Assistance) (September 2)

1948

Anglo-Transjordan Alliance (March 15)
Treaty of Brussels (March 17)
Charter of the Organization of American States
    (April 30)
Geneva Convention on the Prevention and
    Punishment of the Crime of Genocide
    (December 9)

1949

North Atlantic Treaty (April 4)
Geneva Convention Relative to the Treatment of
    Prisoners of War (August 2)

1950

Sino-Soviet Treaty of Friendship, Alliance, and
    Mutual Assistance

1951

Treaty of Paris (April 18)
ANZUS Treaty (September 1)
Japan–United States Security Treaty
    (September 8)
Treaty of Peace with Japan (September 8)

1953

Korean War Armistice (July 27)

United States–South Korea Mutual Defense Treaty (October 10)

1954

Soviet Declaration on the Sovereignty of the German Democratic Republic (March 24)

Geneva Agreements of 1954 (July 15)

South-East Asia Collective Defense Treaty (SEATO) (September 8)

United States–Nationalist Chinese Mutual Defense Treaty (December 2)

1955

Baghdad Pact (February 24)

Warsaw Pact (May 14)

Austrian State Treaty (May 15)

1957

Treaty of Rome

1960

European Free Trade Association Convention (January 4)

Treaty of Mutual Cooperation and Security between the United States and Japan (January 19)

1961

Alliance for Progress

1963

Charter of the Organization of African Unity (May 25)

Hot Line Memorandum (June 20)

Nuclear Test Ban Treaty (August 5)

1968

Treaty on the Non-Proliferation of Nuclear Weapons

1973

Paris Peace Accords (January 27)

Agreement on the Prevention of Nuclear War (June 22)

Joint Communiqué by the United States and the Soviet Union (Détente) (June 25)

1977

Panama Canal Treaty (and Treaty of Neutrality)

1978

Camp David Accords

1981

Convention on Prohibitions or Restrictions on the Use of Certain Conventional Weapons Which May Be Deemed to Be Excessively Injurious or to Have Indiscriminate Effects

1984

Convention against Torture and Other Cruel, Inhuman or Degrading Treatment or Punishment

1987

Montreal Protocol on the Ozone Layer (September 16)

INF (Intermediate-Range Nuclear Force) Treaty (December 8)

1988

HAMAS Covenant

1989

Convention on the Rights of the Child

1990

Charter of Paris for a New Europe (Paris Charter)

1992

Maastricht Treaty (Consolidated Treaty on European Unity) (February 7)

Convention on Climate Change (May 9)

Convention on Biodiversity (June 14)

Rio Declaration (June 14)

North American Free Trade Agreement (NAFTA) (December 17)

1993

Israel–Palestine Liberation Organization Peace Agreements (September 9 and 13)

1994

Vienna Declaration on Human Rights

1995

Protocol on Blinding Laser Weapons to the Convention on Prohibitions or Restrictions on the Use of Certain Conventional Weapons Which May Be Deemed to Be Excessively Injurious or to Have Indiscriminate Effects (October 13)

Dayton Accords (November 21)

1997

Convention on the Prohibition of the Use, Stockpiling, Production, and Transfer of Anti-Personnel Mines and on Their Destruction (Land Mine Ban Treaty) (September 18)

Kyoto Protocol on Climate Change (December 11)

1998

Belfast Agreement (Good Friday Agreement) (April 10)

Rome Statute of the International Criminal Court (July 17)

Israel-Palestine Liberation Organization Agreements (October 23)

1999

International Convention for the Suppression of the Financing of Terrorism (December 9)

2000

Optional Protocol to the Convention on the Rights of the Child on the Involvement of Children in Armed Conflict (May 25)

Optional Protocol to the Convention on the Rights of the Child on the Sale of Children, Child Prostitution and Child Pornography (May 25)

Convention against Transnational Organized Crime (November 15)

Protocol against the Smuggling of Migrants by Land, Sea and Air (November 15)

Protocol to Prevent, Suppress and Punish Trafficking in Persons, Especially Women and Children (November 15)

2001

Protocol against the Illicit Manufacturing of and Trafficking in Firearms, Their Parts and Components and Ammunition

2002

Optional Protocol to the Convention against Torture and Other Cruel, Inhuman or Degrading Treatment or Punishment

2003

Strategic Offensive Reductions Treaty (Treaty of Moscow) (March 10)

Convention against Corruption (October 31)

Protocol on Explosive Remnants of War to the Convention on Prohibitions or Restrictions on the Use of Certain Conventional Weapons Which May Be Deemed to be Excessively Injurious or to Have Indiscriminate Effects (November 28)

FURTHER REFERENCE

GENERAL

Albrecht-Carrie, René. *A Diplomatic History of Europe since the Congress of Vienna.* Rev. ed. New York: Harper and Row, 1970.

Aust, Anthony. *Modern Treaty Law and Practice.* Cambridge and New York: Cambridge University Press, 2000.

Barrett, Scott. *Environment and Statecraft: The Strategy of Environmental Treaty-making.* Oxford and New York: Oxford University Press, 2003.

Bowman, M. J., and D. F. Harris. *Multi-Lateral Treaties: Index and Current Status.* London: Butterworths, 1984.

Carty, Anthony. *The Decay of International Law.* Manchester, England: Manchester University Press, 1986.

Congressional Research Service, Library of Congress. *Treaties and Other International Agreements: The Role of the United States Senate: A Study Prepared for the Committee on Foreign Relations, United States Senate.* Buffalo, N.Y.: W. S. Hein, 2004.

Crandall, Samuel B. *Treaties, Their Making and Enforcement.* 2d ed. Clark, N.J.: Lawbook Exchange, 2005.

Davidson, J. Scott, ed. *The Law of Treaties.* Aldershot, England and Burlington, Vt.: Ashgate/Dartmouth, 2004.

Dehio, Ludwig. *The Precarious Balance: Four Centuries of the European Power Struggle.* Charles Fullman, trans. New York: Alfred A. Knopf, 1962.

Feltham, R. G. *Diplomatic Handbook.* 7th ed. Harlow: Longman, 1998.

Grenville, J. A. S., *The Major International Treaties, 1914–1973.* New York: Stein and Day, 1975.

———, ed. *The Major International Treaties, 1914–1945.* London and New York: Methuen, 1987.

Grenville, John and Bernard Wasserstein, eds., *The Major International Treaties of the Twentieth Century.* New York: Routledge, 2000.

Hinsley, F. H. *Power and the Pursuit of Peace: Theory and Practice in the History of Relations between States.* London: Cambridge University Press, 1967.

Holborn, Hajo. *The Political Collapse of Europe.* Westport, Conn.: Greenwood Press, 1982.

Howard, Michael. *War in European History.* London: Oxford University Press, 1976.

Israel, Fred L., ed. *Major Peace Treaties of Modern History, 1648–2000.* Philadelphia: Chelsea House Publishers, 2002.

Krasner, Stephen. *International Regimes.* Ithaca, N.Y.: Cornell University Press, 1982.

Macmillan, Margaret. *Paris, 1919: Six Months That Changed the World.* New York: Random House, 2002.

Maslen, Stuart. *Commentaries on Arms Control Treaties.* Oxford and New York: Oxford University Press, 2004.

McNair, Lord. *The Law of Treaties.* Oxford: Oxford University Press, 1961.

Morgenthau, Hans J., and Kenneth W. Thompson. *Politics among Nations: The Struggle for Power and Peace.* 6th ed. New York: Alfred A. Knopf, 1985.

Osmanczyk, Edmund Jan. *The Encyclopedia of the United Nations and International Agreements.* Philadelphia: Taylor and Francis, 1985.

Political Handbook and Atlas of the World. New York: Council on Foreign Relations, 1927–.

Rengger, N. J., ed. *Treaties and Alliances of the World.* Detroit: Gale Research, 1990.

Spector, Bertram I., and I. William Zartman, eds. *Getting It Done: Postagreement Negotiation and International Regimes.* Washington, D.C.: United States Institute of Peace Press, 2003.

United Nations. *Treaties Series* (UNTS). New York: United Nations.

Watson, Adam. *Diplomacy: The Dialogue between States.* London: Methuen, 1982.

Watt, Stephen. *The Origins of Alliances.* Ithaca, N.Y.: Cornell University Press, 1987.

Wheeler-Bennett, J. W., et al. *Documents on International Affairs.* Oxford: Royal Institute of International Affairs, 1928–63.

World Treaty Index. 5 vols. Santa Barbara, Calif.: ABC-Clio, 1984.

1—THE ANCIENT WORLD

Errington, R. M. *The Dawn of Empire.* Ithaca, N.Y.: Cornell University Press, 1972.

Grant, Michael. *The World of Rome.* New York: Meridian, 1987.

Kramer, Samuel Nosch. *History Begins at Sumer.* Philadelphia: University of Pennsylvania Press, 1981.

Scarre, Chris, ed. *Smithsonian Timelines of the Ancient World.* Washington, D.C. and New York: Smithsonian Institution/D. Kindersley, 1993.

2—MEDIEVAL ROOTS

Barraclough, Geoffry. *The Medieval Papacy.* London: Thames and Hudson, 1968.

Ganshof, François Louis. *The Middle Ages: A History of International Relations.* New York: Harper and Row, 1971.

Holt, P. M. *The Age of the Crusades.* London: Longman, 1986.

Little, Lester K., and Barbara H. Rosenwein, eds. *Debating the Middle Ages: Issues and Readings.* Malden, Mass.: Blackwell Publishers, 1998.

Kidson, Peter. *The Medieval World.* London: Paul Hamlyn, 1967.

Mango, Cyril. *Byzantium.* London: Weidenfeld and Nicolson, 1980.

McKitterick, Rosamond, ed. *The New Cambridge Medieval History.* Cambridge and New York: Cambridge University Press, 1995–2000.

Wolbrink, Shelley, ed. *Great Lives from History: The Middle Ages, 477–1453.* Pasadena, Calif.: Salem Press, 2005.

3—THE BIRTH OF MODERN DIPLOMACY

Anderson, M. S. *The Rise of Modern Diplomacy, 1450–1919.* London and New York: Longman, 1993.

Constantinou, Costas M. *On the Way to Diplomacy.* Minneapolis: University of Minnesota Press, 1996.

Israel, Jonathan. *The Dutch Republic and the Hispanic World.* Oxford, England: Oxford University Press, 1985.

Langer, Herbert. *The Thirty Years' War.* Poole, Dorset, England: Blandford Press, 1980.

Lewis, W. H. *The Splendid Century.* London: Eyre and Spottiswoode, 1953.

Mattingly, Garrett. *Renaissance Diplomacy.* New York: Russell and Russell, 1970.

Mitford, Nancy. *The Sun King.* London: Hamish Hamilton, 1966.

Parker, Geoffrey. *The Dutch Revolt.* Harmondsworth, England: Penguin Books, 1979.

———. *The 30 Years' War.* London: Routledge and Kegan Paul, 1984.

Walton, Guy. *Louis XIV's Versailles.* London: Viking, 1986.

Wedgwood, C. V. *The King's War.* London: Collins, 1958.

4—AGE OF REASON

Alexander, John T. *Catherine the Great: Life and Legend.* Oxford: Oxford University Press, 1989.

Behrans, C. B. A. *The Ancien Régime.* London: Thames and Hudson, 1967.

Donnert, Erich. *Russia in the Age of Enlightenment.* Alison and Alistair Wightman, trans. Edition Leipzig, Germany: 1986.

Hampson, Norman. *The Enlightenment.* London: Pelican, 1969.

Hubatsch, Wallther. *Frederick the Great: Absolutism and Administration.* London: Thames and Hudson, 1975.

Magdariaga, Isabel de. *Russia in the Age of Catherine the Great.* London: Weidenfeld and Nicolson, 1981.

McKay, D., and H. M. Scott. *The Rise of the Great Powers: 1648–1815.* London: Longman, 1983.

Mitford, Nancy. *Frederick the Great.* London: Hamish Hamilton, 1970.

Sutton, Ian, ed. *The Eighteenth Century: Europe in the Age of Enlightenment.* London: Thames and Hudson, 1968.

Thackeray, Rank W., and John E. Findling, eds. *Events That Changed the World in the Seventeenth Century.* Westport, Conn.: Greenwood Press, 1999.

Van Houdt, Toon, ed. *On the Edge of Truth and Honesty: Principles and Strategies of Fraud and Deceit in the Early Modern Period.* Leiden; Boston: Brill, 2002.

PART 5—A NEW WORLD

Andrews, Kenneth. *Trade, Plunder, and Settlement: Maritime Enterprise and the Genesis of the British Empire, 1480–1630.* New York: Cambridge University Press, 1984.

Armitage, David, and Michael J. Braddick, eds. *The British Atlantic World 1500–1800.* London: Palgrave Macmillan, 2002.

Axelrod, Alan. *Chronicle of the Indian Wars: From Colonial Times to Wounded Knee.* New York: Prentice Hall, 1993.

Bobrick, Benson. *Angel in the Whirlwind: The Triumph of the American Revolution.* New York: Simon and Schuster, 1997.

Cleland, Hugh. *George Washington in the Ohio Valley.* Pittsburgh, Pa.: University of Pittsburgh Press, 1955.

Coupler, Charles J., ed. *Indian Treaties, 1778–1883*. New York: Interland, 1972.

Daniels, Christine, and Michael V. Kennedy, eds. *Negotiated Empires: Centers and Peripheries in the New World, 1500–1820*. New York: Routledge, 2002.

DeVoto, Bernard. *The Course of Empire*. Cambridge, Mass.: Riverside, 1952.

Dippie, Brian W. *The Vanishing American: White Attitudes and U.S. Indian Policy*. Middleton, Conn.: Wesleyan University Press, 1982.

Drinnon, Richard. *Facing West: The Metaphysics of Indian-Hating and Empire Building*. New York: Meridian, 1980.

Dull, Jonathan R. *A Diplomatic History of the American Revolution*. New Haven, Conn.: Yale University Press, 1985.

Eccles, W. J. *France in America*. New York: Harper and Row, 1972.

Egnal, Marc. *A Mighty Empire: Origins of the American Revolution*. Ithaca, N.Y.: Cornell University Press, 1988.

Ellis, Joseph J. *American Sphinx: The Character of Thomas Jefferson*. New York: Alfred A. Knopf, 1997.

Geiter, Mary K., and W. A. Speck. *Colonial America: From Jamestown to Yorktown*. London: Palgrave Macmillan, 2003.

Graymont, Barbara. *The Iroquois in the American Revolution*. Syracuse, N.Y.: University of Syracuse Press, 1972.

Jennings, Francis. *The Invasion of America: Indians, Colonialism, and the Cant of Conquest*. New York: W. W. Norton, 1976.

———. *The Ambiguous Iroquois Empire: The Covenant Chain Confederation of Indian Tribes with English Colonies from Its Beginnings to the Lancaster Treaty of 1744*. New York: W. W. Norton, 1984.

———. *Empire of Fortune: Crowns, Colonies & Tribes in the Seven Years War in America*. New York: W. W. Norton, 1988.

Katz, Stanley N., John Murrin, and Douglas Greenberg, eds. *Colonial America: Essays in Politics and Social Development*. New York: McGraw-Hill, 2000.

Keegan, John. *Fields of Battle: The Wars for North America*. New York: Alfred A. Knopf, 1996.

Lewis, Thomas A. *For King and Country: The Maturing of George Washington, 1748–1760*. New York: HarperCollins, 1993.

McDermott, John Francis, ed. *The French in the Mississippi Valley*. Urbana: University of Illinois Press, 1965.

———. *The Spanish in the Mississippi Valley, 1762–1804*. Urbana: University of Illinois Press, 1974.

Onuf, Peter S. *Statehood and Union: A History of the Northwest Ordinance*. Bloomington: University of Indiana Press, 1987.

Peckham, H. H. *The Colonial Wars, 1689–1762*. Chicago: University of Chicago Press, 1964.

Phillips, Charles, and Alan Axelrod. *Encyclopedia of the American West*. 4 vols. New York: Simon and Schuster Macmillan, 1996.

Prucha, Francis Paul. *The Great Father: The United States Government and the American Indian*. Lincoln: University of Nebraska Press, 1984.

———. ed. *Documents of United States Indian Policy*. Lincoln: University of Nebraska Press, 1990.

Reich, Jerome R. *Colonial America*. 5th ed. Paramus, N.J.: Prentice Hall, 2000.

Sauer, Carl Ortwin. *Sixteenth Century North America: The Land and People as Seen by the Europeans*. Berkeley: University of California Press, 1971.

Sheehan, Bernard W. *Savages and Civilization: Indians and Englishmen in Colonial Virginia*. Cambridge: Cambridge University Press, 1980.

Sword, Wiley. *President Washington's Indian War: The Struggle for the Old Northwest, 1790–1795*. Norman: University of Oklahoma Press, 1985.

Todish, Timothy J. *America's First World War: The French and Indian War, 1754–1763*. Grand Rapids, Mich.: Eagles View, 1987.

Trelease, Allen W. *Indian Affairs in Colonial New York*. Ithaca, N.Y.: Cornell University Press, 1960.

Washburn, Wilcomb E. *Red Man's Land/White Man's Law: A Study of the Past and Present Status of the American Indian*. New York: Scribner's, 1971.

Weber, David J. *The Spanish Frontier in North America*. New Haven, Conn.: Yale University Press, 1992.

Zinn, Howard. *A People's History of the United States*. New York: HarperCollins, 1980.

6—EPOCH OF NAPOLEON

Asprey, Robert B. *The Reign of Napoleon Bonaparte*. New York: Basic Books, 2001.

Barnett, Cornelli. *Bonaparte*. New York: Hill and Wang, 1978.

Bergeron, Louis. *France under Napoleon*. Princeton, N.J.: Princeton University Press, 1981.

Chandler, David G. *The Campaigns of Napoleon*. London: Weidenfeld and Nicolson, 1967.

Connelly, Owen. *Napoleon's Satellite Kingdoms*. London: Macmillan, 1965.

———. ed. *Historical Dictionary of Napoleonic France*. London: Aldwych, 1985.

Cooper, Duff. *Talleyrand*. New York: Fromm, 1986.

DeConde, Alexander. *The Quasi-War: The Politics and Diplomacy of the Undeclared War with France*. New York: Charles Scribner's Sons, 1966.

Delamater, Matt. *An Introduction to the Age of Napoleon*. Atglen, Pa.: Stackpole, 2001.

Doyle, William. *Origins of the French Revolution*. Oxford: Oxford University Press, 1980.

Durant, Will, and Ariel Durant. *The Story of Civilization.* Vol. 11: *The Age of Napoleon: A History of European Civilization from 1789 to 1815.* New York: Simon and Schuster, 1980.

Herold, J. Christopher. *The Age of Napoleon.* New York: Columbia University Press, 1963.

Honsbawm, E. J. *The Age of Revolution.* London: Weidenfeld and Nicolson, 1962.

Horne, Alistair. *Napoleon, Master of Europe.* London: Weidenfeld and Nicolson, 1979.

Lefebvre, G. *Napoleon.* New York: Columbia University Press, 1969.

Lynch, John. *The Spanish American Revolutions.* New York: W. W. Norton, 1986.

Mansel, Philip. *The Eagle in Splendor.* London: George Philip, 1987.

Markham, F. *Napoleon and the Awakening of Europe.* London: Macmillan, 1965.

Mowat, R. B. *The Diplomacy of Napoleon.* London: Russell and Russell, 1971.

Roberts, J. M. *The French Revolution.* Oxford: Oxford University Press, 1978.

Schama, Simon. *Citizens: A Chronicle of the French Revolution.* New York: Alfred A. Knopf, 1989.

Sutherland, D. M. G. *France 1789–1815: Revolution and Counterrevolution.* New York: Oxford University Press, 1986.

Thompson, J. M. *Napoleon Bonaparte.* Oxford: Blackwell, 1988.

Tulard, J. *Napoleon: The Myth of the Savior.* London: Widenfeld and Nicolson, 1984.

7—WILDERNESS DIPLOMACY AND CONTINENTAL EXPANSION

Aquila, Richard. *The Iroquois Restoration: Iroquois Diplomacy on the Colonial Frontier, 1701–1754.* Lincoln: University of Nebraska Press, 1997.

Axelrod, Alan. *Chronicle of the Indian Wars: From Colonial Times to Wounded Knee.* New York: Prentice Hall, 1993.

Baily, Lynn R. *The Long Walk.* Los Angeles: Westernlore Press, 1964.

Coupler, Charles J., ed. *Indian Treaties, 1778–1883.* New York: Interland, 1972.

Dangerfield, George. *The Era of Good Feelings.* New York: Harcourt, Brace, 1952.

DeConde, Alexander. *The Quasi-War: The Politics and Diplomacy of the Undeclared War with France.* New York: Charles Scribner's Sons, 1966.

———. *This Affair of Louisiana.* Baton Rouge: Lousiana State University Press, 1976.

De Puy, Henry Farr. *A Bibliography of the English Colonial Treaties with the American Indians, Including a Synopsis of Each Treaty.* Clark, N.J.: Lawbook Exchange, 2001.

DeVoto, Bernard. *The Course of Empire.* Cambridge, Mass.: Riverside, 1952.

Dippie, Brian W. *The Vanishing American: White Attitudes and U.S. Indian Policy.* Middleton, Conn.: Wesleyan University Press, 1982.

Drinnon, Richard. *Facing West: The Metaphysics of Indian-Hating and Empire Building.* New York: Meridian, 1980.

Eisenhower, John S. D. *So Far from God: The U.S. War with Mexico, 1846–1848.* New York: Doubleday, 1989.

Ehle, John. *Trail of Tears: The Rise and Fall of the Cherokee Nation.* New York: Anchor Books, 1988.

Ellis, Joseph J. *American Sphinx: The Character of Thomas Jefferson.* New York: Alfred A. Knopf, 1997.

Fay, Bernard. *The Revolutionary Spirit in France and America.* New York: Cooper Square, 1966.

Gibson, Arnell. *The Chickasaws.* Norman: University of Oklahoma Press, 1971.

Hickey, Donald R. *The War of 1812: A Forgotten Conflict.* Urbana: University of Illinois Press, 1989.

Keegan, John. *Fields of Battle: The Wars for North America.* New York: Alfred A. Knopf, 1996.

Meinig, D. W. *The Shaping of America.* Vol. 2: *Continental America, 1800–1867.* New Haven, Conn.: Yale University Press, 1993.

Miller, John Chester. *The Wolf by the Ears.* New York: Macmillan, 1977.

Phillips, Charles, and Alan Axelrod. *Encyclopedia of the American West.* 4 vols. New York: Simon and Schuster, Macmillan, 1996.

Prucha, Francis Paul. *The Great Father: The United States Government and the American Indian.* Lincoln: University of Nebraska Press, 1984.

———. ed. *Documents of United States Indian Policy.* Lincoln: University of Nebraska Press, 1990.

Remini, Robert V. *Andrew Jackson and the Course of American Empire.* 3 vols. New York: Harper and Row, 1977–84.

Rogin, Paul. *Fathers and Children: Andrew Jackson and the Subjugation of the American Indian.* New York: Random House, 1975.

Smith, Joseph Burkholder. *James Madison's Phony War: The Plot to Steal Florida.* New York: Arbor House, 1983.

Sprague, Marshall. *So Vast, So Beautiful a Land: Louisiana and the Purchase.* Boston: Little, Brown, 1974.

Stagg, J. C. *Mr. Madison's War.* Princeton, N.J.: Princeton University Press, 1983.

Washburn, Wilcomb E. *Red Man's Land/White Man's Law: A Study of the Past and Present Status of the American Indian.* New York: Scribner's, 1971.

Wilson, Lyon E. *Louisiana in French Diplomacy, 1759–1804.* Norman: University of Oklahoma Press, 1974.

Zinn, Howard. *A People's History of the United States.* New York: HarperCollins, 1980.

8—THE AMERICAN CIVIL WAR

Berlin, Ira, ed. *Freedom: A Documentary History of Emancipation, 1861–1867.* 2 vols. Cambridge, Mass.: Harvard University Press, 1982.

Bernath, Stuart L. *Squall Across the Atlantic: American Civil War Prize Cases and Diplomacy.* Berkeley: University of California Press, 1970.

Bowman, John S., ed. *The Civil War Almanac.* New York: Facts On File, 1983.

———. *Mr. Lincoln's Army.* Garden City, N.Y.: Doubleday, 1951.

———. *This Hallowed Ground: The Story of the Union Side of the Civil War.* Garden City, N.Y.: Doubleday, 1951.

Catton, Bruce. *Glory Road.* Garden City, N.Y.: Doubleday, 1952.

———. *A Stillness at Appomattox.* Garden City, N.Y.: Doubleday, 1953.

———. *Grant Moves South.* Boston: Little, Brown, 1960.

———. *Grant Takes Command.* Boston: Little, Brown, 1968.

Foote, Shelby. *The Civil War: A Narrative.* 3 vols. New York: Random House, 1958, 1963, 1974. 40th Anniversary rev. ed., 14 vols. Alexandria, Va.: Time-Life Books, 1999–2000.

Hehrenbacher, Don E. *The Dred Scott Case: Its Significance in Law and Politics.* New York: Oxford University Press, 1978.

Hubbard, Charles M. *The Burden of Confederate Diplomacy.* Knoxville: University of Tennessee, 2000.

Jones, Howard. *Abraham Lincoln and a New Birth of Freedom: The Union and Slavery in the Diplomacy of the Civil War.* Lincoln: University of Nebraska Press, 2002.

Mahin, Dean B. *One War at a Time: The International Dimensions of the American Civil War.* New York: Brassey's, 1999.

McPherson, James M. *Ordeal by Fire: The Civil War and Reconstruction.* New York: Oxford University Press, 1982.

———. *Battle Cry of Freedom: The Civil War Era.* New York: Oxford University Press, 1988.

Nevins, Allan. *The Ordeal of the Union.* 2 vols. New York: Scribner, 1947.

———. *The Emergence of Lincoln.* 2 vols. New York: Scribner, 1950.

———. *The War for the Union.* 4 vols. New York: Scribner, 1959–1971.

Phillips, Charles, and Alan Axelrod. *My Brother's Face: Portraits of the Civil War.* 1993. Reprint, New York: Barnes and Noble, 1998.

Time-Life Books, eds. *The Civil War.* 28 vols. Alexandria, Va.: Time-Life Books, 1987.

9—THE NEW IMPERIALISM

Anderson, M. S. *The Ascendancy of Europe, 1815–1914.* New York: Longman, 1985.

Bayly, Christopher, ed. *Atlas of the British Empire.* London: Hamlyn/Amazon, 1989.

Beale, Howard K. *Theodore Roosevelt and the Rise of America to World Power.* New York: Macmillan, 1962.

Beeching, Jack. *The Chinese Opium Wars.* London: Hutchison, 1975.

Chamberlain, M. E. *The Scramble for Africa.* London: Longman, 1974.

Crossman, Carl L. *The China Trade.* Princeton, N.J.: Pyne Press, 1972.

Daws, Gavan. *Shoals of Time: A History of the Hawaiian Islands.* Honolulu: University of Hawaii Press, 1968.

Duignan, Peter, and Lewis H. Gann. *Colonialism in Africa 1870–1960.* New York and Cambridge: Cambridge University Press, 1974.

Dulles, F. R. *America's Rise to World Power.* New York: Harper, 1955.

Ferguson, Niall. *Empire: The Rise and Demise of the British World Order and the Lessons for Global Power.* New York: Basic Books, 2004.

Foner, Philip. *The Spanish-Cuban-American War and the Birth of American Imperialism.* 2 vols. New York: Monthly Review Press, 1972.

Grenville, J. A. S. *Europe Reshaped: 1848–1878.* London: Fontana Harvester Press, 1976.

Hardt, Michael, and Antonio Negri. Empire. Cambridge, Ma.: Harvard University Press, 2001.

Healy, David. *U.S. Expansion: The Imperialist Urge in the 1890s.* Madison: University of Wisconsin Press, 1970.

Hibbert, Christopher. *The Great Mutiny, 1857.* London: Penguin, 1980.

Holt, Edgar. *The Opium Wars in China.* London: Putnam, 1964.

Howard, Michael. *The Franco-Prussian War.* London: Kart-Davis, 1962.

Hsü, Immanuel C. Y. *The Rise of Modern China.* Oxford: Oxford University Press, 1986.

Keegan, John. *The Price of Admiralty.* New York: Viking, 1988.

Kent, George O. *Bismarck and His Times.* Carbondale: Southern Illinois University Press, 1978.

Lafeber, Walter. *The New Empire: An Interpretation of American Expansion.* Ithaca, N.Y.: Cornell University Press, 1963.

Lewis, Davis L. *The Race for Fashoda.* New York: Weidenfeld and Nicolson, 1987.

Massie, Robert K. *Dreadnought: Britain, Germany, and the Coming of the Great War.* New York: Random House, 1991.

Moon, Sir Penderel. *The British Conquest and Domination of India.* London: Duckworth, 1989.

Morris, James. *Farewell the Trumpets*. London: Penguin, 1979.

———. *Heaven's Command*. London: Penguin, 1979.

———. *Pax Britannica*. London: Penguin, 1979.

Mosse, W. E. *Liberal Europe: The Age of Bourgeois Realism: 1848–1875*. London: Thames and Hudson, 1974.

O'Connor, Richard. *The Spirit Soldiers: A Historical Narrative of the Boxer Rebellion*. New York: G.P. Putnam's Sons, 1973.

Pakenham, Thomas. *The Boer War*. New York: Random House, 1979.

Pflance, Otto. *Bismarck and the Development of Germany*. Princeton, N.J.: Princeton University Press, 1963.

Ryn, Claes G. *America the Virtuous: The Crisis of Democracy and the Quest for Empire*. New Brunswick, N.J.: Transaction Publishers, 2003.

Said, Edward W. *Culture and Imperialism*. New York: Vintage, 1994.

Simon, W. M. *Germany in the Age of Bismarck*. London: Allen and Unwin, 1970.

Sowell, Thomas. *Conquests and Cultures: An International History*. New York: Basic Books, 1999.

Stone, Norman. *Europe Transformed: 1878–1919*. London: Fontana, 1983.

Wiebe, R. H. *The Search for Order*. London: Macmillan, 1967.

Williams, William Appleman. *The Roots of the Modern American Empire*. New York: Random House, 1969.

10—EPOCH OF THE GREAT WAR

Albertini, Luigi. *The Origins of the War of 1914*. 3 vols. Oxford, England: Oxford University Press, 1952–57.

Berghahn, V. R. *Germany and the Approach of the War of 1914*. London: Macmillan, 1973.

Cavallaro, Gaetano V. *The Beginning of Futility: The Most Complete Work of Diplomacy and Warfare on the Austro-Italian Front During World War I*. Chicago: Ex-Libris, 2003.

Debijer, V. *The Road to Sarajevo*. London: MacGibbon and Kee, 1967.

Dutton, David. *The Politics of Diplomacy: Britain, France and the Balkans in the First World War*. London: I. B. Tauris, 1998.

Egerton, George W. *Great Britain and the Creation of the League of Nations: Strategy, Politics, and International Organization, 1914–1919*. Chapel Hill: University of North Carolina Press, 1978.

Ferguson, Niall. *The Pity of War: Explaining World War I*. New York: Basic Books, 1999.

Ferro, M. *The Great War 1914–18*. London: Routledge, 1973.

Fleming, Thomas. *The Illusion of Victory: America in World War I*. New York: Basic Books, 2004.

Hunt, B., and A. Preston, eds. *War Aims and Strategic Policy in the Great War, 1914–18*. London: Croom Helm, 1977.

Joll, James. *The Origins of the First World War*. New York: Longman, 1984.

Kann, B., K. Kiraly, and P. S. Fichtner, eds. *The Habsburg Empire in World War I*. New York: Columbia University Press, 1977.

Kedourie, E. *England and the Middle East: The Destruction of the Ottoman Empire, 1914–21*. New York: Harvester, 1977.

Keegan, John. *The First World War*. New York: Alfred K. Knopf, 1999.

Lafore, Laurence. *The Long Fuse: An Interpretation of the Origins of World War I*. Philadelphia: Lippincott, 1965.

Lee, Dwight E. *The Outbreak of the First World War: Causes and Responsibilities*. 4th ed. Lexington, Mass.: Heath, 1975.

Macmillan, Margaret. *Paris 1919 : Six Months That Changed the World*. New York: Random House, 2002.

Marwick, A. *The Deluge: British Society and the First World War*. London: Macmillan, 1973.

Maurer, John H. *The Outbreak of the First World War: Strategic Planning, Crisis Decision Making, and Deterrence Failure*. New York: Praeger, 1995.

May, E. R. *The World and American Isolation, 1914–17*. New York: Times Books, 1966.

Mayer, Arno J. *Political Origins of the New Diplomacy, 1917–1918*. New York: H. Fertig, 1969.

Rothwell, V. H. *British War Aims and Peace Diplomacy*. Oxford: Oxford University Press, 1971.

Schmitt, Bernadotte E., and Harold C. Vedeler. *The World in Crucible, 1914–1919*. New York: Harper and Row, 1984.

Steiner, Zara S. *Britain and the Origins of the First World War*. London: Macmillan, 1973.

Stevenson, D. *First World War and International Politics*. New York: Oxford University Press, 1987.

Stevenson, David. *Cataclysm: The First World War As Political Tragedy*. New York: Basic Books, 2004.

Walworth, Arthur. *America's Moment, 1918: American Diplomacy at the End of World War I*. New York: Norton, 1977.

Zeman, Z. A. B. *The Gentleman Negotiators* (U.K. title *A Diplomatic History of the First World War*). London: Weidenfeld and Nicolson, 1971.

11—PEACE IN OUR TIME, PRELUDE TO WAR

Adamthwaite, Anthony P. *France and the Coming of the Second World War, 1936–1939*. Totowa, N.J.: Biblio Distribution Center, 1977.

———. *The Making of the Second World War*. 2d ed. Boston: Allen and Unwin, 1979.

Aldcroft, Derek H. *From Versailles to Wall Street, 1919–1929*. London: Allen Lane, 1977.

Campbell, F. Gregory. *Confrontation in Central Europe: Weimar Germany and Czechoslovakia*. Chicago: University of Chicago Press, 1975.

Churchill, Winston. *The Gathering Storm*. Boston: Houghton Mifflin, 1985.

Connell-Smith, Gordon. *The United States and Latin America: An Historical Analysis of Inter-American Relations*. London: Heinemann Educational, 1974.

Craig, Gordon A., and Felix Gilbert, eds. *The Diplomats: 1919–1939*. 2 vols. Princeton, N.J.: Princeton University Press, 1971–72.

Dallek, Robert. *Franklin D. Roosevelt and American Foreign Policy, 1932–1945*. New York: Oxford University Press, 1995.

Davis, Richard. *Anglo-French Relations Before the Second World War: Appeasement and Crisis*. London: Palgrave Macmillan, 2001.

Gilbert, Martin. *The Roots of Appeasement*. London: Weidenfeld and Nicolson, 1966.

Hoff-Wilson, Joan. *Ideology and Economics: U.S. Relations with the Soviet Union, 1918–1933*. Columbia: University of Missouri Press, 1974.

Iriye, Akira. *After Imperialism: The Search for a New Order in the Far East, 1921–1931*. Cambridge, Mass.: Harvard University Press, 1965.

Jacobson, Jon. *Locarno Diplomacy: Germany and the West, 1925–1929*. Princeton, N.J.: Princeton University Press, 1972.

Jonas, Manfred. *Isolationism in America, 1935–1941*. Ithaca, N.Y.: Cornell University Press, 1966.

Kennan, George F. *Russia and the West Under Lenin and Stalin*. 1961.

Kershaw, Ian. *Hitler, 1889–1936: Hubris*. New York: W. W. Norton, 1999.

Keynes, Maynard. *The Economic Consequences of the Peace*. New York: Harcourt Brace, 1971.

Leffler, Melvyn P. *The Elusive Quest: America's Pursuit of European Stability and French Security, 1919–1923*. Chapel Hill: University of North Carolina Press, 1979.

Levin, N. Gordon, Jr. *Woodrow Wilson and World Politics: America's Response to War and Revolution*. New York: Oxford University Press, 1968.

MacDougall, Walter A. *France's Rhineland Diplomacy, 1914–1924: The Last Bid for a Balance of Power in Europe*. Princeton, N.J.: Princeton University Press, 1978.

Maier, Charles S. *Recasting Bourgeois Europe: Stabilization in France, Germany, and Italy in the Decade after World War I*. Princeton, N.J.: Princeton University Press, 1975.

McDonough, Frank. *Hitler, Chamberlain and Appeasement*. Cambridge and New York: Cambridge University Press, 2002.

Mayer, Arno J. *Politics and Diplomacy of Peacemaking: Containment and Counterrevolution at Versailles, 1919–1919*. London: Weidenfeld and Nicolson, 1968.

Marks, Frederick W. *Wind over Sand: The Diplomacy of Franklin Roosevelt*. Athens: University of Georgia Press, 1990.

Nicolson, Harold. *Peacemaking, 1919*. New York: Grosset and Dunlap, 1965.

Offner, Arnold A. *The Origins of the Second World War: American Foreign Policy and World Politics, 1917–1941*. Maldor, Fla.: R.E. Kreiger, 1986.

Parker, Robert A. *Chamberlain and Appeasement: British Policy and the Coming of the Second World War*. London: Bedford/St. Martins, 1993.

Schuker, Stephen A. *The End of French Predominance in Europe: The Financial Crisis of 1924 and the Adoption of the Dawes Plan*. Chapel Hill: University of North Carolina Press, 1976.

Scott, George. *The Rise and Fall of the League of Nations*. New York: Macmillan, 1974.

Shen, Peijian. *Age of Appeasement: The Evolution of British Foreign Policy in 1930's*. London: Alan Sutton, 2000.

Silverman, Dan P. *Reconstructing Europe after the Great War*. Cambridge, Mass.: Harvard University Press, 1982.

Sontag, Raymond J. *A Broken World, 1919–1939*. New York: Harper and Row, 1971.

Taylor, Telford. *Munich: The Price of Peace*. Garden City, N.Y.: Doubleday, 1979.

Thomas, Hugh. *The Spanish Civil War*. New York: Simon and Schuster, 1994.

Trachtenberg, Marc. *Reparation in World Politics: France and European Economic Diplomacy, 1916–1923*. New York: Columbia University Press, 1980.

Ulam, Adam B. *Expansion and Coexistence: Soviet Foreign Policy, 1917–73*. 2d ed. New York: Praeger, 1974.

Walters, F .P. *A History of the League of Nations*. 2 vols. Westport, Conn.: Greenwood Press, 1986.

Wandycz, Piotr S. *France and Her Eastern Allies, 1919–1925: French-Czechoslovak-Polish Relations from the Paris Peace Conference to Locarno*. Westport Conn.: Greenwood Press, 1974.

Watt, Donald Cameron. *Too Serious a Business: European Armed Forces and the Approach to the Second World War*. London: Temple Smith, 1975.

Weinberg, Gerhard L. *The Foreign Policy of Hitler's Germany: Diplomatic Revolution in Europe, 1933–36*. Atlantic Highlands, N.J.: Humanities Press, 1994.

White, Stephen. *The Origins of Detente: The Genoa Conference and Soviet-Western Relations, 1921–1922*. New York: Cambridge University Press, 1985.

Wiskeman, Elizabeth. *The Rome-Berlin Axis: A Study of the Relations between Hitler and Mussolini*. Rev. ed. London: Collins, 1966.

12—THE WORLD AT WAR

Beschloss, Michael R. *The Conquerors: Roosevelt, Truman and the Destruction of Hitler's Germany, 1941–1945.* New York: Simon and Schuster, 2002.

Buhite, Russel H. *Decisions at Yalta: An Appraisal of Summit Diplomacy.* Wilmington, Del.: Scholarly Resources, 1986.

Bullock, Alan. *Hitler: A Study in Tyranny.* Rev. ed. New York: Harper and Row, 1964.

———. *Hitler and Stalin: Parallel Lives.* New York: Alfred A. Knopf, 1992.

Breitman, Richard. *The Architect of Genocide: Himmler and the Final Solution.* New York: Alfred A. Knopf, 1991.

Dawidowicz, Lucy S. *The War against the Jews: 1933–1945.* New York: Penguin, 1999.

Divine, Robert A. *Roosevelt and World War II.* Baltimore, Md.: Johns Hopkins Press, 1969.

———. *The Reluctant Belligerent: American Entry into World War II.* 2d ed. New York: Wiley, 1979.

Edmonds, R. *The Big Three: Churchill, Roosevelt, and Stalin.* New York: Penguin, 1992.

Feis, Herbert. *Between War and Peace.* Princeton, N.J.: Princeton University Press, 1960.

———. *Churchill, Roosevelt, Stalin: The War They Waged and the Peace They Sought.* 2d ed. Princeton, N.J.: Princeton University Press, 1967.

Freidlander, Saul. *Nazi Germany and the Jews.* New York: HarperCollins, 1997.

Giovannitti, L., and F. Freed. *The Decision to Drop the Bomb.* London: Metheun, 1967.

Hildebrand, Klaus. *The Foreign Policy of the Third Reich.* Anthony Fothergill, trans. London: Batsford, 1973.

Keegan, John. *The Second World War.* New York: Viking, 1989.

Knox, MacGregor. *Mussolini Unleashed, 1939–1941: Politics and Strategy in Fascist Italy's Last War.* Cambridge: Cambridge University Press, 1982.

Kolko, Gabriel. *The Politics of War: The World and United States Foreign Policy, 1943–5.* New York: Pantheon, 1990.

Krug, Hans-Joachim, Yoichi Hirama, Berthold J. Sander-Nagashima, and Axel Niestle. *Reluctant Allies: German-Japanese Naval Relations in World War II.* Annapolis, Md.: Naval Institute Press, 2002.

Leiss, Amelia Catherine. *European Peace Treaties after World War II: Negotiations and Texts of Treaties with Italy, Bulgaria, Hungary, Rumania, and Finland.* Reprint. New York: Kraus, 1976.

Louis, W. R. *Imperialism at Bay, 1941–5: The United States and the Decolonization of the British Empire.* Oxford: Oxford University Press, 1978.

McNeill, William H. *America, Britain, and Russia: Their Cooperation and Conflict, 1941–1946.* Reprint, New York: Johnson Reprint, 1970.

Meacham, Jon. *Franklin and Winston: An Intimate Portrait of an Epic Friendship.* New York: Random House, 2003.

Read, Anthony, and David Fisher. *Deadly Embrace: Hitler, Stalin and the Nazi-Soviet Pact, 1939–1941.* New York: Norton, 1988.

Renouvin, Pierre. *World War II and Its Origins: International Relations, 1929–1945.* Rémy Inglis Hall, trans. New York: Harper and Row, 1968.

Rhodes, Richard. *The Making of the Atomic Bomb.* New York: Simon and Schuster, 1986.

Rosenbaum, Ron. *Explaining Hitler.* New York: HarperCollins, 1999.

Rozek, E. J. *Wartime Diplomacy: A Pattern in Poland.* New York: Wiley, 1958.

Slavinsky, Boris, and Geoffrey Jukes. *The Japanese-Soviet Neutrality Pact: A Diplomatic History, 1941–45.* London: Routledge/Curzon, 2004.

Steinhart, M. G. *Hitler's War and the Germans.* Columbus: Ohio University Press, 1977.

Stoler, Mark A. *Allies and Adversaries: The Joint Chiefs of Staff, the Grand Alliance, and U.S. Strategy in World War II.* Chapel Hill: University of North Carolina Press, 2000.

Woodward, Sir Llewellyn. *British Foreign Policy in the Second World War.* 5 vols. London: Her Majesty's Stationery Office, 1962–70.

Wright, Gordon. *The Ordeal of Total War, 1939–1945.* New York: Harper and Row, 1968.

Wylie, Neville. *European Neutrals and Non-Belligerents during the Second World War.* Cambridge: Cambridge University Press, 2001.

Yoshitsu, Michael M. *Japan and the San Francisco Peace Settlement.* New York: Columbia University Press, 1983.

13—COLD WAR, PEACEFUL COEXISTENCE

Blair, Clay. *The Forgotten War: America in Korea, 1950–1953.* New York: Random House, 1987.

Cook, D. *Forging the Alliance: The Birth of the NATO Treaty and the Dramatic Transformation in American Foreign Policy between 1945 and 1950.* London: Secker and Warburg, 1989.

Davison, W. P. *The Berlin Blockade: A Study in Cold War Politics.* Princeton, N.J.: Princeton University Press, 1958.

Divine, Robert A. *Blowing on the Wind: The Nuclear Test Ban Debate, 1954–1960.* New York: Oxford University Press, 1978.

Dupuy, Trevor N. *Elusive Victory: The Arab-Israeli Wars, 1947–1974.* 3rd ed. Dubuque, Iowa: Kendall/Hunt, 1992.

Feeland, Richard M. *The Truman Doctrine and the Origins of McCarthyism: Foreign Policy, Domestic Politics, and Internal Security, 1946–1948.* New York: Alfred A. Knopf, 1972.

Gaddis, John Lewis. *The United States and the Origins of the Cold War, 1941–1947*. New York: Columbia University Press, 1972.

———. *Strategies of Containment: A Critical Appraisal of Post-War American National Security Policy*. Oxford: Oxford University Press, 1982.

———. *We Now Know: Rethinking Cold War History (A Council on Foreign Relations Book)*. Oxford and New York: Oxford University Press, 1998.

Grosser, A. *The Western Alliance: European-American Relations since 1945*. London: Macmillan, 1980.

Halberstam, David. *The Best and the Brightest*. New York: Penguin, 1983.

Haley, Edwar P. *Arms Control and the End of the Cold War: An Oral History of the Negotiations on Conventional Armed Forces in Europe*. Claremont, Calif.: Keck Center for International and Strategic Studies, 2002.

Hargreaves, John D. *The End of Colonial Rule in West Africa*. New York: Barnes and Noble Books, 1979.

Horowitz, David. *The Free World Colossus: A Critique of American Foreign Policy in the Cold War*. New York: Hill and Wang, 1971.

Iriye, Arika. *The Cold War in Asia: A Historical Introduction*. New York: Prentice Hall, 1974.

Jugler, Richard L. *Commitment to Purpose: How Alliance Partnership Won the Cold War*. Washington, D.C.: Rand Corporation, 1993.

Karnow, Stanley. *Vietnam: A History*. 2nd rev. and updated ed. New York: Penguin Books, 1997.

Kolko, Gabriel. *The Roots of American Foreign Policy: An Analysis of Power and Purpose*. New York: Pantheon, 1969.

———. *Anatomy of a War: Vietnam, the United States, and the Modern Historical Experience*. New York: Pantheon, 1985.

Laquer, Walter. *The Rebirth of Europe*. New York: Holt, Rinehart and Winston, 1970.

Low, Alfred. *The Sino-Soviet Dispute: An Analysis of the Polemics*. Rutherford, N.J.: Fairleigh Dickinson University Press, 1976.

Mastny, V. *Russia's Road to the Cold War*. New York: Columbia University Press, 1979.

Mayne, Richard. *The Recovery of Europe from Devastation to Unity*. New York: Harper and Row, 1970.

Morley, M. H. *Imperial State and Revolution: The United States and Cuba, 1952–1986*. Cambridge: Cambridge University Press, 1987.

Neilson, Keith, and Ronald G. Haycock, eds. *The Cold War and Defense*. New York: Praeger, 1990.

Ovendale, Ritchie. *The Origins of the Arab-Israeli Wars*. New York: Longman, 1984.

Reed, Thomas. *At the Abyss: An Insider's History of the Cold War*. Novato, Calif.: Presidio Press, 2004.

Rees, David. *Korea: The Limited War*. New York: St. Martin's Press, 1964.

Schmidt, Gustav, ed. *A History of NATO—The First Fifty Years*. London: Palgrave Macmillan, 2001.

Schulzinger, Robert D. *A Companion to American Foreign Relations*. London: Blackwell, 2003.

Seaborg, Glenn T. *Kennedy, Khrushchev, and the Test Ban*. Berkeley: University of California Press, 1981.

Seabury, Paul. *The Rise and Decline of the Cold War*. New York: Basic Books, 1967.

Thomas, Hugh. *Suez Affair*. Harmondsworth, England: Penguin, 1967.

———. *Armed Truce: The Beginnings of the Cold War, 1945–46*. North Pomfret, Vt.: Trafalgar Square: 1986.

Yergin, David. *Shattered Peace: The Origins of the Cold War and the National Security State*. London: Penguin, 1977.

Walker, Martin. *The Cold War: A History*. New York: Owl Books, 1995.

Williams, Ann. *Britain and France in the Middle East and North Africa, 1914–1967*. London: Macmillan, 1968.

Williams, William Appleman. *The Tragedy of American Diplomacy*. 2d rev. ed. New York: Dell, 1972.

14—NEW WORLD ORDER

Ambrose, S. E. *Rise to Globalism: American Foreign Policy since 1938*. New York: Penguin, 1991.

Armstrong, D. *The Rise of International Organisations*. London: Macmillan, 1982.

Batt, J. *East Central Europe from Reform to Transformation*. London: Royal Institute for International Affairs, 1991.

Bertram, Christoph. *Europe in the Balance: Securing the Peace Won in the Cold War*. Washington, D.C.: Carnegie Endowment for International Peace, 1995.

Brown, Seyom. *The Faces of Power: Constancy and Change in United States Foreign Policy from Truman to Reagan*. New York: Columbia University Press, 1983.

Croft, Stuart. *The Conventional Armed Forces in Europe Treaty: The Cold War Endgame*. Aldershot, U.K., and Brookfield, Vt. : Dartmouth Publishing Group, 1994.

Dawisha, K. *Eastern Europe, Gorbachev, and Reform*. Cambridge: Cambridge University Press, 1990.

Freedman, Lawrence, and Efraim Karsh. *The Gulf Conflict, 1990–1991: Diplomacy and War in the New World Order*. Princeton, N.J.: Princeton University Press, 1993.

Gasteyger, Curt. *Searching for World Security: Understanding Global Armament and Disarmament*. New York: St. Martin's Press, 1985.

Glenny, M. *The Rebirth of History: Eastern Europe in the Age of Democracy*. New York: Penguin, 1990.

Kennedy, Paul. *The Rise and Fall of the Great Powers.* New York: Random House, 1987.

Kirkendall, R. S. *A Global Power: America since the Age of Roosevelt.* 2nd ed. New York: Alfred A. Knopf, 1980.

Krasner, Stephen D. *Structural Conflict: The Third World against Global Liberalism.* Berkeley: University of California Press, 1985.

LaFeber, Walter. *The Panama Canal: The Crisis in Historical Perspective.* Oxford: Oxford University Press, 1984.

McCausland, Jeffrey D. *The CFE Treaty: A Cold War Anachronism?* Carlisle, Pa.: Strategic Studies Institute, U.S. Army War College, 1995.

Medvedev, Roy. *China and the Superpowers.* Harold Shukman, trans. Oxford: Blackwell, 1986.

Nassar, Jamal R., and Roger Heacock, eds. *Intifada: Palestine at the Crossroads.* New York: Praeger, 1990.

Papacosma, S. Victor, and Mary Ann Heiss, eds. *NATO in the Post–Cold War Era: Does It Have a Future?* London: Palgrave Macmillan, 1995.

Pinder, J. *European Community: The Building of a Union.* New York: Oxford University Press, 1991.

Rafael, Gideon. *Destination Peace: Three Decades of Israeli Foreign Policy.* New York: Stein and Day, 1981.

Romberg, Alan D., and Tadishi Yamamoto, eds. *Same Bed, Different Dreams: America and Japan: Societies in Transition.* New York: Council on Foreign Relations, 1990.

Rubin, B. *Paved with Good Intentions: The American Experience in Iran.* New York: Penguin, 1981.

Sakwa, R. *Gorbachev and His Reforms, 1986–1990.* London: Philip Alan, 1990.

Schoultz, Lars. *Human Rights and United States Policy toward Latin America.* Princeton, N.J.: Princeton University Press, 1981.

Smith, Gaddis. *Morality, Reason, and Power: American Diplomacy in the Carter Years.* New York: Hill and Wang, 1986.

Smith, Mark. *NATO Enlargement During the Cold War: Strategy and System in the Western Alliance.* London: Palgrave Macmillan, 2000.

Smith, Martin A. *NATO in the First Decade After the Cold War.* Dordrecht, Netherlands: Kluwer Academic Publishers, 2000.

Spector, L. S. *Nuclear Proliferation Today.* New York: Random House, 1984.

Urwin, D. W. *The Community of Europe: A History of European Integration since 1945.* New York: Longman, 1991.

15—INTERNATIONAL THREATS, GLOBAL OPPORTUNITIES

Akdeniz, Yaman. *Internet Child Pornography and the Laws Response: National and International.* Aldershot, England: Ashgate, 2005.

Allison, Graham. *Nuclear Terrorism: The Ultimate Preventable Catastrophe.* New York: Times Books, 2004.

Bales, Kevin. *Disposable People: New Slavery in the Global Economy.* Berkeley: University of California Press, 2000.

Boulden, Jane, and Thomas George Weiss. *Terrorism and the UN: Before and After September 11.* Bloomington: Indiana University Press, 2004.

Hochschild, Arlie Rissell, and Barbara Ehrenreich, eds. *Global Woman: Nannies, Maids, and Sex Workers in the New Economy.* New York: Owl Books, 2004.

Holliday, Walker T. *Governmental Principles and Statutes on Child Pornography.* Hauppague, N.Y.: Nova Science Publishers, 2003.

Kempadoo, Kamala, and Jo Doezema. *Global Sex Workers: Rights, Resistance, and Redefinition.* London and New York: Routledge, 1998.

Klain, Eva J. *Prostitution of Children and Child-Sex Tourism: An Analysis of Domestic and International Responses.* Lake Park, Fla.: National Center for Missing and Exploited Children, 1999.

Kyle, David, and Rey Koslowski. *Global Human Smuggling: Comparative Perspectives.* Baltimore, Md.: Johns Hopkins University Press, 2001.

Lilley, Peter. *Dirty Dealing: The Untold Truth About Global Money Laundering, International Crime and Terrorism.* 2d ed. London: Kogan Page, 2003.

Masika, Rachel. *Gender, Trafficking and Slavery.* London: Oxfam, 2002.

McGill, Craig. *Human Traffic: Sex, Slaves, and Immigration.* London: Vision Paperbacks, 2003.

National Commission on Terrorist Attacks. *The 9/11 Commission Report: Final Report of the National Commission on Terrorist Attacks upon the United States.* New York: Norton, 2004.

Primakov, E. M. *A World Challenged: Fighting Terrorism in the Twenty-first Century.* Washington, D.C.: Brookings Institution Press, 2004.

Robinson, Jeffrey. *The Laundrymen: Inside the World's Third Largest Business.* New York: Simon and Schuster, 1998.

———. *The Merger: The Conglomeration of International Organized Crime.* New York: Overlook Press, 2000.

Scheuer, Michael. *Imperial Hubris: Why the West Is Losing the War on Terror.* New York and London: Brassey's, 2004.

Seabrook, Jeremy. *No Hiding Place: Child Sex Tourism and the Role of Extra-Territorial Legislation.* London: Zed Books, 2000.

Skrobanek, Siriporn, Nattaya Boonpakdi, and Chutima Janthakeero. *The Traffic in Women: Human Realities of the International Sex Trade.* London: Zed Books, 1997.

Staloff, Robert B. *The Battle of Ideas in the War on Terror: Essays on U.S. Public Diplomacy in the Middle East.* Washington, D.C.: Washington Institute for Near East Policy, 2004.

Taillon, J. Paul de B. *The Evolution of Special Forces in Counter-Terrorism: The British and American Experiences.* New York: Praeger, 2000.

Taillon, J. Paul de B. *Hijacking and Hostages: Government Responses to Terrorism.* New York: Praeger, 2002.

U.S. House of Representatives. *The Role of Public Diplomacy in Support of the Anti-terrorism Campaign: Hearing Before the Committee on International Relations.* Washington, D.C.: U.S. Government Printing Office, 2001.

U.S. Senate. *Diplomacy and the War on Terrorism: Hearing Before the Committee on Foreign Relations, United States Senate.* Washington, D.C.: U.S. Government Printing Office, 2003

INDEX

Boldface page numbers denote texts of documents.

C

Y

Z